PERCEPTION: MECHANISMS AND MODELS

Readings from

SCIENTIFIC AMERICAN

PERCEPTION: MECHANISMS AND MODELS

with introductions by

Richard Held and Whitman Richards

Massachusetts Institute of Technology

W. H. Freeman and Company

San Francisco

Most of the SCIENTIFIC AMERICAN articles in *Perception: Mechanisms and Models* are available as separate Offprints. For a complete list of more than 900 articles now available as Offprints, write to W. H. Freeman and Company, 660 Market Street, San Francisco, California 94104

Printed in the United States of America

Library of Congress Catalog Card Number: 70-190437

Standard Book Number: 0-7167-0853-1 (cloth)
0-7167-0852-3 (paper)

9 8 7 6 5

PREFACE

That we see, hear, feel, taste, and smell is obvious, but a systematic understanding of the perceptual phenomena associated with these senses is difficult to achieve. The very notion of what constitutes systematic knowledge in this area is often subject to controversy. The articles from SCIENTIFIC AMERICAN included here were selected because we felt that they reflect either actual or potential increases in our scientific understanding of the phenomena of perception. Implicit in this choice are certain assumptions about what constitutes progress in the field; our biases are reflected both by our selection of articles and by our discussions of them.

As the title of the book indicates, the emphasis is upon descriptions of the various modes of operation of perceptual systems. Some of these descriptions, particularly those concerned with the more peripheral mechanisms, are now part of the permanent cumulation of science; others are more exploratory, and have only a conditional validity; and a few may be actually wrong, but represent interesting approaches toward explanations. Because the whole field is in a phase of expansion, we can only hope that the more tenuous models of perceptual systems discussed here represent the kind of programmatic approach that will, in the future, result in more convincing explanations of perceptual processes.

For several years, we have used this collection of articles (in the form of SCIENTIFIC AMERICAN Offprints) as the sole assigned reading material in a course on perception. SCIENTIFIC AMERICAN articles are problem-centered and are written in a lively fashion that engages the reader's curiosity. For the most part, their authors are active researchers in various fields, and they bring to their accounts the questing and questioning attitudes that are an essential part of the development of science. Student response has borne out our enthusiasm for these readings.

In the introductions to the six sections of this book, we have attempted to provide some essential background material and to indicate the relations among the reprinted articles, very much as we have done in our own course. Section I provides an overview of the field, as we define it, together with a discussion of the possible kinds of models of perceptual systems. Section II covers the sensory transducers, the organs that convert stimulus energy into neural impulses. These transducers constitute the first stage in a perceptual process. Section III deals with the early stages of analysis by the nervous system of transduced sensory stimulation. In Section IV, we consider certain perceptual processes that seem amenable to explanations in terms of known properties of the nervous system, along with the residual difficulties posed by such explanations. Section V, by contrast, reviews classic perceptual problems that are more recalcitrant to explanation in terms of known properties of the nervous system. Finally, Section VI treats the development and modification of perception as it bears on the elucidation of the mechanisms of perception.

Clearly, those who study perception have many unanswered questions. The field is open both to conceptual clarification and to experimental test, and we have tried to indicate those areas that need further research. The field is ripe for new advances, and they are coming at a quickening rate.

Richard Held
Whitman Richards

December 1971

CONTENTS

I THE ORGANIZATION OF PERCEPTUAL SYSTEMS

II SENSORY SYSTEMS

III PHYSIOLOGICAL ANALYZERS

IV PERCEPTUAL PROCESSES

V ILLUSIONS AND CONSTANCIES

VI DEVELOPMENT AND MODIFICATION

Note on cross-references: References to articles included in this book are noted by the title of the article and the page on which it begins; references to articles that are available as Offprints, but are not included here, are noted by the article's title and Offprint number; references to articles published by SCIENTIFIC AMERICAN, but which are not available as Offprints, are noted by the title of the article and the month and year of its publication.

PERCEPTION: MECHANISMS AND MODELS

I

THE ORGANIZATION OF PERCEPTUAL SYSTEMS

I

THE ORGANIZATION OF PERCEPTUAL SYSTEMS

INTRODUCTION

The naive observer believes that he correctly perceives the objects and events in the world and that is all that there is to perception. Doubts begin to arise only when properties that do not correspond to apparent reality are assigned to these objects and events: this happens when the world is analyzed in terms of geometry, physics, and other sciences. Objects then have mathematically definable sizes and shapes, such physically definable properties as motion, mass, and spectral reflectance, and events have duration and other temporal properties. Questions about perception are then raised: How do these objectively defined properties of objects and events relate to our perceptions of those objects and events? For example, is the measured size of an object directly proportional to its perceived size? Is the apparent speed of motion of a body exactly proportional to its actual velocity? That the answer to such questions is frequently "no" is apparent from our everyday experience: the remote figure of a man may appear to be no larger than an ant; after viewing a moving scene, an observer may perceive a truly stationary one to move in the opposite direction. The relation between objective descriptions of the world and perceptual effects is not simple; it is, in fact, the subject matter of a scientific approach to perception. Our attempts to find the laws underlying this relation are embodied in the mechanisms and models that are the subject matter of this book.

The Inverted Image. Our internal representation of a real object is never identical to that external object. Consider the image in the eye of an object in space: such an image will be inverted and much smaller. Clearly, the image is not identical with the object; but if the observer is not to be continually deceived, some semblance must be preserved. Historically, a major question has been the preservation of a point-to-point projection from object to image, the maintenance of uprightness, and the achievement of a single percept from two separate images—one from each of the two retinas. The modern counterparts of this problem are attempts to find a topological representation of external objects in the cortex. A. C. Crombie, in his article "Early Concepts of the Senses and the Mind," characterizes such efforts as misguided attempts to answer the question "How do we see?"

Crombie then describes how scientific thought developed into a commitment to the study of mechanisms, leaving the intangibles to philosophy. There were a number of advantages to this mechanistic approach. First, the relevant issues became those that were amenable to quantitative interpretation. Extent, quantity, and motion were primary; the rest—color, sound, taste, and smell—were figments of the observer's mental processes provoked by the sensory effects of the primary properties. Thus, in the seventeenth century, the model for scientific understanding became the mathematical law of the sort set by the science of mechanics. Under such influences, Johannes Kepler carried out the correct analysis of the optics of the eye, showing that, in fact, an object has an inverted image on the retina. Thus, Kepler dissociated his analysis from the separate issue of how an inverted retinal image can be reconciled with our perception of an upright world.

Key Themes. If we are to apply Kepler's lesson today, then our principal efforts should be directed toward an objective analysis of the properties of perceptual processes rather than towards attempting to find an internal portrait of the external world. Several major advances in our understanding of perceptual systems are possible once such limitations are imposed. First, a knowledge of neurology, physiology, and the anatomy of the nervous system allows us to constrain unnecessary speculations about perceptual processing, and it enables us to theorize about what extent certain perceptual processes are functionally independent. Of course the relation between perception and the nervous system is a two-way street: our knowledge of perception allows us, in turn, to speculate about how the nervous system is constructed.

A second lesson from Kepler is that the senses and the nervous system do not convey an exact representation of the object exciting the senses, but only an abstraction: the nervous system transmits messages about certain features of the object. This point was explicitly recognized by Descartes, and is a precursor to the modern idea of "feature detectors"—that individual neurons in the brain are activated only by stimuli with very specific characteristics, such as a certain frequency or a line in a particular orientation.

The third lesson is the importance of recognizing that a completely mechanistic account of perception can be achieved only by tracing the consequences of sensory excitation through the nervous system to its end product: an overt response measurable by the experimenter. From our point of view, the virtue of considering such input–output relations lies in the implication that perceptual processing is not merely sensory analysis: confirmation of this analysis by an overt action, sensed by the subject himself, is a necessary part of perception. The full development of perceptual systems requires such feedback. Consequently, a satisfactory approach to perception is one in which the perceptual processes are regarded as systems—or better, as sets of systems—whose functions range from receptor input to muscular output, which, in turn, restimulate the senses through feedback loops traversing the environment. By considering these external feedback loops, we may seek more sophisticated and more significant answers to the question "How do we see?"

Model Building. Underlying the development of modern scientific analyses is the development of models. Models serve several functions: they can summarize, in an elegant way, certain general properties of systems; at the same time, they also provide a framework for relating factual information. By examining models of particular systems, we put ourselves in a better position to begin the testing and development of hypotheses of how these systems are organized.

All of these advantages apply to models of perceptual systems. Of initial interest will be the general, overall principles of organization that apply to many different kinds of sensory and perceptual systems. Later, we will consider more detailed models for specific phenomena, such as movement, color, or brightness contrast.

Consider first the problem of modeling a whole perceptual system. Such a system will receive some kind of input (stimulus) from its environment; it will process this input and react by producing a particular output (response):

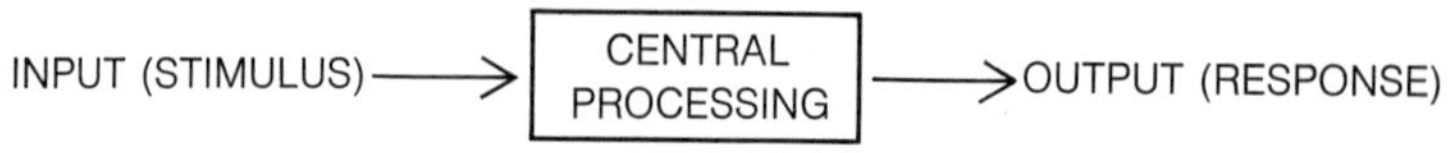

The act of perception includes the internal processing of sensory inputs and the internal code that the processor uses for that purpose. The carriers of this code are the neurons, which respond in an all-or-none manner by propagating pulses or "spikes" of electrical energy. The code itself consists both in the firing patterns of the neurons and in the spatial organization of those neurons. Thus, the internal code used by an organism in processing a sensory input is an internal space–time representation of the external signals that constitute the input.

Clearly, an organism cannot process all the external signals that it receives. In man, in the visual system alone, there are more than a million channels. If every group of ten of these channels is assumed to be independent of every other such group, then, with a maximum firing rate of the neurons of 100 pulses or "spikes" per second, the neural channels could be handling up to $10^6(10^2/10) = 10^7$ pulses per second. If each pulse provides one "bit" of information about the input, then the brain could be bombarded by 10^7 bits of information per second. This figure far exceeds our capacity to deal with information, which is limited to about 25 "bits" of binary information per second. Thus, the information reaching the brain must be whittled down considerably in order to abstract the most relevant data. This is the principal function of the initial stages in neural processing: to abstract certain important features from the external signals and to eliminate redundancy. Many examples of this abstracting (or feature-encoding) appear in the articles that follow. Occasionally, this encoding process—which, by necessity, imposes structure upon the input—will lead to ambiguities, or "illusions."

Limited Input and Basic Code. If there is only one major central processor, it is clear that, regardless of the actual variety of inputs and outputs, a common code will be used. Thus, it may be possible to obtain some insight into the basic principles of eoding and the organization of the processor by examining any one of the many possible types of input–output systems. George Miller's article "Information and Memory" demonstrates one kind of analysis that reveals some major encoding principles. One of the most important of these is revealed by studying our immediate recall of lists of random numbers or letters. The length of the list is approximately the same whether we use letters, numbers, or more complex "alphabets." Clearly, the limitation is of the number of symbols, rather than of the total number of pieces or "bits" of information contained in those symbols. In fact, if we wish to remember a long string of binary digits (0, 1), we can recode the string into another base in order to reduce the total number of symbols to be stored. Sensory processing in the visual, somesthetic, and auditory pathways appears to proceed in an entirely analogous manner. Apparently, the brain cannot process more than a very limited number of items at one time; therefore, it is important, for the sake of efficiency, that each item sent to it carries as much information as possible.

The very limited capacity of the brain to handle a large volume of inputs is seen time and again. The more isolated the input—that is, the fewer the points of reference for that input—then the harder it is to process. As Miller suggests in his article, this limitation for making absolute judgments may be approximated by the "magical" number seven.

There are several ways in which the brain can overcome this limitation imposed upon absolute judgments. The most obvious is by insuring that inputs in a given group share the same general frame of reference, so that their differences, relative to that frame, help to identify them. Under such circumstances, the ability of the brain to detect differences between simultaneous inputs is exceedingly good. In fact, under controlled laboratory conditions, the differential performance of sensory systems may be almost as good as that of the best physical detector. Thus, sensory and perceptual systems are better suited to detect and to process differences between absolute values, rather than the values themselves.

Selective Attention. Still another important method by which the brain increases its ability to handle a large volume of incoming signals is the selection of those inputs that are most relevant to the task at hand. As Descartes recognized, the brain has the ability to attend selectively to one sensory modality at the expense of another: thus, for example, as the figure on page 14 illustrates, attending to a visual stimulus impairs one's perception of an olfactory one. A tribute to the power of selective attention, however, is that it may operate effectively upon a group of inputs within a single sensory modality. The "cocktail-party" problem, mentioned by Donald E. Broadbent in his article "Attention and the Perception of Speech," is a good illustration of the fineness of the filtering mechanism of the human brain, whereby attention can be paid to one voice among many. Because the mechanism that makes possible this neural filtering action is not understood—and because of its universal importance—it warrants considerably more study.

Parallel Processing. One obvious explanation for the brain's remarkable ability to attend selectively to various inputs is that incoming information is processed in parallel, rather than serial, order. Clearly, the anatomical separation of the visual, olfactory, and cutaneous sensory apparatus provides a good basis for the expectation that the brain is capable of "tuning in" only one of these channels at a time. Thus, selective attention between modalities could be accomplished merely by gating the input:

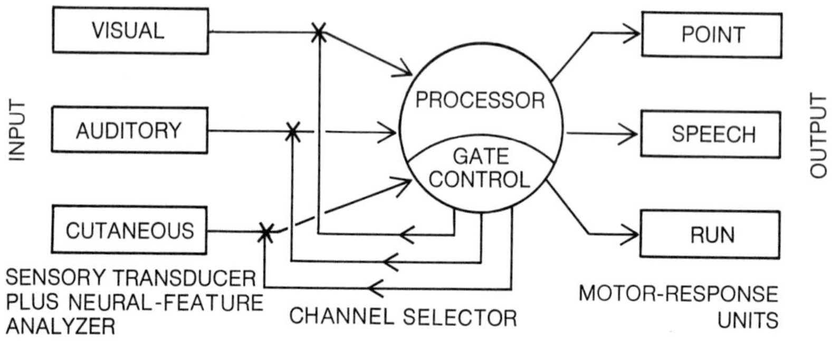

Similarly, we may wish to introduce complementary switching points at the output side of the processor, or perhaps further refine the selection of incoming sensory inputs within each modality. Regardless of what refinements or modifications we may conceive of, however, our first thought is to allow the various inputs to flow into only one central processor. In this way, various sensory inputs may be easily paired with any number of possible motor outputs, merely by opening and shutting the appropriate gates.

Michael S. Gazzaniga's article "The Split Brain in Man" suggests that our flow diagram should not be so simple. In fact, we may have erred at a very crucial point—namely, in the assumption that there is but one central processor. When the cerebrum is divided surgically, it seems to function as two independent brains. Each "hemibrain" has its own inputs and—most importantly—its own optimal outputs or ways of responding. Thus, the left hemisphere will react best to visual input with a verbal response, whereas the right hemisphere prefers a tactual or pointing response. This finding suggests that at least two major processors are involved in linking the visual input to a motor-response output. Is it possible that the brain is merely constructed from a large set of such parallel-processing systems, each of which has its own optimal input and its own optimal output?

There is mounting evidence, in fact, that a brain is basically a set of parallel-processing systems, each system analyzing the input to detect the presence or absence of a particular "trigger" feature, which will release a stereotyped pattern of behavior. In lower animals, such a system is called an "innate releasing mechanism." Some of these releasers are extremely simple: In frogs, the triggering mechanism can be activated by a color (see the article by Muntz in Section III), and in fish or gulls, by a colored spot (see "Behavior of the Stickleback" and "Behavior in Gulls" by N. Tinbergen, available as SCIENTIFIC AMERICAN Offprints 414 and 456, respectively). In ducklings, the releaser is more complex—namely, a simple pattern that must move in a particular direction. Obviously, the more complex the animal, the greater the possibilities for behavior patterns and releasers. Is it still possible, nevertheless, that information handling in the human brain is a continuation and elaboration of this deterministic and largely innate parallel-processing scheme used by lower animals? There is a surprising amount of evidence (some of which is reported in the articles in this collection) that suggests that it is.

REFERENCES

Barlow, H. B. The reduction of redundancy and intelligence. In National Physical Laboratory, *Mechanisation of thought processes.* Vol. II. London: Her Majesty's Stationery Office, 1959.

Broadbent, D. E. *Perception and communication.* New York: Pergamon Press, 1958.

Gazzaniga, M. *The bisected brain.* New York: Appleton-Century Crofts, 1970.

Miller, G. A. The magical number seven, plus or minus two: some limits on our capacity for processing information. *Psychological Review*, 1956, **63**, 81–97.

Treisman, A. M. Selective attention in man. In J. M. Foley, R. A. Lockhart, and D. M. Messick (Eds.), *Contemporary readings in psychology.* New York: Harper & Row, 1970.

1

EARLY CONCEPTS OF THE SENSES AND THE MIND

A. C. CROMBIE

May 1964

A ferment that stirred in men's thoughts about natural phenomena during the 17th century moved a scientist of the time to enthusiasm. Henry Power, an English physician and naturalist who was elected to the Royal Society in its infancy, wrote in his *Experimental Philosophy* of 1664: "These are the days that must lay a new Foundation of a more magnificent Philosophy, never to be overthrown: that will Empirically and Sensibly canvass the *Phaenomena* of Nature, deducing the Causes of things from such Originals in Nature, as we observe are producible by Art, and the infallible demonstration of Mechanicks: and certainly, this is the way and no other, to build a true and permanent Philosophy.... And he that will give a satisfactory Account of those *Phaenomena,* must be an Artificer, indeed, and one well skill'd in the Wheelwork and Internal Contrivance of such Anatomical Engines."

In those words Power characterized the program for research into living things set by the new "mechanical philosophy," which had been established earlier in the century by several investigators, notably Galileo Galilei and René Descartes. The philosophy was at the root of one of the most fruitful ideas guiding the modern study of the senses and the mind: the idea that the body is a mechanism. That idea was first successfully exploited in the experimental and theoretical inquiries made during the 17th century into the mechanisms of the sense organs, particularly the eye and the ear.

I shall argue the thesis that this "mechanistic hypothesis" made it possible to formulate and, as far as was technically possible, to solve the problems of how the sense organs worked; that moreover the hypothesis pointed the way to a new approach to the altogether different problem of how the information conveyed by the senses is transformed into perceptions. Two things about the hypothesis accounted for its achievements. The first was its ruthless commitment of the investigator, before he made any observations, to asking only one kind of question. Thereby the hypothesis provided the initial key to success by isolating the kind of problem that would yield to it. In a world that was assumed to be simply a system of mechanisms, the problem was to discover the particular mechanisms concerned.

Second, the commitment forced the recognition, as nothing less ruthless could, of its own limits. Once the full extent of the mechanistic commitment had become clear in the 17th century, it was comparatively easy to see that there were several different kinds of question involved in the inquiries into sensation and perception. By the end of the century clear distinctions had been made between three such kinds of question. One was physical and physiological: By what mechanisms are external physical motions transformed into internal physical motions of the sense organs, the nerves and the brain? Another question concerned the link between physiology and psychology: How do the physical motions of the sense organs, the nerves and the brain effect sensations in what Galileo called the "animate and sensitive body"? Finally there was the psychological problem of perception: What information does a person receive in visual, auditory and other perceptions; what sensory cues are necessary for him to have these perceptions?

My argument is that the mechanistic hypothesis, applied as an instrument of thought, was the key to the success of 17th-century investigators because it transformed not the techniques, or even at the beginning most of the essential facts, but the formulation of traditional problems so that the essential distinctions described above could be made. The advances produced by the hypothesis began with, and gradually intensified, the recognition that these distinctions existed and that they required different modes of attack. In setting forth the argument I shall use as illustrations the study of vision, hearing and the coordination of sensory information and behavior.

Students of vision up until the 17th century never clearly recognized that there were at least three different kinds of question to be asked. Ancient and medieval authors on the subject invariably made their treatment of the physiology of the eye and of the means by which vision is effected serve as an explanation of how we see. In other words, they dealt with the problem as if it involved only a single question.

This can be seen in the theory of vision most widely accepted before Johannes Kepler arrived in 1604 at the explanation that is the basis of the modern understanding of vision. (Francesco Maurolico had arrived at a similar explanation earlier, but it was published posthumously after Kepler's.) The pre-Kepler theory was that of the Arab philosopher Ibn al-Haitham, better

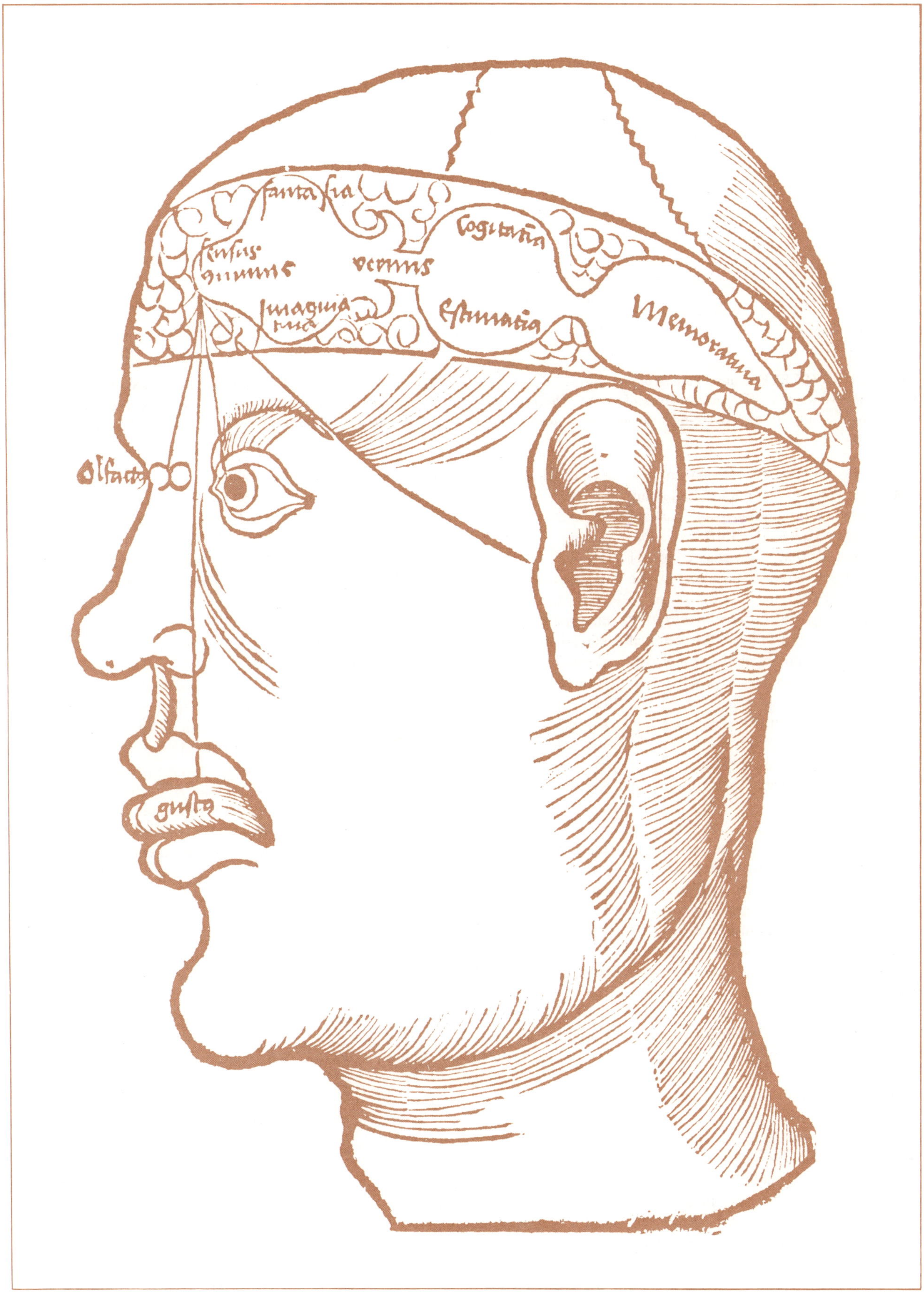

DIVISIONS OF BRAIN according to a traditional early concept are shown in an illustration from Gregor Reisch's *Margarita Philosophica,* published in 1504. In the frontal cavity was the "common sensory," connected by nerves to the sense organs; that cavity also was the site of fantasy and imagination. The middle cavity was the seat of thought and judgment; the rear cavity, of the memory.

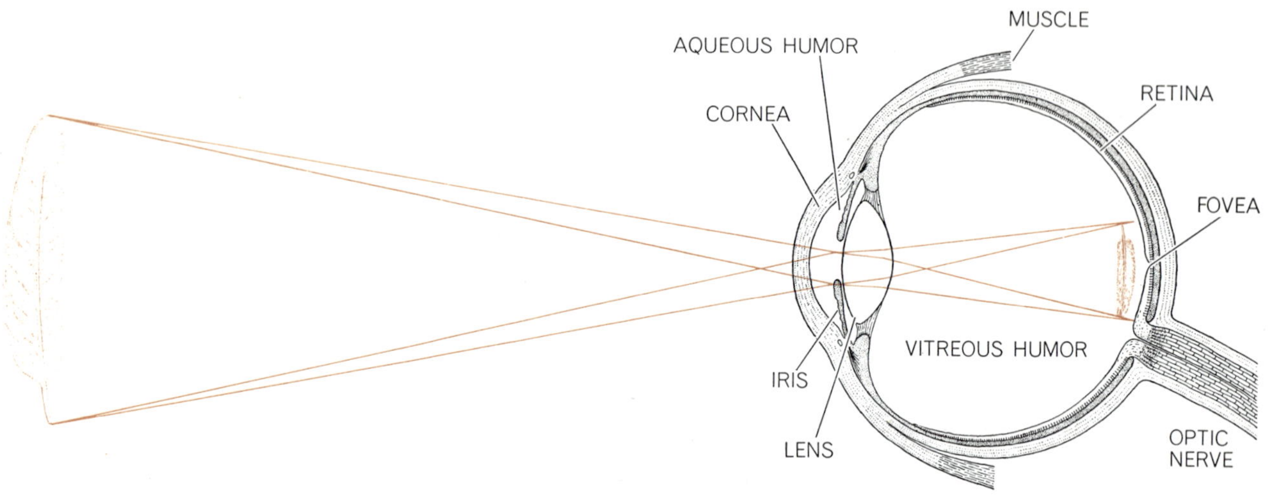

STRUCTURE OF EYE as now understood is portrayed as a contrast to the views of earlier investigators of vision. The inversion of the image as a result of refraction by the lens was a phenomenon that gave them particular difficulty. Even some investigators who were aware that inversion must occur concluded that a process within the eye preserved the erect image that is apparently seen.

known in the West as Alhazen, the Latin version of his name. Following the theories of his predecessors, particularly Euclid, Galen and Ptolemy, Alhazen supposed that a "visual cone" of rays extended from the object to the eye and that the lens was the sensitive organ [*see top illustration on opposite page*]. He then proposed the original theory that the image of the object was propagated by physical rays sent from each point on the object to a corresponding point on the sensitive forward surface of the lens, which thus brought about a perception of the whole object through the separate perceptions of each of its points.

This geometrical treatment of images enabled Alhazen to offer at once a solution to an ancient and puzzling problem: how the images of large objects got into the diminutive pupil of the eye. It also raised some difficulties. First, if each sensitive point on the lens was stimulated by every ray reaching it from all points on the object, the lens would not be able to distinguish different colors coming from different parts of the object. To overcome this difficulty Alhazen introduced the hypothesis that only the rays that struck the lens perpendicularly and without being weakened by refraction stimulated it fully. This made it necessary for him to suppose further that in the optical system of the eye the center of curvature of the cornea, of the aqueous humor and of the front surface of the lens all coincided at the center of the eyeball.

A second difficulty shows even more clearly how Alhazen's thinking was put on the wrong track by his attempt to make the mechanism by which the image is formed explain immediately how we see. He agreed with Galen that vision was not completed in the lens but that "the act of vision is accomplished in such a way that the visual image received by the crystalline lens passes through to the optic nerve." He also described an experiment with a camera obscura in which when a number of candles were set up outside "an opening leading into a dark place, with an opaque wall or body opposite the opening, the images of these candles appear on the body or wall, each distinctly."

Alhazen used this experiment simply to show that the images all passed in straight lines through the same hole unaffected by one another; this, he said, "is to be understood for all transparent bodies, including the transparent parts of the eye." His difficulty was that he knew that in an optical system such as the eye the image would be inverted unless some refraction occurred. "The image cannot proceed from the surface of the crystalline lens to the hollow [optic] nerve along straight lines," he wrote, "and still preserve the proper order of its parts. For all the lines intersect at the center of the eye, and if they continued straight on, their order of position beyond the center would be reversed: What is right would become left and vice versa, what is up would be down, and down up." So in order to preserve the erect image that he thought was necessary for the eye to cause us to see as we do, he supposed that the rays would be refracted at the back surface of the lens in such a way that they did not intersect. The two erect images formed at corresponding points in each of the eyes then united at the junction of the two optic nerves to form a single image that was conveyed by the "visual spirit" sent out from the brain to the "ultimate seat of sensation" in the cerebral cavity, the location of the "common sensory."

It was a stroke of genius for Alhazen to impose geometrical optics on anatomy. His difficulties arose because he was not resolute enough. Plainly it was a change of concept that gave Kepler success where Alhazen and several later investigators fell short. Kepler's new concept was based on a complete willingness to exploit the mechanistic hypothesis.

Several brilliant attempts to explain vision failed for want of complete commitment to the mechanistic approach. Alhazen was unable to see in the camera obscura a model for the formation of the image in the eye. Leonardo da Vinci compared the eye to a camera obscura and introduced what could be called an engineering approach to the problem of vision with a proposal to investigate it by means of models using glass balls, but like Alhazen and for the same reason he found it necessary to arrange the optics to suit the demand for an erect image [*see bottom illustration on opposite page*]. Giambattista della Porta made the same error, but it was he who gave Kepler the idea that the eye is a camera obscura. Felix Plater, who in 1583 put forward the fundamental idea that the retina and not the lens is the sensitive organ of vision and who published a greatly improved eye anatomy to which Kepler referred, drew from Kepler the comment: "Compare the true mechanism of vision as given by me with that given by Plater, and you will see that this famous man is no farther from the truth than is consonant with being a medical man who has not studied mathematics."

All the necessary knowledge was available before Kepler. He succeeded by seeing the problem in a new way. A year after the publication in 1604 of *Ad Vitellionem Paralipomena,* in which he gave his explanation, Kepler wrote of his cosmology: "My goal is to show that the heavenly machine is not a kind of divine living being but similar to a clockwork." His strategic judgment about vision, in keeping with this cosmological judgment, was to restrict the problem in the first place to discovering how the eye operates as an optical instrument like any other.

He solved this purely optical problem by showing that the formation of the image in the eye must be analyzed geometrically not as a cone of rays extending from a base on the object to a vertex in the eye but in terms of a multitude of cones coming from vertexes at every point on the object to a common base on the lens [*see illustration on next page*]. The physical process of seeing he described as follows: "Vision is brought about by a picture of the thing seen being formed on the white concave surface of the retina. That which is to the right outside is depicted on the left on the retina, that to the left on the right, that above below, and that below above.... Green is depicted green, and in general things are depicted by whatever color they have."

Kepler went a significant step further: he recognized that a physical description of the eye's operation carried the explanation of vision only part of the way, and that there were other questions the mechanistic approach could not answer. The psychophysiological question of how the physical processes of the eye effect sensations lay outside his mathematical solution. "I leave it," he said, "to natural philosophers."

By asking questions that were answerable because they involved physical and mathematical analysis rather than philosophical speculation, Kepler opened the way to the solution of further problems of vision by purely physiological methods. Soon his own analysis of vision was amplified by others. Christoph Scheiner observed the formation of images on retinas by removing the

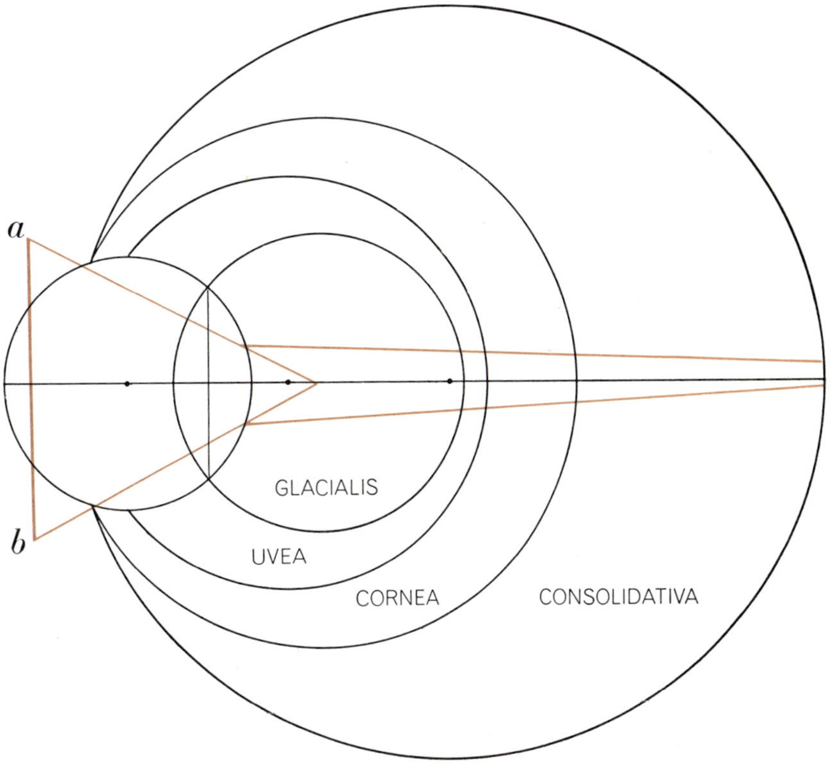

GEOMETRICAL MODEL OF EYE shows curvatures of refracting media according to Alhazen's theory of vision. A visual pyramid (*color*) had the object sighted (*a-b*) as its base; its apex was the center of the eye, which also was the center of curvature of the cornea, the *glacialis,* or lens, and the aqueous humor. Alhazen said that rays from the object struck forward surface of lens perpendicularly, so undergoing no refraction, but at rear of lens were refracted away from center of eye, thus keeping image erect. Dots show, from left, centers of curvature of vitreous humor; uvea, or choroid, and *consolidativa,* or sclera.

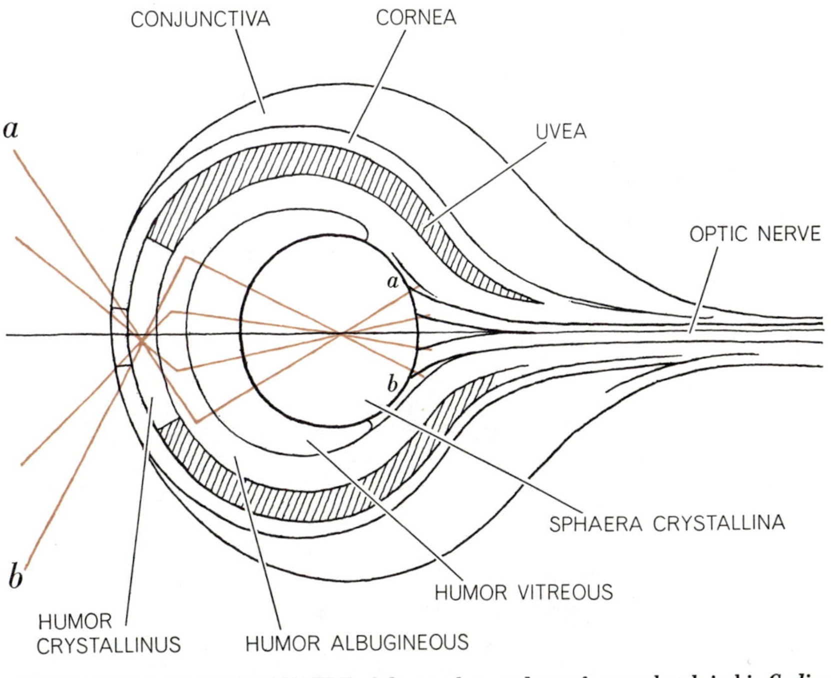

LEONARDO DA VINCI'S CONCEPT of the eye, here redrawn from a sketch in his *Codice Atlantico* with legends supplied from other passages, also arranged the physics of vision to preserve an erect image. Rays from an object sighted were, according to his theory, refracted by the *humor albugineous,* or aqueous humor, and then refracted again in the *sphaera crystallina,* or lens. Therefore they appeared upright on back of lens, as with rays *a* and *b*. Da Vinci, like other early investigators, thought lens was the sensitive organ.

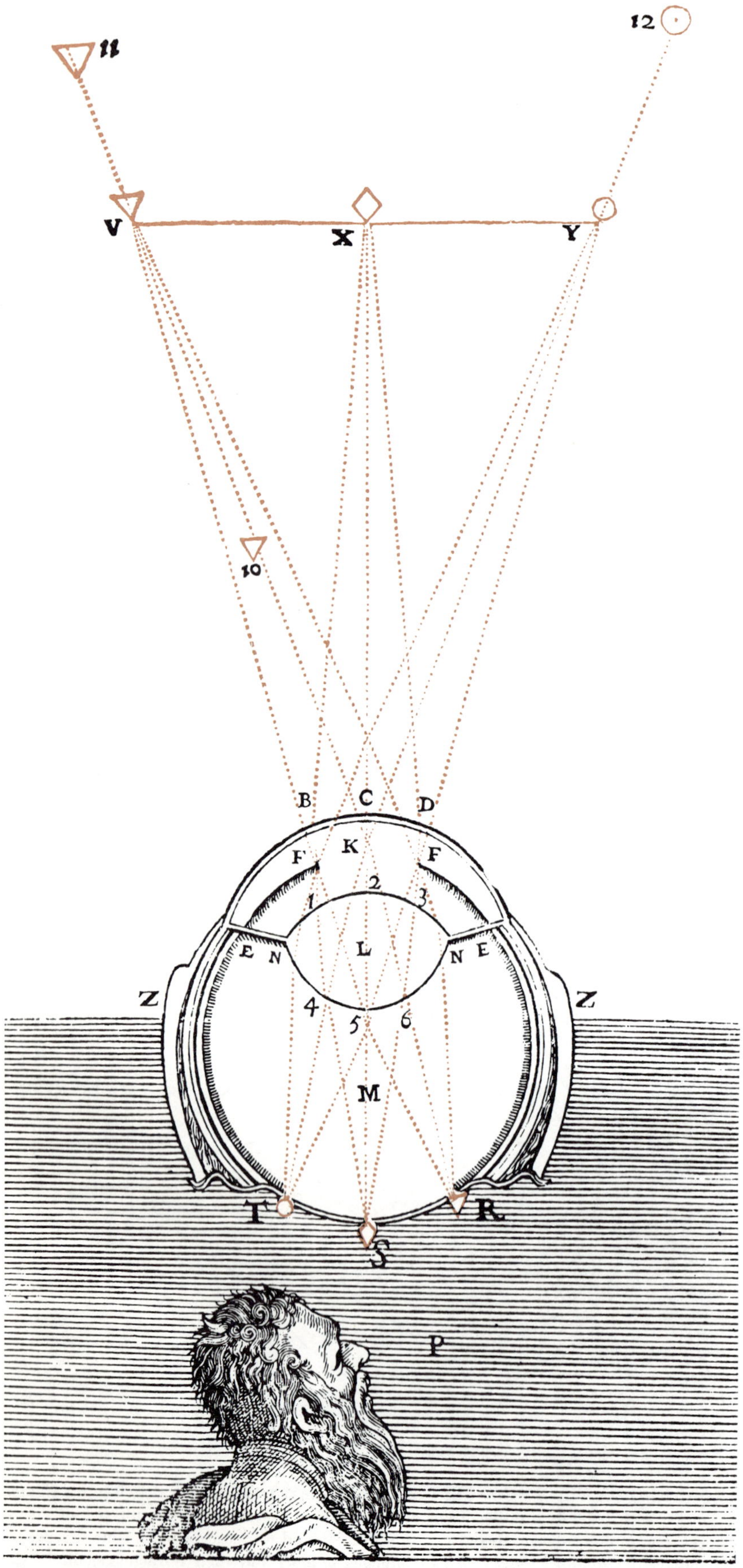

OPTICAL GEOMETRY according to Johannes Kepler explained the inverted image. This illustration of Kepler's optics is from René Descartes's *La Dioptrique*. The man looking at a retina in a camera obscura sees an inverted image (*RST*) of the sighted object (*VXY*).

backs from the eyes of men and oxen shortly after death. Descartes corrected Kepler's optical analysis by using the newly discovered sine law of refraction and treating the lens in its actual flattened shape rather than as the sphere Kepler had described; he also attributed visual accommodation to changes in the shape and not in the position of the lens. By the end of the century the work of Christian Huygens, Isaac Newton and many others had established physiological optics as a discipline in which investigators were confident of how to proceed.

The study of hearing was at a considerable disadvantage compared with that of vision because of the primitive state of acoustics. The anatomists who began the investigation anew in the 16th century had at their disposal only an elementary, qualitative theory of sound and of hearing inherited from Greek and medieval sources; it in no way compared with the well-developed discipline of geometrical optics. Even so, here again the mechanistic program, once grasped and reinforced by the successful model presented by the inquiry into the mechanism of vision, offered a clear definition of problems for study. These involved three kinds of investigation: into the anatomy of the ear and its neural connections with the brain, into the physics of sound and into the problem of relating the results of these investigations in a theory of the auditory mechanism.

Anatomical research, beginning in Italy in the early 16th century not far from where Galen had left off, had by the early 17th century clarified and in large part discovered the principal elements of the auditory mechanism [*see top illustration on page 13*]. Full descriptions were eventually published by Thomas Willis in 1672 and by Joseph Guichard Duverney in 1683.

According to the theory of hearing inherited by these anatomists from ancient and medieval sources, a sounding body transmitted its motion to the contiguous air, which in turn propagated the motion to the ear, where the beating of the external air on the drum produced a corresponding motion of the "internal air" enclosed in the ear. As anatomical knowledge progressed, discussion centered on the identification of the organ sensitive to sound and the mode of operation of the other parts believed to modulate and transmit the pulses received from the external air and to present what the Dutch anatomist Volcher Coiter called "the image of the sound"

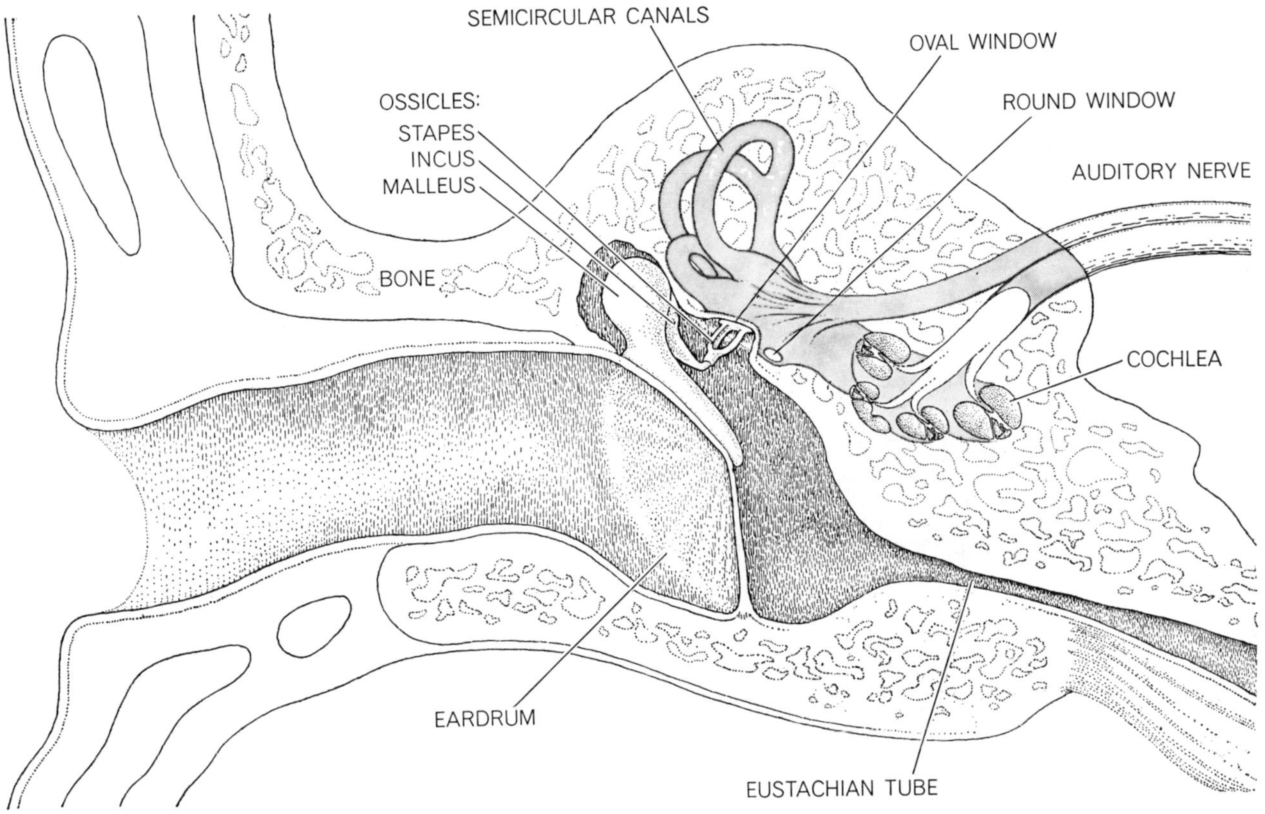

ANATOMY OF EAR as now known is presented for comparison with the ideas put forward by ancient, medieval and renaissance students of hearing. Vibrations of sound produce vibrations of the eardrum, which are transmitted by the small, articulated bones of the ossicles to the oval window at the base of the cochlea. Vibrations of the fluid in the cochlea are converted into nerve impulses.

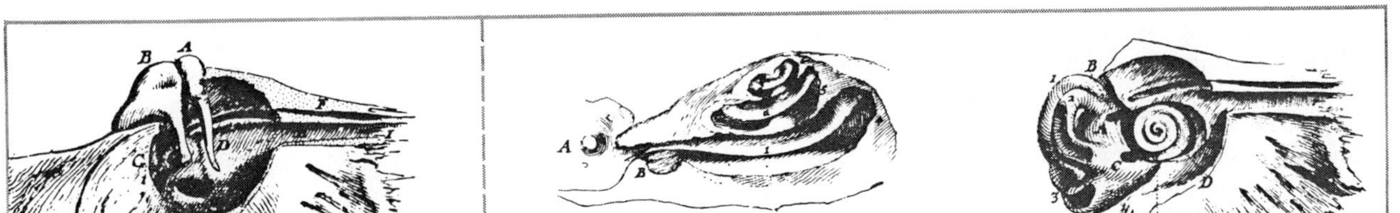

17TH-CENTURY CONCEPT of the ear is shown in illustrations from Joseph Duverney's *Traité de l'organe de l'ouïe*, published in 1683. At left are structures of the tympanic cavity, or middle ear, including the bones of the ossicles. At right are inner-ear structures, including at top right cochlea and semicircular canals. Other drawings show details of inner ear. Some of the structures are enlarged.

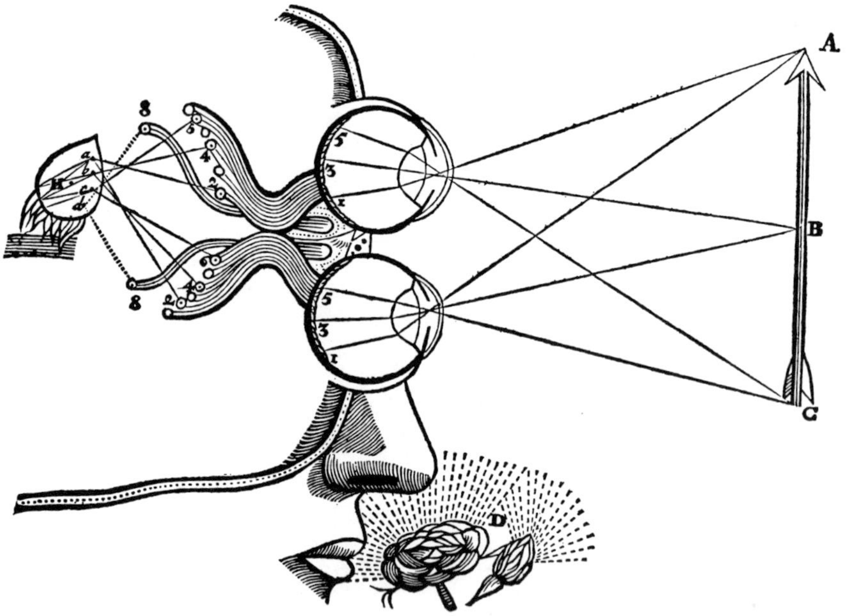

COORDINATION OF SENSES in Descartes's view was a wholly mechanistic and neurological process. In this illustration, from his *L'Homme*, the visual stimulus going from the arrow to the coordinating pineal gland (*H*) prevents attention to the smell of the flower.

to the sensitive organ for transmission to the "common sensory" in the brain. These different parts were thought to correspond to analogous parts in the eye. After a succession of opinions, beginning with the ancient view that the sensitive organ was the "internal air" itself and followed by the view that it must be the termination of the auditory nerve corresponding to the expansion of the optic nerve into the retina, Willis finally argued in his *De Anima Brutorum* in 1672 that the proper organ was the membranous spiral lamina of the cochlea. Along the length of the spiral the auditory nerve terminated in slender threads, so that here "the audible Species may be impressed on the Fibers and the ends of the sensible Nerves, inserted in this place, not at once or at large, but by little and little, and as it were in a just proportion and dimension." Hence it was here that "the proper Sensory of Hearing ought to be placed; for there is the sense, where the Nerve receiving the Idea of Sensation, is implanted." Willis could not, however, explain how the sensitive organ worked.

Similarly, opinion remained uncertain and unclear about the function of the middle-ear ossicle system in transmitting the drum's motion, in spite of comparisons made between the control of the tension of the drum by the ossicles and the tension exerted by the muscles in the eye in focusing or in altering the size of the pupil.

For many years the more critical investigators had been well aware of how little they understood the functions of the structures they were discovering. The essential requirements were recognized in the 17th century by Marin Mersenne: first, the combining of anatomy with the quantitative study of the physics of sound, and then the separation of the physiological problem of the mechanism of the sense organ from the psychological and philosophical problems arising from sensation and perception. Mersenne undertook studies of the speed of sound, the correlation of pitch with the frequency of vibration of strings, consonance and dissonance, and harmonic induction. Some years later, in 1677, Claude Perrault undertook a program of research in the Académie Royale des Sciences in Paris "to examine to the bottom everything concerned with the sense of hearing." The program was carried out with remarkable scientific sophistication by a group of physicists and anatomists who made intelligent use of the comparative method. With Duverney, aided by the physicist Edmé Mariotte, it yielded what Willis had been unable to provide: a theory based on an exact acoustical law (the law of harmonic induction) explaining how sound is received by the sensitive organ. With his elegant *Traité de l'organe de l'ouïe* in 1683 Duverney became, as far as was technically possible, the Kepler of hearing.

Duverney based his theory on a model: the vibrations induced in specific strings of a lute when those of a neighboring lute are plucked. Because the sound transmitted from one lute to another through a solid table is louder than it is when it is transmitted through the air, he argued that the ossicles, and not the air enclosed in the middle ear, played the major role in transmitting the vibrations of the drum to the oval window and so to the "implanted air" that he thought filled the labyrinth of the inner ear. On the grounds of its anatomy and neural connections he argued, as had Willis, that the membranous spiral lamina was the sensitive organ that responded to the vibrations transmitted to the "implanted air." Dividing the cochlea longitudinally into two separate spirals connected respectively with the oval window and the round window, he said that "this lamina is not only capable of receiving the vibrations of the [implanted] air, but its structure must make us think that it can respond to all their different characteristics." He thought it might respond to the lower notes at the wider bottom end and to higher notes as it narrowed upward. In this he was anticipating Hermann von Helmholtz' 19th-century resonance theory of hearing, which is now generally accepted.

By contemporary criteria of certification, however, Duverney himself recognized that his theory could not then be firmly established inside testable scientific knowledge; he presented it simply as a "conjecture" that he hoped was "credible." This of course it remained, even in the new form given to it when Domenico Cotugno showed in 1760 that the labyrinth including the cochlea was filled with fluid and not with air, until eventually technical scientific advances allowed Helmholtz to bring it within range of testability.

I turn now to the second part of my thesis: that by first successfully restricting the inquiry to specifically limited problems, the mechanistic hypothesis made it possible in the 17th century to recognize systematically the three different kinds of question involved in the phenomena of the "animate and sensitive body." The distinguishing of these kinds of question came about largely through the inquiries of Descartes into the coordination of sensory information and behavior.

Kepler in his *Paralipomena,* as already mentioned, explicitly put aside the problem of how vision is effected by the body's sensory organs. In his later *Dioptrice,* however, he attempted once more to deal with the problem traditionally. He offered an account of the causation of sensation by means of a "representative image," which was simply a more mechanistic version of the ancient theory already used by Alhazen. Kepler wrote: "To see is to feel the stimulation of the retina, however it is stimulated. The retina is painted with the colored rays of visible things.... But this picture does not complete the act of vision until the image so received by the retina passes through the continuity of the spirits to the brain, and is there delivered to the threshold of the faculty of the soul." He suggested that the image might be transmitted from the eye to the "common sensory" in the brain through the visual spirit in the optic nerve as a wave is transmitted across water.

One of the great contributions made by Descartes, and by Mersenne, was that they clarified this problem by using a "representative image" that they kept rigorously mechanical. Thereby they were able to show that the traditional formulation of vision confused two quite different questions.

They began by distinguishing the case of animals from that of men. Kepler had treated the living eye as a dead optical instrument; Descartes in his *Traité de l'homme* and Mersenne in his *Harmonie universelle* extended this concept physiologically by treating the whole living animal body as a dead machine. Ruthlessly they allowed only one kind of question: What physical motions follow each preceding physical motion? They asserted that when the motion of light or sound impresses a physical image on the eye or ear, this is transmitted through a physical "animal spirit" to the brain, and that eventually through the physical structure of the neuromuscular system a physical response takes place—coordinated with other built-in responses.

In this approach the study of animal behavior was therefore the study of the coordination of physical states without sensation. As Mersenne put it: "Animals have no knowledge of these sounds, but only a representation, without knowing whether what they apprehend is a sound or a color or something else; so one can say that they do not act so much as are acted upon, and that objects make an impression upon their senses from which their action necessarily follows, as the wheels of a clock necessarily follow the weight or spring which drives them."

The crucial point about this approach is the argument that Descartes and Mersenne derived from it. The argument was that in this "animal machine" science had to deal only with purely physiological questions, separate from all psychological questions about sensation. They recognized that physiology faced a scientific and technical frontier. Thereafter advances in knowledge of sensory physiology were restricted only by scientific and technical limitations. It was these that prevented real advances in the understanding of what happens behind the retina and the cochlea until the 19th century. Then progress became possible because of progress in physical optics and acoustics—in histology with the improved achromatic microscope and new chemical stains, and in electrophysiology with the work of Johannes Müller's pupils in Berlin, above all that of Helmholtz.

Having clarified this physiological frontier in the study of the animal body, Descartes then had no difficulty arguing that the question of how sensations are caused in men was a different kind of question encountering a different kind of frontier. He argued in *La Dioptrique* that an account of the "representative image" type did not touch the central problem (recognized clearly since Plato's time) of passing from a physical motion or image, produced by external stimuli in the sensory mechanisms, to a sensation in the sentient being. Discussing how he had removed the backs of the eyes of newly dead men or animals and placed a piece of paper or eggshell over the opening in order to watch the images produced on the retina, he went on to say: "While this picture, in thus passing into our head, always retains some degree of resemblance to the objects from which it proceeds, yet we need not think ... that it is by means of

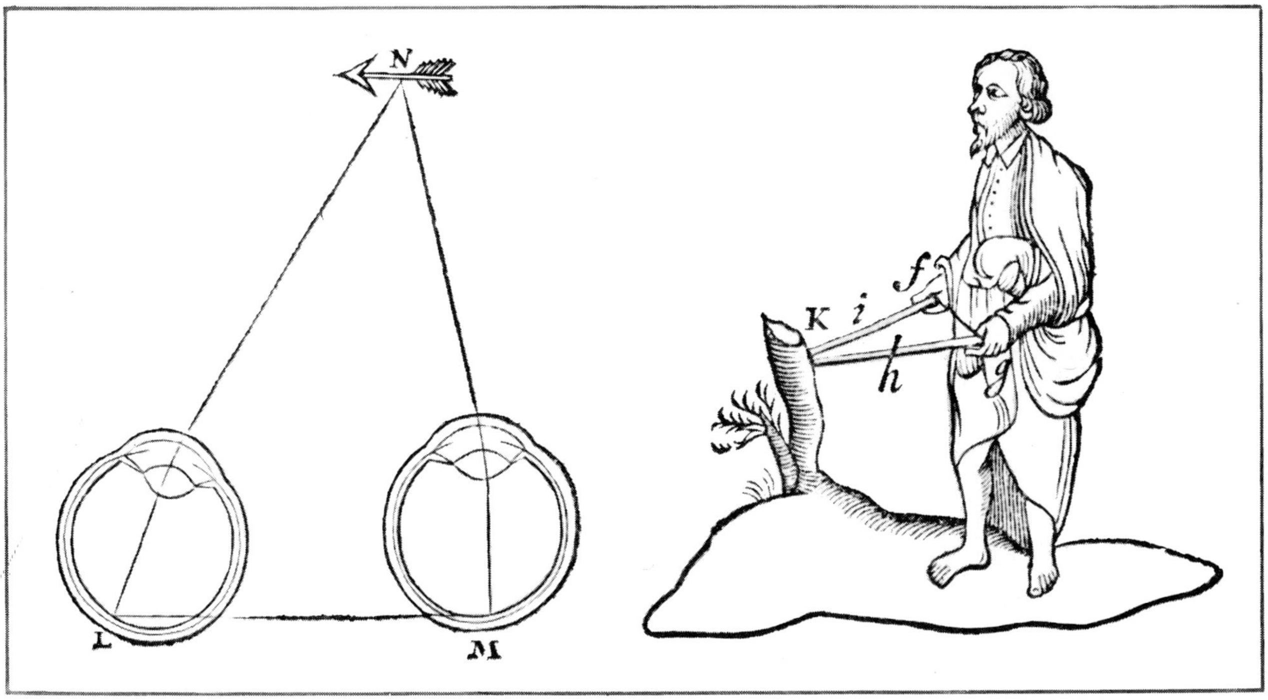

PERCEPTION OF DISTANCE according to Descartes is illustrated by these drawings from his *L'Homme*, published in 1664. He thought the mind perceived distance by means of the angle formed by the axes of the eyes in the sighting of an object (*left*), just as a blind man could calculate the distance to an object by the angle, or the separation, between two sticks of known lengths (*right*).

this resemblance that the picture makes us perceive the objects...: Rather we must hold that the movements that go to form the picture, acting immediately on our soul inasmuch as it is united to our body, are so ordained by nature as to give it such sensations."

Thus Descartes's main argument against the "representative image" theory was that it was irrelevant because it took the physiological image as being the object instead of the means of sensing. He behaved then as though he recognized that the question of how physiological motions cause sensations belonged to a type to be explicitly classified by John Locke as in principle unanswerable because it concerns relations between different categories of subject. Descartes simply avoided the frontier Kepler had attempted to cross from motions to sensations: a philosophical frontier of knowledge established by what cannot be known. Instead he directed his attack wholly against a quite different frontier, reached by asking a different, answerable question: What physical and physiological clues determine different sensations? He pointed out that even in vision the image was not a strict representation of the object but more like a two-dimensional engraving that could suggest with a few strokes many different qualities, including not strictly visual ones; still less was the image strictly representative in the other senses. So, he wrote, "the only question we need raise is that of knowing how the images can supply to the soul the means of sensing all the diverse qualities of the objects to which they stand related."

The contribution I claim for Descartes and his stronger successors is, then, that they were able by their use of the mechanistic hypothesis to separate explicitly the answerable questions of physiology and of psychophysiological correlation from the unanswerable questions about the causation of perception that they had inherited from ancient and medieval sources. The mechanistic hypothesis in its brutal Cartesian form brought the exact lines of the scientific frontier of potentially testable propositions out into the open and so offered a clear view of what to do next to extend the area of scientific knowledge. The pushing back of this frontier by the direct study of living things led in turn to the recognition of the diversity of the answerable questions to be discovered in the subject matter of the "animate and sensitive body."

2

INFORMATION AND MEMORY

GEORGE A. MILLER

August 1956

Some things are easy to remember. A short poem is easier to memorize than a long one; an interesting story is better recalled than a dull one. But brevity and wit are not all that is involved. Equally important is the way things fit together. If a new task meshes well with what we have previously learned, our earlier learning can be transferred with profit to the novel situation. If not, the task is much harder to master.

Imagine that you are teaching geometry to children. You have covered the business of calculating the length of the hypotenuse of a right-angled triangle when the base and the altitude are given. Now you are about to take up the problem of finding the *area* of a right triangle when the base and the hypotenuse are given. Suppose you were given your choice of the following two methods of teaching the children to solve the problem. In method A you would help them to discover that the area of a right triangle is half that of a rectangle with the same base and altitude, that the unknown altitude of the triangle in this case can be calculated from the given base and hypotenuse by use of the Pythagorean theorem, and that the area of the triangle can therefore be found by deriving the altitude, computing the area of the rectangle and then taking half of that. In method B you would simply tell the class to memorize six steps: (1) add the length of the base to the length of the hypotenuse; (2) subtract the length of the base from the length of the hypotenuse; (3) multiply the first result by the second; (4) extract the square root of this product; (5) multiply the positive root by the length of the base; (6) divide this product by 2.

Which method of teaching would you choose? Probably no one but an experimental psychologist would ever consider method B. Method A is productive and insightful; method B is stupid and ugly.

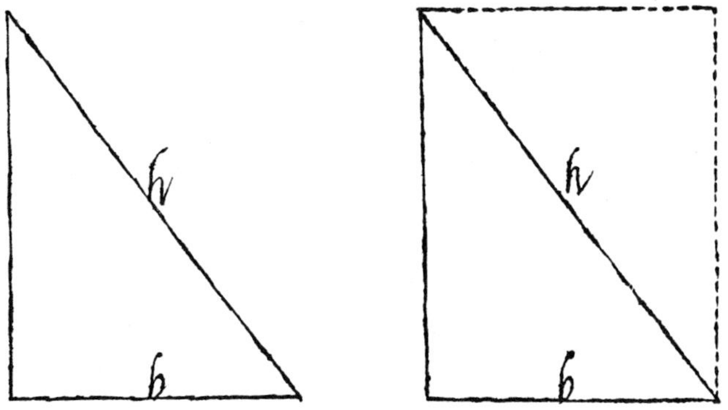

TWO METHODS may be used to teach children how to find the area of a right-angled triangle. The method associated with the triangle at left has the following algebraic steps: (1) $h + b = v$, (2) $h - b = w$, (3) $v \times w = x$, (4) $\sqrt{x} = \pm y$, (5) $+ y \times b = z$, (6) $z/2 =$ area. The method associated with the triangle at right proceeds: (1) find altitude by the Pythagorean theorem, (2) find area of rectangle from base and altitude, (3) area of triangle is half the area of rectangle. The first method is considered ugly and the second efficient. Why?

But just why do we find method B repulsive? What is repugnant about a procedure that is logically impeccable and that leads always to the correct answer? This question is raised by the psychologist Max Wertheimer in his provocative little book, *Productive Thinking*. An obvious answer is that a child taught by method A will understand better what he is doing. But until we can say what it means to understand what one is doing, or what profit there is in such understanding, we have not really answered Wertheimer's question.

It is helpful to consider the interesting fact that method B is the procedure we would use to instruct a computing machine of the present-day type. The machine is able to perform arithmetical operations such as addition, subtraction, multiplication, division and the extraction of roots. Instruction for the machine consists in writing a "program"—like the series of steps used in method B except that the computer's program must be even more explicit and detailed, with even less hint of the basic strategy. Computing machine engineers have their hearts set on some day designing machines which will construct programs for themselves: that is, given the strategy for handling a problem, the machine will understand the problem well enough to create all the appropriate operations or subroutines required to solve it. The desirability of such a development is obvious. In the first place, at present it takes many hours of drudgery to write the detailed instructions for all the steps a computer must take. Then, after the instructions have been written, they must be stored in the machine in some easily accessible form. In a large machine the number of subroutines may run into the thousands; it might actually

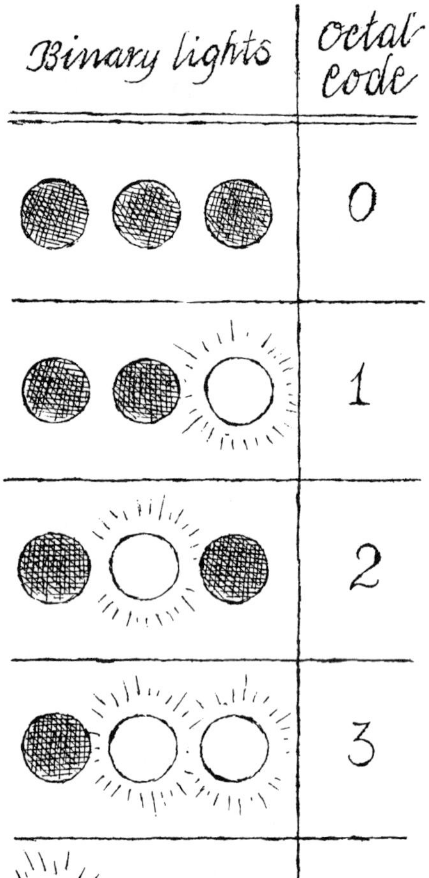

COMPUTER LIGHTS are quickly read by engineers using the code illustrated here.

be more economical to equip the machine with the ability to create them on demand rather than to build the necessary storage and access machinery. In other words, in a very elaborate computer it would be more efficient to store rules from which subroutines could be generated than to store the routines themselves.

It seems, therefore, that even the computing machine realizes that method B is ugly. Each subroutine is an isolated operation that must be stored in its proper place, and no attempt is made to tie these steps to other information available to the machine. So we can see that one superiority of method A lies in the fact that it makes more efficient use of the capacity for storing information. In the teaching of geometry to a child, method A highlights the relations of the new problem to things that the child has already learned, and thus it provides the rules by which the child can write his own subroutines for computation. In essence the ugly method is less efficient because it requires the child to master more new information.

The intimate relation between memory and the ability to reason is demonstrated every time we fail to solve a problem because we fail to recall the necessary information. Since our capacity to remember limits our intelligence, we should try to organize material to make the most efficient use of the memory available to us. We cannot think simultaneously about everything we know. When we attempt to pursue a long argument, it is difficult to hold each step in mind as we proceed to the next, and we are apt to lose our way in the sheer mass of detail. Three hundred years ago René Descartes, in an unfinished treatise called *Rules for the Direction of the Mind*, wrote:

"If I have first found out by separate mental operations what the relation is between the magnitudes A and B, then that between B and C, between C and D, and finally between D and E, that does not entail my seeing what the relation is between A and E, nor can the truths previously learned give me a precise knowledge of it unless I recall them all. To remedy this I would run them over from time to time, keeping the imagination moving continuously in such a way that while it is intuitively perceiving each fact it simultaneously passes on to the next; and this I would do until I had learned to pass from the first to the last so quickly, that no stage in the process was left to the care of memory, but I seemed to have the whole in intuition before me at the same time. This method will relieve the memory, diminish the sluggishness of our thinking, and definitely enlarge our mental capacity."

Descartes's observation is familiar to anyone who has ever memorized a poem or a speech, or mastered a mathematical proof. Rehearsal or repetition has the very important effect of organizing many separate items into a single unit, thus reducing the load our memory must carry and leaving us free for further thinking. In terms of logic, the process is like the substitution of a single symbol for a longer expression which would be clumsy to write each time we wanted to use it.

The practical advantages of this unitizing process were vividly illustrated for me the first time I saw one of those digital computing machines that have small neon lights to show which relays are closed. There were 20 lights in a row, and I did not see how the men who ran the machine could grasp and remember a pattern involving so many elements. I quickly discovered that they did not try to deal with each light as an individual item of information. Instead, they translated the light pattern into a code. That is to say, they grouped the lights into successive triplets and gave each possible triplet pattern a number as its name, or symbol. The pattern all three lights off (000) was called 0; the pattern off-off-on (001) was called 1; off-on-off (010) was called 2, and so forth. Having memorized this simple translation, the engineers were able to look at a long string of lights such as 011000101001111 and break it down into triplets (011 000 101 001 111) which they immediately translated into 30517. It was much easier to remember these five digits than the string of 15 lit and unlit lights.

Reorganization enabled the engineers to reduce the original complexity to something easily apprehended and remembered without changing or discarding any of the original data. There is an analogy between this simple trick and the process described by Descartes. Each step in a complex argument is like a single light in the binary sequence. Rehearsal organizes the steps into larger units similar to the engineers' triplets. Repeated rehearsal patterns the long argument into larger and larger units which are then replaced in thought by simpler symbols.

The first person to propose an experimental test of the span of a man's instantaneous grasp seems to have been Sir William Hamilton, a 19th-century Scottish metaphysician. He wrote: "If you throw a handful of marbles on the floor, you will find it difficult to view at once more than six, or seven at most, without confusion." It is not clear whether Hamilton himself actually threw marbles on the floor, for he remarked that the experiment could be performed also by an act of imagination, but at least one reader took him literally. In 1871 the English economist and logician William Stanley Jevons reported that when he threw beans into a box, he never made a mistake when there were three or four, was sometimes wrong if the number was five, was right about half the time if the beans numbered 10 and was usually wrong when the number reached 15. Hamilton's experiment has been repeated many times with better instrumentation and control, but refined techniques serve only to confirm his original intuition. We are able to perceive up to about six dots accurately without counting; beyond this errors become frequent.

But estimating the number of beans or dots is a perceptual task, not necessarily related to concepts or thinking. Each step in the development of an argument is a particular thing with its own structure, different from the other steps and quite different from one anonymous bean in Jevons's box. A better test of "apprehension" would be the ability to remember various symbols in a given sequence. Another Englishman, Joseph Jacobs, first performed this experiment with digits in 1887. He would read aloud a haphazard sequence of numbers and ask his listeners to write down the sequence from memory after he finished. The maximum number of digits a normal adult could repeat without error was about seven or eight.

From the first it was obvious that this span of immediate memory was intimately related to general intelligence. Jacobs reported that the span increased between the ages of 8 and 19, and his test was later incorporated by Alfred Binet, and is still used, in the Binet intelligence test. It is valuable principally because an unusually short span is a reliable indicator of mental deficiency; a long span does not necessarily mean high intelligence.

A person who can grasp eight decimal digits can usually manage about seven letters of the alphabet or six monosyllabic words (taken at random, of course). Now the interesting point about this is that six words contain much more information, as defined by information theory, than do seven letters or eight digits. We are therefore in a position analogous to carrying a purse which will hold no more than seven coins—whether pennies or dollars. Obviously we will carry more wealth if we fill the purse with silver dollars rather than pennies. Similarly we can use our memory span most efficiently by stocking it with informationally rich symbols such as words, or perhaps images, rather than with poor coin such as digits.

The mathematical theory of communication developed by Norbert Wiener and Claude Shannon provides a precise measure of the amount of information carried. In the situation we are considering, the amount of information per item is simply the logarithm (to the base two) of the number of possible choices. Thus the information carried by a binary digit, where there are two alternatives, is $\log_2 2 = 1$ bit. In the case of decimal digits the amount of information per digit is $\log_2 10 = 3.32$ bits. Each letter of the alphabet carries $\log_2 26 = 4.70$ bits of information. When we come to make the calculation for words, we must take into account the size of the dictionary from which the words were drawn. There are perhaps 1,000 common monosyllables in English, so a rough estimate of the informational value of a monosyllabic word selected at random might be about 10 bits.

A person who can repeat nine binary digits can usually repeat five words. The informational value of the nine binary digits is nine bits; of the five words, about 50 bits. Thus the Wiener-Shannon measure gives us a quantitative indication of how much we can improve the efficiency of memory by using informationally rich units. The computer engineers who group the relay lights by threes and translate the triplets into a code can remember almost three times as much information as they would otherwise.

It is impressive to watch a trained person look at 40 consecutive binary digits, presented at the rate of one each second, and then immediately repeat the sequence without error. Such feats are called "mnemonic tricks"—a name that reveals the suspicious nature of psychologists. The idea that trickery is involved, that there is something bogus about it, has discouraged serious study of the psychological principles underlying such phenomena. Actually some of the best "memory crutches" we have are called laws of nature. As for the common criticism that artificial memory crutches are quickly forgotten, it seems to be largely a question of whether we have used a stupid crutch or a smart one.

When I was a boy I had a teacher who told us that memory crutches were only

SIR WILLIAM HAMILTON, a 19th-century Scottish philosopher (not to be confused with Sir William Rowan Hamilton, the mathematician), observed: "If you throw . . . marbles on the floor, you will find it difficult to view at once more than six . . . without confusion."

Binary (1 bit)	Decimal (3.3 bits)	Alphabetic (4.7 bits)	Syllabic (10 bits)
110100	4972	XJR	for, line
0100110	86515	AYCZ	nice, it, act
10010011	021942	EDLYG	time, who, to, air
101100010	3776380	QJPEVJ	by, west, cent, or, law
0010101110	28201394	DLXBAHC	boy, sea, ten, red, ask, mob
11010001011	918374512	HOKOMSFB	go, how, ice, save, hat, sue, way
101001110110	1038204665	FQGUJRZVM	odd, gas, call, at, ant, pay, get, was
0001010111011	57048621937	DNKSNWJUWT	by, game, log, free, so, you, car, big, why

SPAN OF IMMEDIATE MEMORY depends mainly on the number of items to be memorized and is relatively independent of the amount of information per item. In this table the amount of information is measured in "bits," or binary digits. A binary digit can be 1 or 0, and hence conveys a minimum amount of information. A person who can repeat nine binary digits can usually memorize seven decimal digits, six letters or five words (*row above broken line*). The other rows compare the span for other groups of items.

one grade better than cheating, and that we would never understand anything properly if we resorted to such underhanded tricks. She didn't stop us, of course, but she did make us conceal our method of learning. Our teacher, if her conscience had permitted it, no doubt could have shown us far more efficient systems than we were able to devise for ourselves. Another teacher who told me that the ordinate was vertical because my mouth went that way when I said it and that the abscissa was horizontal for the same reason saved me endless confusion, as did one who taught me to remember the number of days in each month by counting on my knuckles.

The course of our argument seems to lead to the conclusion that method A is superior to the ugly method B because it uses better mnemonic devices to represent exactly the same information. In method A the six apparently arbitrary steps of method B are organized around three aspects of the total problem so that each aspect can be represented by symbols which the student has already learned. The process is not essentially different from the engineers' method for recoding a sequence of binary lights.

It is conceivable that all complex, symbolic learning proceeds in this way. The material is first organized into parts which, once they cohere, can be replaced by other symbols—abbreviations, initial letters, schematic images, names, or what have you—and eventually the whole scope of the argument is translated into a few symbols which can all be grasped at one time. In order to test this hypothesis we must look beyond experiments on the span of immediate memory.

Our question is: Does the amount of information per item (*i.e.*, the number of possible alternative choices per item) affect the number of items we can remember when there is a large amount of material to be mastered? For example, is it more difficult to memorize a random sequence of 100 monosyllabic words than 100 digits or 100 letters of the alphabet? The question is important because it has a bearing on how we can organize material most efficiently for learning.

In an exploratory study that S. L. Smith and I devised at the Harvard University Psychological Laboratories, the subjects were required to memorize three different kinds of lists of randomly chosen items. One list was constructed from a set of 32 alternatives (all the alphabet except Q plus the numerals 3, 4, 5, 6, 7, 8 and 9), another from a set of eight alternatives, and the third from just two alternatives. The subject read a test list at the rate of one item every second and then had to write down as much of the list as he could remember in the correct order. The lists ran to 10, 20, 30 or 50 items. If the subject failed to reproduce the list exactly, it was presented again. The number of presentations required before the first perfect reproduction measured the difficulty of the task.

We were not greatly surprised to find that the subjects did somewhat better (*i.e.*, needed about 20 per cent fewer trials) on the binary-choice lists than on the other types. After all, a run of, say, six zeros or six ones is easy to remember and therefore in effect shortens the list. But on the other two types of lists (eight alternatives and 32 alternatives) the subjects' performances were practically indistinguishable. In other words, it was just as easy to memorize a list containing a lot of information as one of the same length containing less information.

Very similar results have been obtained at the University of Wisconsin by W. J. Brogden and E. R. Schmidt, who did their experiments for other reasons and without knowledge of the hypothesis Smith and I were trying to test. They used verbal mazes with either 16 or 24 choice points and they varied the number of alternatives per choice point from two to 12. Here again the length of the list of points that had to be learned, and not the number of alternatives offered at each choice point, determined the difficulty of the test—with the same excep-

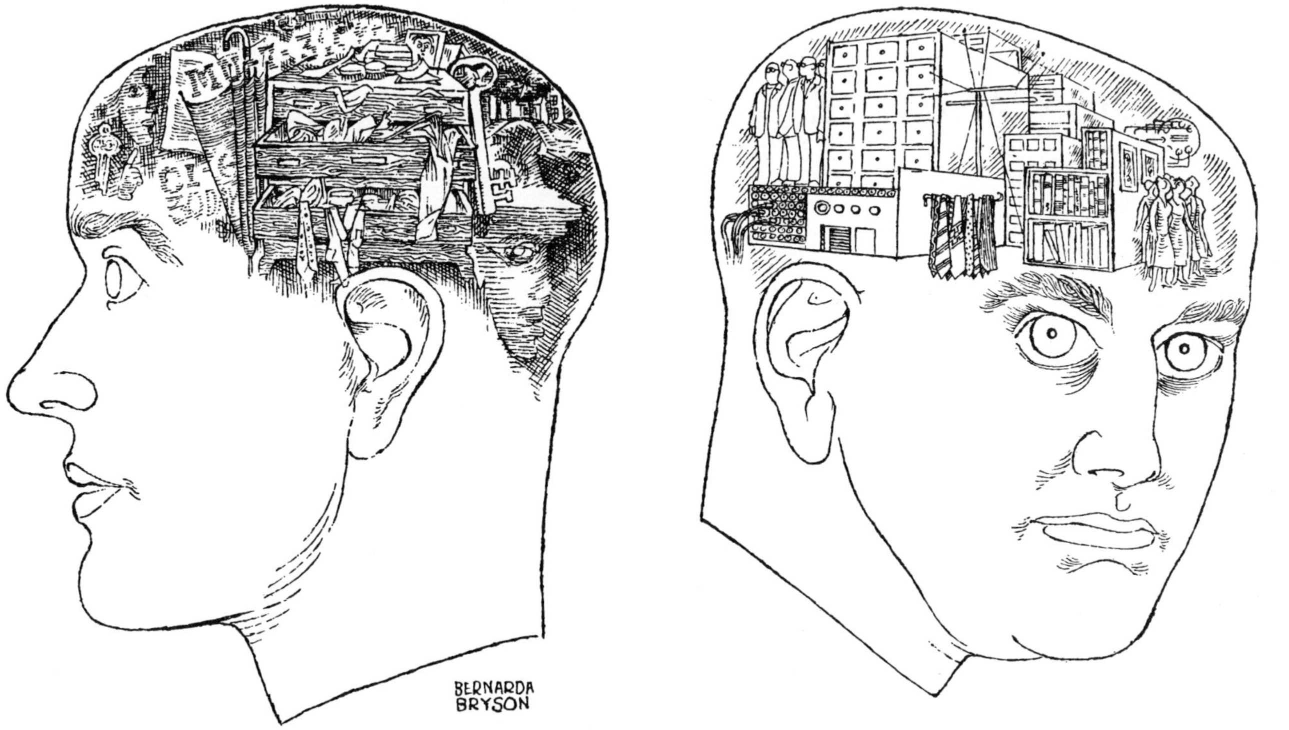

FANCIFUL HEADS were drawn by Bernarda Bryson to depict René Descartes's *Rules for the Direction of the Mind*, described in the text of the article. The individual at left has presumably not had the benefit of the rules, whereas the man at right has.

tion that we found, namely, that it was slightly easier to remember where only two choices were offered.

Tentatively, therefore, we are justified in assuming that our memories are limited by the number of units or symbols we must master, and not by the amount of information that these symbols represent. Thus it is helpful to organize material intelligently before we try to memorize it. The process of organization enables us to package the same total amount of information into far fewer symbols, and so eases the task of remembering.

How much unitizing and symbolizing must we do, and how can we decide what the units are? The science of linguistics may come to our aid here. Language has a hierarchical structure of units—sounds, words, phrases, sentences, narratives—and it is there that one should seek evidence for a similar hierarchy of cognitive units.

It has been estimated that English sentences are about 75 per cent redundant: that is, about four times as long as they would need to be if we used our alphabet with maximum efficiency. At first glance this fact seems paradoxical. If length is our major source of difficulty, why do we deliberately make our sentences longer than necessary? The paradox arises from a confusion about the definition of sentence length. Is a sentence 100 letters, or 25 words, or 6 phrases, or one proposition long? The fact that all our books contain 75 per cent more letters than necessary does not mean that 75 per cent of the ideas could be deleted. And it is those larger subjective units, loosely called ideas, that we must count to determine the psychological length of any text.

A sequence of 25 words in a sentence is easier to recall than a sequence of 25 words taken haphazardly from the dictionary. The sentence is easier because the words group themselves easily into familiar units. In terms of psychological units, a 25-word sentence is shorter than a sequence of 25 unrelated words. This means that the word is not the appropriate unit for measuring the psychological length of a sentence. Perhaps linguistic techniques for isolating larger units of verbal behavior will provide an objective basis for settling the question.

When we memorize a sentence, all our previous familiarity with the lexicon and grammar of the language comes to our aid. It is one of the clearest possible examples of the transfer of previous learning to a new task. And the transfer is profitable because it serves to reduce the effective length of the material to be remembered. By learning the language, we have already acquired automatic habits for unitizing those sequences that obey the rules of the language.

There are three stages in the unitizing process. All three were described in the 17th century by John Locke in his famous *Essay Concerning Human Understanding:* "Wherein the mind does these three things: first, it chooses a certain number [of specific ideas]; secondly, it gives them connexion, and makes them into one idea; thirdly, it ties them together by a name." Men form such complex ideas, Locke said, "for the convenience of communication," but the combination of ideas sometimes leads to confusion because it is "the workmanship of the mind, and not referred to the real existence of things." The development in the 20th century of a mathematical theory of communication enables us to see more clearly how this process serves the convenience of communication and, coupled with the fact that it is the length, not the variety of the material that limits our memories, gives us an important insight into the economics of cognitive organization.

Organizing and symbolizing are pervasive human activities. If we can learn to perform them more efficiently, perhaps we shall indeed be able, as Descartes promised, to "relieve the memory, diminish the sluggishness of our thinking, and definitely enlarge our mental capacity."

3

ATTENTION AND THE PERCEPTION OF SPEECH

DONALD E. BROADBENT

April 1962

Paying attention—and not paying attention—are surely two of the most important abilities of human beings. Yet in spite of their crucial role in learning, and in a host of other intelligent activities, psychologists for many years did not consider them proper topics of study. Attention seemed a subjective quality, associated historically with the introspective method of investigation. That method tends to give inconsistent results and so fell into disrepute among experimental psychologists. Correspondingly, most respectable theorists failed to make use of any concept resembling attention; and, since research in psychology tends to be dominated by theory, there was little experimentation along lines that might have revived the idea.

In the past 10 years, however, the concept of attention has begun to force itself on the attention of psychologists in various ways. One is through studies of the efficiency of control systems such as those concerned with the regulation of air traffic at airports. A major cause of failure in these systems is that the human operator has too much information to handle simultaneously, or that he reacts to an unimportant signal when he should be dealing with an important one. These problems require some understanding of phenomena that would commonly be described under the heading of "attention." There is now accumulating a wide variety of experimental results that clarify these phenomena, although the larger part of the work remains to be done. In this article I shall describe some of the research on attention to spoken messages.

One of the earliest findings, and one that agrees with everyday experience, is that it is harder to understand two messages arriving simultaneously than two messages arriving one after the other. One might be tempted to explain this as a purely physical interference between the two stimuli; for example, the louder passages of one message might drown out the softer passages of the other and vice versa, rendering them both unintelligible. Actually the matter is not so simple. By recording the messages on tape and playing them for different subjects instructed to respond in different ways, the intelligibility is shown to depend on psychological factors. Specifically, either message becomes understandable if the listener is instructed to ignore the other. But the two messages together cannot both be understood, even though the necessary information is available to the ear. Another way of making the same point is to insert the words of one message into spaces between the words from the other: "Oh God say save can our you gracious see Queen." Each message is hard to understand, but each word is spoken separately and is fully audible. The difficulty evidently lies inside the nervous system, which somehow prevents an adequate response to signals that are "heard" satisfactorily.

Further experiments demonstrate that comprehension improves if the two messages differ in certain physical characteristics. For instance, it is better if a man speaks one message and a woman speaks the other; or if the loudspeaker removes the lower tones from one voice but not the other. Spatial separation of the two voices gives the best result of all. The different messages should not come through the same loudspeaker or even from separate speakers mounted one above the other; the two speakers should be separated as far as possible from each other in the horizontal plane. Interestingly enough, a listener also comprehends simultaneous spoken messages better when they come from a stereophonic system than when they are played over a single loudspeaker. (This effect, rather than the doubtful gain in realism, is for many people the main advantage of stereophonic high-fidelity systems: the listener can pay attention to different musical instruments played at the same time.)

Physical distinctions are most helpful in promoting understanding when one message has no importance for the listener and does not have to be answered. It would seem that the differences allow the brain to filter the incoming sounds and select some for response while ignoring others.

The need to throw away part of the available information can perhaps be understood by comparing the brain with man-made communication systems. Engineers nowadays talk of capacity for transmitting information, by which they mean the number of equally probable messages of which one can be sent in a specified time. Suppose, for example, that two complicated military plans have been prepared and an order is to be sent to carry out one of them. A simple communication system consisting of a red and a green lamp can transmit the message with maximum efficiency by the lighting of a single lamp. If there were four plans instead of two, however, it would be impossible to give the order by lighting one of the two lamps no matter how simple each plan might be. Either there must be more lamps or more time is needed for sending the order. In the most efficient code for two lamps, two successive flashes of the red lamp would mean one plan, a red flash followed by a green flash would mean another, and so on. One of four possible messages can be transmitted with two lamps, but only by taking two units of time. With eight possible messages the code would call for three flashes of the two lamps, taking three units of time; 16 possible messages would require four flashes, and so forth.

Although the human brain has far more than the two states represented by the red and the green lamp, the number of its possible states is presumably limited. One would expect, then, that there is a limit to the number of different possibilities among which it can distinguish in a given time. Indeed, a number of experiments suggest a close parallel with the two-lamp system: in many cases a man's reaction time in responding to one of several possible signals increases by an equal amount every time the number of possible signals is doubled. Since there is a maximum speed at which one signal can be distinguished from others, the brain limits the number of possibilities being considered at any one time by selecting only part of the information reaching the ears. Therefore the degree of difficulty in dealing with two simultaneous spoken messages depends on the number of other messages that might have arrived instead of the two that did arrive. If only a few other messages are possible, the two messages together may not exceed the capacity of the brain and the listener may understand both. On the other hand, if each message is drawn from a very large range of possibilities, it may be all the listener can do to respond appropriately to one of them.

Several studies support these conclusions. John C. Webster and his associates at the U.S. Navy Electronics Laboratory in San Diego, Calif., observed that control-tower operators in San Diego could sometimes identify two aircraft call signs arriving at the same time but could understand only one of the two messages that followed. The call signs penetrated because the operators knew pretty well which aircraft might call. They did not know what the pilots would say.

An experiment at the Applied Psychology Research Unit in Cambridge, England, required a listener to answer a rapid series of questions while pressing a key in response to an intermittent buzzer. The interference produced by the buzzer in the ability to answer questions increased after the subject had been told that he would also have to respond to a bell. Even when the bell did not ring, the subject found the questions harder to answer than when he was expecting only the buzzer.

These results help to explain why a person can sometimes listen to two things at once and sometimes cannot pay atten-

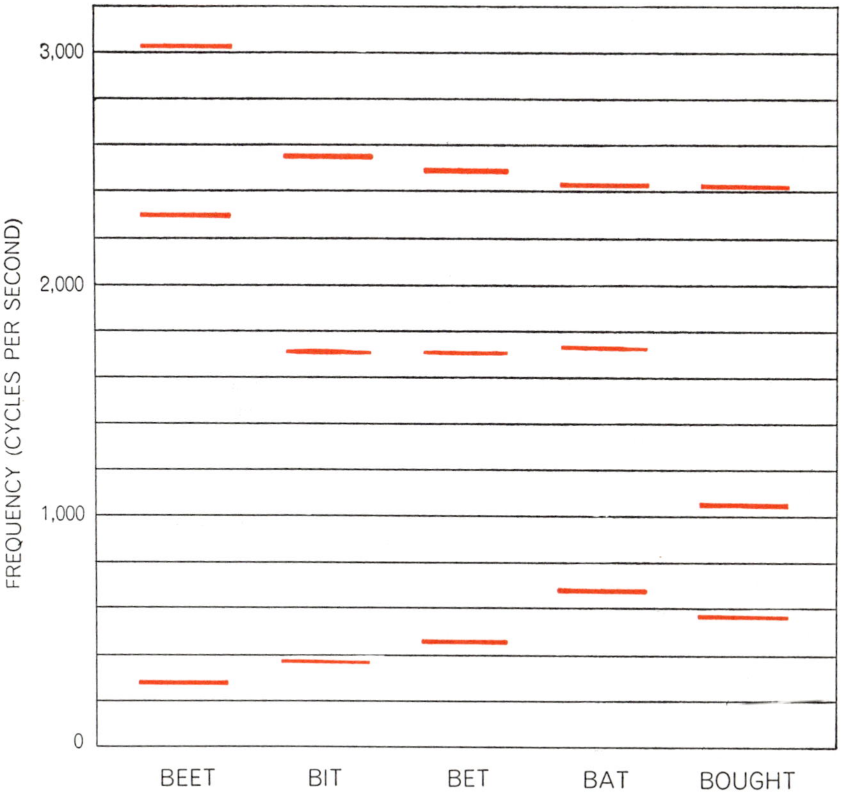

VOWEL FORMANTS, or frequencies that make up each vowel sound, are shown here for five different vowels. The values given are averages for male voices. Actually they differ from person to person. Although three formants are shown here for each sound, quite recognizable vowels can be produced by mechanisms using two filters to make two formants.

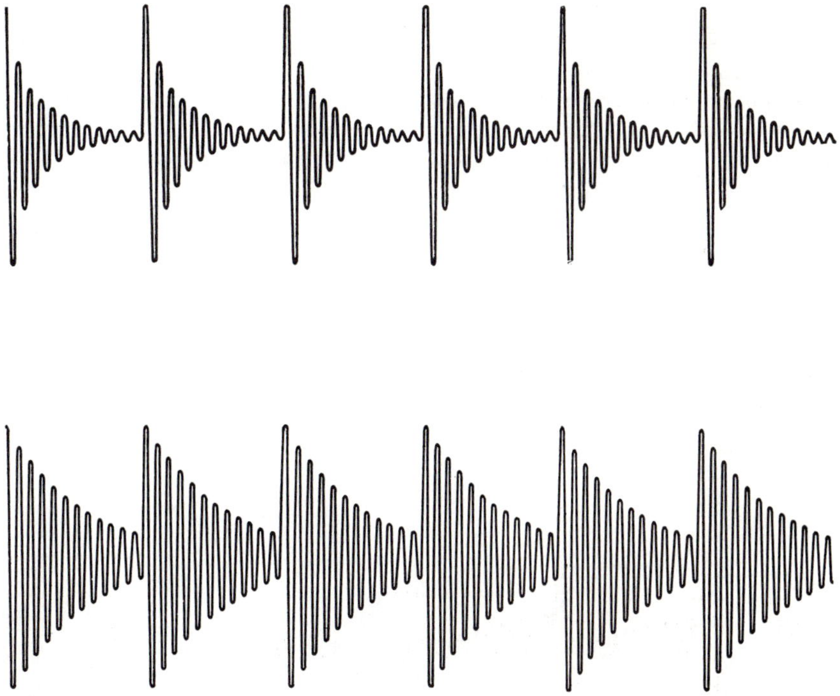

DECAY RATE of pulses from vocal cords affects quality of speech. Waves of highest amplitude mark beginning of each pulse. At top, pulses decay rapidly, helping to give the voice a crisp or sharp sound. At bottom, the decay is much slower, giving the voice a mellow quality. In both cases the frequencies of the pulses and the vibrations are exactly the same.

tion to more than one. When the listener is thoroughly familiar with a situation, so that he knows to within a small number of alternatives what each message will be, he can comprehend two simultaneous messages. But when one or both messages are drawn from a large number of possibilities, the filter in the brain lets only one message come through.

How does the filter work? As yet the answer is not known. Enough is known, however, about the physical characteristics of speech and the physiology of hearing to make possible some reasonable speculation. Human speech is produced by the combined action of the vocal cords and the vocal tract, which consists of the cavities of the throat, mouth and nose. Taut vocal cords produce a buzz when air is forced through them. The buzz consists of brief pulses, or puffs of air, at the rate of 100 or more per second, each pulse containing energy at many frequencies. These pulses excite into vibration the air in the cavities of the throat, nose and mouth. The cavities can be tuned to different frequencies by changing the position of the tongue, cheeks, jaw and lips. What emerges is a train of waves that contains a particular group of frequencies and is pulsed about 100 times per second. Each pulse starts out at full strength and decays rapidly until the sound energy is renewed by the next one [*see bottom illustration on preceding page*].

Many vowel sounds contain waves at two or more widely separated frequencies. For example, when the greatest energy is at 375 and 1,700 cycles per second, the vowel sound in the word "bit" is produced; frequencies of 450 and 1,700 cycles per second give the vowel in "bet." (These figures apply to a typical male voice. In the voices of women and children the whole range of frequencies may be higher but the listener takes this into account.) On reaching the ear, the sounds stimulate sense organs arranged along the basilar membrane in the cochlea [*see illustration on page 27*]. Low frequencies stimulate organs at one end of the membrane; high frequencies affect those at the other end. A complex sound made up of several frequencies energizes several different regions of the basilar membrane. Each sense organ on the membrane connects with particular nerve fibers going to the brain; thus the word "bit" stimulates one combination of fibers and the word "bet" another combination.

If both words reach the ear simultaneously, both combinations of fibers would come into play and the brain would have the problem of deciding which belong together. It might seem then that two or more voices would produce so much confusion in the ear that the brain could not select one voice for special attention. Of course, certain obvious features help distinguish one speaker from another: accent, rate of speaking, loudness or softness. But one cannot make use of these features until one knows which frequencies belong to which voice. Thus the problem remains: How does the brain manage to focus attention on one voice? Studies of the artificial generation of speech sounds have begun to throw some light on this problem.

Peter Ladefoged of the University of Edinburgh and I have been experimenting with a device that was developed by Walter Lawrence of the Signals Research Development Establishment in England. Our version of the apparatus sends a series of electrical pulses (analogous to pulses from the vocal cords) through two filter circuits, each of which passes primarily one frequency. The waves from one filter circuit, which are like those from the largest human speech cavity, are mixed with waves from the other, which imitate the frequencies produced by the second largest cavity. To-

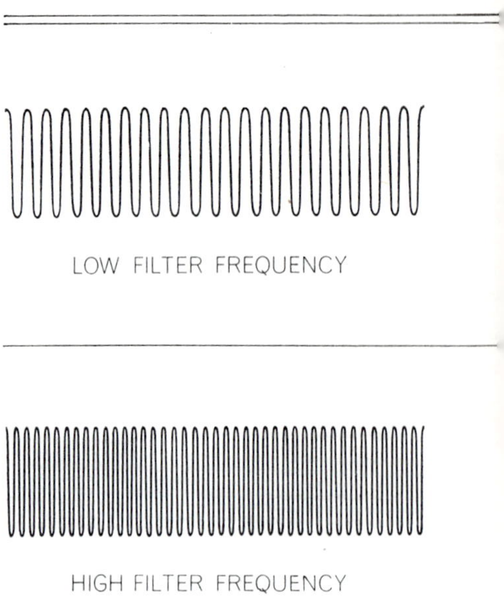

SPEECH SOUNDS consist of pulses of energy from the voice, shown here as high and

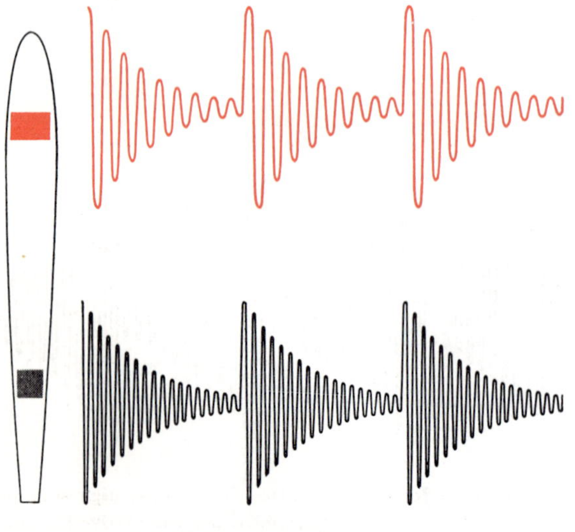

DIFFERENT FILTER FREQUENCIES but same rate of pulsation or modulation from voice excites two different regions of a basilar membrane (*left*). Listener reports he hears one vowel sound.

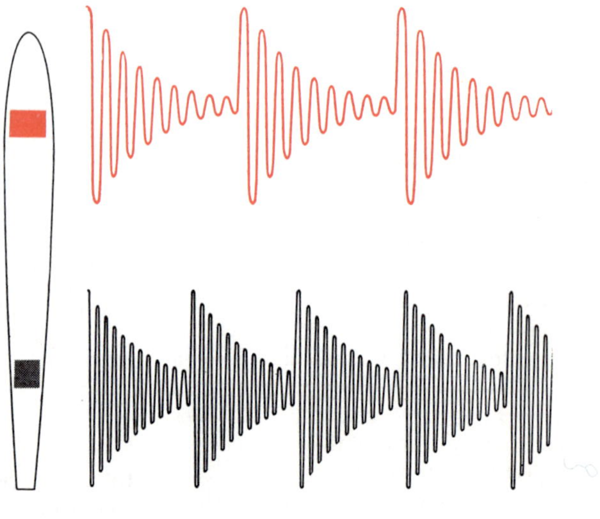

DIFFERENT PULSATION RATES and different filter frequencies make the listener hear two different sounds, even though only one ear or basilar membrane is actually being used for hearing.

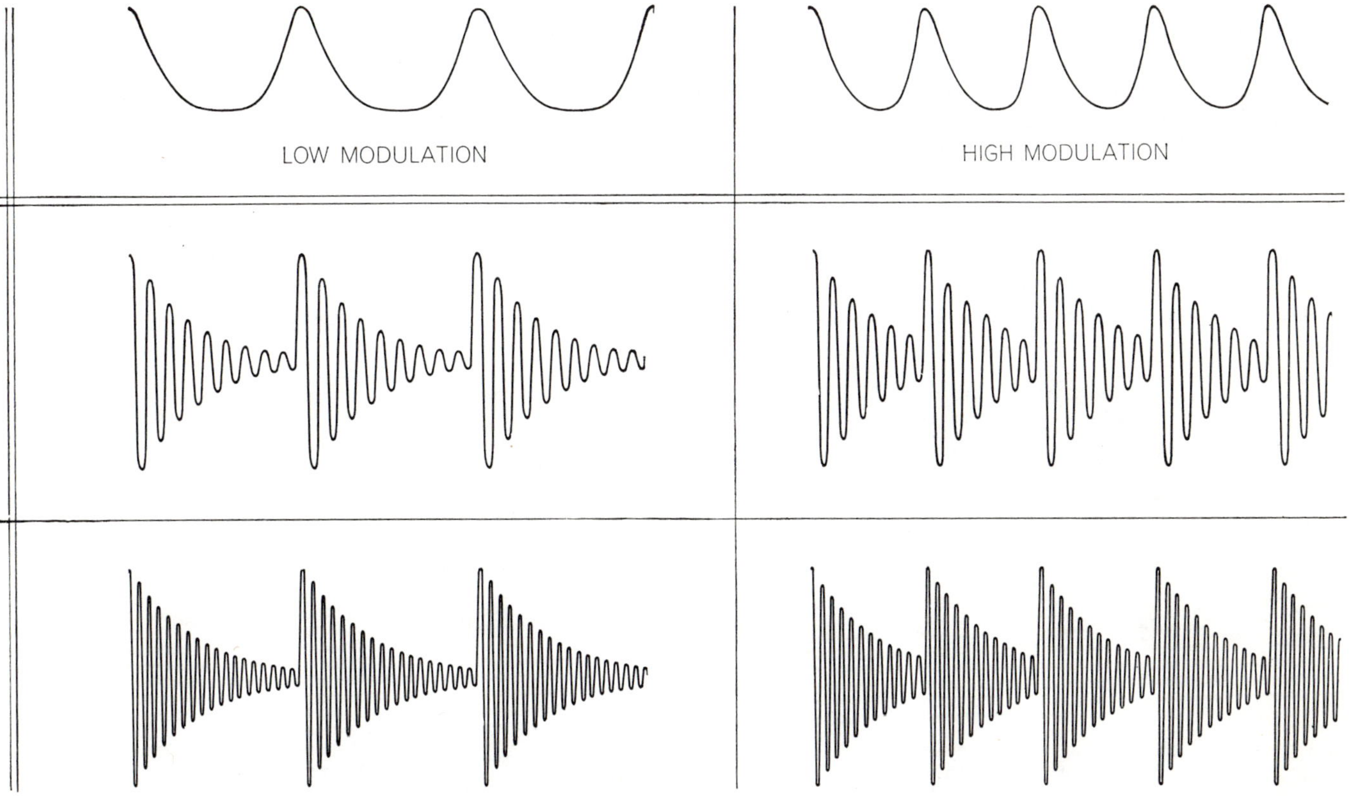

low modulations (*across top*), and of specific frequencies emitted by the mouth and throat "filters," or cavities (*far left*). These two types of wave combine in patterns like those in this diagram. Effects of such waves are shown across bottom of these two pages.

gether the two wave trains are heard as quite acceptable vowel sounds that can be changed by tuning the filters to different frequencies. Varying the pulse rate used to excite the filters alters the apparent pitch or intonation of the "speech": it rises with faster pulse rates and falls with slower ones.

When the same pulses excite both filters, a listener hears the output as readily identifiable vowel sounds. This is true even when the low frequency is fed into one ear and the high frequency into the other. But if the two filters are pulsed at slightly different rates, the "speech" becomes unacceptable and listeners say that they are hearing two sounds coming from two sources rather than a single vowel sound.

Other experiments on the fusion of sounds at the two ears, conducted by Colin A. Cherry and his colleagues at the Imperial College of Science and Technology in London, also support the idea that when the rate of pulsing, or modulation, is the same for two sounds, the hearer perceives them as one sound. It seems reasonable to suppose, therefore, that a man can listen to one person

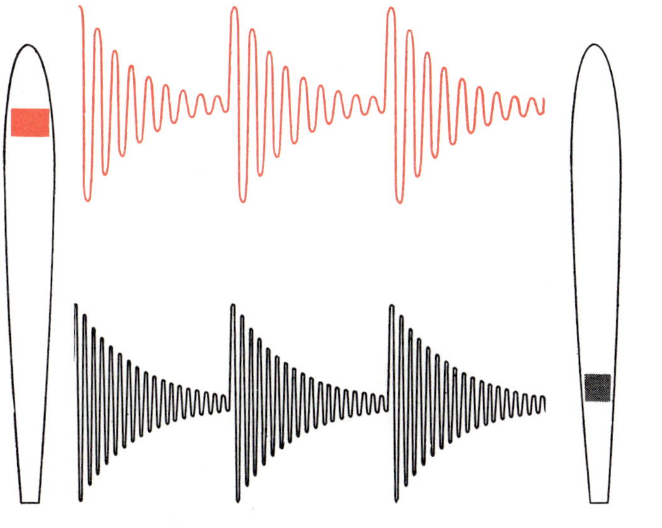

USING BOTH EARS, listener will hear one vowel sound, although right ear hears one filter frequency and left ear hears another. The pulsation or modulation rate has to be the same.

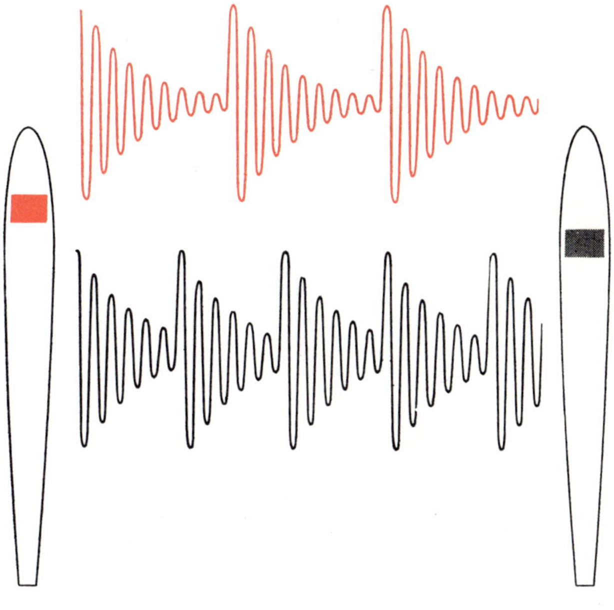

TWO PULSATION RATES, combined with same filter frequency and fed into each ear separately, produce two distinct sounds. The brain evidently focuses its attention on the rate of pulsation.

and ignore another primarily by selecting from the mass of sounds entering his ears all those frequencies that are being modulated at the same rate. Since it is most unlikely that the vocal cords of two speakers would vibrate at exactly the same rate at any moment, modulation would almost always provide an important (if not the sole) means of separating a pair of voices.

It is now a generally accepted principle of neurophysiology that messages traveling along a particular nerve can differ either by involving different nerve fibers or by producing a different number of impulses per second in the fibers. High-frequency and low-frequency sounds stimulate different fibers. It may be that the rate at which the sounds are pulsed controls the rate of firing of the fibers. If so, the brain could pick out one voice from others by focusing its attention on all auditory nerve fibers that are firing at the same rate.

A further indication of the importance of modulation is that it, rather than the frequency of the waves being modulated, seems under certain conditions to determine the pitch of a voice. This can be demonstrated with the artificial speech generator. A filter tuned to, say, 3,000 cycles per second is pulsed at the rate of 100 cycles per second. A listener is asked to match the pitch of the sound with either of two simple sound waves, one at 100 cycles per second and the oth-

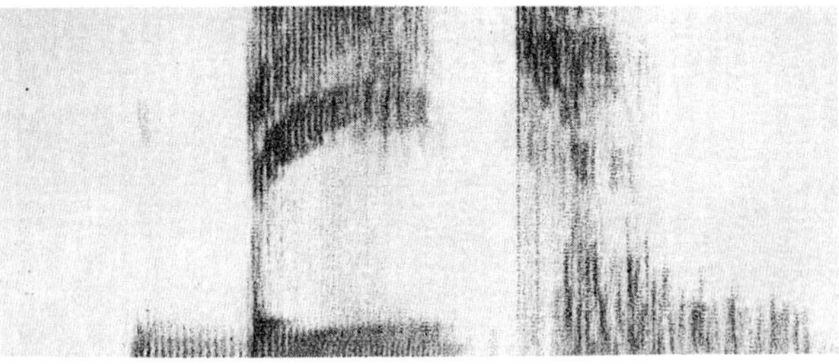
"BEET"

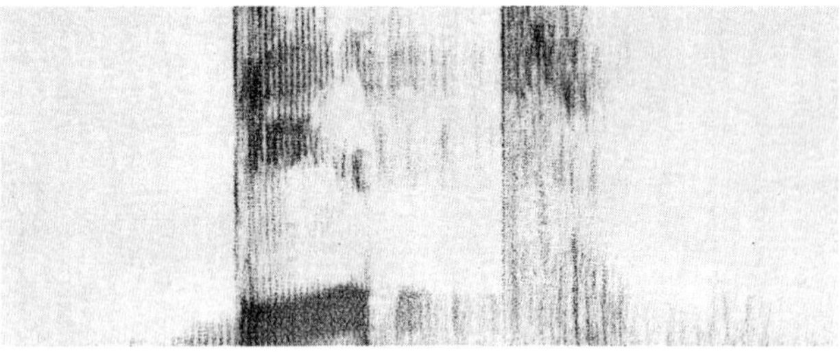
"BIT"

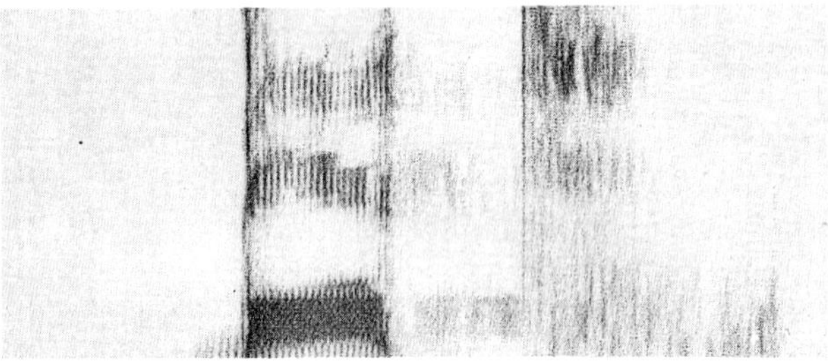
"BET"

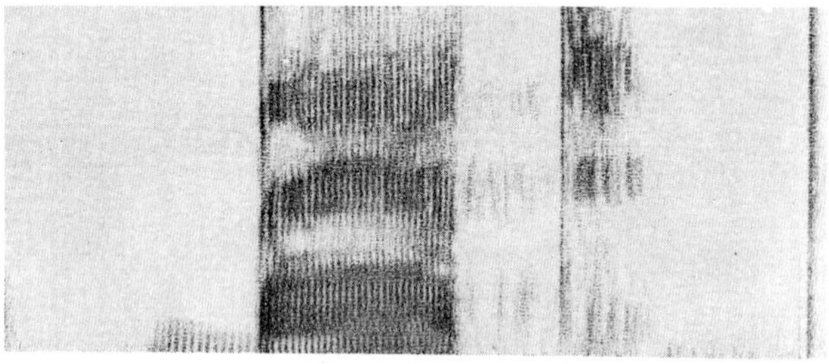
"BAT"

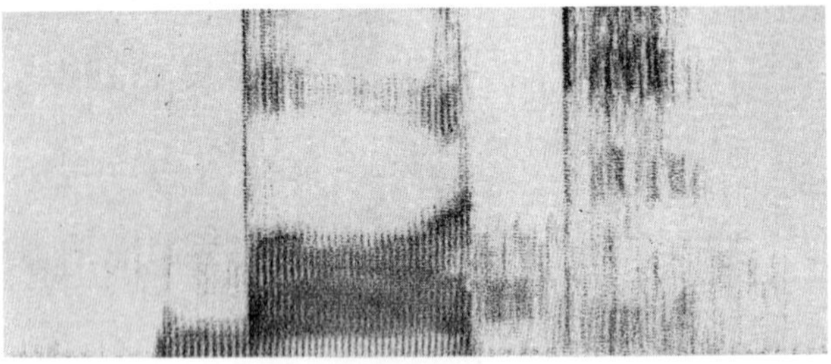
"BOUGHT"

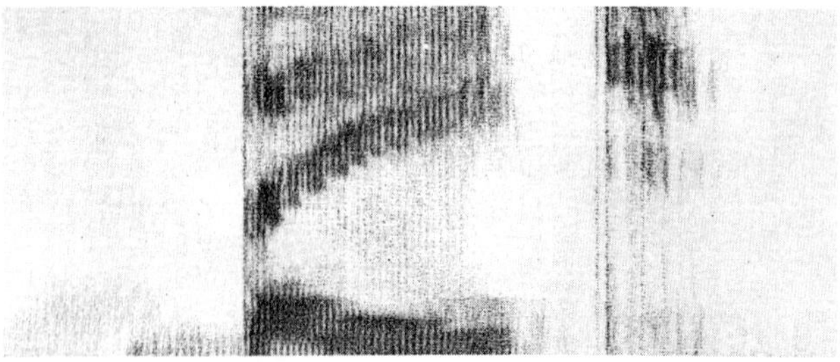
"BATE"

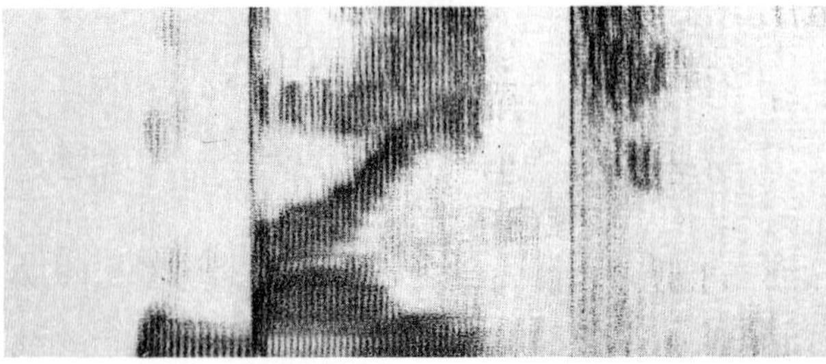
"BITE"

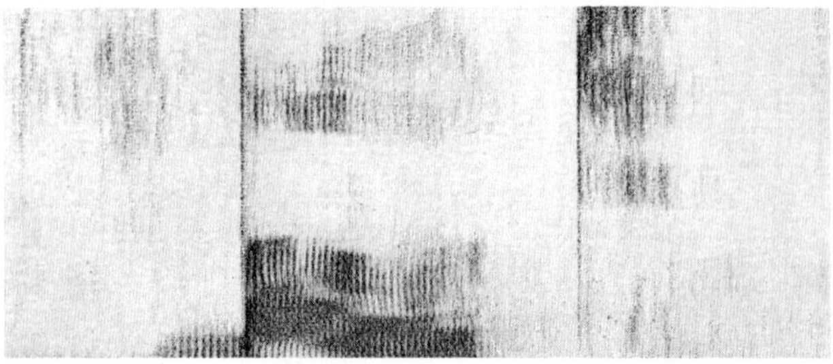
"BOAT"

SOUND SPECTROGRAMS show that various vowel sounds are made of several different frequencies. Time is shown horizontally, frequencies vertically and intensity of sound by relative darkness. The "b" of each word appears at lowest frequency. Vowel begins suddenly as lips open. After vowel there is a quiet period followed by a burst of noise primarily at high frequency as the "t" explodes. Frequency shifts in "bate" and "bite" are diphthongs. Spectrograms were made by H. K. Dunn of Bell Telephone Laboratories.

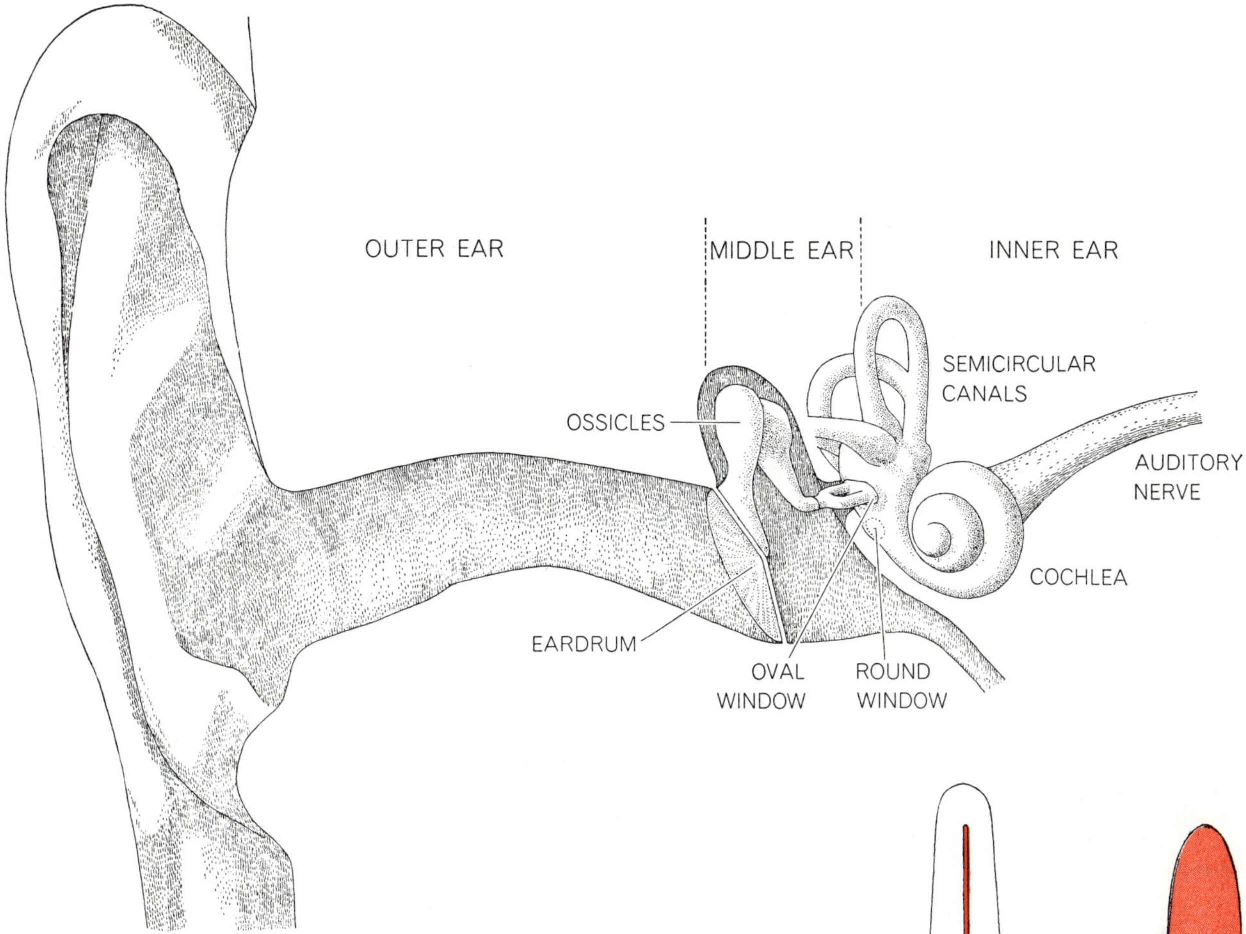

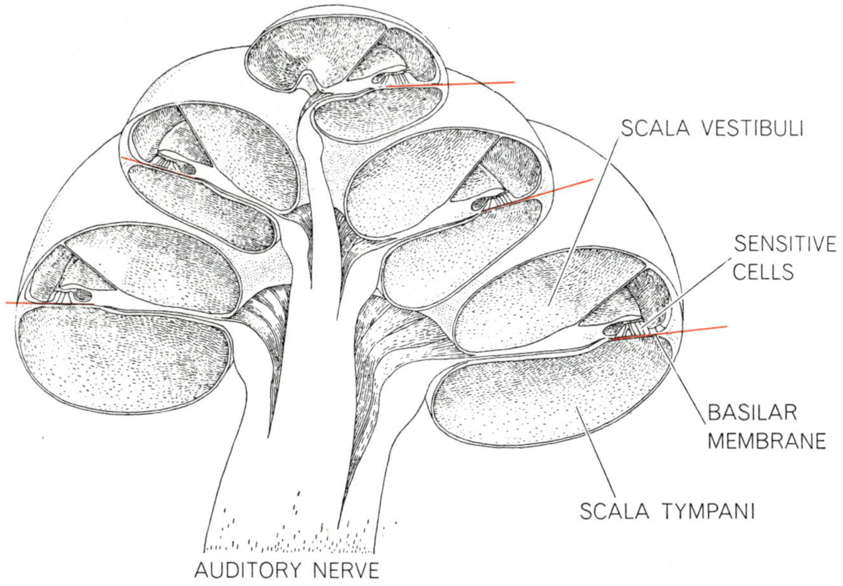

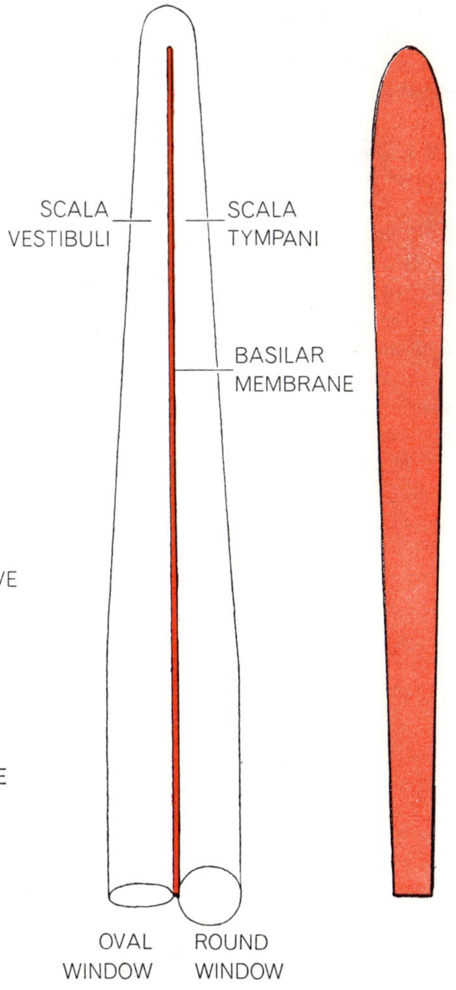

PERCEPTION OF SPEECH begins in the ear, shown at top in simplified cross section. The eardrum transmits sound vibrations to the three small bones called ossicles, which cause waves in fluid in the cochlea. The cochlea, seen in cross section at bottom left, contains the basilar membrane (*color*), on which rest the sensitive cells that excite auditory-nerve fibers. At bottom center cochlea is rolled out, with basilar membrane in side view. Front view of the basilar membrane (*bottom right*) shows that it is wider at one end than the other. The wide region vibrates in response to low frequencies, whereas the narrow region responds to high frequencies.

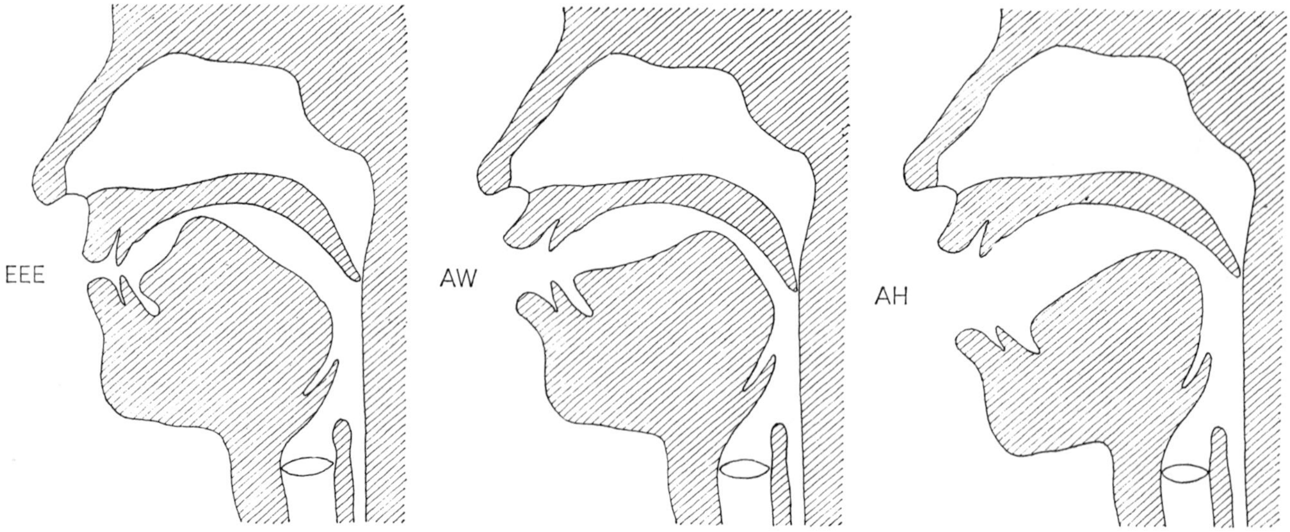

SHAPE OF CAVITIES in the mouth is primarily responsible for the production of different vowel sounds. Three other factors that play a key role in this process are the configuration of the tongue, the size of the opening of the mouth and the position of the lips.

er at 3,000. Usually he selects the 100-cycle sound.

The selection mechanism that has been described is still hypothetical, but I believe that something much like it must exist. There can be no doubt, however, that it is not the only basis for auditory attention. Several experiments have served to make this clear. In one, a listener is equipped with earphones that feed one voice into the right ear and another voice into the left. Normally the subject has no difficulty in understanding the message entering one ear and ignoring the other. But under certain conditions sound from the ear being ignored can break into consciousness. For example, Neville Moray of the University of Oxford has demonstrated that a man fully occupied in listening to speech entering one ear will hear his own name in the other ear even though he remains quite unresponsive to any other word in that ear. Under similar circumstances Anne M. Treisman of the University of Oxford has found that speech entering the rejected ear can break through to the subject's attention if it consists of words that would probably follow the words that have just been heard by the ear that is receiving attention. In these cases the content of the speech has taken precedence over its physical characteristics.

How the brain focuses attention on meaning or content is as yet an almost complete mystery. One thing is clear. If the method proposed for choosing between voices is correct, there must be two attention mechanisms. Selection on the basis of content involves examining a stimulus for its possible appropriateness to a particular set of responses rather than for the presence or absence of a physical marker. At one moment, for example, a person might be ready to write down any of the digits one through nine and highly unready to write anything else, or indeed to respond in any other way. If he hears a sound from any direction or in any voice that can be interpreted as the name of one of the digits, he will respond by writing it down; only if the sound cannot be so interpreted will he not respond. At another time he might be ready to write down letters of the alphabet but not numbers, and so on.

Both types of attention are now the subject of intensive research. The next few years should yield more definite clues to the nature of each and at least a tentative answer to the question of whether or not they depend on different mechanisms.

THE SPLIT BRAIN IN MAN

MICHAEL S. GAZZANIGA

August 1967

The brain of the higher animals, including man, is a double organ, consisting of right and left hemispheres connected by an isthmus of nerve tissue called the corpus callosum. Some 15 years ago Ronald E. Myers and R. W. Sperry, then at the University of Chicago, made a surprising discovery: When this connection between the two halves of the cerebrum was cut, each hemisphere functioned independently as if it were a complete brain. The phenomenon was first investigated in a cat in which not only the brain but also the optic chiasm, the crossover of the optic nerves, was divided, so that visual information from the left eye was dispatched only to the left brain and information from the right eye only to the right brain. Working on a problem with one eye, the animal could respond normally and learn to perform a task; when that eye was covered and the same problem was presented to the other eye, the animal evinced no recognition of the problem and had to learn it again from the beginning with the other half of the brain.

The finding introduced entirely new questions in the study of brain mechanisms. Was the corpus callosum responsible for integration of the operations of the two cerebral hemispheres in the intact brain? Did it serve to keep each hemisphere informed about what was going on in the other? To put the question another way, would cutting the corpus callosum literally result in the right hand not knowing what the left was doing? To what extent were the two half-brains actually independent when they were separated? Could they have separate thoughts, even separate emotions?

Such questions have been pursued by Sperry and his co-workers in a wide-ranging series of animal studies at the California Institute of Technology over the past decade [see "The Great Cerebral Commissure," by R. W. Sperry; SCIENTIFIC AMERICAN Offprint 174]. Recently these questions have been investigated in human patients who underwent the brain-splitting operation for medical reasons. The demonstration in experimental animals that sectioning of the corpus callosum did not seriously impair mental faculties had encouraged surgeons to resort to this operation for people afflicted with uncontrollable epilepsy. The hope was to confine a seizure to one hemisphere. The operation proved to be remarkably successful; curiously there is an almost total elimination of all attacks, including unilateral ones. It is as if the intact callosum had served in these patients to facilitate seizure activity.

This article is a brief survey of investigations Sperry and I have carried out at Cal Tech over the past five years with some of these patients. The operations were performed by P. J. Vogel and J. E. Bogen of the California College of Medicine. Our studies date back to 1961, when the first patient, a 48-year-old war veteran, underwent the operation: cutting of the corpus callosum and other commissure structures connecting the two halves of the cerebral cortex [*see illustration on page 31*]. As of today 10 patients have had the operation, and we have examined four thoroughly over a long period with many tests.

From the beginning one of the most striking observations was that the operation produced no noticeable change in the patients' temperament, personality or general intelligence. In the first case the patient could not speak for 30 days after the operation, but he then recovered his speech. More typical was the third case: on awaking from the surgery the patient quipped that he had a "splitting headache," and in his still drowsy state he was able to repeat the tongue twister "Peter Piper picked a peck of pickled peppers."

Close observation, however, soon revealed some changes in the patients' everyday behavior. For example, it could be seen that in moving about and responding to sensory stimuli the patients favored the right side of the body, which is controlled by the dominant left half of the brain. For a considerable period after the operation the left side of the body rarely showed spontaneous activity, and the patient generally did not respond to stimulation of that side: when he brushed against something with his left side he did not notice that he had done so, and when an object was placed in his left hand he generally denied its presence.

More specific tests identified the main features of the bisected-brain syndrome. One of these tests examined responses to visual stimulation. While the patient fixed his gaze on a central point on a board, spots of light were flashed (for a tenth of a second) in a row across the board that spanned both the left and the right half of his visual field. The patient was asked to tell what he had seen. Each patient reported that lights had been flashed in the right half of the visual field. When lights were flashed only in the left half of the field, however, the patients generally denied having seen any lights. Since the right side of the visual field is normally projected to the left hemisphere of the brain and the left field to the right hemisphere, one might have concluded that in these patients with divided brains the right hemisphere was in effect blind. We found, however, that this was not the case when the patients were directed to point to the lights that had flashed instead of giving a verbal report. With this manual response they were able to indicate when lights had

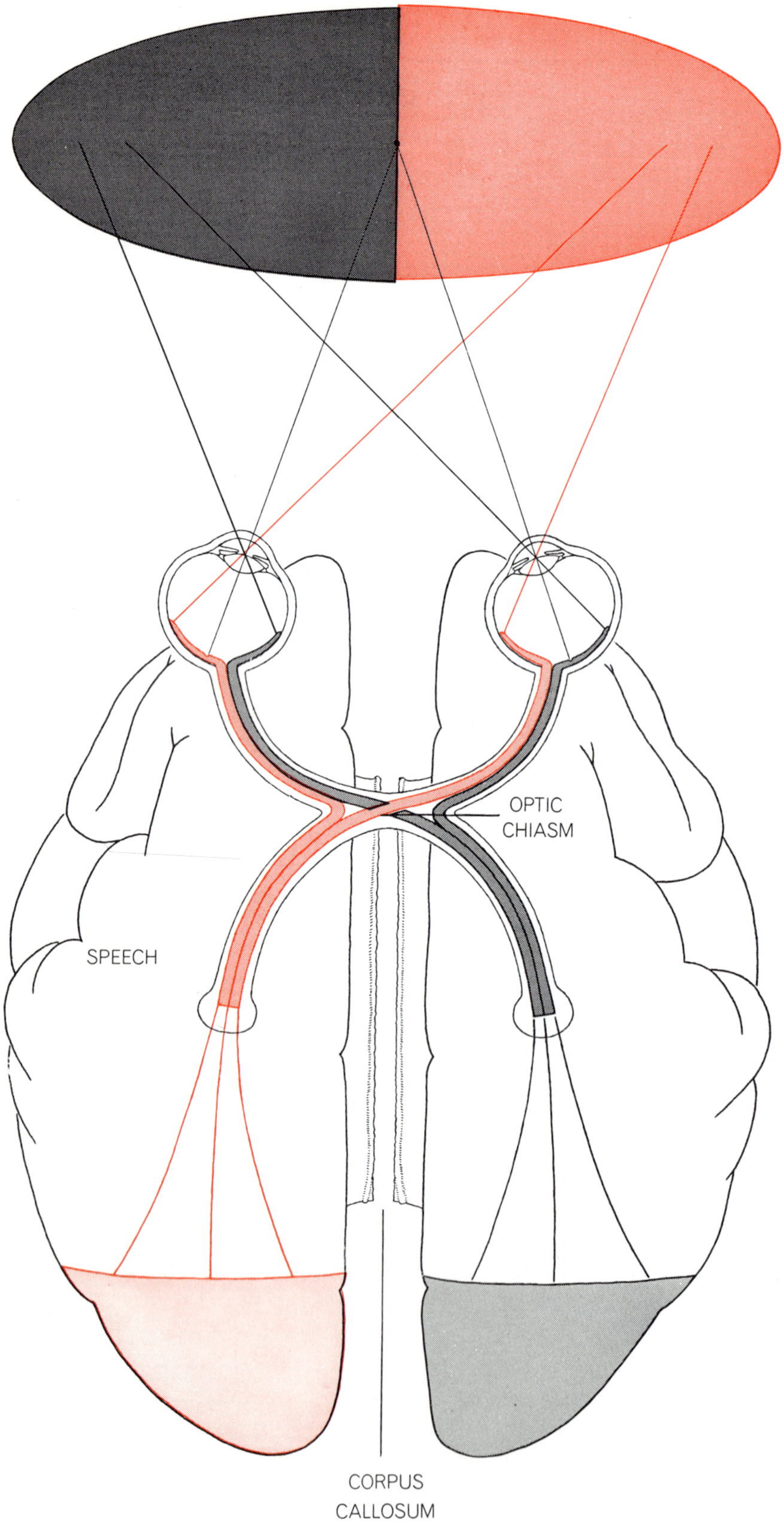

VISUAL INPUT to bisected brain was limited to one hemisphere by presenting information only in one visual field. The right and left fields of view are projected, via the optic chiasm, to the left and right hemispheres of the brain respectively. If a person fixes his gaze on a point, therefore, information to the left of the point goes only to the right hemisphere and information to the right of the point goes to the left hemisphere. Stimuli in the left visual field cannot be described by a split-brain patient because of the disconnection between the right hemisphere and the speech center, which is in the left hemisphere.

been flashed in the left visual field, and perception with the brain's right hemisphere proved to be almost equal to perception with the left. Clearly, then, the patients' failure to report the right hemisphere's perception verbally was due to the fact that the speech centers of the brain are located in the left hemisphere.

Our tests of the patients' ability to recognize objects by touch at first resulted in the same general finding. When the object was held in the right hand, from which sensory information is sent to the left hemisphere, the patient was able to name and describe the object. When it was held in the left hand (from which information goes primarily to the right hemisphere), the patient could not describe the object verbally but was able to identify it in a nonverbal test—matching it, for example, to the same object in a varied collection of things. We soon realized, however, that each hemisphere receives, in addition to the main input from the opposite side of the body, some input from the same side. This "ipsilateral" input is crude; it is apparently good mainly for "cuing in" the hemisphere as to the presence or absence of stimulation and relaying fairly gross information about the location of a stimulus on the surface of the body. It is unable, as a rule, to relay information concerning the qualitative nature of an object.

Tests of motor control in these split-brain patients revealed that the left hemisphere of the brain exercised normal control over the right hand but had less than full control of the left hand (for instance, it was poor at directing individual movements of the fingers). Similarly, the right hemisphere had full control of the left hand but not of the right hand. When the two hemispheres were in conflict, dictating different movements for the same hand, the hemisphere on the side opposite the hand generally took charge and overruled the orders of the side of the brain with the weaker control. In general the motor findings in the human patients were much the same as those in split-brain monkeys.

We come now to the main question on which we centered our studies, namely how the separation of the hemispheres affects the mental capacities of the human brain. For these psychological tests we used two different devices. One was visual: a picture or written information was flashed (for a tenth of a second) in either the right or the left visual field, so that the information was transmited only to the left or to the right brain hemisphere [*see illustration on page 32*]. The other type of test was tactile: an object was placed out of view in the patient's right or left hand, again for the purpose of conveying the information to just one hemisphere—the hemisphere on the side opposite the hand.

When the information (visual or tactile) was presented to the dominant left hemisphere, the patients were able to deal with and describe it quite normally, both orally and in writing. For example, when a picture of a spoon was shown in the right visual field or a spoon was placed in the right hand, all the patients readily identified and described it. They were able to read out written messages and to perform problems in calculation that were presented to the left hemisphere.

In contrast, when the same information was presented to the right hemisphere, it failed to elicit such spoken or written responses. A picture transmitted to the right hemisphere evoked either a haphazard guess or no verbal response at all. Similarly, a pencil placed in the left hand (behind a screen that cut off vision) might be called a can opener or a cigarette lighter, or the patient might not even attempt to describe it. The verbal guesses presumably came not from the right hemisphere but from the left, which had no perception of the object but might attempt to identify it from indirect clues.

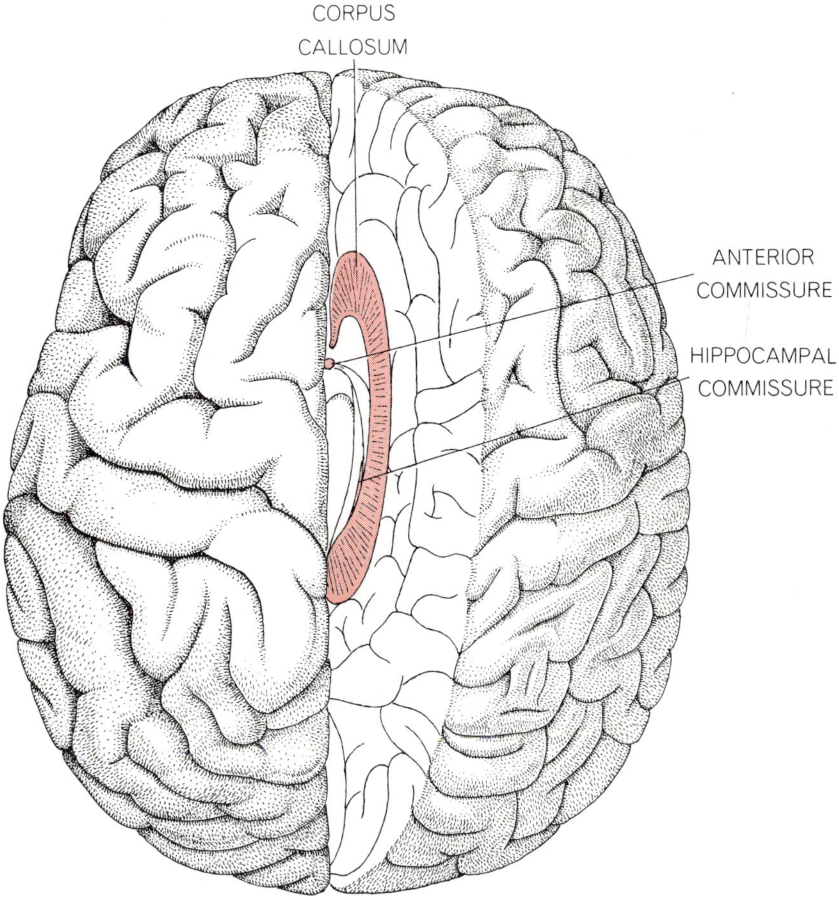

TWO HEMISPHERES of the human brain are divided by neurosurgeons to control epileptic seizures. In this top view of the brain the right hemisphere is retracted and the corpus callosum and other commissures, or connectors, that are generally cut are shown in color.

Did this impotence of the right hemisphere mean that its surgical separation from the left had reduced its mental powers to an imbecilic level? The earlier tests of its nonverbal capacities suggested that this was almost certainly not so. Indeed, when we switched to asking for nonverbal answers to the visual and tactile information presented in our new psychological tests, the right hemisphere in several patients showed considerable capacity for accurate performance. For example, when a picture of a spoon was presented to the right hemisphere, the patients were able to feel around with the left hand among a varied group of objects (screened from sight) and select a spoon as a match for the picture. Furthermore, when they were shown a picture of a cigarette they succeeded in selecting an ashtray, from a group of 10 objects that did not include a cigarette, as the article most closely related to the picture. Oddly enough, however, even after their correct response, and while they were holding the spoon or the ashtray in their left hand, they were unable to name or describe the object or the picture. Evidently the left hemisphere was completely divorced, in perception and knowledge, from the right.

Other tests showed that the right hemisphere did possess a certain amount of language comprehension. For example, when the word "pencil" was flashed to the right hemisphere, the patients were able to pick out a pencil from a group of unseen objects with the left hand. And when a patient held an object in the left hand (out of view), although he could not say its name or describe it, he was later able to point to a card on which the name of the object was written.

In one particularly interesting test the word "heart" was flashed across the center of the visual field, with the "he" portion to the left of the center and "art" to the right. Asked to tell what the word was, the patients would say they had seen "art"—the portion projected to the left brain hemisphere (which is responsible for speech). Curiously when, after "heart" had been flashed in the same way, the patients were asked to point with the left hand to one of two cards—"art" or "he"—to identify the word they had seen, they invariably pointed to "he." The experiment showed clearly that both hemispheres had simultaneously observed the portions of the word available to them and that in this particular case the right hemisphere, when it had had the opportunity to express itself, had prevailed over the left.

Because an auditory input to one ear goes to both sides of the brain, we conducted tests for the comprehension of words presented audibly to the right hemisphere not by trying to limit the original input but by limiting the ability to answer to the right hemisphere. This was done most easily by having a patient use his left hand to retrieve, from a grab bag held out of view, an object named by the examiner. We found that the patients could easily retrieve such objects as a watch, comb, marble or coin. The object to be retrieved did not even have to be named; it might simply be described or alluded to. For example, the command "Retrieve the fruit monkeys like best" results in the patients' pulling out a banana from a grab bag full of plastic fruit; at the command "Sunkist sells a lot of them" the patients retrieve an orange. We knew that touch information from the left hand was going exclusively to the right hemisphere because moments later, when the patients were asked to name various pieces of fruit placed in the left hand, they were unable to score above a chance level.

The upper limit of linguistic abilities in each hemisphere varies from subject to subject. In one case there was little or no evidence for language abilities in the right hemisphere, whereas in the other three the amount and extent of the capacities varied. The most adept patient showed some evidence of even being able to spell simple words by placing plastic letters on a table with his left hand. The subject was told to spell a word such as "pie," and the examiner then placed the three appropriate letters, one at a time in a random order, in his left hand to be arranged on the table. The patient was able to spell even more abstract words such as "how," "what" and "the." In another test three or four letters were placed in a pile, again out of view, to be felt with the left hand. The letters available in each trial would spell only one word, and the instructions to the subject were "Spell a word." The patient was able to spell such words as "cup" and "love." Yet after he had completed this task, the patient was unable to name the word he had just spelled!

The possibility that the right hemisphere has not only some language but even some speech capabilities cannot be ruled out, although at present there is no firm evidence for this. It would not be surprising to discover that the patients are capable of a few simple exclamatory remarks, particularly when under emotional stress. The possibility also remains, of course, that speech of some type could be trained into the right hemisphere. Tests aimed at this question, however, would have to be closely scrutinized and controlled.

The reason is that here, as in many of the tests, "cross-cuing" from one hemisphere to the other could be held responsible for any positive findings. We had a case of such cross-cuing during a series of tests of whether the right hemisphere could respond verbally to simple red or green stimuli. At first, after either a red or a green light was flashed to the right hemisphere, the patient would guess the color at a chance level, as might be expected if the speech mechanism is solely represented in the left hemisphere. After a few trials, however, the score improved whenever the examiner allowed a second guess.

We soon caught on to the strategy the patient used. If a red light was flashed and the patient by chance guessed red, he would stick with that answer. If the flashed light was red and the patient by chance guessed green, he would frown, shake his head and then say, "Oh no, I meant red." What was happening was that the right hemisphere saw the red light and heard the left hemisphere make the guess "green." Knowing that the answer was wrong, the right hemisphere precipitated a frown and a shake of the head, which in turn cued in the left hemisphere to the fact that the answer was wrong and that it had better correct itself! We have learned that this cross-cuing mechanism can become extremely refined. The realization that the neurological patient has various strategies at his command emphasizes how difficult it is to obtain a clear neurological description of a human being with brain damage.

Is the language comprehension by the right hemisphere that the patients exhibited in these tests a normal capability of that hemisphere or was it acquired by learning after their operation, perhaps during the course of the experiments themselves? The issue is difficult to decide. We must remember that we are examining a half of the human brain, a system easily capable of learning from a single trial in a test. We do know that the right hemisphere is decidedly inferior to the left in its overall command of language. We have established, for instance, that although the right hemisphere can respond to a concrete noun such as "pencil," it cannot do as well with verbs; patients are unable to re-

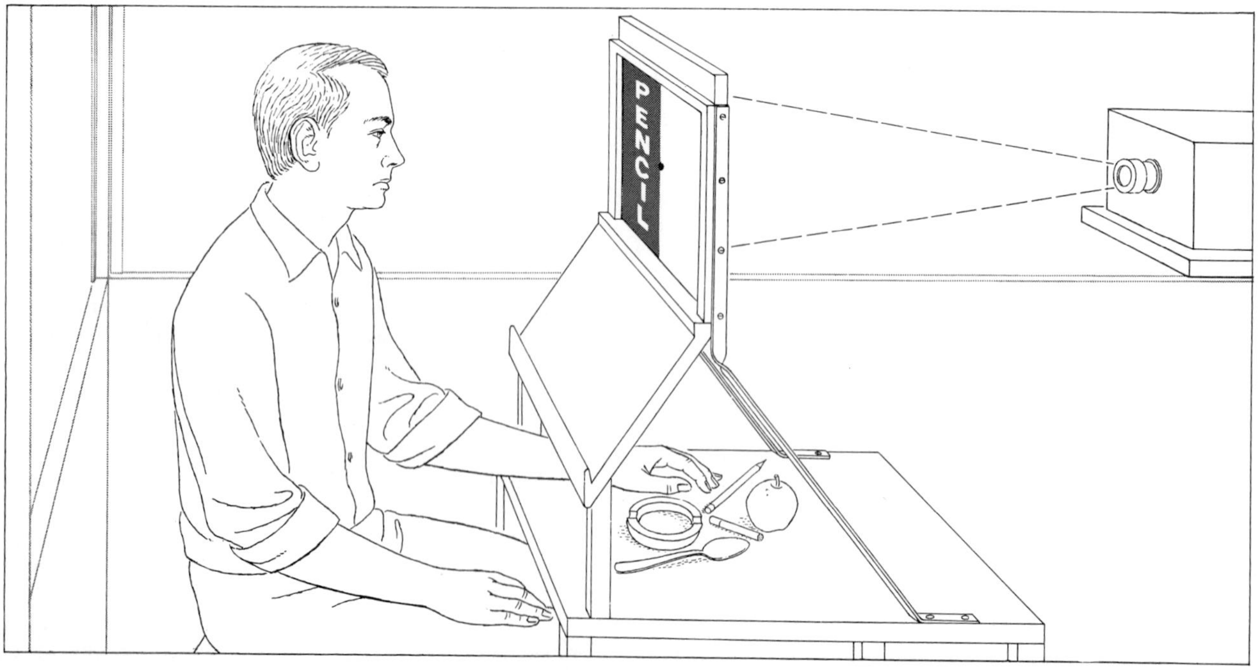

RESPONSE TO VISUAL STIMULUS is tested by flashing a word or a picture of an object on a translucent screen. The examiner first checks the subject's gaze to be sure it is fixed on a dot that marks the center of the visual field. The examiner may call for a verbal response—reading the flashed word, for example—or for a nonverbal one, such as picking up the object that is named from among a number of things spread on the table. The objects are hidden from the subject's view so that they can be identified only by touch.

spond appropriately to simple printed instructions, such as "smile" or "frown," when these words are flashed to the right hemisphere, nor can they point to a picture that corresponds to a flashed verb. Some of our recent studies at the University of California at Santa Barbara also indicate that the right hemisphere has a very poorly developed grammar; it seems to be incapable of forming the plural of a given word, for example.

In general, then, the extent of language present in the adult right hemisphere in no way compares with that present in the left hemisphere or, for that matter, with the extent of language present in the child's right hemisphere. Up to the age of four or so, it would appear from a variety of neurological observations, the right hemisphere is about as proficient in handling language as the left. Moreover, studies of the child's development of language, particularly with respect to grammar, strongly suggest that the foundations of grammar—a ground plan for language, so to speak—are somehow inherent in the human organism and are fully realized between the ages of two and three. In other words, in the young child each hemisphere is about equally developed with respect to language and speech function. We are thus faced with the interesting question of why the right hemisphere at an early age and stage of development possesses substantial language capacity whereas at a more adult stage it possesses a rather poor capacity. It is difficult indeed to conceive of the underlying neurological mechanism that would allow for the establishment of a capacity of a high order in a particular hemisphere on a temporary basis. The implication is that during maturation the processes and systems active in making this capacity manifest are somehow inhibited and dismantled in the right hemisphere and allowed to reside only in the dominant left hemisphere.

Yet the right hemisphere is not in all respects inferior or subordinate to the left. Tests have demonstrated that it excels the left in some specialized functions. As an example, tests by us and by Bogen have shown that in these patients the left hand is capable of arranging blocks to match a pictured design and of drawing a cube in three dimensions, whereas the right hand, deprived of instructions from the right hemisphere, could not perform either of these tasks.

It is of interest to note, however, that although the patients (our first subject in particular) could not execute such tasks

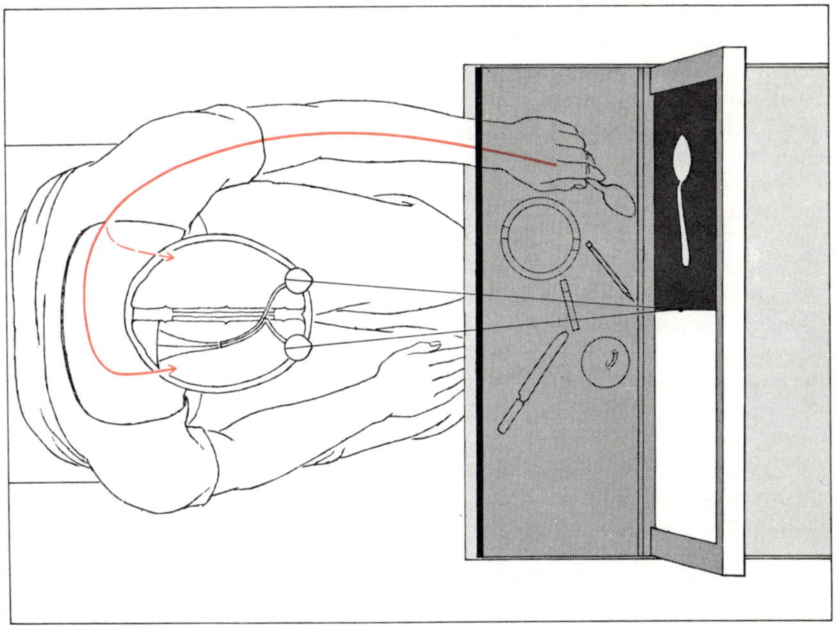

VISUAL-TACTILE ASSOCIATION is performed by a split-brain patient. A picture of a spoon is flashed to the right hemisphere; with the left hand he retrieves a spoon from behind the screen. The touch information from the left hand projects (*color*) mainly to the right hemisphere, but a weak "ipsilateral" component goes to the left hemisphere. This is usually not enough to enable him to say (using the left hemisphere) what he has picked up.

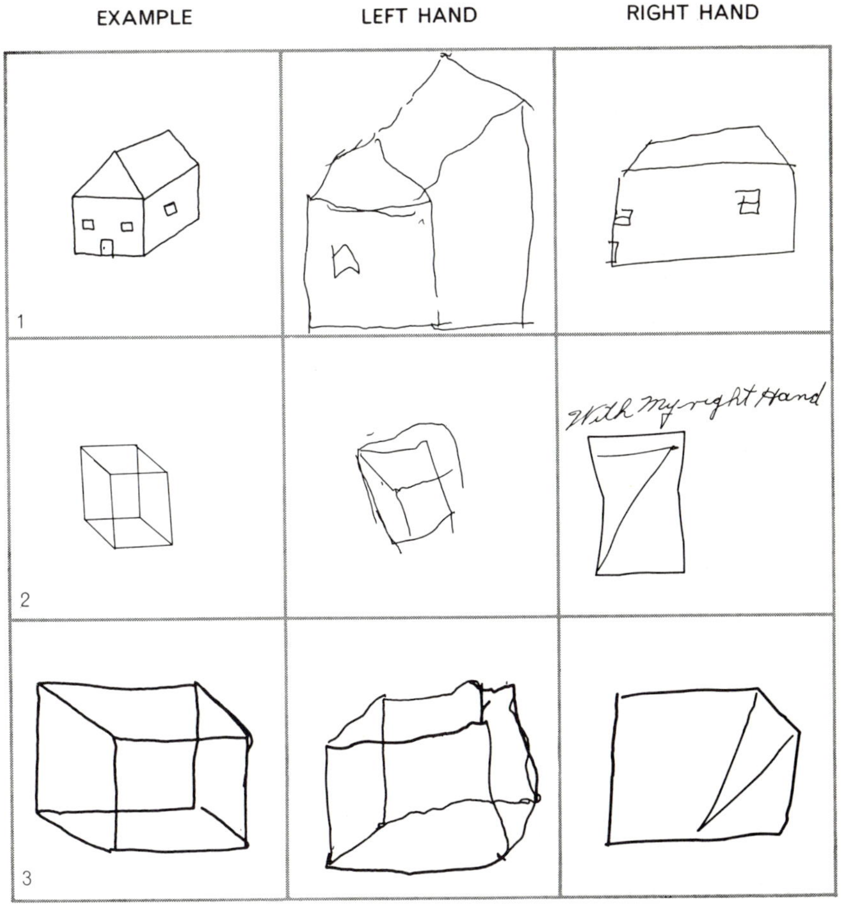

"VISUAL-CONSTRUCTIONAL" tasks are handled better by the right hemisphere. This was seen most clearly in the first patient, who had poor ipsilateral control of his right hand. Although right-handed, he could copy the examples only with his left hand.

with the right hand, they were capable of matching a test stimulus to the correct design when it appeared among five related patterns presented in their right visual field. This showed that the dominant left hemisphere is capable of discriminating between correct and incorrect stimuli. Since it is also true that the patients have no motor problems with their right hand, the patients' inability to perform these tasks must reflect a breakdown of an integrative process somewhere between the sensory system and the motor system.

We found that in certain other mental processes the right hemisphere is on a par with the left. In particular, it can independently generate an emotional reaction. In one of our experiments exploring the matter we would present a series of ordinary objects and then suddenly flash a picture of a nude woman. This evoked an amused reaction regardless of whether the picture was presented to the left hemisphere or to the right. When the picture was flashed to the left hemisphere of a female patient, she laughed and verbally identified the picture as a nude. When it was later presented to the right hemisphere, she said in reply to a question that she saw nothing, but almost immediately a sly smile spread over her face and she began to chuckle. Asked what she was laughing at, she said: "I don't know... nothing... oh—that funny machine." Although the right hemisphere could not describe what it had seen, the sight nevertheless elicited an emotional response like the one evoked from the left hemisphere.

Taken together, our studies seem to demonstrate conclusively that in a split-brain situation we are really dealing with two brains, each separately capable of mental functions of a high order. This implies that the two brains should have twice as large a span of attention—that is, should be able to handle twice as much information—as a normal whole brain. We have not yet tested this precisely in human patients, but E. D. Young and I have found that a split-brain monkey can indeed deal with nearly twice as much information as a normal animal [*see illustration below*]. We have so far determined also that brain-bisected patients can carry out two tasks as fast as a normal person can do one.

Just how does the corpus callosum of the intact brain combine and integrate the perceptions and knowledge of the two cerebral hemispheres? This has been investigated recently by Giovanni Berlucchi, Giacomo Rizzolati and me at the Istituto di Fisiologia Umana in Pisa. We made recordings of neural activity in the posterior part of the callosum of the cat with the hope of relating the responses of that structure to stimulation of the animal's visual fields. The kinds of responses recorded turned out to be similar to those observed in the visual cortex of the cat. In other words, the results suggest that visual pattern information can be transmitted through the callosum. This finding militates against the notion that learning and memory are transferred across the callosum, as has usually been suggested. Instead, it looks as though in animals with an intact callosum a copy of the visual world as seen in one hemisphere is sent over to the other, with the result that both hemispheres can learn together a discrimination presented to just one hemisphere. In the split-brain animal this extension of the visual pathway is cut off; this would explain rather simply why no learning proceeds in the visually isolated hemisphere and why it has to learn the discrimination from scratch.

Curiously, however, the neural activity in the callosum came only in response to stimuli at the midline of the visual field. This finding raises difficult questions. How can it be reconciled with the well-established observation that the left hemisphere of a normal person can give a running description of all the visual information presented throughout the entire half-field projected to the right hemisphere? For this reason alone one is wearily driven back to the conclusion that somewhere and somehow all or part of the callosum transmits not only a visual scene but also a complicated neural code of a higher order.

All the evidence indicates that separation of the hemispheres creates two independent spheres of consciousness within a single cranium, that is to say, within a single organism. This conclusion is disturbing to some people who view consciousness as an indivisible property of the human brain. It seems premature to others, who insist that the capacities revealed thus far for the right hemisphere are at the level of an automaton. There is, to be sure, hemispheric inequality in the present cases, but it may well be a characteristic of the individuals we have studied. It is entirely possible that if a human brain were divided in a very young person, both hemispheres could as a result separately and independently develop mental functions of a high order at the level attained only in the left hemisphere of normal individuals.

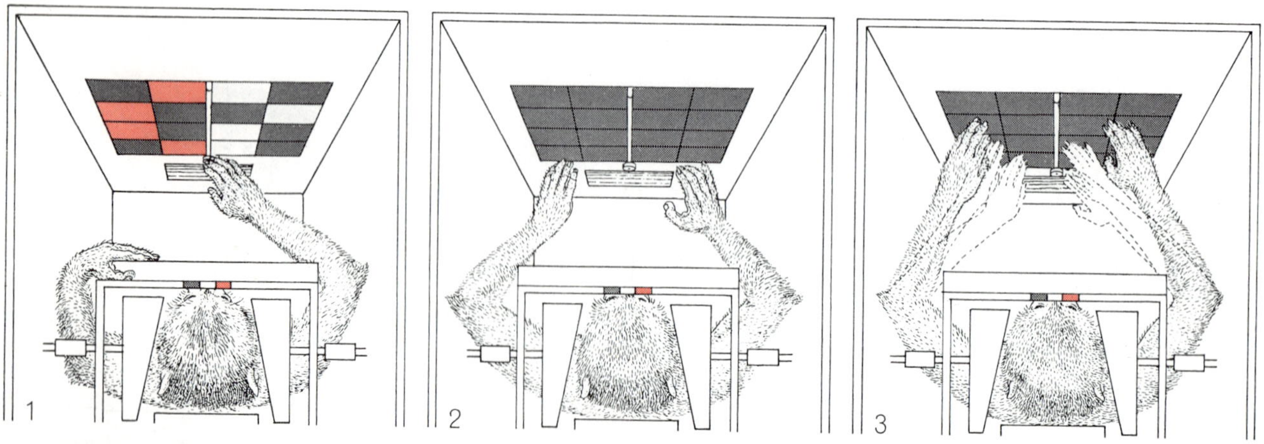

SPLIT-BRAIN MONKEYS can handle more visual information than normal animals. When the monkey pulls a knob (*1*), eight of the 16 panels light momentarily. The monkey must then start at the bottom and punch the lights that were lit and no others (*2*). With the panels lit for 600 milliseconds normal monkeys get up to the third row from the bottom before forgetting which panels were lit (*3*). Split-brain monkeys complete the entire task with the panels lit only 200 milliseconds. The monkeys look at the panels through filters; since the optic chiasm is cut in these animals, the filters allow each hemisphere to see the colored panels on one side only.

II

SENSORY SYSTEMS

II

SENSORY SYSTEMS

INTRODUCTION

In a way, each of our senses is like a sieve, catching only a small fraction of all available information. Our view of the world about us is limited because the range of energies to which we can respond is limited. We can sense directly only those types of energies that our transducers, or sense organs, can detect and convert to neural signals. The kind of information that we are able to "sieve out" is therefore limited by the types of sense organs that we possess.

For example, perception of direct information about the external world as it is conveyed by electromagnetic waves is essentially limited to the visible region of the spectrum—only about one ten-quadrillionth of the total range that we may explore with the aid of physical devices. However, within this narrow band of wavelengths (from about 350 to 750 millimicrons), we find all of the light visible to other animals and all of the light employed by plants in photosynthesis. That living organisms have developed and selected transducers sensitive to this region of the electromagnetic spectrum is not entirely fortuitous. According to George Wald (see his article "Light and Life," available as SCIENTIFIC AMERICAN Offprint 61), the choice is dictated by intrinsic factors, including the general role of energy in chemical reactions, and the nature of the molecules that mediate the utilization of light by living organisms. What ultimately sets the range of useful wavelengths is not only their availability, but their suitability to perform certain tasks. Ultraviolet radiation below 300 millimicrons denatures proteins and depolymerizes nucleic acids, preventing normal cell development. On the other hand, wavelengths in the far-infrared beyond 2000 millimicrons are too "hot" for sustained life. Thus, the wavelengths most suitable for the development of life are those lying in or near the visible region of the spectrum. We are fortunate that the composition of our atmosphere is such that an ozone

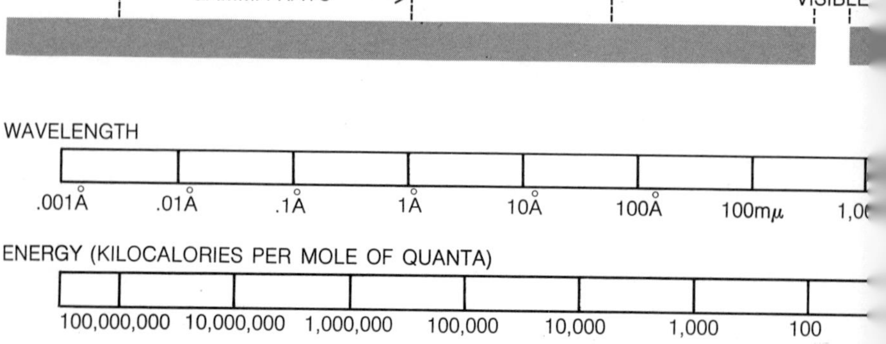

Figure 1. **The electromagnetic spectrum is divided by man into qualitatively different regions (*top bar*), although the only difference between one kind of radiation and another is difference in wavelength (*middle bar*). From gamma rays measured here in Ångstrom units, or hundred-millionths of centimeter (Å), through light waves, measured here in millimicrons, or ten-millionths of a centimeter (mμ), the waves range upward**

layer absorbs the ultraviolet radiation, whereas radiation in the far-infrared and beyond is absorbed almost completely by water vapor, carbon dioxide, and ozone. As shown by Figure 2, the radiation that most effectively penetrates our atmosphere lies near 500 millimicrons—not far from the center of the visible spectrum.

Perhaps it is not surprising, therefore, that the wavelength to which man and other animals have the greatest sensitivity is 510 millimicrons, in the blue-green region of the spectrum. Wald further notes that, of the eleven major phyla of animals, only three have developed well-formed, image-resolving eyes: the arthropods (insects, crabs, spiders), the mollusks (octopus, squid), and the vertebrates. Quite clearly, these three kinds of eyes are analogous (that is, they all perform the same function), but they are not homologous (they do not have the same evolutionary origins—each appears to have been an independent development). Each of the three kinds of eyes, however, possesses a chemistry of the visual process that is very nearly identical to that of the others, a photochemistry that permits maximum sensitivity to the appropriate energies of the electromagnetic spectrum available on earth. Will life and visual systems elsewhere in the universe also be restricted to the same range of wavelengths and develop in a similar manner?

Similar arguments may be made for the selection of other types of sensory transducers. For example, information transmission or communication by sound waves is subject to several kinds of constraints that delimit the optimal frequency band. Obvious constraints are: (1) the size of the sound box (such as the vocal cords in man); (2) the size of the receiver (ear or antenna); (3) the noise spectrum (that is, extraneous, random sounds in the environment that might mask the message-carrying signal); and (4) the desired resolution and distance

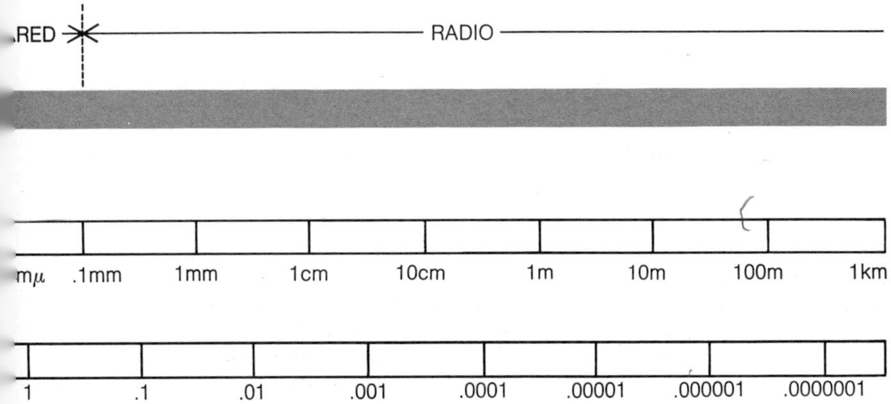

in length to the longest radio waves. The difference in wavelength is associated with a decisive difference in the energy conveyed by radiation at each wavelength. This energy content (*bottom bar*) is inversely proportional to wavelength. [From "Life and Light," by George Wald, *Scientific American*, October 1959.]

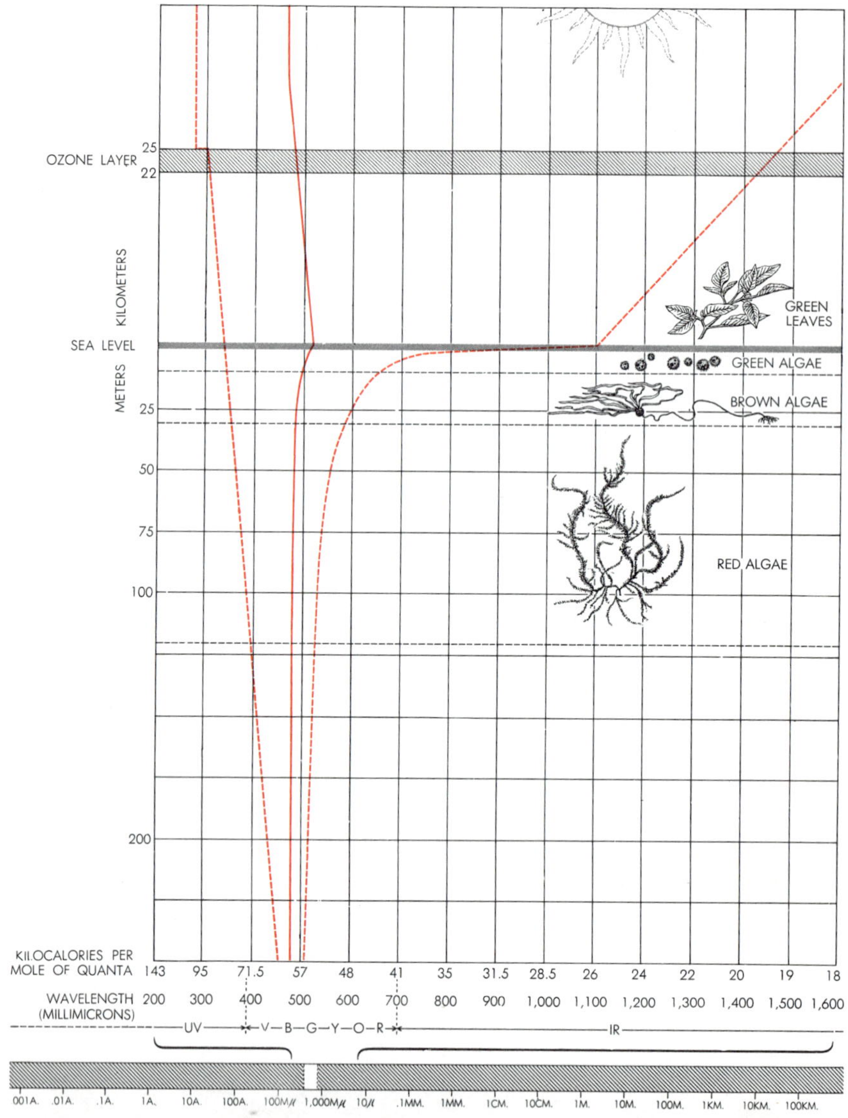

Figure 2. **The spectrum of sunlight at the earth's surface is narrowed by atmospheric absorption to the range of wavelengths (from 320 to 1,100 millimicrons) that are effective in photobiological processes. The sunlight reaching the domain of life in the sea is further narrowed by absorption in the sea water. The solid colored line locates the wavelengths of maximum intensity; the broken colored lines, the wavelength-boundaries within which 90 percent of the solar energy is concentrated at each level in the atmosphere and ocean. The letters above the spectrum of wavelengths at bottom represent ultraviolet (*UV*), violet (*V*), blue (*B*), green (*G*), yellow (*Y*), orange (*O*), red (*R*) and infrared (*IR*). Other usages in the chart are explained in Figure 1. [From "Life and Light," by George Wald, *Scientific American*, October 1959.]**

of communication. If the information rate (which is closely related to resolution) is of principal concern, then the highest possible frequencies should be used. The bat uses the ultrasonic range (20–100 kc) for echolocation. This "choice" was dictated, in part, by the practical requirement that any signal carrier for echolocating should be at least one-tenth the signal length, which may be shorter than 0.5 msec. if phase information is to be extracted. Thus, a lower bound on the frequency range will be about 20 kc. One constraint on the upper frequencies is that the bat is a small animal with limited acoustic power and cannot afford the loss in transmission distance that he would incur by using exceptionally high frequencies. Although signal resolution would be improved by going to higher frequencies, the transmission distances would be limited. Thus, one effective strategy for the bat would be to increase the frequency of the emitted signal as he approaches his prey; there is some evidence that this flexible behavior is a part of the repertory of certain species of bat.

Because the attenuation of sound waves increases roughly as the square of the frequency, the lowest available frequencies are more suitable for communication at a distance. Yet, there are obvious constraints that set a lower bound to suitable frequencies. For example, our body movements and the contractions of our own muscles generate sounds that we can hear when our ears are plugged. These low-frequency noises are near the threshold of the low-frequency portion of our auditory range—our ears are just insensitive enough so that we generally do not hear these kinds of disturbances. For man, frequencies between 200 and 4000 cycle/sec are optimal. Within this range, our ears and vocal cords are exquisitely matched to provide maximum transmittance for speech communication, with a frequency band broad enough to allow us to include frequency modulation as a carrier of information. Less fortunate, however, are smaller animals, such as insects, who are limited to amplitude modulations at a single frequency, or to variations in the duration of the tone burst. But even with such restrictions upon the carrier, acoustical communication can still be used effectively. An elegant example is offered by the bee, who can make about ten distinctly different sounds, some of which can be related to specific activities, such as indicating the distance to food sources (see Adrian M. Wenner's "Sound Communication in Honeybees," available as SCIENTIFIC AMERICAN Offprint 181). Most of these sounds lie in the range of 250–2000 cycle/sec, and hence are heard by us as buzzing.

Less conspicuous to man, however, is the world of insect communication based upon the chemical senses. It is becoming increasingly clear that chemical systems provide the dominant means of communication in many species, particularly insects. The effectiveness of some of these chemical communication systems is astounding: given the proper wind conditions, a female gypsy moth may attract males from more than a mile away. Clearly, molecules that are effective for chemical communication of this sort are subject to certain constraints. Sex attractants, for example, generally have between ten and seventeen carbon atoms and have molecular weights between 180 and 300. According to Edward O. Wilson (see his article "Pheromones," available as SCIENTIFIC AMERICAN Offprint 157), only compounds of roughly this size or greater can meet the two basic requirements for a sex attractant: narrow specificity, so that only members of one species will respond to it; and high potency, so that only a small quantity will be necessary to elicit the appropriate reaction. If the molecular weight is much less than 180, there are not enough possible variations; if the molecules are much larger, then they become difficult to synthesize and are not as volatile, and their range for communication depends upon their volatility. It is interesting to speculate whether or not these constraints may be sufficiently strong to delimit the form of chemical communication throughout the universe, just as physical and organic chemistry has constrained life to utilizing the visible region of the electromagnetic spectrum.

The fact that the world of insect communication—just as many other worlds of animal communication—may be completely ignored by us demonstrates quite forcefully that what is not sensed is not missed. There exists around us a number of chemical communication systems that transmit a large amount of information about the environment, and yet we remain in almost complete ignorance of this chemical world. By analogy, we may infer that even when our principal sensory systems—hearing and vision—are missing some transduction capability, then we are not aware of this loss, unless someone points out to us our failures of discrimination. Thus, the common "blindnesses"—such as color blindness, tone deafness, and taste blindness, which are described by H. Kalmus in his article "Inherited Sense Defects"—have little impact upon one's perceptions of the surrounding world. What is not seen cannot be missed—just as your own blindspot cannot be "seen" except by inference, as when an object known to lie eighteen degrees temporal to the fixation point suddenly disappears in one eye's view.

To those interested in sensory and perceptual systems, the "blindnesses" provide a valuable tool. They help to identify the various possible modes of processing; they suggest how sensory systems may interact in normal individuals; and they can also be used to reveal the adaptive capabilities of an entire sensory system that is forced to compensate for the loss of sensory input.

THE CHEMICAL SENSES

Paradoxically, our most primitive senses—smell and taste—have been the most difficult to explain. We can accurately define and characterize light, touch, and sound by simple physical measurements, but we cannot adequately define taste or smell along any one physical continuum. Yet the subjective dimensions of taste and smell are reasonably clear: we generally recognize four basic tastes—sweet, salty, bitter, and sour; and about seven basic odors—camphoraceous, musky, floral, pepperminty, ethereal, pungent, and putrid. Our descriptions of odors and tastes are generally based upon comparisons with these more familiar categories. However, when we list the physical attributes of those substances that yield a common sensation, we find that there is no single, unidimensional physical property that can be used to define that particular class of sensation.

In the absence of a clear, physical continuum that correlates with olfactory and gustatory sensations, alternate schemes must be devised for classifying these kinds of stimuli. One possible approach is to attempt to identify the basic types of sensations that contribute to smelling and tasting. Two approaches in this direction are obvious: (1) the study of odor and taste "blindnesses," and (2) generalizing to man the forms of chemical transduction used by relatively primitive animals.

The rationale for studying chemoreception in primitive animals, therefore, is the possibility that the same or similar systems may also be used by man. Perhaps by examining the broad categories of stimuli that yield the same behavioral responses in such a simple animal as an insect, various transducers may be identified. For example, those substances that are used by insects to signal alarm show surprising similarities: of the seven alarm substances known in the social insects, six have ten or fewer carbon atoms (see Edward O. Wilson's article "Pheromones," available as SCIENTIFIC AMERICAN Offprint 157). The chemical structure of four alarm substances is shown in Figure 3 (such insect repellents as citronella are composed of mixtures of such compounds). For comparison, six sex substances are shown in Figure 4. Because these latter substances serve as attractants, rather than repellents, it is of interest to note the differences in their structure. Sex pheromones have higher molecular weights; thus, their specificity and potency is increased but their volatility and effective range are decreased. Narrow specificity for attractants is necessary to restrict the response only to members of the species. Further specificity without an increase in weight becomes possible by altering the shape of compounds. The mammalian musks in Figure 4, for example, have distinctly different structures, one consisting of a chain and the other a ring of carbon atoms. This structural difference suggests at least two possible kinds of receptor sites that might differentiate between the two musks. Better substantiated discriminations that are dependent upon chemical structure are discussed by Edward S. Hodgson in his article "Taste Receptors." Two sugar alcohols, inositol and dulcitol, produce two different and dissociable responses in the blowfly—feeding and repulsion, respectively—despite the fact that the two are chemically very similar. The difference is attributable to the configuration of the two molecules: inositol has a ring structure, like the sugars that are most stimulating to the fly, while dulcitol has a chain structure. With luck, perhaps similar dissociations can be made in mammals, including man, by studying response patterns—or their absence, in cases of "odor blindness."

The most sophisticated analysis of stimulus structure and chemotransduction has been made by John E. Amoore and his colleagues James W. Johnston, Jr., and Martin Rubin (see their article "The

DENDROLASIN (*LASIUS FULIGINOSUS*)

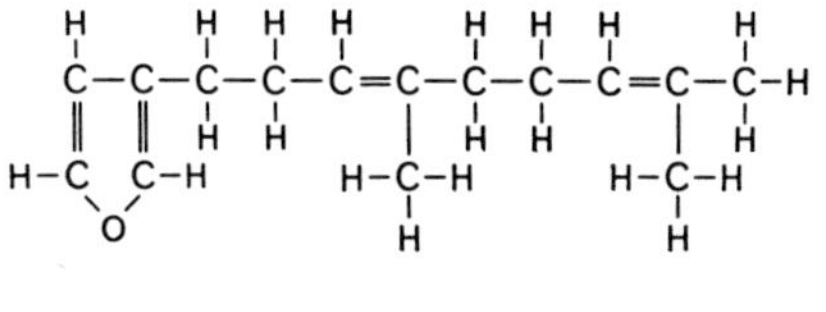

CITRAL (*ATTA SEXDENS*)

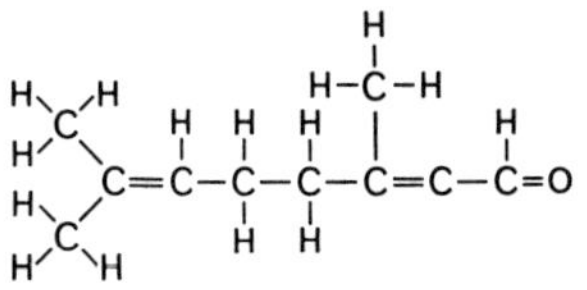

CITRONELLAL (*ACANTHOMYOPS CLAVIGER*)

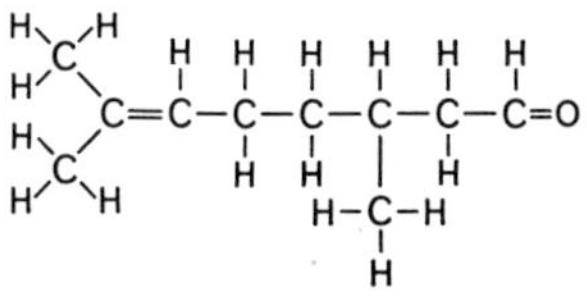

2-HEPTANONE (*IRIDOMYRMEX PRUINOSUS*)

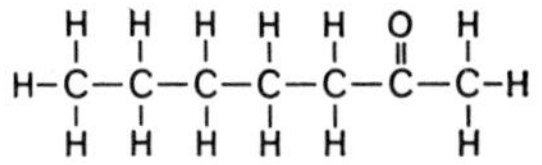

Figure 3. **Four alarm pheromones, given off by the workers of the ant species indicated, have so far been identified. Disturbing stimuli trigger the release of these substances from various glandular reservoirs. [From "Pheromones," by Edward O. Wilson, *Scientific American*, May 1963.]**

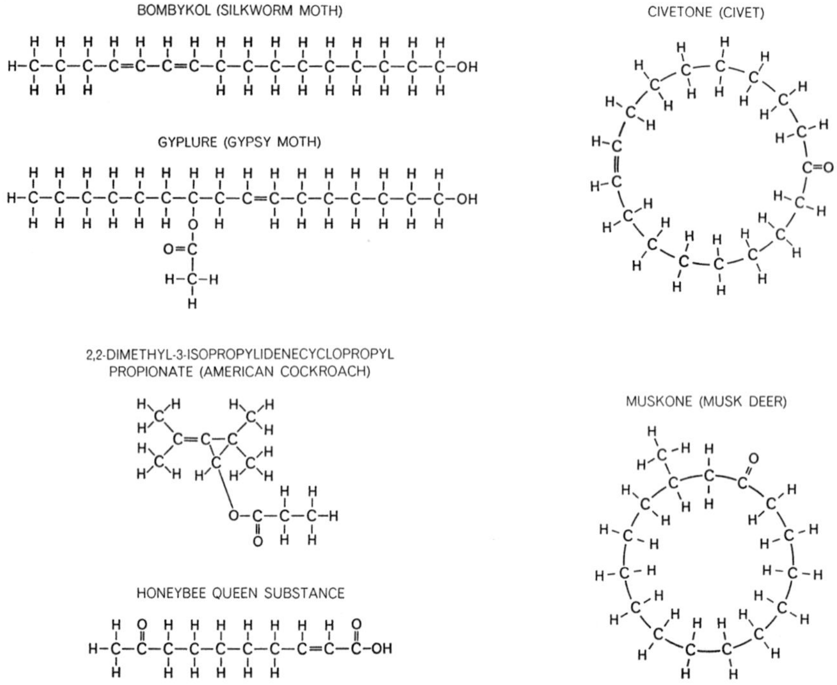

***Figure 4.* Six sex pheromones include the identified sex attractants of four insect species as well as two mammalian musks generally believed to be sex attractants. The high molecular weight of most sex pheromones accounts for their narrow specificity and high potency. [From "Pheromones," by Edward O. Wilson, *Scientific American*, May 1963.]**

Stereochemical Theory of Odor"). The proposal is simple, and was first clearly stated by R. W. Moncrieff (1951): ". . . odorous molecules produce their effects by fitting closely into 'receptor sites.'" Thus, according to this model, the shape and size of the molecule are the most crucial physical correlates. This "lock-and-key" concept is discussed extensively by Amoore and his co-workers in their article, and it is of interest to compare their proposed receptor sites with those required by insects for the perception of attractants and alarm substances.

Unfortunately, as elegant as the scheme proposed by Amoore and his co-workers may be, there is a logical flaw in their method for deciding upon the number of basic receptor sites for olfactory mechanisms. The difficulty is that the number of dimensions that we assign with words to the qualities of our sensations can greatly exceed the number of different transducers that lead to those sensations. We know, for example, that there are only three different kinds of photopigments that subserve color vision (see W. A. H. Rushton's article "Visual Pigments in Man"), but there are at least seven different names commonly used to describe our color sensations: red, orange, yellow, green, blue, violet, and black (or white). Thus, only three different transducers are sufficient to produce seven or more different sensory qualities. In general, we always tend to divide our sensory continua into seven different parts, such as seven labels for color qualities, seven "pitches," and seven basic olfactory sensations. George A. Miller has discussed this frequent occurrence of the magical number seven (± 2) in his article in Section I, and he cites other examples and discusses a possible rationale. The inference is clear: we cannot "deduce" the number of different kinds of peripheral transducers or "sites" from the number of attributes that we assign to the class of sensations associated with them.

Instead, the complex problem of the chemical senses must be solved by further, more direct studies of the peripheral sense organs. Unfortunately, the direct approach is exceedingly difficult in man; thus, most investigators, like Hodgson, have concentrated their efforts upon insects and other submamallian forms of life. One exception, however, is George von Békésy (1967), who has begun a study of the taste sense in man by direct electrical stimulation of the taste buds. In order to investigate the possible relations between the transducer itself and the associated sensations, von Békésy took care to stimulate only one collection of taste buds (on single papillae) at a time. His results, which are summarized in Table 1, show that there

TABLE 1. *A comparison of certain features of two types of papillae, each of which produces a different taste sensation.*

Type of papillae	Shape	Location on tongue	Best frequency of response (cycle/sec)	Response to drugs	
				Gymnemic acid	Miraculous fruit
Sour or salt	rounded top	sides	40	none	sensation abolished
Sweet or bitter	pointed top	tip or back	80	sensation abolished	none

Source: Data from von Békésy (1967).

must be at least two different kinds of transducers, which, when separately stimulated, produce sensations of either bitter and sweet, or salty and sour. Direct stimulation of individual transducers may thus elicit only a limited variety of sensations, suggesting certain basic sensory attributes. But such inferences between transduction and sensation may be made in only one direction: the transducers cannot be inferred from the sensations, but certain sensations may be correlated with particular transducers.

THE MECHANICAL SENSES

There are probably more varieties of sense organs that respond to mechanical stimulation than to any other kind of physical energy. In man alone, there are three major classes of mechanical sense organs: (1) those on the skin or at the joints; (2) the vestibular organs; and (3) the ear. Each of these types of transducers actually evolved quite early, and each appears in very sophisticated forms in many lower animals.

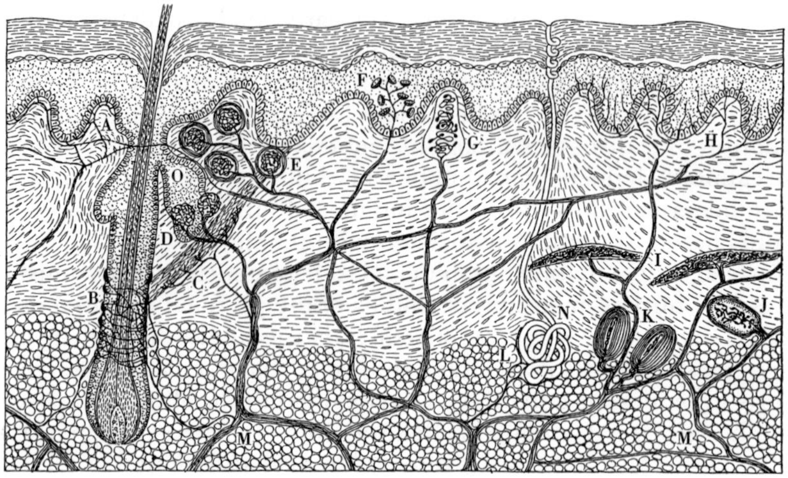

Figure 5. **Nerve endings in the skin are the receptors of touch, heat, cold, and pain. These and other structures are labeled as follows in this schematic drawing of a microscopic cross section of the skin: *A* indicates free nerve endings; *B*, nerve endings around a hair follicle; *C*, sympathetic nerve fibers supplying a small muscle; *D*, Ruffini's endings; *E*, Krause's end bulbs; *F*, Merkel's disks; *G*, Meissner's corpuscles; *L*, sympathetic fibers innervating a sweat gland; *M*, nerve trunks; *N*, sweat gland; *O*, sebaccous gland. The function of each type of ending is not known. [From "What is Pain?" by W. K. Livingston, *Scientific American*, March 1953.]**

Perhaps the simplest mechanical transducer associated with the nervous systems is the free nerve ending itself. In man, the surface of the body contains many such free nerve endings, which are believed to mediate, in part, sensations of pain. For example, the cornea of the eye, from which "painful" sensations can be elicited by even mild contact, relies upon free nerve ends almost exclusively to sense mechanical stimulation.

Various capsules and end organs, which serve to increase the sensitivity of the free nerve ending and to introduce some selectivity of function, appear as refined appendages to the nerve axon. Werner R. Loewenstein, in his article "Biological Transducers," describes one such refinement: the Pacinian corpuscle. This onionlike appendage acts as a mechanical amplifier, creating a novel transducer that will respond to very small amounts of mechanical deformation—as small as one-half micron. In man, this type of nerve ending is common in the joints, and is also believed to subserve vibration sensations originating near the surface of the skin. Other specialized end organs were proposed by M. von Frey at the turn of the century as the principal mediators of other cutaneous sensations, such as touch and warmth and cold. This simple proposal—that specific receptor types underlie different sensations—has failed several crucial tests, however. For example, when spots of maximum sensitivity to warmth and cold are mapped on the skin, the positions of maximum sensitivity do not remain constant from one mapping to the next, which casts doubt on the idea that fixed immobile receptors are responsible for detecting warmth and cold on the skin. Furthermore, once regions of optimal sensitivity to mechanical stimuli have been mapped on the skin, and the surface of the skin is then peeled off and inspected, there is generally no one-to-one relationship between the type of receptors found in a given region and the sensation reported for that region.

In spite of these difficulties, the simplicity and elegance of von Frey's proposal still make it the leading theory of cutaneous sensation. In its modern form, however, an exact one-to-one relation between receptor type and sensation is not the central issue; other factors, such as the spatial and temporal properties of the neuronal activity, are also recognized as significant. Two findings provide strong evidence for the existence of dissociable receptor systems: the application of anaesthesia and the pressure blocking of a nerve (as occurs when an arm "goes to sleep") both result in an ordered, sequential loss of sensations. These findings are of interest because both manipulations progressively incapacitate the nerve fibers according to their size. Thus, anaesthesia affects the smallest fibers first and the largest last, whereas pressure blocking acts in the reverse direction. For both manipulations, the correlation with fiber inactivity and loss of sensitivity is the same. Large fibers seem to be associated with kinesthetic sensations, whereas the smallest fibers appear to subserve pain. The "fiber spectrum," from the largest fibers to the smallest, seems to be correlated with the following "spectrum" of sensations: kinesthesis, touch, pressure, sting, warmth, cold, and deep pain. All of these fibers from the skin go first to the spinal cord, where they synapse upon a second fiber that sends the resulting signal to the brain.

In man and most other animals, the surface of the skin serves primarily as a protective covering and not as a sensitive receiver of mechanical stimulation. More specialized organs are needed to improve the reception of mechanical energy. The most sensitive organs are characterized by a membrane and affiliated hair cells. The most common of these specialized "ears" are the tympanic organs of such insects as the moth and the subgenual organs (in the knee joint) of other arthropods, such as spiders and ants. Sound causes the membrane to vibrate and the vibrations, in turn, bend the hairs on the affiliated nerve cells, resulting in neural activity. Because most tympanic membranes are quite small, their optimal acoustic power usually lies beyond our range of hearing in the ultrasonic region. Such frequencies are an order of magnitude higher than the highest that neurons can follow. Hence, any communication of sound patterns in which tympanic organs are the only receivers is dependent upon amplitude modulations of the carrier. Such a sound-communication pattern used by honeybees is shown in Figure 6. Clearly, even though insect "ears" cannot appreciate the harmonies sensed by the human ear, they are quite capable of distinguishing elaborate patterns of communication that may indicate alarm, the presence of food, or the readiness of other members of the species to mate.

The principal advantage of the human ear over a simple tympanic auditory system is that it is capable of recognizing different tones. Not only does our ability to perform a frequency analysis of a sound pattern give us the capacity for the aesthetic pleasure of music, but it is also a significant factor in our capacity to recognize speech. Some of the complex sound patterns that we produce and recognize are portrayed in sound spectrograms in the article by Broadbent in Section I.

The mechanisms by which we are able to break a sound pattern into its component frequencies (Ohm's Law) is still far from clear. Georg von Békésy's article "The Ear" shows that, even though the ear is a very sensitive detector, the displacements of the vibrating tympanic membrane are quite broad. The problem is to translate these

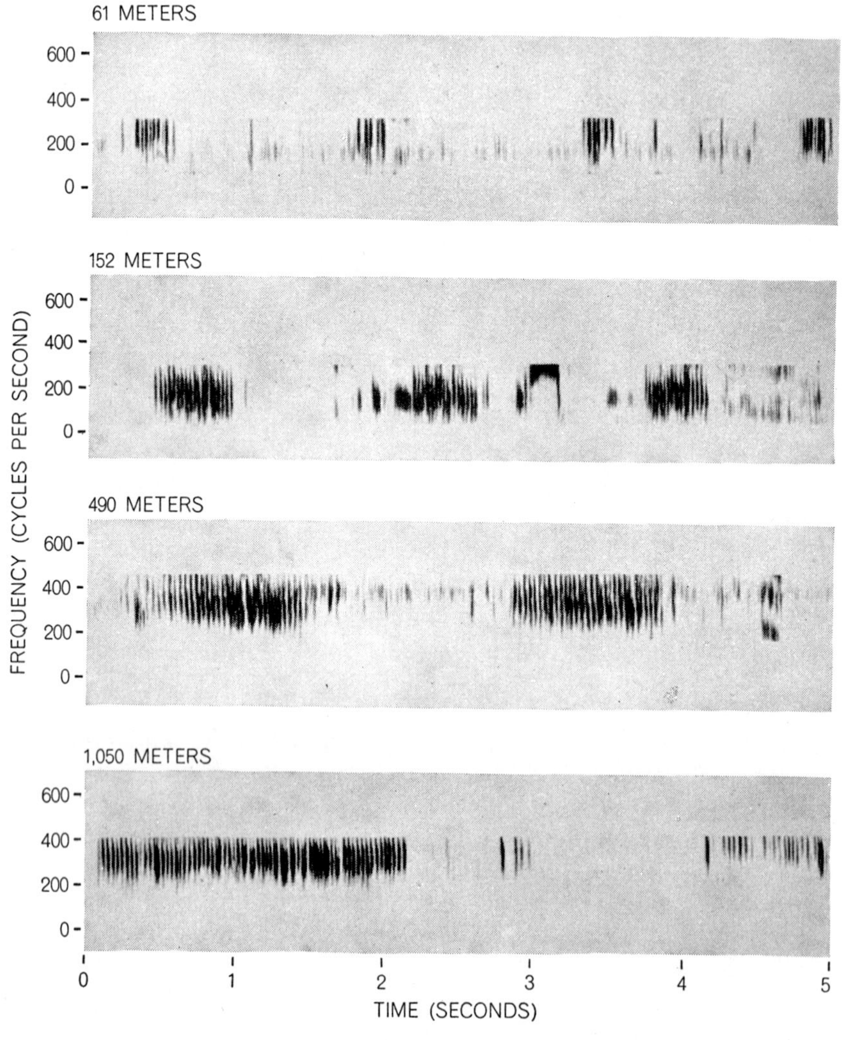

Figure 6. **Worker sounds are shown in these spectrograms. The top tracing illustrates two sounds produced when a hive is disturbed: the sharp burst of a disturbed worker (*left*), followed by two faint beeps, or worker piping. The middle and bottom tracings show "croaking" and "bipping," two sounds that have yet to be related to any specific activity. [Spectrograms by Adrian M. Wenner, from his "Sound Communication in Honeybees," *Scientific American*, April 1964.]**

rather broad vibrations into separate sensations, where each sensation corresponds to a different frequency. The human ear is able to do this by localizing the positions of maximum displacement of the membrane—a process requiring considerable "neural" sharpening of the pattern of vibration of the tympanic membrane. Thus, von Békésy's proposal for frequency discrimination supplements the ability of neurons to "follow" low-frequency signals. The proposal is most significant in that it may also be applied to other sensory surfaces, such as the skin or the retina of the human eye. The general principles of neural image sharpening mentioned by von Békésy will thus reappear in subsequent articles.

THE PHOTO SENSES

The eye is often compared to a camera: it has a shutter (the eyelid), a diaphragm (the iris), and a lens, and it contains a photosensitive surface analogous to film (the retina with its photoreceptors). In his article "Eye and Camera," George Wald discusses these analogies, highlighting the similarities and differences in his historical overview of the development of our knowledge about the human eye. Just as the qualities of the film and resolving power of the camera are of particular interest to photographers, two properties of the "living camera" are of particular interest to those of us who study perception—the sensitivity of the retina and the resolving power of the eye.

One of the striking characteristics of all biological photosensors is that, regardless of the degree of optical complexity that they exhibit, their "film" or "emulsion" is very similar. Thus, the photopigments found in all eyes, from insect to mollusk or from fish to man, are all based on molecules of vitamin A, which are attached to proteins (opsins) that determine the optimal wavelength sensitivity of the pigment. One such photopigment is rhodopsin; found in some fishes and in most higher vertebrates, it allows for vision in very dim light. Rhodopsin is important to human vision, as are three other photopigments that provide different "film speeds" for daylight color vision. Because rhodopsin is found in receptors that resemble rods, whereas the pigments for color vision are usually found in receptors with tapered ends (cones), the term "rod vision" is often used to indicate night vision, and the term "cone vision," to signify vision at high light levels of illumination, in which colors are discriminated. Each of these four photopigments occurs in a different type of receptor. Thus, in addition to the rods, the retina contains three types of cones:

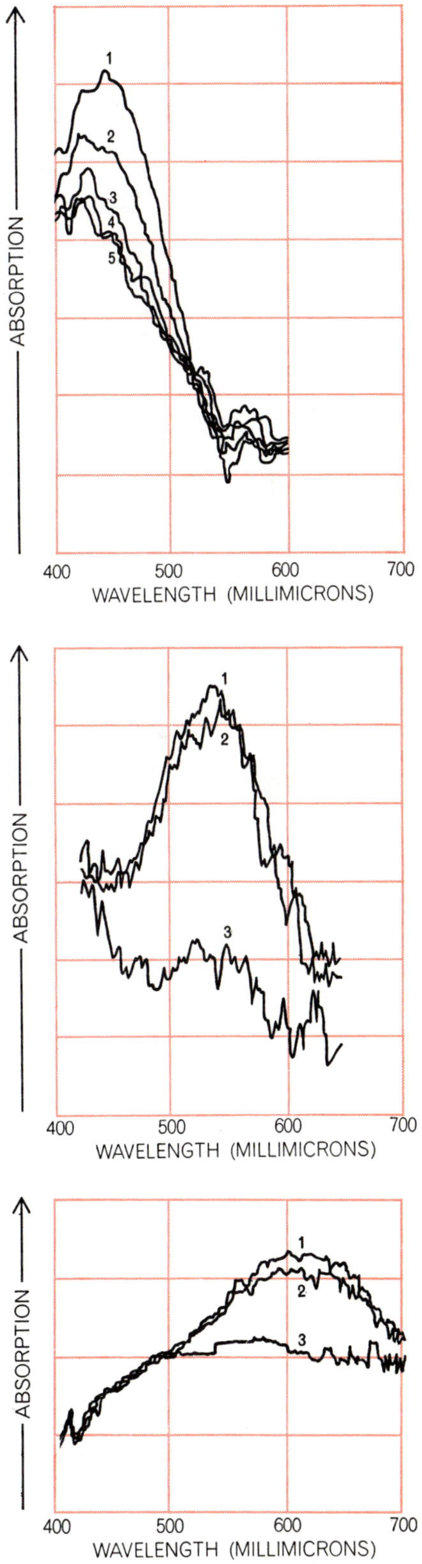

Figure 7. Spectral sensitivities of goldfish cone pigments obtained from individual cones by scanning the visible spectrum with monochromatic bleaching light. Because each scan bleaches the photopigment, successive scans (labelled 1–5 in the figure) yield different curves. The raw data for blue (_top_), green (_middle_), and red (_bottom_) cones were recorded with varying light intensities. The final curves in each figure were recorded after deliberate flash bleaching in white light. Subtracting the last from the first curves yields different spectra, which peak at wavelengths of about 455, 530, and 625 millimicrons, depending upon whether blue, green, or red cones were sampled. [From "Three-Pigment Color Vision," by Edward F. MacNichol, Jr., _Scientific American_, December 1964.]

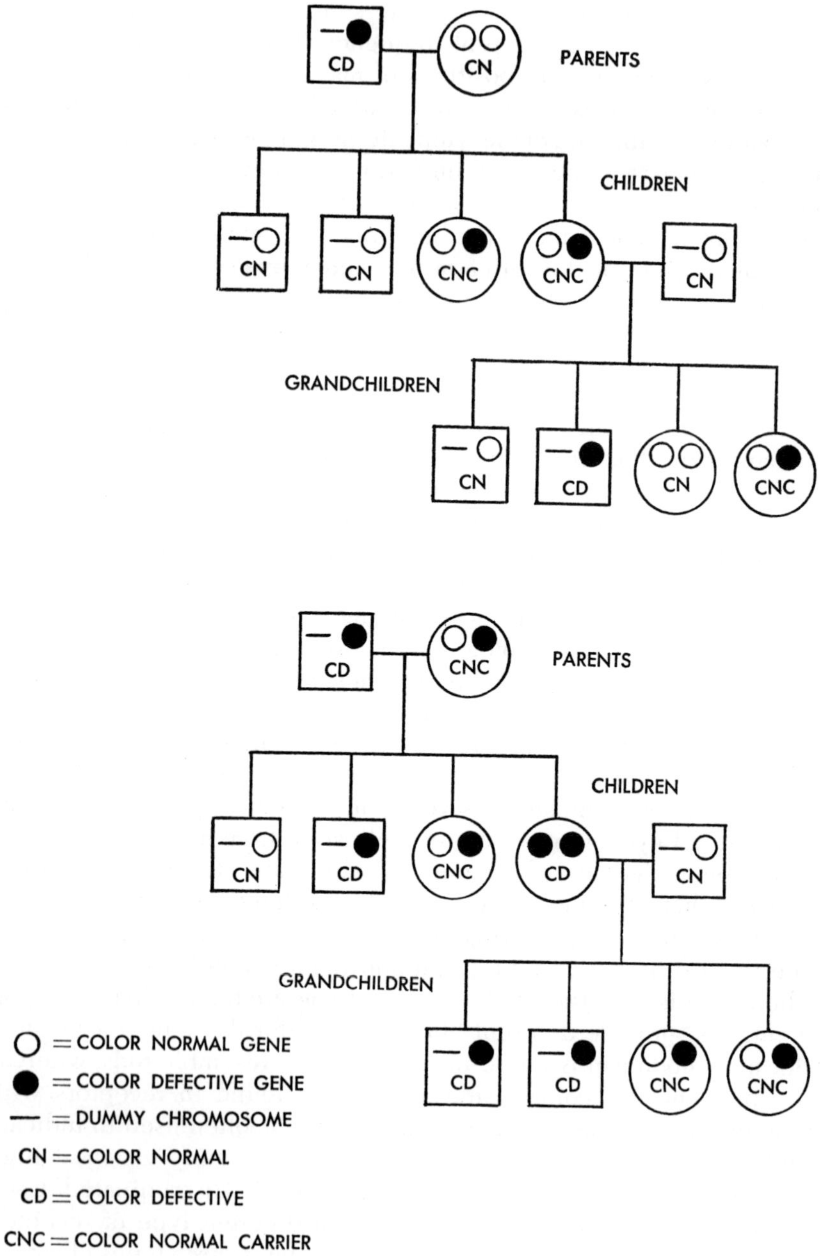

Figure 8. Inheritance of color blindness is sex-linked. Men (*squares*) possess only one color-normal or color-defective gene: women (*circles*), two. The color-defective gene is recessive, which means that women are color-blind only if they possess two of them. The chart at the top of the page shows that a color-blind man passes his defect through his daughters to half of his grandsons. The lower chart shows one of the two rare combinations that will result in a color-blind woman. The lower chart also shows that if a color-blind woman marries a color-normal man, all of their sons are color-blind. [From "Color Blindness," by Alphonse Chapanis, *Scientific American*, March 1951.]

one sensitive to blue light, another to green light, and a third to red light.

Even though it has only been in the past few years that the photopigments for color vision have been shown to be segregated into different receptors (see the article "Three-Pigment Color Vision," by Edward F. MacNichol, Jr., available as SCIENTIFIC AMERICAN Offprint 197), this possibility was raised as early as 1802 by the English physicist Thomas Young. The basis for postulating three different receptor mechanisms for color was twofold: First, it was found that all colors may be matched by suitable combinations of only three primary lights. This finding, demonstrated conclusively by James Clark Maxwell in 1860, suggested that three regions of the spectrum are sampled independently by the eye. Further support for this postulate came from color-blind observers, who required only two primary lights to match all colors. Color-blind observers confuse such colors as red and green, which are easily distinguished by those with normal color vision. Presumably, therefore, the color-blind observer lacks one of the receptor mechanisms, and is obtaining only two independent samples of the visible spectrum. Because no more than three basic types of color-blindness have been found—red-blindness, green-blindness, and blue-blindness—there is the strong implication that normal, trichromatic color vision is based upon three independent receptor mechanisms. The elegant spectrophotometric measurements on single cone cells by Wald's group at Harvard University and MacNichol's group at the Johns Hopkins University provided direct confirmation of Thomas Young's original three-receptor hypothesis.

With the knowledge that normal color vision is based upon the presence of three different cone pigments, we may state a simple rule for human color vision: Whenever the photopigments in the cones are bleached equally by different lights, then those lights will appear to be identical, regardless of their spectral composition. Thus, a broad-band spectral source, such as a fluorescent light, can be matched exactly by three narrow-band line spectra of suitable wavelengths and power. This rule reveals nothing about the color of the matched lights, other than that they appear equally blue-green, or red-orange, or whatever. Instead, the rule only specifies a condition under which spectrally different lights will appear the same. The perceived color of these two matching lights (metamers) may still be changed drastically by altering the color of a surrounding field. Yet the two lights will continue to match despite their physical differences. Clearly, the color match will continue to hold because the absorption of light by the photopigments will remain unchanged in the region of the retina that is illuminated by the matching lights. This simple rule for the apparent equivalence of two light sources is a constraint imposed upon color vision by the properties of the retinal "emulsion." No more than three suitably chosen wavelengths are needed to match any spectral source. A similar rule also applies to color photographic film.

Now that the types of receptors in the retina have been described,

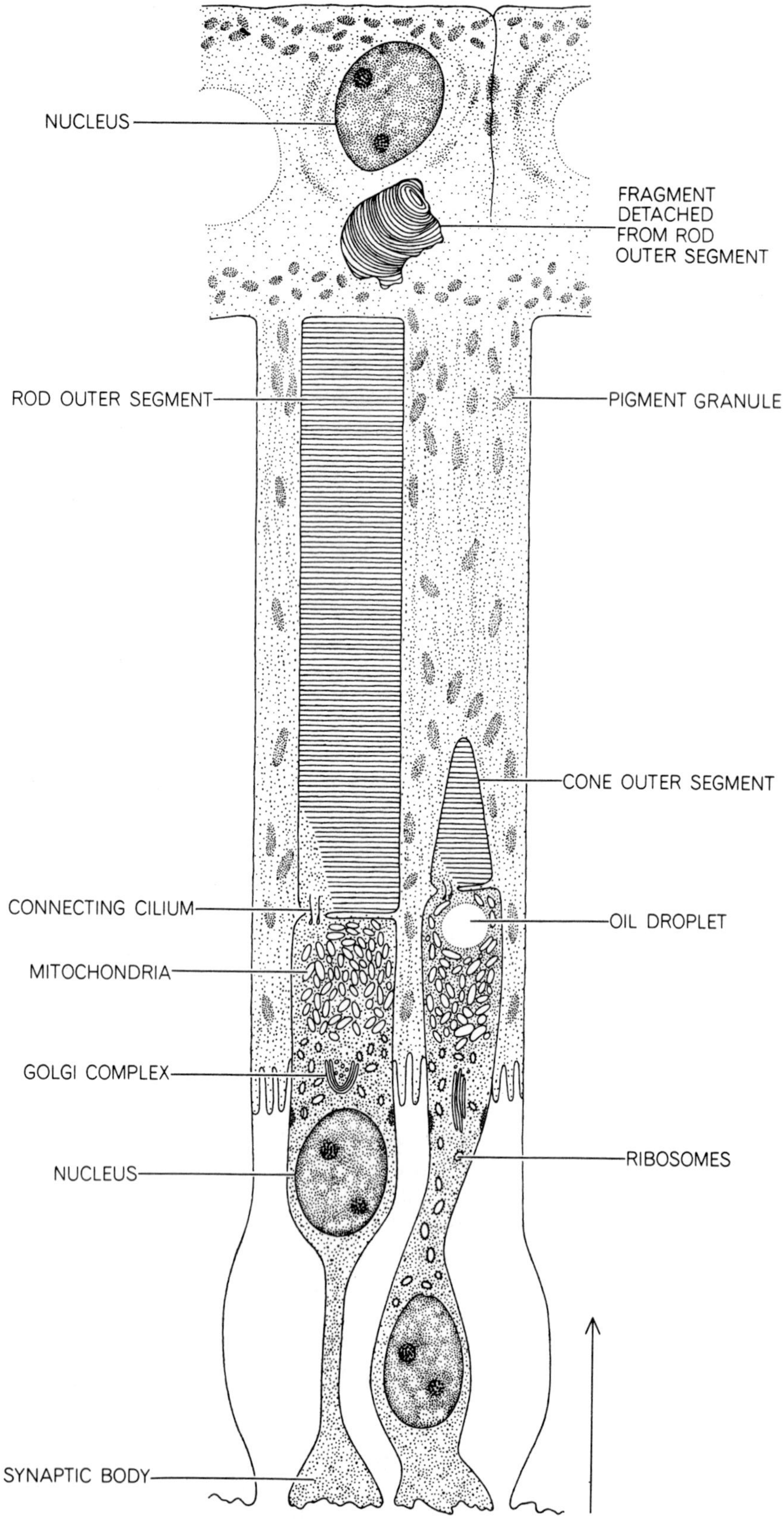

Figure 9. **Metabolic machinery of visual cells is compartmentalized. In the frog's retina the rod *(left)* and the cone *(right)* are oriented parallel to the path of light *(arrow)*, which passes through the transparent parts of the cell and is absorbed by pigment molecules in the disk-shaped membranes of the outer segment. The visual message is transmitted back along the cell to the synaptic body and thence to other retinal cells. Mitochondria supply cell's fuel; ribosomes and Golgi complex manufacture proteins and complex carbohydrates. [From "Visual Cells," by Richard W. Young, *Scientific American*, October, 1970.]**

much research effort is being concentrated on discovering the exact manner in which the light is "caught" by the pigments and transformed by the rods and cones into neural signals. The answer may lie, in part, in the extraordinary structure of the receptor cells. Each visual cell comprises two segments—an inner segment, which contains the substances necessary for the maintenance of the cell, and an outer segment, which contains the visual pigment (see Richard W. Young's article "Visual Cells," available as SCIENTIFIC AMERICAN Offprint 1201). It is the outer segment that traps the light; it is made up of hundreds of thin discs that are stacked on top of each other like pancakes. Light entering the eye first passes through the inner segment and then enters the outer segment to be "caught" by the photosensitive molecules in the discs. The initial absorption of a quantum of light by the visual pigment leads to the isomerization of its component vitamin-A aldehyde, causing the pigment molecule to change its shape. This change in shape presumably "uncorks" a plugged hole in the membrane of the disc, which, in turn, causes an avalanche of ion flow across the membrane. In some way, this signal propagates down the cell and is amplified and transmitted to the fiber and synapse at the base of the receptor. At this point, the signal is a neural one and is passed on to the next neural element (the bipolar cell). This entire sequence of events, from the absorption of the light to the generation of a neural signal, takes place in about three milliseconds. In order to accomplish this feat, the receptor that absorbs one quantum of light must amplify the energy more than a thousandfold—otherwise, there will be insufficient energy to trigger a nerve impulse. The efficiency of this quantum-catching and amplification process in the human eye is so great that, under ideal conditions, we can detect only a few quanta of light.

One of the further mysteries of the visual process is the manner in which the eye performs successfully over a range of light levels of ten-million to one. How many films need you buy in order to photograph scenes equally well in twilight in the forest or in intense sunlight in the desert? Yet the eye uses the same "film" for all purposes. Some years ago, it was believed that the sensitivity of the eye was regulated by the amount of photopigment remaining unbleached in the receptors. In his article "Visual Pigments in Man," W. A. H. Rushton clarifies this problem, making important distinctions between photochemical and neural factors, and concludes that the most significant process is neural feedback. Subsequent work has shown that bleached receptors continue to send their signals upstream, creating a "background" of neural activity. This background activity from the bleached receptors is then fed back so that it controls the gain of the newer, incoming signals. In very dim light, the background activity is low and the sensitivity of the eye is high; in bright light, the signal gain is reduced in order to maintain the same average signal strength. These neural processes occur in a matter of seconds, whereas the actual recovery of bleached photopigment takes many minutes. It is in this manner, through the use of neural mechanisms, that the eye can begin to outperform the camera.

REFERENCES

Geldard, F. A. *The human senses.* New York: John Wiley & Sons, 1953.

Hayashi, T. *Olfaction and taste.* New York: Pergamon Press, 1967.

Hornstein, I., & Teranishi, R. The chemistry of flavor. *Chemical and Engineering News*, 1967, **45**, 97–108.

Macrides, F., & Chorover, S. L. Olfactory bulb units: activity correlated with inhalation cycles and odor quality. *Science*, 1972, **175**, 84–87.

Moncrieff, R. W. *The chemical senses.* London: Leonard Hill, 1951.

Polyak, S. *The vertebrate visual system.* Chicago: University of Chicago Press, 1957.

Ratliff, F. *Mach bands: quantitative studies on neural networks in the retina.* San Francisco: Holden-Day, 1965.

Sinclair, D. *Cutaneous sensation.* London: Oxford University Press, 1968.

von Békésy, G. *Sensory inhibition.* Princeton, N.J.: Princeton University Press, 1967.

Whitfield, I. C. *The auditory pathway.* Baltimore, Md.: Williams & Wilkins, 1967.

Wilson, E. O. *The insect societies.* Cambridge, Mass.: Belknap Press, 1971.

INHERITED SENSE DEFECTS

H. KALMUS
May 1952

All our purposeful behavior, all our awareness of physical "reality," all our ideas about the universe ultimately derive from data which our sense organs alone can provide: *"Nihil est in intellectu, quid non est in sensibus."* Thus for the biologist and the philosopher alike the study of the structure and function of the sense organs is of outstanding importance.

No two animals or people live in exactly the same world, for no two are precisely identical in sense perception. A fish and a snail in the same aquarium actually are living in quite different subjective environments. Because of the differences in their eyes, brains and locomotor systems, they receive totally different impressions from the same stimuli. The snail, having poor visual acuity, will not perceive a hand waved before the tank unless it casts a shadow, but the fish may see every finger. Similarly a blind person lives in a different world from one who sees; the environment of a man differs from that of a bat, for the reason, among others, that he cannot hear supersonic sound as a bat can; and so on.

We shall consider here some differences in sense perception that are inherited, that is, controlled by genes. In the main these differences can be determined only on the basis of the individual's own subjective judgment or his performance in carefully prepared tests, for nobody has yet discovered any morphological difference between, for example, normal and color-blind eyes or normal and tone-deaf ears.

Certain perceptual abnormalities do betray themselves by visible physical signs; some interesting examples of this occur in insects. Among insects there sometimes appear mutant individuals with white eyes, lacking the usual red and brown pigments. These deviant specimens respond to light, but they are unable to react to moving patterns. A white-eyed drone bee cannot find its way back to the hive, and a white-eyed housefly can readily be caught with the hand, because it does not perceive the movement.

In at least one species of fruit fly (*Drosophila subobscura*) this has rather interesting consequences. It has been found impossible to maintain a pure white-eyed stock of such flies, because white-eyed males and females of this species apparently do not find each other or at any rate do not sufficiently excite each other to mate. White-eyed mutants of other fruit-fly species can be bred successfully, however, as they can mate even in complete darkness.

Drosophila flies show another visible sign of a perception defect: absence of antennae, which carry the organs of smell. Flies with the gene responsible for this defect may have only one antenna or none, instead of the normal two, and their sense of smell is impaired.

Genetic sense differences also are known in various strains of mice and

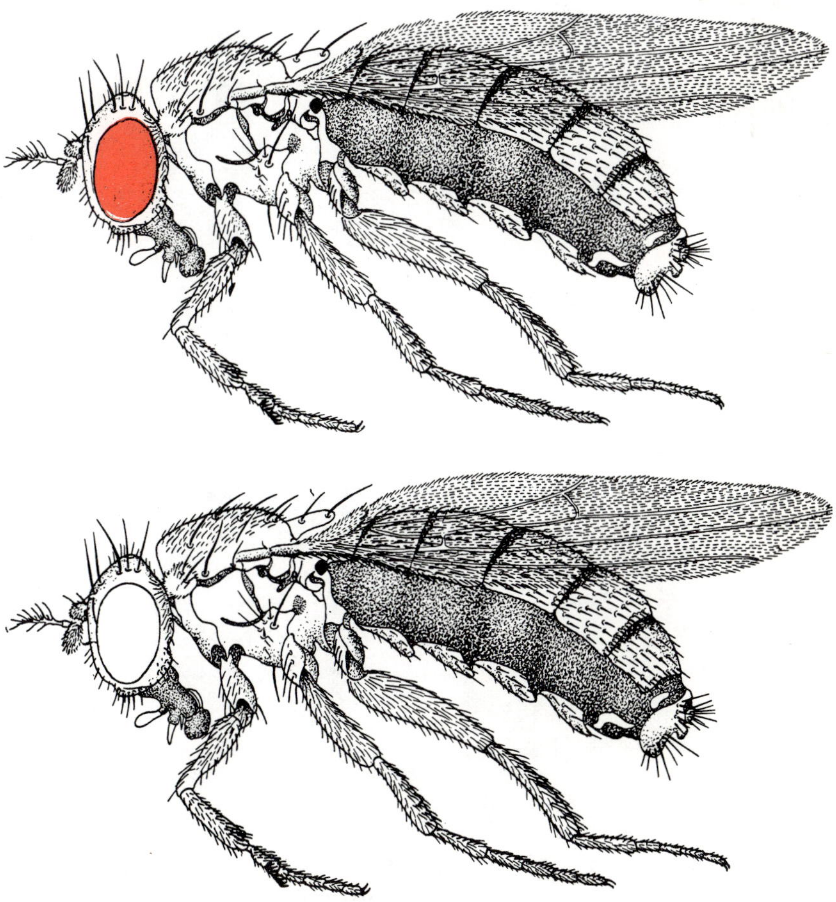

FRUIT FLY normally has a red eye (*top*). Some fruit flies have white eyes (*bottom*) and appear unable to perceive objects that are in motion.

voles. Individuals of certain pure lines of laboratory mice, for instance, are seized with violent fits and may even die when they are exposed to high-pitched sounds, whereas mice of other strains are completely impervious to such treatment. These fits are in some ways very similar to certain types of human epilepsy.

THE CLASSIC example of inherited sense variations in human beings, of course, is color blindness, which was well covered some time ago in SCIENTIFIC AMERICAN ("Color Blindess," by Alphonse Chapanis; March, 1951). Whether individual color blindness occurs in animals other than man is not known. We do know that various animal species differ in color perception. Bees cannot see red and can distinguish only between orange, yellow-green and blue hues; on the other hand, they do see a small range of ultraviolet, which is invisible to man. Many birds have yellow or orange oil globules in their retinas, and it is supposed that this enables them to see objects through a bluish haze better than other animals can. Some people believe that all dogs are color-blind; so far none has ever been trained to distinguish between colors. But this is still a moot question.

During blackout periods in the recent war it was discovered that many people are subject to night blindness. In a night-blind person the rods in the retina take an inordinately long time to become dark-adapted. Such people are quite helpless when they step out suddenly into a dark night, and they may remain unable to see for hours.

The defect exists in various forms, sometimes associated with eye disease of genetic origin, sometimes as an isolated trait. Some night-blind people can improve their dark-adaptation by taking large doses of vitamin A. Night blindness appears to be a sex-linked trait in some cases and linked to nonsex chromosomes in others.

TONE DEAFNESS, which I prefer to call tune deafness, is known to run in families. It is a familiar defect; almost everybody knows of friends who have been removed from a choral group because of inability to sing in tune, or who sing everything in a monotone or in the same off-key pattern, usually a distorted nursery melody. There is the famous story of the general at Queen Victoria's funeral who failed to rise for the national anthem.

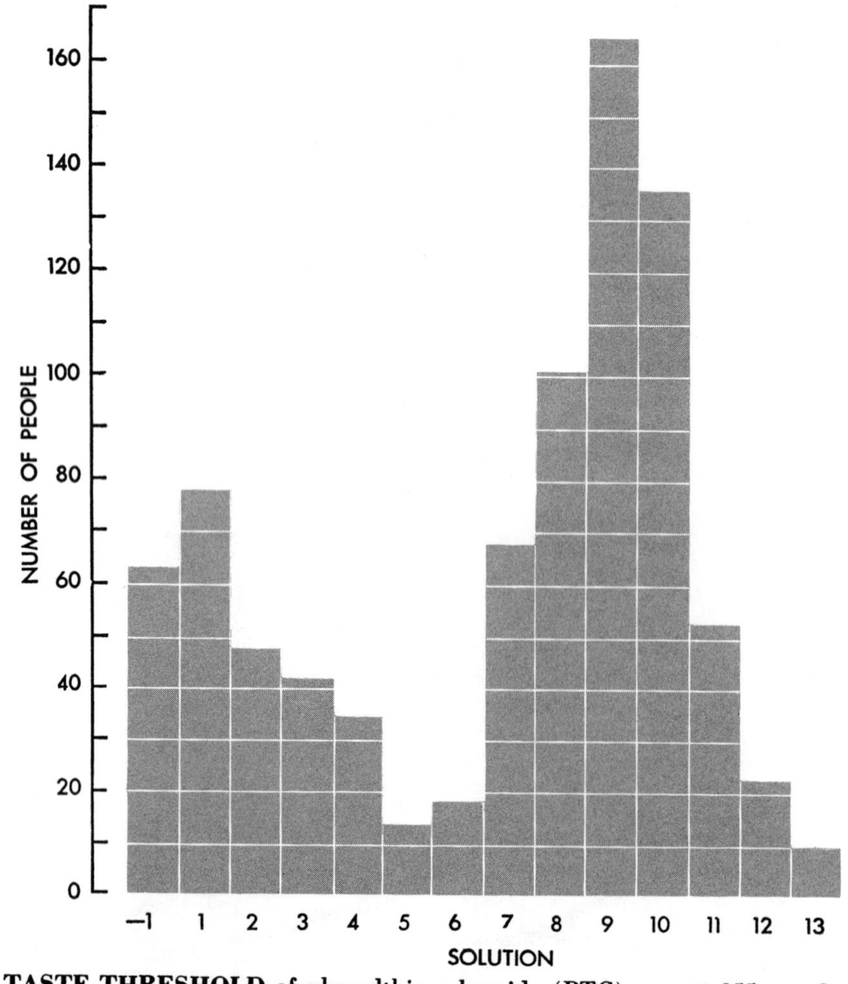

TASTE THRESHOLD of phenylthiocarbamide (PTC) among 855 people was oddly distributed in two peaks. Solution 1 was 1.3 grams of PTC per liter; each number indicates a solution half as strong as the one preceding it.

We do not know for certain whether tune deafness is caused by a single gene difference or controlled by many genetic factors. It is possible that several types of tune deafness exist. The genetical analysis is complicated by the fact that the condition is by no means independent of upbringing. In societies where music is regarded as socially valuable, children are trained to overcome their tune deafness to some extent. In spite of their handicap they can sometimes, if pressed, achieve a reasonable proficiency on the piano. But probably no such person has ever learned to sing tolerably or to play the violin or flute without arousing violent reactions. In general it is unprofitable to make a tune-deaf child take music lessons.

Many tune-deaf people have an acute dislike for music, but others may genuinely enjoy listening to it, especially dance and symphonic music. They can appreciate the rhythm, intensity and polyphonic structure of music, even if not the harmony or melody. Needless to say, tune deafness has nothing to do with intelligence; tune-deaf people may be highly sensitive to other forms of art.

To determine whether an individual is tune-deaf is not easy. Self-ratings are completely worthless. On the one hand there are assertive types, happily unaware of their atrocious performance, who insist that they have a perfect ear. On the other hand there are perfectionists who consider themselves tune-deaf because their singing or playing is slightly imperfect. Nor are the objective tests that have been devised altogether reliable, because test conditions are difficult to standardize and the effects of age and education cannot be separated.

Two points of view have been adopted concerning the physiology of tune deafness. One holds that it is primarily a defect in pitch discrimination or in perception of the melodic line. However, defective pitch discrimination, even where it exists, is probably not the whole story. Apparently auditory thresholds and the discrimination of intensity, length and "color" of sounds are not greatly impaired in tune-deaf people. The other point of view is that the individual notes of a melody are perceived more or less correctly but that their relationship is not accurately perceived. Tests to decide between those two possibilities unfortunately have not been decisive. People who are poor at recognizing melodies usually score low in pitch discrimination and in tonal memory.

Investigation has shown that the inability of tune-deaf people to sing correctly is rarely due to a motor defect but is as a rule caused by a defect in perception, or feedback.

An aspect of tune deafness on which one can only speculate is its possible effect on the history of music. A gene responsible for tune deafness, when brought in by marriage, can break the line of a musical family. This may very well have happened in the families of some famous composers. The family of Johann Sebastian Bach had for generations produced musicians, some of the first rank; 200 or 300 years ago the name Bach was synonymous with musician in Germany. But no great musical ability has been found among the numerous descendants of Johann Sebastian who now live in Germany and in North America.

Another defect on the higher level of perception that may be hereditary is the inability to read, known as dyslexia. People suffering from this defect may clearly perceive the individual letters of a word, but they cannot put them together. While every child experiences some such difficulty during an early phase of its school career, dyslectic children may never overcome it, in spite of high over-all intelligence. Inability to learn to spell correctly usually accompanies the inability to read.

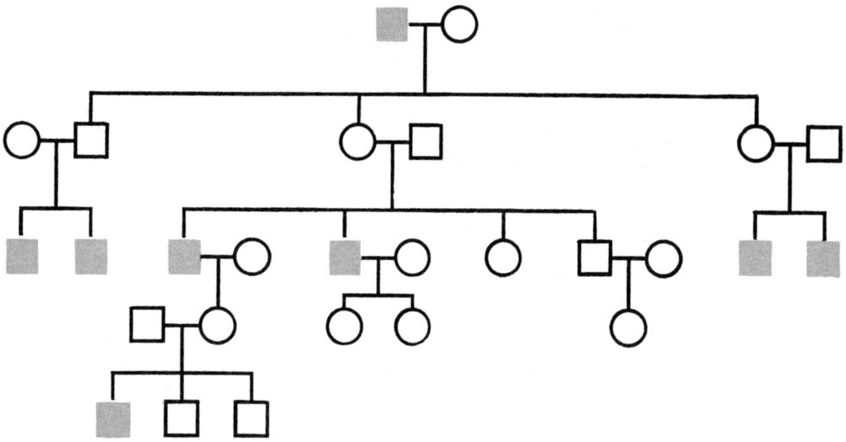

PEDIGREE of one kind of night blindness shows that males (*squares*) and females (*circles*) can transmit defect, but only males are affected by it.

FINALLY, perhaps most interesting of all, there are the recent discoveries about differences in the ability to smell and taste. Although the sense of smell is believed to be less acute in civilized man than in his forebears, it is still very sensitive and plays a large role in our eating, drinking and mating. Variations in sensitivity are wide. The perfumer, the teataster and the winetaster must have very good noses. At the other extreme we know there are people who completely lack ability to perceive any odor. Some can smell only vapors that cause pungent or stinging sensations, but these do not so much stimulate the olfactory end organs as irritate the trigeminal nerve in the nose. Total inability to smell is usually caused by infection or injury; only rarely does it affect more than one member of a family.

An interesting difference between men and women in odor perception has recently been described by some French authors. They claim that certain compounds which are related to the sex hormones are not perceived by men but have a musklike odor for adult women, especially during certain phases of the menstrual cycle. Confirmation of this is still lacking.

Some 20 years ago a chance discovery concerning the sense of taste started a long chain of investigations which have provided us with a most fascinating problem in sense perception, genetics and metabolism in general. The U. S. chemist Arthur L. Fox discovered that the crystals of a certain substance, phenylthiocarbamide (PTC), appeared very bitter to some people but tasteless to others. Using various dilutions of the substance in water, he found that the differences in tasting were graded. The range of minimum concentration tasted by various individuals varied by more than 10,000-fold. In general, however, people could be divided into two groups: tasters and nontasters. Whereas the distribution of taste thresholds for most other substances would show one peak, situated somewhere in the middle, the frequency diagram for PTC thresholds shows two, representing in effect the tasters and the nontasters.

It is perhaps worth while to describe in some detail how such threshold measurements are taken. Originally each person being examined was simply asked whether a series of given solutions tasted bitter or not, and the threshold was determined in this way. However, it soon developed that this purely subjective and verbal approach did not produce data worthy of statistical analysis. After some trial and error the following method emerged: The examiner first uses the old method to obtain a preliminary opinion as to the lowest concentration the subject can taste. Then a little of this solution is poured into each of four tumblers. These four are shuffled with four other tumblers containing only water, so that the subject does not know which contain the solution. He is asked to separate them according to taste. If he separates them correctly, the test is repeated with progressively weaker solutions until the subject can no longer detect the solution with any accuracy. This procedure yields more accurate results on actual ability to taste the substance.

THE percentage of people who cannot taste PTC varies greatly among different populations. In European, North American and Australian populations about a third fail to taste the substance in dilution; in many peoples of non-European origin the proportions of nontasters are much smaller. If this is a truly genetic trait, the gene for nontasting must vary in frequency from more than a half in "European" populations down to almost nil in certain isolated tribes. Some day, when the genetics of tasting are fully elucidated, it may be possible to trace human migrations by comparing taster frequencies.

The division of people into tasters and nontasters of PTC poses a unique problem. In most cases of perceptual differences we can describe one class as normal and the other as abnormal. Color-blind people, for example, are a small minority. The nontasters of PTC, on the other hand, form up to one-third of our population, and the gene responsible for the trait must be more frequent than the taster gene, since it is present in many individuals without expressing itself. Under the circumstances it is impossible to say what is normal and what abnormal—whether one "ought" to taste PTC or not.

Nontasting has been held to be associated with various diseases, among them diabetes mellitus. The only condition on which there is any undisputed evidence is nodular goiter, which seems to occur somewhat more frequently in nontasters than in tasters.

PTC is by no means the only substance that divides people into tasters and nontasters. Most other compounds with the same carbon-nitrogen-sulfur group appear bitter to the same people and tasteless to the others. One of these thiocarbamides, known as "ANTU," is a powerful rat poison but is tolerated in relatively large doses by mice and men. Another is the substance called Antabuse, which is being used to fight alcoholism because it prevents the normal destruction of alcohol in the blood and produces very unpleasant aftereffects. Great caution is advisable, however, in administering such a drug.

IT APPEARS that the vast majority of the substances having dual taste thresholds inhibit the formation of thyroxine in the thyroid gland. Some of them, derivatives of thiouracil, are now widely used to treat overactivity of the thyroid. All this and other pieces of evidence would seem to support the idea that nontasting and goiter are somehow related. Endemic goiter has usually been attributed to lack of iodine in food and water. But some features of the occurrence of goiter remain unexplained, and it may well be that certain substances in food help account for the high incidence of the condition in given regions. Regional differences in the proportion of nontasters may be responses to specific differences in diet. Many points in this intriguing complex of problems are still obscure. We do not know, for instance, whether the ability or lack of ability to taste these substances has anything to do with food preferences.

All in all, even the small amount of work that has been done in the study of sense differences makes clear that it is a broad, important subject which should not be pursued piecemeal.

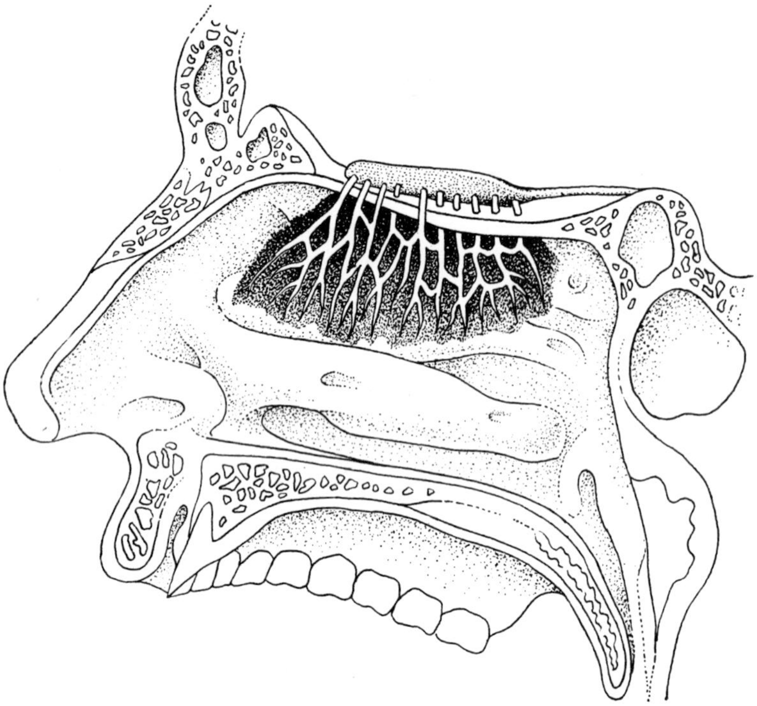

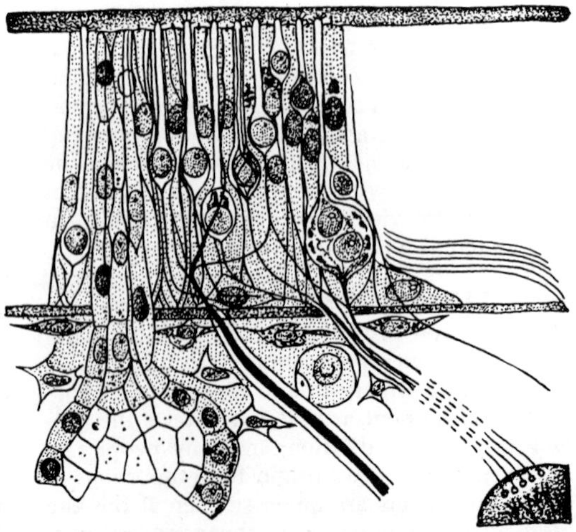

SMELL RECEPTORS are in a spongy region at the top of the nasal cavity, a cross section of which is shown at the top of this illustration. At the bottom is a microscopic cross section of the cells in the olfactory mucous membrane. [From "Smell and Taste," by A. J. Haagen-Smit, *Scientific American*, March, 1952.]

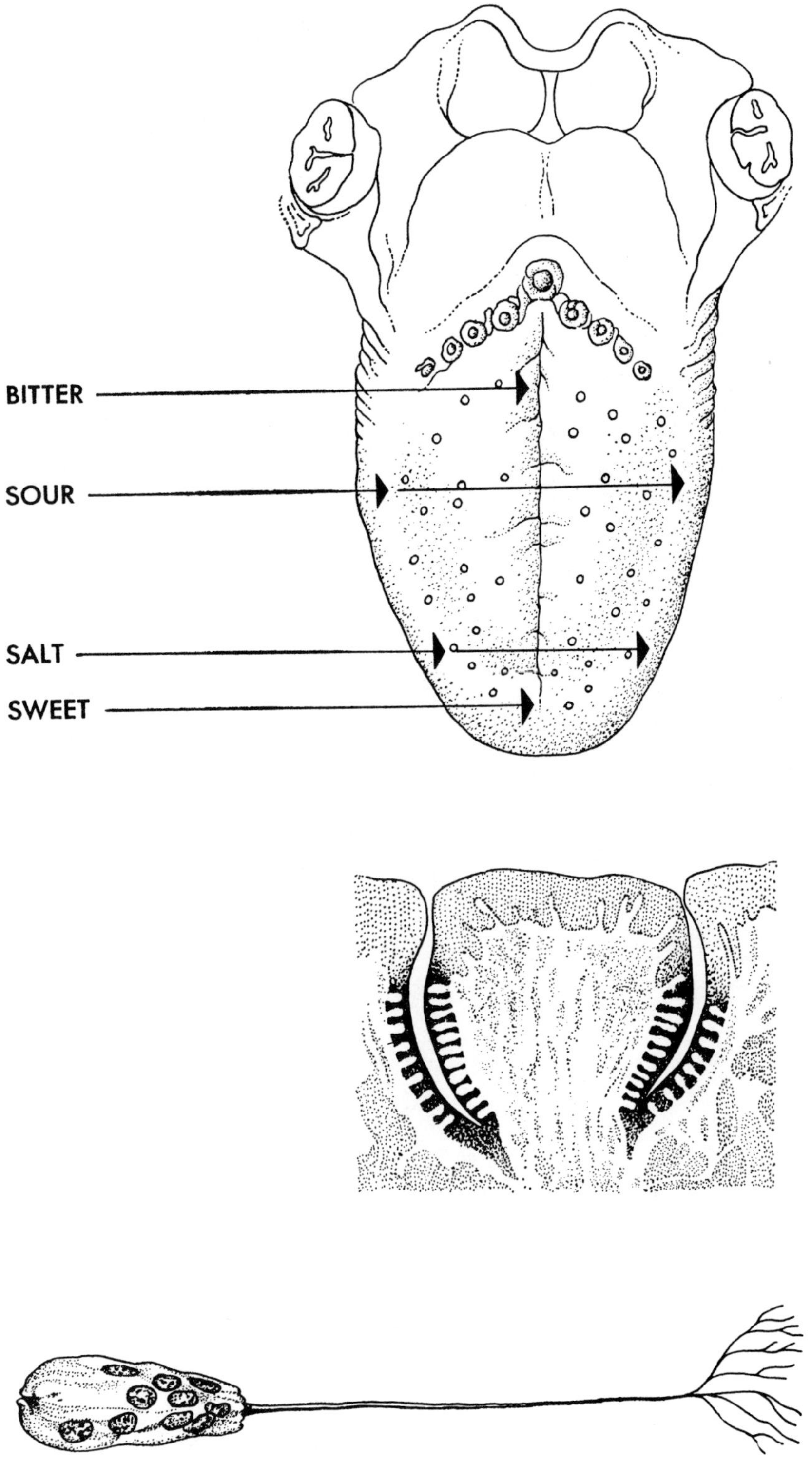

TASTE RECEPTORS are located in the tongue, the top of which is shown in the drawing at the top of this illustration. On the surface of the tongue are numerous round structures called papillae; the larger of these are indicated by the small circles in the drawing. A cross section of one of the largest papillae is shown in the drawing at the middle of the illustration. The small white structures adjoining the fissure around the papilla are the taste buds. An individual taste bud *(left)* and its nerve fiber *(right)* are shown in the drawing at the bottom. Some areas of the tongue are more sensitive to certain tastes than others; these areas are indicated by the arrows on the top drawing. [From "Smell and Taste," by A. J. Haagen-Smit, *Scientific American*, March, 1952.]

6

TASTE RECEPTORS

EDWARD S. HODGSON
May 1961

The severed head of a fly, a lump of wax and a minute glass tube filled with salt water were the novel ingredients of the experiment. The other items, including an amplifier, a cathode-ray oscilloscope and a motion-picture camera, were conventional tools for exploring the workings of the nervous system. When this improbable collection was appropriately hooked up, it provided the long-sought means of measuring directly the electrical impulses by which a single taste cell sends a taste sensation to the brain. At last the workings of one of the least understood types of sensory receptor cell could be subjected to direct observation.

Blowflies began losing their heads to such good purpose in 1955, when I collaborated in a study of taste mechanisms with Jerome Y. Lettvin of the Massachusetts Institute of Technology and Kenneth D. Roeder of Tufts University. In our experiments we fastened the fly's head upside down to the lump of wax and subjected the head to slight pressure, causing the proboscis to extend. Then, using a micromanipulator, we could slip the water-filled glass tube over one of the fine sensory hairs on the tip of the proboscis. A silver wire inserted into the other end of the tube connects it with the amplifier and the oscilloscope.

BLOWFLY PROBOSCIS with water-filled glass tube slipped over a single hair (*right*) is in position for experiment. The shiny horizontal object is a staple that keeps the proboscis extended. Part of one of the fly's eyes is just below the staple (*right of center*).

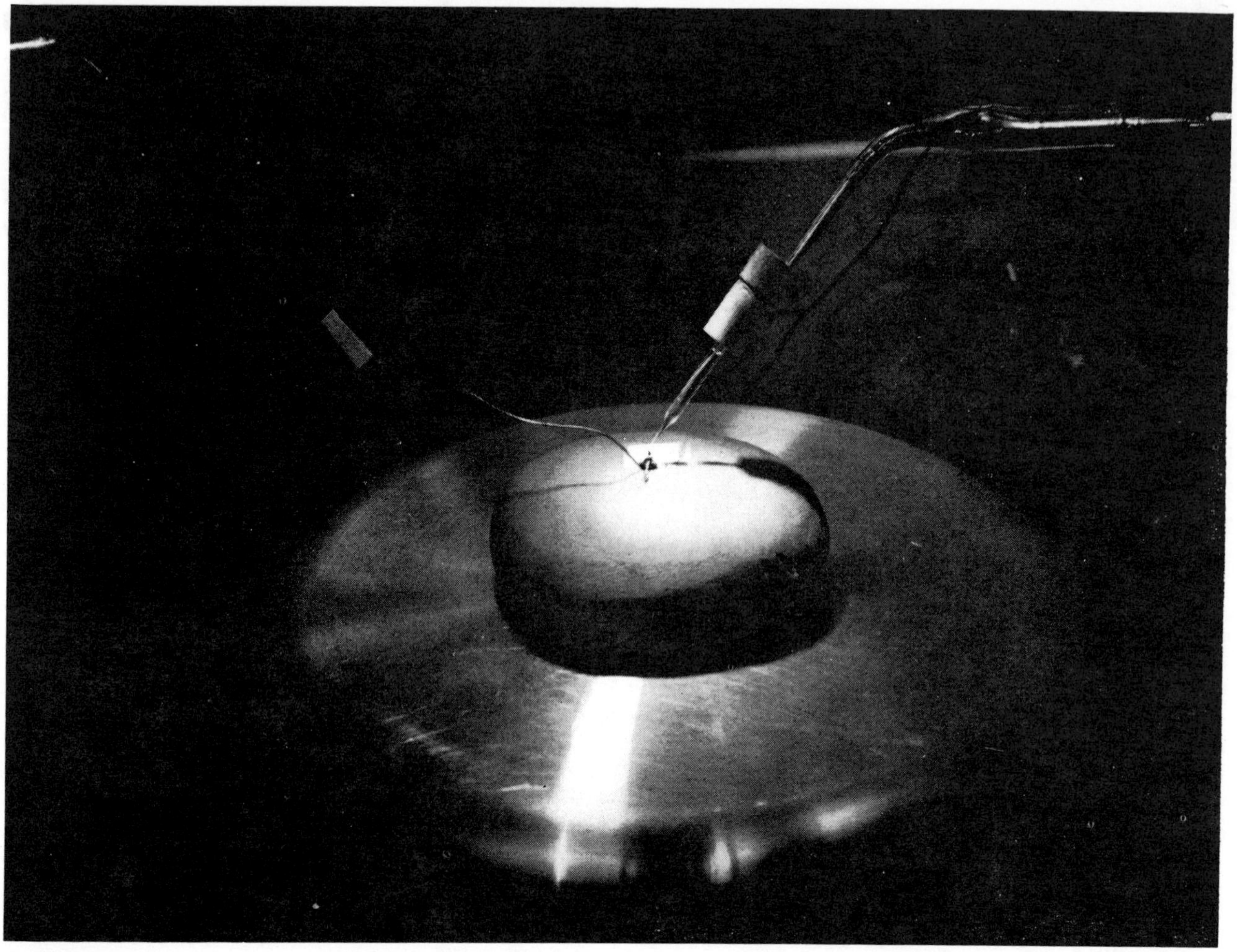

ELECTRICAL CONNECTION carries impulse from taste cells. Blowfly head is on lump of wax. Electrode at right is glass tube filled with salt water. Electrode at left, connected to amplifier, is implanted in severed head to complete the electrical circuit.

COMPLETE LABORATORY SETUP for measuring impulses from blowfly taste cells includes microscope, micromanipulators (*at left and right of center stand*) and oscilloscope (*right*). Electrodes that make contact with fly's head are just above lump of wax.

To complete the circuit, another wire from the amplifier is inserted into the fly's head. Contact between the sensory hair and the solution in the tube causes the taste nerve to produce a series of electrical impulses that register as a fleeting trace on the face of the oscilloscope tube. This visible image of the nerve impulse is recorded by the motion-picture camera.

Although the chemical senses—taste and smell—may seem less important than other sensory systems in man, they have always had a central role in the behavior of other animals. Cells particularly sensitive to the chemical environment were among the earliest to appear, no doubt because the murky aquatic environments that were the scene of so much evolutionary history made chemical perception essential for survival. Chemical detectors are found in one of the oldest of multicellular creatures: the jellyfish. In flatworms, the simplest bilaterally symmetrical animals, chemoreceptors on the sides of the head direct the search for food. Knowledge of the operation of these primitive receptors is so meager, however, that the concepts of "smell" and "taste" must be reserved for the animals that evolved later.

When animals emerged from the water, they continued to depend heavily on the chemical senses. In most insects and in many other land animals, taste and smell play a key part in detecting a suitable environment, finding sustenance and initiating reproductive behavior. The chemical senses do much more than provide pleasurable sensations for gourmets: they are essential to the survival of many animal species.

The study of taste and smell not only sheds light on one of the fundamental processes in nature; it also can be of help in combating insects and other pests that share with man a taste for certain foods. By understanding the mechanism of the chemical senses, man may be able to interfere with their operation, to anesthetize them or even to exploit them with chemicals that attract or repel pests.

Quantitative studies of the chemical senses largely awaited the development of equipment sensitive enough to measure nerve impulses. The first such study was made less than three decades ago by E. D. Adrian and C. Ludwig at the University of Cambridge. They recorded impulses from the olfactory stalk of a catfish brain while flushing the fish's nasal sac with fluid from decaying earthworms or from a putrefying alligator head. They found that the olfactory nerves carry some impulses even without stimulation. The fluid from decaying meat greatly increases the number of impulses, which signal the brain that food is nearby. Adrian and Ludwig also discovered that the olfactory stalk will not show a response to stimulation twice in quick succession: full sensitivity reappears only after a recovery period. (Nerve physiologists would say that the olfactory system is "slow-adapting.") Subsequent studies have shown that the chemoreceptor systems of most animals, including many only distantly related to the catfish, have the same general characteristics.

From the point of view of the investigator, however, the taste and smell receptors of vertebrate animals usually share certain drawbacks. The actual receptor cells are too small or too inconveniently located to be probed with electrodes; hence recordings of nerve impulses are customarily taken from nerve fibers connected to the receptor cells rather than from the receptors themselves. Since each nerve fiber is connected to several receptor cells, the original messages must be condensed and delayed by the time they reach the recording electrodes. The situation can be further complicated by a layer of mucus over the receptor cell; it is extremely difficult even to estimate the time it takes a stimulating chemical to penetrate the mucus or wash out of it.

The line of investigation that was eventually to lead to the making of direct and convenient contact with single receptor cells began even before the work of Adrian and Ludwig. In the 1920's D. E. Minnich of the University of Minnesota applied a sugar solution to the sensory hairs on the mouth parts of flies and on the feet of butterflies. When the solution touched even a single hair, the proboscis would extend as if the insect were trying to feed. Each hair seemed to be a taste receptor.

More recently V. G. Dethier, working at Johns Hopkins University, dipped the feet of blowflies into a variety of solutions. He observed which solutions caused extension of the proboscis and so was able to compile a long list of molecules that the fly apparently found tasty. By 1950, largely as a consequence of Dethier's work, more was known about the taste receptors of blowflies than about those of any other organism, including man.

The taste hairs of the fly are merely the inert housings of the living taste-receptor cells. By means of microscopic studies of thin sections of the hairs and the surrounding tissue, Dethier found that each sensory hair on the proboscis of the blowfly has three receptor cells at its base. Two of the cells send thin filaments through the hollow shaft of the hair to its tip. Dethier concluded that these two cells are the taste receptors because when he rolled a droplet

LIVING AUSTRALIAN SHEEP BLOWFLY is shown here with proboscis (*between two front legs*) extended. The fly, which lays its eggs on sheep, is a serious pest in Australia.

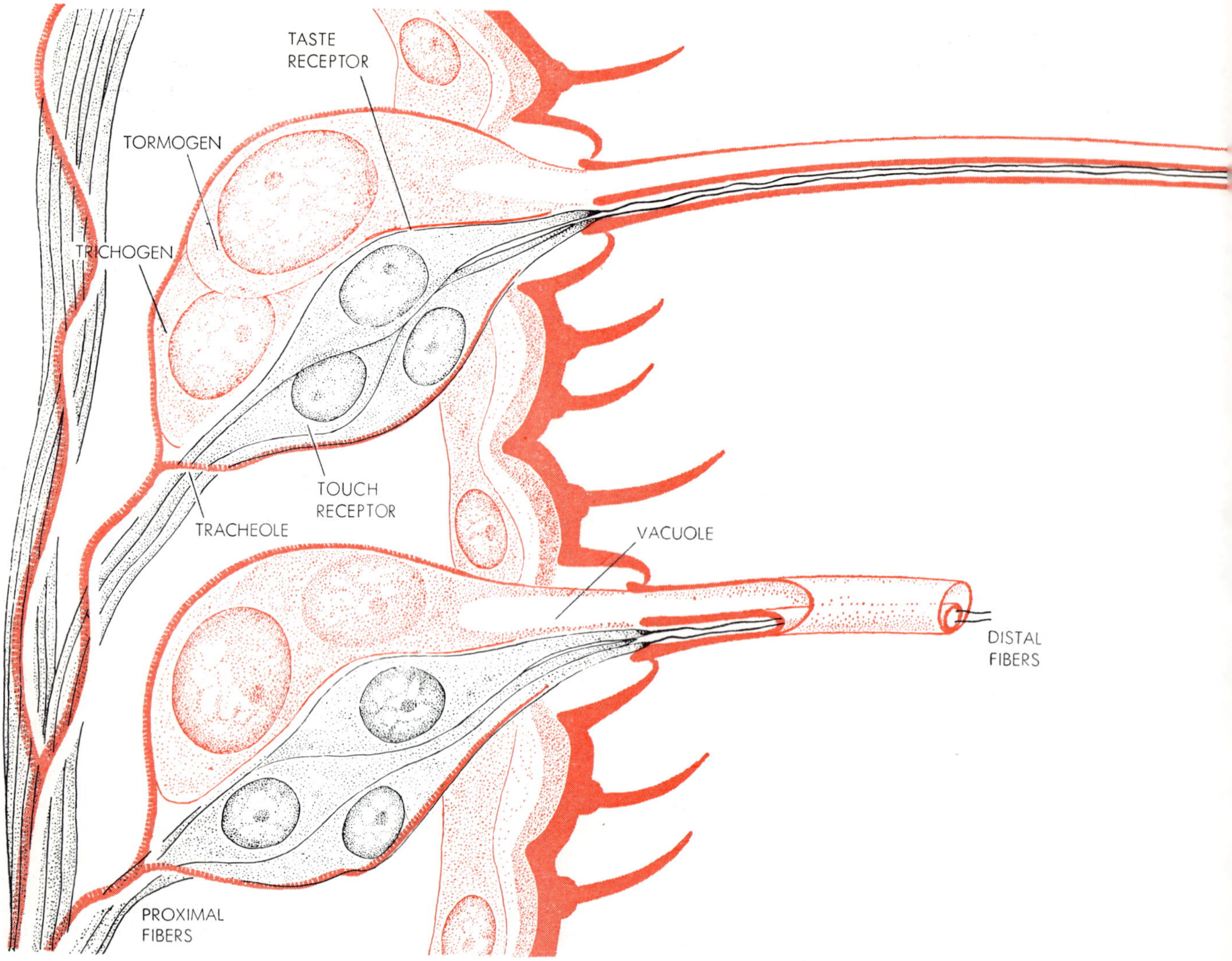

SENSORY HAIR of blowfly proboscis ends in papilla (*far right*) capable of detecting chemicals. A "bag" of cells (*left*) lies at base of each hair. The smaller cells in the bag are the two taste receptors, which send filaments ("*distal fibers*") through hollow hair, and between them is a touch receptor. The tormogen and trichogen are not receptors but give rise to the hair structure. The proximal fibers connect the taste and touch receptors directly with the brain. The entire chemoreception system is shown in black.

of sugar water along the shaft of the hair, the proboscis extended only after the solution had reached the tip. The third receptor cell, which sends no filament into the hair, was found by Myron L. Wolbarsht and Dethier to be a touch receptor, sensitive to the bending of the hair. From each of the three cells an extension goes directly to the brain.

The blowfly's two taste-receptor cells, made accessible to external stimuli by the extension of their sensitive filaments in hairs outside the body, seemed to offer an ideal opportunity for observing the chemoreceptor mechanism. No mucus or saliva flows over the cells. Moreover, the hairs on the end of the proboscis are so far apart that experiments on a single hair do not disturb neighboring hairs.

One important difficulty remained to be overcome: making an electrical connection to detect the nerve impulse. Near the tip of a sensory hair the filaments from each receptor are only about a ten-thousandth of a millimeter in diameter—too small to generate much voltage or withstand conventional techniques of making electrical connections with cells. At its largest the diameter of the receptor-cell body may be 22 thousandths of a millimeter, but this part of the cell lies buried at the base of the hair, shielded by the tough, nonconducting waxy cuticle of the hair wall and by the surrounding proboscis tissue.

A clue to the technique for making the electrical connection without injuring the delicate receptor cell came from a beautifully simple experiment performed by Eleanor H. Slifer at the State University of Iowa. By dipping hairs on the antenna of a grasshopper into water containing a dye she showed that aqueous solutions penetrate the tips of sensory hairs. These antenna hairs resemble in miniature the taste hairs of the blowfly proboscis. Lettvin, Roeder and I guessed that if water passes through the cuticle at the tip of a sensory hair, a solution that conducts electricity might pick up a nerve impulse through the same permeable spot. Perhaps the solution could both stimulate the taste-receptor cell and provide a workable connection between the receptors inside the fly hair and the electrical recording system outside. Thus it was that we performed the experiment described at the beginning of this article.

As we had hoped, the salt water in the tiny glass tube at once stimulated the receptors and conducted a current away from them. Now that we could record messages directly from the taste receptors, we were able to attack the more interesting problem of how the receptors work. Their reactions to various chemical stimuli would, we felt, provide im-

SENSORY PAPILLA

portant clues to the chemical events that generate the electrical impulses in the receptors.

We were especially curious to see if both of the taste receptors in a sensory hair are sensitive to the same kinds of chemical. It quickly became apparent that they are not. Salts, acids, most alcohols and most other compounds, except sugars, elicited electrical impulses with a constant amplitude of about 300 microvolts (300 millionths of a volt). Test solutions of sucrose and many other sugars, mixed with a trace of salt to provide electrical conductivity, elicited predominantly smaller impulses, about 200 microvolts in amplitude. Since a given nerve cell normally produces impulses of only one amplitude, the two distinct amplitudes from the taste hair provided a way to tell the response of one cell from that of the other. Actually the impulse amplitudes varied somewhat in recordings from different hairs, but the impulses of the two taste cells were usually distinguishable.

For easy reference we called the cell producing the larger impulses the "L" receptor and the cell producing the smaller impulses the "S" receptor. Our first generalization was that the S cell appears to be a sugar receptor and the L cell a less specific nonsugar receptor. Since blowflies feed on sugars and avoid most of the chemicals that stimulate the L receptor, the electrical activity of the nerves seemed to match the flies' feeding behavior.

Further work in my laboratory at Columbia University supported the idea that compounds "acceptable" to the fly stimulate the S receptor, whereas "unacceptable" compounds stimulate the L receptor. We found that the electrical recordings from L and S receptors in single hairs correlate well with the proboscis behavior that follows stimulation of single hairs with a droplet of each test solution. For example, fructose and glucose, both sugars that trigger proboscis extension, strongly stimulate S receptors, even when applied in relatively low concentration. Two other sugars, cellobiose and mannose, must be applied in high concentration or to many sensory hairs in order to produce a proboscis response. Correspondingly, they evoke only a few S impulses when observed electrically.

The most striking correlation between taste-receptor activities and behavior occurs with four polyhydric alcohols. All these compounds are composed of exactly the same atoms; only the arrangement of the atoms differs. Sorbitol, dulcitol and mannitol stimulate the L receptor. Inositol, however, strongly stimulates the S receptor; it is also the only one of these alcohols that evokes the feeding response of the proboscis. These reactions indicate that the architecture of a stimulating molecule plays a part in the function of the S receptor, because inositol is the only polyhydric alcohol with a ring-shaped molecule, resembling the sugars we found to be most stimulating.

The selective response of the S receptor suggests that enzymes mediate the chemical reaction that triggers the impulse. These biological catalysts are

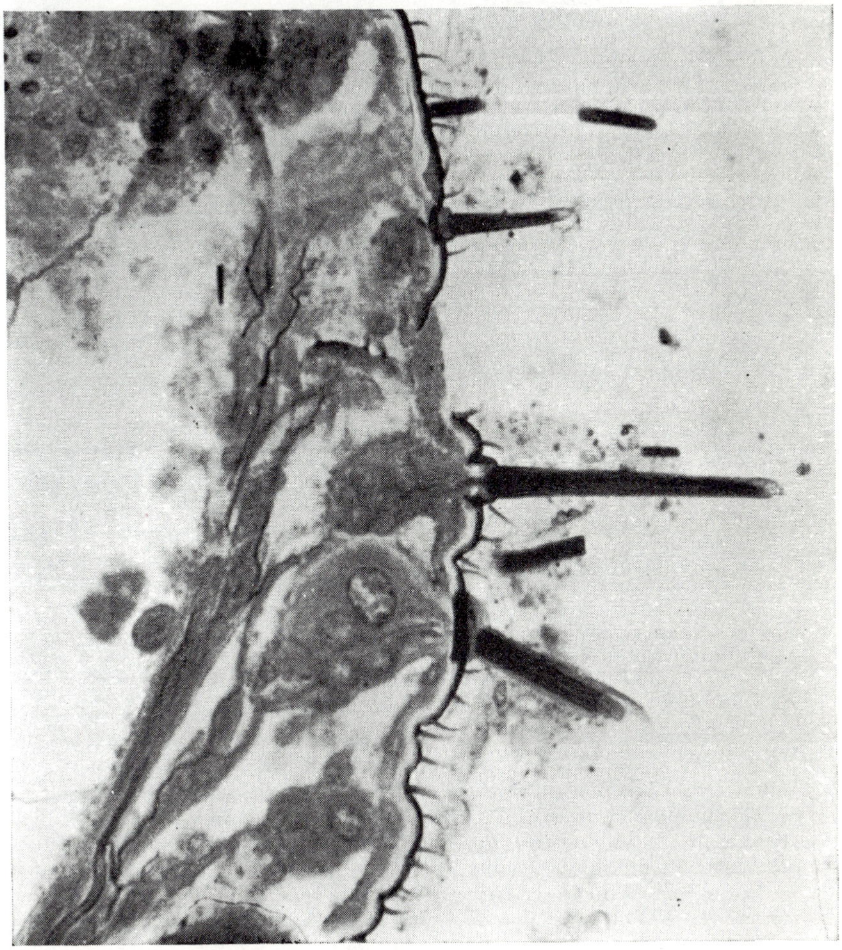

SENSORY HAIRS AND CELLS of blowfly proboscis are shown in section in photomicrograph by V. G. Dethier of University of Pennsylvania. Magnification is 600 diameters.

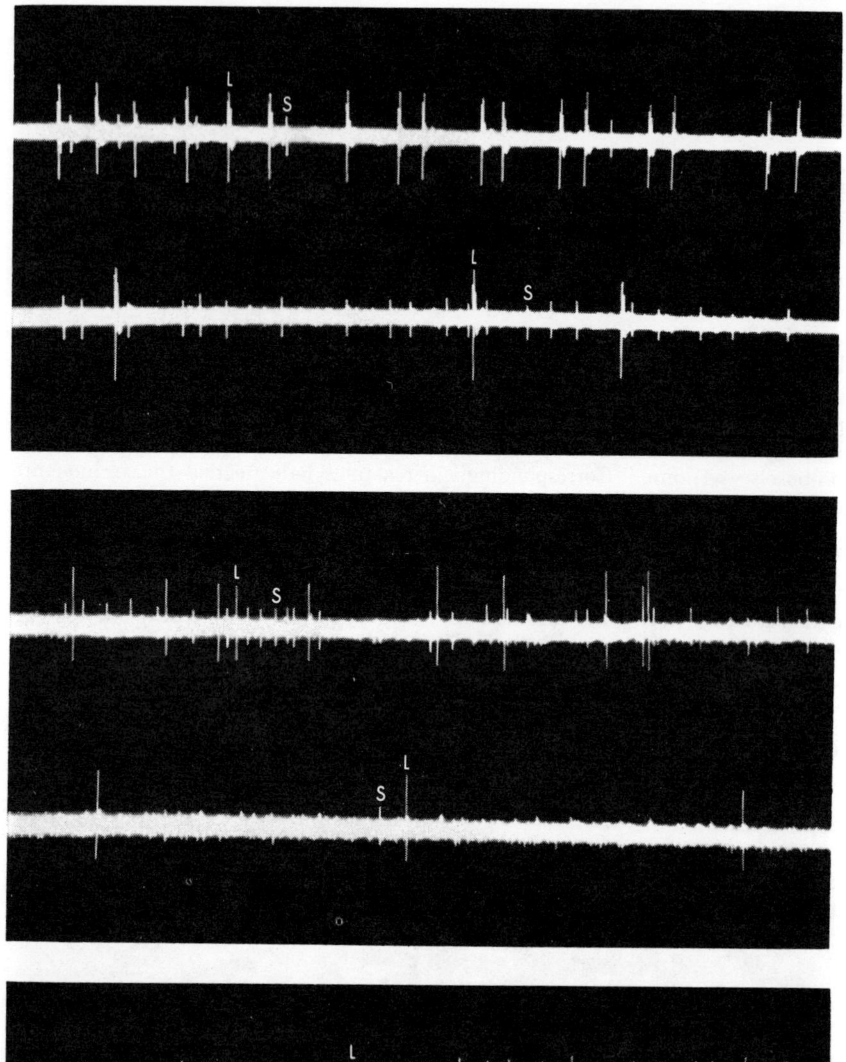

OSCILLOSCOPE TRACES show reactions of taste hairs to various chemicals. Each hair has two receptors, one giving an "L" (large amplitude) response on the oscilloscope, and one giving an "S" (small) response. In top picture top trace resulted from application of the sugar raffinose, which caused many L impulses, while bottom trace shows reaction of same hair to fructose, which caused mote S than L impulses. Middle picture shows how another hair reacted to fructose (*top trace*) and to another sugar, ribose (*bottom trace*). Ribose stimulated scarcely any impulses. The bottom pair of traces was made by a third hair exposed to two polyhydric alcohols. The alcohol dulcitol (*top trace*) strongly stimulated L impulses, whereas inositol, made up of same atoms in a different arrangement, primarily stimulated S responses. At bottom is time scale for traces; it has 100 peaks a second.

highly specific in their activity. The far less specific responses of the L receptor, which is stimulated by salts and a variety of other nonsugars, suggest that a different mechanism is involved here. It might be sufficient for ions of the stimulating compounds to become loosely bound to the surface of the L receptor. This possibility is particularly interesting, because the same mechanism has been postulated for the salt-taste receptors in mammals.

Further support for the idea of different mechanisms of S and L activity comes from experiments that Lindsay Barton-Browne and I performed on the Australian sheep blowfly at the Australian National University and at the Australian Commonwealth Scientific and Industrial Research Organization. We were able to measure the time interval between the applications of the stimulus and the first receptor impulse in 141 individual taste-receptor cells. It happens that the oscilloscope beam shows a slight deflection the instant our experimental circuit is closed by contact between the stimulating solution and the sensory hair [*see bottom illustration on opposite page*]. The deflection is followed by a briet interval before the taste cell fires the impulse that goes to the brain. We found that the impulses from the L receptors appear within as little as a millisecond (a thousandth of a second) after a salt solution is applied. With S receptors, however, the delay after contact with a sugar solution is always at least five milliseconds. (These speeds are only a fourth to a 20th as long as those generally observed in experiments with vertebrates, showing again the value of making recordings as close as possible to the site of receptor stimulation.) The sugar molecules would be expected to move slower than the salt ions to the receptor site. Only part of the difference in the response times of S and L receptors can, however, be explained on this basis alone, and some fundamental difference in their mechanism of operation again seems indicated.

Of course, a fly does not normally encounter chemicals in the pure forms employed in our experiments. In nature, feeding behavior may depend on the proportions of L and S impulses reaching the brain. Experiments at Columbia have shown that mixtures seldom produce impulses that are the simple sum of the impulses obtained when the chemicals are tried singly. The addition of sucrose to a solution of sodium chloride, for example, not only activates the S receptor; it also lowers the frequency of the L impulses caused by the salt. This may be due in part to interactions of the ions and molecules in solution. Whatever the mechanism, this effect tends to increase the discrepancy between frequencies of L and S impulses, enhancing the contrast between acceptable and unacceptable chemicals. Thus the fly's taste receptors would signal the brain that a substance is either "very acceptable" or "very unacceptable."

The individual sensory hairs on the fly's mouth parts exhibit further refinements that provide additional information to the brain. Barton-Browne and I found that the receptors in some hairs are slow in responding to stimuli and are relatively inexcitable, while those in other hairs always fire rapidly. Thus strong stimulation that would virtually inactivate the sensitive receptors would still be affecting the less active receptors. The reverse would be true of barely perceptible stimuli.

Temperature changes of less than a degree can also modulate the frequency of firing of some receptors during a period of otherwise regular discharge. This temperature effect is not produced at the tips of the hairs and apparently does not involve the chemosensory processes occurring there. Since the bending of a sensory hair can also provide information about tactile properties of the environment, the range of sensations provided by even a single sensory hair can be wide indeed.

It is amusing to imagine the sensations experienced by the living fly when a taste receptor hair is stimulated in various ways. In contact with heated sirup a single hair might signal not only a strong and acceptable taste but the temperature and stickiness of the sirup as well. Other situations and the sensations they excite are not too difficult to imagine. The wire tapping that brings the nerve impulse to the oscilloscope has probably provided far more accurate information about the fly's taste sensations than could be obtained if the insect could talk.

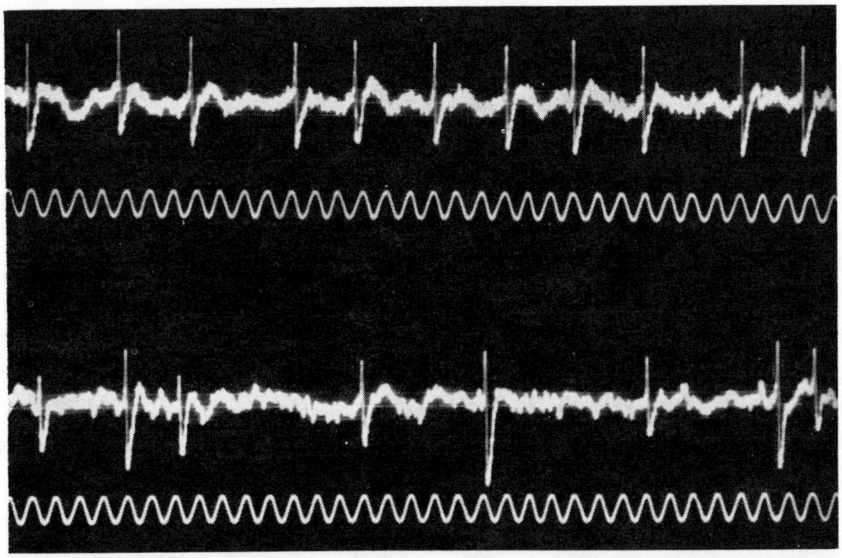

ONLY L FIBER RESPONDS when solution consists of sodium chloride alone (*top*). A much weaker salt solution plus the sugar sucrose causes five S and only three L impulses in same time period (*bottom*). The time scales here contain 100 peaks to the second.

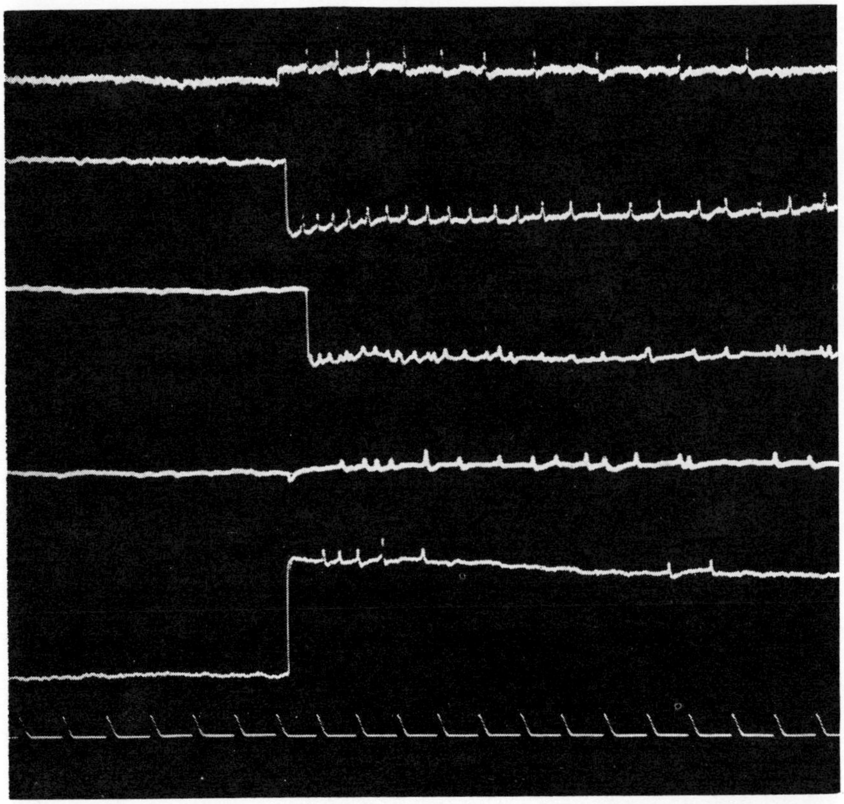

TIME OF RESPONSE after application of stimulus can be seen on these tracings. Each peak on time scale (*bottom*) marks passage of 10 one-thousandths of a second. First deflection of beam indicates application of stimulus. Second deflection is first receptor response. The three top traces show response of L receptors to salt. The two bottom traces, showing response of S receptors to sucrose, illustrate how the S receptor reacts slower.

Although microelectrodes attached to the tip of a fly's taste hairs have revealed a great deal about nerve cells sensitive to chemicals, they have failed to detect one of the very first steps that was expected to occur in the process of tasting: the initial electrical changes that trigger the fly's taste cell to send an impulse to the brain. Recently two Japanese investigators, Hiromichi Morita and Satoru Yamashita of Kyushu University, reached this objective. Through an opening in the side wall of a fly's sensory hair they managed to connect a microelectrode to the filaments inside. Before being stimulated, the receptor-cell filaments registered some spontaneous activity like that found by Adrian and Ludwig in the catfish olfactory stalk. More important, Morita and Yamashita have demonstrated that, upon stimulation, a relatively slow change in electrical potential in the filament precedes and leads to the generation of the brief but much stronger impulse going to the brain. These slow electrical changes occur only in the filaments that lie within

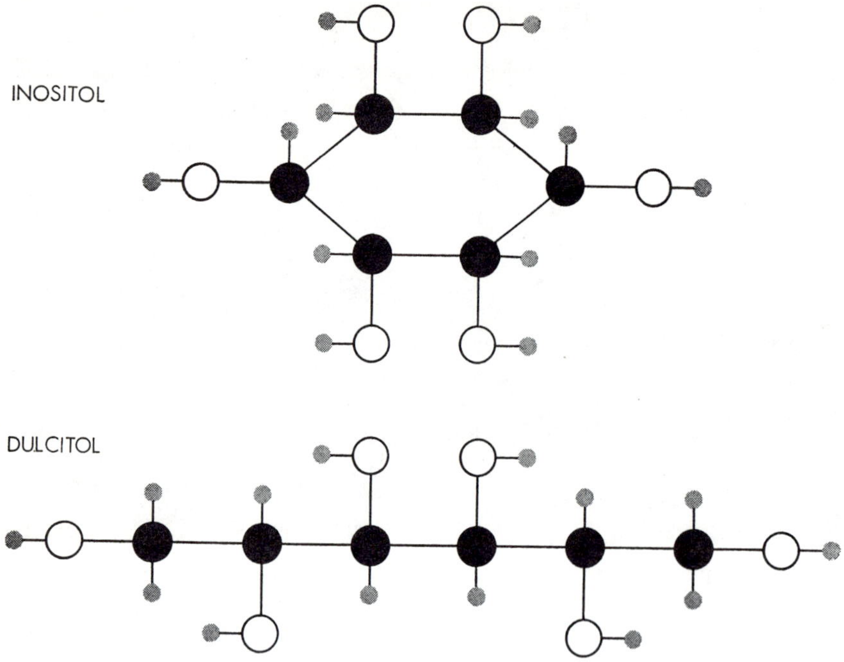

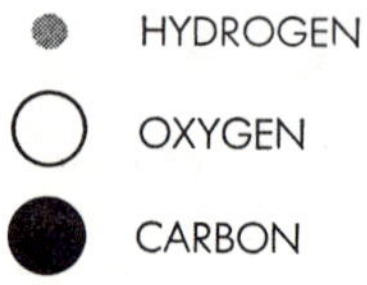

POLYHYDRIC ALCOHOL MOLECULES are made of same atoms in different arrangements. Because of its ring structure, which resembles that of stimulating sugars, inositol evokes feeding response in blowflies. Dulcitol, which has no ring, tends instead to repel the fly.

the shaft of the sensory hair and are elicited by chemical reaction with the stimulating chemical. They correspond to the "generator" potentials observed in other receptor cells, which cause the main bodies of the cells to fire impulses into the central nervous system [see the article "Biological Transducers, by Werner R. Loewenstein, beginning on page 75]. Further study of these generator potentials in taste-receptor cells will undoubtedly lead to a more complete description of the mechanisms of the chemical senses.

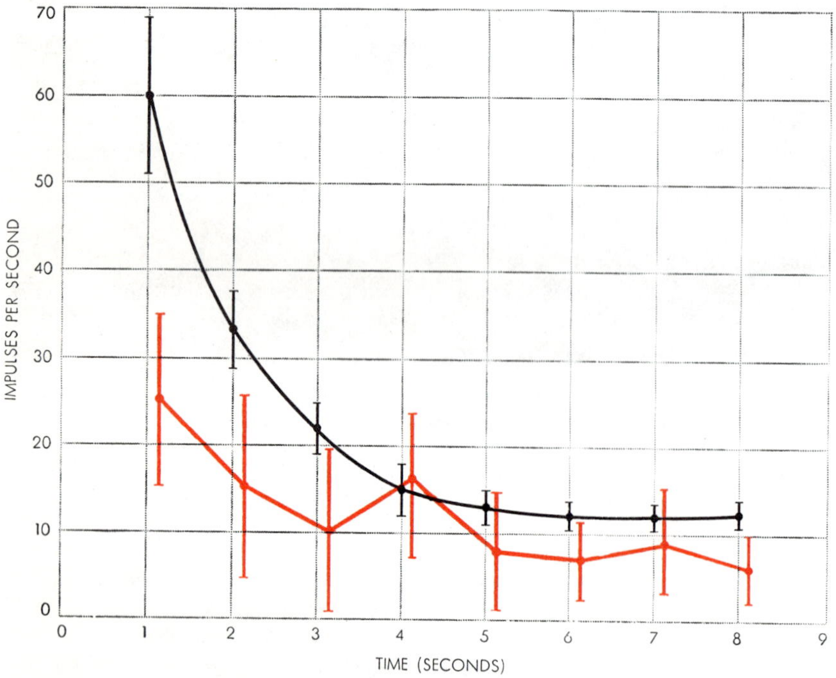

TASTE CELLS "ADAPT" to stimulus by decreasing number of impulses sent to brain. L receptor (*black line*) sends more impulses than S receptor (*color*) and rate decreases faster. The vertical lines indicate the range of impulses found in repeated tests on one hair.

THE STEREOCHEMICAL THEORY OF ODOR

JOHN E. AMOORE, JAMES W. JOHNSTON, JR., AND MARTIN RUBIN

February 1964

A rose is a rose and a skunk is a skunk, and the nose easily tells the difference. But it is not so easy to describe or explain this difference. We know surprisingly little about the sense of smell, in spite of its important influence on our daily lives and the voluminous literature of research on the subject. One is hard put to describe an odor except by comparing it to a more familiar one. We have no yardstick for measuring the strength of odors, as we measure sound in decibels and light in lumens. And we have had no satisfactory general theory to explain how the nose and brain detect, identify and recognize an odor. More than 30 different theories have been suggested by investigators in various disciplines, but none of them has passed the test of experiments designed to determine their validity.

The sense of smell obviously is a chemical sense, and its sensitivity is proverbial; to a chemist the ability of the nose to sort out and characterize substances is almost beyond belief. It deals with complex compounds that might take a chemist months to analyze in the laboratory; the nose identifies them instantly, even in an amount so small (as little as a ten-millionth of a gram) that the most sensitive modern laboratory instruments often cannot detect the substance, let alone analyze and label it.

Two thousand years ago the poet Lucretius suggested a simple explanation of the sense of smell. He speculated that the "palate" contained minute pores of various sizes and shapes. Every odorous substance, he said, gave off tiny "molecules" of a particular shape, and the odor was perceived when these molecules entered pores in the palate. Presumably the identification of each odor depended on which pores the molecules fitted.

It now appears that Lucretius' guess was essentially correct. Within the past few years new evidence has shown rather convincingly that the geometry of molecules is indeed the main determinant of odor, and a theory of the olfactory process has been developed in modern terms. This article will discuss the stereochemical theory and the experiments that have tested it.

The nose is always on the alert for odors. The stream of air drawn in through the nostrils is warmed and filtered as it passes the three baffle-shaped turbinate bones in the upper part of the nose; when an odor is detected, more of the air is vigorously sniffed upward to two clefts that contain the smelling organs [*see the illustration on page 75*]. These organs consist of two patches of yellowish tissue, each about one square inch in area. Embedded in the tissue are two types of nerve fiber whose endings receive and detect the odorous molecules. The chief type is represented by the fibers of the olfactory nerve; at the end of each of these fibers is an olfactory cell bearing a cluster of hairlike filaments that act as receptors. The other type of fiber is a long, slender ending of the trigeminal nerve, which is sensitive to certain kinds of molecules. On being stimulated by odorous molecules, the olfactory nerve endings send signals to the olfactory bulb and thence to the higher brain centers where the signals are integrated and interpreted in terms of the character and intensity of the odor.

From the nature of this system it is obvious at once that to be smelled at all a material must have certain basic properties. In the first place, it must be volatile. A substance such as onion soup, for example, is highly odorous because it continuously gives off vapor that can reach the nose (unless the soup is im-

PRIMARY ODOR	CHEMICAL EXAMPLE	FAMILIAR SUBSTANCE
CAMPHORACEOUS	CAMPHOR	MOTH REPELLENT
MUSKY	PENTADECANOLACTONE	ANGELICA ROOT OIL
FLORAL	PHENYLETHYL METHYL ETHYL CARBINOL	ROSES
PEPPERMINTY	MENTHONE	MINT CANDY
ETHEREAL	ETHYLENE DICHLORIDE	DRY-CLEANING FLUID
PUNGENT	FORMIC ACID	VINEGAR
PUTRID	BUTYL MERCAPTAN	BAD EGG

PRIMARY ODORS identified by the authors are listed, together with chemical and more familiar examples. Each of the primary odors is detected by a different receptor in the nose. Most odors are composed of several of these primaries combined in various proportions.

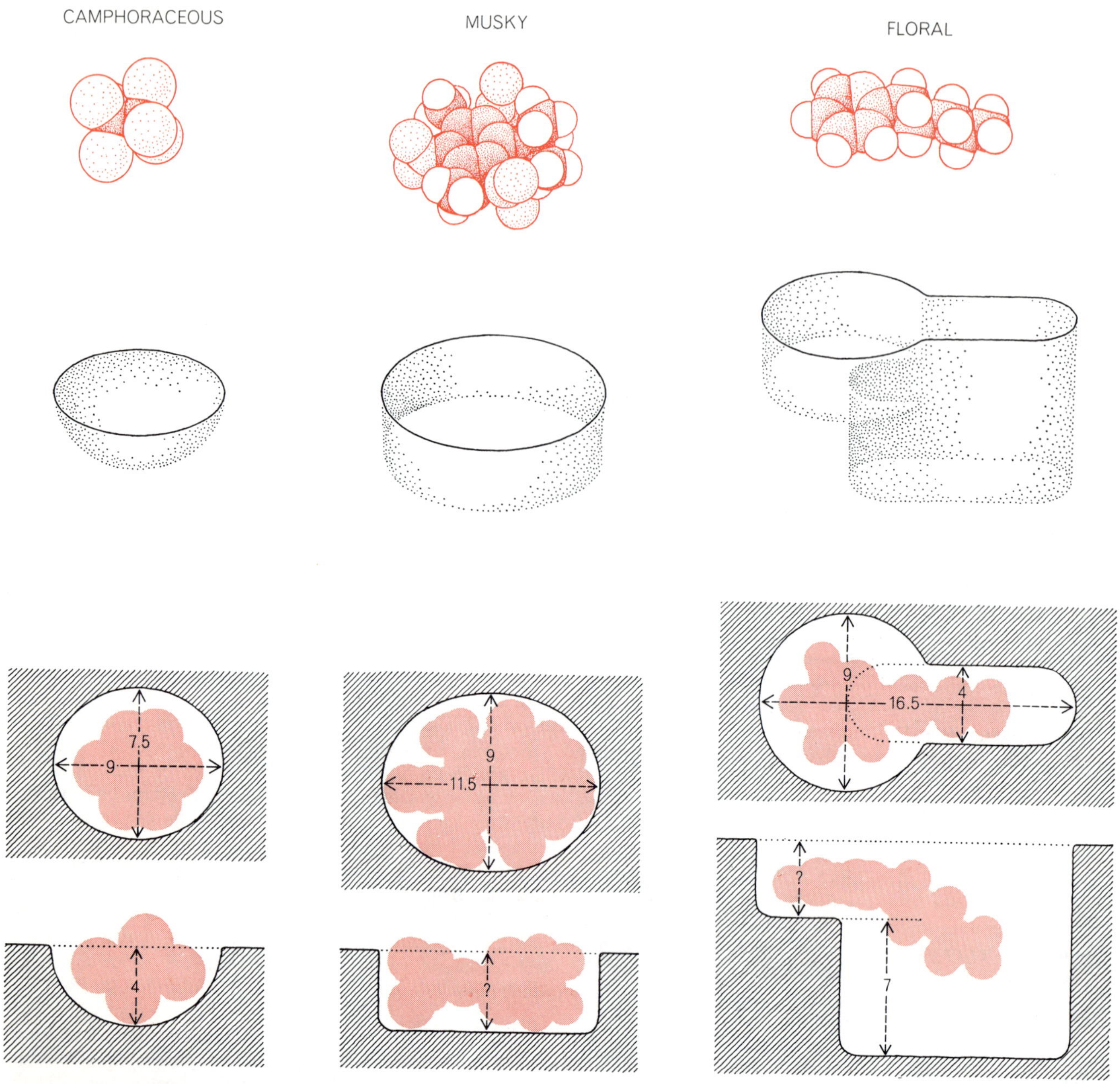

OLFACTORY RECEPTOR SITES are shown for each of the primary odors, together with molecules representative of each odor. The shapes of the first five sites are shown in perspective and (with the molecules silhouetted in them) from above and the side;

prisoned in a sealed can). On the other hand, at ordinary temperatures a substance such as iron is completely odorless because it does not evaporate molecules into the air.

The second requirement for an odorous substance is that it should be soluble in water, even if only to an almost infinitesimal extent. If it is completely insoluble, it will be barred from reaching the nerve endings by the watery film that covers their surfaces. Another common property of odorous materials is solubility in lipids (fatty substances); this enables them to penetrate the nerve endings through the lipid layer that forms part of the surface membrane of every cell.

Beyond these elementary properties the characteristics of odorous materials have been vague and confusing. Over the years chemists empirically synthesized a wealth of odorous compounds, both for perfumers and for their own studies of odor, but instead of clarifying the properties responsible for odor these compounds seemed merely to add to the confusion. A few general principles were discovered. For instance, it was found that adding a branch to a straight chain of carbon atoms in a perfume molecule markedly increased the potency of the perfume. Strong odor also seemed to be associated with chains of four to eight carbon atoms in the molecules of certain alcohols and aldehydes. The more chemists analyzed the chemical structure of odorous substances, however, the more puzzles emerged. From the standpoint of chemical composition and structure the substances showed some remarkable inconsistencies.

Curiously enough, the inconsistencies themselves began to show a pattern. As an example, two optical isomers—molecules identical in every respect except that one is the mirror image of the other—may have different odors. As another

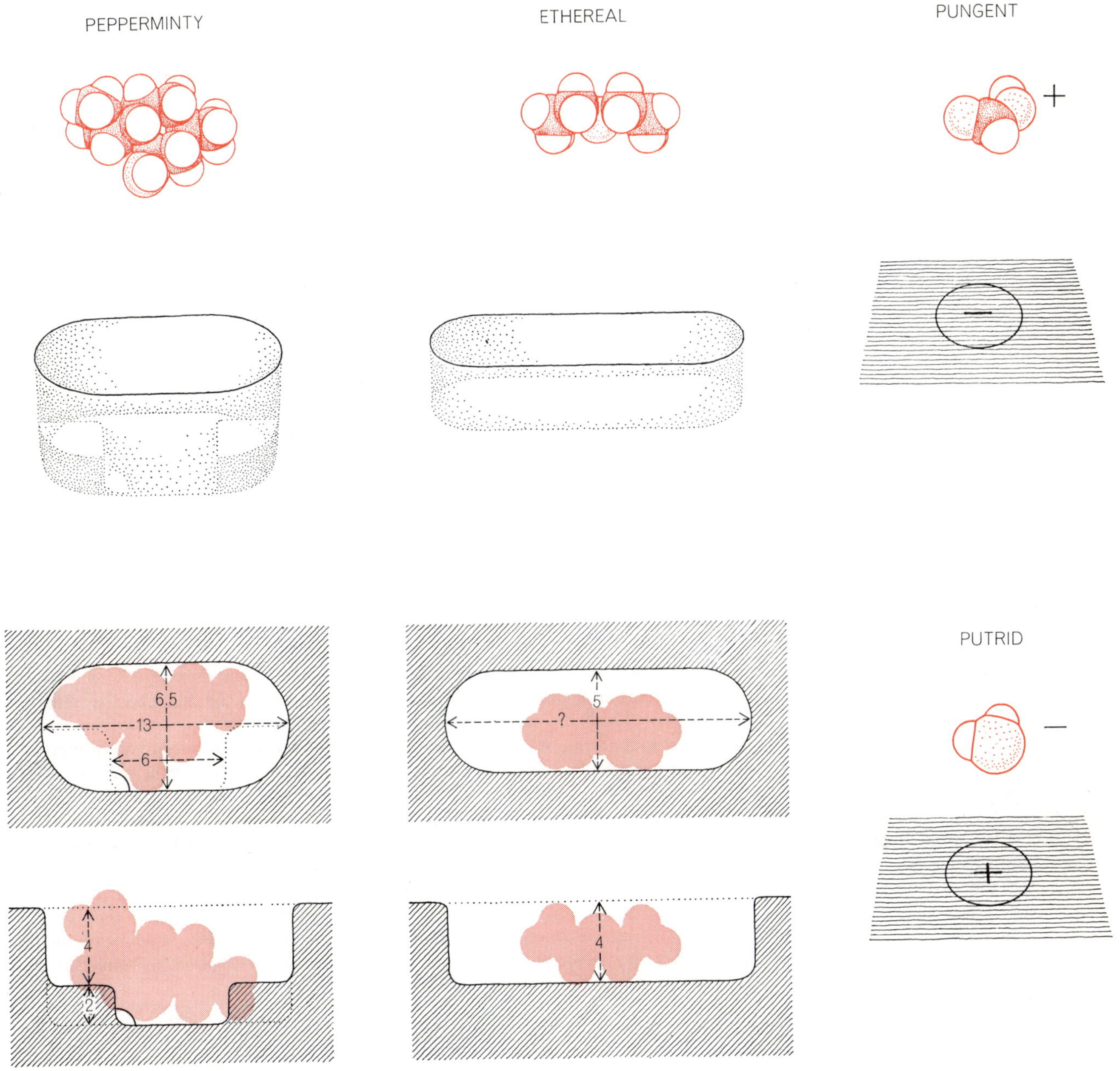

known dimensions are given in angstrom units. The molecules are (*left to right*) hexachloroethane, xylene musk, alpha-amylpyridine, *l*-menthol and diethyl ether. Pungent (formic acid) and putrid (hydrogen sulfide) molecules fit because of charge, not shape.

example, in a compound whose molecules contain a small six-carbon-atom benzene ring, shifting the position of a group of atoms attached to the ring may sharply change the odor of the compound, whereas in a compound whose molecules contain a large ring of 14 to 19 members the atoms can be rearranged considerably without altering the odor much. Chemists were led by these facts to speculate on the possibility that the primary factor determining the odor of a substance might be the over-all geometric shape of the molecule rather than any details of its composition or structure.

In 1949 R. W. Moncrieff in Scotland gave form to these ideas by proposing a hypothesis strongly reminiscent of the 2,000-year-old guess of Lucretius. Moncrieff suggested that the olfactory system is composed of receptor cells of a few different types, each representing a distinct "primary" odor, and that odorous molecules produce their effects by fitting closely into "receptor sites" on these cells. His hypothesis is an application of the "lock and key" concept that has proved fruitful in explaining the interaction of enzymes with their substrates, of antibodies with antigens and of deoxyribonucleic acid with the "messenger" ribonucleic acid that presides at the synthesis of protein.

To translate Moncrieff's hypothesis into a practical approach for investigating olfaction, two specific questions had to be answered. What are the "primary odors"? And what is the shape of the receptor site for each one? To try to find answers to these questions, one of us (Amoore, then at the University of Oxford) made an extensive search of the literature of organic chemistry, looking for clues in the chemical characteristics of odorous compounds. His search resulted in the conclusion that there were seven primary odors, and in 1952 his findings were summed up in a stereochemical theory of olfaction that identified the seven odors and gave a detailed description of the size, shape and chemical affinities of the seven corresponding receptor sites.

To identify the primary odors Amoore started with the descriptions of 600 organic compounds noted in the literature as odorous. If the receptor-site hypothesis was correct, the primary odors should be recognized much more frequently than mixed odors made up of two or more primaries. And indeed, in the chemists' descriptions certain odors turned up much more commonly than others. For instance, the descriptions mentioned more than 100 compounds as having a camphor-like odor, whereas only about half a dozen were put in the category characterized by the odor of cedarwood. This suggested that in all likelihood the camphor odor was a primary one. By this test of frequency, and from other considerations, it was possible to select seven odors that stand out as probable primaries. They are: camphoraceous, musky, floral, pepperminty, ethereal (ether-like), pungent and putrid.

From these seven primaries every known odor could be made by mixing them in certain proportions. In this respect the primary odors are like the three primary colors (red, green and blue) and the four primary tastes (sweet, salt, sour and bitter).

To match the seven primary odors there must be seven different kinds of olfactory receptors in the nose. We can picture the receptor sites as ultramicroscopic slots or hollows in the nerve-fiber membrane, each of a distinctive shape and size. Presumably each will accept a molecule of the appropriate configuration, just as a socket takes a plug. Some molecules may be able to fit into two different sockets—broadside into a wide receptor or end on into a narrow one. In such cases the substance, with its molecules occupying both types of receptor, may indicate a complex odor to the brain.

The next problem was to learn the shapes of the seven receptor sites. This was begun by examining the structural formulas of the camphoraceous compounds and constructing models of their molecules. Thanks to the techniques of modern stereochemistry, which explore the structure of molecules with the aid of X-ray diffraction, infrared spectroscopy, the electron-beam probe and other means, it is possible to build a three-dimensional model of the molecule of any chemical compound once its structural formula is known. There are rules for building these models; also available are building blocks (sets of atomic units) on a scale 100 million times actual size.

As the models of the camphoraceous molecules took form, it soon became clear that they all had about the same shape: they were roughly spherical. Not only that, it turned out that when the models were translated into molecular dimensions, all the molecules also had about the same diameter: approximately seven angstrom units. (An angstrom unit is a ten-millionth of a millimeter.) This meant that the receptor site for camphoraceous molecules must be a hemispherical bowl about seven angstroms in diameter. Many of the camphoraceous molecules are rigid spheres that would inevitably fit into such a bowl; the others are slightly flexible and could easily shape themselves to the bowl.

When other models were built, shapes and sizes of the molecules representing the other primary odors were found [*see illustration on preceding two pages*]. The musky odor is accounted for by molecules with the shape of a disk about 10 angstroms in diameter. The pleasant floral odor is caused by molecules that have the shape of a disk with a flexible tail attached—a shape somewhat like a kite. The cool pepperminty odor is produced by molecules with the shape of a wedge, and with an electrically polarized group of atoms, capable of forming a hydrogen bond, near the point of the wedge. The ethereal odor is due to rod-shaped or other thin molecules. In each of these cases the receptor site in the nerve endings presumably has a shape and size corresponding to those of the molecule.

The pungent and putrid odors seem to be exceptions to the Lucretian scheme of shape-matching. The molecules responsible for these odors are of indifferent shapes and sizes; what matters in their case is the electric charge of the molecule. The pungent class of odors is produced by compounds whose molecules, because of a deficiency of electrons, have a positive charge and a strong affinity for electrons; they are called electrophilic. Putrid odors, on the other hand, are caused by molecules

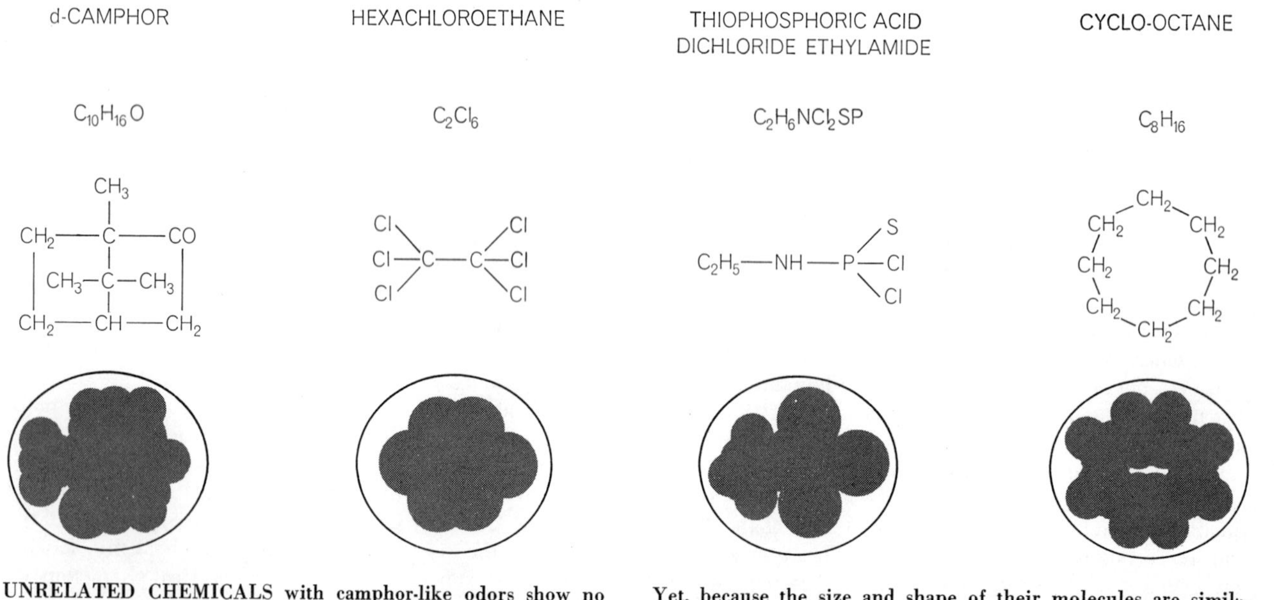

UNRELATED CHEMICALS with camphor-like odors show no resemblance in empirical formulas and little in structural formulas. Yet, because the size and shape of their molecules are similar, they all fit the bowl-shaped receptor for camphoraceous molecules.

that have an excess of electrons and are called nucleophilic, because they are strongly attracted by the nuclei of adjacent atoms.

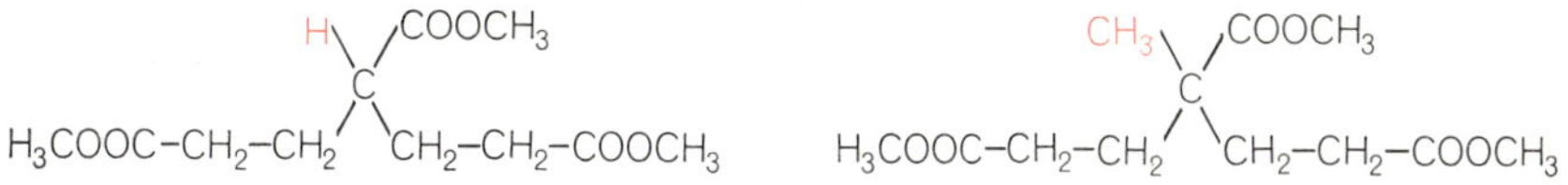

CHANGE IN SHAPE of a molecule changed its odor. The molecule at left smelled fruity because it fitted into three sites. When it was modified (*right*) by the substitution of a methyl group for a hydrogen, it smelled somewhat ethereal. Presumably the methyl branch made it fit two of the original sites less well but allowed it still to fit the ethereal slot.

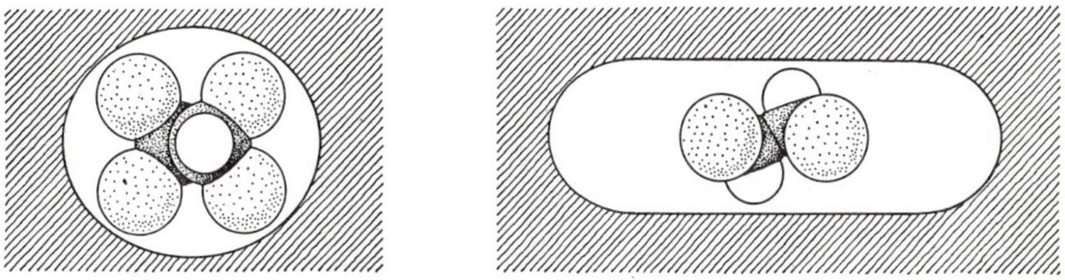

SINGLE CHEMICAL has more than one primary odor if its molecule can fit more than one site. Acetylenetetrabromide, for example, is described as smelling both camphoraceous and ethereal. It turns out that its molecule can fit either site, depending on how it lies.

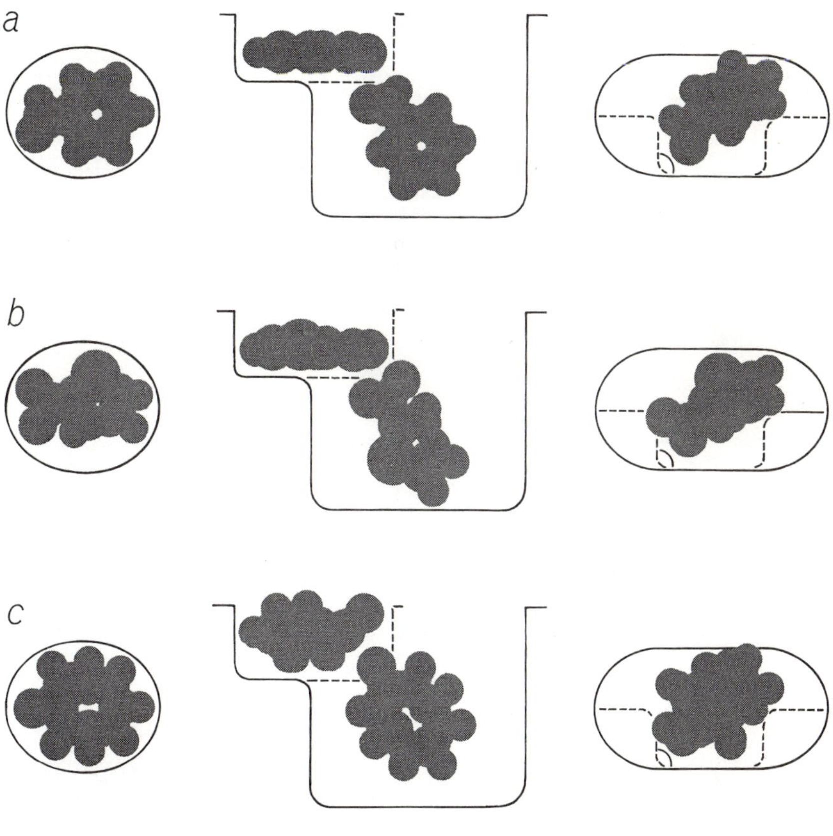

COMPLEX ODORS are made up of several primaries. Three molecules with an almond odor are illustrated: benzaldehyde (*a*), alpha-nitrothiophen (*b*) and cyclo-octanone (*c*). Each of them fits (*left to right*) camphoraceous, floral (with two molecules) and pepperminty sites.

A theory is useful only if it can be tested in some way by experiment. One of the virtues of the stereochemical theory is that it suggests some very specific and unambiguous tests. It has been subjected to six severe tests of its accuracy so far and has passed each of them decisively.

To start with, it is at once obvious that from the shape of a molecule we should be able to predict its odor. Suppose, then, that we synthesize molecules of certain shapes and see whether or not they produce the odors predicted for them.

Consider a molecule consisting of three chains attached to a single carbon atom, with the central atom's fourth bond occupied only by a hydrogen atom [*see top illustration at right*]. This molecule might fit into a kite-shaped site (floral odor), a wedge-shaped site (pepperminty) or, by means of one of its chains, a rod-shaped site (ethereal). The theory predicts that the molecule should therefore have a fruity odor composed of these three primaries. Now suppose we substitute the comparatively bulky methyl group (CH_3) in place of the small hydrogen atom at the fourth bond of the carbon atom. The introduction of a fourth branch will prevent the molecule from fitting so easily into a kite-shaped or wedge-shaped site, but one of the branches should still be able to occupy a rod-shaped site. As a result, the theory predicts, the ether smell should now predominate.

Another of us (Rubin) duly synthesized the two structures in his laboratory at the Georgetown University School of Medicine. The third author (Johnston), also working at the Georgetown School of Medicine, then submitted the products to a panel of trained smellers. He used an instrument called the olfactometer, which by means of valves and controlled air streams delivers carefully measured concentrations of odors, singly or mixed, to the observer. The amount of odorous vapor delivered was measured by gas chromatography. A pair of olfactometers was used, one for each of the two compounds under test, and the observer was asked to sniff alternately from each.

The results verified the predictions. The panel reported that Compound A had a fruity (actually grapelike) odor, and that Compound B, with the methyl group substituted for the hydrogen atom, had a pronounced tinge of the ether-like odor. This experiment, and the theory behind it, make understandable the earlier finding that the odor of certain benzene-ring compounds changes sharply when the position of a group of atoms is shifted. The change in odor is due to the change in the over-all shape of the molecule.

A second test suggested itself. Could a complex odor found in nature be matched by putting together a combination of primary odors? Taking the odor of cedarwood oil as a test case, Amoore found that chemicals known to

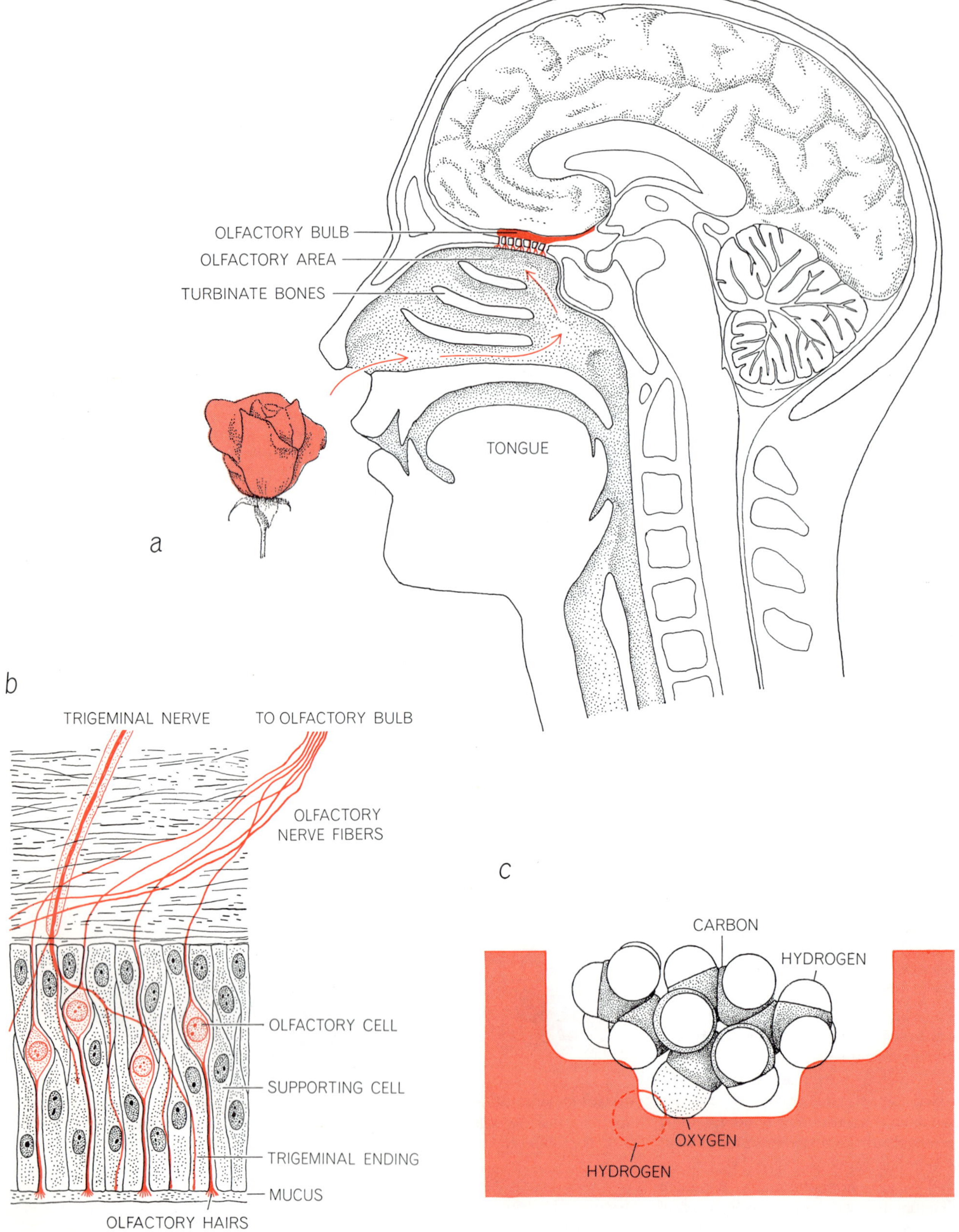

ANATOMY of the sense of smell is traced in these drawings. Air carrying odorous molecules is sniffed up past the three baffle-shaped turbinate bones to the olfactory area (*a*), patches of epithelium in which are embedded the endings of large numbers of olfactory nerves (*color*). A microscopic section of the olfactory epithelium (*b*) shows the olfactory nerve cells and their hairlike endings, trigeminal endings and supporting cells. According to the stereochemical theory different olfactory nerve cells are stimulated by different molecules on the basis of the size and shape or the charge of the molecule; these properties determine which of various pits and slots on the olfactory endings it will fit. A molecule of *l*-menthone is shown fitted into the "pepperminty" cavity (*c*).

possess this odor had molecular shapes that would fit into the receptor sites for the camphoraceous, musky, floral and pepperminty odors. Johnston proceeded to try various combinations of these four primaries to duplicate the cedarwood odor. He tested each mixture on eight trained observers, who compared the synthetic odor with that of cedarwood oil. After 86 attempts he was able to produce a blend that closely matched the natural cedarwood odor. With the same four primaries he also succeeded in synthesizing a close match for the odor of sandalwood oil.

The next two tests had to do with the identification of pure (that is, primary) odors. If the theory was correct, a molecule that would fit only into a receptor site of a particular shape and size, and no other, should represent a primary odor in pure form. Molecules of the same shape and size should smell very much alike; those of a different primary shape should smell very different. Human subjects were tested on this point. Presented with the odors from a pair of different substances whose molecules nonetheless had the same primary shape (for example, that of the floral odor), the subjects judged the two odors to be highly similar to each other. When the pair of substances presented had the pure molecular traits of different categories (for instance, the kite shape of the floral odor and the nucleophilic charge characteristic of putrid compounds), the subjects found the odors extremely dissimilar.

Johnston went on to make the same sort of test with honeybees. He set up an experiment designed to test their ability to discriminate between two odors, one of which was "right" (associated with sugar sirup) and the other "wrong" (associated with an electric shock). The pair of odors might be in the same primary group or in different primary groups (for example, floral and pepperminty). At pairs of scented vials on a table near the hive, the bees were first conditioned to the fact that one odor of a pair was right and the other was wrong. Then the sirup bait in the vials was replaced with distilled water and freshly deodorized scent vials were substituted for those used during the training period. The visits of the marked bees to the respective vials in search of sirup were counted. It could be assumed that they would tend to visit the odor to which they had been favorably conditioned and to avoid the one that had been associated with electric shock, provided that they could distinguish between the two.

So tested, the honeybees clearly showed that they had difficulty in detecting a difference between two scents within the same primary group (say pepperminty) but were able to distinguish easily between different primaries (pepperminty and floral). In the latter case they almost invariably chose the correct scent without delay. These experiments indicate that the olfactory system of the honeybee, like that of human beings, is based on the stereochemical principle, although the bee's smelling organ is different; it smells not with a nose but with antennae. Apparently the receptor sites on the antennae are differentiated by shape in the same way as those in the human nose.

A fifth test was made with human observers trained in odor discrimination. Suppose they were presented with a number of substances that were very different chemically but whose molecules had about the same over-all shape. Would all these dissimilar compounds smell alike? Five compounds were used for the test. They belonged to three different chemical families differing radically from one another in the internal structure of their molecules but in all five cases had the disk shape characteristic of the molecules of musky-odored substances. The observers, exposed to

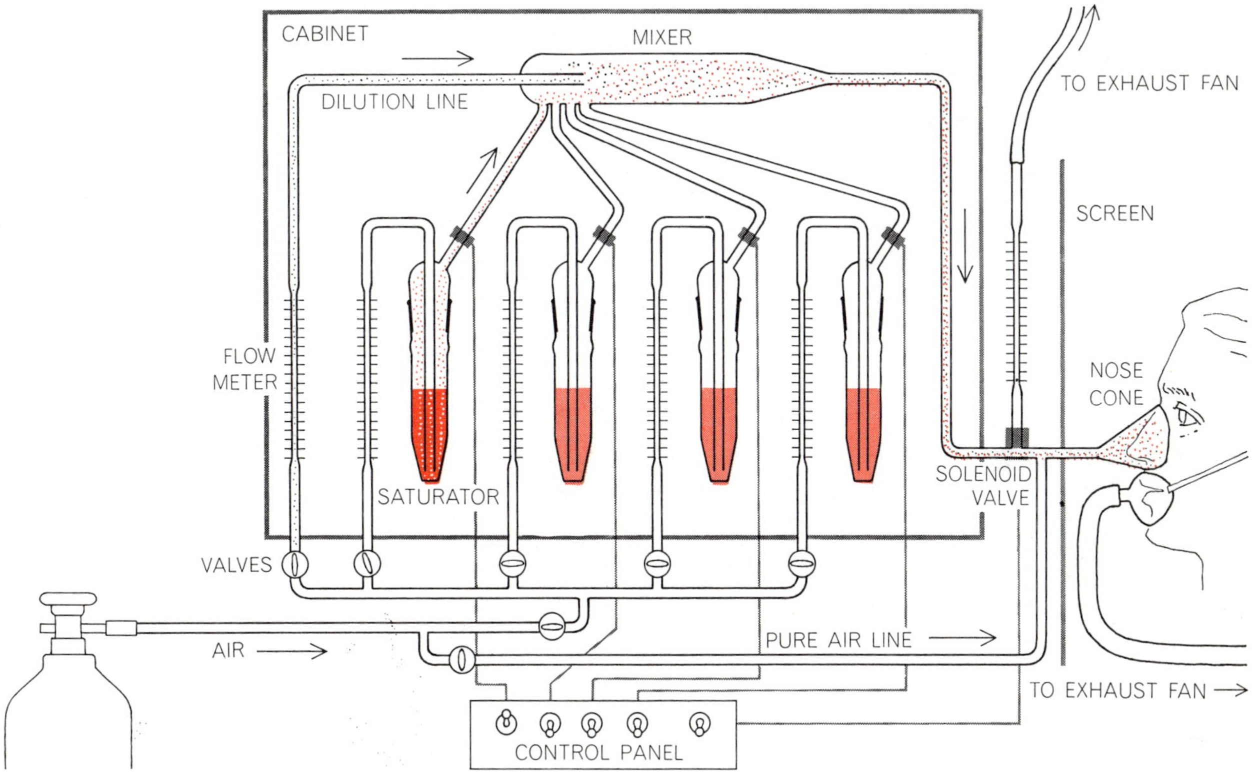

OLFACTOMETER developed by one of the authors (Johnston) mixes odors in precise proportions and delivers them to a nose cone for sampling. This schematic diagram shows the main elements. Air bubbles through a liquid in one of the saturators, picks up odorous molecules and is then diluted with pure air or mixed with air carrying other odors. The experimenter controls the solenoid valves.

CONSTANT-TEMPERATURE CABINET maintains the olfactometer parts at 77 degrees Fahrenheit. The photograph shows the interior of the cabinet, containing two units of the type diagramed on the opposite page. Several of the saturators are visible, as are two mixers (*horizontal glass vessels*), each of them connected by tubing to a nose cone at right.

the vapors of these five chemicals among many others by means of the olfactometer, did indeed pick out and identify all five as musky. By the odor test, however, they were often unable to distinguish these five quite different chemicals from one another.

Basically all this evidence in favor of the stereochemical theory was more or less indirect. One would like some sort of direct proof of the actual existence of differentiated receptor sites in the smelling organ. Recently R. C. Gesteland, then at the Massachusetts Institute of Technology, searched for such evidence. He devised a way to tap the electric impulses from single olfactory-nerve cells by means of microelectrodes. Applying his electrodes to the olfactory organ of the frog, Gesteland presented various odors to the organ and tapped the olfactory cells one by one to see if they responded with electric impulses. He found that different cells responded selectively to different odors, and his exploration indicated that the frog has about eight such different receptors. What is more, five of these receivers correspond closely to five of the odors (camphoraceous, musky, ethereal, pungent and putrid) identified as primary in the stereochemical theory! This finding, then, can be taken as a sixth and independent confirmation of the theory.

Equipped now with a tested basic theory to guide further research, we can hope for much faster progress in the science of osmics (smell) than has been possible heretofore. This may lead to unexpected benefits for mankind. For man the sense of smell may perhaps have become less essential as a life-and-death organ than it is for lower animals, but we still depend on this sense much more than we realize. One can gain some appreciation of the importance of smell to man by reflecting on how tasteless food becomes when the nose is blocked by a head cold and on how unpleasantly we are affected by a bad odor in drinking water or a closed room. Control of odor is fundamental in our large perfume, tobacco and deodorant industries. No doubt odor also affects our lives in many subtle ways of which we are not aware.

The accelerated research for which the way is now open should make it possible to analyze in fine detail the complex flavors in our food and drink, to get rid of obnoxious odors, to develop new fragrances and eventually to synthesize any odor we wish, whether to defeat pests or to delight the human nose.

BIOLOGICAL TRANSDUCERS

WERNER R. LOEWENSTEIN

August 1960

Aristotle's maxim "Nothing is in the mind that did not pass through the senses" is questioned by some schools of philosophy. If "brain" is substituted for "mind," however, and the statement is made a physiological rather than a philosophical one, it then becomes literally true. For higher organisms the sensory receptor furnishes the only means of gaining information about the surrounding world.

This is not the case with primitive one-celled organisms; the cell is directly excited by the environmental stimulus and responds through movement, secretion and so on. But as organisms became more complex in the course of evolution, many of their body cells lost direct contact with the outside world. Certain cells appeared that specialize in the reception of external stimuli. They are, in general, attuned to a single type of stimulus: the rods and cones in the retina respond to light, the thermal receptors in the skin respond to heat and cold, and the mechanoreceptors in muscle respond to mechanical stimuli such as stretching and pressure. The specialized receptor is an outgrowth of a nerve cell, or is in intimate contact with one. Environmental stimuli of the appropriate kind excite the receptor, and the excitation is conveyed to other parts of the organism along nerve circuits of varying complexity.

From the physical point of view the sensory receptors are transducers, that is, they convert one form of energy into another. The various types of receptor convert the particular form of energy to which each is attuned into the electrical energy of the nerve impulse. One may compare them with the transducer devices which modern technology has developed in great variety for automatic control of machines and factories—devices that measure temperature, pressure, rate of flow and so on, and feed their measurements into the artificial nerve-circuits of the control system. The biological transducers that nature took somewhat longer to develop have remarkable sensitivity and efficiency.

The mechanoreceptors were among the earliest to evolve; they enabled primitive marine animals to maintain their orientation with respect to gravity, to detect obstacles and to sense vibrations produced by other animals. The evolution of life on land brought the development of mechanoreceptors sensitive to vibrations of the air; with the growth of specialized internal organs and the need for fast regulatory mechanisms came the development of receptors sensitive to internal mechanical stimuli. Vertebrates possess mechanoreceptors in all organs in which active or passive movements occur, including the digestive tract, the lungs, the heart and the blood vessels, as well as the skin and the skeletal muscles. These receptors feed into the nervous system information about movement, tension and pressure.

The transducer mechanism in the mechanoreceptor was first demonstrated in 1950 by Bernhard Katz of University College London. He discovered that the stretching of a muscle spindle (a mechanoreceptor built into skeletal muscle) generates a local electric current. When the current reaches a certain intensity, he found, it triggers the firing of an impulse in the nerve fiber leading from the muscle spindle to the higher nerve-centers [see "The Nerve Impulse," by Bernhard Katz; SCIENTIFIC AMERICAN Offprint 20].

This result did not come as a complete surprise. Since the time of Luigi Galvani and Alessandro Volta, physiologists have used electric currents to trigger impulses in nerve fibers. But the current that tripped the nerve impulse in Katz's experiment did not come from a battery or any other external power supply; it came from within the muscle spindle itself. Several other workers soon obtained similar results in experiments on mechanoreceptors from organisms as diverse as the crayfish and the cat.

In all these receptors mechanical stimulation produces a weak local current. It is known as the generator current, because it in turn triggers the nerve impulse. The generator current is the earliest detectable step in the transducer sequence. In a typical mammalian mechanoreceptor the current follows the stimulus within a thousandth of a second. Moreover, the generator current increases in direct relation with the increase in the energy of the stimulus. This relation between the input and output of energy resembles that of a good mechanoelectric transducer of the type represented by a carbon microphone. In the microphone mechanical deformation of the disk of carbon by the impinging sound wave reduces its electrical resistance, permitting the electric current to flow through it in strength proportional to the intensity of the sound. The output current from the biological and from the man-made transducer thus conveys a measurement of the strength of the stimulus and of the sound.

With this much known about the mechanoreceptor, the next problem was to discover which of its several structural components is the transducer element. I became interested in the question in 1955, and looked for an appropriate receptor with which to look into it. The Pacinian corpuscle—found in the skin, muscles, tendons and joints of mammals—occurs in an especially accessible

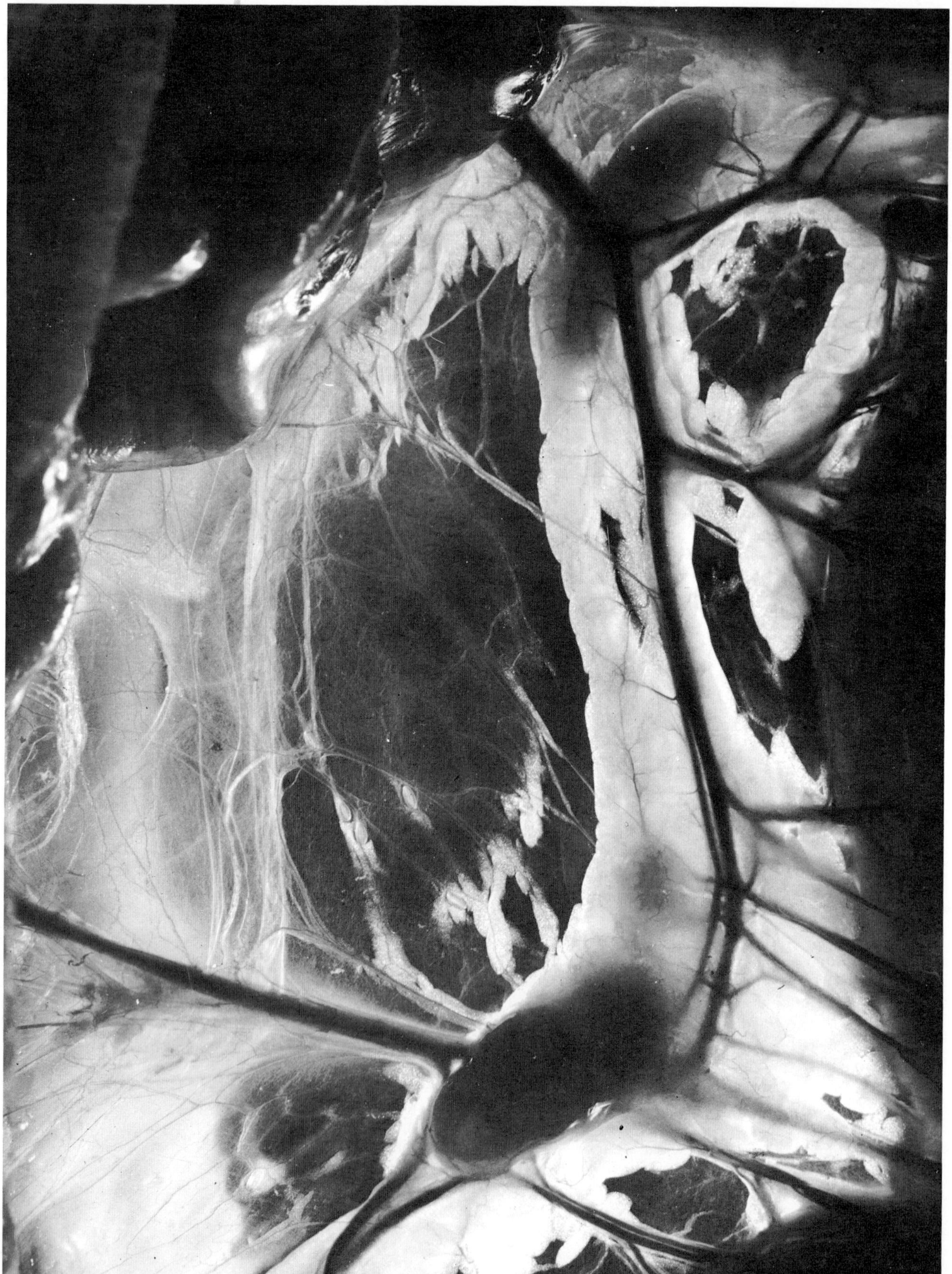

PACINIAN CORPUSCLES are small ellipsoidal bodies, three of which are visible at the lower left side of the dark area in the center of this photograph. Here the corpuscles are located in the mesentery (a thin membrane attached to the intestine) of a cat. They are enlarged some four diameters. In actual size each corpuscle is about one millimeter long and .6 millimeter thick.

form in the mesentery of the cat, that is, the fold of tissue that connects the intestine to the rear wall of the abdomen. From the mesentery it can be easily removed and kept alive for hours in a suitable salt solution. Moreover, John Gray and his colleagues at University College London had already shown that the corpuscle can be stimulated mechanically and the resulting current recorded through an electrode attached to its nerve fiber. But the greatest experimental advantage of the Pacinian corpuscle is its large size. It is truly a giant among receptors, measuring almost one millimeter long and .6 millimeter thick. Under the microscope it looks like an onion: it consists of many concentric layers, or lamellae, ultimately enclosing a nerve ending. The nerve fiber leading from it can be kept functioning along with the corpuscle. This easily manageable unit became our experimental subject.

For mechanical stimulation of the corpuscle we used a piezoelectric crystal of the type employed in phonograph pickups. In its familiar applications such a crystal converts mechanical energy into electrical energy. But it can also be used to convert electrical energy into mechanical; it deflects when a voltage is applied across it, the deflection increasing linearly with voltage. In our experiment a glass stylus transmitted the deflection to the corpuscle as a readily measurable stimulus.

To locate the transducer site in the corpuscle, R. Rathkamp and I adopted a direct approach; we removed pieces of its structure in the hope that we might isolate the part essential to the transducer process. We peeled off the outer layers of the corpuscle, stimulating it after each step of dissection. It soon became clear that more than 99.9 per cent of the mass of the corpuscle could be dissected away without impairing the transducer function. A preparation consisting of the nerve ending surrounded only by a thin sheath of "inner core" was as good a transducer as the intact corpuscle. When stimulated mechanically, it produced generator currents which, if the outgoing nerve fiber was left intact, triggered the firing of nerve impulses in the normal manner.

Since the transducer mechanism had to be somewhere within the inner core, the nerve ending appeared to be the most likely site. We tried to strip away the inner core around the nerve ending, but did not succeed because the tissue here is only about .01 millimeter thick and is too intimately attached to the

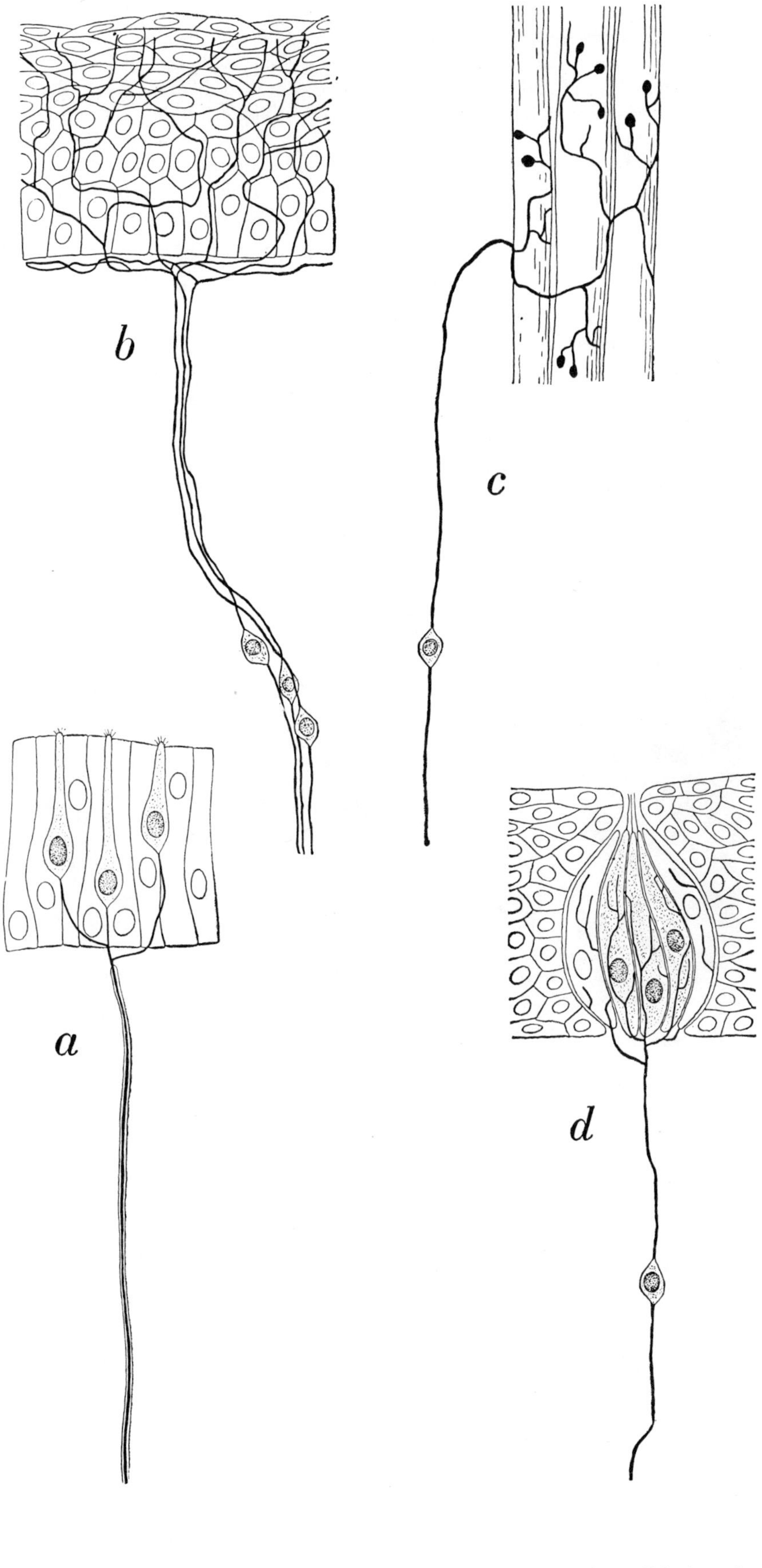

SENSORY NERVES such as olfactory receptors of the nose (*a*) have their cell body at the periphery; pain receptors of the skin (*b*), mechanoreceptors of muscle (*c*) and taste receptors of the tongue (*d*) have their cell bodies buried in the organism. All of them act as biological transducers. The muscle receptors end in leaflike structures; the others are bare.

nerve. However, with a pair of micromanipulators we were able to tease off the outer layers, cut out a few pieces of the remaining layers and puncture the rest with a fine glass needle. This preparation, in which the nerve ending was the only intact structure, was still a good transducer, producing currents as in the intact organ.

Thus we could not yet say whether the core tissues or the nerve ending produced the current. Since the technique of microdissection could not completely free the nerve ending from the surrounding core material, we decided to try the opposite tack. We prepared an "endingless" core by severing the nerve fiber of the corpuscle in the living animal and allowing the nerve ending to degenerate. When this preparation was removed two or three days later and stimulated, it failed to produce a generator current, indicating that the nerve ending was indeed the transducer site.

Investigators have now begun to take a closer look at the mechanosensitive nerve-ending with the electron microscope. The two different types, the Pacinian corpuscle and the muscle spindle, that have been examined so far have three characteristics in common: (1) the absence of the insulating sheath of myelin found in nerve-circuit cells; (2) the presence, characteristic of cells that must produce large amounts of energy, of a relatively large number of mitochondria, the small bodies associated with metabolic activity; and (3) the presence of many small, round structures of unknown function that resemble certain structures found in motor-nerve endings.

The generator current produced by the nerve ending in the mechanoreceptor does not itself travel along the nerve fiber. It serves merely to trigger the nerve impulse which does propagate along the nerve circuit, often for considerable distances. Generator current and nerve impulse originate at different places in the corpuscle. Rathkamp and I located the site at which the impulse originates by blocking the activity of selected portions of the nerve fiber. The myelin sheath that covers this fiber extends well into the corpuscle, and is interrupted at intervals of about .25 millimeter by small gaps known as the nodes of Ranvier. In a dissected preparation several nodes and the nerve ending are visible under the microscope; the first node lies within the corpuscle. We applied pressure to the nodes with a wisp of glass about .004 millimeter in diameter, blocking the electric activity of each one in turn. The nerve continued to fire its impulse in response to mechanical stimulation of the nerve ending and to the resulting generator current until we blocked the first node. Plainly the first node is the point at which the nerve impulse starts.

The production of the nerve impulse could now be visualized as a two-step

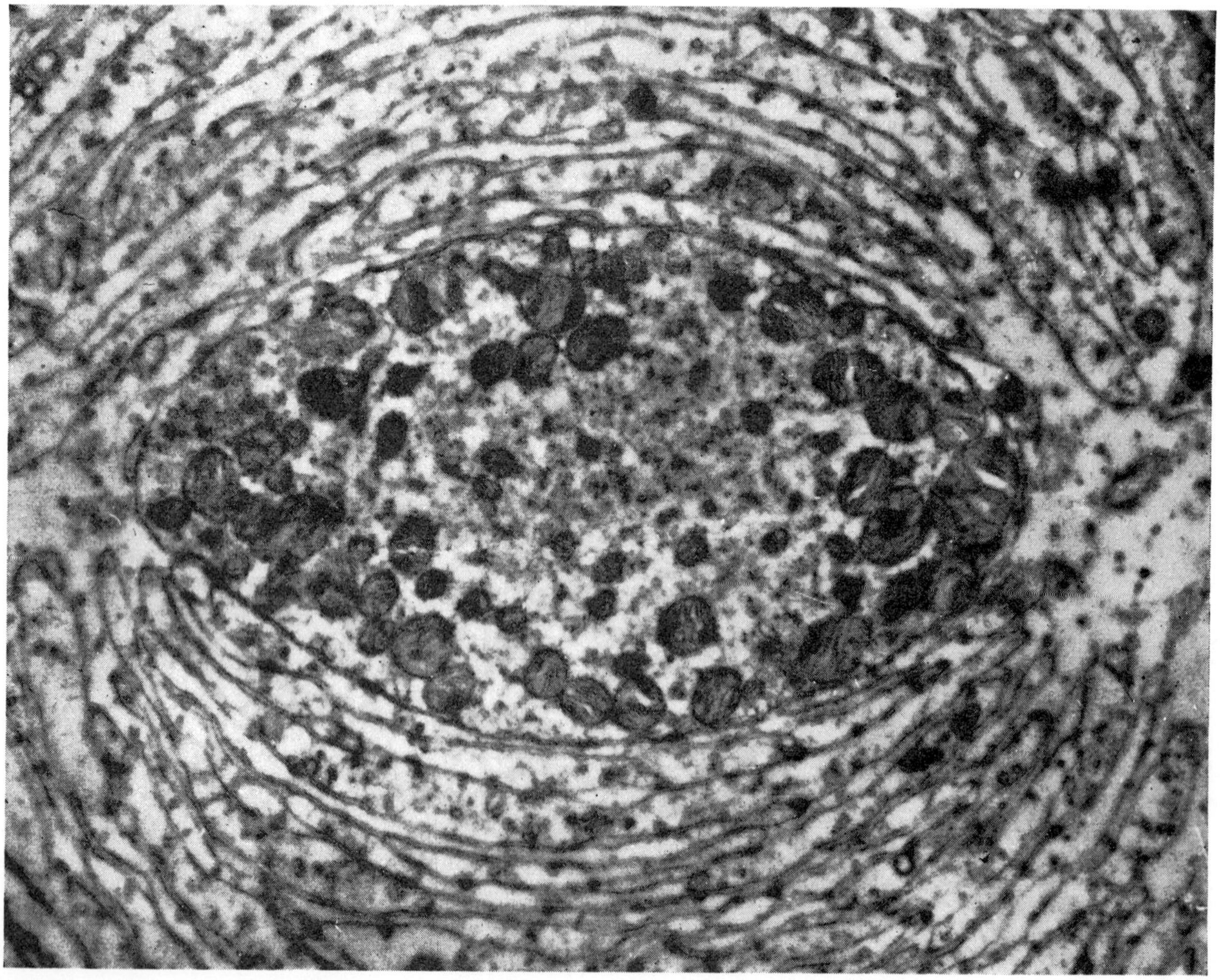

NERVE ENDING of the Pacinian corpuscle is enlarged some 20,000 diameters in this electron micrograph made by D. C. Pease and T. A. Quilliam of the University of California. The section cuts across the long axis of the ending, which is the oval area in the center. The round, dark bodies within this area are mitochondria. Around the area are the layers, or lamellae, of the corpuscle core.

process, each step related to a particular structure. Under resting conditions there is a potential across the "receptor" membrane or the nerve ending in the corpuscle; the inside of the ending is several tenths of a volt negative with respect to the outside. This potential appears to be produced and maintained by unequal concentrations of ions (that is, charged atoms or molecules) on the two sides of the membrane. The ending thus resembles other excitable—nerve and muscle—tissues. It differs markedly from such tissues, however, in its high sensitivity to mechanical stimulation: deformation of the receptor membrane leads to a drop in resting potential. Under resting conditions the membrane resistance is so high that no appreciable net ion current leaks through it. Distortion produces a decrease in resistance which allows ions to move along their concentration gradients across the membrane, causing the resting potential to drop. Mechanical stimulation thus results in a transfer of charges across the receptor membrane; this constitutes the generator current. Part of the generator current flows through the first node, where it triggers the nerve impulse [*see illustration on page 81*]. Apparently the generator current must be of a minimal intensity and must reach this intensity at a minimal rate in order to have this effect.

The nerve impulse has been far more thoroughly studied than has the generator current. It is the signal which in the sensory nerve fibers travels from the periphery to the nerve centers, conveying information about color, shape, texture, temperature, sound and so on; and in the motor and secretory fibers in the opposite direction, conveying orders for contraction of muscles or for secretion of glands. No basic qualitative differences are known to exist among these fibers. The nerve impulse is a pulse of current that under equal conditions and in any given fiber is of the same size and duration [see "The Nerve Impulse," by Bernhard Katz; SCIENTIFIC AMERICAN Offprint 20]. In the case of the fiber that leads out of the Pacinian corpuscle, the generator current excites the membrane of the first node of Ranvier. The node responds with a change in permeability to certain ions, and the result is an abrupt surge of current through the membrane lasting for a thousandth of a second or so. From here on propagation of the nerve impulse follows the pattern of other myelin-insulated nerve fibers. Part of the current set up at the first node flows through the second node, and this current is more than sufficiently strong to trip off a current pulse of the same magnitude in the next node. In this manner the impulse regenerates itself at each node and propagates at full amplitude to the nerve centers. That amplitude bears no relation, however, to the intensity of the generator current that triggered it at the first node.

Here one encounters an apparent difficulty. The receptor chain begins with a mechanical stimulus of a given energy content; the stimulus is transformed into a generator current with an energy content proportional to that of the stimulus, and now the chain ends in a signal—the nerve impulse—with an energy content that bears no relationship to either of the preceding events. How can the all-or-none signal of the nerve impulse convey quantitative information about the strength of the stimulus along the nerve fiber?

A clue is furnished by the fact that many man-made information systems operate with all-or-none signals. Digital computers send and store information by all-or-none pulses, and the telegraph transmits messages of the most varied content with dots and dashes, two types of all-or-none pulses. Biological sensory systems operate on the same digital principle and use only dots. As long ago as 1926 E. D. Adrian of the University of Cambridge recorded the signals from skin and muscle receptors and made the far-reaching discovery that the frequency—not the amplitude—of the nerve impulses varies with the strength of the stimulus. Adrian and his colleagues soon broke the code of other sensory systems, and investigators in many parts of the world took up the task of decoding the rest. All turned out to be frequency-modulating systems which translate an increase in the intensity of the stimulus into an increase in the frequency of the nerve impulse. In fibers connected to mechanoreceptors it has been found that the impulse frequency varies with the intensity of the generator current and with the rate at which it increases.

For the student of biological transducers the most interesting and still not completely answered question is how the receptor produces a generator current that varies with the strength of the stimulus and serves to measure it. If the membrane were a carbon microphone, current would flow only in the region distorted by the stimulus, and this would explain the linear relationship between the flow of current and the strength of the stimulus. But physiologists deal with information systems in which signals are carried by ions through conduction lines composed chiefly of water and salts. In a

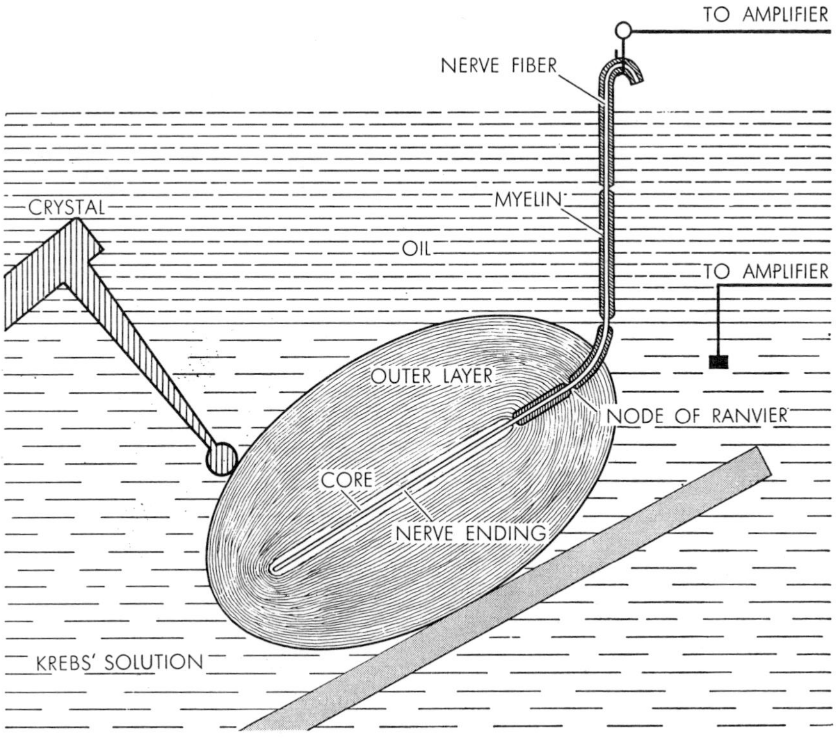

ISOLATED PACINIAN CORPUSCLE was stimulated by a rod attached to a vibrating phonograph crystal (*left*). The resulting nerve impulse was picked up by a pair of electrodes (*right*). This illustration also schematically depicts the corpuscle and its various parts.

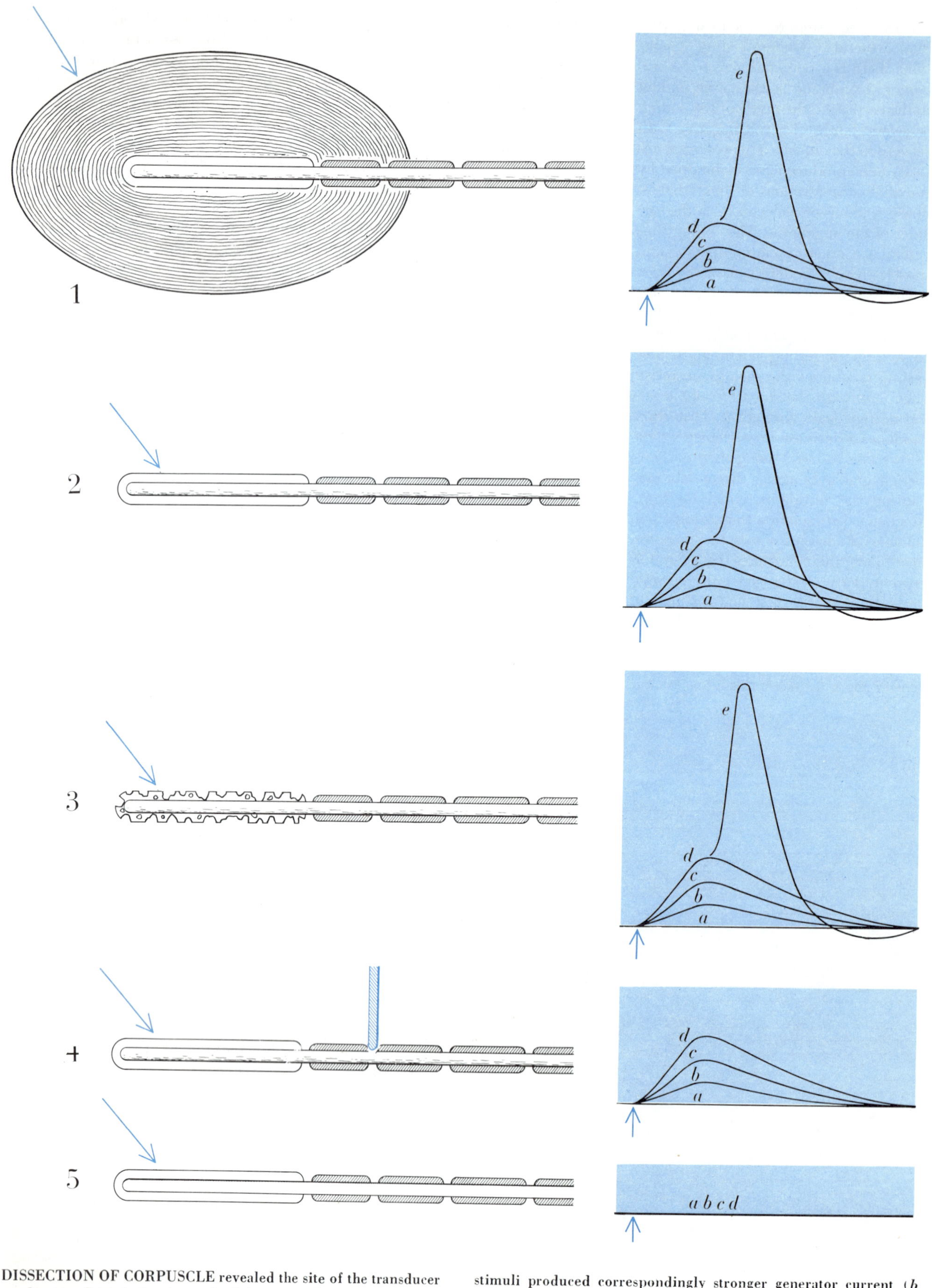

DISSECTION OF CORPUSCLE revealed the site of the transducer mechanism. Stimulation (*arrow*) of the corpuscle when intact (1), with outer layers removed (2) or after partial destruction of the core sheath (3) produced the same responses. A weak stimulus produced a weak generator current (*a*); progressively stronger stimuli produced correspondingly stronger generator current (*b* and *c*); the threshold stimulus (*d*) fired an all-or-none nerve impulse (*e*). When the first node of Ranvier was blocked (4), no all-or-none impulse could be induced. After degeneration of nerve ending (5), receptor did not respond at all to stimuli.

typical conductile nerve-fiber a region of membrane cannot remain unexcited for long next to an excited one. The excited region generates an electric current that is more than sufficient to excite the neighboring region; this region in turn excites the next, and so on. In this manner excitation sweeps in a wave over the entire membrane. Such is the behavior of the nerve fiber. Does the transducer membrane in the corpuscle act like a carbon microphone or like a nerve fiber? Or, to rephrase the question, is current generated throughout the membrane, or generated only in the mechanically distorted region?

A technique worked out in my laboratory at Columbia University provided an approach to this question. We applied a mechanical pulse to a tiny patch of membrane, about .03 millimeter in diameter, and measured the resulting generator currents at varying distances from the stimulated site. We found that the current decreases exponentially with the distance. This is precisely what one would expect if the excitation were restricted to the stimulated region of the membrane. Some of the generator current leaks into the unexcited regions, but the unexcited membrane acts like a passive cable in which signals fade out with distance. The experiment showed clearly that excitation in the receptor membrane is confined to the mechanically distorted region.

I have recently succeeded in exciting two generator currents in the same nerve ending by simultaneously stimulating two spots on the membrane separated by about .5 millimeter. This experiment brought to light a most significant effect: Two such independently generated currents sum to produce a single large generator-current.

The summation of two or more currents, each generated at a separate active site on the membrane, thus promised to explain why the intensity of the generator current is proportional to the strength of the stimulus. To test this hypothesis we applied a series of mechanical stimuli of progressively increasing strength to part of the nerve ending and scanned the membrane with a microelectrode. We found that as the stimulus strength increased, deforming progressively more of the receptor membrane, the excitation spread over a correspondingly greater area.

This opened the rather attractive possibility that the receptor membrane might contain a great number of tiny active sites that show the conventional all-or-none response to mechanical stimulation, and yet give rise to a continuously variable generator current which represents the sum of the currents generated by each of these sites. Theoretically this model can account for the entire input-output response of the mechanoreceptor, and it is alluring because of its simplicity. Unfortunately it must remain rather tentative because there may still be an intensity factor at work. A membrane node that fits the experimental results just as well is one that operates on the basis of spatial summation and in which each active site generates a variable current. We have as yet no way to distinguish between these two possibilities. The only evidence of excitation that can be traced at present is the flow of electric current through the membrane. Current flow is a good index, but a rather blurred one. Even the finest microelectrode is far too large to discrimi-

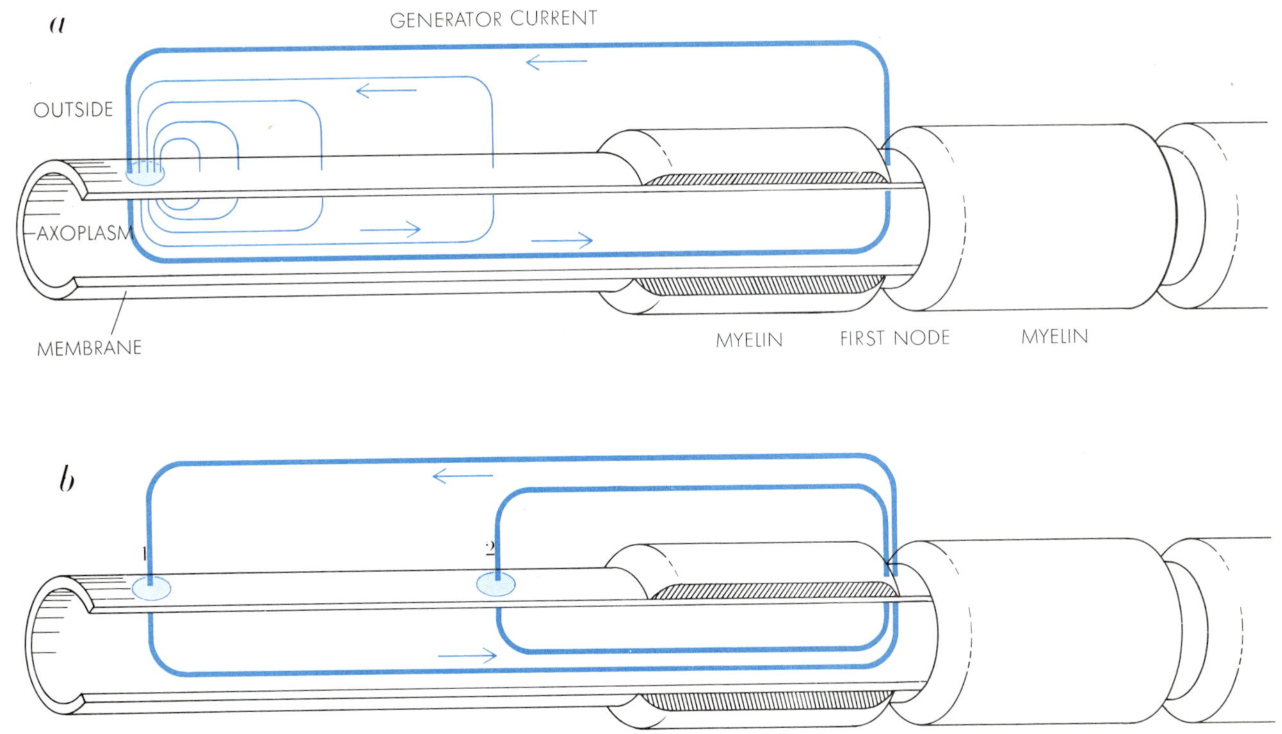

GENERATOR CURRENT arises in limited region of the receptor membrane of the nerve ending (*at left in top diagram*) in response to mechanical stimulation of that area. This current dies out quickly over the nonstimulated area of the membrane, but if sufficient current reaches the first node of the conducting fiber (*at right*) it triggers a nerve impulse. Two or more generator currents produced by stimulation of separate membrane regions (*bottom diagram*) sum to produce a strong current at the first node.

nate changes in the molecular structure of the membrane which apparently account for the flow of electric charges.

The finding that current flow increases with the area of membrane deformed by the stimulus suggested that the excitation might be a statistical process. In other words, the deformation of a given area of membrane might be expected to excite a statistically fluctuating number of active sites, producing a statistically fluctuating generator current. The fluctuations proved, upon measurement, to be large. My colleague Nobusada Ishiko and I were able to show that a constant mechanical stimulus elicits a generator current that fluctuates at random, and that these fluctuations increase with stimulus strength as predicted by the spatial-summation model.

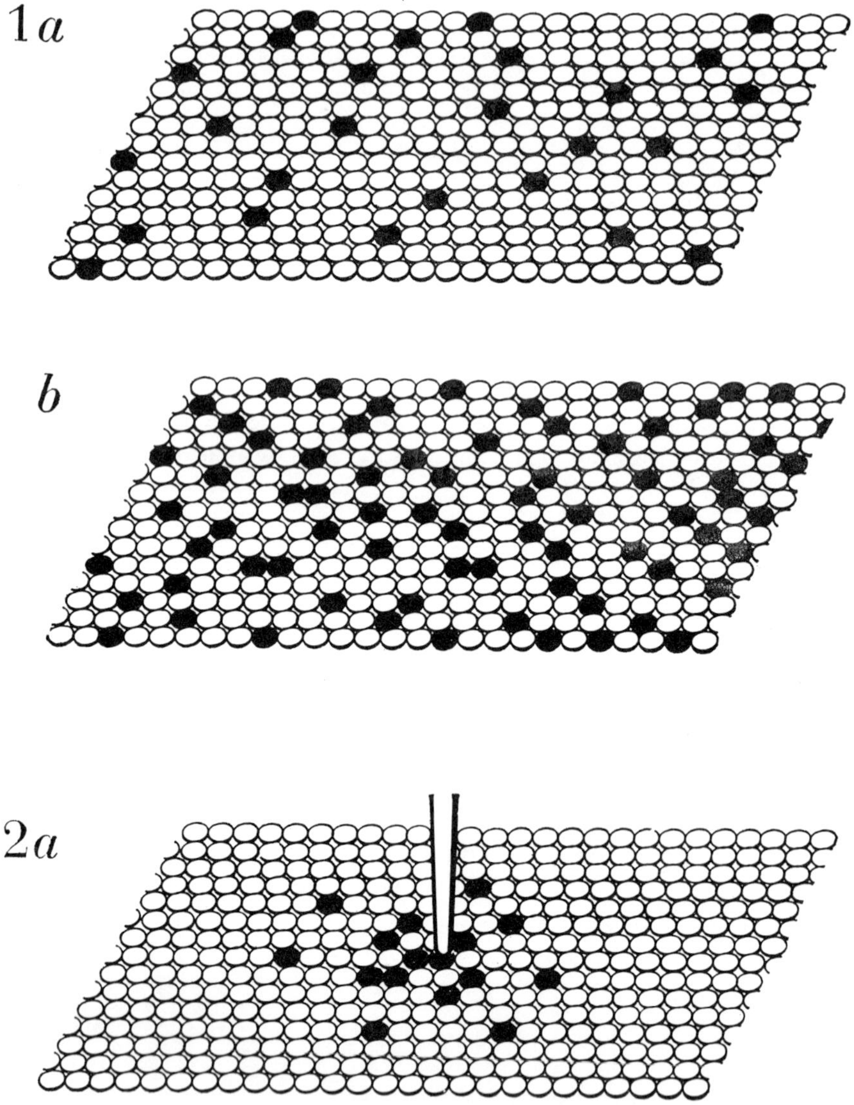

EXCITED REGIONS (*black*) on receptor membranes increase in number as strength of stimulus increases. A possible pattern of spread with increase in stimulus strength is shown for the case in which the stimulus is distributed rather uniformly over the entire membrane, as probably occurs in the intact Pacinian corpuscle (*1a* and *b*), and for the case in which a small area of membrane is stimulated by means of a fine stylus (*2a* and *b*).

One may now perhaps picture the receptor as a membrane in which there is a number of tiny holes. In the resting state the holes are too small for certain ions to pass. Mechanical deformation of a given area opens (excites) a statistically determined number of holes, and the ions move through these, setting up the generator current. The opening may occur directly—through stretching, for example—or indirectly, through some biochemical process. As the stimulus strength increases, an increasing number of holes opens up and a correspondingly increasing number of ions passes through the membrane.

A glance at an electron micrograph of the receptor suggests that the number of ions available for transfer must be limited. The lamellae of the receptor core, which are formidable barriers for ion diffusion, are tightly wrapped around the ending, leaving little fluid space between the receptor membrane and the first lamella [*see illustration on page 78*]. This prompted Stanley Cohen and me to see whether the receptor could be "depleted" of ions by repeated stimulation. We found that the reduction of responsiveness is considerable. For example, a stimulus that produces a generator current of 100 units in the fully rested receptor produces a current of barely 10 units after the application of 5,000 stimuli (at the rate of 500 per second) and none at all after 7,000. The effect is now being studied in our laboratory by Sidney J. Socolar and Masayasu Sato. Preliminary results suggest that the transfer of charges across the membrane depends on the interplay of two competing processes: the depletion and the restoration of something, or the inactivation and reactivation of something. But what this something is—whether it is ions or some chemical precursor—is not yet clear.

The linear relationship between stimulus and response observed in the mechanoreceptor is characteristic of all sensory receptors, and in all sensory circuits the rise in the intensity of the generator current increases the frequency of the nerve impulses dispatched to the higher nerve centers. Another important factor reinforcing the correspondence between input and output in the sensory system is the fact that the receptors occur in groups. Thus a weight pressing on the skin excites many Pacinian corpuscles; light shining into the eye excites a large number of photoreceptors. The greater the strength of the stimulus, the greater the number of excited receptors; if the light is brightened or the pressure on the skin is increased, more receptors are excited, and hence more parallel nerve-fibers fire off impulses to higher centers. Moreover, since several receptor endings are generally the twigs of a single nerve-fiber, there will be considerable convergence of impulses in the common fiber. Thus when a strong stimulus increases the number of activated receptors, this also increases the frequency of impulses traveling along the fiber.

The higher nerve-centers may decipher a receptor message and estimate the strength of the stimulus in at least two ways: by counting the number of parallel information channels engaged in impulse traffic, and by gauging the frequency and sequence patterns of impulses transmitted in each information channel. However, the nature of the mechanisms that decode and store such information is still one of the many open questions on the brain-mind frontier.

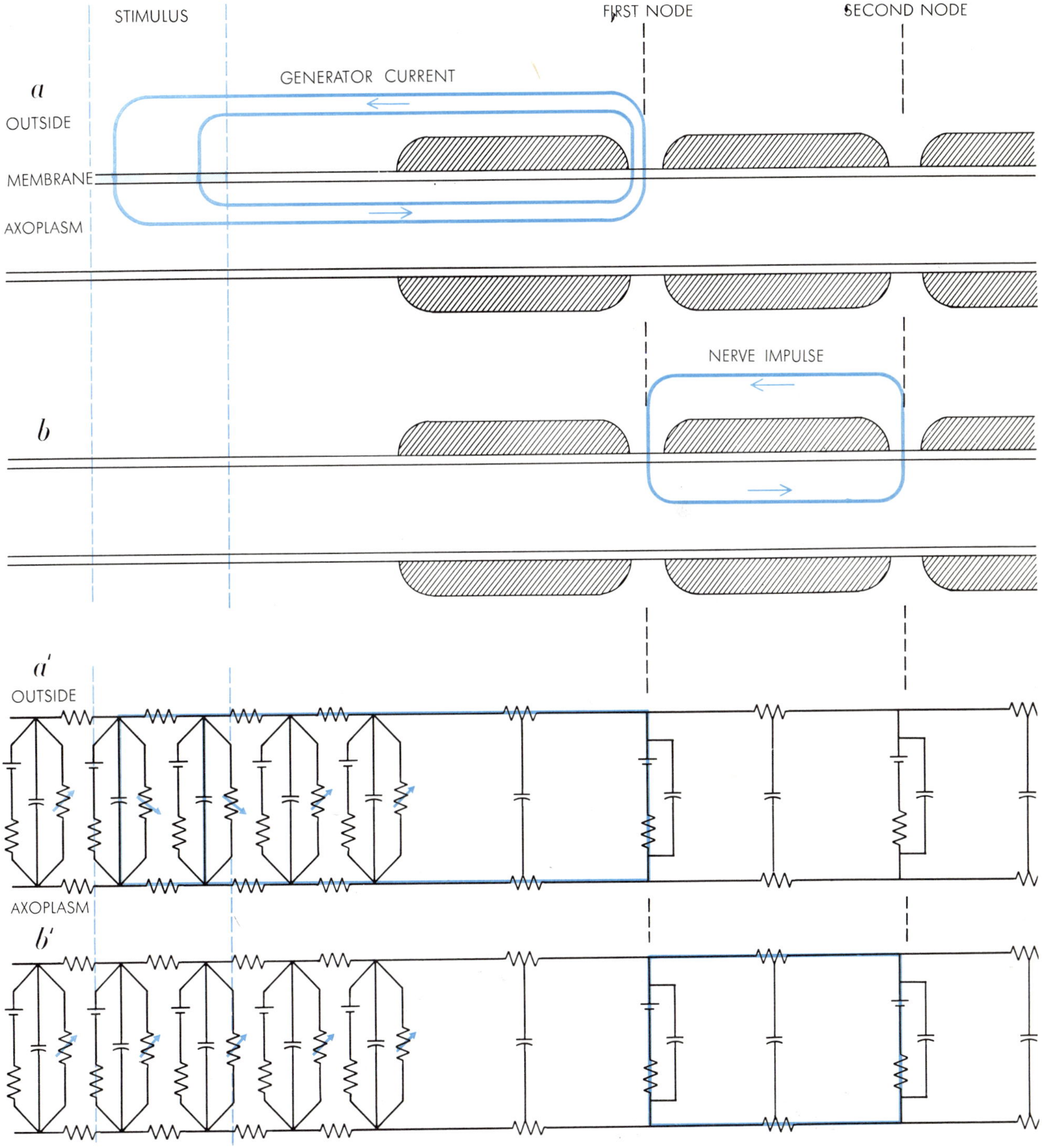

MECHANISM OF TRANSDUCER can be explained by analogy with an electrical circuit. Stimulating a portion of the receptor membrane (*colored area*) causes a drop in the resistance of this membrane region to ion movement. This leads to a transfer of charge, a drop in membrane potential and the generation of current (*colored loops*) in that region. The current flows through the first node of Ranvier and triggers a nerve impulse, the current of which in turn excites the second node (*b*) and so on. In the electrical equivalent (*a'* and *b'*), membrane potential is represented by battery units, and membrane resistance and capacitance is distributed uniformly over a large number of units. (Only five are shown here.) Excitation of a unit causes its resistance to drop (*colored arrows*) and starts events indicated by colored loops. Current discharging into inactive receptor membrane is omitted.

9

THE EAR

GEORG VON BÉKÉSY
August 1957

Even in our era of technological wonders, the performances of our most amazing machines are still put in the shade by the sense organs of the human body. Consider the accomplishments of the ear. It is so sensitive that it can almost hear the random rain of air molecules bouncing against the eardrum. Yet in spite of its extraordinary sensitivity the ear can withstand the pounding of sound waves strong enough to set the body vibrating. The ear is equipped, moreover, with a truly impressive selectivity. In a room crowded with people talking, it can suppress most of the noise and concentrate on one speaker. From the blended sounds of a symphony orchestra the ear of the conductor can single out the one instrument that is not performing to his satisfaction.

In structure and in operation the ear is extraordinarily delicate. One measure of its fineness is the tiny vibrations to which it will respond. At some sound frequencies the vibrations of the eardrum are as small as one billionth of a centimeter—about one tenth the diameter of the hydrogen atom! And the vibrations of the very fine membrane in the inner ear which transmits this stimulation to the auditory nerve are nearly 100 times smaller in amplitude. This fact alone is enough to explain why hearing has so long been one of the mysteries of physiology. Even today we do not know how these minute vibrations stimulate the nerve endings. But thanks to refined electro-acoustical instruments we do know quite a bit now about how the ear functions.

What are the ear's abilities? We can get a quick picture of the working condition of an ear by taking an audiogram, which is a measure of the threshold of hearing at the various sound frequencies. The hearing is tested with pure tones at various frequencies, and the audiogram tells how much sound pressure on the eardrum (*i.e.*, what intensity of sound) is necessary for the sound at each frequency to be just barely audible. Curiously, the audiogram curve often is very much the same for the various members of a family; possibly this is connected in some way with the similarity in the shape of the face.

The ear is least sensitive at the low frequencies: for instance, its sensitivity for a tone of 100 cycles per second is 1,000 times lower than for one at 1,000 cycles per second. This comparative insensitivity to the slower vibrations is an obvious physical necessity, because otherwise we would hear all the vibrations of our own bodies. If you stick a finger in each ear, closing it to air-borne sounds, you hear a very low, irregular tone, produced by the contractions of the muscles of the arm and finger. It is interesting that the ear is just insensitive enough to low frequencies to avoid the disturbing effect of the noises produced by muscles, bodily movements, etc. If it were any more sensitive to these frequencies than it is, we would even hear the vibrations of the head that are produced by the shock of every step we take when walking.

On the high-frequency side the range that the ear covers is remarkable. In childhood some of us can hear well at frequencies as high as 40,000 cycles per second. But with age our acuteness of hearing in the high-frequency range steadily falls. Normally the drop is almost as regular as clockwork: testing several persons in their 40s with tones at a fixed level of intensity, we found that over a period of five years their upper limit dropped about 80 cycles per second every six months. (The experiment was quite depressing to most of the participants.) The aging of the ear is not difficult to understand if we assume that the elasticity of the tissues in the inner ear declines in the same way as that of the skin: it is well known that the skin becomes less resilient as we grow old—a

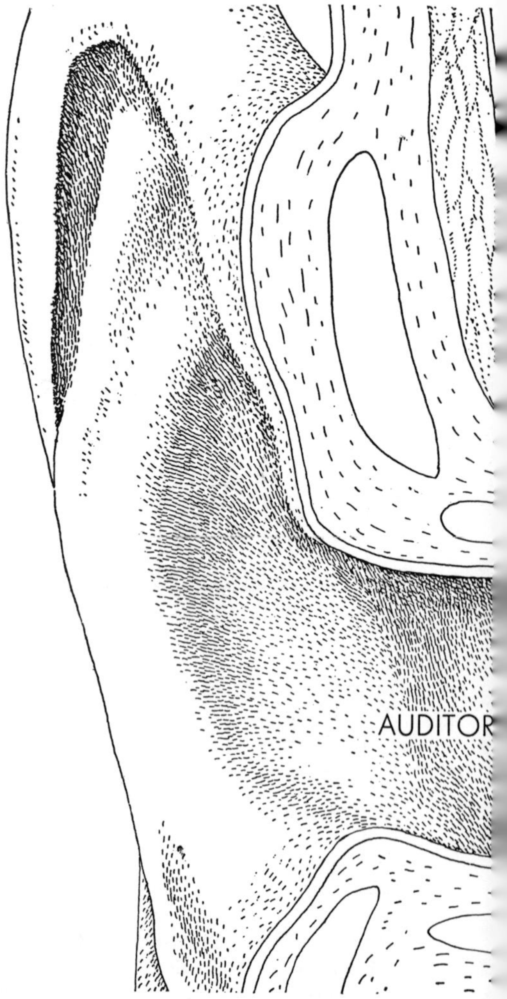

PARTS OF THE EAR are illustrated in somewhat simplified cross section. Be-phenomenon anyone can test by lifting the skin on the back of his hand and measuring the time it takes to fall back.

However, the loss of hearing sensitivity with age may also be due to nerve deterioration. Damage to the auditory nervous system by extremely loud noises, by drugs or by inflammation of the inner ear can impair hearing. Sometimes after such damage the hearing improves with time; sometimes (*e.g.*, when the damaging agent is streptomycin) the loss is permanent. Unfortunately a physician cannot predict the prospects for recovery of hearing loss, because they vary from person to person.

Psychological factors seem to be involved. Occasionally, especially after an ear operation, a patient appears to improve in hearing only to relapse after a short time. Some reports have even suggested that operating on one ear has improved the unoperated ear as well. Since such an interaction between the two ears would be of considerable neurological interest, I have investigated the matter, but I have never found an improvement in the untreated ear that could be validated by an objective test.

Structure of the Ear

To understand how the ear achieves its sensitivity, we must take a look at the anatomy of the middle and the inner ear. When sound waves start the eardrum (tympanic membrane) vibrating, the vibrations are transmitted via certain small bones (ossicles) to the fluid of the inner ear. One of the ossicles, the tiny stirrup (weighing only about 1.2 milligrams), acts on the fluid like a piston, driving it back and forth in the rhythm of the sound pressure. These movements of the fluid force into vibration a thin membrane, called the basilar membrane. The latter in turn finally transmits the stimulus to the organ of Corti, a complex structure which contains the endings of the auditory nerves. The question immediately comes up: Why is this long and complicated chain of transmission necessary?

The reason is that we have a formidable mechanical problem if we are to extract the utmost energy from the sound waves striking the eardrum. Usually when a sound hits a solid surface, most of its energy is reflected away. The problem the ear has to solve is to absorb this energy. To do so it has to act as a kind of mechanical transformer, converting the large amplitude of the sound pressure waves in the air into more forceful vibrations of smaller amplitude. A hydraulic press is such a transformer: it multiplies the pressure acting on the surface of a piston by concentrating the force of the pressure upon a second piston of smaller area. The middle ear acts exactly like a hydraulic press: the tiny footplate of the stirrup transforms the small pressure on the surface of the eardrum into a 22-fold greater pressure on the fluid of the inner ear. In this way the

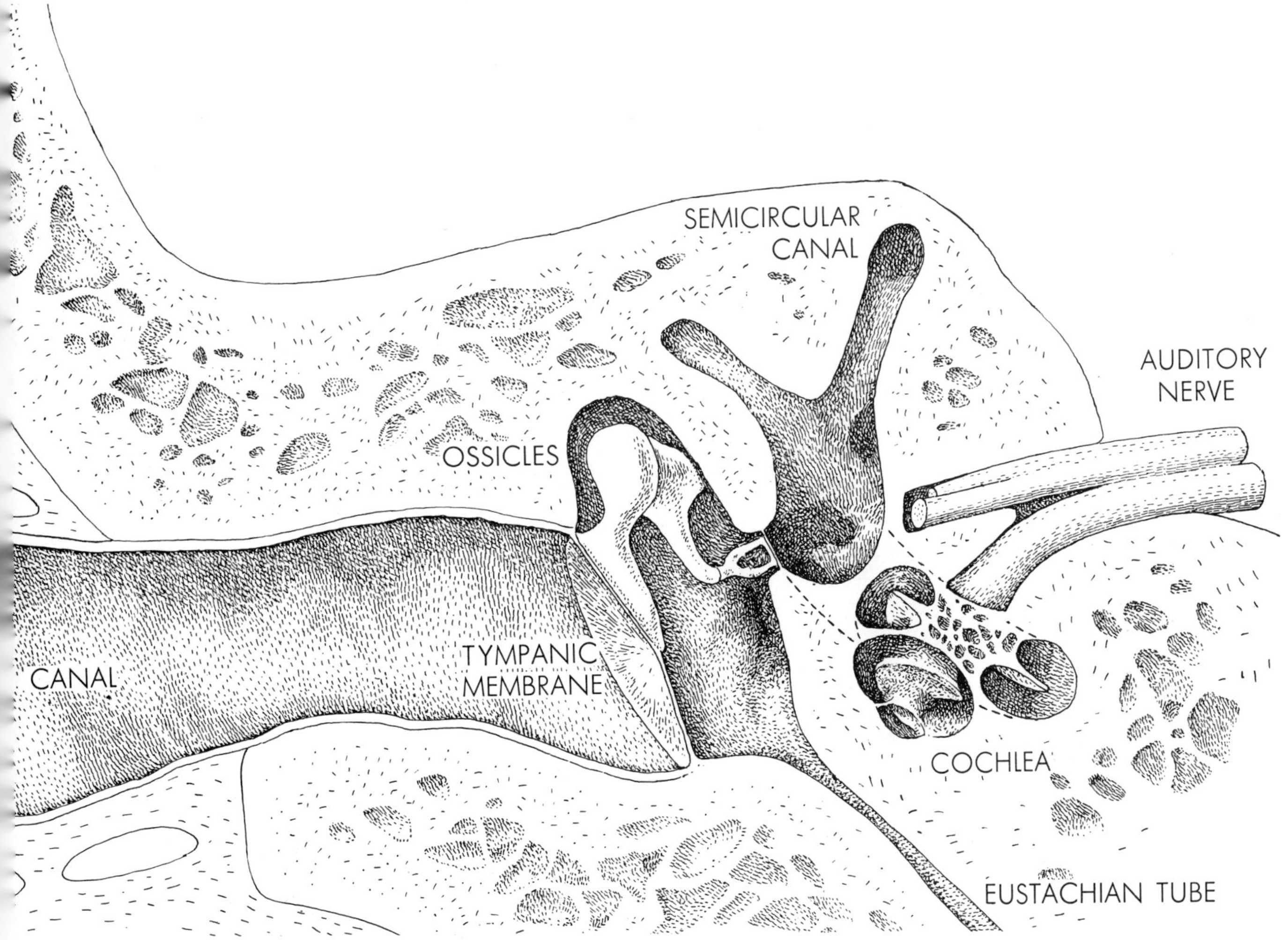

tween the eardrum (tympanic membrane) and the fluid-filled inner ear are the three small bones (ossicles) of the middle ear. The auditory nerve endings are in an organ (*not shown*) between the plate of bone which spirals up the cochlea and the outer wall of the cochlea.

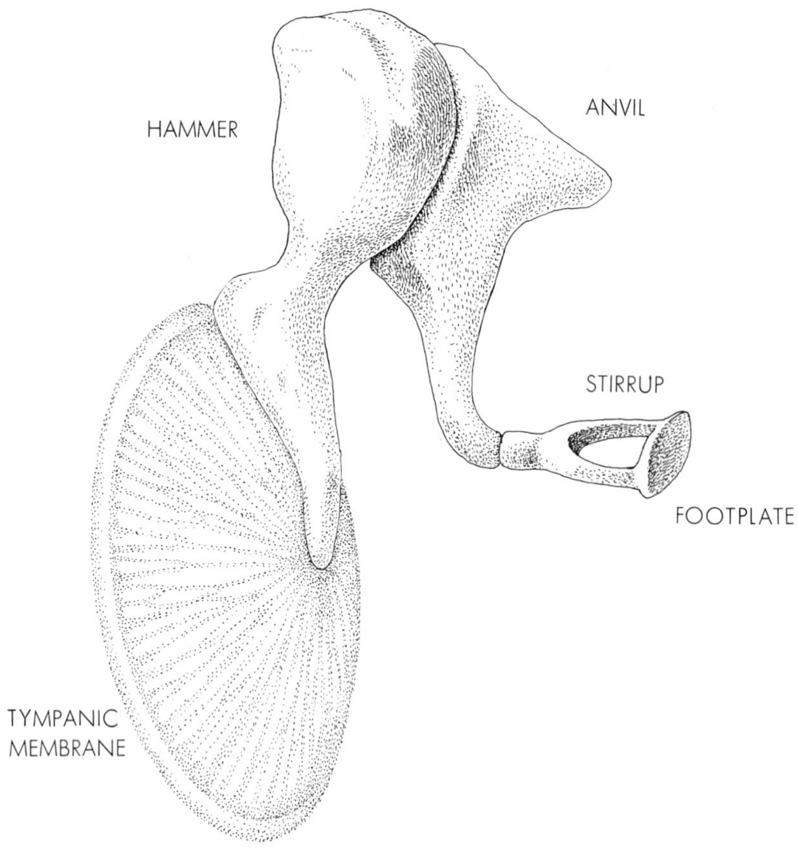

THREE OSSICLES transmit the vibrations of the tympanic membrane to the inner ear. The footplate of stirrup, surrounded by a narrow membrane, presses against inner-ear fluid.

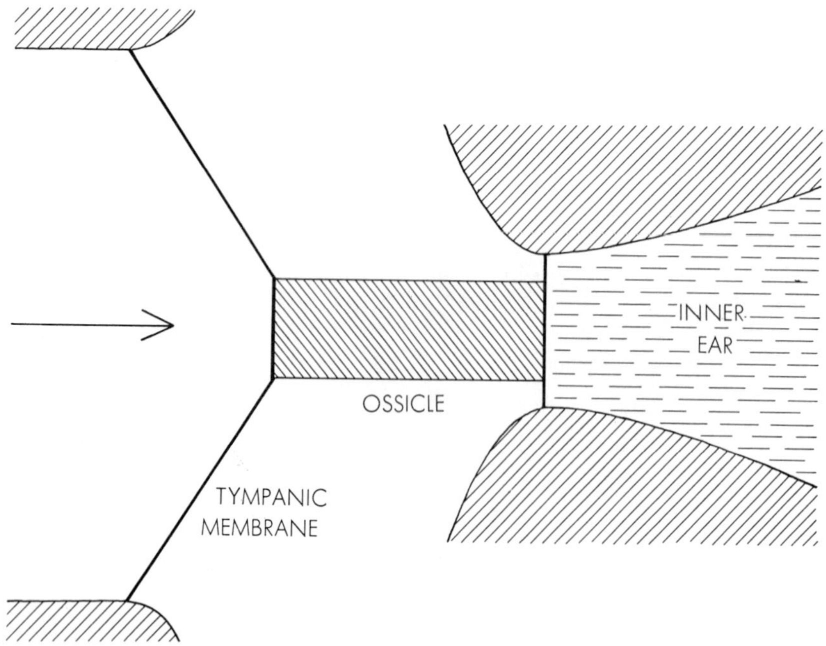

HOW OSSICLES ACT as a piston pressing against the fluid of the inner ear is indicated by this drawing. Pressure of the vibrations of tympanic membrane are amplified 22 times.

ear absorbs the greater part of the sound energy and transmits it to the inner ear without much loss.

But it needs another transformer to amplify the pressure of the fluid into a still larger force upon the tissues to which the nerves are attached. I think the ear's mechanism for this purpose is very ingenious indeed. It is based on the fact that a flat membrane, stretched to cover the opening of a tube, has a lateral tension along its surface. This tension can be increased tremendously if pressure is applied to one side of the membrane. And that is the function of the organ of Corti. It is constructed in such a way that pressure on the basilar membrane is transformed into shearing forces many times larger on the other side of the organ [*see diagram at bottom of opposite page*]. The enhanced shearing forces rub upon extremely sensitive cells attached to the nerve endings.

The eardrum is not by any means the only avenue through which we hear. We also hear through our skull, which is to say, by bone conduction. When we click our teeth or chew a cracker, the sounds come mainly by way of vibrations of the skull. Some of the vibrations are transmitted directly to the inner ear, by-passing the middle ear. This fact helps in the diagnosis of hearing difficulties. If a person can hear bone-conducted sounds but is comparatively deaf to air-borne sounds, we know that the trouble lies in the middle ear. But if he hears no sound by bone conduction, then his auditory nerves are gone, and there is no cure for his deafness. This is an old test, long used by deaf musicians. If a violin player cannot hear his violin even when he touches his teeth to the vibrating instrument, then he knows he suffers from nerve deafness, and there is no cure.

Speaking and Hearing

Hearing by bone conduction plays an important role in the process of speaking. The vibrations of our vocal cords not only produce sounds which go to our ears via the air but also cause the body to vibrate, and the vibration of the jawbone is transmitted to the ear canal. When you hum with closed lips, the sounds you hear are to a large degree heard by bone conduction. (If you stop your ears with your fingers, the hum sounds much louder.) During speaking and singing, therefore, you hear two different sounds—one by bone conduction and the other by air conduction. Of course another listener hears only the air-conducted sounds. In these sounds

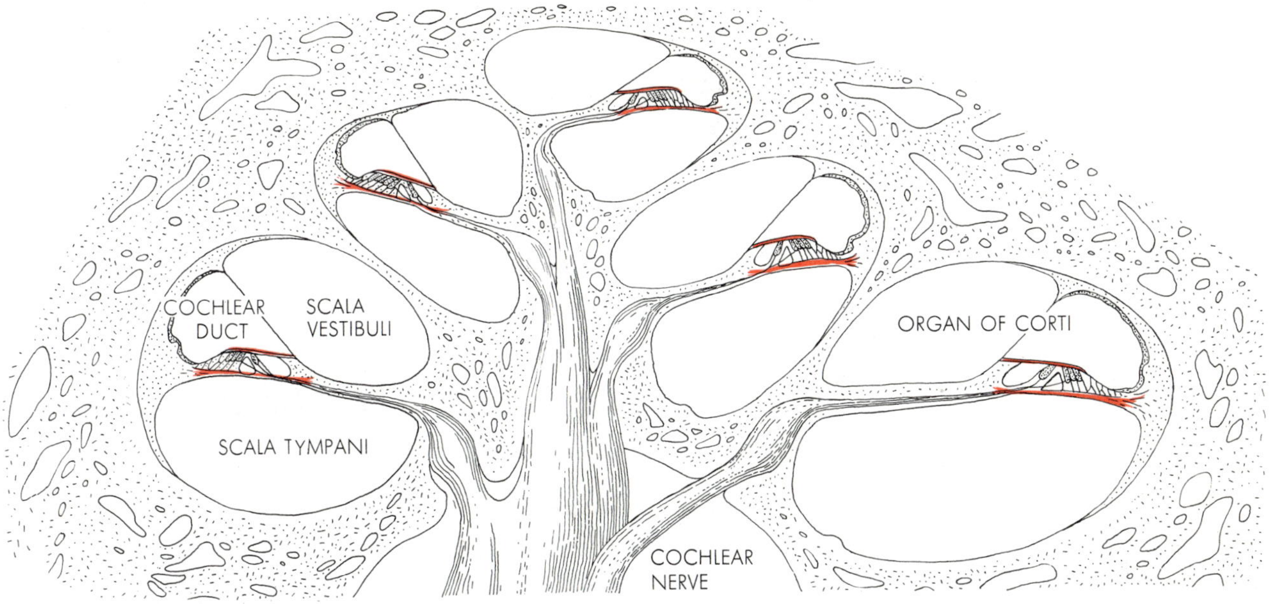

TUBE OF THE COCHLEA, coiled like the shell of a snail, is depicted in cross section. The plate of bone which appears in the cross section on pages 84 and 85 juts from the inside of the tube. Between it and the outside of the tube is the sensitive organ of Corti.

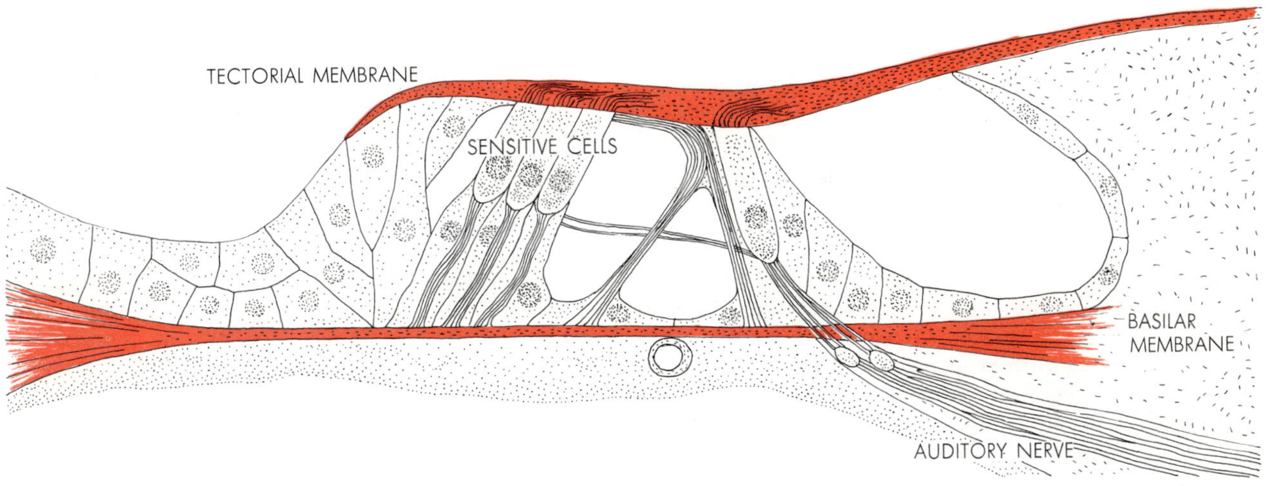

ORGAN OF CORTI lies between the basilar and tectorial membranes. Within it are sensitive cells which are attached to a branch of the auditory nerve *(lower right)*. When fluid in scala tympani *(see drawing at top of page)* vibrates, these cells are stimulated.

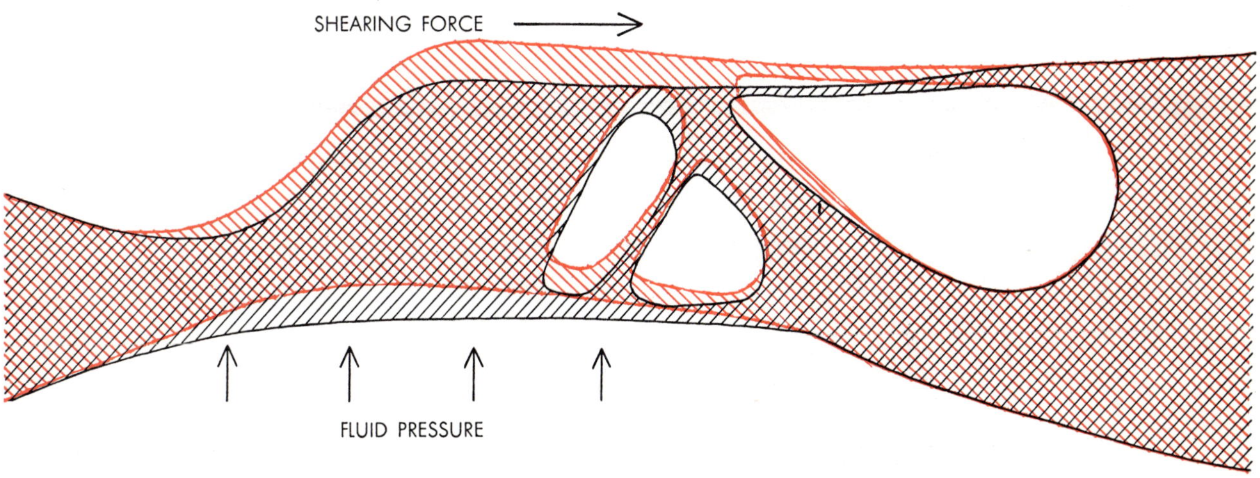

HOW VIBRATION FORCES ARE AMPLIFIED by the organ of Corti is indicated by this drawing. When the vibration of the fluid in the scala tympani exerts a force on the basilar membrane, a larger shearing force is brought to bear on tectorial membrane.

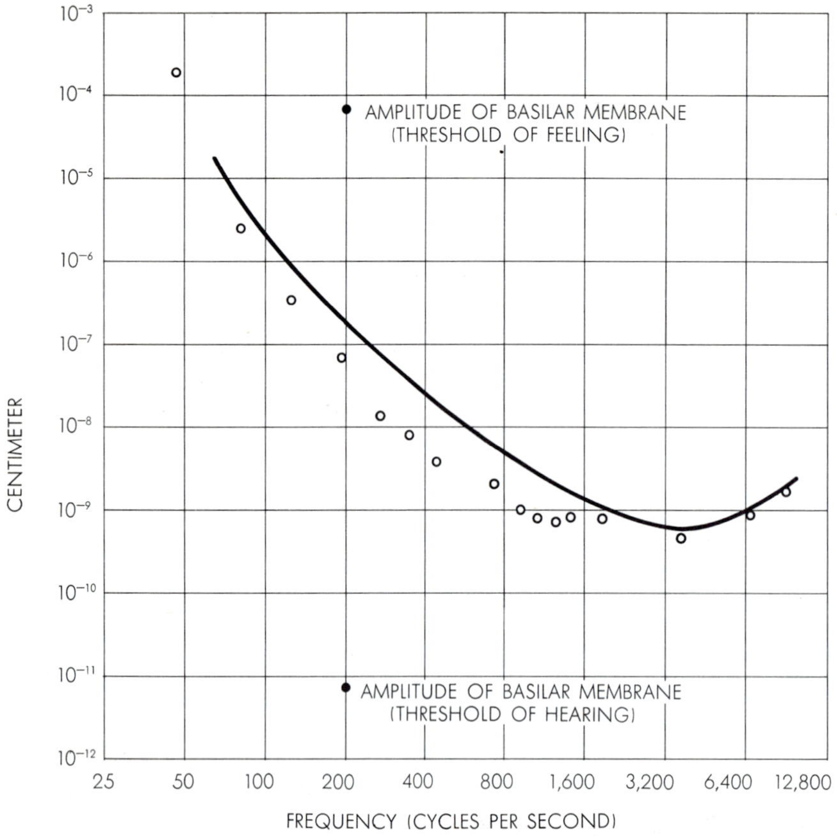

SENSITIVITY OF THE EAR is indicated by this curve, in which the amplitude of the vibrations of the tympanic membrane in fractions of a centimeter is plotted against the frequency of sound impinging on the membrane. Diameter of hydrogen atom is 10^{-8} centimeter.

some of the low-frequency components of the vocal cords' vibrations are lost. This explains why one can hardly recognize his own voice when he listens to a recording of his speech. As we normally hear ourselves, the low-frequency vibrations of our vocal cords, conducted to our own ears by the bones, make our speech sound much more powerful and dynamic than the pure sound waves heard by a second person or through a recording system. Consequently the recording of our voice may strike us as very thin and disappointing. From this point of view we have to admire the astonishing performance of an opera singer. The singer and the audience hear rather different sounds, and it is a miracle to me that they understand each other so well. Perhaps young singers would progress faster if during their training they spent more time studying recordings of their voices.

Feedback to the Voice

The control of speaking and singing involves a complicated feedback system. Just as feedback between the eyes and the muscles guides the hand when it moves to pick up an object, so feedback continually adjusts and corrects the voice as we speak or sing. When we start to sing, the beginning of the sound tells us the pitch, and we immediately adjust the tension of the vocal cords if the pitch is wrong. This feedback requires an exceedingly elaborate and rapid mechanism. How it works is not yet entirely understood. But it is small wonder that it takes a child years to learn to speak, or that it is almost impossible for an adult to learn to speak a foreign language with the native accents.

Any disturbance in the feedback immediately disturbs the speech. For instance, if, while a person is speaking, his speech is fed back to him with a time delay by means of a microphone and receivers at his ears, his pronunciation and accent will change, and if the delay interval is made long enough, he will find it impossible to speak at all.

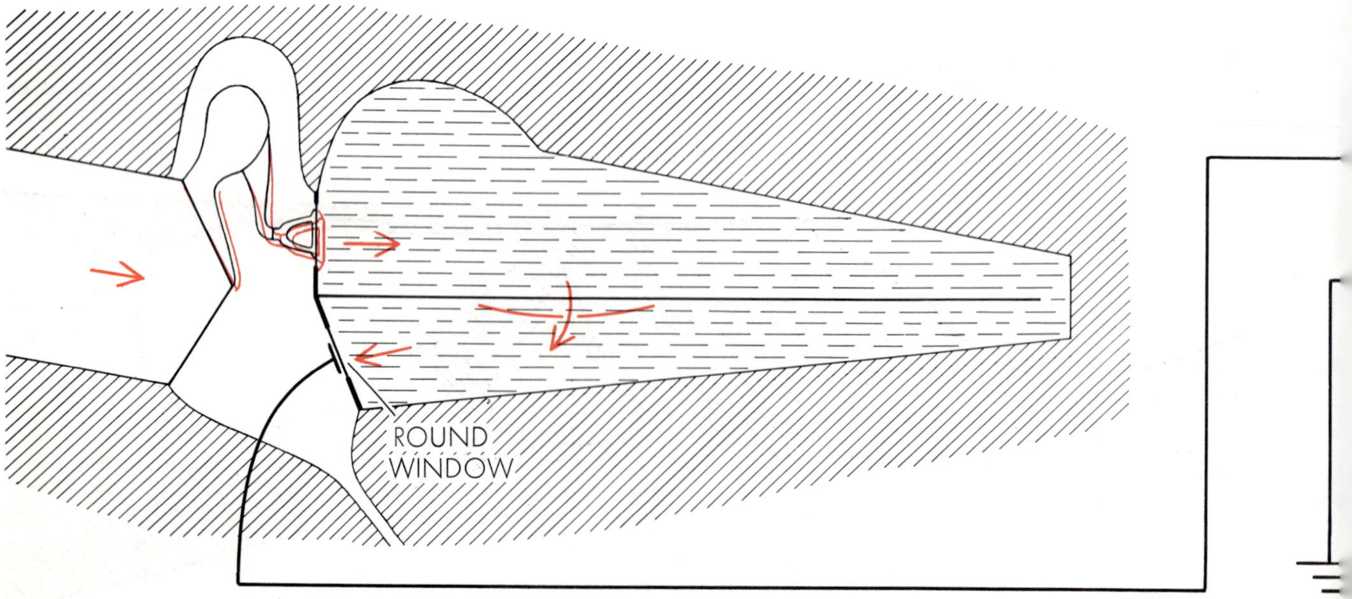

ELECTRICAL POTENTIALS of the microphonic type generated by the inner ear of an experimental animal can be detected by this arrangement. At left is a highly schematic diagram of the ear; the cochlea is represented in cross section by the fluid-filled chamber and the organ of Corti by the horizontal line in this chamber. When the vibrations of the eardrum are transmitted to the organ of Corti,

This phenomenon affords an easy test for exposing pretended deafness. If the subject can continue speaking normally in the face of a delayed feedback through the machine to his ears, we can be sure that he is really deaf.

The same technique can be used to assess the skill of a pianist. A piano player generally adjusts his touch to the acoustics of the room: if the room is very reverberant, so that the music sounds too loud, he uses a lighter touch; if the sound is damped by the walls, he strengthens his touch. We had a number of pianists play in a room where the damping could be varied, and recorded the amplitude of the vibrations of the piano's sounding board while the musicians played various pieces. When they played an easy piece, their adjustment to the acoustics was very clear: as the sound absorption of the room was increased, the pianist played more loudly, and when the damping on the walls was taken away, the pianist's touch became lighter. But when the piece was difficult, many of the pianists concentrated so hard on the problems of the music that they failed to adjust to the feedback of the room. A master musician, however, was not lost to the sound effects. Taking the technical difficulties of the music in stride, he was able to adjust the sound level to the damping of the room with the same accuracy as for an easy piece. Our rating of the pianists by this test closely matched their reputation among musical experts.

In connection with room acoustics, I should like to mention one of the ear's most amazing performances. How is it that we can locate a speaker, even without seeing him, in a bare-walled room where reflections of his voice come at us from every side? This is an almost unbelievable performance by the ear. It is as if, looking into a room completely lined with mirrors, we saw only the real figure and none of the hundreds of reflected images. The eye cannot suppress the reflections, but the ear can. The ear is able to ignore all the sounds except the first that strikes it. It has a built-in inhibitory mechanism.

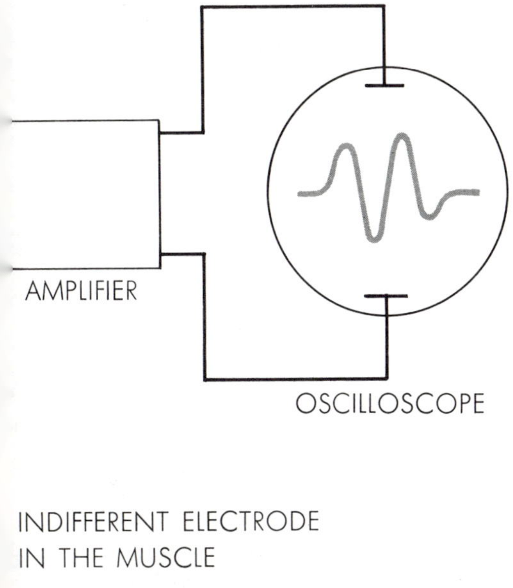

its microphonic potentials can be picked up at the round window of the cochlea and displayed on the face of an oscilloscope (*right*).

Suppressed Sounds

One of the most important factors that subordinate the reflected sounds is the delay in their arrival; necessarily they come to the ear only after the sound that has traveled directly from the speaker to the listener. The reflected sounds reinforce the loudness and tone volume of the direct sound, and perhaps even modify its localization, but by and large, they are not distinguishable from it. Only when the delay is appreciable does a reflected sound appear as a separate unit—an echo. Echoes often are heard in a large church, where reflections may lag more than half a second behind the direct sound. They are apt to be a problem in a concert hall. Dead walls are not desirable, because the music would sound weak. For every size of concert room there is an optimal compromise on wall reflectivity which will give amplification to the music but prevent disturbing echoes.

In addition to time delay, there are other factors that act to inhibit some sounds and favor others. Strong sounds generally suppress weaker ones. Sounds in which we are interested take precedence over those that concern us less, as I pointed out in the examples of the speaker in a noisy room and the orchestra conductor detecting an errant instrument. This brings us to the intimate collaboration between the ear and the nervous system.

Any stimulation of the ear (*e.g.*, any change in pressure) is translated into electrical messages to the brain via the nerves. We can therefore draw information about the ear from an analysis of these electrical impulses, now made possible by electronic instruments. There are two principal types of electric potential that carry the messages. One is a continuous, wavelike potential which has been given the name microphonic. In experimental animals such as guinea pigs and cats the microphonics are large enough to be easily measured (they range up to about half a millivolt). It

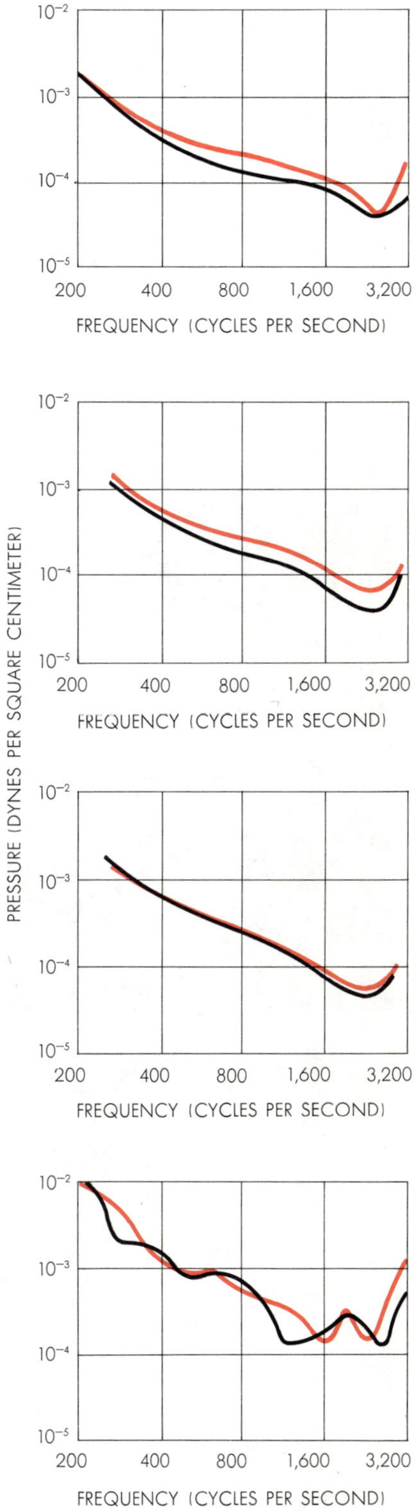

AUDIOGRAMS plot the threshold of hearing (in terms of pressure on the tympanic membrane) against the frequency of sound. The first three audiograms show the threshold for three members of the same family; the fourth, the threshold for an unrelated person. The black curves represent the threshold for one ear of the subject; the colored curves, for the other ear of the same subject. The audiogram curves indicate that in normal hearing the threshold in both ears, and the threshold in members of the same family, are remarkably similar.

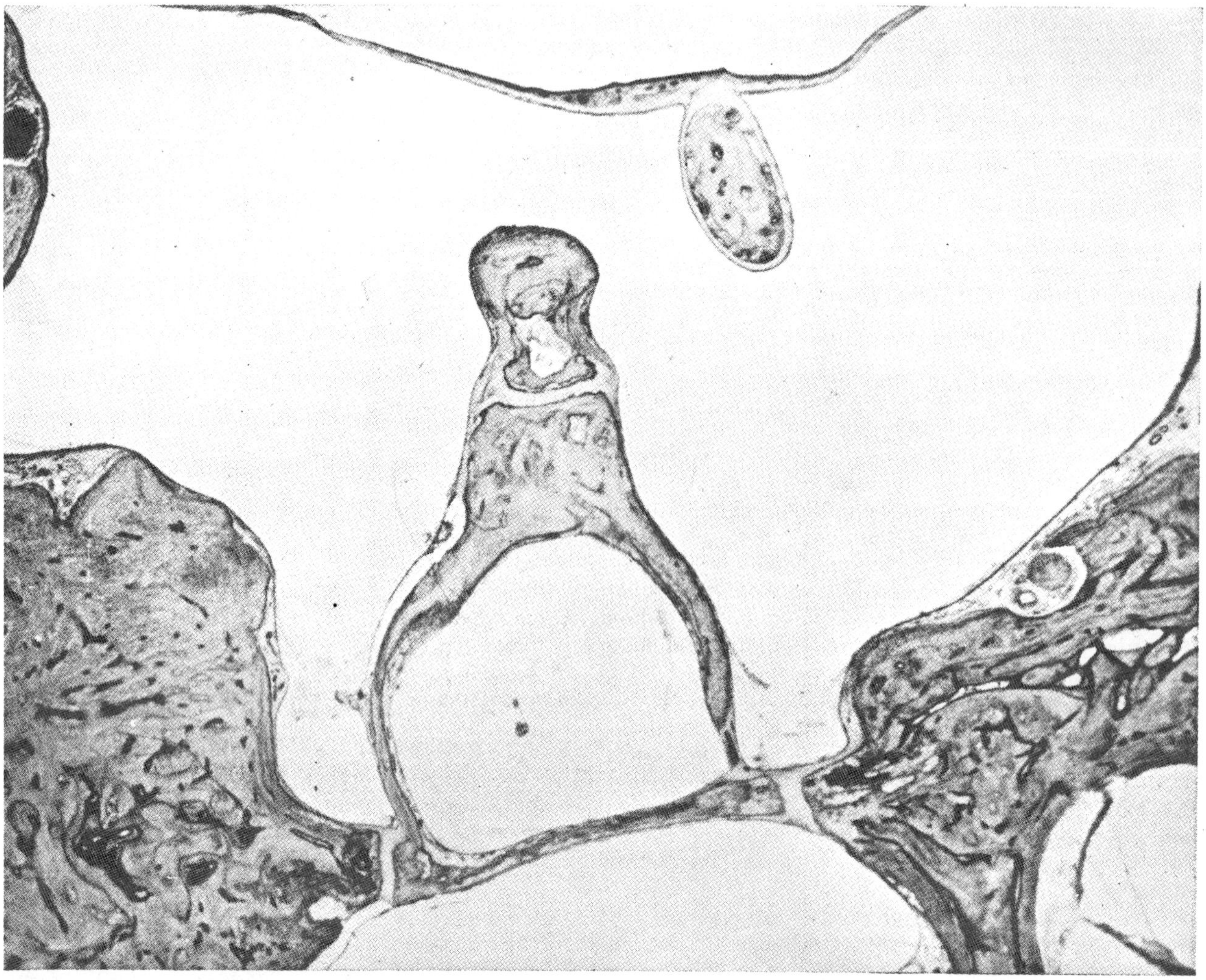

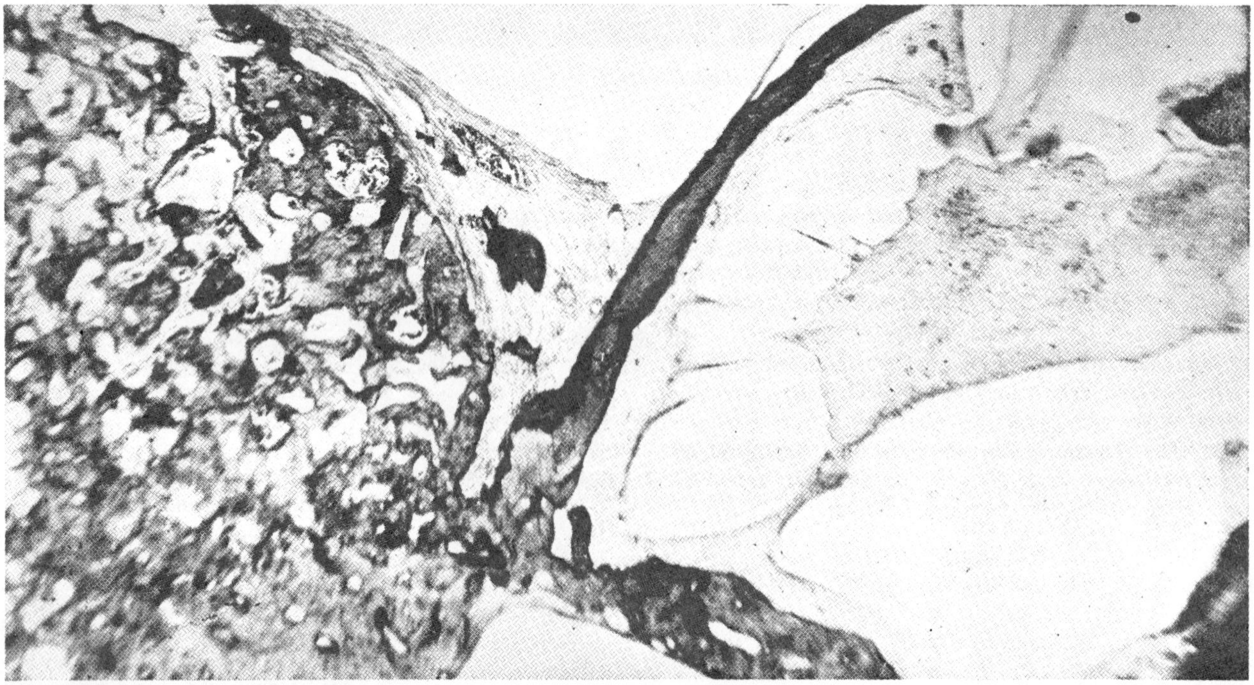

STIRRUP of the normal human ear is enlarged 19 times in the photograph at the top of this page. The thin line at the top of the photograph is the tympanic membrane seen in cross section. The hammer and anvil do not appear. The narrow membrane around the footplate of the stirrup may be seen as a translucent area between the footplate and the surrounding bone. The photograph at the bottom shows the immobilized footplate of an otosclerotic ear. In this photograph only the left side of the stirrup appears; the footplate is the dark area at the bottom center. The membrane around the footplate has been converted into a rigid bony growth.

has turned out that the magnitude of the microphonics produced in the inner ear is directly proportional to the displacements of the stirrup footplate that set the fluid in the inner ear in motion. The microphonics therefore permit us to determine directly to what extent the sound pressure applied to the eardrum is transmitted to the inner ear, and they have become one of the most useful tools for exploring sound transmission in the middle ear. For instance, there used to be endless discussion of the simple question: Just how much does perforation of the eardrum affect hearing? The question has now been answered with mathematical precision by experiments on animals. A hole of precisely measured size is drilled in the eardrum, and the amount of hearing loss is determined by the change in the microphonics. This type of observation on cats has shown that a perforation about one millimeter in diameter destroys hearing at the frequencies below 100 cycles per second but causes almost no impairment of hearing in the range of frequencies above 1,000 cycles per second. From studies of the physical properties of the human ear we can judge that the findings on animals apply fairly closely to man also.

The second type of electric potential takes the form of sharp pulses, which appear as spikes in the recording instrument. The sound of a sharp click produces a series of brief spikes; a pure tone generates volleys of spikes, generally in the rhythm of the period of the tone. We can follow the spikes along the nerve pathways all the way from the inner ear up to the cortex of the brain. And when we do, we find that stimulation of specific spots on the membrane of the inner ear seems to be projected to corresponding spots in the auditory area of the cortex. This is reminiscent of the projection of images on the retina of the eye to the visual area of the brain. But in the case of the ear the situation must be more complex, because there are nerve branches leading to the opposite ear and there seem to be several auditory projection areas on the surface of the brain. At the moment research is going on to find out how the secondary areas function and what their purpose is.

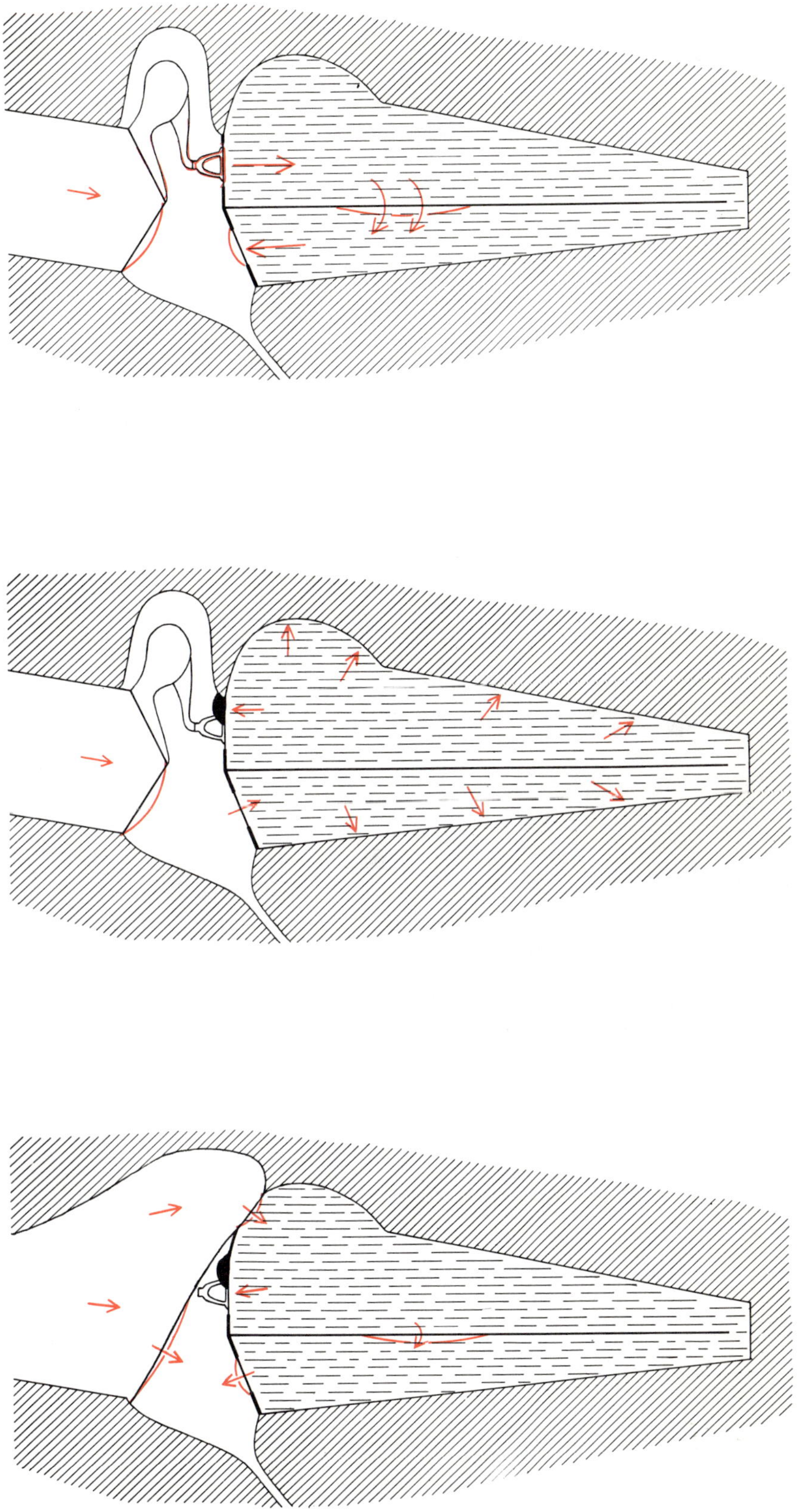

FENESTRATION OPERATION can alleviate the effects of otosclerosis. The drawing at the top schematically depicts the normal human ear as described in the caption for the illustration on page 88 and 89. The pressure on the components of the ear is indicated by the colored arrows. The drawing in the middle shows an otosclerotic ear; the otosclerotic growth is represented as a black protuberance. Because the stirrup cannot move, the pressure on the tympanic membrane is transmitted to the organ of Corti only through the round window of the cochlea; and because the fluid in the cochlea is incompressible, the organ of Corti cannot vibrate. The drawing at the bottom shows how the fenestration operation makes a new window into the cochlea to permit the organ of Corti to vibrate freely.

Detecting Pitch

The orderly projection of the sensitive area of the inner ear onto the higher brain levels is probably connected with the resolution of pitch. The ear itself can analyze sounds and separate one tone from another. There are limits to this

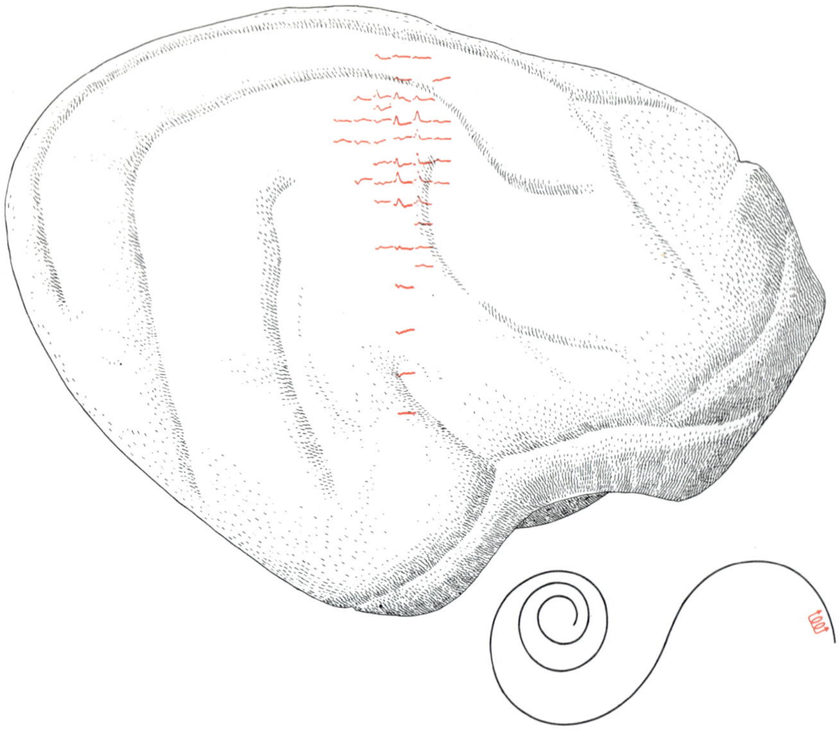

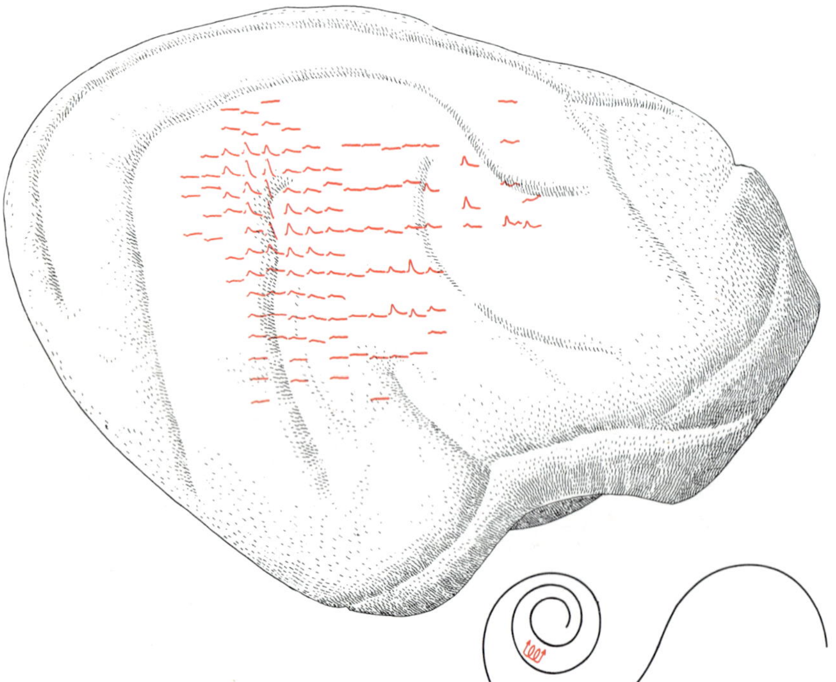

NERVE IMPULSES due to the electrical stimulation of the organ of Corti were localized on the surface of the brain of a cat. The spirals below each of these drawings of a cat's brain represent the full length of the organ of Corti. The pairs of colored arrows on each spiral indicate the point at which the organ was stimulated. The colored peaks superimposed on the brains represent the electrical potentials detected by an electrode placed at that point.

ability, but if the frequencies of the tones presented are not too close together, they are discriminated pretty well. Long ago this raised the question: How is the ear able to discriminate the pitch of a tone? Many theories have been argued, but only within the last decade has it been possible to plan pertinent experiments.

In the low-frequency range up to 60 cycles per second the vibration of the basilar membrane produces in the auditory nerve volleys of electric spikes synchronous with the rhythm of the sound. As the sound pressure increases, the number of spikes packed into each period increases. Thus two variables are transmitted to the cortex: (1) the number of spikes and (2) their rhythm. These two variables alone convey the loudness and the pitch of the sound.

Above 60 cycles per second a new phenomenon comes in. The basilar membrane now begins to vibrate unequally over its area: each tone produces a maximal vibration in a different area of the membrane. Gradually this selectivity takes over the determination of pitch, for the rhythm of the spikes, which indicates the pitch at low frequencies, becomes irregular at the higher ones. Above 4,000 cycles per second pitch is determined entirely by the location of the maximal vibration amplitude along the basilar membrane. Apparently there is an inhibitory mechanism which suppresses the weaker stimuli and thus sharpens considerably the sensation around the maximum. This type of inhibition can also operate in sense organs such as the skin and the eye. In order to see sharply we need not only a sharp image of the object on the retina but also an inhibitory system to suppress stray light entering the eye. Otherwise we would see the object surrounded by a halo. The ear is much the same. Without inhibitory effects a tone would sound like a noise of a certain pitch but not like a pure tone.

We can sum up by saying that the basilar membrane makes a rough, mechanical frequency analysis, and the auditory nervous system sharpens the analysis in some manner not yet understood. It is a part of the general functioning of the higher nerve centers, and it will be understood only when we know more about the functioning of these centers. If the answer is found for the ear, it will probably apply to the other sense organs as well.

Deafness

Now let us run briefly over some of

the types of hearing disorders, which have become much more understandable as a result of recent experimental researches.

Infections of the ear used to be responsible for the overwhelming majority of the cases of deafness. Ten years ago in a large city hospital there was a death almost every day from such infections. Thanks to antibiotics, they can now be arrested, and, if treated in time, an ear infection is seldom either fatal or destructive of hearing, though occasionally an operation is necessary to scoop out the diseased part of the mastoid bone.

The two other principal types of deafness are those caused by destruction of the auditory nerves and by otosclerosis (a tumorous bone growth). Nerve deafness cannot be cured: no drug or mechanical manipulation or operation can restore the victim's hearing. But the impairment of hearing caused by otosclerosis can usually be repaired, at least in part.

Otosclerosis is an abnormal but painless growth in a temporal bone (*i.e.*, at the side of the skull, near the middle ear). If it does not invade a part of the ear that participates in the transmission of sound, no harm is done to the hearing. But if the growth happens to involve the stirrup footplate, it will reduce or even completely freeze the footplate's ability to make its piston-like movements; the vibrations of the eardrum then can no longer be transmitted to the inner ear. An otosclerotic growth can occur at any age, may slow down for many years, and may suddenly start up again. It is found more often in women than in men and seems to be accelerated by pregnancy.

Immobilization of the stirrup blocks the hearing of air-borne sound but leaves hearing by bone conduction unimpaired. This fact is used for diagnosis. A patient who has lost part of his hearing ability because of otosclerosis does not find noise disturbing to his understanding of speech; in fact, noise may even improve his discrimination of speech. There is an old story about a somewhat deaf English earl (in France it is a count) who trained his servant to beat a drum whenever someone else spoke, so that he could understand the speaker better. The noise of the drum made the speaker raise his voice to the earl's hearing range. For the hard-of-hearing earl the noise of the drum was tolerable, but for other listeners it masked what the speaker was saying, so that the earl enjoyed exclusive rights to his conversation.

Difficulty in hearing air-borne sound can be corrected by a hearing aid. Theoretically it should be possible to compensate almost any amount of such hearing loss, because techniques for amplifying sound are highly developed, particularly now with the help of the transistor. But there is a physiological limit to the amount of pressure amplification that the ear will stand. Heightening of the pressure eventually produces an unpleasant tickling sensation through its effect on skin tissue in the middle ear. The sensation can be avoided by using a bone-conduction earphone, pressed firmly against the surface of the skull, but this constant pressure is unpleasant to many people.

Operations

As is widely known, there are now operations (*e.g.*, "fenestration") which can cure otosclerotic deafness. In the 19th century physicians realized that if they could somehow dislodge or loosen the immobilized stirrup footplate, they might restore hearing. Experimenters in France found that they could sometimes free the footplate sufficiently merely by pressing a blunt needle against the right spot on the stirrup. Although it works only occasionally, the procedure seems so simple that it has recently had a revival of popularity in the U. S. If the maneuver is successful (and I am told that 30 per cent of these operations are) the hearing improves immediately. But unfortunately the surgeon cannot get a clear look at the scene of the operation and must apply the pushing force at random. This makes the operation something of a gamble, and the patient's hearing may not only fail to be improved but may even be reduced. Moreover, the operation is bound to be ineffectual when a large portion of the footplate is fixed. There are other important objections to the operation. After all, it involves the breaking of bone, to free the adhering part of the stirrup. I do not think that bone-breaking can be improved to a standard procedure. In any case, precision cutting seems to me always superior to breaking, in surgery as in mechanics. This brings us to the operation called fenestration.

For many decades it has been known that drilling a small opening, even the size of a pinhead, in the bony wall of the inner ear on the footplate side can produce a remarkable improvement in hearing. The reason, now well understood, is quite simple. If a hole is made in the bone and then covered again with a flexible membrane, movements of the fluid in, for instance, the lateral canal of the vestibular organ can be transmitted to the fluid of the inner ear, and so vibrations are once again communicable from the middle to the inner ear. In the typical present fenestration operation the surgeon bores a small hole in the canal wall with a dental drill and then covers the hole with a flap of skin. The operation today is a straightforward surgical procedure, and all its steps are under accurate control.

Hazards to Hearing

I want to conclude by mentioning the problem of nerve deafness. Many cases of nerve deafness are produced by intense noise, especially noise with high-frequency components. Since there is no cure, it behooves us to look out for such exposures. Nerve deafness creeps up on us slowly, and we are not as careful as we should be to avoid exposure to intense noise. We should also be more vigilant about other hazards capable of producing nerve deafness, notably certain drugs and certain diseases.

We could do much to ameliorate the tragedy of deafness if we changed some of our attitudes toward it. Blindness evokes our instant sympathy, and we go out of our way to help the blind person. But deafness often goes unrecognized. If a deaf person misunderstands what we say, we are apt to attribute it to lack of intelligence instead of to faulty hearing. Very few people have the patience to help the deafened. To a deaf man the outside world appears unfriendly. He tries to hide his deafness, and this only brings on more problems.

10

EYE AND CAMERA

GEORGE WALD
August 1950

OF all the instruments made by man, none resembles a part of his body more than a camera does the eye. Yet this is not by design. A camera is no more a copy of an eye than the wing of a bird is a copy of that of an insect. Each is the product of an independent evolution; and if this has brought the camera and the eye together, it is not because one has mimicked the other, but because both have had to meet the same problems, and frequently have done so in much the same way. This is the type of phenomenon that biologists call convergent evolution, yet peculiar in that the one evolution is organic, the other technological.

Over the centuries much has been learned about vision from the camera, but little about photography from the eye. The camera made its first appearance not as an instrument for making pictures but as the *camera obscura* or dark chamber, a device that attempted no more than to project an inverted image upon a screen. Long after the optics of the camera obscura was well understood, the workings of the eye remained mysterious.

In part this was because men found it difficult to think in simple terms about the eye. It is possible for contempt to breed familiarity, but awe does not help one to understand anything. Men have often approached light and the eye in a spirit close to awe, probably because they were always aware that vision provides their closest link with the external world. Stubborn misconceptions held back their understanding of the eye for many centuries. Two notions were particularly troublesome. One was that radiation shines out of the eye; the other, that an inverted image on the retina is somehow incompatible with seeing right side up.

I am sure that many people are still not clear on either matter. I note, for example, that the X-ray vision of the comic-strip hero Superman, while regarded with skepticism by many adults, is not rejected on the ground that there are no X-rays about us with which to see. Clearly Superman's eyes supply the X-rays, and by directing them here and there he not only can see through opaque objects, but can on occasion shatter a brick wall or melt gold. As for the inverted image on the retina, most people who learn of it concede that it presents a problem, but comfort themselves with the thought that the brain somehow compensates for it. But of course there is no problem, and hence no compensation. We learn early in infancy to associate certain spatial relations in the outside world with certain patterns of nervous activity stimulated through the eyes. The spatial arrangements of the nervous activity itself are altogether irrelevant.

It was not until the 17th century that the gross optics of image formation in the eye was clearly expressed. This was accomplished by Johannes Kepler in 1611, and again by René Descartes in 1664. By the end of the century the first treatise on optics in English, written by William Molyneux of Dublin, contained several clear and simple diagrams comparing the projection of a real inverted image in a "pinhole" camera, in a camera obscura equipped with a lens and in an eye.

Today every schoolboy knows that the eye is like a camera. In both instruments a lens projects an inverted image of the surroundings upon a light-sensitive surface: the film in the camera and the retina in the eye. In both the opening of the lens is regulated by an iris. In both the inside of the chamber is lined with a coating of black material which absorbs stray light that would otherwise be reflected back and forth and obscure the image. Almost every schoolboy also knows a difference between the camera and the eye. A camera is focused by moving the lens toward or away from the film; in the eye the distance between the lens and the retina is fixed, and focusing is accomplished by changing the thickness of the lens.

The usual fate of such comparisons is that on closer examination they are exposed as trivial. In this case, however, just the opposite has occurred. The more we have come to know about the mechanism of vision, the more pointed and fruitful has become its comparison with photography. By now it is clear that the relationship between the eye and the camera goes far beyond simple optics, and has come to involve much of the

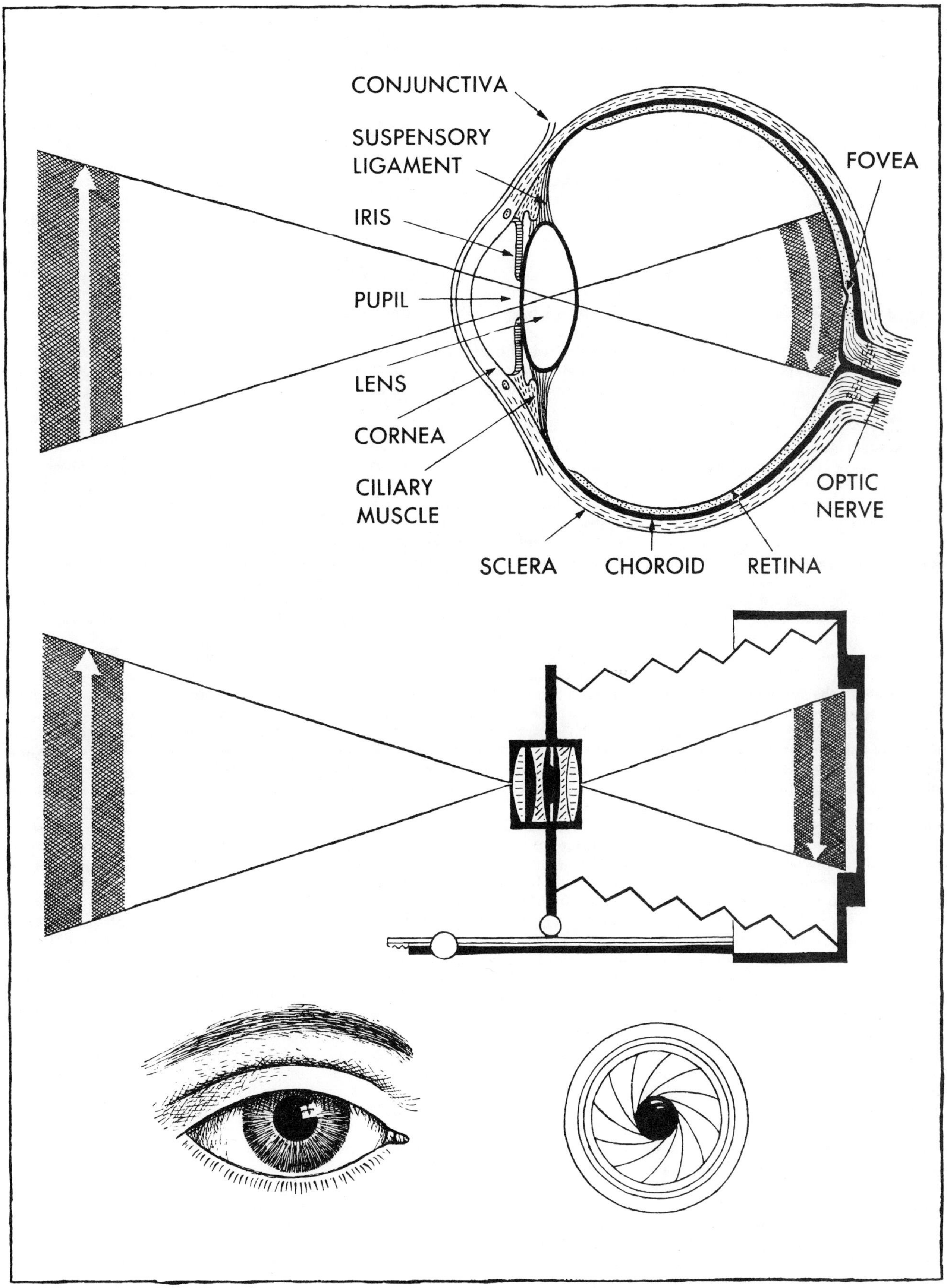

OPTICAL SIMILARITIES of eye and camera are apparent in their cross sections. Both utilize a lens to focus an inverted image on a light-sensitive surface. Both possess an iris to adjust to various intensities of light. The single lens of the eye, however, cannot bring light of all colors to a focus at the same point. The compound lens of the camera is better corrected for color because it is composed of two kinds of glass.

essential physics and chemistry of both devices.

Bright and Dim Light

A photographer making an exposure in dim light opens the iris of his camera. The pupil of the eye also opens in dim light, to an extent governed by the activity of the retina. Both adjustments have the obvious effect of admitting more light through the lens. This is accomplished at some cost to the quality of the image, for the open lens usually defines the image less sharply, and has less depth of focus.

When further pressed for light, the photographer changes to a more sensitive film. This ordinarily involves a further loss in the sharpness of the picture. With any single type of emulsion the more sensitive film is coarser in grain, and thus the image cast upon it is resolved less accurately.

The retina of the eye is grainy just as is photographic film. In film the grain is composed of crystals of silver bromide embedded in gelatin. In the retina it is made up of the receptor cells, lying side by side to form a mosaic of light-sensitive elements.

There are two kinds of receptors in the retinas of man and most vertebrates: rods and cones. Each is composed of an inner segment much like an ordinary nerve cell, and a rod- or cone-shaped outer segment, the special portion of the cell that is sensitive to light. The cones are the organs of vision in bright light, and also of color vision. The rods provide a special apparatus for vision in dim light, and their excitation yields only neutral gray sensations. This is why at night all cats are gray.

The change from cone to rod vision, like that from slow to fast film, involves a change from a fine- to a coarse-grained mosaic. It is not that the cones are smaller than the rods, but that the cones act individually while the rods act in large clumps. Each cone is usually connected with the brain by a single fiber of the optic nerve. In contrast large clusters of rods are connected by single optic nerve fibers. The capacity of rods for image vision is correspondingly coarse. It is not only true that at night all cats are gray, but it is difficult to be sure that they are cats.

Vision in very dim light, such as starlight or most moonlight, involves only the rods. The relatively insensitive cones are not stimulated at all. At moderately low intensities of light, about 1,000 times greater than the lowest intensity to which the eye responds, the cones begin to function. Their entrance is marked by dilute sensations of color. Over an intermediate range of intensities rods and cones function together, but as the brightness increases, the cones come to dominate vision. We do not know that the rods actually stop functioning at even the highest intensities, but in bright light their relative contribution to vision falls to so low a level as to be almost negligible.

To this general transfer of vision from rods to cones certain cold-blooded animals add a special anatomical device. The light-sensitive outer segments of the rods and cones are carried at the ends of fine stalks called myoids, which can shorten and lengthen. In dim light the rod myoids contract while the cone myoids relax. The entire field of rods is thus pulled forward toward the light, while the cones are pushed into the background. In bright light the reverse occurs: the cones are pulled forward and the rods pushed back. One could scarcely imagine a closer approach to the change from fast to slow film in a camera.

The rods and cones share with the grains of the photographic plate another deeply significant property. It has long been known that in a film exposed to light each grain of silver bromide given enough developer blackens either completely or not at all, and that a grain is made susceptible to development by the absorption of one or at most a few quanta of light. It appears to be equally true that a cone or rod is excited by light to yield either its maximal response or none at all. This is certainly true of the nerve fibers to which the rods and cones are connected, and we now know that to produce this effect in a rod—and possibly also in a cone—only one quantum of light need be absorbed.

It is a basic tenet of photochemistry that one quantum of light is absorbed by, and in general can activate, only one molecule or atom. We must attempt to understand how such a small beginning can bring about such a large result as the development of a photographic grain or the discharge of a retinal receptor. In the photographic process the answer to this question seems to be that the absorption of a quantum of light causes the oxidation of a silver ion to an atom of metallic silver, which then serves as a catalytic center for the development of the entire grain. It is possible that a similar mechanism operates in a rod or a cone. The absorption of a quantum of light by a light-sensitive molecule in either structure might convert it into a biological catalyst, or an enzyme, which could then promote the further reactions that discharge the receptor cell. One wonders whether such a mechanism could possibly be rapid enough. A rod or a cone responds to light within a small fraction of a second; the mechanism would therefore have to complete its work within this small interval.

One of the strangest characteristics of the eye in dim light follows from some of these various phenomena. In focusing the eye is guided by its evaluation of the sharpness of the image on the retina. As the image deteriorates with the opening of the pupil in dim light, and as the retinal capacity to resolve the image falls with the shift from cones to rods, the ability to focus declines also. In very dim light the eye virtually ceases to adjust its focus at all. It has come to resemble a very cheap camera, a fixed-focus instrument.

In all that concerns its function, therefore, the eye is one device in bright light and another in dim. At low intensities all its resources are concentrated upon sensitivity, at whatever sacrifice of form; it is predominantly an instrument for seeing light, not pattern. In bright light all this changes. By narrowing the pupil, shifting from rods to cones, and other stratagems still to be described, the eye sacrifices light in order to achieve the utmost in pattern vision.

Images

In the course of evolution animals have used almost every known device for forming or evaluating an image. There is one notable exception: no animal has yet developed an eye based upon the use of a concave mirror. An eye made like a pinhole camera, however, is found in Nautilus, a cephalopod mollusk related to the octopus and squid. The compound eye of insects and crabs forms an image which is an upright patchwork of responses of individual "eyes" or ommatidia, each of which records only a spot of light or shade. The eye of the tiny arthropod Copilia possesses a large and beautiful lens but only one light receptor attached to a thin strand of muscle. It is said that the muscle moves the receptor rapidly back and forth in the focal plane of the lens, scanning the image in much the same way as it is scanned by the light-sensitive tube of a television camera.

Each of these eyes, like the lens eye of vertebrates, represents some close compromise of advantages and limitations. The pinhole eye is in focus at all distances, yet to form clear images it must use a small hole admitting very little light. The compound eye works well at distances of a few millimeters, yet it is relatively coarse in pattern resolution. The vertebrate eye is a long-range, high-acuity instrument useless in the short distances at which the insect eye resolves the greatest detail.

These properties of the vertebrate eye are of course shared by the camera. The use of a lens to project an image, however, has created for both devices a special group of problems. All simple lenses are subject to serious errors in image formation: the lens aberrations.

Spherical aberration is found in all lenses bounded by spherical surfaces. The marginal portions of the lens bring rays of light to a shorter focus than the central region. The image of a point in

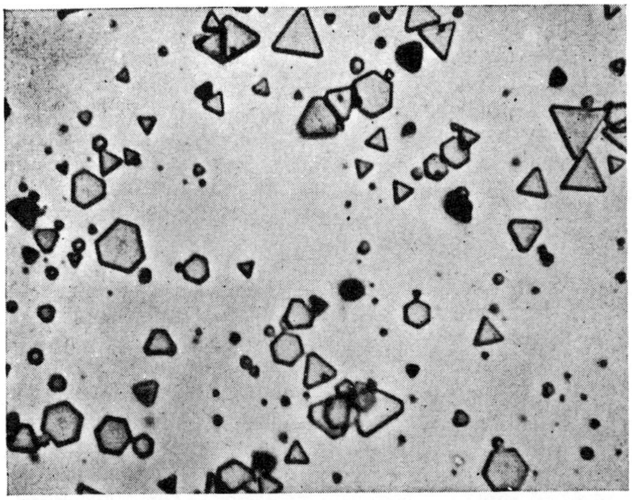

GRAIN of the photographic emulsion, magnified 2,500 times, is made up of silver-bromide crystals in gelatin.

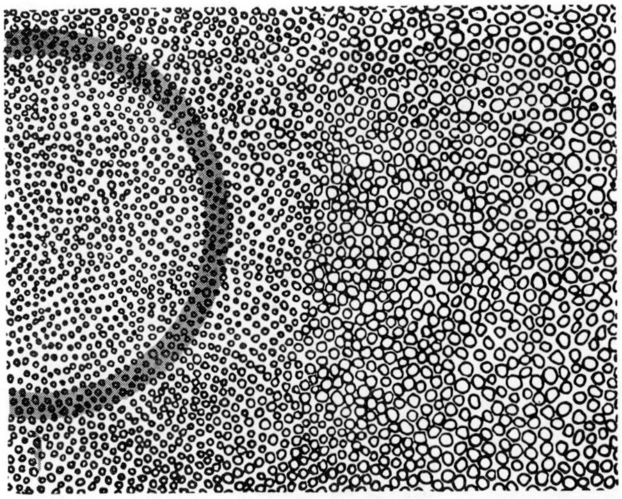

"GRAIN" of the human retina is made up of cones and rods (*dots at far right*). Semicircle indicates fovea.

space is therefore not a point, but a little "blur circle." The cost of a camera is largely determined by the extent to which this aberration is corrected by modifying the lens.

The human eye is astonishingly well corrected—often slightly overcorrected—for spherical aberration. This is accomplished in two ways. The cornea, which is the principal refracting surface of the eye, has a flatter curvature at its margin than at its center. This compensates in part for the tendency of a spherical surface to refract light more strongly at its margin. More important still, the lens is denser and hence refracts light more strongly at its core than in its outer layers.

A second major lens error, however, remains almost uncorrected in the human eye. This is chromatic aberration, or color error. All single lenses made of one material refract rays of short wavelength more strongly than those of longer wavelength, and so bring blue light to a shorter focus than red. The result is that the image of a point of white light is not a white point, but a blur circle fringed with color. Since this seriously disturbs the image, even the lenses of inexpensive cameras are corrected for chromatic aberration.

It has been known since the time of Isaac Newton, however, that the human eye has a large chromatic aberration. Its lens system seems to be entirely uncorrected for this defect. Indeed, living organisms are probably unable to manufacture two transparent materials of such widely different refraction and dispersion as the crown and flint glasses from which color-corrected lenses are constructed.

The large color error of the human eye could make serious difficulties for image vision. Actually the error is moderate between the red end of the spectrum and the blue-green, but it increases rapidly at shorter wavelengths: the blue, violet and ultraviolet. These latter parts of the spectrum present the most serious problem. It is a problem for both the eye and the camera, but one for which the eye must find a special solution.

The first device that opposes the color error of the human eye is the yellow lens. The human lens is not only a lens but a color filter. It passes what we ordinarily consider to be the visible spectrum, but sharply cuts off the far edge of the violet, in the region of wavelength 400 millimicrons. It is this action of the lens, and not any intrinsic lack of sensitivity of the rods and cones, that keeps us from seeing in the near ultraviolet. Indeed, persons who have lost their lenses in the operation for cataract and have had them replaced by clear glass lenses, have excellent vision in the ultraviolet. They are able to read an optician's chart from top to bottom in ultraviolet light which leaves ordinary people in complete darkness.

The lens therefore solves the problem of the near ultraviolet, the region of the spectrum in which the color error is greatest, simply by eliminating the region from human vision. This boon is distributed over one's lifetime, for the lens becomes a deeper yellow and makes more of the ordinary violet and blue invisible as one grows older. I have heard it said that for this reason aging artists tend to use less blue and violet in their paintings.

The lens filters out the ultraviolet for the eye as a whole. The remaining devices which counteract chromatic aberration are concentrated upon vision in bright light, upon cone vision. This is good economy, for the rods provide such a coarse-grained receptive surface that they would be unable in any case to evaluate a sharp image on the retina.

As one goes from dim to bright light, from rod to cone vision, the sensitivity of the eye shifts toward the red end of the spectrum. This phenomenon was described in 1825 by the Czech physiologist Johannes Purkinje. He had noticed that with the first light of dawn blue objects tend to look relatively bright compared with red, but that they come to look relatively dim as the morning advances. The basis of this change is a large difference in spectral sensitivity between rods and cones. Rods have their maximal sensitivity in the blue-green at about 500 millimicrons; the entire spectral sensitivity of the cones is transposed toward the red, the maximum lying in the yellow-green at about 562 millimicrons. The point of this difference for our present argument is that as one goes from dim light, in which pattern vision is poor in any case, to bright light, in which it becomes acute, the sensitivity of the eye moves away from the region of the spectrum in which the chromatic aberration is large toward the part of the spectrum in which it is least.

The color correction of the eye is completed by a third dispensation. Toward the center of the human retina there is a small, shallow depression called the fovea, which contains only cones. While the retina as a whole sweeps through a visual angle of some 240 degrees, the fovea subtends an angle of only about 1.7 degrees. The fovea is considerably smaller than the head of a pin, yet with this tiny patch of retina the eye accomplishes all its most detailed vision.

The fovea also includes the fixation point of the eye. To look directly at something is to turn one's eye so that its image falls upon the fovea. Beyond the boundary of the fovea rods appear, and they become more and more numerous as the distance from the fovea increases. The apparatus for vision in bright light is thus concentrated toward the center of the retina, that for dim light toward its periphery. In very dim light, too dim to excite the cones, the fovea is blind. One can see objects then only by looking at them slightly askance

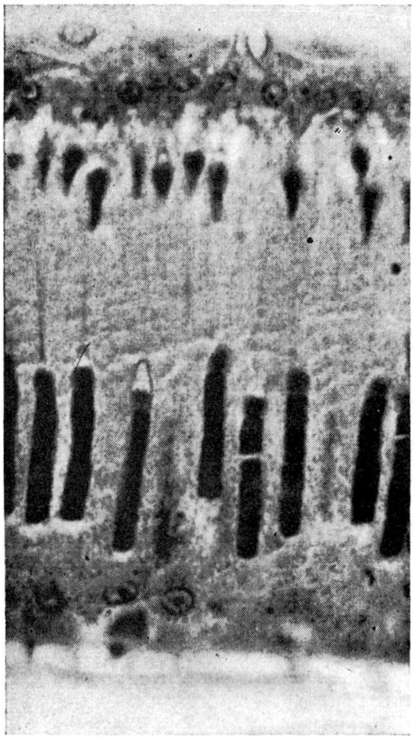

CONES of the catfish *Ameiurus* are pulled toward the surface of the retina (*top*) in bright light. The rods remain in a layer below the surface.

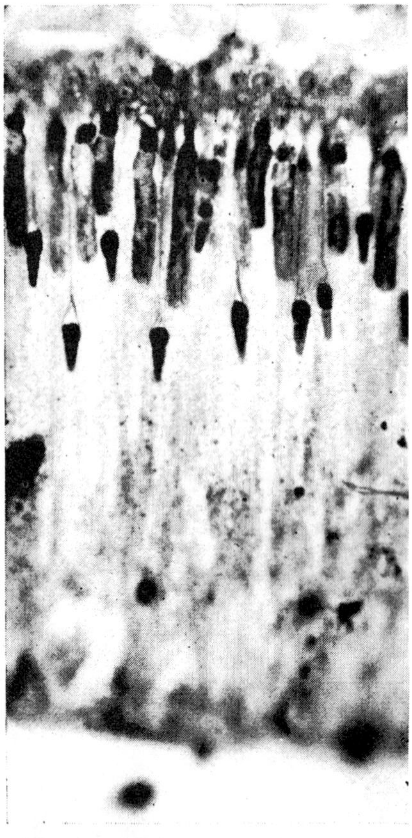

RODS advance and cones retreat in dim light. This retinal feature is not possessed by mammals. It is peculiar to some of the cold-blooded animals.

to catch their images on areas rich in rods.

In man, apes and monkeys, alone of all known mammals, the fovea and the region of retina just around it is colored yellow. This area is called the yellow patch, or *macula lutea*. Its pigmentation lies as a yellow screen over the light receptors of the central retina, subtending a visual angle some five to 10 degrees in diameter.

Several years ago in our laboratory at Harvard University we measured the color transmission of this pigment in the living human eye by comparing the spectral sensitivities of cones in the yellow patch with those in a colorless peripheral area. The yellow pigment was also extracted from a small number of human maculae, and was found to be xanthophyll, a carotenoid pigment that occurs also in all green leaves. This pigment in the yellow patch takes up the absorption of light in the violet and blue regions of the spectrum just where absorption by the lens falls to very low values. In this way the yellow patch removes for the central retina the remaining regions of the spectrum for which the color error is high.

So the human eye, unable to correct its color error otherwise, throws away those portions of the spectrum that would make the most trouble. The yellow lens removes the near ultraviolet for the eye as a whole, the macular pigment eliminates most of the violet and blue for the central retina, and the shift from rods to cones displaces vision in bright light bodily toward the red. By these three devices the apparatus of most acute vision avoids the entire range of the spectrum in which the chromatic aberration is large.

Photography with Living Eyes

In 1876 Franz Boll of the University of Rome discovered in the rods of the frog retina a brilliant red pigment. This bleached in the light and was resynthesized in the dark, and so fulfilled the elementary requirements of a visual pigment. He called this substance visual red; later it was renamed visual purple or rhodopsin. This pigment marks the point of attack by light on the rods: the absorption of light by rhodopsin initiates the train of reactions that end in rod vision.

Boll had scarcely announced his discovery when Willy Kühne, professor of physiology at Heidelberg, took up the study of rhodopsin, and in one extraordinary year learned almost everything about it that was known until recently. In his first paper on retinal chemistry Kühne said: "Bound together with the pigment epithelium, the retina behaves not merely like a photographic plate, but like an entire photographic workshop, in which the workman continually renews the plate by laying on new light-sensitive material, while simultaneously erasing the old image."

Kühne saw at once that with this pigment which was bleached by light it might be possible to take a picture with the living eye. He set about devising methods for carrying out such a process, and succeeded after many discouraging failures. He called the process optography and its products optograms.

One of Kühne's early optograms was made as follows. An albino rabbit was fastened with its head facing a barred window. From this position the rabbit could see only a gray and clouded sky. The animal's head was covered for several minutes with a cloth to adapt its eyes to the dark, that is to let rhodopsin accumulate in its rods. Then the animal was exposed for three minutes to the light. It was immediately decapitated, the eye removed and cut open along the equator, and the rear half of the eyeball containing the retina laid in a solution of alum for fixation. The next day Kühne saw, printed upon the retina in bleached and unaltered rhodopsin, a picture of the window with the clear pattern of its bars.

I remember reading as a boy a detective story in which at one point the detective enters a dimly lighted room, on the floor of which a corpse is lying. Working carefully in the semidarkness, the detective raises one eyelid of the victim and snaps a picture of the open eye. Upon developing this in his darkroom he finds that he has an optogram of the last scene viewed by the victim, including of course an excellent likeness of the murderer. So far as I know Kühne's optograms mark the closest approach to fulfilling this legend.

The legend itself has nonetheless flourished for more than 60 years, and all of my readers have probably seen or heard some version of it. It began with Kühne's first intimation that the eye resembles a photographic workshop, even before he had succeeded in producing his first primitive optogram, and it spread rapidly over the entire world. In the paper that announces his first success in optography, Kühne refers to this story with some bitterness. He says: "I disregard all the journalistic potentialities of this subject, and willingly surrender it in advance to all the claims of fancy-free coroners on both sides of the ocean, for it certainly is not pleasant to deal with a serious problem in such company. Much that I could say about this had better be suppressed, and turned rather to the hope that no one will expect from me any corroboration of announcements that have not been authorized with my name."

Despite these admirable sentiments we find Kühne shortly afterward engaged in a curious adventure. In the nearby town of Bruchsal on November 16, 1880, a young man was beheaded by guillotine. Kühne had made arrangements to receive the corpse. He had prepared a dimly lighted room screened with red and yellow glass to keep any rhodopsin left in the eyes from bleaching further. Ten minutes after the knife had fallen he obtained the whole retina from the left eye, and had the satisfaction of seeing and showing to several colleagues a sharply demarcated optogram printed upon its surface. Kühne's drawing of it is reproduced at the bottom of page 101. To my knowledge it is the only human optogram on record.

Kühne went to great pains to determine what this optogram represented. He says: "A search for the object which served as source for this optogram remained fruitless, in spite of a thorough inventory of all the surroundings and reports from many witnesses. The delinquent had spent the night awake by the light of a tallow candle; he had slept from four to five o'clock in the morning; and had read and written, first by candlelight until dawn, then by feeble daylight until eight o'clock. When he emerged in the open, the sun came out for an instant, according to a reliable observer, and the sky became somewhat brighter during the seven minutes prior to the bandaging of his eyes and his execution, which followed immediately. The delinquent, however, raised his eyes only rarely."

Color

One of the triumphs of modern photography is its success in recording color. For this it is necessary not only to graft some system of color differentiation and rendition upon the photographic process; the finished product must then fulfill the very exacting requirement that it excite the same sensations of color in the human eye as did the original subject of the picture.

How the human eye resolves colors is not known. Normal human color vision seems to be compounded of three kinds of responses; we therefore speak of it as trichromatic or three-color vision. The three kinds of response call for at least three kinds of cone differing from one another in their sensitivity to the various regions of the spectrum. We can only guess at what regulates these differences. The simplest assumption is that the human cones contain three different light-sensitive pigments, but this is still a matter of surmise.

There exist retinas, however, in which one can approach the problem of color vision more directly. The eyes of certain turtles and of certain birds such as chickens and pigeons contain a great predominance of cones. Since cones are the organs of vision in bright light as well as of color vision, these animals necessarily function only at high light intensities. They are permanently night-blind, due

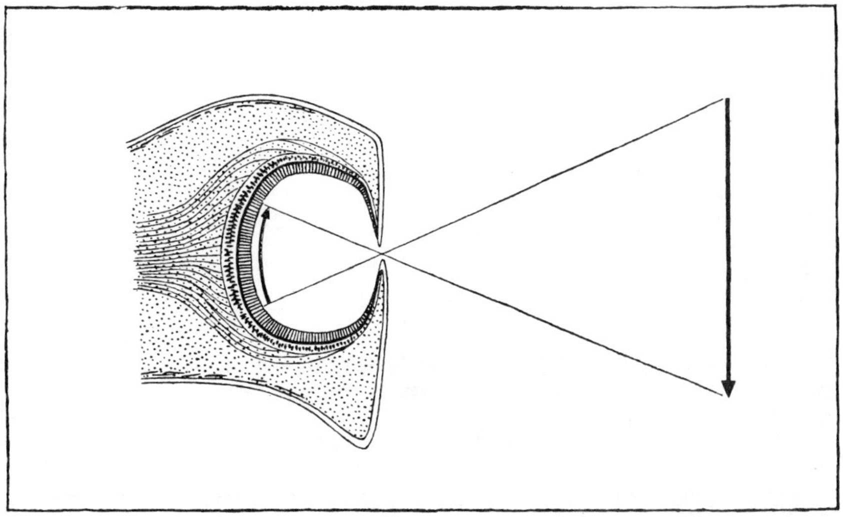

PINHOLE-CAMERA EYE is found in Nautilus, the spiral-shelled mollusk which is related to the octopus and the squid. This eye has the advantage of being in focus at all distances from the object that is viewed. It has the serious disadvantage, however, of admitting very little light to the retina.

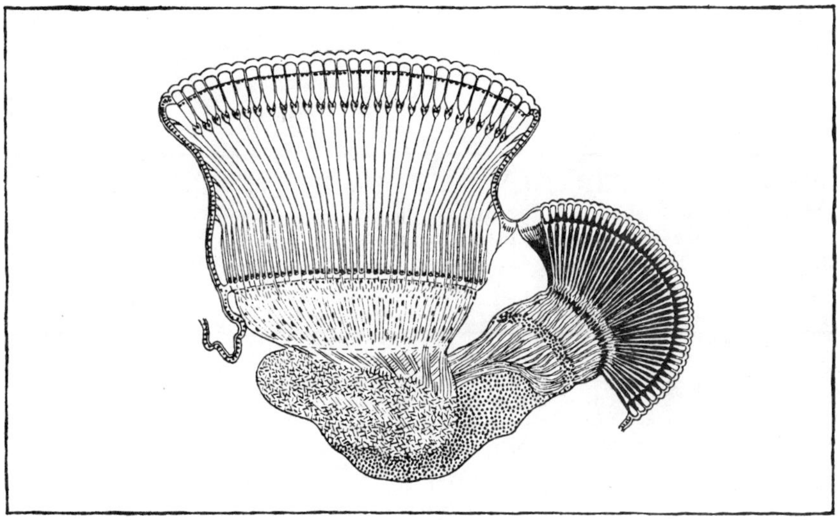

COMPOUND EYE is found in insects. Each element contributes only a small patch of light or shade to make up the whole mosaic image. This double compound eye is found in the mayfly *Chloeon*. The segment at the top provides detailed vision; the segment at the right, coarse, wide-angled vision.

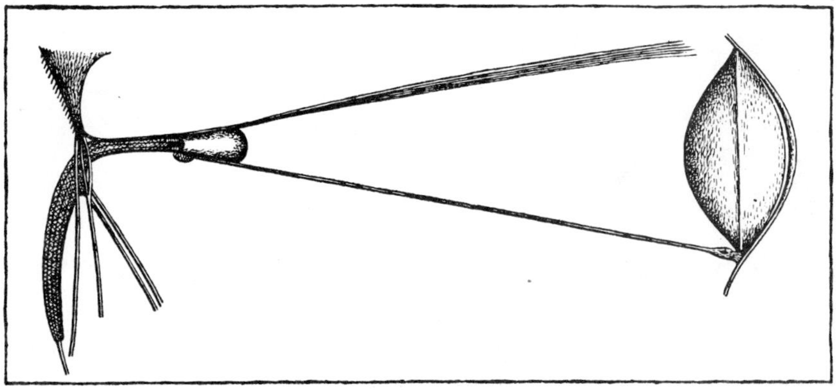

SCANNING EYE is found in the arthropod Copilia. It possesses a large lens (*right*) but only one receptor element (*left*). Attached to the receptor are the optic nerve and a strand of muscle. The latter is reported to move the receptor back and forth so that it scans the image formed by the lens.

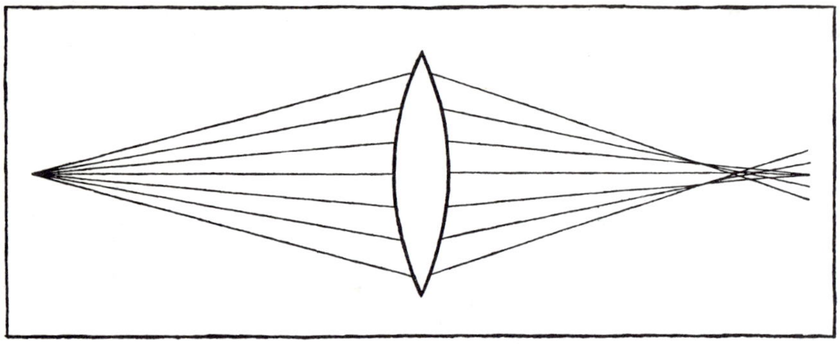

SPHERICAL ABERRATION occurs when light is refracted by a lens with spherical surfaces. The light which passes through the edge of the lens is brought to a shorter focus than that which passes through the center. The result of this is that the image of a point is not a point but a "blur circle."

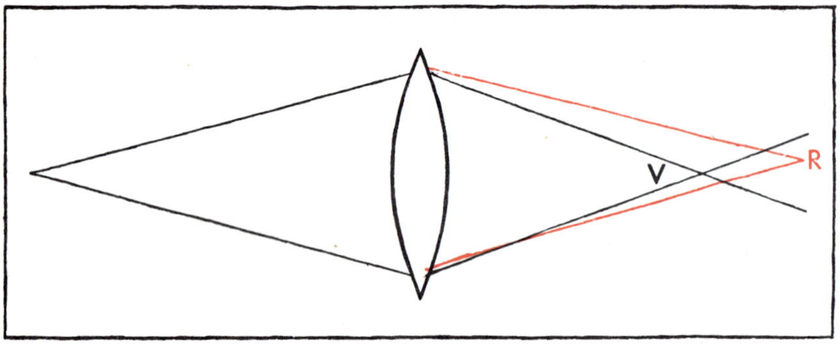

CHROMATIC ABERRATION occurs when light of various colors is refracted by a lens made of one material. The light of shorter wavelength is refracted more than that of longer wavelength, *i.e.*, violet is brought to a shorter focus than red. The image of a white point is a colored blur circle.

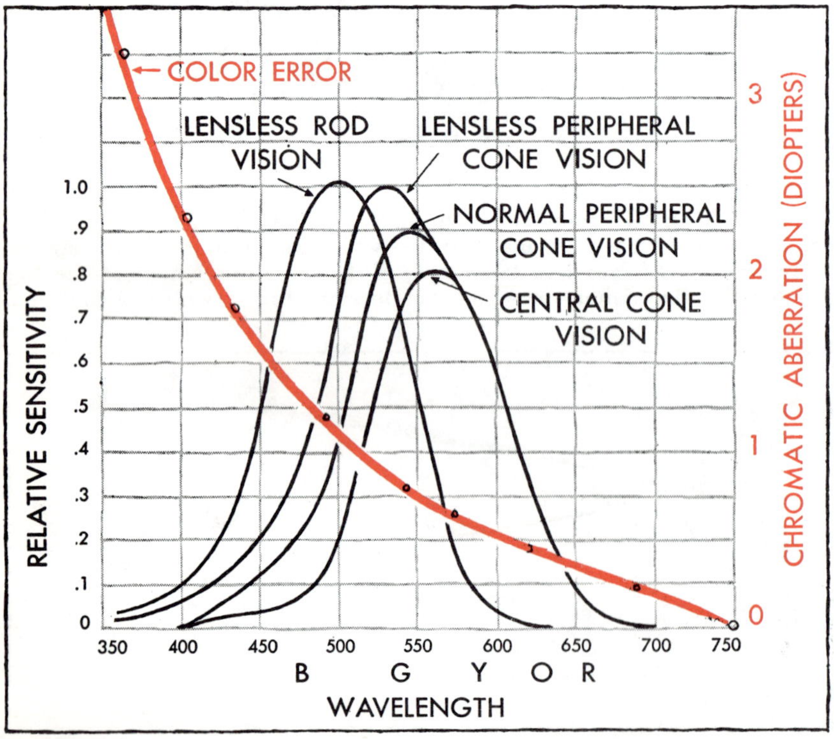

CHROMATIC ABERRATION of the human eye is corrected by various stratagems which withdraw the cones from the region of maximum aberration, *i.e.*, the shorter wavelengths. The horizontal coordinate of this diagram is wavelength in millimicrons; the colors are indicated by initial letters.

to a poverty or complete absence of rods. It is for this reason that chickens must roost at sundown.

In the cones of these animals we find a system of brilliantly colored oil globules, one in each cone. The globule is situated at the joint between the inner and outer segments of the cone, so that light must pass through it just before entering the light-sensitive element. The globules therefore lie in the cones in the position of little individual color filters.

One has only to remove the retina from a chicken or a turtle and spread it on the stage of a microscope to see that the globules are of three colors: red, orange and greenish yellow. It was suggested many years ago that they provide the basis of color differentiation in the animals that possess them.

In a paper published in 1907 the German ophthalmologist Siegfried Garten remarked that he was led by such retinal color filters to invent a system of color photography based upon the same principle. This might have been the first instance in which an eye had directly inspired a development in photography. Unfortunately, however, in 1906 the French chemist Louis Lumière, apparently without benefit of chicken retinas, had brought out his autochrome process for color photography based upon exactly this principle.

To make his autochrome plates Lumiere used suspensions of starch grains from rice, which he dyed red, green and blue. These were mixed in roughly equal proportions, and the mixture was strewn over the surface of an ordinary photographic plate. The granules were then squashed flat and the interstices were filled with particles of carbon. Each dyed granule served as a color filter for the patch of silver-bromide emulsion that lay just under it.

Just as the autochrome plate can accomplish color photography with a single light-sensitive substance, so the cones of the chicken retina should require no more than one light-sensitive pigment. We extracted such a pigment from the chicken retina in 1937. It is violet in color, and has therefore been named iodopsin from *ion*, the Greek word for violet. All three pigments of the colored oil globules have also been isolated and crystallized. Like the pigment of the human macula, they are all carotenoids: a greenish-yellow carotene; the golden mixture of xanthophylls found in chicken egg yolk; and red astaxanthin, the pigment of the boiled lobster.

Controversy thrives on ignorance, and we have had many years of disputation regarding the number of kinds of cone concerned in human color vision. Many investigators prefer three, some four, and at least one of my English colleagues seven. I myself incline toward three. It is a good number, and sufficient unto the day.

The appearance of three colors of oil globule in the cones of birds and turtles might be thought to provide strong support for trichromatic theories of color vision. The trouble is that these retinas do in fact contain a fourth class of globule which is colorless. Colorless globules have all the effect of a fourth color; there is no doubt that if we include them, bird and turtle retinas possess the basis for four-color vision.

Latent Images

Recent experiments have exposed a wholly unexpected parallel between vision and photography. Many years ago Kühne showed that rhodopsin can be extracted from the retinal rods into clear water solution. When such solutions are exposed to light, the rhodopsin bleaches just as it does in the retina.

It has been known for some time that the bleaching of rhodopsin in solution is not entirely accomplished by light. It is started by light, but then goes on in the dark for as long as an hour at room temperature. Bleaching is therefore a composite process. It is ushered in by a light reaction that converts rhodopsin to a highly unstable product; this then decomposes by ordinary chemical reactions—"dark" reactions in the sense that they do not require light.

Since great interest attaches to the initial unstable product of the light reaction, many attempts were made in our laboratory and at other laboratories to seize upon this substance and learn its properties. It has such a fleeting existence, however, that for some time nothing satisfactory was achieved.

In 1941, however, two English workers, E. E. Broda and C. F. Goodeve, succeeded in isolating the light reaction by irradiating rhodopsin solutions at about −73 degrees Celsius, roughly the temperature of dry ice. In such extreme cold, light reactions are unhindered, but ordinary dark processes cannot occur. Broda and Goodeve found that an exhaustive exposure of rhodopsin to light under these conditions produced only a very small change in its color, so small that though it could be measured one might not have been certain merely by looking at these solutions that any change had occurred at all. Yet the light reaction had been completed, and when such solutions were allowed to warm up to room temperature they bleached *in the dark*. We have recently repeated such experiments in our laboratory. With some differences which need not be discussed, the results were qualitatively as the English workers had described them.

These observations led us to re-examine certain early experiments of Kühne's. Kühne had found that if the retina of a frog or rabbit was thoroughly dried over sulfuric acid, it could be exposed even to brilliant sunlight for long periods without bleaching. Kühne concluded that dry rhodopsin is not affected by light, and this has been the common understanding of workers in the field of vision ever since.

It occurred to us, however, that dry rhodopsin, like extremely cold rhodopsin, might undergo the light reaction, though with such small change in color as to have escaped notice. To test this possibility we prepared films of rhodopsin in gelatin, which could be dried thoroughly and were of a quality that permitted making accurate measurements of their color transmission throughout the spectrum.

We found that when dry gelatin films of rhodopsin are exposed to light, the same change occurs as in very cold rhodopsin. The color is altered, but so slightly as easily to escape visual observation. In any case the change cannot be described as bleaching; if anything the color is a little intensified. Yet the light reaction is complete; if such exposed films are merely wetted with water, they bleach in the dark.

We have therefore two procedures—cooling to very low temperatures and removal of water—that clearly separate the light from the dark reactions in the bleaching of rhodopsin. Which of these reactions is responsible for stimulating rod vision? One cannot yet be certain, yet the response of the rods to light occurs so rapidly that only the light reaction seems fast enough to account for it.

What has been said, however, has a further consequence that brings it into direct relation with photography. Everyone knows that the photographic process also is divided into light and dark components. The result of exposing a film to light is usually invisible, a so-called "latent image." It is what later occurs in the darkroom, the dark reaction of development, that brings out the picture.

This now appears to be exactly what happens in vision. Here as in photography light produces an almost invisible result, a latent image, and this indeed is probably the process upon which retinal excitation depends. The visible loss of rhodopsin's color, its bleaching, is the result of subsequent dark reactions, of "development."

One can scarcely have notions like this without wanting to make a picture with a rhodopsin film; and we have been tempted into making one very crude rhodopsin photograph. Its subject is not exciting—only a row of black and white stripes—but we show it at the right for what interest it may have as the first such photograph. What is important is that it was made in typically photographic stages. The dry rhodopsin film was first exposed to light, producing a latent image. It was then developed in the dark by wetting. It then had to be fixed; and, though better ways are known, we fixed this photograph simply

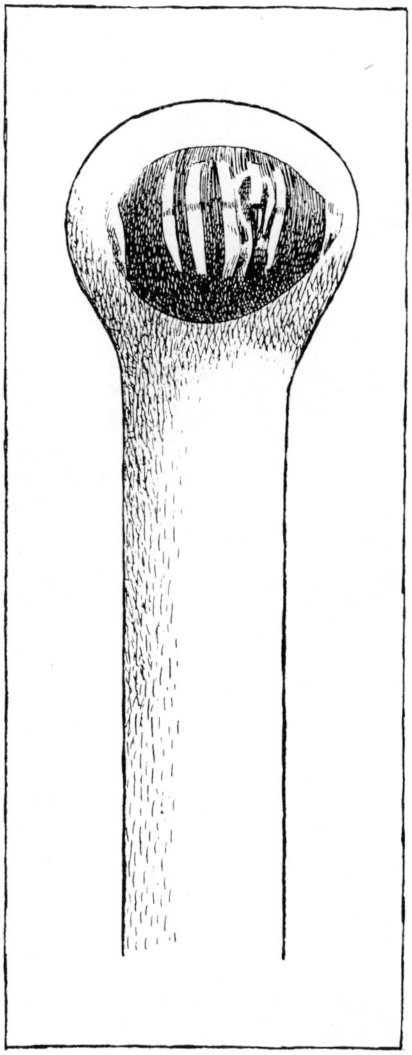

FROG OPTOGRAM showing a barred pattern was made by the German ophthalmologist Siegfried Garten. The retina is mounted on a rod.

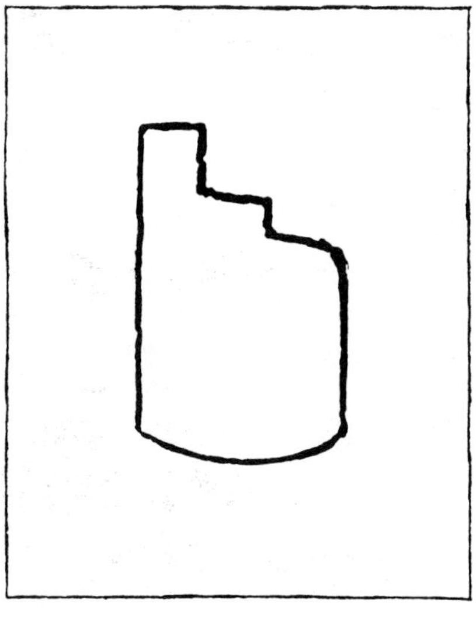

HUMAN OPTOGRAM was drawn by Kühne after he had removed the retina of a beheaded criminal. Kühne could not determine what it showed.

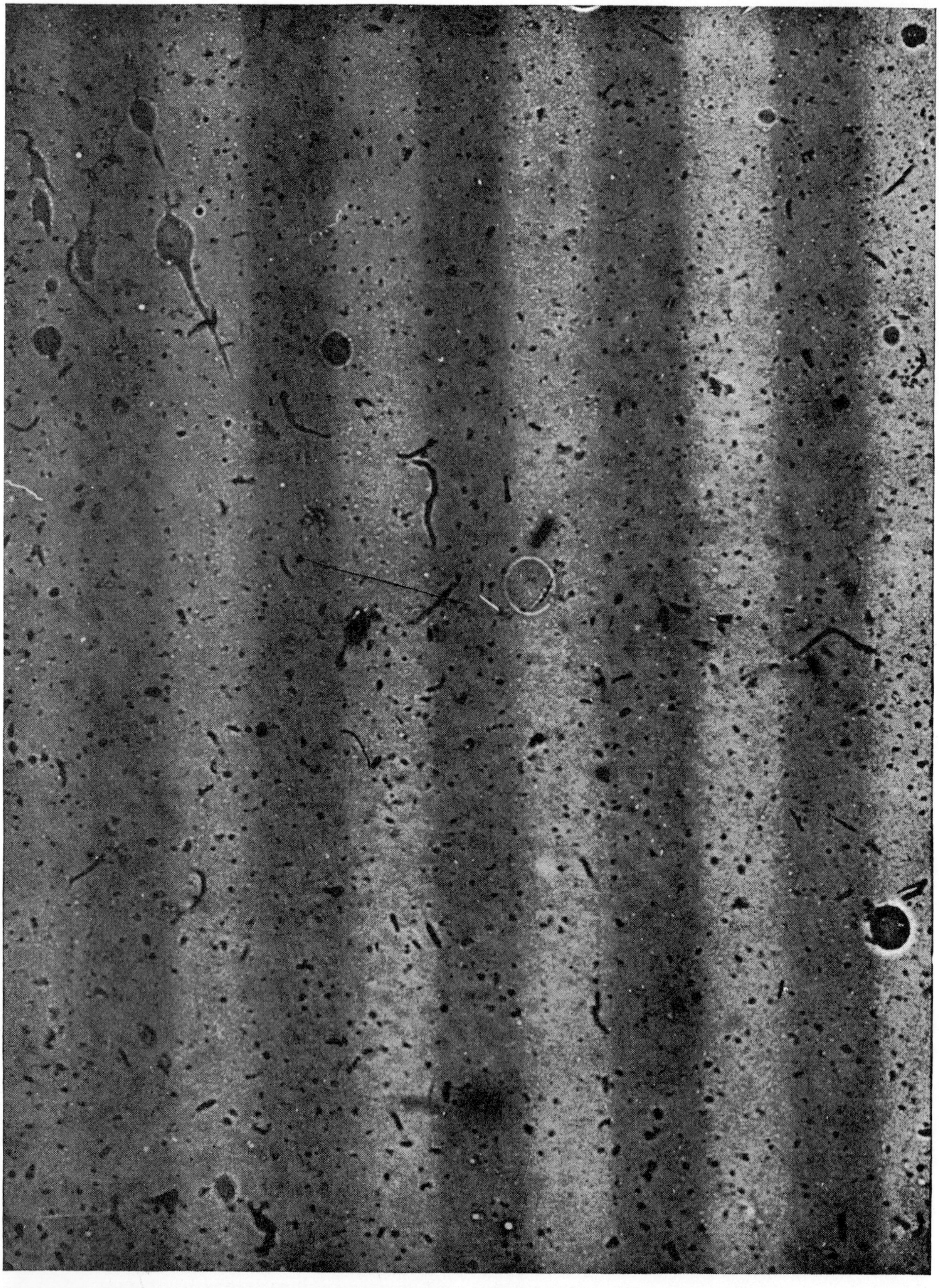

RHODOPSIN PHOTOGRAPH was made by the author and his associates Paul K. Brown and Oscar Starobin. Rhodopsin, the light-sensitive red pigment of rod vision, had been extracted from cattle retinas, mixed with gelatin and spread on celluloid. This was then dried and exposed to a pattern made up of black and white stripes. When the film was wetted in the dark with hydroxylamine, the rhodopsin bleached in the same pattern.

by redrying it. Since irradiated rhodopsin bleaches rather than blackens on development, the immediate result is a positive.

Photography with rhodopsin is only in its first crude stages, perhaps at the level that photography with silver bromide reached almost a century ago. I doubt that it has a future as a practical process. For us its primary interest is to pose certain problems in visual chemistry in a provocative form. It does, however, also add another chapter to the mingled histories of eye and camera.

RETINAL PHOTOGRAPH, or an optogram, was drawn in 1878 by the German investigator Willy Kühne. He had exposed the eye of a living rabbit to a barred window, killed the rabbit, removed its retina and fixed it in alum.

11

VISUAL PIGMENTS IN MAN

W. A. H. RUSHTON
November 1962

Everyone knows that the eye is a camera—more properly a television camera—that not only forms a picture but also transmits it in code via the optic nerves to the brain. In this article I shall not discuss how the lens forms an image on the retina; it does so in virtually the same way that the lens of a photographic camera forms an image on a piece of film, and the process needs no explanation here. Nor shall I treat of the encoding of nerve messages in the eye, still less of their decoding in the brain, because on those topics reliable information remains extremely scanty. I shall deal rather with the light-sensitive constituents of the retina of the eye—the "silver bromide" of vision—and their relation to the perception of light and color.

It is no use taking a snapshot with color film if the illumination is poor; the only hope of getting a picture is to use sensitive black-and-white film. If the light signal is only sufficient to silhouette outlines, it cannot provide additional information for the discrimination of color. Thus for a camera to be well equipped to extract the maximum information from any kind of scene it must be provided with sensitive black-and-white film for twilight and color film for full daylight. The eye is furnished with a retina having precisely this dual purpose. The saying goes, "In the twilight all cats are gray," but by day some cats are tortoise-shell.

We cannot slip off our daylight retina and wind on the twilight roll; the two films must remain in place all the time. They are not situated one behind the other but are mixed together, the grains of the two "emulsions" lying side by side. The color grains are too insensitive to contribute to the twilight picture, which is therefore formed entirely by the black-and-white grains; these, on the other hand, give only a rather faint picture, which in daylight is quite overpowered by the color grains.

Of course the actual grains in the retina are not inorganic crystals such as silver bromide but are the specialized body cells known as rods and cones. The rods and cones do, however, contain a photosensitive pigment that is laid down in a molecular array so well ordered as to be quasi-crystalline. The rods are the grains responsible for twilight vision, and their photosensitive pigment is rhodopsin, often called visual purple. The cones are the grains of daylight vision, and the photosensitive pigments they contain will be one of the topics of this article.

It was first noticed almost a century ago that if a frog's eye was dissected in dim light and if the excised retina was then brought out into diffuse daylight, the initial rose-pink color of the retina would gradually fade and become almost transparent. The fading of the retina was the more rapid the stronger the light to which it was exposed; hence the term "bleaching" is used to describe the chemical change brought about when light falls on the photosensitive constituents of the rods and cones. If a microscope is employed to observe the retina as it bleaches, one can see that the pink color resides only in the rods. The cones appear to possess no colored pigment at all.

The presence of a photosensitive pigment in the rods does not prove that this is the chemical that catches the light with which we see; the pigment may be doing something quite different. There is one rather strict test that must be satisfied if rhodopsin, the pink pigment, is the starting point of vision. Since the pigment looks pink by transmitted light, it obviously absorbs green and transmits red (and some blue). With a spectrophotometer it is quite easy to measure the absorption of a rhodopsin solution at various wavelengths. When this is done, one obtains a bell-shaped curve with a peak close to a wavelength of 500 millimicrons, in the blue-green region of the spectrum. If rhodopsin catches the light we see in twilight, we should see best precisely those wavelengths that are best caught. In other words, the spectral absorption curve of rhodopsin should coincide with the spectral sensitivity curve of human twilight vision. Actual measurements of the twilight sensitivity of the eye at various wavelengths leave no doubt that rhodopsin is indeed the pigment that enables us to see at night [*see illustration on page 108*].

The eye is able to discriminate differences in brightness efficiently over a range in which the brightest light is a billion times more intense than the dimmest. Any instrument that can do that must have a variable "gain," or sensitivity-multiplying factor, and some means of adjusting the gain to match the level of signal to be discriminated. It is common experience that the eye adjusts its gain so smoothly that when the sun goes behind a cloud, the details of the scene appear just as distinct as before, and indeed we have so little clue to the eye's automatic compensation that when (as in photography) we want an estimate of the light intensity, it is safer to use a photoelectric meter. The change in gain of the eye is called visual adaptation.

It is plain that visual adaptation adjusts itself automatically to the prevailing brightness. To explain how this could occur Selig Hecht of Columbia Uni-

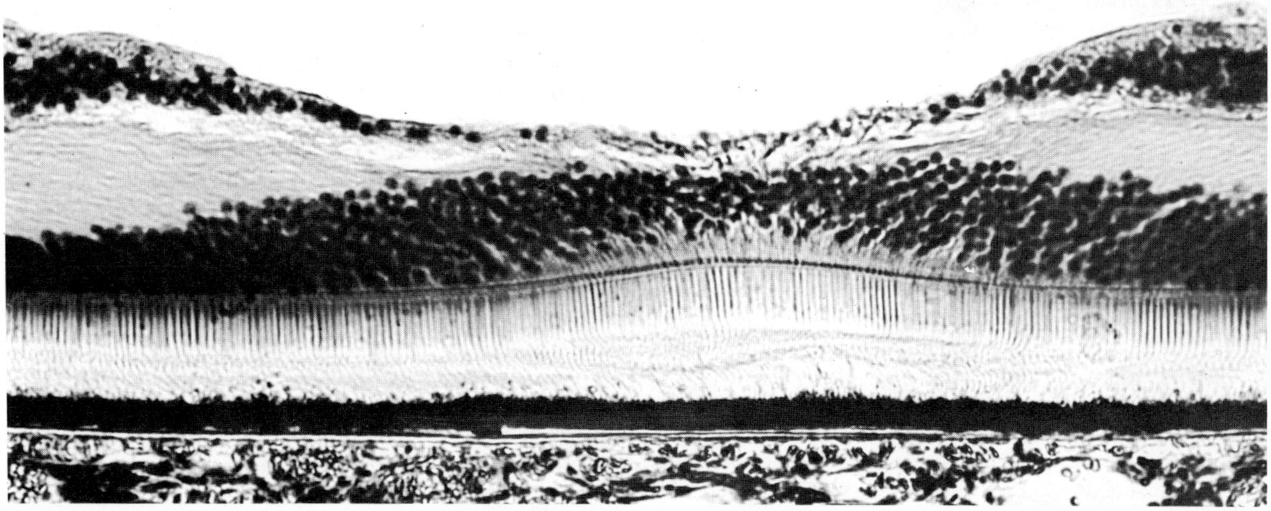

HUMAN RETINA, magnified about 370 diameters, is shown sectioned through the fovea, the tiny central region responsible for acute vision. The rods and cones, the photoreceptor cells containing the visual pigments, are the closely packed vertical stalks extending across the picture. Above the rods and cones are several layers composed chiefly of nerve cells that relay signals from the retina to the brain. At the fovea, which contains few if any rods, these layers are much thinned out to expose the light-sensitive part of the cones to incident light. This micrograph was made by C. M. H. Pedler of the Institute of Ophthalmology at University of London.

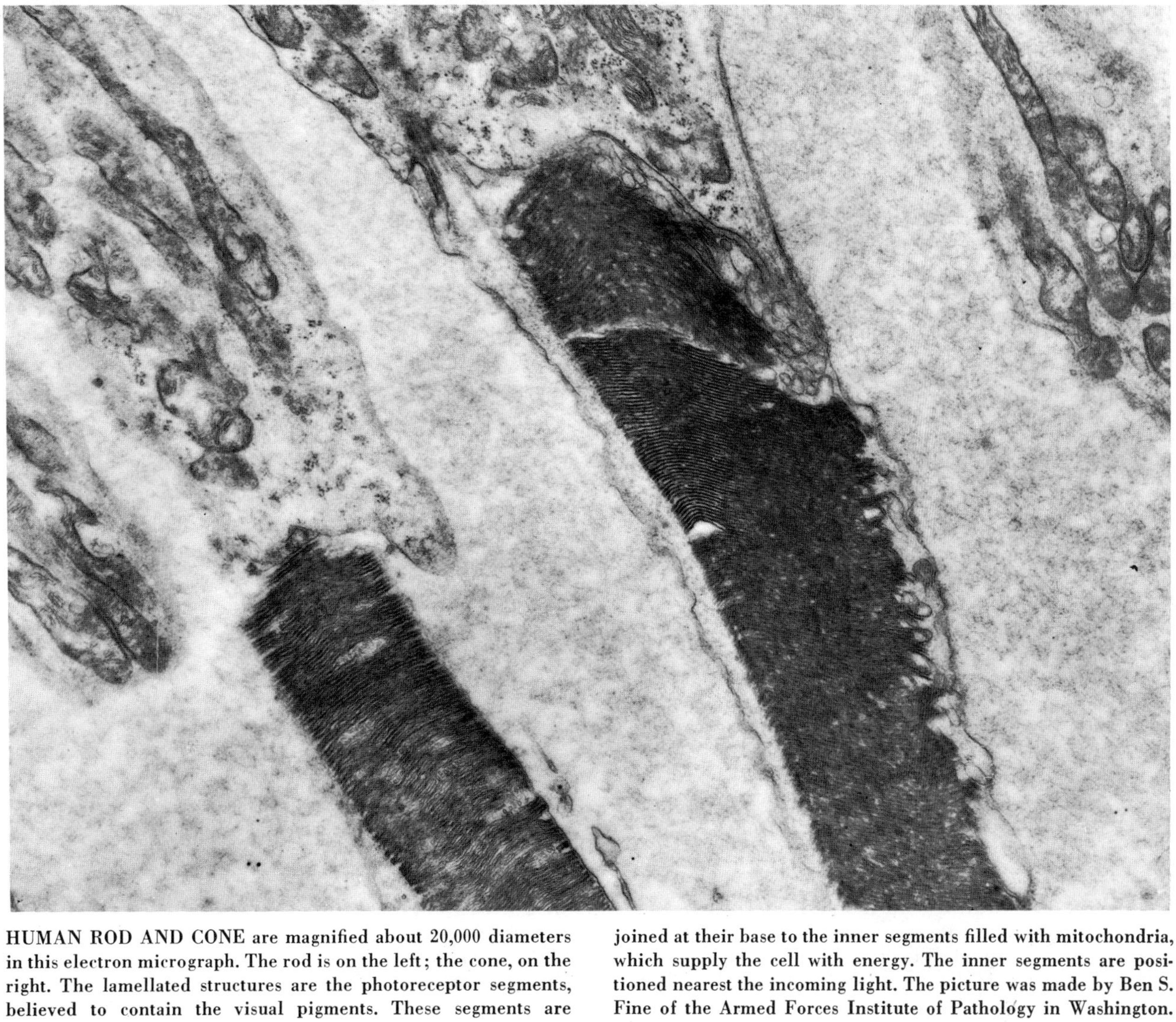

HUMAN ROD AND CONE are magnified about 20,000 diameters in this electron micrograph. The rod is on the left; the cone, on the right. The lamellated structures are the photoreceptor segments, believed to contain the visual pigments. These segments are joined at their base to the inner segments filled with mitochondria, which supply the cell with energy. The inner segments are positioned nearest the incoming light. The picture was made by Ben S. Fine of the Armed Forces Institute of Pathology in Washington.

versity 40 years ago drew attention to the visual pigments and suggested that their color intensity seems to vary with the level of light. He hypothesized that in bright light these pigments are somewhat bleached and that in the dark they are regenerated from precursors stored in the eye or conveyed by the blood. Under steady illumination a balance will be struck between these two processes, and the equilibrium level of rhodopsin will be lower the stronger the bleaching light is. Hecht suggested that the level of rod adaptation is controlled by the level of the rhodopsin in the rods.

One difficulty in accepting this rather plausible suggestion is that until one can measure the actual rhodopsin level in the eye and correlate it with the corresponding state of visual adaptation, the idea remains speculative and very insecure. This indeed was the situation for some 30 years, but now it is possible to measure rhodopsin and cone pigments in the normal human eye by a procedure requiring only about seven seconds. As a result one can now follow the time course of bleaching and regeneration and test Hecht's suggestion.

Most people have at one time or another seen the eyes of a cat in the glare of an automobile headlight. The brilliant yellow-green eyes shining out of the darkness are a striking sight. The effect is caused simply by the reflection of light from the back of the cat's eye. What is important for our purpose is that these rays are reflected from behind the cat's retina and have therefore passed twice through the retina and the rhodopsin contained in the retina. This by itself would make the eye look pink, as it does in the case of the dissected frog retina. The cat, however, has a brilliant green backing to its retina and it is this backing that colors the returning light. To see the color of rhodopsin itself we need an animal whose retina has a white backing. If instead of a cat there were an alligator in the road, we should see the eye-shine colored pink by rhodopsin.

By using a photocell to analyze the returning light one can measure the rhodopsin no matter whether the eye is backed by green as it is in the cat, by white as in the alligator or even by black as in man. Regardless of its color, the reflectivity of the rear surface is unchanging, whereas the rhodopsin lying in front can be bleached away by strong light. It follows that if one measures not the color but the intensity of the returning light, one can find how much of the light was absorbed by rhodopsin.

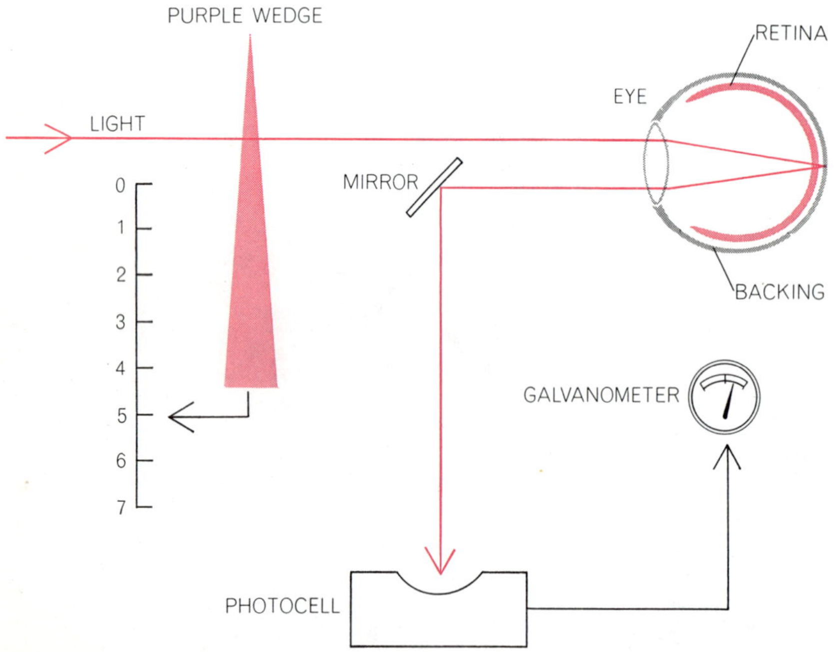

METHOD OF MEASURING VISUAL PIGMENTS depends on the bleaching produced by light. Light enters the eye through a purple wedge, and the amount reflected is measured by a photocell. When the pigment rhodopsin, or "visual purple," is bleached from the retina, an equivalent amount of wedge is inserted in the light beam to keep the electric output the same after bleaching as before. The change in pigment is measured by the wedge displacement; a change of one unit means reflectivity of the eye has changed by a factor of 10.

The illustration on this page shows schematically the instrument used to measure the bleaching of human eye pigments in my laboratory at the University of Cambridge. Light enters the eye through the upper half of the pupil, which has been dilated by a drug to allow more light to pass. It returns after reflection from the black rear surface, having twice traversed the retina. A small mirror intercepts the light from the lower half of the pupil and deflects it into a photomultiplier tube, which provides a measure of the light absorbed by the retinal pigments. If a powerful light is shined into the eye, the light bleaches away some of the pigment. This leaves less pigment to absorb the light traversing the retina; consequently the photocell output will be greater than before. The output can be returned to its former value by reduction of the measuring light. This is done by interposing a purple wedge in the beam of light entering the eye. The initial photocell output is restored when the amount of purple added by the wedge exactly matches the visual purple—the rhodopsin—removed by bleaching. The change in rhodopsin is thus measured simply by the change in wedge thickness that replaces it. The wedge scale is calibrated so that the reading is zero when all the rhodopsin is bleached away. Therefore the wedge setting for constant photocell output gives the rhodopsin density at that moment.

The intensity of the light reaching the photocell is only about a 20,000th of that falling on the eye, and the light striking the eye has to be so weak that it will not appreciably bleach the pigment it measures. Thus the equipment needs some rather careful compensations if measurements are to be reliable. We are not concerned here, however, with the technique of measurement but with the results in relation to the physiology of vision, and in particular with the question of the relation of rhodopsin level to visual adaptation.

The top illustration on page 109 shows the first measurements of this kind. They were made on my eye by F. W. Campbell at the University of Cambridge in 1955. The black dots show the wedge readings when a moderately bright bleaching light (one "bleaching unit") was applied to the dark-adapted eye. The pigment at first bleaches fast, then more slowly, and in five minutes it levels out, either because all the pigment is now bleached or because bleaching is just counterbalanced by the regeneration

EYE OF THE ALLIGATOR, which has a white reflecting layer behind the retina, illustrates how rhodopsin bleaches in the light and regenerates in the dark. The eye of the alligator above is light-adapted; the light of a stroboscopic-flash lamp, reflected from the white layer through the retina, is essentially colorless. The eyes of the alligator below are dark-adapted; the light reflected is red. The photographs were made at the New York Zoological Park with the kind assistance of Herndon G. Dowling and Stephen Spencook.

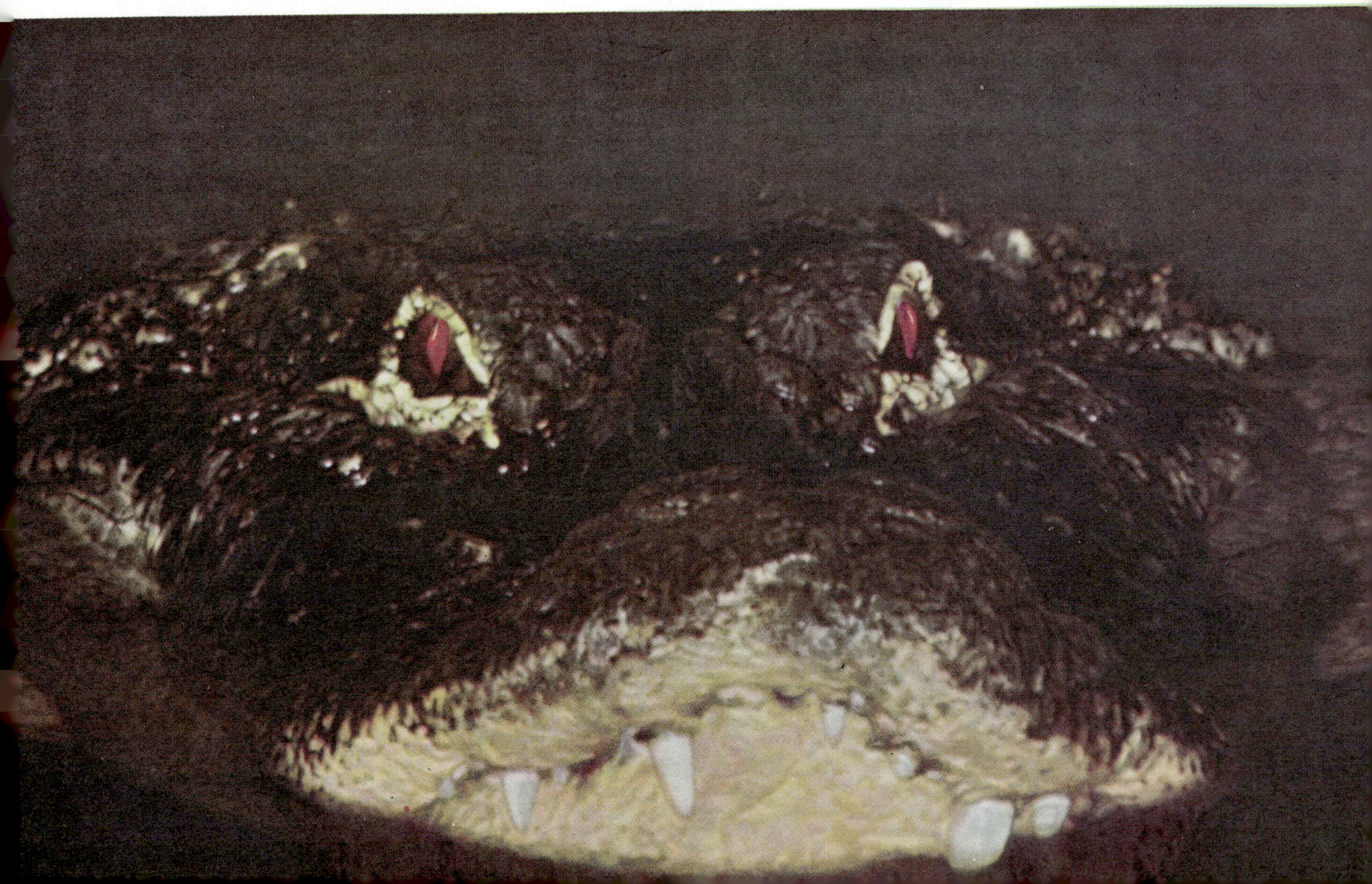

process. The latter is obviously the correct explanation, since by increasing the intensity of the bleaching light fivefold, further bleaching occurs and a lower level of equilibrium is achieved. In fact, a further increase of a hundredfold is needed to bleach the pigment entirely. The rate of pigment regeneration in the dark following total bleaching is plotted by the colored dots in the illustration. The regeneration follows an exponential curve and is about 90 per cent complete in 15 minutes.

Let us now examine Hecht's suggestion that it is the level of rhodopsin in the rods that defines the state of adaptation in twilight vision. But before doing so we must distinguish two quite different visual processes that are often designated by the word "adaptation." One process is exemplified by the quick changes in sensitivity that occur at night when the moon is fitfully obscured by passing clouds. This can be called field adaptation. When, on the other hand, we have got well adapted to bright light and then go into the dark—from sunlight into a theater, for instance—a different process occurs, which can be called adaptation of bleaching.

Now, field adaptation has nothing to do with the level of rhodopsin in the rods (or of visual pigments in the cones); the light intensity involved is only about a 100,000th of the bleaching unit referred to earlier, so that no appreciable bleaching can have occurred. Moreover, the time of adjustment to the new light level when the moon pops in and out of cloud is of the order of two seconds, rather than the 1,000 seconds required for the regeneration of rhodopsin. This rapid change of gain is in all likelihood produced entirely by the activity of nerve cells. Conceivably a feedback mechanism in the neural system maintains a constant signal strength by exchanging sensitivity for space-time discrimination. The adaptation of bleaching, on the other hand, turns out to be tightly linked to the level of rhodopsin in the rods.

The simplest way to examine this relation is to illuminate the eye with a powerful beam of light, a beam having an intensity of 100 bleaching units. After a minute or two all the rhodopsin will be bleached away and the course of pigment regeneration can be followed. The experiment is now repeated, but instead of measuring rhodopsin we determine the threshold of the eye by finding what is the weakest flash that can be detected at various intervals as the pigment regenerates. This is conveniently done by inserting a gray wedge to reduce the flash to threshold strength. The wedge displacement will now give the threshold directly on a logarithmic scale. A plot of this threshold yields the well-known dark-adaptation curve, shown in the bottom illustration on the next page.

As can be seen, the curve for the normal eye consists of two branches, the first of which corresponds to the log threshold of cones; the second, to the log threshold of rods. Only the rod threshold is related to rhodopsin, and it is a serious drawback that so much of this curve is hidden by the cone branch. Fortunately the complete rod curve can be obtained by using test subjects with a rare congenital abnormality in which rods are normal but cones entirely lack function. The dark-adaptation curve for such a subject is the black curve in the bottom illustration on the next page. It can be seen that the curve exactly follows the time course of the regeneration of rhodopsin, whether measured in the same subject or in a normal subject. It is therefore plain that the increase in light sensitivity of the rods waits precisely on the return of rhodopsin in the rods. What is far from plain, however, is what the increase in sensitivity waits for.

The change of sensitivity gain by nerve feedback in field adaptation is purposeful and efficient. The coupling of gain to the regeneration of rhodopsin in the adaptation of bleaching seems both pointless and clumsy. I have a far greater faith in nature, however, than in myself. I am sure that someone with deeper insight will eventually show that the deficiencies in dark adaptation, which to me seem unnecessary, are in fact inevitable.

The rapid and unconscious change of gain that makes absolute levels of light intensity hard to judge applies to cones as well as to rods, but in cones there is also the appreciation of color, which has its own adaptations. In judging brightness we estimate the brightness of parts with respect to the mean brightness of the whole. Thus the actual intensity of light reflected from black print in the noonday sun is far greater than that from white paper after sunset, yet the first looks black and the second white.

In color judgments wavelengths en-

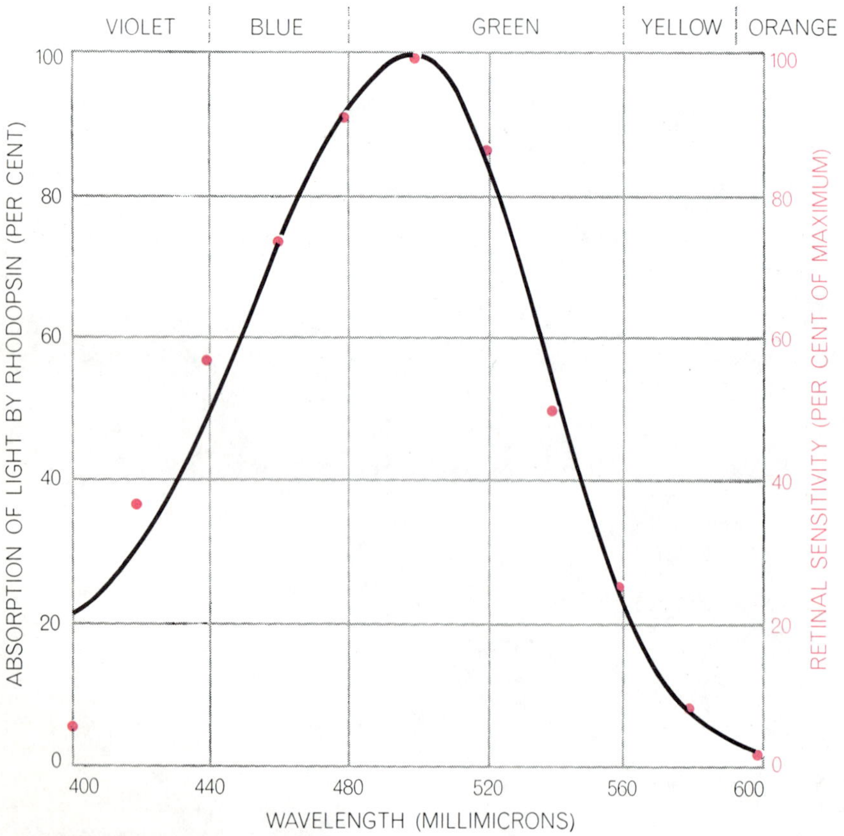

MEASUREMENTS OF RHODOPSIN show it to be the pigment responsible for twilight vision. The black curve indicates how a solution of rhodopsin, obtained from retinal rods, absorbs light of various wavelengths. Dots show sensitivity of the eye in twilight.

ter in, and we estimate the color of parts of a scene in relation to the mean wavelength of the whole. The fact that our perceptions of color can be independent of wavelength to a surprising degree has been brought into great prominence by the striking demonstrations of Edwin H. Land of the Polaroid Corporation [see "Experiments in Color Vision," by Edwin H. Land, beginning on page 286]. Land has shown, for example, that two superimposed images of a scene, made on black-and-white film through different filters, will appear to contain a large range of color when one image is projected by red light and the other by white light. To say that the eye uses the average wavelength of such a red-and-white projection to judge the color of its parts is not meant to "explain" the Land phenomena, still less to suggest that no explanation is needed. It is merely a reminder that owing to some sort of adaptation—which Land has recently shown to be instantaneous—the eye is almost as bad at making absolute judgments of color as it is of brightness.

What the eye can do very well, however, is to make color *matches*, and these remain good even in the conditions of Land's projections. For instance, if monochromatic beams of red and green light are superimposed by projection on a screen, they can be made to match the yellow of a sodium lamp exactly, just by suitably adjusting the intensity of the red and of the green. If this red-green mixture is now substituted for the sodium yellow in one of Land's two-color projections, the colored picture resulting is exactly what it was before. Although many strange things appear in Land's pictures, one thing is clear: If red and green match yellow in one situation, they will match it in every other situation. Why, we may ask, are color matches stable under conditions where color appearance changes so greatly, and what colors can be matched by a mixture of others? A century ago James Clerk Maxwell showed that all colors could be matched by a suitable mixture of red, green and blue primaries, and indeed that any three colors could be chosen as primaries provided that no one of them could be matched by a mixture of the other two. The trichromaticity of color implies that the cones have three and only three ways of catching light. It seems reasonable, therefore, that there may be three and only three different cone pigments.

Since the rods have only one pigment,

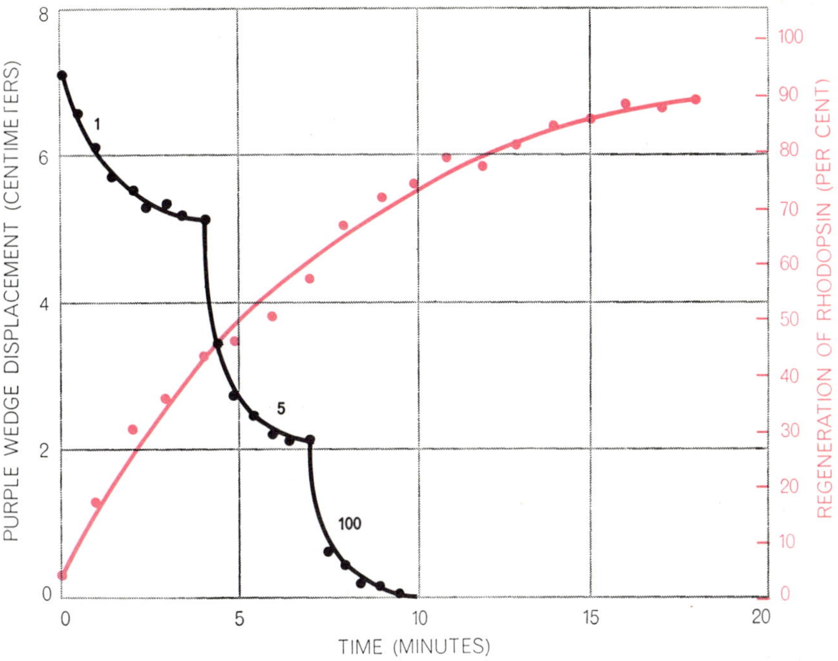

BLEACHING AND REGENERATION OF RHODOPSIN are shown in the two curves obtained by the method illustrated on page 106. The black curve records the time course of bleaching for a light of moderate intensity *(1)* and for lights five and 100 times brighter. In the dark, rhodopsin regenerates as shown by the colored curve. The measurements were made on the eye of the author by F. W. Campbell at the University of Cambridge.

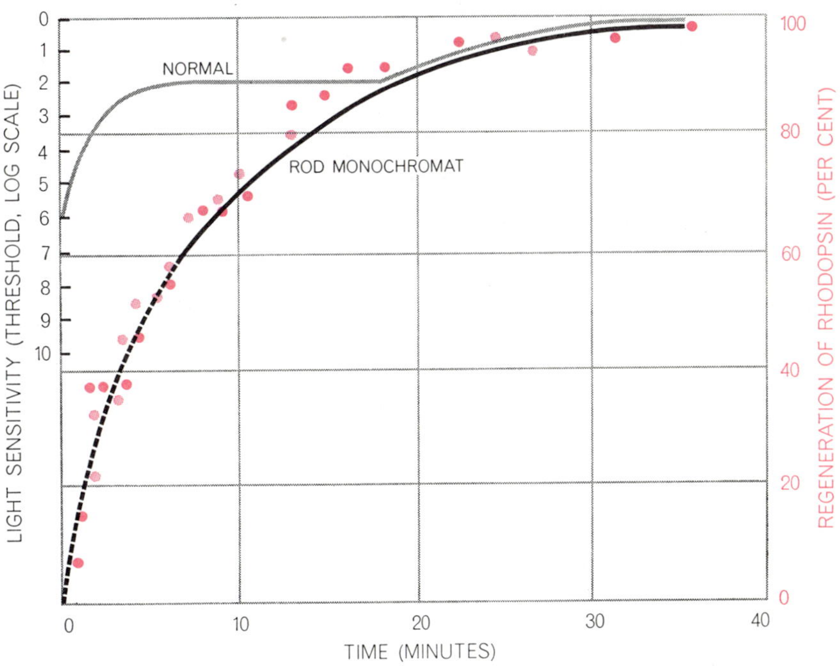

ROD AND CONE LIGHT SENSITIVITY can be distinguished by comparing a normal eye with that of a "rod monochromat," a person whose retinal cones do not function. The rhodopsin is fully bleached and the weakest detectable flash of light is measured. As the rhodopsin regenerates, the eye detects flashes that are weaker and weaker. The light sensitivity of the normal eye follows a discontinuous curve. The initial sensitivity increase is due to cones; the final increase is due to rods. In the rod monochromat the sensitivity rises more slowly but in a smooth curve. Independent measurements with the purple-wedge technique show that rhodopsin regeneration goes hand in hand with increased light sensitivity in the rod monochromat (*dark-colored dots*). In the normal eye, however, rhodopsin regeneration (*light-colored dots*) follows only the rod branch of the light-sensitivity curve.

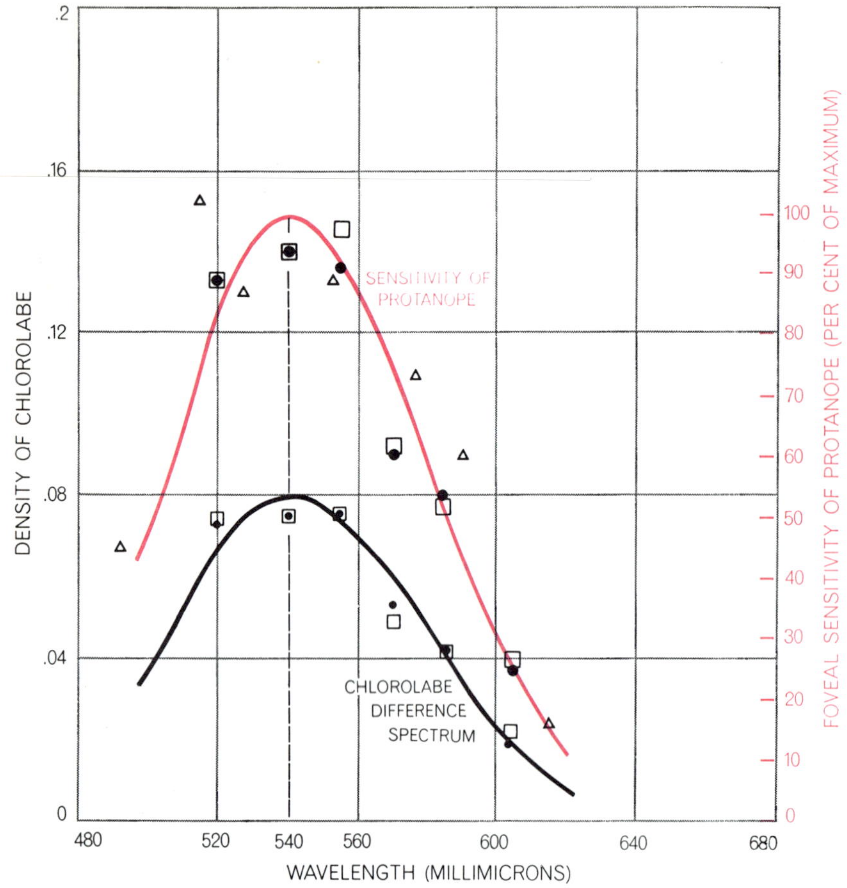

GREEN-CATCHING PIGMENT, called chlorolabe, can be measured in the eye of a protanope, the name given to a person who is red-blind. The pigment in the fovea of a protanope is partially bleached with red light and the change in reflectivity is measured at six wavelengths (*small dots*). The reflectivity change is then measured after partial bleaching with blue-green light (*small squares*). Since the protanope's fovea responds in the same way to both bleaches, it evidently contains only one pigment. The two sets of measurements define the difference spectrum of chlorolabe. Bleaching with white light, which shows total pigment present, shifts the foveal reflectivity upward at each wavelength (*larger squares and dots*). White-bleaching measurements coincide well with measurements of the protanope's sensitivity to white light (*colored curve*), made by F. H. G. Pitt of Imperial College. Still another way to measure bleaching, described in text, defines the "action spectrum" (*triangles*). It also supports the view that cones of the protanope contain one pigment.

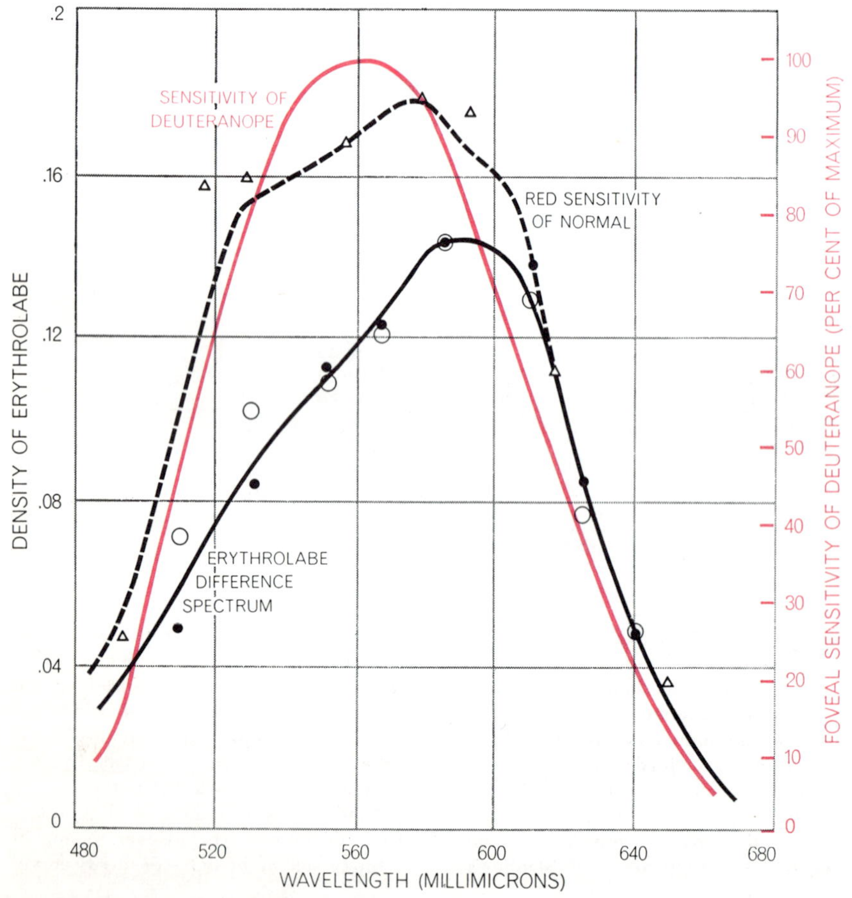

RED-CATCHING PIGMENT, erythrolabe, can be measured in the eye of a deuteranope, a person who is green-blind. The experiments are similar to those performed on the protanope. The black dots show the change in reflectivity of the fovea after partial bleaching with red light, the open circles after partial bleaching with blue-green light. The curve fitted to the two sets of circles is the difference spectrum of erythrolabe, the single visual pigment in the foveal cones of the deuteranope. The erythrolabe difference spectrum, however, does not coincide well with measurements by Pitt showing the deuteranope's sensitivity to white light (*colored curve*). This suggests that erythrolabe forms a colored photoproduct when bleached, which reduces foveal reflectivity below the values expected. The efficacy of bleaching as measured by the action spectrum comes closer to matching the deuteranope's visual sensitivity. It also agrees well with the sensitivity of the normal eye to red light alone (*broken curve*).

two lights of different wavelength composition will appear identical if they are scaled in intensity so that both are equally absorbed by rhodopsin. By the same token it should be possible to scale the intensity of two lights of different composition so that they will be absorbed equally by any one cone pigment. To that pigment the two lights would appear to have the same color. The scaling that will deceive the red pigment, however, will be detected by the green and blue pigments. It needs rather careful adjustment of two different color mixtures if they are to match; that is, if they are to deceive all three cone pigments at the same time. When this is achieved, the two inputs to the eye are in fact identical, and no one—not even Land—has the magic to show as different what all three cone pigments agree is the same.

Now we see why color matches are stable although color appearances change. Matches depend simply on the wavelength and intensity of light striking the three pigments and on the absorption spectra of these three chemicals. But appearances are subject to the whole complex of nervous interaction, not only between cone and cone in the retina but also between sensation and preconception in the mind. Let us therefore leave the rarefied atmosphere of color appearance and return to the solid ground of cone pigments.

If the cones contain three visual pigments, it should be possible to detect them and measure some of their properties by the method described for rhodopsin. To be sure, the human retina, like that of the frog, contains such a preponderance of rhodopsin that it is hard to measure anything else. Fortunately the fovea, that precious central square millimeter of the retina that we use for reading, contains no rods. It is also deficient in blue cones. Therefore if pigment-absorption measurements are confined to this tiny area, they should reveal the properties of just the red and green cones. One can simplify even further.

The common red-green color blindness is of two kinds: in one the color-blind individual is red-blind, in the other he is not. It turns out that the first individual lacks the red-sensitive pigment and that the second lacks the green-sensitive pigment. Therefore by measuring the fovea of the red-blind person, or protanope, we obtain information about the green-sensitive pigment only. The results of an analysis of this kind are set forth in the top illustration on the opposite page.

It will be recollected that what we do is to adjust the wedge so that the output of the photocell is the same after bleaching as it was before. For the protanope experiment we use a gray wedge and express this displacement in terms of the corresponding change in optical density of the cone pigment. Since light passes through the pigment twice, once on entering and once on returning, measurements indicate a "double density" of pigment. Such measurements, made in lights of six wavelengths, are shown by the squares and dots in the illustration. The change in the reflectivity of the fovea, caused by bleaching, is maximal when measured with light that has a wavelength of 540 millimicrons and diminishes on each side. The small squares represent change in the reflectivity after bleaching with blue-green light; the small dots, after bleaching with very bright red light. These changes define a curve that we call a difference spectrum. The fact that both curves coincide means that there is only one pigment present. If there had been a mixture, the more red-sensitive of the two would have shown a greater change after bleaching with red light; the other, after bleaching with blue-green light. A second series of measurements made after bleaching with a bright white light shows the total pigment present.

To discover whether or not this photosensitive pigment is indeed the basis of cone vision in the protanope we apply the test discussed earlier for rhodopsin. We simply ask: Does the spectral absorption coincide with the spectral sensitivity? The colored curve in the top illustration on the facing page shows how the cone sensitivity of the protanope does in fact correspond to the absorption measurements. We may conclude, therefore, that the protanope in daylight sees by this pigment, which is called chlorolabe, after the Greek words for "green-catching."

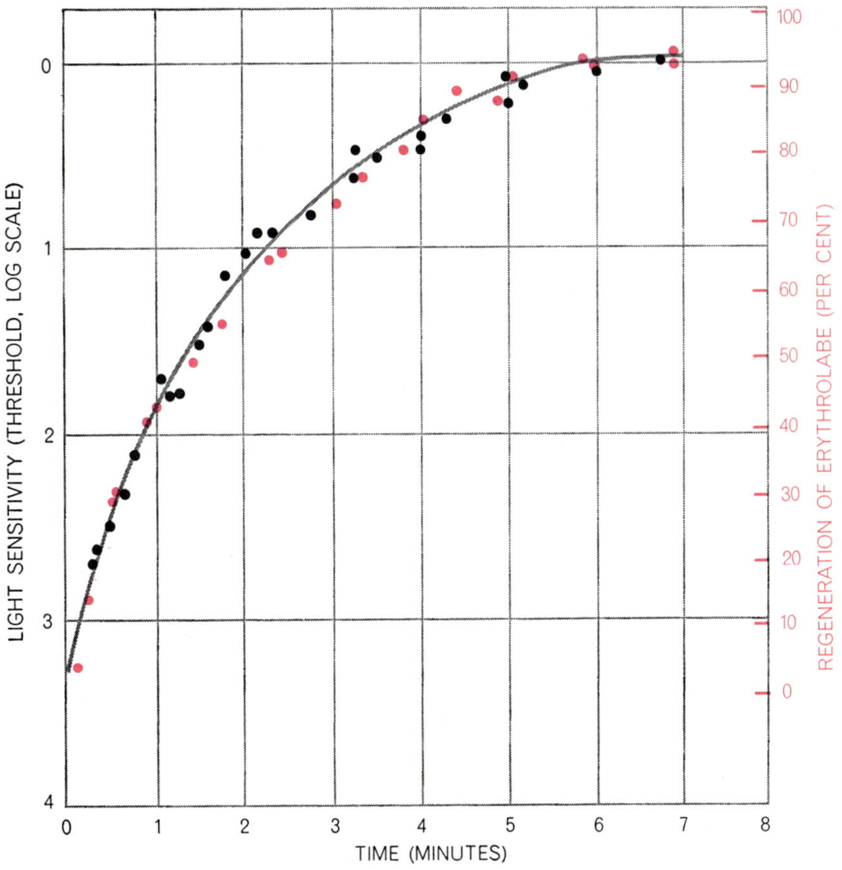

LIGHT SENSITIVITY AND REGENERATION OF ERYTHROLABE follow the same time course. The black dots show how the deuteranope's fovea becomes increasingly sensitive to brief flashes of light as the eye becomes dark-adapted. The colored dots are separate measurements made after the erythrolabe has been fully bleached. They show that the foveal pigment regenerates in seven minutes. The coincidence of the two sets of measurements implies that cones, like rods, have dark adaptation linked to pigment regeneration.

The other type of color-blind person, lacking chlorolabe, is known as a deuteranope. That he also has a single foveal pigment is established by the similar change in foveal reflectivity produced by either deep red light or blue-green light, as shown in the bottom illustration on page 110. It is plain that this pigment, which is called erythrolabe ("red-catching"), has a difference spectrum extending much further into the red than chlorolabe. If erythrolabe is the pigment that catches the light by which the deuteranope sees, he ought to be able to see further into the red end of the spectrum than the protanope can. This indeed is the case, but it is also apparent that the difference spectrum of chlorolabe does not coincide too well with the spectral sensitivity of the deuteranope, shown by the colored curve. Therefore the matter needs to be studied further.

If erythrolabe is the cone pigment of the deuteranope, lights of various wavelengths adjusted in intensity so that each appears equally bright to the deuteranope ought also to prove equivalent in the rate at which they bleach erythrolabe. Measurements of bleaching efficacy for lights of various wavelengths produce an "action spectrum," shown by triangles in the two illustrations on page 110. It can be seen in the bottom illustration that the action spectrum coincides reasonably well with the sensitivity of the deuteranope and also with the sensitivity of the red mechanism in the normal eye, shown by the broken curve. Thus there is fair agreement between sensitivity and bleaching power, and erythrolabe has a strong claim as the visual pigment of the deuteranope and of the normal red color mechanism.

It is also possible to measure the time required for the erythrolabe in the deuteranope's fovea to regenerate after bleaching. The curve in the illustration at the left resembles that for rhodopsin but rises about four times faster. It can be seen that the light sensitivity of the deuteranope, also plotted, increases precisely in step with the return of erythrolabe. So we are reasonably confident that erythrolabe is the pigment with which the deuteranope catches light.

Now we are in a position to prove that the normal fovea contains both green-sensitive chlorolabe and red-sensitive erythrolabe. The pertinent measurements are shown in the illustration below. The black dots show the bleaching produced by deep red light, and it is evident that they define a curve identical to the difference spectrum of erythrolabe, as measured in the deuteranope.

If in the deuteranope we changed the bleaching light from red to blue-green, no alteration would occur, since both lights bleach the deuteranope's single pigment equally. But when blue-green light is used to bleach the normal eye, one discovers that additional bleaching takes place, which cannot be attributed to erythrolabe. This additional bleaching is shown by the open circles in the illustration. Since no change in erythrolabe can contribute to this increment, it must represent the pure change in a second pigment in the normal eye. To see if this pigment is chlorolabe we draw on the same chart the difference spectrum of chlorolabe, as measured in the protanope, and we find that it closely follows the open circles. Thus the normal fovea is seen to contain both erythrolabe and chlorolabe.

A person with normal color vision can distinguish colors in the red-orange-yellow-green range of the spectrum because all of these colors affect the pigments erythrolabe and chlorolabe in different proportions. In this range protanopes and deuteranopes have only the one, or only the other, of these pigments; hence they have no more means of distinguishing these colors by day than a person with normal vision has by night. They can see only one color because they have only one pigment.

The reader will ask: What about the blues? Is there a "blue-catcher"—a cyanolabe—to complete the triad of cone pigments? I think there is, but it is much harder than the others to measure and there is not much at present to be said about it.

Practically all the ideas in this article have been entertained long ago by acute investigators; they have also often been disputed. What the measurement of pigments in man has done is to bring some degree of exactness and security to ideas that were enticing but speculative. The precision of measurement, however, lies not in the investigator who turns the knobs but in the subjects who sit with clamped head and fixed eye gazing steadfastly 20 minutes at a time through flashing and gloom. These are my students, some normal, some color-blind—volunteers from the classes in physiology in the University of Cambridge.

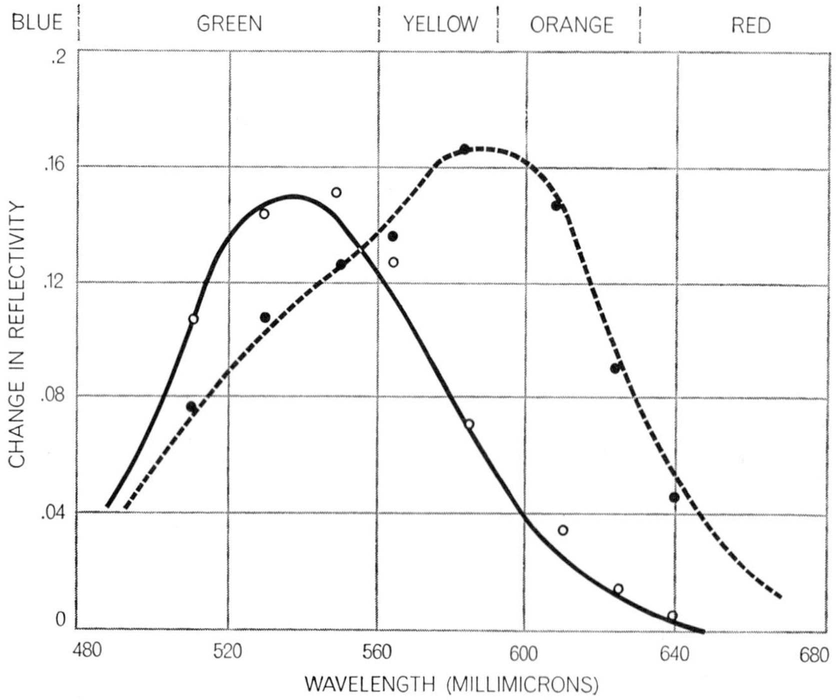

TWO PIGMENTS IN NORMAL CONES are demonstrated by bleaching the eye with deep red light, then with blue-green light and recording the change in reflectivity of the fovea at eight wavelengths. Bleaching with red light gives the results shown by black dots and coincides with the erythrolabe difference spectrum *(broken curve)* found in the deuteranope *(see bottom illustration on page 110)*. When the bleaching light is blue-green, the reflectivity of the fovea increases beyond that observed when the bleach is red. The additional reflectivity is shown by open circles and conforms to the difference spectrum of chlorolabe *(solid curve)*, as measured in the protanope *(see top illustration on page 110)*.

III

PHYSIOLOGICAL ANALYZERS

III

PHYSIOLOGICAL ANALYZERS

INTRODUCTION

Perhaps the most fundamental property of sensory and perceptual mechanisms is that they respond better to changes of input and to new events than to relatively monotonous occurrences in the environment. When one's hand is immersed and held still in a tub of water, for example, the most obvious sensations are first a change in temperature and then the surface ripple of the water against the skin. It is the transitions that are most striking, not the uniform pressure of the water beneath the surface. Analogous effects may be observed in all modalities: the steady hum of an air conditioner eventually fades away and is lost, until the unit is switched off and the hum suddenly becomes conspicuous by its absence; perfumes and scents that may be detectable in the tiniest concentrations when we first smell them tend to fade into the background after prolonged exposure; or a change in illumination from sunlight to incandescent lighting indoors, which, although it will be noted by the human visual system as a change, will be ignored so that the colors and brightnesses of objects appear unchanged. These are examples of the power of the most primitive analyzing mechanism: lateral inhibition.

The basic features of lateral inhibition in neural networks are the same for a wide range of species, as is obvious from the articles by Donald Kennedy ("Inhibition in Visual Systems") and William H. Miller, Floyd Ratliff, and H. K. Hartline ("How Cells Receive Stimuli"). Because these articles deal exclusively with visual systems, it is not immediately apparent that exactly the same mechanisms also appear in the cutaneous (skin), auditory, and gustatory modalities. Thus, in Figure 1, which depicts the contrast-sensitive ganglion cells in the cat's retina, the visual receptors (cones) could be replaced by the hair cells of the organ of corti, or the receptors of the skin, and the description would be appropriate for the auditory or the cutaneous

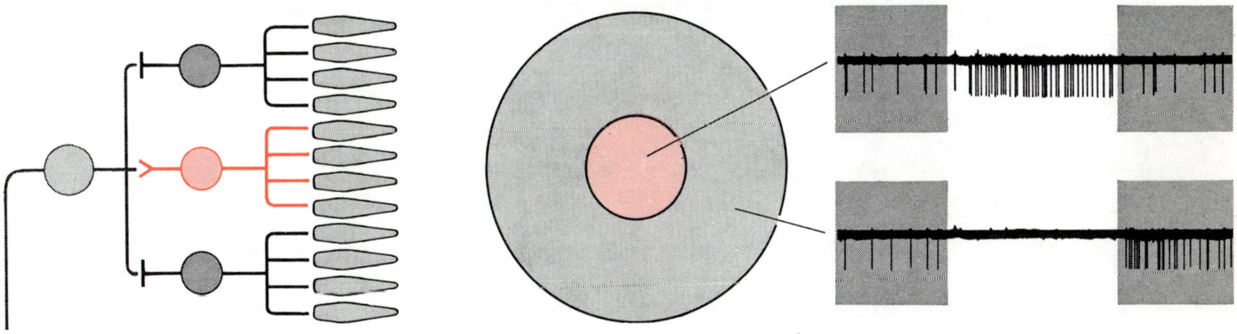

Figure 1. Contrast-sensitive ganglion cells in the cat's retina have fields with a concentric organization. The oscilloscope records _(right)_ show that a spot of light in the center of the receptive field _(middle)_ of this "on"-center ganglion cell excites the cell; stimulation of the surround inhibits it. (The responses would be reversed if this were an "off"-center cell.) Presumably there are two types of bipolar cell, excitatory _(color)_ and inhibitory _(black)_, that collect information from receptors in the two parts of the field _(left)_. [From "Retinal Processing of Visual Images," by Charles R. Michael, _Scientific American_, May 1969.]

Figure 2. In Spillmann's illusion, light regions are seen at the intersections of dark bars on a light background and dark regions are seen at the intersections of light bars on a dark background. Note that the illusion may disappear as the distance of the pattern from the eye is changed. The optimal visual angle of the bars is somewhere between 6 and 18 minutes of arc, suggesting that the excitatory region of human receptive fields is of this magnitude near the fovea. [From "Contrast Enhancement in a Hermann Grid with a Variable Figure–Ground Ratio," by L. Spillmann and J. Levine, *Experimental Brain Research*, Vol. 13, 1971.]

senses, respectively. Lateral inhibition in each of these sense modalities also serves a similar function—namely, to enhance contours or differences and to ignore uniform fields or steady-state activities.

The effects of lateral interactions may be understood most easily by considering the behavior of a simple "on–off" unit, as found in the cat's retina. In 1953, while recording from a ganglion cell, Stephen Kuffler found that a light stimulus that illuminated a region of the retina above the cell had two different effects, depending upon the exact position of the illuminated portion of the retina. When the receptors directly above the ganglion cell were illuminated, the cell responded with a burst of activity, whereas light falling on the surrounding region shut the cell off. However, once the light was removed from the surrounding region, the cell would fire briefly. Such a cell was identified as an "on-center–off-surround" unit. Other cells were found with reciprocal properties.

When such "on–off" cells are exposed to an edge or a step of light, they will be either excited or inhibited, depending upon whether the central part of the field of the cell lies on the bright or dark side of the edge. However, when the entire field of the "on–off" cell lies on one side of the edge—either the bright or the dim side—the cell will not fire. When such a cell lies entirely on the bright side of the edge, both its central (excitatory) region and the surrounding (inhibitory) region will be activated equally, cancelling each other. Thus, the ganglion cell will not respond to a uniform field. Instead, the strongest stimulus for an "on-center–off-surround" ganglion cell would be a bright central disc of light surrounded by a black annulus. Of course, in order for it to obtain the optimal stimulus, it is important that the disc of light just match the size of the central, excitatory region of the cell's receptive field. Figure 2, which was designed by Lothar Spillmann, may be used to estimate the size of these excitatory regions in the human eye.

Mechanisms of lateral inhibition similar to that found in the eye also appear in the auditory and cutaneous modalities, sharpening the senses of pitch and touch. Fibers may be found along the auditory pathway that respond only to bands of sound frequencies whose half bandwidths are less than an octave. Yet it is obvious from von Békésy's article on the ear in Section II that an acoustic stimulus causes a large displacement of the basilar membrane, which, in fact, innervates almost all of the underlying hair cells. The explanation proposed by von Békésy was that the activities of the hair cells would reciprocally inhibit one another in such a manner that only the most active channel would survive inhibition by its neighbors. In this manner, the diffuse and shallow gradients of neural activity would cancel one another out, leaving only the activities of cells in the regions of the steepest gradients and rates of change. Because the position of the steepest gradient moves along the basilar membrane as the frequency of the auditory signal is changed, the neural signals not filtered out by inhibition will accurately reflect the frequency of the stimulus tone.

A similar effect occurs on the skin. If a small probe is vibrated on the arm, the skin will be distorted not only at the point of impact of the probe, but also on the opposite side of the arm. The wave of distortion may actually encompass the entire circumference of the arm, and yet be felt only at the point of impact. Once again, the neural network enhances the sharpest stimulus gradient, which is located in the region nearest the probe, and inhibits the activities of the surrounding receptors, which are stimulated less fully. The mechanism is the same as in the visual system: inhibition between adjacent neural channels.

The examples of lateral inhibition cited above, as well as those described in the articles by Kennedy and Miller, Ratliff, and Hartline, are mainly examples of inhibition leading to the enhancement of contrast. Such inhibitory effects are generally not directional—in fact, they may be quite diffuse and disordered and still function effectively. Once directionality is imposed upon the nature of lateral inhibition, however, then the subsequent neural unit may become more specialized, responding to a smaller class of stimuli. Consider, for example, the model for directional selectivity to movement shown in Charles R. Michael's article "Retinal Processing of Visual Images" on page 143. Here, the inhibition of the receptor activities is communicated from right to left via a horizontal cell. Because the intermediate horizontal cell also interposes a time delay, the activity reaching the ganglion cell depends upon the sequence in which the receptors are activated. The result is a "motion detector," whereby the ganglion cell will respond only to stimuli moving opposite to the direction of lateral inhibition.

Inhibitory networks whose structure is still more elaborate, such as those having neurons activated specifically by lines of different lengths and orientation, are described in detail by David H. Hubel in his article "The Visual Cortex of the Brain." These classic studies provide extensive insight into the specificity of connections necessary to create high-level neural analyzers. Hubel and his colleague T. N. Wiesel proposed that, by cascading feature extractions performed at one level with subsequent neural interactions at the next, a group of the simple "on–off" retinal cells discovered by Kuffler may together constitute a line detector in the cortex. Such cascading of outputs requires the preservation of spatial order and suggests a hierarchical organization of building blocks for feature extraction.

Cascades of feature analysis may occur simultaneously along several parallel channels in the brain. Of what advantage is such parallel processing? One answer is suggested by the article "Vision in Frogs." In this article, W. R. A. Muntz reviews some of the simple analyzing mechanisms found in the visual pathways of these animals. Two mechanisms are particularly apparent: one that analyzes movement and a second that analyzes spectral composition or color. Muntz takes pains to demonstrate that, depending upon the color of the object, the response of the frog will change; thus, different response patterns may be elicited by similar moving objects. It is important that, in each case, the abrupt presence of a particular feature (color or direction of movement) triggers a stereotyped response. Such a consistent relation between a given feature and a stereotyped response suggests that each feature analyzer may drive a different channel or pathway that, in turn, may set up or regulate a very complex pattern of motor activity. The frog is by no means unique in these respects, however: an analogous anatomical separation between channels for color vision and channels for movement detection in the ground squirrel is discussed by Michael in his article in this section. Thus, we see that two quite distant relatives have anatomically dissociated certain of their feature-extracting mechanisms, which, in the case of the frog, undoubtedly provides the basis for different stereotyped patterns of behavior. Is it possible that the anatomical dissociation of simple analyzing mechanisms is universal, and that these separate feature-extracting mechanisms also trigger stereotyped patterns of behavior in man?

REFERENCES

Barlow, H. B., & Levick, W. R. The mechanism of directionally selective units in rabbit's retina. *Journal of Physiology*, 1965, **178**, 477–504.

Brindley, G. S. *Physiology of the retina and the visual pathways.* (2nd ed.) London: Edward Arnold, 1970.

Granit, R. The visual pathway. In H. Davson (Ed.), *The eye.* Vol. II. *The visual processes.* New York: Academic Press, 1962.

Gray, J. A. B. Initiation of impulses at reception. In American Physiological Society, *Handbook of physiology.* Section I. *Neurophysiology.* Vol. II. Baltimore, Md.: Williams & Wilkins, 1959.

Hubel, D. H., & Wiesel, T. N. Receptive fields, binocular interaction and functional architecture in the cat's visual cortex. *Journal of Physiology*, 1962, **160**, 106–154.

Hubel, D. H., & Wiesel, T. N. Receptive fields and functional architecture of monkey striate cortex. *Journal of Physiology*, 1968, **195**, 215–243.

Kuffler, S. W. Discharge patterns and functional organization of mammalian retina. *Journal of Neurophysiology*, 1953, **16**, 37–68.

Michael, C. R. Receptive fields of single optic nerve fibers in a mammal with an all-cone retina. *Journal of Neurophysiology*, 1968, **31**, 249–282.

Rosenblith, W. A. (Ed.) *Sensory communications.* New York: John Wiley & Sons, 1961.

12

INHIBITION IN VISUAL SYSTEMS

DONALD KENNEDY
July 1963

The familiar analogy of the eye to the camera serves nicely to describe the physical basis of vision. It does not, however, begin to present a complete picture of the physiology of vision now emerging from comparative studies of the visual organs of mammals, insects and other arthropods and lower invertebrates. The simplistic physical model suggests that the image-forming eye acts as a straightforward transducer of the energy of light, converting a pattern of light inputs into a matching pattern of electrical energy in the form of nerve impulses. This does not account for the fact that the retina produces nerve impulses in response to shadows as well. Nor does it explain the performance of the light-receptors of certain aquatic organisms. A feather worm living in its tube in the crevice of a rock in a Pacific tide pool, or a clam with its siphon peeping unprotected from its open shell, may care little what time dawn comes or what the neighborhood looks like. But any sedentary, bottom-dwelling aquatic animal has a variety of reasons for being concerned about shadows. To such an animal a shadow may represent a cruising predator, a potential meal or even—for some fresh-water mollusks—an inviting host for the strings of parasitic larvae the organism is ready to extrude on demand. If a receptor is to respond to shadows, it must be, in a real functional sense, the opposite of a light-receptor: it must respond to the onset of darkness.

The photoreceptors of this odd assortment of animals do not look much like eyes. Investigation of their physiology, however, has produced some unexpected dividends. In addition to explaining the sensory basis of some interesting behavior, this work has had a bearing on two general aspects of vision. The first is the growing realization that in many animals nerve cells—although often responsible for other functions—may be brought into service as light-receptors by being equipped with an appropriate photosensitive pigment. The second involves the question of how such rudimentary receptors serve as "shadow-sensitive" visual organs. Since they must necessarily function in response to the input of light—not to the "input" of darkness—it may be postulated that in some cases at least the energy of light might cause the discharge of nerve impulses to be inhibited and then, upon termination of the stimulus, to be released as an effective signal. Just such an "off-receptor" has been found in some mollusks.

The demonstration of this mechanism in a mollusk lends the "off-response" an unexpected universality and illuminates its importance in higher visual systems.

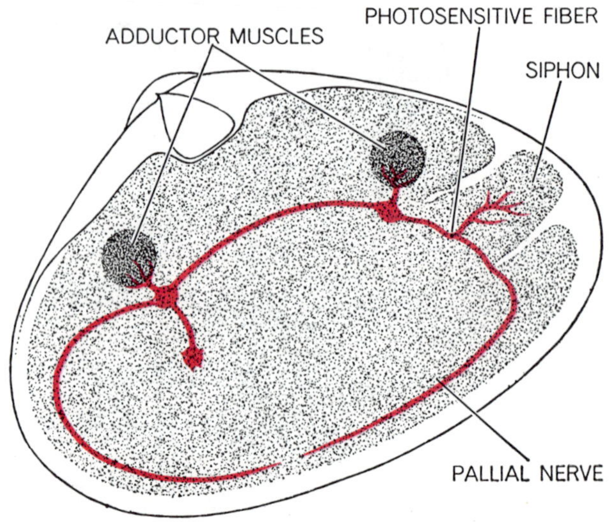

SURF CLAM (*Spisula*) abruptly withdraws its siphon and closes its shell (*left*) when a shadow passes over it. A photosensitive fiber in the pallial nerve at the base of the siphon (*right*) seems to mediate this response, which is fairly common among mollusks.

In the case of the mammalian eye it is now well established that some single fibers of the optic nerve, which conducts impulses from the eye to the brain, discharge impulses when illumination of the retina ceases. This signal is mediated by an interesting linkage in the circuitry of the retina itself. Each fiber of the optic nerve collects impulses from a receptive field that occupies a circle of retina about one millimeter in diameter, an area containing several thousand receptor cells. Activity generated in the receptor cells converges, through intermediate neurons called bipolar cells, on the neurons that form the optic nerve. The kinds of connections they make with one another depend on their location in the receptive field. In some receptive fields the center, when stimulated with a tiny patch of light, produces discharges in the optic nerve at "on"; the periphery produces discharges only when the stimulus is extinguished, or at "off." Stimulation of the peripheral zone simultaneously with the center produces both on- and off-discharges but at diminished frequency [*see top illustration on page 123*]. In essence the evidence indicates that interaction of the retinal nerve cells blocks the on-discharges from some of the light-receptors by inhibition at the synaptic junctions between the cells; the generation of off-discharges in response to a shadow results from the release of inhibition in these cells. This interaction of the retinal cells plays a vital role in the perception of movement across the visual field, in the accentuation of contrast and in the perception of shape. The off-discharge in the visual apparatus of certain mollusks arises, as will be seen, from a quite different and perhaps simpler mechanism, but the ability to "see" shadows plays a no less vital role in their life history.

Much of the work in this field stems from the original achievement of H. K. Hartline of the Rockefeller Institute, who in 1932 was the first to record impulses from single optic nerve fibers in the vertebrate eye. More recently, with his colleagues Floyd Ratliff and William H. Miller, he has shown how the responses of ommatidia, or single elements, in the compound eye of the horseshoe crab, *Limulus,* are integrated to furnish this animal with an impressively detailed view of its environment. Each ommatidium in the *Limulus* eye contains a group of eight retinula cells, which, when illuminated, evoke discharges in a single, large eccentric cell. A single independent channel of information—the eccentric cell axon—passes from each ommatidium to the brain. Each axon is connected, however, to many of its neighbors in a network of circuits located just below the bases of the ommatidia. These connections are inhibitory; activity in each ommatidium tends to suppress that in adjoining ones in much the same way as parts of the retinal receptive field in vertebrates inhibit other regions. By appropriately varying the geometry of the stimulus and the conditions of illumination Hartline and his colleagues have been able to synthesize discharges from single *Limulus* axons that mimic with remarkable fidelity the "off" and "on-off" discharges found in many vertebrate optic nerve fibers [see "How Cells Receive Stimuli," by William H. Miller, Floyd Ratliff and H. K. Hartline, beginning on page 127].

The fruitfulness of this work with *Limulus* has stimulated a number of in-

SCALLOP (*Pecten*) has a row of bright blue eyes along the mantle edge of each shell. The eyes of this mollusk are similar in structure to the image-forming eyes of vertebrate animals.

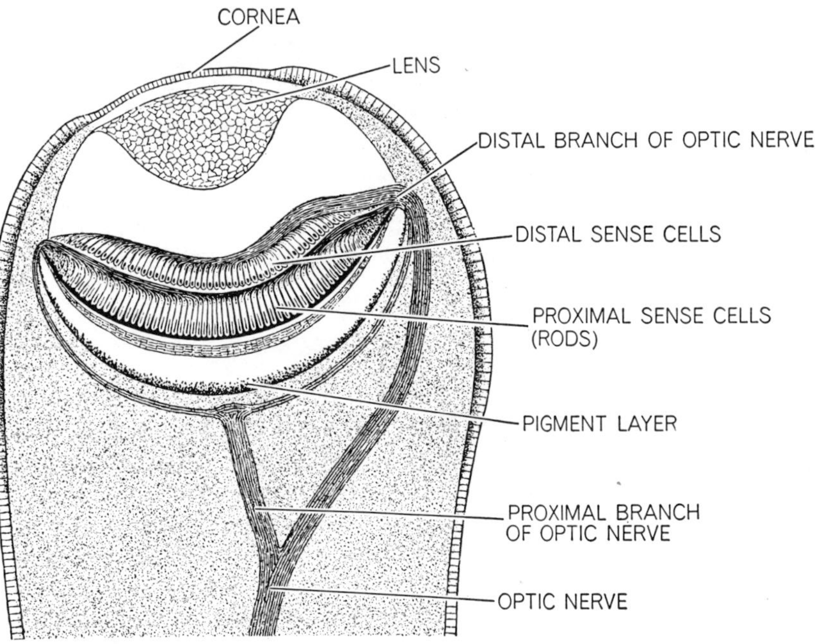

DETAIL OF SCALLOP EYE shows its peculiar double-layered retina. The proximal layer discharges impulses when illuminated; the distal layer discharges when illumination ceases.

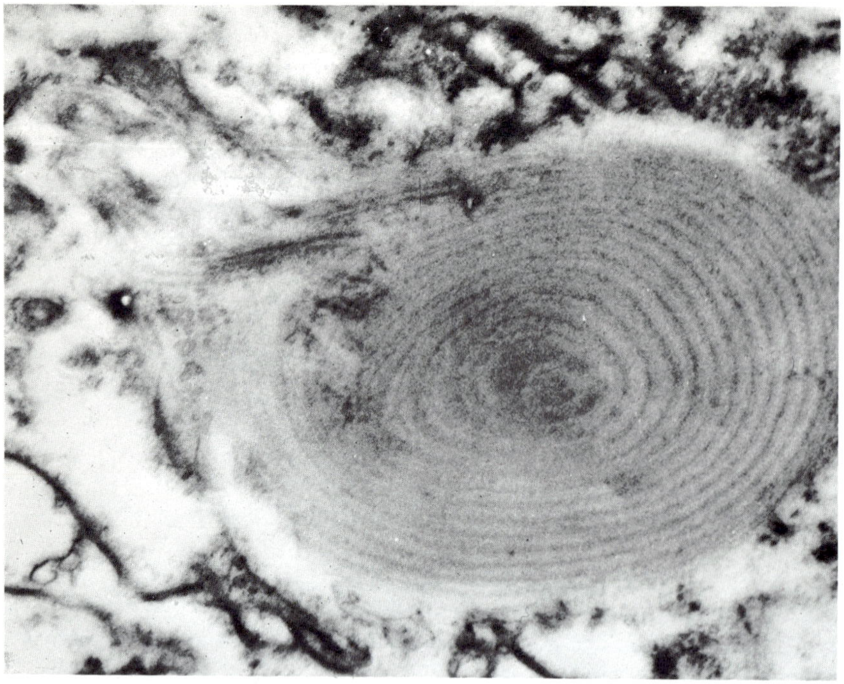

ELECTRON MICROGRAPH made in 1958 by William H. Miller of the Rockefeller Institute showed that the "shadow-sensitive" cells in the distal layer of the scallop retina are true photoreceptors. The large oval structure is an organelle located on the surface of a single distal cell. The small dark objects at the left are ciliary stalks, simpler structures from which the organelles are derived. This mode of construction is typical of many other photoreceptors, including the retinal rods of vertebrate eyes. Magnification is 20,000 diameters.

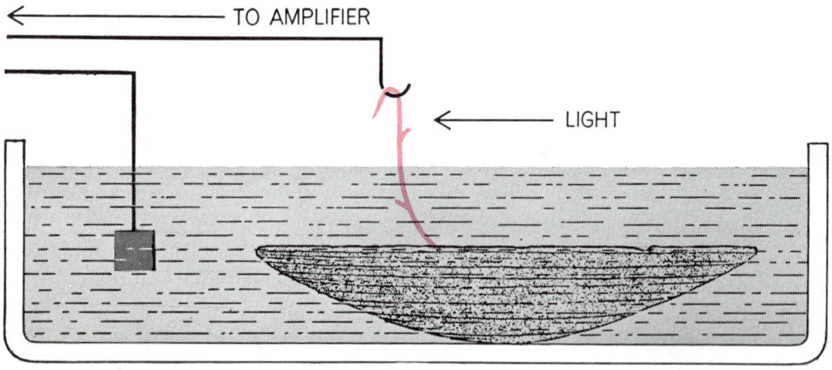

IMPULSES ARE MEASURED by excising one end of a *Spisula* pallial nerve and placing it across an electrode. Another electrode leads from the salt-water bath in which the clam is immersed. Impulses are amplified before being displayed on a cathode ray oscilloscope.

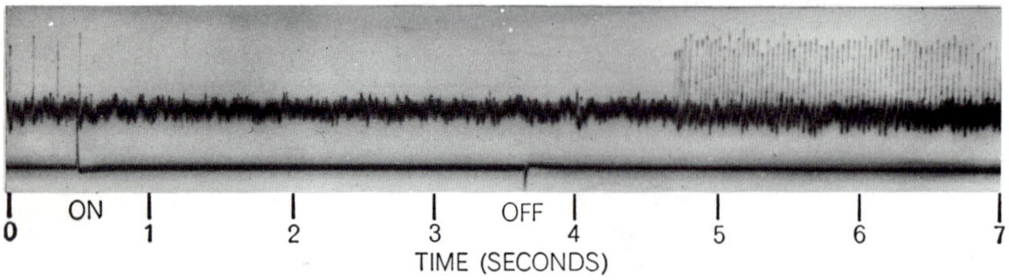

OSCILLOSCOPE TRACE obtained by the procedure described above reveals the effects of inhibition in the *Spisula* visual system. In the dark the photosensitive fiber of the pallial nerve discharges at a constant frequency of about five impulses per second. When the fiber is illuminated ("on"), this discharge ceases abruptly; shortly after the light is extinguished ("off"), a high-frequency burst of impulses (about 35 per second) passes through the fiber.

vestigators to look into the physiology of the simpler photoreceptors found in other marine invertebrates. My own particular interest in them has been to determine whether or not the "off" discharges generated by some of these primitive systems are organized in the same way as those of the vertebrate retina. A long history of investigation suggested that the bivalve mollusks were a good group in which to tackle this problem. Seventy years ago the German zoologist Wilibald A. Nagel observed that many mollusks showed pronounced reactions whenever shadows were passed over them: they would abruptly withdraw their siphons and close their valves. During the 1920's mollusks played a distinguished role in the development of understanding of the relation between photochemistry and visual response. The late Selig Hecht of Columbia University used the withdrawal response of *Mya*, the familiar soft-shell clam, to make several extraordinary predictions about the chemical processes involved in vision.

More recently, at the Marine Biological Laboratory in Woods Hole, Mass., and at Syracuse University, I have been attempting to learn something about the electrophysiological responses of the visual receptors of several species of clams including *Mya*. It proved fairly easy to record impulses in fine branches of the nerves from the siphon by the usual technique of placing them across electrodes and displaying the amplified "action potentials" on an oscilloscope. When the siphon was illuminated, grouped discharges of impulses occurred in a number of nerve fibers, both at "on" and at "off." These results were consistent with previous findings of multiple sensory endings, assumed to be photoreceptors, in the siphon well of *Mya*.

A surprise came, however, when the same kind of experiment was tried with the surf clam *Spisula*. From this bivalve, which exhibits particularly pronounced behavioral reactions to shadows, it was impossible to evoke any kind of discharge in the siphon nerves by illuminating the siphon—or anything else. But light did have a remarkable effect on the activity of a single nerve fiber of the pallial nerve. This nerve tract is a roughly circular one, passing around the edge of the mantle and past the base of the siphon into the visceral ganglion [*see illustration on page 120*]. The first observations, which were made on live clams with one end of the pallial nerve dissected for electrical recording, showed that in the dark a single nerve fiber in the tract discharges at a remarkably constant frequency of about five impulses per second. When the nerve was illuminated, the discharge ceased abruptly. When the light was turned off, however, or when a shadow passed over the animal, a high-frequency burst of impulses appeared in the fiber [*see bottom illustration on page 122*].

It was quickly established that this response is not mediated by sensory endings in the siphon, as in the case of *Mya;* instead a nerve cell in the pallial circuit seemed to act as the receptor. A segment of pallial trunk removed from the animal and tested in the same way was found to produce the response, whereas illumination of the siphon alone, or of neighboring tissues, failed to produce it in the intact animal. Clearly a part of the nervous system itself is involved in receiving the light energy and responding to it. It does so with a sensitivity that is impressive even when compared with that of much more highly organized receptors; the threshold for inhibiting the dark discharge of the neuron is about the same as that for stimulating the cone cells of the human retina.

Many kinds of nerve cells, when released from inhibition, give one or several quick "rebound" impulses. The off-response of the *Spisula* receptor neuron is so high in frequency and so long-lasting, however, that such an explanation seemed inadequate to account for it. A clue to the mechanism actually involved came from experiments in which colored lights of high spectral purity were employed to stimulate the receptor. When blue light was used, the off-discharges of impulses were weak or even entirely absent. Moreover, if the intensity of the blue light was high enough, it produced an inhibitory blockade that halted the resumption of the low-frequency beat of the nerve for a full minute or more after the stimulus was shut off. Stimulation by red light, on the other hand, produced very strong off-responses that lasted many seconds after the light was turned off and before the nerve resumed its regular output of five discharges per second. It appeared possible, therefore, that the whole response of the nerve cell was the sum of excitatory and inhibitory components, each one mediated by a different light-sensitive pigment. According to this hypothesis the inhibitory process was particularly sensitive to short (blue) wavelengths, whereas the excitatory process was more responsive to long (red) wavelengths. During exposure to

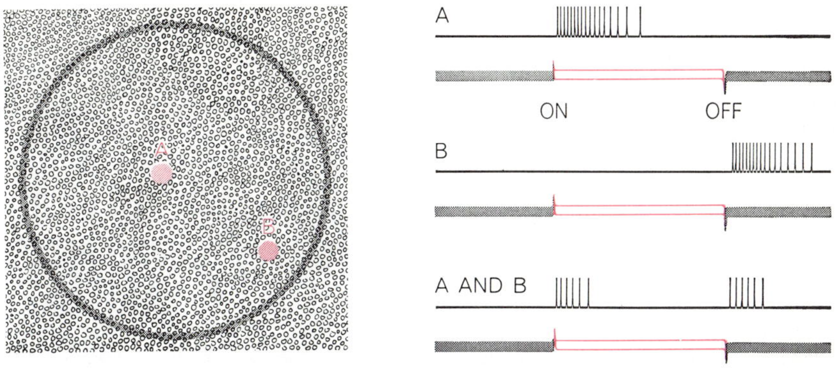

INHIBITION IN MAMMALIAN EYE is demonstrated in this schematic drawing of a small area on the surface of a cat's retina. The tiny open circles represent the tips of rods and cones, the photoreceptor cells of the retina. The large gray circle indicates the extent of the "receptive field" served by a single optic nerve fiber. This field is about one millimeter in diameter and contains several thousand receptor cells. When a beam of light is focused on receptors near the center of the field (*colored dot at A*), the fiber discharges a burst of impulses at "light on"; when the beam strikes receptors at the periphery of the field (*colored dot at B*), the fiber discharges at "light off." When the center and the periphery are illuminated simultaneously, mutual inhibition takes place in the network of neurons that connect the receptors to the optic fiber, causing diminished discharges at both "on" and "off."

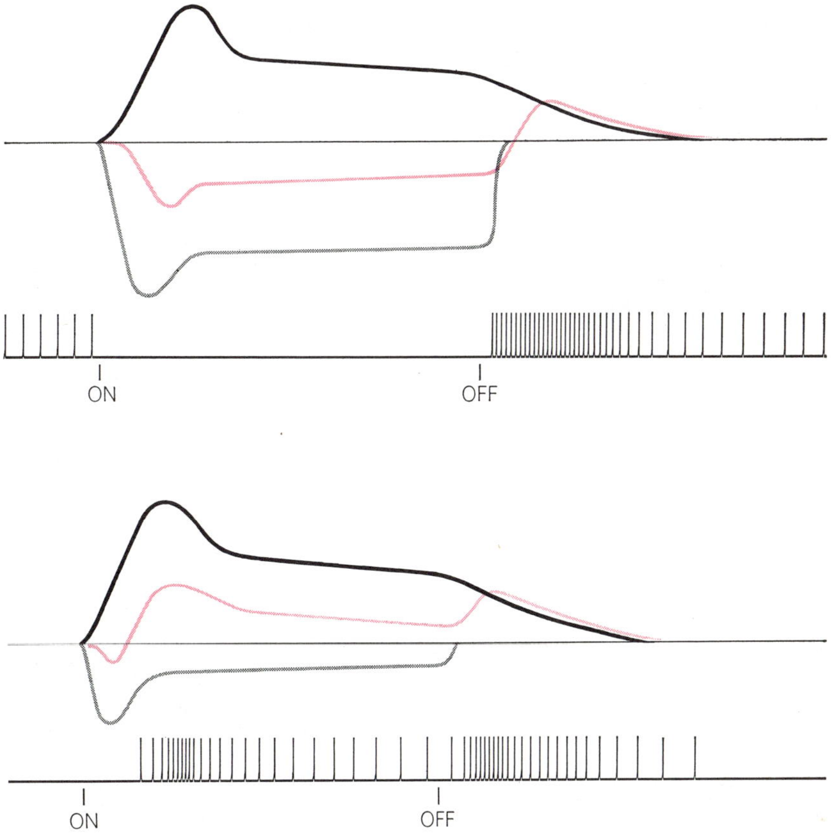

INHIBITION IN *SPISULA* PHOTORECEPTOR contributes to the characteristic "shadow response" of this mollusk. When the pallial nerve is illuminated with white light (*graph at top*), the inhibitory response (*gray curve*) dominates the excitatory response (*black curve*); the net sum of these two responses (*colored curve*) remains below the "firing threshold" (*horizontal line*) and no impulses are discharged during illumination. At "off," however, the slower-decaying excitatory response raises the net sum above the firing threshold, producing a high-frequency burst of impulses in the nerve. When the pallial nerve is illuminated with red light following prolonged preadaptation to blue (*graph at bottom*), the inhibitory response, mediated by the depleted blue pigment, is accordingly reduced and the net sum of the two responses produces bursts of impulses at both "on" and "off."

illumination the inhibitory process predominated; it decayed, however, more rapidly when the light was shut off, leaving a residual, slowly decaying excitation in its wake that produced the off-response [*see bottom illustration on page 123*]. In other words, firing of the neuron occurs only when the net sum of inhibitory and excitatory processes exceeds the firing level or threshold of the cell. These observations and deductions suggested that the inhibitory process in *Spisula* is mediated by a blue-sensitive pigment and the excitatory process by a red-sensitive one, with the two pigments overlapping considerably in absorption.

Support for this hypothetical scheme was obtained by taking advantage of the contrasting specificity of response shown by the nerve to wavelengths at opposite ends of the spectrum. All photosensitive pigments in the light-receptors of animals undergo a change when they absorb light; that is how they communicate excitation. This "bleaching" of the pigments, although reversible, can temporarily desensitize the receptor by reducing its supply of light-sensitive pigment. Thus in the familiar phenomenon of light adaptation our own eyes become less sensitive following exposure to intense illumination. By exposing the *Spisula* nerve to intense blue light for a minute or so, it was possible to reduce the inhibitory component, presumably by the bleaching of the blue-absorbing pigment. When the cell was now exposed to a red stimulus, it produced impulses at "light on" as well as at "light off." Within limits, the extent of the on-response to red light increased as the preadaptation to blue was lengthened. That the red wavelengths also excite the inhibitory process is demonstrated by the decay of the on-response under continued illumination. There seems no reason, therefore, to doubt that the off-discharge (or "shadow response") of the receptor neuron is a positive result of excitation remaining after the stimulus, although it is masked during the stimulus by a more sensitive inhibitory process. By selectively reducing the latter one reveals the former.

The neuron that produces the discharges recorded in these experiments is a single cell. What guarantee is there that these opposing processes are really taking place within this cell itself? Might it not be equally likely that the active cell is actually secondary, receiving and integrating primary neural messages from receptors or other nerve cells in which the inhibitory and excitatory events are segregated? Anatomical considerations suggest otherwise; the area of pallial nerve over which these responses may be produced by light is very small, and there is no evidence for the presence of any accessory receptors. Fixed, stained sections of the region do not reveal the required cluster of cells; usually a single nerve cell body appears—the likely, although not established, candidate for the photoreceptor element.

It is highly probable, then, that in the off-receptor of *Spisula* inhibition is a primary event, involving a kind of coupling between mechanisms of energy reception and transmission that is the reverse of the one usually associated with sense organs. There is another case, also involving a mollusk, in which a similar conclusion can be reached ex post facto. More than 20 years ago Hartline became interested in the strange photoreceptors of the scallop *Pecten*. These small eyes, bright blue in color,

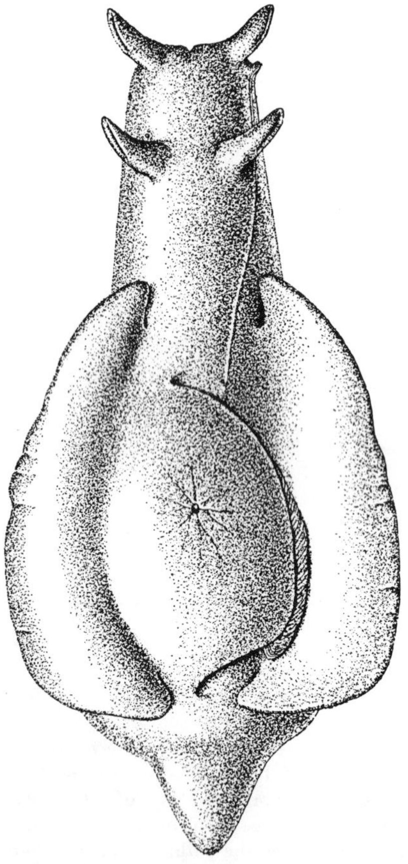

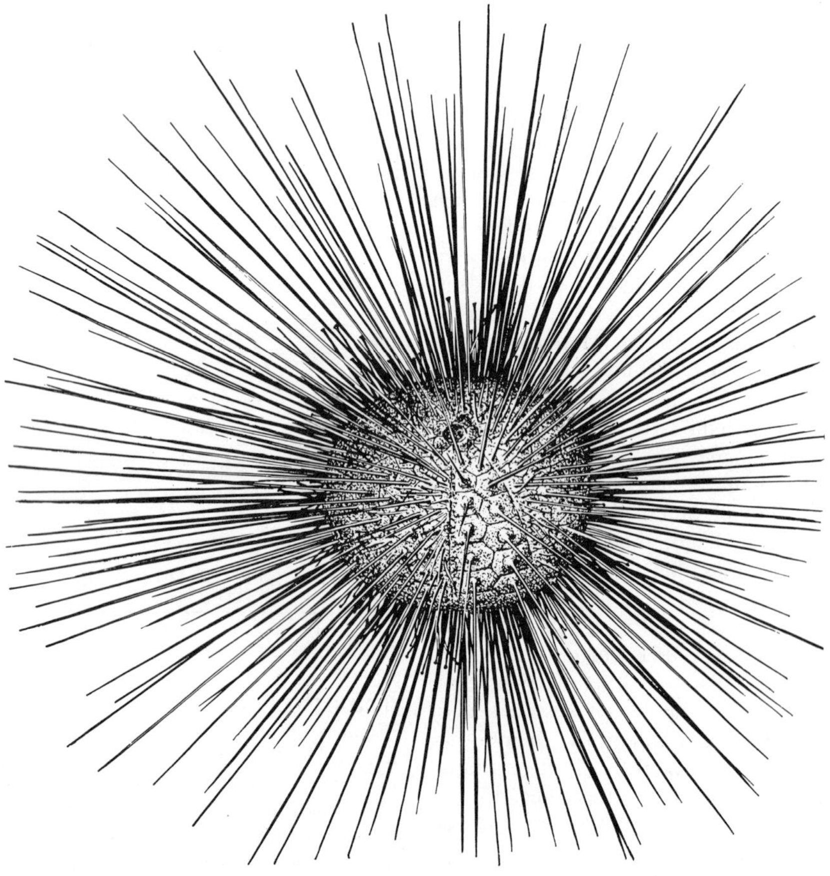

TWO MARINE INVERTEBRATES whose photoreceptive systems resemble that of *Spisula* are depicted. Neurons located within the central nervous system of the shell-less mollusk *Aplysia* (*left*) discharge impulses both at the onset and at the cessation of illumination. The long spines of the sea urchin *Diadema* (*right*) move in response to shadows falling across certain peripheral nerves.

stud the edge of the scallop's mantle; each one has a tiny lens, a reflecting pigment coat and a double-layered retina. Both layers contribute bundles of fibers to the optic nerve. Hartline was able to dissect single fibers from each set, and he showed that whereas those from the inner layer discharge impulses at "on," those from the outer layer respond only to shadows. At the time it was not possible to decide whether the outer layer was truly made up of receptor cells or whether instead it consisted of a layer of second-order nerve cells. Electron micrographs made recently at the Rockefeller Institute by Miller, however, seem to answer the question. They show clearly that the outer layer is composed of primary sensory cells, which contain the typical lamellar organelles characteristic of all other photoreceptors. It is hard to avoid the conclusion that in this case too inhibition—and shadow responses—are the primary result of the absorption of light energy by the receptor. In *Limulus* or mammalian retinas, in contrast, inhibition arises as a secondary effect through the interaction of receptor cells, all of which produce on-discharges.

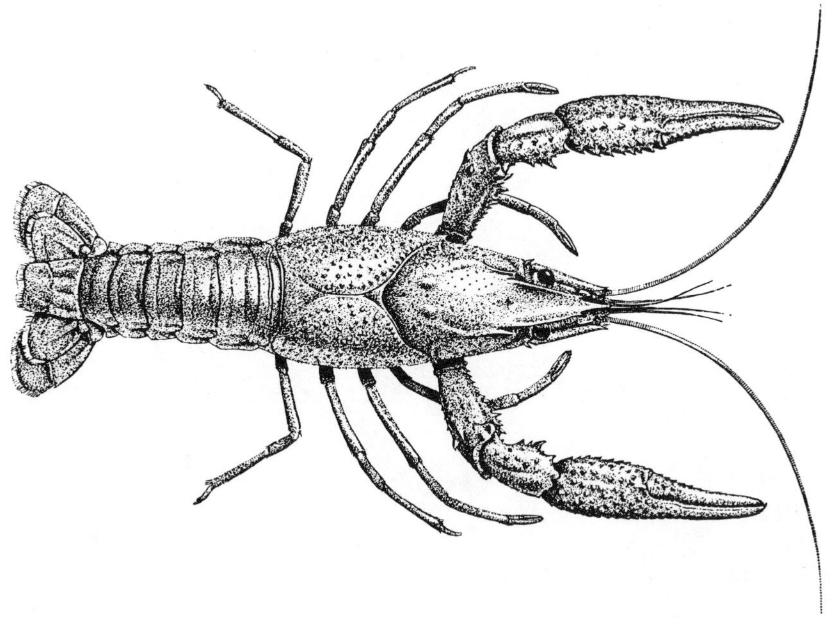

CRAYFISH (*Cambarus*) has, in addition to its typical arthropod eyes, two photosensitive nerve fibers located near the under surface of its segmented abdomen. Light passing through the translucent exoskeleton activates a pair of neurons in the last abdominal ganglion; these also serve as relays for impulses originating in the sensory hairs of the tail.

It is significant in connection with the evolution of vision that the receptor element in *Spisula* is a nerve cell. The idea that neurons—and other "excitable" cells—can respond to light is not new. In their laboratories at Lyons and in Monaco, A. Arvanitaki and her husband, N. Chalazonitis, have found that in the mollusk *Aplysia,* as in *Spisula* and others, neurons within central ganglia often possess a rich variety of intracellular pigments. Some of these neurons change the frequency of spontaneously discharged impulses when they are illuminated. In certain cells the effect is excitatory; in others light appears to reduce the impulse frequency. Such findings form a kind of precedent for the operation of the photoreceptor system I have described. It may be that *Spisula* has merely taken advantage of a general property of its neurons by moving one to the periphery, making it more sensitive and using it as a functional receptor.

If this has happened in one mollusk, why not in others? It would be of great advantage if receptors could be found that combine the accessibility and large size of the *Aplysia* neurons and the interesting sensory properties of the *Spisula* cell. In such a system one might hope to correlate impulse discharge (or the lack of it) with those local changes in membrane potential that are known to control the generation of conducted impulses in nerve cells. We are hopeful that the right organisms have now been found: John Barth of our laboratory at Stanford University has succeeded in recording with microelectrodes from inside single receptor neurons in the eyespots of several species of Pacific coast nudibranchs. These gastropod mollusks have no shell; their eyespots sit above the brain, and they generally consist of a tiny lens with a cluster of a dozen or more large nerve cells beneath it. The cells may depolarize and fire impulses when the light goes on, just as primary sensory cells from a variety of other systems do. In some cases, however, they exhibit complex changes in membrane potential, including increases as well as decreases. When increases in membrane potential occur, the cells are inhibited from discharging spikes; and in some cells the interaction of these opposite effects produces off-responses much like those in *Spisula.* Like *Spisula,* some nudibranchs also show pronounced behavioral responses to shadows. Barth is now working out the wavelength dependence of these responses.

Light sensitivity on the part of neurons raises a still more interesting prospect. It may be that photosensitivity is not the unique endowment of highly specialized receptor cells with a complex fine structure but a much more basic property. In the sea urchin *Diadema,* for example, N. Millott of the University of London has shown that the spine movements with which the animal responds to shadows are elicited only when the stimuli fall directly on certain peripheral nerves.

At Stanford we have also been working on certain neurons in the ventral nerve cord of the crayfish. Although these cells function as perfectly conventional interneurons, relaying impulses to the brain from mechanically sensitive receptors on the tail, they have the additional function of responding to light that falls on the last abdominal ganglion through the translucent exoskeleton. Thus the same element serves as a second-order unit for one sensory system and as a primary receptor for another. Only one nerve fiber in each half of the nerve cord exhibits these responses; we are now able to isolate the specific fiber by fine dissection from the nerve. The endowment of photosensitivity is no "accident"; in every case the same interneuron (in terms of its other functions) serves as the photoreceptor.

Nor does this complete the list of excitable cells that show "incidental" photosensitivity. The heart muscle of certain snails, muscle fibers in the pupil of many vertebrates, the brain cells of some insects, and even smooth-muscle cells from the walls of arterioles in mammalian skin are all light-sensitive. The ubiquity of this property, surely only partly represented by our present inventory, may perhaps urge physiologists to look for relations between normal pigmented constituents of cells and the important events that lead to the excitation of nerve and muscle membranes.

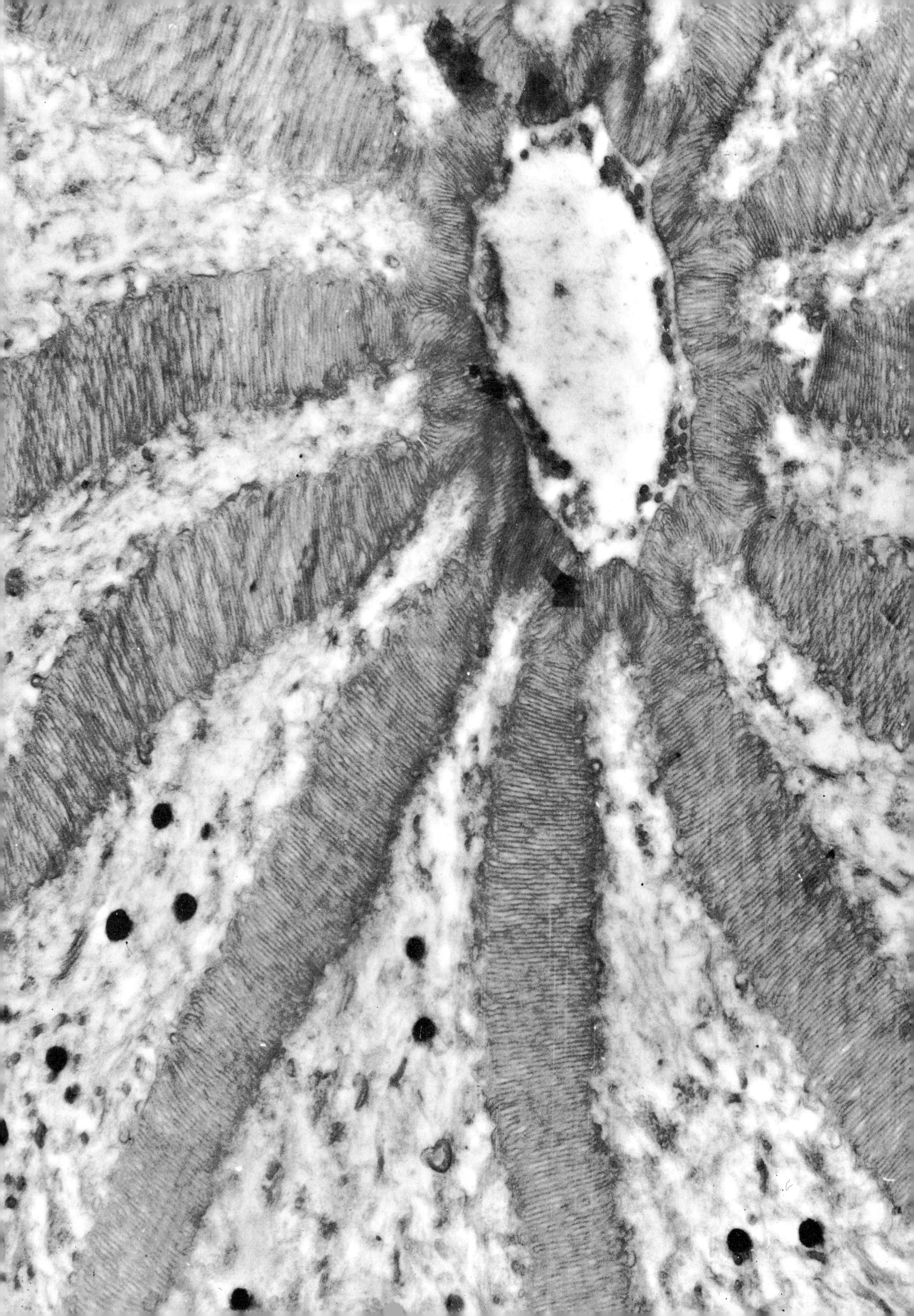

HOW CELLS RECEIVE STIMULI

WILLIAM H. MILLER, FLOYD RATLIFF AND H. K. HARTLINE

September 1961

The survival of every living thing depends ultimately on its ability to respond to the world around it and to regulate its own internal environment. In most multicellular animals this response and regulation is made possible by specialized receptor cells that are sensitive to a wide variety of physical, chemical and mechanical stimuli.

In many animals, including man, these receptors provide information that far exceeds that furnished by the traditional five senses (sight, hearing, smell, taste and touch). Sense organs of which we are less aware include equally important receptors that monitor the internal environment. Receptor organs in the muscles, called muscle spindles, provide a continuous measure of muscle stretch, and other receptors sense the movement of joints. Without such receptors it would be difficult to move or talk. Receptor cells in the hypothalamus, a part of the brain, are sensitive to the temperature of the blood; pressure-sensitive cells in the carotid sinus measure the blood pressure. Still other internal receptors monitor carbon dioxide in special regions of the large arteries. Pain receptors, widely distributed throughout the body, respond to noxious stimuli of almost any nature that are likely to cause tissue damage.

VISUAL RECEPTOR of the horseshoe crab *(Limulus)* is enlarged 19,000 diameters in the electron micrograph on the opposite page. Called an ommatidium, it is one of about 1,000 photoreceptor units in the compound eye of *Limulus*. Here the ommatidium is seen in cross section; the individual receptor cells are arranged radially like segments of a tangerine around a nerve filament (dendrite) arising from an associated nerve cell *(see illustration on page 131)*. The dark ring around the dendrite and spokelike areas may contain photosensitive pigment. The electron micrograph was made by William H. Miller, one of the authors.

Receptor cells not only have diverse functions and structures but also connect in various ways with the nerve fibers channeling into the central nervous system. Some receptor cells give rise directly to nerve fibers of their own; others make contact with nerve fibers originating elsewhere. All receptors, however, share a common function: the generation of nerve impulses. This does not imply that impulses necessarily occur in the receptor cells themselves. For example, in the eyes of vertebrates no one has yet been able to detect impulses in the photoreceptor cells: the rods and cones. Nevertheless, the rods and cones, when struck by light, set up the physicochemical conditions that trigger impulses in nerve cells lying behind them. Typical nerve impulses are readily detected in the optic nerve itself, which is composed of fibers of ganglion cells separated from the rods and cones by at least one intervening group of nerve cells.

Eventually physiologists hope to unravel the detailed train of events by which a receptor cell gives rise to a discharge of nerve impulses following mechanical deformation, absorption of light or heat, or stimulation by a particular molecule. In no case have all the events been traced out. In our discussion we will begin with the one final event common to all sensory reception—the generation of nerve impulses. We will then examine in some detail the events occurring in one particular receptor: the photoreceptor of *Limulus*, the horseshoe crab. Finally, we will describe some characteristics of the output of receptors acting singly and in concert with others.

The nerve fiber, or axon, is a thread-like extension of the nerve-cell body. The entire surface membrane of the cell, including that of the axon, is electrically polarized; the inside of the cell is some 70 millivolts negative with respect to the outside. This potential difference is called the membrane potential. In response to a suitable triggering event the membrane potential is momentarily and locally altered, giving rise to a nerve impulse, which is then propagated the whole length of the axon [see "How Cells Communicate," Offprint 98].

In any particular nerve fiber the impulses are always of essentially the same magnitude and form and they travel with the same speed. This has been known for some 30 years, since the pioneering studies of E. D. Adrian at the University of Cambridge. He and his colleagues found that varying the intensity of the stimulus applied to a receptor cell affects not the size of the impulses but the frequency with which they are discharged; the greater the intensity, the greater the frequency of nerve impulses generated by the receptor. Thus all sensory messages—concerning light, sound, muscle position and so on—are conveyed in the same code of individual nerve impulses. The animal is able to decode the various messages because each type of receptor communicates to the higher nerve centers only through its own private set of nerve channels.

Adrian and others have investigated the problem of how the receptor cell triggers sensory nerve impulses. Adrian suggested that the receptor must somehow diminish the resting membrane potential of its nerve fiber; that is, it must locally depolarize the axon membrane. The existence of local potentials in the eye has been known since 1865, and much later similar potentials were recorded in other sense organs. But the relationship of these gross electrical changes to the discharge of nerve impulses was not clear. For some simple eyes, however, the polarity of the local potential changes in the receptors is such that they appear to depolarize the sensory nerve fibers. This led Ragnar Granit of the Royal Caroline Institute in Stockholm to propose that they be called "generator" potentials. The present view is that stimulation of the receptor cell gives rise to a sustained local depolarization of the sensory nerve fiber, which thereupon generates a train of impulses.

Some of the first direct evidence for generator potentials at the cellular level was produced in 1935 by one of the authors of this article (Hartline), then working at the Johnson Research Foundation of the University of Pennsylvania. He found what appeared to be a generator potential when he recorded the activity of a single optic nerve fiber and its receptor in the compound eye of *Limulus*. Superimposed on the potential was a train of nerve impulses [*see illustration on page 132*].

In 1950 Bernhard Katz of University College London obtained unmistakable evidence for a generator potential in a somewhat simpler receptor: the vertebrate muscle spindle. When the spindle was stretched, a small, steady depolarization could be recorded in the nerve fiber coming from the spindle. As viewed on the oscilloscope, it appeared that the base line of the recorded signal had been shifted slightly upward. Superimposed on the shifted signal, or local potential, was a series of "spikes" representing individual nerve impulses. The stronger or the more rapid the stretch, the greater the magnitude of the potential shift and the greater the frequency of the impulses [*see illustration on page 130*]. Analysis of many such records showed that in the steady state the frequency of nerve impulses depends directly on the magnitude of the altered potential. If a local anesthetic is applied to the spindle, the impulses are abolished but the potential shift remains. Katz concluded that this potential shift is an essential link between the stretching of the spindle and the discharge of nerve impulses; indeed, that it is the generator potential. Moreover, the potential can be detected only very close to the spindle, showing that it is conducted passively—which is to say poorly—along the nerve fiber.

Important confirmation of the role of the generator potential was provided by the work of Stephen W. Kuffler and

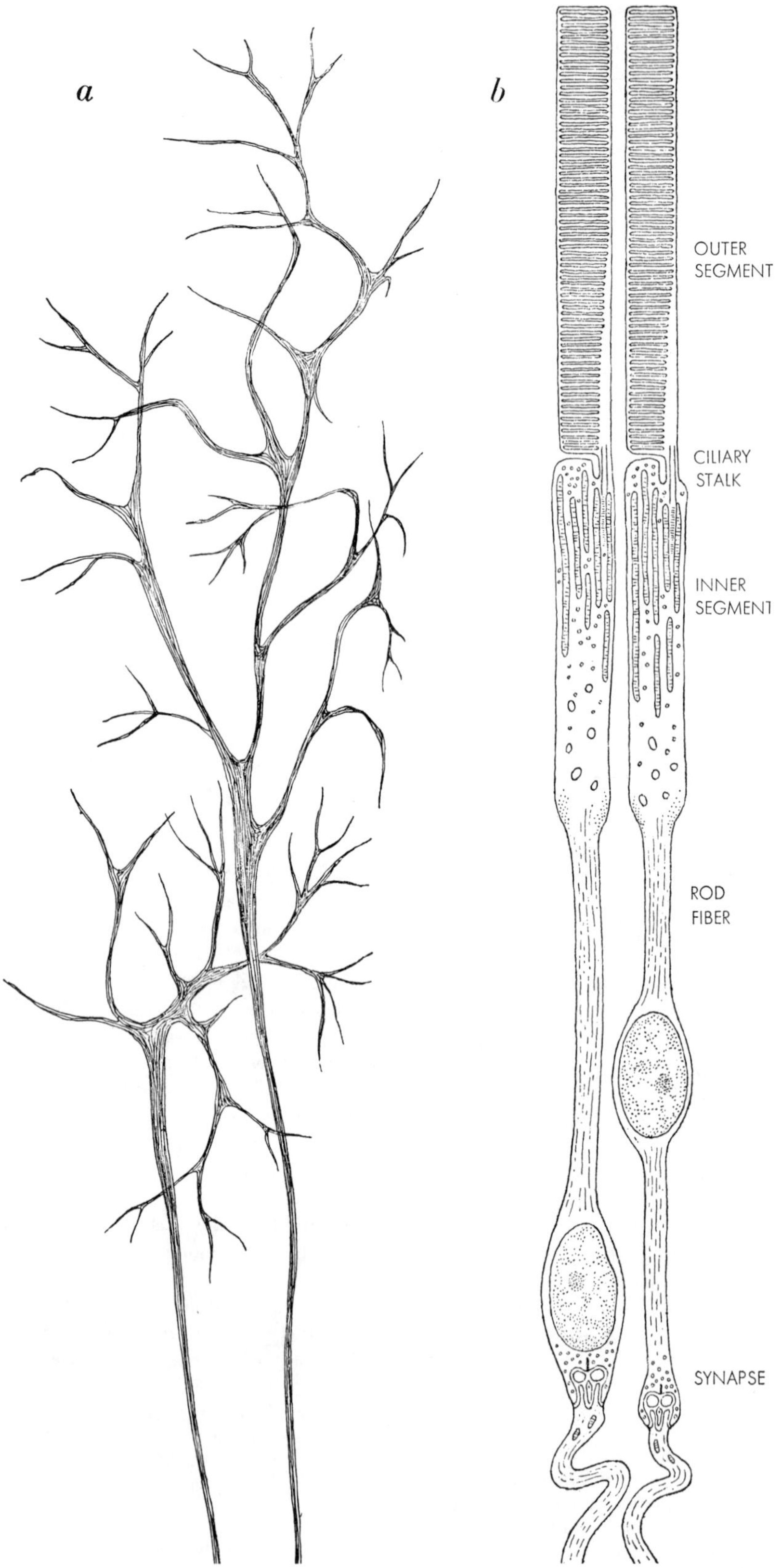

RECEPTOR CELLS, typical of those found in vertebrates, respond to a variety of stimuli: heat, light, chemicals and mechanical deformation. The "pit" on the head of the pit viper contains a network of free nerve endings (*a*) that are sensitive to heat and help the viper locate its prey. Rods (*b*) are light-sensitive cells in the retina of the eye; photosensitive pigment is in the laminar structure at top of drawing. Taste buds (*c*) are chemoreceptor cells embedded in the tongue. The cochlea, a spiral tube in the inner ear, contains thousands of

c

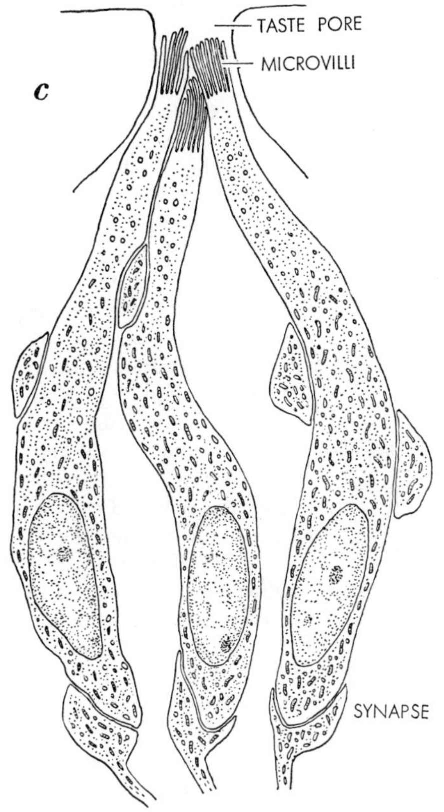

d

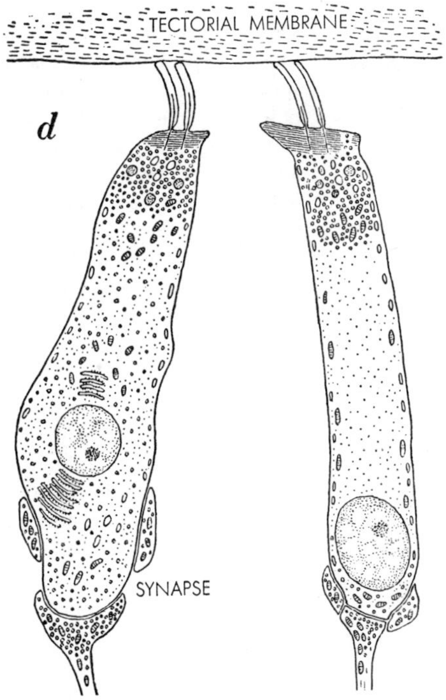

e

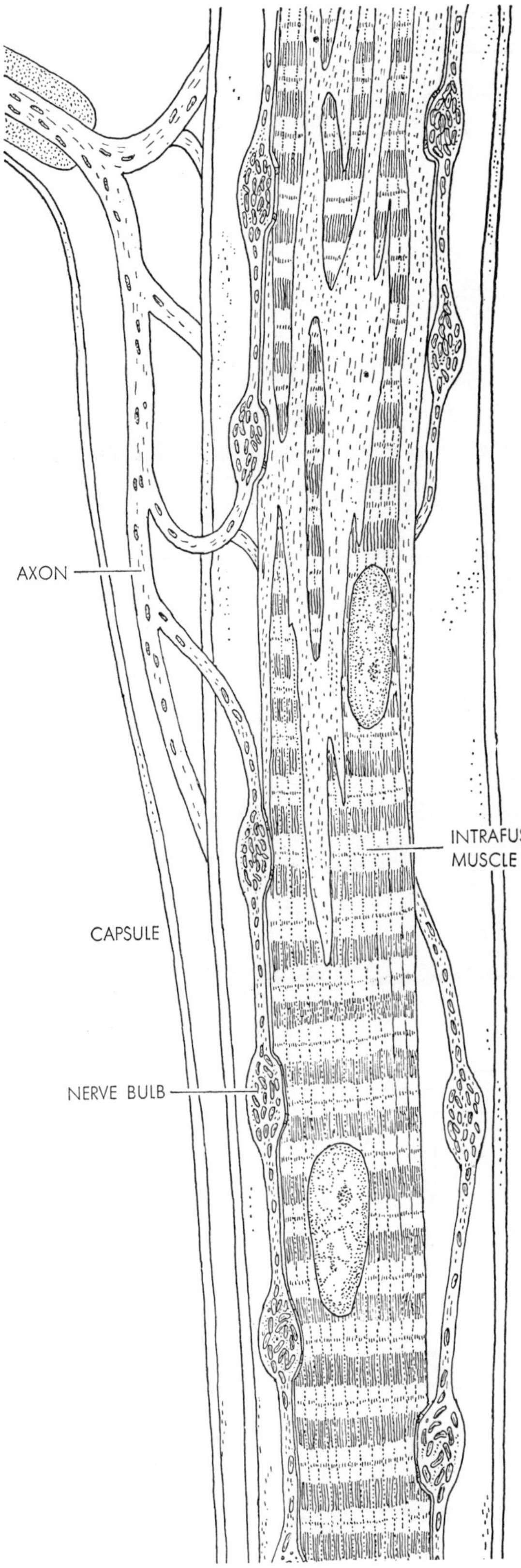

sensitive cells (*d*) in the so-called organs of Corti. When the hairlike bristles of these cells are mechanically deformed by sound vibrations, impulses are generated in the auditory nerve fibers leading to brain. Muscle spindle (*e*) contains a number of nerve endings that respond sensitively to stretching of muscle fibers surrounding them. These illustrations of receptor cells are based on the work of the following investigators: Theodore H. Bullock of the University of California at Los Angeles (*a*), Fritiof Sjöstrand of the same institution (formerly of the Karolinska Institute, Stockholm) (*b*), A. J. de Lorenzo of the Johns Hopkins School of Medicine, Baltimore, Md. (*c*), Salvatore Iurato of the University of Milan (*d*) and Bernhard Katz of University College London (*e*).

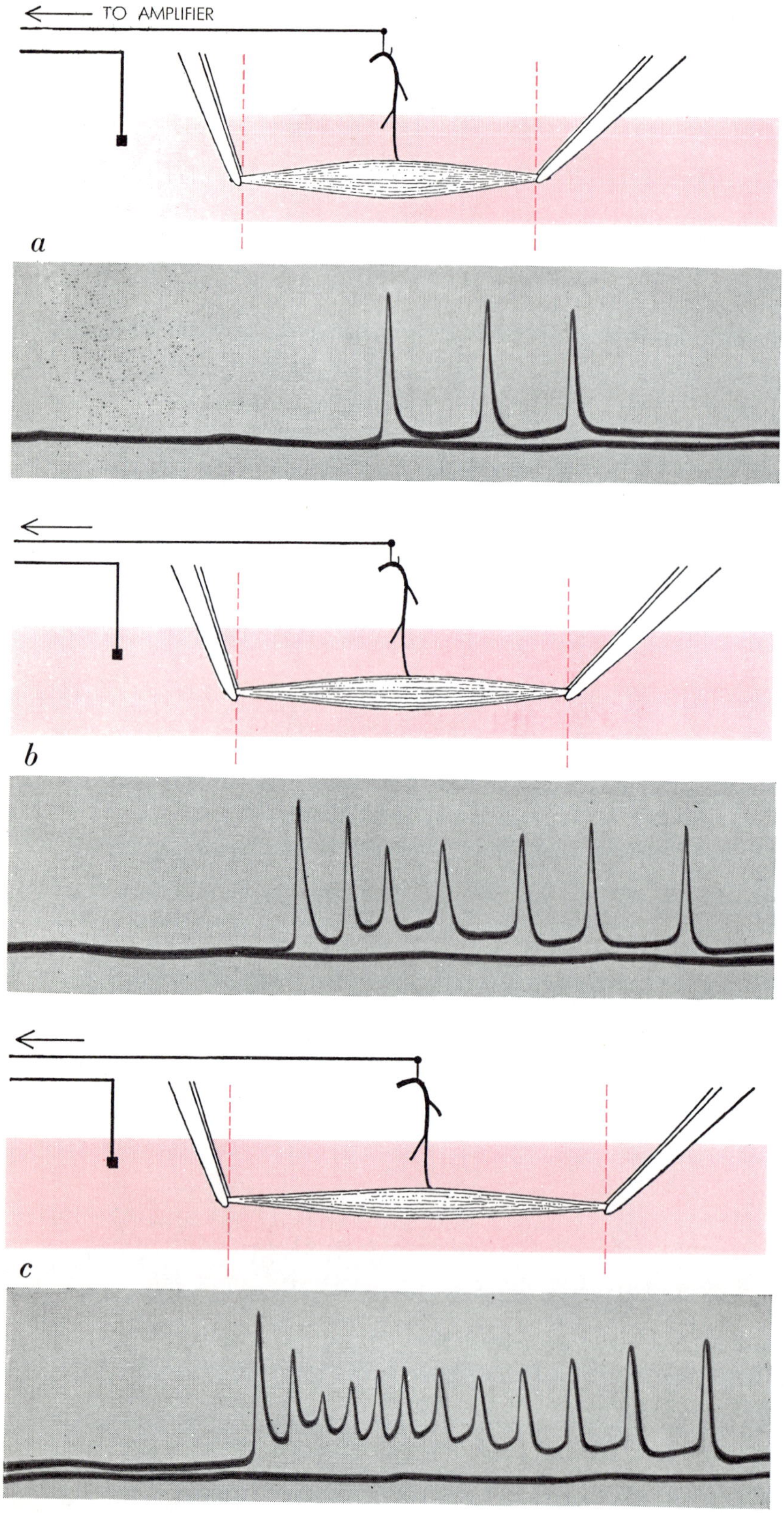

MUSCLE SPINDLE responds to stretch by firing nerve impulses at a rate proportional to the degree and speed of stretching. These recordings made by Bernhard Katz of University College London were the first to show that stretching causes depolarization of the nerve near the spindle (*base line shifted upward in the traces*) and that this depolarization is the precondition for the firing of nerve impulses. The shift is called the generator potential.

Carlos Eyzaguirre, then at Johns Hopkins University, using the so-called Alexandrowicz stretch-receptor cells in crustaceans. These are large single receptor cells with dendrites (short fibers) that are embedded in specialized receptor muscles. Kuffler was able to insert a microelectrode within the cell and record its membrane potential as well as the nerve impulses in its axon. He found that when he distorted the cell's dendrites by stretching the receptor muscle, the cell body became depolarized and the depolarization spread passively to the site of impulse generation, which is probably in the axon close to where it emerges from the cell body. When this generator potential reached a critical level, the cell fired a train of nerve impulses; the greater the depolarization of the axon above this critical level, the higher the frequency of the discharge.

There is now abundant evidence that a receptor cell triggers a train of nerve impulses by locally depolarizing the adjacent nerve fiber—either its own fiber or one provided by another cell. With few exceptions, a fiber of a nerve trunk will not respond repetitively if one passes a sustained depolarizing current through it; it responds only briefly with one to several impulses and then accommodates to the stimulus and responds no more. Evidently that part of the sensory nerve fiber close to the receptor must be specialized so that it does not speedily accommodate to the generator potential. It is nonetheless true that a certain amount of accommodation, or adaptation, almost always takes place when a receptor cell is exposed to a sustained stimulus. In any event, the initiation of nerve impulses in the axons of receptor cells by means of a generator potential appears to be a general phenomenon.

The question still remains: How does the external stimulus produce the generator potential? In most of the receptors studied there is no evidence whatever on this point. Only in the photoreceptor do we have precise knowledge of the first step in the excitation of the sense cell. Yet the study of the photoreceptor is beset by special difficulties. In most eyes the receptors are small and densely packed, and their associated neural structures are complex and highly organized. A fortunate exception is the compound eye of *Limulus,* which provided early evidence for the generator potential. In this eye the receptor cells are large and the neural organization is relatively simple.

The coarsely faceted compound eye

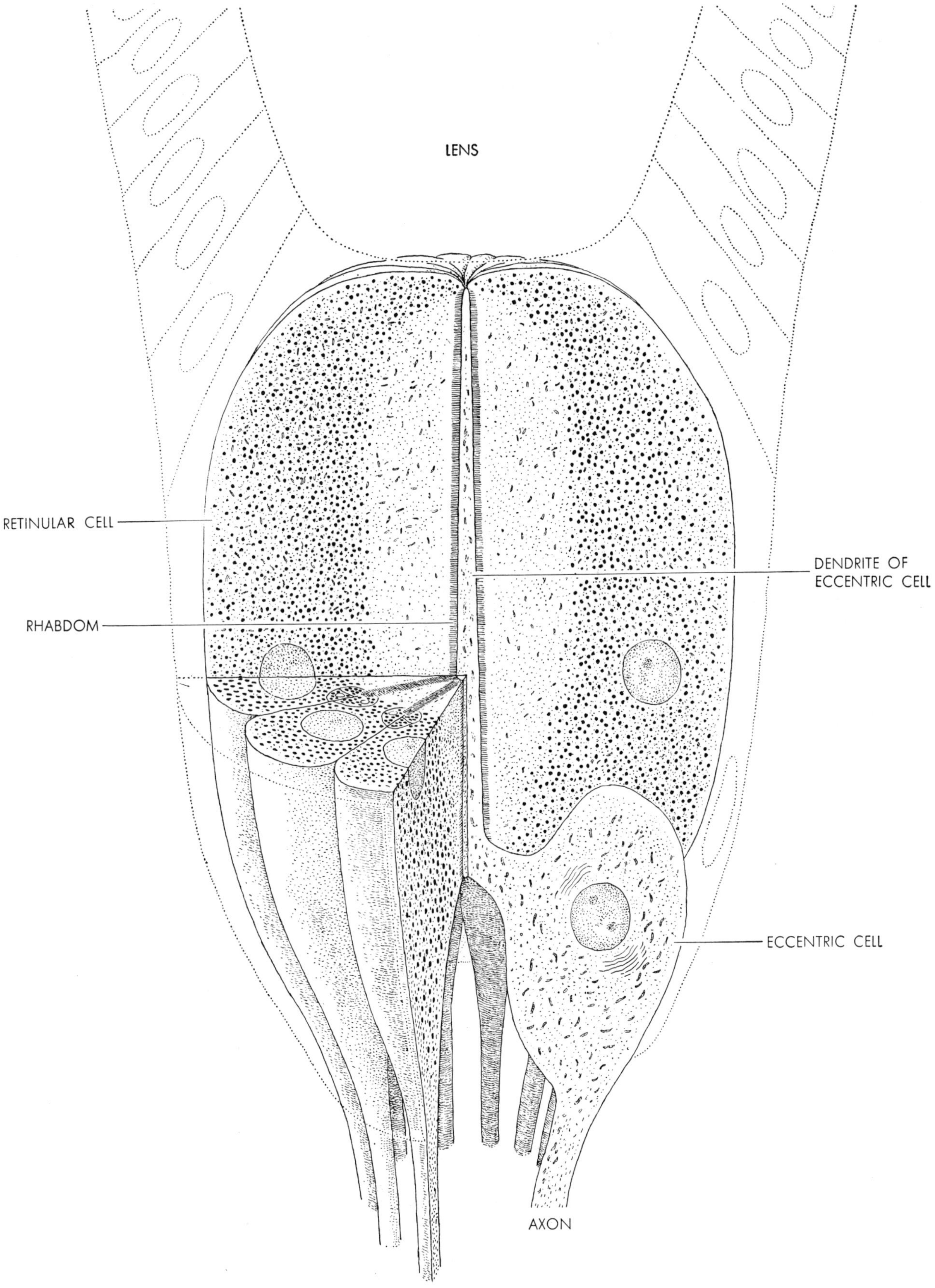

OMMATIDIUM OF LIMULUS is a remarkable structure roughly the size of a pencil lead. About 1,000 form the crab's compound eye. The ommatidium consists of about 12 wedge-shaped retinular cells clustered around a central fiber, which is the dendrite (sensitive process) of a nerve cell, the eccentric cell shown at lower right. When light strikes the ommatidium (*at the top*), the eccentric cell gives rise to nerve impulses (*see illustration on next page*). Photosensitive pigment rhodopsin is believed to be in the rhabdom.

of *Limulus* has some 1,000 ommatidia ("little eyes"), each of which contains about a dozen cells. The cells in each ommatidium have a regular arrangement. The retinular cells—the receptors—are arranged radially like the segments of a tangerine around the dendrite of an associated neuron: a single eccentric cell within each ommatidium [*see illustration on preceding page*].

Hartline, H. G. Wagner and E. F. MacNichol, Jr., working at Johns Hopkins University, found by the use of microelectrodes that the eccentric cell gives rise to the nerve impulses that can be recorded farther down in the nerve strand leaving the ommatidium. The microelectrode also records the generator potential of the ommatidium. Because of the anatomical complexity of the ommatidium, the site of origin of the generator potential has not been identified with certainty. Nor has activity yet been detected in the axons of the retinular cells. As in the vertebrate and invertebrate stretch receptors, local anesthetics extinguish the nerve impulses without destroying the generator potential. Moreover, as in the stretch receptors, there is a proportional relationship between the degree of depolarization and the frequency of nerve impulses.

Recently M. G. F. Fuortes of the National Institute of Neurological Diseases and Blindness has shown that illumination increases the conductance of the eccentric cell. He postulates that the increase is produced by a chemical transmitter substance that is released by the action of light and acts on the eccentric cell's dendrite. Presumably the increased conductance of the dendrite results in a depolarization that spreads passively to the site of impulse generation, where it acts as the generator potential.

In photosensory cells—alone among all receptors—there exists direct experimental evidence of the initial molecular events in the receptor process. It has been known for about a century that visual receptor cells in both vertebrates and invertebrates have specially differentiated organelles containing a photosensitive pigment. In vertebrates this reddish pigment, called rhodopsin, can be clearly seen in the outer segments of rods. The absorption spectrum of human rhodopsin corresponds closely to the light-sensitivity curve for human vision under conditions of dim illumination, when only the rods of the retina are operative. This is strong evidence that rhodopsin brings about the first active event in rod vision: the absorption of light by the photoreceptor structure. (There is evidence for similar pigments in the outer segments of cones, but they have proved more difficult to isolate and study.)

The visual pigments are known to be complex proteins, but the light-absorbing part of the pigment, called the chromophore, has been found to be a relatively simple substance: vitamin A aldehyde. Because it contains a number of double chemical bonds in its make-up, vitamin A aldehyde can exist in various molecular configurations known as "*cis*" and "*trans*" isomers. We know from the work of Ruth Hubbard, George Wald and their colleagues at Harvard University that the absorption of light changes the chromophore from

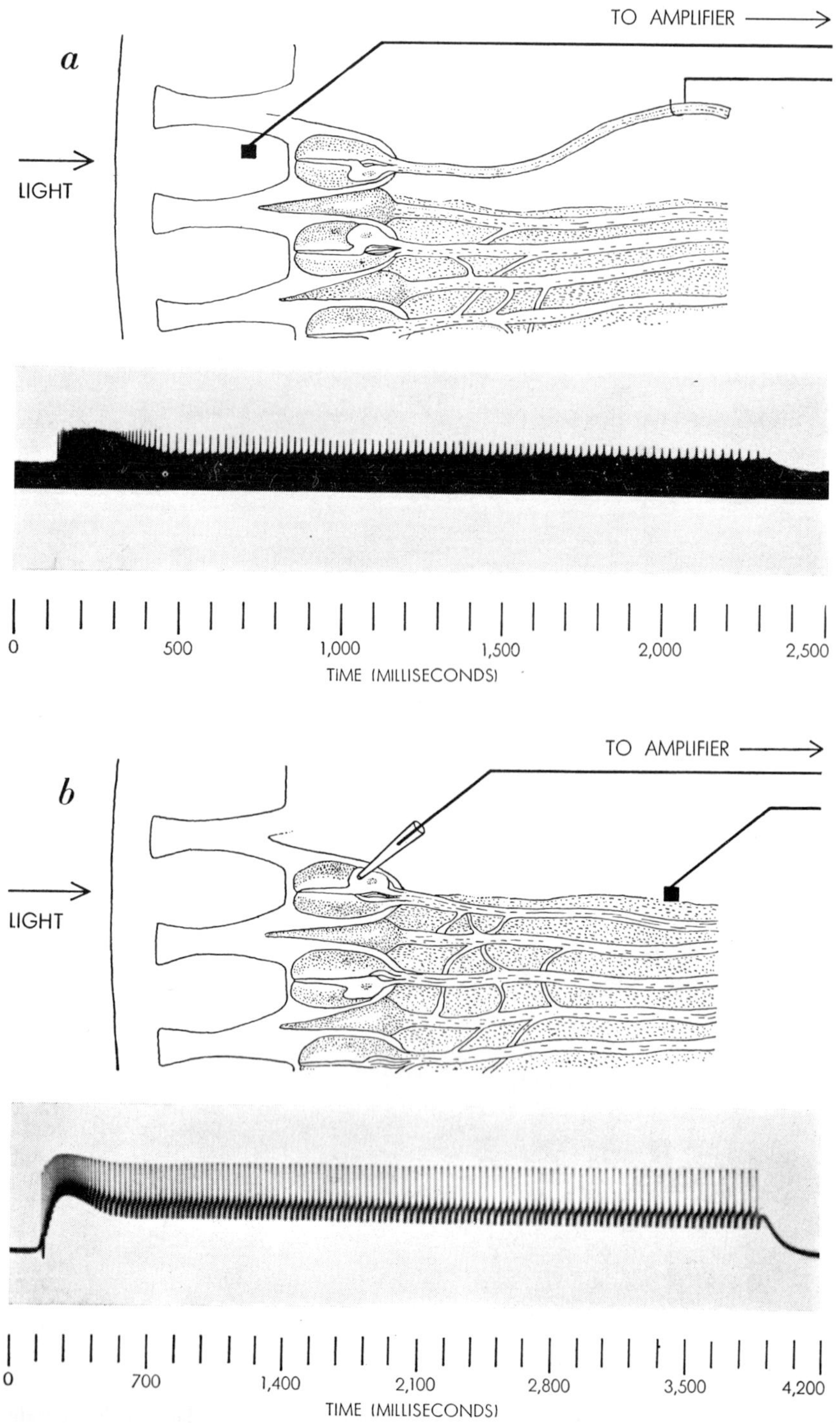

RECORDINGS FROM OMMATIDIA show trains of nerve impulses evoked by light. The upper recording from a nerve bundle (*a*) was made by one of the authors, H. K. Hartline, some 25 years ago. Shift of base line underlying nerve spikes is the generator potential. Lower recording, made with microelectrode (*b*), shows generator potential more clearly.

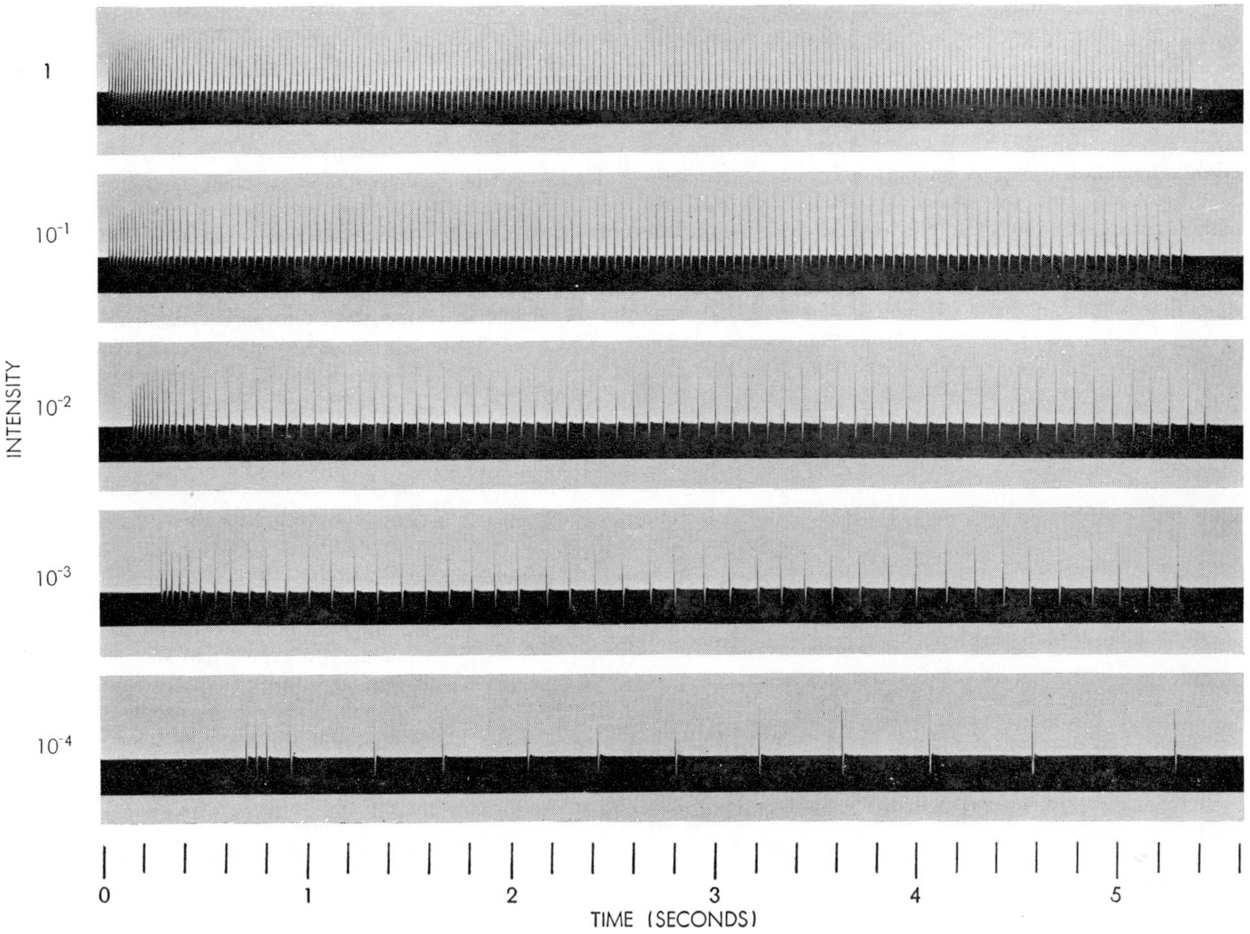

NERVE IMPULSES TRIGGERED BY LIGHT are directly related to intensity of steady light falling on the *Limulus* eye. Recordings were made from the optic nerve fiber arising from one ommatidium. At high light intensity (*top*) the nerve fires about 30 times per second. As intensity is reduced by factors of 10, firing is reduced in uniform steps, falling to a low of two or three impulses per second.

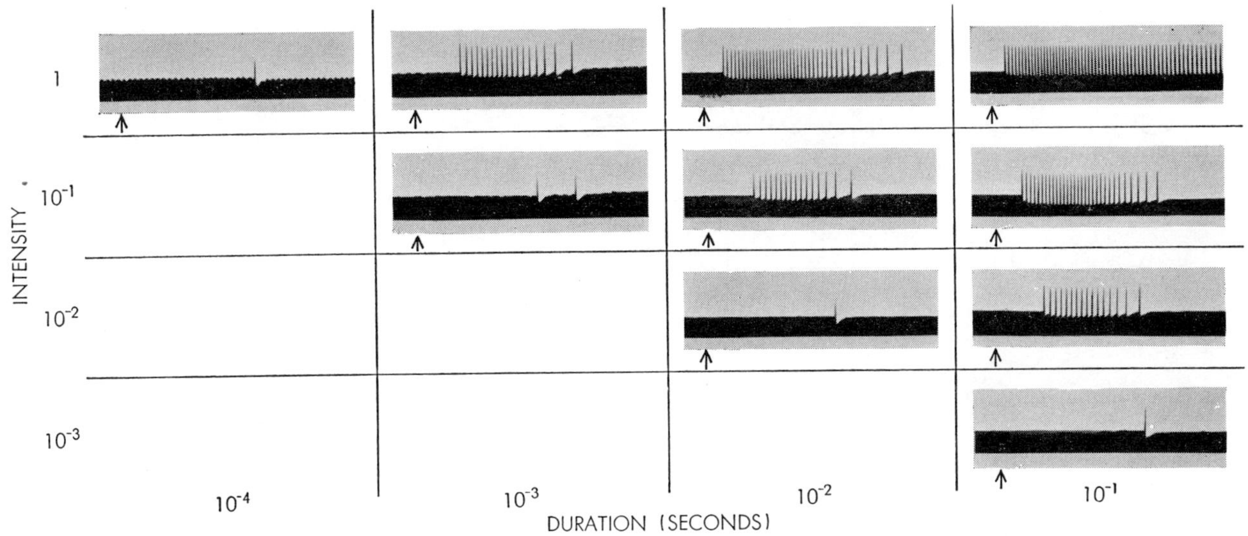

DURATION AND INTENSITY OF LIGHT have equivalent effect on the *Limulus* eye. Evidently the receptor responds to the total amount of energy received in a brief flash (*arrows*) regardless of how the energy is "packaged" in duration and intensity. Thus a brief intense flash (*top left*) evokes about the same response as a flash a 1,000th as bright lasting 1,000 times longer (*bottom right*).

11-*cis* vitamin A aldehyde to the *trans* configuration. This photochemical reaction is the first step that leads, through a chain of chemical and physical events as yet unknown, to the initiation of the generator potential of the receptor cell and finally to the discharge of impulses in the optic nerve. This is the only case in which the specific molecular mechanism is known whereby a receptor cell detects environmental conditions.

Supporting evidence that rhodopsin governs the response to a light stimulus can be found by comparing the absorption spectrum of *Limulus* rhodopsin with the sensitivity of the *Limulus* eye at various wavelengths. In 1935 Clarence H. Graham and Hartline measured the intensity of flashes at several wavelengths required to produce a fixed number of impulses in the *Limulus* optic nerve. When a sensitivity curve obtained from this experiment is superimposed on the absorption curve found by Hubbard and Wald for *Limulus* rhodopsin, the two match almost perfectly. At a wavelength of about 520 angstrom units, where rhodopsin absorbs light most strongly, the *Limulus* eye generates the highest number of impulses for a given quantity of light energy received. It turns out that the wavelength sensitivity of the *Limulus* eye is close to that of the human eye in dim light when rod vision dominates.

Many other familiar sensory experiences are manifestations of the properties of individual sense cells. Perhaps the most elementary experience is our ability to perceive when a stimulus has been increased in intensity. Under such circumstances we can be sure that the sensory fibers conveying information to the brain are firing more rapidly as the stimulus is increased. We are also familiar with the experience of sensory adaptation; for example, a strong odor usually seems to decrease in intensity after a time, although objective measurements would show that its intensity has remained constant.

We know from photography that shutter speed and lens opening can be interchanged to produce a constant exposure, which is the same as saying that intensity and duration of illumination can be interchanged (within limits) to produce a constant photochemical effect. The same equivalence holds for the human eye exposed to short flashes of light, and the equivalence can be demonstrated in the photoreceptor of *Limulus*. About the same number of nerve impulses are produced by exposing the ommatidium to a weak light for a 10th of a second as by exposing it to light 10 times as bright for a 100th of a second [*see bottom illustration on page 133*].

We also know from watching motion pictures or television that a light flickering at a high rate appears not to be flickering at all. A neural basis for this phenomenon can be seen in the generator potentials and nerve impulses recorded when a *Limulus* ommatidium is exposed to a light flickering at various rates [*see illustration at left*]. Flicker is detectable as fluctuations in the generator potential, which in turn gives rise to bursts of impulses. As the repetition rate increases, the rate of discharge becomes steadier and finally is indistinguishable from a response to continuous illumination. As can be seen from the records, this "flicker fusion" is directly attributable to the generator potential, which becomes smooth at the highest repetition rates.

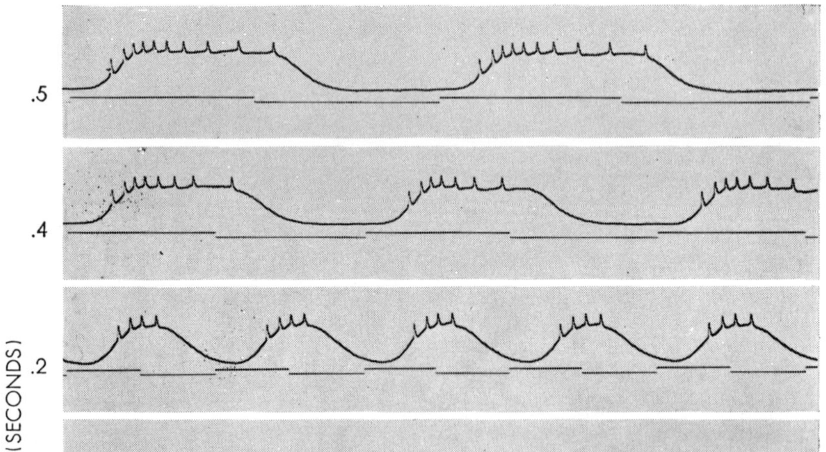

EFFECT OF FLICKERING LIGHT on the *Limulus* ommatidium provides a basis for explaining "flicker fusion": the inability to perceive a rapid flicker. The recordings show the response of the ommatidium to a light flickering at various rates; when the horizontal line is raised, the light is on. At low flicker rates the generator potential, indicated by a rise in base potential, rises and falls. As flicker rate increases, the generator potential no longer falls between flashes, and spacing between nerve impulses becomes more uniform.

The experiments described so far were carried out on single cells or single sensory units. In the eye, ear and other organs, however, receptor cells are grouped close together and usually act in concert. In fact, modern studies show that receptor cells of complex sense organs seldom act independently. In such organs the receptor cells are interconnected neurally and as a result of these connections new functional properties arise.

Although the compound eye of *Limu-*

lus is much less complex than the eyes of vertebrates, it still shows clearly the effects of neural interaction. In *Limulus* the activity of each photoreceptor unit is affected to some degree by the activity of adjacent ommatidia. The frequency of discharge of impulses in an optic nerve fiber from a particular ommatidium is decreased—that is, inhibited—when light falls on its neighbors. Since each ommatidium is a neighbor of its neighbors, mutual inhibition takes place. This inhibition is brought about by a branching array of nerve axons that make synaptic contact with each other in a feltwork of fine fibers behind the ommatidia. The inhibition probably results from a decrease in the magnitude of the generator potential at the site of origin of the nerve impulses, as a consequence of which the rate of firing is slowed down.

When two adjacent ommatidia are illuminated at the same time, each discharges fewer impulses than when it receives the same amount of light by itself [*see illustrations on this page*]. The magnitude of the inhibition exerted on each ommatidium (in the steady state) depends only on the frequency of the response of the other. The more widely separated the ommatidia, the smaller the mutual inhibitory effect. When several ommatidia are illuminated at the same time, the inhibition of each is given by the sum of the inhibitory effects from all others.

Inhibitory interaction can produce important visual effects. The more intensely illuminated retinal regions exert a stronger inhibition on the less intensely illuminated ones than the latter do on the former. As a result differences in neural activity from differently lighted retinal regions are exaggerated. In this way contrast is heightened and certain significant features of the retinal image tend to be accentuated at the expense of fidelity of representation.

This has been shown by illuminating the *Limulus* compound eye with a "step" pattern: a bright rectangle next to a dimmer one [*see illustration on page 136*]. The eye was masked so that only one ommatidium "observed" the pattern, which was moved to various positions on the retinal mosaic. At each position the steady-state frequency of discharge was measured. The result was a faithful reproduction (in terms of frequency of impulses) of the form of the pattern. Then the eye was unmasked so that all the ommatidia observed the pattern, and a recording was again made from the single ommatidium. This time

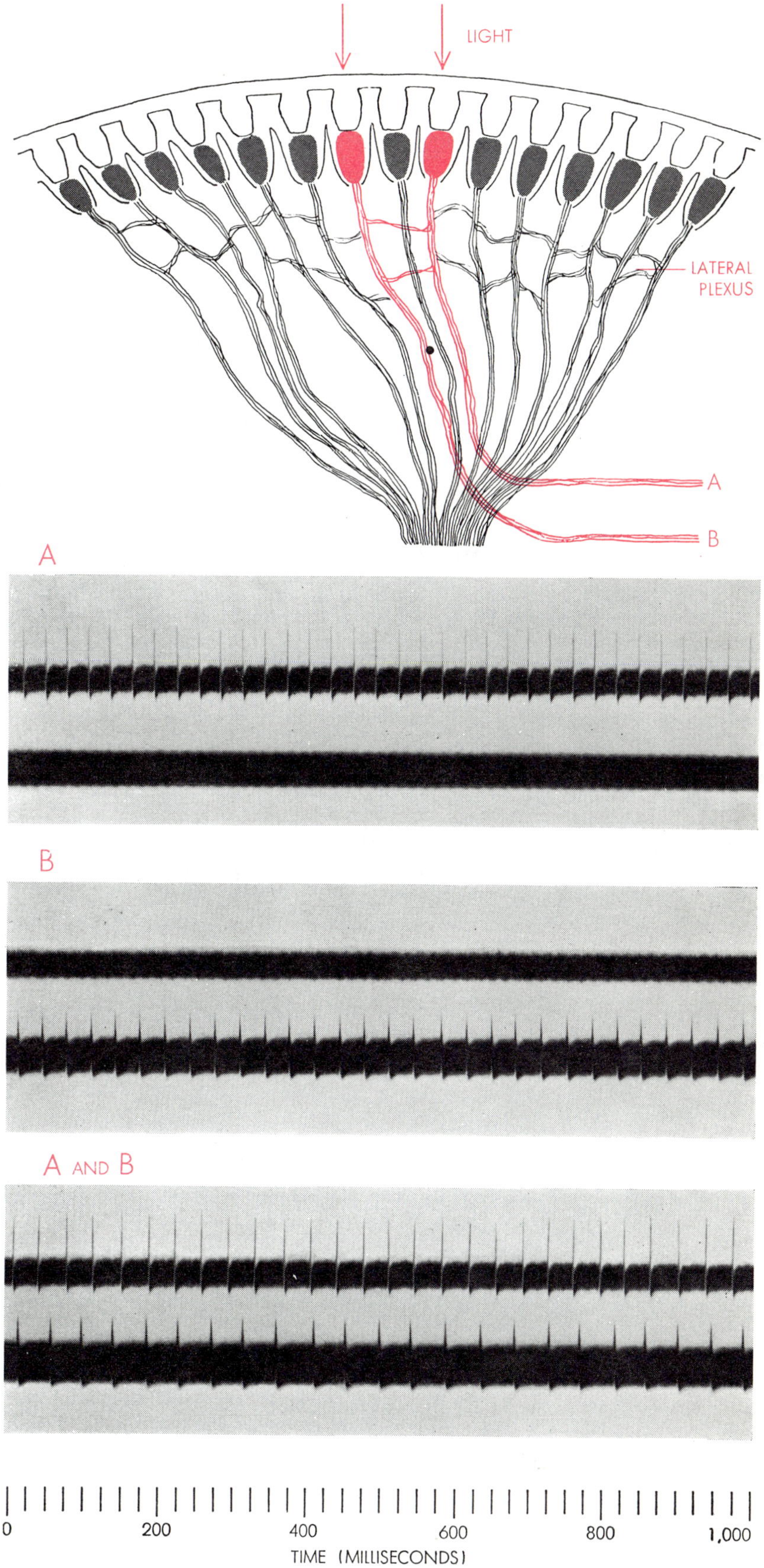

MUTUAL INHIBITION results when two neighboring ommatidia are illuminated at the same time (*top*). The inhibition is exerted by cross connections among nerve fibers. When ommatidia attached to fiber *A* and fiber *B* were illuminated separately, 34 and 30 impulses were recorded respectively in one second. Illuminated together, they fired less often.

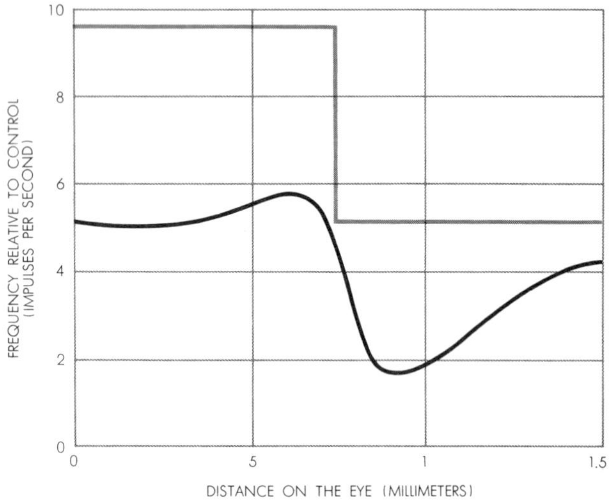

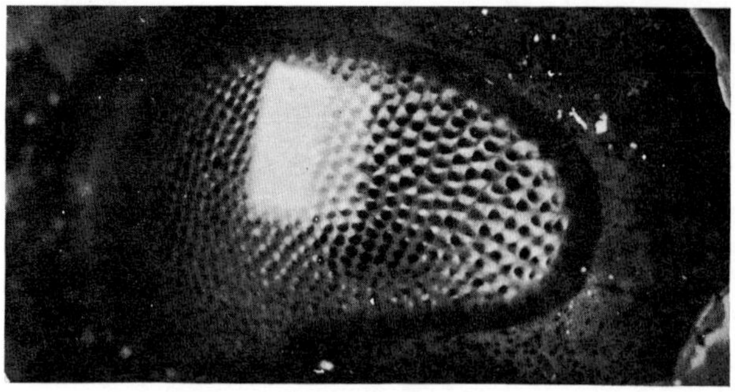

CONTRAST HEIGHTENING AT CONTOURS is demonstrated by letting "step" pattern of light, a bright area next to a darker one, fall on *Limulus* compound eye (*right*). If eye is masked so light strikes only one ommatidium, a recording of its output forms a simple step-shaped curve (*left*) as the pattern moved across the eye. If the eye is unmasked, the output of the single ommatidium is inhibited in varying degrees by the light striking its neighbors. The net effect (*lower curve*) is to heighten the contrast at light-dark boundaries.

the frequency increased on the bright side of the step and decreased near the dim side. This is expected because near the bright side of the step the neighboring ommatidia illuminated by the dim part of the step pattern have a low frequency of firing and therefore do not exert much inhibition. Consequently the frequency of discharge of the receptors on the bright side of the step is higher than its equally illuminated but more distant neighbors. Similar reasoning explains the decrease in frequency on the dim side of the step. The net effect of this pattern of response is to enhance contours, an effect we can easily demonstrate in our own vision by looking at a step pattern consisting of a series of uniform gray bands graded from white to black. Artists are quite familiar with the existence of "border contrast" and may even heighten it in their paintings. And as we all know, significant information is conveyed by contours alone, as is demonstrated by cartoons and other line drawings. Georg von Békésy of Harvard University has suggested that a similar reciprocal inhibition in the auditory system would lead to a sharpening of the sense of pitch.

There is also evidence that in many sense organs the response can be modified by neural influences exerted back onto them by higher centers of the nervous system. Thus the sensitivity of the vertebrate stretch receptor or muscle spindle is established by variations in the length of the spindle fibers, and this length is dependent both on the output of the receptor and on its interaction with higher centers. The sensitivity of the vertebrate olfactory receptors can also be altered, in all probability, by the flow of impulses from above. Similar influences, not yet well understood, also seem to be at work in the retina of the eye.

It is evident, then, that the responses of complex sense organs are determined by the fundamental properties of the individual receptor cells, by the influences they exert on one another and by control exerted on them by other organs. In this way the activity of the receptor cells is integrated into complex patterns of nervous activity that enable organisms to survive in a world of endless variety and change.

RETINAL PROCESSING OF VISUAL IMAGES

CHARLES R. MICHAEL

May 1969

In the eye of vertebrate animals an image of the external world is focused on the retina by the cornea and the lens. The light is absorbed by the visual pigments of the retinal receptor cells, the electrical activity of which varies with the quantity of light they receive. The conversion of light into electrical activity is not the only function of the retina, however. The retina is more than just the biological equivalent of a photographic emulsion. The transformation of the visual image into nerve impulses traveling along the optic nerve calls for a considerable amount of processing. Activity in the optic nerve is not related simply to the intensity of illumination falling on each retinal receptor but rather to specific aspects of the visual image, and some aspects are emphasized at the expense of others. The information transmitted to the brain is related not so much to patterns of light and dark as to such properties as contrast at borders, the movement of an object or its color.

It is now clear that the degree of retinal transformation varies among species. Curiously, the degree of transformation does not parallel the evolutionary development of the vertebrates. For example, the retina of primates (monkeys, apes and man) is simpler in terms of both anatomy and physiology than the retina of the frog. On the other hand, some mammals, such as the rabbit and the ground squirrel, have retinas that are almost as complex as the frog's. In each species there is a close correlation between the anatomy and the physiology of the retina. Furthermore, there appears to be a direct relation between the complexity of an animal's retina and the development of the visual centers of its brain.

A brief description of the structure and interactions of neurons, or nerve cells, is necessary for a clear understanding of the retina's organization and operation. A number of fine processes called dendrites radiate from the cell body of each neuron [*see illustration below*]. In addition there usually is a single long process—an axon—that extends some distance from the cell body. Messages, in the form of brief electrical nerve impulses that vary in frequency but not in amplitude, travel from the cell body along the axon to its endings, which come in contact with the dendrites or the cell body of another neuron at junctions known as synapses. Information is transmitted from one neuron to another at the synapses, usually by the release of a chemical substance from tiny vesicles, or sacs, in the axon endings. The release of the chemical is initiated by the arrival of a nerve impulse.

There are two basic types of chemical synapse. In one type the substance diffusing from the axon has an excitatory effect on the dendrite or cell body beyond the synapse and makes it more likely that the postsynaptic cell will discharge. In the other type the chemical has an inhibitory effect on the postsynaptic process and renders the cell less likely to discharge. The interplay of the excitatory and the inhibitory synaptic activity impinging on a single cell strongly influences its pattern of discharge.

In the vertebrate retina the cell bodies of the neurons are arrayed in three distinct layers [*see illustration on page 144*]. The outermost layer (the one farthest from the lens of the eye) consists of the receptor cells containing the light-absorbing visual pigments. The next layer includes the bipolar cells (which conduct messages from the receptors to the cells in the third layer) and the horizontal and amacrine cells, which appear to be involved in the lateral transmission of information. The third layer contains the ganglion cells, whose axons form the optic nerve, the sole output of the retina. In between the three layers of cell bodies are two synaptic layers in which the different cell processes come in close contact. One might think a system containing only two layers of synapses and five types of cell could not accomplish much in terms of the analysis of the retinal image. The richness of the synaptic connections in the retina, however, makes possible a variety of integrative mechanisms.

John E. Dowling of the Wilmer Ophthalmological Institute of the Johns Hopkins University School of Medicine has

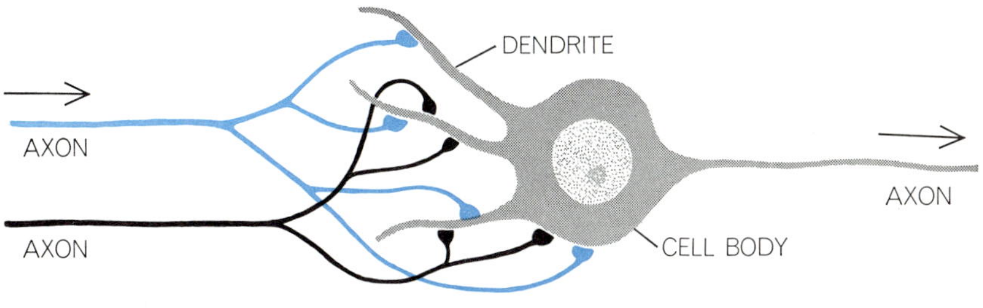

INFORMATION is transmitted from an axon ending of one nerve cell to the cell body or dendrite of another by a chemical transmitter substance that diffuses across the synaptic gap. Impulses from an excitatory cell (*color*) tend to make the cell beyond the synapse (*gray*) fire. Impulses from inhibitory endings (*black*) make it less likely that the cell will fire.

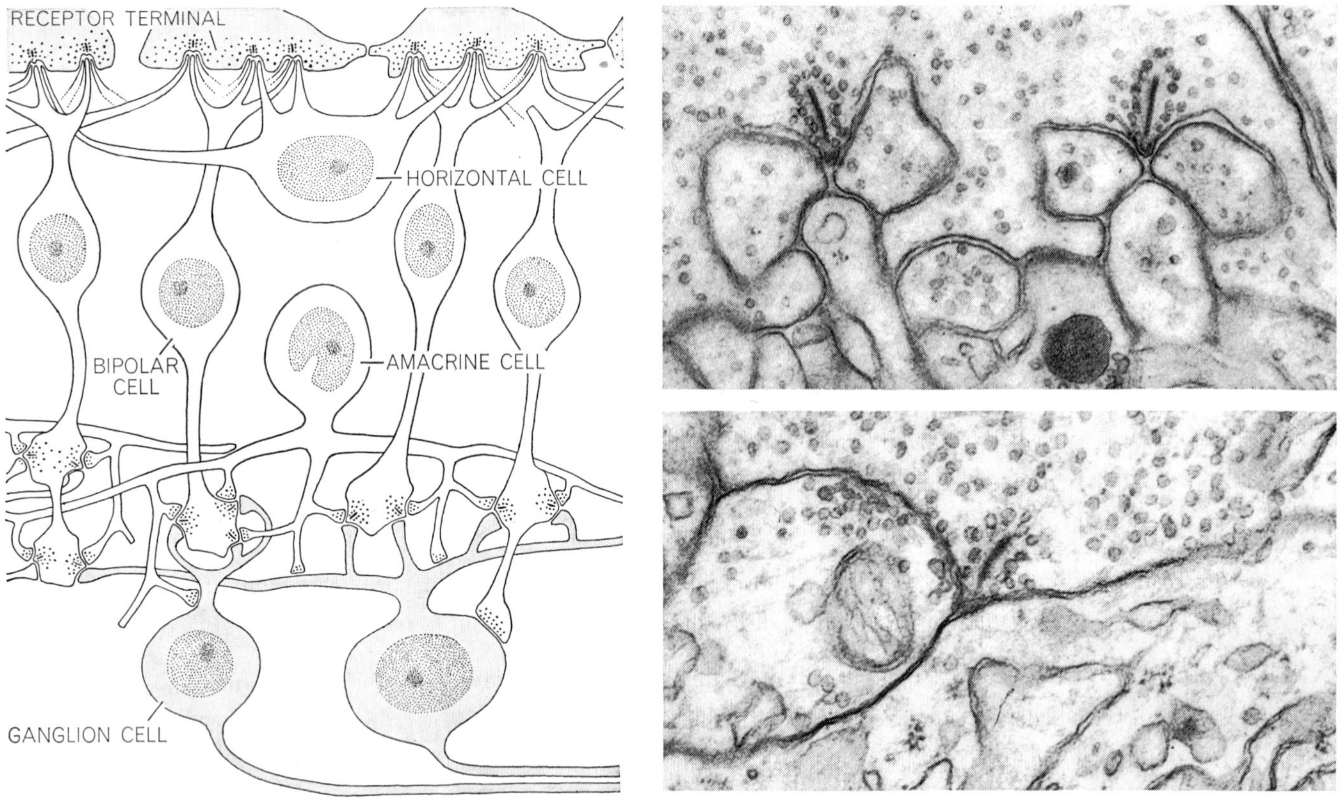

PRIMATE RETINA'S synaptic organization is diagrammed (*left*) on the basis of electron micrographs made by Dowling, two of which are reproduced (*middle*) and mapped (*right*). Two "ribbon" synapses in the base of a receptor in a monkey's retina are enlarged 45,000 diameters (*top*); at each of them a bipolar-cell dendrite and two horizontal-cell processes make contact. The small spheroidal objects are sacs containing transmitter substances. An axon ending of a bipolar cell in a human retina, enlarged 35,000

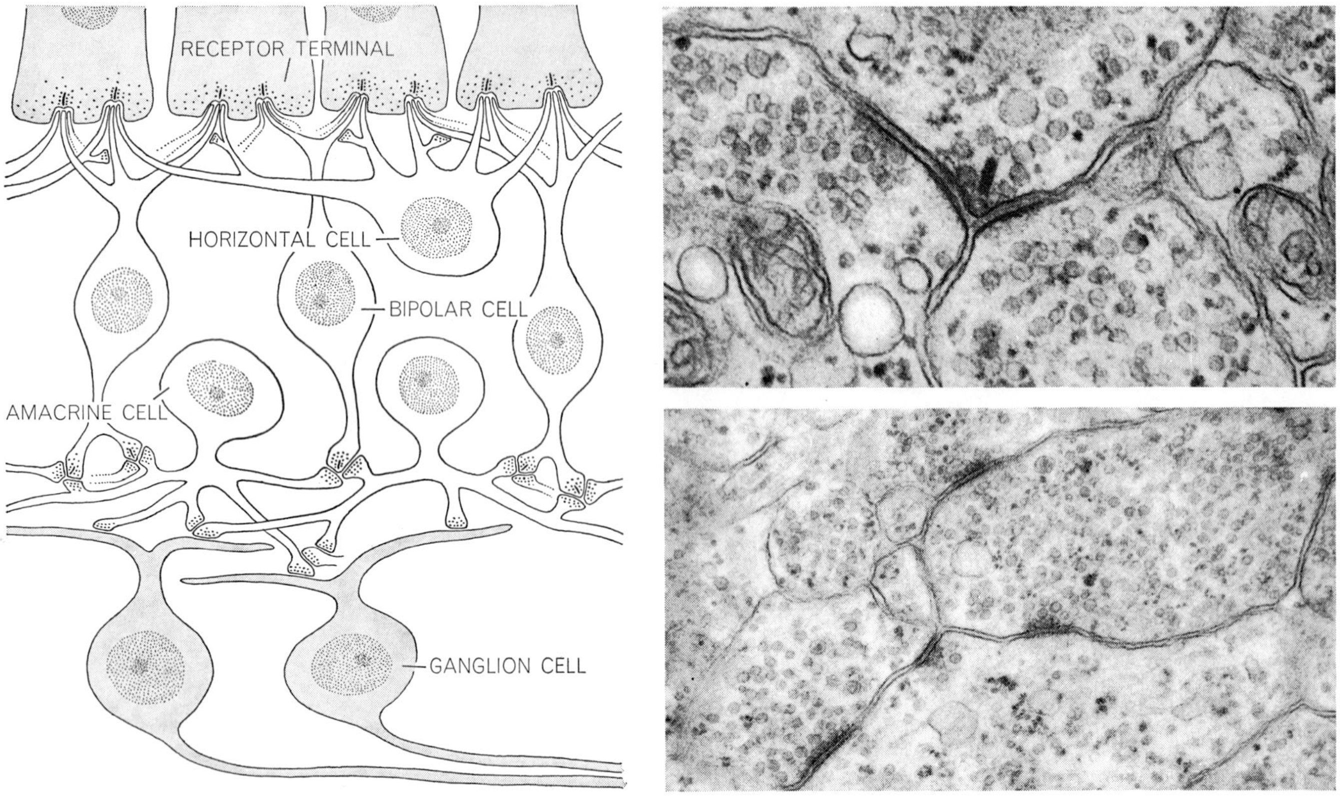

FROG RETINA'S synaptic contacts are illustrated. In the two electron micrographs a bipolar-cell axon (enlarged 60,000 diameters) synapses with two amacrine-cell processes (*top*), and four amacrine cells (enlarged 30,000 diameters) synapse serially with one another (*bottom*). In the frog's retina horizontal cells not only connect receptors but also synapse on bipolar-cell processes.

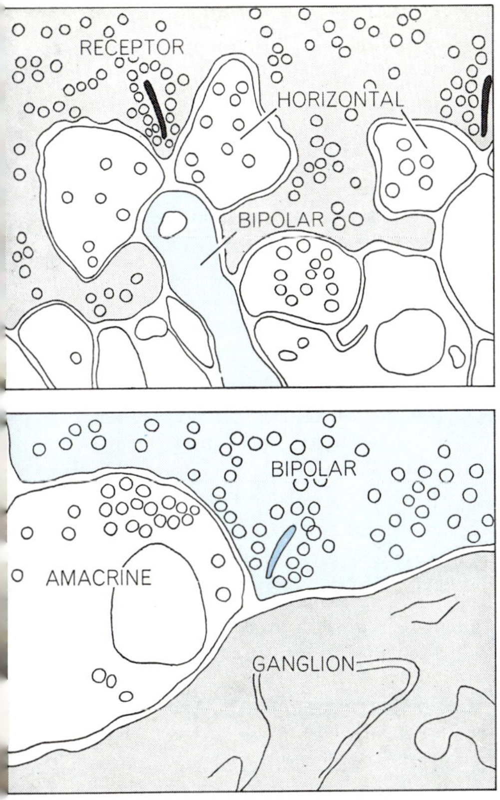

diameters (*bottom*), synapses with processes from an amacrine cell and a ganglion cell. In the primate retina the signal from a receptor is conducted directly to a ganglion cell.

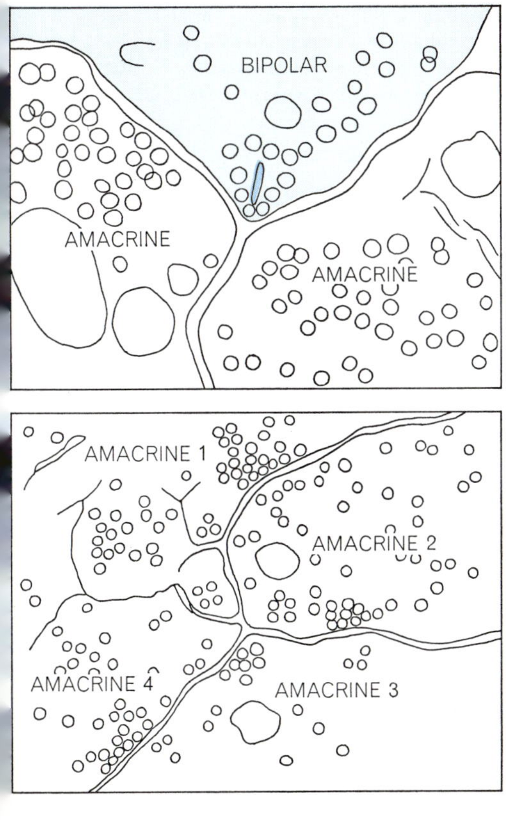

Signals from receptors are conducted not directly to ganglion cells but rather to amacrine cells and from them to ganglion cells.

carried out a detailed electron-microscope study of the synaptic organization of the retina [*see illustrations on these two pages*]. In the outer synaptic layer of all the retinas he has studied the terminals in the bases of the receptors form synapses with bipolar-cell dendrites and horizontal-cell processes. The horizontal cells connect neighboring receptors; the bipolar cells send information to the inner synaptic layer. In the retinas of the frog, the pigeon and the rabbit there are additional connections: horizontal-cell processes also form synapses with other horizontal cells and with bipolar-cell dendrites.

In the inner synaptic layer of the primate retina each bipolar terminal forms synapses with two processes, a ganglion-cell dendrite and an amacrine-cell process. The tangential processes of the amacrine cells extend as much as one millimeter along the inner synaptic layer and are most likely involved in the lateral transmission of information across the retina. In the inner synaptic layer of the frog's retina the bipolar terminals make contact only with amacrine cells, which in turn form synapses with ganglion cells; the frog's ganglion cells are therefore primarily influenced by amacrine rather than by bipolar cells. In fact, in the frog's retina anywhere from one to five amacrine cells may be interposed between a given bipolar cell and the ganglion cell with which it is associated. Through these serially arranged amacrine cells there is the possibility of considerable neural interaction in the inner synaptic layer of the frog.

It appears that it is primarily the pattern of organization in the two synaptic layers that distinguishes the retinas of different species. How is it that the retina of primates is simpler than that of the frog, an animal much lower on the evolutionary scale, and that the frog and the pigeon, which are widely separated in terms of overall development, have remarkably similar retinas? As we shall see, the synaptic complexity of these retinas is reflected in their analytical capacity.

By some unknown mechanism the absorption of light produces an electrical response in the receptors that is transmitted to the bipolar cells. These neurons in turn transmit information to the retinal ganglion cells, whose axons form the optic nerve. Since the optic nerve is the only connection between the retina and the brain, the information it carries represents the total integrative capacity of the retina. It would be ideal if one could study the electrical activity of each of the five types of neuron in the retina and thus learn the function of each and how they interact with one another. Unfortunately it is difficult to record the electrical activity of any individual neurons in the retina other than the ganglion cells. Most investigators have therefore studied ganglion cells or their axons, the individual fibers of the optic nerve. This type of study enables one to determine the overall analytical powers of a retina, and in some cases to deduce the individual steps of the processing.

A given retinal ganglion cell receives information from a rather small population of receptor cells. The area covered by these receptors is called the receptive field of that ganglion cell. In other words, the receptive field of a cell in the visual system is the area of the retina that, when stimulated, influences the electrical activity of the cell in either an excitatory or an inhibitory manner. In an experiment a microelectrode is inserted into the retina or the optic nerve of an anesthetized animal until the electrical activity of a single ganglion cell or optic nerve fiber is recorded. The eye is presented with a series of test stimuli, projected directly onto the retina or onto a white screen the animal is facing, while the microelectrode is simultaneously advanced through the optic nerve or the retina. Often it is necessary to try a large variety of stimuli before finding the one that will evoke the strongest response from a cell. The search may take several hours, but in all cases it is eventually possible to map a cell's receptive field and define precisely the type of stimulus to which it responds.

In 1938 H. K. Hartline, working at the University of Pennsylvania, studied the receptive fields of the frog's ganglion cells and for the first time succeeded in mapping the receptive fields of cells in a visual system. (For such pioneering investigations Hartline received a Nobel prize in 1967.) In 1953 Stephen W. Kuffler, then at the Wilmer Institute, found that the receptive fields of the cat's retinal ganglion cells were organized in a concentric manner, with a circular central area surrounded by a ring-shaped outer zone. In some instances a spot of light in the central region excited a cell (an "on" response), whereas light falling on the surround inhibited any spontaneous discharge and a burst of impulses followed when the illumination ceased (an "off" response). In other cells the situation was reversed: illumination of the center produced an "off" response, and stimulation of the surround an "on" response. Stimuli that simultaneously covered both the center and the surround had little effect on a cell's discharge. What each of these ganglion cells was doing, in other words, was comparing the illumination of the center of its receptive field with that of the surround. Ganglion cells with this type of receptive field have been found in the retinas of every vertebrate that has been studied.

Several years later Jerome Y. Lettvin and his colleagues at the Massachusetts Institute of Technology decided to reexamine the receptive fields of ganglion cells in the retina of the frog. They found that the frog's retina is much more complex than the cat's. It appears to have at least five classes of ganglion cells, including some that respond only to convex edges or only to changes in contrast. For example, the convex-edge detectors respond to the positive curvature of an edge that is darker than the background. Straight edges are poor stimuli, but any perceptible convexity or projecting angle evokes a discharge; in general, the greater the curvature of the edge, the larger the response.

These cells respond to moving stimuli as well as to those that are stationary within the receptive field. The response to a stationary dark spot lasts for many minutes, but it ceases immediately when the background light is turned off and does not appear again when it is turned on. Similarly, when a stimulus is brought into the receptive field in total darkness and the background light is then turned on, there is no response. Apparently an additional requirement for the discharge of these cells is that the object be "seen" during its movement into the field.

The frog is primarily interested in catching flying insects, and so most of its ganglion cells, including the convex-edge detectors, are organized to respond to small moving objects. Cells with such sophisticated discriminatory properties have never been seen in the cat's retina. The complexity of the ganglion cells' behavior in the frog may be related to the extensive serial synapses among amacrine cells interposed between the bipolar axons and the ganglion-cell dendrites.

For the past 10 years David H. Hubel and Torsten N. Wiesel of the Harvard Medical School have been studying the receptive fields of cells in the visual system of cats and monkeys [see the article "The Visual Cortex of the Brain," by David H. Hubel, beginning on page

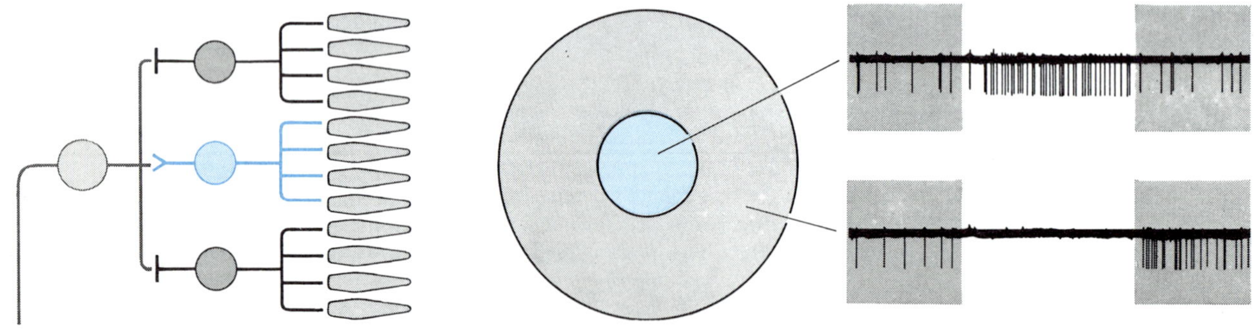

CONTRAST-SENSITIVE ganglion cells in the cat's retina have fields with a concentric organization. The oscilloscope records (*right*) show that a spot of light in the center of the receptive field (*middle*) of this "on"-center ganglion cell excites the cell; stimulation of the surround inhibits it. (The responses would be reversed if this were an "off"-center cell.) Presumably there are two types of bipolar cell, excitatory (*color*) and inhibitory (*black*), that collect information from receptors in the two parts of the field (*left*).

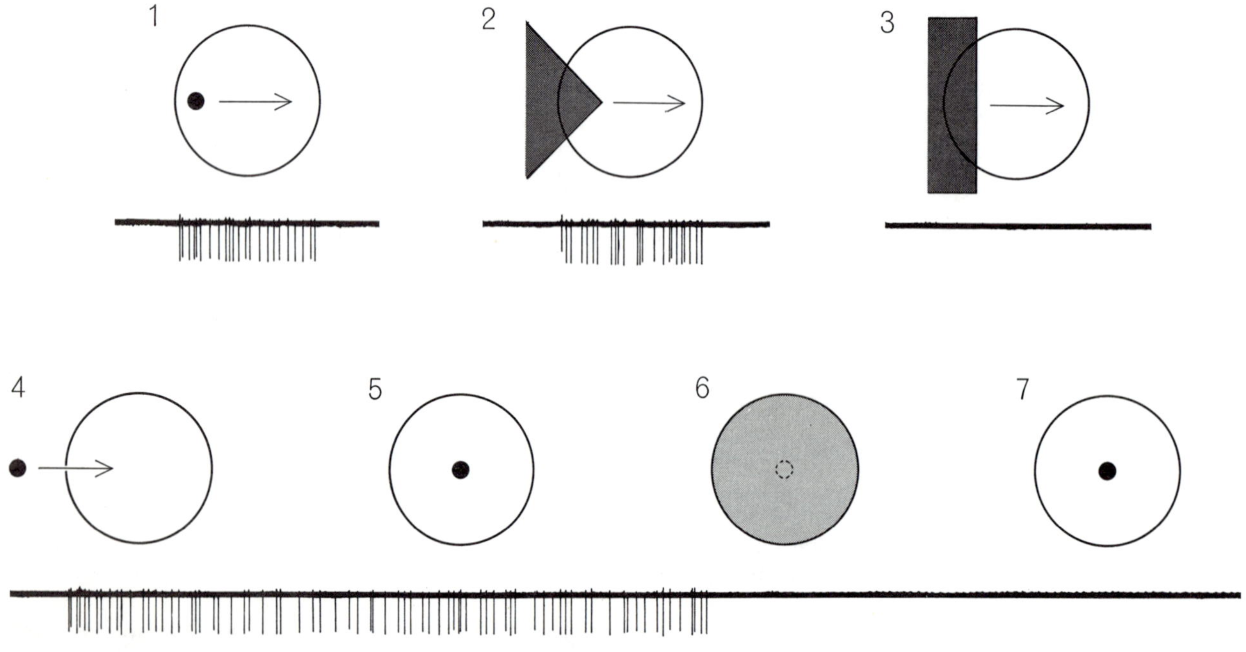

CONVEX-EDGE DETECTORS in the frog's retina respond to a moving stimulus that has a positive curvature (*1*) or contains an angle (*2*) but not to a moving straight edge (*3*). The response to an object entering the field (*4*) continues when the object stops within the field (*5*). The response ceases when the background light goes off (*6*) and does not recur if the light goes on again (*7*).

148]. In the course of their investigations farther along the visual pathway they have found that the receptive fields of neurons in the visual cortex of the brain are organized so that the cells are most sensitive to line stimuli, such as white or black bars or straight edges separating light areas from dark ones. In all cases the size, shape, position and orientation of the stimulus is highly critical for an optimum response.

So far Hubel and Wiesel have identified three major classes of form-sensitive cortical cells [*see illustrations at right*]. The first, called simple cells, have receptive fields that can be mapped with stationary stimuli. The fields are subdivided into excitatory and inhibitory regions separated by boundaries that are straight and parallel. The neurons next highest in order, the complex cells, have receptive fields that cannot be mapped into "on" and "off" regions and are best studied with moving stimuli. Unlike the simple cells, the complex ones respond with sustained firing to movement throughout their receptive fields, and the response is usually directionally selective.

The highest order of cortical neurons studied, the hypercomplex cells, are most effectively activated by a properly oriented line stimulus that is limited in its length at one end or both ends. The receptive fields consist of a central orientation-sensitive "activation" area flanked on one side or on opposite sides by orientation-sensitive "antagonistic" regions. The hypercomplex cells respond only to moving stimuli, again usually in a directionally selective manner. Cells with receptive fields of these three types occur only in the cortex of the cat and the monkey, not in the retina. Moreover, of these three types of cortical cell only the hypercomplex ones have functional properties that approach in sophistication the retinal ganglion cells of the frog.

From the work of Kuffler, Lettvin, Hubel and Wiesel one might have concluded that it is only in lower animals such as frogs that the visual image is analyzed to a significant extent in the retina, and that cells with complicated response properties and receptive fields are found only at the cortical level in the mammalian visual system. Recent investigations—by Horace B. Barlow and William R. Levick at the University of California at Berkeley on the rabbit's retina and by me at Harvard University and Johns Hopkins on the retina of the ground squirrel—make it clear that such a conclusion is not justified. In certain mammals complex analysis of sensory information does occur in the retina, be-

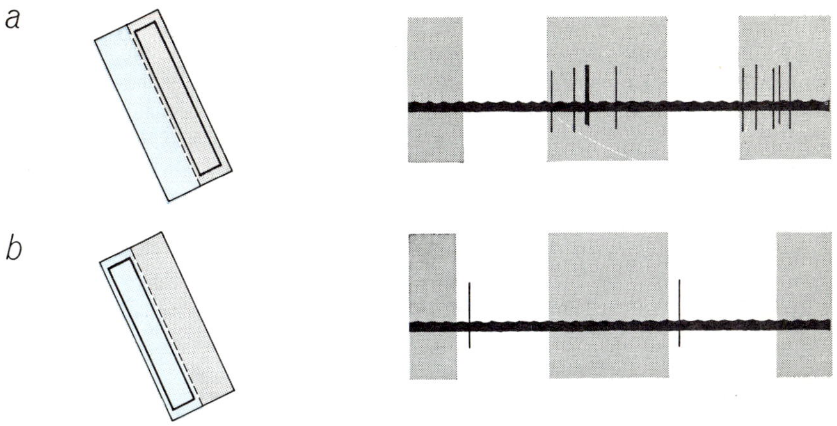

SIMPLE CELL in the cat's visual cortex has a field with excitatory (*color*) and inhibitory regions separated by straight, parallel boundaries. This one gives an "off" response to a slit stimulus in one region (*a*) and a small "on" response to a stimulus in the other region (*b*).

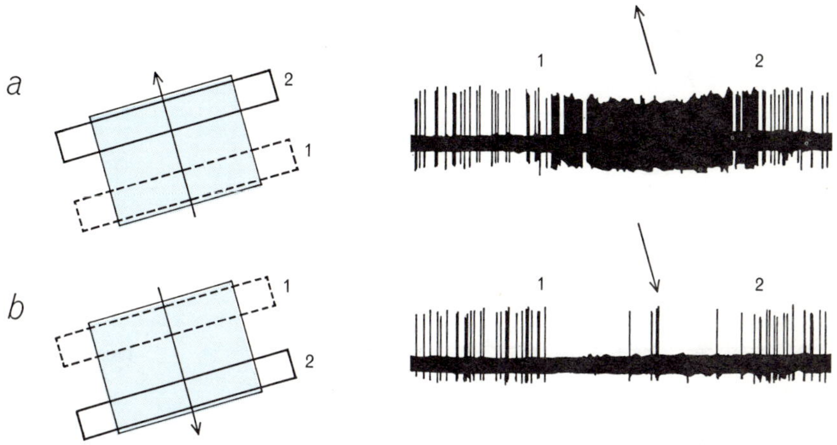

COMPLEX CELL in the cat's cortex responds continuously to a properly oriented stimulus moving across its entire field. This spontaneously active cell responds vigorously to movement in one direction (*a*) and is largely inhibited by movement in the other direction (*b*).

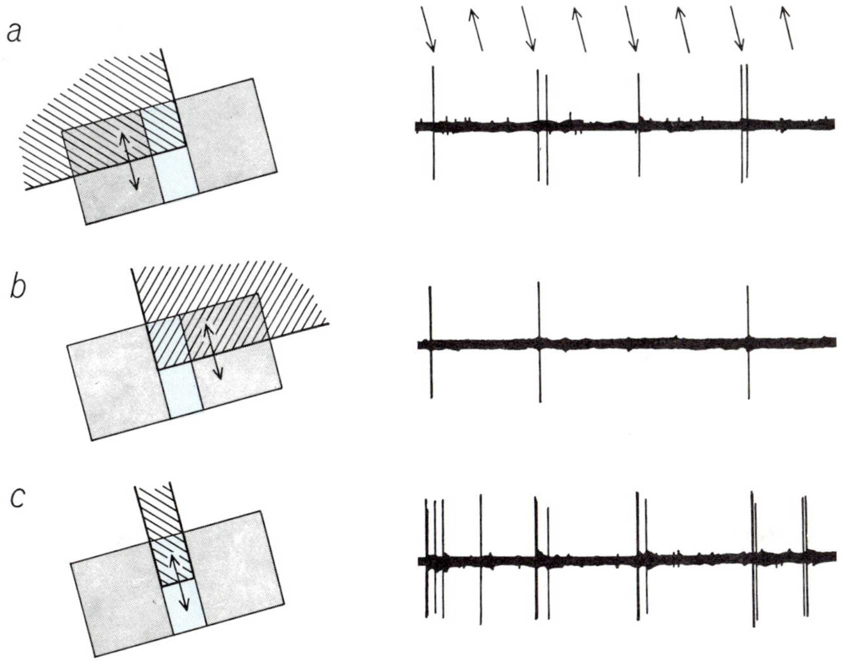

HYPERCOMPLEX CELL has a field with a central activation region (*color*) and antagonistic flanks (*gray*). It responds best to stimuli that are limited in length. Here the longer stimuli affect both kinds of region (*a*, *b*), the most limited one only the activation area (*c*).

fore the neural activity moves on to the higher nervous centers. Some mammalian retinas, in fact, appear to be capable of a complexity of neural integration that in the cat and the monkey is attained only in the visual cortex.

We find that the retina of the rabbit and that of the ground squirrel (*Citellus mexicanus*) contain many types of ganglion cell, each specifically sensitive to a particular aspect of the stimulus such as color, convex edges or oriented lines. The most thoroughly investigated of these cells are the directionally selective neurons found in both animals. They are vigorously excited by a stimulus moving in one direction (the "preferred" direction) across their receptive fields and are inhibited by motion in the reverse direction (the "null" direction). The directionally selective response is independent of the velocity of movement of the stimulus, its shape, the contrast between it and the background and the level of the background illumination [*see upper illustration below*]. Smaller stimuli are more effective than larger ones, indicating that a powerful antagonistic region surrounds the center of the receptive field. The activity of these cells would seem to provide a basis for discriminating the direction of motion of small objects in the animal's visual field.

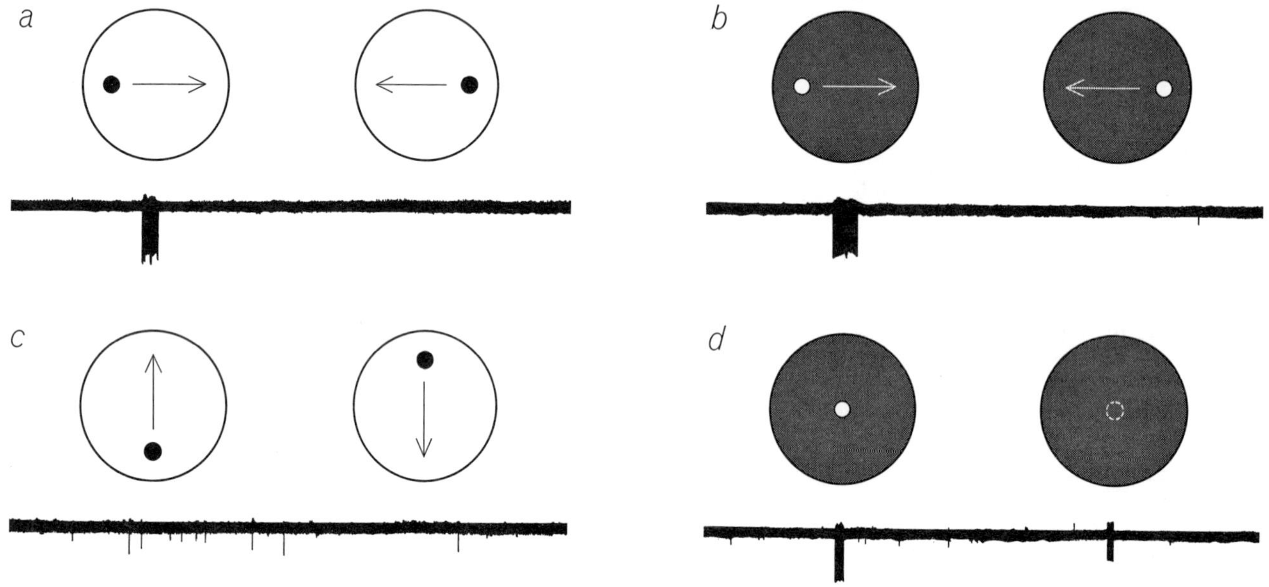

DIRECTIONALLY SELECTIVE ganglion cells in the ground squirrel's retina respond to movement in one direction but not in the opposite direction (*a*). A change in contrast makes no difference (*b*). Movement at a right angle does not produce a clear response (*c*). A stationary spot evokes a brief discharge when the light goes on and another discharge when the light goes off (*d*).

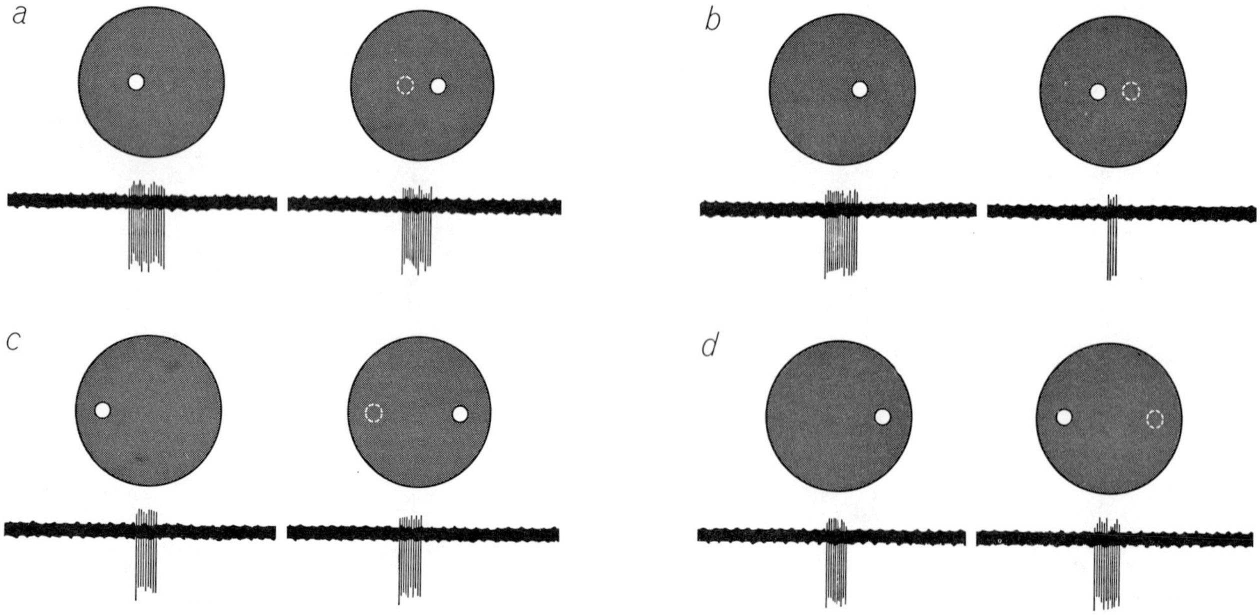

SEQUENCE-DISCRIMINATION is the basis of directional selectivity. When two spots close together are flashed sequentially in the preferred direction, there is a good "on-off" response to each flash (*a*). (In this illustration only "on" responses are shown.) When they are flashed in the opposite direction, the response to the second flash is much weakened (*b*), apparently because of inhibition from the first flash. When the two spots are farther apart, however, the sequence of illumination makes no difference (*c, d*).

We have established that this directional selectivity is accomplished primarily by an inhibitory mechanism. The most direct evidence for inhibition was the cessation of the discharge of spontaneously active units during null movements. Most of the directionally sensitive ganglion cells are not spontaneously active, however. For such "quiet" cells a light spot anywhere in the field center produced a short burst of impulses when it was turned on and another when it was turned off; if the same spot was moved in the null direction, it produced no such response—even though the movement of its leading and trailing edges should be equivalent to the turning on and off of a stationary spot. Apparently a wave of inhibition precedes the null-moving stimulus, preventing or counteracting an excitatory response that would occur if the spot were stationary.

By working with two independent stationary stimuli instead of one moving stimulus we learned more about the inhibitory mechanism and its spatial extent. When two small white spots were positioned next to each other on the directional axis, each spot by itself produced the expected "on-off" response [*see bottom illustration on opposite page*]. When the spots were flashed sequentially in the preferred direction, the response to the second spot was as large as or larger than the response to the first one. When they were flashed sequentially in the null direction, however, only the first spot produced a strong "on-off" discharge; the second response was weak or absent. Apparently any potential response to the second spot was partially or completely inhibited by the first flash. It must therefore be the sequence of changes in the illumination of points along the directional axis that determines the response to a moving stimulus.

The next step was to move the two white spots away from each other. When the separation was small, there was a clear indication of inhibition for the null sequence of illumination. When the separation reached 20 minutes of arc, however, the second response was as strong as the first regardless of the sequence of illumination. This showed that the complete mechanism for discriminating the sequence of excitation is contained within an area extending about 15 minutes of arc along the directional axis, a distance corresponding to about 30 microns (30 thousandths of a millimeter) on the retina. Since the diameter of the field centers ranged between 30 and 60 minutes of arc, the mechanism

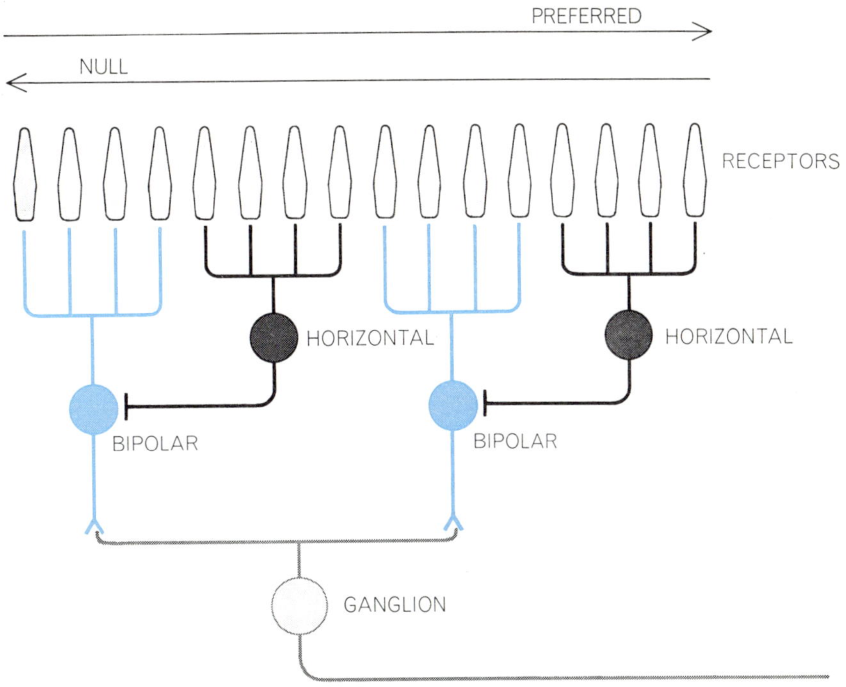

MECHANISM for directional selectivity is suggested. Each bipolar cell is connected to two groups of receptors—to one directly and to the other by way of an inhibitory horizontal cell. A stimulus moving to the right (preferred direction) excites the bipolar cells, which in turn excite the ganglion cell. A stimulus moving to the left (null direction), however, first excites the horizontal cells, inhibiting any subsequent response from the bipolar cells.

for directional selectivity clearly does not require movement over the entire center in order to operate effectively.

Barlow and Levick proposed a mechanism to explain the directional selectivity of these cells, and their conclusions were confirmed and extended by my own work on the ground squirrel's retina. The results from both laboratories suggest that a directionally selective ganglion cell must be excited by a group of sequence-discriminating subunits that share the same preferred direction of motion. This must be the case because the experiments with two spots showed that sequence discrimination involved distances considerably smaller than the size of the ganglion cell's field center. The directionally selective mechanism must therefore be located at an earlier stage than the retinal ganglion cells, and it seems likely that the bipolar cells are the subunits.

Suppose a given bipolar cell is connected to two groups of receptors, to one set directly and to the other by way of an interneuron, probably a horizontal cell [*see illustration above*]. The receptors have an excitatory effect on the horizontal or bipolar cell with which they are in contact, but the horizontal cell makes an inhibitory synapse with the bipolar cell. The sequence of excitation of the two populations of receptors will determine the response of the bipolar cell. A stimulus moving in the preferred direction will first excite the bipolar cell through the directly connected receptors. Although the horizontal cell will subsequently be activated, its inhibitory effect will be too late to prevent the bipolar cell's excitatory response. A spot moving in the null direction, on the other hand, will first stimulate the receptors connected to the horizontal cell, thereby inhibiting the bipolar-cell activity that would otherwise be excited by the directly connected receptors. Thus the bipolar cells distinguish between the null and the preferred sequences of excitation of the two neighboring receptor populations with which they are associated. A ganglion cell receives excitatory inputs from a number of these sequence-discriminating bipolar cells and therefore is itself excited by preferred motion. Since any spontaneous discharges by ganglion cells are inhibited by null movement, such spontaneous activity is probably produced by a constant excitatory bombardment from the bipolar cells. Any null movement inhibits the bipolar cells, and so the spontaneous activity of the ganglion cell ceases.

This proposed mechanism needs further study, but so far it is supported by all the physiological experiments performed independently in Barlow's labo-

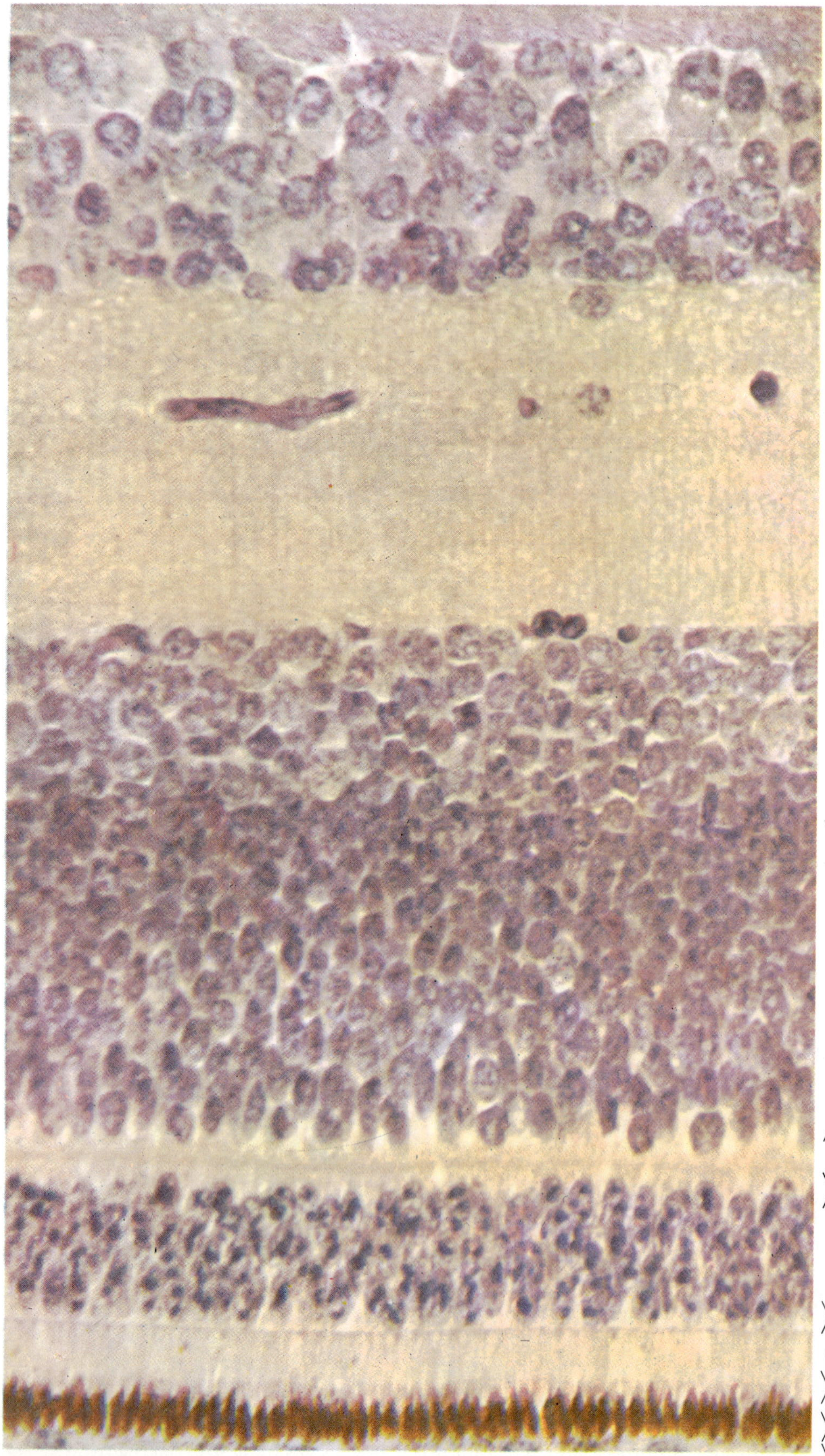

RETINA of the ground squirrel is enlarged 800 diameters in a photomicrograph made by John E. Dowling of the Johns Hopkins University School of Medicine from a section prepared by Richard L. Sidman of the Harvard Medical School. Light striking the retina passes back (*down in the micrograph*) through the cell layers and is absorbed by visual pigments in the receptors. Depending on the pattern of retinal synapses, the resulting nerve activity excites or inhibits horizontal, bipolar and amacrine cells and ultimately the ganglion cells. The output of the ganglion cells constitutes all the information that is conducted to the brain along the optic nerve.

ratory and in my own. Moreover, the theory's requirement of connections between horizontal and bipolar cells receives anatomical confirmation from Dowling's discovery of horizontal-cell processes in the rabbit's retina that synapse on the dendrites and cell bodies of the bipolar cells. The lateral extent of these processes is in the same range as the dimensions of the subunit systems, measured physiologically. To be sure, these are preliminary microscopic observations, but the organization of the rabbit's outer synaptic layer does seem to support the proposed mechanism for directional selectivity.

Let us now turn to another aspect of the visual image, the perception of color. It is surely one of the most fascinating sensory capacities man possesses, and he shares it with few other animals. Among the mammals only man and some of the Old World monkeys have complete color vision as we know it; some New World monkeys, the tree shrew and the ground squirrel have partial color vision. Any animal that does see color must have two or more visual pigments in its retina. These pigments are contained in the receptors called cones. (The other photoreceptor cells of vertebrates, the rods, function in dim illumination and their visual pigment is not involved in color perception.) Since the ground squirrel's retina contains only cones, it is not surprising that many of its ganglion cells code and relay color information.

The ground squirrel appears to have two cone visual pigments, one that absorbs maximally in the green region of the spectrum and another that is most sensitive in the blue. The ganglion cells concerned with color coding are "opponent color" cells. They are either excited by green light and inhibited by blue or excited by blue light and inhibited by green. It seems probable that a given ganglion cell receives information from two classes of bipolar cells, one connected only with cones containing the green-sensitive pigment and the other only with cones containing the blue-sensitive pigment. Presumably one type of bipolar cell excites the ganglion cell and the other inhibits it. As one would expect, these ganglion cells are poorly responsive to white light, which contains all wavelengths and therefore stimulates both the excitatory and the inhibitory inputs.

A series of experiments revealed that

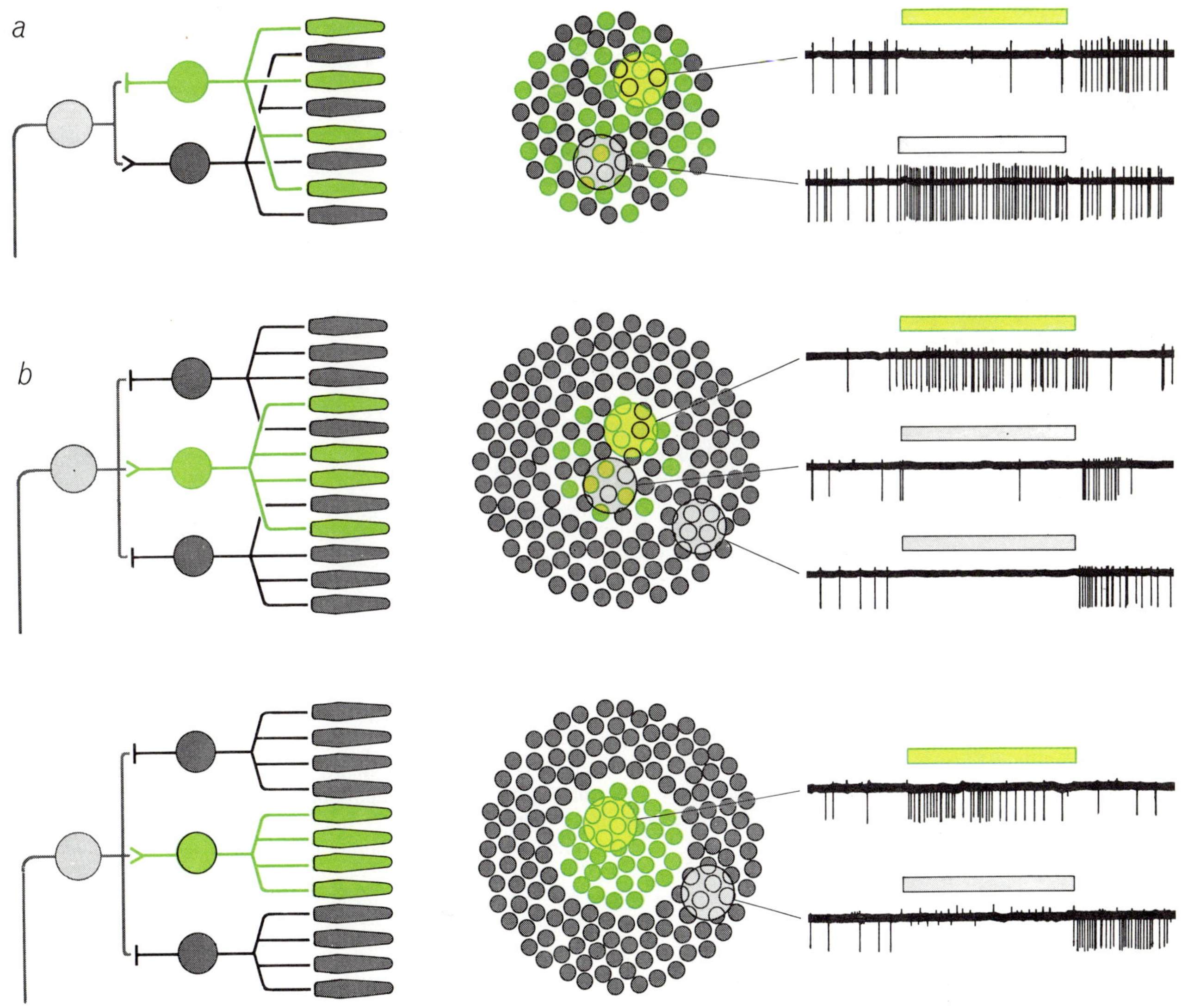

GROUND SQUIRREL'S RETINA seems to have two cone pigments, one more sensitive to green light and the other to blue (*shown here as gray*). Three types of color-coded ganglion cell (*left*) have been identified: some with receptive fields (*middle*) in which two cone populations overlap completely (*a*), some in which they are partially segregated (*b*) and some in which they are completely segregated (*c*). Probably each ganglion cell receives information from some bipolar cells connected to green-sensitive cones and others connected to blue-sensitive cones. The bipolar cells have opposite effects: one excites a ganglion cell and the other inhibits it.

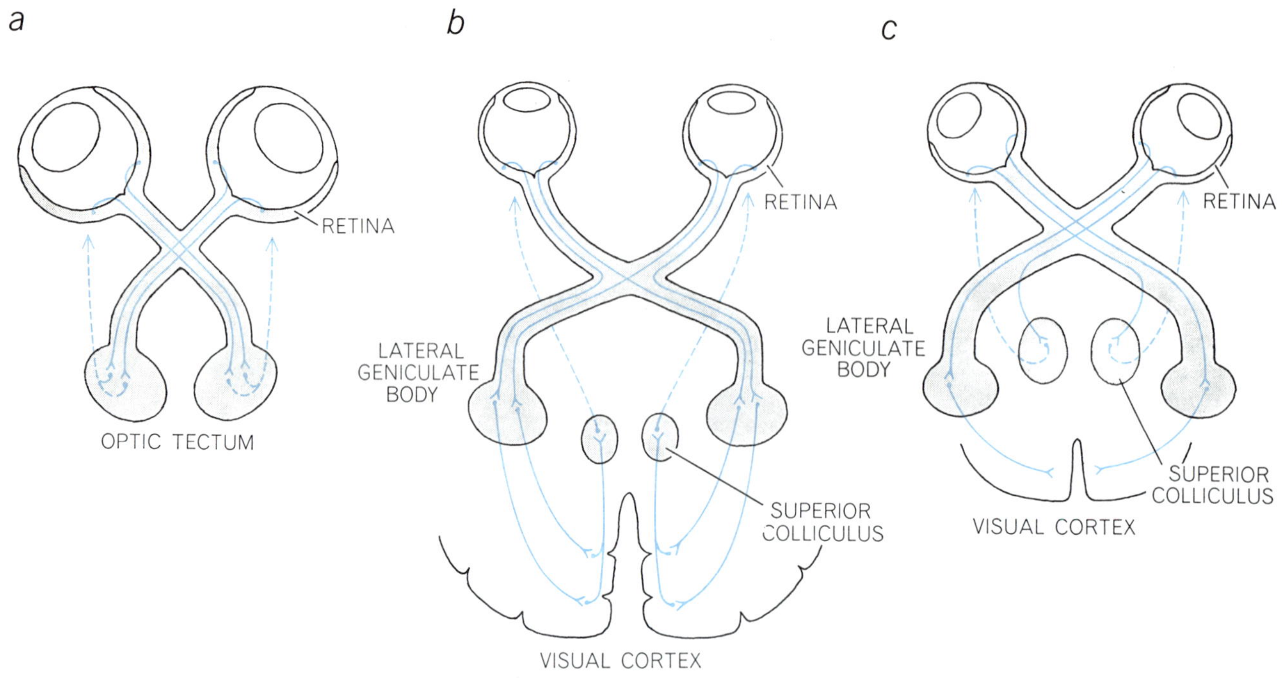

OPTIC NERVE FIBERS have different destinations in different species. The frog and the pigeon have no cortex, and almost all the fibers project to the optic tectum (*a*). In the cat and primates almost all the fibers go to the lateral geniculate nucleus, where signals are relayed to the well-developed visual cortex (*b*). The ground squirrel may be a special intermediate case. Some fibers (the more sophisticated, directionally selective ones) go to the superior colliculus; the remainder go to the lateral geniculate, which projects to the cortex (*c*). From the colliculus (or tectum) signals travel to the muscles controlling eye movement (*broken arrows*).

the receptive fields of the ground squirrel's opponent-color cells are divided into several classes [*see illustration on preceding page*]. In many cases the field seemed not to be organized into a center and a surround but instead gave opponent-color responses throughout its extent; apparently the green-sensitive and the blue-sensitive cones feeding into these cells had identical spatial distributions. Another class of cells had a field center and a surround; only the center received inputs from green-sensitive cones, whereas both the center and the surround were influenced by blue-sensitive cones. The third group also had a center-surround organization, but here the center was driven only by green-sensitive cones and the surround only by blue-sensitive ones; in this last type of field there was complete spatial separation of the two color systems.

The color-coded responses of ganglion cells were first studied in the goldfish by Edward F. MacNichol, Jr., of Johns Hopkins and Henry G. Wagner and Myron L. Wolbarsht of the Naval Medical Research Institute [see "Three-Pigment Color Vision," by Edward F. MacNichol, Jr.; Scientific American Offprint 197]. Recently Hubel and Wiesel have mapped the receptive fields of several types of opponent-color cells in the monkey's lateral geniculate nucleus, the neural way station between the retina and the visual cortex. In all the animals studied the receptive fields of most of the color-coded cells are organized in such a way that they can deal with both color and contrast information. In other words, there are opponent-color and opponent-spatial mechanisms influencing the activity of a single cell. This means that the optimum stimulus must be specified not only in terms of color but also in size and shape.

It appears to be a general rule that the retinal processing of information involves a comparison by a ganglion cell of the signals from two sets of receptors. What the contrast-sensitive units in the cat are doing is comparing the information received from receptors in the field center with information from other receptors located in the surround. The directionally selective cells in the rabbit's and the ground squirrel's retina are collecting data from subunits sensitive to the sequence in which two separate sets of receptors are illuminated. Finally, the opponent-color units in the ground squirrel are comparing the excitatory and inhibitory signals from two populations of cones that have different spectral sensitivities and often different spatial distributions. For each type of cell there is an antagonistic interaction of the excitatory and inhibitory effects of two groups of receptors, and so a generalized stimulus is far less effective than one that is quite specific in contrast, movement or color.

One can see, then, that there are two principal types of visual system. The first is typified in the frog, the rabbit and the ground squirrel. (The work of Humberto R. Maturana in Chile on the pigeon's retina indicates that it too belongs in this group.) The individual ganglion cells of these animals are usually highly specialized in terms of stimulus requirements, and such fundamental variables as edges, color, contrast, orientation and directional movement are processed intensively within the retina. The second type of visual system is the one found in cats, monkeys and presumably man. Here the ganglion cells at the retinal level are concerned only with the simultaneous contrast between the centers and the surrounds of their receptive fields, and in some cases with color information. The aspects of edge detection, orientation and directional selectivity are dealt with only later in the visual cortex, and there in a most detailed and precise manner.

Why should some animals process visual information so intensively within the retina whereas others put off this integration until farther along the visual pathway? One major factor may be the presence or absence of a visual cortex and, if it is present, its level of development. The frog and the pigeon, for instance, have no visual cortex; almost all their optic nerve fibers go to the optic tectum. The cat and the monkey have a highly developed cortex; almost all their optic nerve fibers go to the lateral geniculate nucleus, whose neurons in turn project their axons to the visual cortex. The ground squirrel has a visual cortex, but it is one that lacks the extensive convoluted surface characteristic of the cat's and the primate's cortex and presumably has not developed functionally to the same degree as it has in the higher mammals. And, as one might have predicted, in the ground squirrel about half of the optic nerve fibers project to the lateral geniculate nucleus and the rest go to the superior colliculus, the mammalian analogue of the optic tectum [*see illustration on page 146*].

The ground squirrel, then, represents an interesting intermediate situation. It has some highly specialized retinal ganglion cells, the directionally selective neurons. These, I have found, project to the superior colliculus just as the sophisticated neurons of the frog's and the pigeon's retina go to the analogous optic tectum. On the other hand, the ground squirrel's retina also contains some simpler ganglion cells, the contrast-sensitive and opponent-color neurons. As in the cat and primates, these cells project to the lateral geniculate nucleus, where the information is relayed to the visual cortex. It appears that, regardless of the presence or absence of a visual cortex or of its degree of development, highly specialized retinal ganglion cells always project to the superior colliculus (or the optic tectum). Since the superior colliculus is associated with eye movements, it is not surprising that the information on directional movement is sent there. Nor is it surprising that the contrast and color information goes to the cortex, which is involved in the conscious perception of the visual image.

This parceling out of information occurs in a different way in the cat and the primate, whose retinas are simpler. In these animals one of the major outputs of the visual cortex is to the superior colliculus, perhaps providing a route for information related to the voluntary control of eye movements. This suggests a functional unity amid anatomical diversity. The colliculus has not lost its importance with the extensive development of the cortex in higher mammals; rather, its relative position in the visual system has simply been shifted.

15

THE VISUAL CORTEX OF THE BRAIN

DAVID H. HUBEL
November 1963

An image of the outside world striking the retina of the eye activates a most intricate process that results in vision: the transformation of the retinal image into a perception. The transformation occurs partly in the retina but mostly in the brain, and it is, as one can recognize instantly by considering how modest in comparison is the achievement of a camera, a task of impressive magnitude.

The process begins with the responses of some 130 million light-sensitive receptor cells in each retina. From these cells messages are transmitted to other retinal cells and then sent on to the brain, where they must be analyzed and interpreted. To get an idea of the magnitude of the task, think what is involved in watching a moving animal, such as a horse. At a glance one takes in its size, form, color and rate of movement. From tiny differences in the two retinal images there results a three-dimensional picture. Somehow the brain manages to compare this picture with previous impressions; recognition occurs and then any appropriate action can be taken.

The organization of the visual system —a large, intricately connected population of nerve cells in the retina and brain —is still poorly understood. In recent years, however, various studies have begun to reveal something of the arrangement and function of these cells. A decade ago Stephen W. Kuffler, working with cats at the Johns Hopkins Hospital, discovered that some analysis of visual patterns takes place outside the brain, in the nerve cells of the retina. My colleague Torsten N. Wiesel and I at the Harvard Medical School, exploring the first stages of the processing that occurs in the brain of the cat, have mapped the visual pathway a little further: to what appears to be the sixth step from the retina to the cortex of the cerebrum. This kind of work falls far short of providing a full understanding of vision, but it does convey some idea of the mechanisms and circuitry of the visual system.

In broad outline the visual pathway is clearly defined [*see bottom illustration on opposite page*]. From the retina of each eye visual messages travel along the optic nerve, which consists of about a million nerve fibers. At the junction known as the chiasm about half of the nerves cross over into opposite hemispheres of the brain, the other nerves remaining on the same side. The optic nerve fibers lead to the first way stations in the brain: a pair of cell clusters called the lateral geniculate bodies. From here new fibers course back through the brain to the visual area of the cerebral cortex. It is convenient, although admittedly a gross oversimplification, to think of the pathway from retina to cortex as consisting of six types of nerve cells, of which three are in the retina, one is in the geniculate body and two are in the cortex.

Nerve cells, or neurons, transmit messages in the form of brief electrochemical impulses. These travel along the outer membrane of the cell, notably along the membrane of its long principal fiber, the axon. It is possible to obtain an electrical record of impulses of a single nerve cell by placing a fine electrode near the cell body or one of its fibers. Such measurements have shown that impulses travel along the nerves at velocities of between half a meter and 100 meters per second. The impulses in a given fiber all have about the same amplitude; the strength of the stimuli that give rise to them is reflected not in amplitude but in frequency.

At its terminus the fiber of a nerve cell makes contact with another nerve cell (or with a muscle cell or gland cell), forming the junction called the synapse. At most synapses an impulse on reaching the end of a fiber causes the release of a small amount of a specific substance, which diffuses outward to the membrane of the next cell. There the substance either excites the cell or inhibits it. In excitation the substance acts to bring the cell into a state in which it is more likely to "fire"; in inhibition the substance acts to prevent firing. For most synapses the substances that act as transmitters are unknown. Moreover, there is no sure way to determine from microscopic appearances alone whether a synapse is excitatory or inhibitory.

It is at the synapses that the modification and analysis of nerve messages take place. The kind of analysis depends partly on the nature of the synapse: on how many nerve fibers converge on a single cell and on how the excitatory and inhibitory endings distribute themselves. In most parts of the nervous system the anatomy is too intricate to reveal much about function. One way to circumvent this difficulty is to record impulses with microelectrodes in anesthetized animals, first from the fibers coming into a structure of neurons and then from the neurons themselves, or from the fibers they send onward. Comparison of the behavior of incoming and outgoing fibers provides a basis for learning what the structure does. Through such exploration of the different parts of the brain concerned with vision one can hope to build up some idea of how the entire visual system works.

That is what Wiesel and I have undertaken, mainly through studies of the visual system of the cat. In our experiments the anesthetized animal faces a wide screen 1.5 meters away, and we shine various patterns of white light on the screen with a projector. Simultaneously we penetrate the visual portion of the cortex with microelectrodes. In that way we can record the responses of individual cells to the light patterns. Sometimes it takes many hours to find the region of the retina with which a particular visual cell is linked and to work out the optimum stimuli for that cell. The reader should bear in mind the relation between each visual cell—no matter how far along the visual pathway it may be—and the retina. It requires an image on the retina to evoke a meaningful response in any visual cell, however indirect and complex the linkage may be.

The retina is a complicated structure, in both its anatomy and its physiology, and the description I shall give is highly simplified. Light coming through the lens of the eye falls on the mosaic of receptor cells in the retina. The receptor cells do not send impulses directly through the optic nerve but instead connect with a set of retinal cells called bipolar cells. These in turn connect with retinal ganglion cells, and it is the latter set of cells, the third in the visual pathway, that sends its fibers—the optic nerve fibers—to the brain.

This series of cells and synapses is no simple bucket brigade for impulses: a receptor may send nerve endings to more than one bipolar cell, and several receptors may converge on one bipolar cell. The same holds for the synapses between the bipolar cells and the retinal ganglion cells. Stimulating a single receptor by light might therefore be expected to have an influence on many bipolar or ganglion cells; conversely, it should be possible to influence one bipolar or retinal ganglion cell from a number of receptors and hence from a substantial area of the retina.

The area of receptor mosaic in the retina feeding into a single visual cell is called the receptive field of the cell. This term is applied to any cell in the visual system to refer to the area of retina with which the cell is connected—the retinal area that on stimulation produces a response from the cell.

Any of the synapses with a particular cell may be excitatory or inhibitory, so that stimulation of a particular point on the retina may either increase or decrease the cell's firing rate. Moreover, a single cell may receive several excitatory and inhibitory impulses at once, with the result that it will respond according to the net effect of these inputs. In considering the behavior of a single cell an observer should remember that it is just one of a huge popu-

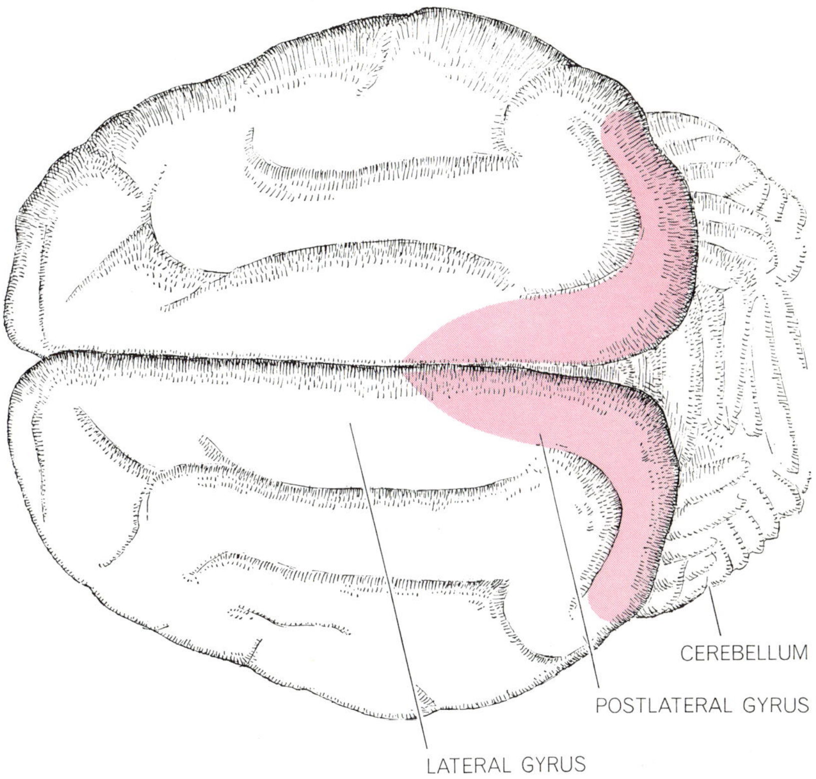

CORTEX OF CAT'S BRAIN is depicted as it would be seen from the top. The colored region indicates the cortical area that deals at least in a preliminary way with vision.

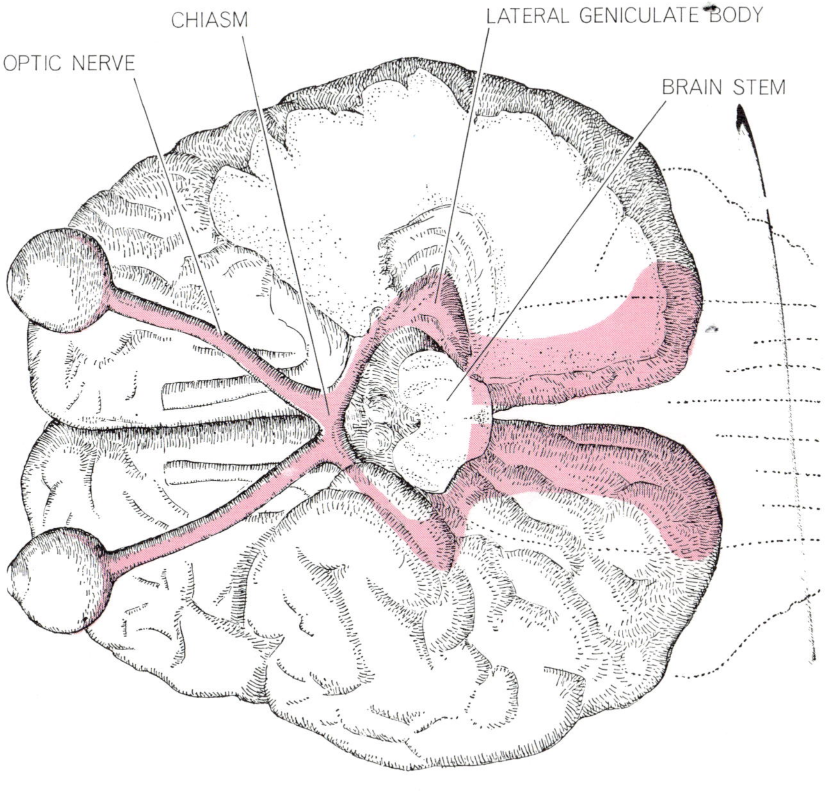

VISUAL SYSTEM appears in this representation of the human brain as viewed from below. Visual pathway from retinas to cortex via the lateral geniculate body is shown in color.

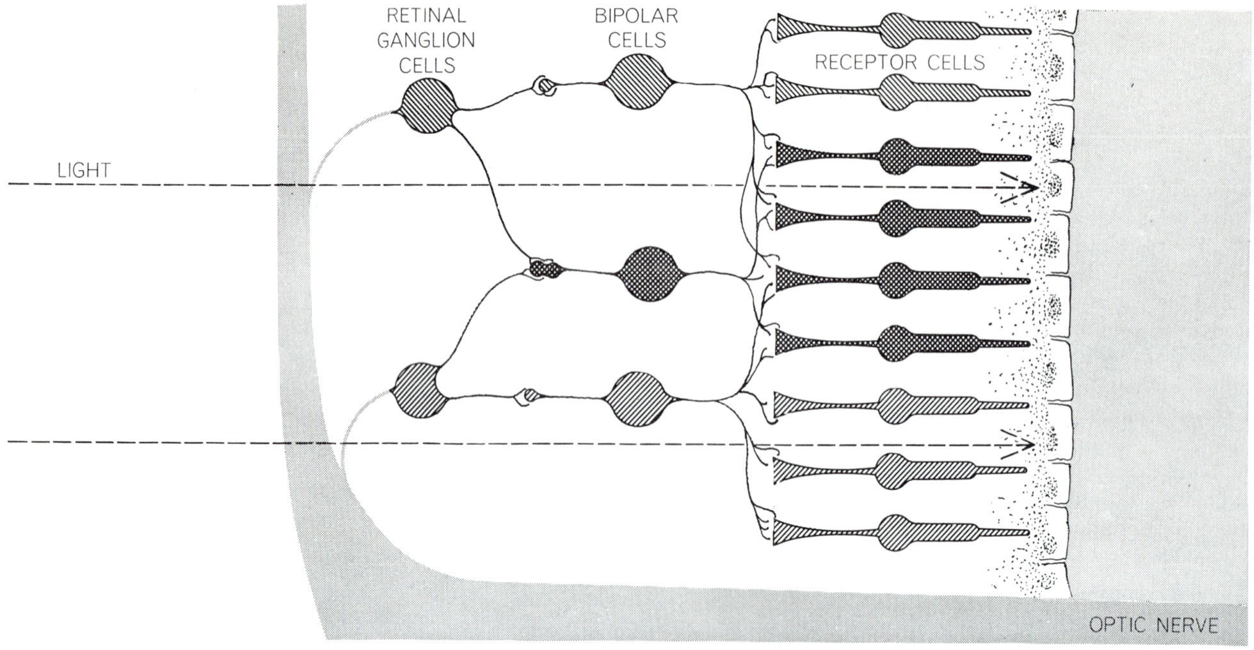

STRUCTURE OF RETINA is depicted schematically. Images fall on the receptor cells, of which there are about 130 million in each retina. Some analysis of an image occurs as the receptors transmit messages to the retinal ganglion cells via the bipolar cells. A group of receptors funnels into a particular ganglion cell, as indicated by the shading; that group forms the ganglion cell's receptive field. Inasmuch as the fields of several ganglion cells overlap, one receptor may send messages to several ganglion cells.

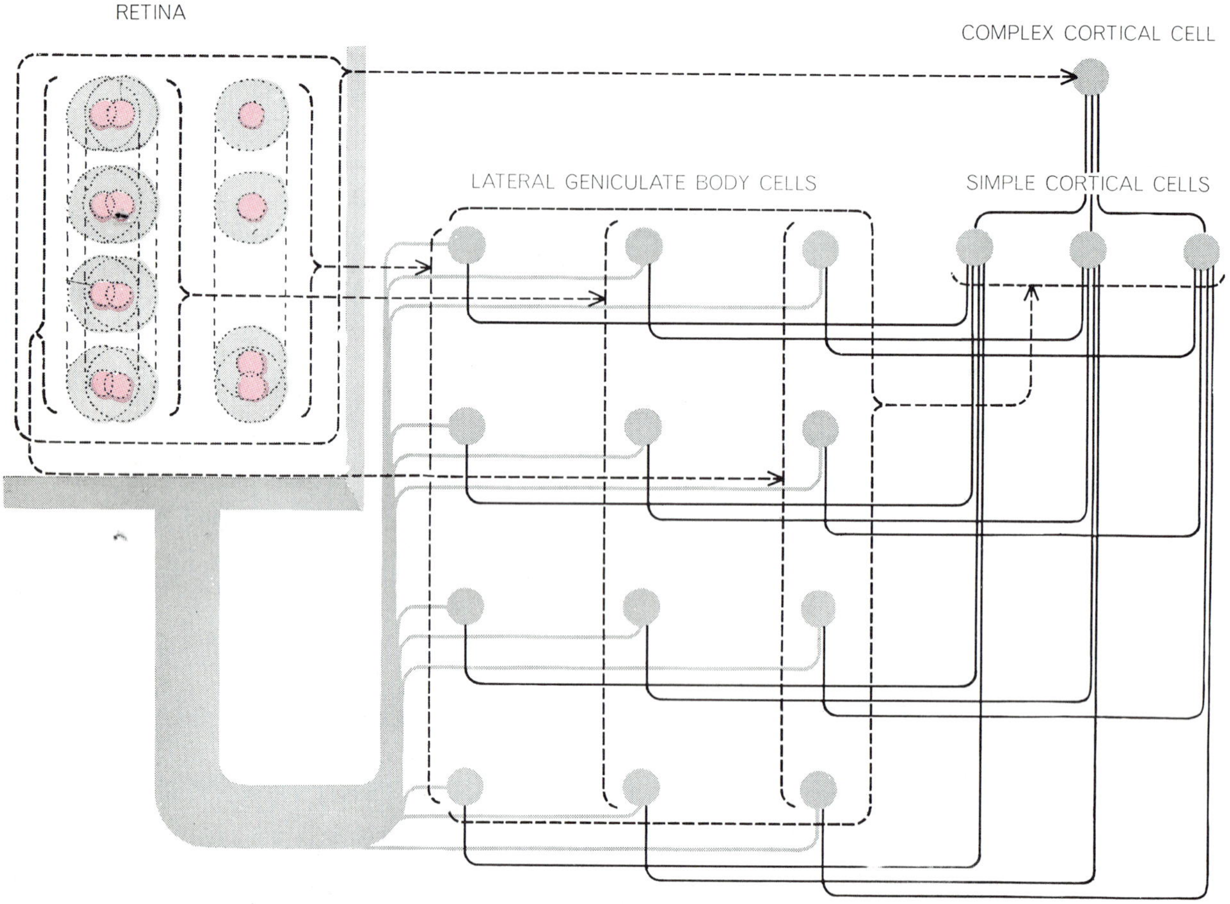

VISUAL PROCESSING BY BRAIN begins in the lateral geniculate body, which continues the analysis made by retinal cells. In the cortex "simple" cells respond strongly to line stimuli, provided that the position and orientation of the line are suitable for a particular cell. "Complex" cells respond well to line stimuli, but the position of the line is not critical and the cell continues to respond even if a properly oriented stimulus is moved, as long as it remains in the cell's receptive field. Broken lines indicate how receptive fields of all these cells overlap on the retina; solid lines, how several cells at one stage affect a single cell at the next stage.

lation of cells: a stimulus that excites one cell will undoubtedly excite many others, meanwhile inhibiting yet another array of cells and leaving others entirely unaffected.

For many years it has been known that retinal ganglion cells fire at a fairly steady rate even in the absence of any stimulation. Kuffler was the first to observe how the retinal ganglion cells of mammals are influenced by small spots of light. He found that the resting discharges of a cell were intensified or diminished by light in a small and more or less circular region of the retina. That region was of course the cell's receptive field. Depending on where in the field a spot of light fell, either of two responses could be produced. One was an "on" response, in which the cell's firing rate increased under the stimulus of light. The other was an "off" response, in which the stimulus of light decreased the cell's firing rate. Moreover, turning the light off usually evoked a burst of impulses from the cell. Kuffler called the retinal regions from which these responses could be evoked "on" regions and "off" regions.

On mapping the receptive fields of a large number of retinal ganglion cells into "on" and "off" regions, Kuffler discovered that there were two distinct cell types. In one the receptive field consisted of a small circular "on" area and a surrounding zone that gave "off" responses. Kuffler termed this an "on"-center cell. The second type, which he called "off"-center, had just the reverse form of field—an "off" center and an "on" periphery [*see top illustration on this page*]. For a given cell the effects of light varied markedly according to the place in which the light struck the receptive field. Two spots of light shone on separate parts of an "on" area produced a more vigorous "on" response than either spot alone, whereas if one spot was shone on an "on" area and the other on an "off" area, the two effects tended to neutralize each other, resulting in a very weak "on" or "off" response. In an "on"-center cell, illuminating the entire central "on" region evoked a maximum response; a smaller or larger spot of light was less effective.

Lighting up the whole retina diffusely, even though it may affect every receptor in the retina, does not affect a retinal ganglion cell nearly so strongly as a small circular spot of exactly the right size placed so as to cover precisely the receptive-field center. The main concern of these cells seems to be the contrast in illumination between one retinal region and surrounding regions.

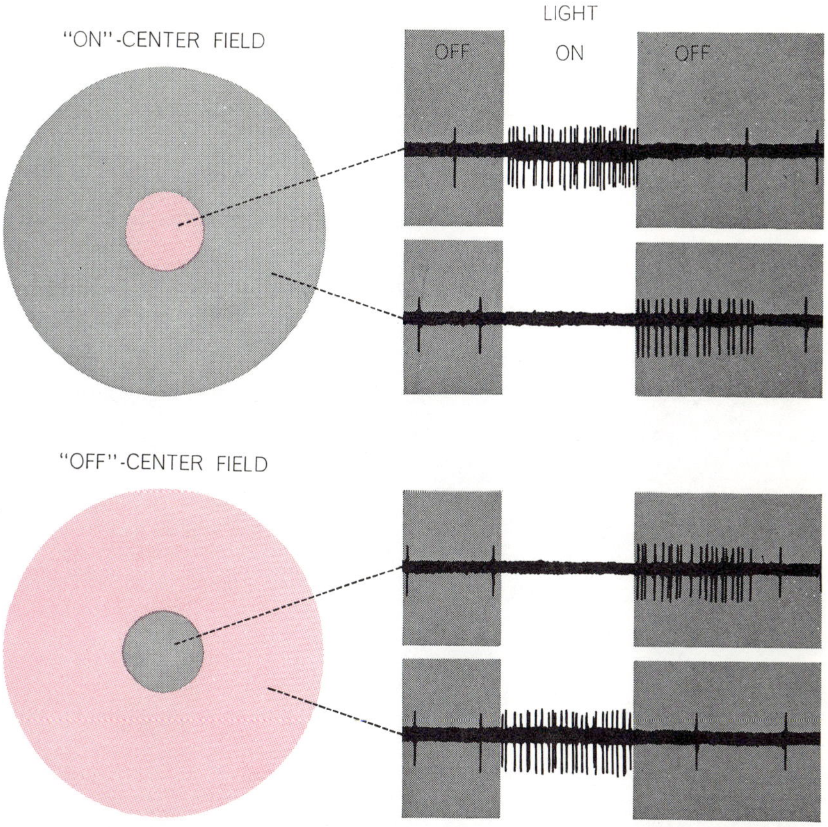

CONCENTRIC FIELDS are characteristic of retinal ganglion cells and of geniculate cells. At top an oscilloscope recording shows strong firing by an "on"-center type of cell when a spot of light strikes the field center; if the spot hits an "off" area, the firing is suppressed until the light goes off. At bottom are responses of another cell of the "off"-center type.

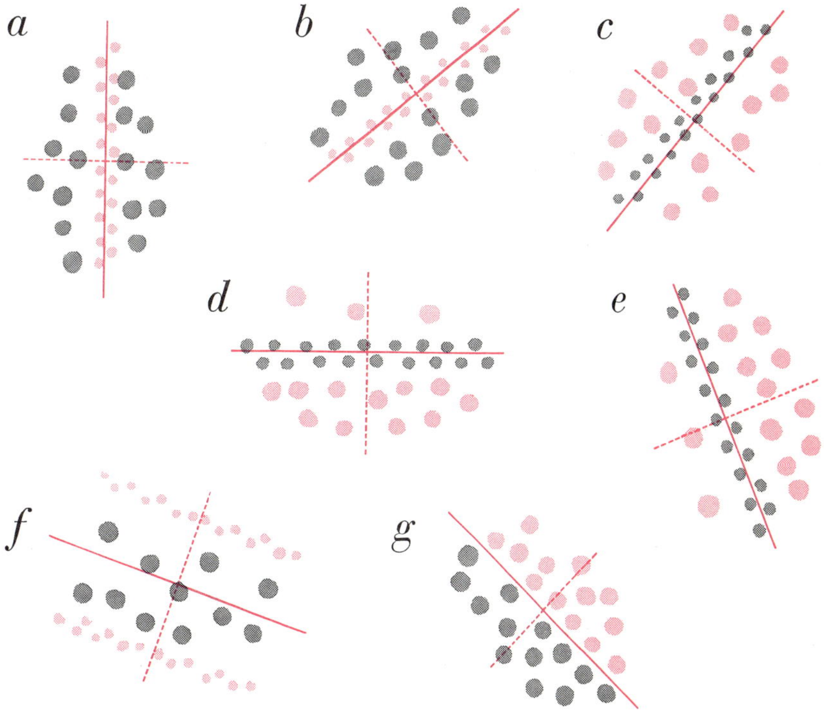

SIMPLE CORTICAL CELLS have receptive fields of various types. In all of them the "on" and "off" areas, represented by colored and gray dots respectively, are separated by straight boundaries. Orientations of fields vary, as indicated particularly at *a* and *b*. In the cat's visual system such fields are generally one millimeter or less in diameter.

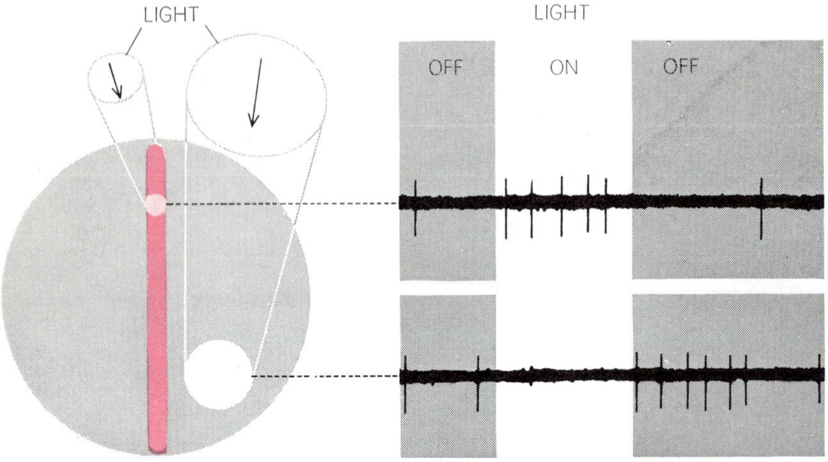

RESPONSE IS WEAK when a circular spot of light is shone on receptive field of a simple cortical cell. Such spots get a vigorous response from retinal and geniculate cells. This cell has a receptive field of type shown at *a* in bottom illustration on preceding page.

IMPORTANCE OF ORIENTATION to simple cortical cells is indicated by varying responses to a slit of light from a cell preferring a vertical orientation. Horizontal slit *(top)* produces no response, slight tilt a weak response, vertical slit a strong response.

Retinal ganglion cells differ greatly in the size of their receptive-field centers. Cells near the fovea (the part of the retina serving the center of gaze) are specialized for precise discrimination; in the monkey the field centers of these cells may be about the same size as a single cone—an area subtending a few minutes of arc at the cornea. On the other hand, some cells far out in the retinal periphery have field centers up to a millimeter or so in diameter. (In man one millimeter of retina corresponds to an arc of about three degrees in the 180-degree visual field.) Cells with such large receptive-field centers are probably specialized for work in very dim light, since they can sum up messages from a large number of receptors.

Given this knowledge of the kind of visual information brought to the brain by the optic nerve, our first problem was to learn how the messages were handled at the first central way station, the lateral geniculate body. Compared with the retina, the geniculate body is a relatively simple structure. In a sense there is only one synapse involved, since the incoming optic nerve fibers end in cells that send their fibers directly to the visual cortex. Yet in the cat many optic nerve fibers converge on each geniculate cell, and it is reasonable to expect some change in the visual messages from the optic nerve to the geniculate cells.

When we came to study the geniculate body, we found that the cells have many of the characteristics Kuffler described for retinal ganglion cells. Each geniculate cell is driven from a circumscribed retinal region (the receptive field) and has either an "on" center or an "off" center, with an opposing periphery. There are, however, differences between geniculate cells and retinal ganglion cells, the most important of which is the greatly enhanced capacity of the periphery of a geniculate cell's receptive field to cancel the effects of the center. This means that the lateral geniculate cells must be even more specialized than retinal ganglion cells in responding to spatial differences in retinal illumination rather than to the illumination itself. The lateral geniculate body, in short, has the function of increasing the disparity—already present in retinal ganglion cells—between responses to a small, centered spot and to diffuse light.

In contrast to the comparatively simple lateral geniculate body, the cerebral cortex is a structure of stupendous complexity. The cells of this great plate of

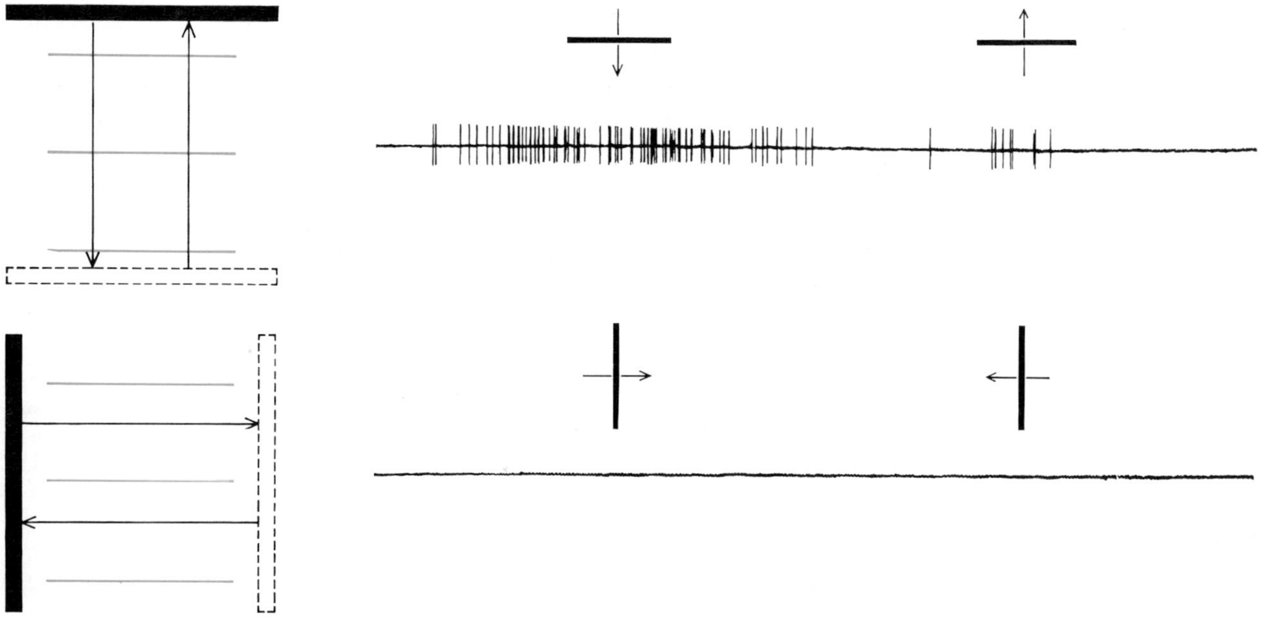

COMPLEX CORTICAL CELL responded vigorously to slow downward movement of a dark, horizontal bar. Upward movement of bar produced a weak response and horizontal movement of a vertical bar produced no response. For other shapes, orientations and movements there are other complex cells showing maximum response. Such cells may figure in perception of form and movement.

gray matter—a structure that would be about 20 square feet in area and a tenth of an inch thick if flattened out—are arranged in a number of more or less distinct layers. The millions of fibers that come in from the lateral geniculate body connect with cortical cells in the layer that is fourth from the top. From here the information is sooner or later disseminated to all layers of the cortex by rich interconnections between them. Many of the cells, particularly those of the third and fifth layers, send their fibers out of the cortex, projecting to centers deep in the brain or passing over to nearby cortical areas for further processing of the visual messages. Our problem was to learn how the information the visual cortex sends out differs from what it takes in.

Most connections between cortical cells are in a direction perpendicular to the surface; side-to-side connections are generally quite short. One might therefore predict that impulses arriving at a particular area of the cortex would exert their effects quite locally. Moreover, the retinas project to the visual cortex (via the lateral geniculate body) in a systematic topologic manner; that is, a given area of cortex gets its input ultimately from a circumscribed area of retina. These two observations suggest that a given cortical cell should have a small receptive field; it should be influenced from a circumscribed retinal region only, just as a geniculate or retinal ganglion cell is. Beyond this the anatomy provides no hint of what the cortex does with the information it receives about an image on the retina.

In the face of the anatomical complexity of the cortex, it would have been surprising if the cells had proved to have the concentric receptive fields characteristic of cells in the retina and the lateral geniculate body. Indeed, in the cat we have observed no cortical cells with concentric receptive fields; instead there are many different cell types, with fields markedly different from anything seen in the retinal and geniculate cells.

The many varieties of cortical cells may, however, be classified by function into two large groups. One we have called "simple"; the function of these cells is to respond to line stimuli—such shapes as slits, which we define as light lines on a dark background; dark bars (dark lines on a light background), and edges (straight-line boundaries between light and dark regions). Whether or not a given cell responds depends on the orientation of the shape and its position on the cell's receptive field. A bar shone vertically on the screen may activate a given cell, whereas the same cell will fail to respond (but others will respond) if the bar is displaced to one side or moved appreciably out of the vertical. The second group of cortical cells we have called "complex"; they too respond best to bars, slits or edges, provided that, as with simple cells, the shape is suitably oriented for the particular cell under observation. Complex cells, however, are not so discriminating as to the exact position of the stimulus, provided that it is properly oriented. Moreover, unlike simple cells, they respond with sustained firing to moving lines.

From the preference of simple and complex cells for specific orientation of light stimuli, it follows that there must be a multiplicity of cell types to handle the great number of possible positions and orientations. Wiesel and I have found a large variety of cortical cell responses, even though the number of individual cells we have studied runs only into the hundreds compared with the millions that exist. Among simple cells, the retinal region over which a cell can be influenced—the receptive field—is, like the fields of retinal and geniculate cells, divided into "on" and "off" areas. In simple cells, however, these areas are far from being circularly symmetrical. In a typical example the receptive field consists of a very long and narrow "on" area, which is adjoined on each side by larger "off" regions. The magnitude of an "on" response depends, as with retinal and geniculate cells, on how much either type of region is covered by the stimulating light. A long, narrow slit that just fills the elongated "on" region produces a powerful "on" response. Stimulation with the slit in a different orientation produces a much weaker effect, because the slit is now no longer illuminating all the "on" region but instead includes some of the antagonistic "off" region. A slit at right angles to the optimum orientation for a

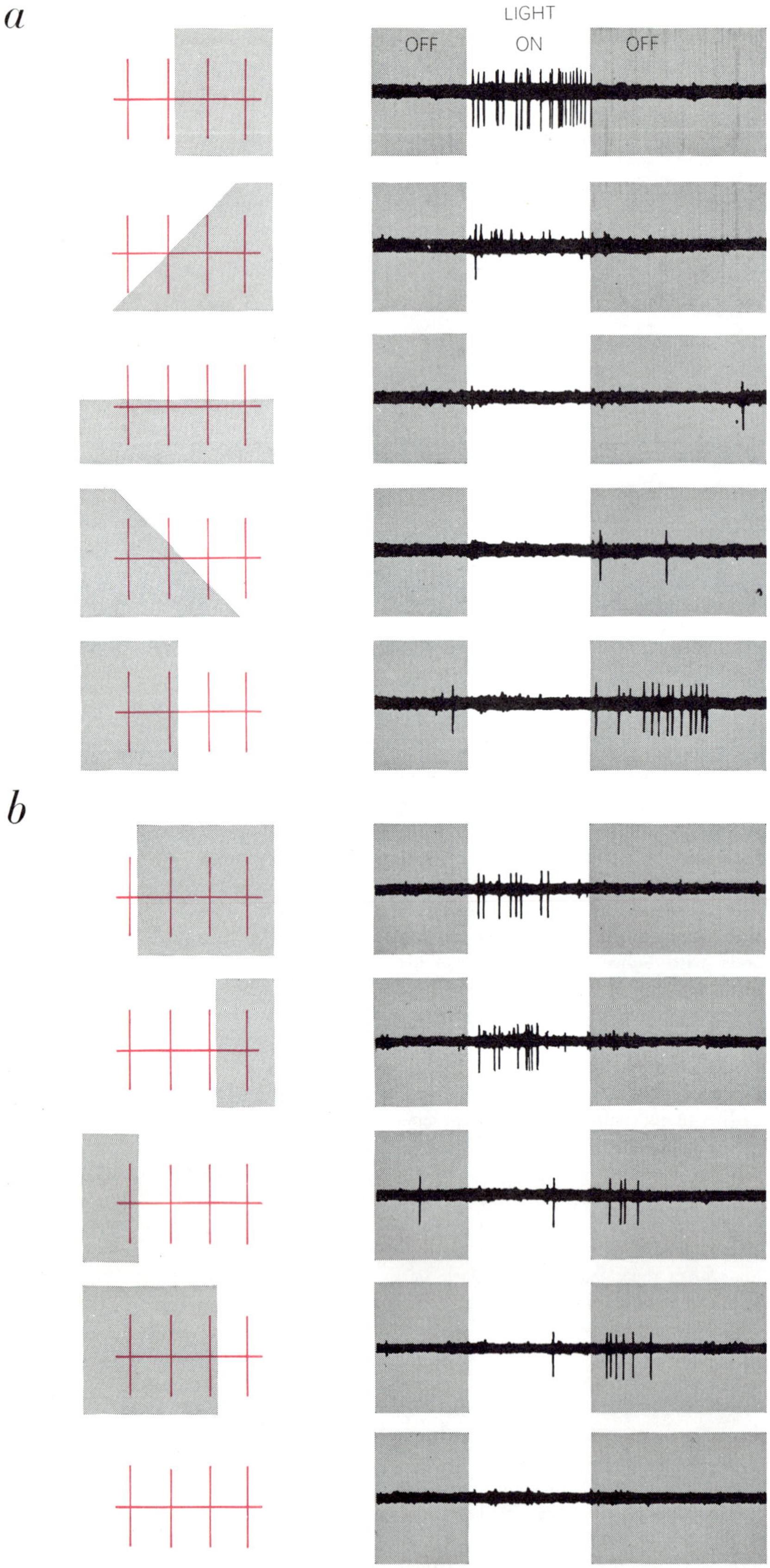

SINGLE COMPLEX CELL showed varying responses to an edge projected on the cell's receptive field in the retina. In group *a* the stimulus was presented in differing orientations. In group *b* all the edges were vertical and all but the last evoked responses regardless of where in the receptive field the light struck. When a large rectangle of light covered entire receptive field, however, as shown at bottom, cell failed to respond.

cell of this type is usually completely ineffective.

In the simple cortical cells the process of pitting these two antagonistic parts of a receptive field against each other is carried still further than it is in the lateral geniculate body. As a rule a large spot of light—or what amounts to the same thing, diffuse light covering the whole retina—evokes no response at all in simple cortical cells. Here the "on" and "off" effects apparently balance out with great precision.

Some other common types of simple receptive fields include an "on" center with a large "off" area to one side and a small one to the other; an "on" and an "off" area side by side; a narrow "off" center with "on" sides; a wide "on" center with narrow "off" sides. All these fields have in common that the border or borders separating "on" and "off" regions are straight and parallel rather than circular [*see bottom illustration on page 151*]. The most efficient stimuli—slits, edges or dark bars—all involve straight lines. Each cell responds best to a particular orientation of line; other orientations produce less vigorous responses, and usually the orientation perpendicular to the optimum evokes no response at all. A particular cell's optimum, which we term the receptive-field orientation, is thus a property built into the cell by its connections. In general the receptive-field orientation differs from one cell to the next, and it may be vertical, horizontal or oblique. We have no evidence that any one orientation, such as vertical or horizontal, is more common than any other.

How can one explain this specificity of simple cortical cells? We are inclined to think they receive their input directly from the incoming lateral geniculate fibers. We suppose a typical simple cell has for its input a large number of lateral geniculate cells whose "on" centers are arranged along a straight line; a spot of light shone anywhere along that line will activate some of the geniculate cells and lead to activation of the cortical cell. A light shone over the entire area will activate all the geniculate cells and have a tremendous final impact on the cortical cell [*see bottom illustration on page 150*].

One can now begin to grasp the significance of the great number of cells in the visual cortex. Each cell seems to have its own specific duties; it takes care of one restricted part of the retina, responds best to one particular shape of stimulus and to one particular orientation. To look at the problem from the opposite direction, for each stimulus—each area of the retina stimulated, each type of line (edge, slit or bar) and each orientation of stimulus—there is a particular set of simple cortical cells that will respond; changing any of the stimulus arrangements will cause a whole new population of cells to respond. The number of populations responding successively as the eye watches a slowly rotating propeller is scarcely imaginable.

Such a profound rearrangement and analysis of the incoming messages might seem enough of a task for a single structure, but it turns out to be only part of what happens in the cortex. The next major transformation involves the cortical cells that occupy what is probably the sixth step in the visual pathway: the complex cells, which are also present in this cortical region and to some extent intermixed with the simple cells.

Complex cells are like simple ones in several ways. A cell responds to a stimulus only within a restricted region of retina: the receptive field. It responds best to the line stimuli (slits, edges or dark bars) and the stimulus must be oriented to suit the cell. But complex fields, unlike the simple ones, cannot be mapped into antagonistic "on" and "off" regions.

A typical complex cell we studied happened to fire to a vertical edge, and it gave "on" or "off" responses depending on whether light was to the left or to the right. Other orientations were almost completely without effect [*see illustration on opposite page*]. These responses are just what could be expected from a simple cell with a receptive field consisting of an excitatory area separated from an inhibitory one by a vertical boundary. In this case, however, the cell had an additional property that could not be explained by such an arrangement. A vertical edge evoked responses anywhere within the receptive field, "on" responses with light to the left, "off" responses with light to the right. Such behavior cannot be understood in terms of antagonistic "on" and "off" subdivisions of the receptive field, and when we explored the field with small spots we found no such regions. Instead the spot either produced responses at both "on" and "off" or evoked no responses at all.

Complex cells, then, respond like simple cells to one particular aspect of the stimulus, namely its orientation. But when the stimulus is moved, without changing the orientation, a complex cell differs from its simple counterpart chiefly in responding with sustained firing. The firing continues as the stimulus is moved over a substantial retinal area, usually the entire receptive field of the cell, whereas a simple cell will respond to movement only as the stimulus crosses a very narrow boundary separating "on" and "off" regions.

It is difficult to explain this behavior by any scheme in which geniculate cells project directly to complex cells. On the other hand, the findings can be explained fairly well by the supposition that a complex cell receives its input from a large number of simple cells. This supposition requires only that the simple cells have the same field orientation and be all of the same general type. A complex cell responding to vertical edges, for example, would thus receive fibers from simple cells that have vertically oriented receptive fields. All such a scheme needs to have added is the requirement that the retinal positions of these simple fields be arranged throughout the area occupied by the complex field.

The main difficulty with such a scheme is that it presupposes an enormous degree of cortical organization. What a vast network of connections must be needed if a single complex cell is to receive fibers from just the right simple cells, all with the appropriate field arrangements, tilts and positions! Yet there is unexpected and compelling evidence that such a system of connections exists. It comes from a study of what can be called the functional architecture of the cortex. By penetrating with a microelectrode through the cortex in many directions, perhaps many times in a single tiny region of the brain, we learned that the cells are arranged not in a haphazard manner but with a high degree of order. The physiological results show that functionally the cortex is subdivided like a beehive into tiny columns, or segments [*see illustration on next page*], each of which extends from the surface to the white matter lower in the brain. A column is de-

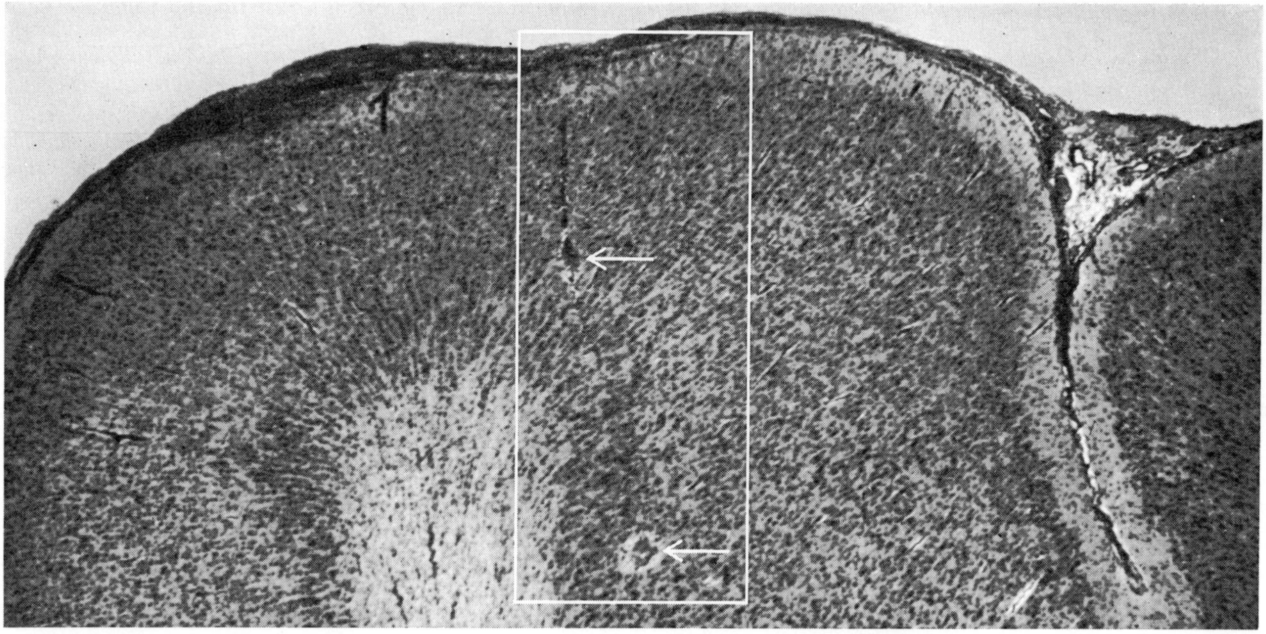

SECTION OF CAT'S VISUAL CORTEX shows track of microelectrode penetration and, at arrows, two points along the track where lesions were made so that it would be possible to ascertain later where the tip of the electrode was at certain times. This section of cortex is from a single gyrus, or fold of the brain; it was six millimeters wide and is shown here enlarged 30 diameters.

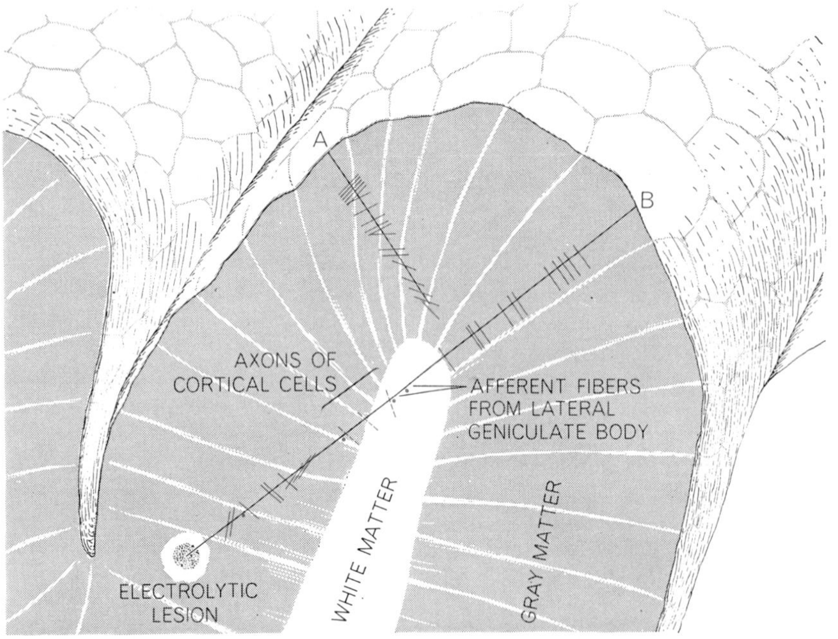

FUNCTIONAL ARRANGEMENT of cells in visual cortex resembled columns, although columnar structure is not apparent under a microscope. Lines *A* and *B* show paths of two microelectrode penetrations; colored lines show receptive-field orientations encountered. Cells in a single column had same orientation; change of orientation showed new column.

fined not by any anatomically obvious wall—no columns are visible under the microscope—but by the fact that the thousands of cells it contains all have the same receptive-field orientation. The evidence for this is that in a typical microelectrode penetration through the cortex the cells—recorded in sequence as the electrode is pushed ahead—all have the same field orientation, provided that the penetration is made in a direction perpendicular to the surface of the cortical segment. If the penetration is oblique, as we pass from column to column we record several cells with one field orientation, then a new sequence of cells with a new orientation, and then still another.

The columns are irregular in cross-sectional shape, and on the average they are about half a millimeter across. In respects other than receptive-field orientation the cells in a particular column tend to differ; some are simple, others complex; some respond to slits, others prefer dark bars or edges.

Returning to the proposed scheme for explaining the properties of complex cells, one sees that gathered together in a single column are the very cells one should expect to be interconnected: cells whose fields have the same orientation and the same general retinal position, although not the same position. Furthermore, it is known from the anatomy that there are rich interconnections between neighboring cells, and the preponderance of these connections in a vertical direction fits well with the long, narrow, more or less cylindrical shape of the columns. This means that a column may be looked on as an independent functional unit of cortex, in which simple cells receive connections from lateral geniculate cells and send projections to complex cells.

It is possible to get an inkling of the part these different cell types play in vision by considering what must be happening in the brain when one looks at a form, such as, to take a relatively simple example, a black square on a white background. Suppose the eyes fix on some arbitrary point to the left of the square. On the reasonably safe assumption that the human visual cortex works something like the cat's and the monkey's, it can be predicted that the near edge of the square will activate a particular group of simple cells, namely cells that prefer edges with light to the left and dark to the right and whose fields are oriented vertically and are so placed on the retina that the boundary between "on" and "off" regions falls exactly along the image of the near edge of the square. Other populations of cells will obviously be called into action by the other three edges of the square. All the cell populations will change if the eye strays from the point fixed on, or if the square is moved while the eye remains stationary, or if the square is rotated.

In the same way each edge will activate a population of complex cells, again cells that prefer edges in a specific orientation. But a given complex cell, unlike a simple cell, will continue to be activated when the eye moves or when the form moves, if the movement is not so large that the edge passes entirely outside the receptive field of the cell, and if there is no rotation. This means that the populations of complex cells affected by the whole square will be to some extent independent of the exact position of the image of the square on the retina.

Each of the cortical columns contains thousands of cells, some with simple fields and some with complex. Evidently the visual cortex analyzes an enormous amount of information, with each small region of visual field represented over and over again in column after column, first for one receptive-field orientation and then for another.

In sum, the visual cortex appears to have a rich assortment of functions. It rearranges the input from the lateral geniculate body in a way that makes lines and contours the most important stimuli. What appears to be a first step in perceptual generalization results from the response of cortical cells to the orientation of a stimulus, apart from its exact retinal position. Movement is also an important stimulus factor; its rate and direction must both be specified if a cell is to be effectively driven.

One cannot expect to "explain" vision, however, from a knowledge of the behavior of a single set of cells, geniculate or cortical, any more than one could understand a wood-pulp mill from an examination of the machine that cuts the logs into chips. We are now studying how still "higher" structures build on the information they receive from these cortical cells, rearranging it to produce an even greater complexity of response.

In all of this work we have been particularly encouraged to find that the areas we study can be understood in terms of comparatively simple concepts such as the nerve impulse, convergence of many nerves on a single cell, excitation and inhibition. Moreover, if the connections suggested by these studies are remotely close to reality, one can conclude that at least some parts of the brain can be followed relatively easily, without necessarily requiring higher mathematics, computers or a knowledge of network theories.

16

VISION IN FROGS

W. R. A. MUNTZ
March 1964

The analogy between the eye and the camera has helped to clarify the process by which the lens of the eye, its aperture regulated by the iris, casts an image on the light-sensitive screen of the retina. On this basis the optic nerve connects the retina to the central nervous system in such a way that a map of the retina is formed on the surface of the brain. The analogy can be carried too far. Students of the visual system came to assume that the retina was like a photographic film, its individual receptor cells responding to light and its absence like the grains of silver salt in a photographic emulsion; that the whole function of the eye and the optic nerve was to form and then transmit a mosaic of the visual world to the brain, there to form the basis of visual perception.

Anatomical investigations have shown, however, that there are many more receptor cells in the retina than there are fibers in the optic nerve. It is thus impossible for every receptor cell to send a separate message to the brain, and the concept that the array of receptor cells is equivalent to the grain of a photographic emulsion must be abandoned. The very intricacy of the retina, the cells of which are variously specialized and richly interconnected, hints at a role more complex than the mere relaying of a visual map. The fact is that the retina is more filter than film. It discriminates: it sends on to the brain only the most useful information.

What is useful varies from animal to animal. Consider, for example, the frog. From the frog's point of view the most relevant objects are the insects on which it feeds. Any small moving object is therefore likely to be important and calls for a specific set of fast responses; no such responses are required by small stationary objects such as pebbles. According to the earlier theories an image of the object—whether moving or stationary, important or unimportant—was sent to the brain, where the meaningful distinctions were made at some later stage.

It now appears that the retina itself makes the distinctions. Certain nerve fibers leaving the retina have been found to respond specifically to small moving objects and not to stationary objects or even to large moving ones. Such "bug-detectors" can be disadvan-

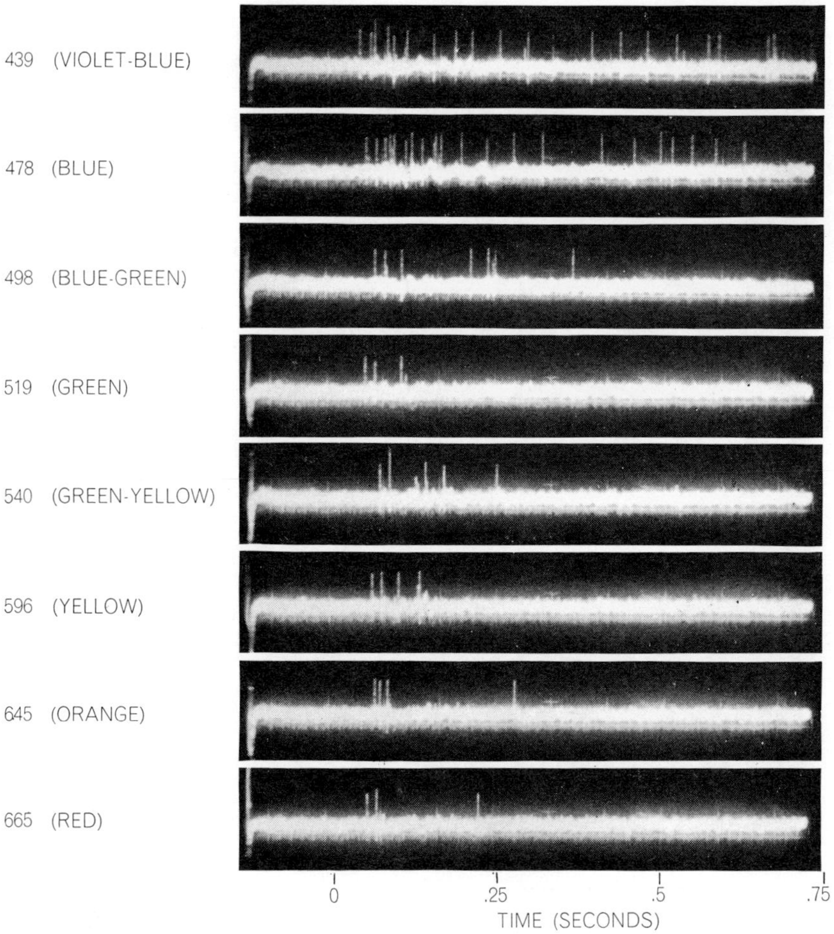

IMPULSES from an "on" fiber are picked up by a microelectrode and recorded on an oscilloscope. Each spike represents response by fiber to stimulation by light of various wavelengths (*shown in millimicrons*). Fibers responded strongly to blue and weakly to green.

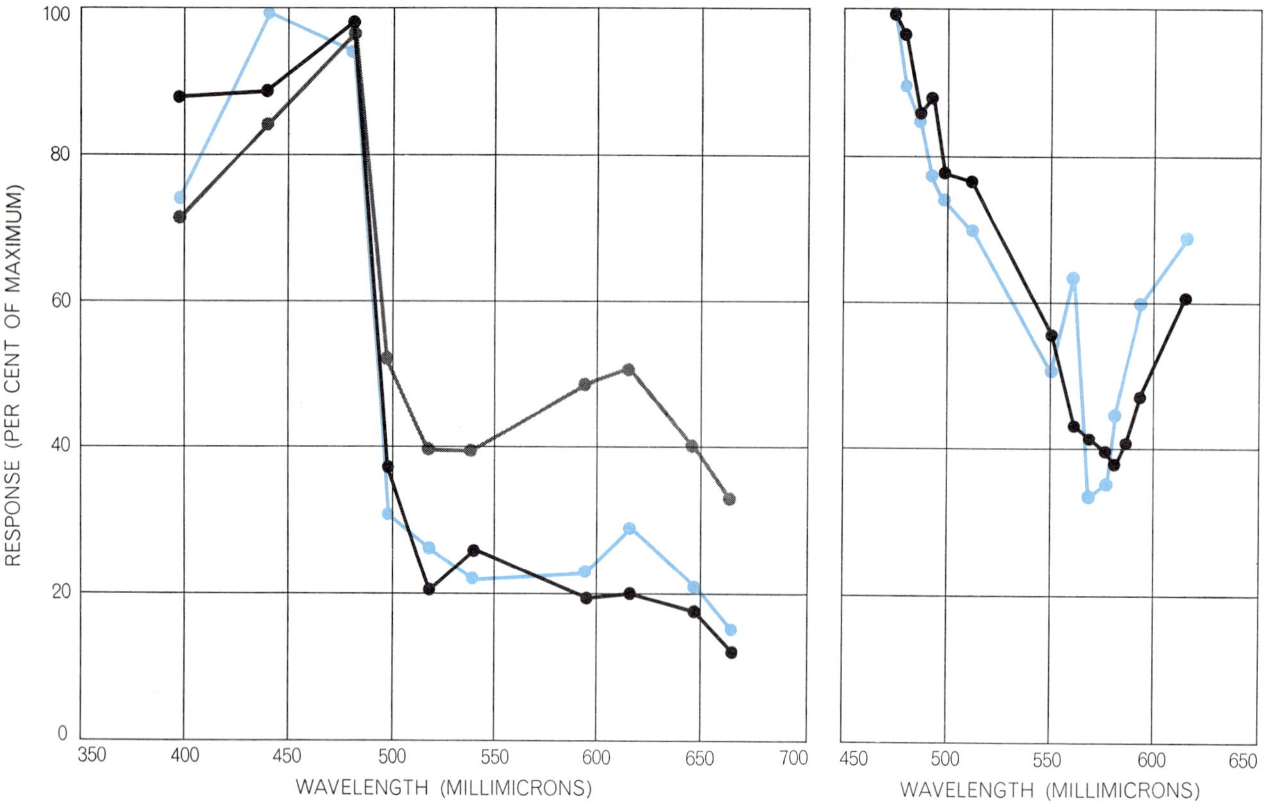

RESPONSES of three on-fibers to 10 different colored lights are compared in the curves at left. The "maximum response" was the largest number of spikes counted in a 1/2-second period. These colors, obtained from interference filters, were quite pure. Unsaturated, or impure, colors had about the same effect, however, as shown by the responses of two fibers to 14 colored papers (*right*).

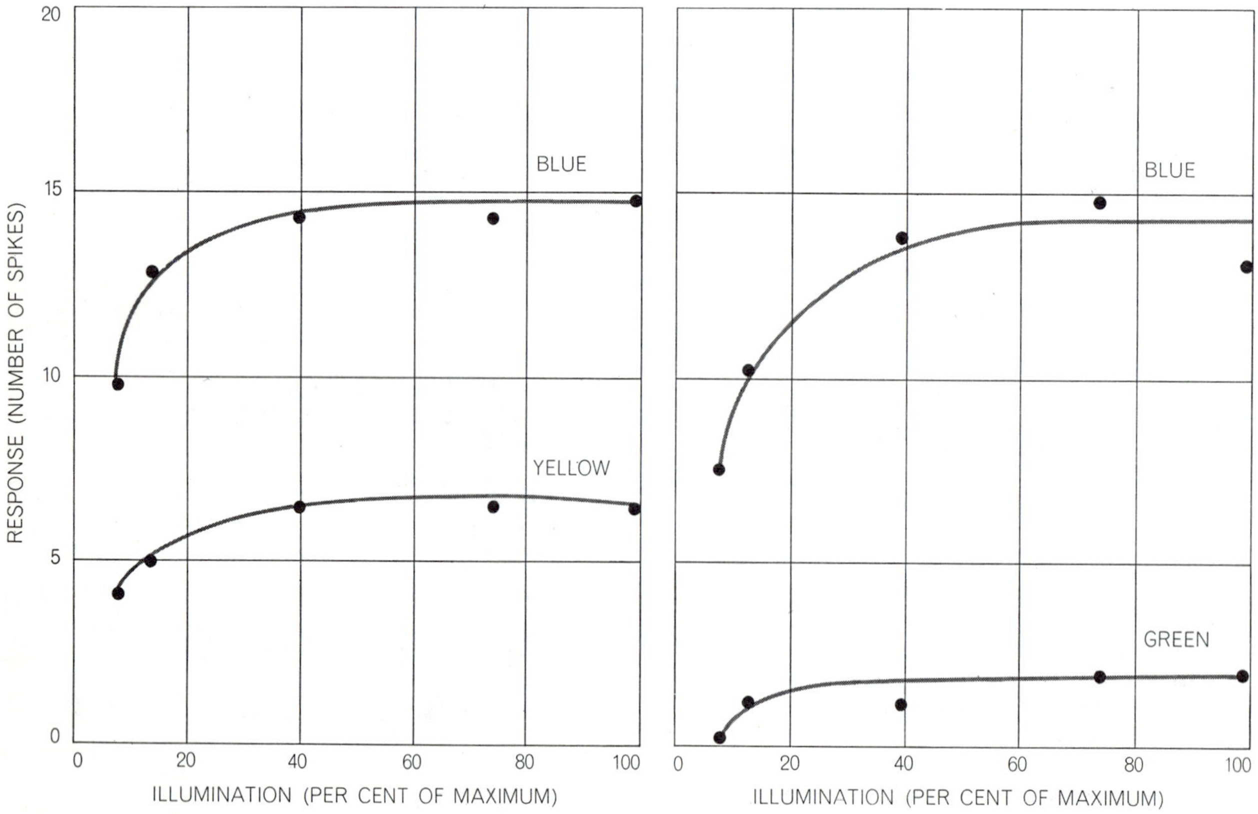

INTENSITY of the stimulating light was not a major factor. The curves at left are for light reflected from colored papers, those at right for filtered light. In both instances blue brought a greater response than yellow or green even when only a tenth as bright.

tageous under unusual conditions: a frog will starve to death surrounded by dead flies. In the ordinary circumstances of a frog's life, however, the early filtering of significant information by the retina makes for efficient utilization of the limited number of optic nerve fibers.

Each fiber, then, reports not whether illumination is present but whether some rather complex situation—such as the approach of a bug—exists in a given part of the visual field. The eye is not a physical instrument like a camera but a biological instrument adapted to meet the animal's needs; to understand the function of the frog's eye it is necessary to consider the frog's point of view. To this end several investigators have studied the nature of some of the messages sent by the frog's eye to the frog's brain and have undertaken to correlate the properties of individual optic nerve fibers with the behavior of the whole animal.

The first recordings of the activity of single optic nerve fibers in the retina of a vertebrate were made by H. K. Hartline at Johns Hopkins University in 1938. Under the microscope he teased a single fiber out of the inner surface of the retina of a frog, placed an electrode under the fiber and then amplified and displayed on an oscilloscope the nerve impulses that resulted when the eye was stimulated by various visual events. Hartline found three types of fiber in the frog's retina: those responding only to the onset of illumination, which he called "on" fibers, those responding only to the end of illumination ("off" fibers), and "on-off" fibers, which responded to both events. The subsequent perfection of microelectrodes made it possible to confirm and extend Hartline's findings without dissecting out the individual fibers; this was done by H. B. Barlow of the University of Cambridge and Ragnar A. Granit of the Royal Caroline Medico-Surgical Institute in Sweden. Their experiments, like Hartline's, were performed on the isolated retina of the frog and therefore demonstrated the retina's analytical capabilities.

From the retina most of the optic nerve fibers pass to the optic tectum, the chief visual center in the frog, where they project a map—not a one-to-one reproduction of the visual world as it appears on the retina but a selective map. At the Massachusetts Institute of Technology Jerome Y. Lettvin, Humberto R. Maturana, Warren S. McCulloch and W. H. Pitts were able to determine that four specific attributes of the visual field elicit responses in four specific types of fiber and are emphasized in the map projected on the optic tectum. Each fiber ends in a dense mass of small branches that makes contact with the cells of the tectum; Lettvin and his colleagues, recording nerve impulses in these "terminal arbors" with a special microelectrode, located each type of fiber at a different level.

Fibers ending in the surface layers of the tectum responded to the presence of any sharp edge in the visual field whether the edge was moving or stationary. Fibers ending slightly deeper proved to be the bug-detectors: they responded to small, dark moving objects but not to large or stationary objects. Neither of these groups reacted to a change in general illumination: switching a light on or off did not affect them. They had probably eluded discovery by earlier investigators of isolated retinas because they lack the fatty myelin sheathing of most nerve fibers and are hard to isolate by dissection.

Probing deeper into the optic tectum, the investigators found the myelinated fibers detected earlier by Hartline. The first of these responded to either the onset or the end of illumination, and they fitted his category of on-off fibers. They responded even more markedly to the movement of a linear shape, however, and therefore they are called "moving-edge detectors." Deeper still Lettvin came on fibers that responded to the cessation of illumination: Hartline's off-fibers.

The M.I.T. workers, to sum up, identified in the tectum four different kinds of optic nerve fiber, each carrying information about an attribute of the visual world that the animal requires in its daily life. They did not find a tectal projection of Hartline's on-fibers. Anatomical studies had shown that not all the frog's optic nerve fibers pass to the tectum; some go instead to a secondary visual center in the dorsal thalamus. This thalamic system is of particular interest because it is the forerunner of the visual system in higher animals, including man. In the human brain the tectal network is small

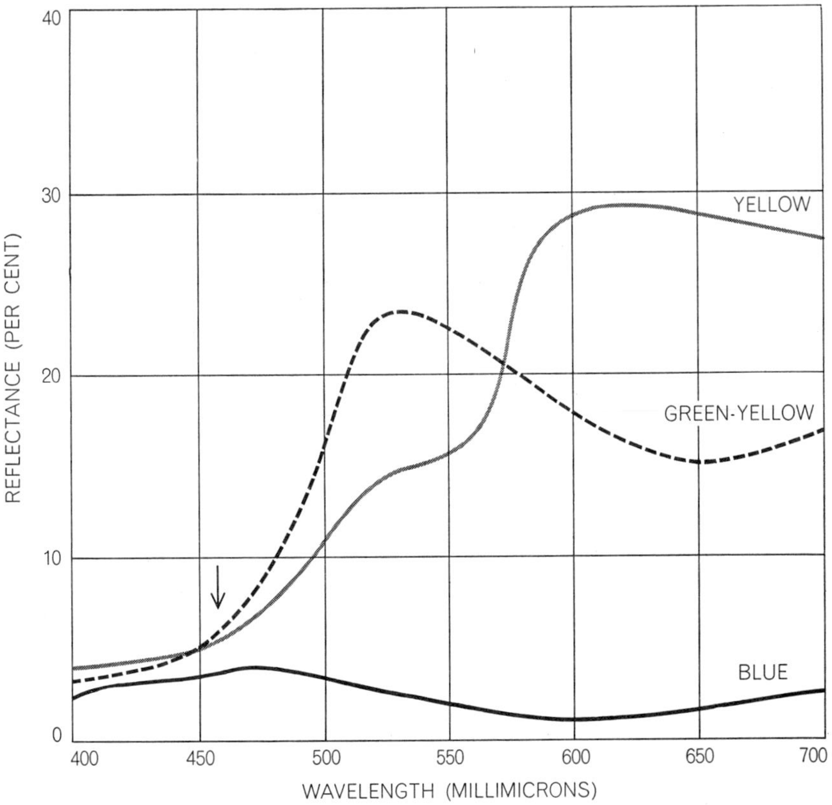

DIM BLUE LIGHT in an experiment such as the one graphed at bottom left on the opposite page had the characteristics of the bottom curve in this graph. It is compared with a green and a yellow light 10 times brighter and has less energy in the blue region (*arrow*) than either. It nevertheless stimulated a greater response. This demonstrates that the sensitivity of the thalamic fibers to blue cannot be due to any single visual pigment in the retina.

and relatively unimportant; most of the fibers carry signals from the retina, by way of the lateral geniculate nucleus in the dorsal thalamus, to the visual area of the cerebral cortex [see the article "The Visual Cortex of the Brain," by David H. Hubel, beginning on page 148].

In Lettvin's laboratory at M.I.T. I applied his microelectrode methods to an exploration of the optic nerve endings in the dorsal thalamus of the frog. When I displayed various targets in the visual field of a frog, the record of responses showed that all the optic fibers running to the thalamus were sensitive to the onset of illumination and to no other stimulus; they are the on-fibers. Clearly the frog's eye transmits messages about objects primarily to the tectum and sends information from light-detectors primarily to the dorsal thalamus. The information does not become mixed, since four kinds of optic nerve fibers go only to the tectum and one kind only to the thalamus. There are opportunities for interaction at a subsequent stage, however, through a rich network of nerve fibers that connects the optic tectum and the dorsal thalamus.

The light-detectors of the dorsal thalamus proved to be sensitive not only to the presence or absence of light but also to the color of the light. Every fiber I tested in this area responded much more strongly to blue light than to light of any other color. Exposure to blue light brought a rapid burst of nerve impulses that often lasted for several seconds, but in response to green, yellow or red light there was only a brief burst of a few impulses [*see illustration on page 157*].

In considering this selective response to blue the first question to be settled was whether it represented mere color-dependence or true color vision. Any visual receptor responds only to the light it absorbs, and receptors absorb different wavelengths depending on the visual pigment they contain. For example, the retinal cells called rods, which are responsible for vision in faint light, contain a pigment (rhodopsin, or visual purple) that strongly absorbs blue-green light. Consequently rod vision is much more sensitive to blue-green than to other colors; it is color-dependent. The rods, however, are not capable of color vision, because they cannot distinguish between a low-intensity blue-green and, say, a high-intensity yellow. Although a blue-green barn may appear lighter than a red one in the moonlight, it will appear gray rather than blue-green. True color vision distinguishes among different wavelengths regardless of the intensity or the purity of the stimulating light.

What was manifested in the blue-sensitive system of the frog's dorsal thalamus: color-dependence ("spectral sensitivity") or color vision ("wavelength discrimination")? The question had an important biological aspect in view of the eminently useful nature of the information delivered to the optic tectum by the bug-detectors and similar fibers. The information about blue light supplied to the dorsal thalamus might be similarly significant, but not unless it was true color vision. That is, to be useful it must respond differentially not only to the pure colors I obtained from interference filters in my first experiments but also to the impure colors of nature. In addition it must also distinguish among colors regardless of their brightness, making the distinction, for example, between a dim blue and a bright green.

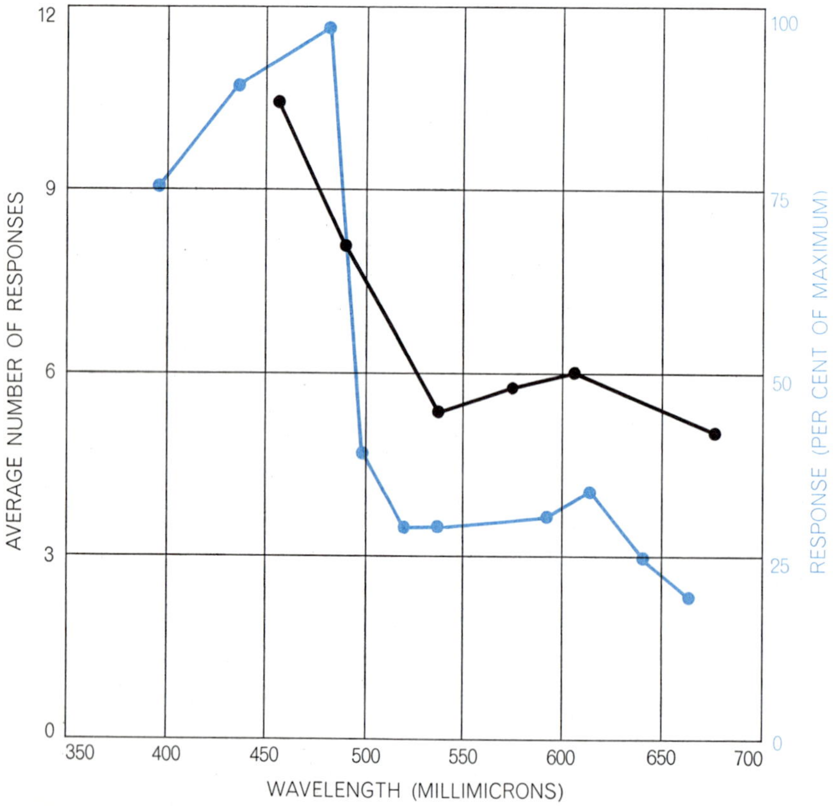

BEHAVIORAL EXPERIMENT showed that frogs preferred a blue light to other colors when they were tested in the apparatus illustrated on the opposite page. Six colors were displayed, each paired with one another and with darkness. Black curve shows average number of times frogs jumped toward each color out of a possible maximum of 12. The results are similar to those obtained in the earlier experiment on thalamic fibers (*colored curve*).

A series of experiments demonstrated that the on-fibers do indeed respond in just this manner, emitting a prolonged burst of impulses on exposure to anything that looks blue to the human eye. This was true, first of all, in the case of light transmitted by gelatin filters that passed a rather broad portion of the spectrum in contrast to the narrow band passed by the interference filters. Next the retina was exposed to light reflected from a series of colored papers. All of these were highly unsaturated—that is, they reflected light at all wavelengths with only a slight peak at the dominant wavelength of their apparent color—but they nevertheless stimulated the differential response to blue [*see top illustration on page 158*]. Finally, when I varied the intensity of the light reflected from these papers or passed by interference filters, there was a much stronger response to dim blue light than to bright yellow or green [*see bottom illustration on page 158*]. This was true even when the blue paper was illuminated only a tenth as brightly as the green, at which point the unsaturated green actually contained more blue than did the light from the blue paper [*see illustration on preceding page*]. This proved that the re-

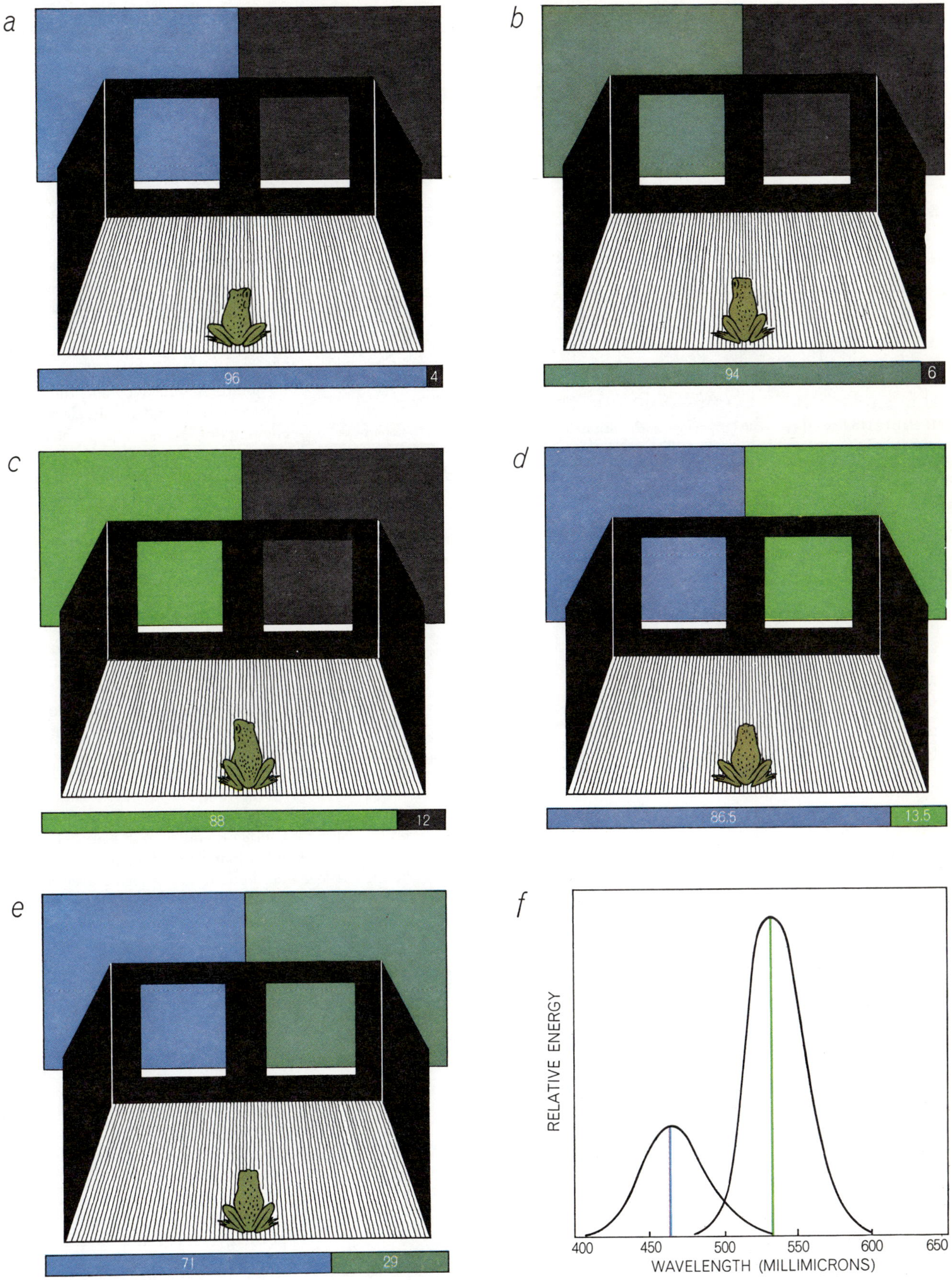

COLOR PREFERENCE of frogs was tested by placing them in a small box, drawn here with the top and back wall removed. The animals faced two windows backed by a screen. The part of the screen visible through each window was illuminated with a different color or left dark; the investigators recorded the number of times the frogs jumped toward each color. In the experiment illustrated here the colors were blue and green and an additive mixture of the two. The frogs preferred blue to darkness on 96 per cent of the occasions (*a*) and preferred blue-green and green to darkness as shown (*b*, *c*). They preferred blue to green (*d*) and even to the mixture of blue plus green (*e*). Ten frogs were tested several times on each pair of colors, which appeared at left or right at random. The wavelengths and relative intensities of the blue and green are shown by the two curves (*f*).

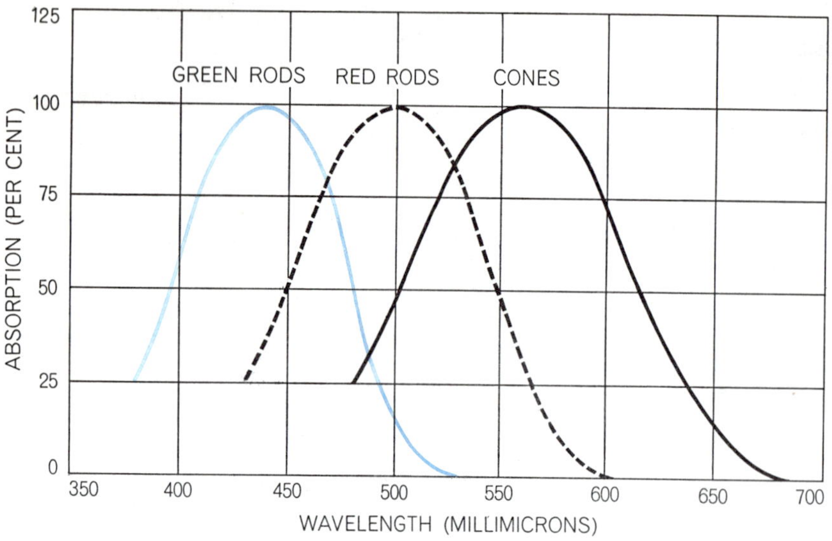

AMPHIBIANS have three visual pigments, each with its own absorption pattern. The peak sensitivity of the green rods is at 440 millimicrons, that of the red rods at 502. The cone pigment has not yet been extracted but is believed to have its peak sensitivity at about 560.

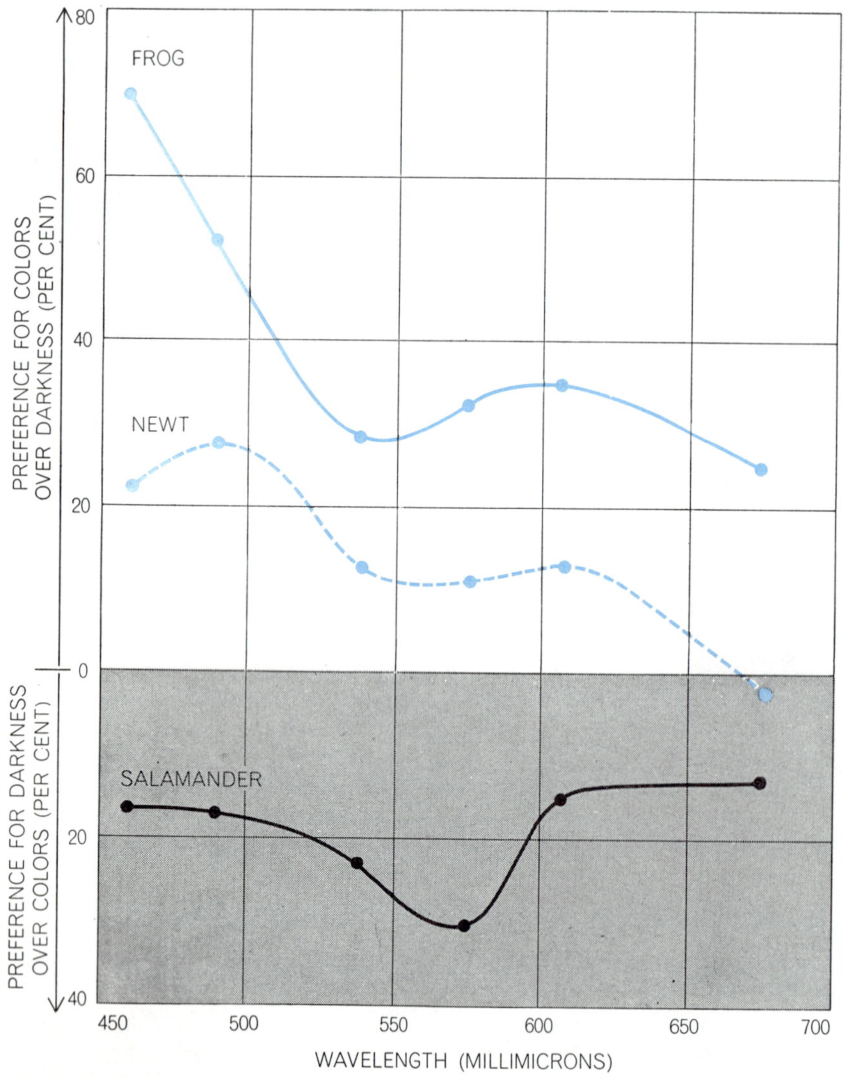

COLOR PREFERENCES of three amphibians are compared on the basis of jumping or swimming behavior. Scores for each color and darkness were converted to percentages. Frog and newt have green rods; they seek light and are most sensitive to blue. Salamander lacks green rods; it seeks darkness and is most sensitive to green light rather than to blue.

sponse to blue was genuine hue discrimination and that the on-fibers of the thalamus were indeed capable of true color vision.

Does the frog use this information? Zoologists have known for many years that frogs tend to jump toward the light and that this "phototactic" behavior is stimulated particularly by blue light. In my laboratory at the University of Oxford we undertook to confirm this blue-seeking behavior and to find out if it was caused by the retinal signals carried by on-fibers to the dorsal thalamus. To test frogs for color preference we built a simple black box with two windows through which the animal could jump. A screen behind the windows was illuminated in turn with different pairs of colors. A frog placed in the box invariably jumped (sometimes a gentle poke was required) through one of the windows; we recorded the number of times each frog chose a certain color or a dark window. The experiment confirmed the frog's reputed preference for blue, and the curve for the behavioral response was very similar to the one for the electrophysiological response of the thalamic fibers [*see illustration on page 160*].

Subsequent experiments demonstrated clearly that the animals' behavior involved genuine color vision. For one thing, the degree of preference for blue was largely unaffected by variations in the intensity of the stimulating lights. In another parallel to the earlier tests of individual fibers, the frogs preferred a blue light to other colors even when it contained only about a tenth as much energy. The most striking demonstration involved various paired combinations of a blue and a green light [*see illustration on page 161*]. The green was almost three times brighter than the blue, but when the two were opposed the green was chosen on only 13.5 per cent of the occasions. Furthermore, adding the green to the blue reduced the attractiveness of the blue. When the blue and the blue-green were opposed, the frogs chose the pure blue 71 per cent of the time in spite of the fact that the additive mixture of blue and green contained nearly four times more energy and just as much blue. Like the colored-paper experiment, this ruled out the possibility that mere sensitivity is involved, because no visual pigment can exist that will absorb more of a pure blue light than it will of the same blue light plus green.

The frog shows a simple type of color vision: it is capable of distinguish-

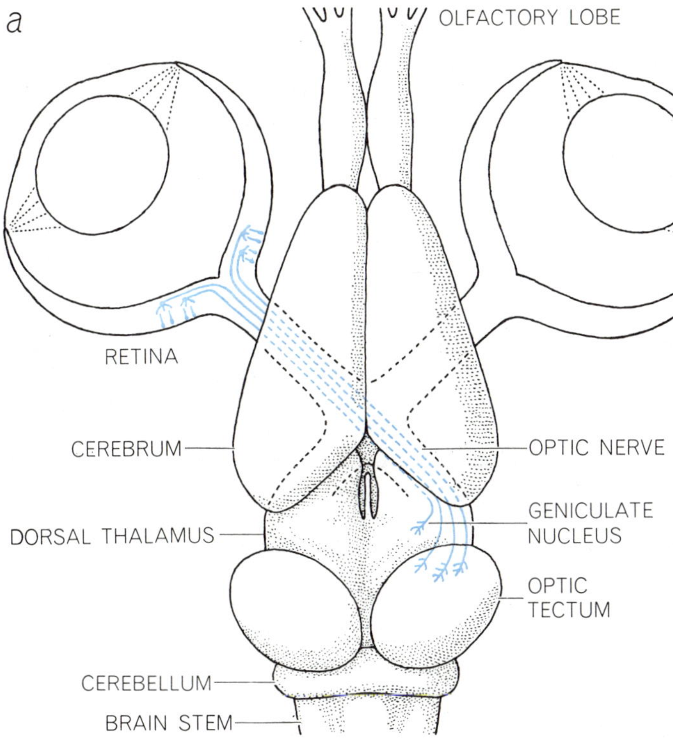

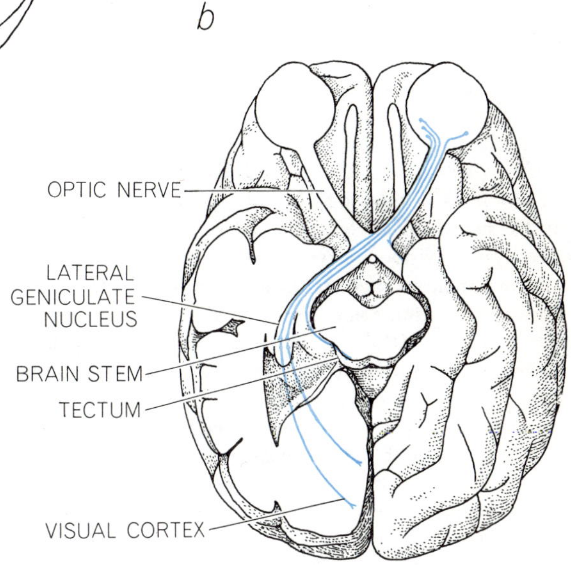

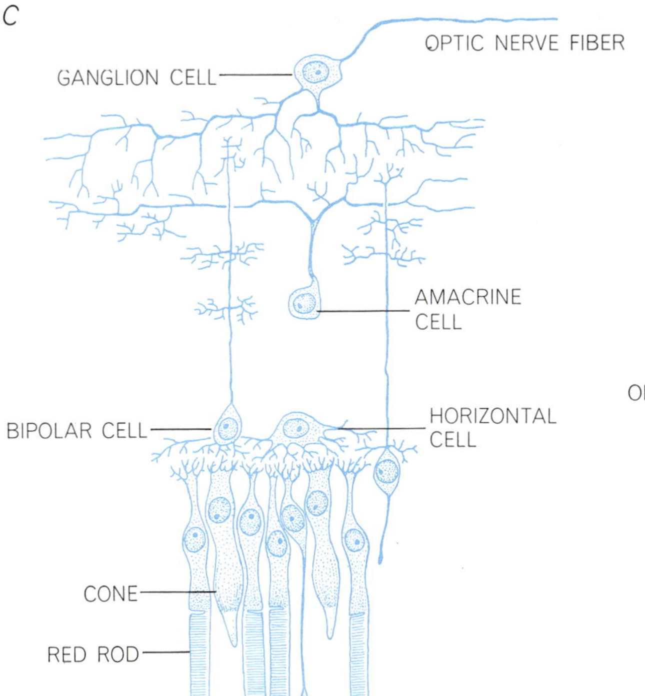

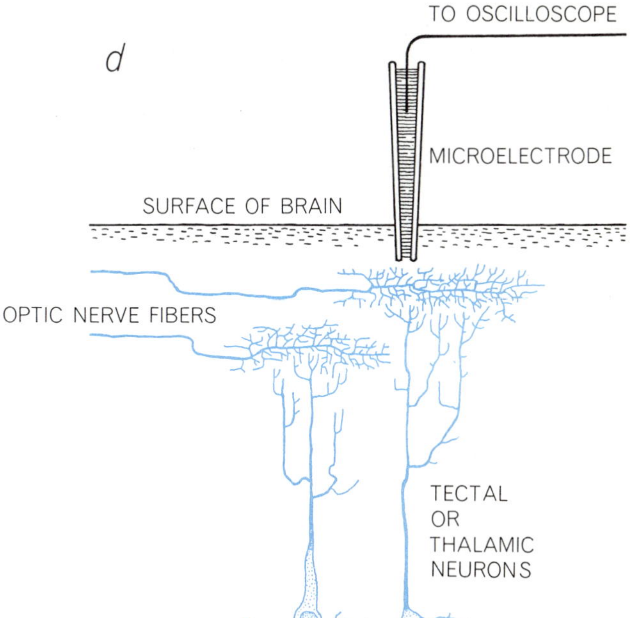

VISUAL PATHWAYS are traced in color in these drawings. In the frog (*a*) an image of the visual world formed on the retina is transmitted by optic nerve fibers to the optic tectum and, to a lesser extent, to the geniculate nucleus in the dorsal thalamus. In man (*b*) the tectum is unimportant; most of the fibers go, via the geniculate nucleus, to the visual cortex. The frog retina (*c*) contains about a million receptors (rods and cones), three million connecting cells (bipolar, amacrine and horizontal) and 500,000 ganglion cells leading to optic nerve fibers. In the brain (*d*) these fibers end as small branches that intermingle with the neurons of the optic tectum and dorsal thalamus. A microelectrode records impulses from these terminal arbors of the optic nerve fibers.

ing blue from other colors. The parallelism between the blue-seeking behavior and the response of the fibers running to the dorsal thalamus is strong evidence that it is these thalamic fibers that underlie the behavior. Such a simple example of color vision merits close attention, because it should be possible to learn in detail how the retina performs the color analysis in the frog and perhaps to derive general principles that apply to other animals as well. We have made a small start in this direction by comparing the frog's color sensitivity with that of some other amphibians.

The spectral sensitivities of the visual pigments in the frog's receptor cells must account for at least the first stage of its color vision system. There are three pigments, each with a characteristic absorption curve [*see top illustration on page 162*]. The pigment contained by the green rods is most sensitive at a wavelength of about 440 millimicrons and is therefore presumably implicated in the blue color vision. If it is, we reasoned, the blue-seeking behavior should not occur in certain amphibians that lack green rods. We tested two closely related amphibians: the European newt (*Triturus cristatus*), which has green rods, and the fire salamander (*Salamandra salamandra*), which does not. The testing apparatus differed from the frogs' jumping box in several respects, in particular in that it was filled with water and the animals swam toward the target screens.

When they were tested with the same colored lights that had been used with the frogs, the newts showed much the same behavior: they chose blue more often than other colors [*see the bottom illustration on page 162*]. (The newt's response curve, however, is shifted bodily toward the red end of the spectrum, probably because of a difference in the spectral sensitivity of the receptors; it is known that the rods of the newt have their maximum sensitivity at longer wavelengths than the peak sensitivity of the frog's rods, and it is likely that the same displacement toward the red occurs for the other receptors as well.) The salamander behaves quite differently, shunning light instead of seeking it. Our salamanders swam away from colors and toward a dark screen whenever they could. And the color to which they were apparently most sensitive—the one they most avoided—was green, not blue.

These results supported the finding that the green rod is a basic factor in blue color vision. It cannot, however, be the only receptor involved. Since no single visual pigment can be more sensitive to pure blue than to the same blue plus green, no one kind of receptor can underlie the blue-seeking behavior. There must be some inhibitory element at work to account for the fact that adding green light to blue renders the blue less effective. We are investigating the nature of this inhibitory receptor and have some preliminary evidence that it may be the red rod.

As was suggested earlier, an efficient color vision system should offer some biological advantage to the animal. Why should a frog need to distinguish blue? I think it is quite possible that the function of the blue-sensitive system is to direct the jump of a frightened frog in such a way that it will leap into the water to avoid its predators. Frogs normally live at the edges of ponds, in the grass or under trees. The predominant color around the frog will therefore be green. In the direction of the water, however, there is likely to be less vegetation, and there may also be more blue light from the open sky. Since blue light is effective in guiding the direction of the jump and green light is very ineffective—even less effective than yellow or red—when the frog is frightened it will tend to jump away from the vegetation toward the open space and thus into the water. On this view the important point is that green is particularly ineffective in stimulating the blue-sensitive system, so that light from any other source will be more effective than the green light from the vegetation. Although ponds are not necessarily blue and the sky may be overcast, still the light from the open sky over the pond will contain more blue and less green than the light reflected from the vegetation.

A number of studies in the past few years have demonstrated that the frog's retina responds selectively to various attributes of the visual world, filters out information significant to the animal and sends it along to different areas of the brain. What happens to the messages when they reach the brain, however, is still largely unknown. Even at the retinal level there is much to be learned about how the different cells are interconnected to perform their complex tasks of reception and analysis. What the retina of the frog does is fairly clear; how it does its work remains to be investigated.

IV

PERCEPTUAL PROCESSES

IV

PERCEPTUAL PROCESSES

INTRODUCTION

Perception is the process of knowing objects and events in the world by means of the senses. Historically and popularly, men have thought of the process of perception as the transmission of a copy (picture) of an object to a sense organ and thence to the seat of consciousness in the brain. But from previous discussions of the action of the sensory systems, it is already clear that nothing like a replica is maintained in transmission, not even a replica of the spatio-temporal pattern of energy distributed over such a receptor surface as the retina. The processes upon which perception depends are governed by certain principles, including those of lateral inhibition, convergence and divergence of neural pathways, and encoding of inputs into neural impulses (which precludes the transmission of unaltered patterns). In a modern view, these facts are recognized, and perception is regarded as the outcome of the nervous system's processing of the information that comes to it through the senses. From this point of view, it may be argued that animals with different processing equipment may well have disparate perceived "worlds." The relations between stimulus input and perception are indirect, complex, and often dependent upon the current state of the system, and this is precisely what makes the study of perception both difficult and challenging.

The study of perception can be approached from an empty-organism (sometimes called black-box) point of view, in which the aim of any given investigation is to discover the stimulus or class of stimuli that, presented to the senses, will produce a given percept. Some of the classic studies in psychophysics were made from this point of view. But more can be attempted: From a knowledge of effective stimuli, it is possible to theorize about processing mechanisms. Theories of color vision based on color mixture are excellent examples of this sort of model building. It is also possible to theorize about perceptual processing from a partial knowledge of the neural processes upon which perception is known to depend. From a convergence of these approaches, progress has been made and will certainly continue to be made.

OBSERVATION AND INFERENCE ABOUT MECHANISMS

Having reviewed some of the transducer processes and primitive neural processes, we are prepared to consider more complex neural functioning and its relation to certain aspects of perception. In his article "Texture and Visual Perception," Bela Julesz applies some very sophisticated techniques to a classic problem: How are single objects distinguished in complexly textured fields? The generality of this problem is apparent to anyone simply glancing about a room: different objects lie in different planes and appear to overlap each other when viewed from one perspective; the effect is a complex and variegated set of textured surfaces. How are these objects segregated and identified by the perceiver out of the mass of texture? (When an observer fails in this, the effect is called camouflage, but the very difficulty of camouflaging real objects demonstrates the efficiency with which we segregate and identify objects in complex fields.) The question was most explicitly raised by the gestalt psychologists, a group of investigators, most of them German, whose work, which cohered around the contributions of three men—Wolfgang Köhler, Kurt Koffka, and Max Wertheimer—began during the period of World War I. A very old answer to that question was that familiarity and meaningfulness somehow produce the segregation, out of the welter of visual input, of clusters of texture that represent objects; but the gestaltists were not satisfied with this answer, and they attempted, by many demonstrations, to show its inadequacy (see examples of proximity and similarity in Roy M. Pritchard's article "Stabilized Images on the Retina"). They believed, instead, that the process of perception was intrinsically organizing—in the sense of forming aggregates—and that perceived form was one outcome of this organizing tendency. Julesz's ingenious use of the pseudorandom output of a computer gives his explorations a much more rigorous base than previous attempts. In accord with the gestaltists, he concludes, from his studies, that clusters formed of adjacent items of similar properties—hue, brightness, or spatial value—are crucial to the delineation of perceived form.

In his article on the stabilized retinal image, Pritchard deals with questions about the perception of form not unlike those discussed by Julesz. He claims, however, to have found evidence for the influence of meaningful interpretations of forms, as well as for that of gestalt factors, and for a kind of fragmentation of forms into pieces not unlike the clusters of Julesz. In interpreting the influence of meaning, Pritchard appeals to past experience. From the point of view of a naive observer, a letter—or printed word—is an arbitrary and conventional form; its significance must be acquired during the education of the growing child. On the other hand, perception of such figures as circle and triangle may result from a simple ordering intrinsic to perceptual processing and, hence, may show more resistance to fragmentation than more complexly ordered figures. Finally, the tendencies of figures to fragment into line segments is interpreted by Pritchard as revealing the existence of the cell assemblies postulated some twenty-odd years ago by the Canadian psychologist Donald Hebb. Hebb speculated that the perception of line segments and angles develops slowly as the result of the young observer's tendency to scan along edges to fixate successively on the corners of objects in his field of vision. An essentially associative process can then build up cell assemblies in the nervous system that, in turn, allow of the rapid recognition of line and corner elements in the mature perceiver. Hebb's insights were interesting percursors of the recent discoveries of visual feature detectors in the nervous systems of many animals.

FEATURE DETECTION

Against the background of ideas discussed above, the neurophysiological discoveries, beginning in the later fifties, of David Hubel and Torsten Wiesel (discussed in Hubel's article in Section III), of Jerome Lettvin (mentioned by Michael in his article in Section III), and other investigators have made an enormous impression on psychologists of perception. Between the global notions of gestalt and the atomistic ideas of sensation, there seemed to be no middle ground; yet the need for analysis of properties of the visible environment in terms of features of intermediate size was becoming ever more apparent from several perspectives. Attempts to build computer-aided devices for recognition—which Oliver G. Selfridge and Ulric Neisser discuss in their article "Pattern Recognition by Machine"—emphasized the economy to be achieved by carefully chosen intermediate steps in analyses of sensory input. Perceptual evidence for fragmentation into gross units, as discussed by Pritchard and Julesz, was accumulating, and certain theorists attempted to model the process of form discrimination in animals by assuming the existence of neural analyzers of specific properties of stimulation. The realization that sensory inputs to the central nervous system comprise appallingly large amounts of information clearly led to the inference that signal compression, reencoding, or other means of reducing this amount of information must occur to a previously unanticipated degree. This prepared the way for the welcome reception accorded the finding that certain neural units—presumably single cells—have a specificity of responsiveness to particular fragments out of the welter of information that impinges upon the retina. In turn, many perceptual phenomena appear to gain simple interpretations in terms of the properties of the central feature-detecting units inferred to exist in the human visual system. The illusions discussed by Whitman Richards in his article "The Fortification Illusions of Migraines" represent an unusually direct implication of the existence of such units; other, less direct inferences about the operations of such units are discussed in Section V. In simpler animals, features of stimulation that trigger discharges of particular cells appear to simulate real objects and events of importance to the organism (see the articles by Michael and Muntz in Section III).

One major aspect of the new neurophysiology is the finding of receptive fields subtending large areas of the retina including hundreds and even thousands of receptor units (see Michael's article). This result carries the implication that the output of many visual receptors converges onto single ganglion cells in the retina. To this may be added the further convergence implied by Hubel and Wiesel's findings higher up in the visual nervous system (see Hubel's article in Section III).

Taken by itself, neural convergence suggests the possibility that some of the information is lost in transmission from receptors to ganglion cells. A useful analogy in this connection is that, in a sample of water taken from a river downstream from several tributaries, it is impossible to determine, without other knowledge, from which particular tributary a given water molecule originated. This sort of loss of information would begin to account for the reduction of the amount of information that is available at the receptor surface. However, several considerations suggest that this interpretation be applied cautiously. As Hubel shows in his diagram of the columns of the visual cortex, particular regions of the retina are represented over and over again in partially overlapping receptive fields. Given such multiple representation, information about the locus of origin of stimuli on the retina may, in theory, be recovered to a degree of resolution far finer than the size of the more complex receptive fields. In other words, the ultimate resolution of a *set* of cortical receptive fields may be much better than that of its constituent units, provided that further processing is possible. Such further processing has been suggested by Hubel and Wiesel to account for the existence of hypercomplex receptive fields, which have been reported in recent publications (see Michael's article in Section III). They found two sorts of optimal stimuli for triggering the units that have such fields, which they called the single-stopped edge and the double-stopped edge—or, in other words, "corners" and "tongues," respectively. They derived the specific action of these units from a combination of excitation by a complex unit and inhibition by one or two flanking units maximally activated by an edge of the same orientation.

In addition to this mode of maintaining resolution, it is conceivable that neural pathways other than the geniculostriate system preserve information lost in the projections to the striate and extrastriate cortex. For example, a fraction (which varies from one vertebrate species to another) of the fibers of the optic nerve terminate in the superior colliculus, a midbrain structure homologous to part of the tectum found in the frog brain (see diagrams on pp. 146 and 163 in the articles by Michael and Muntz, respectively). Finally, even though the functional anatomy of the system suggests information reduction, reencoding of the information into other properties of neural firing—into a frequency-modulation code, for example—cannot be precluded.

Apart from the analysis of static, spatially distributed stimulation at the retina, certain evidence—discussed by Michael—points to the extraction of information about moving stimuli and colored stimuli. Such information may be sent from the retina to different centers in the brain for further analysis. The model for motion detection proposed by Barlow and Levick that Michael mentions in his article is one of the most interesting of its kind in the literature. The model—which draws upon neuroanatomical layout and physiological processes of inhibition and conduction velocity—is testable, at least in principle.

Single-unit studies indicate that our stream-flow analogy is inadequate: they suggest that—in the terms of the analogy—each tributary stream (input neuron) splits into many branches, each of which empties into one of several different rivers. Information about the precise origin of the waters in a given river is lost, but each river contains a sample, combined from a set of tributaries, that defines a receptive field. By this means, many features are extracted from the input in accord with a logic we are only beginning to understand.

SINGLE UNITS AND RELEASING STIMULI

The responses of single units in some animal species show greater specificity than might be expected from a consideration of the selectivity of orientation, size, and motion found by Hubel and Wiesel. The ganglion cells of the frog retina (discussed in the articles by Michael and by Muntz in Section III) are a case in point. One class of these cells is characterized as the "bug detector"; another class might be termed the "shadow detector," for reasons that are self-evident. Muntz also found that the frog's visual system is sensitive to blue. Taken together, this set of characters provides a basis for the survival of the individual frog, because they provide triggering information necessary to the acquisition of food (bugs), the detection of predators (the shadows of predatory birds), and the location of sanctuary (water). Given the motor responses appropriate to these inputs, the frog is capable of performing the requisite actions. To this repertory should be added recent fascinating findings about hearing in the bullfrog and about the behavior in that species that is contingent upon the mating call. Robert Capranica and his associates discovered that the croak of a male bullfrog tends to elicit croaking in other males of that species. Critical to this effect are a low-frequency band and a high-frequency band that are constituents of the croak; sound of intermediate frequencies inhibits the croaking response. Consistent with these behavioral results, single units in the bullfrog's auditory system have shown excitability peaks when the frog is stimulated by sound in the critical frequency bands. This discovery broadens our knowledge of the reproductive behavior of the bullfrog, and it supplements our list of those characters upon which the frog's chances for survival are based.

Our discussion of the feature detectors of the frog and their relation to the animal's behavioral repertory has already suggested a correlation between life style and neural equipment. However, there are several other respects in which the feature-detecting equipment of an animal varies with the grosser aspects of its anatomy, which, in turn, is adapted to the life style of the animal.

PREY AND PREDATOR

Those animals that rely mainly on vision to warn them of the approach of predators have developed panoramic vision in the course of evolution. The optic axes of their eyes tend to point laterally so that their fields of vision encompass wide regions to the sides and back of the body. Taken together, the right and left fields of such an animal may yield a visual angle of nearly 360°. The fields may overlap in front by only a few degrees or not at all. The advantage of such panoramic vision is obvious; the more of the world continuously surveyed by the retina, the better the warning system. On the other hand, the less the overlap of the fields, the less stereoscopic is the animal's vision, and it is stereopsis that allows discrimination of fine differences in depth. This trade-off between panoramic vision and stereopsis would appear to have played an important role in the evolution of visual systems. Stereopsis is usually best developed in those animals that have fine control of their movements, particularly their manipulative actions; the primates – including men and monkeys – provide obvious examples. If the value of stereopsis is not evident to the reader, let him try to thread a needle with one of his eyes shut, and then compare that with his performance of the same task with both eyes open.

Accompanying increased stereopsis in vertebrate species is a change in the central projection of the visual nervous system. An indication of this is given by the diagrams of the visual pathways in Muntz's article (see p. 163). All of the fibers in the optic nerve of the frog are shown crossing (decussating) the midline of the brain to synapse in the lateral geniculate nucleus and optic tectum on the side opposite the eye from which they originate. On the other hand, in the visual system of man, approximately half of the fibers originating in, say, the right eye remain on the right side of the brain, synapsing, for the most part, in the lateral geniculate. The proportion of non-crossing fibers increases with the amount of overlap of the visual fields. One of the functions of this curious change in the central projections of the visual nervous system is to bring together the projections of corresponding parts of the two retinas: for example, fibers from the left half of the retina of the left eye join those from the left half of the retina of the right eye. It is this convergence of inputs from corresponding regions of the two eyes that is essential to stereopsis. A special class of Hubel-Wiesel units, called binocular-difference detectors, are receptive to the combined inputs from the two eyes. They are discussed in the next section.

It has also been suggested that differences, among species, in the complexity of feature detectors at low levels in the nervous system (in the retina, in particular) may be accounted for by differences in the degree of overlap of the visual fields. When there is a large binocular overlap, it may be more efficient to delay complex feature extraction until the inputs from corresponding regions in the fields of both eyes have converged. In such animals as the frog and the rabbit, whose visual fields overlap little or not at all, such a delay would not improve the efficiency of visual perception.

AUDITORY LOCALIZATION AND BINAURAL DIFFERENCES

Hearing – like vision – begins with paired organs of reception. The fate of the information entering the nervous system by way of the two ears makes an interesting chapter in the psychology of the senses. Observation and experiment have made it quite clear that the most precise spatial localization of acoustic events (sources of sound) is dependent upon binaural stimulation. Just as small spatial differences in binocular inputs allow for the visual perception of depth (stereoscopy), it is differences in the intensity and in the time of arrival of binaural inputs that provide information about the location of sound sources. As Mark R. Rosenzweig emphasizes in his article "Auditory Localization," the ear and its nervous system are specialized to provide high resolution in the time domain. It is this power of analysis that is used by the system for the most precise mode of locating sources of sound.

Rosenzweig discusses some of the evidence for the existence of feature detectors specifically responsive to binaural differences; this evidence has been considerably increased in recent years. In a number of nuclei in the auditory nervous system, including the olivary nucleus and higher centers, single units have been discovered that are specifically responsive to binaural differences in time and intensity; they provide an analogue to the binocular-difference detectors of the visual nervous system.

COMPARISONS AMONG SPECIES

As we mentioned previously, phylogenetic considerations aid in assessing the significance of neural mechanisms. The number and diversity of the receptive organs of a given animal species may be correlated both with the type and degree of responsivity to the environment shown by that species and with the complexity of its behavioral repertory. More germane to consideration of the higher processes of perception in vertebrate animals is the relation of the peripheral to the central processing equipment of the organism. Among the vertebrates—fish, amphibians, reptiles, birds, and mammals—the typical number of sensory systems and associated receptor organs does not differ greatly, but much evidence points to differences from class to class in the complexity of neural processing of the several sensory inputs. Differences in perceptual abilities that accompany degrees of complexity of neural processing can provide clues to the function and operation of neural mechanisms.

An extreme example of the correlation of stimulus filtering with behavioral repertory is shown by the male silkworm moth. Upon emergence from the pupa, the male moth has but one purpose—to find and mate with a female of the species. The male moth is remarkably capable of accomplishing his purpose: he may detect and approach his mate from a distance of more than a mile. Experiments have shown that this behavior is controlled by the sense of smell. But how can the male distinguish the particular scent of the female from among the vast number of odors to which he is exposed? Electrophysiological studies have shown that the moth has no need to distinguish: his olfactory system responds solely to a specific substance secreted by the female.

An example of a protective device whose operation appears to depend upon a very simple receptor and neural mechanism is the sensitivity of the scallop to the shadow of a potential predator (see Kennedy's article in Section III). Such specialization is, of course, not to be found in vertebrate species whose evolution has not, in general, led to such extreme simplicity of function and structure.

THE PERCEPTION OF FORM

Much of the interest in feature detectors in the nervous system stems from the question of how advanced animals—man, in particular—perceive form. This question has its origins (as the problem of universals) in classical philosophy. How, despite the enormous range of variation, does a perceiver identify a particular tree as a member of the class of trees, a particular chair as a chair, any writer's penned "a" as an instance of that letter, and so on. Given the brute capability of detecting entities in the visual field as they are defined by gradations of light intensity or by texture differences, how do such entities come to be characterized as members of the particular sets we call forms? The problem is no less important in hearing: How do the members of a given species identify those sounds that serve that species in communication? The great variety, from one speaker to the next, of all the acoustic properties of any phrase in any given language does not preclude recognition of the words and their meaning by any normal person who also speaks that language. The astonishing ellipses that occur in common speech further complicate the problem of specifying the stimulus properties that allow different phrasings of the same thought to be grouped together by the listener as having a common meaning.

STIMULUS EQUIVALENCE

Psychologists refer to similar stimuli as equivalent when they elicit the same response from an organism. But the term "stimulus equivalence" doesn't call attention to a number of important differences among the various sets of stimuli that may be said to exhibit that property. For example, metamers (that is, color stimuli that may be seen as identical under certain conditions but that have different spectrophotometric characters) exhibit stimulus equivalence; an observer cannot possibly detect the wavelength differences between two such colors. On the other hand, many different objects—such as particular fruits, tables, faces, and so on—are recognized as members of their respective classes, even though they may be readily distinguished from each other. Here, the problem of classification according to some principle of a selected dimension of comparison becomes important. Between these two extreme types of equivalence lie many intermediates. Traditionally, the observation that many shapes are immediately recognized, despite wide variations in position on the retina, size, rotation, and other perspectival transformations, led to their characterization as equivalent stimuli and the characterization of the process as one of the perceptual constancies. However, as the reader will recognize, the ability to classify and analogize merges with cognition, problem solving, and even with scientific discovery. The ability of the perceiver to detect those invariant properties that underlie equivalences of form is perhaps the most ubiquitous and difficult problem with which perceptionists have to deal.

The advent of the high-speed digital computer has lent new hope, in recent years, to those who would find a machine analogy for the form-recognizing ability of the human perceiver. The article "Pattern Recognition by Machine," by Oliver C. Selfridge and Ulric Neisser, summarizes one of the important pioneering efforts to develop computer programs for detecting equivalent forms. It is perhaps not surprising that the first step in computer recognition consists of breaking the form up into smaller bits, some of which are shared by each member of the set of forms to be distinguished. From an historical point of view, it is interesting that the discovery of feature detectors in the nervous system was more or less simultaneous with the conclusion by investigators of form-recognizing devices that their programs should initially analyze figures into elements of a complexity intermediate between the whole figure and the mosaic of punctate receptors stimulated at the retina.

If we return now to a consideration of neural units of the Hubel-Wiesel type, it is easy to see how they might be interpreted as edge detectors and used in the initial stages in establishing the equivalence of simple forms. Combinations of the outputs of four properly oriented complex edge detectors and four hypercomplex corner detectors could readily be taken to represent a rectangle over considerable ranges of size and position on the retina. It is tempting to identify specific neural units known from microelectrode studies of the nervous systems with the feature detectors inferred to account for form perception. In that spirit, Hubel and Wiesel term these units the "building blocks of perception." As yet, however, there is only the slimmest direct evidence that such is the case.

If we accept the view that form perception is based upon piecemeal feature detection, we are still left with the question of how decisions about form are arrived at from the collection of features into which a pattern is reduced. Selfridge and Neisser discuss two alternative modes of processing features: parallel and sequential. This distinction recurs in the article "Eye Movements and Visual Perception," by David Noton and Lawrence Stark. Noton and Stark wish to implicate scanning movements of the eye in the creation of an internal representation of an object and in the later recognition of that object. Constant change of the retinal image, a difficulty for the static-image theory of form perception (see the article by Neisser in Section V), becomes an asset in this theory.

Scanning an object that subtends a large visual angle is essential in order to bring details of that object into focus in the foveal region. But as Noton and Stark acknowledge, small objects may be recognized without overt eye movements, or when exposures are short enough to preclude the effects of eye movements. To account for recognition under such conditions, resort must be made to some sort of internal scan carried out within the visual nervous system. Such sequential processing in the recognition of form is plausible whether or not explicit eye movements are involved in the initial survey of the form. But this sort of process is but one among many alternative schemata that have been proposed to account for form recognition. Thus far, no convincing general theory has been advanced.

REFERENCES

Capranica, R. *The evoked vocal response of the bullfrog.* Cambridge, Mass.: M.I.T. Press, 1965.

Hebb, D. *The organization of behavior.* New York: John Wiley & Sons, 1949.

Köhler, W. *Gestalt psychology.* New York: Liveright, 1929.

Lettvin, J. Y., Maturana, H. R., McCulloch, W. S., & Pitts, W. H. What the frog's eye tells the frog's brain. *Proceedings of the Institute of Radio Engineers,* 1959, **47**, 1940–1951.

17

STABILIZED IMAGES ON THE RETINA

ROY M. PRITCHARD
June 1961

In normal vision the eye is constantly in motion. Small involuntary movements persist even when the eye is "fixed" on a stationary object. As a result the image of the object on the retina of the eye is kept in constant motion. One movement of the eyeball makes the image drift slowly away from the center of the fovea, the region of maximum visual acuity in which the cone receptor cells are most densely concentrated. The drifting motion terminates in a flick that brings the image back toward the center of the fovea. Superimposed on the drift motion is a tremor with frequencies up to 150 cycles per second and an amplitude of about half the diameter of a single cone receptor.

These three involuntary movements of the eyeball, all much smaller than the voluntary movements involved in looking at the visual world or in reading, have been known to physiologists for many years. During the past decade Lorrin A. Riggs of Brown University and R. W. Ditchburn of the University of Reading in England succeeded in measuring them with great accuracy. Though the movements cannot be stopped without incapacitating the subject or endangering the eye, Ditchburn and Riggs found ways to circumvent them and so make an image stand still on the retina. They were thereby able to show that the motion of the image plays a significant role in the sensory function of the eye. When an image is stabilized on the retina by one means or another, it soon fades and disappears. Just how this happens is not yet completely understood.

It was also observed, however, that the stabilized image regenerates after a time and again becomes visible to the subject in whole or in part. The image—or fragments of it—alternately fades and regenerates over prolonged periods of observation. This finding has attracted the attention of psychologists interested in the perceptual aspects of vision, those aspects which involve the functioning of the brain as well as the cells of the retina. At McGill University, D. O. Hebb, Woodburn Heron and I have been investigating the stabilized visual image as a source of data for the formulation of a comprehensive theory of visual perception. We have found that the fragmentation, or the alternate partial fading and partial regeneration, of the image is related to the character and content of the image itself.

Our evidence supports to some extent the "cell assembly" idea that experience is needed to develop the innate potential of perception: a pattern is perceived through the combination in the brain of separate neural impressions that have been established there and correspond to various learned elements. But the evidence also sustains the Gestalt, or holistic, theory, which holds that perception is innately determined: a pattern is perceived directly as a whole and without synthesis of parts, a product of unlearned capacity to perceive "form," "wholeness" and "organization." It is becoming apparent that the complete explanation of perception must be sought in a resolution of these opposing views.

We stabilize the image by attaching the target to be viewed to the eyeball itself. The device we use for this purpose consists of a tight-fitting contact lens on which is mounted a tiny, self-contained optical projector [*see illustration on opposite page*]. With the subject lying on a couch, the device is set in place on the cornea and focused to project an image on the retina. The experimenter changes the target film from time to time, and he keeps a continuous record of the subject's report of what he sees.

What the subject sees, before fading sets in, is an image located at apparent infinity and subtending a visual angle of two degrees in a patch of light that subtends an angle of five degrees in the surrounding darkness. Provided that the contact lens does not slip on the cornea, the image remains fixed on the retina and does not move with movement of the eyeball.

After a few seconds of viewing, the image disappears progressively and bit by bit, leaving a structureless gray field of light. Later this gray field may darken, and with complete loss of sensation of light the field becomes intensely black. When the image disappears or reappears the uninitiated subject at first rotates his eyes in an effort to bring the image or a center of interest in the image back to the center of the fovea. These movements are, of course, futile because they cannot change the geometrical relationship between the target, the lens of the eye and the retina. Soon the subject learns to view the image passively and discovers that he can still transfer his attention from point to point over the limited visual field.

In general we have found that the image of a simple figure, such as a single line, vanishes rapidly and then reappears as a complete image. A more complex target, such as the profile of a face or a pattern of curlicues, may similarly disappear and reappear as a whole; on the other hand, it may vanish in fragments, with one or more of its parts fading independently. We have found in addition that the length of time an image persists is also a function of its complexity. A single line may be visible for only 10 per cent of the aggregate view-

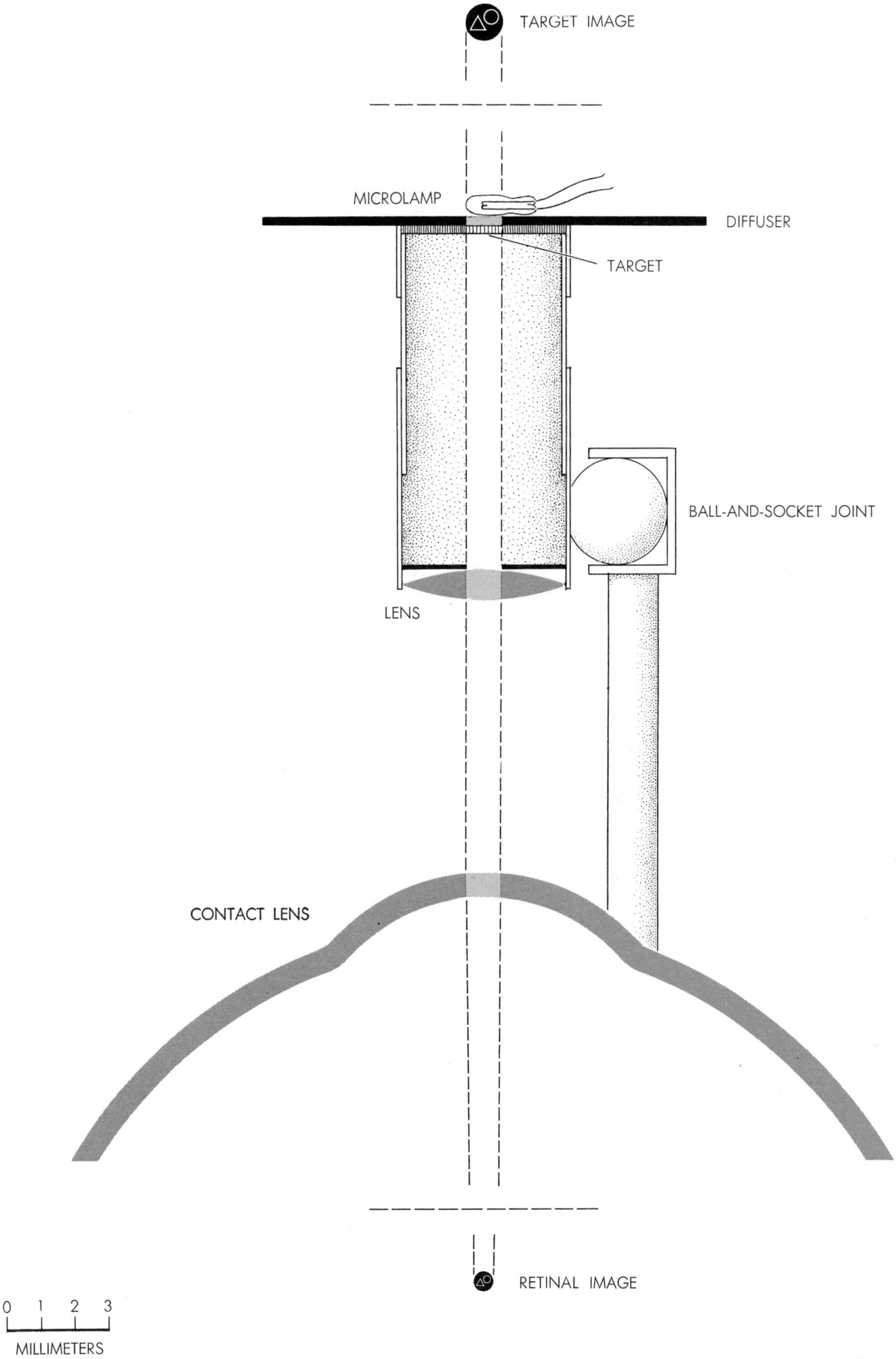

STABILIZED-IMAGE DEVICE is a tiny projector mounted on a contact lens worn by the subject. The contact lens moves with every movement of the eyeball; so, therefore, does the projector, and as a result the target image (*at top of illustration*) is kept fixed at one point on the retina (*as suggested at bottom of illustration*). The convex lens focuses parallel rays of light on the retina, so the target is viewed by the subject as if it were at an infinite distance. The entire optical system weighs only .25 gram.

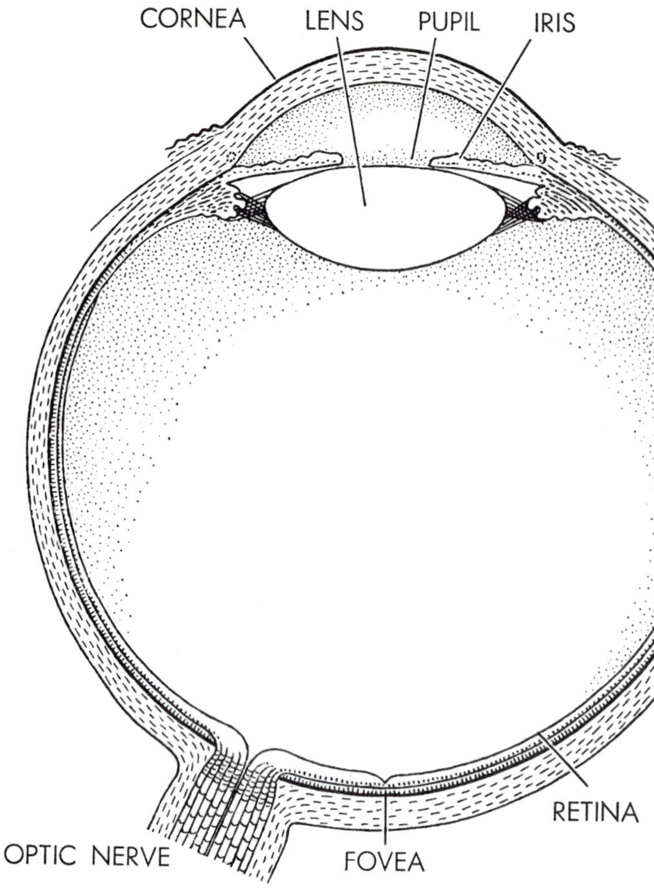

HUMAN EYE, seen here in horizontal cross section, works much like a camera. Light entering through the pupil is focused by the lens upon the retina's light-sensitive receptor cells, from which impulses travel via the optic nerve to the brain. The fovea, the area of most acute vision, is 1.5 millimeters in diameter and subtends a visual angle of five degrees.

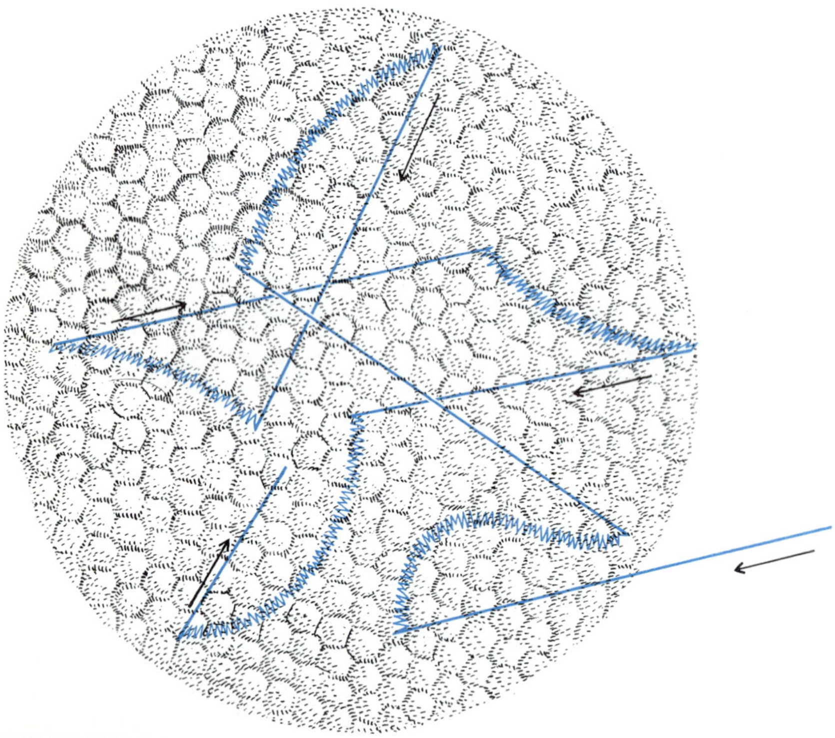

EYE MOVEMENTS that are halted in stabilized vision normally carry an image across the receptors of the retina as shown here. The three movements are a drift (*curved lines*) away from the center of vision, a faster flick (*straight lines*) back toward the center and a high-frequency tremor superimposed on the drift. The magnitude of all these movements is very small; the diameter of the patch of the fovea shown above is only .05 millimeter.

ing time, whereas a more complex figure may remain visible in whole or in part for as much as 80 per cent of the time.

The contrasting manner in which complex images fade and regenerate lends support to the role of learning in perception. For example, the figure of the human profile invariably fades and regenerates in meaningful units. The front of the face, the top of the head, the eye and the ear come and go as recognizable entities, separately and in various combinations. In contrast, on first presentation a meaningless pattern of curlicues is described as extremely "active"; the individual elements fade and regenerate rapidly, and the subject sees almost every configuration that can be derived from the original figure. After prolonged viewing, however, certain combinations of curlicues become dominant and these then disappear and reappear as units. The newly formed groupings persist for longer periods than other combinations, and the figure can no longer be considered unorganized and meaningless.

In the cell-assembly approach to a theory of perception these observations are explained in terms of "perceptual elements," as opposed to purely sensory elements. The "organized," "meaningful" or "recognizable" parts of the image correspond to perceptual elements previously learned or established by experience. The parts of the human profile would thus function as perceptual elements at the outset in the behavior of the stabilized image. Given time for learning, parts of the originally meaningless curlicue pattern become recognizable in turn and operate as perceptual elements. These elements may be excited, it is argued, by the minimum retinal stimulation provided by the stabilized image. To evoke and maintain the image of the entire figure would require the additional information normally supplied by the movement of the image across the retinal receptors.

This interpretation gains additional support from what subjects report about the stabilized images of monograms that combine such symbols as the letters *H* and *B*. One or the other letter, or a fragment such as *P*, constitutes the unit that is perceived from one period to the next, with periods of complete fade-out intervening. When entire words are presented, the partial fragmentation of letters can cause different words to be perceived [*see bottom illustration on opposite page*]. In a figure that presents a meaningful symbol such as *B* obscured by hatching lines, the subject sees either the intact *B* or the hatching lines independently. He may also on occasion see the two elements together, but then the *B* appears to float in a plane in front of the one containing the hatching lines. There is nothing haphazard about the fading of such figures, and these effects cannot be attributed to random fluctuation of threshold in various parts of the retina. Even if such fluctuation is thought to occur in the retinal system, the organized or meaningful unit remains visible longer than the unorganized one, in keeping with the presumed importance of learning in visual perception.

But the Gestalt psychologist can argue that it is unnecessary to bring learning and experience into the explanation of these effects. The same effects show up in experiments with meaningless or only semimeaningful figures and can be explained in terms of the Gestalt concept of perception as a process that works by "the whole." If an irregular shape, like that of an amoeba, is obscured by hatching lines, for example, the subject may report the same unitary and separate fading of the amoeba shape and of the hatching lines that he reports in the case of a letter of the alphabet. The two parts of the complete figure may also appear separated in different planes. More commonly in this case, however, parts of both the amoeba shape and the obscuring lines disappear together, and the remaining elements amalgamate to form a new composite figure. The hybrid is a more compact, tidy figure, with fewer disrupting elements.

When the amoeba shape is presented alone, parts of the figure tend to disappear. One or more of the bulges in the figure fade from view, and a line or lines are hallucinated to seal off the gaps produced by their disappearance. The limb or limbs that fade are invariably the grosser or more distorted features of the figure, and their disappearance, together with the closures, produces a "better" or more rounded figure. Any other comparatively irregular or jagged figure similarly appears unstable on first

STABILIZED IMAGES typically fade as in the illustrations on this and the following two pages. The parts of a profile drawing that stay visible are invariably specific features or groups of features, such as the front of the face or the top of the head.

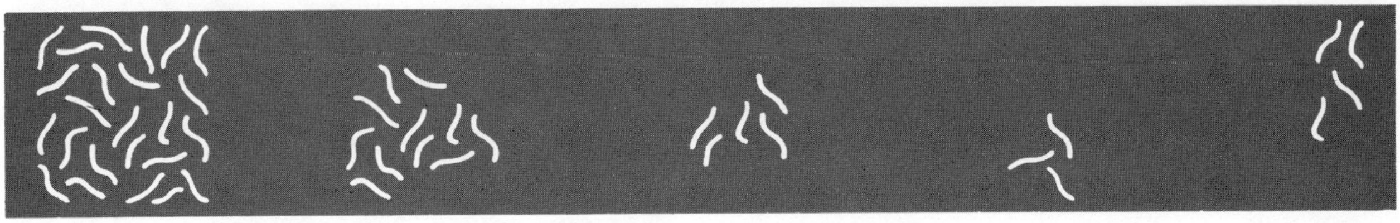

MEANINGLESS CURLICUES first come and go in random sequence. But after a while small groups of curlicues organized in recognizable patterns start to behave as units. This suggests that they have themselves become meaningful perceptual elements.

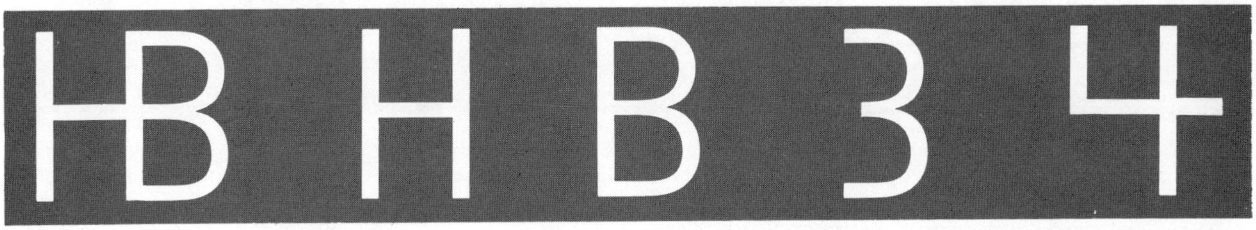

MONOGRAM formed of the letters *H* and *B* also seems to illustrate the importance of elements that are meaningful because of past experience. When the monogram breaks up it is the recognizable letters and numbers within it that come successively into view.

WORDS containing other words behave in much the same manner as the monogram. Here, for example, the subject sees new words made up of letters and parts of letters in the original. He is far less likely to report seeing meaningless groups of letters such as *EER*.

viewing. Its individual elements come and go until the holistic "editing" process reduces it to a more rounded configuration. A smooth, rounded figure, in contrast, appears more stable at the outset and tends to operate more as a whole in the alternate process of fading and regeneration.

As Gestalt theory would predict, contiguity and similarity strongly determine the functioning of the groups as entities isolated from the total figure. A target consisting of rows of small squares usually fades to leave one whole row—horizontal, diagonal or vertical—visible. Similarly a random collection of dots will fade to leave only those dots which lie approximately in a line, and it is the disappearance of the remainder that reveals this linear association. At the same time it must be emphasized that the original figure as well as each configuration that can be derived from it may function as a single unit, disappearing and reappearing as a whole.

Our experiments with stabilized images have thus produced evidence to sustain both of the major theoretical approaches to visual perception, which have for so long been considered mutually exclusive. It may be, however, that the two concepts are really complementary. As in the historic clash of the wave and the particle concepts in physics, the apparent opposition may arise solely from a difference in approach to the same problem. We have performed a number of experiments that conform equally well to both interpretations. This supports our expectation that a modern theory of perception will eventually result from a mating of the two systems.

In experiments with simple straight-line figures the cell-assembly approach is supported by the observation that the line is the apparent unit of perception just as the line is the unit of structure in the figure. It is always the whole line that fades or reappears, independently or in association with others, and the breaking, when fading occurs, is always at the intersection of lines. In fact, the overwhelmingly independent action of

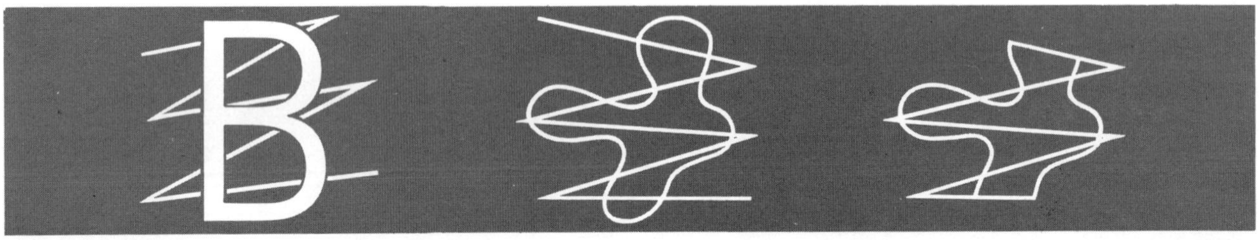

OBSCURING LINES drawn over a figure act in various ways. In the case of the *B*, the lines often drop into a plane behind the meaningful letter. But lines over a less meaningful amoeba shape usually combine with the amoeba to form a more compact figure.

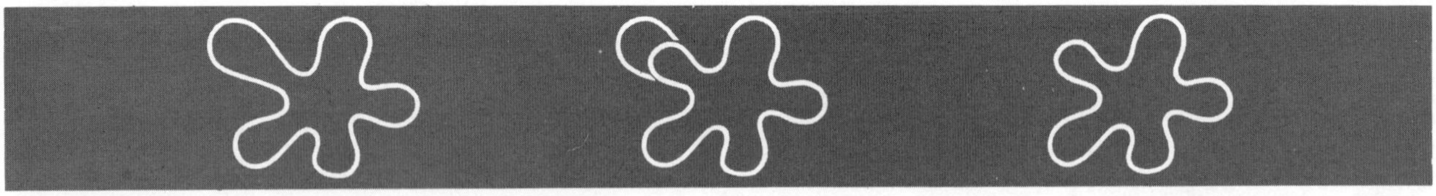

AMOEBA SHAPE standing alone usually fades by losing one or more bulges. What fades, as in this case, is always the most distorted feature, and it is replaced by a new closure "ghosted" by the subject and tending to form a more symmetrical and rounded figure.

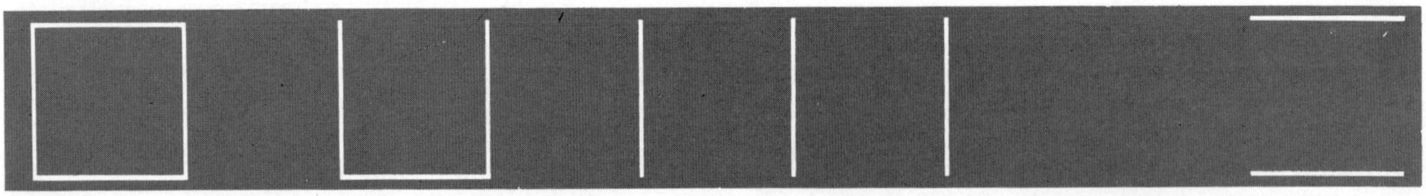

LINES act independently in stabilized vision, with breakage in the fading figure always at an intersection of lines. Adjacent or parallel lines may operate as units. This independent action of lines tends to support the cell-assembly theory of perception.

PLANES operate as units in three-dimensional figures. In this Necker cube (which gives an illusion of reversing in stabilized as well as in normal vision) a line may act alone. But usually lines defining a plane operate together, leaving parallel planes.

lines makes inevitable the inclusion of some cell-assembly concepts in any complete theory of perception.

In a figure composed of a circle and a triangle, either the circle or the triangle may fade to leave the other visible. One could take this independent action of meaningful figures as evidence for the role of learning in perception. On the other hand, the Gestalt psychologist can just as readily explain the unitary action of the circle or triangle as evidence of the behavior of wholes.

But the fading process may also dissect the figure in other ways—for example, it may leave only one side of the triangle and the segment of the circle closest or most nearly parallel to it in view. Gestalt theory explains this report by the so-called field effect. The minimal sensory stimulus provided by the stabilized image is said to excite a perceptual response that goes well beyond the region of actual stimulation. In straight-line figures, furthermore, there is a tendency for noncontiguous parallel lines to operate together, and lines of the Necker cube [*see bottom illustration on preceding page*] usually vanish to leave parallel planes visible in space, with one of the planes in advance of the other. These observations can also be advanced as evidence of a field effect.

Most figures are seen as three-dimensional when viewed as a stabilized image. Most line drawings appear at some stage as "wires" suspended in space. The small squares in a repetitive pattern are perceived as protrusions or depressions. And a simple hexagon has been reported to be the outline of a cube in three dimensions that "reverses" in the same manner as the Necker cube.

In the case of figures drawn in solid tones as distinguished from those drawn in outline, the behavior of the stabilized image seems more consistent with cell-assembly theory. The corner now replaces the line as the unit of independent action. A solid square will fade from its center, and the fading will obliterate first one and then another corner, leaving the remaining corners sharply outlined and isolated in space. Regeneration

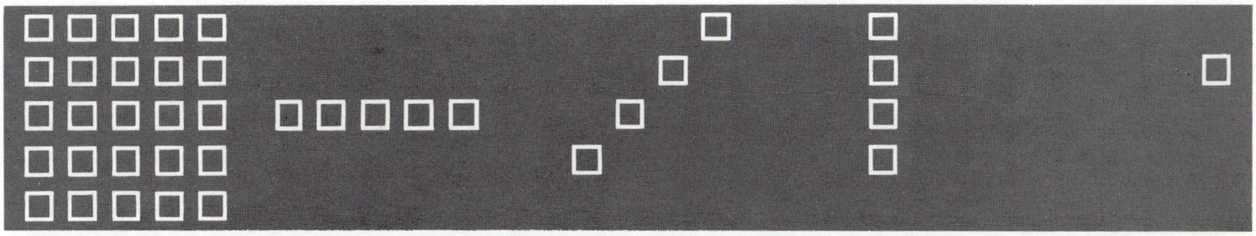

LINEAR ORGANIZATION is emphasized by the fading of this target composed of rows of squares. The figure usually fades to leave one whole row visible: horizontal, diagonal or vertical. In some cases a three-dimensional "waffle" effect is also noted.

CIRCLE AND TRIANGLE may fade as units, leaving one or the other in view. When there is partial fading, a side of the triangle may remain in view along with a parallel segment of the circle, suggesting the "field effect" postulated in Gestalt visual theory.

CORNERS are the basic units when solid-tone figures are used. The fading starts in the center and the sharply defined corners disappear one by one. This target, like the others in the series, was presented to subjects both in white-on-black and black-on-white.

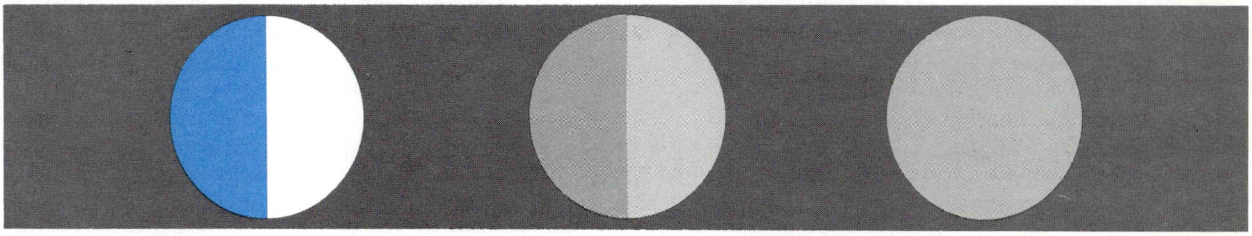

SENSE OF COLOR is lost with particular speed. A two-color field like this fades almost immediately when stabilized, to leave two values of gray; then the brightness difference disappears. The stabilized technique promises to be useful for studying color vision.

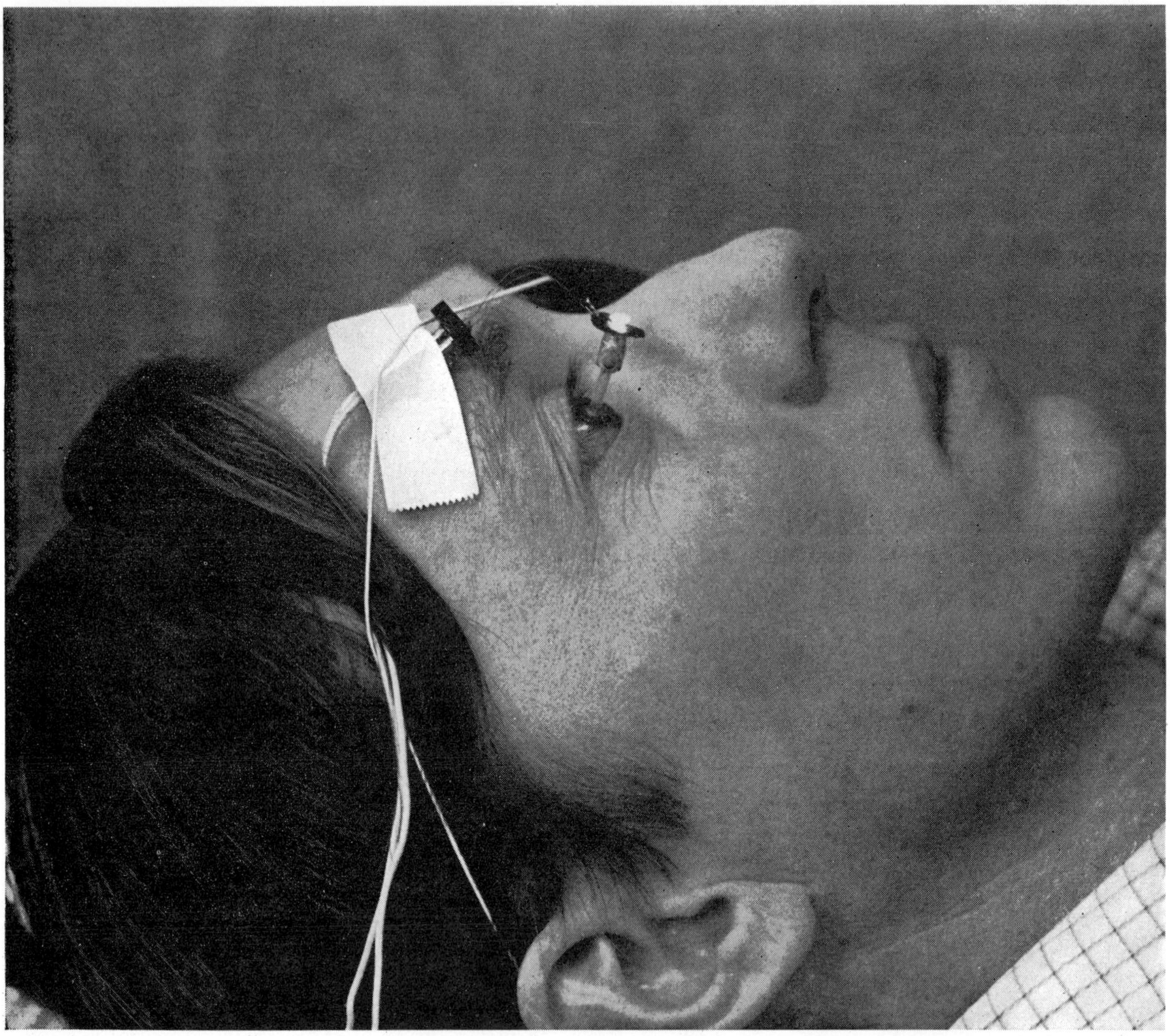

TAKING TURN AS SUBJECT in a stabilized-vision experiment, the author wears on his right eye a contact lens on which the projector is mounted. The other eye is occluded by a patch. Wires lead from the small projector lamp to a battery through a connecting jack taped to his forehead. The experimenter inserts a target film under the diffuser. At first the image is clear to the subject, but it soon fades and then regenerates. The subject makes a continuous report of what he sees, and the experimenter records his comments.

correspondingly begins with the reappearance of first one and then another corner, yielding a complete or partial figure with the corners again sharply outlined.

The basic concepts of Gestalt theory receive strong support in our experiments from the observed importance of field effects, from the dominance of "good" figures and from the action of whole figures and of groups of design elements as perceptual entities. But it is the independent action of the parts and not the whole of a figure that is paramount in stabilized vision. This observation agrees with cell-assembly theory and the perceptual elements it postulates. On the other hand, the perceptual elements themselves appear as organized entities and so conform to Gestalt concepts. Perhaps the Gestalt perception-by-the-whole theory can best be used in interpreting perception in a broad sense, while the cell-assembly idea of perception by parts may turn out to be most useful for analysis of perception in detail.

Meanwhile stabilized images have opened up a promising approach to another significant problem in the field of perception: color vision. Color disappears quickly in the stabilized image of a colored figure. In a field composed of the three primary colors, the red, green and blue hues disappear to leave a colorless field of three different brightnesses. These brightness differences also disappear with time, but it is the color that goes first. This supports the suggestion that the hue of a color is produced by radiation of a given wavelength on the retina and that the perception of hue is maintained by continuous changes in the luminosity of the radiation falling on a receptor cell or cells. Movement of the edges of a patch of color across the retina, produced by normal eye movements, would therefore be necessary for continuous perception of color. We are now making an investigation of the amplitude, frequency and form of movement necessary to sustain or regenerate a particular color.

18

TEXTURE AND VISUAL PERCEPTION

BELA JULESZ
February 1965

Because we are surrounded every waking minute by objects of different sizes, shapes, colors and textures we are scarcely surprised that we can tell them apart. There are so many visual clues to the distinctiveness of objects that we hardly ever make the mistake of believing that two different objects are one object unless we have been deliberately tricked.

Four years ago I became interested in studying the extent to which one can perceive differences in visual patterns when all familiar cues are removed. In this way I hoped to dissociate the primitive mechanisms of perception from the more complex ones that depend on lifelong learned habits of recognition. To obtain suitable patterns for this investigation a computer was used to generate displays that had subtly controlled statistical, topological or other properties but entirely lacked familiar features.

This method is basically different from those employed earlier by workers interested in visual perception. One method that has been widely used is to impoverish or degrade the images presented to the subject. This can be done by adding visual "noise," by presenting the stimuli for a limited time or by otherwise impairing the normal conditions of viewing. Another approach is to study human subjects whose perceptual mechanisms are known to be deficient (such as color-blind people) or animals whose perceptual mechanisms have been altered by surgical operations. I hoped that my approach of "familiarity deprivation" might be a useful addition to these other methods.

In a broad sense I was interested in the same kind of problem that has long concerned psychologists of the *Gestalt* school. One such problem has been to explain why it is that under certain conditions an outline drawing is seen as a unified whole—as a *Gestalt*—and under other conditions is seen as having two or more parts. I undertook to reduce this problem to how one discriminated between the parts (or did not discriminate between them). In my investigations, which have been conducted at the Bell Telephone Laboratories, I have been concerned with two specific questions. First, can two unfamiliar objects connected in space be discriminated solely by differences in their surface texture? Second, can two unfamiliar objects with identical surface texture be discriminated solely on the basis of their separation in space?

To make these questions less abstract let me give examples that could arise in real life. The first question would be involved if you wanted to replace a section of wallpaper and discovered that the original pattern was no longer available. If the pattern happened to be nonrepresentational and irregular, you might be able to find a new pattern that could not easily be discriminated from the old one when the two were placed side by side. Yet if you studied the two patterns closely, you might find that they differed substantially in detail. You would conclude that the matching must be attributable to the similarity of certain critical features in the two patterns.

The second question has its counterpart in aerial reconnaissance to detect objects that have been camouflaged. Flying at a height of several thousand feet, an observer can easily be deceived by the camouflage because normal binocular depth perception is inoperative beyond 100 feet or so. But if he photographs the ground from two points several hundred feet apart and views the resulting pictures stereoscopically, he will usually discover that even a camouflaged object will stand out vividly in three dimensions.

Of course neither of these examples provides an adequate test of the discrimination problems I hoped to examine with artificial displays. The weakness in the wallpaper analogy is that most wallpaper patterns, including irregular ones, have repetitive features and even forms that suggest familiar objects. The aerial reconnaissance example has the important defect that most camouflaged objects have contours

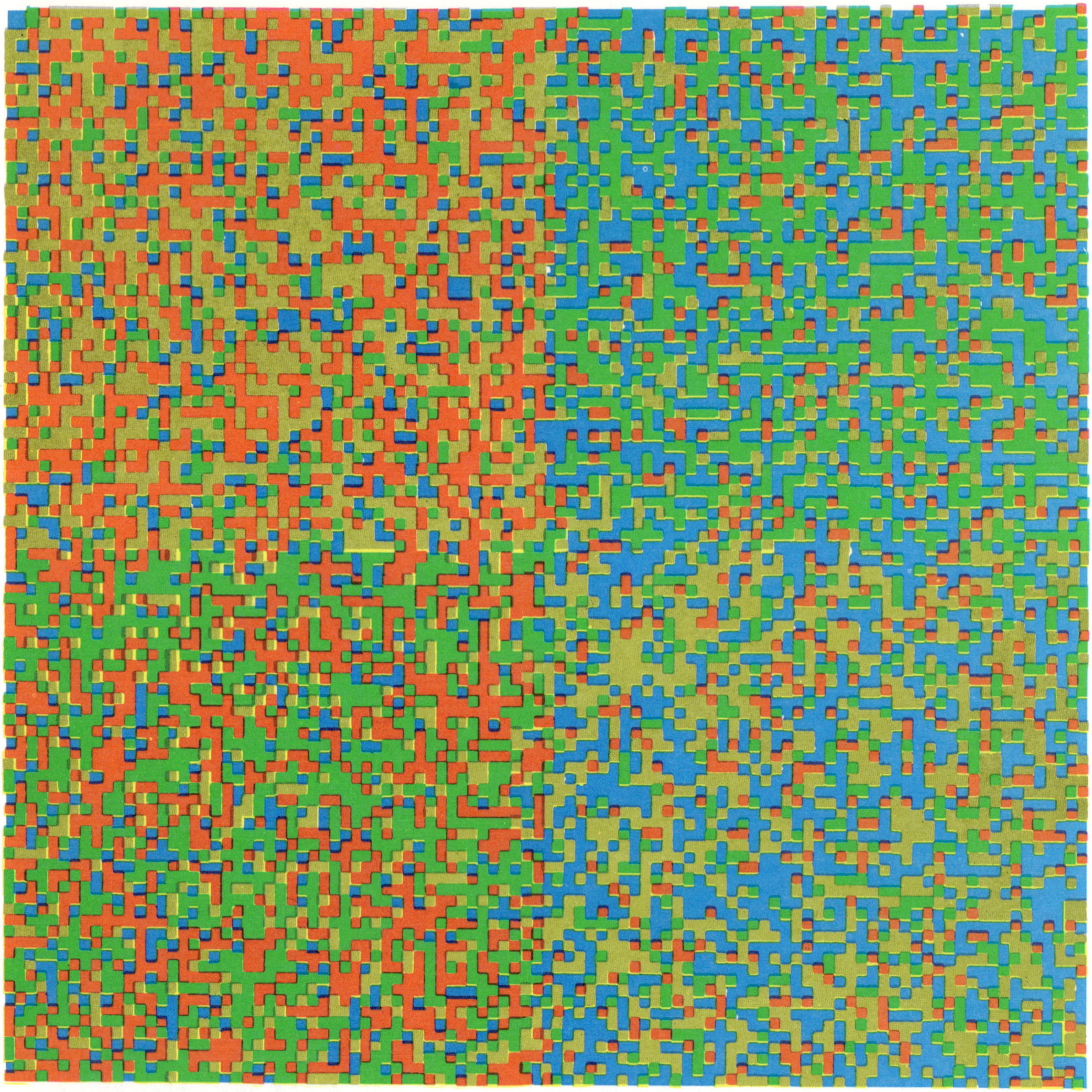

TEXTURE DISCRIMINATION in random fields of colored dots is highly dependent on the way the component colors are paired. The two patterns at the top of the opposite page are basically the same as those shown one above the other in the figure on this page. Neither version adequately reproduces the author's laboratory demonstration, in which the patterns are created by colored lights of equal subjective brightness. To simulate this condition the yellow picture elements above have been reduced in brightness by a fine-mesh overlay of black dots. They have the drawback, however, of making the yellow areas look greenish. In the version on the opposite page the black-dot overlay has been omitted, with the result that the yellow elements are much too bright. On the whole the figure above comes closer to achieving the desired effect, which is to show that a texture composed chiefly of red and yellow dots is readily discriminated from a texture composed chiefly of blue and green dots (top half of figure on this page), whereas a texture composed chiefly of red and green dots is not so readily discriminated from one composed chiefly of blue and yellow dots (bottom half of figure). These paired textures—one easily discriminable, the other less so—are respectively repeated at top left and right on the opposite page. The makeup of each top panel is shown in the four panels below it. The only difference is in the transposition of yellow and green.

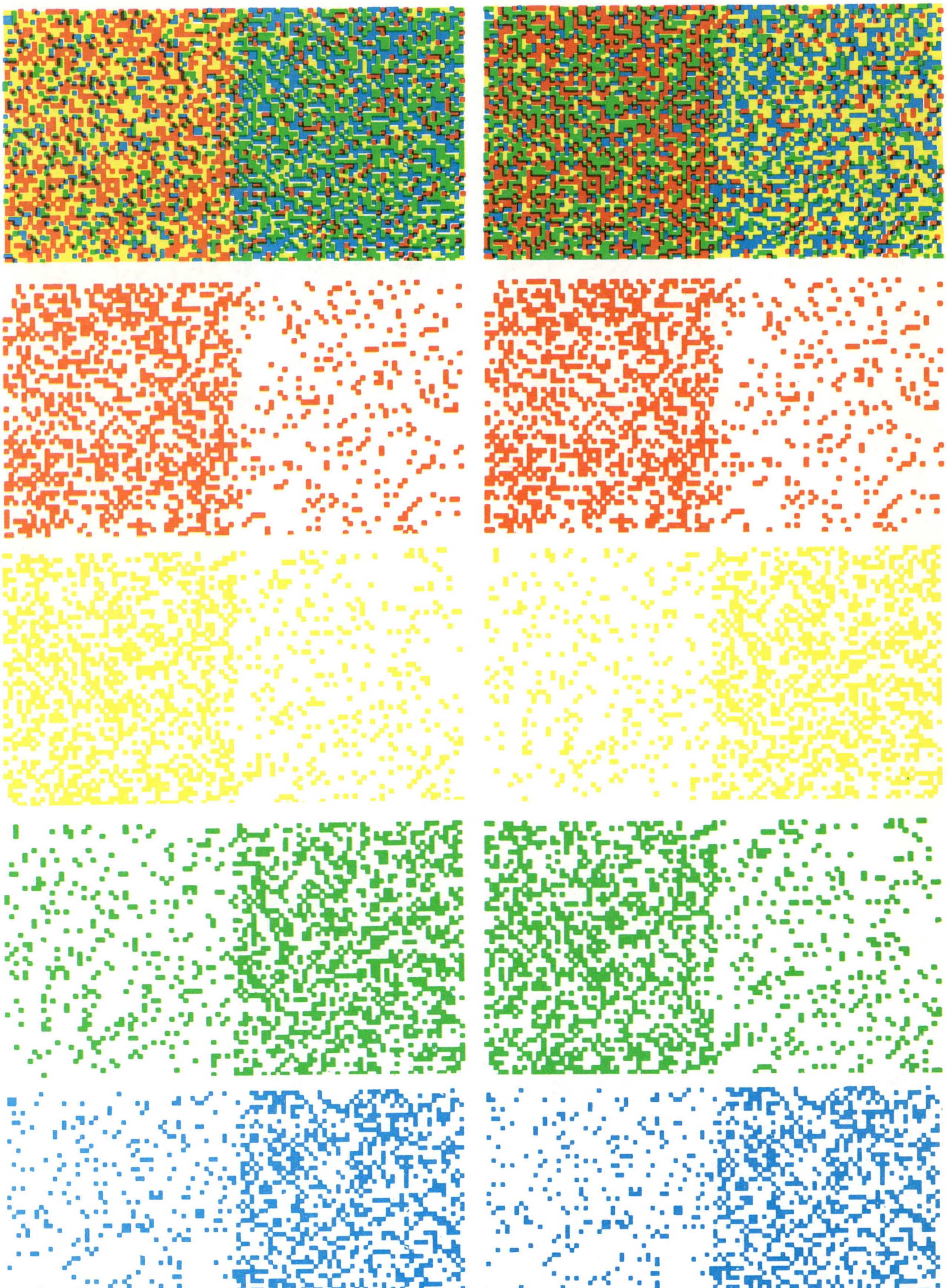

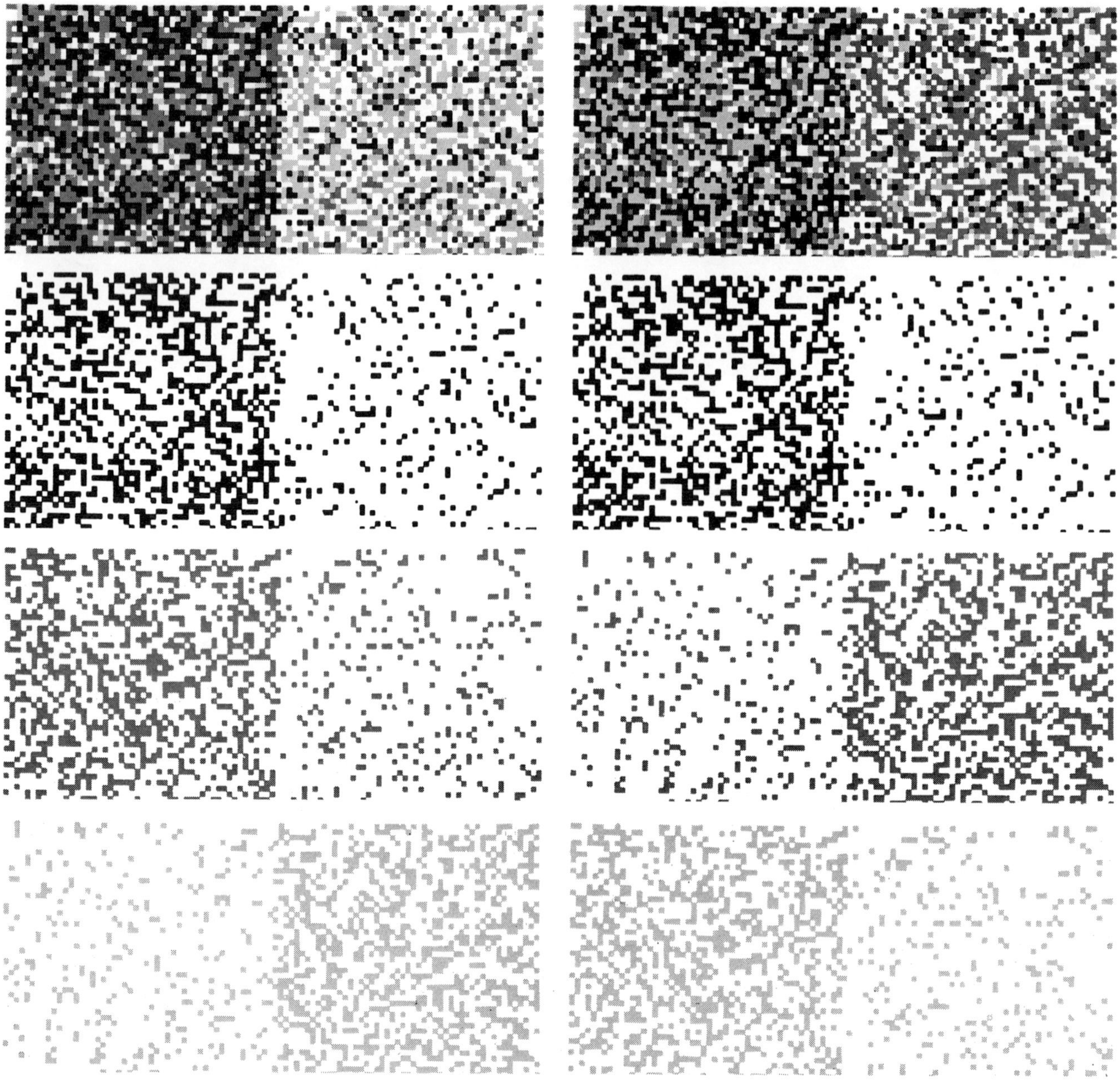

EASE OF DISCRIMINATION in random patterns of various brightness levels seems to depend on whether or not adjacent dots of different values form clusters. The pattern at top left forms two easily discriminated areas because the half field on the left contains mostly black and dark gray dots, which form dark clusters, whereas the half field on the right contains mostly light gray and white dots, which form light clusters. When the dark gray and light gray components are reversed (*top right*), the clustering does not take place and the half fields are not so readily discriminated. The composition of each top pattern is shown in the three panels below it.

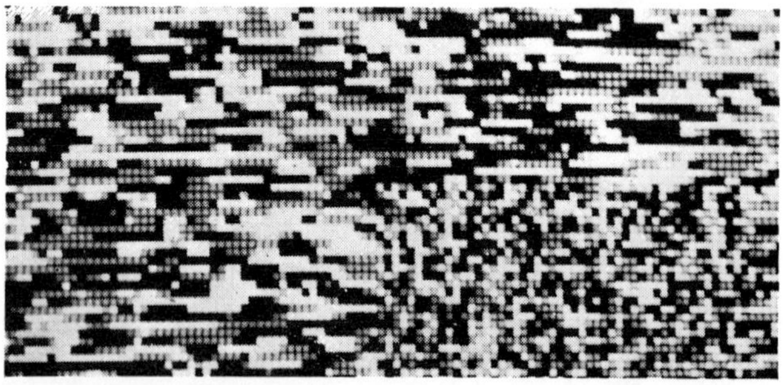

SPONTANEOUS DISCRIMINATION occurs even though the smaller field has the same average tonal quality as the larger field because the granularity of the two fields is different. At a distance the granularity is less noticeable and discrimination more difficult.

SCIENCE	SPECIFY	PRECISE	SUBJECT	MERCURY	GOVERNS	ECNEICS	YFICEPS	ESICERP	TCEJBUS	YRUCREM	SNREVOG
METHODS	RECORDS	OXIDIZE	COLUMNS	CERTAIN	QUICKLY	SDOHTEM	SDROCER	EZIDIXO	SNMULOC	NIATREC	YLKCIUQ
DEPICTS	ENGLISH	CERTAIN	RECORDS	EXAMPLE	SCIENCE	STCIPED	HSILGNE	NIATREC	SDROCER	ELPMAXE	ECNEICS
SUBJECT	PUNCHED	GOVERNS	MERCURY	SPECIFY	PRECISE	TCEJBUS	DEHCNUP	SNREVOG	YRUCREM	YFICEPS	ESICERP
EXAMPLE	QUICKLY	SPECIFY	METHODS	COLUMNS	MERCURY	ELPMAXE	YLKCIUQ	YFICEPS	SDOHTEM	SNMULOC	YRUCREM
SCIENCE	PRECISE	EXAMPLE	CERTAIN	DEPICTS	ENGLISH	ECNEICS	ESICERP	ELPMAXE	NIATREC	STCIPED	HSILGNE
SPECIFY	MERCURY	PUNCHED	QUICKLY	METHODS	EXAMPLE	YFICEPS	YRUCREM	DEHCNUP	YLKCIUQ	SDOHTEM	ELPMAXE
EXAMPLE	GOVERNS	OXIDIZE	ENGLISH	SUBJECT	RECORDS	ELPMAXE	SNREVOG	EZIDIXO	HSILGNE	TCEJBUS	SDROCER
COLUMNS	SUBJECT	PRECISE	MERCURY	PUNCHED	CERTAIN	SNMULOC	TCEJBUS	ESICERP	YRUCREM	DEHCNUP	NIATREC
ENGLISH	RECORDS	EXAMPLE	SUBJECT	OXIDIZE	GOVERNS	HSILGNE	SDROCER	ELPMAXE	TCEJBUS	EZIDIXO	SNREVOG
CERTAIN	PRECISE	PUNCHED	METHODS	ENGLISH	COLUMNS	NIATREC	ESICERP	DEHCNUP	SDOHTEM	HSILGNE	SNMULOC
OXIDIZE	QUICKLY	SCIENCE	DEPICTS	SPECIFY	PRECISE	EZIDIXO	YLKCIUQ	ECNEICS	STCIPED	YFICEPS	ESICERP
DEPICTS	EXAMPLE	ENGLISH	CERTAIN	RECORDS	SCIENCE	STCIPED	ELPMAXE	HSILGNE	NIATREC	SDROCER	ECNEICS
SPECIFY	MERCURY	GOVERNS	PRECISE	QUICKLY	METHODS	YFICEPS	YRUCREM	SNREVOG	ESICERP	YLKCIUQ	SKOHTEM

NONSPONTANEOUS DISCRIMINATION is represented by two half fields that have the same apparent texture and granularity. The left half field, however, contains familiar English words, whereas the right half field contains only random sequences of seven letters.

that can be recognized monocularly as shapes of some sort; they are not, in other words, random patterns.

These and other difficulties are quite easily circumvented by using a computer to generate random-dot patterns in which all familiar cues and other unwanted factors are eliminated. For the purpose of studying the first problem—the role of texture in discrimination—random-dot patterns with different properties were generated side by side. The objective was to determine those pattern properties that make it possible to discriminate between the adjacent visual displays. I was concerned primarily with the discrimination that can be achieved immediately. Such discrimination can be regarded as a spontaneous process and thus can be ascribed to a primitive perceptual mechanism.

An example of spontaneous discrimination is given by the illustration at bottom left on the opposite page. Both fields of the pattern contain black, gray and white dots with equal first-order, or overall, probability; therefore if the pattern is viewed from a distance, both fields appear uniformly gray. When the two fields are viewed at close range, however, they exhibit a different second-order, or detailed, probability. This shows up immediately as a difference in granularity.

The illustration at bottom right on the opposite page represents a case in which there can be no spontaneous discrimination between two fields. In this case discrimination can be achieved only by someone who knows the difference between English words and random sequences of letters. Here discrimination requires a sophisticated kind of pattern recognition. This article is concerned only with discrimination of the spontaneous type.

In the case of random-dot patterns one might expect that discrimination of visual texture is fundamentally governed by variations in the statistical properties of the patterns. That is true in the most general sense, because any two different patterns must differ in some such property. It turns out, however, that simple statistical measurements of brightness distribution are not adequate to describe perceptual performance.

This is demonstrated in the illustration at upper left on this page, which consists of two patterns made up of black, gray and white dots. In one quadrant the dots are distributed with equal probability and completely at random. The surrounding area matches the quadrant in overall brightness, but it also contains small triangular units composed of black, white and gray dots in various arrangements. Although these triangular units occur with equal probability, the only ones observed are those made up entirely of black dots; the others pass unnoticed.

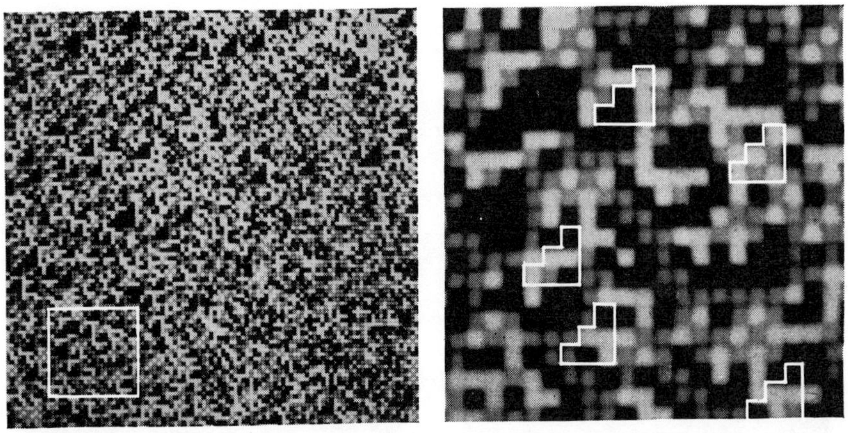

CLUSTER IDENTIFICATION in the pattern at left extends only to triangular shapes made up entirely of black dots. Other equally probable triangles containing dots of mixed brightness do not form clusters. These are marked in the enlargement at right.

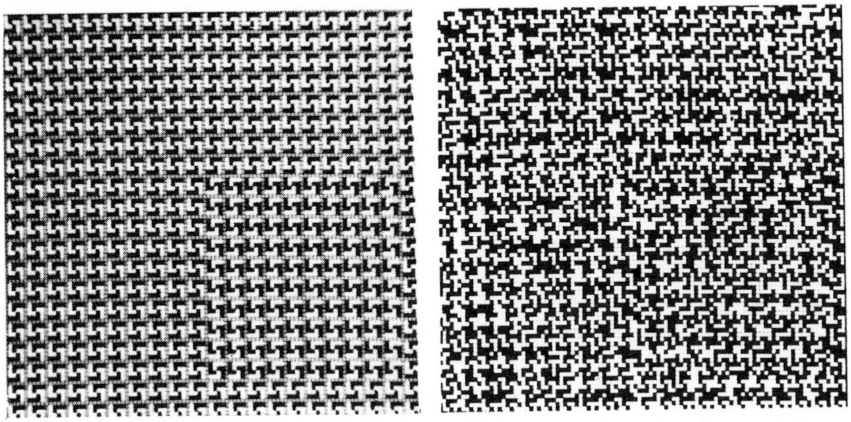

EFFECT OF "NOISE" is demonstrated in these two patterns. In the pattern at left the two subpatterns containing either black or white "S" shapes are easily discriminated. Moreover, every fifth horizontal and vertical row is gray. The pattern at right is identical except that the dots in the gray rows have been made black or white at random. By breaking up the connectivity of the pattern in this way the subpatterns are almost obliterated.

This indicates that discrimination of visual texture is not based on complex statistical analysis of brightness distribution but involves a kind of preprocessing. Evidently the preprocessing extracts neighboring points that have similar brightness values, which are perceived as forming clusters or lines. This process, which should not be confused with the actual spatial connection of objects, might be called connectivity detection. It is on the relatively simple statistics of these clusters and some simple description of them, such as spatial extent, that texture discrimination is really based.

The lower pair of illustrations above shows this connectivity detection even more clearly. In the left member of the pair two textures are easily discriminated; in the right member discrimination is difficult, if not impossible. In the pattern at the left every fifth horizontal and vertical row is gray; in the pattern at the right, which is otherwise identical, every fifth row is randomly peppered black and white. The "noise" added to the pattern at the right has only a minor effect on the statistics of the two subpatterns to be discriminated, yet it breaks up the connectivity of the subpatterns enough for them to merge into one field. The black and white "S" shapes that appear so clearly in the pattern at the left are completely destroyed in the pattern at the right. If the disrupted pattern is viewed at a sharp angle, however, the line clusters reappear and discrimination is facilitated.

The importance of proximity and similarity was emphasized early in the

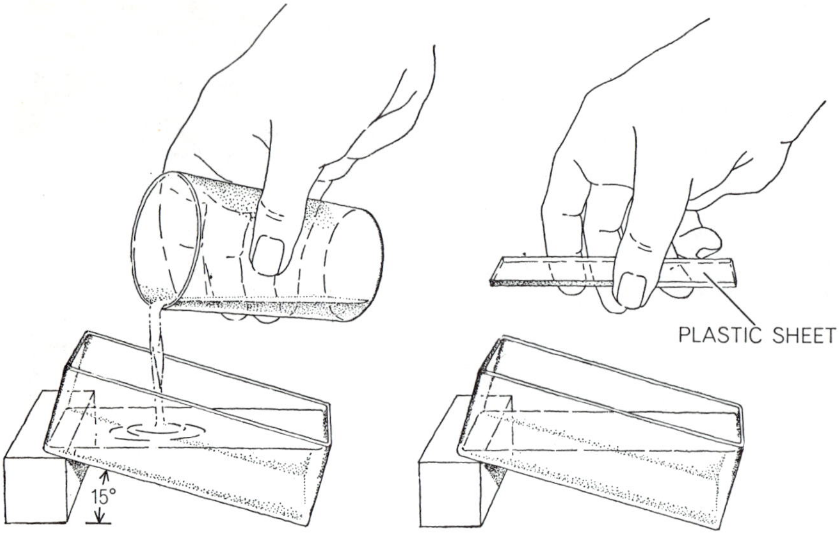

GELATIN PRISM provides a simple stereoscopic viewer. A clear plastic box for holding the gelatin can be obtained at a five-and-ten-cent store. Use five parts of very hot water to one part of household gelatin and mix thoroughly. Tilt the box about 15 degrees and pour in the gelatin solution. In about 30 minutes, when the solution has gelled, dampen the surface and press a rectangular sheet of clear plastic (or glass) against it. The prism will ordinarily work without this top sheet, but images may appear fuzzy.

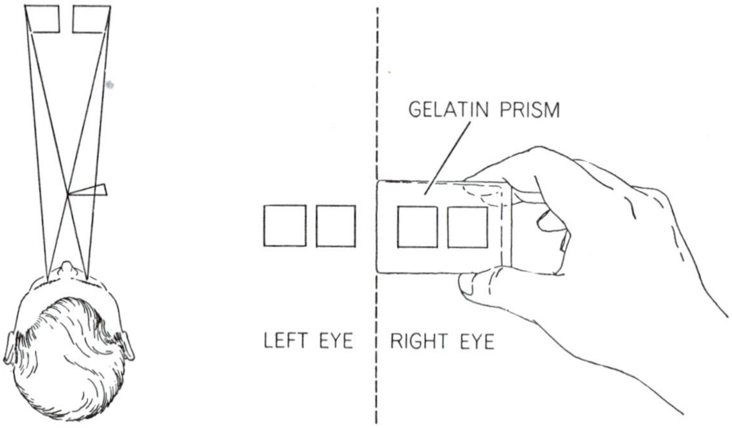

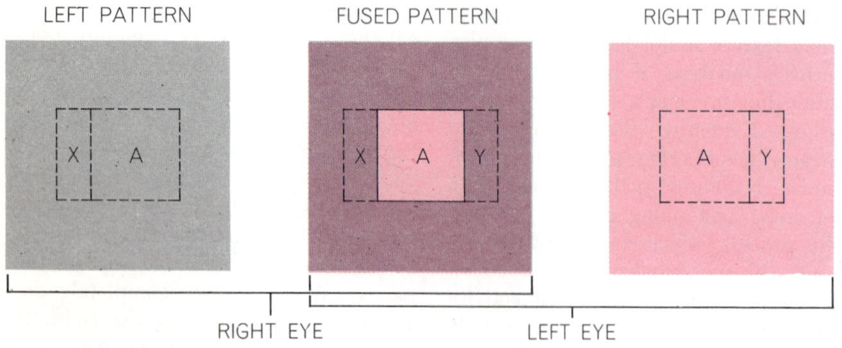

TO USE PRISM hold it about six inches in front of the right eye, thin edge toward the nose. Adjust the prism so that both stereoscopic images can be seen through it. Both images should also be visible to the left eye, as shown in the upper two diagrams. With little difficulty the images should rearrange themselves so that there appear to be only three images, of which the center one is the fused stereoscopic image. Once binocular fusion has occurred the image can be made sharper by moving the prism closer to the right eye.

work of the *Gestalt* psychologists, particularly that of Kurt Koffka and Max Wertheimer. Now, with the help of the random-dot-pattern technique one can give a more precise meaning to these notions. For example, the last experiment, in which the disrupted pattern is viewed at an angle, shows that neighboring points need not touch each other to appear connected. This notion comes as no surprise. On the other hand, when one observes that neighboring points of similar brightness are perceived as clusters, the meaning of "similar brightness" requires further clarification. How dissimilar in brightness can adjacent points be and still be perceived as clusters? In order to examine this question two computer patterns were generated.

In one pattern, shown at top left on page 186, the field at the left is composed chiefly of black and dark grey random dots; the field at the right contains mostly white and light gray dots. As a result the field at the left forms a large dark cluster and the field at the right forms a light cluster, with a fairly sharp boundary between them. In the adjacent pattern the light gray and dark gray dots are transposed so that the field at the left contains chiefly black and light gray dots and the field at the right contains chiefly white and dark gray dots. Here discrimination between the two fields is more difficult. These and similar results suggest that the visual system incorporates a slicer mechanism that separates adjacent brightness levels into two broad categories: dark and light. The level of slicing can be adjusted up and down, but it is impossible to form clusters by shifting our attention to dots that are not adjacent in brightness.

One might argue that the eye could hardly respond otherwise when brightness levels are involved. It can be shown, however, that the same connectivity rules hold for patterns composed of dots of different colors adjusted to have the same subjective brightness. This is the demonstration that is shown on pages 184 and 185. Since these patterns are made up of colored inks that do not reflect light with equal intensity, they do not fully simulate the laboratory demonstration, in which the dots are projected on a screen in such a way that their subjective brightness can be carefully balanced. Nonetheless, the printed demonstration, particularly the one on the cover, is reasonably effective. In the pattern on the cover what one observes is that the top half of the pattern is immediately discriminated into a red-yellow field on the left and a blue-green field on the right, whereas the bottom half of the pattern seems more or less uniform in texture across its entire width. This uniformity in texture is achieved simply by transposing the yellow and green random elements so that the field at the left is composed mostly of red and green dots and the field at the right is composed mostly of blue and yellow dots. The first demonstration shows that red and yellow dots form clusters that are easily discriminated from the clusters formed by blue and green dots. The second demonstration shows that dots of nonadjacent hue, such as red and green or blue and yellow, do not form clusters.

Evidently this clustering, whether it is of adjacent brightness levels or of adjacent hues, represents a preprocessing mechanism of great importance in the visual system. Instead of performing complex statistical analyses when presented with complex patterns, the visual system wherever possible detects clusters and evaluates only a few of their relatively simple properties. One now

STEREOSCOPIC IMAGES investigated by the author consist of random-dot patterns generated by a computer. When these two images are viewed with a stereoscope or with a prism held in front of one eye, a center panel should be seen floating above the background, as illustrated at the far right. The principle employed in making such stereoscopic images is explained below.

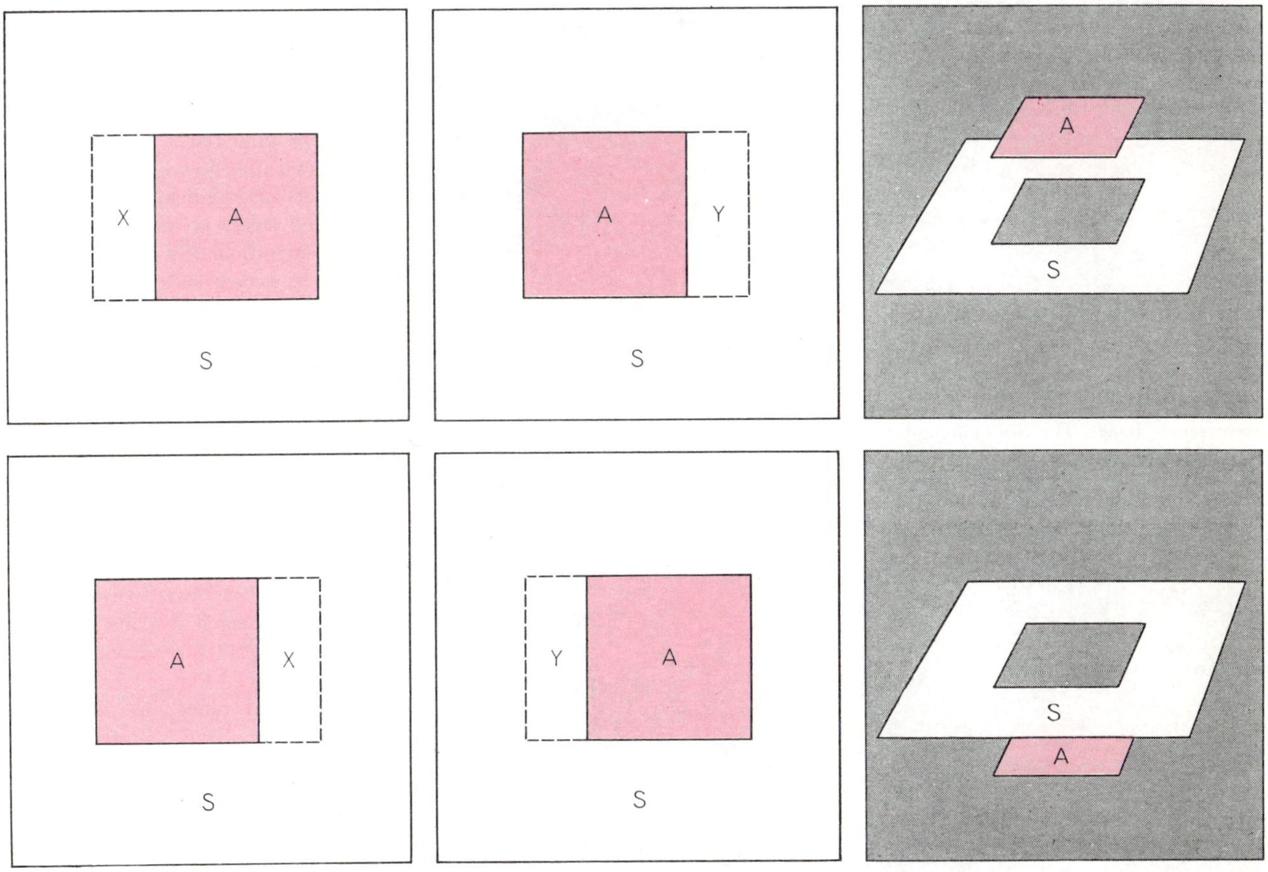

STEREOSCOPIC PRINCIPLE is simply that identical areas that appear in both fields must be shifted horizontally with respect to each other. Because these areas are themselves random-dot patterns they cannot be seen monocularly against a random-dot surround. In these diagrams *A* identifies the area common to both fields. In the upper pair of fields *A* is shifted inward, leaving two areas, *X* and *Y*, that are filled in with different random-dot patterns. When viewed stereoscopically, *A* seems to float above the surround. When *A* is shifted outward as shown in the two lower fields, *A* seems to lie behind the surround.

has a formula for matching wallpaper patterns. As long as the brightness value, the spatial extent, the orientation and the density of clusters are kept similar in two patterns, they will be perceived as one. Even for familiar patterns with recognizable and different forms discrimination can be made very difficult or impossible if the simple rules that govern clustering are observed. Thus a wallpaper pattern made up of seven-letter English words arranged in columns, as in the illustration at bottom right on page 186, would appear to be matched by a similar pattern containing nonsense sequences. The seven-letter nonwords would form clusters that could not be discriminated spontaneously from English words.

These findings answer in the affirmative the first question raised at the beginning. Objects can indeed be discriminated by differences in their surface texture alone even if they are spatially connected and cannot be recognized. The basis of this texture discrimination depends on simple properties of clusters, which are detected according to simple rules. Cluster detection seems to be a quite primitive and general process. Recent neurophysiological studies of frogs and cats have disclosed that their visual systems extract certain basic features of a scene prior to more complex processing [see the articles "Vision in Frogs," by W. R. A. Muntz, beginning on page 157; and "The Visual Cortex of the Brain," by David H. Hubel, beginning on page 148]. The "bug" detector in the frog's visual system and the slit detector in the cat's visual system are special cases of connectivity detection. It will be interesting to see if neurophysiologists can find evidence for cluster detectors of the type suggested by these perception experiments.

We are now ready to consider the second question: Can two unfamiliar objects of identical texture be discriminated solely on the basis of their spatial separation? To study this question it was necessary to create patterns that were unfamiliar, that had the same surface texture and that could be perceived in depth. Again the problem was solved with the help of random-dot patterns generated by a computer. This time the computer was used to generate pairs of patterns that were identical except for a central area that was displaced in various ways. I had hoped that one would obtain a sensation of depth when the two patterns were viewed stereoscopically, and I was delighted when that turned out to be the case. This proved that one can perceive a camouflaged object in depth even when the camouflage is perfect and the hidden object cannot be discerned monocularly. In short, the answer to the second question is also yes.

A pair of these random-dot stereoscopic patterns is shown in the upper illustration on the preceding page. The two patterns are identical except for a center square that is shifted horizontally to the left by six dots in the pattern at the right. By virtue of this shift the

BLURRED IMAGE was produced by defocusing the field at left in the random-dot stereoscopic patterns on the preceding page. The field at right is unchanged. In spite of the blurring the two fields will fuse into a stereoscopic image; moreover, the image looks sharp.

REDUCED IMAGE also does not interfere seriously with the ability to obtain a good stereoscopic image. The two random-dot patterns are again those shown on the preceding page. The stereoscopic field at left, however, has been reduced about 10 percent in size.

NOISY IMAGE (*left*) is produced by breaking up triplets of black dots along one diagonal and white triplets along the other diagonal wherever they occur in the left field on the preceding page. Nevertheless, the two fields will still fuse stereoscopically.

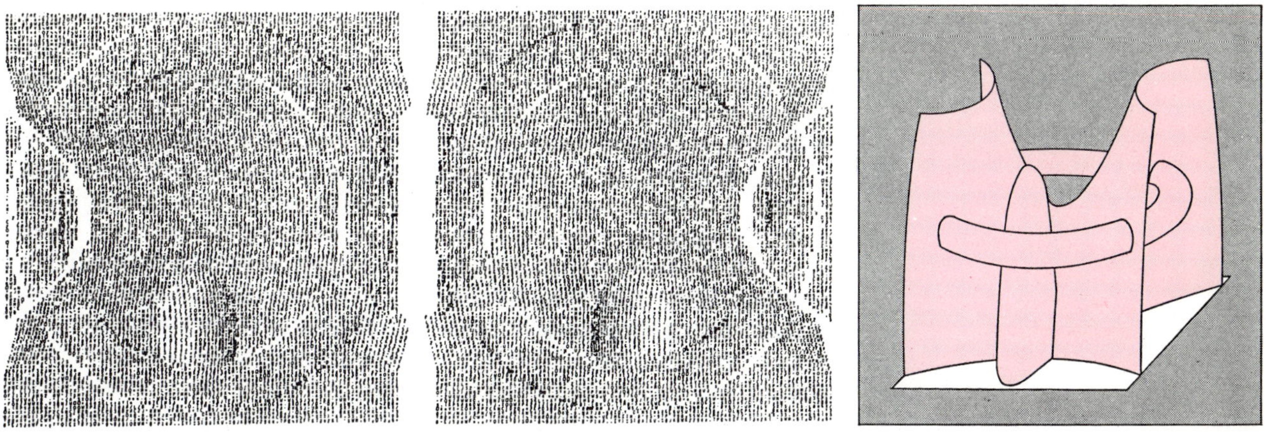

SADDLE-SHAPED FIGURE (*far right*) **was transformed into left and right stereoscopic fields by a computer program devised by the author. The picture elements consist of 64 standard characters randomly selected but paired in the left and right fields.**

square seems to float above the background when it is viewed stereoscopically. If the reader does not have an old-fashioned stereoscopic viewer at hand, by following the instructions on page 188 he can easily make a prism of gelatin that will serve the same purpose.

The phenomenon demonstrated by the binocular fusion of such random-dot patterns has a number of surprising implications. First of all, as the original statement of the problem requires, the stereoscopic picture is completely devoid of all familiarity and depth cues. Although the area selected for stereoscopic displacement in the first example is a simple square, it could be of any shape and it could also give the illusion of having more than one level [*see illustration above*]. The fact that the center square and its surround are horizontally shifted by different amounts in the fields at left and right corresponds to the different depth levels that are perceived. Thus spatial disconnectivity alone is enough for the center square and its surround to be perceived as two distinct objects.

The demonstration also demolishes a long-standing hypothesis of stereopsis, or binocular depth perception, in which it is assumed that the slightly different images that are simultaneously projected on the retinas of the two eyes are first monocularly recognized and then matched. The process was thought to be somewhat analogous to the operation of an optical range finder, in which the corresponding separate images are first recognized and then brought into alignment. This last step corresponds to measuring the amount of displacement between patterns and determining the amount of depth by simple trigonometry (which the range finder performs automatically).

Research in stereopsis has traditionally been devoted to the problem of relating the displacement, or disparity, of images and the perception of depth. It has become increasingly apparent that depth perception involves many cues and cannot be described by trigonometry alone. Little or no attention was paid to the more fundamental problem of how the visual system is able to identify the same object in the separate two-dimensional images formed on each retina. The studies with random-dot patterns have now shown that monocular recognition of shapes is unnecessary for depth perception.

The method of producing random-dot stereoscopic images is shown in the lower illustration on page 189. The surround (*S*) is composed of randomly selected but identical dot patterns in the fields at left and right. The center panel (*A*) is also identical in the two fields but is shifted in one field with respect to the other as if it were a solid sheet. If the shift is inward (toward the nose of the observer), the center panel seems to float in front of the surround. If the shift is in the opposite direction, the panel seems to lie behind the surround. The greater the parallax shift, the greater the perceived depth.

If one simply cut a panel out of a random-dot pattern and shifted it, say, to the left, an empty space would be exposed along the right edge of the panel. The empty region (labeled *Y* in the middle diagram on page 189) is simply filled in with more random dots. A similar region (labeled *X*) must be filled when the panel is shifted to the right. Each region is projected onto only one retina (*X* onto the left retina and *Y* onto the right) and therefore exhibits no displacement. It is curious that these regions are always perceived as being the continuation of the adjacent area that seems to be farthest away.

By further manipulation of the random-dot patterns, it is possible to produce panels whose apparent location in space is ambiguous. If the *X* and *Y* regions described above are filled in with the same random-dot pattern, which we will label *B*, then when the two fields are viewed stereoscopically the center panel *A* may seem to be raised above the surround or area *B* may seem to lie below the surround. The diagram on page 192 illustrates the reason for this ambiguity. If the center panel is to be wider than the parallax shift (that is, wider than *B*), it must contain repeating vertical stripes of *ABAB* and so on in one field and stripes of *BABA* and so on in the other. An ambiguous panel created in this way is shown in the lower pair of stereoscopic images on page 193.

All these depth phenomena can be perceived in a very short interval, provided that the two fields are presented to the observer in reasonable alignment. The presentation time is so short (a few milliseconds) that there is no time for the eye to move and thus no time for a range-finder mechanism to operate. One must therefore conclude that depth perception occurs at some point in the central nervous system after the images projected onto the left and right retinas have been fed into a common neural pathway. This was actually demonstrated as long ago as 1841 by Heinrich Wilhelm Dove of Germany, who used brief electric sparks to illuminate stereoscopic images only three years after Charles Wheatstone of England had first shown how the young art of photography could be used to produce them. Evidently the convergence movements of the eye serve mainly to bring the images on the left and right retinas into approximate register. This does not mean, however, that convergence motions do not influence the perception of depth when the presentation time is of long duration.

The processing in the nervous system that gives rise to depth perception is now more of a mystery than ever. The German physiologist Ewald Hering believed that this processing involves the crossing or uncrossing of images that are initially perceived as double because they lie either in front of or behind the eyes' point of convergence. The extent to which this cue is utilized could not previously be determined because double images were inherent in stereoscopic presentation. The random-dot stereoscopic images, on the other hand, do not contain recognizable images prior to their actual perception in depth; thus it is impossible to perceive double images either before or after fusion.

It could still be argued that although random-dot stereoscopic pairs do not contain recognizable shapes, some similar patterns can be perceived in the two fields and these might serve as the basis for fusion. This possibility can be tested in several ways. In the top stereoscopic pair on page 190 the field at the left has been blurred by being printed out of focus. Even when the patterns are almost obliterated in this way, stereopsis is easily obtained. What is more surprising is that the perceived image resembles the sharp one. The blurred image serves only to convey the required disparity information and is then suppressed.

The bottom stereoscopic pair on page 190 carries the disruption of patterns still further. This is achieved by breaking the diagonal connectivity in the field at the left. Along one diagonal whenever three adjacent dots were black, the middle dot was changed to white, and along the other diagonal whenever three adjacent dots were white, the middle one was changed to black. In the field at the right diagonally adjacent groups of three black or white dots were left unchanged. This procedure changes 20 percent of the picture elements in the field at the left and so removes them from the fusion process. The fact that the two fields look so different when viewed monocularly and yet can be perceived in depth when viewed stereoscopically provides additional evidence that no monocular pattern recognition is necessary and that the ultimate three-dimensional pattern emerges only after fusion has taken place.

Although the random-dot stereoscopic images lack monocular depth cues, which normally augment depth perception, they are actually easier to perceive in depth than stereoscopic images of real objects. The explanation is that each black or white dot in a random pattern contributes depth information, whereas in actual objects there are large homogeneous areas that carry no depth information. Thus random-dot stereoscope fields that differ in size by 10 percent or more can easily be perceived in depth [*see middle illustration on page 190*].

It is probably obvious that these find-

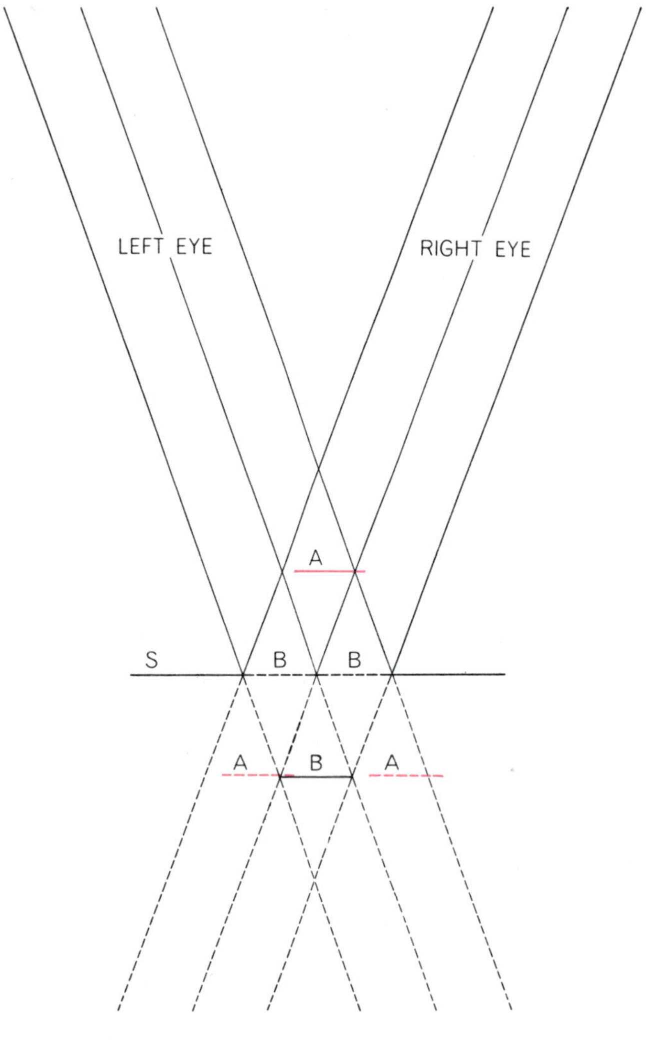

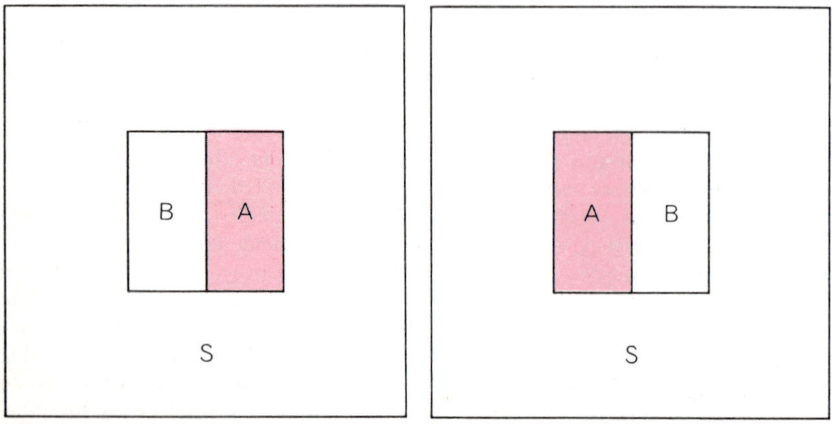

AMBIGUOUS DEPTH EFFECT can be obtained by transposing the *A* and *B* fields in the random-dot patterns. When viewed stereoscopically (*top diagram*), area *A* may seem to be raised above the surround or area *B* may seem to lie below it. In either case the nonfused area seems to be a continuation of the field that looks farthest away.

ings have important implications for *Gestalt* psychology. According to this school stereoptic perception is not a result of disparity in the images projected on the two retinas; rather each eye works up its complex of stimuli into a *Gestalt* and it is the difference between the two *Gestalten* that gives rise to the impression of depth. The fact that stereopsis can be obtained in random-dot images without any monocular cues decisively settles this question, since no *Gestalten* can be worked up.

It might still be argued that *Gestalt* factors may operate after the binocular fusion of the two fields. In this connection it is interesting to look closely at the vertical boundaries of the raised panel formed by the top stereoscopic pair on page 189. The boundaries are fuzzy. The reason is that the black-and-white picture elements along the boundary have an equal probability of being perceived as belonging either to the raised panel or to the surround. Because a square has a "good *Gestalt*" one might expect to perceive these points as forming a straight line. That they do not suggests that perception is governed by simple considerations of probability.

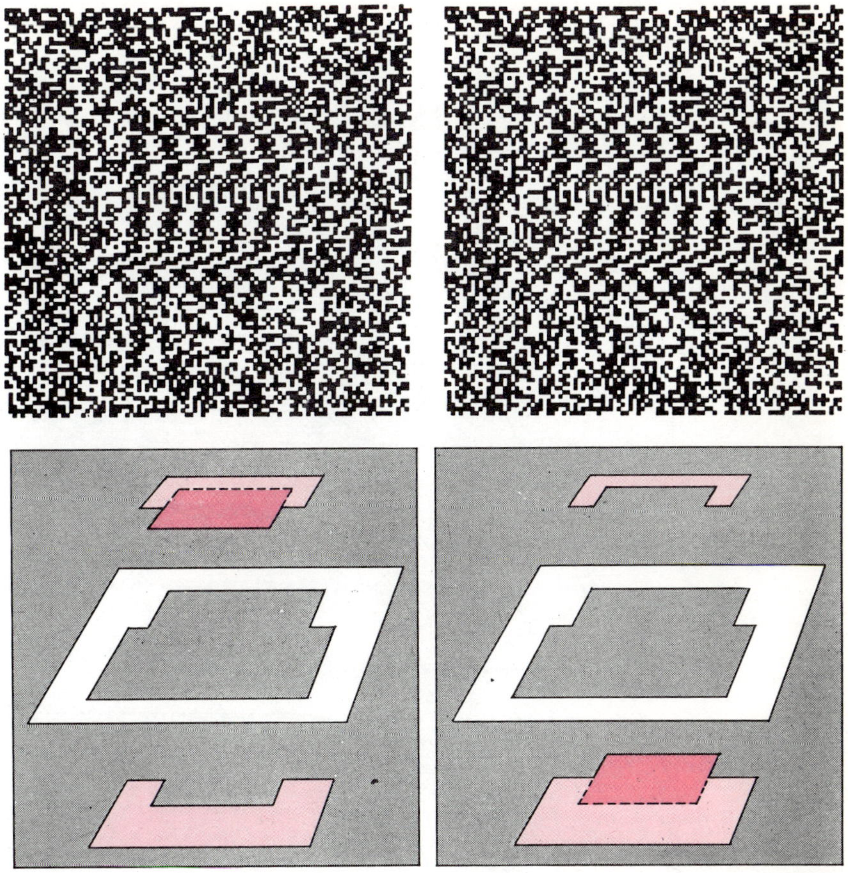

AREA OF AMBIGUOUS DEPTH appears in the middle of this periodically striped stereoscopic pattern. Sometimes it will seem to be a continuation of an elevated panel (*lower left*); at other times it will seem to be part of a depressed panel (*lower right*).

In presenting random-dot stereoscopic pairs for very brief intervals I have found evidence for a restricted but unmistakable kind of subliminal perception. This term refers, of course, to the idea that an individual can be influenced by a stimulus he does not consciously perceive. Efforts to demonstrate this phenomenon by other techniques have been inconclusive and controversial.

The finding was made while I was trying to measure the minimum time needed to perceive stereopsis in random-dot images. The time cannot be measured simply by presenting the images for briefer and briefer periods, for the reason that an afterimage remains on the retina for an indeterminate time. I found that it was possible to "erase" these afterimages by a new technique in which a second stereoscopic pair of random-dot images is flashed onto a screen almost immediately after the first pair.

In these short-interval experiments the first stereoscopic pair flashed onto a screen has a panel that is unmistakably either in front of the surround or behind it. This pair is followed quickly by another in which the location of the panel is ambiguous; under more leisurely viewing conditions it will seem to lie either in front of or behind the surround. Not only were the subjects unaware that the second pair was ambiguous but if the interval between the two presentations was made short enough they were also unaware that they were seeing anything but the second pair. The second pair erased all conscious knowledge of the first. The real presentation time of the first pair could therefore be established because it was governed by the time allowed to elapse before presentation of the second pair.

The main result was that the first stereoscopic pair, although not consciously perceived, can influence the way in which the second pair—the ambiguous pair—is perceived. When the presentation time of the first pair was long enough, the ambiguous panel in the second pair consistently seemed to be at the same depth as the panel in the first pair. A presentation time adequate to produce this result was about 40 milliseconds; it can be regarded as the "minimum perception time" for stereopsis. When the first pair is presented for a shorter time, or when the second pair is delayed by more than a certain interval, which I have called the "attention time," the second pair is removed from the subliminal influence of the first and is perceived ambiguously. These experiments suggest that the first pair serves as a "depth marker" and determines which of the two possible depth organizations in the second pair should be favored. All this processing must take place in the central nervous system because the times are too short for any eye motion to be initiated.

The various studies described in this article indicate that visual texture discrimination and binocular depth perception operate under simpler conditions than has been thought, since they do not require the recognition of form. This finding makes it attractive to try to design a machine that will automatically produce contour maps according to information contained in aerial stereoscopic photographs. As long as it seemed that such a task could only be done by a machine that could recognize complex and virtually unpredictable shapes, the job seemed all but hopeless. On the basis of the new findings I have helped to devise a computer program (called Automap-1) that can be used to compile a three-dimensional contour map from high-resolution stereoscopic images [*see illustration on page 194*]. This computer program not only should be useful for reducing the tedium of pro-

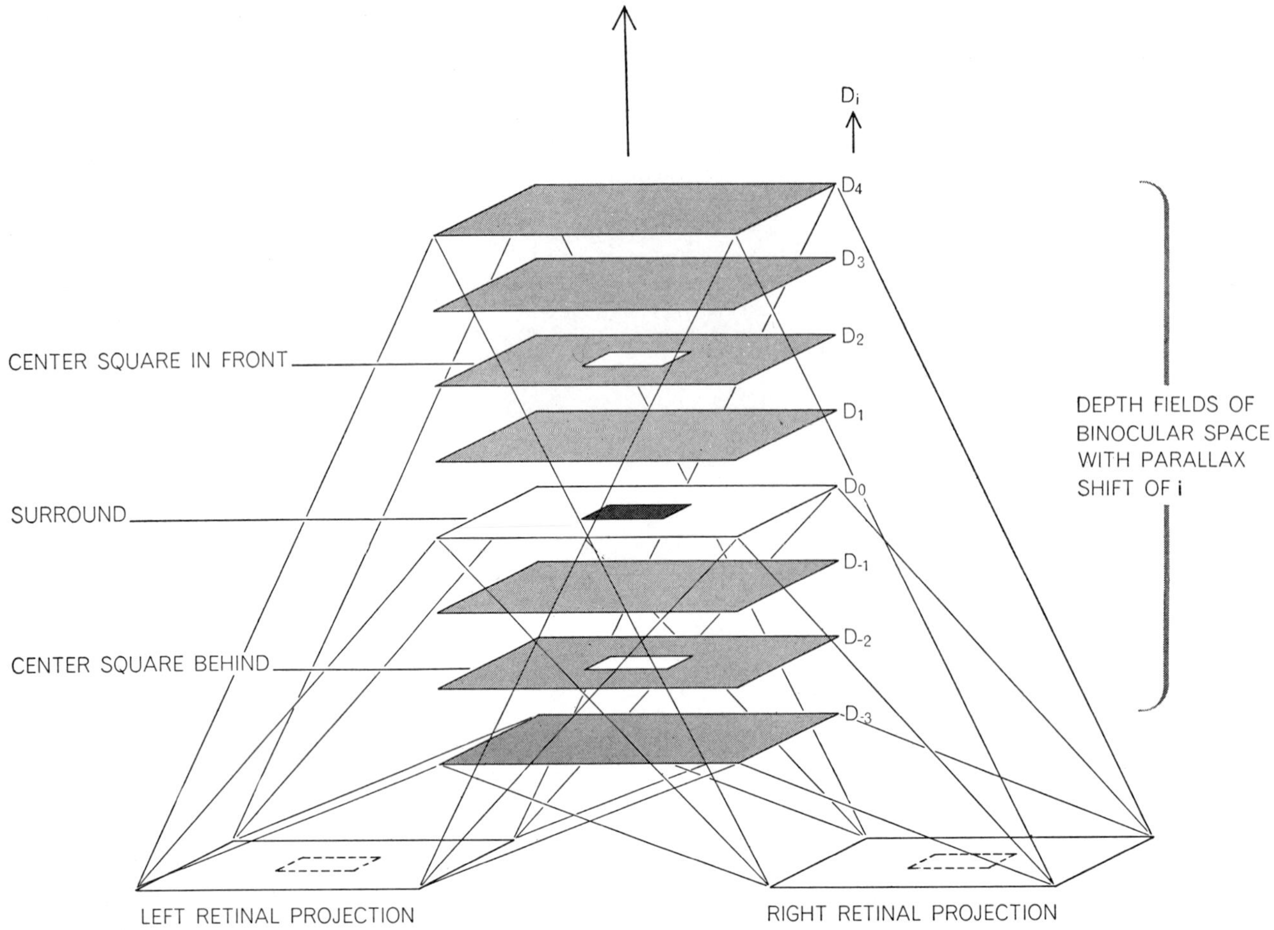

AUTOMAP-1 is a computer program that compiles a three-dimensional contour map from two-dimensional stereoscopic images. The program compares left and right fields point by point and subtracts the brightness of each point from its counterpart. Where the two fields match, the difference is zero, shown above as a white area. Thus the surround (D_0) is white except where there is a shifted center panel. The program repeats the point-by-point comparison after shifting one field horizontally (both left and right) by one unit, two units and so on. This provides an ordered set of depth planes (D_i). When a shift such as D_2 or D_{-2} brings a shifted panel into alignment, the points in the panel cancel and show up as zero (white). Form recognition is not needed.

ducing such maps but since it is based on psychologically observed phenomena it is also a crude model of part of the visual system.

This article has described methods for studying visual texture discrimination and depth perception in their purest form. The methods have shown that connectivity detection is basic to both visual tasks and that it is a more primitive process than form recognition. It remains to be seen if on the psychological level a simpler "explanation" can be given. I hope that the next findings in this area will come from neurophysiologists.

THE FORTIFICATION ILLUSIONS OF MIGRAINES

WHITMAN RICHARDS
May 1971

How does the brain perceive objects in the world outside it? In an effort to answer that question neurophysiologists have for the past 30 years or so been probing animal brains, recording their nerve impulses and thus determining how their neural elements respond to different kinds of stimuli. The resulting data are generally complex and difficult to interpret, with one outstanding exception: data collected from regions of the brain that receive information directly from the sense organs. In these primary receiving areas the data are often remarkably unequivocal; single neural elements are found that respond, in roughly an all or nothing fashion, only to highly specific kinds of stimuli, such as lines of a certain length and orientation [see the article "The Visual Cortex of the Brain," by David H. Hubel, beginning on page 148]. The behavior of single neurons in these areas is usually so stimulus-specific—so dependent on the nature and orientation of the feature that stimulates them—that such neurons are considered to be "feature detectors," and each neuron or neural unit is labeled according to the feature that triggers its activity. By identifying the features that trigger neurons at various levels in the sensory pathways one can begin to reconstruct the method the brain uses to analyze and process incoming information about the external world.

Whereas neurophysiologists have only recently obtained this direct evidence on the stimulus features to which different parts of the animal brain respond, indirect evidence on the abstracting operations performed by the brain has been available for many centuries. What is perhaps the most impressive indirect evidence on feature detectors comes from man's own experience when selected parts of his brain become spontaneously active. Such abnormal internal activity may begin naturally during periods of stress that result in decreased blood flow. One result is a headache; another result may be a change in the ionic balance in a local region of the brain that causes the underlying neurons to discharge spontaneously. This internally generated activity often leads to perceptions.

Some 10 percent of us suffer migraine headaches at one time or another during our lifetime, and about half of the time such headaches involve the visual areas of the brain. In these headaches, when the visual areas become active, the individual sees a spectacular array of scintillating bars and corners; the display as a whole has the appearance of pre-20th-century fortifications seen from above. The form of the fortification figures provides strong clues to the kind of feature extraction conducted by the human visual system. Although reports of these displays go back many centuries, it was only some 100 years ago that their significance was recognized when George Biddell Airy, the British astronomer royal, and his son Hubert Airy, a physician, provided accurate accounts of their own visual displays. In a remarkable paper published in 1870 Hubert Airy related the displays to the known structure of the brain and concluded by recognizing that the spontaneous perceptions probably represented a realistic "photograph" of processing in the brain.

The visual displays that arise during ophthalmic migraines can take several forms, but only the classical type experienced by the Airys and reported in their papers [*see the illustration on page 199*] is sufficiently clear and well documented to provide reliable evidence on feature extraction in the human visual system. I should like to describe this type of display in some detail, basing my quantitative results largely on observations provided by one person (my wife), with supporting data obtained from several other people. One of the others was the late neurophysiologist W. S. McCulloch, who recognized the importance of his own migraines and provided a photograph of a sketch of what he saw during one of his attacks. All these people, and others described in the literature, saw their displays equally well with either eye. In view of the basic neuroanatomy of the visual system, this means that the visual effects must have been the result of neuronal activity in the brain rather than in the eye itself.

The visual disturbance usually precedes the headache and can occur without any headache. It generally begins near the center of the visual field as a small, gray area with indefinite boundaries. If this area first appears during reading, as it often does, then the migraine is first noticed when words are lost in a region of "shaded darkness." During the next few minutes the gray area slowly expands into a horseshoe, with bright zigzag lines appearing at the expanding outer edge. These lines are small at first and grow as the blind area expands and moves outward toward the periphery of the visual field. The rate of expansion of both the arc formed by the zigzag lines and its associated band of blindness is quite slow: some 20 minutes can elapse between their initial appearance near the center of the visual field and their expansion beyond its limit. It is then that the headache usually begins, behind or above the eyes. It is the only unpleasant aftereffect of a spectacular visual display.

Because the band of activity moves so slowly across the visual field, the general shape and overall properties of the fortification are easy to chart. The subject fixes his gaze on a mark on a piece of paper and then sketches the projected outlines of the figures he sees [*see illustration below*]. Combining several such drawings, one can also record the general form the arcs take as they expand across the visual field [*see top illustration on opposite page*]. The arcs drawn by Hubert Airy 100 years ago almost exactly match those of my principal subject, and they are the basis of the whole-field drawings. The only additional feature that has been reported is a slightly more complex arc, shaped somewhat like a double *C*.

A plot of successive arcs resembles a map of an electric field around a point source, and many people have suggested that the expanding arc represents a wave of excitation radiating from a single region of the visual cortex. The noted neuropsychologist K. S. Lashley estimated on the basis of his own experience with migraine fortifications a propagation rate of three millimeters (about an eighth of an inch) per minute. In order to arrive at such an estimate he assumed that the excitation spread at a constant rate even though the arcs themselves appeared to expand with increasing speed as they grew larger. In view of the way the visual field is mapped on the cortex, the assumption is quite reasonable. A constant propagation rate of excitation would indeed cause the larger arcs to grow faster, because the peripheral part of the visual field is represented by a diminishing amount of cerebral cortex: since there is progressively less cortex per degree of visual field as one moves from the field's central region to its outer margin, a wave moving at a constant rate across the cortex will appear to move faster as it moves toward the peripheral field. My own calculation of the maximum rate of propagation of this wave, based on recent electrophysiological maps of the topography of the visual field in the human striate cortex, is 3.3 millimeters per minute, in good agreement with Lashley's earlier estimate.

Although the arc of fortifications is clearly visible at any given instant, the details of the lines comprising the arc itself are hard to fix in the mind or capture on paper. For those of us engaged in analyzing the mechanisms of the brain, it is these details that are of the most interest [*see bottom illustration on opposite page*]. In the simplest type of fortification the arc is serrated and consists of two lines about as bright as an overhead fluorescent lamp. Each member of the pair of lines oscillates in brightness at about five cycles per second, with all the inside lines "on" when all the outside lines are "off," and vice versa. This synchronization causes the entire arc to reverberate with what is described as a "boiling" or "rolling" motion. Such behavior suggests an underlying neural network of reciprocal inhibition, in which the depression of activity in one local region would enhance the spontaneous neural activity in adjacent regions. If this antagonistic activity were triggered by the expanding boundary of the cortical disturbance, then the disappearance of one set of lines at the outside margin of the disturbance would be followed by their reappearance inside the expanding boundary in what had previously been a depressed region.

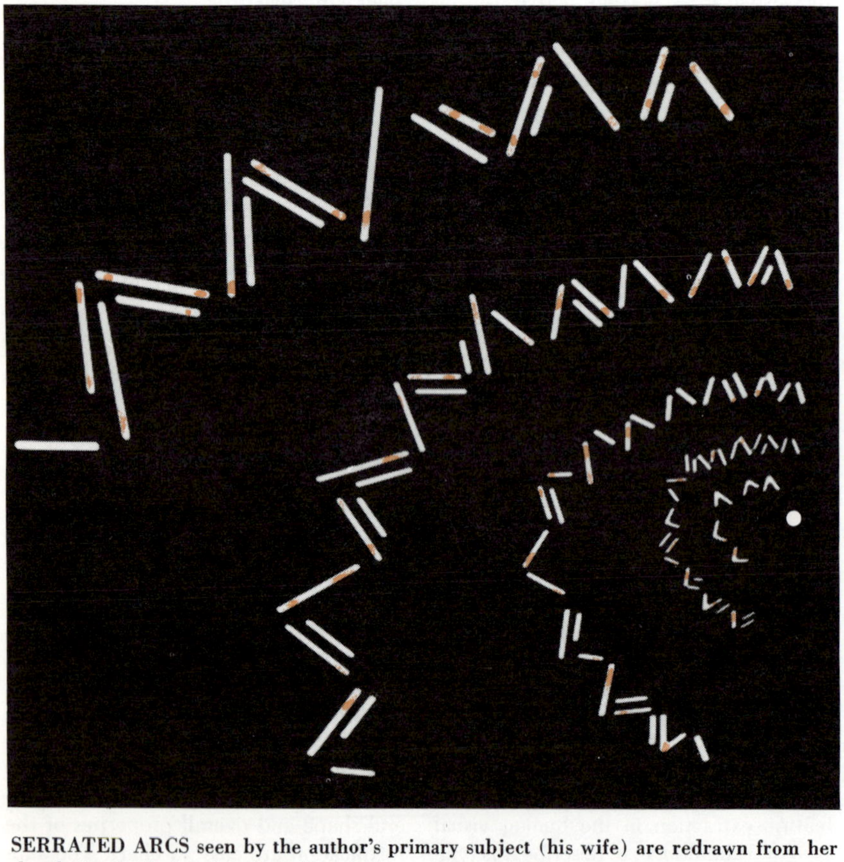

SERRATED ARCS seen by the author's primary subject (his wife) are redrawn from her sketch, in which the white lines have yellow, orange and red segments, particularly near the ends, and a few streaks of blue. Ordinarily one arc is seen at a time, its constituent lines flickering to give a "boiling" or "rolling" motion. The white dot is the point of fixation.

In addition to the obvious spatial properties of the display, such as the increasing size of the lines as the arcs move toward the periphery, there are also subtle effects related to color, line orientation and the spacing between the lines. It is difficult to provide more than qualitative impressions of most of these details. When the fortifications are complex, only a general impression of the display can be recorded; the details are not necessarily accurate. The arc may become a grid: a hatched band that seems to consist of five or six parallel lines, although it is difficult to make an actual count because the bands sweep across the figure toward the advancing margin and are constantly renewed at the inner edge. Between the lines of the grid faint red, yellow and blue streaks often appear, whereas on the lines themselves these colors may be seen only at the tips ("like match heads") when the display is of the simpler variety. Both George Airy and his son reported seeing red, blue and yellow in that order of frequency; they saw green only rarely, and green was never observed by my main subject.

Within each arc of fortification figures there is a transient band of blindness. It becomes apparent when the lines are being sketched because the end of the pencil simply becomes invisible as it enters the band! If the subject is not aware that there is something within the visual field that is not visible, the region of blindness is easy to miss, in part because it may be "filled in." Lashley told of a time when in the course of a conversation he glanced just to the right of his friend's face and the face disappeared. His friend's shoulders and necktie were still visible, but the vertical stripes in the wallpaper behind him now seemed to extend right down to the

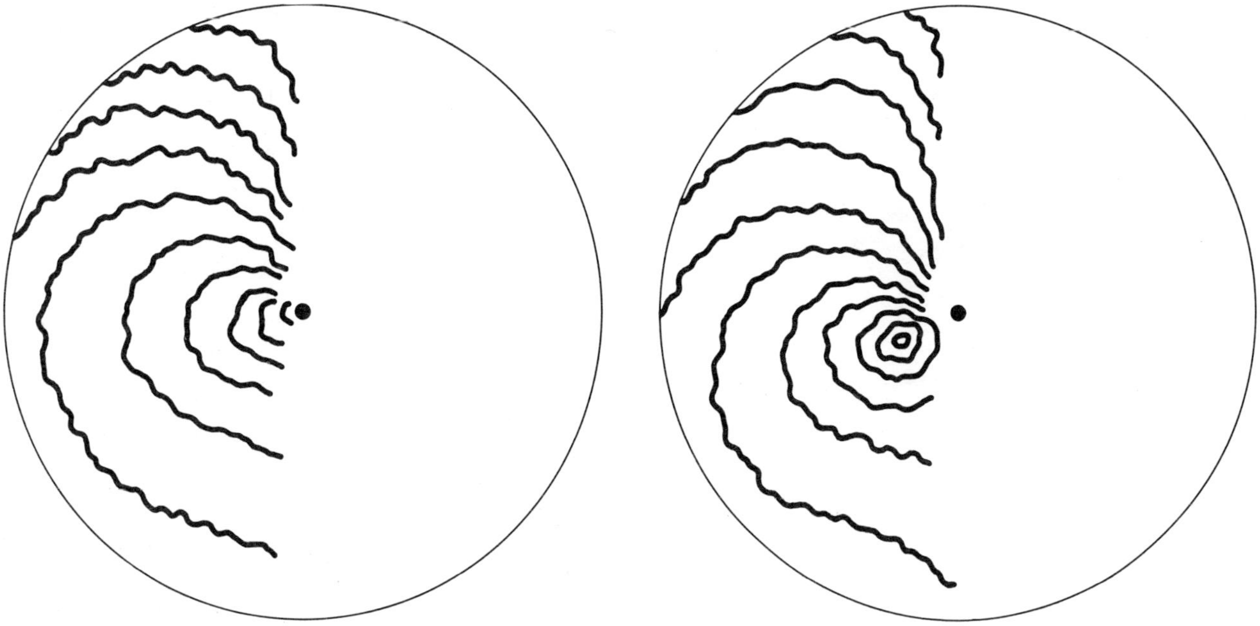

SUCCESSIVE ARCS expand across half of the visual field, as shown in two diagrams based on Airy's two sets of arcs. The disturbance may take 20 or 25 minutes to expand from a fuzzy gray area near the fixation point (*dot*) to the outer limit of the visual field.

necktie. This filling-in phenomenon is the consequence of some higher-level process that presents an interesting and still unsolved puzzle.

Considering the recent direct evidence obtained by the neurophysiologists from single cells in the visual cortex of the cat and monkey brain, it is of interest to compare their description of feature detectors with some of the properties of the fortification figures. For example, David H. Hubel and T. N. Wiesel have shown that one kind of feature extraction conducted by the visual cortex in their experimental animals is the detection of lines of a particular length and orientation. The fortification figures suggest that the human visual system performs a similar type of analysis. The expanding boundary of cortical disturbance is actually a set of discrete lines in visual space. If the length of these lines is charted over a wide range of positions in the visual field, it is seen that the lines are small near the central part of the field and become steadily larger with increasing distance from the center. On the basis of current knowledge of the mapping of the visual field onto the human cortex one can estimate how much distance on the cortex is represented by one of these lines. My calculations yield an estimate of about 1.2 millimeters of cortical distance for each line, regardless of the line's position in the visual field; it simply appears larger farther out.

The constant size of these line lengths on the cortex suggests that the cortex it-

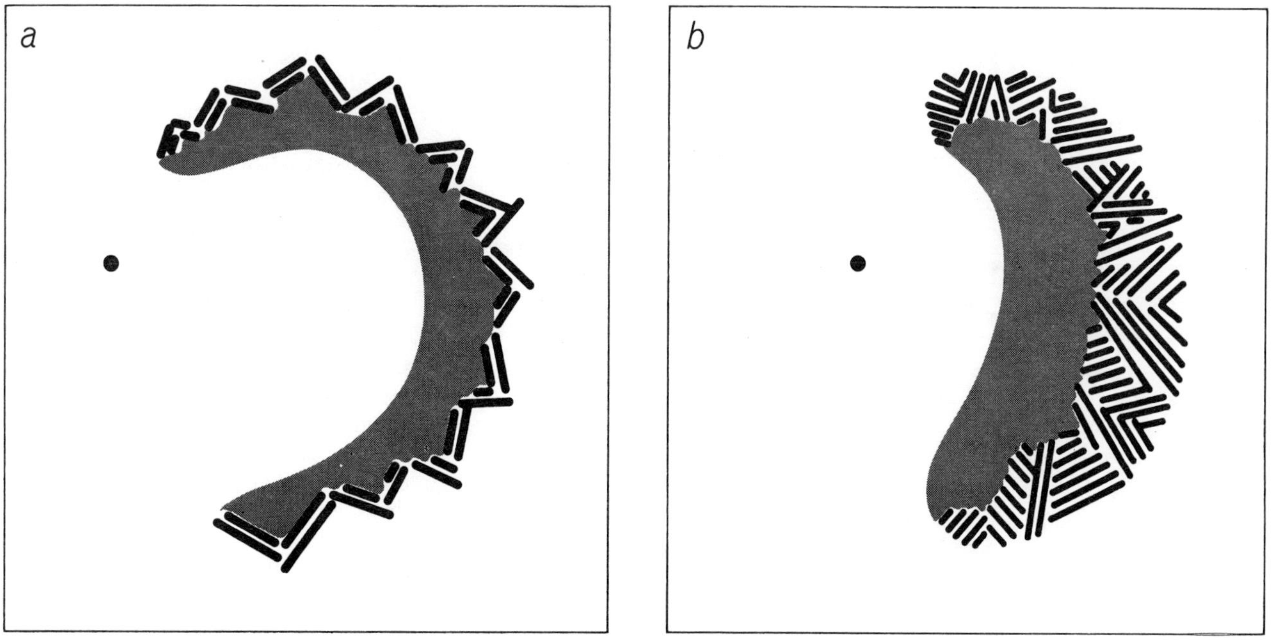

DETAILED FORM of two types of figure is apparent in these diagrams, in which individual fortifications are "stopped," without their customary flickering or rolling motion. The contrast tends to be greater in the simple type of arc (*a*) than in the more complex one (*b*). In each case the gray area represents a transient region of blindness that moves outward roughly parallel to the expanding arc.

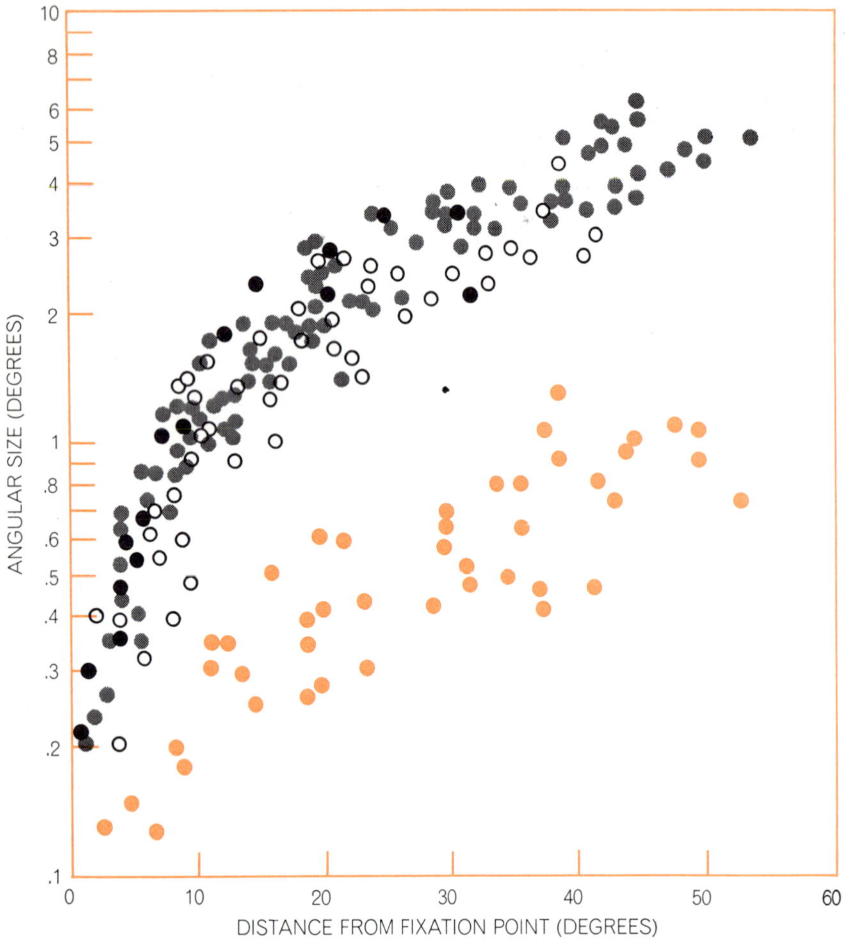

LENGTH AND WIDTH of lines in three displays are plotted for different positions in the visual field. The angular lengths (*black, gray and open circles*) increase with distance from the center of vision but all represent about 1.2 millimeters on the cortex. The width (which is equivalent to the separation between lines) is about a fourth as large (*color*).

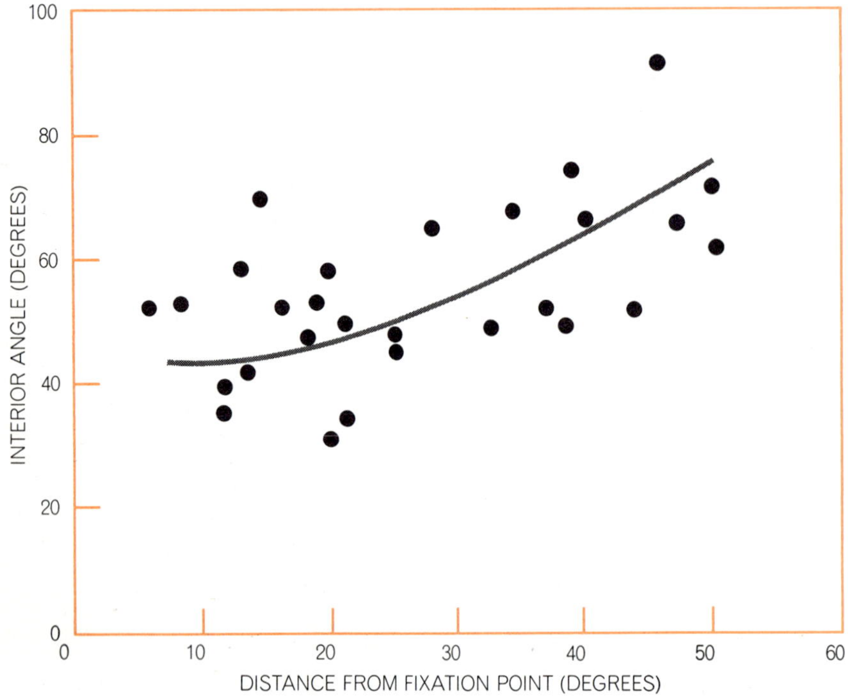

INNER ANGLE between two lines meeting to form a serration was measured at various points in the field. The average angle increased from 45 degrees near the center to 70 degrees.

self is organized into discrete "elements" of constant size. In fact, Vernon Mountcastle, Hubel and Wiesel and others have shown that brain areas in the visual pathway up to and including the cortex seem to possess "columns" of cells that have certain triggering features in common. In the monkey visual area these columns average .2 to .3 millimeter in diameter, or a fifth as large as my estimates based on line length. The discrepancy between the results obtained for the monkey and for man disappears, however, if the line elements seen during migraines represent not the output of individual columns but rather pools of columnar activity—perhaps a summation of or convergence from several columnar units. The size of the units contributing to the pool would presumably be indicated by their smallest dimension, which would be the width or separation of the lines. The distance between the lines is about a fourth of the line length [*see top illustration at left*]; hence the simplest columnar units presumably measure about .3 millimeter in diameter in man.

In addition to "line detectors," neurophysiologists find more complex analyzers ("corner detectors" and "tongue detectors") in the same and neighboring visual areas of the cat and monkey cortex. These complex analyzers do not seem to be present in the human cortex at the level of the migraine disturbance. The serrated edges of the fortifications do give the appearance of corners, but the neurons apparently do not detect corners as such. Most of the lines form not precise corners but rather parts of a disjointed *T*, with one line extending beyond its neighbor. Moreover, only a small fraction of the lines are actually joined at their end points, and the gaps separating the end points seem to be located at random. The gaps are seen most easily when the tips of the lines are colored, and the colors help to show that these are blurred intersections rather than true corners.

An interesting size effect has come to light in this connection. The lines, their colored end points and the gaps between them were seen with more clarity when my subject projected the display onto a surface about eight inches or less from her eyes than when she projected it onto a wall a yard or two away, even though their apparent size was smaller. This sharpening of the visual display was of course not caused by optical factors such as better focusing by the lens; the display is in the brain and not the result of light passing into the eye. The sharpness of the display must have been caused by a change within the brain itself, such as

FORTIFICATIONS drawn in 1870 by a British physician, Hubert Airy, show a characteristic form: bands of bright lines, approximately *C*-shaped, that expand across the visual field (*1–4 and 5–8*). In each case the white dot (*0*) is the point on which the subject's gaze was fixed. The large figure (*9*) shows the detailed form of the bands, which are made up of sets of sharply angled short lines.

a change in the grain of the visual system brought about by the convergence of the eyes.

The reduction of apparent size was to be expected: when the eyes are converged to fixate a near object, there is an illusory reduction in the size of a fixed retinal image, an effect called size micropsia. (The illusion is striking when a card on which an afterimage is projected is brought closer and closer to the eyes.) What is strange in the case of the fortifications is that even though the lines seen during a migraine attack may *appear* to the observer to become smaller when the eyes are converged, their true average angular size (determined by the experimenter's measuring them on a sketch or presenting sample lines for comparison) may actually increase at the nearer fixation distance; the angular eccentricity of the arc increases at the same time. The most accurate measurements indicate that the magnitude of this "reverse size effect" is an enlargement of some 25 percent when fixation is reduced from about 48 inches to about eight inches. Because the changes in the angular size of these internal images are the opposite of the changes seen with images of external objects, one infers that the act of eye convergence leads to modification in the visual pathway at the site of the cortical disturbance or between the eye and the site of the disturbance.

If the serrations in the boundary of a fortification figure do not represent the activity of corner detectors, why is the boundary serrated? Why is it not a smooth line, reflecting the presumably smooth and continuous front of the expanding cortical disturbance? The appearance of serrations supports the notion that the neural substrate of the cortex is organized into discrete elements at a level at or above that of individual neurons. If that is the case, a smooth line traced across the cortex would move from one discrete element to the next,

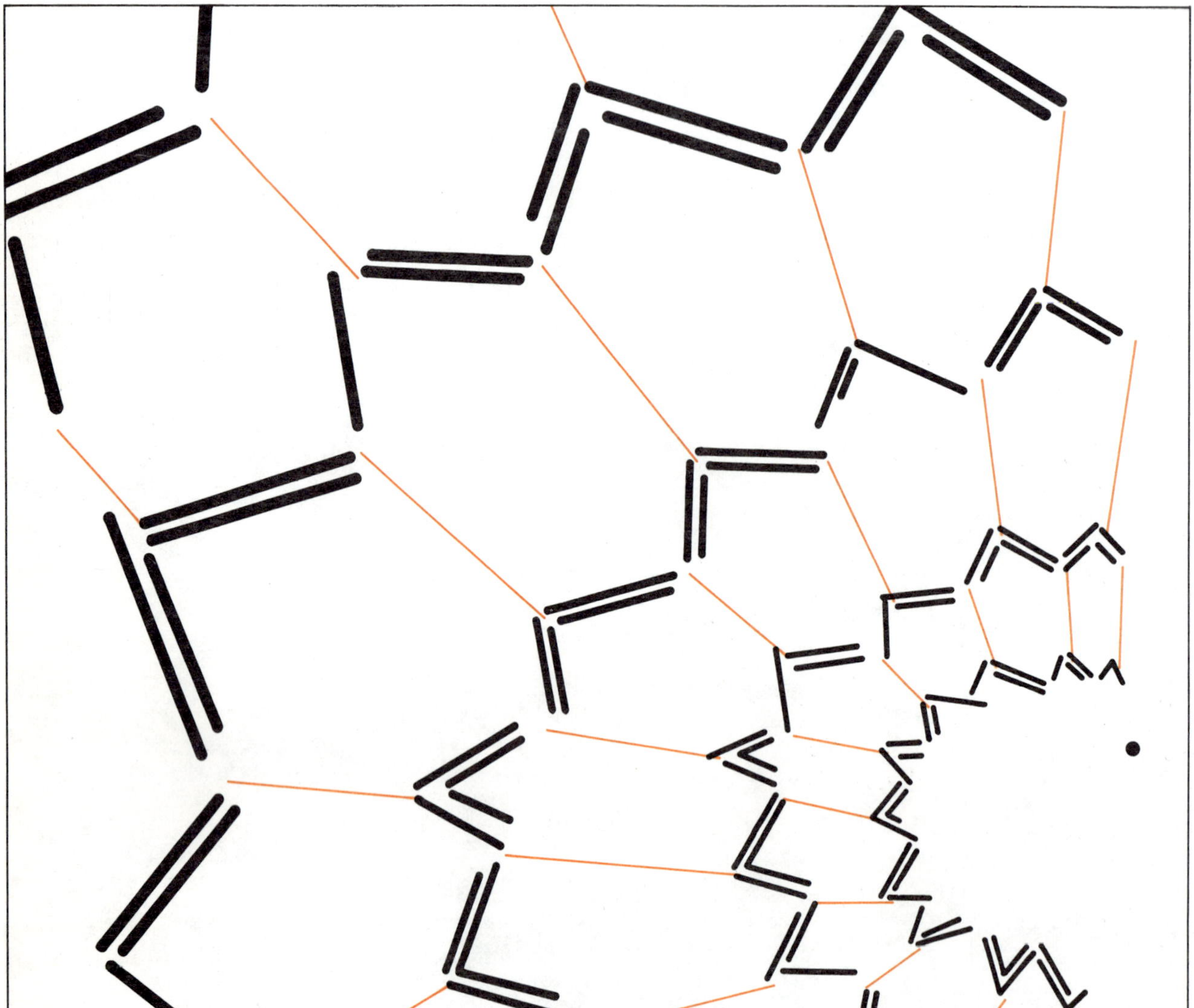

HONEYCOMB PATTERN emerges when a number of arcs are plotted together, following the data from the two illustrations shown on page 198, and approximately radial lines *(color)* are added. The honeycomb and the tendency for the inner angle between lines to approximate 60 degrees are suggestive of hexagonal organization. But why are the sides of the cells *(color)* never seen?

and each element could have an entirely different representation in the visual field. These elements should correspond to clusters of cortical cells that have certain triggering features in common, such as the same line orientation in a given region of the visual field. Neurophysiologists have compiled evidence that such clusters exist, but it has been difficult to map a long succession of clusters with direct recording techniques and thus to determine how the clusters are organized in the cortex. In this respect the migraine fortification is an excellent natural experiment: the advancing waves of disturbance draw continuous traces across the cortex and in less than half an hour reveal part of the secret of its neuronal organization.

All fortification figures have two striking and significant properties. One is revealed when the inner angle between the two lines forming a serration is measured over the entire visual field. The angle is almost always acute; it is about 45 degrees near the center of the field, increases to about 70 degrees at the periphery and averages about 60 degrees [*see bottom illustration on page 198*]. The other property is the absence of radial lines perpendicular to the boundary of the fortifications. The first property suggests that the neuronal substrate of line detectors in the human visual cortex must be organized into a regular lattice such that the relative orientation of each line to its neighbor is about 60 degrees. To the extent that the lattice is regular within a local region of the field, each line element could have only one of three orientations; it would therefore sample visual space in the pattern of an asterisk (*). The second property confirms this notion, because only some such spatial order in the cortex can explain a response so selective that it leaves out all radial lines.

Let me develop this reasoning in more detail. Normally only one serrated arc is seen at a time, but one can plot a succession of the arcs, making both the length of the lines and the angles between them conform to the experimental evidence [*see illustration on preceding page*]. If one then adds radial lines [*color*], a distorted honeycomb structure is revealed. The radial lines, however, are precisely the ones that are never seen. Why? The explanation lies in the nature of perceptual processes, which respond primarily to local differences. For example, it is not the luminous intensity inside a homogeneous square that determines how bright the square appears to be. The critical factor is the magnitude of the step in luminance at the edge of the square. A piece of gray paper therefore appears either dark or light depending on its background [see the article "The Perception of Neutral Colors," by Hans Wallach, beginning on page 278]. In other words, the visual system looks only at both sides of the edge and "fills in" a description of the remaining area by extrapolation or inference.

Now consider a hypothetical wave front of electrical activity advancing across the cortex [*see illustration below*]. The electrical gradient associated with the wave front is defined by the density of plus and minus signs; the circles represent the individual components whose activity is pooled to form the clusters, or line elements, indicated by the colored outlines. Consider three possible orientations of these elements: perpendicular, parallel and oblique to the wave front.

Two adjacent line elements perpendicular to the wave front are likely to have identical electrical activity; there is thus no basis for a differential response between them, and so they are not "seen." Line elements parallel to the wave front—one on each side of it—have

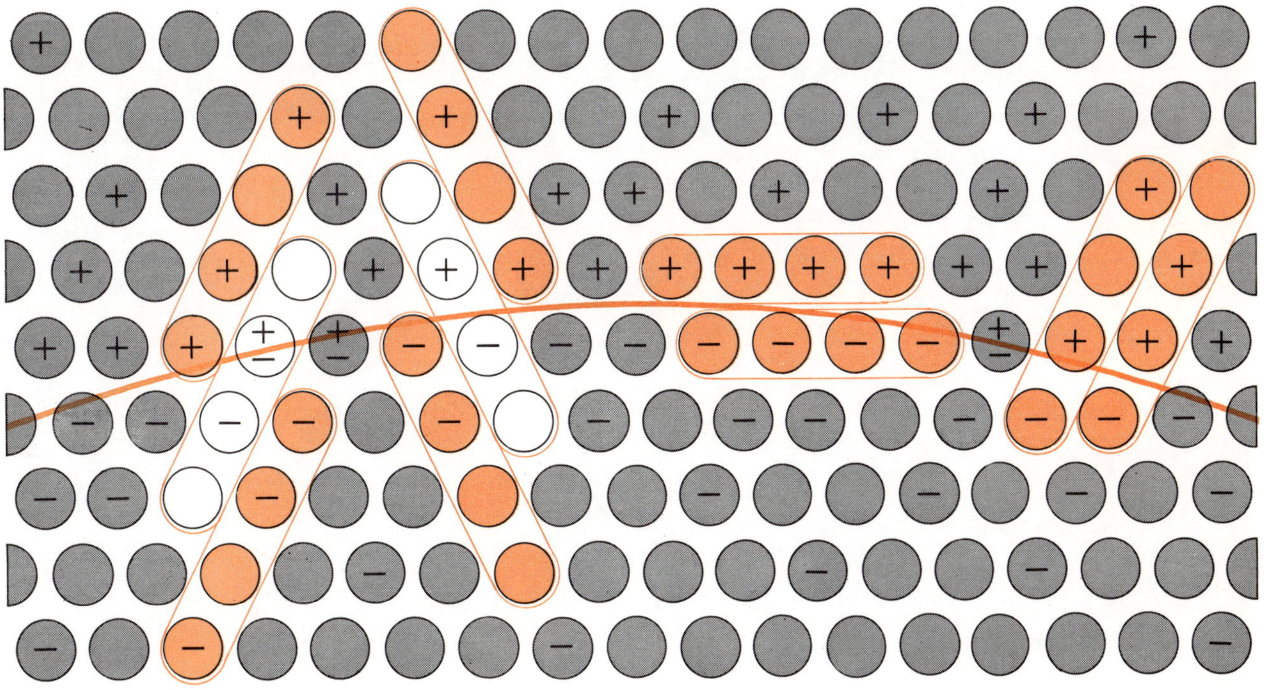

NEURAL SUBSTRATE affected by a migraine disturbance is diagrammed to illustrate how electrical activity results in the perception of lines with only certain orientations. The density of plus and minus signs represents the electrical gradient associated with the expanding wave front (*colored arc*) of the migraine disturbance. The circles are brain cells. Four cells in line form a line element. Two elements (*color*) at the right are perpendicular to the wave front. In this orientation the total activity of the two elements is the same; there is no basis for a differential response in the cortex and such elements are not seen. Elements parallel to the wave front may be seen on occasion, but only when the gradient lies athwart an element, not when it lies between them as shown here. Elements oblique to the wave front (*left*) are the most visible: active elements (*color*) above and below the wave front yield differential responses with respect to the elements with zero net activity (*white*) between them. These are the elements that form the serrations.

quite different electrical activity (are very positive or very negative) and one might expect them to be quite visible. Lines parallel to the expanding arc are actually seen infrequently in fortifications, however. The explanation lies in the nature of the neuronal response to the electrical gradient. Neurons comprising an element are activated when the element has either a positive or a negative ionic imbalance; the polarity at the gradient is immaterial. Therefore when the wave front lies precisely between two parallel elements, the activity of the two elements is equal, there is no basis for a differential response and the two adjacent parallel elements will not be seen. Only when the wave front lies directly on one element should the two neighboring elements be seen, because then their large activity is in contrast to the inactivity of the element between them that is split by the wave front. Since an element will be precisely split only a small fraction of the time, parallel elements will seldom be visible. And if the gradient is shallow, they may not be visible at all.

It is the third kind of element, an element oblique to the wave front, that is most likely to be seen. In this orientation there are two possible active elements, one on the positive side and one on the negative side. There is a clear difference between each such element and the intermediate, neutral one between them. Because the contrast in activity between two such oblique elements is largely independent of the exact position and extent of the electrical gradient, the lines representing their activity should be the ones most commonly observed. They are the lines that form the typical serrations.

Such speculation on the detailed neuronal organization of part of the brain may seem premature, but it is in keeping with everything that is being learned about the visual cortex. In this apparently undifferentiated mass of brain tissue, neuronal specificity appears to be the rule rather than the exception. Moreover, a hexagonal lattice, such as might be represented by the honeycomb structure I have described, is the commonest arrangement for the packing of cellular structures in living systems, as D'Arcy Wentworth Thompson showed so elegantly in his celebrated treatise *On Growth and Form*. Such a structure is indeed a natural consequence of the packing of a well-ordered array of cylindrical elements. Would it be surprising, then, if the neural structure of the human brain also follows this simple, basic pattern?

AUDITORY LOCALIZATION

MARK R. ROSENZWEIG
October 1961

Anyone who has ever gone temporarily deaf in one ear can testify to the advantages of binaural hearing. Sounds heard through one ear only are difficult or impossible to localize, and they lose their quality of depth. For human beings the ability to localize sound is more than a convenience; for some animals it is a necessity. Two ears are better than one if a person is trying to understand one voice against a background of other voices. (This is what acoustical engineers call the cocktail-party problem.) Two ears provide bats and certain night-flying birds with their fantastically sensitive location system.

That a pair of separated receivers should facilitate localization is reasonable enough. Each ear receives a slightly different sound pattern from a given source. The difference is somehow used by the brain to fix the position of the source. For more than 150 years investigators have been trying to find out how. Recently there has been considerable progress, but the process is still far from completely understood.

So far as the records show, the first person to look into the matter was the Italian physicist Giovanni Battista Venturi (1746–1822). Nowadays Venturi is remembered for his research in fluid dynamics. In fact, his name has become a common noun: the venturi, or venturi tube, is a standard device for measuring the flow of fluids. Venturi also turned his talents to many problems outside of physics. He studied visual and auditory perception, wrote on economics and history and was active in politics during the Napoleonic period.

In his work on auditory localization Venturi stationed a blindfolded subject in the middle of an unobstructed meadow. Circling around the subject at a distance of about 150 feet, the experimenter periodically sounded a note on a flute or rang a bell. When the sound came from a direction at right angles to "straight ahead," the listener could easily identify the direction. If he kept his head still, he often confused sounds coming from directly in front of him with sounds coming from behind him. When the source was diagonally in front of him or diagonally in back of him on the same side, the subject frequently was unable to distinguish front from back, but he never had any trouble with right and left. If the test sound was sustained for a few seconds and the listener was allowed to turn his head, he did not make these mistakes.

Venturi also found that a person with one deaf ear could localize sounds, but only if he turned his head while the sound continued. The subject simply turned until the sound was loudest, at which time his good ear directly faced the source. The experimenter noted that subjects with one deaf ear never localized brief sounds accurately.

Venturi concluded that a listener uses the relative intensities of the stimuli arriving at his ears to localize sound. He believed, furthermore, that the process involves judgment, and he denied the possibility of physiological interaction of the neural messages from the ears. "Since we distinguish the two simultaneous sensations of the two ears," he wrote, "and since their different intensities furnish us knowledge of the true direction of the sound, therefore one must conclude that the two sound impressions do not mix together inside the skull." This interpretation was to prevail for more than a century.

Notwithstanding the fact that Venturi published his findings no less than four times between 1796 and 1801—twice in German and once each in French and Italian—they made remarkably little impression. His observations and conclusions were occasionally mentioned in early 19th-century texts, but they were not credited to him. Later they were forgotten altogether. In the 1870's the British physicist Lord Rayleigh repeated essentially the same experiments, with the same results, apparently with no knowledge of Venturi's work. He believed that the observations supported the common view that localization is judged on the basis of the relative intensities of stimulation at the two ears.

Shortly after 1900 a German physician named Stenger devised an ingenious clinical hearing test that effectively demolished the ordinary view of localization, although no one seems to have realized it at the time. The test, which is still in use, was designed to expose people feigning deafness in one ear. Anyone who pretends to be deaf in his right ear, for example, will report hearing a tone if it is presented to his left ear through an earphone. What happens if the tone is now presented to the left ear and simultaneously but more intensely to the right ear? The listener hears the sound as coming from the right. The malingerer will therefore give himself away by saying that he does not hear any sound, in spite of the fact that it is just as intense as before at his admittedly good left ear. The effectiveness of this test makes it clear that the listener hears only a single localized sound and does not compare separate sensations arising at the two ears. Unfortunately the obvious meaning of the clinical discovery was ignored by students of auditory perception.

In 1911 there was published the first suggestion that a different mechanism—small differences in the time of arrival of a sound at the two ears—might influence the apparent location of the source. A sound originating directly to the right side of the head reaches the right ear about .0005 second before it reaches the left ear. A sound originating five degrees to the right of straight ahead or straight back reaches the right ear only .00004 second earlier than the left ear. Could perception of location be based on such minute time differences? During World War I the question was investigated secretly, both in France and Germany, in connection with the development of sound locators to detect airplanes. The tests showed that time differences of the order of .0001 second (with no accompanying differences in intensity) do indeed serve to locate the source of sound. Such intervals are far too small to allow the sound to be heard as separate stimuli by the two ears.

When the results were made public after the war, the judgment theory of localization was finally abandoned and a search was begun for the neural mechanisms underlying the process. During the 1920's there was a good deal of speculation about possible mechanisms. The 1930's saw the beginning of a mounting volume of experimentation on the electrical activity of the nervous system in response to auditory stimulation, as well as a revival of studies of the effect of brain damage on localization. The latter investigations had first been conducted in the 1880's.

Whenever a nerve conducts messages, small changes in electrical potential travel along the fibers of its constituent cells. With suitable equipment experimenters can tap the electrical signals as they travel from each ear up the auditory pathways to the auditory cortex [*see illustration on page 207*]. My colleagues and I have pursued this line of research for a number of years, first at Harvard University and later at the University of California.

Our subjects were anesthetized cats. As sources of stimuli we used independent earphones, one at each ear. Tiny electrodes inserted at various points in the auditory neural pathways fed signals into our amplifier and recorder.

Stimulating the cats' ears with a brief,

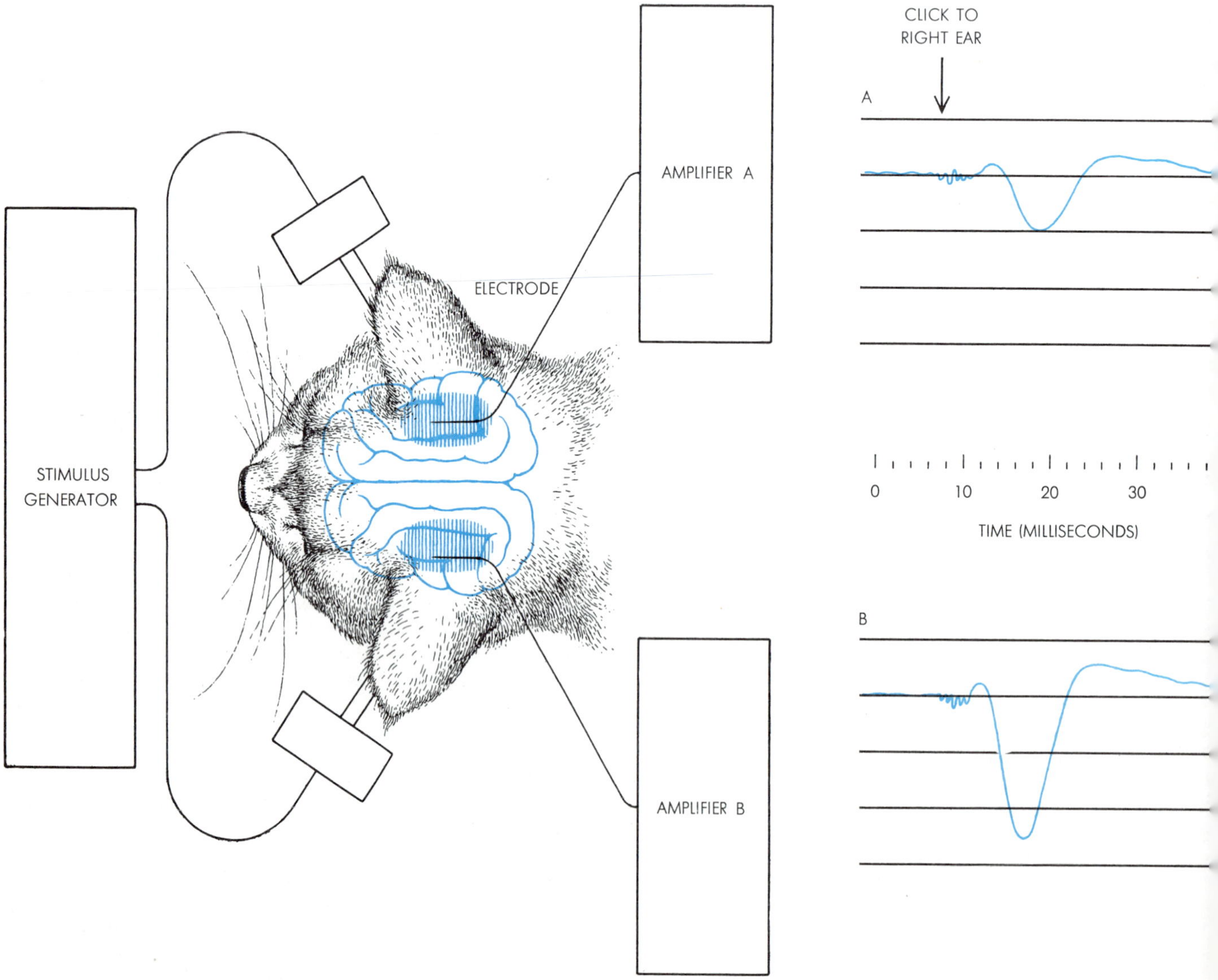

RESPONSES OF AUDITORY CORTEX, recorded through openings in the skull of an anesthetized cat, vary according to the stimulus conditions. Four electrical response curves for the cortex of the right hemisphere appear at top; those for the left cortex, at bottom. When only the right ear is stimulated, there are responses in the auditory cortex on both sides of the brain; response from the left sharp click produced characteristically different electrical responses at each of the levels of the auditory system. Moreover, we found that, at every level in the neural pathways serving each half of the brain, an input to the ear on the opposite side of the body elicited a larger response than it did on the same side [*see illustration on these two pages*]. Most of the neural systems of the body run contralaterally in this way: from one side of the brain to the opposite side of the body. This asymmetry is less pronounced in the auditory system than in most others, but it is clearly present. Because of the asymmetry we could always tell which ear had been stimulated by comparing the responses at the two sides of the brain. A basis for an elementary localization—discrimination of right from left—appeared clearly in the neural responses.

These first experiments corroborated some earlier findings, obtained in a different way. It has been known for many years that nerve cells can be stimulated to activity by small electric currents. In the 1870's physiologists began to map the functional regions of the brain by applying currents to portions of the exposed brain and observing the different bodily responses that were evoked. In this way the British neurologist Sir David Ferrier delimited several sensory regions of the cerebral cortex, including an area devoted to hearing. When Ferrier touched an electrode to the auditory cortex on one side of a monkey's brain, the ear on the other side of the head pricked up, and the animal often turned its eyes or head to that side. In Ferrier's description it was as if a shrill note had been sounded in the ear. Moreover, the "sound" was always on the opposite side of the head from the stimulus.

In the past 25 years or so human testimony has confirmed Ferrier's observations. Patients whose cortex was being mapped in preparation for brain surgery have reported what they felt when electric current was applied to different regions of the brain. A great deal of such information has been obtained by Wilder Penfield and his associates at the Montreal Neurological Institute. When the auditory area is stimulated, patients say they hear sounds, even though no sound waves have reached

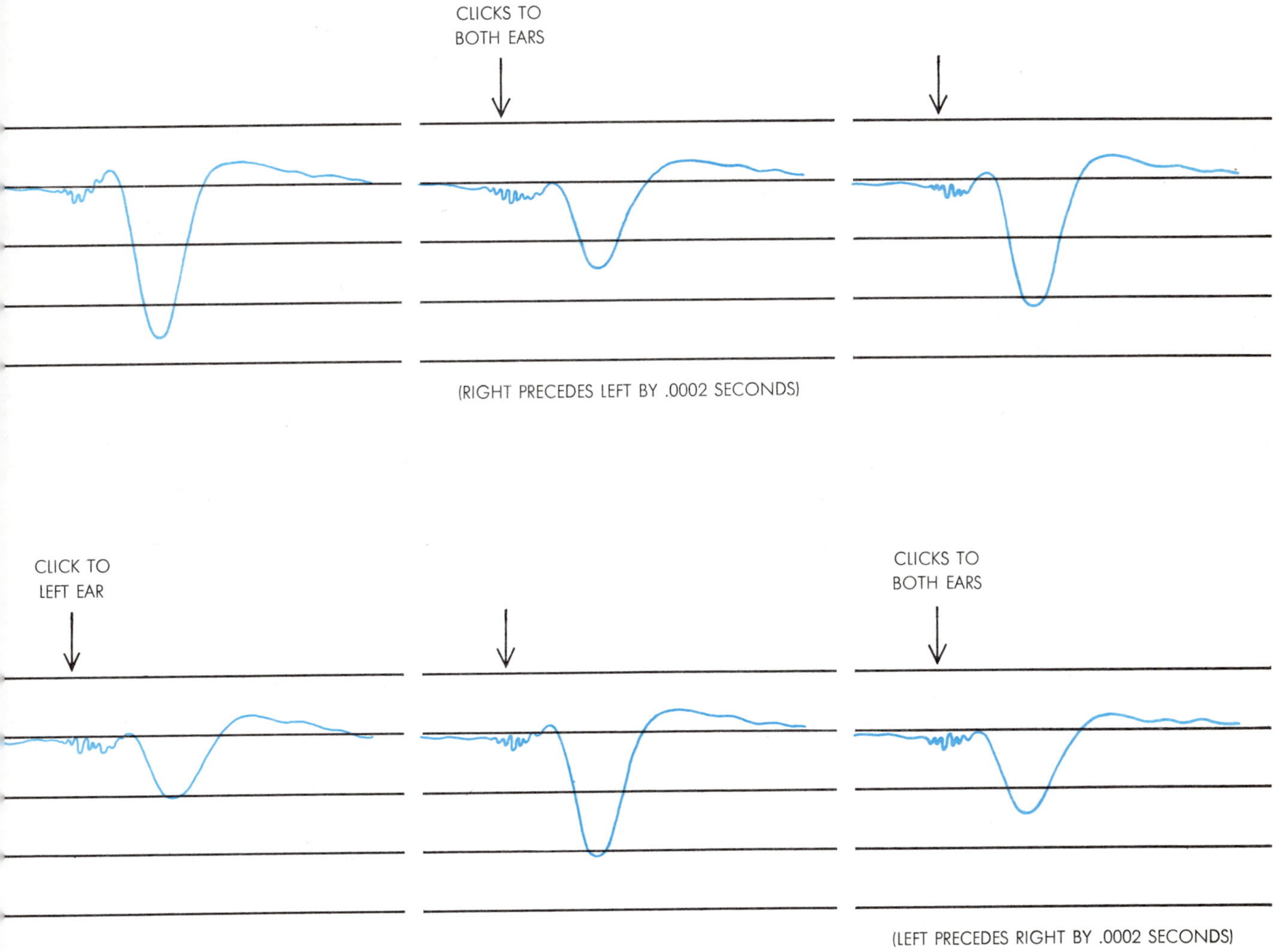

side is larger. When only the left ear is stimulated, the response from the right side is greater. When both ears are stimulated with a small time interval between clicks, the response tends to resemble the response to the prior stimulus alone. Thus when a click to the right ear precedes one to the left by .0002 second, the response from the left side is slightly larger than that from the right, and vice versa.

their ears. When the right side of the brain is stimulated, the patient usually hears the sound as coming from his left; when the left side is stimulated, he hears it as coming from his right. Occasionally the sound seems to come from both sides, but never only from the same side as that on which the brain is stimulated. All the experiments point to the same conclusion: each ear is represented more strongly in the opposite side of the brain than in the same side, and a sound delivered to one ear alone excites more neural activity in the opposite side than in the same side.

Under normal hearing conditions, of course, both ears receive sound, not just one at a time. We extended our experiments with cats by stimulating both ears and recording the electrical activity along the auditory pathways. When we began, it was generally doubted that small differences in the time of arrival of a sound wave at the two ears could be preserved in the neural messages during the 10 milliseconds required for them to travel from the ear to the cerebral cortex. We soon discovered, however, that the electrical pattern does reflect such differences. If the interval was a few milliseconds, long enough so that the two electrical responses showed up separately, the response to the earlier stimulus partially inhibited the response to the later one. With shorter intervals the electrical responses fused into one, but the amplitude was chiefly determined by the first stimulus. Stimulating the ears in the order left-right produced a larger response on the right side of the brain; stimulating in the order right-left, a larger response on the left side. This remained true down to intervals of a tenth of a millisecond, although differences between responses became harder to detect as the interval grew smaller.

Differences in the intensity of stimulation at the two ears were found to produce comparable effects. Feeding a more intense sound to the right ear evoked larger responses on the left side of the brain, and the other way around. The patterns in the nervous system therefore reflect all the differences in the pattern of stimulation—temporal order of stimulation, time interval, and relative intensities of the stimuli at the two ears. (Under ordinary circumstances the temporal and intensity cues reinforce each other. The ear on the side opposite to the source of sound receives not only a later signal but also one of lower intensity, because of the shadowing effect of the head.)

We next carried our investigation down the auditory pathway from the cortex toward the ears. The interaction between the two sides was found to decrease steadily the lower we went. Some interaction can be traced, however, down as far as the olivary nucleus, a group of nerve cells in the medulla that is the next to the last station before each ear. In these nuclei the anatomist W. A. Stotler of the University of Oregon Medical School has found cells that receive connections from both ears [*see illustration on this page*]. At the Walter Reed Army Institute of Research, Robert Galambos and his associates have recently been able to record the activity

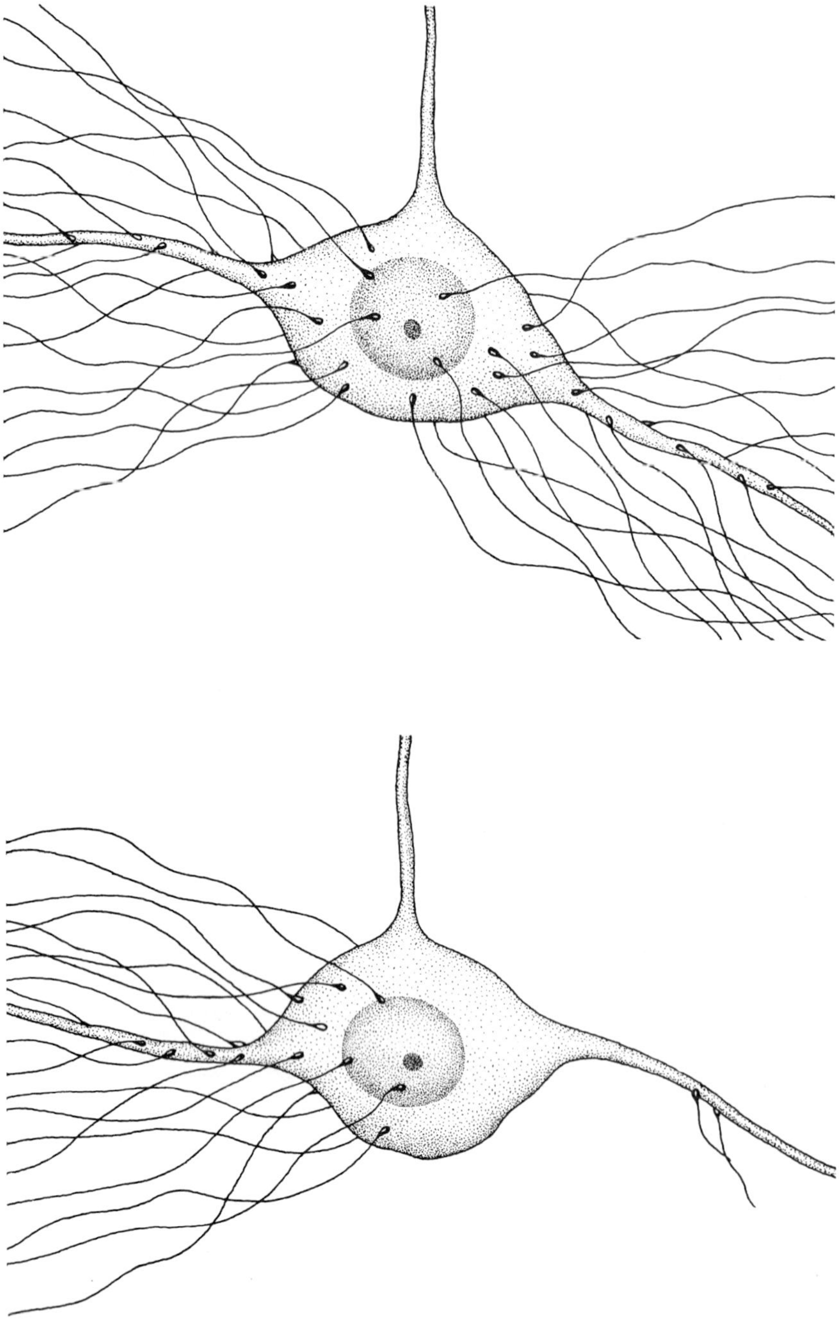

CELLS OF OLIVARY NUCLEUS normally receive connections from the cochlear nuclei of both ears *(see illustration on page 207)*. In a normal cell *(drawing at top)* the incoming fibers *(thin black lines)* from the cochlear nuclei terminate on the dendritic "poles" of the cell. When the cochlear nucleus on one side of the brain stem is destroyed, the fibers leaving that nucleus degenerate; cells of the olivary nucleus lose almost all their connections on that side, demonstrating that each pole receives its connections from the ear on the same side.

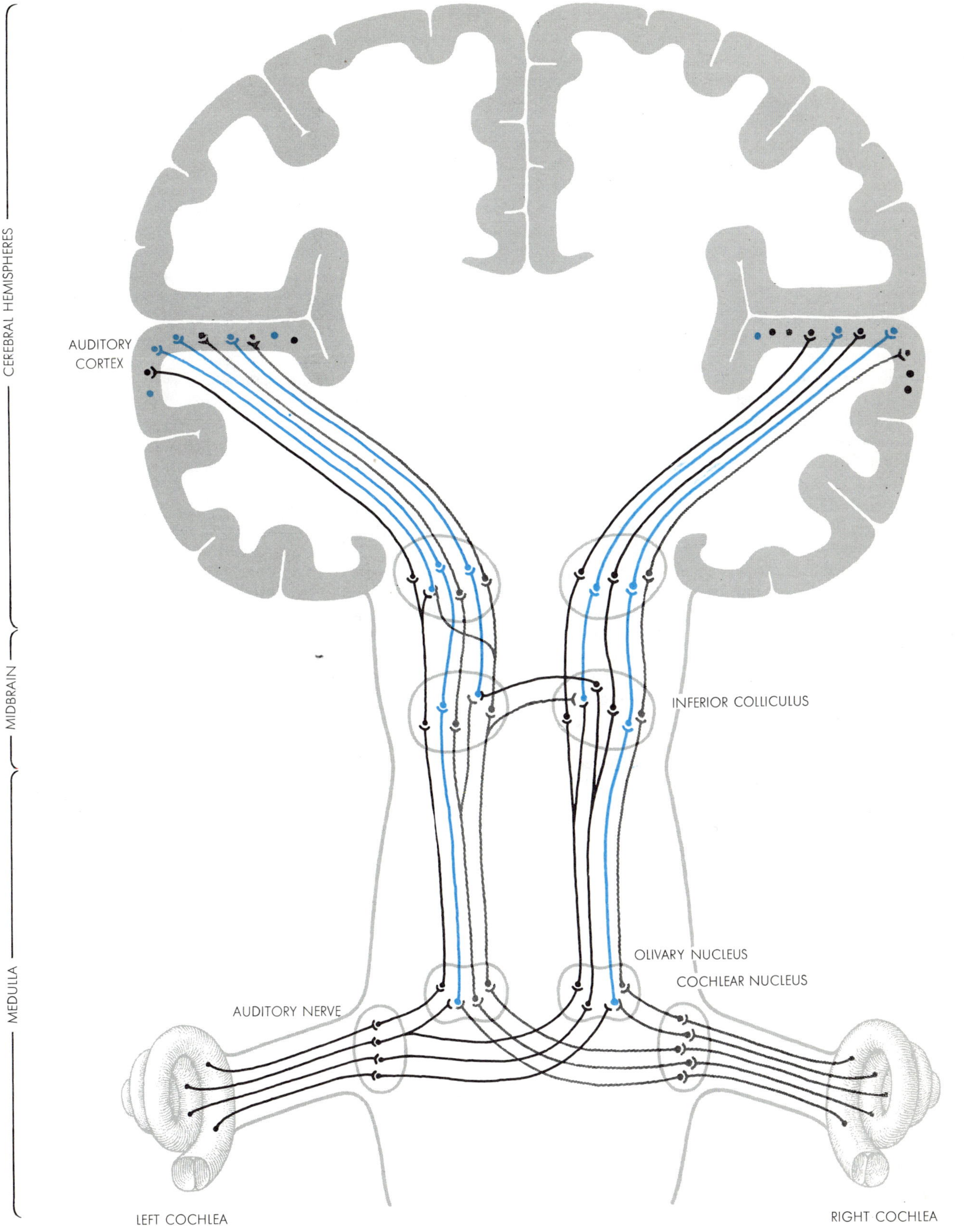

AUDITORY-NERVE PATHWAYS connect the cochlea of each ear with the auditory areas of the cerebral cortex. At the lowest level of the auditory system (the auditory nerves and cochlear nuclei) the pathways are completely separate. (In this greatly simplified diagram of the system the pathways from the left ear are shown in black; those from the right ear are shown in gray.) At the next level (the olivary nucleus in the medulla) some of the nerve fibers from the cochlear nuclei of both ears converge on the same nerve cells. These cells, which thus carry messages from both ears, are shown in color. At successively higher levels of the system there is increasing convergence, and increasing interaction, between messages from the two ears, as is indicated by the larger proportion of cells in color. The majority of nerve pathways starting in one cochlear nucleus cross to the opposite side of the brain.

of single nerve cells in the olivary nucleus. They found that some of the cells respond differently according to which ear receives the earlier stimulus. At the last station before the ear—the cochlear nucleus—there is no indication of binaural interaction.

The picture of increasing interconnection of pathways as they go from lower to higher centers suggests that the higher brain centers may be required for auditory localization. The first direct attempt to test the matter goes back 80 years to the work of an Italian physiologist, Luigi Luciani. Experimenting on dogs, he removed the part of the brain then considered to constitute the auditory cortex. To test the effect on localization he blindfolded the animals and tossed small bits of food on the floor near them, observing how promptly and accurately they retrieved the food. When the operation was performed on only one cerebral hemisphere, the ability to localize was impaired, particularly in the case of sounds originating on the other side of the head. A bilateral operation disrupted localization completely. In the course of time Luciani's studies were generally forgotten. Seen from the vantage point of the present, his results lead to the right answer, but in themselves they are not conclusive. The dogs' ability to localize recovered somewhat several weeks after the operation, perhaps because Luciani never cut away all of what is now known to constitute the auditory cortex.

In the 1930's interest in Luciani's approach revived. Two independent groups reported that cats with the entire cerebral cortex removed could still localize sound. In both experiments, however, the test sound was sustained for several seconds, and the animals were allowed to move their heads. More recent studies by William D. Neff and his collaborators at the University of Chicago served to indicate that the cortex is necessary for auditory localization. From the design of the experiments, however, it was not clear whether the cats had actually lost the ability to localize or had merely lost the ability to keep their attention fixed on the task.

Finally, in 1959, Walter Riss of the State University of New York Downstate Medical Center reported a series of more conclusive experiments. Also working with cats, he removed the auditory cortex in some of the animals and other regions of the cortex in a group of control animals. Both groups were tested with two types of stimulus, one very brief and the other sustained. The brief noise was produced by dropping a food pellet on the platform on which the animal stood; the sustained noise, by rapping the pellet repeatedly against the edge of the platform. He compared the performance of the two groups, recording the accuracy with which the animals turned their heads to face the sound and also measuring the time that they took to reach the food.

In tests with the single brief stimulus the animals without an auditory cortex performed at a random level. The control cats, on the other hand, turned their heads promptly toward the sound every time. With the repetitive stimuli, the performance of the experimental cats was somewhat better. They seemed to sample the sound field by movements of the head and ears. Their first reaction was correct in half the trials. Throughout the tests the experimental animals showed no deficiency of attention, so their poor performance could not be attributed to impairment of this faculty. Riss came to the conclusion that the auditory cortex is necessary for localizing the instantaneous position of a sound—the performance that is characteristic of binaural perception.

What emerges from all the studies so far is a physiological picture—in the higher mammals at least—that partially accounts for the ability to locate a source of sound. Starting at each ear and leading to the cerebral cortex is a chain of neurons. There are several stations along the chain where some neurons end and others begin. At all but the very lowest of these stations the pathways from the two ears overlap to some extent, the degree of overlap increasing as the pathways ascend. Neural impulses from one ear consequently have an increasing probability of encountering impulses from the other as they approach the cortex. Depending on the conditions of stimulation, which in turn depend on the relative positions of the listener and the source of sound, the converging impulses make some groups of nerve cells become more active and others less so. The different patterns of activity that result in the auditory cortex are correlated with different locations of auditory stimuli.

Here, for the present, the story ends. Of course, the cortex in its turn must send neural impulses to further centers so that localization ultimately evokes different patterns of behavior. Exploring this part of the neural pathway is a job for the future.

21

PATTERN RECOGNITION BY MACHINE

OLIVER G. SELFRIDGE AND ULRIC NEISSER

August 1960

Can a machine think? The answer to this old chestnut is certainly yes: Computers have been made to play chess and checkers, to prove theorems, to solve intricate problems of strategy. Yet the intelligence implied by such activities has an elusive, unnatural quality. It is not based on any orderly development of cognitive skills. In particular, the machines are not well equipped to select from their environment the things, or the relations, they are going to think about.

In this they are sharply distinguished from intelligent living organisms. Every child learns to analyze speech into meaningful patterns long before he can prove any propositions. Computers can find proofs, but they cannot understand the simplest spoken instructions. Even the earliest computers could do arithmetic superbly, but only very recently have they begun to read the written digits that a child recognizes before he learns to add them. Understanding speech and reading print are examples of a basic intellectual skill that can variously be called cognition, abstraction or perception; perhaps the best general term for it is pattern recognition.

Except for their inability to recognize patterns, machines (or, more accurately, the programs that tell machines what to do) have now met most of the classic criteria of intelligence that skeptics have proposed. They *can* outperform their designers: The checker-playing program devised by Arthur L. Samuel of International Business Machines Corporation usually beats him. They *are* original: The "logic theorist," a creation of a group from the Carnegie Institute of Technology and the Rand Corporation (Allen Newell, Herbert Simon and J. C. Shaw) has found proofs for many of the theorems in *Principia Mathematica,* the monumental work in mathematical logic by A. N. Whitehead and Bertrand Russell. At least one proof is more elegant than the Whitehead-Russell version.

Sensible as they are, the machines are not perceptive. The information they receive must be fed to them one "bit" (a contraction of "binary digit," denoting a unit of information) at a time, up to perhaps millions of bits. Computers do not organize or classify the material in any very subtle or generally applicable way. They perform only highly specialized operations on carefully prepared inputs.

In contrast, a man is continuously exposed to a welter of data from his senses, and abstracts from it the patterns relevant to his activity at the moment. His ability to solve problems, prove theorems and generally run his life depends on this type of perception. We suspect that until programs to perceive patterns can be developed, achievements in mechanical problem-solving will remain isolated technical triumphs.

Developing pattern-recognition programs has proved rather difficult. One reason for the difficulty lies in the nature of the task. A man who abstracts a pattern from a complex of stimuli has essentially classified the possible inputs. But very often the basis of classification is unknown, even to himself; it is too complex to be specified explicitly. Asked to define a pattern, the man does so by example; as a logician might say, ostensively. This letter is A, that person is mother, these speech sounds are a request to pass the salt. The important patterns are defined by experience. Every human being acquires his pattern classes by adapting to a social or environmental consensus—in short, by learning.

In company with workers at various institutions our group at the Lincoln Laboratory of the Massachusetts Institute of Technology has been working on mechanical recognition of patterns. Thus far only a few simple cases have been tackled. We shall discuss two examples. The first one is MAUDE (for Morse Automatic Decoder), a program for translating, or rather transliterating, hand-sent Morse code. This program was developed at the Lincoln Laboratory by a group of workers under the direction of Bernard Gold.

If telegraphers sent ideal Morse, recognition would be easy. The keyings, or "marks," for dashes would be exactly three times as long as the marks for dots; spaces separating the marks within a letter or other character (mark spaces) would be as long as dots; spaces between characters (character spaces), three times as long; spaces separating words (word spaces), seven times as long. Unfortunately human operators do not transmit these ideal intervals. A machine that processed a signal on the assumption that they do would perform very poorly indeed. In an actual message the distinction between dots and dashes is far from clear. There is a great deal of variation among the dots and dashes, and also among the three kinds of space. In fact, when a long message sent by a single operator is analyzed, it frequently turns out that some dots are longer than some dashes, and that some mark spaces are longer than some character spaces.

With a little practice in receiving code, the average person has no trouble with these irregularities. The patterns of the letters are defined for him in terms of the continuing consensus of experience, and he adapts to them as he listens. Soon he does not hear dots and dashes at all, but perceives the characters as wholes. Exactly how he does so is still obscure, and the mechanism probably varies widely from one operator to another. In any event transliteration is impossible if each mark and space is considered individually. MAUDE therefore uses contextual information, but far less than is available to a trained operator. The machine program knows all the standard Morse characters and a few compound ones, but no syllables or words. A trained operator, on the other hand, hears the characters themselves embedded in a meaningful context.

Empirically it is easier to distinguish between the two kinds of mark than among the three kinds of space. The main problem for any mechanical Morse translator is to segment the message into its characters by identifying the character spaces. MAUDE begins by assuming that the longest of each six consecutive spaces is a character space (since no Morse character is more than six marks long), and the shortest is a mark space. It is important to note that although the former rule follows logically from the structure of the ideal code, and that the latter seems quite plausible, their effectiveness can be demonstrated only by experiment. In fact the rules fail less than once in 10,000 times.

The decoding process proceeds as follows [*see illustration on page 217*]. The marks and spaces, received by the machine in the form of electrical pulses, are converted into a sequence of numbers measuring their duration. (For technical reasons these numbers are then converted into their logarithms.) The sequence of durations representing spaces

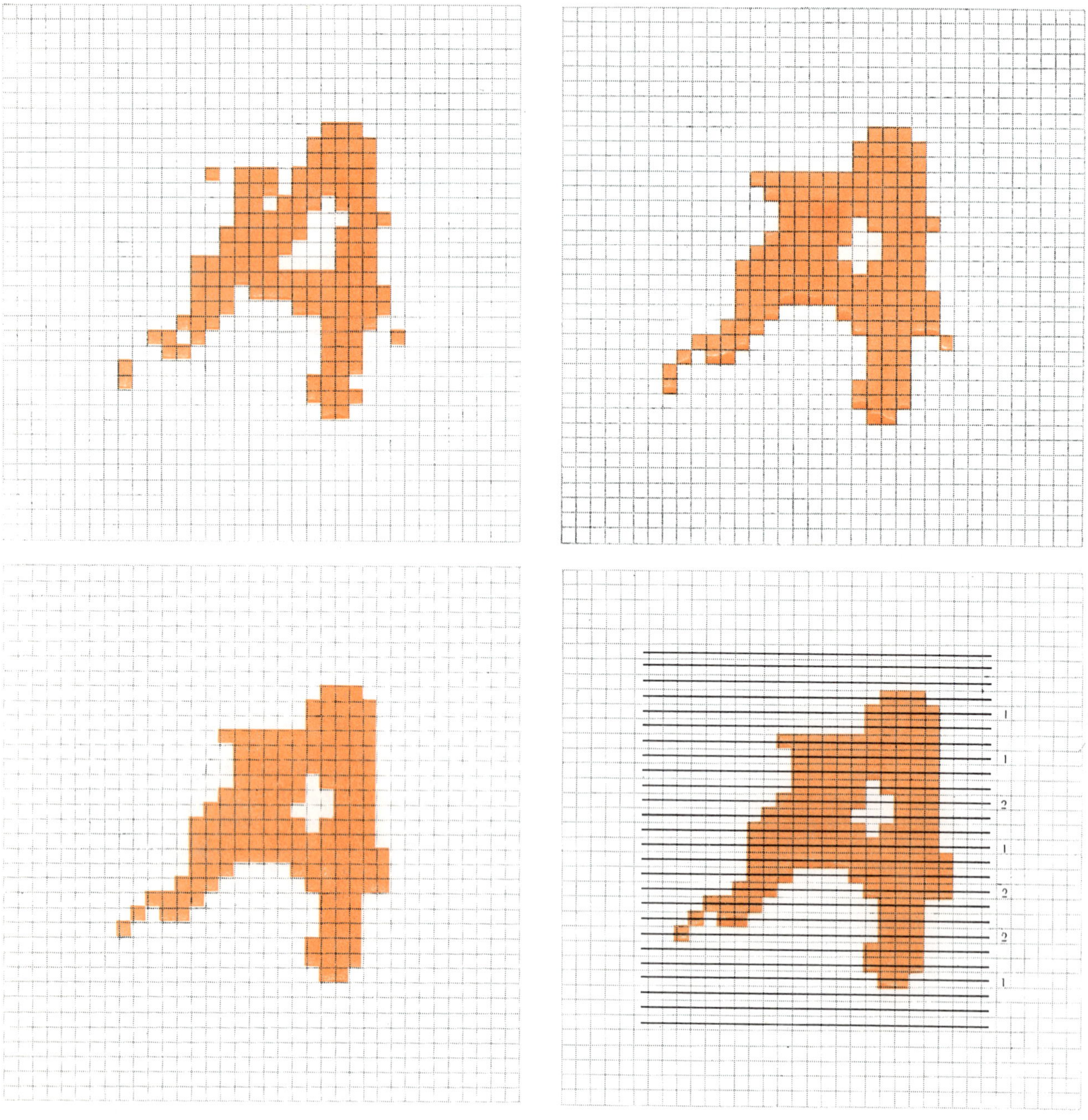

HAND-PRINTED LETTER A is processed for recognition by computer. Original sample is placed on grid and converted to a cellular pattern by completely filling in all squares through which lines pass (*top left*). The computer then cleans up the sample, filling in gaps (*top right*) and eliminating isolated cells (*bottom left*). The program tests the pattern for a variety of features. The test illustrated here (*bottom right*) is for the maximum number of intersections of the sample with all horizontal lines across the grid.

is processed first. The machine examines each group of six (spaces one through six, two through seven, three through eight and so on), recording in each the longest and shortest durations. When this process is complete, about 75 per cent of the character spaces and about 50 per cent of the mark spaces will have been identified.

To classify the remaining spaces a threshold is computed. It is set at the most plausible dividing line between the range of durations in which mark spaces have been found and the range of the identified character spaces. Every unclassified number larger than the threshold is then identified as a character space; every one smaller than the threshold, as a mark space.

Now, by a similar process, the numbers representing marks are identified as dots and dashes. Combining the classified marks and spaces gives a string of tentative segments, separated by character spaces. These are inspected and compared to a set of proper Morse characters stored in the machine. (There are about 50 of these, out of the total of 127 possible sequences of six or fewer marks.) Experience has shown that when one of the tentative segments is not acceptable, it is most likely that one of the supposed mark spaces within the segment should be a character space instead. The program reclassifies the longest space in the segment as a character space and examines the two new characters thus formed. The procedure continues until every segment is an acceptable character, whereupon the message is printed out.

In the course of transmitting a long message, operators usually change speed from time to time. MAUDE adapts to these changes. The computed thresholds are local, moving averages that shift with the general lengthening or shortening of marks and spaces. Thus a mark of a certain duration could be classified as a dot in one part of the message and a dash in another.

MAUDE's error rate is only slightly higher than that of a skilled human operator. Thus it is at least possible for a machine to recognize patterns even where the basis of classification is variable and not fully specified in advance. Moreover, the program illustrates an important general point. Its success depends on the rules by which the continuous message is divided into appropriate segments. Segmentation seems likely to be a primary problem in all mechanical pattern-recognition, particularly in the recognition of speech, since the natural pauses in spoken language do not generally come between words. MAUDE handles the segmentation problems in terms of context, and this will often be appropriate. In other respects MAUDE does not provide an adequate basis for generalizing about pattern recognition. The patterns of Morse code are too easy, and the processing is rather specialized.

Our second example deals with a more challenging problem: the recognition of hand-printed letters of the alphabet. The characters that people print in the ordinary course of filling out forms and questionnaires are surprisingly varied. Gaps abound where continuous lines might be expected; curves and sharp angles appear interchangeably; there is almost every imaginable distortion of slant, shape and size. Even human readers cannot always identify such characters; their error rate is about 3 per cent on randomly selected letters and numbers, seen out of context.

The first step in designing a mechanical reader is to provide it with a means of assimilating the visual data. By nature computers consider information in strings of bits: sequences of zeros and ones recorded in on-off devices. The simplest way to encode a character into such a sequence is to convert it into a sort of half-tone by splitting it into a mesh or matrix of squares as fine as may be necessary. Each square is then either black or white—a binary situation that the machine is designed to handle. Making such half-tones presents no problem. For example, an image of the letter could be projected on a bank of photocells, with the output of each cell controlling a binary device in the computer. In the ex-

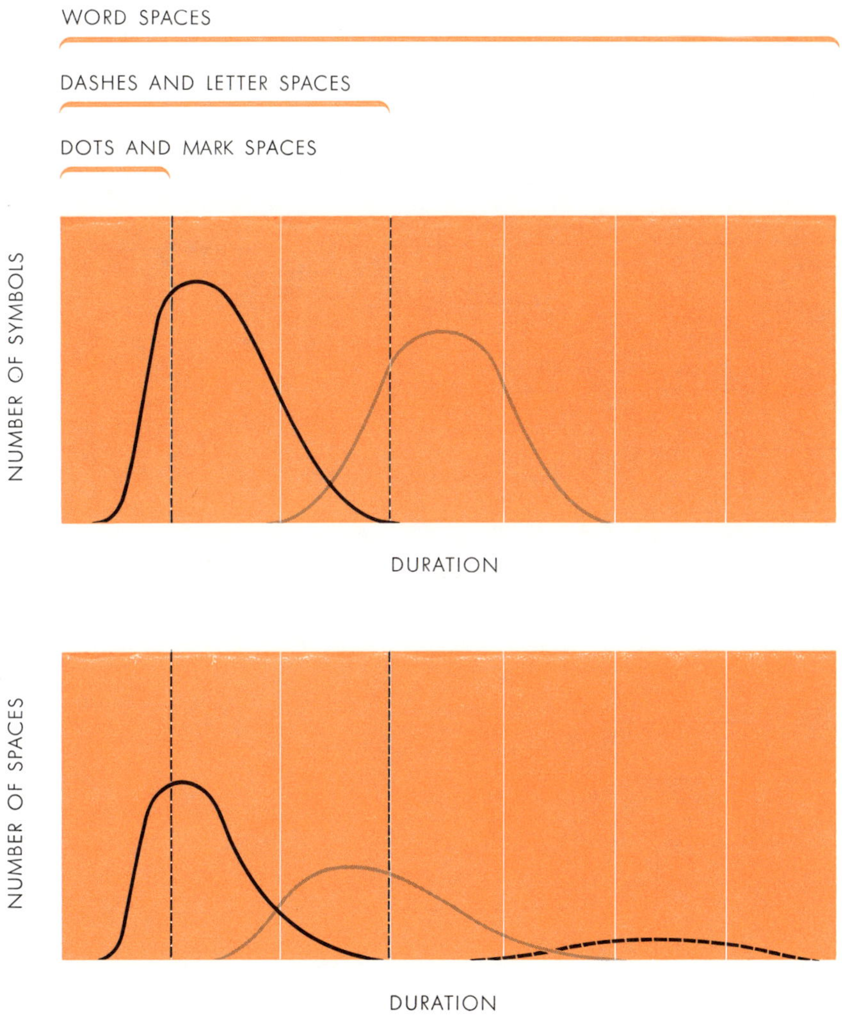

VARIABILITY OF MORSE CODE sent by a human operator is illustrated in these curves. Upper graph shows range of durations for dots (*black curve*) and dashes (*gray curve*) in a message. Lower graph gives the same information for spaces between marks within a character (*solid black curve*), spaces between characters (*gray curve*) and between words (*broken curve*). Ideal durations are shown by brackets at top and vertical broken lines.

periments to be described here the appropriate digital information from the matrix was recorded on punch cards and was fed into the computer in this form.

Once this sequence of bits has been put in, how shall the program proceed to identify it? Perhaps the most obvious approach is a simple matching scheme, which would evaluate the similarity of the unknown to a series of ideal templates of all the letters, previously stored in digital form in the machine. The sequence of zeros and ones representing the unknown letter would be compared to each template sequence, and the number of matching digits recorded in each case. The highest number of matches would identify the letter.

In its primitive form the scheme would clearly fail. Even if the unknown were identical to the template, slight changes in position, orientation or size could destroy the match completely [*see top illustration on page 216*]. This difficulty has long been recognized, and in some character-recognition programs it has been met by inserting a level of information-processing ahead of the template-matching procedure. The sample is shifted, rotated and magnified or reduced in order to put it into a standard, or at least a more tractable, form.

Although obviously an improvement over raw matching, such a procedure is still inadequate. What it does is to compare shapes rather successfully. But letters are a good deal more than mere shapes. Even when a sample has been converted to standard size, position and orientation, it may match a wrong template more closely than it matches the right one [*see bottom illustration on page 216*].

Nevertheless the scheme illustrates what we believe to be an important general principle. The critical change was from a program with a single level of operation to a program with two distinctly different levels. The first level shifts, and the second one matches. Such a hierarchical structure is forced on the recognition system by the nature of the entities to be recognized. The letter A is defined by the set of configurations that people call A, and their selections can be described—or imitated—only by a multilevel program.

We have said that letter patterns cannot be described merely as shapes. It appears that they can be specified only in terms of a preponderance of certain *features*. Thus A tends to be thinner at the top than at the bottom; it is roughly concave at the bottom; it usually has two main strokes more vertical than horizontal, one more horizontal than vertical, and so on. All these features taken together characterize A rather more closely than they characterize any other letter. Singly none of them is sufficient. For example, W is also roughly concave

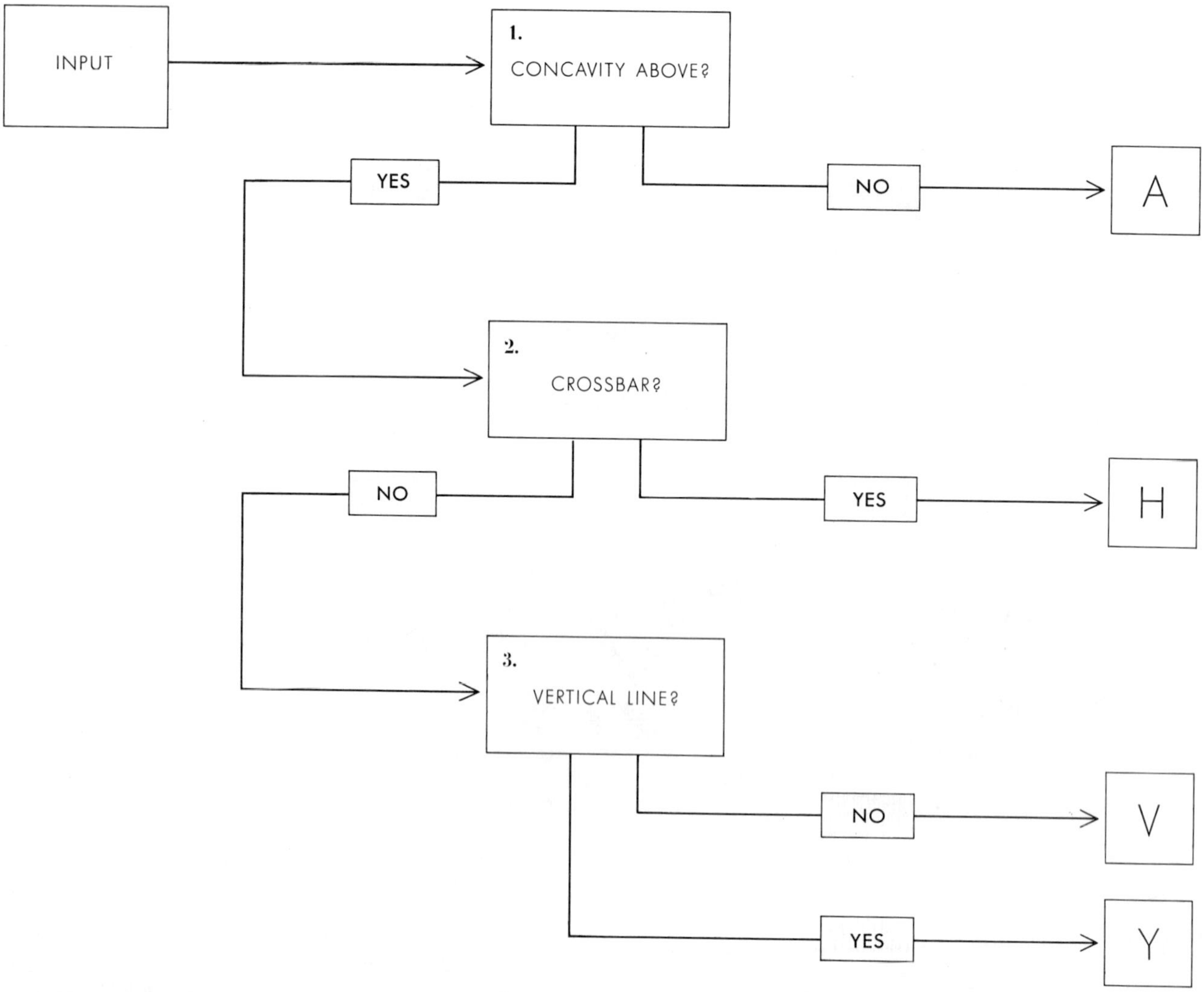

SEQUENTIAL-PROCESSING program for distinguishing four letters, A, H, V and Y employs three test features: presence or absence of a concavity above, a crossbar and a vertical line. The tests are applied in order, with each outcome determining the next step.

at the bottom, and H has a pattern of horizontal and vertical strokes similar to that described for A. Each letter has its own set of probable features, and a successful character recognizer will determine which set is the best fit to an unknown sample.

So far nothing has been said about how the features are to be determined and how the program will use them. The template-matching scheme represents one approach. Its "features," in a sense, are the individual cells of the matrix representing the unknown sample, and its procedure is to match them with corresponding cells in the template. Both features and procedure are determined by the designer. We have seen that this scheme will not succeed. In fact, any system must fail if it tries to specify every detail of a procedure for identifying patterns that are themselves defined only ostensively. A pattern-recognition system must learn. But how much?

At one extreme there have been attempts to make it learn, or generate, everything: the features, the processing, the decision procedure. The initial state of such a system is called a "random net." A large number of on-off computer elements are multiply interconnected in a random way. Each is thus fed by several others. The thresholds of the elements (the number of signals that must be received before the element fires) are then adjusted on the basis of performance. In other words, the system learns by reinforcing some pathways through the net and weakening others.

How far a random net can evolve is controversial. Probably a net can come to act as though it used templates. However, none has yet been shown capable of generating features more sophisticated than those based, like templates, on single matrix-cells. Indeed, we do not believe that this is possible.

At present the only way the machine can get an adequate set of features is from a human programmer. The effectiveness of any particular set can be demonstrated only by experiment. In general there is probably safety in numbers. The designer will do well to include all the features he can think of that might plausibly be useful.

A program that does not develop its own features may nevertheless be capable of modifying some subsequent level of the decision procedure, as we shall see. First however, let us consider that procedure itself. There are two fundamentally different possibilities: sequential and parallel processing. In sequential processing the features are inspected in a predetermined order, the outcome of each test determining the next step. Each letter is represented by a unique sequence of binary decisions. To take a simple example, a program to distinguish the letters A, H, V and Y

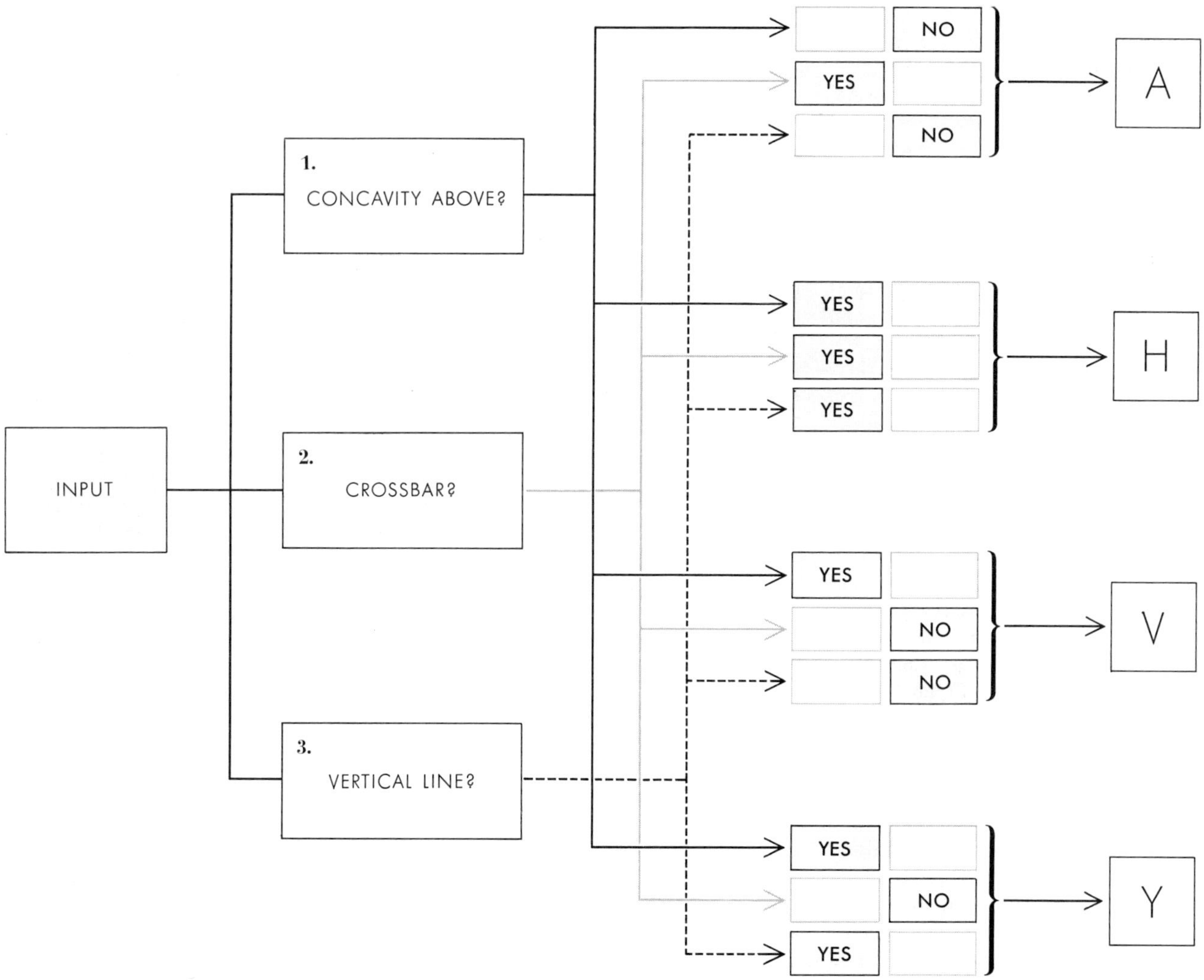

PARALLEL-PROCESSING program uses the same test features as the sequential program on opposite page, but applies all tests simultaneously and makes decision on the basis of the combined outcomes. The input is a sample of one of the letters A, H, V and Y.

LETTER	SAMPLES	OUTCOME 1	2	3	4
A	39		33	6	
E	46	6	35	5	
I	25	25			
L	24	7	17		
M	24			18	6
N	28		2	25	1
O	34		27	7	
R	33		28	4	1
S	38	8	30		
T	39	10	22	7	
TOTAL	330	56	194	72	8

"CENSUS" represents information learned by letter-recognition program during training period. This table summarizes the outcomes of the test for maximum number of intersections with a horizontal line, applied to a total of 330 identified samples in the learning process.

might decide among them on the basis of the presence or absence of three features: a concavity at the top, a crossbar and a vertical line. The sequential process would ask first: "Is there a concavity at the top?" If the answer is no, the sample is A. If the answer is yes, the program asks: "Is there a crossbar?" If yes, the letter is H; if no, then: "Is there a vertical line?" If yes, the letter is Y; if no, V [*see illustration on page 216*].

In parallel processing all the questions would be asked at once, and all the answers presented simultaneously to the decision-maker [*see illustration on preceding page*]. Different combinations identify the different letters. One might think of the various features as being inspected by little demons, all of whom then shout the answers in concert to a decision-making demon. From this conceit comes the name "Pandemonium" for parallel processing.

Of the two systems the sequential type is the more natural for a machine. Computer programs are sequences of instructions, in which choices or alternatives are usually introduced as "conditional transfers": Follow one set of instructions if a certain number is negative (say) and another set of instructions if it is not. Programs of this kind can be highly efficient, especially in cases where any given decision is almost certain to be right. But in "noisy" situations sequential programs require elaborate checking and back-tracking procedures to compensate for erroneous decisions. Parallel processing, on the other hand, need make no special allowance for error and uncertainty.

Furthermore, some features are simply not subject to a reasonable dichotomy. An A very surely has a crossbar, an O very surely has not. But what about B? The most we can say is that it has more of a crossbar than O, and less than A. A Pandemonium program can handle the situation by having the demons shout more or less loudly. In other words, the information flowing through the system need not be binary; it can represent the quantitative preponderance of the various features.

Still another advantage of parallel processing lies in the possibility of making small changes in a network for experimental purposes. In typical sequential programs the only possible changes involve replacing a zero with a one, or vice versa. In parallel ones, on the other hand, the weight given to crossbarness in deciding if the unknown is actually B may be changed by as small an amount as desired. Experimental changes of this kind need not be made by the programmer alone. A program can be designed to alter internal weights as a result of experience and to profit from its mistakes. Such learning is much easier to incorporate into a Pandemonium than into a sequential system, where a change at any point has grave consequences for large parts of the system.

Parallel processing seems to be the human way of handling pattern recognition as well. Speech can be understood if all acoustic frequencies above 2,000 cycles per second are eliminated, but it can also be understood if those below 2,000 are eliminated instead. Depth perception is excellent if both eyes are open and the head is held still; it is also excellent if one eye is open and the head is allowed to move.

A Pandemonium system that learns from experience has been tested by Worthie Doyle of the Lincoln Laboratory. At present it is programmed to identify 10 hand-printed characters, and has been tested on samples of A, E, I, L, M, N, O, R, S and T. The program has six levels: (1) input, (2) clean-up, (3) inspection of features, (4) comparison with learned-feature distribution, (5) computation of probabilities and (6) decision. The input is a 1,024-cell matrix, 32 on a side. At the second level the sample character is smoothed by filling in isolated gaps and eliminating isolated patches [*see illustration on page 210*].

Recognition is based on such features as the relative length of different edges and the maximum number of intersections of the sample with a horizontal line. (The computer "draws" the lines by inspecting every horizontal row in the matrix, and recognizes "intersections" as sequences of ones separated by sequences of zeros.) No single feature is essential to recognition, and various numbers of them have been tried. The particular program shown here [*see illustration on opposite page*] uses 28.

Every letter fed into the machine is tested for each of the features. During the learning phase a number of samples

RECOGNITION PROGRAM for hand-printed letters applies the 28 feature tests listed by code name at left. Names represent such features as maximum intersections with horizontal line (HOMSXC), concavity facing south (SOUCAV) and so on. Figures in right-hand section of table are relative probabilities of all letters for each test outcome. The program decides on the letter with the largest total of all probabilities. In the example shown here the decision is for the letter A, with a probability total of 4.579.

TYPE OF TEST AND DESIGNATION		OUTCOME	A	E	I	L	M	N	O	R	S	T
HORIZONTAL AND VERTICAL CROSS-SECTIONS	HOMSXC	3	.083	.070			.250	.347	.097	.056		.097
	VEMSXC	3	.073	.339			.040		.008	.194	.258	.089
	HORUNS	2111111		.500						.500		
	VERUNS	2111111						1.000				
STROKES	HORSTR	1	.182	.006	.125	.125	.125	.146	.016	.057	.016	.203
	VERSTR	2	.178	.007			.170	.207	.229	.207		
EDGE LENGTHS AND RATIOS	SEDGE	1	.267	.007		.014	.158	.115	.007	.165		.266
	WEDGE	1	.083	.071	.024	.024	.035	.012		.047	.318	.389
	NEDGE	2	.259	.024	.153	.024	.106	.106	.071	.059	.189	.012
	EEDGE	4	.232		.161		.214	.286	.107			
	NO:SOU	4	.513				.205	.077		.128		.077
	EA:WES	1	.055	.400		.309	.018	.036		.163		.018
PROFILES	SOUCAV	3	.150				.800	.050				
	WESCAV	2	.047	.094	.023	.012	.023	.035	.035	.059	.412	.259
	NORCAV	1	.133	.177	.100	.092	.004		.133	.108	.116	.137
	EASCAV	1	.155	.005	.115	.095	.105	.130	.170	.010	.050	.165
	SOUBOT	220	.268	.106		.068	.159	.167	.008	.220	.008	
	WESBOT	221	.030	.030	.061						.364	.515
	NORBOT	121	.290	.145					.354	.042	.042	.125
	EASBOT	121	.326				.020	.102	.266	.020	.245	.020
INTERNAL STRUCTURE	SBOTSG	2	.250	.008		.016	.125	.141	.219	.203	.039	
	WBOTSG	1	.161	.076	.090	.099	.108	.121	.063	.081	.045	.157
	NBOTSG	1	.119	.190	.111	.102	.013	.018	.089	.040	.159	.159
	EBOTSG	1	.147	.058	.098	.103	.103	.121	.062	.071	.076	.061
	SOUBEN	20					.333	.167				.500
	WESBEN	10	.198	.143	.011	.022	.121	.132	.011	.099	.022	.241
	NORBEN	10	.169	.180		.135	.079			.146	.247	.045
	EASBEN	10	.211	.012	.012	.118	.176	.106		.176		.188
TOTAL SCORE			4.579	2.648	1.084	1.358	3.490	3.622	1.945	2.851	2.606	3.823

of each of the 10 letters is presented and identified. For every feature the program compiles a table or "census." It tests each sample and enters the outcome under the appropriate letter. When the learning period is finished, the table shows how many times each outcome occurred for each of the 10 letters. The table on page 214, which refers to maximum intersections with a horizonal line, represents the experience gained from a total of 330 training samples. It shows, for example, that the outcome (three intersections) occurred 72 times distributed among six A's, five E's, 18 M's, 25 N's, seven O's, four R's, seven T's and no other letters. The other possible outcomes are similarly recorded.

TEMPLATE MATCHING cannot succeed when the unknown letter (*color*) has the wrong size, orientation or position. The program must begin by adjusting sample to standard form.

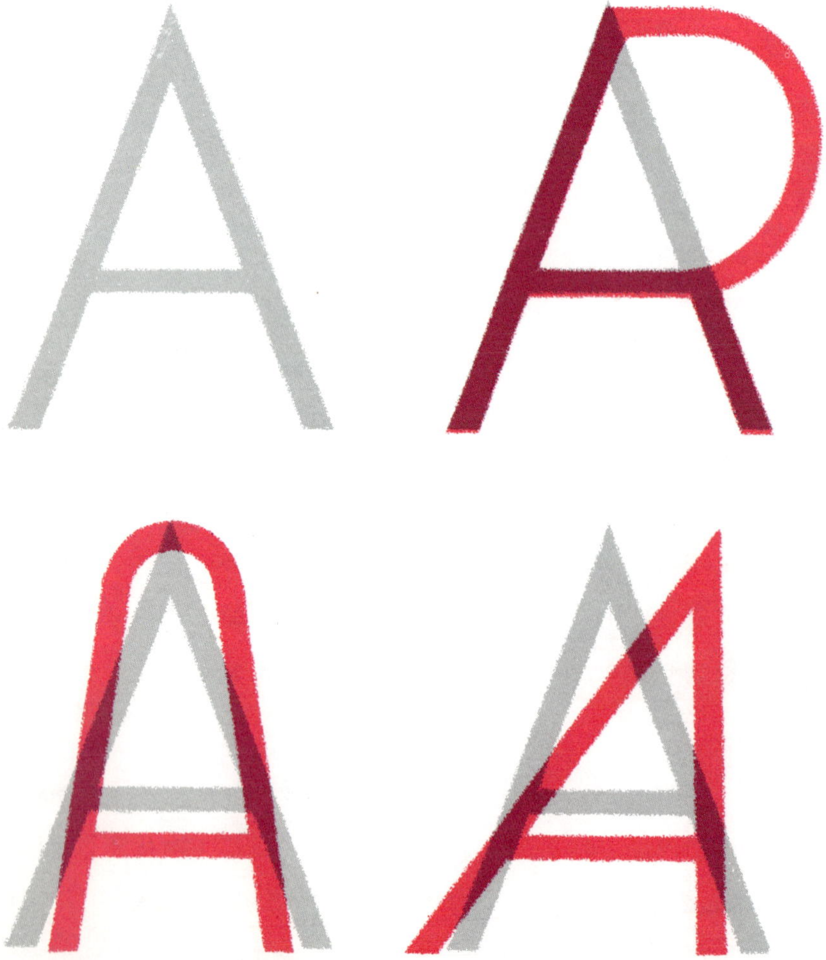

INCORRECT MATCH may result even when sample (*color*) has been converted to standard form. Here R matches A template more closely than do samples of the correct letter.

Next the 28 censuses are converted to tables of estimated probabilities, by dividing each entry by the appropriate total. Thus the outcome—three intersections—comes from an A with a probability of .083 (6/72); an E, with a probability of .070 (5/72), and so on.

Now the system is ready to consider an unknown sample. It carries out the 28 tests and "looks up" each outcome in the corresponding feature census, entering the estimated probabilities in a table. Then the total probabilities are computed for each letter. The final decision is made by choosing the letter with the highest probability.

This program makes only about 10 per cent fewer correct identifications than human readers make—a respectable performance, to be sure. At the same time, the things it cannot do point to the difficulties that still lie ahead. We would emphasize three general problems: segmentation, hierarchical learning and feature generation.

Characters must be fed in one at a time. The program is unable to segment continuous written material. The problem will doubtless be relatively easy to solve for text consisting of separate printed characters, but will be more formidable in the case of cursive script.

The program learns on one level only. The relation between feature presence and character probability is determined by experience; everything else is fixed by the designer. It would certainly be desirable for a character recognizer to use experience for more general improvements: to change its clean-up procedures, alter the way probabilities are combined and refine its decision process. Eventually we look to recognition of words; at that point the program will have to learn a vocabulary so that it can use context in identifying dubious letters. At the moment, however, neither we nor any other designers have any experience with the interaction of several levels of learning.

The most important learning process of all is still untouched: No current program can generate test features of its own. The effectiveness of all of them is forever restricted by the ingenuity or arbitrariness of their programmers. We can barely guess how this restriction might be overcome. Until it is, "artificial intelligence" will remain tainted with artifice.

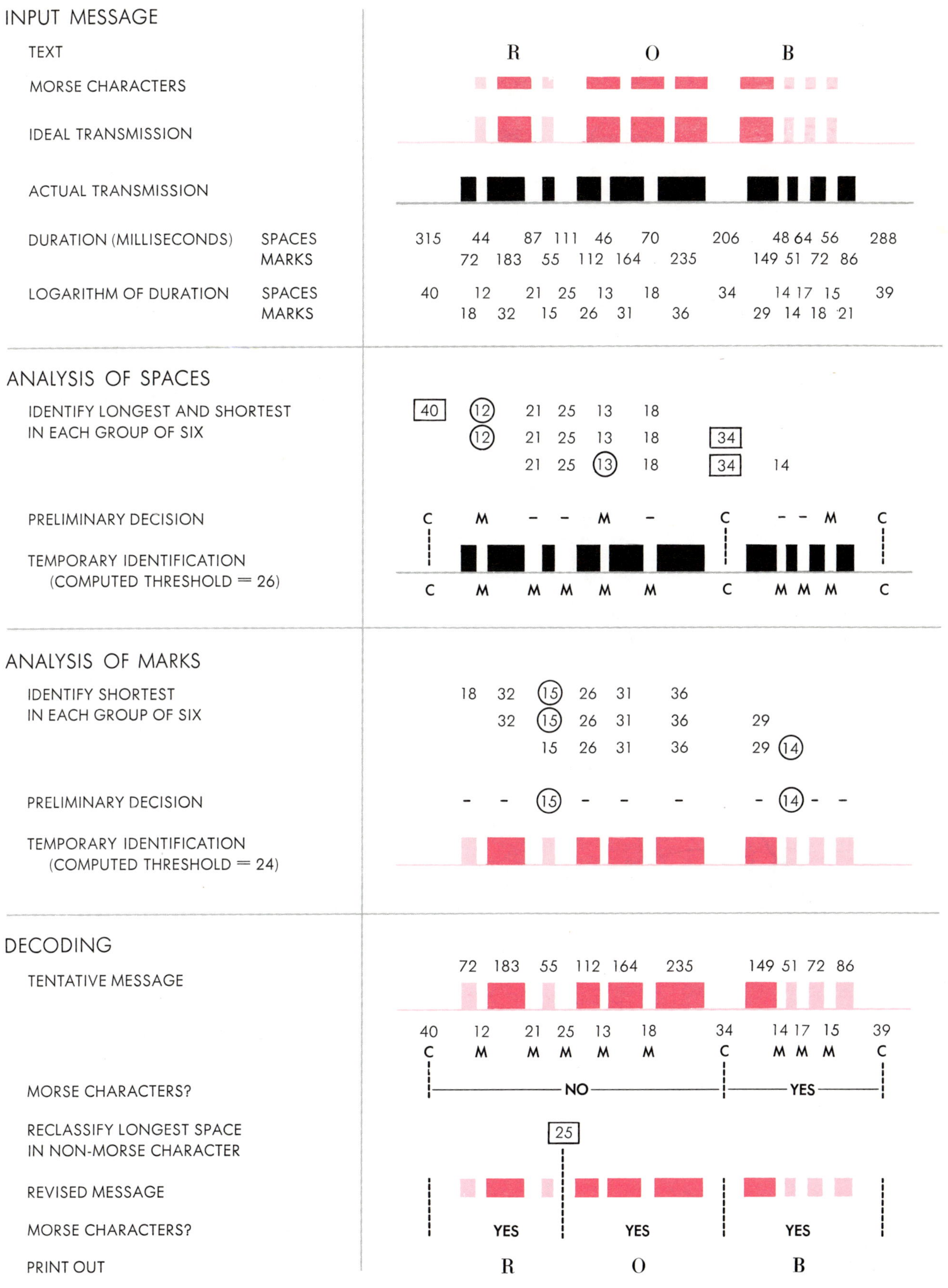

"MAUDE" PROGRAM, described in text, translates Morse code. Marks identified as dots are shown in light color; marks identified as dashes, in dark color. Unidentified marks are in black. Character spaces are denoted by C; mark spaces, by M. A circle around a number indicates that it is the smallest in a group; a rectangle means it is the largest. Analysis of spaces and marks proceeds by an examination of successive groups of six throughout the message. The table shows only the first three such groups in each case.

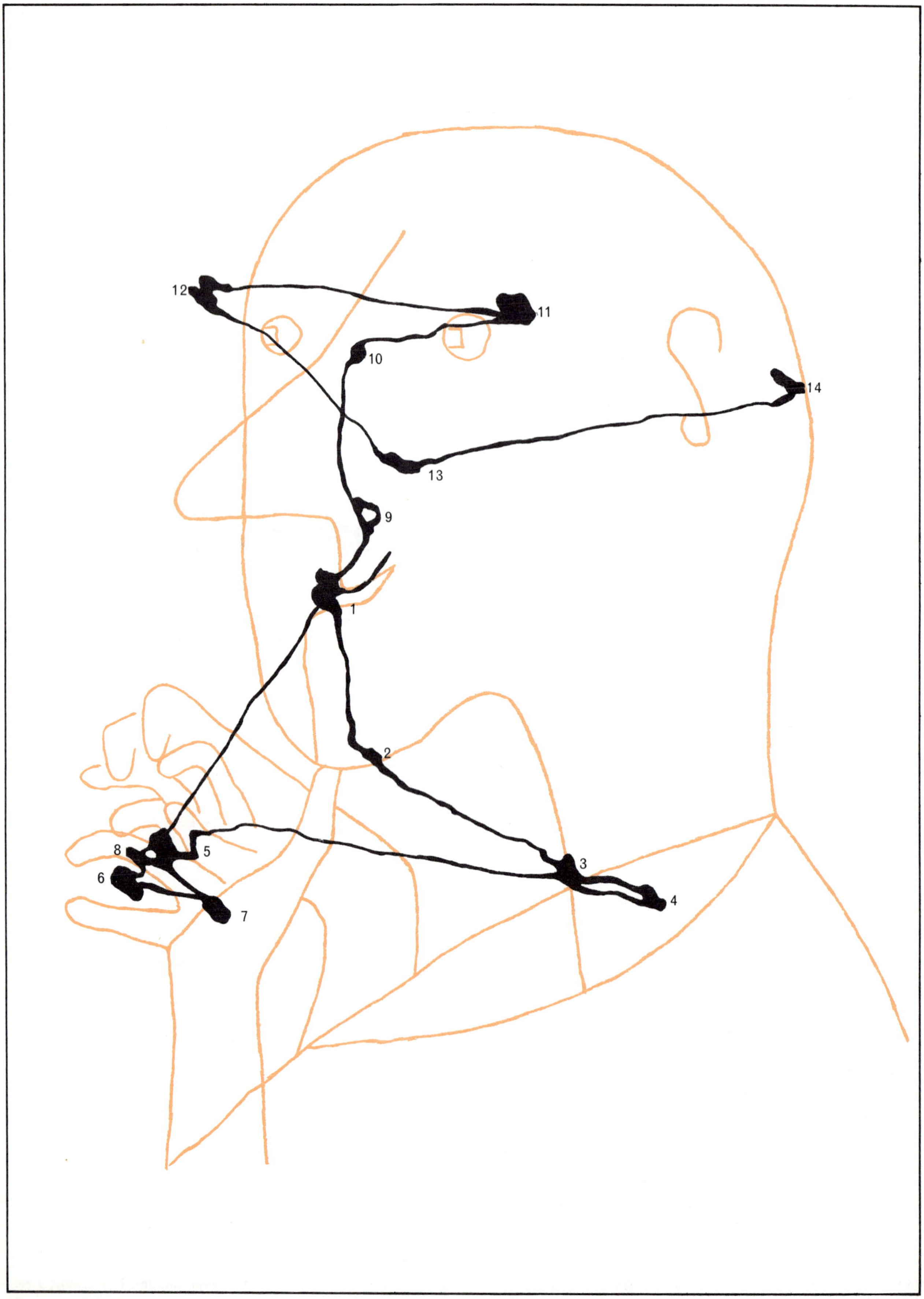

EYE MOVEMENTS made by a subject viewing for the first time a drawing adapted from Paul Klee's "Old Man Figuring" appear in black. Numbers show the order of the subject's visual fixations on the picture during part of a 20-second viewing. Lines between them represent saccades, or rapid movements of eyes from one fixation to the next. Saccades occupy about 10 percent of viewing time.

EYE MOVEMENTS AND VISUAL PERCEPTION

DAVID NOTON AND LAWRENCE STARK

June 1971

The eyes are the most active of all human sense organs. Other sensory receptors, such as the ears, accept rather passively whatever signals come their way, but the eyes are continually moving as they scan and inspect the details of the visual world. The movements of the eyes play an important role in visual perception, and analyzing them can reveal a great deal about the process of perception.

We have recently been recording the eye movements of human subjects as they first inspected unfamiliar objects and then later recognized them. In essence we found that every person has a characteristic way of looking at an object that is familiar to him. For each object he has a preferred path that his eyes tend to follow when he inspects or recognizes the object. Our results suggest a new hypothesis about visual learning and recognition. Before describing and explaining our experiments more fully we shall set the stage by outlining some earlier experiments that have aided the interpretation of our results.

Eye movements are necessary for a physiological reason: detailed visual information can be obtained only through the fovea, the small central area of the retina that has the highest concentration of photoreceptors. Therefore the eyes must move in order to provide information about objects that are to be inspected in any detail (except when the object is quite small in terms of the angle it subtends in the visual field). The eye-movement muscles, under the control of the brain, aim the eyes at points of interest [see "Control Mechanisms of the Eye," by Derek H. Fender, SCIENTIFIC AMERICAN Offprint 187, and "Movements of the Eye," by E. Llewellyn Thomas, SCIENTIFIC AMERICAN Offprint 516].

During normal viewing of stationary objects the eyes alternate between fixations, when they are aimed at a fixed point in the visual field, and rapid movements called saccades. Each saccade leads to a new fixation on a different point in the visual field. Typically there are two or three saccades per second. The movements are so fast that they occupy only about 10 percent of the viewing time.

Visual learning and recognition involve storing and retrieving memories. By way of the lens, the retina and the optic nerve, nerve cells in the visual cortex of the brain are activated and an image of the object being viewed is formed there. (The image is of course in the form of neural activity and is quite unlike the retinal image of the object.) The memory system of the brain must contain an internal representation of every object that is to be recognized. Learning or becoming familiar with an object is the process of constructing this representation. Recognition of an object when it is encountered again is the process of matching it with its internal representation in the memory system.

A certain amount of controversy surrounds the question of whether visual recognition is a parallel, one-step process or a serial, step-by-step one. Psychologists of the Gestalt school have maintained that objects are recognized as wholes, without any need for analysis into component parts. This argument implies that the internal representation of each object is a unitary whole that is matched with the object in a single operation. More recently other psychologists have proposed that the internal representation is a piecemeal affair—an assemblage of parts or features. During recognition the features are matched serially with the features of the object step by step. Successful matching of all the features completes recognition.

The serial-recognition hypothesis is supported mainly by the results of experiments that measure the time taken by a subject to recognize different objects. Typically the subject scans an array of objects (usually abstract figures) looking for a previously memorized "target" object. The time he spends considering each object (either recognizing it as a target object or rejecting it as being different) is measured. That time is normally quite short, but it can be measured in various ways with adequate accuracy. Each object is small enough to be recognized with a single fixation, so that eye movements do not contribute to the time spent on recognition.

Experiments of this kind yield two general results. First, it is found that on the average the subject takes longer to recognize a target object than he does to reject a nontarget object. That is the result to be expected if objects are recognized serially, feature by feature. When an object is compared mentally with the internal representation of the target object, a nontarget object will fail to match some feature of the internal representation and will be rejected without further checking of features, whereas target objects will be checked on all features. The result seems inconsistent with the Gestalt hypothesis of a holistic internal representation matched with the object in a single operation. Presumably in such an operation the subject would take no longer to recognize an object than he would to reject it.

A second result is obtained by varying the complexity of the memorized target object. It is found that the subject takes longer to recognize complex target objects than to recognize simple ones. This result too is consistent with the serial-recognition hypothesis, since more features must be checked in the more complex object. By the same token the result also appears to be inconsistent with the Gestalt hypothesis.

It would be incorrect to give the impression that the serial nature of object recognition is firmly established to the exclusion of the unitary concept advanced by Gestalt psychologists. They have shown convincingly that there is indeed some "primitive unity" to an object, so that the object can often be singled out as a separate entity even before true recognition begins. Moreover, some of the recognition-time experiments described above provide evidence, at least with very simple objects, that as an object becomes well known its internal representation becomes more holistic and the recognition process correspondingly becomes more parallel. Nonetheless, the weight of evidence seems to support the serial hypothesis, at least for objects that are not notably simple and familiar.

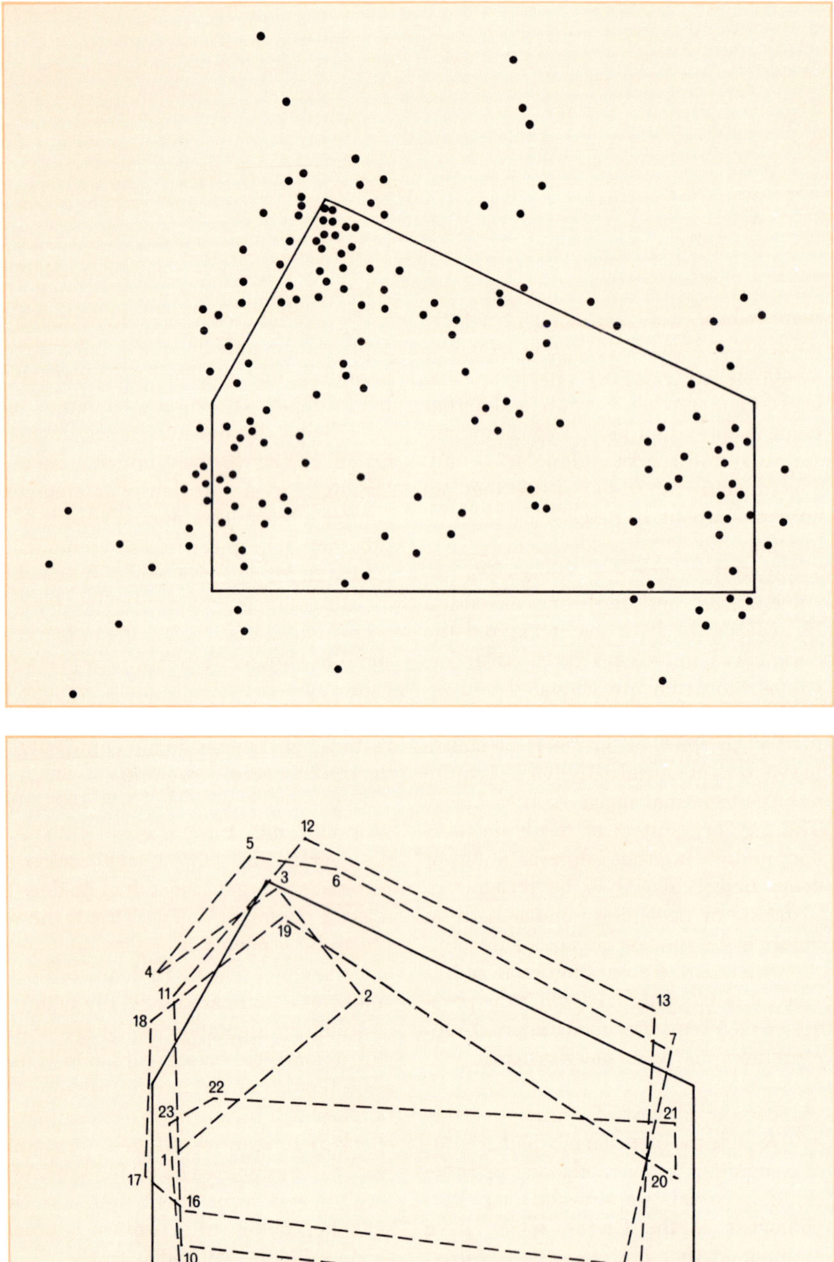

IMPORTANCE OF ANGLES as features that the brain employs in memorizing and recognizing an object was apparent in experiments by Leonard Zusne and Kenneth M. Michels at Purdue University. They recorded fixations while subjects looked at drawings of polygons for eight seconds. At top is one of the polygons; the dots indicate the fixations of seven subjects. Sequence of fixations by one subject in an eight-second viewing appears at bottom.

If the internal representation of an object in memory is an assemblage of features, two questions naturally suggest themselves. First, what are these features, that is, what components of an object does the brain select as the key items for identifying the object? Second, how are such features integrated and related to one another to form the complete internal representation of the object? The study of eye movements during visual perception yields considerable evidence on these two points.

In experiments relating to the first question the general approach is to present to a subject a picture or another object that is sufficiently large and close to the eyes so that it cannot all be registered on the foveas in one fixation. For example, a picture 35 centimeters wide and 100 centimeters from the eyes subtends a horizontal angle of 20 degrees at each eye—roughly the angle subtended by a page of this magazine held at arm's length. This is far wider than the one to two degrees of visual field that are brought to focus on the fovea.

Under these conditions the subject must move his eyes and look around the picture, fixating each part he wants to see clearly. The assumption is that he looks mainly at the parts of the picture he regards as being its features; they are the parts that hold for him the most information about the picture. Features are tentatively located by peripheral vision and then fixated directly for detailed inspection. (It is important to note that in these experiments and in the others we shall describe the subject is given only general instructions, such as "Just look at the pictures," or even no instructions at all. More specific instructions, requiring him to inspect and describe some specific aspect of the picture, usually result in appropriately directed fixations, as might be expected.)

When subjects freely view simple pictures, such as line drawings, under these conditions, it is found that their fixations tend to cluster around the angles of the picture. For example, Leonard Zusne and Kenneth M. Michels performed an experiment of this type at Purdue University, using as pictures line drawings of simple polygons [*see illustration on opposite page*]. From the fixations made by their subjects in viewing such figures it is clear that the angles of the drawings attracted the eyes most strongly.

Our tentative conclusion is that, at least with such line drawings, the angles are the principal features the brain employs to store and recognize the drawing. Certainly angles would be an efficient choice for features. In 1954 Fred Attneave III of the University of Oregon pointed out that the most informative parts of a line drawing are the angles and sharp curves. To illustrate his argument he presented a picture that was obtained by selecting the 38 points of greatest curvature in a picture of a sleeping cat and joining the points with straight lines [*see top illustration at right*]. The result is clearly recognizable.

Additional evidence that angles and sharp curves are features has come from electrophysiologists who have investigated the activity of individual brain cells. For example, in the late 1950's Jerome Y. Lettvin, H. R. Maturana, W. S. McCulloch and W. H. Pitts of the Massachusetts Institute of Technology found angle-detecting neurons in the frog's retina. More recently David H. Hubel and Torsten N. Wiesel of the Harvard Medical School have extended this result to cats and monkeys (whose angle-detecting cells are in the visual cortex rather than the retina). And recordings obtained from the human visual cortex by Elwin Marg of the University of California at Berkeley give preliminary indications that these results can be extended to man.

Somewhat analogous results have been obtained with pictures more complex than simple line drawings. It is not surprising that in such cases the features are also more complex. As a result no formal description of them has been achieved. Again, however, high information content seems to be the criterion. Norman H. Mackworth and A. J. Morandi made a series of recordings at Harvard University of fixations by subjects viewing two complex photographs. They concluded that the fixations were concentrated on unpredictable or unusual details, in particular on unpredictable contours. An unpredictable contour is one that changes direction rapidly and irregularly and therefore has a high information content.

We conclude, then, that angles and other informative details are the features selected by the brain for remembering and recognizing an object. The next question concerns how these features are integrated by the brain into a whole—the internal representation—so that one sees the object as a whole, as an object rather than an unconnected sequence of features. Once again useful evidence comes from recordings of eye movements. Just as study of the locations of fixations indicated the probable nature of the features, so analysis of the order of fixations suggests a format for the interconnection of features into the overall internal representation.

The illustration below shows the fixations made by a subject while viewing a photograph of a bust of the Egyptian queen Nefertiti. It is one of a series of recordings made by Alfred L. Yarbus of the Institute for Problems of Information Transmission of the Academy of Sciences of the U.S.S.R. The illustration

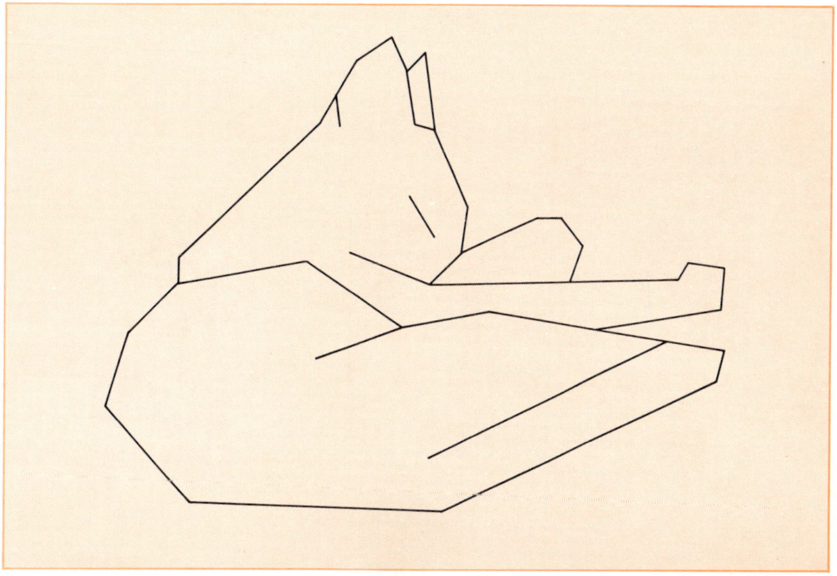

SHARP CURVES are also important as features for visual identification, as shown by Fred Attneave III of the University of Oregon in a picture made by selecting the 38 points of greatest curvature in a picture of a sleeping cat and joining them with straight lines, thus eliminating all other curves. The result is still easily recognizable, suggesting that points of sharp curvature provide highly useful information to the brain in visual perception.

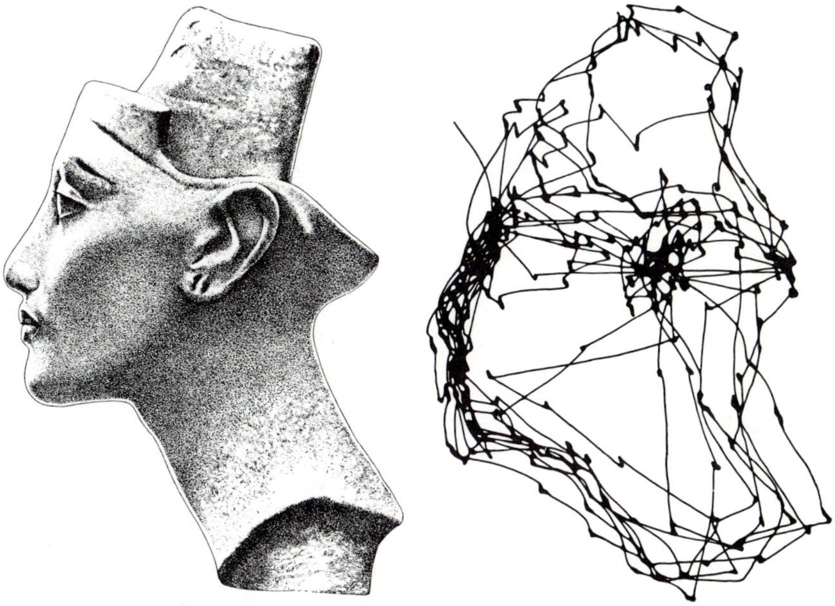

REGULARITIES OF EYE MOVEMENT appear in a recording of a subject viewing a photograph of a bust of Queen Nefertiti. At left is a drawing of what the subject saw; at right are his eye movements as recorded by Alfred L. Yarbus of the Institute for Problems of Information Transmission in Moscow. The eyes seem to visit the features of the head cyclically, following fairly regular pathways, rather than crisscrossing the picture at random.

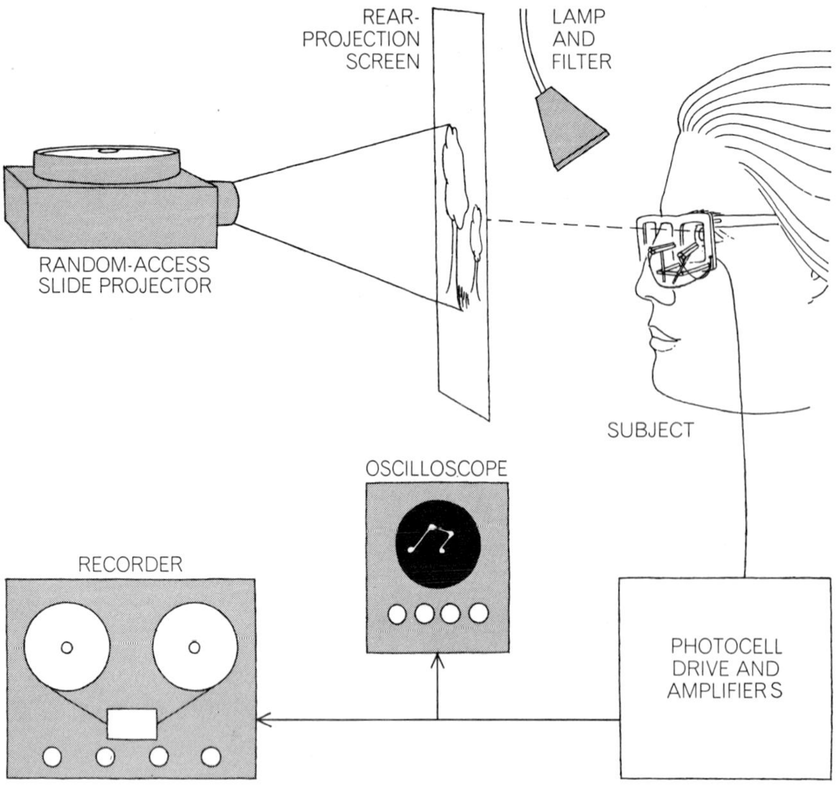

EXPERIMENTAL PROCEDURE employed by the authors is depicted schematically. The subject viewed pictures displayed on a rear-projection screen by a random-access slide projector. Diffuse infrared light was shined on his eyes; his eye movements were recorded by photocells, mounted on a spectacle frame, that detected reflections of the infrared light from one eyeball. Eye movements were displayed on oscilloscope and also recorded on tape.

shows clearly an important aspect of eye movement during visual perception, namely that the order of the fixations is by no means random. The lines representing the saccades form broad bands from point to point and do not crisscross the picture at random as would be expected if the eyes visited the different features repetitively in a random order. It appears that fixation on any one feature, such as Nefertiti's eye, is usually followed by fixation on the same next feature, such as her mouth. The overall record seems to indicate a series of cycles; in each cycle the eyes visit the main features of the picture, following rather regular pathways from feature to feature.

Recently at the University of California at Berkeley we have developed a hypothesis about visual perception that predicts and explains this apparent regularity of eye movement. Essentially we propose that in the internal representation or memory of the picture the features are linked together in sequence by the memory of the eye movement required to look from one feature to the next. Thus the eyes would tend to move from feature to feature in a fixed order, scanning the picture.

Most of Yarbus' recordings are summaries of many fixations and do not contain complete information on the ordering of the fixations. Thus the regularities of eye movements predicted by our hypothesis could not be definitely confirmed from his data. To eliminate this constraint and to subject our hypothesis to a more specific test we recently made a new series of recordings of eye movements during visual perception.

Our subjects viewed line drawings of simple objects and abstract symbols as we measured their eye movements (using photocells to determine the movements of the "white" of the eye) and recorded them on magnetic tape [see illustration above]. We thereby obtained a permanent record of the order of fixations made by the subjects and could play it back later at a lower speed, analyzing it at length for cycles and other regularities of movement. As in the earlier experiments, the drawings were fairly large and close to the subject's eyes, a typical drawing subtending about 20 degrees at the eye. In addition we drew the pictures with quite thin lines and displayed them with an underpowered slide projector, throwing a dim image on a screen that was fully exposed to the ordinary light in the laboratory. In this way we produced an image of low visibility and could be sure that the subject would have to look directly (foveally) at each feature that interested him, thus revealing to our recording equipment the locus of his attention.

Our initial results amply confirmed the previous impression of cycles of eye movements. We found that when a subject viewed a picture under these conditions, his eyes usually scanned it following—intermittently but repeatedly—a fixed path, which we have termed his "scan path" for that picture [*see illustration on opposite page*]. The occurrences of the scan path were separated by periods in which the fixations were ordered in a less regular manner.

Each scan path was characteristic of a given subject viewing a given picture. A subject had a different scan path for every picture he viewed, and for a given picture each subject had a different scan path. A typical scan path for our pictures consisted of about 10 fixations and lasted for from three to five seconds. Scan paths usually occupied from 25 to 35 percent of the subject's viewing time, the rest being devoted to less regular eye movements.

It must be added that scan paths were not always observed. Certain pictures (one of a telephone, for example) seemed often not to provoke a repetitive response, although no definite common characteristic could be discerned in such pictures. The commonest reaction, however, was to exhibit a scan path. It was interesting now for us to refer back to the earlier recordings by Zusne and Michels, where we observed scan paths that had previously passed unnoticed. For instance, in the illustration on page 220 fixations No. 4 through No. 11 and No. 11 through No. 18 appear to be two occurrences of a scan path. They are identical, even to the inclusion of the small reverse movement in the lower right-hand corner of the figure.

This demonstration of the existence of scan paths strengthened and clarified our ideas about visual perception. In accordance with the serial hypothesis, we assume that the internal representation of an object in the memory system is an assemblage of features. To this we add a crucial hypothesis: that the features are assembled in a format we have termed a "feature ring" [*see illustration on page 224*]. The ring is a sequence of sensory and motor memory traces, alternately recording a feature of the object and the eye movement required to reach the next feature. The feature ring establishes a fixed ordering of features and eye movements, corresponding to a scan path on the object.

Our hypothesis states that as a subject views an object for the first time and becomes familiar with it he scans it with his eyes and develops a scan path for it. During this time he lays down the memory traces of the feature ring, which records both the sensory activity and the motor activity. When he subsequently encounters the same object again, he recognizes it by matching it with the feature ring, which is its internal representation in his memory. Matching consists in verifying the successive features and carrying out the intervening eye movements, as directed by the feature ring.

This hypothesis not only offers a plausible format for the internal representation of objects—a format consistent with the existence of scan paths—but also has certain other attractive features. For example, it enables us to draw an interesting analogy between perception and behavior, in which both are seen to involve the alternation of sensory and motor activity. In the case of behavior, such as the performance of a learned sequence of activities, the sensing of a situation alternates with motor activity designed to bring about an expected new situation. In the case of perception (or, more specifically, recognition) of an object the verification of features alternates with movement of the eyes to the expected new feature.

The feature-ring hypothesis also makes a verifiable prediction concerning eye movements during recognition: The successive eye movements and feature verifications, being directed by the feature ring, should trace out the same scan path that was established for the object during the initial viewing. Confirmation of the prediction would further strengthen the case for the hypothesis. Since the prediction is subject to experimental confirmation we designed an experiment to test it.

The experiment had two phases, which we called the learning phase and the recognition phase. (We did not, of

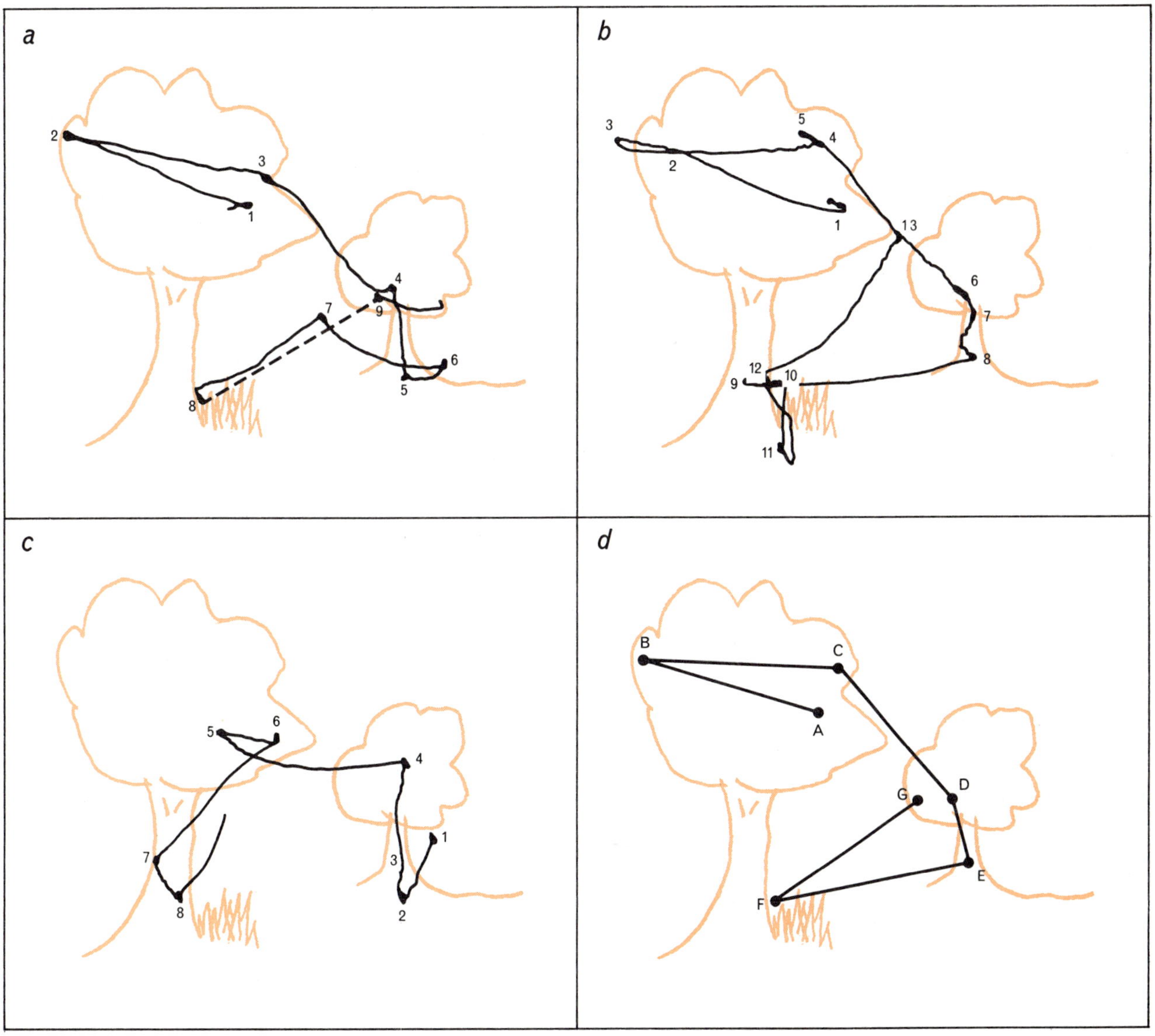

REGULAR PATTERN of eye movement by a given subject viewing a given picture was termed the subject's "scan path" for that picture. Two of five observed occurrences of one subject's scan path as he looked at a simple drawing of trees for 75 seconds are shown here (*a*, *b*). The dotted line between fixations 8 and 9 of *a* indicates that the recording of this saccade was interrupted by a blink. Less regular eye movements made between these appearances of the scan path are at *c*. Subject's scan path is idealized at *d*.

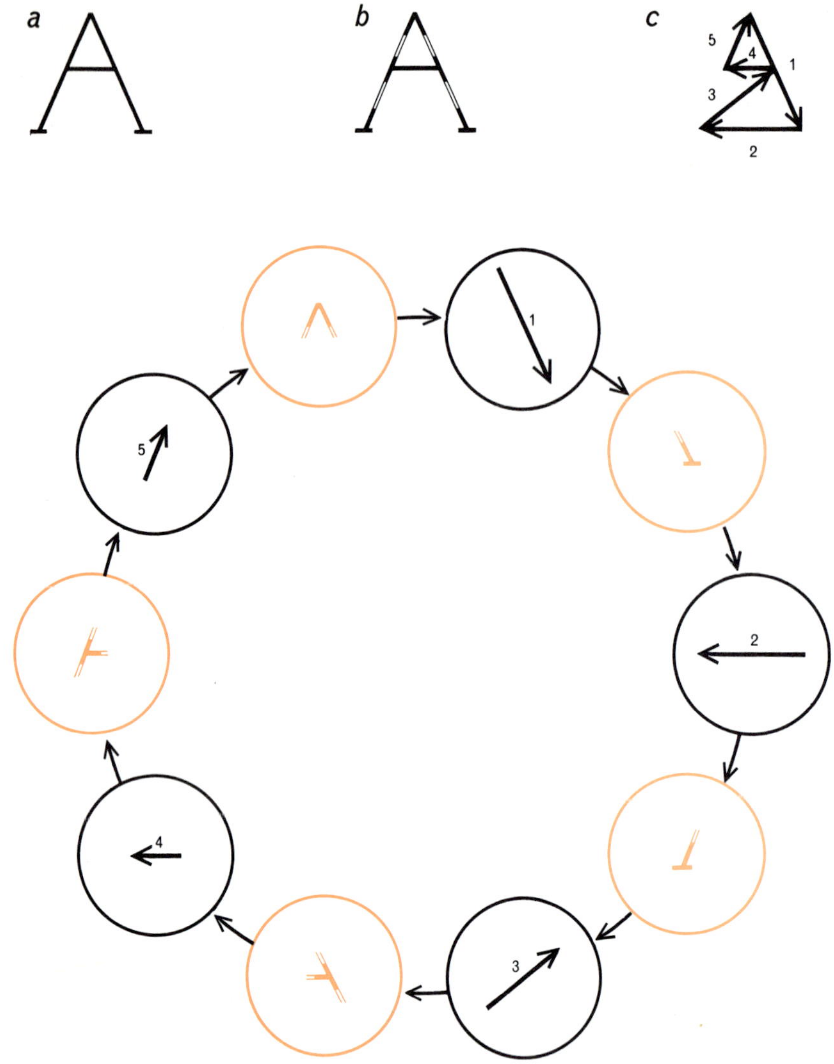

FEATURE RING is proposed by the authors as a format for the internal representation of an object. The object (*a*) is identified by its principal features (*b*) and is represented in the memory by them and by the recollection of the scan path (*c*) whereby they were viewed. The feature ring therefore consists of sensory memory traces (*color*) recording the features and motor memory traces (*black*) of the eye movements from one feature to the next.

course, use any such suggestive terms in briefing the subjects; as before, they were simply told to look at the pictures.) In the learning phase the subject viewed five pictures he had not seen before, each for 20 seconds. The pictures and viewing conditions were similar to those of the first experiment. For the recognition phase, which followed immediately, the five pictures were mixed with five others the subject had not seen. This was to make the recognition task less easy. The set of 10 pictures was then presented to the subject three times in random order; he had five seconds to look at each picture. Eye movements were recorded during both the learning phase and the recognition phase.

When we analyzed the recordings, we were pleased to find that to a large extent our predictions were confirmed. Scan paths appeared in the subject's eye movements during the learning phase, and during the recognition phase his first few eye movements on viewing a picture (presumably during the time he was recognizing it) usually followed the same scan path he had established for that picture during the learning phase [*see illustration on opposite page*]. In terms of our hypothesis the subject was forming a feature ring during the learning-phase occurrences of the scan path; in the recognition phase he was matching the feature ring with the picture, following the scan path dictated by the feature ring.

An additional result of this experiment was to demonstrate that different subjects have different scan paths for a given picture and, conversely, that a given subject has different scan paths for different pictures [*see illustration on page 226*]. These findings help to discount certain alternative explanations that might be advanced to account for the occurrence of scan paths. The fact that a subject has quite different scan paths for different pictures suggests that the scan paths are not the result of some fixed habit of eye movement, such as reading Chinese vertically, brought to each picture but rather that they come from a more specific source, such as learned feature rings. Similarly, the differences among subjects in scan paths used for a given picture suggest that the scan paths do not result from peripheral feature detectors that control eye movements independent of the recognition process, since these detectors might be expected to operate in much the same way in all subjects.

Although the results of the second experiment provided considerable support for our ideas on visual perception, certain things remain unexplained. For example, sometimes no scan path was observed during the learning phase. Even when we did find a scan path, it did not always reappear in the recognition phase. On the average the appropriate scan path appeared in about 65 percent of the recognition-phase viewings. This is a rather strong result in view of the many possible paths around each picture, but it leaves 35 percent of the viewings, when no scan path appeared, in need of explanation.

Probably the basic idea of the feature ring needs elaboration. If provision were made for memory traces recording other eye movements between features not adjacent in the ring, and if the original ring represented the preferred and habitual order of processing rather than the inevitable order, the occasional substitution of an abnormal order for the

RECURRENCE OF SCAN PATH during recognition of an object is predicted by the feature-ring hypothesis. A subject viewed the adaptation of Klee's drawing (*a*). A scan path appeared while he was familiarizing himself with the picture (*b*, *c*). It also appeared (*d*, *e*) during the recognition phase each time he identified the picture as he viewed a sequence of familiar and unfamiliar scenes depicted in similar drawings. This particular experimental subject's scan path for this particular picture is presented in idealized form at *f*.

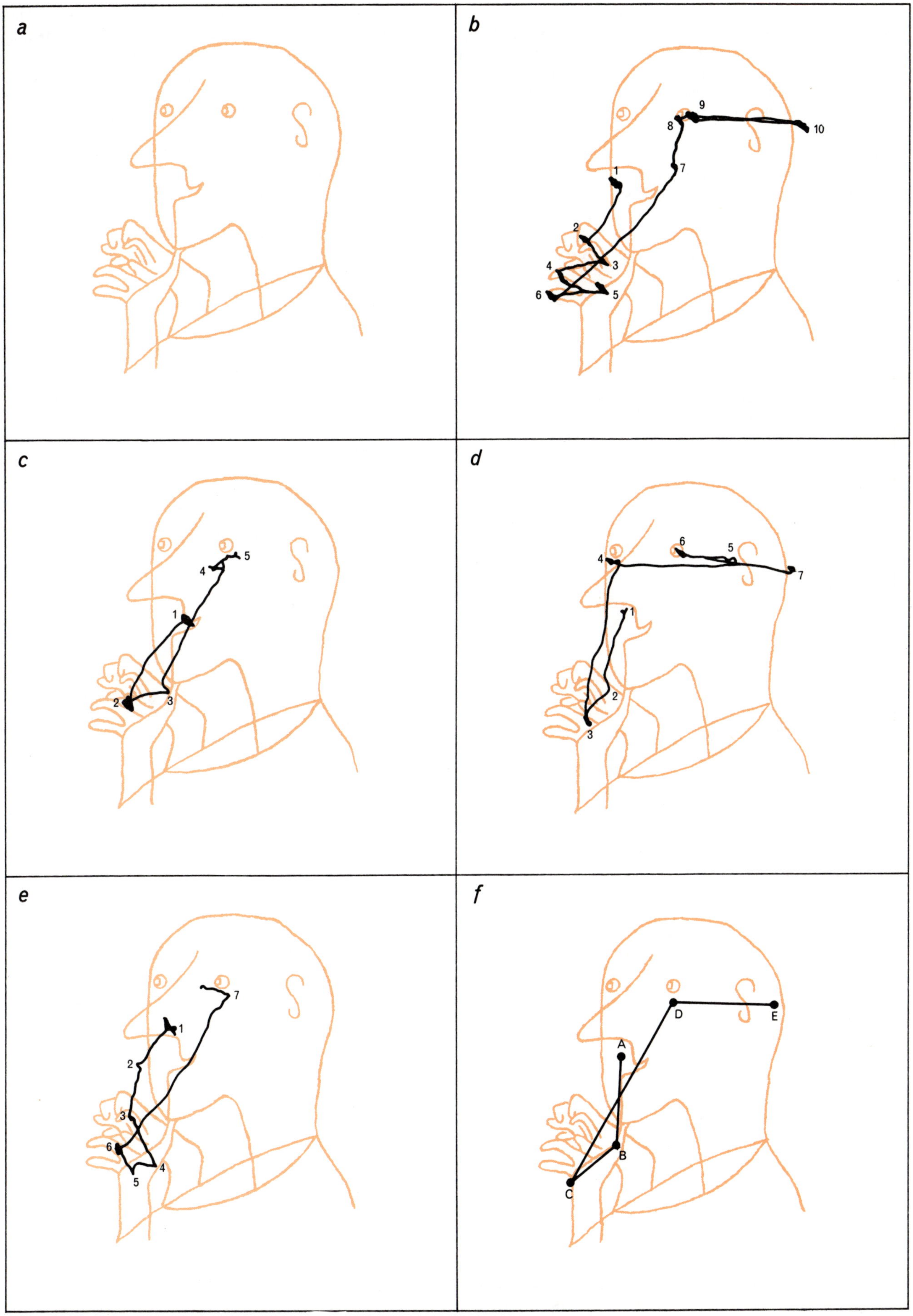
a
b
1
2
3
4
5
6
7
8
9
10
c
1
2
3
4
5
d
1
2
3
4
5
6
7
e
1
2
3
4
5
6
7
f
A
B
C
D
E

scan path would be explained [*see top illustration on opposite page*].

It must also be remembered that the eye-movement recordings in our experiments were made while the subjects viewed pictures that were rather large and close to their eyes, forcing them to look around in the picture to see its features clearly. In the more normal viewing situation, with a picture or an object small enough to be wholly visible with a single fixation, no eye movements are necessary for recognition. We assume that in such a case the steps in perception are parallel up to the point where an image of the object is formed in the visual cortex and that thereafter (as would seem evident from the experiments on recognition time) the matching of the image and the internal representation is carried out serially, feature by feature. Now, however, we must postulate instead of eye movements from feature to feature a sequence of internal shifts of attention, processing the features serially and following the scan path dictated by the feature ring. Thus each motor memory trace in the feature ring records a shift of attention that can be executed either externally, as an eye movement, or internally, depending on the extent of the shift required.

In this connection several recordings made by Lloyd Kaufman and Whitman Richards at M.I.T. are of interest. Their subjects viewed simple figures, such as a drawing of a cube, that could be taken in with a single fixation. At 10 randomly chosen moments the subject was asked

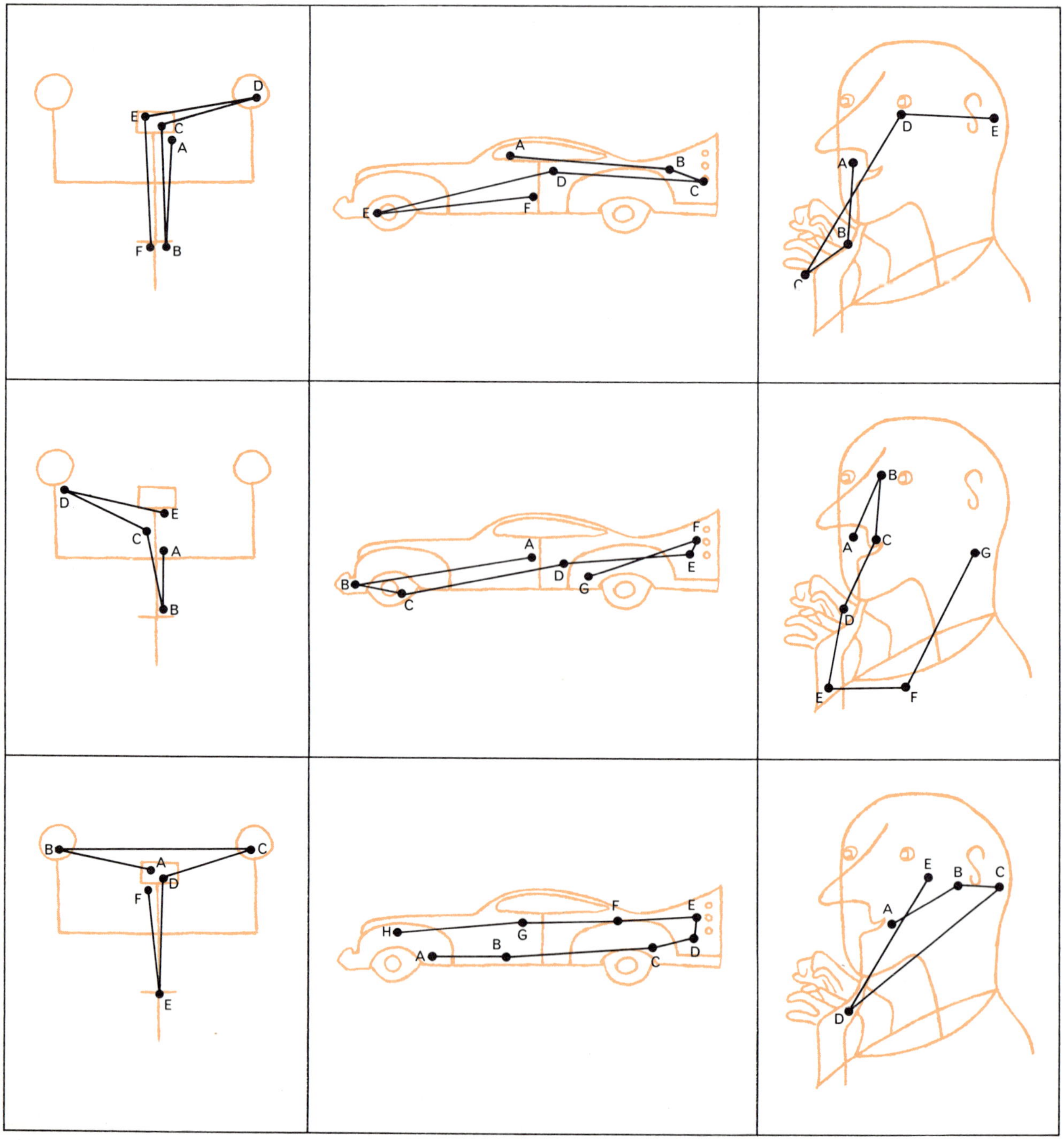

VARIETY IN SCAN PATHS is shown for three subjects and three pictures. Each horizontal row depicts the scan paths used by one subject for the three pictures. Vertically one sees how the scan paths of the three subjects for any one picture also varied widely.

to indicate where he thought he was looking. His answer presumably showed what part of the picture he was attending to visually. His actual fixation point was then recorded at another 10 randomly selected moments [*see bottom illustration at right*]. The results suggest that the subject's attention moved around the picture but his fixation remained fairly steady near the center of the picture. This finding is consistent with the view that smaller objects too are processed serially, by internal shifts of attention, even though little or no eye movement is involved.

It is important to note, however, that neither these results nor ours prove that recognition of objects and pictures is necessarily a serial process under normal conditions, when the object is not so large and close as to force serial processing by eye movements. The experiments on recognition time support the serial hypothesis, but it cannot yet be regarded as being conclusively established. In our experiments we provided a situation that forced the subject to view and recognize pictures serially with eye movements, thus revealing the order of feature processing, and we assumed that the results would be relevant to recognition under more normal conditions. Our results suggest a more detailed explanation of serial processing—the feature ring producing the scan path—but this explanation remains conditional on the serial hypothesis.

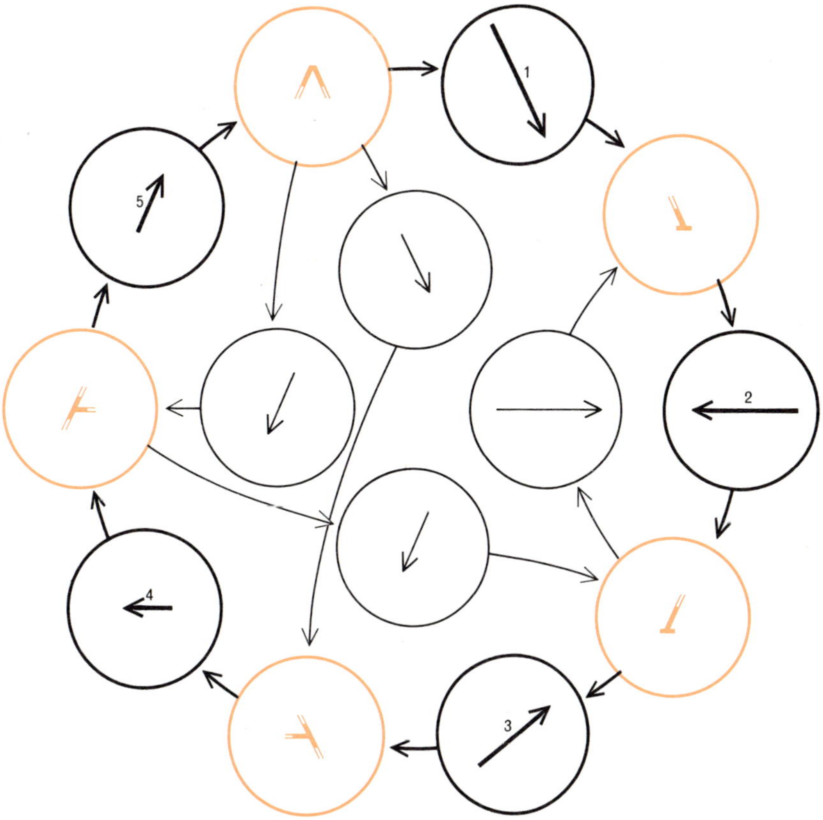

MODIFIED FEATURE RING takes into account less regular eye movements that do not conform to scan path. Several movements, which appeared in 35 percent of recognition viewings, are in center of this ring. Outside ring, consisting of sensory (*color*) and motor memory traces (*black*), represents scan path and remains preferred order of processing.

In sum, we believe the experimental results so far obtained support three main conclusions concerning the visual recognition of objects and pictures. First, the internal representation or memory of an object is a piecemeal affair: an assemblage of features or, more strictly, of memory traces of features; during recognition the internal representation is matched serially with the object, feature by feature. Second, the features of an object are the parts of it (such as the angles and curves of line drawings) that yield the most information. Third, the memory traces recording the features are assembled into the complete internal representation by being connected by other memory traces that record the shifts of attention required to pass from feature to feature, either with eye movements or with internal shifts of attention; the attention shifts connect the features in a preferred order, forming a feature ring and resulting in a scan path, which is usually followed when verifying the features during recognition.

Clearly these conclusions indicate a distinctly serial conception of visual learning and recognition. In the trend to look toward serial concepts to advance the understanding of visual perception one can note the influence of current work in computerized pattern recognition, where the serial approach has long been favored. Indeed, computer and information-processing concepts, usually serial in nature, are having an increasing influence on brain research in general.

Our own thoughts on visual recognition offer a case in point. We have developed them simultaneously with an analogous system for computerized pattern recognition. Although the system has not been implemented in working form, a somewhat similar scheme is being used in the visual-recognition system of a robot being developed by a group at the Stanford Research Institute. We believe this fruitful interaction between biology and engineering can be expected to continue, to the enrichment of both.

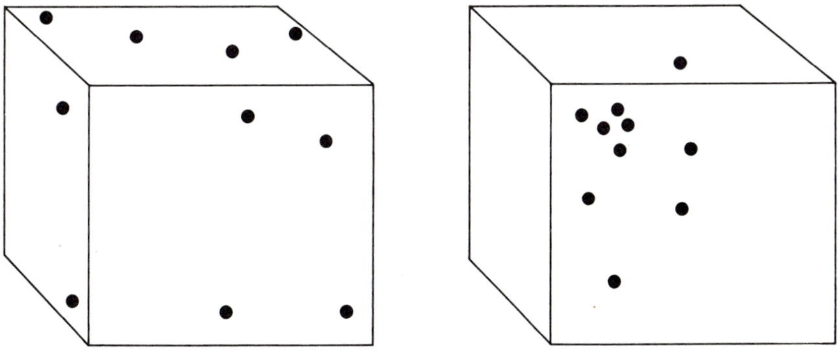

INTERNAL SHIFTS OF ATTENTION apparently replace eye movements in processing of objects small enough to be viewed with single fixation. A subject's attention, represented by statements of where he thought he was looking, moved around picture (*left*), whereas measured fixation point (*right*) remained relatively stationary. Illustration is based on work by Lloyd Kaufman and Whitman Richards at the Massachusetts Institute of Technology.

V

ILLUSIONS AND CONSTANCIES

Figure 1. Complementary test patterns are used to demonstrate the color changes that take place when a negative afterimage of a brightly colored stimulus is formed on the retina. A negative afterimage of the pattern above resembles the pattern below, and vice versa. A positive afterimage of either test pattern retains the colors of the original. Cover one pattern when looking at the other. [From "Afterimages," by G. S. Brindley, *Scientific American*, October 1963.]

V

ILLUSIONS AND CONSTANCIES

INTRODUCTION

The study of feature detection is providing analytic tools for an approach to perception in which neurological, psychological, and simulation techniques complement each other. As yet, however, this approach provides only the beginning of an understanding of the classic problems of perception. This section is concerned with attempts to solve some of these problems.

Crombie's article in Section I indicates the long history of concern about perception. He discusses the vicissitudes of the discovery of the true image-forming properties of the optics of the eye. Identification of the optical image of an object with its percept—the notion that the image should resemble the percept—created a problem that persisted for centuries; the great physicist Johannes Kepler shelved the problem by leaving it to the natural philosophers. As Crombie comments, the science of vision progressed by asking answerable questions about the anatomy and the physiology of sensory systems. Crombie's account of the curious history of the retinal-image concept can give us an insight into the classic problems of perception. Most of them, like that of the retinal image, derive from implicit assumptions that identify perceived qualities with particular properties of stimulation. Under some circumstances, the identification seems to hold, and under others, to fail, thereby creating a puzzle. The illusions of vision constitute an important set of examples that illustrate this point.

ILLUSIONS

Line segments of equal length presented side by side in an otherwise blank field will appear to be equal, but the same lines presented side by side in a context of other lines may not (see the illusion figures in the articles in this section by Kolers and Gregory). But why should such lines ever have been expected to appear to be of equal length in different contexts? Only because of the implicit assumption that equal angular distances across the retina of the observer should correspond to equal perceived distances, irrespective of the context.

Two colored patches presented side by side may appear to be of the same hue, but if one patch is surrounded by an annulus of another color, it will appear to differ in hue from the other patch (see Wallach's article in this section). In the past, this contrast effect was regarded as illusory, because of the supposition that inputs to localized portions of the retina are processed independently of inputs to other portions.

For every illusion, we may find an assumption about an expected correspondence between stimulus and percept. When an illusion is not understood, we should immediately suspect that we do not yet have an adequate understanding of the perceptual mechanisms that prescribe the relation between the percept and the conditions for perceiving.

Some writers say that illusions are examples of nonveridical or incorrect perceptions of objects, whereas normal perception is veridical. Such statements must be regarded as shorthand for saying that the world may look differently under certain circumstances of observation than it does under certain other, perhaps more typical, circumstances. There is simply no test of veridicality, if the term is intended to mean some sort of identity between the object and its appearance. The descriptions of the two—physical on one hand, behavioral on the other—cannot be directly compared.

CONSTANCIES

Perceptual constancies are similar to illusions in the sense that they also violate simple assumptions of correspondence between stimulus and percept. They differ, however, in that they seem to demonstrate correspondence between a percept and its object despite the lack of such a correspondence between the percept and the intermediary stimulation of a receptor organ. Let us consider, for example, the phenomenon of size constancy: Why should retinal images subtending different angles on the retina result in perceptions of objects having the same apparent size? (See Neisser's article in this section.) Taken by itself, this discrepancy might be called an illusion, yet the outcome appears to keep the percept in proper size correspondence with the object. The rule of size constancy says that perceived size, corresponding to a given retinal image, increases with apparent distance. Because this rule is the inverse of the geometrical rule that the size of the retinal image decreases with the distance of the object that produces it, size correspondence is maintained, at least over the range in which apparent distance increases proportionally with geometrical distance.

In brightness constancy (see "The Perception of Neutral Colors," by Hans Wallach), the contrast illusion acts to maintain the constancy of achromatic color; and color (hue) constancy is an accompaniment of color contrast. The brightness and color constancies are, in fact, among the most impressive, because the underlying mechanisms serve to maintain uniform appearances over an enormous range of intensity and despite wide variations in the spectral composition of the illuminant.

As is evident from these examples, illusion and constancy are processes that go hand in hand in the relation between objects, stimuli, and percepts. When stimulus and percept do not correspond, the result is defined as an illusion; but when such noncorrespondence is accompanied by a correspondence between object and percept, the outcome is referred to as a constancy. In this sense, the relation between illusion and constancy is complementary.

Constancies depend upon a kind of stimulus equivalence, because diverse stimuli yield the same percept. Unlike the problem of equivalence of form, some of the constancies have seemed amenable to fairly simple rules.

Size Constancy. Explanations of size constancy range from the old idea of an invariant relation between the size of the retinal image and apparent distance (discussed by Gregory and by Kaufman and Rock in this section and by Bower in Section VI) to James Gibson's assertion of an invariant relation between object size and texture size (discussed by Ulric Neisser in his article "The Processes of Vision"). Richard L. Gregory, in his article "Visual Illusions," explains certain size illusions as the outcome of a size-constancy mechanism in which an apparent difference in distance from the eye (depth) is provided by perspectival cues. In his view, both illusion and constancy are outcomes of the same central process, a process that determines the size of ambiguous stimuli. Lloyd Kaufman and Irvin Rock, in their article "The Moon Illusion," interpret that illusion as an apparent change in size caused by an apparent difference in the distance from the observer of the zenith and horizontal moons.

Apparent distance is influenced by such extravisual information as the convergence angle of the two eyes when they are fixed on a target at some distance (see the article by Crombie in Section I) and also by the output of the accommodative mechanism that adjusts the focus of the retinal image for optimal sharpness. Both of these adjustments of the eyes vary monotonically with the distance of the viewed object from the eye and, consequently, provide further input to size-distance mechanisms, although only over a limited range.

That a purely visual impression is influenced by extraretinal factors has seemed problematic to many thinkers. Consequently, it has been thought that a special learning process must be involved in establishing the connection. George Berkeley, the eighteenth-century philosopher, was one of the first to suppose that spatial qualities learned through touch were responsible for the interpretation of the size of visible objects. Irvin Rock and Charles S. Harris, in their article "Vision and Touch," discuss the possibility that learning about vision may occur through the medium of touch, or, more precisely, the sense of felt position. They argue, on the basis of several sorts of evidence, that when spatial judgments are based upon either visual or tactile information, and the two differ, the visual will tend to dominate. Moreover, there is some evidence that this dominance has an influence that outlasts the duration of the conflicting cues. We shall return to the lasting effects of such conflict—to what is called adaptation to rearranged vision—in the next section.

Depth. It is clear from the articles included in this section that the impression of depth—when depth refers to the perception that one object is in front of or behind another—may be conveyed by many different stimulus conditions. One of these is retinal disparity, a simple result of the geometry of the light rays coming from an object to the eyes, whereby the two retinal images of an object differ slightly in size, shape, and location. When two objects lie at different distances from the eyes, the horizontal distance between their images on the right retina differs from that between their images on the left retina. Such a disparity varies monotonically with the magnitude of the difference in distance of the objects from the eyes, providing the observer with information about their depth in his visual field. Julesz, in his article in Section IV, discusses retinal disparity in conjunction with the production of stereoscopic views, and Ivo Kohler, in his article "Experiments with Goggles," discusses it in connection with chromatic stereoscopy. We may expect that those spatial constancies that depend upon information about depth provided by retinal disparities will be among the most consistent and well ordered of such effects.

In accord with the orderly (and, hence, informative) properties of retinal disparity, single neural units have been discovered in the cortices of cats and monkeys that are maximally excited by particular magnitudes of retinal disparity. These units are of the Hubel-Wiesel type, but their receptive fields differ in position on the two retinas in such manner as to be optimally excited by edges that are either ahead of or behind a frontal surface through the fixation point of the two eyes. They are probably responsible for the exquisite depth discrimination of primates.

Color Constancy. Is it possible to change the appearance of light of constant intensity and wavelength without altering the absorption of the three photopigments of the retina? The change is, in fact, readily produced by contrast. Hans Wallach (see "The Perception of Neutral Colors") demonstrates contrast in a series of experiments that show how the appearance of a disc is altered by changing the light intensity of a surrounding annulus. The brightness of the disc depends largely upon the ratio between its light intensity and that of its surround. The ratio rule can then be used to explain brightness constancy, because the ratio of reflectances of light from adjacent objects is independent of the intensity of the illuminating light over a large range. As a consequence, an object seen against a background should not change its appearance, despite changes in the intensity of light it reflects to the eyes of an observer.

Contrast may be explained in terms of the simple "on–off" receptive fields of the ganglion cells of the retina, which were described in Section III by Miller, Ratliff, and Hartline, by Hubel, and by Michael. The threshold of response of these ganglion cells in the retina is not related to an absolute of illumination, but rather to the light level relative to the surrounding or average illumination.

Consider now the possibility that there are three types of ganglion cells—one innervated by the red mechanism, another by the green, and a third that receives its input primarily from blue cones. Each of these color-coded ganglion cells will then have center and surround properties that are dependent upon the wavelength of the light stimulus. Neurophysiologists have recently found several types of such color-coded neurons; some of these were described in Section III by Michael. Many of these units show reduced or enhanced activity following adaptation to colored lights. For certain types of complex color-coded cells, exposure of the region surrounding the cell is associated with inhibition, while the central region of the cell's receptive field is excitatory. When properly color-coded, such cells are affected by a red–green border in much the same way that achromatic on–off

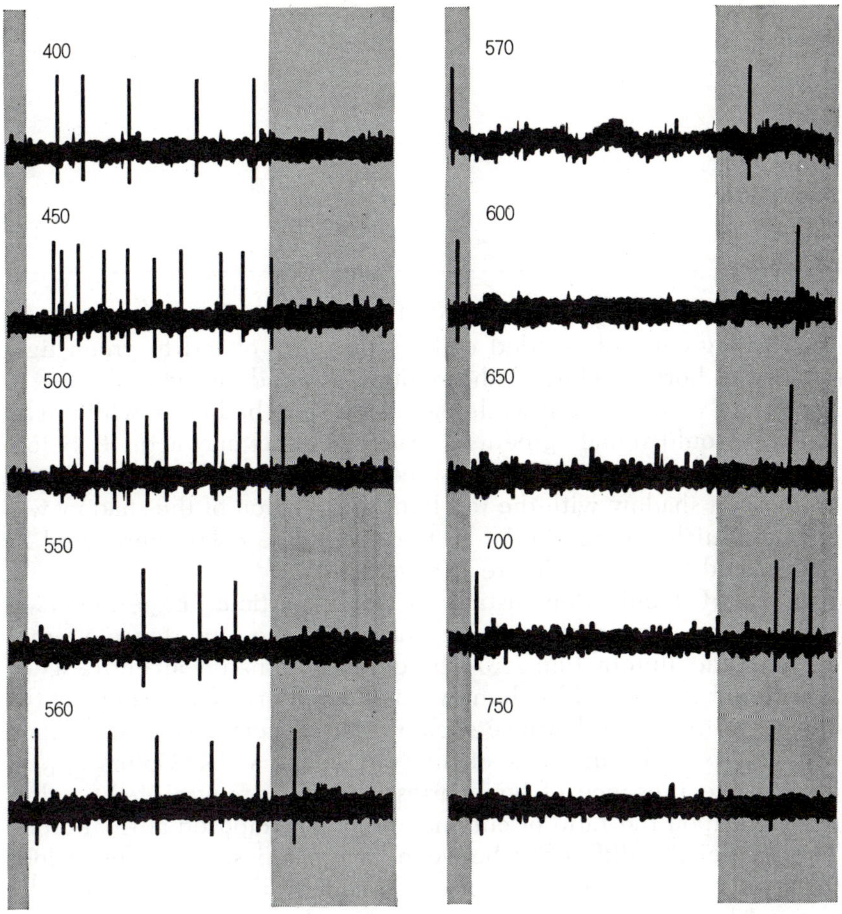

Figure 2. Ganglion-cell response varies with the wavelength of the stimulus, a half-second flash of light (*white area*). At short wavelengths (*left*) there is an "on" response, a burst of impulses during illumination. At long wavelengths (*right*) there is an "off" response instead. (Spikes at left side of some long-wavelength records are from preceding stimuli.) [From "Three-Pigment Color Vision," by Edward F. MacNichol, Jr., *Scientific American*, December 1964.]

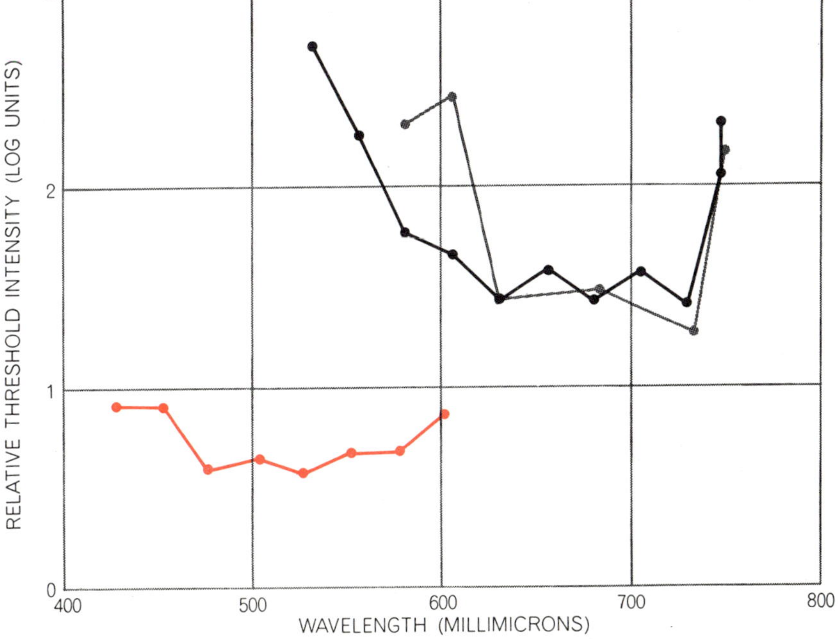

Figure 3. Threshold curves show the intensity necessary to elicit "on" and "off" responses from a ganglion cell at different wavelengths. The "on" response (*color*) was obtained at short wavelengths, the "off" (*black*) at long wavelengths. In the overlap region the "off" response required a higher-intensity stimulus. The gray curves traces the inhibition threshold. [From "Three-Pigment Color Vision," by Edward F. MacNichol, Jr., *Scientific American*, December 1964.]

cells are affected by a black–white border. The relevant stimulus for such red–green color-coded cells is the ratio of red to green light across the border. Thus, if the region surrounding the cell were illuminated with red light while the inside were bathed in white light, the cell would signal "greenish." Such an effect may actually be observed if we illuminate a white screen with red and white lights, and then cast a shadow with the red light. The region of the shadow will appear bluish green, similar to the afterimage colors generated by the colored display in Figure 1 (page 230).

Edwin H. Land's demonstrations (see his article "Experiments in Color Vision") provide a striking example of the importance of ratios of chromatic illumination across borders. Illuminating an entire scene in pale red, green, or blue light will not much distort the colors of the objects in the scene because such a diffuse effect acts equally upon the centers and surrounds of all color-coded cells. Colors appear only in the presence of boundaries, and the strength of the colors depends upon the ratio of chromatic lights juxtaposed at the border. The greater the difference between two juxtaposed spectral colors, the stronger will be the colors signalled by the appropriate color channels. It is this ratio principle that underlies Land's coordinate system, which is shown on page 291). Thus, to a first approximation, when the ratio of neural activities in the three color channels are equal for two colored areas, these areas will appear equal even if their surrounds appear different.

Hyperconstancy. Ivo Kohler's article "Experiments with Goggles" deals with the effects of prolonged exposure to systematically atypical conditions of stimulation. The gradual reduction and (in some cases) elimination of the distortions of normal vision that are produced by prisms add a new dimension to our consideration of the variables that determine perception. Because perception of a stimulus, distorted by optical means and, hence, yielding an erroneous percept, tends to return to its normal undistorted appearance, an adaptive mechanism of some sort must maintain constancy despite perturbations.

Observations on color adaptation showed long ago that sensitivity to hue varies with the duration of the exposure of the eye to light—a presumed result of the depletion of photosensitive pigments. Only in recent years, however, have observations of adaptation to more complex stimuli been taken seriously. As Kohler explains, adaptation to the prismatically induced color fringes cannot be subsumed under ordinary color adaptation. Instead, the hue change is tied to the direction of the brightness gradients produced by sharp changes in luminance at edges. These observations may now be interpreted in accord with other selective sensitivities that have been discovered in studies of the human visual system.

SELECTIVE SENSITIVITIES IN THE HUMAN VISUAL SYSTEM

Much as we should like to know the response characteristics of single units in the human visual system, the barriers to obtaining such knowledge are obvious and formidable. An alternative approach, however, has been taken by many recent investigators. This approach uses psychophysical procedures that have their origins in older work but now gain a new interpretation. Kohler discusses adaptation to the curvature of edges that is produced by viewing the world through wedge prisms. The apparent curvature reduces over time. It has long been known that if an observer scans, for even a minute or two, a set of parallel bars slightly tilted off vertical, and then shifts his gaze to a truly vertical straight line, that line will appear to be tilted off vertical

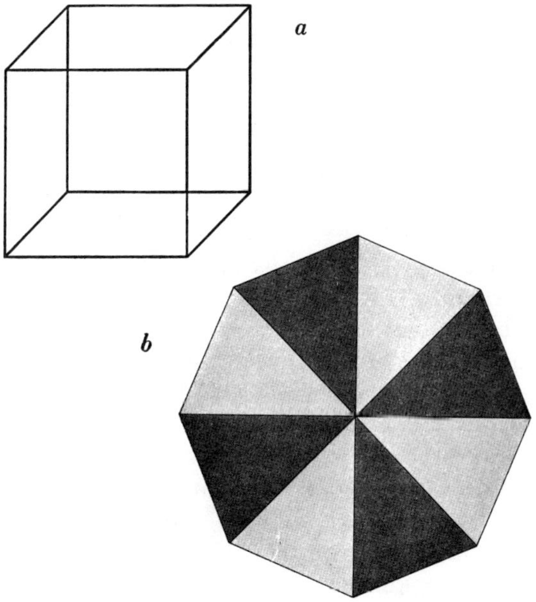

Figure 4. Perceptual anomalies associated with figural aftereffects are shown here. The cube (_a_) and the cross (_b_) periodically reverse with prolonged viewing. Reversability is a special case of a general perceptual process, related to the self-limiting direct-current flow in the brain caused by sensory stimilation and to its effects on the future reactivity of brain tissue. Drawings _c_, _c′_, _d_ and _d′_ demonstrate these effects. Prolonged viewing of the cross in _c_ causes an apparent vertical displacement of the left-hand squares when the gaze is shifted to the cross in _c′_. Similarly, prolonged inspection of the cross in _d_ causes an apparent displacement of the right-hand line in _d′_ when the gaze is shifted to the cross between the parallel lines. Drawing _e_ is the Müller-Lyer illusion, in which the upper half of the line appears shorter than the lower. Brief inspections of this figure, repeated over a period of days, can reverse the original illusion. [From "Aftereffects in Perception," by W. C. H. Prentice, _Scientific American_, January 1962.]

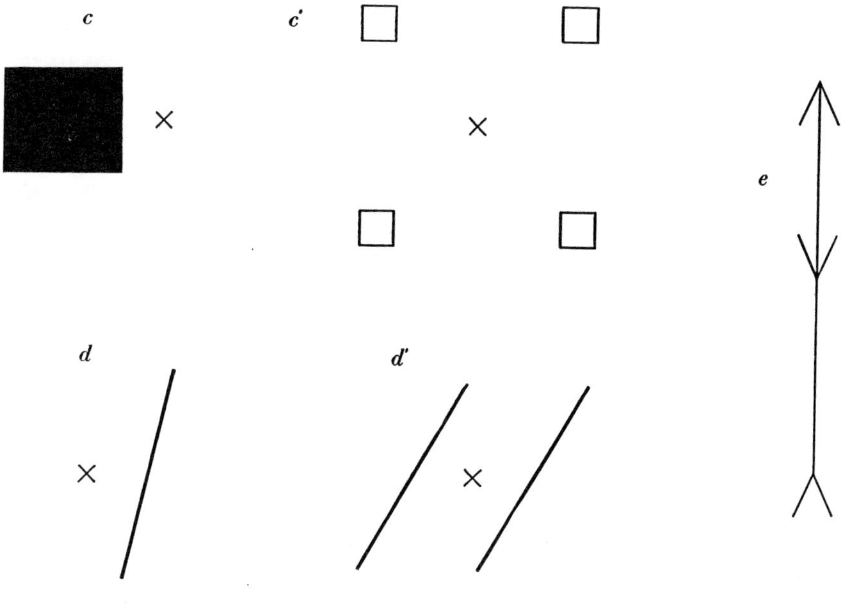

in a direction opposite to the tilt of the bars. This effect—and many others like it, called figural aftereffects—may be said to result from the desensitization of neural elements that are selectively sensitive, normally, to the orientation of edges. Neural models based upon this assumption may be readily constructed to explain the aftereffect.

Each neural element may be assumed to respond to slanting lines or edges over a certain range of orientations, but with peaked excitation at one particular orientation. Perception of the orientation of a given edge may then be assumed to result from a kind of averaging over the set of orientation-sensitive elements that it excites. Prior exposure to a tilted bar or a grating of bars maximally desensitizes certain of the slightly off-vertical elements. Consequently, the average excitation produced by a vertical edge will be biased away from the direction of the tilted adapting edges.

Other experiments using masking techniques are consistent with the results of the aftereffect studies. For example, if a grating consisting of black and white bars is flashed on a screen viewed by an observer, the threshold luminance for detecting a second grating, presented a fraction of a second before or after, will be raised. The maximum threshold rise occurs when the edges of the two gratings are of the same orientation and the effect diminishes rapidly as the difference in orientation increases. Such data confirm the notion that there exist elements in the visual system that are selectively sensitive to the orientation of edges, and, moreover, that they are tuned to a range of edge orientations that extends from maximal sensitivity at their preferred orientation down to zero at roughly twenty degrees on either side.

Similar techniques have revealed selective sensitivities to the spatial frequencies of patterns. Spatial frequency refers to the repetition rate per unit of distance of the periodic (sinusoidal) waxing and waning of luminance. Studies of motion sensitivity have revealed analogous results. To an observer who has just viewed a display moving in one direction, a stationary object will appear to move in the opposite direction. This classic aftereffect of seen motion—another illusion—has also been analyzed in terms of selective sensitivities in the visual system: the existence of elements that are maximally sensitive to certain velocities of motion has been inferred by some workers.

In addition to certain single dimensions of stimulation to which elements of the human nervous system are inferred to be sensitive, combinations of dimensions have been shown to yield aftereffects contingent upon two or even more properties of stimulation. One of the most striking of these is a color aftereffect, discovered by Celeste McCollough, that is dependent upon the orientation and the spatial frequency of a black-and-white test grating upon which it appears. The effect is typically produced by prolonged viewing (five minutes or longer) of a red vertical grating alternated every five seconds with a green horizontal grating (projected slides work best). Complementary hues then appear with maximal saturation on black-and-white gratings of the same orientations (green on vertical, red on horizontal). The edge-specific color adaptation discussed by Kohler is, of course, a close relative of this orientation-specific color aftereffect.

The phenomena of adaptation to the sort of complex stimuli discussed above have important implications for our understanding of perception, although we can only speculate now about their neural mechanism. The adaptive changes indicate that past stimulation of the visual system will partially determine present receptivity. Consequently, the laws that relate stimulus to percept must contain specifications of the history of particular kinds of stimulation. Without some knowledge of the past, we cannot predict present function.

MOTION

Just as a large part of the classic work on the perception of size and shape started with the study of illusions, so most of the research on motion perception has been concerned with what has been called apparent motion. The term "apparent," in this connection, carries the same meaning as the term "illusory"; such motion can be termed illusory because the stimuli that give rise to the perception either do not move or move in an unexpected direction relative to the retina.

In his article "The Illusion of Movement," Paul A. Kolers discusses the apparent motion that results from successive stimulation by two or more separated, stationary stimuli. This phenomenon is, of course, the perceptual basis for the motion observed in cinema photography. Kolers argues convincingly, on the basis of his experiments, that real and apparent motion differ in a number of respects, despite some previous claims to the contrary. Yet there may be an important and basic insight in the older claims: because the visual nervous system consists of discrete units at each stage, the continuous motion of a stimulus traversing the retina must be resolved into a series of discrete excitations. A neural mechanism by means of which these excitations may be analyzed as motion is suggested in Michael's article in Section III. To be sure, it seems very doubtful that the analysis that Michael suggests is carried out in the retinas of higher mammals, but the model could, in principle, be applied to any level of the visual system.

Hans Wallach, in his article "The Perception of Motion," discusses other forms of illusory motion, including the induced motion of a stationary object surrounded by a moving field and the dominant influence of the relative motion, to the neglect of the objective motions, of two objects moving along unparallel trajectories. In his article in this section, Ulric Neisser complements this account with his discussion of the kinetic depth effect, which demonstrates how movements in only two dimensions give rise to the impression of motion in a third—namely, depth. The perceptual resolution of compound movements has been extensively studied by Gunnar Johansson, and expressed by him in laws that Wallach mentions briefly in the second of his two articles in this section.

To sum up this discussion of illusions and constancies, we may say that these phenomena are readily identifiable examples of the operation of the processing mechanisms of perception. Some illusions and constancies have yielded to analysis, and the mechanisms presumably responsible for them are now understood. Certain others, however, are still refractory to such explanation; these provide us with obvious problems for future research.

REFERENCES

Berkeley, G. *An essay towards a new theory of vision.* Dublin: 1709.

Gibson, J. *The perception of the visual world.* Boston: Houghton Mifflin, 1950.

Johansson, G. Perception of motion and changing form. *Scandinavian Journal of Psychology,* 1964, **5**, 181–208.

McCullough, C. Color adaptation of edge-detectors in the human visual system. *Science,* 1965, **149**, 1115–1116.

VISUAL ILLUSIONS

RICHARD L. GREGORY
November 1968

A satisfactory theory of visual perception must explain how the fleeting patterns of light reaching the retina of the eye convey knowledge of external objects. The problem of how the brain "reads" reality from the eye's images is an acute one because objects are so very different from images, which directly represent only a few of the important characteristics of objects. At any instant the retinal image represents the color of an object and its shape from a single position, but color and shape are in themselves trivial. Color is dependent on the quality of the illumination, and on the more subtle factors of contrast and retinal fatigue. Shape, as we all know, can be strongly distorted by various illusions. Since it is obviously not in the best interests of the possessor of an eye to be tricked by visual illusions, one would like to know how the illusions occur. Can it be that illusions arise from information-processing mechanisms that under normal circumstances make the visible world easier to comprehend? This is the main proposition I shall examine here.

Illusions of various kinds can occur in any of the senses, and they can cross over between the senses. For example, small objects feel considerably heavier than larger objects of exactly the same weight. This can be easily demonstrated by filling a small can with sand and then putting enough sand in a much larger can until the two cans are in balance. The smaller can will feel up to 50 percent heavier than the larger can of precisely the same weight. Evidently weight is perceived not only according to the pressure and muscle senses but also according to the expected weight of the object, as indicated by its visually judged size. When the density is unexpected, vision produces the illusion of weight. I believe all systematic-distortion illusions are essentially similar to this size-weight illusion.

Although several visual illusions were known to the ancient Greeks, they have been studied experimentally for only a little more than a century. The first scientific description in modern times is in a letter to the Scottish physicist Sir David Brewster from a Swiss naturalist, L. A. Necker, who wrote in 1832 that a drawing of a transparent rhomboid reverses in depth: sometimes one face appears to be in front and sometimes the other. Necker noted that although changes of eye fixation could induce this change in perception, it would also occur quite spontaneously. This celebrated effect is generally illustrated with an isometric cube rather than with Necker's original figure [*see top illustration on page 243*].

Somewhat later W. J. Sinsteden reported an equally striking effect that must have long been familiar to Netherlanders. If the rotating vanes of a windmill are viewed obliquely or directly from the side, they spontaneously reverse direction if there are no strong clues to the direction of rotation. This effect can be well demonstrated by projecting on a screen the shadow, seen in perspective, of a slowly rotating vane. In the absence of all clues to the direction of rotation the vane will seem to reverse direction spontaneously and the shadow will also at times appear to expand and contract on the plane of the screen. It is important to note that these effects are not perceptual distortions of the retinal image; they are alternative interpretations of the image in terms of possible objects. It is as though the brain entertains alternative hypotheses of what object the eye's image may be representing. When sensory data are inadequate, alternative hypotheses are entertained and the brain never "makes up its mind."

The most puzzling visual illusions are systematic distortions of size or shape. These distortions occur in many quite simple figures. The distortion takes the same direction and occurs to much the same extent in virtually all human observers and probably also in many animals. To psychologists such distortions present an important challenge because they must be explained by a satisfactory theory of normal perception and because they could be important clues to basic perceptual processes.

Distortion Illusions

The simplest distortion illusion was also the first to be studied. This is the horizontal-vertical illusion, which was described by Wilhelm Wundt, assistant to Hermann von Helmholtz at Heidelberg and regarded as the father of experimental psychology. The illusion is simply that a vertical line looks longer than a horizontal line of equal length. Wundt attributed the distortion to asymmetry in the system that moves the eye. Although this explanation has been invoked many times since then, it must be ruled out because the distortions occur in afterimages on the retina and also in normal images artificially stabilized so as to remain stationary on the retina. In addition, distortions can occur in several directions at the same time, which could hardly be owing to eye movements. It is also difficult to see how curvature distortions could be related to eye movements. All the evidence suggests that the distortions originate not in the eyes but in the brain.

Interest in the illusions became general on the publication of several figures showing distortions that could produce errors in the use of optical instruments. These errors were an important concern to physicists and astronomers a centu-

ZÖLLNER ILLUSION was published in 1860 by Johann Zöllner; the first of the special distortion illusions.

ry ago, when photographic and other means of avoiding visual errors were still uncommon. The first of the special distortion figures was the illusion published by Johann Zöllner in 1860 [*see illustration above*]. The same year Johann Poggendorff published his line-displacement illusion [*see middle illustration on page 243*]. A year later Ewald Hering presented the now familiar illusion in which parallel lines appear bowed; the converse illusion was conceived in 1896 by Wundt [*see illustration on page 245*].

Perhaps the most famous of all distortion illusions is the double-headed-arrow figure devised by Franz Müller-Lyer and presented in 15 variations in 1889 [*see illustration on page 246*]. This figure is so simple and the distortion is so compelling that it was immediately accepted as a primary target for theory and experiment. All kinds of theories were advanced. Wundt again invoked his eye-movement theory. It was also proposed that the "wings" of the arrowheads drew attention away from the ends of the central line, thus making it expand or contract; that the heads induced a state of empathy in the observer, making him feel as if the central line were being either stretched or compressed; that the distortion is a special case of a supposed general principle that acute angles tend to be overestimated and obtuse angles underestimated, although why this should be so was left unexplained.

All these theories had a common feature: they were attempts to explain the distortions in terms of the stimulus pattern, without reference to its significance in terms of the perception of objects. There was, however, one quite different suggestion. In 1896 A. Thiery proposed that the distortions are related to the way the eye and brain utilize perspective to judge distances or depths. Thiery regarded the Müller-Lyer arrows as drawings of an object such as a sawhorse, seen in three dimensions; the legs would be going away from the observer in the acute-angled figure and toward him in the obtuse-angled figure. Except for a brief discussion of the "perspective theory" by Robert S. Woodworth in 1938, Thiery's suggestion has seldom been considered until recently.

Woodworth wrote: "In the Müller-Lyer figure the obliques readily suggest perspective and if this is followed one of the vertical lines appears farther away and therefore objectively longer than the other." This quotation brings out the immediate difficulties of developing an adequate theory along such lines. The distortion occurs even when the perspective suggestion is not followed up, because the arrows generally appear flat and yet are still distorted. Moreover, no hint is given of a mechanism responsible for the size changes. An adequate theory based on Thiery's suggestion must show how distortion occurs even though the figures appear flat. It should also indicate the kind of brain mechanisms responsible.

The notion that geometric perspective—the apparent convergence of parallel lines with distance—has a bearing on the problem is borne out by the occurrence of these distortions in photographs of actual scenes in which perspective is pronounced. Two rectangles of equal size look markedly unequal if they are superposed on a photograph of converging railroad tracks [*see illustration on page 244*]. The upper rectangle in the illustration, which would be the more distant if it were a real object lying between the tracks, looks larger than the lower (and apparently nearer) one. This corresponds to the Ponzo illusion [*see bottom illustration on this page*].

Similarly, the eye tends to expand the inside corner of a room, as it is seen in a photograph, and to shrink the outside corners of structures [*see illustration on page 251*]. The effect is just the same as the one in the Müller-Lyer figures, which in fact resemble outline drawings of corners seen in perspective. In both cases the regions indicated by perspective as being distant are expanded, whereas those indicated as being closer are shrunk. The distortions are opposite to the normal shrinking of the retinal image when the distance to an object is increased. Is this effect merely fortuitous, or is it a clue to the origin of the illusions?

Paradoxical Pictures

Before we come to grips with the problem of trying to develop an adequate theory of perspective it will be helpful to consider some curious fea-

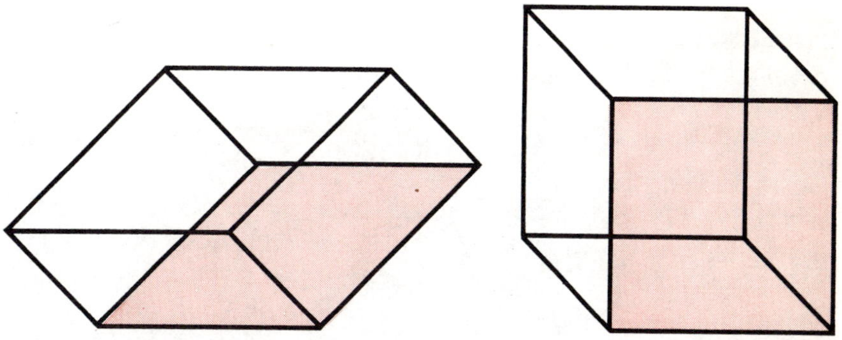

NECKER ILLUSION was devised in 1832 by L. A. Necker, a Swiss naturalist. He noticed that a transparent rhomboid (*left*) spontaneously reverses in depth. The area lightly tinted in color can appear either as an outer surface or as an inner surface of a transparent box. The illusion is now more usually presented as a transparent cube (*right*), known as a Necker cube.

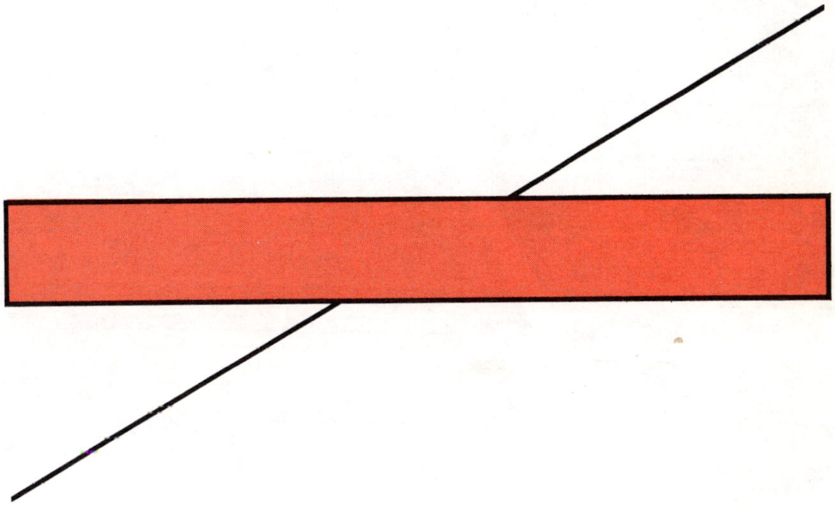

POGGENDORFF ILLUSION was proposed by Johann Poggendorff in 1860, the same year that Johann Zöllner proposed the figure shown on the opposite page. In Poggendorff's figure the two segments of the diagonal line seem to be offset.

PONSO ILLUSION, also known as the railway lines illusion, was proposed by Mario Ponzo in 1913. It is the prototype of the illusion depicted in the photograph on the following page.

ILLUSION INVOLVING PERSPECTIVE is remarkably constant for all human observers. The two rectangles superposed on this photograph of railroad tracks are precisely the same size, yet the top rectangle looks distinctly larger. The author regards this illusion as the prototype of visual distortions in which the perceptual mechanism, involving the brain, attempts to maintain a rough size constancy for similar objects placed at different distances. Since we know that the distant railroad ties are as large as the nearest ones, any object lying between the rails in the middle distance (the upper rectangle) is unconsciously enlarged. Indeed, if the rectangles were real objects lying between the rails, we would know immediately that the more distant was larger.

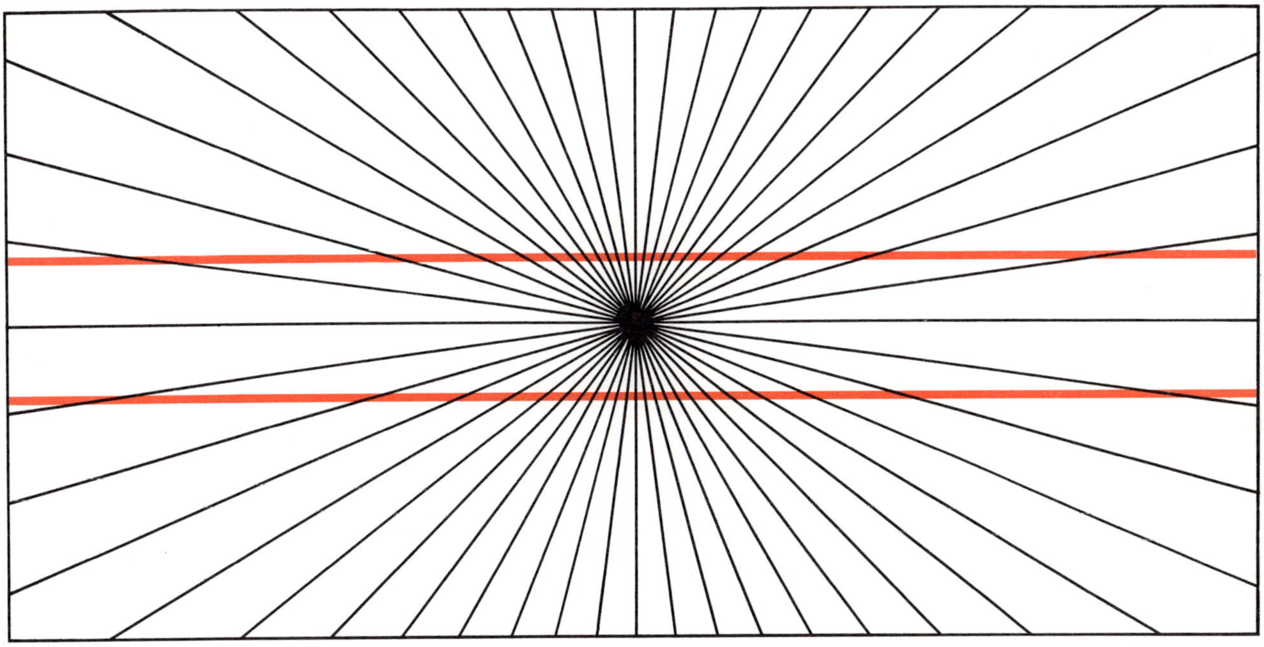

HERING ILLUSION was published in 1861 by Ewald Hering. The horizontal lines are of course straight. Physicists and astronomers of that period took a lively interest in illusions, being concerned that visual observations might sometimes prove unreliable.

tures of ordinary pictures. Pictures are the traditional material of perceptual research, but all pictures are highly artificial and present special problems to the perceiving brain. In a sense all pictures are impossible because they have a dual reality. They are seen both as patterns of lines lying on a flat background and as objects depicted in a quite different three-dimensional space. No actual object can be both two-dimensional and three-dimensional, yet pictures come close to it. Viewed as patterns they are seen as being two-dimensional; viewed as representing other objects they are seen in a quasi-three-dimensional space. Pictures therefore provide a paradoxical visual input. They are also ambiguous, because the third dimension is never precisely defined.

The Necker cube is an example of a picture in which the depth ambiguity is so great that the brain never settles for a single answer. The fact is, however, that any perspective projection could represent an infinity of three-dimensional shapes. One would think that the perceptual system has an impossible task! Fortunately for us the world of objects does not have infinite variety; there is usually a best bet, and we generally interpret our flat images more or less correctly in terms of the world of objects.

The difficulty of the problem of seeing the third dimension from the two dimensions of a picture, or from the

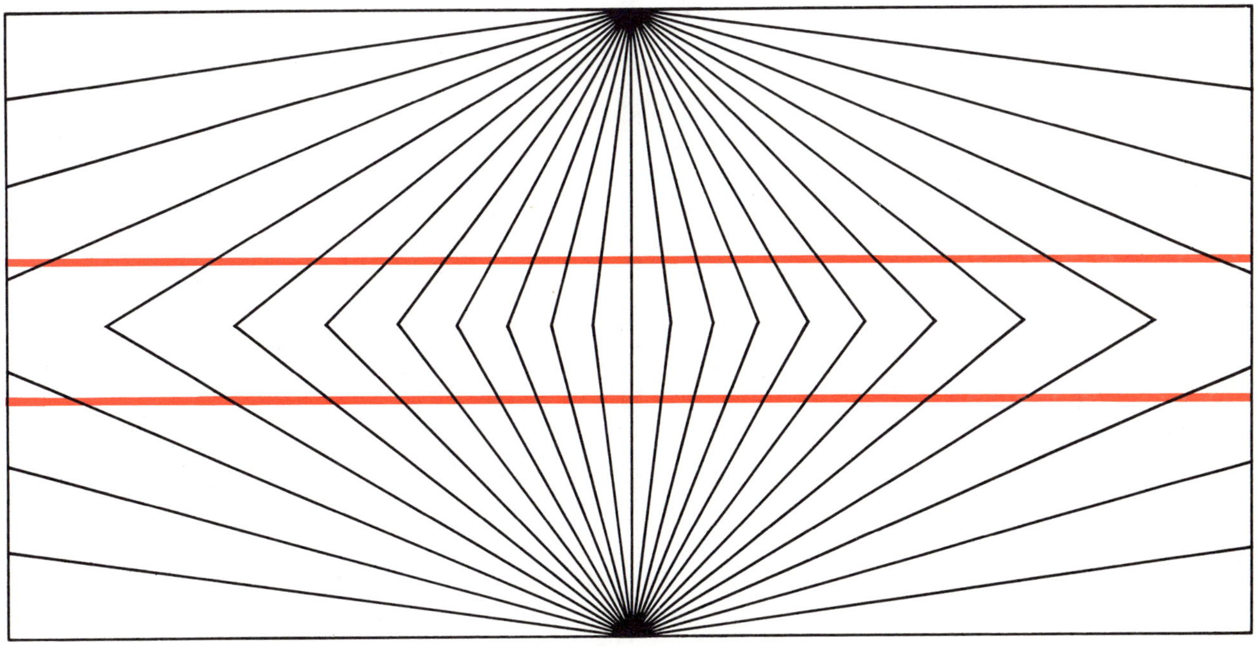

CONVERSE OF HERING ILLUSION was conceived in 1896 by Wilhelm Wundt, who introduced experimentation into psychology. Wundt earlier described the simplest of the visual illusions: that a vertical line looks longer than a horizontal line of equal length.

retinal images of normal objects, is ingeniously brought out by special "impossible pictures" and "impossible objects." They show what happens when clearly incompatible distance information is presented to the eye. The impossible triangle devised by Lionel S. Penrose and R. Penrose cannot be perceptually interpreted as an object in normal three-dimensional space [*see illustration on page 247*]. It is, however, perfectly possible to make actual three-dimensional objects, not mere pictures, that give rise to the same perceptual confusion—provided that they are viewed with only one eye. For example, the Penrose triangle can be built as an open three-dimensional structure [*see top illustration on page 249*] that looks like an impossible closed structure when it is viewed with one eye (or photographed) from exactly the right position [*see bottom illustration on page 249*].

Ordinary pictures are not so very different from obviously impossible pictures. All pictures showing depth are paradoxical: we see them both as being flat (which they really are) and as having a kind of artificial depth that is not quite right. We are not tempted to touch objects shown in a picture through the surface of the picture or in front of it. What happens, however, if we remove the surface? Does the depth paradox of pictures remain?

The Removal of Background

To remove the background for laboratory experiments we make the pictures luminous so that they glow in the dark. In order to deprive the brain of stereoscopic information that would reveal that the pictures are actually flat the pictures are viewed with one eye. They may be wire figures coated with luminous paint or photographic transparencies back-illuminated with an electroluminescent panel. In either case there is no visible background, so that we can discover how much the background is responsible for the depth paradox of pictures, including the illusion figures.

Under these conditions the Müller-Lyer arrows usually look like true corners according to their perspective. They may even be indistinguishable from actual luminous corners. The figures are not entirely stable: they sometimes reverse spontaneously in depth. Nonetheless, they usually appear according to their perspective and without the paradoxical depth of pictures with a background. The distortions are still present. The figure that resembles a double-headed arrow looks like an outside corner and seems shrunk, whereas the figure with the arrowheads pointing the wrong way looks like an inside corner and is expanded. Now, however, the paradox has disappeared and the figures look like true corners. With a suitable apparatus one can point out their depth as if they were normal three-dimensional objects.

Having removed the paradox, it is possible to measure, by quite direct means, the apparent distance of any selected part of the figures. This we do by using the two eyes to serve as a range finder for indicating the apparent depth of the figure, which is visible to only one eye. The back-illuminated picture is placed behind a polarizing filter so that one eye is prevented from seeing the picture by a second polarizing filter oriented at right angles to the first. Both eyes, however, are allowed to see one or more small movable reference lights that are optically introduced into the picture by means of a half-silvered mirror set at 45 degrees to the line of sight. The distance of these lights is given by stereoscopic vision, that is, by the convergence angle of the eyes; by moving the lights so that they seem to coincide with the apparent distance of selected parts of the picture we can plot the visual space of the observer in three dimensions [*see top illustration on page 248*].

When this plotting is done for various angles of the "fin," or arrowhead line, in the Müller-Lyer illusion figure, it becomes clear that the figures are perceived as inside and outside corners. The illusion of depth conforms closely to the results obtained when the magnitude of the illusion is independently measured by asking subjects to select comparison lines that match the apparent length of the central line between two kinds of arrowhead [*see bottom illustration on page 248*]. In the latter experiment the figures are drawn on a normally textured background, so that they appear flat.

The two exeriments show that when the background is removed, depth very closely follows the illusion for the various fin angles. The similarity of the plotted results provides evidence of a remarkably close connection between the illusion as it occurs when depth is not seen and the depth that is seen when the background is removed. This suggests that Thiery was essentially correct: perspective can somehow create distortions. What is odd is that perspective produces the distortions according to *indicated* perspective depth even when depth is *not* consciously seen.

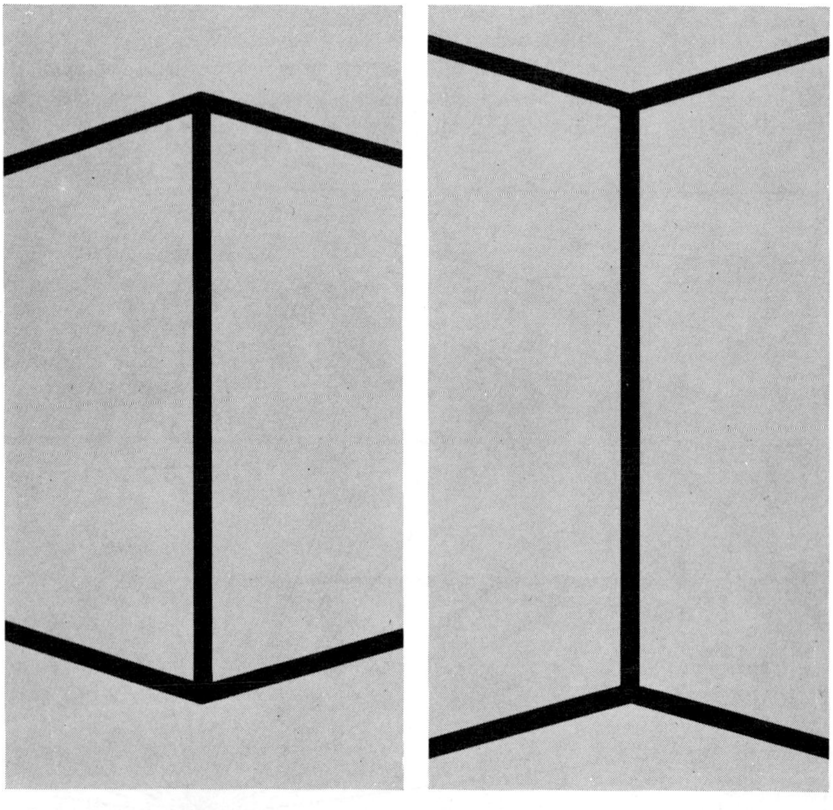

MÜLLER-LYER ILLUSION was devised by Franz Müller-Lyer in 1889. Many theories were subsequently invoked in an attempt to explain why reversed arrowheads (*right*) seem to lengthen a connecting shaft whereas normal arrowheads seem to shrink the shaft (*left*).

Size Constancy

The next step is to look for some perceptual mechanism that could produce this relation between perspective and apparent size. A candidate that should have been obvious many years ago is size constancy. This phenomenon was clearly described in 1637 by René Descartes in his *Dioptrics.* "It is not the absolute size of images [in the eyes] that counts," he wrote. "Clearly they are 100 times bigger [in area] when objects are very close than when they are 10 times farther away, but they do not make us see the objects 100 times bigger. On the contrary, they seem almost the same size, at any rate as we are not deceived by too great a distance."

We know from many experiments that Descartes is quite right. What happens, however, when distance information, such as perspective, is presented to the eye but two components of the scene, one of which should be shrunk by distance, are the same size? Could it be that perspective presented on a flat plane triggers the brain to compensate for the expected shrinking of the images with distance even though there is no shrinking for which to compensate? If some such thing happens, it is easy to see why figures that suggest perspective can give rise to distortions. This would provide the start of a reasonable theory of illusions. Features indicated as being distant would be expanded, which is just what we find, at least for the Müller-Lyer and the Ponzo figures.

It is likely that this approach to the problem was not developed until recently because, although size constancy was quite well known, it has always been assumed that it simply follows apparent distance in all circumstances. Moreover, it has not been sufficiently realized how very odd pictures are as visual inputs. They are highly atypical and should be studied as a special case, being both paradoxical and ambiguous.

Size constancy is traditionally identified with an effect known as Emmert's law. This effect can be explained by a simple experiment involving the apparent size of afterimages in vision. If one can obtain a good afterimage (preferably by briefly illuminating a test figure with an electronic flash lamp), one can "project" it on screens or walls located at various distances. The afterimage will appear almost twice as large with each doubling of distance, even though the size of the image from the flash remains constant. It is important to note, however, that there *is* a change in retinal stimulation for each screen or wall lying at a different distance; their images *do* vary. It is possible that the size change of the afterimage is due not so much to a brain mechanism that changes its scal as to its size on the retina with respect to the size of the screen on which it appears to lie. Before we go any further, it is essential to discover whether Emmert's law is due merely to the relation between the areas covered by the afterimage and the screen, or whether the visual information of distance changes the size of the afterimage by some kind of internal scaling. This presents us with a tricky experimental problem.

As it turns out, there is a simple solution. We can use the ambiguous depth phenomenon of the Necker cube to establish whether Emmert's law is due to a central scaling by the brain or is merely an effect of relative areas of stimulation of the retina. When we see a Necker cube that is drawn on paper reverse in depth, there is no appreciable size change. When the cube is presented on a textured background, it occupies the paradoxical depth of all pictures with visible backgrounds; it does not change in size when it reverses in pseudo-depth.

What happens, however, if we remove the cube's background? The effect is dramatic and entirely repeatable: with each reversal in depth the cube changes its apparent shape, even though there is no change in the retinal image. Whichever face appears to be more distant always appears to be the larger. The use of depth-ambiguous figures in this way makes it possible to separate what happens when the pattern of stimulation of the retina is changed. The answer is that at least part of size constancy, and of Emmert's law, is due to a central size-scaling mechanism in the brain that responds to changes in apparent distance although the retinal stimulation is unchanged.

Apparent size, then, is evidently established in two ways. It can be estab-

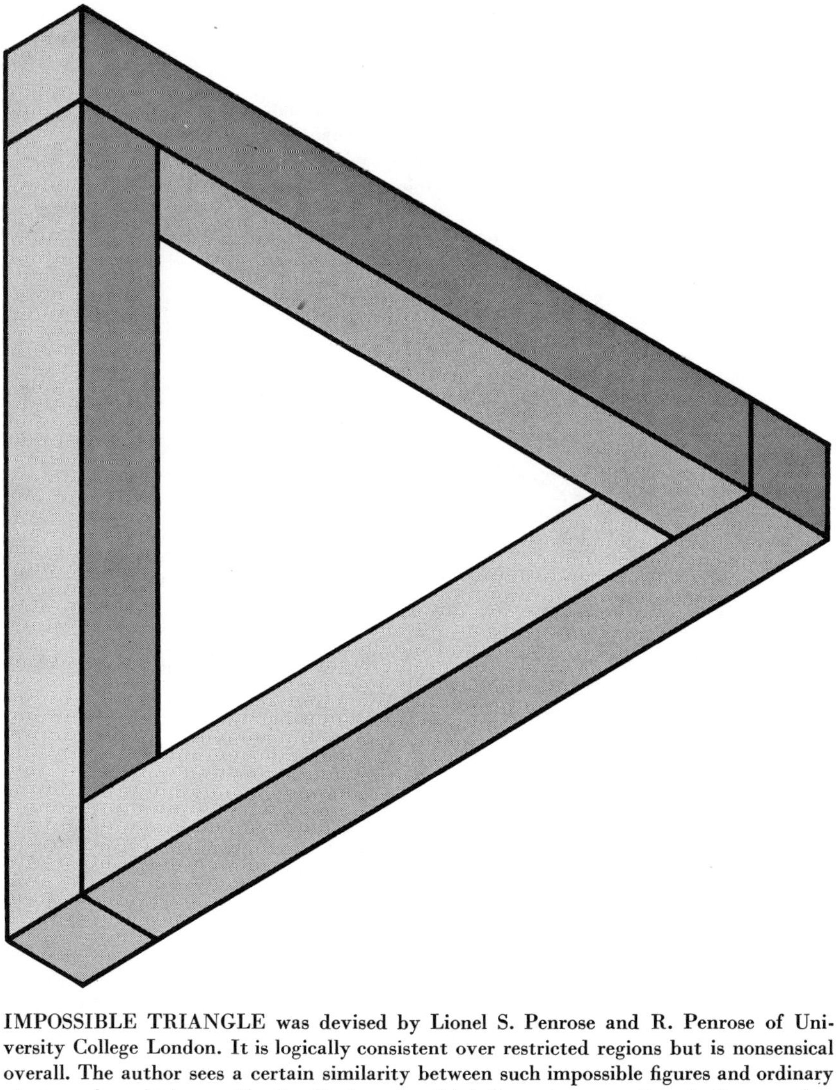

IMPOSSIBLE TRIANGLE was devised by Lionel S. Penrose and R. Penrose of University College London. It is logically consistent over restricted regions but is nonsensical overall. The author sees a certain similarity between such impossible figures and ordinary photographs, which provide the illusion of a third dimension even though they are flat.

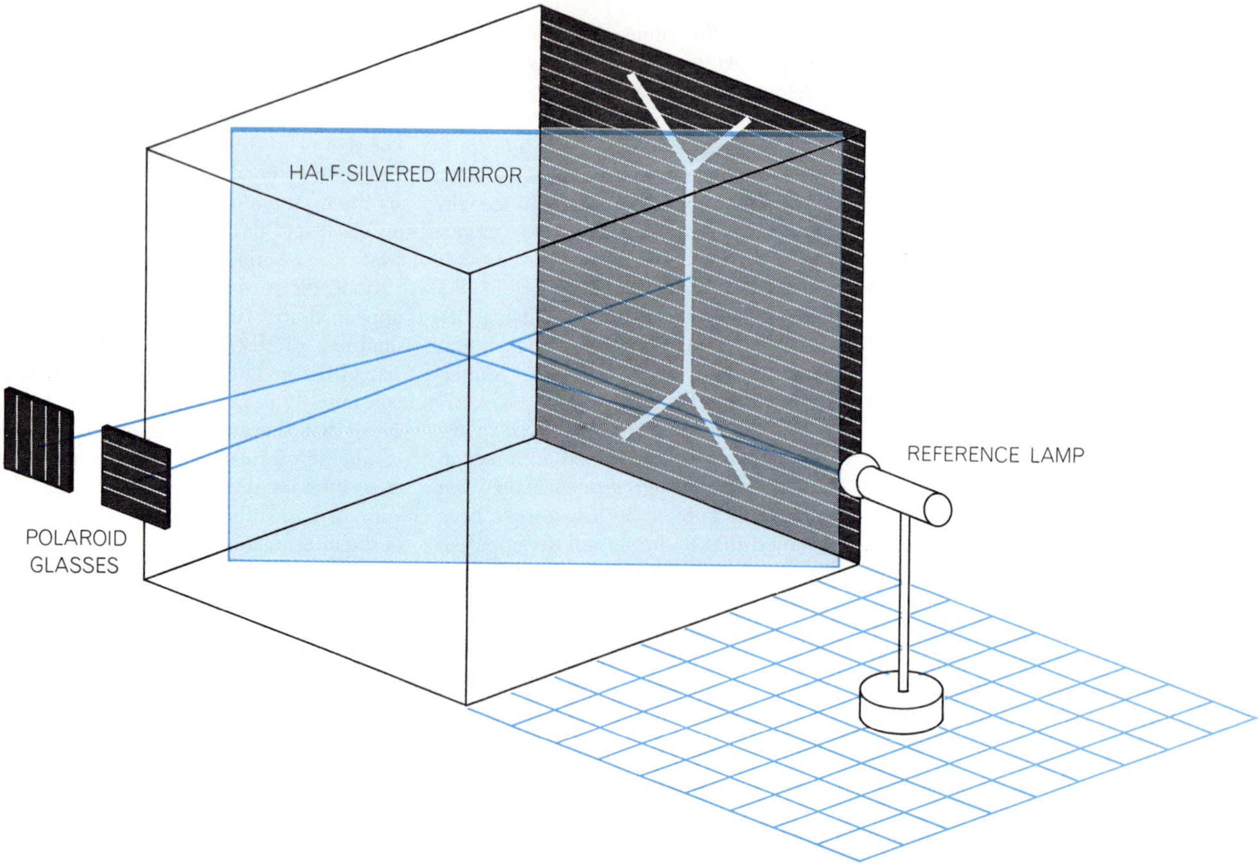

APPARATUS FOR STUDYING ILLUSIONS was devised by the author. The objective is to present figures such as the Müller-Lyer arrows with the background removed so that the figures seem suspended in space. Under these conditions the Müller-Lyer arrows generally look like true corners. The subject can adjust a small light so that it appears to lie at the same depth as any part of the figure. The light, which the subject sees in three-dimensional space with both eyes, is superposed on the illuminated figure by means of a half-silvered mirror. A polarizing filter is placed over the figure and the subject wears polarizing glasses that allow him to see the figure with only one eye. Thus he has no way of telling whether the figure is really two-dimensional or three-dimensional.

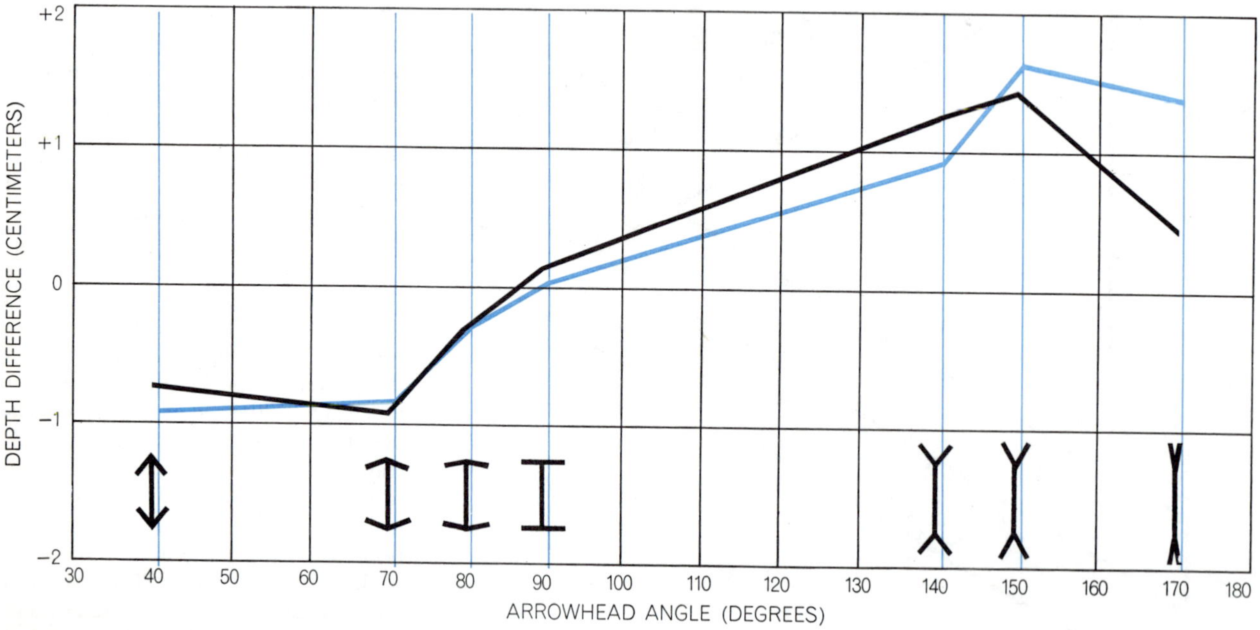

QUANTITATIVE MEASUREMENT OF ILLUSION produced the results plotted here for Müller-Lyer arrows. The black curve shows the average results for 20 subjects who were asked to select a comparison line that matched the length of a central shaft to which were attached arrowheads set at the angles indicated. When arrowheads were set at less than 90 degrees, the comparison lines were as much as one centimeter shorter. When the arrowhead was set at 150 degrees, the comparison line was more than 1.5 centimeters longer. The colored curve shows the maximum depth difference perceived for the same set of arrows when displayed, with the background removed, in the apparatus shown in the illustration at the top of the page. The two curves match quite closely except at the extreme setting of 170 degrees, when the figure no longer resembles a true corner when presented in the light box.

lished purely by apparent distance. It can also be established directly by visual depth features, such as perspective in two-dimensional pictures, even though depth is not seen because it is countermanded by competing depth information such as a visible background. When atypical depth features are present, size scaling is established inappropriately and we have a corresponding distortion illusion.

The size scaling established directly by depth features (giving systematic distortions when it is established inappropriately) we may call "depth-cue scaling." It is remarkably consistent and independent of the observer's perceptual "set." The other system is quite different and more subtle, being only indirectly related to the prevailing retinal information. It is evidently linked to the interpretation of the retinal image in terms of what object it represents. When it appears as a different object, the scaling changes at once to suit the alternative object. If we regard the seeing of an object as a hypothesis, suggested (but never strictly proved) by the image, we may call the system "depth-hypothesis scaling," because it changes with each change of the hypothesis of what object is represented by the image. When the hypothesis is wrong, we have an illusion that may be dramatic. Such alternations in hypotheses underlie the changes in direction, and even size, that occur when one watches the shadow of a rotating vane.

Observers in Motion

The traditional distortion illusions can be attributed to errors in the setting of the depth-cue scaling system, which arise when figures or objects have misleading depth cues, particularly perspective on a flat plane. Although these illusions might occasionally bother investigators making visual measurements, they are seldom a serious hazard. The other kind of illusion—incorrect size-scaling due to an error in the prevailing perceptual hypothesis—can be serious in unfamiliar conditions or when there is little visual information available, as in space flight. It can also be important in driving a car at night or in landing an airplane under conditions of poor visibility. Illusions are most hazardous when the observer is in rapid motion, because then even a momentary error may lead to disaster.

So far little work has been done on the measurement of illusions experienced by observers who are in motion with respect to their surroundings. The ex-

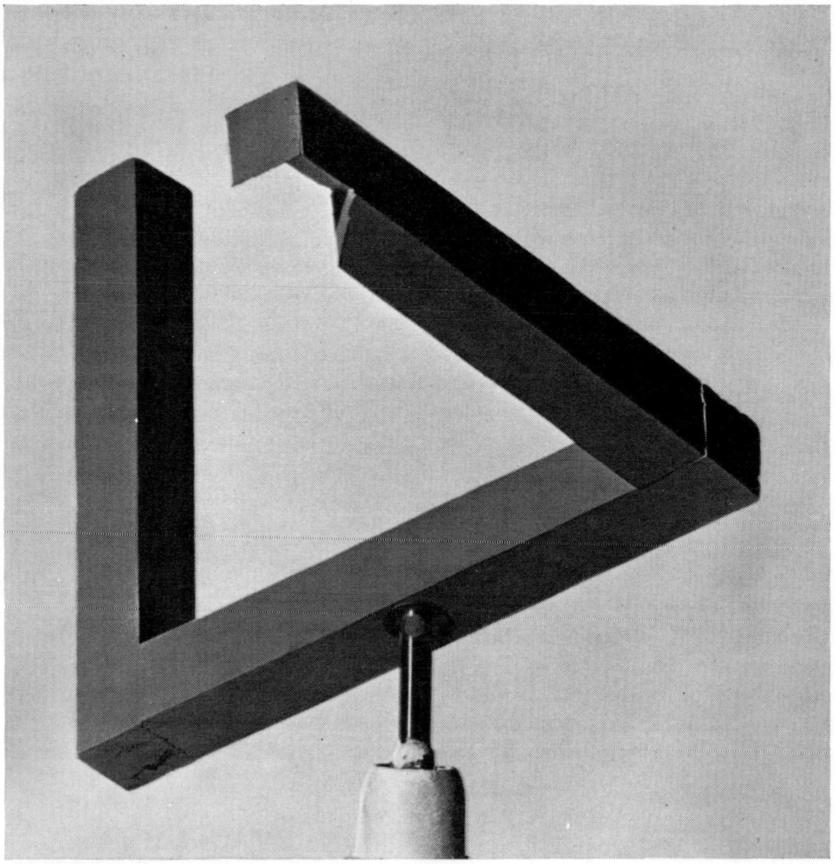

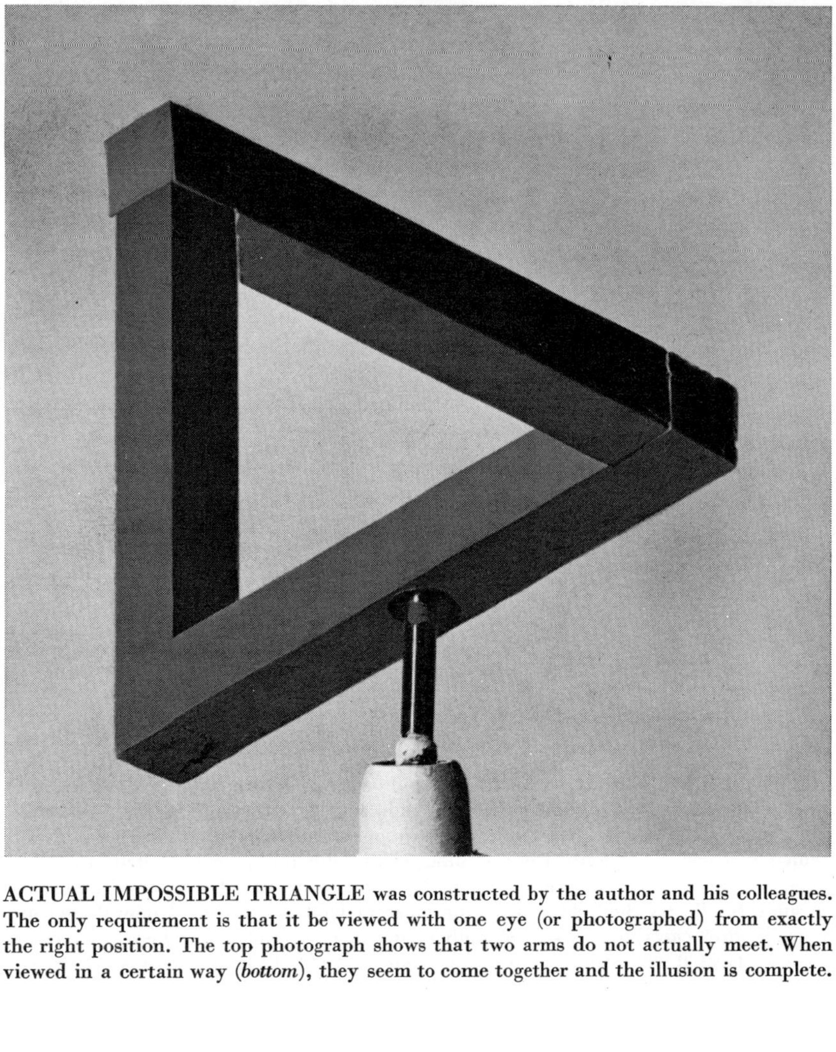

ACTUAL IMPOSSIBLE TRIANGLE was constructed by the author and his colleagues. The only requirement is that it be viewed with one eye (or photographed) from exactly the right position. The top photograph shows that two arms do not actually meet. When viewed in a certain way (*bottom*), they seem to come together and the illusion is complete.

perimental difficulties involved in making such measurements are severe; nevertheless, we have been tackling the problem with support from the U.S. Air Force. The equipment, which is fairly elaborate, can move the observer with controlled velocity and acceleration through various visual environments, including the blackness of space (with or without artificial stars presented optically at infinite distance).

We measure the observer's visual sense of size constancy as he is moving by having him look at a projected display that changes size as he approaches or recedes from it. As he moves away from it, the display is made to expand in size; as he approaches it, the display is made to shrink. The change in size is adjusted until, to the moving observer, the display appears fixed in size. If there were no perceptual mechanism for constancy scaling, the size of the display would have to be adjusted so that its image on the observer's retina would be the same size regardless of his distance from it. If, at the other extreme, the size-constancy effect were complete, we could leave the display unchanged and it would still appear to be the same size regardless of its actual distance from the observer. In practice some size change between these limits provides the illusion of an unchanging display, and this gives us a measure of the size-constancy effect as the observer is moved about.

We find that when the observer is in complete darkness, watching a display that is projected from the back onto a large screen, there is no measureable size constancy when the observer is moving at a fixed speed. When he is accelerated, size constancy does appear but it may be wildly wrong. In particular, if he interprets his movement incorrectly, either in direction or in amount, size constancy usually fails and can even work in reverse. This is rather similar to the reversal of size constancy with reversal of the depth of the luminous Necker cube. In the conditions of space, perception may be dominated by the prevailing hypothesis of distance and velocity. If either is wrong, as it may well be for lack of reliable visual information, the astronaut may suffer visual illusions that could be serious.

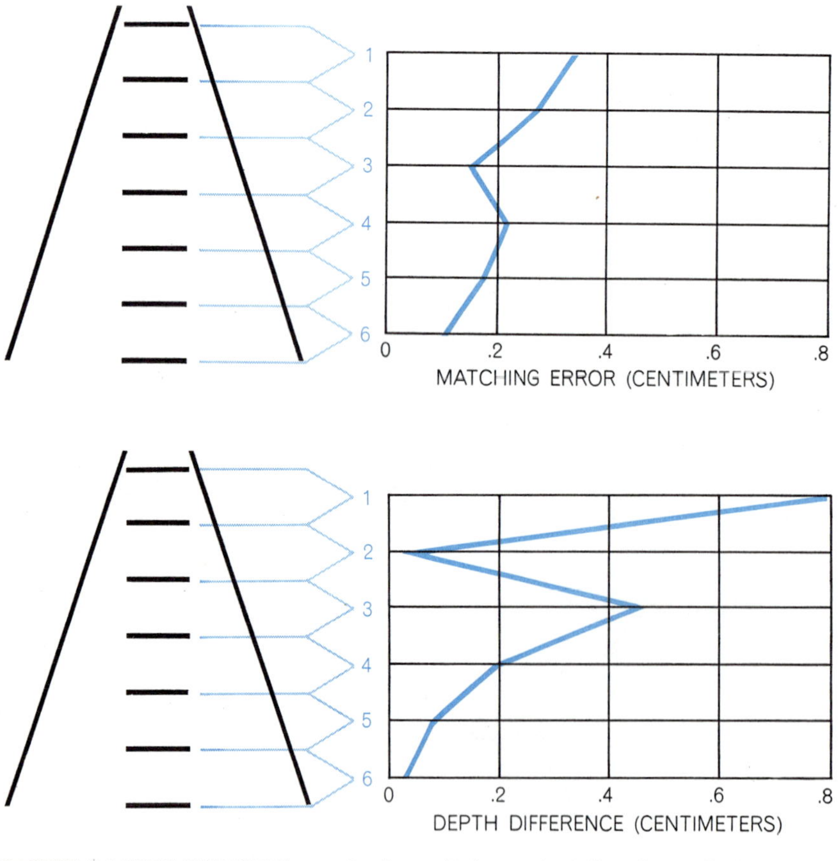

RAILWAY LINES ILLUSION can also be studied quantitatively. The methods are the same as those described in the bottom illustration on page 248. Subjects were presented with a horizontal line at one of the indicated positions and asked to select a second line that seemed to match it in length. The matching error for different pairs is plotted in the top curve. Pairs of lines were then presented in the apparatus shown at the top of page 248 and the subjects adjusted the light to match the apparent depth of each line. Under these conditions (*bottom curve*) the illusion of depth is much more dependent on where a given pair of lines is located with respect to the "rails," but the trend of the top curve is preserved.

The Nonvisual in Vision

Visual perception involves "reading" from retinal images a host of characteristics of objects that are not represented directly by the images in the eyes. The image does not convey directly many important characteristics of objects: whether they are hard or soft, heavy or light, hot or cold. Nonvisual characteristics must somehow be associated with the visual image, by individual learning or conceivably through heredity, for objects to be recognized from their images. Psychologists now believe individual perceptual learning is very important for associating the nonoptical properties of objects with their retinal images. Such learning is essential for perception; without it one would have mere stimulus-response behavior.

Perception seems to be a matter of looking up information that has been stored about objects and how they behave in various situations. The retinal image does little more than select the relevant stored data. This selection is rather like looking up entries in an encyclopedia: behavior is determined by the contents of the entry rather than by the stimulus that provoked the search. We can think of perception as being essentially the selection of the most appropriate stored hypothesis according to current sensory data.

Now, a look-up system of this kind has great advantages over a control system that responds simply to current input. If stored information is used, behavior can continue in the temporary absence of relevant information, or when there is inadequate information to provide precise control of behavior directly. This advantage has important implications for any possible perceptual system, including any future "seeing machine": a robot equipped with artificial eyes and a computer and designed to control vehicles or handle objects by means of artificial limbs. Even when enough direct sensory information is available for determining the important characteristics of surrounding objects (which is seldom the case), it would require a rate of data transmission in excess of that provided by the human nervous system (or current computers) to enable a robot to behave appropriately. Hence there are strong general design reasons for supposing that any effective seeing system—whether biological or man-made—should use current sensory information for selecting performed hypotheses, or models, representing important features of the external world of objects as opposed to controlling behavior directly from sensory inputs.

If we consider the problems of storing information about objects, it soon becomes clear that it would be most uneconomical to store an independent model of each object for every distance and orientation it might occupy in surrounding space. It would be far more economical to store only typical characteristics of objects and to use current sensory information to adjust the selected model to fit the prevailing situation. The model must be continually scaled for distance and orientation if the owner of the perceptual system is to interact with the object.

We might guess that depth-cue scaling represents this adjustment of the selected model in the light of the available depth information. When the available information is inappropriate (as in the case of perspective features on a flat plane), it will scale the perceptual model wrongly. There will be a systematic error: a distortion illusion due to inappropriate depth-cue scaling. There will also be errors—possibly very large ones—whenever a wrong model is selected. We see this happening in a repeatable way in the ambiguous figures, such as the luminous Necker cube, that change shape with each depth reversal even though the sensory input is unchanged.

If this general account of perception as essentially a look-up system is correct, we should expect illusions similar to our own to arise in any effective perceptual system, including future robots. Illusions are not caused by any limitation of our brain. They are the result of the imperfect solutions available to any data-handling system faced with the problem of establishing the reality of objects from ambiguous images.

THEORY OF MÜLLER-LYER ILLUSION favored by the author suggests that the eye unconsciously interprets the arrow-like figures as three-dimensional skeleton structures, resembling either an outside (*left*) or inside corner (*right*) of a physical structure. A perceptual mechanism evidently shrinks the former and enlarges the latter to compensate for distortion caused by perspective.

24

THE PROCESSES OF VISION

ULRIC NEISSER
September 1968.

It was Johannes Kepler who first compared the eye to a "camera" (a darkened chamber) with an image in focus on its rear surface. "Vision is brought about by pictures of the thing seen being formed on the white concave surface of the retina," he wrote in 1604. A generation later René Descartes tried to clinch this argument by direct observation. In a hole in a window shutter he set the eye of an ox, just in the position it would have had if the ox had been peering out. Looking at the back of the eye (which he had scraped to make it transparent), he could see a small inverted image of the scene outside the window.

Since the 17th century the analogy between eye and camera has been elaborated in numerous textbooks. As an account of functional anatomy the analogy is not bad, but it carries some unfortunate implications for the study of vision. It suggests all too readily that the perceiver is in the position of Descartes and is in effect looking through the back of his own retina at the pictures that appear there. We use the same word—"image"—for both the optical pattern thrown on the retina by an object and the mental experience of seeing the object. It has been all too easy to treat this inner image as a copy of the outer one, to think of perceptual experiences as images formed by the nervous system acting as an optical instrument of extraordinarily ingenious design. Although this theory encounters insurmountable difficulties as soon as it is seriously considered, it has dominated philosophy and psychology for many years.

Not only perception but also memory has often been explained in terms of an image theory. Having looked at the retinal picture, the perceiver supposedly files it away somehow, as one might put a photograph in an album. Later, if he is lucky, he can take it out again in the form of a "memory image" and look at it a second time. The widespread notion that some people have a "photographic memory" reflects this analogy in a particularly literal way, but in a weaker form it is usually applied even to ordinary remembering. The analogy suggests that the mechanism of visual memory is a natural extension of the mechanisms of vision. Although there is some truth to this proposition, as we shall see below, it is not because both perception and memory are copying processes. Rather it is because *neither* perception *nor* memory is a copying process.

The fact is that one does not see the retinal image; one sees with the aid of the retinal image. The incoming pattern of light provides information that the nervous system is well adapted to pick up. This information is used by the perceiver to guide his movements, to anticipate events and to construct the internal representations of objects and of space called "conscious experience." These internal representations are not, however, at all like the corresponding optical images on the back of the eye. The retinal images of specific objects are at the mercy of every irrelevant change of position; their size, shape and location are hardly constant for a moment. Nevertheless, perception is usually accurate: real objects appear rigid and stable and appropriately located in three-dimensional space.

The first problem in the study of visual perception is therefore the discovery of the stimulus. What properties of the incoming optic array are informative for vision? In the entire distribution of light, over the retina and over a period of time, what determines the way things look? (Actually the light is distributed over two retinas, but the binocularity of vision has no relevance to the variables considered here. Although depth perception is more accurate with two eyes than with one, it is not fundamentally different. The world looks much the same with one eye closed as it does with both open; congenitally monocular people have more or less the same visual experiences as the rest of us.)

As a first step we can consider the patterns of reflected light that are formed when real objects and surfaces are illuminated in the ordinary way by

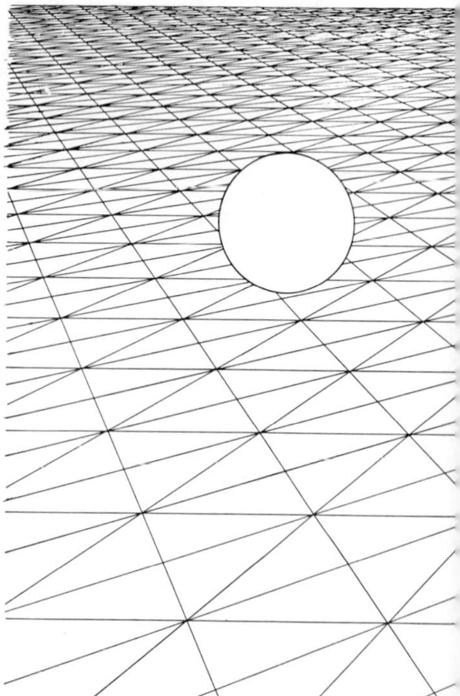

PERCEPTION OF SIZE relies heavily on cues provided by a textured surface. These five disks, if seen alone, would appear to lie

sunshine or lamplight. J. J. Gibson of Cornell University, who has contributed much to our understanding of perception, calls this inquiry "ecological optics." It is an optics in which point sources, homogeneous fields and the other basic elements of classical optics rarely appear. Instead the world we ordinarily look at consists mostly of *surfaces,* at various angles and in various relations to one another. This has significant consequences for the visual input.

One of these consequences (the only one we shall examine here) is to give the visual field a microstructure. Most surfaces have some kind of texture, such as the grain in wood, the individual stalks of grass in a field or the weave in a fabric. These textures structure the light reaching the eye in a way that carries vital information about the layout of environmental objects. In accordance with the principles of perspective the texture elements of more distant surfaces are represented closer to one another on the retina than the elements of surfaces nearby. Thus the microstructure of a surface that slants away from the observer is represented on the retina as a gradient of density—a gradient that carries information about the orientation of the surface.

Consider now an ordinary scene in which discrete figures are superposed on textured surfaces. The gradient of increasing texture density on the retina, corresponding to increasing distance from the observer, gives a kind of "scale" for object sizes. In the ideal case when the texture units are identical, two figures of the same real size will always occlude the same number of texture units, regardless of how far away either one may be. That is, the relation between the retinal texture-size and the dimensions of the object's retinal image is invariant, in spite of changes of distance. This relation is a potentially valuable source of information about the real size of the object—more valuable than the retinal image of the object considered alone. That image, of course, changes in dimension whenever the distance between the object and the observer is altered.

Psychologists have long been interested in what is called "size constancy": the fact that the sizes of real objects are almost always perceived accurately in spite of the linear dependence of retinal-image size on distance. It must not be supposed that this phenomenon is fully explained by the scaling of size with respect to texture elements. There are a great many other sources of relevant information: binocular parallax, shifts of retinal position as the observer moves, relative position in the visual field, linear perspective and so on. It was once traditional to regard these sources of information as "cues" secondary to the size of the object's own retinal image. That is, they were thought to help the observer "correct" the size of the retinal image in the direction of accuracy. Perhaps this is not a bad description of Descartes's situation as he looked at the image on the back of the ox's eye: he may have tried to "correct" his perception of the size of the objects revealed to him on the ox's retina. Since one does not see one's own retina, however, nothing similar need be involved in normal perceiving. Instead the apparent size of an object is determined by information from the entire incoming light pattern, particularly by certain properties of the input that remain invariant with changes of the object's location.

The interrelation of textures, distances and relative retinal sizes is only one example of ecological optics. The example may be a misleadingly simple one, because it assumes a stationary eye, an eye fixed in space and stably oriented in a particular direction. This is by no means a characteristic of human vision. In normal use the eyes are rarely still for long. Apart from small tremors, their

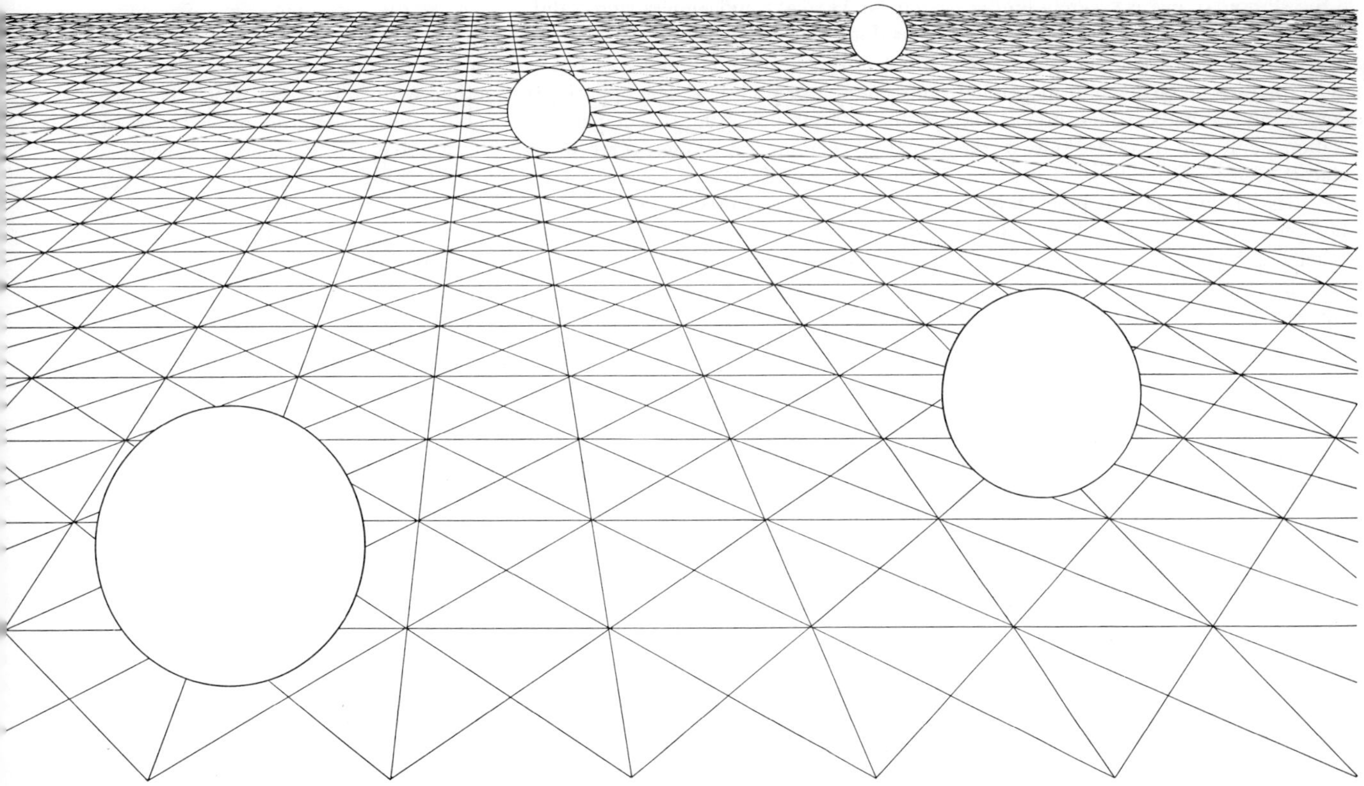

in one plane and be of different sizes. Against this apparently receding surface, however, they seem to lie in five different planes. Since each disk masks the same amount of surface texture, there is a tendency to see them as being equal in size. This illustration, the one at the bottom of the next two pages and the one on page 256 are based on the work of J. J. Gibson of Cornell University.

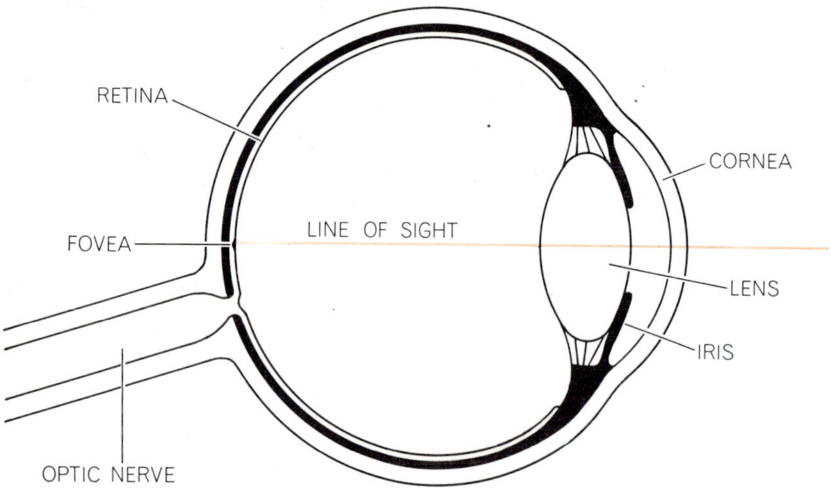

SITE OF OPTICAL IMAGE is the retina, which contains the terminations of the optic nerve. In the tiny retinal depression known as the fovea the cone nerve endings are clustered. Their organization and dense packing make possible a high degree of visual acuity.

most common movement is the flick from one position to another called a "saccade." Saccades usually take less than a twentieth of a second, but they happen several times each second in reading and may be just as frequent when a picture or an actual scene is being inspected. This means that there is a new retinal image every few hundred milliseconds.

Such eye movements are necessary because the area of clear vision available to the stationary eye is severely limited. To see this for oneself it is only necessary to fixate on a point in some unfamiliar picture or on an unread printed page. Only a small region around the fixation point will be clear. Most of the page is seen peripherally, which means that it is hazily visible at best. Only in the fovea, the small central part of the retina, are the receptor cells packed close enough together (and appropriately organized) to make a high degree of visual acuity possible. This is the reason one must turn one's eyes (or head) to look directly at objects in which one is particularly interested. (Animals with nonfoveated eyes, such as the horse, do not find this necessary.) It is also the reason why the eye must make several fixations on each line in reading, and why it roves widely over pictures.

Although it is easy to understand the function of saccadic movements, it is difficult or impossible to reconcile them with an image theory of perception. As long as we think of the perceiver as a homunculus looking at his retinal image, we must expect his experience to be one of almost constant interruption and change. Clearly this is not the case; one sees the page or the scene as a whole without any apparent discontinuity in space or time. Most people are either unaware of their own eye movements or have erroneous notions about them. Far from being a copy of the retinal display, the visual world is somehow *constructed* on the basis of information taken in during many different fixations.

The same conclusion follows, perhaps even more compellingly, if we consider the motions of external objects rather than the motions of the eyes. If the analogy between eye and camera were valid, the thing one looked at would have to hold still like a photographer's model in order to be seen clearly. The opposite is true: far from obscuring the shapes and spatial relations of things, movement generally clarifies them. Consider the visual problem presented by a distant arrow-shaped weather vane. As long as the weather vane and the observer remain motionless, there is no way to tell whether it is a short arrow oriented at right angles to the line of sight or a longer arrow slanting toward (or away from) the observer. Let it begin to turn in the wind, however, and its true shape and orientation will become visible immediately. The reason lies in the systematic distortions of the retinal image produced by the object's rotation. Such distortions provide information that the nervous system can use. On the basis of a fluidly changing retinal pattern the perceiver comes to experience a rigid object. (An interesting aspect of this example is that the input information is ambiguous. The same retinal changes could be produced by either a clockwise or a counterclockwise rotation of the weather vane. As a result the perceiver may alternate between two perceptual experiences, one of which is illusory.)

Some years ago Hans Wallach and D. N. O'Connell of Swarthmore College showed that such motion-produced changes in the input are indeed used as a source of information in perceiving; in fact this kind of information seems to be a more potent determiner of what we see than the traditionally emphasized cues for depth are. In their experiment the subject watched the shadow of a wire form cast on a translucent screen. He could not see the object itself. So long as the object remained stationary the subject saw only a two-dimensional shadow on a two-dimensional screen, as might be expected. The form was mounted in such a way, however, that it could be swiveled back and forth by a small electric motor. When the motor was turned on, the true three-dimensional shape of the form appeared at once, even though the only stimulation reaching the subject's eyes came from a distorting shadow on a flat screen. Here the kinetic depth effect, as it has been called, overrode binocular stereoscopic information that continued to indicate that all the movement was taking place in a flat plane.

In the kinetic depth effect the constructive nature of perception is particularly apparent. What one sees is somehow a composite based on information accumulated over a period of time. The same is true in reading or in any instance where eye movements are involved: information from past fixations is used together with information from the present fixation to determine what is seen. But if perception is a temporally extended act, some storage of information, some kind of memory, must be involved in it. How shall we conceive of this storage? How is it organized? How

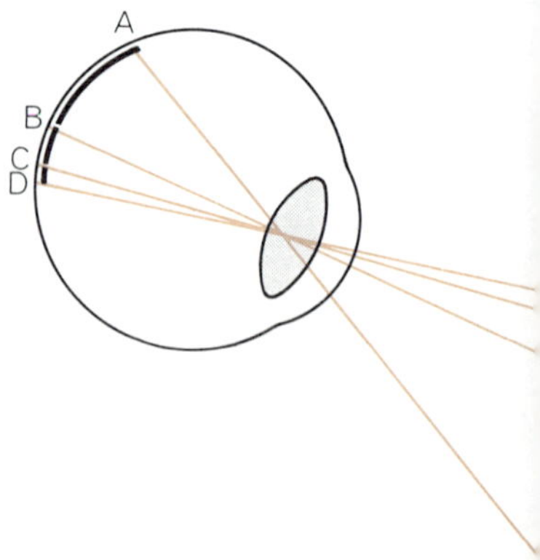

CONTRACTION OF IMAGE takes place as the distance between the viewer and the

long does it last? What other functions might it serve?

With questions like these, we have moved beyond the problem of specifying the visual stimulus. In addition to identifying the sources of information for vision, we want to know how that information is processed. In the long run, perhaps, questions about processes should be answered in neurological terms. However, no such answers can be given at present. The neurophysiology of vision has recently made great strides, but it is still not ready to deal with the constructive processes that are central to perception. We shall have to be content with a relatively abstract account, one that does not specify the neural locus of the implicated mechanisms.

Although seeing requires storage of information, this memory cannot be thought of as a sequence of superposed retinal images. Superposition would give rise only to a sort of smear in which all detail is lost. Nor can we assume that the perceiver keeps careful track of his eye movements and thus is able to set each new retinal image in just the right place in relation to the older stored ones. Such an alignment would require a much finer monitoring of eye motion than is actually available. Moreover, the similar synthesis of information that is involved in the kinetic depth effect could not possibly be explained that way. It seems, therefore, that perceiving involves a memory that is not representational but schematic. During a series of fixations the perceiver synthesizes a model or schema of the scene before him, using information from each successive fixation to add detail or to extend the construction. This constructed whole is what guides his movements (including further eye movements in many cases) and it is what he describes when he is being introspective. In short, it is what he sees.

Interestingly enough, although the memory involved in visual synthesis cannot consist simply of stored retinal afterimages, recent experiments indicate that storage of this kind does exist under certain circumstances. After a momentary exposure (too short for eye movement) that is followed by a blank field the viewer preserves an iconic image of the input pattern for some fraction of a second. George Sperling of the Bell Telephone Laboratories has shown that a signal given during this postexposure period can serve to direct a viewer's attention to any arbitrary part of the field, just as if it were still present.

The displays used in Sperling's experiments consisted of several rows of letters—too many to be reported from a single glance. Nevertheless, subjects were able to report any *single row,* indicated by the postexposure signal, rather well. Such a signal must come quickly; letters to which the observer does not attend before the brief iconic memory has faded are lost. That is why the observer cannot report the entire display: the icon disappears before he can read it all.

Even under these unusual conditions, then, people display selectivity in their use of the information that reaches the eye. The selection is made from material presented in a single brief exposure, but only because the experimental arrangements precluded a second glance. Normally selection and construction take place over a series of glances; no iconic memory for individual "snapshots" can survive. Indeed, the presentation of a second stimulus figure shortly after the first in a brief-exposure experiment tends to destroy the iconic replica. The viewer may see a fusion of the two figures, only the second, or an apparent motion of the figures, depending on their temporal and spatial relations. He does not see them separately.

So far we have considered two kinds of short-term memory for visual information: the iconic replica of a brief and isolated stimulus, and the cumulative schema of the visible world that is constructed in the course of ordinary perception. Both of these processes (which may well be different manifestations of a single underlying mechanism) involve the storage of information over a period of time. Neither of them, however, is what the average man has in mind when he speaks of memory. Everyday experience testifies that visual information can be stored over long periods. Things seen yesterday can be recalled today; for that matter they may conceivably be recalled 20 years from now. Such recall may take many forms, but perhaps the most interesting is the phenomenon called visual imagery. In a certain sense one can see again what one has seen before. Are these mental images like optical ones? Are they revived copies of earlier stimulation? Indeed, does it make any sense at all to speak of "seeing" things that are not present? Can there be visual experience when there is no stimulation by light?

To deal with these problems effectively we must distinguish two issues: first, the degree to which the mechanisms involved in visual memory are like those involved in visual perception and, second, the degree to which the perceiver

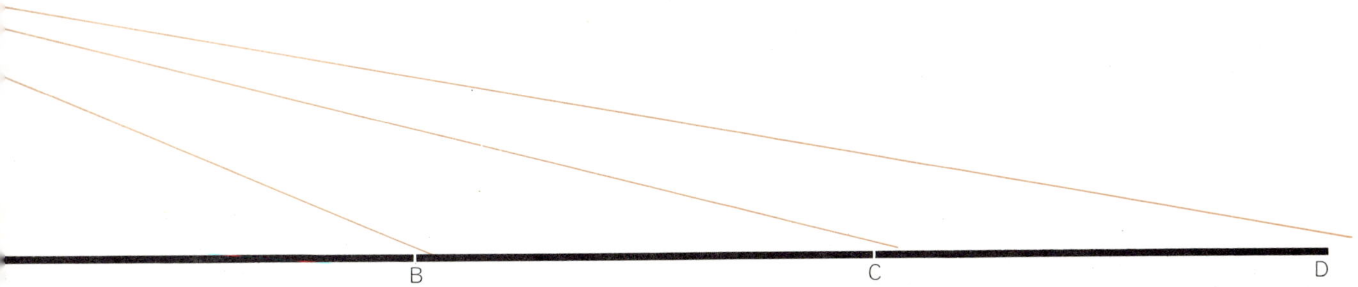

object in view increases. The texture elements of a distant surface are also projected closer together than similar elements nearby. Thus a textured surface slanting away from the viewer is represented optically as a density gradient (*see illustration on next page*).

is willing to say his images look real, that is, like external things seen. Although the first issue is perhaps the more fundamental—and the most relevant here—the second has always attracted the most attention.

One reason for the perennial interest in the "realness" of images is the wide range of differences in imaging capacity from person to person and from time to time. When Francis Galton conducted the first empirical study of mental imagery (published in 1883), he found some of his associates skeptical of the very existence of imagery. They assumed that only poetic fancy allowed one to speak of "seeing" in connection with what one remembered; remembering consisted simply in a knowledge of facts. Other people, however, were quite ready to describe their mental imagery in terms normally applied to perception. Asked in the afternoon about their breakfast table, they said they could see it clearly, with colors bright (although perhaps a little dimmer than in the original experience) and objects suitably arranged.

These differences seem to matter less when one is asleep; many people who report little or no lifelike imagery while awake may have visual dreams and believe in the reality of what they see. On the other hand, some psychopathological states can endow images with such a compelling quality that they dominate the patient's experience. Students of per-

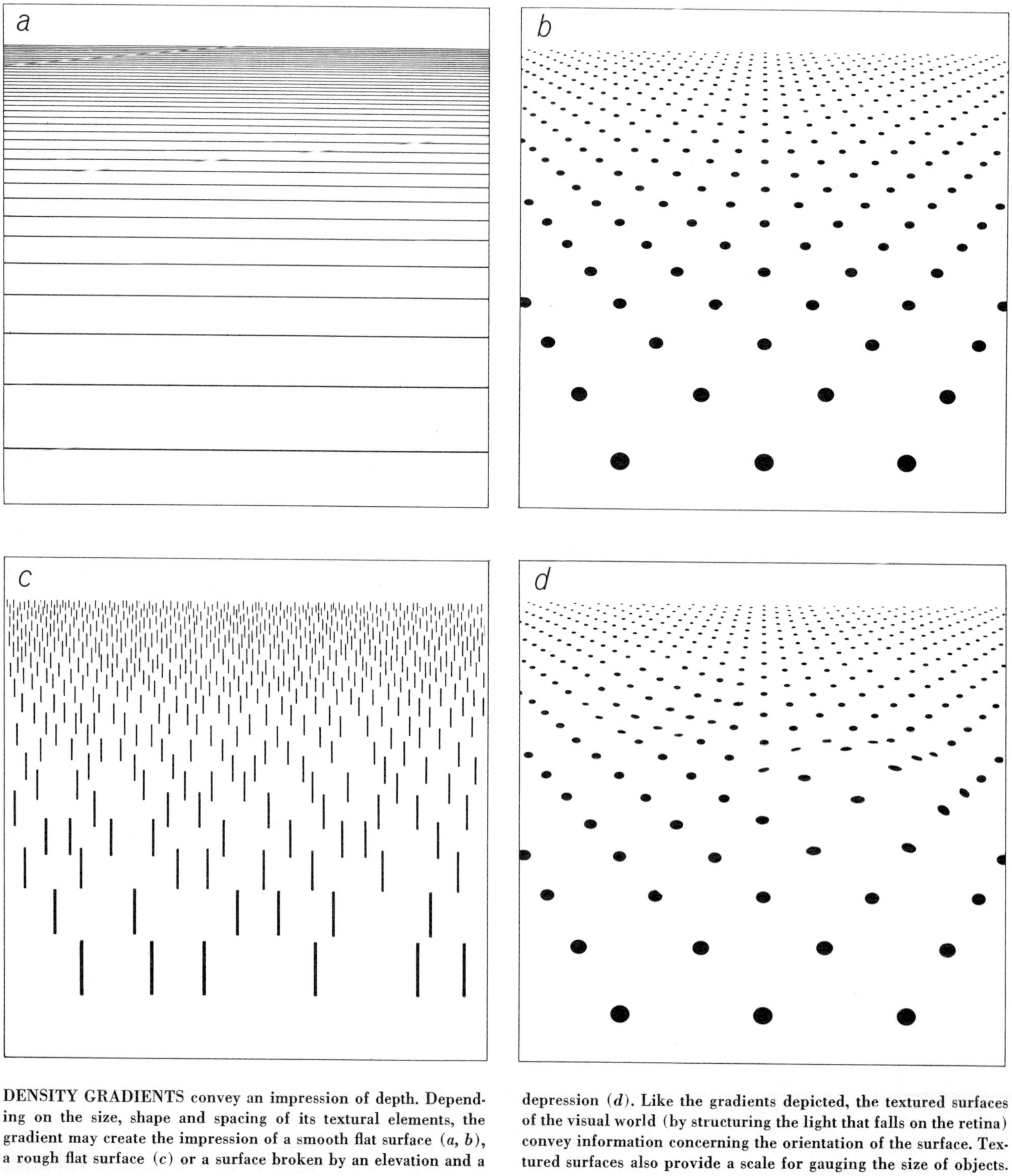

DENSITY GRADIENTS convey an impression of depth. Depending on the size, shape and spacing of its textural elements, the gradient may create the impression of a smooth flat surface (*a*, *b*), a rough flat surface (*c*) or a surface broken by an elevation and a depression (*d*). Like the gradients depicted, the textured surfaces of the visual world (by structuring the light that falls on the retina) convey information concerning the orientation of the surface. Textured surfaces also provide a scale for gauging the size of objects.

ception have often disregarded dreams and phantasms, considering them "hallucinatory" and thus irrelevant to normal seeing. However, this is a difficult position to defend either logically or empirically. Logically a sharp distinction between perception and hallucination would be easy enough if perceptions were copies of the retinal image; hallucinations would then be experiences that do *not* copy that image. But since perception does more than mirror the stimulus (and since hallucinations often incorporate stimulus information), this distinction is not clear-cut. Moreover, a number of recent findings seem to point up very specific relations between the processes of seeing and of imagining.

Perhaps the most unexpected of these findings has emerged from studies of sleep and dreams. The dreaming phase of sleep, which occurs several times each night, is regularly accompanied by bursts of rapid eye movements. In several studies William C. Dement and his collaborators have awakened experimental subjects immediately after a period of eye motion and asked them to report their just-preceding dream. Later the eye-movement records were compared with a transcript of the dream report to see if any relation between the two could be detected. Of course this was not possible in every case. (Indeed, we can be fairly sure that many of the eye movements of sleep have no visual significance; similar motions occur in the sleep of newborn babies, decorticated cats and congenitally blind adults.) Nevertheless, there was appreciably more correspondence between the two kinds of record than could be attributed to chance. The parallel between the eye movements of the dreamer and the content of the dream was sometimes striking. In one case five distinct upward deflections of the eyes were recorded just before the subject awoke and reported a dream of climbing five steps!

Another recent line of research has also implicated eye movements in the processes of visual memory. Ralph Norman Haber and his co-workers at Yale University reopened the study of eidetic imagery, which for a generation had remained untouched by psychological research. An eidetic image is an imaginative production that seems to be external to the viewer and to have a location in perceived space; it has a clarity comparable to that of genuinely perceived objects; it can be examined by the "*Eidetiker*," who may report details that he did not notice in the original presentation of the stimulus. Most *Eidetikers*

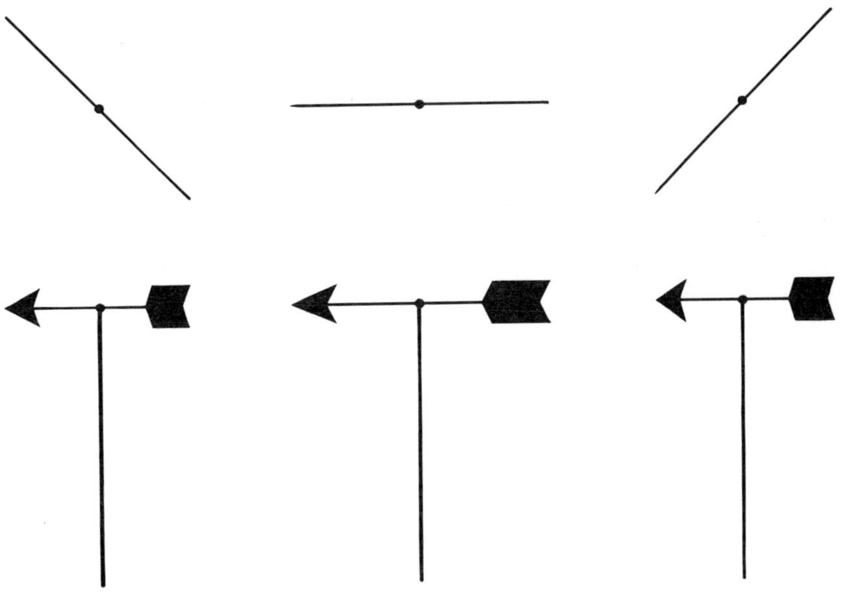

AMBIGUOUS VISUAL INPUT can arise from a stationary weather vane. The weather vane in three different orientations is shown as it would be seen from above (*top*) and in side view (*bottom*). If the vane begins to rotate, its real length will become apparent.

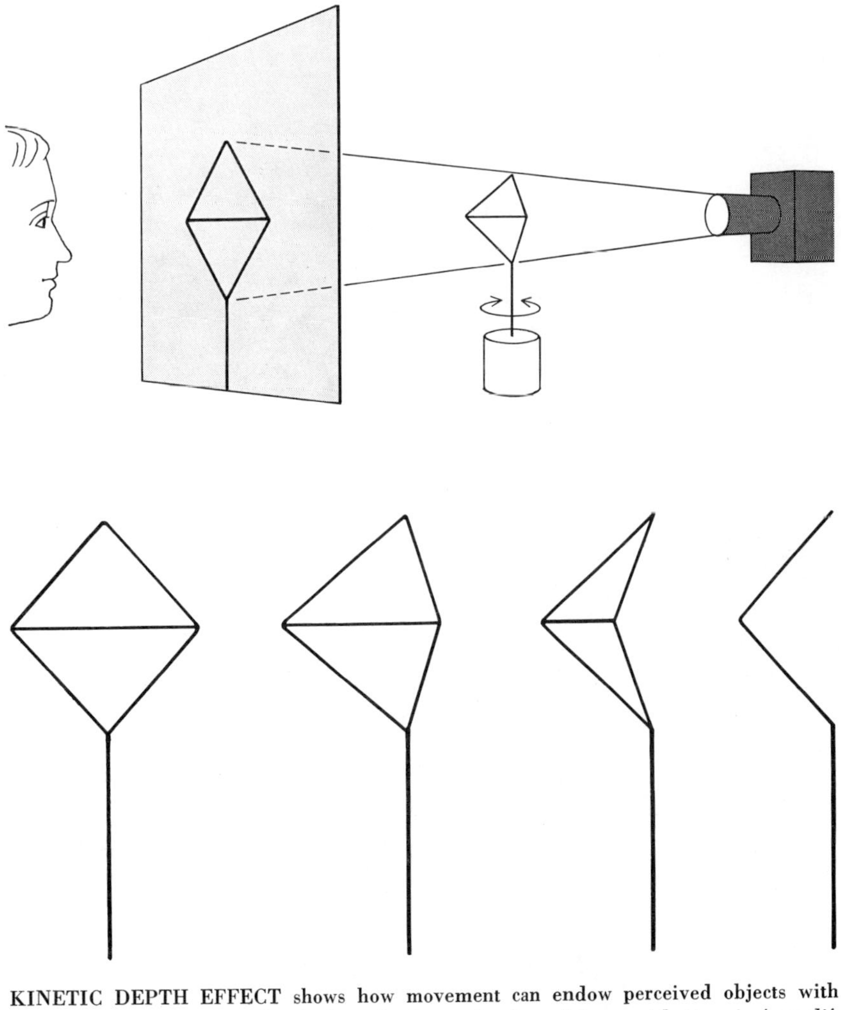

KINETIC DEPTH EFFECT shows how movement can endow perceived objects with three-dimensional shape. The shadow of a bent wire form (*shown at bottom in four different orientations*) looks as flat as the screen on which it is cast so long as the form remains stationary. When it is swiveled back and forth, the changing shadow is seen as a rigid rotating object with the appropriate three-dimensionality. The direction of rotation remains ambiguous, as in the case of the weather vane in the illustration at top of the page.

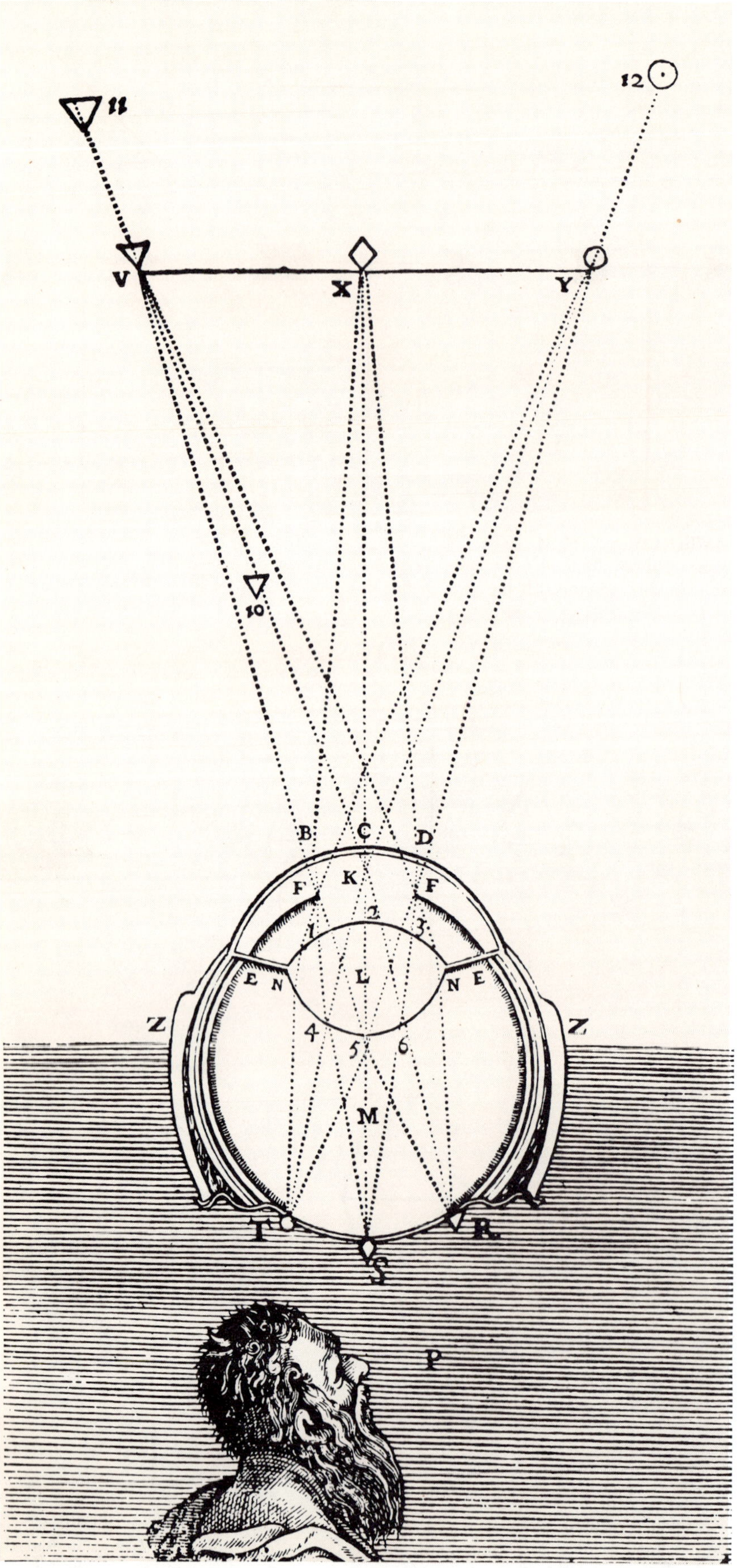

OPTICAL ANALYSIS BY DESCARTES included an experiment in which he removed the eye of an ox, scraped the back of the eye to make it transparent and observed on the retina the inverted image of a scene. The illustration is from Descartes's essay *La Dioptrique.*

are children, but the developmental course of this rather rare ability is not well understood. What is most interesting about these images for the present argument is that the *Eidetiker* scans them with his eyes. Asked about a detail in one or another corner of the image, he moves his eyes to look at the appropriate part of the blank wall on which he has "projected" it. That is, he does just what anyone would do who was really looking at something.

Are these esoteric phenomena really relevant to the study of vision? It might be argued that they do not provide a safe basis for inference; dreaming is a very special physiological state and eidetic imagery is restricted to very special types of people. It is not difficult, however, to show that similar processes occur in persons who do not have vivid visual imagery at all. A simple demonstration suggested by Julian Hochberg of New York University helps to make this point: Try to remember how many windows there are in your own house or apartment.

If you have never considered this question before, it will be hard to find the answer without actively looking and counting. However, you will probably not need to look at the windows themselves. Most people, even those who say they have no visual imagery, can easily form and scan an *internal representation* of the walls, counting off the windows as they appear in them. This process evidently uses stored visual information. It seems to involve mechanisms much like those used for seeing and counting real windows.

We can draw three conclusions from this demonstration. First, seeing and imagining employ similar—perhaps the same—mechanisms. Second, images can be useful, even when they are not vivid or lifelike, even for people who do not have "good imagery." Third, mental images are constructs and not copies. This last point may have been obvious in any case—you might just as well have been asked to imagine a gryphon and to count its claws—but it bears further emphasis. All the windows could not have been optically imaged on the retina simultaneously, and they may not even have appeared there in rapid succession. The image (or series of images) developed in solving this problem is new; it is not a replica of any previous stimulus.

The first two of these points have received additional confirmation in a recent experiment by Lee R. Brooks of McMaster University, whose method puts imagery and visual perception in direct competition. In one of his studies the subjects were shown a large block *F* and told to remember what it looked like. After the *F* was removed from view they were asked to describe the succession of corner points that would be encountered as one moved around it, responding "Yes" for each point that was either on the extreme top or the bottom of the *F*, and "No" for each point in between. This visual-memory task proved to be more difficult when the responses were made by *pointing* to a printed series of yeses and noes than when a spoken "Yes" or "No" was allowed. However, the difficulty was not intrinsic to the act of pointing; it resulted from the conflict between pointing and simultaneously visualizing the *F*. In another of Brooks's tasks the subjects had to respond "Yes" for each noun and "No" for each non-noun in a memorized sentence. In this case they tended to rely on verbal-auditory memory rather than visual memory. As a result spoken response was the more difficult of the two.

We would not have been surprised to find a conflict between visually guided pointing and corner-counting on an *F* the viewer was *looking at*. After all, he could not be expected to look in two places at once. Even if the *F* had appeared on the same sheet of paper with the yeses and noes, interference would have been easy to understand: the succession of glances required to examine the corners of the *F* would have conflicted with the visual organization needed to point at the right succession of responses. What Brooks has shown, rather surprisingly, is that this conflict exists even when the *F* is merely imagined. Visual images are apparently produced by the same integrative processes that make ordinary perception possible.

In short, the reaction of the nervous system to stimulation by light is far from passive. The eye and brain do not act as a camera or a recording instrument. Neither in perceiving nor in remembering is there any enduring copy of the optical input. In perceiving, complex patterns are extracted from that input and fed into the constructive processes of vision, so that the movements and the inner experience of the perceiver are usually in good correspondence with his environment. Visual memory differs from perception because it is based primarily on stored rather than on current information, but it involves the same kind of synthesis. Although the eyes have been called the windows of the soul, they are not so much peepholes as entry ports, supplying raw material for the constructive activity of the visual system.

25

THE MOON ILLUSION

LLOYD KAUFMAN AND IRVIN ROCK
July 1962

When the moon hangs low over the horizon, it looks much bigger than when it is high in the sky. Yet in photographs its image has essentially the same size no matter where the camera finds it. Of course this is equally true of the images in the eye. The change in size is not an optical effect but a psychological one. It is therefore known as the moon illusion.

Men have recognized the moon illusion (as well as the corresponding sun illusion) since antiquity. Many explanations for it have been advanced, but only two deserve serious consideration. One can be called the apparent-distance theory and the other the angle-of-regard theory. According to the former the horizon moon looks bigger because it seems farther away; according to the latter the high moon looks smaller because the viewer raises his eyes or head to look at it.

The apparent-distance theory seems to be the older, going back at least to the second-century astronomer and geometer Ptolemy. He proposed that any object seen through filled space, such as the moon seen across terrain at the horizon, is perceived as being more distant than an object just as far away but seen through empty space, such as the moon at the zenith. If the images of these objects in the eye are in fact of equal size, the one that appears farther away will seem larger.

This follows from the geometrical relationship between size and distance [*see top illustration on page 262*]. If two objects at unequal distances from the observer form images of the same size on the retina, the more remote object must be the larger. It is well known to psychologists that an observer perceiving two equal images, and receiving sensory information that one object is farther away than the other, correctly sees the farther one to be the larger. The reader can demonstrate this fact for himself by looking at a sharply contrasted object against a uniform background long enough to form a clear, persistent afterimage on the retina. This afterimage is of course constant in size. But when the gaze is shifted between two surfaces at different distances, the image appears larger when it is projected on the farther surface.

Similarly, if the moon seems farther away when it is on the horizon than when it is higher in the sky, it should look larger. Some years ago Edwin G. Boring and his colleagues at Harvard University subjected the apparent-distance theory to what he considered a critical test. He asked people to judge the relative distances of the zenith and horizon moons. Most of his subjects said the horizon moon seemed nearer—the opposite of what the theory called for. So Boring sought another explanation.

He proposed that the postural changes involved in looking at the zenith moon might somehow be responsible for the moon illusion (the angle-of-regard theory). Although he could find no explanation of why this might be so, he and his colleagues carried out a series of experiments that seemed to connect the apparent size of the moon with the elevation of the observers' eyes. They used a number of methods; the major one was designed to measure the illusion as follows. The subjects were asked to match the moon, as they saw it, with one of a series of disks of light projected on a nearby screen. Looking at the horizon moon with eyes level, most observers selected a disk one and a half or two times larger than the one they chose when their eyes were raised 30 degrees to view the zenith moon. When they tilted their heads so that they could look at the zenith moon with eyes level, their choice indicated that they experienced no illusion. Two subjects lay supine so that they could see the zenith moon "straight ahead," and, by bending their necks backward, could see the horizon moon with eyes "elevated." For them the illusion was reversed, the zenith moon appearing the larger.

In spite of the apparent persuasiveness of these results, the authors of the present article, working at the New School for Social Research and at Yeshiva University, decided some five years ago to reopen the subject. For one thing, we ourselves saw no significant change in size whether we looked at the moon with our eyes level or elevated. For another, we questioned Boring's method of determining the moon's apparent size.

In effect he was asking his subjects to compare things that are not really commensurable. It is difficult to say how large the moon appears to be. Its virtually infinite distance gives it a large but more or less indeterminate size. The comparison disks, on the other hand, were nearby, so that the observer could easily make a judgment as to their actual size. He then had to match a circle of indeterminate size with one having a diameter of some specific number of inches. We felt that such a comparison was extremely difficult to make.

We decided to try a more direct approach, in which two artificial moons seen against the sky could be compared with each other. (The actual illusion involves the same sort of comparison, although the two real moons are separated by a considerable interval of time as well as space.) In our artificial moon appara-

MOON ILLUSION, in which the horizon moon appears larger than the zenith moon, is simulated in these photographs. An artificial moon has been placed high in the empty sky (*above*) and another, of the same size, has been placed low on the horizon (*below*). Some people note a slight illusion even in the photographs; the illusion is a common phenomenon for most people viewing an actual scene.

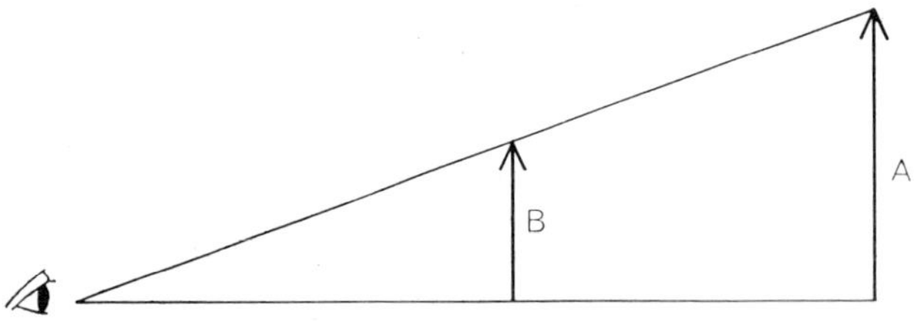

DISTANCE AND SIZE are related in the manner shown here. Although arrows *A* and *B* subtend the same visual angle at the observer's eye and therefore produce images of the same size on his retina, arrow *A* is seen to be farther away and hence actually to be larger.

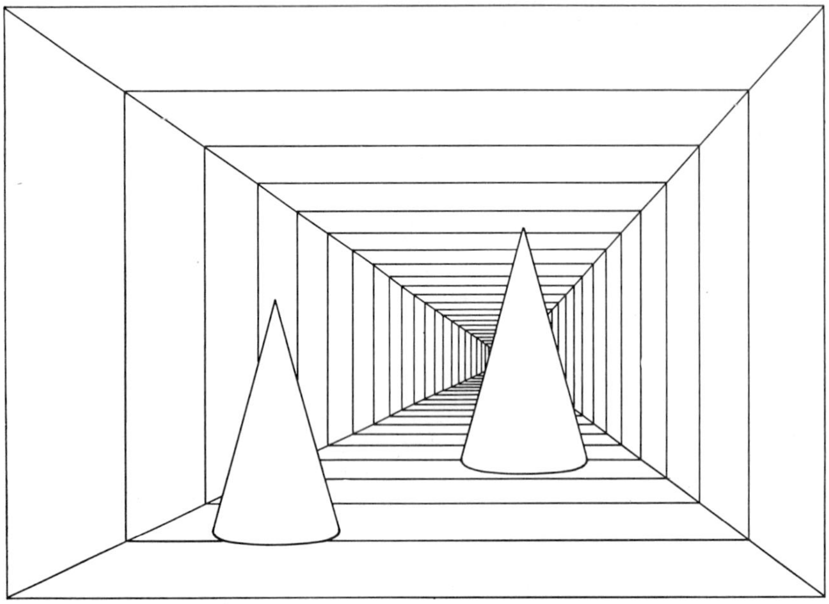

DISTANCE-SIZE RELATIONSHIP is automatically taken into account by an observer. If two objects that are actually the same size are perceived as being at different distances, the one that seems to be farther away will look larger. The figure at the right is perceived as being larger than the identical figure at the left only because it seems to be farther away.

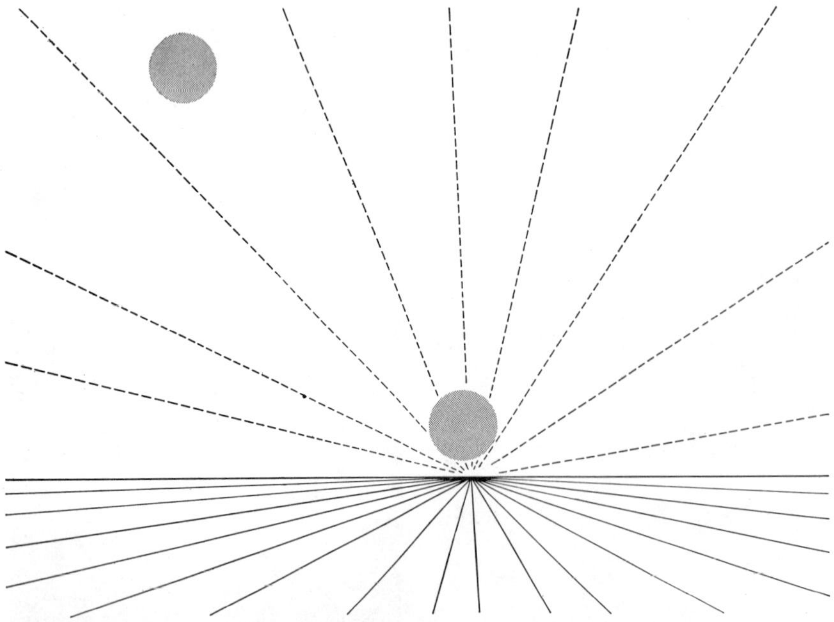

APPARENT-DISTANCE THEORY holds that this is what happens in the case of the moon illusion. The horizon moon appears to be farther away, although it is not. The viewer automatically takes the apparent distance into account. He then unconsciously applies the rule that, of two objects forming images of equal size, the more distant must be the larger.

tus light rays from a lamp pass through a circular aperture and are made parallel by a lens. The parallel rays fall on a piece of glass or a half-silvered mirror tilted at an angle of 45 degrees. An observer looking into the glass sees a bright disk against the sky, which is also visible through the glass [*see illustrations on page 264*].

With two such devices, one pointed toward the horizon and the other pointed toward the zenith, we could test the illusion both qualitatively and quantitatively. Each device was equipped with a set of circular apertures of different sizes; thus the aperture in one could be changed until the subject said that the size of the "moon" matched that in the other. The ratio of the zenith aperture to the horizon aperture gave a numerical value for the illusion. A ratio of one would mean no illusion; a ratio greater than one would indicate that the illusion was present in its usual form.

First we set out to test the eye-elevation hypothesis by our new method. In one experiment 10 subjects viewed the artificial horizon moon normally and compared it with a zenith moon that they saw either with eyes elevated or, by tilting their heads, with their eyes level. We obtained an illusion both ways. The ratio of the horizon moon's apparent diameter to that of the zenith moon was 1.48 with eyes elevated and 1.46 without eye elevation—an insignificant difference. Then we had the subjects compare two moons in the same region of the sky, one viewed with eyes level and the other with eyes elevated. The ratio between the sizes of the two moons was only 1.04. There was no illusion to speak of. We concluded that Boring's findings on eye elevation were peculiar to the methods employed.

Before abandoning the angle-of-regard theory completely, we rechecked one other phenomenon that seemed to support it. Many years ago the German psychologist Erna Schur found she could produce the illusion indoors, in a large dark space such as a zeppelin hangar, by projecting disks of light on the wall and ceiling. Moreover, Boring and Alfred H. Holway reported a sun illusion even when the subject looked at the sun through a dense filter that blanked out everything but the bright disk itself. In both cases no terrain was visible to differentiate horizon from zenith. We repeated Schur's experiment in the Hayden Planetarium in New York and got a ratio of only 1.03 between horizon and zenith. Next we set up our

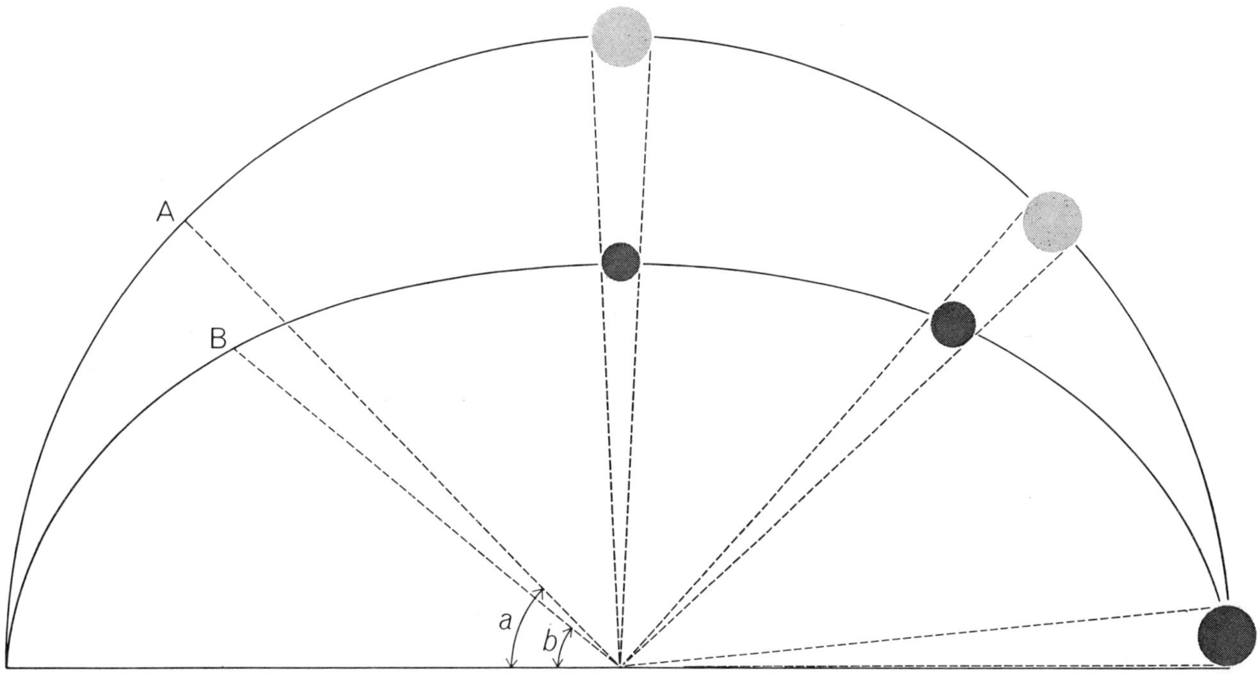

EFFECT OF APPARENT DISTANCE on the moon's apparent size is diagramed. The true positions of the moon are along the upper curve; its apparent positions, if the horizon seems more distant than the zenith, would be along the lower curve. The perceived size of the moon would accordingly vary as shown by the darker disks. Measurement of the half-arc angles (*a*, *b*) to the mid-points (*A*, *B*) of the actual and apparent arcs from zenith to horizon indicates that most people see the sky as "flattened," confirming the theory.

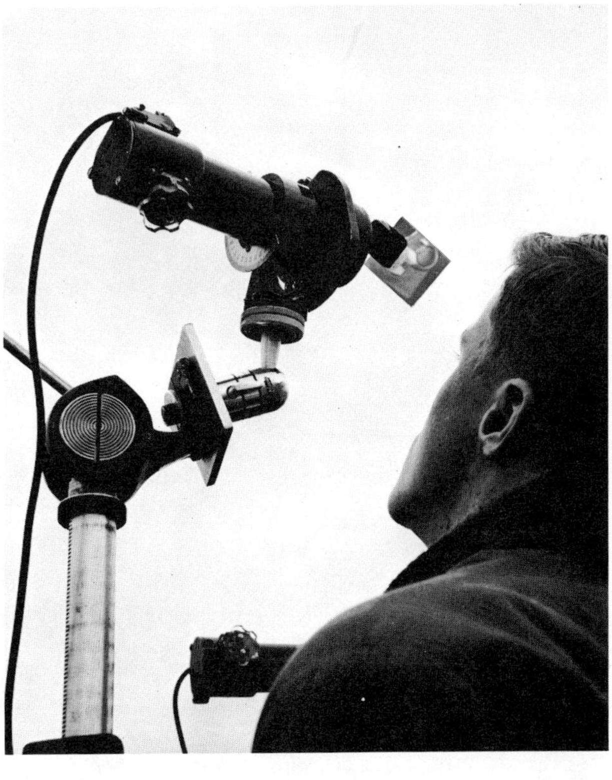

VIEWING ZENITH MOON, an observer looks through the mirror of a device that combines the reflected image of an infinitely distant moon with the background sky (*left*). Then he looks through a device aimed at the horizon (*right*). The size of the horizon moon is adjusted until the observer says it is the same as that of the zenith moon. The ratio between the two sizes measures the illusion.

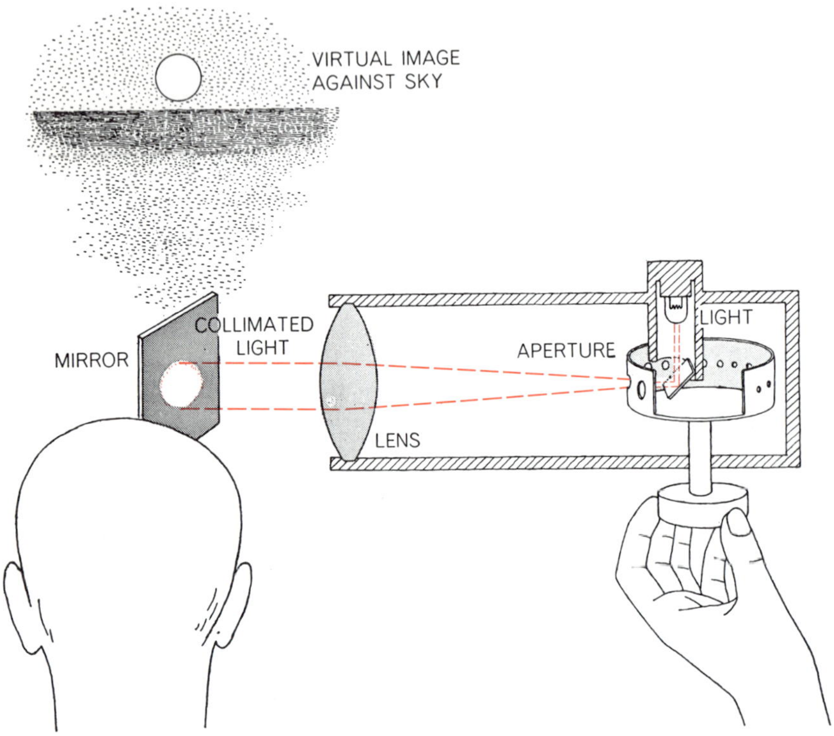

MOONS WERE SIMULATED by an optical apparatus, shown here schematically. Light passing through one of a series of apertures of different sizes is collimated (rendered parallel) by a lens and falls on a half-silvered mirror. An observer looking into the mirror sees against the sky, as if at an infinite distance, a virtual image of the luminous aperture.

VIEW THROUGH MIRROR shows a "moon" against the sky. The observer's eye is placed much nearer the glass than the camera that made photograph, so edge of mirror is not seen.

artificial moon apparatus in a totally dark room and repeated our eye-elevation experiment. In this case the moons were each seen at optical infinity, one at the zenith and one straight ahead. Again the ratio turned out to be 1.03. Considering that T. G. Hermans of the University of Washington has recently reported approximately the same ratio in studying the effect of eye elevation in apparent size, and that we came very close to it (1.04) in our outdoor observations of two moons in the same part of the sky, eye elevation would appear to exert a slight effect. Why this should be so is by no means clear, but in any case it cannot really account for the moon illusion.

We therefore turned to the apparent-distance theory. Boring had rejected it because his subjects said that the horizon moon appeared to be nearer than the zenith moon. But, we wondered, did they really see the horizon moon as nearer? Or were they judging it to be nearer precisely because it looked bigger, effectively turning the reasoning upside down? In that case the reported distance would be a secondary phenomenon, an artifact of the very illusion it was supposed to test. To check this possibility we showed our subjects pairs of artificial moons of different diameters and instructed them to compare their relative distances. Whenever the zenith moon was larger, the subjects said it was nearer than the horizon moon; when it was smaller, they said it was farther away.

Therefore we next undertook to elicit a judgment of distance without regard to the moon. We asked people to scan a moonless sky and to try to see it as a surface. Then they were to say whether the surface seemed farther away immediately over the horizon or at the zenith. Nine out of 10 observers answered that the horizon sky was the more distant; the tenth could see no difference. From this experiment we conclude that the horizon sky does appear farther away whether the observer realizes it or not when the moon is present.

This evidence is supported by a number of observations, dating back to the English mathematician Robert Smith in 1738, on the "half-arc angle." Most people, when they are asked to point along the line that bisects the arc of sky from horizon to zenith, indicate a direction considerably less than 45 degrees from the horizontal. The vault of the heavens looks flattened, like a semiellipsoid, rather than hemispherical. Accordingly the horizon seems farther away than the zenith. If the moon is perceived on the

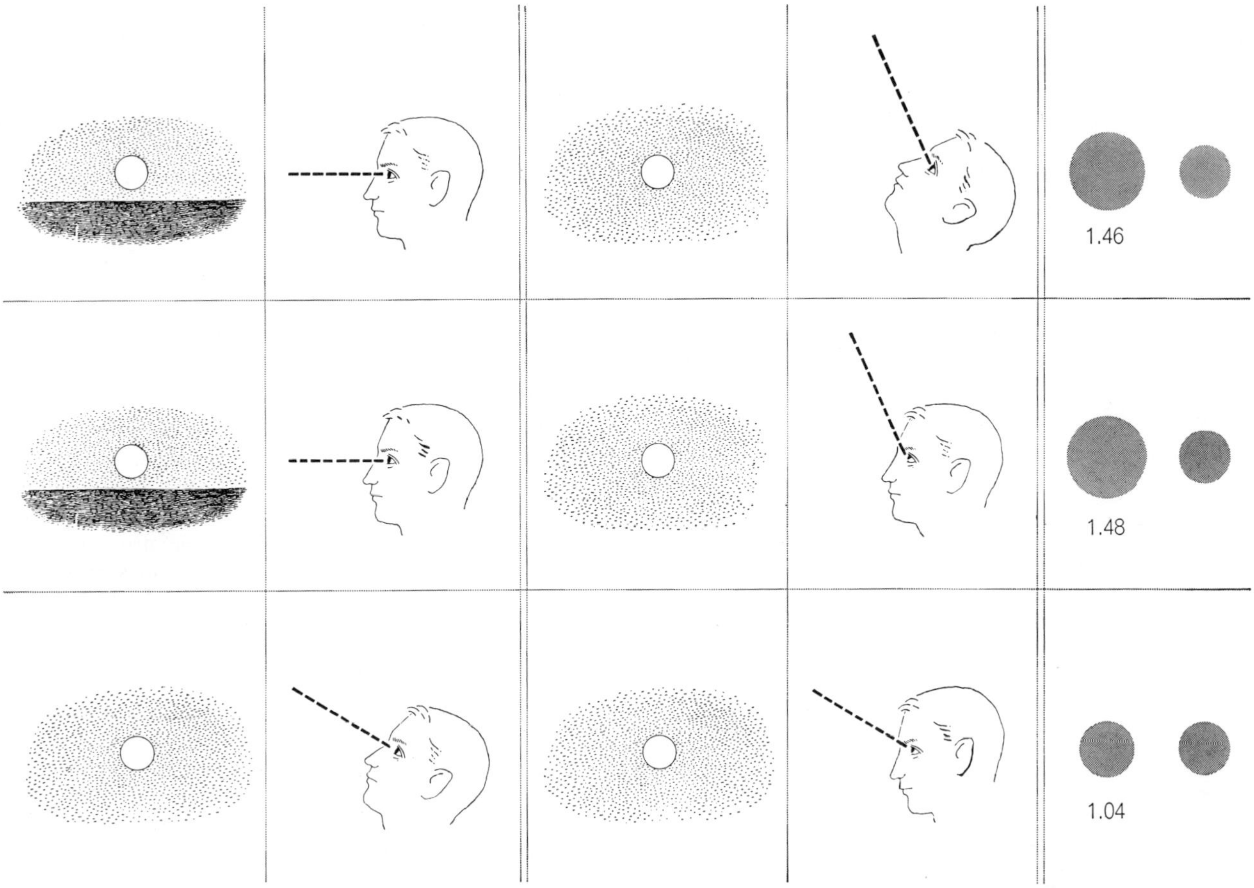

EYE-ELEVATION HYPOTHESIS was tested by having subjects view simulated horizon and zenith moons in various ways. A horizon moon was compared with a zenith moon seen with eyes level (*top row*) and also with eyes elevated (*middle row*). As shown by the ratios between the perceived sizes of the horizon and zenith moons (*right*), the illusion was present in both cases and was almost the same in spite of the different angles of regard. Then subjects were asked to compare two moons in the same part of the sky, raising their heads so that their eyes were level in one case and lowering their heads so that their eyes were elevated in the other case (*bottom row*). Changing the angle of regard had no significant effect on the size of the two moons, as shown by the 1.04 ratio.

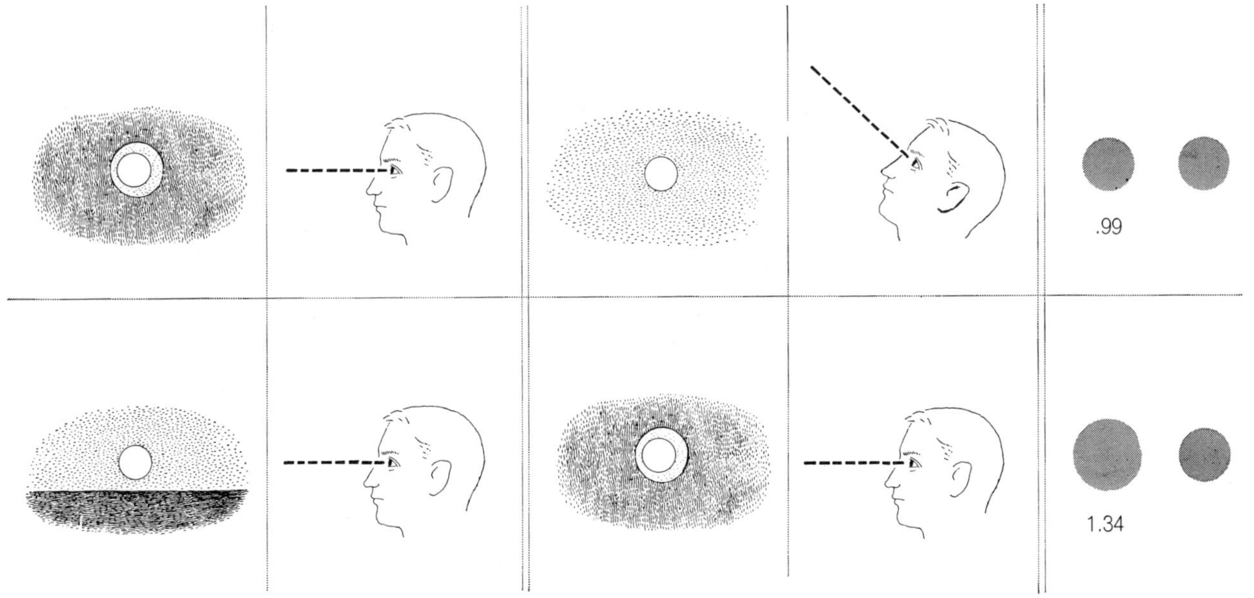

EFFECT OF TERRAIN was shown by an experiment in which the landscape beneath the horizon moon could be masked, leaving the moon visible through an aperture. When this masked horizon moon was compared with a zenith moon, there was no illusion (*top row*). When a normal horizon moon with terrain was compared with the masked horizon moon, substantial illusion resulted (*bottom row*).

"surface" of the semiellipsoid, it too will appear more distant, and therefore larger, at the horizon [*see illustration below*]. All this convinced us that the apparent-distance theory was perfectly tenable on logical grounds, and we set out to test it directly.

Pointing our artificial-moon apparatus at the horizon, we had observers view the "moon" through a hole in a sheet of cardboard that masked the terrain. Under these circumstances the illusion vanished: the horizon moon looked no larger than the zenith moon. Then we pointed two of our devices at the horizon; in one the moon was viewed through a mask and in the other the moon was seen over unobstructed terrain. The illusion appeared, just as the apparent-distance theory predicts; to make the two disks appear equal the masked aperture had to be made 1.34 times larger than the aperture of the moon over terrain [*see bottom illustration on page 265*]. This was quite comparable with the ratios that were obtained in the ordinary illusion experiment carried out at the same site with different subjects.

If, as was beginning to seem likely, the horizon moon looks larger only because it is seen over terrain, it should be possible to reverse the illusion by moving the terrain overhead with a mirror or prism. We arranged a mirror at a 45-degree angle so that by looking into it a subject could see the horizon and its moon high in the sky. By looking straight ahead into another mirror he saw an image of the zenith sky and moon in a horizontal direction. As we had expected, the illusion did reverse: the moon on an overhead horizon appeared to be larger than the moon at a horizontal zenith, with a ratio of 1.34 [*see illustrations on this page*].

At this point we could no longer doubt that terrain plays the major role in the moon illusion, but the nature of its role had not been established. Perhaps it was acting in some way other than by giving a sense of greater distance. We now located our apparatus at a site where the visible horizon was about two miles away in one direction and no more than 2,000 feet away 30 degrees to the left, providing a direct test of the effect of distance. The illusion was distinctly greater when the low-lying artificial moon was seen over the more distant horizon.

In this same experiment we also controlled for cloud conditions. Hermann von Helmholtz and others had speculated that cloudiness might increase the apparent flattening of the sky, and in fact recent observations have indicated that the half-arc angle varies inversely with the degree of cloudiness. If the effect exists, and if the apparent-distance theory is correct, then cloudiness should magnify the moon illusion.

Accordingly we split our experiment into three parts. One group of subjects viewed the artificial moons against a completely overcast sky, one against partial cloud cover and one against a clear sky. The illusion increased significantly both with distance to the horizon and with the degree of cloudiness. Taking all

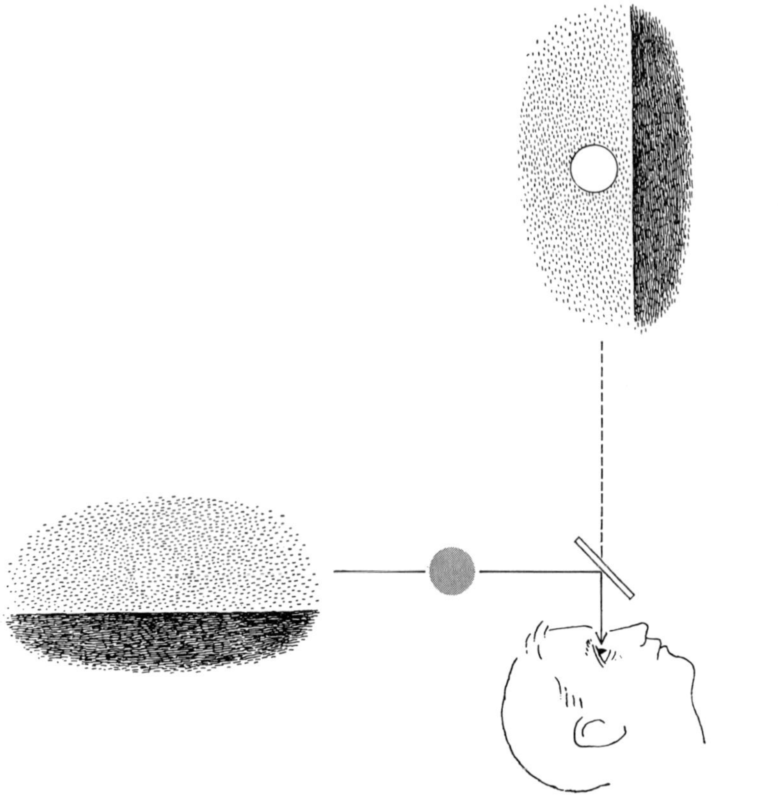

TERRAIN'S IMPORTANCE **was confirmed by using mirrors to reverse the positions of the horizon and zenith moons. By looking up into a mirror (*above*) the observer saw the horizon terrain and its moon overhead. Looking into another mirror (*below*) he saw a patch of zenith sky and its moon, but in a horizontal direction. The illusion was thereupon reversed: the overhead moon appeared 1.34 times larger than the one seen straight ahead.**

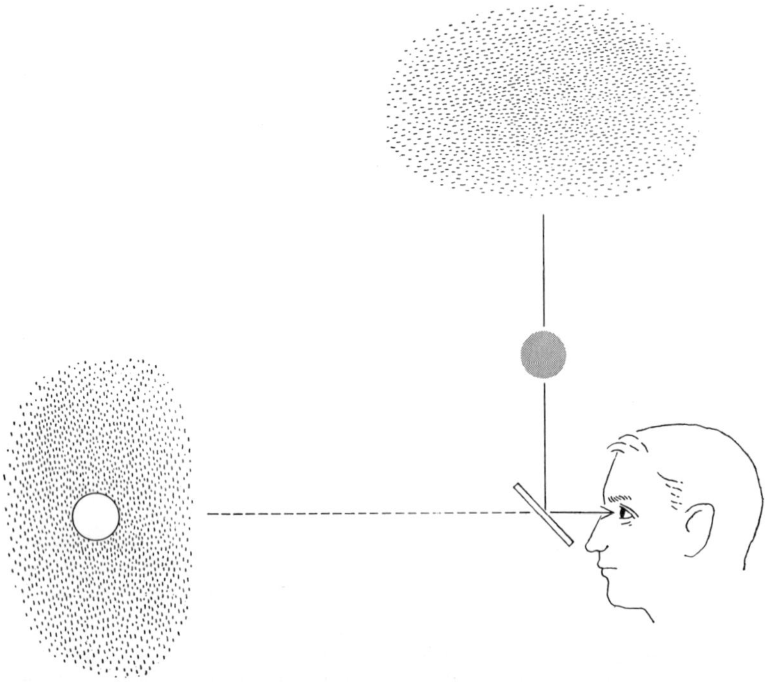

cloud conditions together, the illusion for the far horizon was 1.51 and for the near horizon 1.36. Combining the observations on far and near horizons, the illusion averaged 1.52 in an overcast, 1.45 under partial clouds and 1.34 in a clear sky.

A further test of the apparent-distance theory was provided by turning the horizon upside down with prisms. Inversion is known to lessen the impression of distance, and so we expected it to reduce the size of the moon illusion. Here too our expectations were confirmed: with the horizon inverted the ratio of horizon to zenith moon was 1.28; for the same set of observers under normal conditions it was 1.66. The result probably explains why people have noted a reduced illusion when they view the moon with head down, looking backward between their legs. The image would be inverted. Our inversion observations, incidentally, were carried out on a New York City rooftop, with the horizon moon seen framed between tall buildings. The high value of the ratio for the normal illusion supports the idea that a framing effect can enhance the size of the horizon moon, as many city dwellers have speculated.

The apparent-distance theory was by now supported by a considerable body of experimental evidence, but it remained to be shown that no other factors are involved in the illusion. Two that have been frequently proposed are color and brightness. Often the horizon moon is much redder than the zenith moon be-

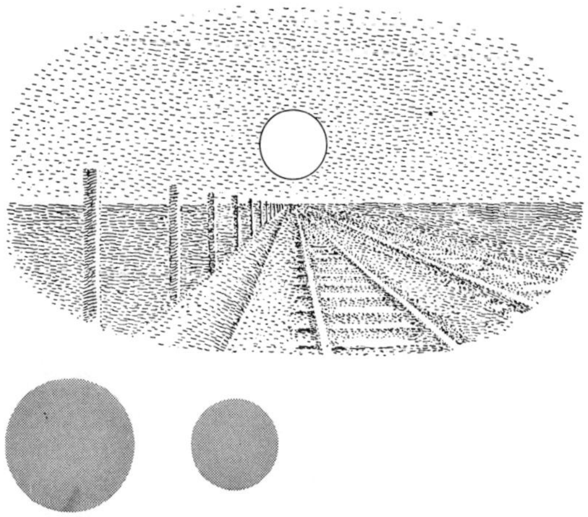

1.51

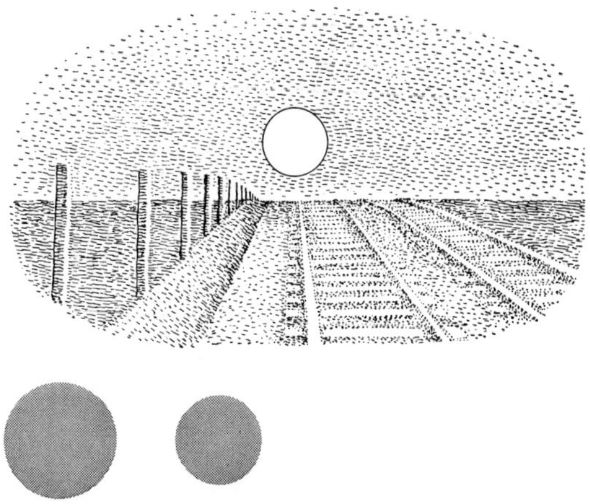

1.36

EFFECT OF DISTANCE was tested more directly by comparing two horizon moons with a zenith moon. One horizon moon was placed where the visible horizon was far off (*left*); the other was over a nearby horizon (*right*). The illusion varied significantly with distance. (The railroad tracks, added here to emphasize the difference in distance, were not actually in the experimental scene.)

1.66

1.28

IMPRESSION OF DISTANCE is known to be lessened by inversion of a scene. Two horizon moons were compared with a zenith moon. In one case the horizon moon was seen normally between tall buildings; in the other case the skyline was inverted by a prism. The moon illusion was significantly smaller in the case of the inverted skyline, confirming the importance of distance as a factor.

cause of the selective scattering by the atmosphere of the shorter wavelengths of light. Many people have suggested that the color difference produces a difference in apparent size. We tried putting a minus-blue filter in front of our artificial horizon moon and found that the resulting reddening had no effect on the illusion.

The Irish metaphysician George Berkeley, among others, attributed the illusion to the dimness of the full horizon moon in the twilight sky compared with the brighter zenith moon in the dark night sky. Again we duplicated the conditions in our apparatus. Neither decreasing the relative brightness of the artificial horizon moon nor increasing the contrast of the zenith moon against its background had any measurable effect on this illusion.

In sum, we have demonstrated that the moon illusion depends on the presence of terrain and specifically on the distance effect of the terrain. Eye elevation, color and apparent brightness evidently have nothing to do with the phenomenon.

The theory we have been defending should not be confused with a deceptively similar explanation that has often been ventured. The horizon moon, it is said, can be compared with objects adjacent to its image along the terrain. If the moon is seen next to a distant house and if its image is about the same size as the house, then it appears as large as a house; since the house is quite large, the moon must be large. This explanation is incorrect because the illusion can be obtained over water or desert, where there are no familiar terrestrial objects for comparison. The apparent-distance theory, on the other hand, stresses the impression of distance created by the terrain considered merely as a plane extending outward from the observer—a distance impression that in turn affects the moon's apparent size according to well-understood relationships.

Eighteen hundred years after Ptolemy we have tested his hypothesis and provided evidence that it is correct. Oddly enough, there is no part of our technique that could not have been carried out centuries ago. But experimentation in psychology is a fairly recent development. So too is the theory of size perception, in which apparent distance is now understood to play a basic role.

26

VISION AND TOUCH

IRVIN ROCK AND CHARLES S. HARRIS

May 1967

A visual perception is not simply a copy of the image on the retina. The image has two dimensions, the perceived object three. The image is upside down, but the object is seen right-side up. An image of a given size can be projected on the retina either from a small object that is nearby or from a large object that is distant, and yet one usually perceives the actual size of the object quite accurately. The image is received by millions of separate light-sensitive cells in the retina, but one sees a unified object with a definite shape.

The striking differences between the retinal image and perception have led many philosophers and psychologists to assume that one must learn how to see. If the retinal image supplies only distorted and incomplete information, one must at first make use of some other source of information about the properties of objects. The most likely source has been considered the sense of touch. In the 18th century the philosopher George Berkeley proposed that an infant discovers by touching an object that it is a distinct, three-dimensional body of a certain size and shape in a certain location and orientation. Thus touch presumably educates vision, adding meaning to the initially meaningless jumble of retinal images.

We have investigated this assumption and have concluded on the basis of several experiments that it is wrong. The sense of touch does not educate vision; vision is totally dominant over touch. As an example, one of our experiments shows that if a subject looks at his hand through a prism, so that the hand appears to be several inches to the right of where it really is, he soon comes to believe the hand is where it appears to be, in spite of nerve messages to the contrary that must be traveling from the hand to his brain. Indeed, one can now turn the traditional argument around and suggest that vision shapes the sense of touch.

We should emphasize that in referring to the sense of touch we mean more than the sensations of contact with the skin that one experiences when touching an object. Touch includes several other components, of which the one most significant for this discussion is the position sense: the sense that enables us to know the position of our body parts when our eyes are closed. It is touch in this broad definition that has been so widely believed to educate vision.

The arguments for the belief rest not only on the recognition of the differences between a retinal image and a visual perception but also on observable evidence. For instance, people who gain sight after having been blind since birth seem at first to have trouble seeing correctly. The phenomenon has been interpreted as suggesting that they must learn to see on the basis of information from touch.

Similar implications have been drawn from experiments by a number of psychologists. A classic experiment was conducted in 1895 by George M. Stratton of the University of California. He spent several days wearing lenses that turned everything upside down. Ivo Kohler of the University of Innsbruck has conducted similar experiments and has also used prisms that reverse right and left. Experiments with prisms that displace the retinal image to one side were carried out in the 19th century by Hermann von Helmholtz and recently by Richard Held of the Massachusetts Institute of Technology [see the article "Plasticity in Sensory-Motor Systems," by Richard Held, beginning on page 372].

In these studies the subject at first saw the world upside down, reversed or displaced, and he acted accordingly. He tried to duck under objects he should have climbed over, he made wrong turns, he missed when he reached for things. After a while, however, he adapted: he behaved normally again, reacting appropriately in spite of the abnormal retinal image.

Such adaptations create the impression that they involve radical adjustments in vision so that the subject again sees the world as normal. Indeed, the adaptations would not be surprising if visual perception is derived from touch. If an infant must learn how to see, an adult could be expected to relearn how to see when his sense of touch tells him that his eyes are deceiving him.

Let us now, however, consider some arguments against the proposition that visual perception is based on touch. In the first place, the same reasoning that seems to rule out innate visual perception also argues against any innate sense of touch on which to build visual perception. Why should one assume that the separate tactile and position components of touch are innately organized into an impression of a solid object with a particular shape? Second, the sense of touch seems far too imprecise to be the source of the accurate perception of form and space that is achieved through vision.

Third, a considerable body of recent evidence suggests that vision is well developed at birth or very soon thereafter. Eleanor J. Gibson of Cornell University and Richard D. Walk of George Washington University found, for example, that babies, chicks and other infant animals have good depth perception before they have had any opportunity to learn it in any way [see "The 'Visual Cliff,'" by Eleanor J. Gibson and Richard D. Walk, beginning on page 341], T. G. R. Bower of Harvard University found that human infants see the size and shape of things in the same way adults do [see "The Visual World of Infants," by T. G. R. Bower, beginning on page 349].

A fourth argument is provided by our own experiments. Even though we have worked separately and have used somewhat different techniques, we have both arrived at essentially the same conclusion, namely that when vision and touch provide contradictory information, perception is dominated by the information from vision. (Similar experiments by Charles R. Hamilton at the California Institute of Technology and by Julian Hochberg, John C. Hay and Herbert Pick, Jr., at Cornell have led them to similar conclusions.)

One of us (Rock) has been investigating perception of size and shape in collaboration with Jack Victor, a graduate student at Yeshiva University. By using a lens that reduces the size of an object's retinal image we can present a subject with contradictory information from vision and from touch [*see illustration at right*]. If he grasps an object while viewing it through the reducing lens, vision should tell him the object is a certain size and touch should tell him it is much larger.

We wanted to find out what the subject would experience under these conditions. Would he be aware that he was seeing an object of one size and feeling an object of another size? Or would he somehow reconcile the conflicting sensory information to achieve a unified perception or impression? If the latter were the case, which sense would have the most influence—vision or touch?

We considered it essential that the subject remain ignorant of the actual situation, otherwise the experiment might be reduced to a conscious decision about which sense to rely on. Because the subject would know that vision can be optically distorted but touch cannot, he would undoubtedly judge the size of the object in terms of what he felt. Accordingly we did not tell the subject that he was looking through a reducing lens. Moreover, we arranged matters so that he saw nothing through the lens except a one-inch white square made of hard plastic.

The subject grasped the square from below through a cloth so that he could not see his own hand; if he could have seen it, he might have deduced that he was looking through a reducing lens, since he would be familiar with the visual size of his hand. To be certain that the subject would not make measurements, such as laying off the side of the square against his finger, we did not ask him anything until after he had been exposed to the conflicting information for five seconds. Each subject was exposed to such a situation only once.

In assessing the subject's perception we could not ask him what was the size of the object he saw or what was the size of the object he felt; either question would prejudice the outcome. Instead we asked him to give his impression of the size of the square. We measured the impression in several ways [*see illustration on page 271*]. Some subjects were asked to draw the size of the square as accurately as they could; drawing involves both vision and touch. We asked others to pick out a matching square from a series of squares presented only visually. Still others were asked to choose a matching square from a series of squares that could be grasped but not seen.

The results of all the tests were clear. Most of the subjects were not even aware that they were receiving conflicting sensory information. This in itself is a most interesting fact. The subjects had a definite unitary experience of the size of the square, and the experience agreed closely with the illusory visual appearance of the square. The average size drawn or matched was about the same when the square was both seen and felt as when, in a control experiment, it was only seen. That size was consistently smaller than the size in another control experiment in which the square was only touched. Thus touch had almost no effect on the perceived size.

We then performed an experiment on the perception of shape. For this test we used a cylindrical optical device that made things seem narrower, so that a square looked like a rectangle with sides in the proportion of two to one. What would happen when the subject simultaneously saw and touched an object that looked like a rectangle but felt like a square?

The result was again quite clear. Vision was completely dominant. In fact, it was so dominant that most subjects said the square actually felt the way it looked. If subjects closed their eyes while grasping the object, they often thought they felt it changing its shape from a rectangle to a square.

A similar domination of touch by vision has been found by Hay, Pick and

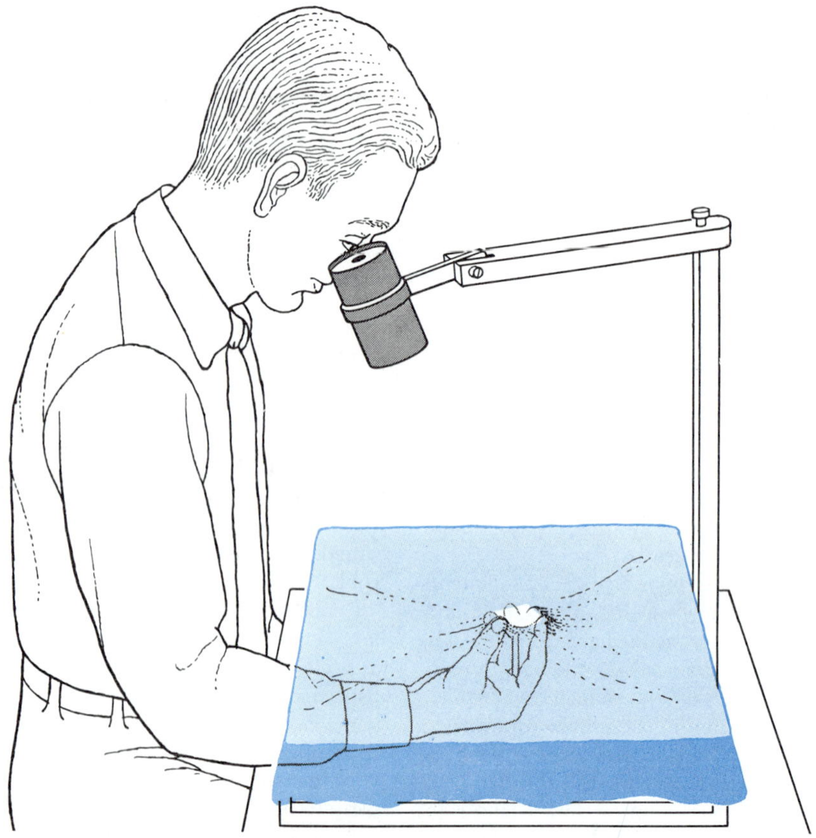

EXPERIMENTAL ARRANGEMENT used to test the effect of a reducing lens on a subject's impression of size included the lens, a cloth over the subject's hand so that he would not deduce from the small appearance of his hand that he was looking through a reducing lens, and a square made of hard plastic. In this test he looked at square and simultaneously grasped it.

Karren Ikeda, working at Smith College. They had each subject rest one hand on a table and look at it through wedge prisms that displaced its visual image to one side. When the subject was asked to reach under the table and make a mark directly below the forefinger of his upper hand, a task he could perform quite accurately when blindfolded, he marked a location about as far from the finger's actual location as the prism-displaced image. Subjects did the same even when they were urged to rely entirely on where they felt the fingertip to be and to ignore its visual appearance. The investigators used for this effect of vision on touch the vivid term "visual capture."

Visual capture had also been observed 30 years earlier by James J. Gibson (then also at Smith but now at Cornell). He noted that when subjects ran their hand along a straight rod while looking through prisms that made the rod look curved, the rod felt curved. Torsten Nielsen of the University of Copenhagen recently demonstrated a similar form of visual capture without using any prisms. His subjects inserted one arm into a box and ran a pencil along a straight line while looking through a peephole. What they actually saw, however, was not their own hand but the experimenter's, reflected in a mirror so that it appeared to be in the same location as theirs. At first both the subject and the experimenter moved their hand back and forth along the line in time to a metronome. Then the experimenter started veering off the line. Strangely enough, few of Nielsen's subjects realized even then that the hand was not their own. They felt that their own hand was uncontrollably moving in a curve in spite of their efforts to stay on the line.

All these experiments show that when vision and touch provide conflicting information, the visual information dominates. Still, this is an immediate effect. Those who believe vision is originally educated by touch are thinking about the long-term result of continuous experience with the two senses. Perhaps, therefore, the experiments we have described are not crucial to the argument. A more pertinent question is: What happens after a period of exposure that is long enough to allow a genuine change in perception to take place?

In the experiments we have cited it could be that vision suppresses touch only temporarily, with the result that as soon as a person closes his eyes his touch perceptions return to normal. It could even be that although vision is at first dominant, it eventually changes to match touch. On the other hand, the converse could be true: with sufficient exposure the sense of touch may be altered so that misperceptions by touch persist even after vision is blocked. With this issue in mind, we shall now consider experiments in which changes in perception might be expected to occur because the exposure to the conflict is continued over a period of time.

Experiments by Helmholtz, Held and others using goggles fitted with sideways-displacing prisms do demonstrate

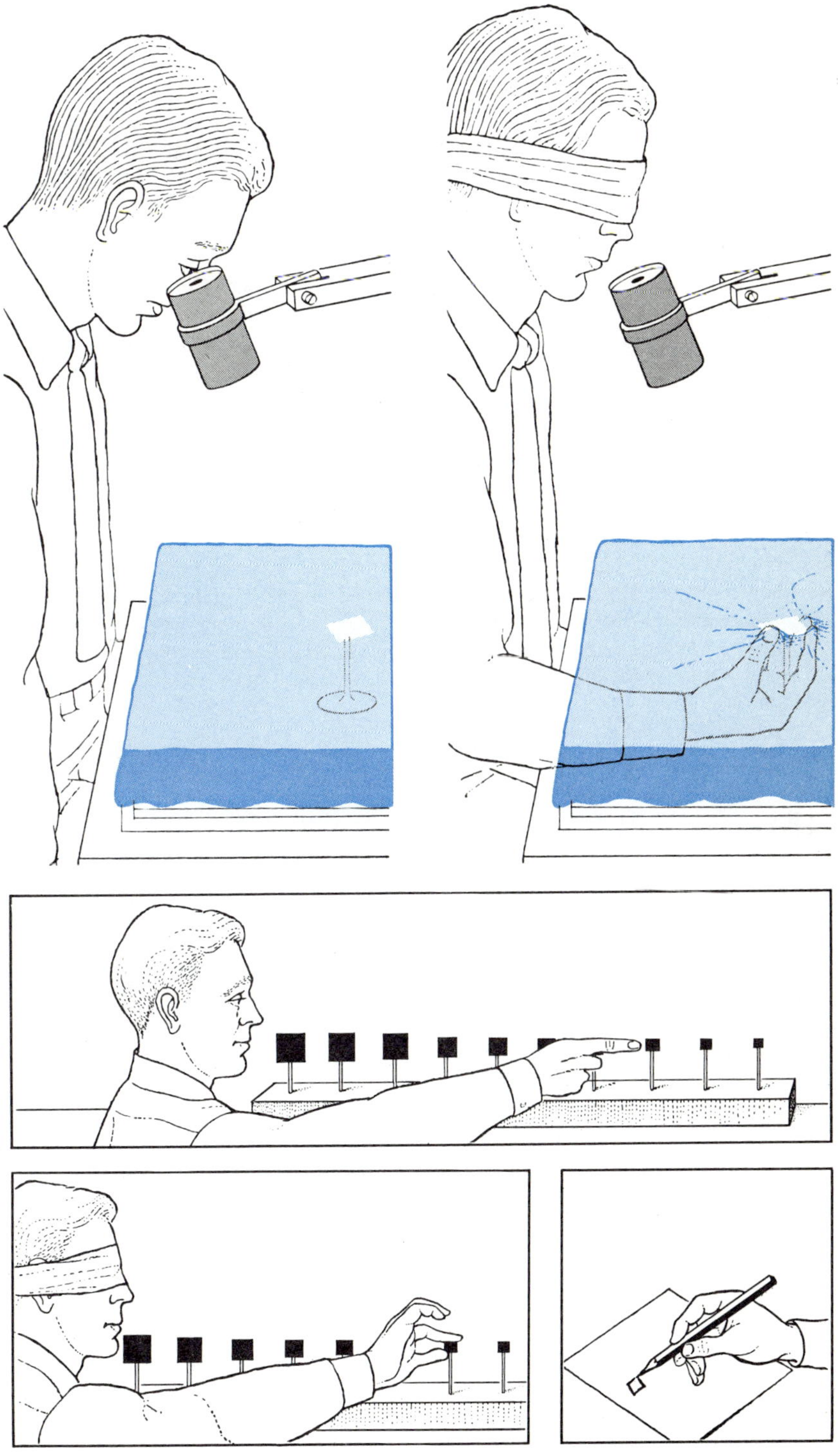

VARIETY OF TESTS determined what size a subject perceived a square to be when he was receiving conflicting data from vision and touch. In control tests he looked at the square without touching it (*top left*) and touched it without seeing it (*top right*). Then he matched it against squares shown only visually (*center*), matched it by touch alone (*bottom left*) and drew it (*bottom right*). In the tests the illusory visual size of the square predominated.

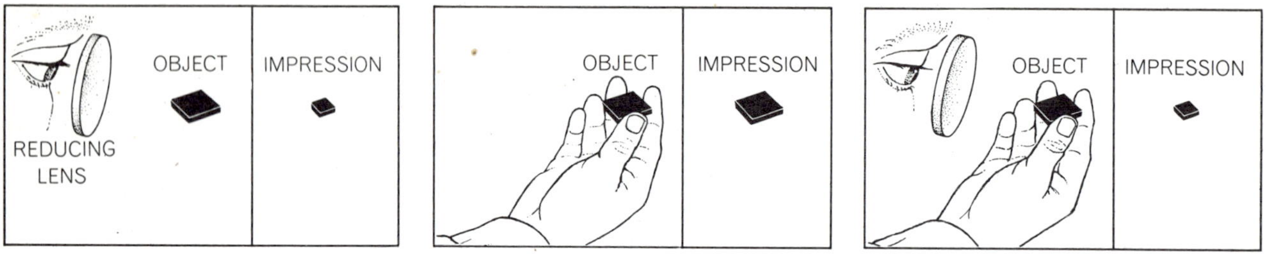

SUBJECT'S IMPRESSIONS in various experiments involving the reducing lens are indicated. In some cases (*left*) he merely saw an object through the lens; in some (*center*) he only felt the object, and in others (*right*) he simultaneously saw an object and felt it.

that appropriate exposure to a conflict between vision and touch produces aftereffects. When an observer first puts on the prisms and tries to point rapidly at an object, he misses. After several minutes of looking at his moving hand through the prisms, however, he points much more accurately even though his retinal images are still displaced. This adaptation is evident even if the subject's view of his hand is blocked during the pointing tests, thus preventing him from steering his seen hand to the seen target.

What does this adaptation show? It could be that the subject's visual perception has changed. He may be pointing more accurately because he is now seeing the object's location more accurately in spite of the displaced retinal image. If so, it could be contended that touch, which remained correct, had educated vision.

Conversely, it could just as well be that the subject is still seeing the object as displaced but now mistakenly feels that his hand is displaced when it is actually pointing straight ahead. This would mean that the adaptive change is in the sense of touch, specifically the sense of where one part of the body is with respect to the rest—the position sense. With continued exposure to the prisms the sensation of where the hand is may more closely approximate its observed location. The subject's misperception of his hand would compensate for his visual misperception of the object, enabling him to point fairly accurately.

To find out which explanation of the adaptation to sideways displacement is correct, one of us (Harris) carried out a series of experiments (some in collaboration with his wife, Judith R. Harris). The apparatus we used consisted of a glass surface that was just below the eye level of a seated subject and had as targets a row of lettered rods standing upright on the glass [*see illustration below*]. The experiments had three parts: pretest, adaptation and retest. In the pretest a black cloth was thrown over the glass surface so that the subject could see the targets but not his hand below the glass, and he was asked to

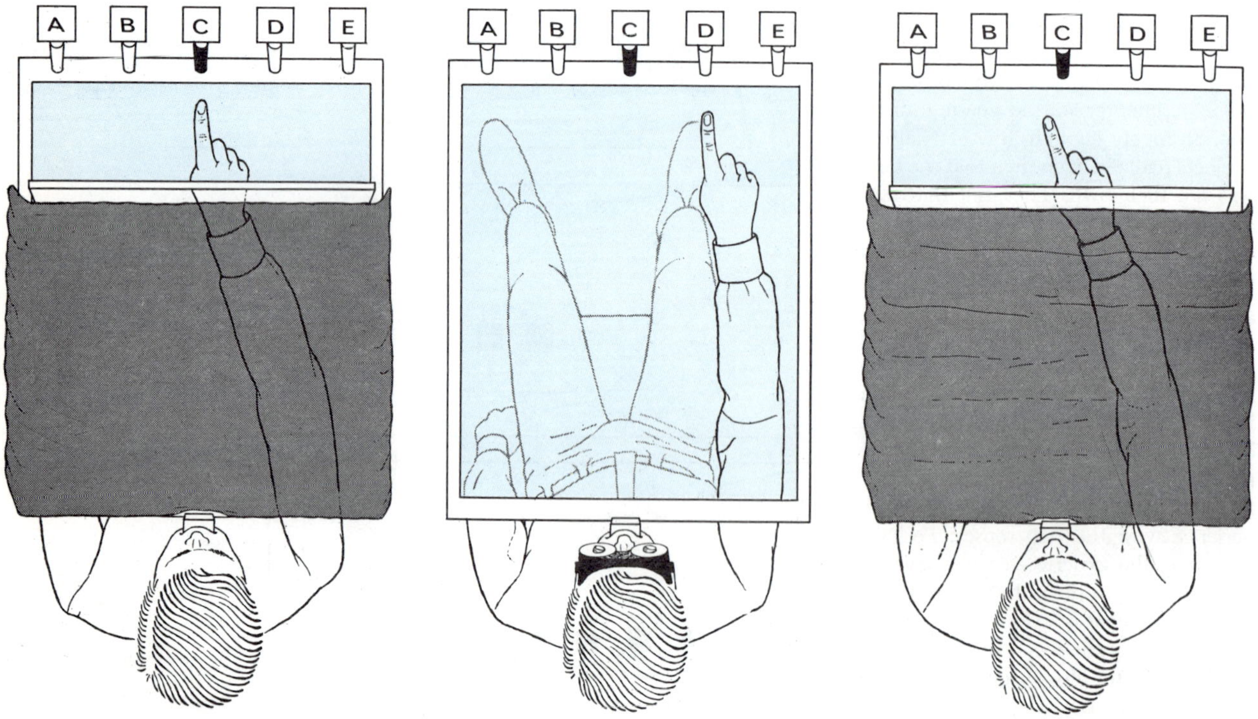

DISPLACED VISION was tested with this apparatus. First (*left*) the subject pointed at lettered rods without being able to see his hand; this pretest determined his normal responses. Then (*center*) he wore prism goggles that displaced his vision about four inches to one side, in this case to the right; while wearing them he was asked to point repeatedly at the center target with one hand. He usually missed at first because of the goggles. Finally (*right*) with the goggles off he was asked to point at various targets. Subjects typically showed an adaptation, or shift in pointing, with the hand used while wearing goggles but little or none with the other hand. Experiment suggested that his sense of the position of the adapted arm had changed. Biting device kept the subject's head steady.

point at various targets from below the glass. The pretest determined the subject's normal responses to the tests he would be given after adapting.

During adaptation the subject wore prism goggles for three minutes. The prisms shifted his visual field 11 degrees to the right or the left; the shift amounted to about four inches at arm's length. The subject's task was to point repeatedly with one hand at the center target. The cloth was removed during this phase so that the subject could see his hand through the glass. At first, because of the prisms, he tended to miss the target, but he quickly became more accurate.

For the retest we needed more than one kind of measurement in order to decide between the alternative explanations for the adaptive change in pointing by the subjects. The tests we chose were (1) pointing at visual targets seen without prisms, (2) pointing in the direction of sounds and (3) pointing in whatever direction the subject thought was straight ahead. During the nonvisual tests, of course, the subject kept his eyes closed.

We found that the subjects showed a large shift in pointing with the adapted hand on all three retests [*see bottom illustration at right*]. In contrast, there was little or no adaptive shift when a subject pointed with his unadapted hand —the one he had not seen through prisms. Each of these results has been obtained in at least one other laboratory, although there are still some unanswered questions about the effects of changing certain details of the experimental procedure.

This pattern of results is consistent with the conclusion that the adaptation involved a change in the position sense of the adapted arm. If the adapted subject feels that he is pointing straight ahead when he is actually pointing about five degrees to one side, he will make the same error no matter what he is pointing at: a visual object, a sound source or the straight-ahead direction. With his unadapted hand, however, he will show no error in pointing.

The findings clearly rule out the possibility that the adaptation is a change in visual perception. First, if the subject had learned to perceive the visual target in a new location, he should point at that new place with either hand. What actually happened was that when our subjects were asked to point at a target, they pointed in one direction with one hand and in a different direction with the other. Second, if adaptation were

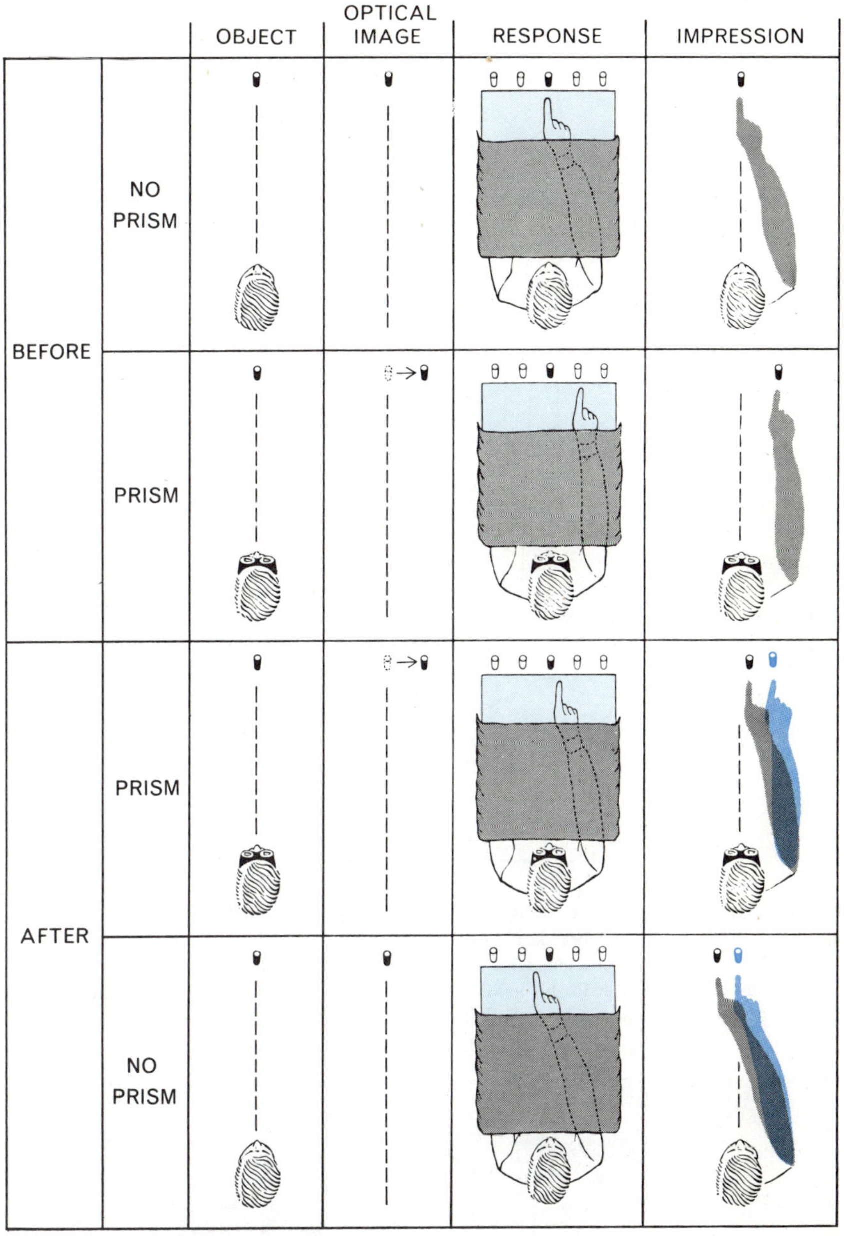

RESULTS OF TESTS with displacing prisms are charted before and after adaptation. "Object" column shows actual location of a target viewed by the subject; "image" column, how prisms displaced the target; "response," how the subject pointed. His impression of where the object was and where he was pointing is in last column. Experiment sought to find if pointing change after adaptation arose because he saw target differently (*gray*) or because he felt the position of his arm differently (*color*). Results showed that it was the latter.

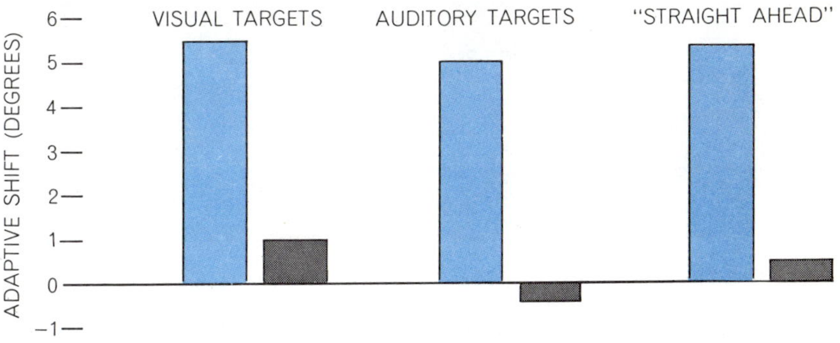

SHIFT IN RESPONSE was made by eight subjects after they had pointed at an object with one hand while wearing prisms that displaced vision to the side. Their shifts in subsequent pointing without prisms are shown for adapted hand (*color*) and unadapted hand (*gray*).

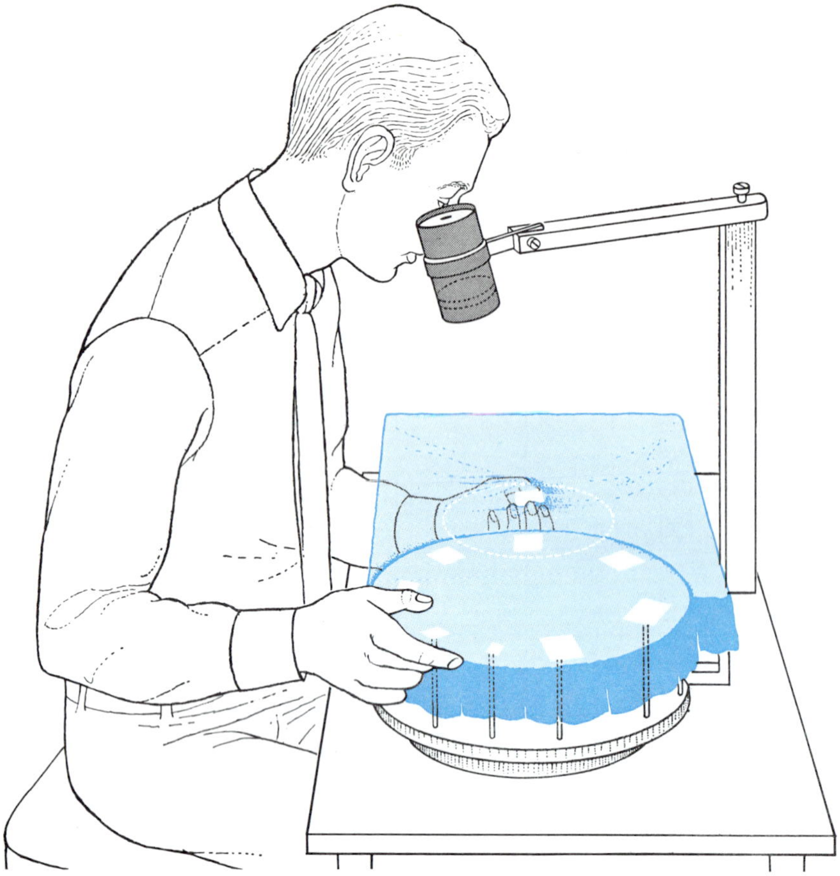

PROLONGED EXPOSURE to conflicting data from vision and touch was achieved with this apparatus. The revolving wheel held squares of various sizes. For 30 minutes the subject looked through the reducing lens while grasping one square after another through a cloth that prevented him from seeing his hand. Tests were given before and after the 30-minute exposure. Aim of experiment was to find if visual perception or touch perception changed.

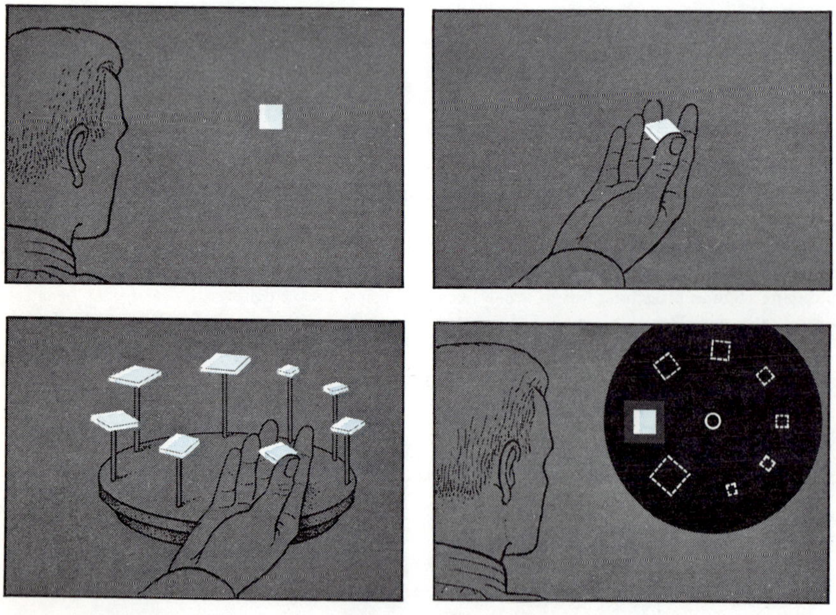

MATCHING TESTS given before and after 30-minute exposure to conflicting data included asking a subject to look at a square in a dark room (*top left*) and to match it by touch from a set of squares he could not see (*bottom left*). He was also asked to feel a square (*top right*) and to match it from a set displayed visually (*bottom right*). Use of reducing lens made subjects choose by touch a larger square than before as matching the visual standard; by vision they chose a smaller square than before as matching a square they had touched.

only a change in visual perception, it should have no effect on tests performed with the subject's eyes closed. Yet we found large adaptive shifts in pointing in the direction of a sound or in the straight-ahead direction—about as large as in pointing at visual targets. Third, if the adaptation is a change in visual perception, it should be revealed by tests of visual localization in which pointing is not involved, but no such effect has been found in this type of experiment.

Another potential explanation of adaptation to prisms (and it is a popular one among psychologists) is that adaptation is the learning of new motor responses: the subject simply learns to make movements appropriate to the altered visual stimulus. A person could correct his movements without any changes in perception. In fact, it may be that in some earlier experiments this is what happened. For example, it is quite clear that Stratton, who wore lenses that inverted the retinal image, did gradually learn to avoid the motor errors he initially made so often. The improvement does not, however, in itself demonstrate that he underwent any perceptual changes, such as learning to see normally through the inverting lenses. In our experiments too it could be that the adaptive shifts in pointing indicate only changes in motor response rather than in perception of where the arm is located.

To find out whether the change is in the subject's position sense or just in the movements he makes, we need a condition in which he judges the location of his hand without moving it. In one such test we had the subject estimate the distance between his hands while he was blindfolded. He made these judgments before and after one arm had been adapted. The adaptation procedure was the same as in the earlier experiment: the subject undertook to point repeatedly with his right hand at a visual target seen through prisms. During the pretest and retest, however, he was blindfolded and his right hand was moved by the experimenter to a predetermined location on the table in front of him. The subject was asked to place his unadapted left hand at a specified distance from his right hand. The right hand was then moved by the experimenter to a new location and the process was repeated.

We knew from the earlier results that the unadapted left hand had not been affected by the adaptation procedure, and during this test the adapted right hand was given no opportunity to execute any new responses it might have learned. Thus the subjects were forced to rely on their position sense in judging how far apart their hands felt. Their judgments indicated that after their right hand had been adapted to prisms that shifted the visual field to the right, the subjects felt that, at a given physical distance, their hands were farther apart than before. After adapting to a visual shift to the left, they felt that their hands were closer together. The results show that the subject's position sense had indeed been altered to the point that he misperceived the location of his adapted hand with respect to the location of his other hand.

The observations with the reducing lens mentioned earlier at first seem to contradict this finding. Although vision was dominant over touch when both senses were active, in that experiment touch returned to normal as soon as the subject closed his eyes. Would the change in touch outlast the conflict situation if the conflict situation were continued for a longer time? This question was investigated in experiments by one of us (Rock) in collaboration with Arien Mack, A. Lewis Hill and Laurence Adams. Over a 30-minute period the subject handled squares of various sizes while looking at them through a reducing lens [*see top illustration on opposite page*]. A cloth prevented the subject from seeing his hand during this time.

Two matching tests administered before and after the 30-minute period showed that the subject's perception of size had changed. In one test we showed him a standard square that he could see but not touch and asked him to select by touch a matching square from a set he could touch but not see. After the 30-minute period with the reducing lens subjects typically selected by touch a larger square than before as matching the visual standard. When they were given a standard square to touch without being able to see it, they typically chose a smaller matching square from a set that was displayed visually. (In both tests the squares were coated with luminous paint and presented in the dark so that there would be no familiar objects to which a square could be compared.)

Both results demonstrate that after exposure to the conflicting information the subject matches felt size with seen size differently than he did before. For a felt object and a seen object to seem equal to him the visual object has to be smaller than before. These results do not reveal, however, which sense has changed to yield the new match. Did the subject pick a smaller seen square because seen objects now looked larger or because felt objects now felt smaller? Although the immediate result of the conflict between vision and touch is a dominance of vision, the correct information provided by touch may still be having an effect, even if it does not enter the consciousness. In that case the square might look larger after adaptation, perhaps ultimately reaching its true size. If, on the other hand, the visual size of the square were to serve as the crucial information and the square were to come to feel smaller than it is, we would have an example consistent with all our other findings.

To determine whether it was vision or touch that had changed, we used a "remembered standard" test. In the test of visual size we first had the subject practice looking at a one-inch square and then matching it visually from immediate memory. Then, after the 30 minutes of looking through the reducing lens, we asked him to select visually a square the same size as he remembered the standard square to be. The selection was again done in the dark with luminous squares.

If visual size has undergone a change, the subject should now (without the reducing lens) select a smaller square as matching the standard one than he did before the exposure to the conflict situation; the smaller square should now look larger than it is. The result, however, was that the subject selected a square that was the same size on the average as the one he chose before exposure to the conflict situation. In other words, there was no change in the visual perception of size.

We used a similar procedure to find out if touch had changed. Before exposure to the conflict the subject practiced feeling the standard square and matching it by touch from immediate recollection. After exposure to the conflict situa-

REVERSING-PRISM EXPERIMENTS called for a subject to doodle (*top*) while looking through a prism that reversed right and left. Before exposure to the prisms every subject wrote numbers and letters as shown at bottom left; after use of the prisms the subjects often wrote as shown at bottom right. Vision was blocked in writing tests. Subjects often thought the letters they had written backward were normal and normal letters were backward.

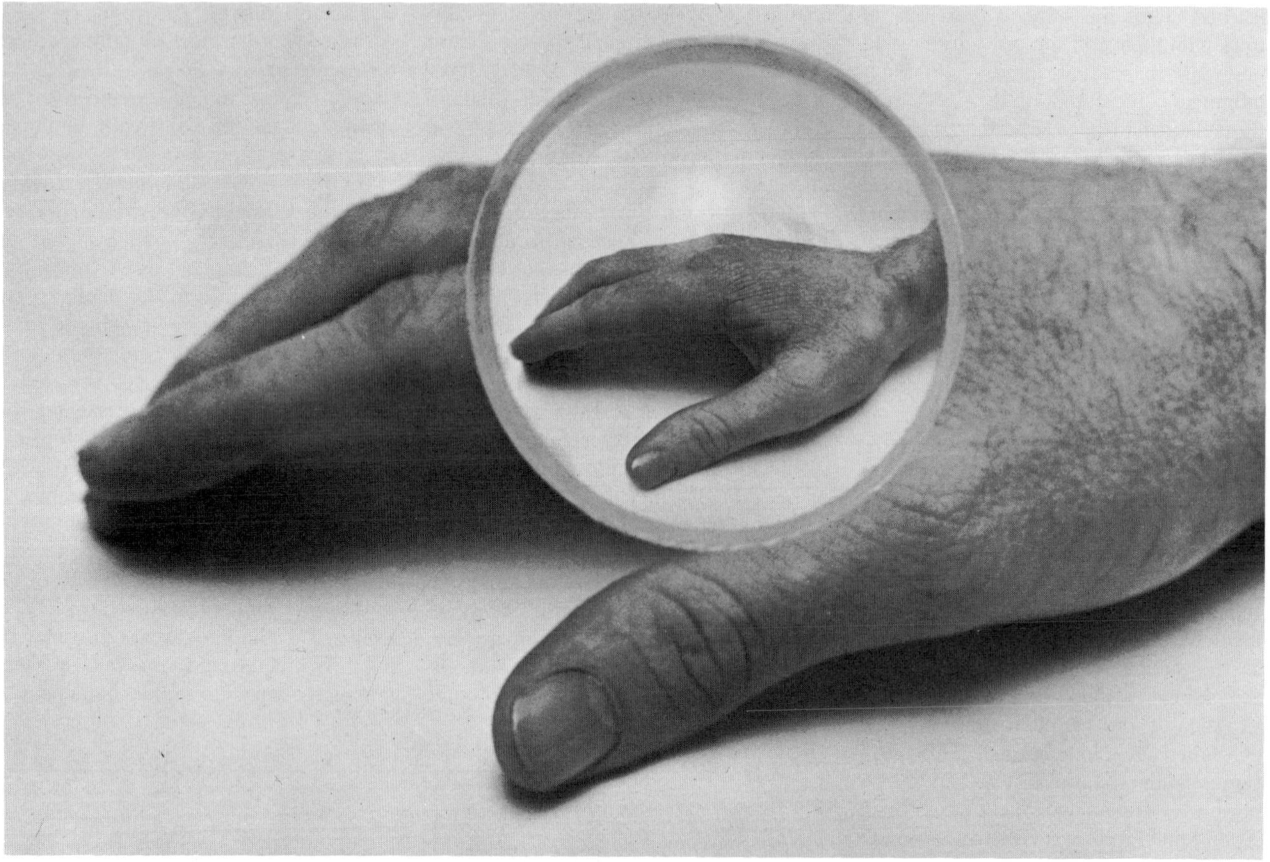

OPTICAL DEVICES were used in experiments to determine whether vision or touch would have the stronger effect on a subject to whom they were providing conflicting information. A reducing lens (*top*) made an object look half its actual size; a prism (*bottom*) reversed left and right. When subjects looked through such a lens or prism and also used touch, they received conflicting sensory data.

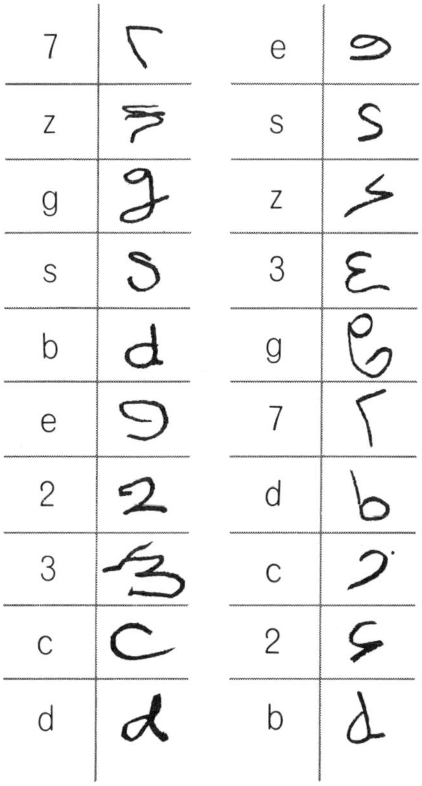

WRITING ABERRATIONS of two subjects after exposure to reversing prisms are represented. The letters and numbers they were asked to write are at left; what they wrote is at right. In the second sample only the *S* is normal; that was the only letter the subject thought she had written backward.

tion he selected by touch alone a square that he felt was the same size as the previously experienced one-inch square. The great majority of subjects chose a larger square as matching the standard than they had before. The larger square now felt smaller than it was.

What would happen if there were a more dramatic conflict between vision and touch, as in experiments on inversion or reversal of the retinal image? If a subject looks through reversing prisms, for example, while moving his hand from left to right, could he be misled into feeling it as moving right to left? An experiment undertaken by one of us (Harris) and Judith Harris showed that vision is powerful enough to accomplish even this radical a misperception.

We had the subject look through a right-angle prism, which acts like a mirror, reversing the visual field right for left [*see the illustration on page 275*]. The prism was attached to a rigid frame. The subject watched his hand through the prism, while drawing and doodling, for 15 minutes a day on four different days. For reasons that will soon become evident, he was not allowed to write or see any letters or numbers while looking through the prism.

For most subjects there was no immediate visual capture. When they felt their hand move in one direction, they saw it stubbornly going in the opposite direction. The felt hand and the seen hand seemed to be separate things.

Within a matter of minutes, however, visual capture took over. Most subjects no longer experienced any discrepancy between how they saw their hands move and how they felt them move. They no longer had trouble drawing or doodling or reaching for locations indicated by the experimenter.

In order to determine if there was an aftereffect of this visual capture, we hit on the following simple procedure. At the end of each prism period we slid a metal plate in front of the prism, blocking the subject's view. We then asked him to quickly write 10 letters and numbers as we dictated them. We had previously told the subjects that the adaptation procedure might make them write an occasional letter backward and that they must be sure to tell us whenever they thought they had done so.

Actually a subject could have two kinds of misperception. He could believe a letter was normal when it was really backward, and he could believe a letter was backward when it was really normal. We found that both kinds of misperception occurred; every one of our eight subjects made at least one such error. In fact, immediately after looking through the prism the subjects misperceived fully 30 percent of the letters and numbers they wrote. (In the pretests given before the use of the prism, of course, no subject ever misperceived what he was writing.) The results, some of which are shown in the illustration on this page, are particularly surprising in view of the fact that writing normal letters and numbers is such a highly practiced skill.

Our experiments all show, then, that when a subject's sense of touch conveys information that disagrees with what he is seeing, the visual information determines his perception. What happens during such a conflict to the information the sense of touch is providing? Is it blocked before it reaches the brain, is it ignored or is it transformed? After sufficient exposure to an intersensory disagreement there is a change in the sense of touch itself. Since the subject continues to misperceive by touch even with his eyes closed, he cannot be blocking or ignoring the information provided by touch. It is therefore a reasonable guess that the information is not blocked or ignored when his eyes are open either. Instead it must be transformed into new touch perceptions that are consistent with visual perception.

The further implications of our experiments are less clear, particularly for situations that are more normal than the restricted conditions under which our subjects worked. What kind of adaptation to altered retinal images takes place when a subject can move about freely and can see much more of his environment than our subjects saw? The experimental data are still fragmentary enough to allow us to disagree on this point.

One of us (Rock) believes visual perception can change if a person subjected to optical distortion has adequate visual information about the distortion. For example, the world might look upside down through reversing prisms, but if the subject can see his own body—the image of which would also be inverted—he realizes that the world is not upside down in relation to himself. Similarly, if a seated subject looks at a straight vertical line through prisms that at first make it appear curved and he then stands up, the appearance of the line will change in a way that would not be the case if the line were really curved. Hence he may come to see that the line is straight. This argument maintains that a change in visual perception can occur but acknowledges that information from touch alone is insufficient to cause such a change.

The other of us (Harris) thinks all substantial adaptation to optical distortions probably results from changes in the sense of the position of the limbs, the head or the eyes. If a person felt that his arms and legs were where he saw them through inverting or reversing prisms, he would make responses like those reported by Stratton and Kohler. If he felt that his eyes were pointing directly ahead or tracing a straight path when they were actually pointing somewhat to one side or tracing a curved path, he would show the kind of adaptation to displacement or curvature that is found in some other experiments.

Our disagreement does not affect the basic points demonstrated by our separate experiments. Those points are that there is no convincing evidence for the time-honored theory that touch educates vision and that there is strong evidence for the contrary theory. Further experiments along these lines can be expected to clarify the points that remain obscure.

27

THE PERCEPTION OF NEUTRAL COLORS

HANS WALLACH

January 1963

Most investigations of color perception deal with the relation between the spectral composition of light—the assortment of wavelengths in it—and the color sensations it evokes. But there is a family of colors the quality of which does not depend on wavelength or combinations of wavelengths. These are the achromatic, or neutral, colors—white, the various grays and black—which differ from one another only in degree of lightness or darkness. The scale of lightness, in other words, is the only dimension of the neutral colors, although it is one dimension (along with hue and saturation) of the chromatic colors as well. The perception of neutral colors is therefore a basic problem in visual perception that needs to be understood in its own right and that at the same time has implications for color vision in general.

The fact that lightness does not depend on a property of light itself is not only a semantic paradox but also a major complication in the study of neutral-color perception. Light can appear dim or bright but not light or dark. It can be blue or yellow or red but not gray. Lightness or darkness is a property of surfaces, and the investigator of neutral-color perception must concern himself with white or gray or black surfaces. Now, the physical property of a surface that corresponds to a perceived neutral color is reflectance. A surface deserves to be called white if it reflects diffusely about 80 per cent of the visible light of any wavelength that falls on it, and it is called black if it reflects only 4 or 5 per cent of the incident light. The various shades of gray range between these extreme reflectance values. The big problem in understanding the perception of neutral colors is that the amount of light reflected by a neutral surface depends not only on its reflectance but also on the intensity of the illuminating light. As the illumination varies over a broad range, the intensity of the light reflected by a surface of a given neutral color will vary just as much. The light message that is received from a reflecting surface is therefore an ambiguous clue to its reflectance—to its "actual" color.

How then can one account for the fact that perceived neutral colors are usually in good agreement with the reflectance of the surface on which they appear—that a dark gray object, for example, tends to look dark gray in all sorts of light? This "constancy" effect, as psychologists call it, can be simply demonstrated by an experiment that David Katz, a German psychologist, devised more than 30 years ago. Two identical gray samples are fastened to a white background and a screen is so placed that it casts a shadow on one of the samples and on its surround [*see illustration below*]. The sample in the shadow does indeed appear to be a somewhat darker gray than the sample in direct illumination. That is to say,

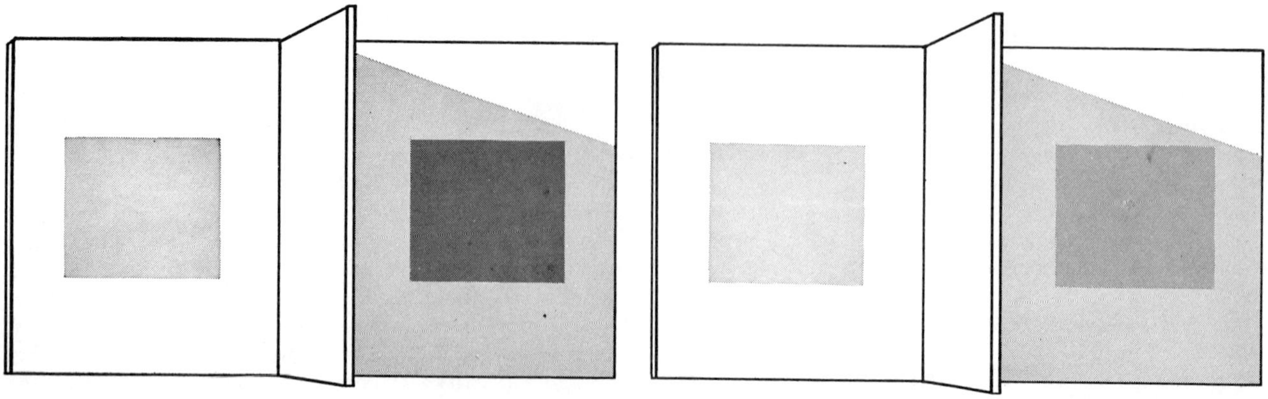

CONSTANCY of neutral colors is demonstrated by this experiment. When one of two identical gray samples is placed in shadow, it looks to an observer only a little darker than its brightly illuminated counterpart although, as the drawing shows, it reflects a lot less light (*left*). The color of the shadowed sample is then lightened until it looks the same as the well-lighted one; it still reflects much less light (*right*). In each situation constancy is at work, making the grays appear more equal than the actual light intensities they reflect would warrant. The drawing reproduces these actual light intensities, not the apparent colors of the samples.

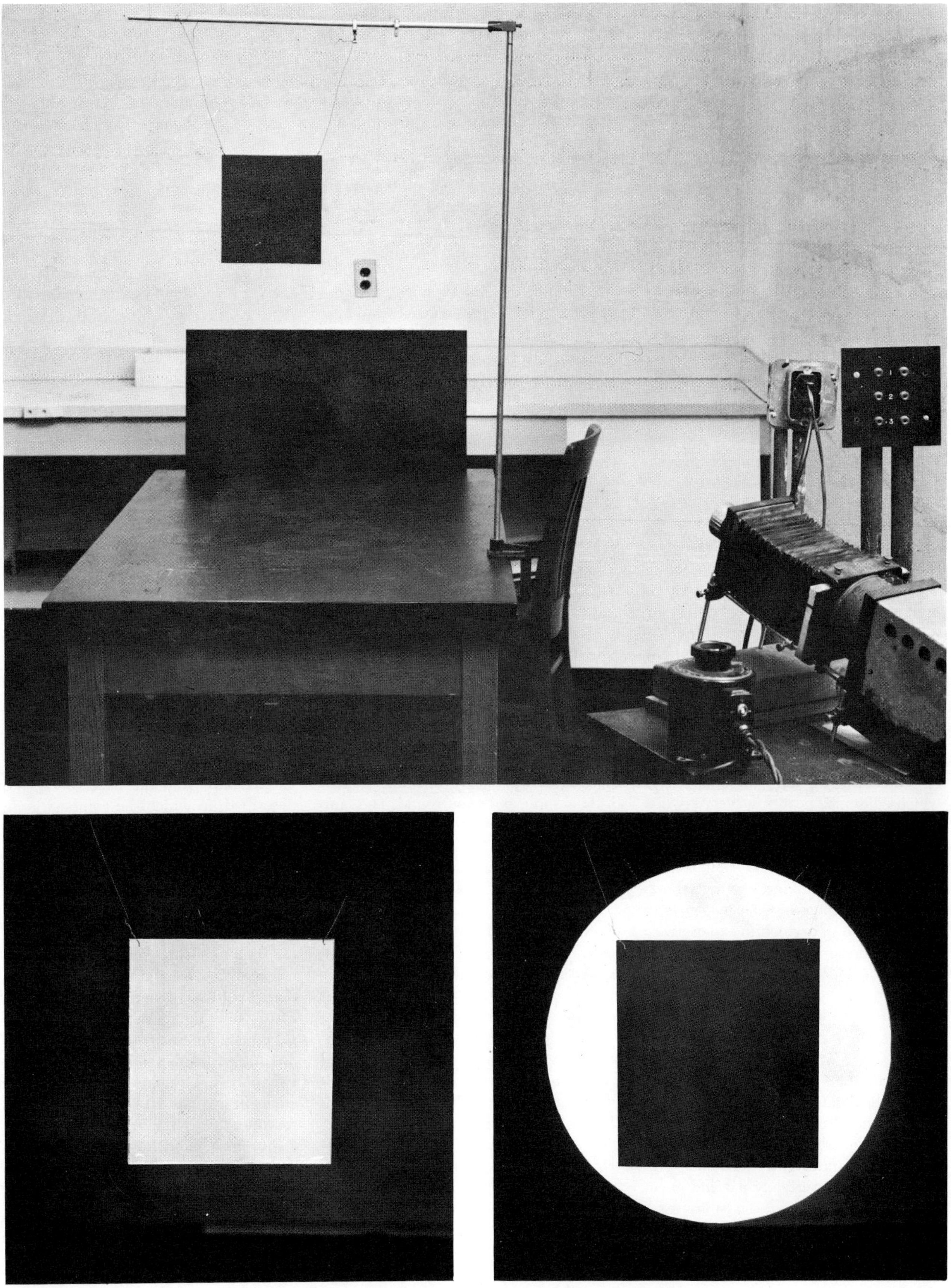

IMPRESSIVE DEMONSTRATION of constancy can be given with the setup illustrated in the top photograph. A dark gray sample suspended before a light-colored wall is illuminated by a projection lantern. When the sample hangs alone, any change in room illumination or lantern intensity changes its apparent color. At the bottom left, for example, it appears almost white. But if a white surround is placed behind the sample within the lantern beam, the sample immediately looks gray again (*bottom right*). It stays gray in spite of changes in the lantern intensity or room illumination. The bottom photographs simulate the apparent colors of the sample.

constancy is not complete. But the shadowed sample by no means looks as much darker as the difference in the actual light intensities reflected by the two samples would warrant, which is to say that there is a constancy effect. When the shadowed sample is replaced by a patch of lighter gray so chosen that the two surfaces appear to be the same in spite of their different illuminations, the shadowed sample will still reflect a good deal less light than the directly illuminated one. This difference in the actual light intensity compatible with apparent equality of color represents the constancy effect. Any explanation of this effect must account eventually not only for its presence but also for its incompleteness as demonstrated in the first part of the experiment.

For a long time the standard explanation of constancy has been that the viewer takes illumination into account when he evaluates the intensity of the light reflected by a surface. The difficulty with this is that illumination is never given independently. It manifests itself only by way of the light that the various surfaces in the visual field reflect. One variable, the intensity of the reflected light, depends on both the incident illumination and the reflectances of the surfaces—and is in turn the only direct clue to both of these factors.

The Katz demonstration had the virtue of simulating the conditions under which constancy occurs in everyday life, but it is not amenable to as much manipulation as an experimental situation worked out by Adhémar Gelb of the University of Frankfort. In my laboratory at Swarthmore College some 15 years ago we undertook to explore with Gelb's setup some of the inconsistencies of the orthodox explanation of constancy.

We suspend a dark gray sample some distance from a light-colored wall and illuminate it with a projection lantern so placed that the bright spot formed where the beam hits the wall is concealed behind a door or curtain. With the room nearly dark, the dark gray sample appears brightly luminous, provided that it is perfectly flat and evenly illuminated so that no shiny high lights show. As the general illumination—and hence the illumination on the light wall behind the suspended sample—is raised, the luminous appearance of the sample disappears and it becomes a white surface. Remember that the sample is really dark gray; in this situation constancy is clearly absent. A further increase in room illumination changes the appearance of the sample to a light gray. Obviously the wrong illumination is being taken into account! The light reflected by the dark sample is being evaluated in terms of the general illumination on the wall; the strong light from the projector is being ignored. The reason for this, proponents of the standard explanation would say, is that the strong light from the lantern is visible on only one object, the dark gray sample, the surround of which reflects only the dimmer general illumination; constancy would be restored if the light from the lantern showed in the surround. And so it is. When a piece of white cardboard, somewhat larger than the sample but small enough to fit into the beam, is hung behind the dark sample, the sample looks dark gray. The orthodox explanation is that the white cardboard surround makes it possible to take into account the effect of the lantern light on the intensity of the light reflected by the dark sample.

What happens when we vary the intensity of the lantern beam? With the gray sample alone intercepting the beam, every reduction in the intensity of the light causes a change in the apparent color of the sample, which can be altered in this manner all the way from white to dark gray. With constancy restored by the addition of the white cardboard, however, the same changes in light intensity hardly affect the color of the sample and its surround. The sample remains dark gray and the surround white, although the latter looks more or less strongly luminous as the lantern light is varied. This "luminousness" is a special aspect of neutral-color perception, as will be seen; in so far as the neutral colors as such are concerned, however, the combination of dark gray surface with white surround is resistant to changes in illumination.

It is difficult to see how this demonstration of constancy can be explained by any mechanism that takes the illumination into account. The amount of light the white cardboard reflects, after all, gives information about the intensity of the illumination only when the cardboard is correctly assumed to be white. But there is no cue for such an assumption. What if the cardboard were not white? As a matter of fact a surround of any other color fails to produce constancy, that is, to cause a dark gray sample to be perceived as dark gray. If, with the walls of the room dark, the white cardboard is replaced by a medium gray one, the surround again appears luminously white in the lantern beam, whereas the dark gray sample looks light gray. Although the color is now incorrectly perceived, the combination of sample and surround is still resistant to illumination changes. The intensity of the beam can be moved through a broad range and the sample remains light gray.

If taking illumination into account is not the explanation of constancy, what is? Some years ago Harry Helson, then at Bryn Mawr College, proposed an entirely different approach, invoking the mechanism of adaptation by which the eye adjusts itself to wide variations in the amount of light available. To account for the fact that constancy prevails when different illuminations are visible simultaneously, he suggested that incoming light intensities are evaluated in terms of a "weighted average" of stimulation in different parts of the retina, the light-sensitive screen at the back of the eye. It seems to me that there is implicit in this notion of regional adaptation an assumption of some sort of interaction of processes arising in different parts of the retina, and such interaction would appear to be a requirement in any explanation of constancy. Helson's explanation was advanced as part of a general theory of sensation that has been quite successful, and he did not describe a specific mechanism for interaction.

Speculating on the observations just described, in which the combination of gray sample and cardboard background proved resistant to changes in illumination, I wondered if a ratio effect might be at the heart of the matter. Since any neutral surface reflects a constant fraction of the available illumination, the light intensities reflected by two different surfaces under the same illumination should stand in a constant ratio no matter how the illumination is changed. If one could demonstrate that perceived neutral colors depend on the ratio between the light intensities reflected from adjacent regions, all the foregoing observations, and in fact neutral-color constancy in general, would be explained. The following experiments show that this is indeed the case.

The first experiment calls for a darkened room, a white screen and two identical slide projectors the light intensity of which can be altered by measured amounts. In an otherwise dark room one lantern projects a disk of light on the screen and the other lantern a ring of light that fits closely around the disk. The light intensity of the disk is kept constant; variation of the intensity of the ring then changes the appearance of the disk through the entire range of neutral colors. When the ring intensity is half or a quarter that of the disk, the disk looks white. When the ring intensity is higher than that of the disk, the disk becomes gray. Its shade deepens from light to medium to dark gray as the ring light is made first twice as intense as and then four and eight times more intense than the light in the disk. When the relative intensity of the ring is raised still further, the disk even appears black. This experiment shows clearly that the neutral color of an area does not depend on the intensity of the reflected light as such, because with the intensity of the illumination of the disk held constant its color nevertheless ranges all the way from white to black as the intensity of its surround is increased. Obviously what matters is the relation of the intensity of the light reflected from the disk to the intensity of the light reflected from the surrounding ring.

Another experiment demonstrates that a particular gray is produced largely by a specific ratio between the intensity of the ring and that of the disk. A second pair of lanterns is added to project an identical ring-and-disk pattern on a second screen. If the ring and disk in each pattern are illuminated with the intensities in the same ratio but with the absolute intensity in one pattern reduced to, say, a third or a quarter of the intensity in the other, almost the same gray is perceived in both disks. Whenever the intensity of one of the disks is varied until the grays of the two disks appear to be truly equal, the disk intensities turn out to be almost equal fractions of the intensities in their respective rings.

The discovery that the various gray colors depend approximately on the ratio between light intensities stimulating adjacent regions of the retina goes a long way toward explaining neutral-color constancy in general. The ratio principle can account for the observed constancy in the Katz experiment, where a sample in shadow is compared with one in direct illumination. The combination of sample and background is resistant to differences in illumination because the ratio between the intensities reflected by sample and background is constant. It will be recalled, however, that constancy was not complete in the Katz experiment. A ring-and-disk demonstration explains this also. The ratio principle operates best only when the ring and disk are presented against

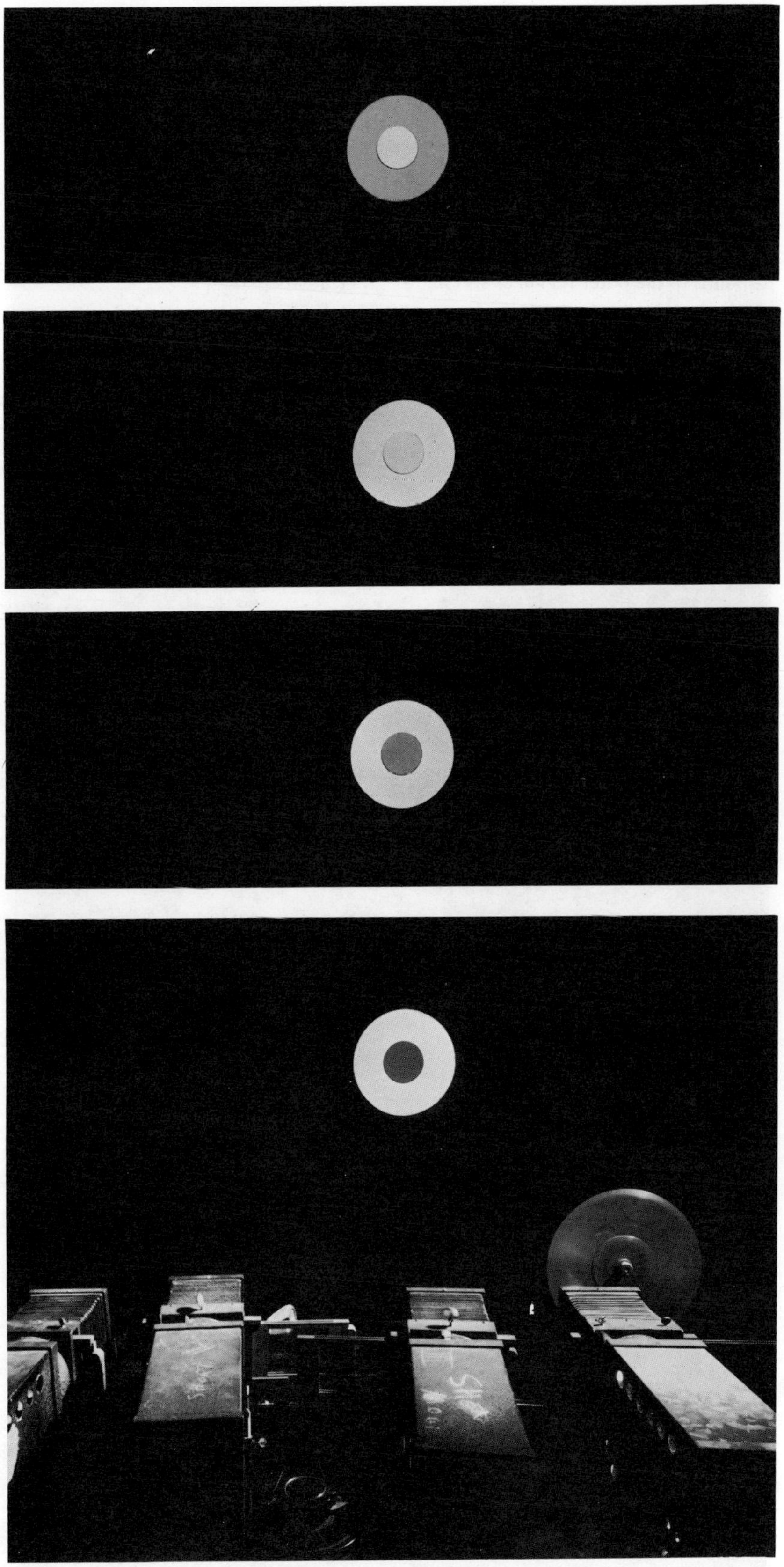

NEUTRAL-COLOR PERCEPTION depends largely on the ratio between two different light intensities in adjacent regions, as demonstrated with a ring-and-disk pattern projected by two lanterns in a dark room. In this experiment the light in the disk is kept constant but the ring light is increased, changing the appearance of the disk from white to dark gray. The ring-to-disk ratios are *(top to bottom)* one to three, two to one, four to one and eight to one. These photographs show how the ring and disk colors appear to an observer.

a dark background or when the ring is enlarged to fill the whole visual field. If, instead, the ring is surrounded by an area of still higher intensity, the disk assumes a darker color. And this is in essence what happens in the Katz setup: the gray sample and background in the shadow correspond to the disk and ring, and the portion of the background that remains under direct illumination corresponds to the outer region of still higher illumination that makes a disk appear darker. It is largely because the shaded region and the area under direct illumination are adjacent that constancy is incomplete. Were they widely separated, as they are in the presentation of two ring-and-disk patterns, much better constancy would result, because the ratio principle would then operate as nearly perfectly as it did in the projector experiments.

Although perception of illumination may not be very accurate and does not account for the constancy of neutral colors, it cannot be denied that people do perceive conditions of illumination. A room looks generally brighter near the window than it does far from the window; there is a bright area on the wall near a lighted table lamp and there are shadows on other walls; one side of the house across the street appears brightly

RATIO PRINCIPLE is confirmed by projecting a second pattern from two more projectors. The ratio between ring and disk light intensities is made the same in both patterns but the absolute intensities in the pattern at the left are four times greater than those at the right. In spite of the variation in absolute intensity, the grays perceived in the two disks look remarkably similar to an observer. The photograph, however, approximately reproduces the true light intensities rather than the apparent disk colors.

illuminated by the sun. How, in view of the ratio principle, is one to account for the fact that the shadow on the gray wall does not look exactly like a darker gray or black but has a somewhat translucent appearance; that the wall near the lamp does not seem to be lighter in color but merely looks brighter and less opaque; that the sunlit wall of the house looks outright luminous? All of these examples have one thing in common: the typical quality of a surface of neutral color is either completely replaced by a luminous appearance or is modified in the direction of what can be considered a partially luminous quality. The two-projector experiment, as already noted, also produces examples of this luminousness and of a translucent quality in the grays that is the low-intensity counterpart of the same effect.

When the intensity of the light reflected from the disk is two to four times higher than the intensity of that reflected from the ring, the disk looks white; when the intensity of the disk is lower than that of the ring, the disk looks gray or black depending on the ratio between the two intensities. If the intensities of ring and disk are reversed, however, the appearance of the ring is very different from that of the disk under corresponding conditions. Under illumination of the higher of the two intensities, the ring appears not white but plainly luminous, like the glass globe of a not too bright lamp. Under illumination of the lower intensity the ring does look gray, but the gray has a peculiar quality. It lacks the opaqueness of an ordinary surface; it seems rather to be somewhat translucent, as if there were a light source behind it. As a matter of fact it resembles an extended shadow, which also lacks the opaqueness of a dark surface color, although to a lesser degree. With the ring eliminated altogether, the dark region surrounding the disk does not look like an opaque black surface but like a dark expanse. The distinction between the two kinds of darkness is pointed up vividly when the disk is eliminated and a ring of light is projected alone on a dark field. The area inside the ring has a black surface color quite different from the dark expanse outside the ring.

LUMINOUS QUALITY is produced by a reduction in the degree of contact with an area of contrasting light intensity. In this pattern of bars of alternating high and low intensity, the two outside bars look somewhat luminous to an observer (the effect is not apparent in a photograph) because they have only half as much contact with contrasting bars.

Several factors seem to account for the sensation of luminosity. The larger of two contrasting areas, in the first place, tends to appear luminous. In our experiments the ring was usually larger than the disk. With the ring reduced in width so that its area is smaller than that of the disk, the appearance of luminosity and translucence transfers to the disk. The degree of contact between two surfaces reflecting different light intensities also plays a part in this effect. Surrounded completely by the ring, the disk tends to look more like an opaque surface. The ring, which tends to assume the luminous quality, is in contact with the disk on one side only and is bordered on its outer perimeter by the darkness of the room, from which there is minimum stimulation. Lack of contact also explains the luminousness or translucence observed when the disk or the ring is presented alone.

To isolate the effect of difference in contact we have projected two sets of bars, one from each lantern, so that bars of high and low intensity alternate in the pattern on the screen. The two outside bars, one white and one gray, appear somewhat luminous, whereas all the other bars show opaque colors. Since the areas of each bar and of each intensity are exactly equal, the luminous look can only be attributed to the diminished contact of the outer bars with areas of different intensities. A special case of reduced contact occurs when an intensity gradient replaces the sharp border between two areas of different intensities. Such gradients appear in the penumbrae of shadows, where the grays assume the quality of translucence that belies the opacity of the surface under inspection.

Regardless of size or degree of contact, when the intensity difference becomes greater than about four to one, the area of higher intensity becomes somewhat luminous as well as white; with very large differences it loses all whiteness. An illuminated disk in an otherwise dark field never looks white or gray; depending on its intensity, it is brightly or dimly luminous. The most familiar illustration of this laboratory finding is the contrast between the appearance of the moon by day and by night. In a bright blue sky the moon looks white. As the setting of the sun reduces the intensity of the blue sky the moon's light becomes relatively more intense and the moon appears more and more luminous, even though the intensity of the light arriving from the direction of the moon certainly does not increase.

It can be concluded, therefore, that a region reflecting the higher of two light intensities will appear white or luminous, whereas an adjacent region of lower intensity will appear gray or black. Every change of the intensity ratio causes a change in the color of the area of lesser intensity along the scale of grays. As for the area of higher intensity, it appears white when the intensity ratio is small and becomes luminously white and finally luminous as the ratio is increased. If the contact between surfaces of different intensities is reduced, neutral colors become less dense and opaque and even somewhat luminous. The same effect is seen in a region that is larger than an adjacent one of different intensity.

It seems to me that these facts can be explained by considering that stimulation with light gives rise to two different perceptual processes. One process causes luminousness and the other produces the various opaque colors. The first process is directly dependent on intensity of stimulation and the state of adaptation of the eye. The second is an interaction process: an area of the retina that receives a higher intensity of stimulation induces a sensation of gray or black in a neighboring region of lower intensity, with the particular color roughly dependent on the ratio of the two intensities; conversely, the region stimulated at a lower intensity induces a white color in the region of higher intensity. If the intensity ratio is too high, however, if the relative size of the inducing surface is too small or if the contact between two regions of different intensities is too small, the interaction process may give way to the process that gives rise to the sensation of luminosity, or the sensation of color and luminosity may be experienced simultaneously.

CHROMATIC COLORS also vary in lightness depending on the intensity of the illumination in an adjacent region. The experiment simulated here shows how the appearance of a disk of orange light changes with the intensity of a neutral surround. In this case increasing the intensity of the ring changes the apparent color of the disk to brown.

The processes of neutral-color perception have their counterparts in the perception of chromatic colors. This is not surprising; the neutral colors are continuous with the chromatic colors: for any sample of a greatly desaturated chromatic color a closely similar gray can be found. A final experiment with the two projectors demonstrates that the lightness of chromatic colors depends on a relation between the intensities of stimulation in neighboring regions. When a disk of chromatic light is surrounded by a ring of white light, variation in the intensity of the latter changes the lightness of the chromatic color in the disk. In this way a bright pink, for example, can be changed to a dark magenta. The same experiment performed with a yellow or orange disk yields a surprising result: surrounding the disk with a ring of high-intensity white light transforms the disk into a deep brown. This serves to demonstrate that brown is a dark shade of yellow or orange. It also dramatizes the point that the shades and tints of chromatic colors, as well as the neutral colors, are the result of an interaction process.

Even the luminous appearance that results from stimulation with light from a neutral surface has its counterpart in the sensation of chromatic colors. For many years psychologists have distinguished a number of "modes of appearance" of chromatic colors, including surface colors, expanse colors and aperture colors. Surface colors are the opaque colors of objects, the hued counterparts of the neutral surface colors. Expanse colors, of which the clear blue sky is a good example, occur in extended homogeneous regions and lack the density and opaqueness of surface colors. That is, expanse colors have a luminous appearance, which may be caused by a relatively high intensity of stimulation or because they are greatly extended in relation to an adjacent region of different intensity. Aperture colors are observed when one looks through a hole in a screen at a chromatic surface some distance beyond the screen. Under these conditions the surface is transformed into a seemingly transparent chromatic film stretched across the hole.

The aperture mode has been attributed to the peculiarities of the laboratory arrangement in which it is usually observed. It can be shown, however, that this effect too is a product of specific ratios of stimulation intensities. The "transparent film" appears only when the intensity of the light reflected from the chromatic surface seen through the hole is high in relation to that of the light reflected from the screen. Raising the illumination on the screen transforms the film into a surface color, so that the hole comes to look like a piece of colored paper attached to the screen.

Such a change can be observed easily out of doors on a clear morning. Cut a small hole in a large sheet of white cardboard. Hold the sheet up so that the sky is visible through the hole. The sky will appear in the hole as a blue transparent film. Now turn until the white cardboard reflects the direct light of the sun. When the cardboard is brightly illuminated, the hole seems to be replaced by an opaque bluish-gray patch, notable for its lack of saturation. This transformation of the strongly saturated expanse color of the sky into a surface color of medium lightness by the provision of a relatively large surface of contrastingly high light-intensity shows how desaturated the blue of the sky really is. It suggests that the sky looks very blue not only because the blue wavelengths of sunlight are scattered by the atmosphere but also—and perhaps largely—because the sky is so bright.

28

EXPERIMENTS IN COLOR VISION

EDWIN H. LAND
May 1959

From childhood onward we enjoy the richness of color in the world around us, fascinated by the questions: "How do we see color? How do you know you see the same color I do? Why do colors sometimes mix to give quite different colors?" Since 1660, when Isaac Newton discovered the properties of the visible spectrum, we have slowly been learning the answers; and we are finding that the beauty of the outer world is fully matched by the technical beauty of the mechanisms whereby the eye sees color.

No student of color vision can fail to be awed by the sensitive discernment with which the eye responds to the variety of stimuli it receives. Recently my colleagues and I have learned that this mechanism is far more wonderful than had been thought. The eye makes distinctions of amazing subtlety. It does not need nearly so much information as actually flows to it from the everyday world. It can build colored worlds of its own out of informative materials that have always been supposed to be inherently drab and colorless.

Perhaps the best way to begin the story is to consider two sets of experiments. The first is the great original work of Newton, which set the stage for virtually all research in color vision since that time. The second is an apparently trivial modification that reverses some of his basic conclusions.

As is so often the case with truly revolutionary insights, the simplicity of Newton's discovery causes one to wonder why no one before him had made it. He passed a narrow beam of sunlight through a prism and found that it fanned out into the band of colors we know as the visible spectrum: red, orange, yellow, green, blue, indigo and violet. When he reversed the process, gathering the beam together with a second prism, the colors vanished and white light reappeared. Next he tried recombining only parts of the spectrum, inserting a slotted board to cut off all but certain selected bands [*see diagram on page 290*]. When he combined two such bands of color, letting the rays mix on a screen, a third color appeared, generally one matching a color lying between the bands in the spectrum.

Let us repeat this last experiment, placing the openings in the board just inside the ends of the narrow yellow band in the spectrum. When these two yellow beams strike the screen, they combine, as Newton observed, to produce yellow.

Now for our modification. In front of the slits we place a pair of black-and-white photographic transparencies. Each shows the same scene: a collection of variously colored objects. There is, of course, no color in the photographs. There are simply lighter and darker areas, formed by black silver grains on transparent celluloid. A glance at the two shows that they are not absolutely identical. Some of the objects in the scene are represented by areas which are lighter in the first photograph than in the second. Others are darker in the first and lighter in the second. But all that either photograph can do is to pass more or less of the light falling on its different regions.

The yellow beams pass through these transparencies and fall on the screen. But now they are not yellow! Somehow, when they are combined in an image, they are no longer restricted to producing their spectral color. On the screen we see a group of objects whose colors, though pale and unsaturated, are distinctly red, gray, yellow, orange, green, blue, black, brown and white [*see bottom photograph on page 288*]. In this experiment we are forced to the astonishing conclusion that the rays are not in themselves color-making. Rather they are bearers of information that the eye uses to assign appropriate colors to various objects in an image.

The Old Theory

This conclusion is diametrically opposed to the main line of development of color theory, which flows from Newton's experiments. He and his successors, notably Thomas Young, James Clerk Maxwell and Hermann von Helmholtz, were fascinated by the problem of simple colors and the sensations that could be produced by compounding them. Newton himself developed quite good rules for predicting the colors that would be seen when various spectral rays were mixed to form a spot of light on a screen. These rules can be summarized in geometrical diagrams, one of the oldest of which is the color triangle [*see diagram at top of page 14*]. On modern versions of it we can read off the result of com-

COLORED OBJECTS in the top picture on the opposite page were photographed with the special dual camera which appears at left. Here the two ground-glass screens of the camera are left uncovered to show that one image is photographed through a green filter and the other through a red filter. The images are photographed on ordinary black-and-white film; then black-and-white positive transparencies are made from the negatives. In the bottom photograph the "red" transparency is projected through a red filter and the "green" without a filter. When the two images are superimposed on the screen at right, they reproduce the objects in a full range of color.

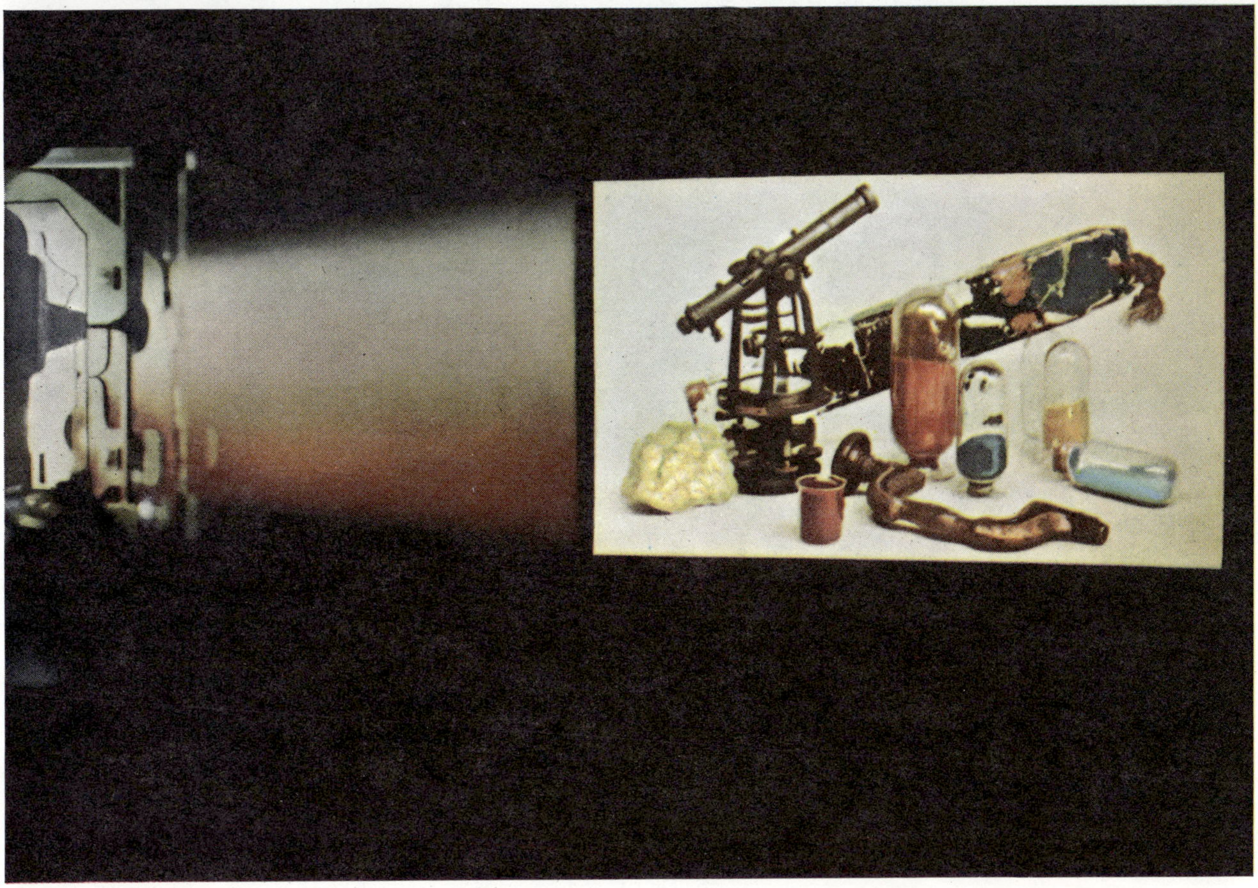

535
589

579
599

bining so many parts of color A with so many of color B.

Once it was discovered that light is a wave motion, the classical investigations of color acquired a deeply satisfying logical basis. The order of colors in the spectrum follows wavelength, the longest visible wavelength falling at the red end of the spectrum and the shortest at the violet end. A pure color would be a single wavelength; compound colors would be mixtures of pure colors.

In trying to match colors by mixing spectral stimuli Maxwell and Helmholtz found that three different wavelengths were enough to effect all matches, and that those wavelengths had to be chosen from the red, green and blue bands of the spectrum. Accordingly red, green and blue came to be called the primary colors. On the basis of this evidence they proposed a three-color theory of color vision. We need not go into the details here. The central idea is that the eye responds to three different kinds of vibration, and that all color sensation is the result of stimulating the three responses in varying degrees of strength. Thus it has become an article of faith in standard theory that the color seen at any point in a field of view depends on what wavelengths are issuing from that point and upon their relative strengths or intensities.

Now, as we have seen in our modification of Newton's experiment, the light at any point on the screen was composed of only two "yellow" wavelengths, yet the image was fully colored. And, as we shall see later, the colors in images will be remarkably stable even when the over-all relative strengths or intensities of the two wavelengths are varied.

Natural Images

Is something "wrong" with classical theory? This long line of great investigators cannot have been mistaken. The answer is that their work had very little to do with color as we normally see it. They dealt with spots of light, and particularly with pairs of spots, trying to match one to another. The conclusions they reached were then tacitly assumed to apply to all of color sensation. This assumption runs very deep, and has permeated all our teaching, except for that of a few investigators like E. Hering, C. Hess and the contemporary workers Dorothea Jameson and Leo M. Hurvich (who have studied the effect produced on a colored spot by a colored surround).

The study of color vision under natural conditions in complete images (as opposed to spots in surrounds) is thus an unexplored territory. We have been working in this territory—the natural-image situation, as we call it—for the past five years. In the rest of this article I shall describe some of the surprises we have encountered.

To form the image in our modification of Newton's experiment we needed two sets of elements: a pair of different photographs of the same scene, and a pair of different wavelengths for illuminating them. It is possible to make the pictures different by tinkering in the laboratory, arbitrarily varying the darkness of their different areas. But, as every photographer will have recognized at this point, a simple way to produce the two pictures is to make "color separations", that is, to photograph the scene through two filters that pass different bands of wavelengths. In this way the film is systematically exposed to longer wavelengths coming from the scene in one case, and to shorter wavelengths in the other. In our investigations we usually use a red filter for the longer wavelengths and a green filter for the shorter.

Now when we illuminate the transparencies with practically any pair of wavelengths and superimpose the images, we obtain a colored image. If we send the longer of the two through the long-wave photograph and the shorter through the short-wave photograph, we

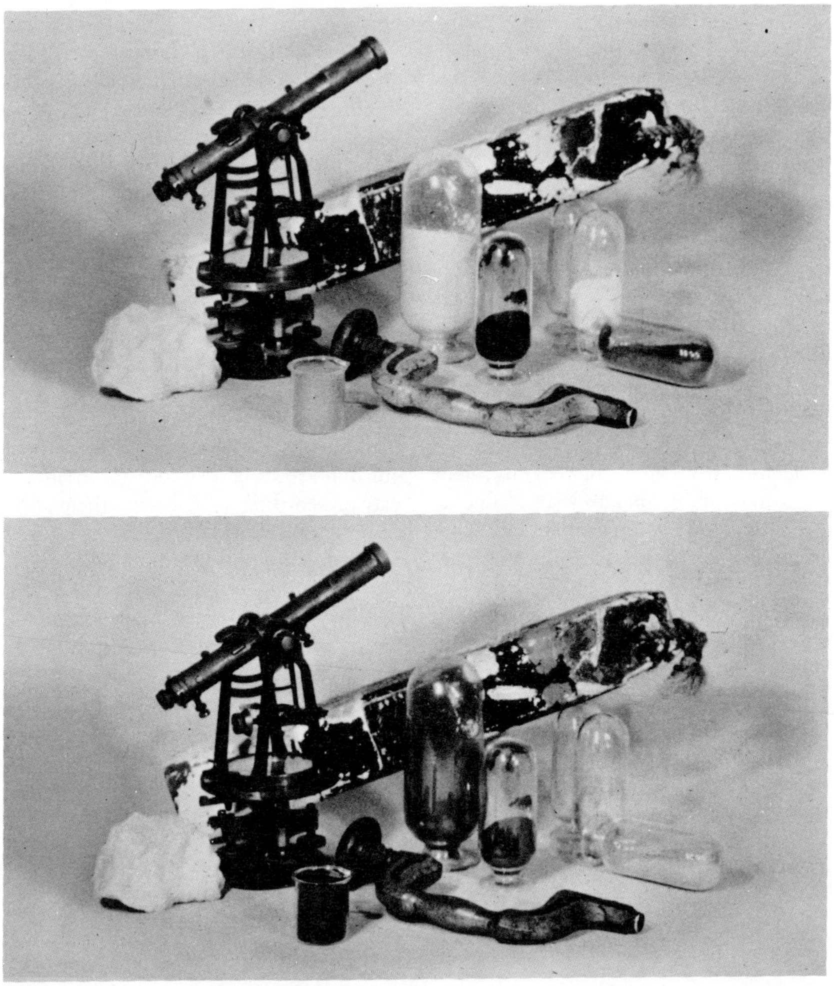

LONG AND SHORT RECORDS are provided by transparencies of these black-and-white photographs made through a red filter (*top*) and a green filter (*bottom*). In projection the long record (*top*) is illuminated by the longer of two wavelengths or bands of wavelengths, and the short record is illuminated by the shorter wavelength or band of wavelengths.

COLORS SEEN when long and short records are illuminated by closely spaced narrow bands of wavelengths are reproduced in these "Flexichrome" photographs. The illuminating wavelengths are indicated by arrows on the spectrum under each photograph. These images could not be photographed directly; the response of color film to the limited range of wavelengths used here is very different from that of the eye. SCIENTIFIC AMERICAN has artificially reproduced the colors seen by the eye by adjusting the color in a Flexichrome print.

obtain most or all of the colors in the original scene and in their proper places. If we reverse the process, the colors reverse, reds showing up as blue-greens and so on.

Long Wavelengths *v.* Short

It appears, therefore, that colors in images arise not from the choice of wavelength but from the interplay of longer and shorter wavelengths over the entire scene. Let us now test this preliminary hypothesis by some further experiments.

There are several more convenient ways to combine images than in the arrangement of Newton's experiment. One of the simplest is to place the transparencies in two ordinary projectors, using filters to determine the illuminating wavelengths. The color photograph at the bottom of page 287 shows images formed in this way.

When we work with filters, we are not using single wavelengths, but rather bands of wavelengths; the bands have more or less width depending on the characteristics of each filter. It turns out that the width of the band makes little difference. The only requirement is that the long-wavelength photograph, or, as we call it, the "long record," should be illuminated by the longer band and the "short record" by the shorter band. Indeed, one of the bands may be as wide as the entire visible spectrum. In other words, it may be white light. The lower photograph on page 287 shows the result of using a red filter for the long record and no filter (that is, white light) for the short record.

One advantage of this arrangement is that an observer can test the truth of our hypothesis in a simple and dramatic way. According to classical theory the combination of red and white can result in nothing but pink. With no photograph in either projector, and with a red filter held in front of one of them, the screen is indeed pink. Now the transparencies are dropped into place and the view changes instantly to one of full, vivid color. If the red filter is taken away, the color disappears and we see a black-and-white picture. When the filter is put back, the colors spring forth again.

An incidental advantage in using red for the long record and white for the short lies in the fact that the colors produced look about the same to color film as they do to the eye. Thus the image can be photographed directly. With more restricted bands of wavelengths the film, which does not have the newfound versatility of the eye, cannot respond as the eye does, and reproductions must be prepared artificially [*see photographs on page 288*].

The projectors afford a simple way of testing another variable: brightness. By placing polarizing filters in front of the projector's lenses we can vary the amount of light reaching the screen from each source. With no transparencies in the projector, but with the red filter still over one lens, the screen displays a full range of pinks, from red to white, as the strengths of the two beams are changed. When the photographs are in place, the colors of the image on the screen hold fast over a very considerable range of relative intensities.

Let us pause for a moment to consider the implications of this last demonstration. Remember that the photographs

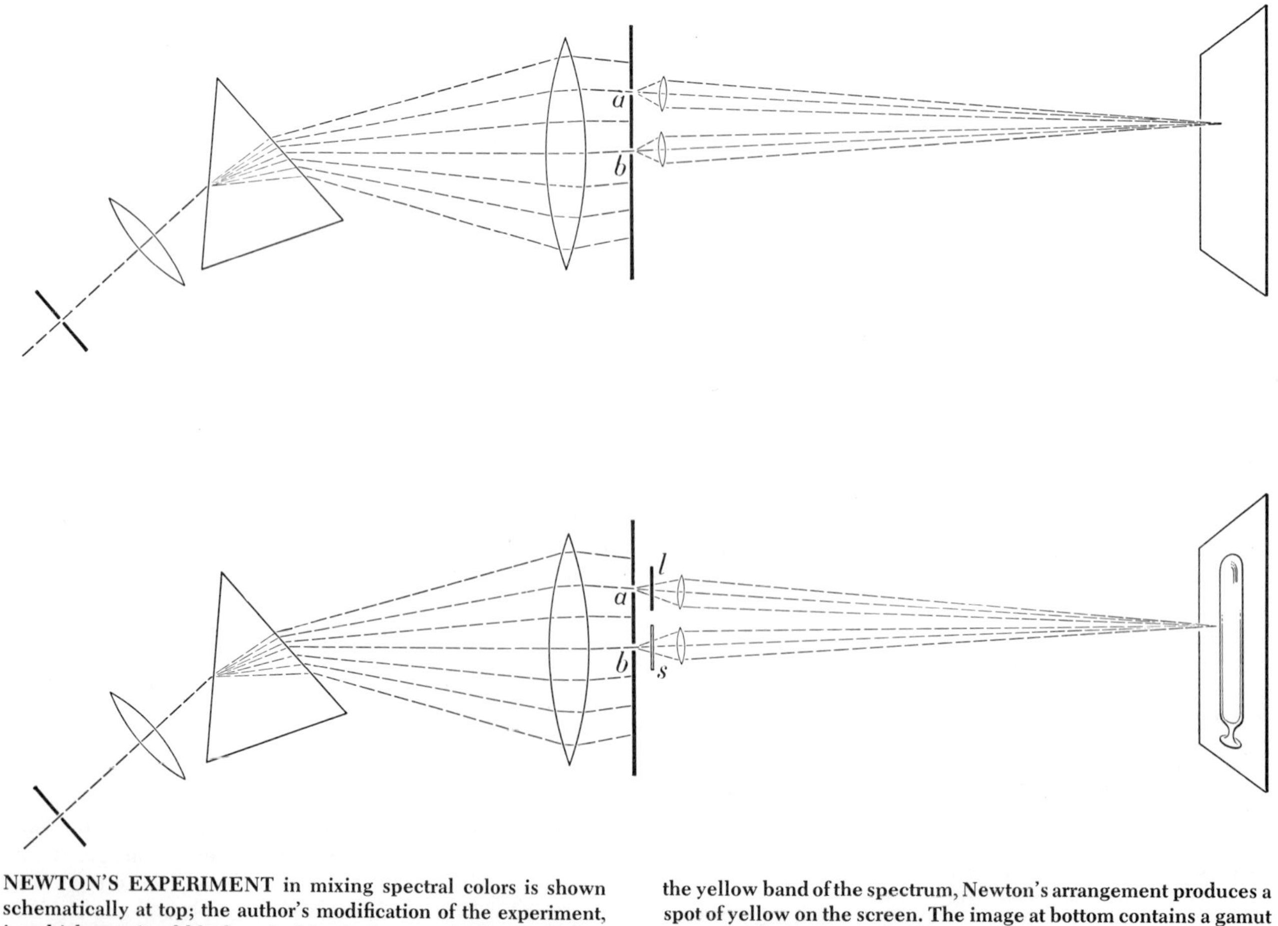

NEWTON'S EXPERIMENT in mixing spectral colors is shown schematically at top; the author's modification of the experiment, in which a pair of black-and-white transparencies is inserted in the beams, is diagrammed at bottom. When slits *a* and *b* are both in the yellow band of the spectrum, Newton's arrangement produces a spot of yellow on the screen. The image at bottom contains a gamut of color. The letters *l* and *s* in this diagram and others in this article refer, respectively, to the long record and the short record.

are nothing but pieces of celluloid treated to pass more light in some places than in others. All they can do to the red and white beams is to change relative intensities from point to point. In doing so they stimulate a complete gamut of color. Yet when we vary the relative intensities of the beams over the whole field of view, the colors stay constant. Evidently, even though the eye needs different brightness ratios, distributed over various parts of the image, to perceive color, the ratios that the eye is interested in are not simple arithmetic ones. Somehow they involve the entire field of view. Just how they involve it we shall see a little later.

The dual-projector system is convenient, but it is not a precision instrument. The wavelengths it can provide are limited by the characteristics of available filters. Narrow band-width filters may be used, but they seriously restrict the quantity of light. My colleague David Grey has therefore designed for me a dual image-illuminating monochromator [*see illustration on page 296*]. This instrument contains a pair of spectroscopes which allow us to light our transparencies with bands as narrow as we choose and of precisely known wavelength. By blocking off the spectroscopes and using filters, we can also obtain white light or broad bands. The two images are combined by means of a small, semitransparent mirror; light from one record passes through the mirror, and light from the other is reflected from its top surface. The intensity of each light source can be closely controlled.

With the dual monochromator we have confirmed our broad hypothesis: Color in natural images depends on a varying balance between longer and shorter wavelengths over the visual field. We have also been able to mark out the limits within which color vision operates. It turns out that there must be a certain minimum separation between the long-record wavelength and the short. This minimum is different for different parts of the spectrum. Any pair of wavelengths that are far enough apart (and the minimum distance is astonishingly small) will produce grays and white, as well as a gamut of colors extending well beyond that expected classically from the stimulating wavelengths. Many combinations of wavelengths produce the full gamut of spectral colors, plus the nonspectral color sensations such as brown and purple. All this information has been summarized in a color map showing the limitations on the sensations produced by different pairs of wave-

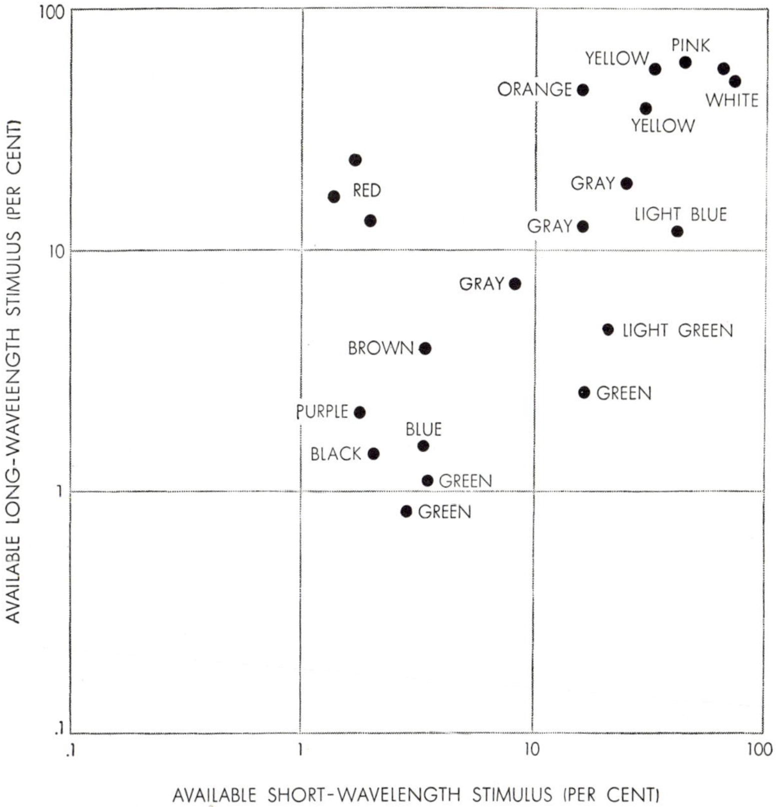

COORDINATE SYSTEM predicts colors in natural images. Axes are dimensionless, each measuring illumination at every point as a percentage of the maximum that could be there.

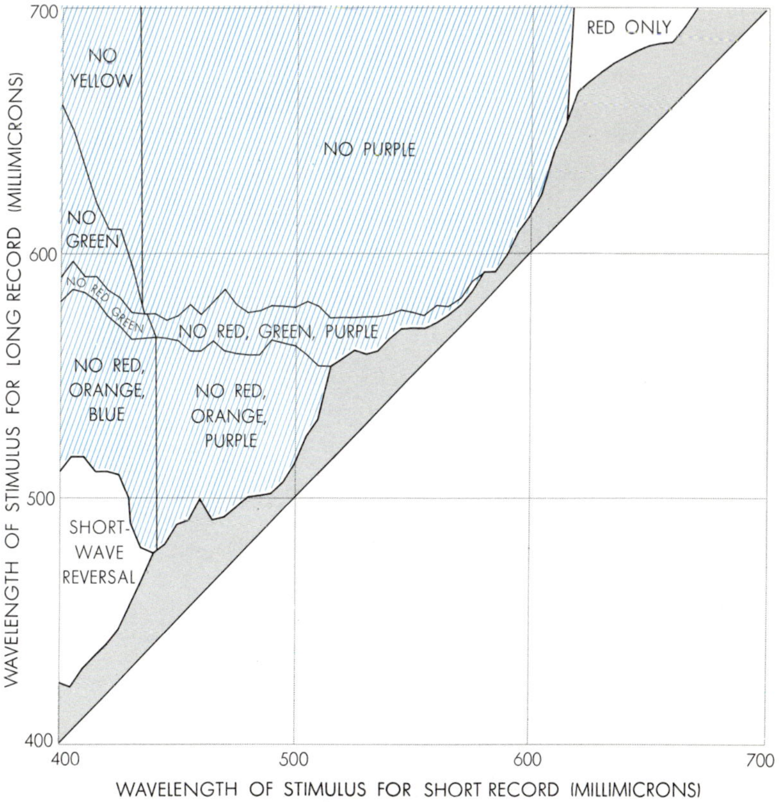

COLOR MAP shows limits on color obtainable with different pairs of wavelengths. The gray area is an achromatic region in which wavelengths are too close together to produce any kind of color. In the region marked "short-wave reversal" the colors are normal, but the short wavelengths act as the stimulus for the long record and the long wavelengths as the stimulus for the short record. The blank area below the diagonal is a region of reversed color obtained by illuminating the short record with long wavelengths and *vice versa*.

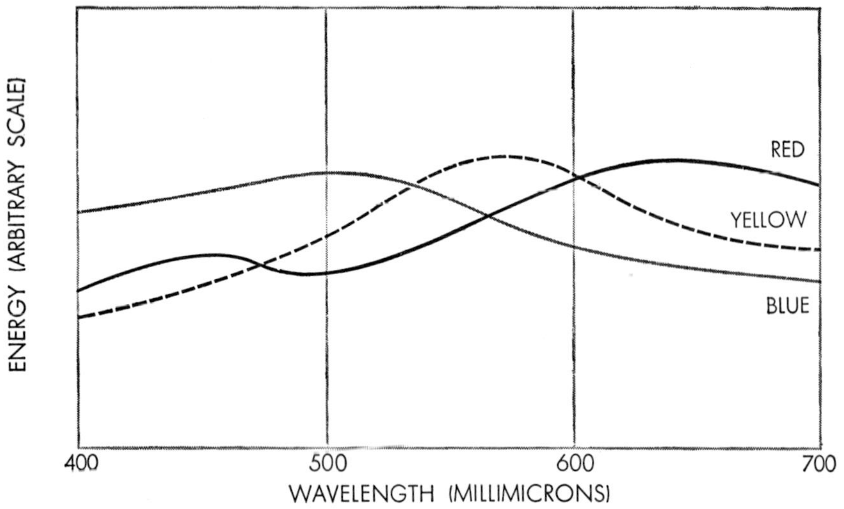

PIGMENTS IN OUR WORLD have broad reflection characteristics. Each pigment reflects some energy from wavelengths across the visible spectrum (400 to 700 millimicrons).

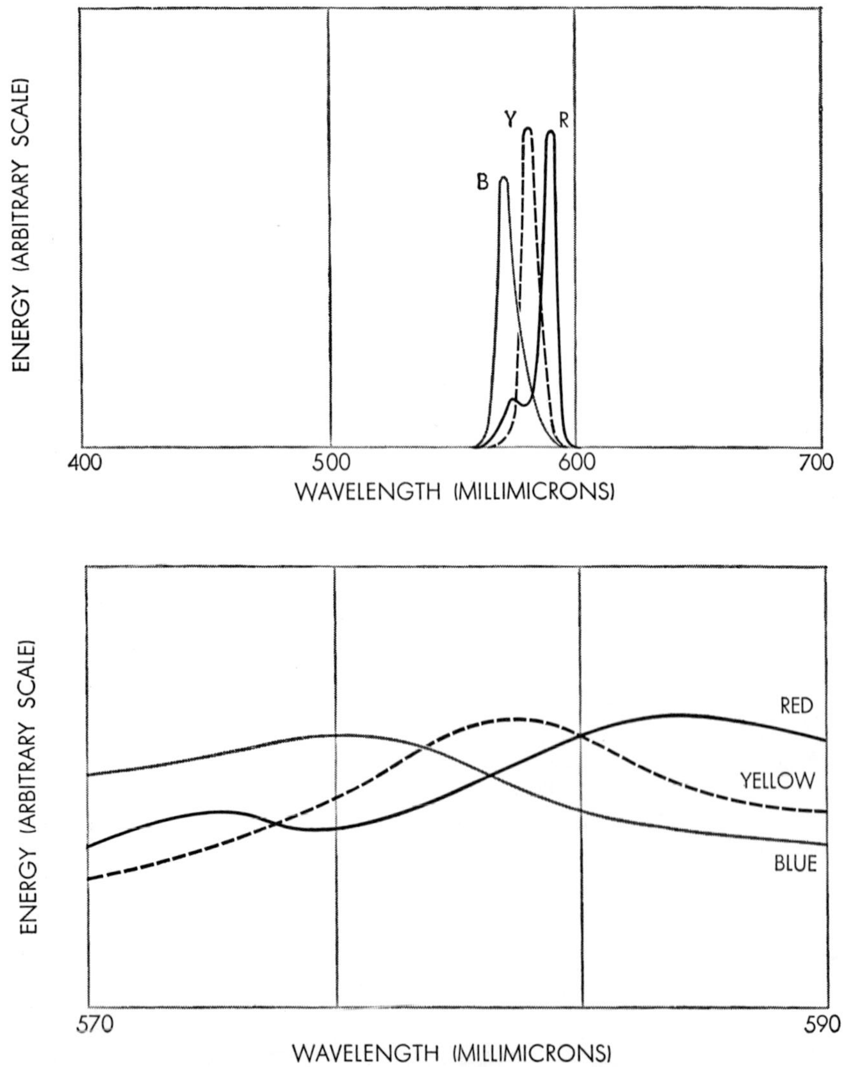

PIGMENTS IN AN IMAGINARY WORLD, whose available light is limited to a band of wavelengths extending only from about 570 millimicrons to 590 millimicrons, would have to be much more sharply selective. Upper curves show reflection curves of pigments which would give full color in such a world. Lower curves represent the same curves stretched out so that the 570-590 band covers the same width as the 400-700 band of the visible spectrum.

lengths [*see illustration at bottom of preceding page*]. We have also investigated the limits on relative brightness. With some pairs the colors are maintained over enormous ranges of brightness; with others they begin to break down with smaller changes. Again, the result depends on the wavelengths we are using. A table showing the stability of various colors for a sample pair of wavelengths appears on page 297.

A New Coordinate System

The color map tells us what we will *not* see when we combine a pair of images at various wavelengths. Can we now make a positive prediction? Given a pair of records of the same scene, and a pair of wave bands with which to illuminate them, what color will appear at each specific point on the combined image? In other words, we want a set of rules that will do for images what the color triangle does for color-matching experiments (and what most of us have mistakenly supposed it does for images as well).

We have formed a new coordinate system that does for the first time predict the colors that will be seen in natural images. Perhaps the best way to approach it is through an actual experiment. Let us set up the dual projector (or the monochromator) for any pair of "long" and "short" bands, say red and white, that can produce full color. We know that local variations in the relative brightness of the two records must somehow give rise to the color. Yet we have also found that changing all the brightness ratios in a systematic way, for example by cutting down the total light from the red projector, has no effect. Therefore we look for a way of describing the brightness in terms that are independent of the total light available in either image.

This can be done as follows: We turn on the "long" projector alone, setting its brightness at any level. Now we find the spot on the red image corresponding to the point at which the long black-and-white record lets through the most light. We measure the intensity at that point and call it 100 per cent. It tells us the maximum available energy for the long waves. Next we measure the intensity of the light all over the rest of the red image, marking down for each point the red intensity as a per cent of the maximum available. Then we turn off the "long" projector, turn on the "short" one and follow the same procedure for the short wavelengths (in this case the full

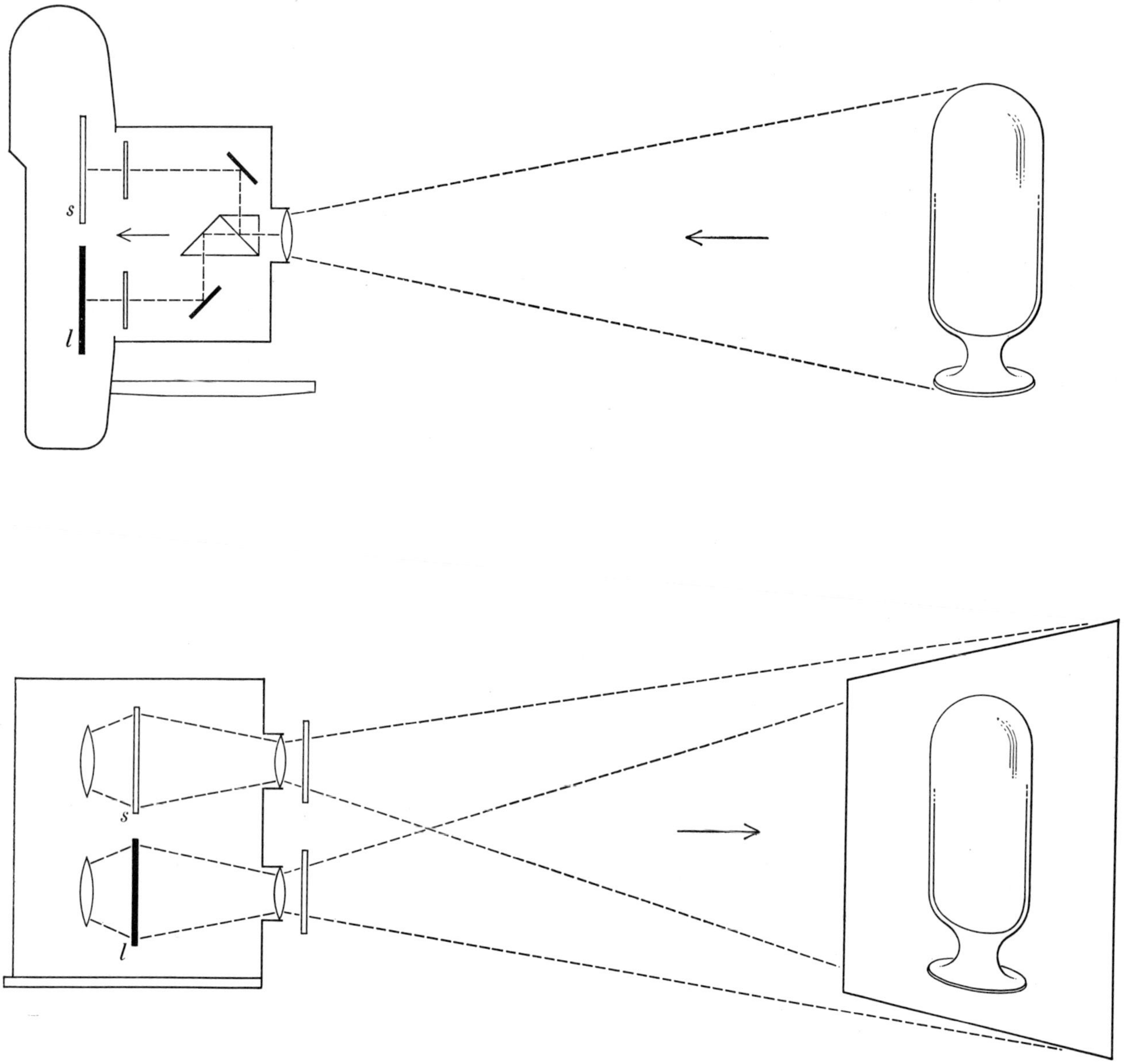

LONG AND SHORT RECORDS are prepared by photographing a scene with the dual camera diagrammed at top. Small open rectangles represent colored filters; the filter in front of the long record is red and the one in front of the short record is green. A composite image is formed by superimposing long and short records (*labeled l and s*) on a screen by means of a dual projector (*bottom*).

spectral band). Now we draw up a two-dimensional graph [*top of page 291*], plotting the percentage of available long wavelengths on one axis and the percentage of available short wavelengths on the other. Every point on the image can be located somewhere on this graph. Each time we plot a point, we note next to it the color it had on the image.

What emerges is a map of points, each associated with a color. When it is finished, we can see that the map is divided into two sections by the 45-degree line running from lower left to upper right. This is the line of gray points. If we had put the same transparency in each projector, all the points would fall on the gray line, since the percentage of available light would be the same at every point on the image for both projectors. The other colors arrange themselves in a systematic way about the 45-degree line. Warm colors are above it; cool colors are below. Thus it seems that the important visual scale is not the Newtonian spectrum. For all its beauty the spectrum is simply the accidental consequence of arranging stimuli in order of wavelength. The significant scale for images runs from warm colors through neutral colors to cool colors.

Repeating our experiment with different illuminating wavelengths or bands, we find that for every pair that produces full color the position of the colors on the coordinate graph remains the same. Thus we have the rule we were looking for, a rule that tells us in advance what color we shall find at any point in an image. We can take any pair of transparencies and measure their percentage of transmission in various regions of the picture. Then, before projecting them, we can predict the colors these areas will have. We will be right provided that the illuminating wavelengths are capable of stimulating all the colors. In cases where they are not, we must change the coordinate map accordingly. Thus the full set of rules consists of a group of coordinate color plots, one for each section of the color map at the bottom of page 291.

Note that each coordinate system is

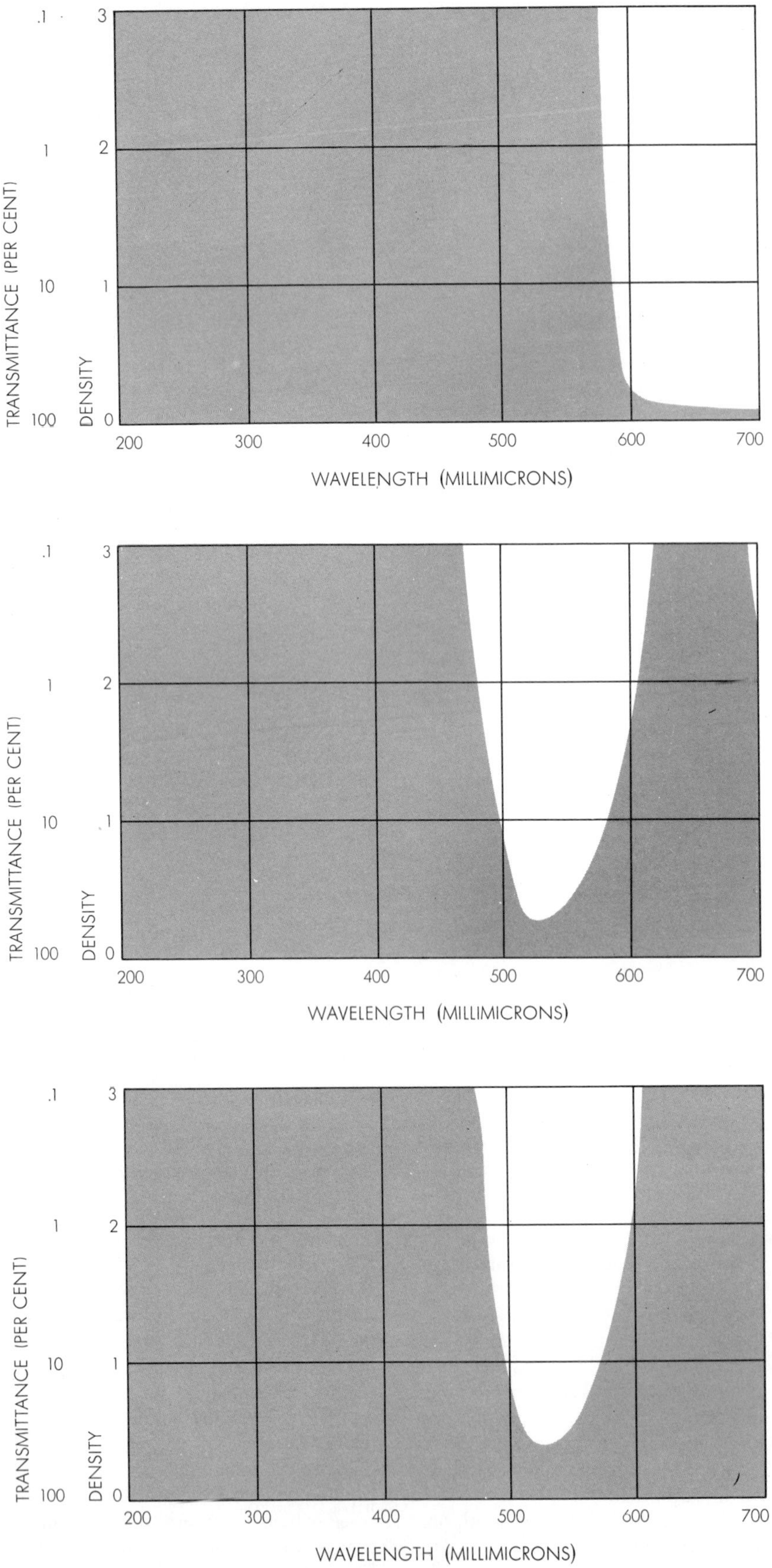

WAVELENGTHS PASSED BY FILTERS used in various experiments described by the author are shown in these curves. At top is the transmittance curve for the red filter used in photographing long record; below it is transmittance curve of green filter for preparing short record. At bottom is curve for the green filter used in the sodium-viewer experiment.

itself dimensionless. The axes do not measure wavelength, brightness or any other physical unit. They express a ratio of intensities at a single wavelength or for a broad band of wavelengths. The axes have another interesting property: they are stretchable. Suppose we superimpose two identical long-wavelength photographs in the slide holder of the "long" projector and leave a single short-wavelength photograph in the holder of the "short" projector. We find that this combination still does not alter the colors on the screen. What sort of change have we made? Every point in the long record that transmitted 1/2 of the available light now transmits 1/4, points that transmitted 1/5 now transmit 1/25 and so on. On the logarithmic scale of our graph this corresponds to stretching the long-record axis to twice its former length. The 45-degree line now shifts to a new direction, but all the color points shift with it, maintaining their relative positions [*see diagram on opposite page*].

Randomness

Our studies of the coordinate graph have uncovered another interesting and subtle relationship. As we plotted graphs for various experiments we began to suspect that any arrangement which yielded points falling on a straight line, or even on a simple smooth curve, would be colorless. To test this idea we tried putting a negative photograph in one projector and a positive of that negative in the other. Such a pair of images will plot as a straight line running at right angles to the 45-degree gray line. The image is indeed virtually colorless, showing only the two "colors" of the stimuli involved in projection and a trace of their Newtonian mixture.

If an image is to be fully colored, its coordinate graph must contain points distributed two-dimensionally over a considerable area. But even this is not enough. The points must fall on the graph in a somewhat random manner, as they do in the plot of any natural scene. This requirement can be demonstrated in a very striking experiment. Suppose we put a "wedge" filter in the slide holder of the red projector. The effect of the filter is to change the intensity of the beam continuously from left to right. That is, when the red projector is on and the white projector off, the left side of the screen is red and the right side is dark, with gradations in between. Now we place a similar wedge, but vertically, in the white projector so that the top of the screen is white and the bottom is dark. With both projectors turned on we now have an infinite variety of red-to-white ratios on the screen, duplicating all those that could possibly occur in a colored image. However, they are arranged in a strictly ordered progression. There is no randomness. And on the screen there is no color—only a graded pink wash.

To repeat, then, the colors in a natural image are determined by the relative balance of long and short wavelengths over the entire scene, assuming that the relationship changes in a somewhat random way from point to point. Within broad limits, the actual values of the wavelengths make no difference, nor does the over-all available brightness of each.

The independence of wavelength and color suggests that the eye is an amazingly versatile instrument. Not only is it adapted to see color in the world of light in which it has actually evolved, but also it can respond with a full range of sensation in much more limited worlds. A dramatic proof of this is provided by another series of experiments.

Color Worlds

In these we use a pair of viewing boxes that superimpose fairly large images by means of semitransparent mirrors [*see diagram at bottom of page 297*]. Each box contains tungsten lamps, which produce white light, to illuminate one record and a sodium lamp to illuminate the other. We turn on one viewer, inserting the long and short transparencies and placing a red filter over the tungsten lamp. The composite image is fully colored, containing greens and blues, although the shortest wavelength coming from the mirror lies in the yellow part of the spectrum. Now we turn on the second viewer, inserting a green filter over the white light-source. Again the image contains a gamut of color, including red. The observer can see the images in both viewers at once—each showing the same range of color, but representing different visual worlds. In the first the sodium light (with a wavelength of 589 millimicrons) serves as the shortest available wavelength and helps to stimulate the green and blue. In the second it is the longest wavelength and stimulates red. If the observer stands back far enough from the viewer, he can also see the "natural" colors in the room around him. Here then is a third world in which yellow is "really" yellow.

Another way to use the green filter in the second sodium viewer is to hold it

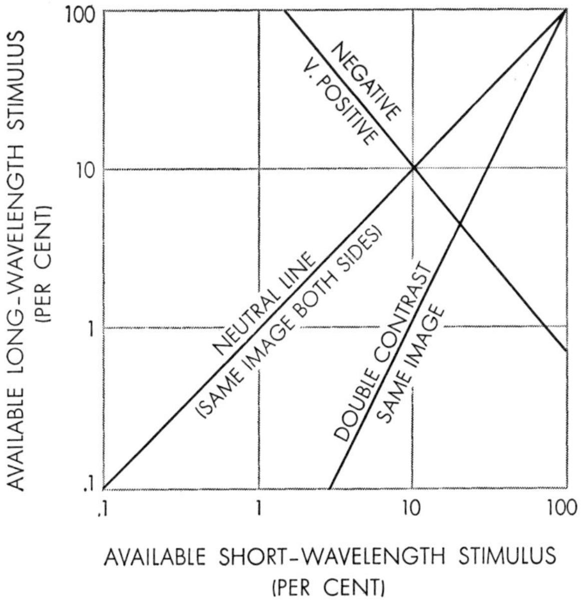

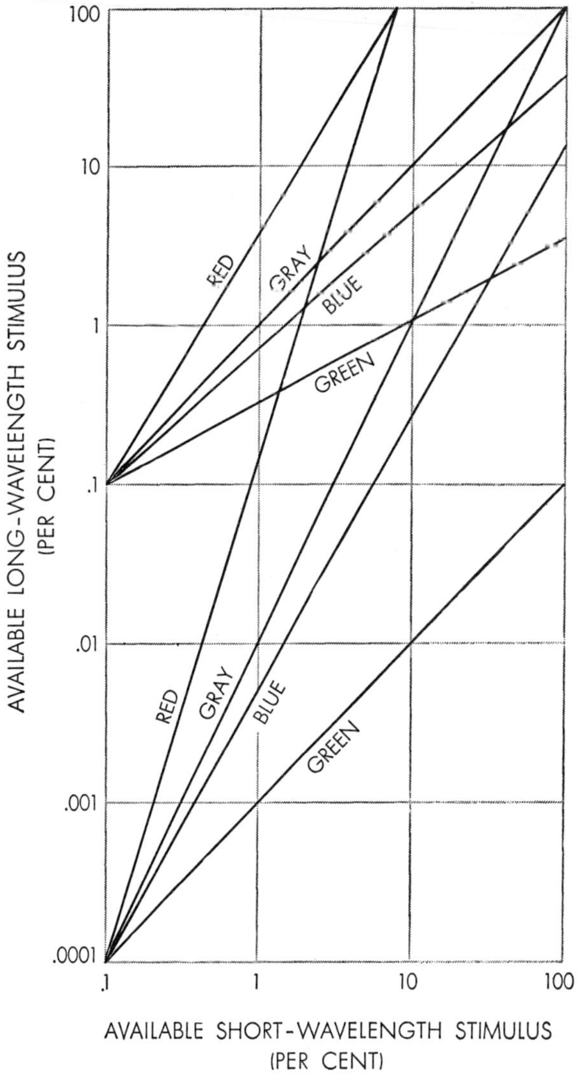

PROPERTIES OF COORDINATE SYSTEM are illustrated in these diagrams. At left are the graphs of experimental situations which do not produce a gamut of color in the image. Such situations appear to graph as straight lines. At right the axes are shown to be stretchable. When gray line dividing warm and cool colors is displaced, colors move but maintain their relative positions.

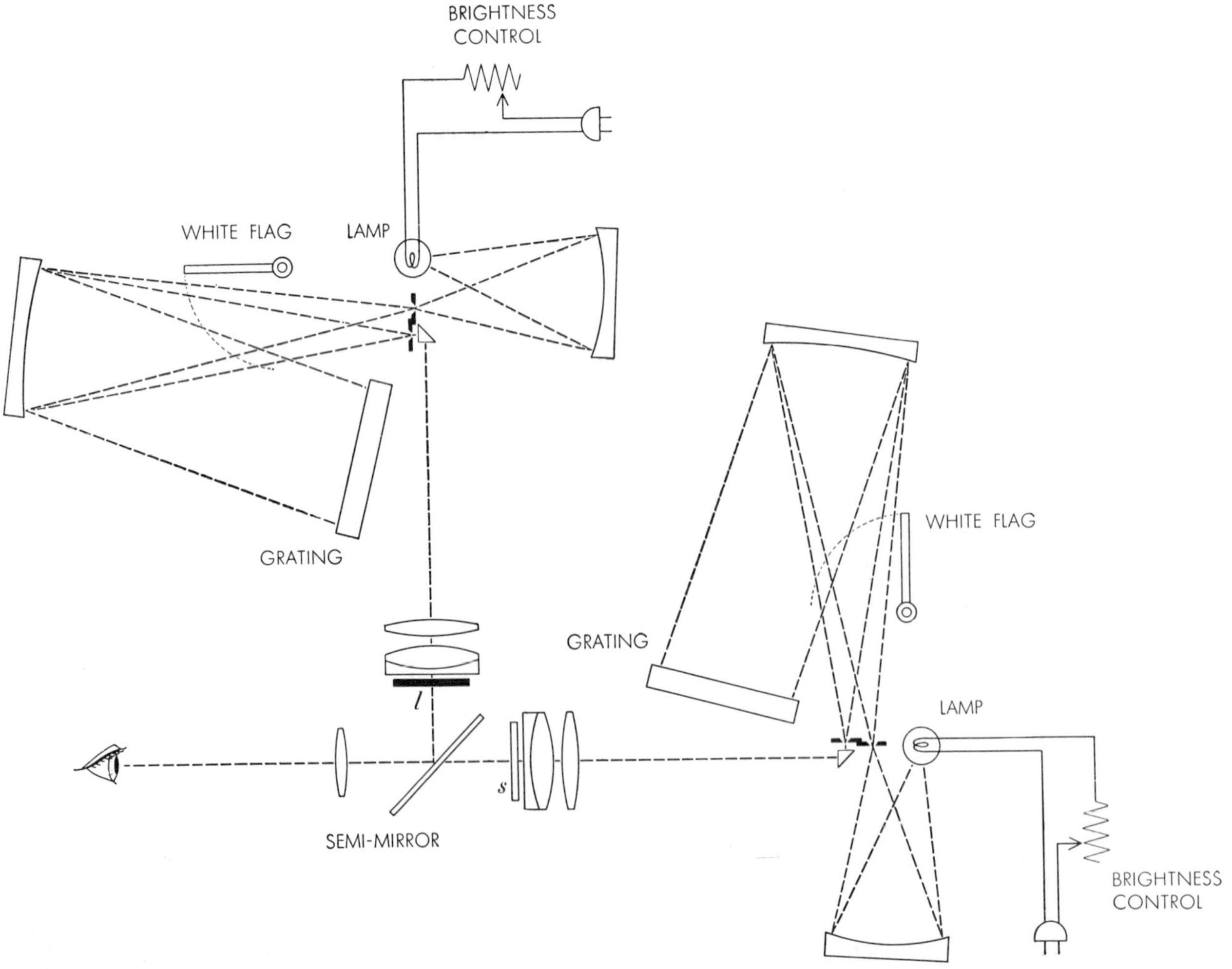

DUAL MONOCHROMATOR is seen in schematic diagram at bottom and in photograph at top. Very narrow bands of wavelengths from any part of the visible spectrum are produced by the two gratings. White flags can be inserted to give white light. Narrow rectangles marked *l* and *s* represent the black-and-white transparencies that serve as the long record and the short record respectively.

up to the eye instead of placing it in front of the tungsten lamps. This filter passes both the sodium wavelength and the green band [*see bottom graph on page 294*]. When he looks around the room, the observer sees red objects as black and the rest of the colors as washed-out green. But when he looks at the picture in the second viewing box, he sees it quite full of color, including red.

The color worlds of the viewers are produced by pictures. Could we make physical models of these worlds, populating them with real objects which would show the same colors as the images in the viewers under the same conditions of illumination? We could if only we had the proper pigments. The pigments in the world around us are the best we have been able to find that look colored in our lighting: a spectrum of visible wavelengths from 400 to 700 millimicrons. Each of these pigments reflects a broad band of wavelengths, and its peak is not sharp [*see diagram at top of page 292*].

Thus our coloring materials do not distinguish clearly between wavelengths that are fairly close together. If we could find pigments with much narrower response curves, we would suspect that these might provide full color in a more restricted world of light—a world, for example, lighted by the wavelengths that pass through the green filter. In the absence of such coloring materials, we might content ourselves with creating this world photographically, if we could show that this is possible. A moment's study of the diagrams on page 292 will show the exciting fact that a two-color separation photograph in a world of any band-width is the same as a two-color photograph in a world of any other band-width—including our own, provided that we postulate that a correctly proportioned change in the absorption bands of the pigments goes along with a change in the band-width of the world. Therefore we can use our regular long and short pictures, taken through the red and green filters, to transport ourselves into new worlds with their new and appropriately narrow pigments.

COLORS SEEN	RANGE OVER WHICH SEEN	VARIATION IN COLOR OVER THIS RANGE
GRAY	200 TO 1	LITTLE VARIATION
BROWN	100 TO 1	YELLOW-BROWN TO DARK BROWN
WHITE	100 TO 1	YELLOWISH-WHITE TO BLUISH-WHITE
YELLOW	30 TO 1	YELLOW TO OFF-WHITE
YELLOW-GREEN	30 TO 1	YELLOW-GREEN TO YELLOW ORANGE
BLUE	10 TO 1	BLUE-VIOLET TO BLUE GREEN
GREEN	6 TO 1	BLUE-GREEN TO GRAY-GREEN
RED	5 TO 1	DARK RED TO DARK ORANGE-RED
ORANGE	5 TO 1	YELLOW TO RED-ORANGE

LIMITS OF STABILITY of colors under variation in relative brightness of a sample pair of long and short stimuli are summarized in this typical chart. Second column shows the mechanism ratio (changing the brightness of either or both of the stimuli) for which color at left is recognizable. Pair of stimuli used was 450 millimicrons and 575 millimicrons.

The Visual Mechanism

The sodium-viewer demonstration suggests an important consideration that we have not previously mentioned, although it is implicit in what has already been said. If the eye perceives color by comparing longer and shorter wavelengths, it must establish a balance point or fulcrum somewhere in between, so that all wavelengths on one side of it are taken as long and all on the other side as short. From the evidence of the viewer we can see that the fulcrum must shift, making sodium light long in one case and short in the other.

Where is the fulcrum in the ordinary, sunlit world? Experiments on a large number of subjects indicate that it is at a wavelength of 588 millimicrons. When we use this wavelength in one part of the dual monochromator and white light in the other, the image is nearly colorless. With a wavelength shorter than 588 millimicrons, white serves as the longer stimulus in producing color; with a wavelength longer than 588 millimicrons, white becomes the short record.

From the dual-image experiments we learn that what the eye needs to see color is information about the long and short wavelengths in the scene it is viewing. It makes little difference on what particular bands the messages come in. The situation is somewhat similar to that in broadcasting: The same information can be conveyed by any of a number of different stations, using different carrier frequencies. But a radio must be tuned to the right frequency. Our eyes are always ready to receive at any frequency

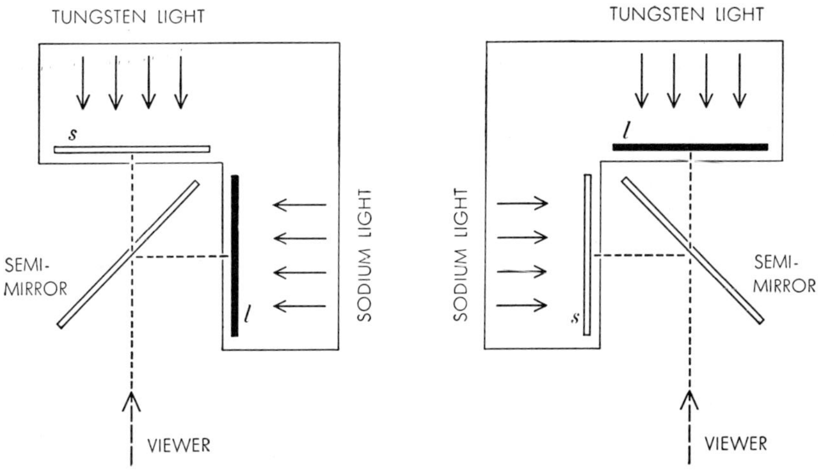

SODIUM-VIEWING BOXES are diagrammed schematically. Each of these instruments produces a large composite image by means of the semitransparent mirror. Tungsten light is white, and is restricted to narrower bands of wavelengths by means of colored filters.

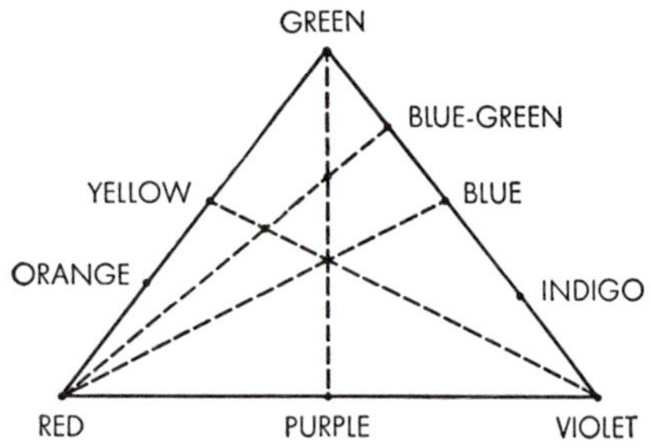

COLOR TRIANGLE of classical theory is shown in an early schematic form. Points of intersection of lines represent colors obtained by mixing spectral wavelengths in amounts proportional to distances from sides of triangle. Central point is equal mixture of primaries and is therefore white.

in the visible spectrum. And they have the miraculous ability to distinguish the longer record from the shorter, whatever the frequencies and the band-widths. Somehow they establish a fulcrum and divide the incoming carrier waves into longs and shorts around that point.

In our experiments we provide a single photograph averaging all the long wavelengths and a single photograph averaging all the short. What happens in the real world, where the eyes receive a continuous band of wavelengths? We are speculating about the possibility that these wavelengths register on the retina as a large number of individual color-separation "photographs," far more than the three that Maxwell thought necessary and far more than the two that we have shown can do so well. The eye-brain computer establishes a fulcrum wavelength; then it averages together all the photographs on the long side of the fulcrum and all those on the short side. The two averaged pictures are compared, as real photographic images are compared in accordance with our coordinate system.

Finally I should like to make clear that, although our experiments deal with two photographs and our coordinate system is two-dimensional, we have not been describing a two-color theory of vision. When we use a band of wavelengths for either or both of the records, we have light of many wavelengths coming from each point on the screen. And if classical three-color theory holds, it should describe the color of each of these points. This, as we have seen, it completely fails to do. It is true, however, that our experiments deal with two packages of information. We have demonstrated that the eye can do almost everything it needs to do with these two packages. The significance of what a third package will add is far from obvious. We are building a triple image-illuminating monochromator to find out.

A third picture may provide better information at the photographic level or an additional and useful interaction with the stimuli from two images. However, there is not a very big gap in the sensation scale to be filled by the third picture. In a given image a particular combination of two stimuli might not provide an electrically intense blue or a delicately yellowish green, but it is still likely to provide more than enough for the animal to live with. Nevertheless we do expect that the richness of many colors will be increased by the interplay of a third stimulus. Whatever we learn by adding a third picture, the visual process will remain an amazing one from the evolutionary point of view. Why has a system that can work so well with two packages of information evolved to work better with three? And who knows whether it will not work better still with four, or five or more?

What does the eye itself do in the everyday world of the full spectrum? Does it make only two averages? Or does it put to better use the new ability we have discovered—the ability to distinguish sharply between images at closely spaced wavelengths? Perhaps it creates many sets of averages instead of just two or three.

Even if more than two information channels are used, we feel that the big jump is obviously from one to two. Most of the capability of our eyes comes into play here. And whatever may be added by more channels, the basic concept will remain. Color in the natural image depends on the random interplay of longer and shorter wavelengths over the total visual field.

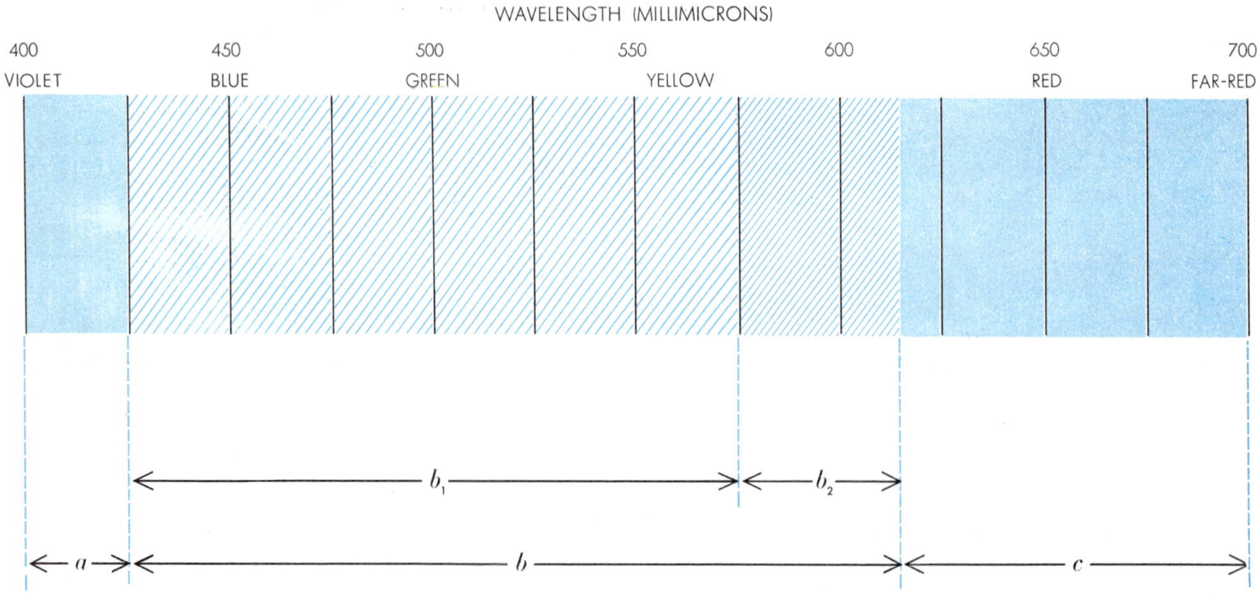

WAVELENGTH AND COLOR are independent of each other, except for the long-short relationship. This diagram shows the roles that various wavelengths can play. Those in the interval *a* can serve only as the short-record stimulus; those in *b* may be either long or short; those in *c* can only be long. If the wavelengths in b_1 are used as short-record stimuli, they will combine with a longer wavelength to produce the full gamut of color. If they are used as long-record stimuli, they will produce a more limited range. Wavelengths in b_2 will produce full color, serving as the stimuli for either the long record or for the short record. When both stimuli come from between 405 and 520 millimicrons, "short-wave reversal" occurs *(see color map on page 291)*.

29

EXPERIMENTS WITH GOGGLES

IVO KOHLER
May 1962

Of all the senses the one most intensively studied is undoubtedly vision. Much has been learned about the physical and physiological basis of visual perception, but understanding of the process remains primitive. Vision is perhaps the most complex of the senses; nonetheless it offers the investigator a tantalizing opportunity to learn how the brain processes sensory data and constructs an effective image of the outside world. Presumably this image is the result of an unconscious learning process; the image is "better" than it should be, considering the known defects in the visual system. For example, the lens of the eye is not corrected for spherical aberration; hence straight lines should look slightly curved. By the same token, lines of a certain curvature should appear straight. It is also well known that the eye is not corrected for color; as a result different wavelengths of light—originating at a common point—do not come to a common focus on the retina. One would expect this defect, called chromatic aberration, to have a noticeable effect on vision, but it does not, except under special conditions.

One way to explore the unconscious learning process that goes on in normal vision is to investigate how the visual system responds to images that are systematically distorted by specially constructed goggles. In this article I shall describe some of our studies, conducted at the University of Innsbruck in Austria, which show that the eye has a remarkable ability to discount or adapt to highly complex distortions involving both spatial geometry and color. But we have been surprised to discover that the eye does not adapt to certain other distortions that seem, superficially at least, less severe than those to which the eye does adapt. Some of these findings appear to be incompatible with traditional theories of vision in general and of color vision in particular.

In addition to contributing to the understanding of vision, experiments with goggles have immediate practical importance for ophthalmologists. If the ophthalmologist knows the extent to which the visual system can adapt to "wrongly" constructed experimental glasses, he will be less reluctant to prescribe strong glasses for his patients. The stronger a glass, meaning the higher its refractive power, the greater its capacity to distort images and produce a fringe of color around them. The ophthalmologist can tell a patient in need of strong glasses that the initially disagreeable distortions and rainbow fringes will disappear if he wears the glasses faithfully for several weeks. Or, to give another example, an operation to repair a detached retina sometimes leaves a fold in the retina that causes a bulge in the patient's visual world. On the basis of goggle experiments, the physician can assure the patient that the bulge will become less noticeable with time and will probably disappear altogether. The fold in the retina will remain, but the patient's vision will gradually adapt to discount its presence. What this implies, of course, is that an individual born with a fold or similar imperfection in his retina may never be aware of it.

We conclude, therefore, that sense organs are not rigid machines but living and variable systems, the functioning of which is itself subject to variation. If a sensory system is exposed to a new and prolonged stimulus situation that departs from the one normally experienced, the system can be expected to undergo a fundamental change in its normal mode of operation.

The use of distorting goggles seems to be the simplest way of producing novel and prolonged visual-stimulus situations. The volunteer subject can be said to be wearing the laboratory on his nose; he cannot leave the laboratory unless he closes his eyes or removes the goggles. The entire visual system, including the manifold projection regions in the brain of which we still know so little, is subjected in a certain way to a completely novel and disturbing situation. Finally it "breaks down"; established habits are abandoned and the visual system begins to respond in a new manner.

When we make the system break down and learn a new way of functioning, we do not believe we are forcing the system to function artificially or abnormally. We assume, rather, that a single mechanism is at work at all times. The mechanism that removes or minimizes an artificially created disturbance is the same one that brings about a normal

UNDISTORTED VIEW of the Union Carbide Building in New York can be compared with distorted images on page 310.

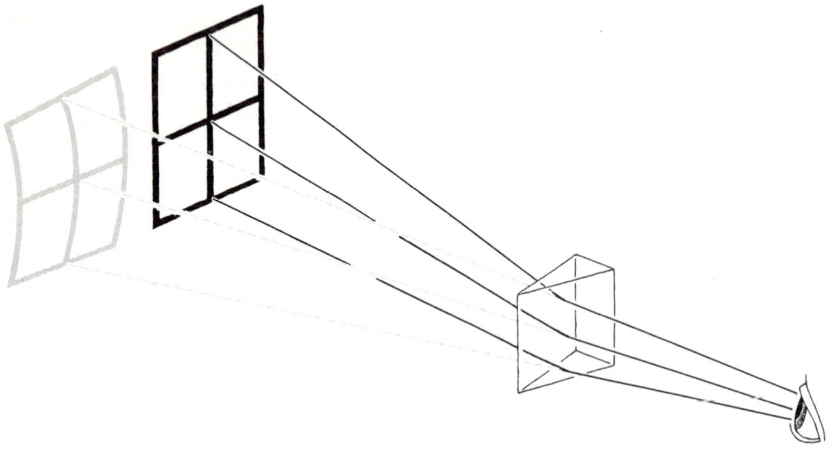

CURVATURE OF LINES is observed when looking through a prism because light rays entering the prism obliquely are bent more than those entering at right angles. A prism that has its base to the right displaces images to the left and bends the top and bottom of vertical lines still farther to the left. As a result vertical lines seem to bow to the right.

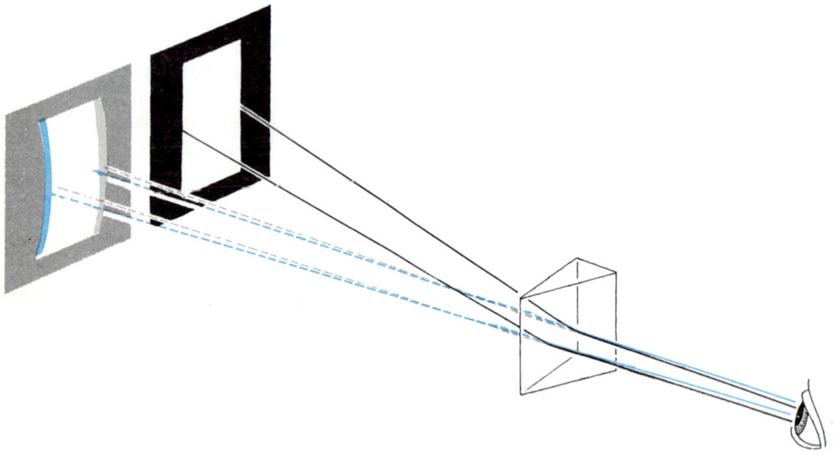

FRINGE OF COLOR borders light-colored objects because a prism bends short wavelengths of light more than long wavelengths. If the prism base is to the right, blue rays, being bent the most, are seen as a blue fringe along the left-hand border. Similarly, a yellow-red fringe of color (*shown here in gray*) appears along the right-hand border of the object.

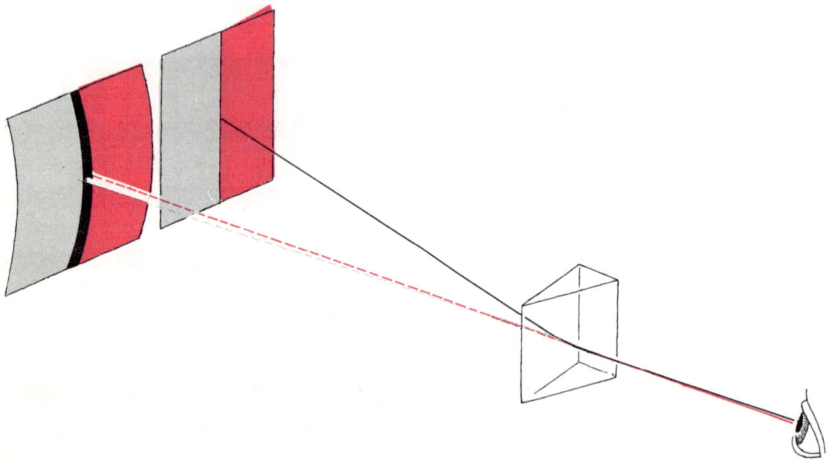

COLOR DISPLACEMENT is another consequence of the differential bending of light rays having different wavelengths. The diagram shows what happens if the green-red figure on the opposite page is viewed through a prism, base to right. The green area (*gray here*) is displaced to the left more than the red area, leaving an empty dark space between the two.

functioning of the sensory system under normal conditions. If this assumption is correct, the development of the normal visual system—in so far as its development depends on the environment—can be explored by the goggle method.

The application of distorting goggles to the study of visual adaptation dates back to the work of G. M. Stratton of the University of California, who used himself as a subject. Primarily because of the difficulty of finding subjects willing to wear goggles for days, weeks or even months, the method was little employed until about 1928. Then, independently and simultaneously, goggle experiments were undertaken by Theodor Erismann at the University of Innsbruck and by James J. Gibson at Smith College. Gibson's subjects wore goggles that placed a glass wedge, or prism, in front of each eye. Erismann experimented not only with prism goggles but also with more elaborate devices that transposed the visual field from right to left or from top to bottom. Another device allowed the subject to see only directly to the rear, as if he had eyes in the back of his head. After several weeks of wearing goggles that transposed right and left, one of Erismann's subjects became so at home in his reversed world that he was able to drive a motorcycle through Innsbruck while wearing the goggles.

Although Gibson's subjects wore goggles for only a few days at a time, they were the first to discover adaptation to the color fringes and line curvature that a prism produces. Depending on the extent to which the front and rear faces of a prism depart from the parallel, light rays passing through the glass are bent to a greater or lesser degree. This property is called the deviation of the prism. The deviation angle is approximately half the angle between the two faces. Deviations between five and 15 degrees are most useful for goggle experiments. Color fringes arise because light of short wavelength, such as blue light, is bent more than light of longer wavelength. As a result the line marking the edge of an object is spread out into a small spectrum, which becomes more noticeable the greater the contrast between the brightness of the object and that of its background [*see top illustration on opposite page*].

The curvature of lines is part of a more general prism effect that produces a variable change in the curvature, angle and distance of observed objects. The effect arises because the angle of deviation varies with the direction of the light reaching the front face of the prism.

COLOR FRINGES appear (*right*) when a simple white-on-black figure is viewed through a prism having its base to the right. The prism also bends vertical lines. The undistorted figure is shown at the left. These prismatic distortions are explained in the upper two illustrations on the opposite page. After a subject has worn prism goggles for a few days the color fringes and line curvature largely disappear. When he removes the goggles, he sees fringes of a complementary color and lines having a reverse curvature.

TEST FIGURE shows how colors are differentially shifted by a prism. When viewed through a prism with base to the right, the greater shift of the green image leaves a thin black void at the color boundary (*see bottom illustration on opposite page*). When the prism is turned around, green overlaps red, producing a thin white border. An eye with prismatic defects will see similar effects.

COLORED GOGGLES devised by the author create a blue-tinted world when the wearer looks to the left and a yellow-tinted world when he looks to the right. If the goggles are worn for several weeks, the eye adapts and the color distortions tend to disappear. Somehow the visual system learns to introduce the proper correction according to whether the eyes are turned to the left or right.

Rays entering at an oblique angle are bent more than rays entering at a right angle. Consequently straight lines appear curved, right angles seem to be acute or obtuse and distances seem to be expanded or foreshortened [*see illustrations on page 300*].

To a subject wearing prism goggles these assorted distortions produce a visual world whose appearance changes drastically as he turns his head. One of our subjects reported that it is "as if the world were made of rubber." When the head is turned to right or left, objects become broader or narrower, producing a "concertina" effect. When the head is moved up or down, objects seem to slant first one way, then the other. We have called this the rocking-chair effect.

Although the distortions arising from prism movement are severe, they might present the eye with a straightforward adaptation problem if the prism were held in rigid alignment with the central axis of the eye. In this case the rays reaching any particular area of the retina would always be deflected by the same amount and would therefore maintain a fixed angular relationship to rays striking adjacent retinal areas. Such a rigid relationship between prism and eye could be achieved if the prism could be worn as a contact lens resting directly on the cornea.

In the Erismann and Gibson experiments, however, as well as in our more recent ones, there is a small distance between the eye and the prism. As a result the eye can, and frequently does, move with respect to the glasses. Two kinds of relative motion arise. In one case the eye can be fixed on a given object while the head and goggles move. In the second case the head and goggles remain fixed while the eye moves. If one analyzes the geometry of the rays striking the retina, one finds that the adaptation problem is much more severe than if the prism and the eye could be held in rigid relationship. Let us consider a single retinal area, for example the important small region called the fovea, near the center of the retina, where the eye has its maximum acuity. The images reaching the fovea will be distorted more when the eye is looking obliquely through the prism than they will be when it is looking straight ahead. In fact, the distortion changes with every change in the angle that the axis of the eye makes in relation to the prism.

COLOR-STEREO EFFECT refers to a visual phenomenon in which colors appear to be located at different depths, according to wavelength. It is a special case of color displacement. The reader should be able to obtain the effect by looking at the opposite page with the outer half of each eye shielded with a card, as shown in the drawing on the next page. Blue and green squares should appear to float above those of other colors; red should seem farthest away.

In the accounts of his experiments Gibson neglected the free mobility of the eyes with respect to the glasses. Since his experiments were of short duration it is not clear how much adaptation took place among his subjects. He refers specifically only to adaptation to color fringes and to the curvature of lines. The latter is often called the Gibson effect.

In our much longer experiments, which extended the investigations begun by Erismann, a finely differentiated adaptation can be observed. Like Gibson's subjects, ours adapt rather quickly to color fringes and line curvature. We refer to these as constant distortions because they are essentially independent of head and eye movement. After wearing prism goggles for several weeks, however, our subjects also adapt to the more complex variable distortions, which are generated partly by movement of the head and goggles and partly by movement of the eyes behind the goggles.

I should like to stress the distinction between constant and variable distortions. Adaptation to the latter category apparently involves a process more complex than all previously known processes of visual adaptation. Let us suppose that the subject is provided with goggles that have prisms whose bases point to the right. When, at the start of the experiment, the subject turns his head to the left and glances to the right, he sees an image that contracts in its horizontal dimensions. Conversely, when he turns his head to the right and glances to the left, he sees an expanding image. After several weeks, however, an adaptation occurs that counteracts both of these forms of distortion. This process of double adaptation tends ultimately to eliminate the concertina effect. What seems so remarkable is that this takes place in spite of the fact that the fovea and other retinal areas have been exposed to a random mixture of these variable images. Somehow the visual system has learned a general rule: a contracted image must be expanded and an expanded image must be contracted, depending on the respective position of head and eyes.

If, after weeks or months, the subject is allowed to remove his goggles, the adaptation continues to operate when he views the normal world. The result is an apparent squeezing of images when he glances one way and an expansion when he glances the other. It is as if he were looking for the first time through prisms that have an orientation exactly opposite to those he has been wearing for so long. Moreover, all the other distortions, such as the rocking-chair effect, to which his eyes have slowly become adapted now appear in reverse when the goggles are removed. These aftereffects in their turn diminish in strength over a period of days, and the subject finally sees the stable world he used to know.

Both adaptation and aftereffects are vividly reported by our subjects. But in addition we have built devices that provide an objective measurement of the phenomena. These devices, for example, present the subject with a variety of horizontal and vertical lines that he can adjust in orientation and curvature until they look "right." Another device allows the subject to look through prisms and select the one with the strength appropriate to cancel the aftereffects induced by wearing prism goggles.

Let us now consider the adaptation to the color fringes a prism produces. If a prism with base to the right is placed before the eye and one looks at a white card on a black background, one sees a blue border along the left vertical edge of the card and a yellow-orange border along the right edge. The explanation is that the various colors of light reflected from the card and carrying its image no longer overlap precisely after passing through the prism. The result is a whole series of slightly offset colored images: yellow to left of red, green to left of yellow and blue to left of green. Across most of the area of the white card the multiplicity of colored images is not apparent because the various colors recombine to form white light. But at the left edge, where the card meets the black background, the blue image, which is shifted farthest to the left, can be seen as a blue border. Similarly, the red image appears along the right edge. (When the prism is weak, the right border looks yellow or orange rather than red because red and yellow lie so close together in the spectrum.

If one views the world through goggles with their prism bases fixed in the same direction, the rainbow fringes diminish rather quickly in intensity and within a few days virtually disappear. Here again, as a result of adaptation, a complementary aftereffect appears when the glasses are removed. The adaptation that has canceled the blue fringe on objects produces a yellowish fringe and vice versa. This complementary aftereffect, which we call the rainbow phantom, can appear after goggles have been worn for less than a day.

At first consideration the rainbow phantom may not seem surprising. Everyone is familiar with the complementary afterimage that can be induced by staring for about 20 seconds at a brightly colored pattern. Evidently the retinal elements that have been intensively exposed to a given color change in some manner, so that when they are subsequently stimulated by a neutral light, they produce a different signal from adjacent elements that are still fresh. In accordance with the work of the German psychologist Ewald Hering, we ascribe such phenomena to a process of self-regulation. The sensory response becomes shifted in such a way as to make a persisting color stimulus appear more and more neutral. As a result a second color stimulus that had previously seemed neutral now appears shifted along the spectrum; for example, toward the blue-green if the first stimulus was red.

The puzzling aspect of the rainbow phantom is that blue and yellow are themselves complementary colors. Moreover, the small foveal area, which provides most of the eye's sensitivity to color, is randomly exposed to both yellow and blue stimuli during prism-goggle experiments. Consequently the response of the fovea should become equally modified to both colors, and since each is the complement of the other their aftereffects should cancel.

Nevertheless, the rainbow adaptation and its aftereffect, the rainbow phantom, do take place. How can they be explained? As in the case of adaptation to variable distortions of geometry, we must evidently assume a similar kind of multiple (at least double) adaptation for color vision also. The two aspects are the distortion itself and the context or situation in which the distortion occurs. I have already indicated that adaptation to the concertina effect requires the visual system to learn that images contract when one looks in one direction and expand when one looks in the other. In the case of color fringing the distortion is related to a brightness gradient. The subject looking at the world through prisms that have their bases facing to the right unconsciously learns a new rule: The boundary between a dark field on the left and a light field on the right always has a fringe of blue; when the dark field lies to the right of the light field, the fringe is always yellow. We must assume that the total adaptation process requires simultaneous adjustment to these two conditions. The rainbow phantom, which appears when the goggles are removed, can then be explained as a direct consequence of the complex adaptation process.

Once we had arrived at this explanatory concept, we undertook a further exploration of "situational color adaptation." For this purpose we designed goggles in which each lens was made up of two differently colored half-segments. For example, each lens might be half blue and half yellow [*see bottom illustration on page 301*]. Wearing such goggles, a subject sees a blue-tinted world when he looks to the left and a yellow-tinted world when he looks to the right. If the two colors are complementary, the situation is somewhat analogous to the rainbow effect of prism goggles. The difference is that the colors are related not to a brightness gradient but to specific positions of the head and eyes; in other words, to a "kinesthetic" gradient.

The experimental results were in accord with those obtained with prism goggles. As before, we found that the visual system adapts to complementary color stimuli so long as the colors are invariably associated with a particular situation—in this case, particular head-and-eye positions. The illustrations on pages 306 and 307 show the results of measuring color adaptation on the first day and on the 60th day of an experiment with blue-yellow glasses. The measurements are obtained through the use of an illuminated window whose color can be varied by turning a dial. The subject first looks at the window through the yellow half of his glasses and turns the dial until the window appears white or neutral in color. To achieve this condition the window must actually be made somewhat blue. The amount of blue light required is automatically recorded. The subject then readjusts the color of the window while looking through the blue half of his glasses. Finally he views the window without glasses, with his eyes turned first to the right and then to the left.

When the subject eventually removes his two-color goggles after wearing them continuously for 60 days, there is no doubt that his visual world is tinged distinctly yellow when he looks in the direction that his goggles had been blue and blue in the direction that his goggles had been yellow. The movement of the eyes, either to right or left, seems to act as a signal for the foveal area to switch over in its color response, compensating for a yellow image in one case and a blue image in the other.

At this point in our investigations everything seemed reasonably clear, but suddenly a new and mystifying phenomenon appeared, the implications of which have not yet been fully explored. During our prism experiments we had also constructed glasses in which the prisms in front of each eye were mounted with their bases pointed in opposite directions. Similar glasses are regularly prescribed by ophthalmologists to correct strabismus, also known as squinting. People with strabismus are unable to focus both eyes on the same object because the eyes turn either inward or outward; crossed eyes are an example. Ophthalmologists are often reluctant to prescribe corrective prism glasses for strabismus because of their concern that the patient may be disturbed by the distortions and color fringes that such glasses produce.

It was partly this prejudice that prompted our experiments. Because our subjects did not have strabismus they

COLORS ACQUIRE DEPTH if viewed with the eyes partially covered by two cards *(left)*, which exploit the chromatic aber-

found the wearing of "squint glasses" difficult until they learned to squint; that is, to turn their eyes either inward or outward, depending on the orientation of the prisms. We found, nevertheless, that adaptation is possible and that it occurs just as rapidly as it does with our usual prismatic goggles.

Our interest, however, was soon drawn to some special effects produced by squint glasses. Because the prism bases face in opposite directions, the glasses create novel stereoscopic effects in addition to those normally seen in binocular vision. The stereoscopic effects involve geometric figures and, more important, colors. If one looks at a vertical rod with prism glasses of the type described earlier, the rod will seem to bend either to the left or to the right, depending on which way the prism bases face. If the same rod is viewed with squint glasses equipped with prism bases facing outward, the rod will appear to be bent away from the observer. Similarly, plane surfaces will look concave.

But it was the stereoscopic effects involving color that took us most by surprise. On September 10, 1952, the first day of an extended experiment with squint glasses, one of our subjects described his discovery as follows.

"In the course of a trip through town, I made the following peculiar observations: multicolored posters, traffic signs, people wearing multicolored clothes, and so on, did not appear as before to lie in one plane, but blue seemed to protrude far beyond the object plane, whereas red seemed to recede, depending on whether the background was bright or dark. A woman carrying a red bag slung over her back seemed to be transparent, and the bag to be inside her, somewhere near her stomach.... Most peculiar was a woman wearing a red blouse. She had no upper body, and the red blouse seemed to be following her about a pace behind, moving its empty sleeves in rhythm with the movement of her arms."

After explaining to ourselves this "color-stereo" effect, we were impatient to learn whether or not the subject's eyes would ultimately adapt and restore colored objects to their proper place. The explanation is not difficult. Each prism deflects colors differentially according to wavelength but in opposite directions since the prism bases are in opposition. When the bases face outward, the blues are deflected outward more than other colors and the eyes must actually converge more to bring blue images into focus than to focus red images, which are deflected less by the two prisms. As a result, blue images seem closer to the observer than red images, and images in other colors seem to lie somewhere between the two, according to wavelength [*see illustration below*].

Again we were surprised by the outcome of the experiment. We have discovered that there is not the slightest adaptation to the color-stereo effect. This was true even in our longest test, in which a subject wore squint glasses for 52 days.

The reader can see the color-stereo effect for himself by viewing the illustration on page 302. Although the effect is more vivid with two prisms, or even one, it can be observed by making use of the chromatic aberration present in the normal eye. The procedure was described almost a century ago by the German physicist Hermann von Helmholtz. One covers the outer half of each

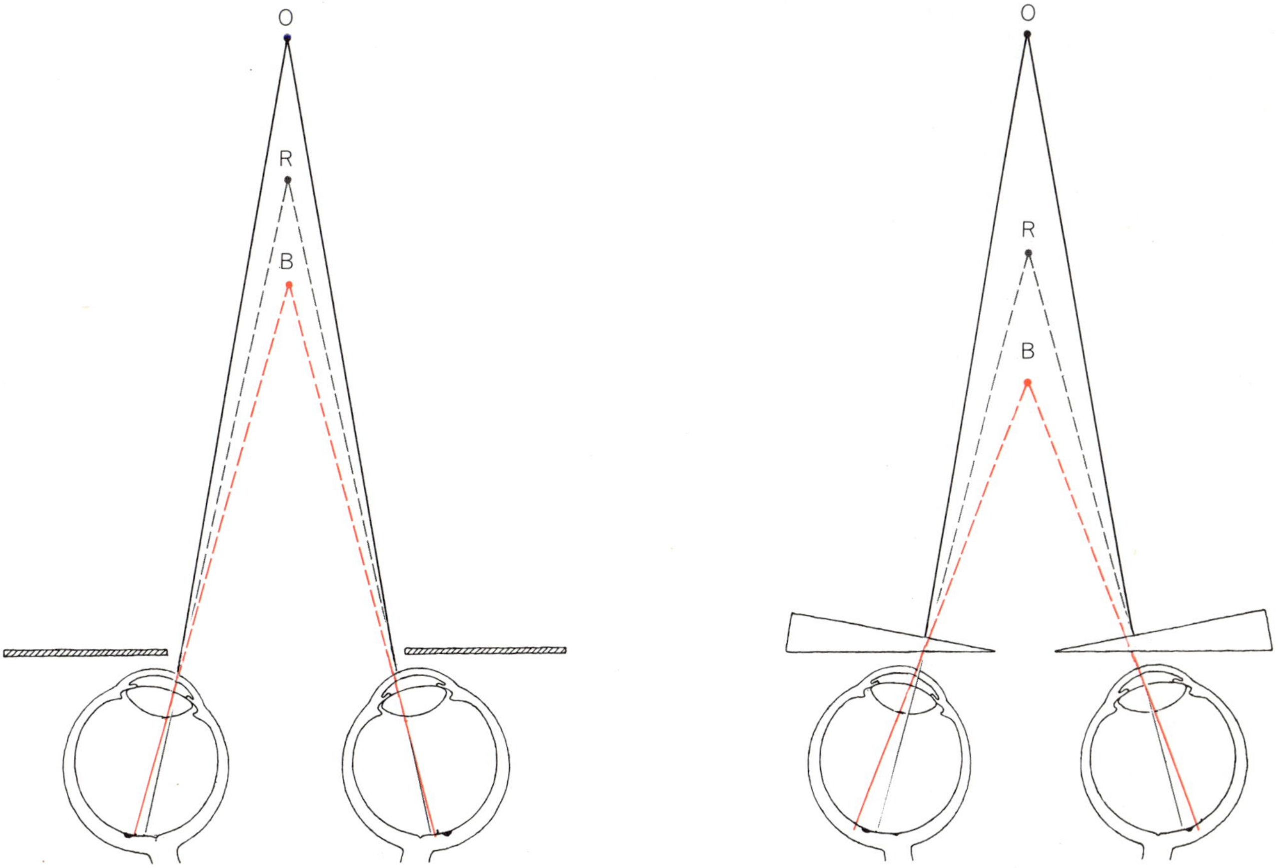

ration of the eye and simulate the effect of looking through prisms whose bases are opposed. The stereo effect works best when strong colors appear against a black background, as on page 302. If light originating at *O* is blue (B), it is bent more than red light (R) in passing through the shielded eye *(center)* or a prism *(right)*. The displacement makes the colors appear to be at different depths.

pupil, using two fingers or two pieces of paper. With the outer half of each lens covered, light passes only through the inner halves, which act as if they were prisms with bases facing outward. If the inner halves of the two lenses are covered, a reverse stereo effect takes place and red objects look closer than blue ones. (The reverse effect is difficult to obtain with prisms because it is hard to force the eyes to diverge enough when the bases of the prisms face inward.)

In a small percentage of people the prismatic defects of the eye are large enough so that they can obtain a color-stereo effect even without prisms or the use of Helmholtz' procedure. A sensitive check for such defects can be made with the help of the green-red figure in the middle of page 301. The figure is to be viewed with each eye separately. To a normal eye the green and red halves of the figure meet cleanly, without any noticeable peculiarity. A defective eye, however, will see either a thin black line or a thin white line where the two colors meet. A black line indicates that the green area is being displaced slightly farther to the left than the red, as it would be by a prism having its base to the right. A white line indicates that the green is being deflected to the right as by a prism with base to the left. When the green shifts to the right, it overlaps the red image, and the combination of green and red reflected light creates a white boundary. People with prismatic defects of the eye have a certain advantage over people with normal eyes, for they can differentiate colors not only by hue but also by the color-stereo effect.

Although it may not be immediately obvious, the color-stereo effect does not depend on the ability of the eye to see color. Like a prism, the lens of the eye bends light according to wavelength regardless of the hue we have come to associate with any particular wavelength. For example, if one photographed the colored pattern on page 302 in black and white using a stereoscopic camera equipped with a suitably oriented prism in front of each lens, one would obtain two pictures that would look three-dimensional when viewed through a stereoscope. The colored squares of the pattern would appear in various shades of gray, lying at various depths according to the wavelength of the original colors. It follows from this that one could enable a color-blind person to discriminate colors by providing him with prism glasses. He could be taught, for example, that the green in a traffic light will look closer to him than

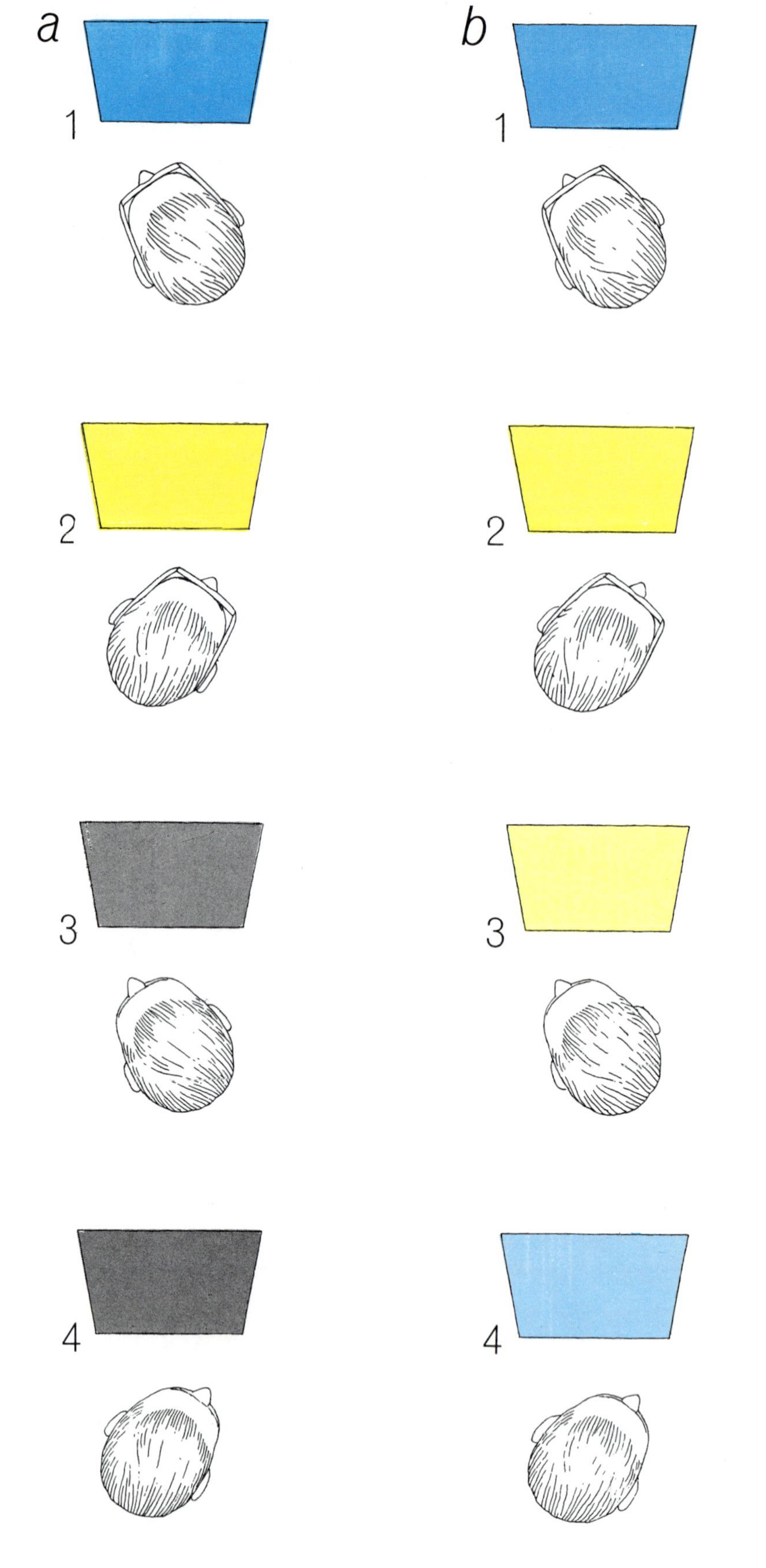

EXPERIMENTS WITH COLORED GOGGLES determine the adaptation to a split-color field, blue on the left, yellow on the right. On the first day of the experiment (*a*) the subject adjusts the color of a glass screen (*see top illustration on opposite page*) until it looks neutral through the yellow half of the goggles (*1*), the blue half (*2*) and with goggles removed (*3 and 4*). After goggles have been worn 60 days the results are different (*b*).

ADAPTATION-MEASURING DEVICE consists of a glass screen or panel whose color can be adjusted by the test subject. The setting of the color-selection dial is automatically transmitted to a pen recorder *(far right)*. The subject is viewing the window through the yellow half of goggles that are half yellow and half blue, as shown at the bottom of page 302. His task is to make the window look neutral gray in color, which requires, in this case, that it be adjusted to look blue as seen by the normal eye.

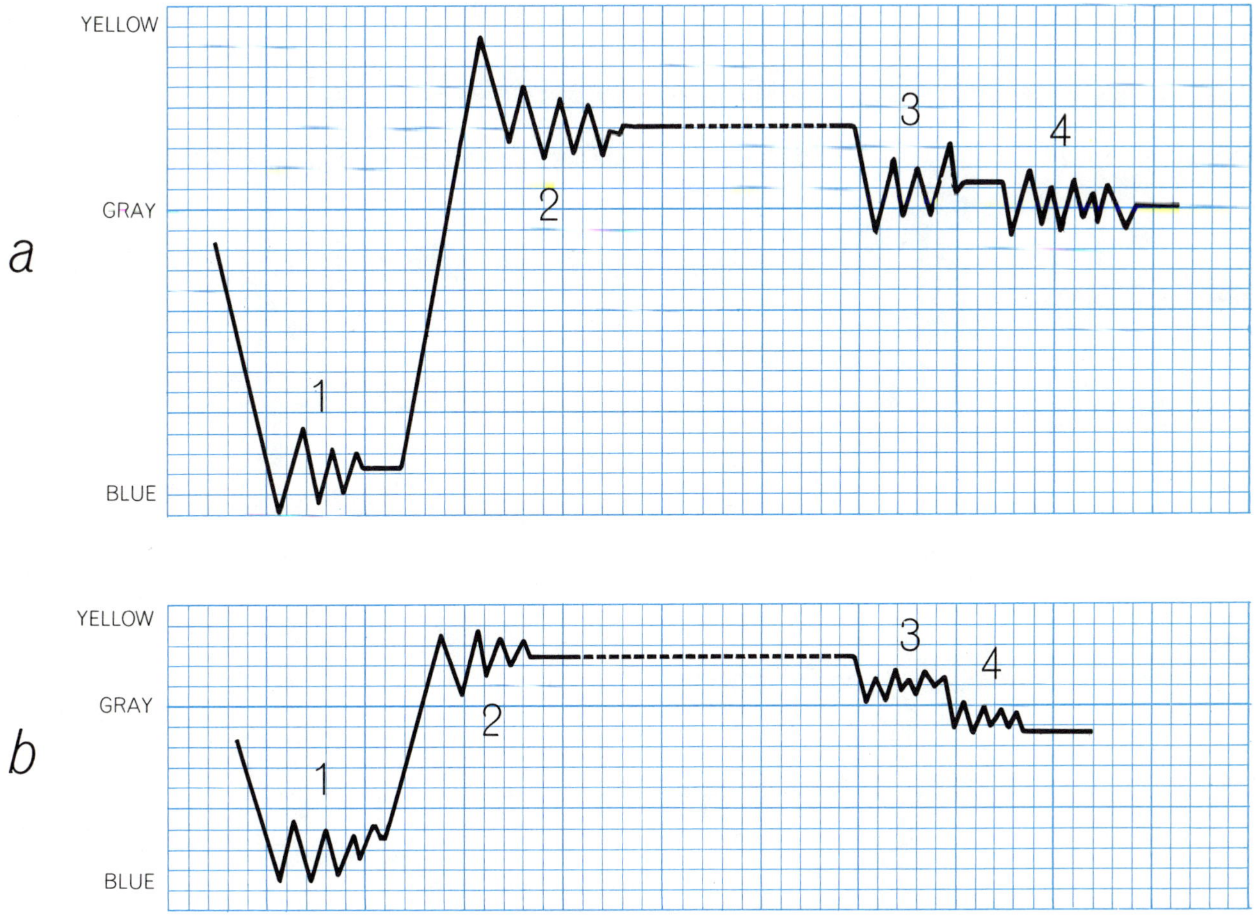

RESULTS OF COLOR-ADAPTATION TEST are shown by chart records made on the first day (*a*) and 60th day (*b*) of the experiment with blue-yellow goggles. On the first day the window of the test apparatus must be made strongly blue (*1*) to compensate for the yellow tint of the goggles and yellow (*2*) to compensate for the blue tine. When the goggles are removed after several hours, the aftereffects are negligible (*3*, *4*). By the 60th day, however, the eye has adapted significantly to the color distortions produced by the goggles (*b1*, *b2*), and when the goggles are removed the complementary aftereffects are significant (*b3*, *b4*).

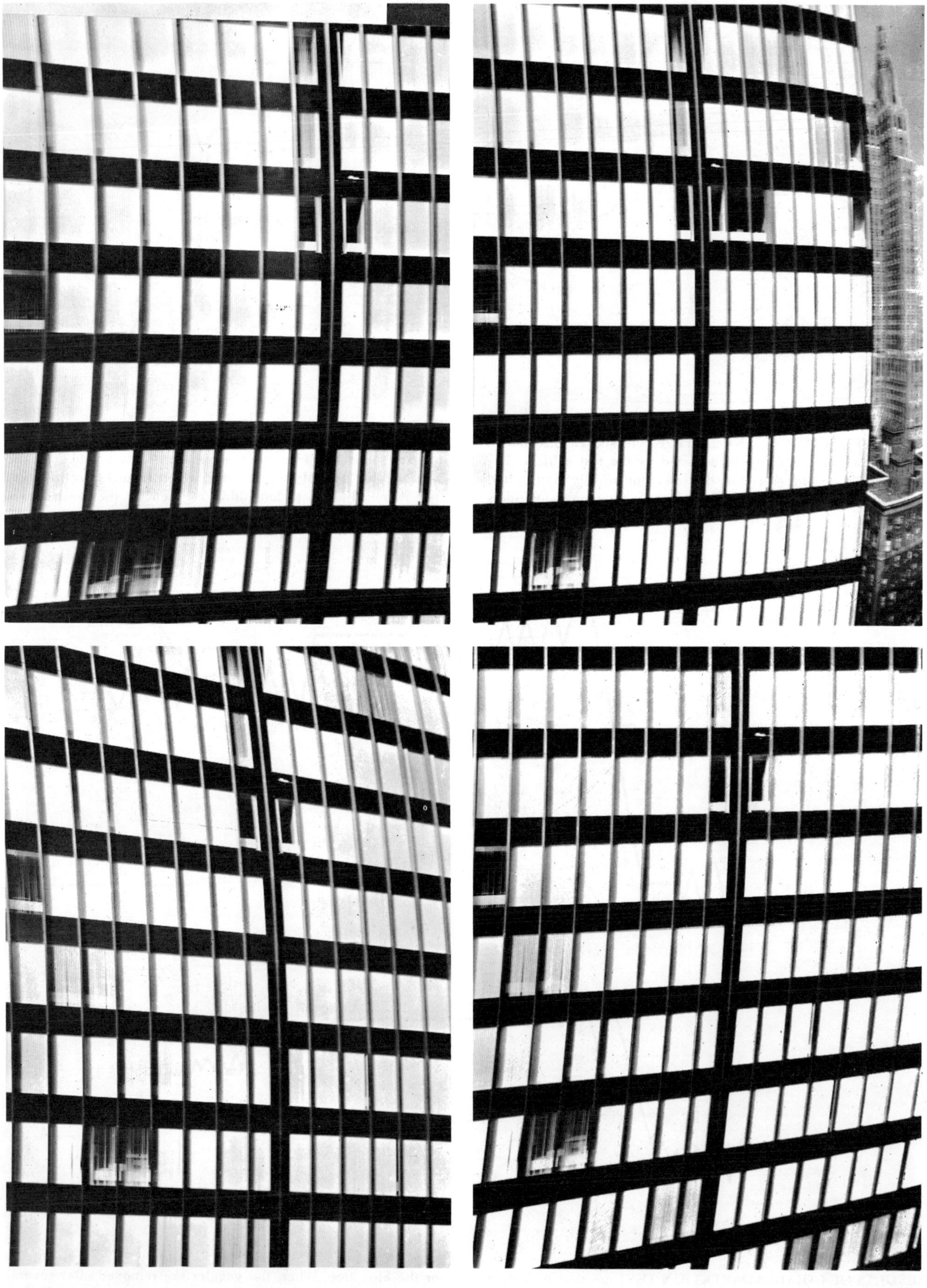

"RUBBER WORLD" is created by prism goggles. These photographs show what the eye would see through a prism with its base held to the right. If the head is turned to the right while glancing to the left, the image expands toward the left *(top left)*. If head and eye movements are reversed, the image shrinks *(top right)*. If the head is moved up and down, vertical and horizontal lines tilt so as to produce a "rocking chair" effect *(two bottom pictures)*. For an undistorted view of this building see page 301.

REAR-LOOKING "GOGGLES," actually a mirror device, were used in early experiments by Theodor Erismann at the University of Innsbruck. Here Erismann is testing the responses of a subject.

INVERTING GOGGLES, which transposed up and down, were also devised by Erismann. This subject is balancing on a springboard to help relate the upside-down world to his bodily sensations.

yellow and that yellow will look closer than red.

The color-stereo effect may also have general implications for biology. It has always seemed strange that in the eyes of most animals, including man, the fovea lies to one side of the optical axis of the lens system. This lack of alignment may combine with the eye's chromatic aberration to produce prismatic effects that are opposite for the left and right eyes, thereby producing a weak color-stereo effect. When we consider that these defects—off-center fovea and chromatic aberration—have persisted through millions of generations of animals without being "corrected" by evolution, we cannot refrain from speculating that the defects may have functional utility. Perhaps in the development of the vertebrate eye the color-stereo effect provided the first form of color discrimination, the colors being associated not with hue but with subtle differences in the depth of images. As a matter of fact, cats, mice and other animals, which are known to be color-blind, sometimes puzzle psychologists by their apparent ability to distinguish a few strong colors in visual tests. Although this color sensitivity is likely to be demonstrated by only a few animals in any experimental group, the ability cannot be ignored, and the explanation may well be that the unusual animals possess a heightened sensitivity to the color-stereo effect.

My colleague Anton Hajos can be credited with showing, by rigorous measurement, that not the slightest adaptation to the color-stereo effect occurs among subjects wearing squint glasses. He also conceived the idea of intensifying the stereo effect to see if it heightened the sensation of color. To test this idea we were fortunate to find in Innsbruck a man who had lost his color vision as the result of an accident. When he put on a pair of our squint glasses, he reported that he was instantly able to see all the colors he had not seen for years. When he removed the glasses, the colors disappeared again. We are carrying on a further investigation of this and related cases.

What shall we make of the finding that the eye adapts rather readily to various intense distortions of geometry and color but fails totally to adapt to the type of distortion embodied in the color-stereo effect? One possible explanation is that in all cases where adaptation occurs the eye is provided with certain systematic clues as to the nature of the distortion. Straight lines always curve in the same direction; blue or yellow color fringes occur in fixed relation to light-dark boundaries; blue and yellow glasses present the eye with color fields that remain consistently either on the right or on the left; even the rubber world is rubbery in a consistent way. The color-stereo effect, however, presents the visual mechanism with a random and nearly unpredictable assortment of displaced images. As the focus of the eye shifts from one point to another, it is just as likely to encounter one color as another, and, depending on wavelength, brightness and background, the stereoscopic position of the colored image is shifted forward or back. Although the eye might conceivably learn to correlate color and displacement and thereby use the former as a basis for correcting the latter, the task is evidently beyond the power of the eye's adaptation mechanism. There is, however, an alternative possibility: the color-stereo effect may represent a primitive way of identifying colors. The failure of the visual system to adapt to this effect, when presented in exaggerated form by squint glasses, may be evidence that spatial displacement of colors indeed played such an evolutionary role.

30

THE PERCEPTION OF MOTION

HANS WALLACH
July 1959

Most of us have had the experience of staring from a waiting train at a train on an adjacent track and sensing momentarily and mistakenly that it was our train that had started to move forward. Alternatively we have idly gazed at a branch reaching upward from a running stream and have seen the branch apparently drift upstream. Or we have looked at the moon through wind-swept, broken clouds, framed in treetops, and have wondered as the moon appeared to sail through the sky against the motion of the clouds.

These are familiar instances of a peculiar aspect of our visual perception of motion. As strictly defined by the physicist, motion is the displacement of one object relative to other objects. But the physicist does not help us to clarify our perception of motion, for he will add that motion is a matter of definition. Which object is displaced and which serves as the frame of reference is an arbitrary choice. Visually perceived, however, motion has no such relative aspect; it is an attribute of the moving object, even if only a temporary one. We say that an object is at rest when this property is absent. Thus, in experience, motion and rest are absolutes, inherent in the object perceived. We sense this absolute quality of motion especially when we must correct a first impression. Though we can certainly make ourselves aware of the displacement of a moving object in relation to other objects in our field of vision, this awareness is by no means a genuine part of the perceived motion, which remains entirely an affair of the moving object.

It is tempting to ascribe this absolute, nonrelativistic aspect of experienced motion to the manner in which the experience is caused. Is not motion perceived when an object changes its position in relation to the observer, causing the eyes to pursue it? The perception of motion would thus seem to accord with the conditions of stimulation, quite independent of the presence of other objects in the visual field. But matters are not quite so simple. We also experience motion when it is caused by the displacement of one object relative to another. At first glance it might seem impossible to distinguish between these two modes of perception, for the displacement of one object in relation to another must always involve the displacement of at least one object in relation to the observer. The distinction may be proved, however, by experiment. As everyone who has watched the hour hand of a clock knows, motion may be too slow to be perceived; one may notice change of position, but not motion. With a luminous dot in a homogeneous dark field, we can measure the threshold of velocity at which motion is perceived. But if we now light up a second, stationary dot near the moving one, we discover that the threshold is lowered considerably. Motion at a lower velocity will be seen so long as the two dots do not move too far apart. We may thus distinguish between motion perceived on the basis of an "angular displacement" of an object relative to the observer and of an "object-relative displacement" of one object in relation to another.

This experiment reveals a further interesting fact. When the moving dot moves too slowly to excite perception of motion by virtue of its angular displacement, object-relative displacement will lead the viewer to experience the motion of one dot or of the other or of both in various patterns, as shown in the illustration on this page. The results reported by observers are as varied as the ambiguity of the situation would suggest. We may now ask a useful question: How do perceived motion and rest in such a situation distribute themselves among the objects that are being displaced relative to one another? The

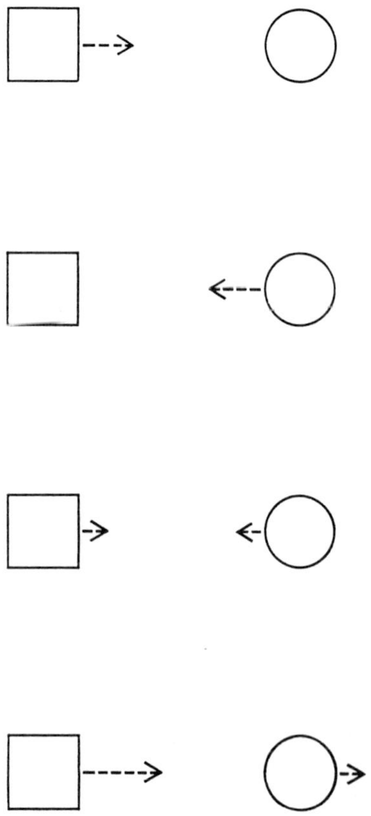

OBJECT-RELATIVE MOTION may give a viewer perceptions of motion quite different from the objective motion. Relative dis-

question suggests further experiments which reveal some significant principles that rule the visual assignment of the properties of motion and rest to the objects perceived.

Consider what happens when one of the two objects surrounds the other, the first object in effect forming the background of the second. For example, the viewer is presented with a dot surrounded by a circle. No matter which object is moved by the experimenter, the result is invariably the same: the viewer sees the dot move and sees the circle remain at rest.

This rule is rather strict and pervasive. It even holds under conditions in which it gives rise to experiences that are at variance with the objective situation. For example, the viewer is presented with a dot surrounded by a rectangle which is in turn surrounded by a ring. If the rectangle is now moved, the viewer perceives motion in both the dot and the rectangle and sees the ring remain stationary. The perceived motion of the rectangle is in the direction of its objective motion, while the motion of the dot is in the opposite direction. But this distribution of motion and rest among the objects is quite inappropriate. That the dot appears to move and the ring does not is inconsistent with the fact that there is no objective displacement between the dot and the ring. The nature of this discrepancy is clarified by removing the ring from the picture. Without the ring only the dot is seen to move. The addition of the ring adds the motion of the rectangle to that of the dot, for the rectangle is now a surrounded object. Thus the two motions perceived arise from the two different relative displacements.

The rule that the surrounded object appears to move holds even when the surrounding object is moved at a velocity above the threshold for perception of angular displacement. In the ring, rectangle and dot experiment, the stationary dot still appears to move in the direction opposite that of the objectively moving rectangle. The ring, however, is no longer a necessary part of the situation, because the motion of the rectangle can now be perceived in the absence of the ring. We have here, in fact, the scheme of the illusion of the sailing moon or of the drifting branch. The moon corresponds to the dot, and the clouds represent the rectangle. The trees or rooftops in our line of vision may serve as the ring, but their presence is not essential because the clouds are moving above the angular-displacement threshold. Similarly the objectively stationary branch in the stream is the surrounded object, and leaves or other debris on the sliding surface of the stream are analogous to the moving rectangle.

This illusion is usually called "induced" movement. The term has been in use a long time; it has been commonly assumed that the induced movement is caused merely by the perceived movement in the environment, and that it is always in the opposite direction. But as

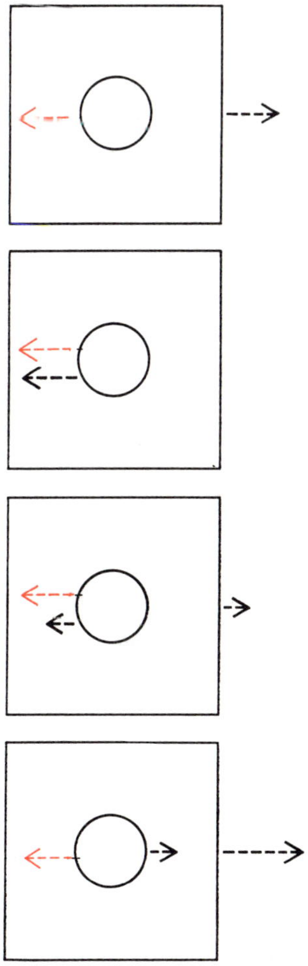

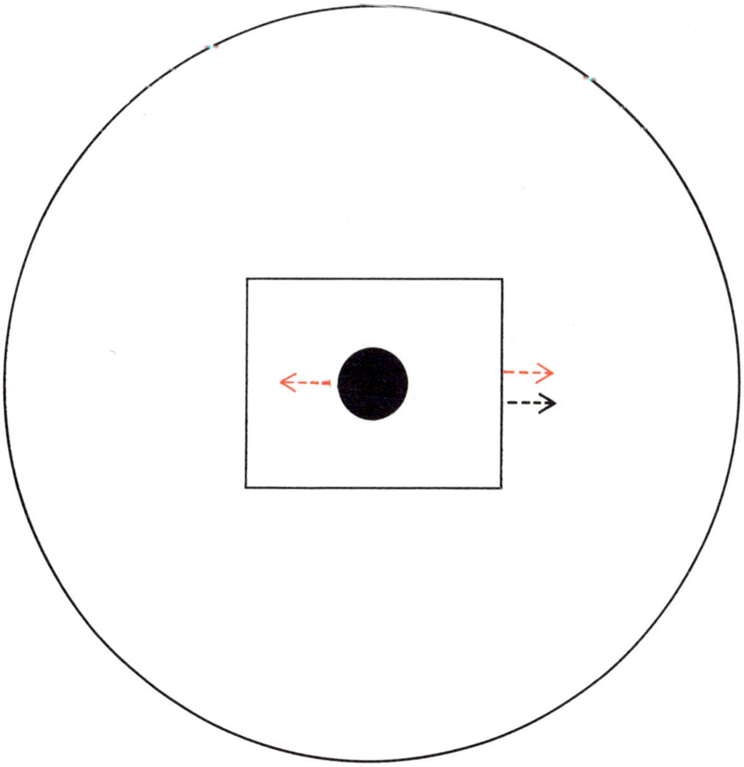

placement of the circle and square at left, produced in four different ways, may be experienced as any of the three upper combinations of motion. A surrounded object, as in center panel, takes on uniform perceived motion (*colored arrows*) despite varying combinations of objective motion (*black arrows*). If surrounded object is itself surrounded (*right*), it too acquires perceived motion.

our experiments have already suggested, this simple view of the matter is inadequate. The crucial element in the picture is the relationship of the surrounded object to the surrounding object. We can, in fact, contrive an experiment in which induced movement is not opposite to the perceived movement of the surrounding object. The dot, rectangle and ring again provide the elements of the picture, but this time the ring is moved downward as the rectangle is moved to the right (in each case at a velocity below the threshold for perception of angular displacement). These objective movements produce a displacement of the rectangle upward and to the right in relation to the ring, and a displacement of the dot horizontally leftward in relation to the rectangle [*see illustration below*]. As in the previous experiments, the perceived motions correspond to these relative displacements: the rectangle is seen to move obliquely upward to the right and the dot horizontally to the left. Under certain conditions the leftward motion of the dot may be slightly oblique in the upward direction. But what has become of the induced motion of the dot relative to the perceived motion of the rectangle? In accord with the original notion of induced motion, the dot should move obliquely downward and to the left, since the perceived motion of the rectangle carried it upward and to the right. But the dot is never seen to do so. Its induced motion relative to the rectangle is fundamentally determined by the fact that the rectangle surrounds it. The displacement of the surrounded object relative to its surrounding remains unaffected by the secondary displacement of the surrounding object relative to a third object or to the observer.

Once we recognize the effectiveness of the object-relative condition of stimulation, we find it playing an ascendant role, even in situations that might otherwise seem to be dominated by perception of angular displacement. Consider, for example, our judgment of speed, taking this term to stand for the perceptual counterpart of objectively measured velocity. A crucial discovery was made in 1927 by J. F. Brown, then working at the University of Berlin. He had his subjects, in a darkened room, observe the speed of a small black disk moving up or down in a lighted aperture. They were to match the speed of the disk by adjusting the speed of a smaller disk moving up or down in a lighted aperture half the size of the first. The experiment yielded a result that at the time was quite unexpected. It turned out that, in order to match the speeds of the two disks, the velocity of the disk in the smaller aperture had to be set at a little more than half that of the larger disk. This transposition of velocity in accord with the relative size of the two fields held over a wide range of velocities, from as little as two inches per second to as much as 10 inches per second. It also held over larger contrasts of field size, although the ratio of matching velocities tended to depart from the ratio of field sizes when the difference in size became very large. When the room was fully lighted, however, and common frames of reference became visible to the experimental subjects, the transposition of velocity became a good deal less exact.

We can explain these results quite readily in terms of the object-relative mode of motion perception. With no general frame of reference available, the judgment of speed in this experiment depends upon the size of the field in which it is observed. Speeds in two different fields are seen to be

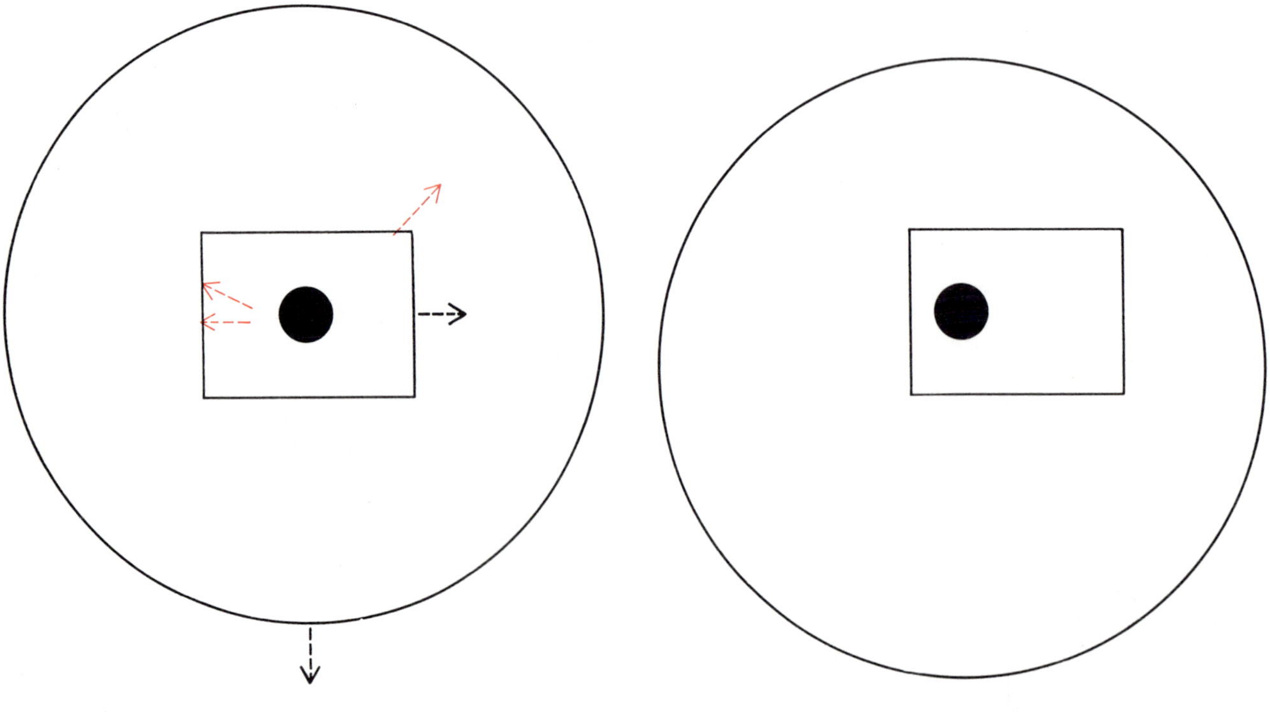

SURROUNDING OBJECT plays the decisive role in determining what motion is perceived and in allocating perceived motion to various objects in the visual field. Here the ring and rectangle at left are moved (*black arrows*) to new positions (*right*). The perceived motion of the rectangle (*colored arrow*) is the outcome of these two motions. The central spot, objectively motionless, acquires perceived motion in either one of two directions: with reference to the rectangle alone or with reference to the circle as well.

the same when the moving disks traverse equal fractions of the apertures in the same unit time. The transpositions are not, of course, 100 per cent perfect. This is because the perception of angular displacement also plays some role in our estimate of speed. But the close match of velocity ratios with the ratios of aperture sizes indicates the preponderant role of the object-relative mode of motion perception.

The important factor of form enters the discussion at this point; it plays a critical role in perception of object-relative motion. A pattern of visual stimulation may be transformed in a number of ways without changing the form. The most familiar, and the one relevant here, is the transformation of size. Two apertures of different size, each with moving disks at the same relative point, present identical forms to the observer. As the disks move at matched speeds, the two forms go through identical changes.

Whereas a change in size does not affect perceived form, another simple transformation produces surprisingly impressive changes in our perception of form. A pattern may change its form entirely when its orientation to the upright is altered. Turn a square through 45 degrees and it looks so different that it commands a different word in our language. The same is true of such a simple configuration as a pair of dots, because the dots produce, in their perceptual relationship to each other, an impression of direction [*see middle illustrations at right*]. Our perception of motion reflects this quality of form perception. For example, if two dots are moved in the same direction at the same velocity below the threshold for perception of angular displacement, they do not appear to move at all. There being no change in the distance between them, there is no object-relative displacement. On the other hand, if one dot is held stationary and the other is moved around it in a circular path, one or the other or both dots are seen in motion. Although the change in form here does not involve change in distance, it acts exactly like object-relative displacement and produces perceived motion.

Our perceptual dependence upon object-relative displacement and form change accounts for a number of engaging phenomena. Frequently the movement of an object along a given path gives rise to the experience of two simultaneous movements. We produce an impressive experience of this kind if we place a light source on the rim of a wheel

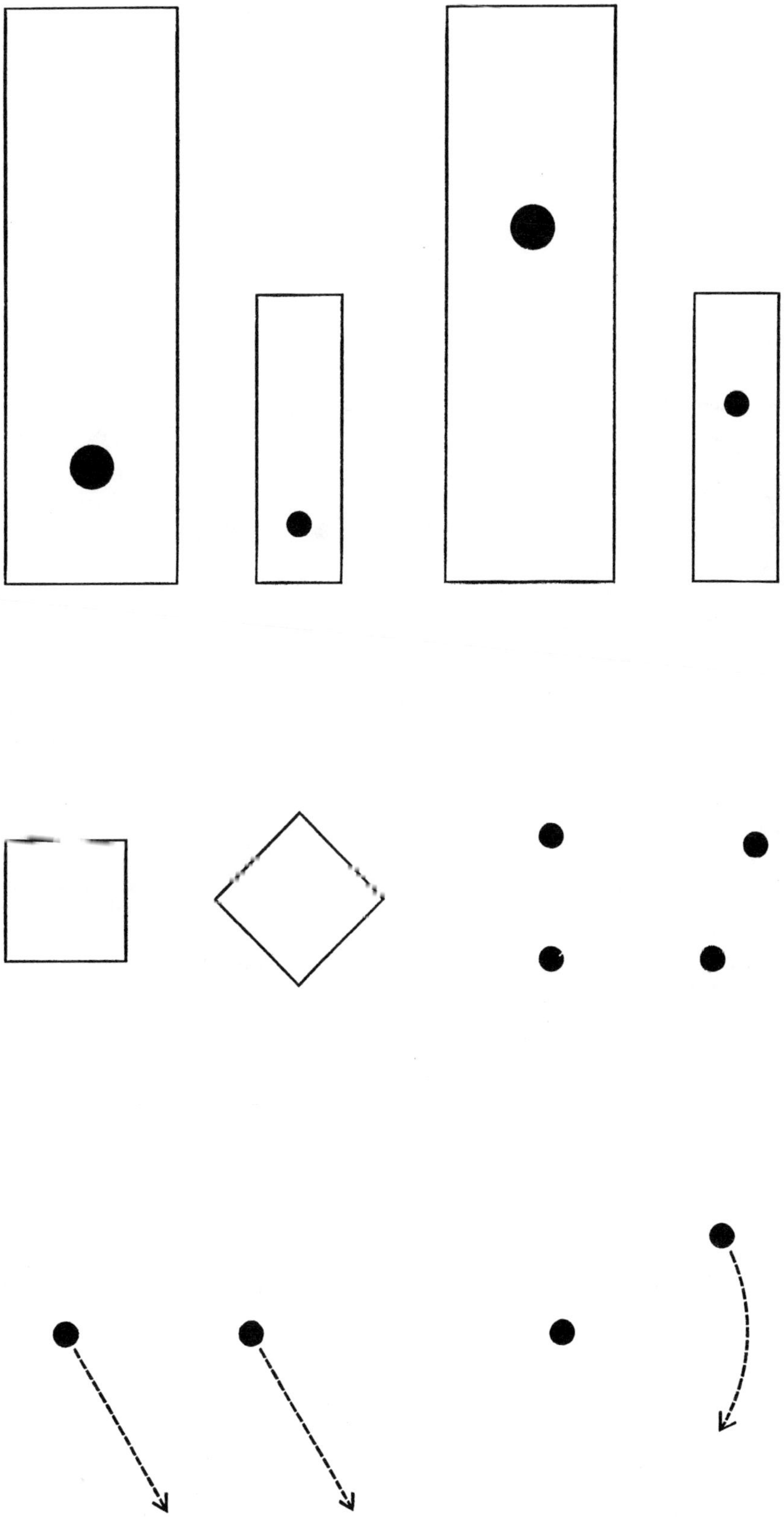

FORM PERCEPTION plays an important role in the perception of motion. At top the motion of the spots in the two similar rectangles appears to be at the same speed because the patterns are identical (*as at right*) at each stage of motion. Rotating a square through 45 degrees makes it into a "diamond." Similarly a change in the position of two dots (*right middle*) conveys quite a different sense of form. If two dots move slowly in the same direction (*bottom left*), no motion is perceived. However, circular motion of one dot (*bottom right*) causes a change of form and excites definite perception of motion (which may involve both dots).

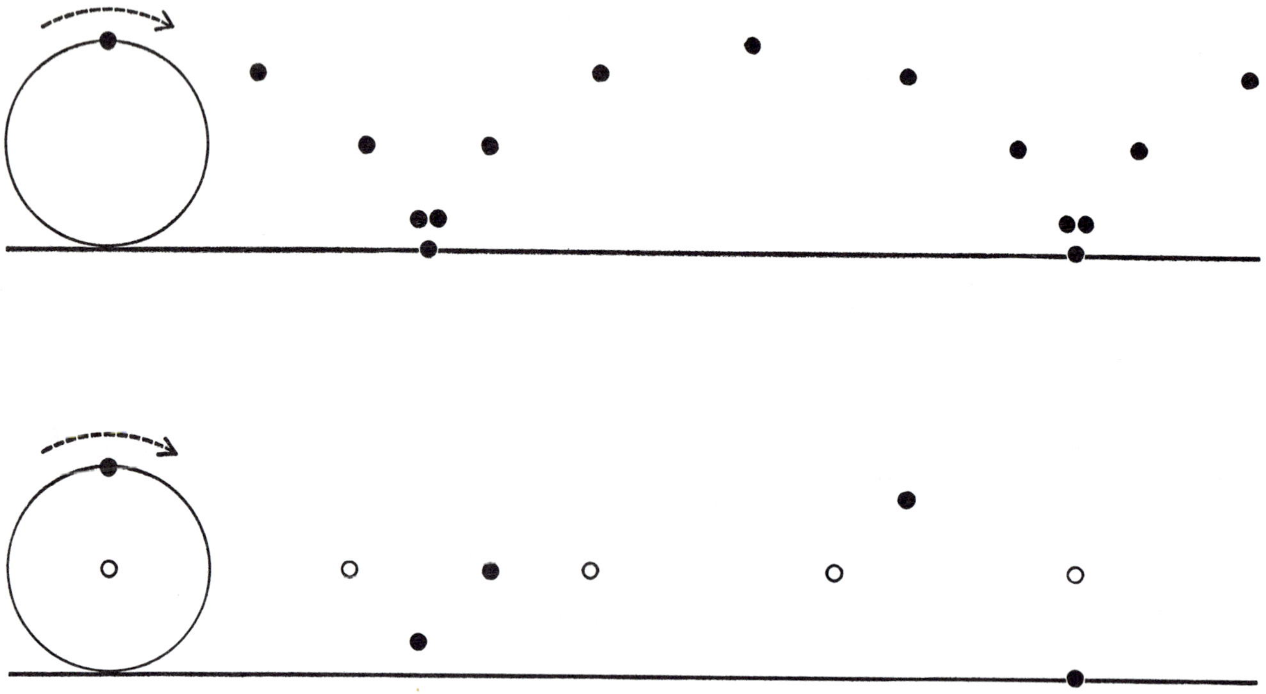

DIFFERENT EXPERIENCES in the observer are caused by the same objective motion of light on the rim of a rolling wheel. At top, the perceived motion (*on a cycloidal curve*) fits the objective motion. However, if the hub is lighted (*bottom*), this perceived motion gives way to a compound motion: the light on the rim now seems to rotate about the hub as the wheel rolls from left to right.

and another at its hub and observe the wheel rolling in the dark. The light on the wheel is seen to move in a circle around the hub and to travel forward along with the light at the hub. If we turn out the light at the hub, both of these motions disappear entirely. The perceived movement of the light at the rim now resembles its objective path, moving along through successive arches of a cycloidal curve [*see illustration at top of this page*].

The experience of two simultaneous movements of a single object can be obtained under even simpler conditions. In an experiment, first performed by Gunnar Johansson, then at the Psychological Institute of the Stockholm Högskola, two round spots are moved along the legs of a right angle toward its apex, and then back to their starting position [*see illustration below*]. Observers invariably see the two spots moving straight toward each other as they travel a slanting path together, and then moving apart as they retrace the same slanting path. Each spot appears to be going through two simultaneous motions. One motion is in the direction of the other spot; the other motion is at right angles to the first and parallel to the slanting path on which the two spots converge. It is as if the true objective motion of the spot were the resultant of the vectors of these two motions. Observers usually find the movement of the spots toward and away from each other to be much the more conspicuous of the two simultaneous motions. About 35 per cent must be prompted before they perceive the second motion and "confirm its presence without hesitation."

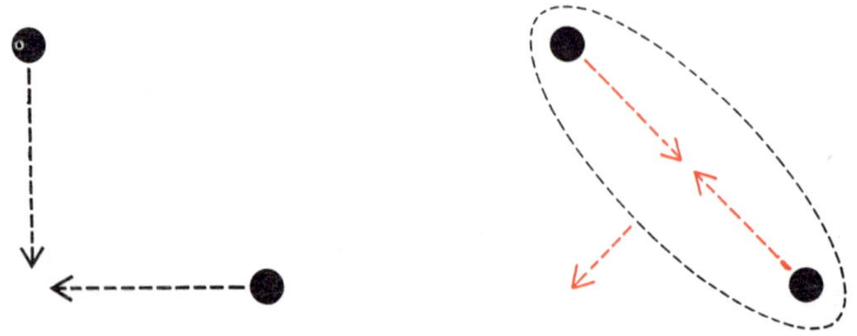

COMPOUND MOTION is perceived in two dots which objectively move (*black arrows*) along straight lines at right angles (*left*). To an observer, however, the dots seem to move (*colored arrows*) toward one another and simultaneously to move as a unit obliquely downward. Observers often fail to note the second component of this compound motion.

To the extent that one's awareness of one's own motion is mediated by visual perception, it may be subject to the vagaries illustrated in these experiments. The illusion of motion experienced when the train on the neighboring track pulls out is an example of induced motion in the perceiver. If the scene that fills the observer's field of vision is in some manner displaced with respect to him, he will feel himself in motion and perceive his environment at rest, even when some large objects in the foreground are not displaced. The visually induced sensation of locomotion seems quite indistinguishable from that which arises from kinesthetic stimuli and on these occasions overwhelms them. This is another instance of our paradoxical tendency to experience motion as an absolute rather than a relative process, even though its perception depends upon relative displacement. In allocating the qualities of motion and of rest to ourselves and to our environment, visual perception follows the rule that keeps the surrounding at rest and bestows motion upon the object surrounded.

31

THE ILLUSION OF MOVEMENT

PAUL A. KOLERS
October 1964

The effort to explain how perceptions are formed by the nervous system has attracted investigators from many disciplines. An important and often elusive aspect of the problem is ascertaining how the physical stimulation of sensory organs is transformed into perceptual information: into objects seen, sounds heard and things touched. In the study of perceptions the examination of illusions has proved helpful. Illusions, in contrast with other perceptions, furnish erroneous reports about the environment. It is through these errors that illusions provide insight into the mechanism of perception. I shall discuss briefly the general subject of illusions and then concentrate on describing some experiments my colleagues and I have conducted with the illusion of movement that can be created under controlled conditions with a suitably timed flashing of lights. Finally, I shall set forth some of the conclusions suggested by the experiments.

Illusions have not always had good standing among the investigators of perception. When perceptual illusions were introduced as a topic of study in the 19th century, the prevailing attitude about them was that they were interesting parlor tricks—minor imperfections or errors in the working of man's perceptual apparatus. The German psychologist Oswald Külpe, writing near the end of the century, called them "subjective perversions of the contents of objective perception." The notion of error Külpe had in mind implied that there is some "real world" faithfully reported by the senses. Few contemporary investigators take this view. Instead of thinking of illusions as errors in perceiving they regard them as genuine perceptions that do not stand up when their implications are tested. Moreover, illusions are now regarded as putting in question any belief in "objective" perception.

The principal property of an illusion is that it is convincing. A person who experiences an illusion usually has had what seems to be a vivid perception. An illusion is illusory for this very reason: it looks or feels exactly like something else. It is only when the individual attempts to verify his experience by predicting what should follow from it that he can say wherein his experience was illusory. For example, if one sees an object that appears to be moving, placing another object in its path will quickly show whether the movement is real or illusory; no collision will occur with illusory movement.

Although the most familiar illusions are the perceptual ones, illusions are not restricted to perceptions. There are illusions of memory; one is *déjà vu,* in which a person has the compelling sense that he is experiencing something he has experienced before, although all objective checks indicate that he could not possibly have experienced it. There are illusions of insight: a person who goes to sleep with a problem on his mind sometimes awakes in the night with the

TYPICAL ILLUSION OF MOVEMENT is represented by the arrows in this electric sign. When one looks at the sign as it operates, one seems to see a stream of arrows in flight.

conviction that he has the answer, whereupon he goes happily to sleep again only to find himself confronted in the morning with a meaningless cliché or (if he has taken the trouble to write down his insight) with an unintelligible scrawl or words that have no relation to the problem. More than one of my colleagues has remarked that the elation attending a "brainstorm" is often a signal that the accompanying idea is likely to be fruitless. Similar illusions are occasionally experienced by people inhaling an anesthetic. Just before "going under" they have a profound experience of insight; it often takes the form of a sentence or two that seem to be the key to an understanding of the universe. On regaining consciousness, however, the patient is usually unable to recall his insight. William James told such a story about himself, and he remembered the sentence. It was: "The universe is permeated with the intense smell of kerosene."

There is another aspect of insight: a person may solve a problem without realizing that he has solved it, and so he continues long afterward to work on it. Some computer programmers have in their office a collection of wastebaskets, each labeled with the name of a day. Every day they put into the appropriate basket the rejected results of the day's work so that the material can be kept for a week, because the programmer may realize on Thursday that he solved the problem on Monday. The point to be made about such phenomena is that there is nothing in an experience that testifies to its correspondence with "reality," nothing in a perception that guarantees its truth. Judgments of reality and truth must come from sources other than the experience or the perception.

Even though illusions occur in a wide range of circumstances, they are not random events. They are certainly not results of an operational failure in perceiving. The little that is known about them indicates that they occur under particular conditions, which differ for different kinds of illusion. For example, in unsystematic investigations I have obtained many more reports of the *déjà vu* experience from adolescents and young adults than from children and older adults, and many of the illusions of insight and understanding seem to be associated with fatigue or the use of drugs.

Having indicated the broad range of illusions, I turn to the perceptual illusions, which have been the most thoroughly studied, and in particular to the visual illusions, among which are the illusions of movement. Several visual illusions, involving the effects of lines, are illustrated on the next page. Look at the drawings first, taking note of what you see. The figures are illusory because what you see does not reflect the physical relations described in the caption. These figures also provide further examples of the limited conditions under which illusions occur. Some of the illusions in the illustration can be explained by the functional anatomy of the eye, others cannot. Some of them can be presented piecemeal in time or to the two eyes without losing their illusory nature, others cannot. These observations suggest that visual illusions are not all processed in the same way or by the same part of the visual system [see the article "The Visual Cortex of the Brain," by David H. Hubel, beginning on page 148].

A visual illusion that has been extensively studied is the illusion of movement. This illusion has a special place in the history of psychology: the systematic account of it in 1912 by Max Wertheimer, who was then in Germany and later came to the U.S., was the manifesto of Gestalt psychology. Wertheimer's thesis was that students of the mind should look at wholes rather than at bits of data: at a melody, for example, rather than at its notes. To put the matter another way, his view was

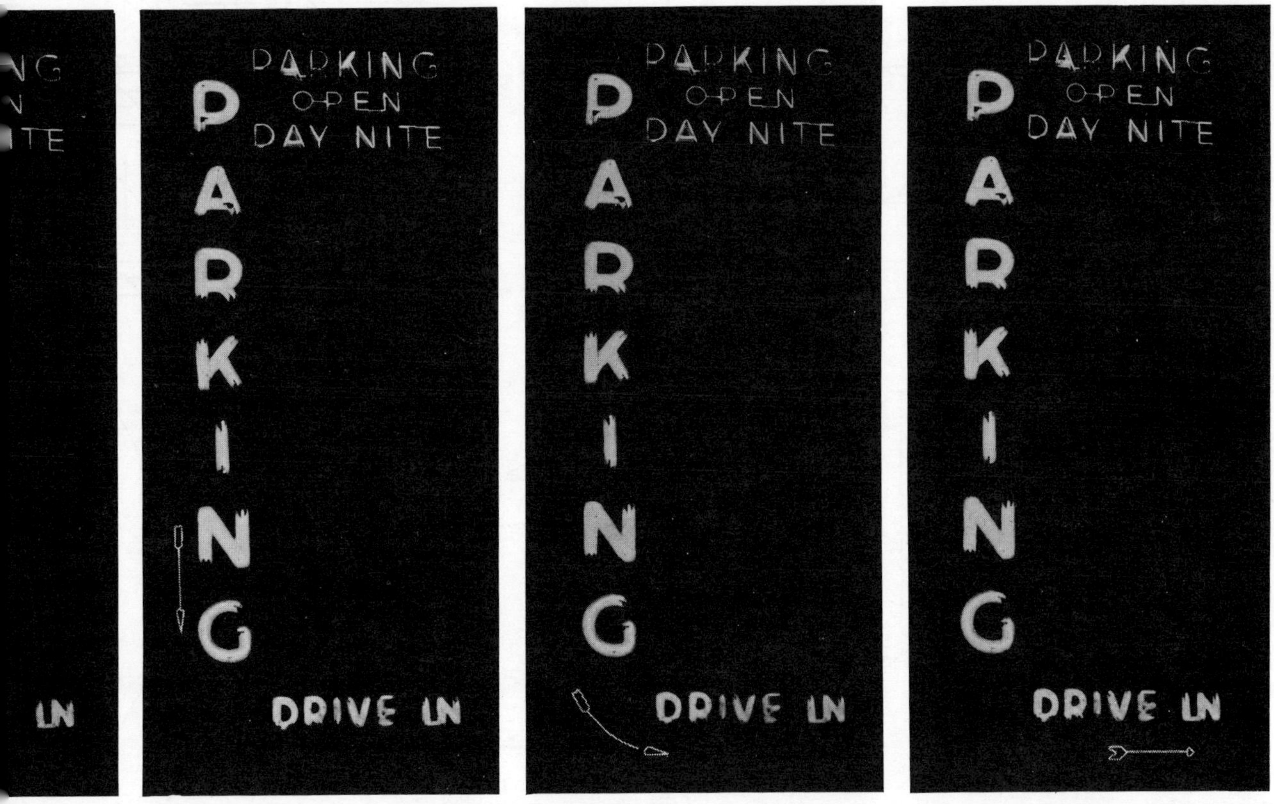

The apparent motion is, of course, an illusion created by flashing individual arrows on and off sequentially. An even more vivid illusion of moving light can be created under controlled conditions and used for the study of the mechanisms of perception.

that the central object of study should be the manner in which the nervous system organizes the stimulation presented to it. The illusion of movement that can be produced with two lights, he said, clearly went beyond the data presented to the eyes and so was an illustration of the organizational activities of the nervous system. The illusion is interesting both for its vividness (under proper laboratory conditions it is a striking, even amusing, thing to observe) and for the fact that it clearly identifies several fundamental and still unsolved problems about the way the human visual system works to deliver a representation of the outside world.

The illusion can be produced in several ways, of which the following is the easiest and best known. Two small gas-discharge lamps are placed a short distance apart and turned on and off in sequence. Each "on" time is about 50 milliseconds, but the interval of time between the turning off of one lamp and the turning on of the other is varied. When the interval is brief, say 10 milliseconds, most observers see the two lamps as being on simultaneously. When the interval is "long," say one second, most people see first one lamp and then the other come on and go off. The illusion occurs when the time interval is manipulated in the lower part of the range, between about 25 and 400 milliseconds. As the interval is increased gradually from 25 milliseconds, the appearance of simultaneity (itself an illusion, since the lamps are actually lighted in sequence) gives way to that of movement. The first lamp appears to move part of the distance toward the second and then disappears; then the second lamp appears, displaced toward the first, and moves toward its own actual location [*see top illustration on opposite page*]. With further increases in the time interval between the two flashes, the distance between the disappearance of the first lamp and the appearance of the second diminishes until the observer perceives what is called optimal movement: a single lamp moving smoothly and continuously across the space from its origin to its terminus. Many people report that the change from partial movements across the screen to optimal movement gives the appearance that the two lamps grow out from their respective locations until they join. So vivid is this appearance of growth and joining that Wertheimer, and subsequently many others, argued that it reflects an increase in excitation of neighboring areas in the brain to the point where they produce a "short circuit." This explanation did not find much favor among investigators not committed to the Gestalt theory.

As the time interval between flashes is increased still further, optimal movement continues to be seen, but its speed grows successively slower. Finally one no longer sees an object moving across the space. Instead most observers have a sense of movement itself: objectless, "pure" movement, which Wertheimer called "phi movement." (From this term came "phi phenomenon," the name sometimes used generically for the entire phenomenon of apparent movement.) The last stage of the perception is a slow sequence of flashes as first one and then the other lamp comes on and goes off. To sum up: Small variations in the interval of time between the two flashes produce five distinctly different perceptions—simultaneity, partial movement, optimal movement, phi movement and succession.

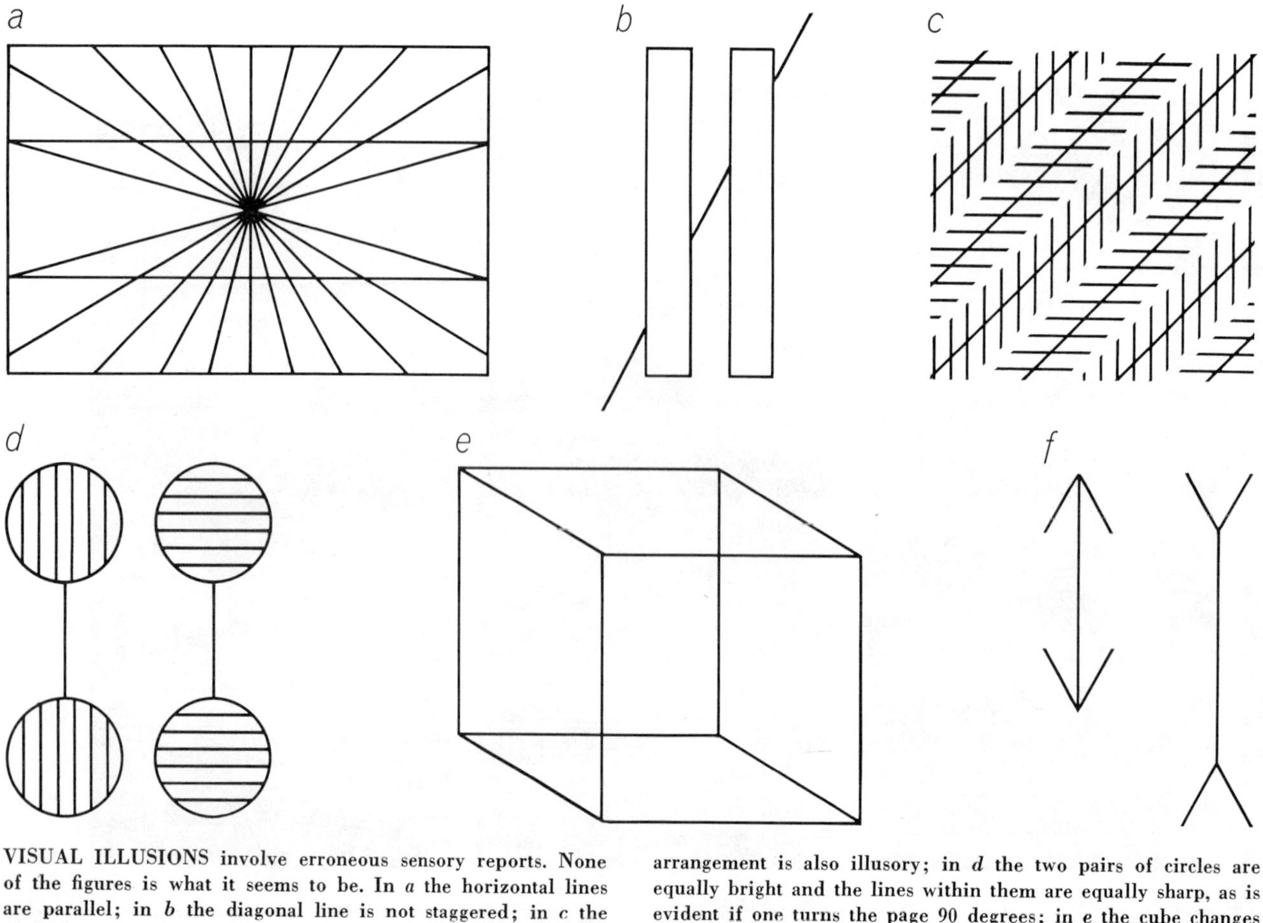

VISUAL ILLUSIONS involve erroneous sensory reports. None of the figures is what it seems to be. In *a* the horizontal lines are parallel; in *b* the diagonal line is not staggered; in *c* the diagonal lines are parallel, and the appearance of a steplike arrangement is also illusory; in *d* the two pairs of circles are equally bright and the lines within them are equally sharp, as is evident if one turns the page 90 degrees; in *e* the cube changes perspective as one stares at it; in *f* the vertical lines are equal.

The phenomenon of apparent movement is frequently encountered in everyday life, in such forms as electric signs with arrows that appear to move and horses that appear to run. In some ways motion pictures incorporate this illusion; one perceives movement in them from a succession of still pictures flashed at certain optimal rates. There is in fact a story to the effect that it was while contemplating the physiological aspect of the motion picture that Wertheimer recognized the problems for psychology the phenomenon of apparent movement provides.

Although there has been no agreement on the cause of the illusion, most observers agree that optimal apparent movement cannot be distinguished in appearance from real movement. This correspondence led many psychologists to argue that the neural mechanisms that give rise to the two perceptions must themselves be identical. The argument further states that the only stimuli necessary to produce a perception of movement are the illumination and darkening of two separated regions of the retina with an appropriate time interval.

In rebuttal it must be said that the perception of movement depends on more than the speed of a target's displacement. Moreover, the conditions that produce real and illusory movement differ in several ways, four of which I shall enumerate. First, apparent movement occurs only at certain rates of stimulation, namely speeds that calculation reveals to be in the region of 15 to 25 degrees per second across the observer's visual field. That is far smaller than the range of real movement, where an object can be seen at speeds between about half a degree and 125 degrees per second. Second, the image of an object moves across the retina when the movement is real, but there is no motion across the retina in the illusion. A third difference is that real movement produces a blur when the movement is rapid, whereas the blurry appearance of phi movement (the illusory appearance of rapid movement) occurs under the opposite circumstances: when the time interval between the turning off of one light and the turning on of the next is made longer than that required for optimal movement. Finally, although an observer cannot distinguish between the appearance of real and illusory movement, apparent movement tends to be slower than real movement: the speed of an object in real movement has to be less than the calculated speed of an

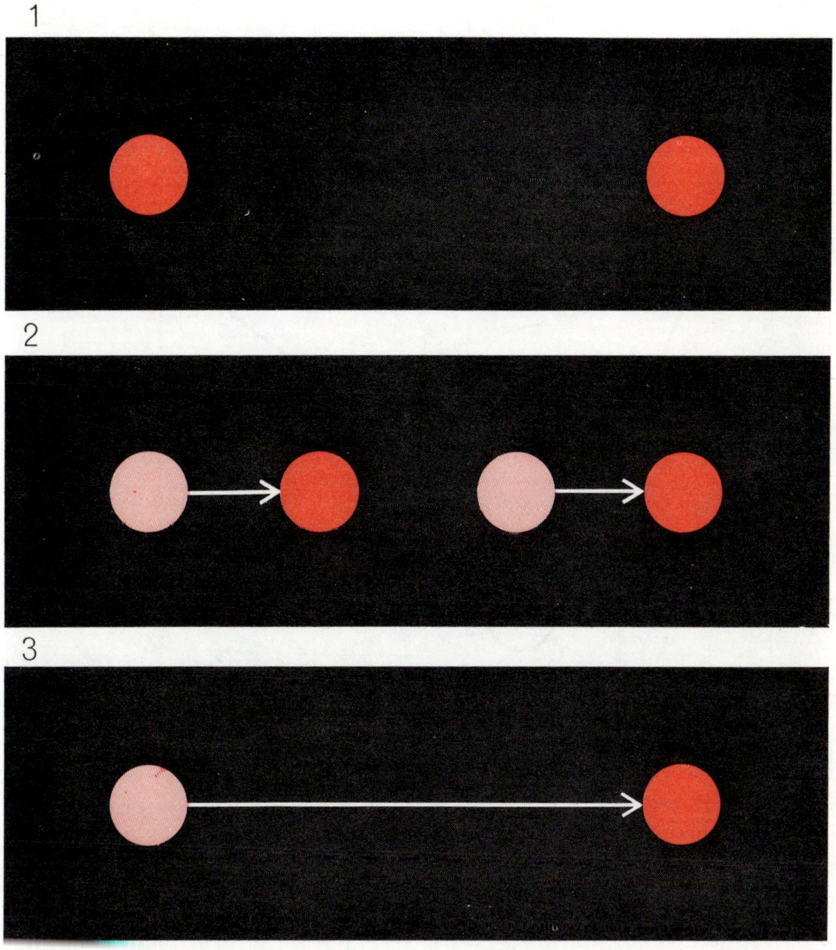

ILLUSION OF MOVEMENT can be created with two lamps flashed sequentially. If the time interval between flashes is very short, the two lamps appear to be on continuously, as at *1;* with a longer interval one sees partial movement, as at *2;* as the interval is further lengthened one sees smooth, continuous movement of a single object, as at *3.*

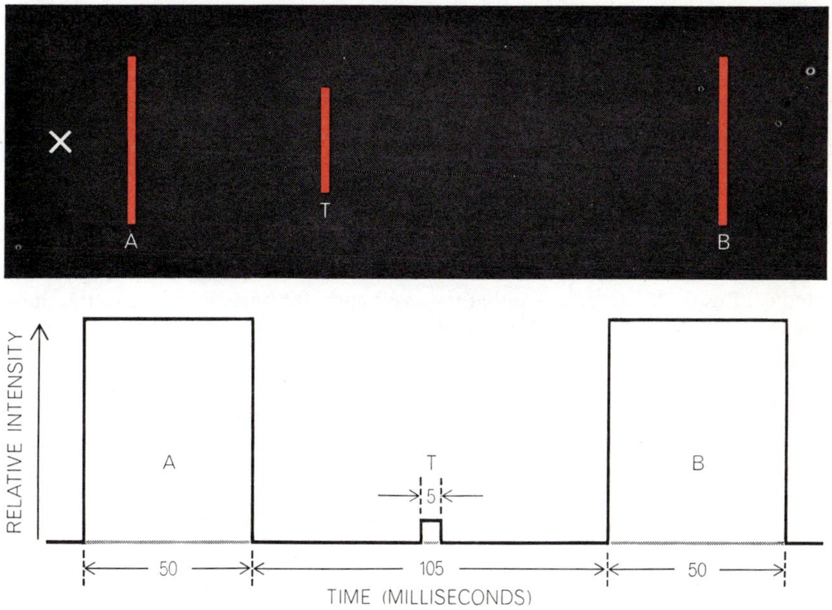

EXPERIMENT IN PERCEPTION involves a line of light in illusory movement, created by sequential flashing of lines *A* and *B*, and a small target light *T* flashed briefly (*top*) as subject looks at point *X*. Typical characteristics of flashes are shown at bottom. The experiment determines the effect of illusory movement on perception of the target light.

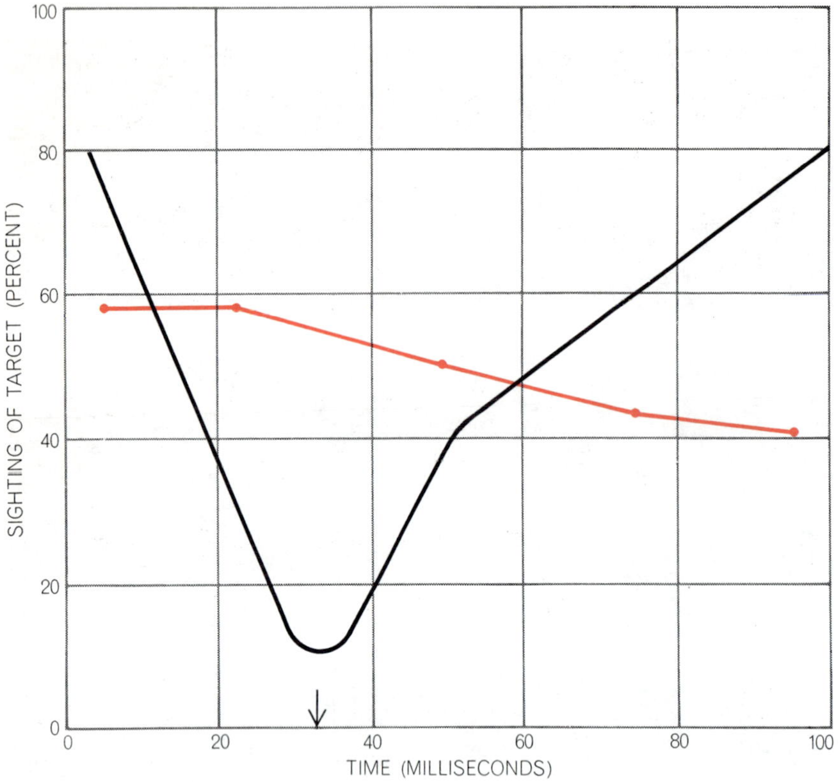

CONTRASTING EFFECTS of illusory and real movement on the perceptibility of a target are indicated. The colored curve shows the perceptibility of a target light presented as indicated by the dots; the light appeared in the "path" of an apparently moving line, which would have been closest to the target at the moment indicated by the arrow. The time scale refers to the intervals between flashes of the two lines used to create the illusion of movement. A line in real movement has a different effect, shown by black curve.

object in illusory movement in order for the two speeds to appear the same.

Over the years these differences between the two types of perception have tended to be overlooked, neglected or gainsaid, with the result that most investigators have stressed the similarities of real and apparent movement. Accordingly many of them have adopted the view that the mechanisms of the two perceptions must be the same. Dissatisfaction with this argument from appearance to mechanism was the starting point for my own investigation, which has been conducted at the U.S. Naval Medical Research Laboratory and at the Harvard University Center for Cognitive Studies. The outcome of my studies was the finding that the neural mechanisms for the two types of perception must be quite different, because these identical perceptions seem to be constructed in the nervous system according to different rules. I shall discuss experiments that showed three such differences.

The experiments leading to the discovery of the first difference grew out of some earlier work in which my colleagues and I found that both the detectability and the brightness of a target form are drastically reduced when a different form is presented briefly within certain intervals of the appearance of the target. The nearer in time and space the different form is presented with respect to the target form, the more difficult it is to see the target form. This phenomenon goes by the name of visual masking. In one variation of it, called backward masking, the second presentation makes it harder to see the first even when the two are separated by as much as 250 milliseconds—an interval that is brief by many standards but in this instance is between 10 and 100 times longer than the duration of the flashes.

On the basis of these experiments we made a prediction about a masking flash that was moving. The prediction was that a small, stationary line of light in the path of a larger moving line should be harder to see the closer the two are, and that the brighter the moving line, the less able one should be to see the stationary one. This in fact is what happens and is our control experiment. Assuming that this result would occur, we asked what would happen to the stationary target if the line of light were in apparent rather than real motion. Would the target be affected by the "position" of the illusory line? The illusion of a moving line can be produced by a process similar to that described for the two flashes: the illusion will appear when two lines—an "origin" and a "terminus"—are turned on and off briefly, their onsets separated by an appropriate pause. Our apparatus presented the lines by means of photographic negatives that were between the light source and the observer's eye, so that the stimuli appeared as lines of light on a dark background [*see bottom illustration on preceding page*]. At various times during the dark interval between the offset of the origin and the onset of the terminus—in other words, at various points along the "path" of the apparently moving line—we presented a fixed target light.

In order to measure the effect of the apparently moving line on the stationary target, we first found the luminance at which the observer was able to detect the target about 90 percent of the time when it was presented without the line for about five milliseconds. Then we determined how often the observer reported seeing the target when the line in apparent movement was also present. Typical results are presented in the illustration on this page, together with the data that would have resulted if the moving line had been real rather than illusory. It is evident from the illustration that the trend of the data differs for the two kinds of line. When the line is in real movement, the probability that the observer will detect the target is least when the line and the target are closest. When the line is in illusory movement, the probability that the observer will see the target is least immediately before the terminus of apparent movement is flashed on—a time when the illusory movement puts the line well past the target. Checking this result with control experiments, in which only the origin or the terminus was presented, we found that the variation in seeing the target was caused by the backward-masking effect of the terminus.

By the series of experiments I have described we were led to our first finding of a difference between the neural mechanisms for the processing of real and apparent movement. A line in real movement affects the perceptibility of objects in its path; a line in illusory movement does not. In other words, real and illusory movement, notwithstanding their identical appearance, differ at least in the way they affect other events going on in the visual nervous system.

Next we sought to ascertain whether other differences exist or whether the one just described was an isolated phenomenon. Brief, neighboring flashes of light are rather rare events in nature, and it might be that our experiments had led us to a finding of little relevance to the understanding of perception. Since the human mind was capable of inventing the phenomenon of illusory movement, however, it might have other criteria for distinguishing that phenomenon from real movement.

To test that possibility we conducted an experiment on the effect of extending the period of observation of illusory movement. We based the experiment on an observable fact about real movement: if you look fixedly at a point marking one end of a pendulum's swing while the pendulum oscillates at about three cycles per second, you may look for three or four minutes without ever losing the perception of a moving object. That is not the case with apparent movement, as we found in our experiment. Observers who looked fixedly at a point adjacent to the "path" of a line of light oscillating in apparent movement at about three cycles per second found that the perception of movement disappeared: they saw only the two terminal lines flash on and off. The perception of movement would return briefly from time to time and then disappear again. These alternations occurred between five and 10 times in two minutes of viewing, the number varying from person to person.

Our initial hypothesis about these alternations was that the threshold for the perception was changing slightly during observation—a not uncommon finding in visual experiments. When we tried to "track" the apparent movement by slightly varying the time interval that produces the effect, however, we found that small changes in the interval of time between the two lines never affected the number of alternations perceived, provided that we stayed within the bounds of optimal movement. Evidently it was not a change in threshold that was causing the alternation but some more complex perceptual function. Here, then, was a second difference in the treatment of real and illusory movement by the neural system of vision.

In further experiments varying the interval between origin and terminus we found a third criterion for distinguishing between real and illusory movement. When the origin and terminus are flashed for 50 milliseconds each and the intervals between them are 100 milliseconds, the observer usually sees a single form oscillating in a plane. If one of the intervals is reduced to about 75 milliseconds, however, the observer continues to see movement in the plane during the shorter interval, but during the longer interval he sees a bow-shaped movement. The object appears to come out in front of the plane of oscillation or to go behind it. If the object were in real movement, it would appear to change its speed rather than its distance from the observer.

Having thus established that the perceptual apparatus deals with illusory movement in at least three ways that differ from how it deals with real movement, we turned to the question of whether or not two illusions can affect each other. We studied this question with two illusions of spatial displacement. One was apparent movement. The other involved a phenomenon that can be seen when one stares at a drawing of a cubelike figure. The phenomenon can be observed in the illustration below, which presents a shape derived from a figure first described some 130 years ago by the Swiss naturalist L. A. Necker. Most people who stare at such a figure see it in three dimensions. As they continue to stare, say for about a minute, they find that the orientation of the cube changes repeatedly. These apparent changes vary in rate with the duration for which one stares. The rate slowly increases, reaches a plateau and then declines a little; the particular values depend on contrast, size, light intensity and other physical variables as well as on what psychologists call the observer's set, or attitude.

Our purpose, as I have said, was to find whether or not these two kinds of illusory spatial displacement—apparent movement and the alternation of a Necker cube—would affect each other. We began by presenting a Necker cube in apparent movement to see what effect this would have on the rate of alterna-

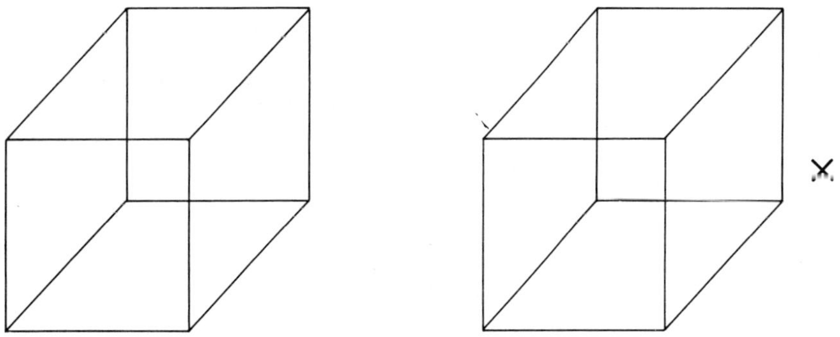

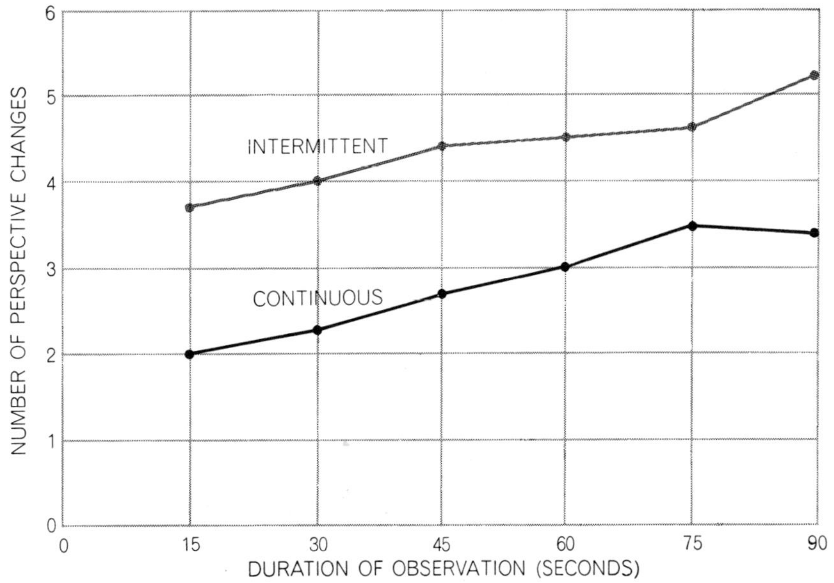

PERSPECTIVE CHANGES were examined in an experiment with two cubes. The cubes were presented either continuously or intermittently, the latter method producing an illusion of a single cube in oscillation. Subject looked at point *X* and pressed a buzzer when the perspective of the right-hand cube seemed to change. Chart at bottom shows an average of the number of perspective changes seen in each 15-second interval by several subjects.

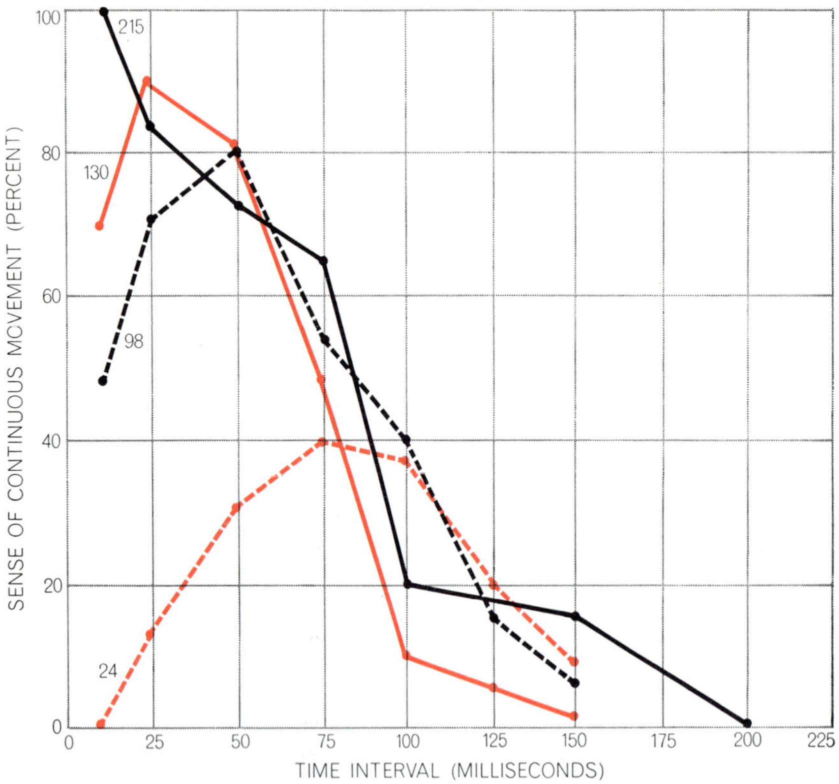

VARIATION OF CONDITIONS produced variations in the perception of illusory movement. Two lines of light were flashed at a constant intensity and spatial separation, but the duration of each flash and the time interval between flashes were varied. Numerals at the beginning of each curve show, in milliseconds, duration of individual flashes.

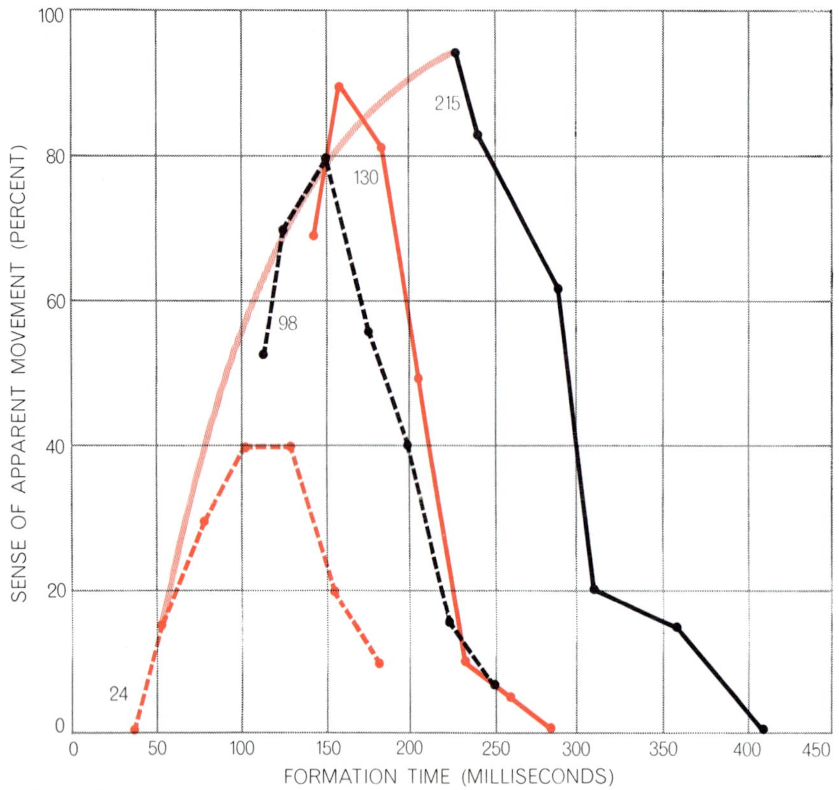

BASIC PROCESS of figure-forming in the visual system is suggested by the broad curve. The other curves replot the data shown in the top illustration on this page by summing the duration of the first flash and the time interval between flashes to give an image-formation time. Broad curve shows a hypothetical function tapped by individual curves.

tion. The method of producing the apparent movement was similar to that described for lights and lines: we presented two cubes alternately, each for 50 milliseconds, with a pause of about 100 milliseconds between them. The entire cycle occurred at a rate of 3.3 cycles per second. For comparison we also had the observers look at a continuously presented cube.

The results were that the apparently moving cube changed perspective more than the continuously presented cube. On the other hand, a control experiment with a single cube presented for 50 milliseconds at a rate of 3.3 times per second produced an equally large number of perspective changes. The experiment demonstrated that the illusions themselves did not interact but that a rate of intermittency required to produce one illusion (apparent movement) was also a rate that increased the frequency of another (reversals of a Necker cube). It was evident that the rate of about three cycles per second plays an important role in the visual system. I shall return to this point, but first I wish to make a corollary observation and to discuss another experiment.

When two Necker cubes are exposed at a rate of about three cycles per second, most observers see a single cube moving back and forth between the termini. This apparent cube changes perspective not only at the two termini, where it is physically present, but also in the space between the termini, where it never "really" exists. These transformations of the illusory cube are consistent with what the observer would have seen if the cube had been physically present in that space. In other words, under certain conditions the observer performs an impletion, or filling in. By doing so he supplies himself with information that is not present in the stimulus array—information that acts to rationalize his perceptions, or make them coherent. What the observer sees is consistent with what he thinks he is seeing. He does not fill in these perceptions ad libitum, however: the impletions occur, for apparent movement, only at certain rates of stimulation. The importance of these rates emerged more fully from the next experiment.

The experiment grew out of interest in a set of relations discovered half a century ago for the intensity, spatial separation and temporal separation of flashes of light that produced apparent movement. Named for the German psychologist Adolf Korte, they have been recognized for some time as approximations rather than laws. Our interest was directed in particular to two of them.

The first was that in order to maintain optimal movement an increase in the spatial separation between flashes required that the time interval be increased if the intensity were held constant. The second was that if the spatial separation were held constant, an increase in the intensity of the flashes required a decrease in the time interval. We found, as had others, that the "law" for spatial separation does not hold for small distances, say .75 degree to 5.25 degrees. In fact, within that range we found no variations at all in the occurrence of apparent movement: the time interval and the intensity required for apparent movement to be seen remained identical over that range. The relation describing intensity and temporal interval, however, held good in the range we measured, up to certain interesting limiting values.

Holding distance and intensity constant, we found that the probability of the subject's reporting apparent movement varied as the duration of the flashes and the temporal interval between them were varied. We also confirmed an earlier finding that the properties of the second flash were practically irrelevant in establishing movement; as long as the second flash was visible, its intensity and duration seemed to be of no consequence. The important things that occurred were in the first flash.

The top illustration on the opposite page shows the proportion of positive responses an experienced subject gave when there was a fixed spatial separation between two flashes but their duration and the temporal interval between them were varied. When the flashes are weak, say 24 milliseconds long at the moderate luminance of about five millilamberts, apparent movement occurs only a limited number of times—at best somewhat less than half the time. Increasing the duration of the flashes increases the probability that apparent movement will be seen.

When the data are replotted to add the duration of the first flash and the time interval between the flashes, we obtain what we believe to be the basic curve describing the formation of the illusion of movement. The curve is shown in the bottom illustration on the opposite page; the thin lines indicate the proportion of times the observer saw apparent movement for each of several flash durations. The broad, tinted line represents a hypothetical function fitted to the data; we believe it describes a single process in the visual system that is tapped by each of the separate curves. It rises steadily to a maximum where the flash duration is about 250 milliseconds. Subsequent checking experiments suggested that this "parent curve" reaches a plateau, at which it stays through flash durations of about 300 to 350 milliseconds and then descends rapidly.

This account of apparent movement, although still incomplete, relates the phenomenon to two mechanisms in human perception. One is the amount of time the visual system requires to form the perception of simple figures. The other is impletion.

From many experiments we know that the visual system takes about 300 milliseconds to form the perception of a simple object one is prepared to see. In other words, one can form certain visual perceptions at an optimum rate of about three per second—the rate I spoke of earlier as having particular significance. Many kinds of simple stimuli that occur within 300 milliseconds, which is to say at faster than the optimum rate, can interact so that the occurrence of each affects the appearance of the other. For example, sequences of letters presented at such a rate can be confused by the observer; he may detect the letters but confuse their sequence. Thus there is something special to the human visual system about rates in the region of three cycles per second. One of the results is the illusion of movement.

In sum, what our experiments reveal, in addition to several behavioral criteria that distinguish real and apparent movement, is that the "mechanism" for illusory movement has more in common with the "mechanism" controlling the formation of simple visual figures than it has with real movement. What one sees "moving" in an illusion is the result of an impletion, but the impletion occurs only at the rates of stimulation associated with forming the perception of simple visual figures. The more difficult problem remaining is to elaborate the rules that govern impletions.

Experiments of this kind also support a hypothesis that has been advanced tentatively in the past few years. It is that perceptions are constructed by means of a number of different operations occurring at different times and places in the nervous system. This could be called an "assembly line" model of visual perception. We look forward to learning if subsequent experiments bear out such a concept.

VI

DEVELOPMENT AND MODIFICATION

DEVELOPMENT AND MODIFICATION

INTRODUCTION

The notion that perception develops in humans early in life was explicitly formulated by the British empiricist philosophers in the seventeenth century. In the eighteenth century, one of them, George Berkeley, wrote what is often referred to as the first systematic treatise on the learning of vision, *An Essay Towards a New Theory of Vision* (see the article by Rock and Harris in Section V). Although the mechanism of acquiring vision was not Berkeley's primary concern, his association theory laid the groundwork for later conceptions of the original development of perception in infancy and the modifiability of perception in later life.

Classic statements to the effect that perceptual abilities are acquired by experience were countered with assertions of their innateness. These arguments of the eighteenth and nineteenth centuries constitute what is known as the nativist-empiricist controversy. After Darwin and the geneticists of the latter part of the nineteenth century, the controversy involved the new dichotomy between abilities that are genetically fixed and those that are acquired or modified in the course of the development of the individual (sometimes referred to as instinctive and learned capabilities, respectively).

How do these arguments bear on our discussion of the mechanisms of vision? To the extent that vision is innate, differences among individuals can be accounted for only by inheritance. To the extent that vision is either acquired, perfected, or simply maintained by informative contact with the environment during the life of an individual, modifiability of the system is implied. In the latter case, the mechanisms must have provision for change, and the study of such change can inform us of their workings. Of course, we exclude such environmental dependencies as nutrition and respiration, although they are obviously essential to survival. Our concern is with the informational aspects of the interaction between the nervous system, on the one hand, and the stimulus world, on the other, as they bear on later use of sensory information to determine the actions of the organism.

Historically, there have been two approaches to the study of these problems: (1) observation and experimental testing of human infants and newborn animals as soon after birth as possible; and (2) control of environmental conditions during earliest development with the aim of testing the influence of environmental contact in determining the functioning of perceptual mechanisms.

TESTING THE NEWBORN

If a behavior is present immediately after birth, the possibility that its development is attributable to contact with the extrauterine environment can be eliminated. Accordingly, considerable ingenuity has been devoted to the study and testing of the newborn. The greatest difficulty in studying many species of newborn mammals is the immaturity of their responses. For example, the human infant cannot talk and his motor coordination is generally poor, making the measure of his capabilities difficult. In such altricial animals, considerable postnatal development occurs in response systems, as a result either of intrinsically controlled growth or of environmentally determined growth—or, most likely, of some combination of both. There are important exceptions, however, that have been exploited to test the use of sensory information. A few responses (unconditioned) can be reliably elicited by particular stimuli without prior training; others require conditioning procedures to establish dependency on stimuli.

UNCONDITIONED RESPONSES

Robert L. Fantz (see his article "The Origin of Form Perception") has taken advantage of the mobility of the eyes of infants to measure their looking behavior. Using this indicator, he has shown that infants only a few weeks old will selectively attend to forms. Moreover, he regards this selection as an essential precursor to learning by experience.

Several important questions are raised by the sort of observations that Fantz has made: How soon after birth must testing be carried out in order to be certain that interaction with the environment has not influenced the function of perceptual mechanisms? The answer depends upon how rapid one conceives the action of the environment to be; at this time, we have no clear answers to the question. Some types of skill learning may take training regimens of many months—even years—to insure precision of performance, whereas imprinting—the tendency of the young of certain species (ducks, for example) to follow, and continue to follow, the first large moving object they encounter—may occur within hours, or even minutes.

Fantz equates "seeing" with "looking"—literally, orienting the eyeball. But is this identification appropriate? When we speak of the act of seeing, we assume that what is seen may be discriminated by any one of a large set of responses—naming, pressing the correct button, reaching, and so on—in addition to looking. Is it reasonable to conclude that an infant—or, for that matter, an animal subject or an adult human—who looks selectively will be capable of using any available response for this purpose? An affirmative answer assumes that there is a single central processor that does the discriminating and can then control any available response. Is this assumption correct for a normal human observer? We know that it is not correct for a human patient with a split callosum (see the article by Gazzaniga in Section I). Is it possible that there is a mechanism (presumably, a subcortical one) that directs the eyes selectively but that may be incapable of directing other responses? We do not have a complete answer at this time, although some evidence favors this possibility.

Besides "looking" behavior, a number of other apparently unconditioned responses have been reliably elicited in human infants. These include optokinetic nystagmus (the involuntary back-and-forth movements of the eye as it views a continuously moving scene) sucking, and heart-rate change. Together, they provide a repertory of simple responses sufficient to answer many of the questions that can be asked about the perceptual capabilities of newborn animals in general, and human infants in particular. Of course, the inventory of infant perception is far from complete at this time.

The maturation of the behavior of animals and human infants on the visual cliff is said by Eleanor J. Gibson and Richard D. Walk (see their article "The 'Visual Cliff'") to proceed independently of trial-and-error learning (a form of conditioning) but to require, at least in the kitten, a period of exposure to light. This observation, among many similar ones, makes it clear that the contact with the sense-stimulating environment that is required for normal development may be of many types, ranging from simple exposure to light through movement-produced stimulation to the type of training regimens common in conditioning procedures. Such a conclusion would be obvious but for the argument—now, for the most part, only a matter of history—that all effects of environmental contact are of the conditioning type.

CONDITIONED RESPONSES

Although conditioning is not to be regarded as a model for all effects of interaction with the environment, it is a useful technique for exploring responsiveness to certain aspects of sensory stimulation. Stimuli to which the newborn are not intrinsically responsive may be made to elicit responses through conditioning. Such a procedure was adopted by T. G. R. Bower in his study of infant vision. As he reports in his article "The Visual World of Infants," Bower used the head-turning response of the infant, and, reinforcing it with a "peekaboo" from the experimenter, he succeeded in demonstrating that the infant's responses in extinction were most frequently given to the object of the same physical size as that to which it was initially conditioned, despite the remoteness (and the smaller retinal image) of the object. From this evidence, he concluded that there is a size-constancy mechanism operating in infants at a very early age. Using the same experimental technique, Bower also presents evidence for shape constancy and the completion phenomena in human infants.

Two cautions are important to the proper interpretation of conditioning studies of human infants and newborn animals. The first, and more important, is the possibility that a conditioning procedure, which is presumed to demonstrate an ability developed independently of experience, may have allowed the organism to obtain some essential experience, unbeknownst to the investigator. The second, which may be a corollary of the first, is that the older the subject when a test for a particular capacity proves to be conclusive, the more likely it is that the subject has had an opportunity to acquire that capacity through the undetermined effects of contact with the environment. Prolonged training procedures are particularly suspect.

NEUROLOGICAL TESTS

Yet another method of testing newborn animals has recently come into prominence. To the extent that anatomical or physiological properties of the nervous system can be identified with perceptual performances, their presence or absence in the newborn may inform us about perceptual capabilities. Only recently have investigations of the nervous system become sufficiently subtle to give promise of the definitiveness of such an approach. A prime example comes from the work of Hubel and Wiesel, who studied the receptive-field properties of single units in the cortex of very young kittens prior to exposure to a patterned environment. They have reported that the responses of these units were strikingly similar to those of adult cats (see the article by Hubel in Section III), although somewhat more sluggish and with their orientation selectivity not as precise as those of the adult. To the extent that the operation of these units is necessary and sufficient for visual perception, we might conclude that the kitten possesses the ability to perceive visually. But caution is in order, because we do not yet know the precise role of the neural units in the perception of form, not to mention their importance in other visually controlled responses. As we shall see, the pioneering work of Hubel and Wiesel, which has demonstrated a congenital function that is presumed to be essential to perception, has led (oddly enough) to the discovery that, for these same animals, later exposure to the environment is very critical to the proper development of that function.

DEPRIVATION AND ENHANCEMENT

The original logic of the deprivation experiment supposed that those difficulties of studying the newborn that are a consequence of their neurological immaturity could be overcome by studying neurologically mature but experientially naive animals. This logic assumes, of course, that maturation and exposure to the sense-stimulating environment are independent. Were that true, then the development of an ability first exhibited by an animal after deprivation cannot be attributed to any interaction with environment that was precluded by deprivation. On the other hand, if a behavior is absent, its loss may be attributed to a lack of exposure to the environment. Unfortunately for easy interpretation, the results of many years of deprivation research belie the assumption of the independence of exposure and maturation.

Deprivation studies began with observations on the recovery of vision in people who had suffered blindness for long periods, and the development of vision in people who had been blind from birth. (Surgical procedures for the removal of cataracts have been used for centuries, and other operative procedures to correct certain kinds of blindness have been developed in recent decades.) These observations make up a fascinating but confusing literature. Several decades ago, experimental work on the effects of visual deprivation was begun at the Yerkes Laboratories of Primate Biology under the guidance of Karl Lashley. Austin H. Riesen, who has been a principal investigator in this work, reviews the outcomes of a number of the experiments carried out at that laboratory in his article "Arrested Vision."

One of the initial results was the discovery of retinal abnormalities in animals that had undergone prolonged deprivation of light. The retina—the most peripheral part of the visual system—had either not matured or had been degraded by the absence of light stimulation. Blindness of retinal origin would, of course, preclude developmental changes at higher levels of the visual nervous system. Following these early results, studies were made of animals subjected to less severe deprivations—deprivations insufficient to produce retinal changes. Animals exposed to diffused light without pattern did not show the same retinal changes as those reared without any light. Nonetheless, they showed behavioral deficits, which led Riesen to claim that patterned stimulation was also required for adequate development and maintenance of visual function.

These experiments set a pattern for later work on sensory deprivation. Increasingly subtle forms of deprivation were studied by Riesen and other investigators, beginning with deprivation of pattern but not of light flux, going on to deprivation of body movement in the presence of patterned stimulation, and leading to comparison of active with passive movement (see Held's article in this section), in which the incidence of visual stimulation, as such, is no different for deprived and undeprived subjects.

TRANSFORMATION

Closely related to experimental deprivation is the procedure of systematically transforming some aspect of normal stimulation into an abnormal form and observing its effects upon experimental subjects. Such transformation can be accomplished by several means: The relation between the world of objects and the input of stimuli to the nervous system can be rearranged either by optical means—through the use of prisms or other rearranging devices, as in the experiments described by Held and by Hess in their articles in this section, and by Kohler and by Rock and Harris in their articles in Section V—or, in some animals, by actually rotating or exchanging eyeballs, as in the experiments described by Sperry in his article in this section. In addition, animals may be reared in an atypical environment built by the experimenter—for example, a cage whose walls are covered with vertical bars.

The informational consequences of such experimental manipulation may be of two kinds. The first of these is a systematic change in the relation between movements of the body and contingent visual changes: hence, an altered correlation between bodily movement and visual consequence. This change contrasts with deprivation that either eliminates the correlation or produces a de-correlation, according to its type and severity. An intermediate degree of de-correlation can be produced optically by prisms of continually varying power (see Held's article). The second kind of informational consequence of experimental manipulation is one that entails changed incidence of certain properties of stimulation. The curvature induced by prisms (see Held's article and Kohler's article in Section V) is a case in point.

The long-term response of organisms to rearrangement has been taken as an index of the plasticity or modifiability of behavior and of the nervous system that controls it. As he points out in his article

"The Eye and the Brain," R. W. Sperry has used it to demonstrate the strength of inherent developmental patterning and the relative absence of modification by experience in amphibians. The ability of the nervous system to reestablish connections despite the disorder produced by severing the optic nerve and moving the eyeball argues strongly for the intrinsic control of development.

Eckhard H. Hess ("Space Perception in the Chick") used prism rearrangement for a purpose very similar to Sperry's. Hess preferred the rearrangement technique to deprivation for studying newly hatched chicks for a very important reason: as we have previously mentioned, deprivation often causes abnormal development of the retina and other parts of the visual nervous system. Hess argued, from the absence of adaptation in his chicks, that development is purely intrinsic, but, in the light of more recent research, this conclusion appears to have been premature. Patrick Rossi, in a renewed study of the chick's ability to adapt to prisms, has shown that, after their removal, the chick will peck with an error opposite to that induced by the prisms. Hess's failure to obtain evidence of modification in chicks required to wear prisms did not preclude its discovery when the prisms were removed.

Richard Held and his collaborators have used the rearrangement technique to study plasticity in adult human subjects (see Held's article "Plasticity in Sensory-Motor Systems"). They have been particularly concerned with the exposure factors that lead to modification of visual-motor coordination. Such factors are then hypothesized to be important for the maintenance and development of function; Kohler, in his article in Section V, made a similar argument. The differences between the development of visual-motor coordination in active kittens and its development in passively transported kittens, when the visual exposure for both is the same, demonstrates an effect of environmental interaction that is not simply visual. If motor-visual feedback is required for such acquisition, then we should expect that visual-motor deficits should also appear in animals reared under purely visual deprivation. Held and his collaborators have shown that it is possible to factor out elements of experience that are essential to particular functions. In addition to the active–passive difference discussed by Held, many other parallels between conditions adequate for development and for adaptation to rearrangement have since been shown. The evidence suggests that the types of information gained from contact with the environment play roles in both kinds of modification, although the underlying processes may differ. Insofar as deprivations of motor-visual feedback have been studied, the deficiencies appear to be reversible, unlike the effects of some of the more severe deprivations of vision, which lead to permanent visual and visual-motor deficits.

As we mentioned in a previous section, recent neurophysiological work by Hubel and Wiesel may have begun to inform us about the perceptual systems of kittens (and about those of other newborn mammals, by implication). Hubel and Wiesel have gone a step further to study the effects of pattern deprivation on the receptive-field properties of cortical cells in the kitten. They find that rearing a kitten without patterned light in both its eyes for several months after birth leaves the receptive fields elicited by stimulation of the retina fairly normal. Such deprivation of only one eye, however, leads to a drastic loss of the ability to arouse cortical cells through stimulation of that eye, though not, of course, through stimulation of the undeprived eye. Curiously enough, deprivation of one eye has much more drastic effects than that of both eyes: it appears as if the two eyes compete in some way for central connections with cortical cells. But these modifications occur only during the first few months of the kitten's life. In terms of loss or recovery of function, only limited changes occur in the neurophysiology of receptive fields after the age of three months. There are hints, in the most recent literature, that the receptive field structure is even more surprisingly modifiable during the early period of plasticity than most researchers had supposed. These results strongly reinforce the view that whatever may be the initial capability of the nervous system at birth and whatever its native capacity for maturation, there is an important component in development that is environmentally determined. If maturation is taken to mean the intrinsically controlled growth of connections in the nervous system, then evidence is available that exposure of the retina to stimulation by light and to stimulation by patterned light influences this growth. On the other hand, the demonstration that there are critical periods during which environmentally produced stimulation is effective proves that the state of maturation of the nervous system is also relevant to the effects of such stimulation. In other words, maturation and exposure codetermine growth. The real issue is the discovery of the process of interaction between the intrinsic design of the nervous system and the extrinsic influences upon it.

Viewed in this light, the deprivation procedure is a double-edged sword. It not only precludes exposure, but it may also alter the properties of the nervous system. From a practical point of view, it is desirable to know that interaction with the environment is critical, irrespective of its mechanism. The procedures of deprivation can tell us about the influences of the environment, which may often be masked by the very universality of conditions of exposure. In order to develop our understanding of mechanism, however, we shall have to develop more subtle experimental techniques.

The history of deprivation studies over the last few decades shows a progression from the grossest forms of deprivation (the elimination of light and patterned light) to more subtle deprivations, such as the elimination of movement-coupled sensory feedback. One goal in this progression has been to preclude the neural changes that have been shown to result from various forms of deprivation. We have already mentioned that gross deprivation of light produces an altered retina. Such peripheral neural changes have been regarded as indications that deprivation degrades the nervous system: an experimental animal deprived of visual stimulation is, in effect, blind—hence, the effects of its early experiences are not tested at all. More recently, with changes in central connectivity being discovered, the effects of deprivation cannot be discounted as artifacts that simply preclude normal function. These effects do, in fact, appear to be the central correlate of the impaired function that results from inadequate experience during rearing. Hubel and Wiesel's discovery, a few years ago, of functioning cortical cells in inexperienced kittens reinforced a nativist bias on the part of many perceptual psychologists. Quite recently, however, the discovery of plasticity in these same cells is pushing the pendulum back towards the position espoused by Donald Hebb many years ago (see the Introduction to Section IV). The next few years will undoubtedly witness major discoveries in this field.

REFERENCE

Rossi, P. J. Adaptation and negative aftereffect to lateral optical displacement in newly hatched chicks. *Science*, 1968, **160**, 430–432.

32

THE ORIGIN OF FORM PERCEPTION

ROBERT L. FANTZ
May 1961

Long before an infant can explore his surroundings with hands and feet he is busy exploring it with his eyes. What goes on in the infant's mind as he stares, blinks, looks this way and that? Does he sense only a chaotic patchwork of color and brightness or does he perceive and differentiate among distinctive forms? The question has always fascinated philosophers and scientists, for it bears on the nature and origin of knowledge. At issue is the perennial question of nature *v.* nurture. On one side is the nativist, who believes that the infant has a wide range of innate visual capacities and predilections, which have evolved in animals over millions of years, and that these give a primitive order and meaning to the world from the "first look." On the other side is the extreme empiricist, who holds that the infant learns to see and to use what he sees only by trial and error or association, starting, as John Locke put it, with a mind like a blank slate.

It has long been known that very young infants can see light, color and movement. But it is often argued that they cannot respond to such stimuli as shape, pattern, size or solidity; in short, that they cannot perceive form. This position is the last stronghold of the empiricist, and it has been a hard one to attack. How is one to know what an infant sees? My colleagues and I have recently developed an experimental method of finding out. We have already disposed of the basic question, that of whether babies can perceive form at all. They can, at least to some degree, although it appears that neither the view of the simple nativist nor that of the simple empiricist tells the whole story. Now we are investigating the further question of how and when infants use their capacity to perceive form to confer order and meaning on their environment.

The technique grew out of studies with lower animals, which are of importance in themselves. They were undertaken in 1951 at the University of Chicago with newly hatched chicks. Paradoxically, chicks can "tell" more directly what they see than higher animals can. Soon after they break out of the shell they go about the business of finding things to peck at and eat. Their purposeful, visually dominated behavior is ideally suited for observation and experiment.

We presented the chicks with a number of small objects of different shapes.

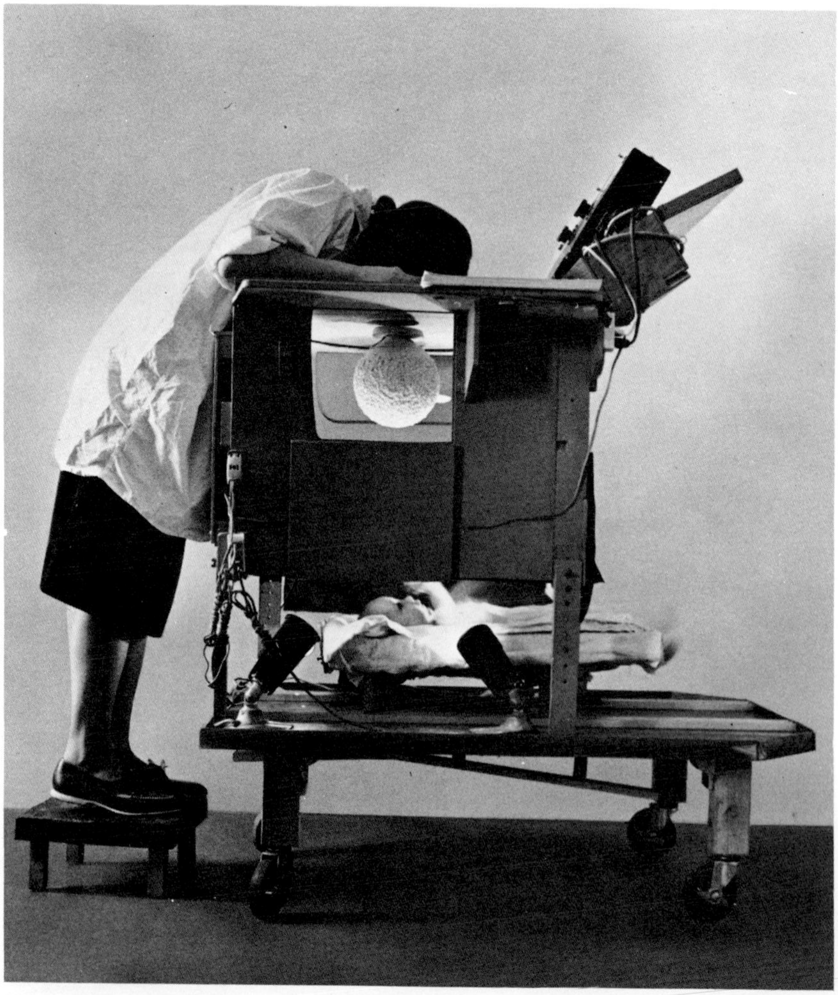

"LOOKING CHAMBER" was used to test the visual interests of chimpanzee and human infants. Here a human infant lies on a crib in the chamber, looking at objects hung from the ceiling. The observer, watching through a peephole, records the attention given each object.

Each object was enclosed in a clear plastic container to eliminate the possible influence of touch, smell or taste, but this did not prevent the chicks from pecking at preferred forms for hours on end. An electrical circuit attached to each container recorded the number of pecks at it.

More than 1,000 chicks were tested on some 100 objects. To exclude any opportunity for learning, the chicks were hatched in darkness and tested on their first exposure to light, before they had had any experience with real food. Presented with eight objects of graded angularity, from a sphere to a pyramid, the subjects pecked 10 times oftener at the sphere than they did at the pyramid. Among the flat forms, circles were preferred to triangles regardless of comparative size; among circles, those of ⅛-inch diameter drew the most attention. In a test of the effect of three-dimensionality the chicks consistently selected a sphere over a flat disk.

The results provided conclusive evidence that the chick has an innate ability to perceive shape, three-dimensionality and size. Furthermore, the chick uses the ability in a "meaningful" way by selecting, without learning, those objects most likely to be edible: round, three-dimensional shapes about the size of grain or seeds. Other birds exhibit similar visual capacity. For example, N. Tinbergen of the University of Oxford found selective pecking by newly hatched herring gulls. These chicks prefer shapes resembling that of the bill of the parent bird, from which they are fed [see "The Evolution of Behavior in Gulls," by N. Tinbergen; SCIENTIFIC AMERICAN Offprint 456].

Of course, what holds true for birds does not necessarily apply to human beings. The inherent capacity for form perception that has developed in birds may have been lost somewhere along the evolutionary branch leading to the primates, unlikely as it seems. Or, more plausibly, the primate infant may require a period of postnatal development to reach the level of function of the comparatively precocious chick.

When we set out to determine the visual abilities of helpless infants, the only indicator we could find was the activity of the eyes themselves. If an infant consistently turns its gaze toward some forms more often than toward others, it must be able to perceive form. Working on this premise, we developed a visual-interest test, using as our first subjects infant chimpanzees at the Yerkes Laboratories of Primate Biology in Orange Park, Fla.

A young chimpanzee lay on its back in a comfortable crib inside a "looking chamber" of uniform color and illumination. We attached to the ceiling of the chamber pairs of test objects, slightly separated from each other. They were exposed to view, alternately at right and left, in a series of short periods. Through a peephole in the ceiling we could see tiny images of the objects mirrored in the subjects' eyes. When the image of

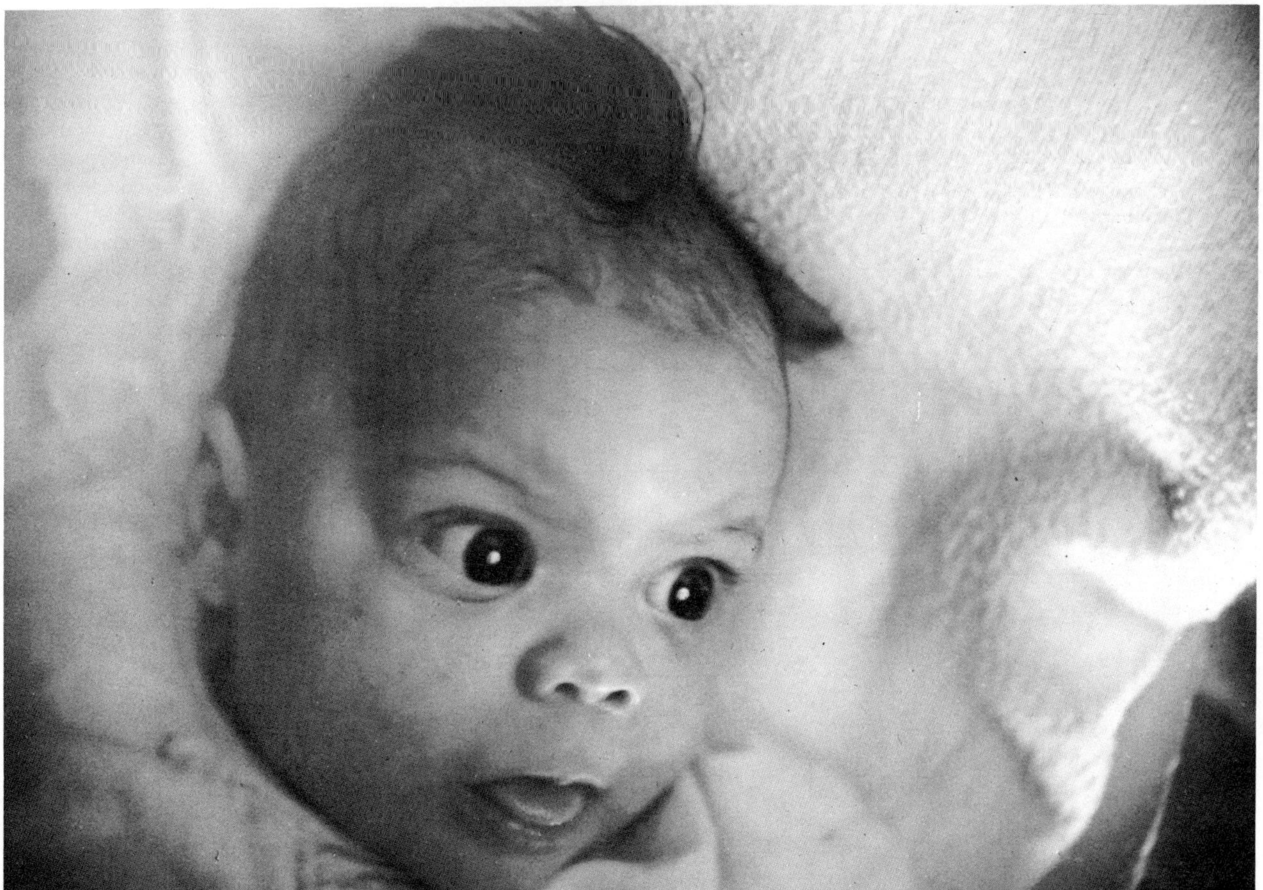

VISUAL INTEREST in various shapes was determined by noting reflections in the subject's eyes. In this case, with the reflection over the center of the infant's eye, the reflected object is being fixated, or looked at directly. (Because this young infant's binocular coordination is poor, only the right eye is fixating the object.) The length of each such fixation was recorded electrically.

PATTERN PREFERENCE of newly hatched chicks is studied by recording their pecks at each of a number of different shapes in plastic containers set into the wall of a test box.

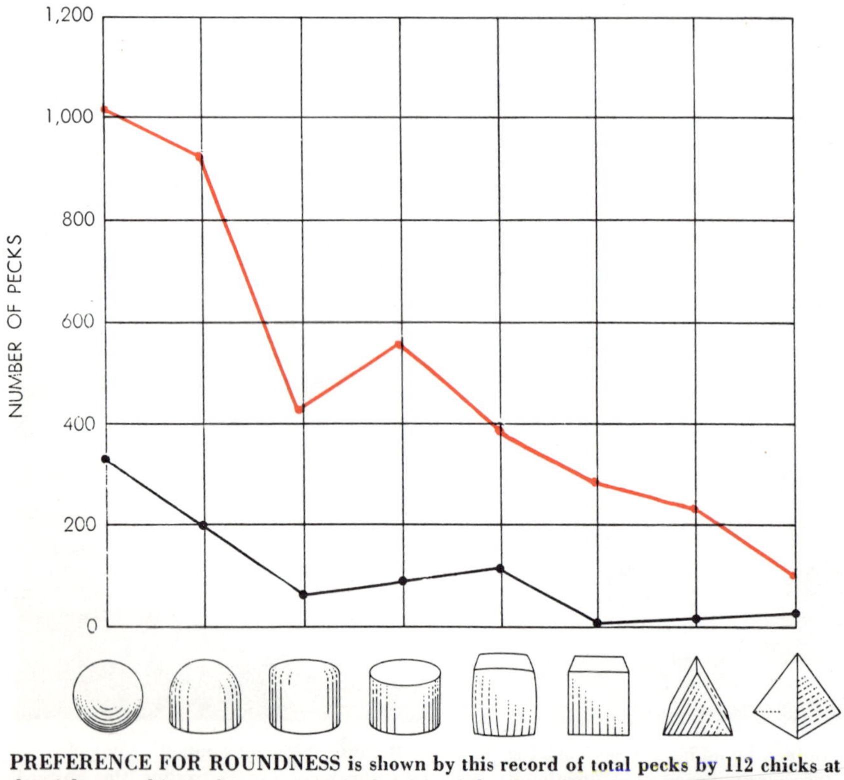

PREFERENCE FOR ROUNDNESS is shown by this record of total pecks by 112 chicks at the eight test objects shown across the bottom of the chart. The results are for the chicks' first 10 minutes (*black line*) and first 40 minutes (*colored line*) of visual experience.

one of the objects was at the center of the eye, over the pupil, we knew the chimpanzee was looking directly at it. The experimenter recorded on an electric timer the amount of attention given each target. The results were then analyzed to determine their statistical significance. Our first subject was a five-month-old chimpanzee. Later we followed a chimpanzee from birth, keeping it in darkness except during the tests. In both cases we found a definite preference for certain objects, indicating an inborn ability to distinguish among them.

Turning to human infants, we made no major change in our procedure except that we did not tamper with their everyday environment. The experiments did not disturb the infants but they did demand great patience of the investigators. Human infants are more rapidly bored than chimpanzees and they tend to go to sleep.

In the first experiment we tested 30 infants, aged one to 15 weeks, at weekly intervals. Four pairs of test patterns were presented in random sequence. In decreasing order of complexity they were: horizontal stripes and a bull's-eye design, a checkerboard and two sizes of plain square, a cross and a circle, and two identical triangles. The total time spent looking at the various pairs differed sharply, the more complex pairs drawing the greater attention. Moreover, the relative attractiveness of the two members of a pair depended on the presence of a pattern difference. There were strong preferences between stripes and bull's-eye and between checkerboard and square. Neither the cross and circle nor the two triangles aroused a significant differential interest. The differential response to pattern was shown at all ages tested, indicating that it was not the result of a learning process. The direction of preference between stripes and bull's-eye, on the other hand, changed at two months of age, due either to learning or to maturation.

Later we learned that a Swiss pediatrician, F. Stirnimann, had obtained similar results with still younger infants. He held cards up to the eyes of infants one to 14 days old and found that patterned cards were of more interest than those with plain colors.

Clearly some degree of form perception is innate. This, however, does not dispose of the role of physiological growth or of learning in the further development of visual behavior. Accordingly we turned our attention to the influence of these factors.

By demonstrating the existence of form perception in very young infants we had already disproved the widely held notion that they are anatomically incapable of seeing anything but blobs of light and dark. Nevertheless, it seems to be true that the eye, the visual nerve-pathways and the visual part of the brain are poorly developed at birth. If this is so, then the acuteness of vision—the ability to distinguish detail in patterns—should increase as the infant matures.

To measure the change in visual acuity we presented infants in the looking chamber with a series of patterns composed of black and white stripes, each pattern paired with a gray square of equal brightness. The width of the stripes was decreased in graded steps from one pattern to the next. Since we already knew that infants tend to look longer and more frequently at a patterned object than at a plain one, the width of the stripes of the finest pattern that was preferred to gray would provide an index to visual acuity. In this modified version the visual-interest test again solved the difficulties involved in getting infants to reveal what they see.

The width of the finest stripes that could be distinguished turned out to decrease steadily with increasing age during the first half-year of life. By six months babies could see stripes 1/64 inch wide at a distance of 10 inches—a visual angle of five minutes of arc, or 1/12 degree. (The adult standard is one minute of arc.) Even when still less than a month old, infants were able to perceive ⅛-inch stripes at 10 inches, corresponding to a visual angle of a little less than one degree. This is poor performance compared to that of an adult, but it is a far cry from a complete lack of ability to perceive pattern.

The effects of maturation on visual acuity are relatively clear and not too hard to measure. The problem of learning is more subtle. Other investigators have shown that depriving animals of patterned visual stimuli for a period after birth impairs their later visual performance, especially in form perception [see the article "Arrested Vision," by Austin H. Riesen, beginning on page 358]. Learned behavior is particularly vulnerable, but even innate responses are affected. For example, chicks kept in darkness for several weeks after hatching lose the ability to peck at food.

Research is now under way at Western Reserve University on this perplexing problem. We have raised monkeys in darkness for periods varying from one to 11 weeks. In general, the longer the period of deprivation, the poorer the performance when the animals were finally exposed to light and the more time they required to achieve normal responses. When first brought into the light, the older infant monkeys bumped into things, fell off tables, could not locate objects visually—for all practical purposes they were blind. It sometimes took weeks for them to "learn to see."

Monkeys kept a shorter time in the dark usually showed good spatial orientation in a few hours or days. Moreover, they showed normal interest in patterned objects, whereas the animals deprived of light for longer periods seemed more interested in color, brightness and size.

These results cannot be explained by innate capacity, maturation or learning alone. If form perception were wholly innate, it would be evident without experience at any age, and visual deprivation would have no effect. If maturation were the controlling factor, younger infant animals would be inferior rather than superior to older ones with or without visual experience. If form perception were entirely learned, the same period of experience would be required regardless of age and length of deprivation.

Instead there appears to be a complex interplay of innate ability, maturation

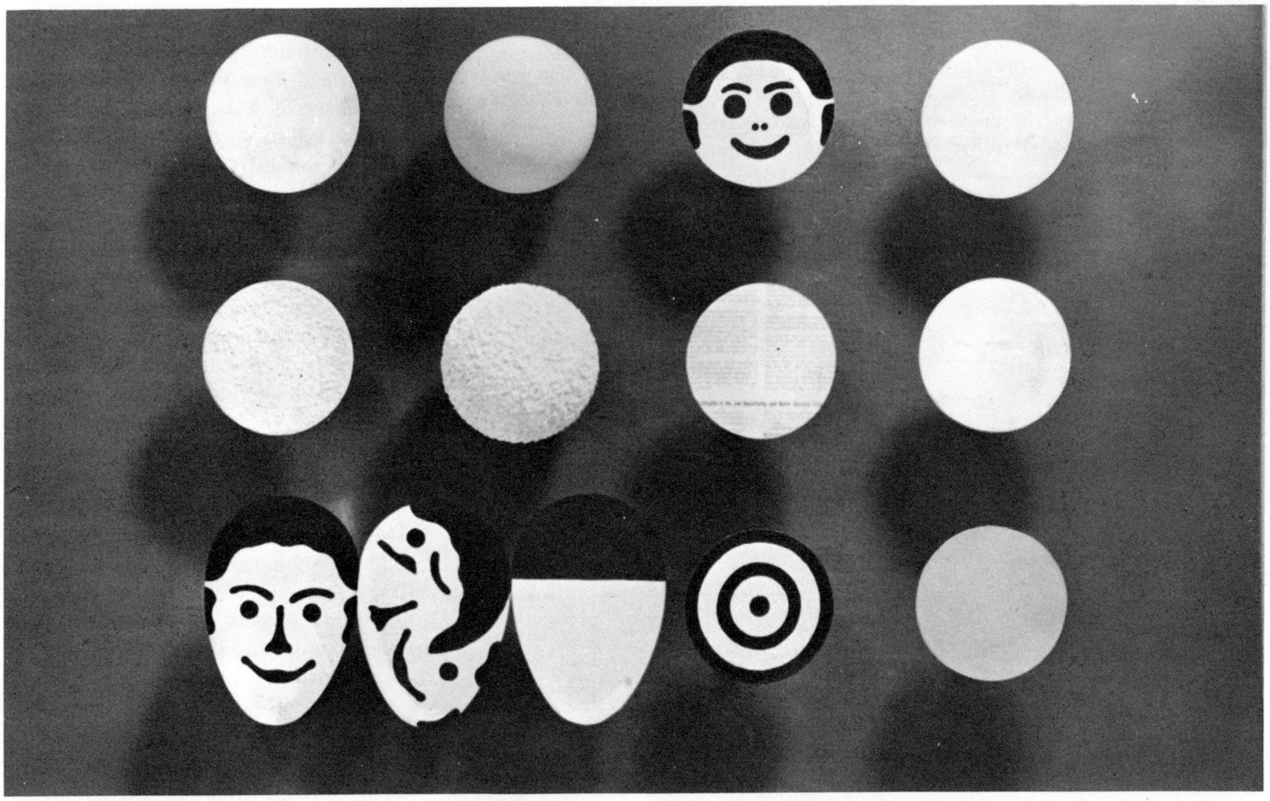

TEST OBJECTS included smooth and textured disks and spheres (*upper left*) to check interest in solidity. Attention to faces was tested with three patterns at lower left. The six round patterns at the right included (*top to bottom, left to right*) a face, a piece of printed matter, a bull's-eye, yellow, white and red disks. Round objects are six inches in diameter; "faces," nine inches long.

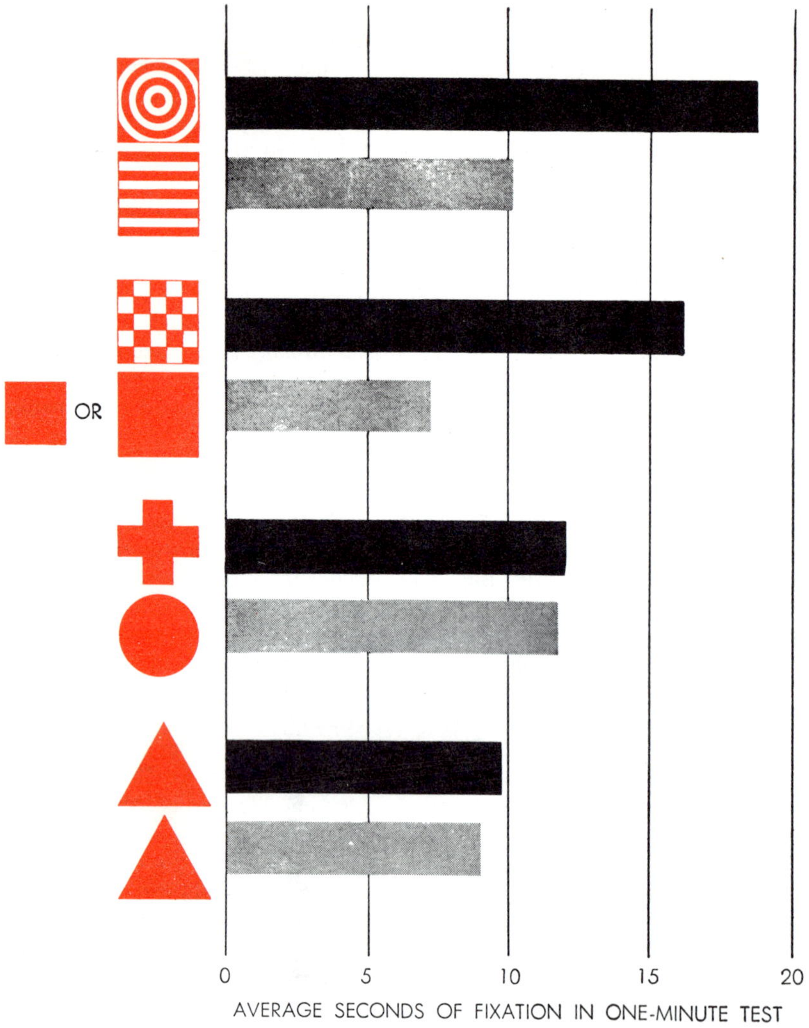

INTEREST IN FORM was proved by infants' reactions to various pairs of patterns (*left*) presented together. (The small and large plain squares were used alternately.) The more complex pairs received the most attention, and within each of these pairs differential interest was based on pattern differences. These results are for 22 infants in 10 weekly tests.

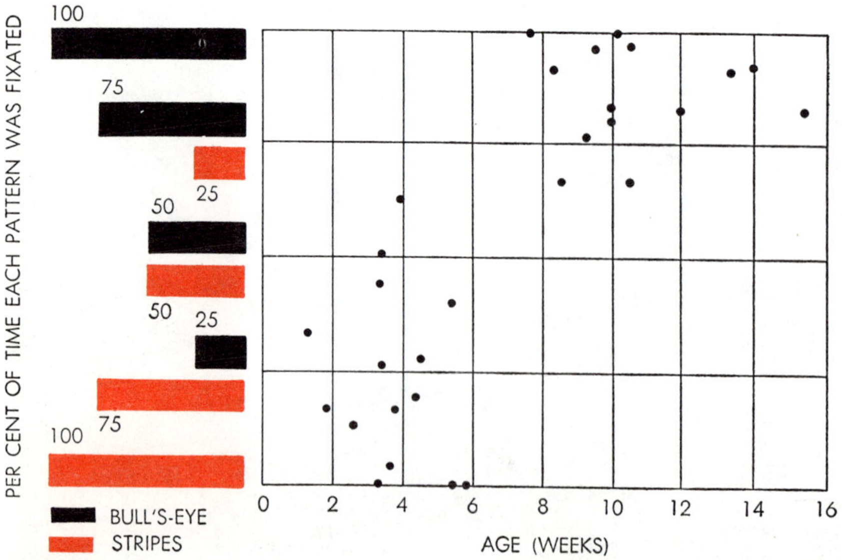

REVERSAL OF INTEREST from the striped pattern to the bull's-eye was apparent at two months of age. Each dot is for a single infant's first test session. It shows the time spent looking at the bull's-eye and at the stripes as a per cent of the time spent looking at both.

and learning in the molding of visual behavior, operating in this manner: there is a critical age for the development of a given visual response when the visual, mental and motor capacities are ready to be used and under normal circumstances will be used together. At that time the animal will either show the response without experience or will learn it readily. If the response is not "imprinted" at the critical age for want of visual stimulus, development proceeds abnormally, without the visual component. Presented with the stimulus later on, the animal learns to respond, if it responds at all, only with extensive experience and training. This explanation, if verified by further studies, would help to reconcile the conflicting claims of the nativist and the empiricist on the origin of visual perception.

To return to human infants, the work described so far does not answer the second question posed earlier in this article: whether or not the infant's innate capacity for form perception introduces a measure of order and meaning into what would otherwise be a chaotic jumble of sensations. An active selection process is necessary to sort out these sensations and make use of them in behavior. In the case of chicks such a process is apparent in the selection of forms likely to be edible.

In the world of the infant, people have an importance that is perhaps comparable to the importance of grain in the chick's world. Facial pattern is the most distinctive aspect of a person, the most reliable for distinguishing a human being from other objects and for identifying him. So a facelike pattern might be expected to bring out selective perception in an infant if anything could.

We tested infants with three flat objects the size and shape of a head. On one we painted a stylized face in black on a pink background, on the second we rearranged the features in a scrambled pattern, and on the third we painted a solid patch of black at one end with an area equal to that covered by all the features. We made the features large enough to be perceived by the youngest baby, so acuity of vision was not a factor. The three objects, paired in all possible combinations, were shown to 49 infants from four days to six months old.

The results were about the same for all age levels: the infants looked mostly at the "real" face, somewhat less often at the scrambled face, and largely ignored the control pattern. The degree of preference for the "real" face to the other one was not large, but it was

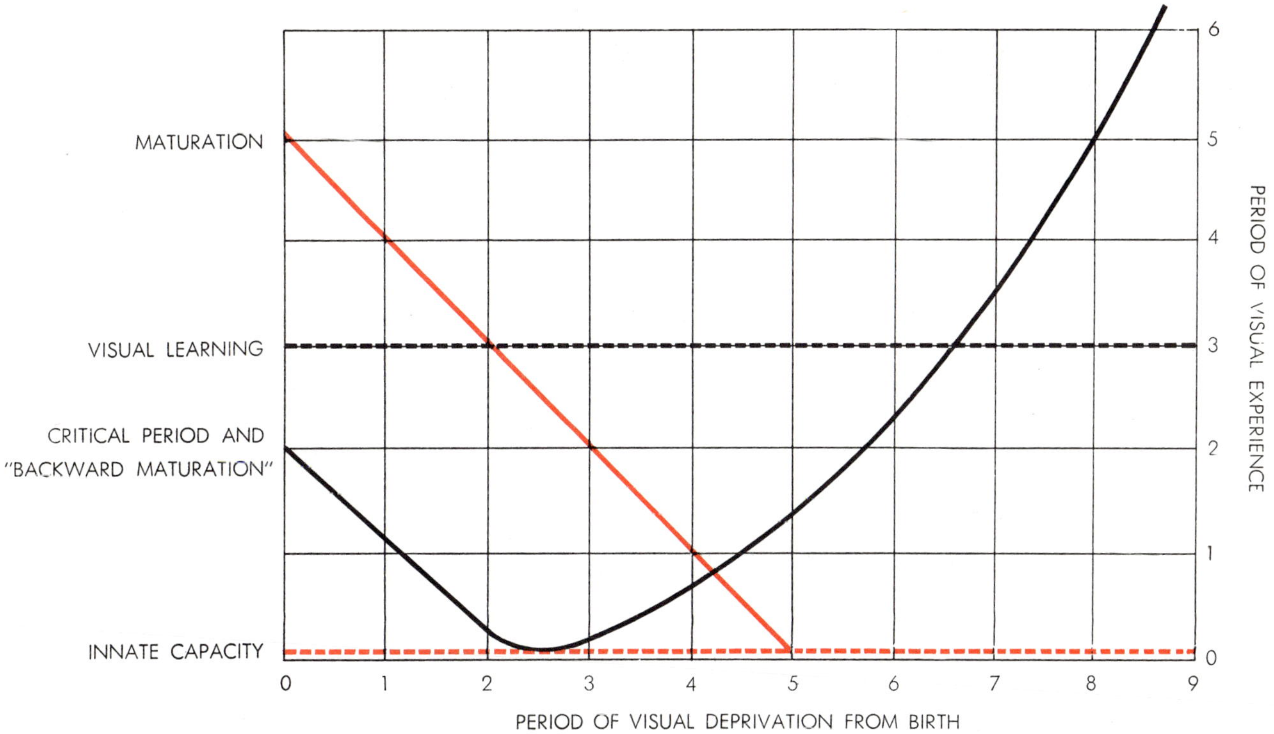

HYPOTHETICAL RESULTS that might be expected if any one developmental factor operated alone are plotted. The horizontal axis shows the period of rearing without visual experience; the vertical axis, the time subsequently required in the light until a given response is shown. Units of time are arbitrary. If innate capacity alone were effective, the response would always come without any experience (*broken colored line*). If maturation were necessary, the response would not be shown before a certain age, in this case five units, regardless of deprivation (*solid colored line*). If learning alone were operative, the required amount of experience would be constant (*broken black line*). Actually tests with chicks and monkey infants suggest the result shown by the solid black curve: after a short period of maturation, a "critical period" is reached when innate capacity can be manifested; more deprivation brings on "backward maturation," in which more and more experience is required before a response is shown.

consistent among individual infants, especially the younger ones. The experiment suggested that there is an unlearned, primitive meaning in the form perception of infants as well as of chicks.

Further support for the idea was obtained when we offered our infant subjects a choice between a solid sphere and a flat circle of the same diameter. When the texture and shading clearly differentiated the sphere from the circle —in other words, when there was a noticeable difference in pattern—the solid form was the more interesting to infants from one to six months old. This unlearned selection of a pattern associated with a solid object gives the infant a basis for perceiving depth.

The last experiment to be considered is a dramatic demonstration of the interest in pattern in comparison to color and brightness. This time there were six test objects: flat disks six inches in diameter. Three were patterned—a face, a bull's-eye and a patch of printed matter. Three were plain—red, fluorescent yellow and white. We presented them, against a blue background, one at a time in varied sequence and timed the length of the first glance at each.

The face pattern was overwhelmingly the most interesting, followed by the printing and the bull's-eye. The three brightly colored plain circles trailed far behind and received no first choices. There was no indication that the interest in pattern was secondary or acquired.

What makes pattern so intrinsically interesting to young infants? It seems to me that the answer must lie in the uses of vision for the child and adult.

One of these functions is the recognition of objects under various conditions. The color and brightness of objects

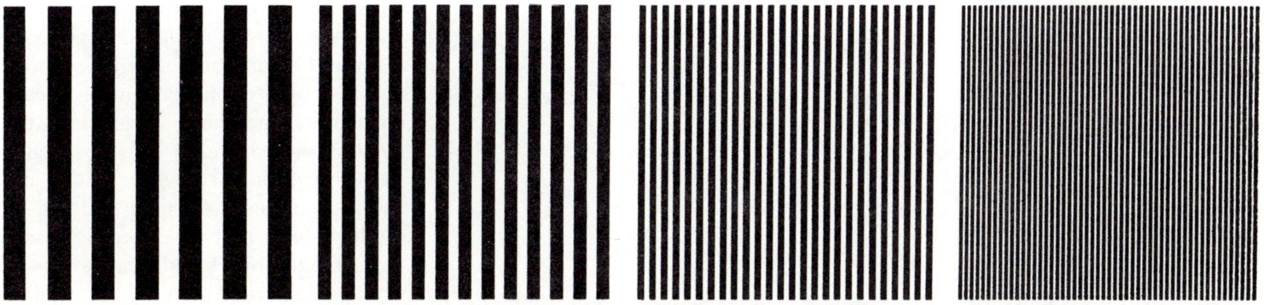

VISUAL ACUITY was tested with these stripes: 1/8, 1/16, 1/32 and 1/64 inch wide. Each pattern was displayed with a gray square of equal brightness 10 inches from the infants' eyes. The finest pattern consistently preferred to gray showed how narrow a stripe the infant could perceive. Infants under a month old could see the 1/8-inch stripes and the six-month-olds could see 1/64-inch stripes.

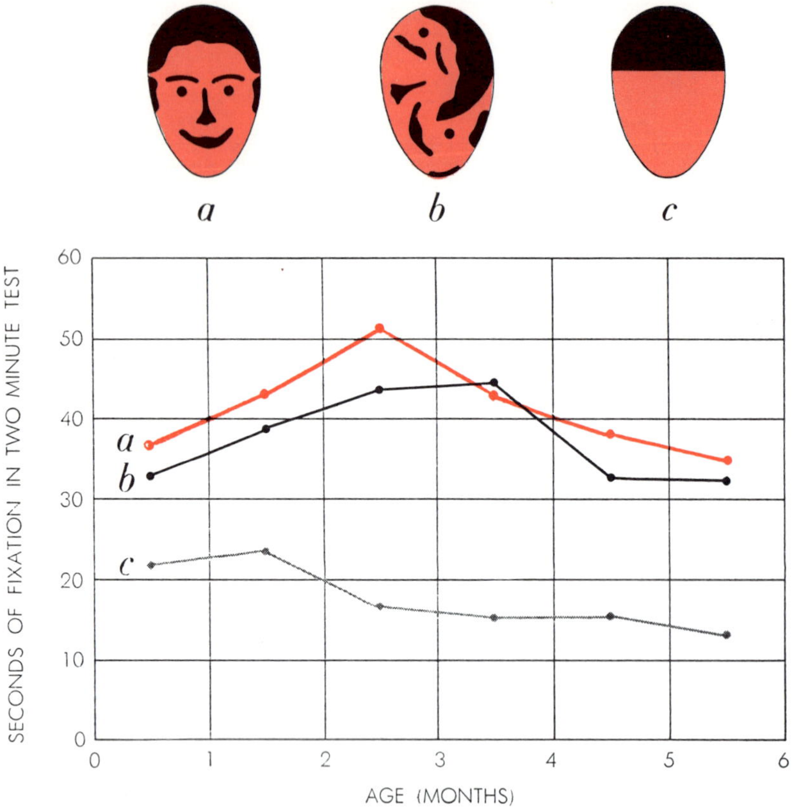

ADAPTIVE SIGNIFICANCE of form perception was indicated by the preference that infants showed for a "real" face (*a*) over a scrambled face (*b*), and for both over a control (*c*). The results charted here show the average time scores for infants at various ages when presented with the three face-shaped objects paired in all the possible combinations.

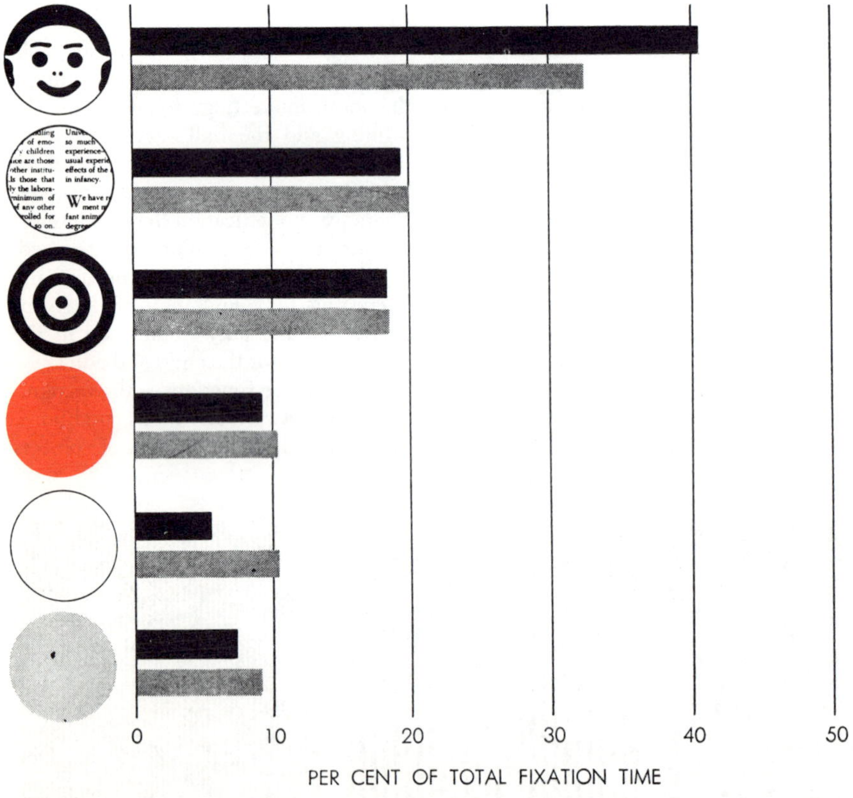

IMPORTANCE OF PATTERN rather than color or brightness was illustrated by the response of infants to a face, a piece of printed matter, a bull's-eye and plain red, white and yellow disks. Even the youngest infants preferred patterns. Black bars show the results for infants from two to three months old; gray bars, for infants more than three months old.

change with illumination; apparent size changes with distance; outline changes with point of view; binocular depth perception is helpful only at short range. But the pattern of an object—the texture, the arrangement of details, the complexity of contours—can be relied on for identification under diverse conditions.

A good example is social perception. As noted earlier, the general configuration of a face identifies a human being to an infant. At a later age a specific person is recognized primarily by more precise perception of facial pattern. Still later, subtle details of facial expression tell the child whether a person is happy or sad, pleased or displeased, friendly or unfriendly.

Another important function of vision is to provide orientation in space. For this purpose James J. Gibson of Cornell University has shown clearly the importance of a specific type of pattern: surface texture. For example, texture indicates a solid surface, whereas untextured light usually indicates air or water. Gradual changes in texture show whether a surface is vertical or horizontal or oblique, flat or curved or angular—and therefore indicate whether it can be walked on, walked around or climbed over. Discontinuities in texture mark the edges of objects and abrupt changes in surfaces.

From these few examples there can be no question of the importance of visual pattern in everyday life. It is therefore reasonable to suppose that the early interest of infants in form and pattern in general, as well as in particular kinds of pattern, play an important role in the development of behavior by focusing attention on stimuli that will later have adaptive significance.

Further research is necessary to pin down this and other implications more concretely, but the results to date do require the rejection of the view that the newborn infant or animal must start from scratch to learn to see and to organize patterned stimulation. Lowly chicks as well as lofty primates perceive and respond to form without experience if given the opportunity at the appropriate stage of development. Innate knowledge of the environment is demonstrated by the preference of newly hatched chicks for forms likely to be edible and by the interest of young infants in kinds of form that will later aid in object recognition, social responsiveness and spatial orientation. This primitive knowledge provides a foundation for the vast accumulation of knowledge through experience.

THE VISUAL CLIFF

ELEANOR J. GIBSON AND RICHARD D. WALK

April 1960

Human infants at the creeping and toddling stage are notoriously prone to falls from more or less high places. They must be kept from going over the brink by side panels on their cribs, gates on stairways and the vigilance of adults. As their muscular coordination matures they begin to avoid such accidents on their own. Common sense might suggest that the child learns to recognize falling-off places by experience—that is, by falling and hurting himself. But is experience really the teacher? Or is the ability to perceive and avoid a brink part of the child's original endowment?

Answers to these questions will throw light on the genesis of space perception in general. Height perception is a special case of distance perception: information in the light reaching the eye provides stimuli that can be utilized for the discrimination both of depth and of receding distance on the level. At what stage of development can an animal respond effectively to these stimuli? Does the onset of such response vary with animals of different species and habitats?

At Cornell University we have been investigating these problems by means of a simple experimental setup that we call a visual cliff. The cliff is a simulated one and hence makes it possible not only to control the optical and other stimuli (auditory and tactual, for instance) but also to protect the experimental subjects. It consists of a board laid across a large sheet of heavy glass which is supported a foot or more above the floor. On one side of the board a sheet of patterned material is placed flush against the undersurface of the glass, giving the glass the appearance as well as the substance of solidity. On the other side a sheet of the same material is laid upon the floor; this side of the board thus becomes the visual cliff.

We tested 36 infants ranging in age from six months to 14 months on the visual cliff. Each child was placed upon the center board, and his mother called him to her from the cliff side and the shallow side successively. All of the 27 infants who moved off the board crawled out on the shallow side at least once; only three of them crept off the brink onto the glass suspended above the pattern on the floor. Many of the infants crawled away from the mother when she called to them from the cliff side; others cried when she stood there, because they could not come to her without crossing an apparent chasm. The experiment thus demonstrated that most human infants can discriminate depth as soon as they can crawl.

The behavior of the children in this situation gave clear evidence of their dependence on vision. Often they would peer down through the glass on the deep side and then back away. Others would pat the glass with their hands, yet despite this tactual assurance of solidity would refuse to cross. It was equally clear that their perception of depth had matured more rapidly than had their locomotor abilities. Many supported themselves on the glass over the deep side as they maneuvered awkwardly on the board; some even backed out onto the glass as they started toward the mother on the shallow side. Were it not for the glass some of the children would have fallen off the board. Evidently infants should not be left close to a brink, no matter how well they may discriminate depth.

This experiment does not prove that the human infant's perception and avoidance of the cliff are innate. Such an interpretation is supported, however, by the experiments with nonhuman infants. On the visual cliff we have observed the behavior of chicks, turtles, rats, lambs, kids, pigs, kittens and dogs. These animals showed various reactions, each of which proved to be characteristic of their species. In each case the reaction is plainly related to the role of vision in the survival of the species, and the varied patterns of behavior suggest something about the role of vision in evolution.

In the chick, for example, depth perception manifests itself with special rapidity. At an age of less than 24 hours the chick can be tested on the visual cliff. It never makes a "mistake" and always hops off the board on the shallow side. Without doubt this finding is related to the fact that the chick, unlike many other young birds, must scratch for itself a few hours after it is hatched.

Kids and lambs, like chicks, can be tested on the visual cliff as soon as they can stand. The response of these animals is equally predictable. No goat or lamb ever stepped onto the glass of the deep side, even at one day of age. When one of these animals was placed upon the glass on the deep side, it displayed characteristic stereotyped behavior. It would refuse to put its feet down and would back up into a posture of defense, its front legs rigid and its hind legs limp. In this state of immobility it could be pushed forward across the glass until its head and field of vision crossed the edge of the surrounding solid surface, whereupon it would relax and spring forward upon the surface.

At the Cornell Behavior Farm a group of experimenters has carried these experiments with kids and goats a step further. They fixed the patterned material to a sheet of plywood and were thus able to adjust the "depth" of the deep side. With the pattern held immediately beneath the glass, the animal would move about the glass freely. With the optical floor dropped more than a foot below the glass, the animal would immediately freeze into its defensive posture. Despite repeated experience of the tactual solidity of the glass, the animals never learned to function without optical support. Their sense of security or danger continued to depend upon the visual cues that give them their perception of depth.

The rat, in contrast, does not depend predominantly upon visual cues. Its nocturnal habits lead it to seek food largely by smell, when moving about in the dark, it responds to tactual cues from the stiff whiskers (vibrissae) on its snout. Hooded rats tested on the visual cliff show little preference for the shallow side so long as they can feel the glass with their vibrissae. Placed upon the

KITTEN'S DEPTH PERCEPTION **also manifests itself at an early age. Though the animal displays no alarm on the shallow side (*top*), it "freezes" when placed on the glass over the deep side (*bottom*); in some cases it will crawl aimlessly backward in a circle.**

glass over the deep side, they move about normally. But when we raise the center board several inches, so that the glass is out of reach of their whiskers, they evince good visual depth-discrimination: 95 to 100 per cent of them descend on the shallow side.

Cats, like rats, are nocturnal animals, sensitive to tactual cues from their vibrissae. But the cat, as a predator, must rely more strongly on its sight. Kittens proved to have excellent depth-discrimination. At four weeks—about the earliest age that a kitten can move about with any facility—they invariably choose the shallow side of the cliff. On the glass over the deep side, they either freeze or circle aimlessly backward until they reach the center board [*see illustrations on opposite page*].

The animals that showed the poorest performance in our series were the turtles. The late Robert M. Yerkes of Harvard University found in 1904 that aquatic turtles have somewhat poorer depth-discrimination than land turtles. On the visual cliff one might expect an aquatic turtle to respond to the reflections from the glass as it might to water and so prefer the deep side. They showed no such preference: 76 per cent of the aquatic turtles crawled off the board on the shallow side. The relatively large minority that choose the deep side suggests either that this turtle has poorer depth-discrimination than other animals, or that its natural habitat gives it less occasion to "fear" a fall.

All of these observations square with what is known about the life history and ecological niche of each of the animals tested. The survival of a species requires that its members develop discrimination of depth by the time they take up independent locomotion, whether at one day (the chick and the goat), three to four weeks (the rat and the cat) or six to 10 months (the human infant). That such a vital capacity does not depend on possibly fatal accidents of learning in the lives of individuals is consistent with evolutionary theory.

To make sure that no hidden bias was concealed in the design of the visual cliff we conducted a number of control experiments. In one of them we eliminated reflections from the glass by lighting the patterned surfaces from below the glass (to accomplish this we dropped the pattern below the glass on both sides, but more on one side than on the other). The animals—hooded rats—still consistently chose the shallow side. As a test of the role of the patterned surface we

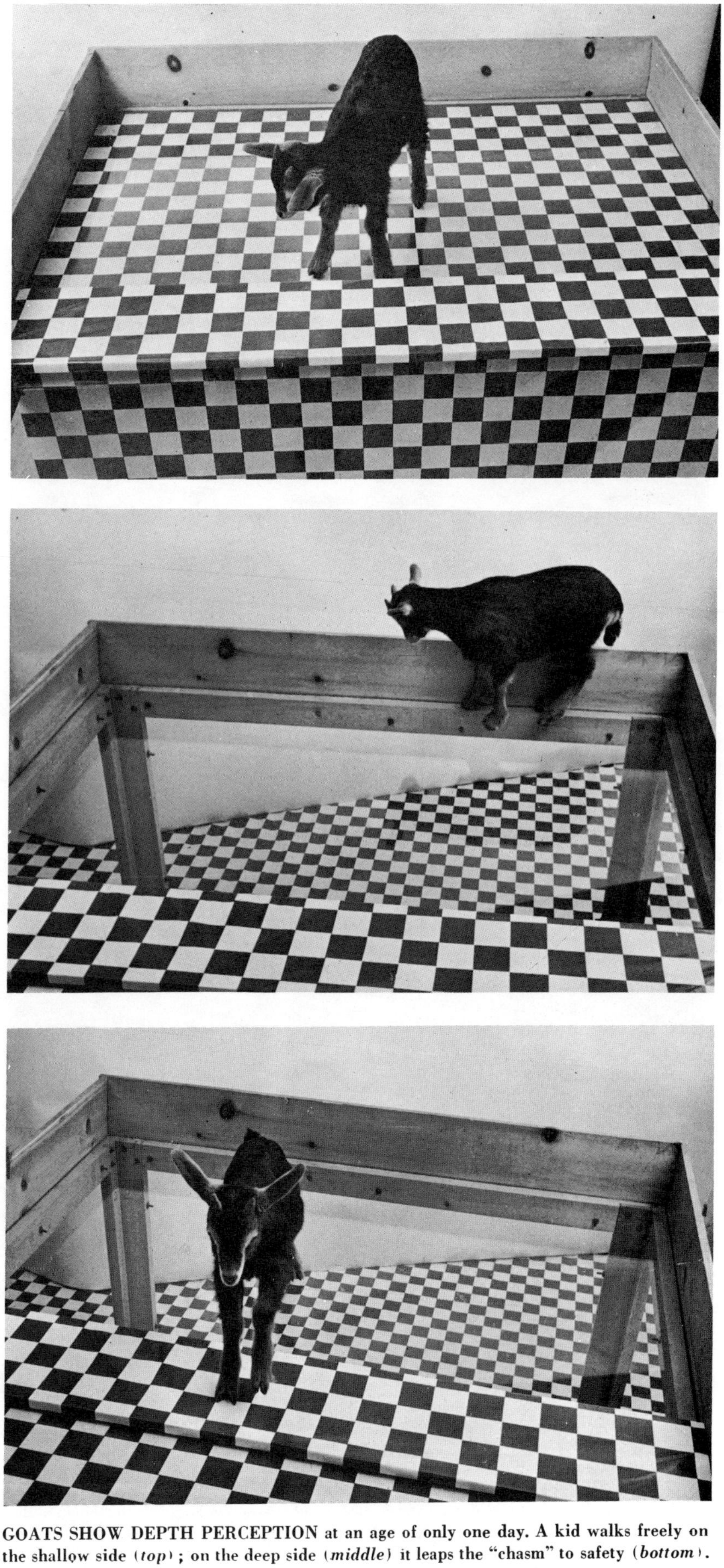

GOATS SHOW DEPTH PERCEPTION at an age of only one day. A kid walks freely on the shallow side (*top*); on the deep side (*middle*) it leaps the "chasm" to safety (*bottom*).

CHILD'S DEPTH PERCEPTION is tested on the visual cliff. The apparatus consists of a board laid across a sheet of heavy glass, with a patterned material directly beneath the glass on one side and several feet below it on the other. Placed on the center board (*top left*), the child crawls to its mother across the "shallow" side (*top right*). Called from the "deep" side, he pats the glass (*bottom left*), but despite this tactual evidence that the "cliff" is in fact a solid surface he refuses to cross over to the mother (*bottom right*).

replaced it on either side of the centerboard with a homogeneous gray surface. Confronted with this choice, the rats showed no preference for either the shallow or the deep side. We also eliminated the optical difference between the two sides of the board by placing the patterned surface directly against the undersurface of the glass on each side. The rats then descended without preference to either side. When we lowered the pattern 10 inches below the glass on each side, they stayed on the board.

We set out next to determine which of two visual cues plays the decisive role in depth perception. To an eye above the center board the optical pattern on the two sides differs in at least two important respects. On the deep side distance decreases the size and spacing of the pattern elements projected on the retina. "Motion parallax," on the other hand, causes the pattern elements on the shallow side to move more rapidly across the field of vision when the animal moves its position on the board or moves its head, just as nearby objects seen from a moving car appear to pass by more quickly than distant ones [*see illustration on following page*]. To eliminate the potential distance cue provided by pattern density we increased the size and spacing of the pattern elements on the deep side in proportion to its distance from the eye [*see top illustration at right*]. With only the cue of motion parallax to guide them, adult rats still preferred the shallow side, though not so strongly as in the standard experiment. Infant rats chose the shallow side nearly 100 per cent of the time under both conditions, as did day-old chicks. Evidently both species can discriminate depth by differential motion alone, with no aid from texture density and probably little help from other cues. The perception of distance by binocular parallax, which doubtless plays an important part in human behavior, would not seem to have a significant role, for example, in the depth perception of chicks and rats.

To eliminate the cue of motion parallax we placed the patterned material directly against the glass on either side of the board but used smaller and more densely spaced pattern-elements on the cliff side. Both young and adult hooded rats preferred the side with the larger pattern, which evidently "signified" a nearer surface. Day-old chicks, however, showed no preference for the larger pattern. It may be that learning plays some part in the preference exhibited by the rats, since the young rats were tested at a somewhat older age than the chicks. This supposition is supported by the results of our experiments with animals reared in the dark.

The effects of early experience and of such deprivations as dark-rearing represent important clues to the relative roles of maturation and learning in animal behavior. The first experiments along this line were performed by K. S. Lashley and James T. Russell at the University of Chicago in 1934. They tested light-reared and dark-reared rats on a "jumping stand" from which they induced animals to leap toward a platform placed at varying distances. Upon finding that both groups of animals jumped with a force closely correlated with distance, they concluded that depth perception in rats is innate. Other investigators have pointed out, however, that the dark-reared rats required a certain amount of "pretraining" in the light before they could be made to jump. Since the visual-cliff technique requires no pretraining, we employed it to test groups of light-reared and dark-reared hooded rats. At the age of 90 days both groups showed the same preference for the shallow side of the apparatus, confirming Lashley's and Russell's conclusion.

Recalling our findings in the young rat, we then took up the question of whether the dark-reared rats relied upon motion parallax or upon contrast in texture density to discriminate depth. When the animals were confronted with the visual cliff, cued only by motion parallax, they preferred the shallow side, as had the light-reared animals. When the

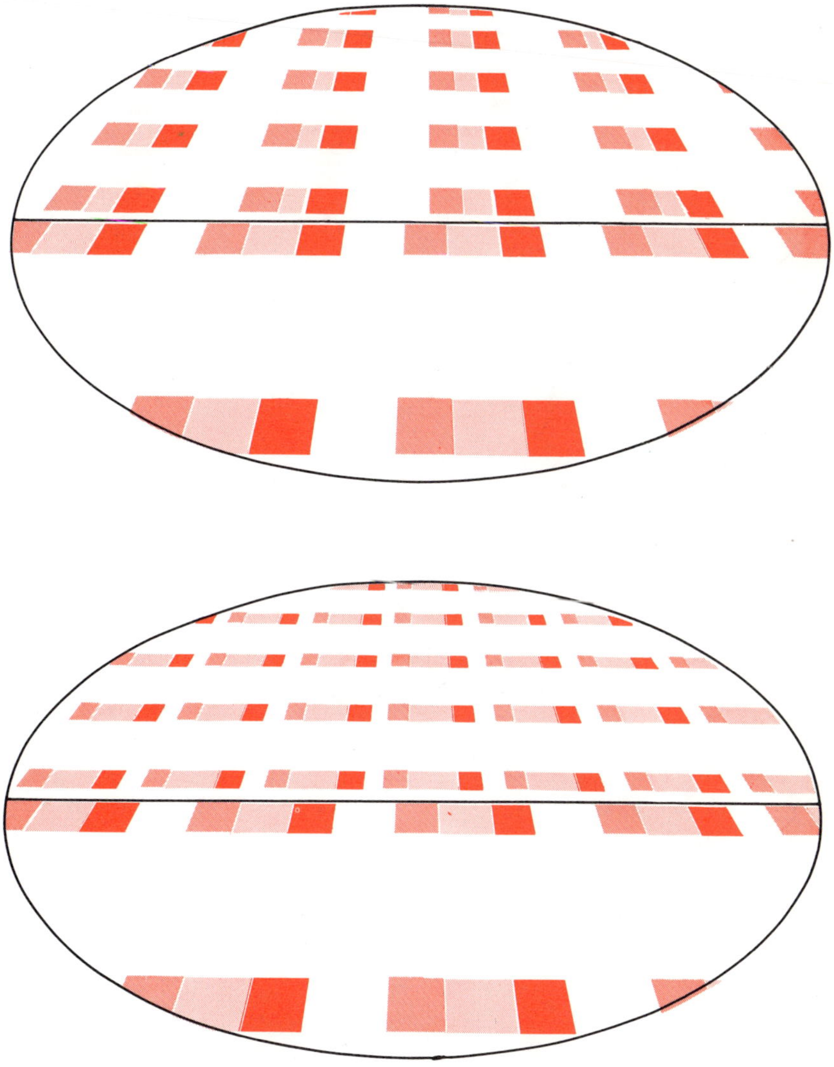

SEPARATION OF VISUAL CUES is shown in these diagrams. Pattern density is held constant (*top*) by using a larger pattern on the low side of the cliff; the drop in optical motion (motion parallax) remains. Motion parallax is equalized (*bottom*) by placing patterns at same level; the smaller pattern on one side preserves difference in spacing.

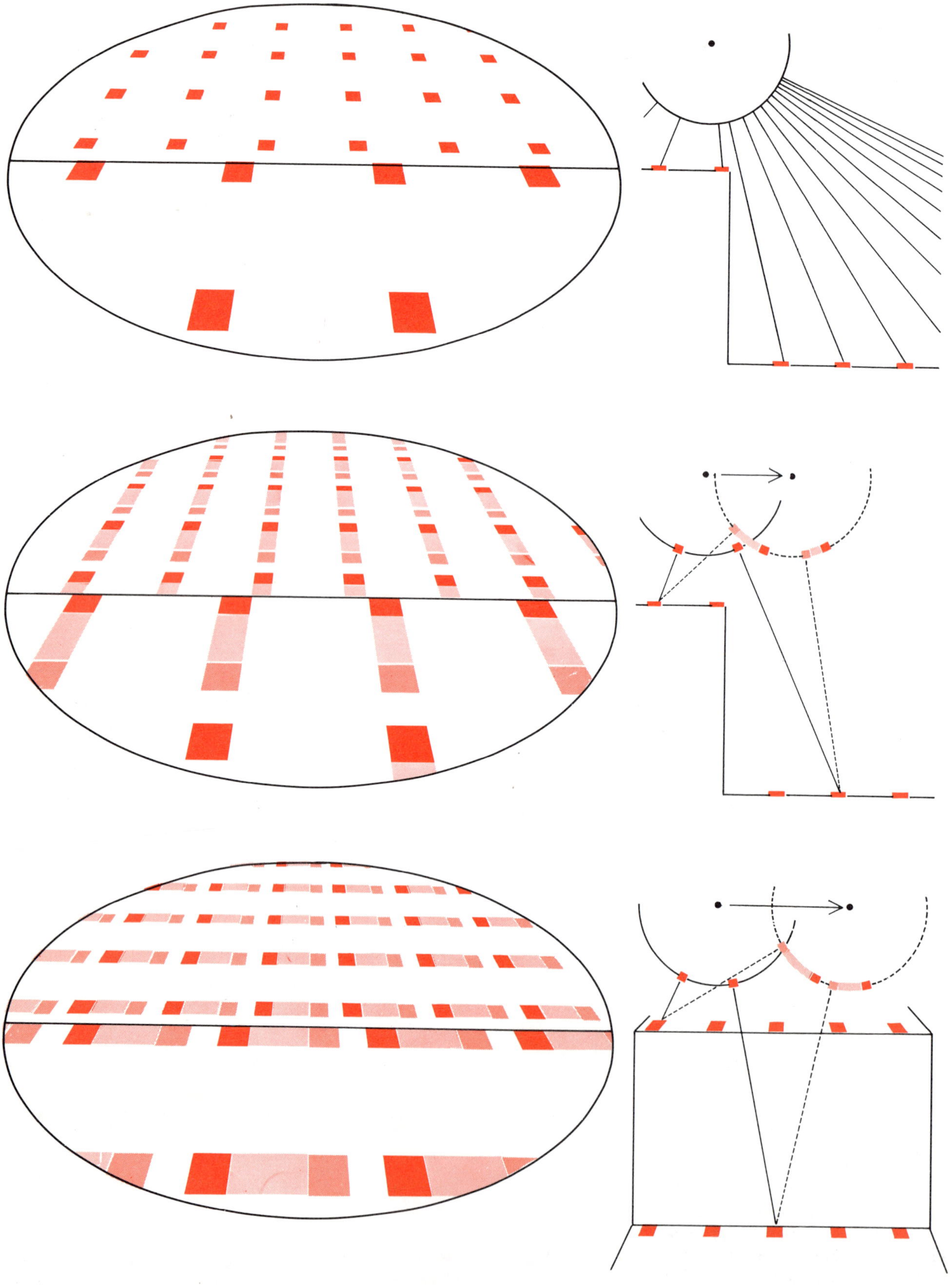

TWO TYPES OF VISUAL DEPTH-CUE are diagrammed schematically on this page. Ellipses approximate the visual field of an animal standing near the edge of the cliff and looking toward it; diagrams at right give the geometrical explanation of differences in the fields. The spacing of the pattern elements (*solid color*) decreases sharply beyond the edge of the cliff (*top*). The optical motion (*shaded color*) of the elements as the animal moves forward (*center*) or sideways (*bottom*) shows a similar drop-off.

IMPORTANCE OF PATTERN in depth perception is shown in these photographs. Of two patterns set at the same depth, normal rats almost invariably preferred the larger (*top row and bottom left*), presumably because it "signified" a nearer and therefore safer surface. Confronted with two patternless surfaces set at different depths, the animals displayed no preference (*bottom right*).

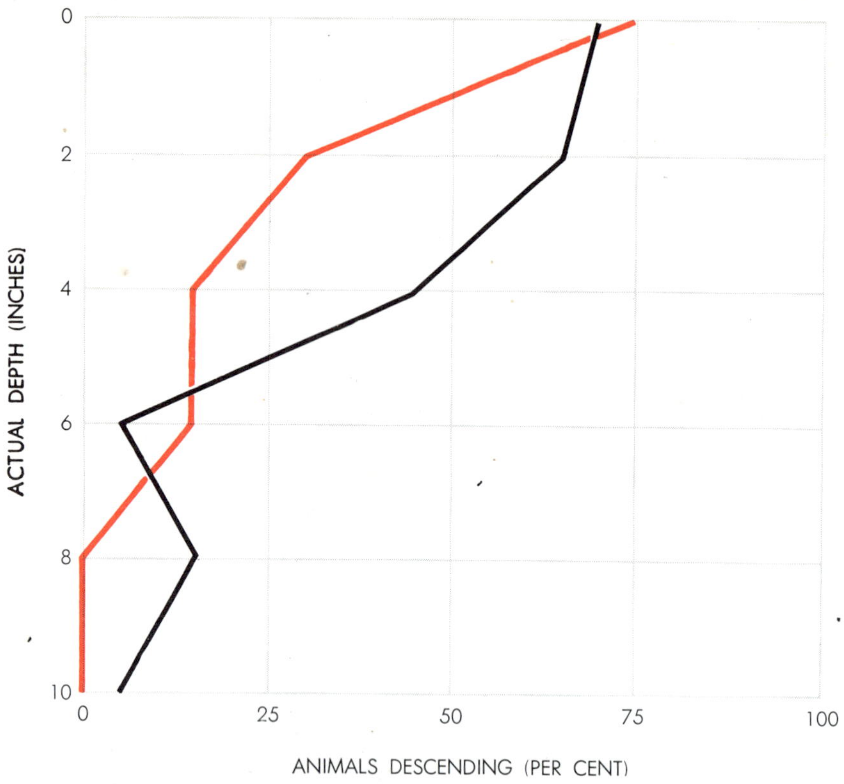

CONTROL EXPERIMENT measured the effect on rats of reflections on the glass of the apparatus. The percentage of animals leaving the center board decreased with increasing depth in much the same way, whether glass was present (*black curve*) or not (*colored curve*).

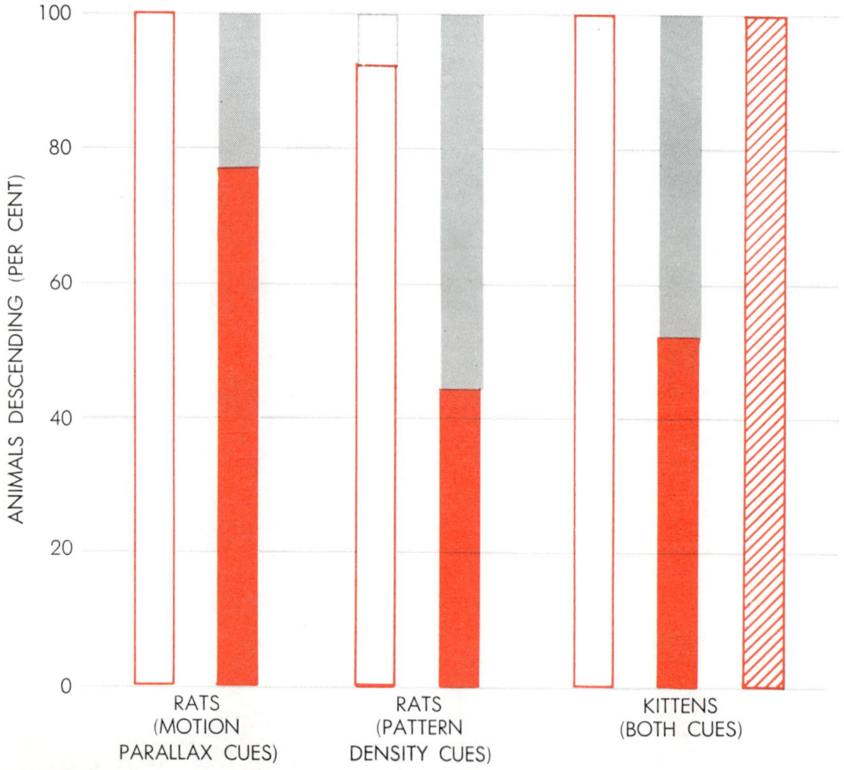

DARK-REARING EXPERIMENTS reveal the order in which different depth-cues are utilized as animals mature. Animals reared in the light (*open bars*) all strongly preferred the shallow side (*color*) to the deep side (*gray*). Dark-reared rats (*solid bars*), utilizing motion parallax alone, still preferred the shallow side; pattern density alone elicited no preference. Dark-reared kittens also showed no preference, because of temporary blindness. After seven days in the light all of them chose the shallow side (*hatched bar*).

choice was cued by pattern density, however, they departed from the pattern of the normal animals and showed no significant preference [*see bottom illustration at left*]. The behavior of dark-reared rats thus resembles that of the day-old chicks, which also lack visual experience. It seems likely, therefore, that of the two cues only motion parallax is an innate cue for depth discrimination. Responses to differential pattern-density may be learned later.

One cannot automatically extrapolate these results to other species. But experiments with dark-reared kittens indicate that in these animals, too, depth perception matures independently of trial and error learning. In the kitten, however, light is necessary for normal visual maturation. Kittens reared in the dark to the age of 27 days at first crawled or fell off the center board equally often on the deep and shallow sides. Placed upon the glass over the deep side, they did not back in a circle like normal kittens but showed the same behavior that they had exhibited on the shallow side. Other investigators have observed equivalent behavior in dark-reared kittens; they bump into obstacles, lack normal eye movement and appear to "stare" straight ahead. These difficulties pass after a few days in the light. We accordingly tested the kittens every day. By the end of a week they were performing in every respect like normal kittens. They showed the same unanimous preference for the shallow side. Placed upon the glass over the deep side, they balked and circled backward to a visually secure surface. Repeated descents to the deep side, and placement upon the glass during their "blind" period, had not taught them that the deep side was "safe." Instead they avoided it more and more consistently. The initial blindness of dark-reared kittens makes them ideal subjects for studying the maturation of depth perception. With further study it should be possible to determine which cues they respond to first and what kinds of visual experience accelerate or retard the process of maturation.

From our first few years of work with the visual cliff we are ready to venture the rather broad conclusion that a seeing animal will be able to discriminate depth when its locomotion is adequate, even when locomotion begins at birth. But many experiments remain to be done, especially on the role of different cues and on the effects of different kinds of early visual experience.

THE VISUAL WORLD OF INFANTS

T. G. R. BOWER
December 1966

What does an infant see as he gazes at the world around him—an ordered array of stable objects or a random flux of evanescent shadows? There are proponents of both answers. Some psychologists have maintained that the ability to perceive the world is as much a part of man's genetic endowment as the ability to breathe; others have contended that perception is an acquired capacity, wholly dependent on experience and learning. The nativists have argued that a baby sees about what adults see; empiricists have held that an infant's visual world must be—in William James's words—"buzzing confusion."

At the heart of the argument there is a genuine scientific question: how to account for the discrepancy between the richness of perception and the poverty of its apparent cause—the momentary retinal image. First of all, there is the problem of space perception. The world as perceived seems to have one more dimension—the dimension of depth—than the retinal image does. Then there are the spatial "constancies," the tendency of an object to retain its size regardless of changes in viewing distance (even though the size of the retinal image changes) and to retain its shape even when its orientation (and therefore its retinal image) is changed. In other words, perception seems faithful to the object rather than to its retinal image.

Most psychologists have given empiricist answers to the problems of space perception and constancy. They have assumed that the infant's perceptual world mirrors the sequence of momentary retinal images that creates it. The chaotic two-dimensional ensemble of changing shapes is slowly ordered, in this view, by various mechanisms. The retinal image contains many cues to depth; for example, far-off objects are projected lower on the retina than nearby objects (which is why they appear higher to us). Supposedly a baby learns that it must crawl or reach farther to get to such a higher image, and so comes to correlate relative height with relative distance. A similar correlation is presumably made in the case of the many other distance cues.

Once these theories have accounted for space perception they must go on to endow infants with the constancies. The oldest theory of constancy learning stems from Hermann von Helmholtz. He argued that by seeing an object at different distances and in a variety of orientations one learns the set of retinal projections that characterize it, so that on encountering a familiar retinal projection one can infer the size, shape, distance and orientation of the object producing it. According to this theory, however, there could be no constancy with an unfamiliar object. To avoid this prediction a different (but still empiricist) theory was developed from a suggestion made by the Gestalt psychologist Kurt Koffka. It assumes that a child who has acquired space perception will notice that there is a predictable relation between the distance of an image and its size, and a predictable relation between the orientation of an image and its shape. Once these relations have been inferred the child should be able to predict the size an image would have if its distance were changed and the shape it would have if its orientation were changed. The child could achieve shape constancy by predicting what shape a slanted image would have if it were rotated to lie directly across his line of sight. This means that the constancies could be attained with any object, familiar or not.

Note that this theory makes an assertion about the course of perceptual development that is also an assertion about the sequence of events in perception: Before an infant can attain size and shape constancy he must be able to register distance or orientation and projective size or shape; before an adult can compute true size or shape he must register projective size and shape and distance and orientation. There were many attempts to validate this theory of development by testing adult subjects. In a typical experiment adults were shown shapes in various orientations and asked to report true shape, projective shape and orientation. If the theory were correct, one should be able to predict a subject's true-shape judgments from the other two. This turned out to be impossible. Subjects' judgments of true shape were often far more accurate than any deduction from their judgments of projective shape and slant could have been; they often got the true shape right and, say, the orientation completely wrong. This apparent disproof of the theory was explained away by supposing the process of deduction from retinal projection and orientation to true shape had become so automatic with long practice that the premises of the deduction had become subconscious.

So-called completion effects are another puzzle created by the characteristics of the retinal image. If one object is partly occluded by another, the two-dimensional retinal image of the first object is transformed in bizarre ways. Koffka argued that when an adult looks at a book on a table, he can see the table under the book. Similarly, if one looks at a triangle with a pencil across it, one can still see that there is a triangle under the pencil. In the retinal image, of course, there is a gap in the table and a gap in the triangle. Empiricists argue that ex-

BINOCULAR PARALLAX is one of two "primary" cues to distance. Because the right and left eyes are some distance apart, each registers a somewhat different view of the same scene. In the two drawings at the left the lower, or nearer, cube is farther to the left in the right eye's view than in the left eye's view. If the two images are combined stereoscopically (with the aid of a prism to superpose one image on the other, for example), the scene acquires a third dimension. The result is simulated by the drawing at the right.

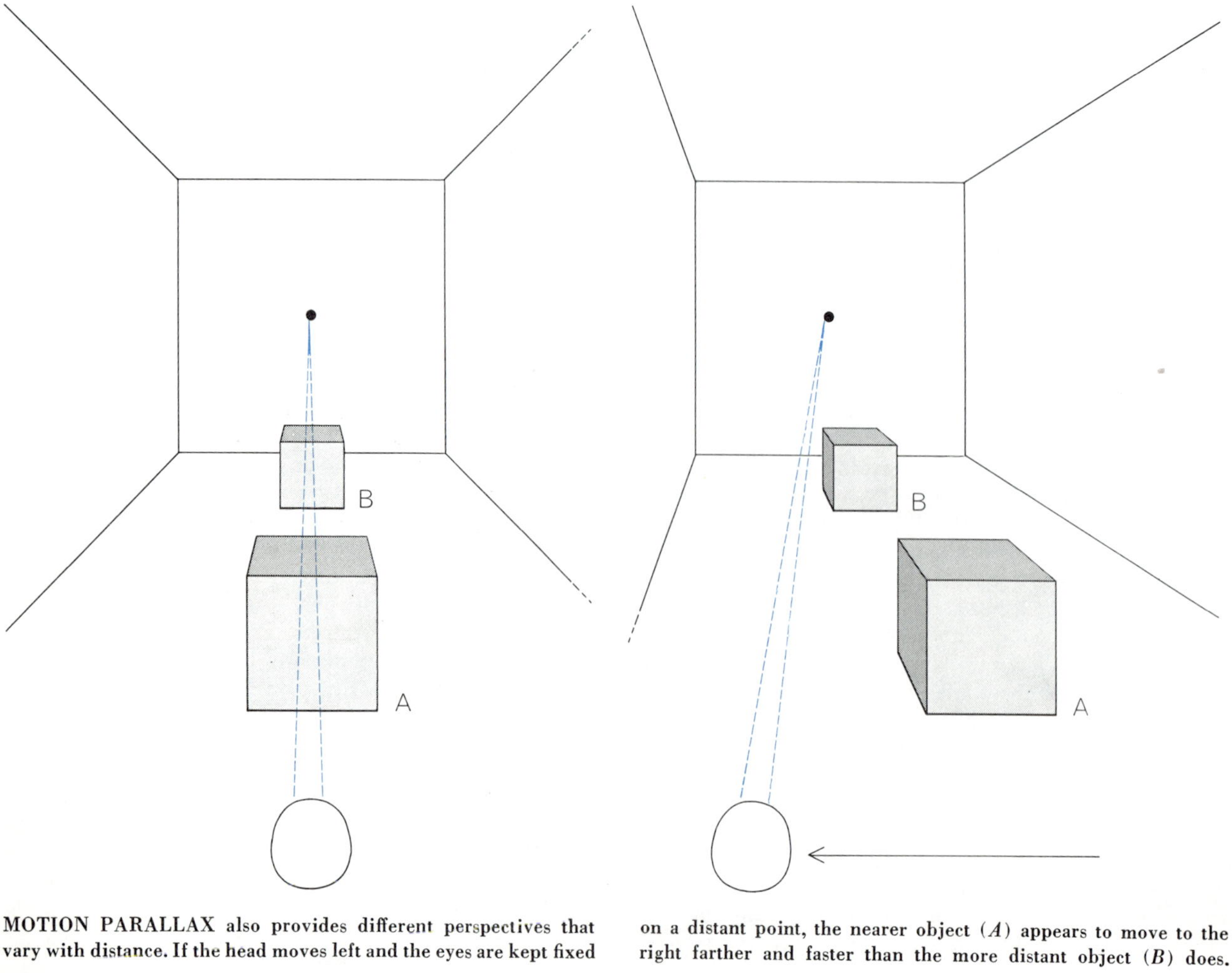

MOTION PARALLAX also provides different perspectives that vary with distance. If the head moves left and the eyes are kept fixed on a distant point, the nearer object (*A*) appears to move to the right farther and faster than the more distant object (*B*) does.

perience and learning are necessary for these retinal deficiencies to be corrected. They argue that one *learns* the shape of a triangle, after which, on seeing a partly covered triangle, one can infer what the hidden parts look like.

This short review of problems will give the reader some idea of what the perceptual world of the infant should be if empiricist theory is correct. William James's description of it as buzzing confusion is then too mild; it should be a chaotic, frightening flux in which nothing stays constant, in which sizes, shapes and edges change, disappear and reappear in a confusing flow. Yet the theories described above are at least serious attempts to handle the problems of space perception, spatial constancies and completion effects. Nativist theories in contrast make a rather poor showing. Too often a nativist theory has merely been an argument against empiricism, not an attempt at genuine explanation.

The nativism-empiricism issue has remained open largely because there have seemed to be no ways to investigate the perceptual world of infants. How is one to get an answer from an organism as helpless as a young human infant, capable of few responses of any kind and of even fewer spatially directed responses? One obvious solution is the use of the operant-conditioning methods that were devised by B. F. Skinner: one selects some response from an organism's repertory and delivers some "reinforcing" agent contingent on the occurrence of that response. If reinforcement is delivered only in the presence of a certain stimulus, the response soon occurs only in the presence of that "conditioned" stimulus. It is then possible, among other things, to introduce new stimuli to be discriminated from the conditioned stimulus. Using manipulations of this kind, one can discover a great deal about the perceptual worlds of pigeons, fishes and even worms.

For some years, first at Cornell University and more recently at Harvard University, I have been applying operant-conditioning techniques to investigate perception in human infants. The major block to applying these methods to infants had been the necessity of a reinforcing agent. The agent is ordinarily either food or water, and it is usually withheld for some time before the experiment; a pigeon working for grain is kept at 80 percent of its normal body weight. One could hardly inflict such privation on infants. Fortunately less drastic methods are available. As

OPERANT-CONDITIONING technique requires that an infant be trained to respond to the presentation of a certain stimulus. In this experiment in shape perception the stimuli are plywood rectangles and trapezoids placed at various angles to the infant's line of sight. The object is to see how well the infant can differentiate among the shapes and orientations.

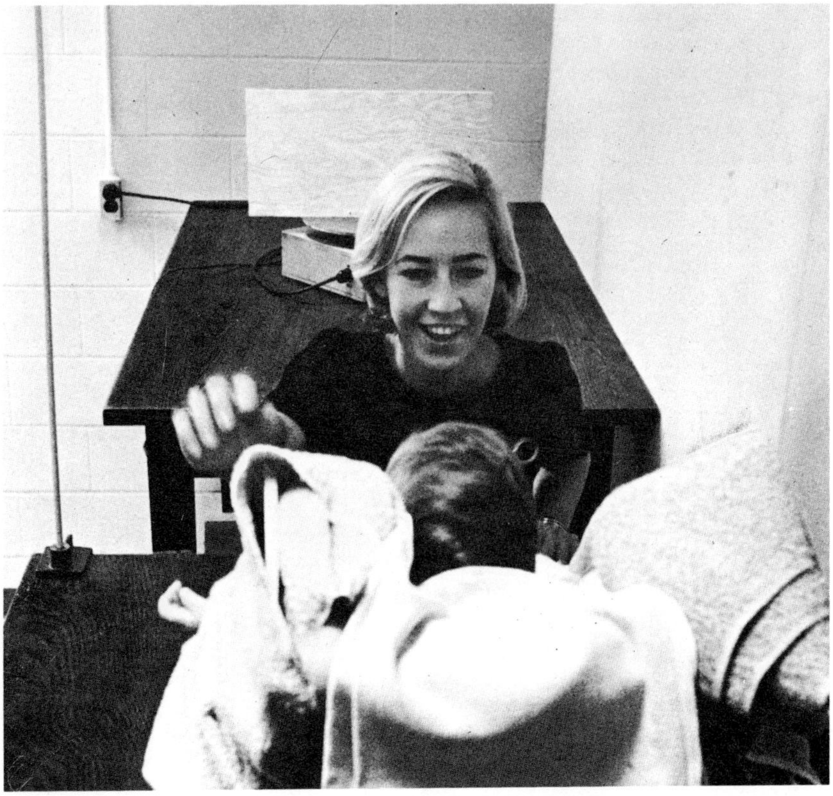

"REINFORCEMENT," part of the training program, is delivered when the infant responds correctly. The usual reinforcement in animal experiments is food or water. The author uses a "peekaboo": as shown, an experimenter pops up, cooing and smiling, then disappears.

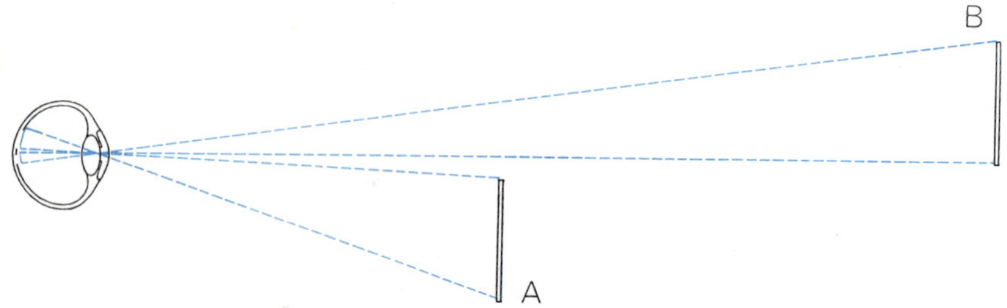

RETINAL IMAGE varies with distance. Objects *A* and *B* are the same size but *A* projects a larger image on the retina. In spite of this, adults usually see such objects as being the same size. One of the author's objectives was to see if infants too have this "size constancy."

Skinner pointed out, any change in surroundings, even the simple rustling of a newspaper, seems to reinforce an infant's responses. The reinforcement we use is a little game that adults often play with infants called "peekaboo": the adult pops out in front of the infant, smiling and nodding, and speaks to him (sometimes patting him on the tummy if he is unresponsive) and then quickly disappears from view. Infants between two and 20 weeks old seem to find this event highly reinforcing and will respond for 20 minutes at a time to make it occur. The situation can be made even more reinforcing by altering the schedule of reinforcement.

A lesser problem is deciding what response to use. Infants have few responses available; most of these require substantial effort and would quickly tire the subject of an experiment. The one used in the present investigations is a turn of the head. The infant reclines with his head between two yielding pads. By turning his head as little as half an inch to the left or right he closes a microswitch that operates a recorder. This response requires scant effort; even infants as young as two weeks old can give 400 such responses with no apparent fatigue.

The first experiment carried out with these techniques was aimed at discovering whether or not infants can perceive distance and are capable of size constancy. An infant between six and eight weeks old, too young to be capable of the spatial behavior of reaching and crawling, reclined in an infant seat on a table, with the peekabooing experimenter crouching in front of him and the stimuli beyond the experimenter. A translucent screen could be raised for rest periods and stimulus changes. The conditioned stimulus in the first experiment was a white cube 30 centimeters (12 inches) on a side, placed one meter from the infant's eyes.

After training an infant to respond only in the presence of the cube, we gradually changed the reinforcement schedule to a variable one in which every fifth response, on the average, was reinforced. After one experimental hour on this schedule we began perceptual testing by introducing three new stimuli. These were the 30-centimeter cube placed three meters away, a 90-centimeter cube placed one meter away and the same 90-centimeter cube placed three meters away. These three stimuli and the conditioned stimulus were each presented for four 30-second periods in counterbalanced order and the number of responses elicited by each stimulus was recorded. During the testing period no reinforcement was given.

On any theory, the conditioned stimulus could be expected to elicit more responses than any of the other stimuli. The stimulus eliciting the next highest number of responses should be the one that appears to the infant to be most like the conditioned stimulus. If the empiricist hypothesis that infants do not perceive distance and do not have size constancy is correct, the stimulus that should have appeared most similar was the third stimulus, the 90-centimeter cube placed three meters away; it was three times the height and width of the conditioned stimulus but also three times as far away, so that it projected a retinal image of the same size. If infants can perceive distance but still lack size constancy, stimulus 3 should still have seemed more like the conditioned stimulus than stimulus 1, the 30-centimeter cube at three meters. Both were at the same distance, but stimulus 3 projected a retinal image with the same area as the conditioned stimulus, whereas stimulus 1 projected an image with only one-ninth the area. If the infants had been unable to discriminate distance at all, stimulus 2 would have elicited as many responses as stimulus 1, since stimulus 2 projected an image with nine times the area of the conditioned stimulus and stimulus 1 projected an image one-ninth as large. If they had been sensitive to distance or its cues but had lacked size constancy, stimulus 2 would have elicited more responses than stimulus 1, since stimulus 2 was at the same distance as the conditioned stimulus. If, on the other hand, the infants had been able to perceive distance and had size constancy, stimuli 1 and 2 should have elicited about the same number of responses, since stimulus 1 differed from the conditioned stimulus in distance and stimulus 2 differed in size; stimulus 3 should have elicited the lowest number of responses, since it differed from the conditioned stimulus in both size and distance [*see illustration at left*].

To sum up the predictions, according to empiricism stimulus 3 should be as effective as or more effective than stimu-

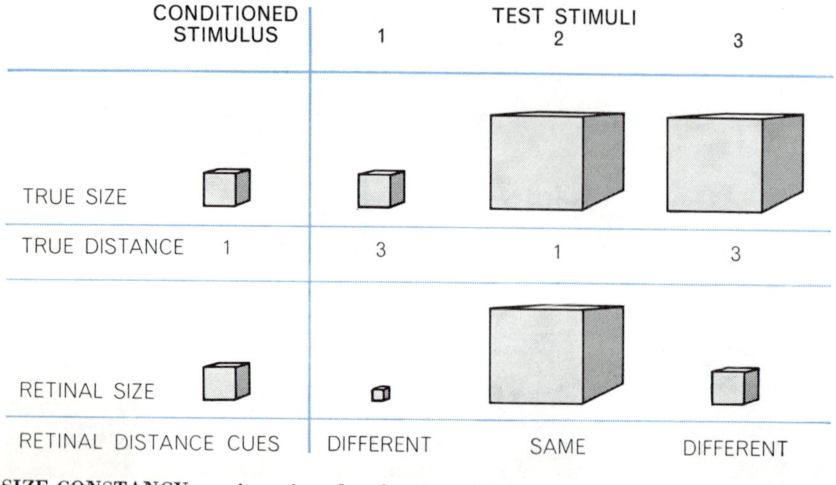

SIZE CONSTANCY was investigated with cubes of different sizes placed at different distances from the infants. The conditioned stimulus was 30 centimeters on a side and one meter away, test stimuli 30 or 90 centimeters on a side and one or three meters away. The chart shows how test stimuli were related to the conditioned stimulus in various respects.

lus 2, which should in turn get more responses than stimulus 1; if retinal distance cues are not taken into account, 3 should be clearly superior to 2. According to nativism the order should be the reverse: more responses to 1 than to 2, more to 2 than to 3. What happened was that the conditioned stimulus elicited an average of 98 responses; stimulus 1, 58 responses; stimulus 2, 54 responses, and stimulus 3, 22 responses. It therefore seems that the retinal image theory cannot be correct. These infants' responses were affected by real size and real distance, not by retinal size or by retinal distance cues.

What stimulus variables were being used by these infants to gauge depth? Two cues, binocular parallax and motion parallax, are called "primary" because they are the most reliable of all the cues. The first of these is available because a human being's eyes are set some distance apart and therefore receive slightly different views of the same scene. This binocular disparity produces an immediate impression of distance, at least in adults. Motion parallax is a similar cue: by moving one's head from side to side, one picks up a sequence of slightly differing perspectives of a scene. Moreover, near objects are displaced farther and faster than far objects. Are binocular parallax and motion parallax "primary" in a developmental sense, however? The presumptive cause of perception is the momentary retinal image of a single eye. As soon as two eyes are introduced for binocular parallax there arises the problem of integrating the two images; as soon as a sequence of images is brought in for motion parallax there is the question of how the visual system integrates multiple images spread out over time. Since these presumably complex integration processes must come into play before the two kinds of parallax can acquire spatial meaning, it is little wonder that these variables have seemed poor candidates for development early in infancy. This drawback does not apply to the host of pictorial cues that are implicit in the momentary retinal image of a single eye. These are the cues—shading, perspective, texture and so on—a painter exploits to produce the illusion of depth on a canvas without benefit of the parallaxes. It has seemed possible that these cues are recognized early in development as having differential value and so become endowed early with spatial meaning.

To discover which cues should be called primary, we tested three new

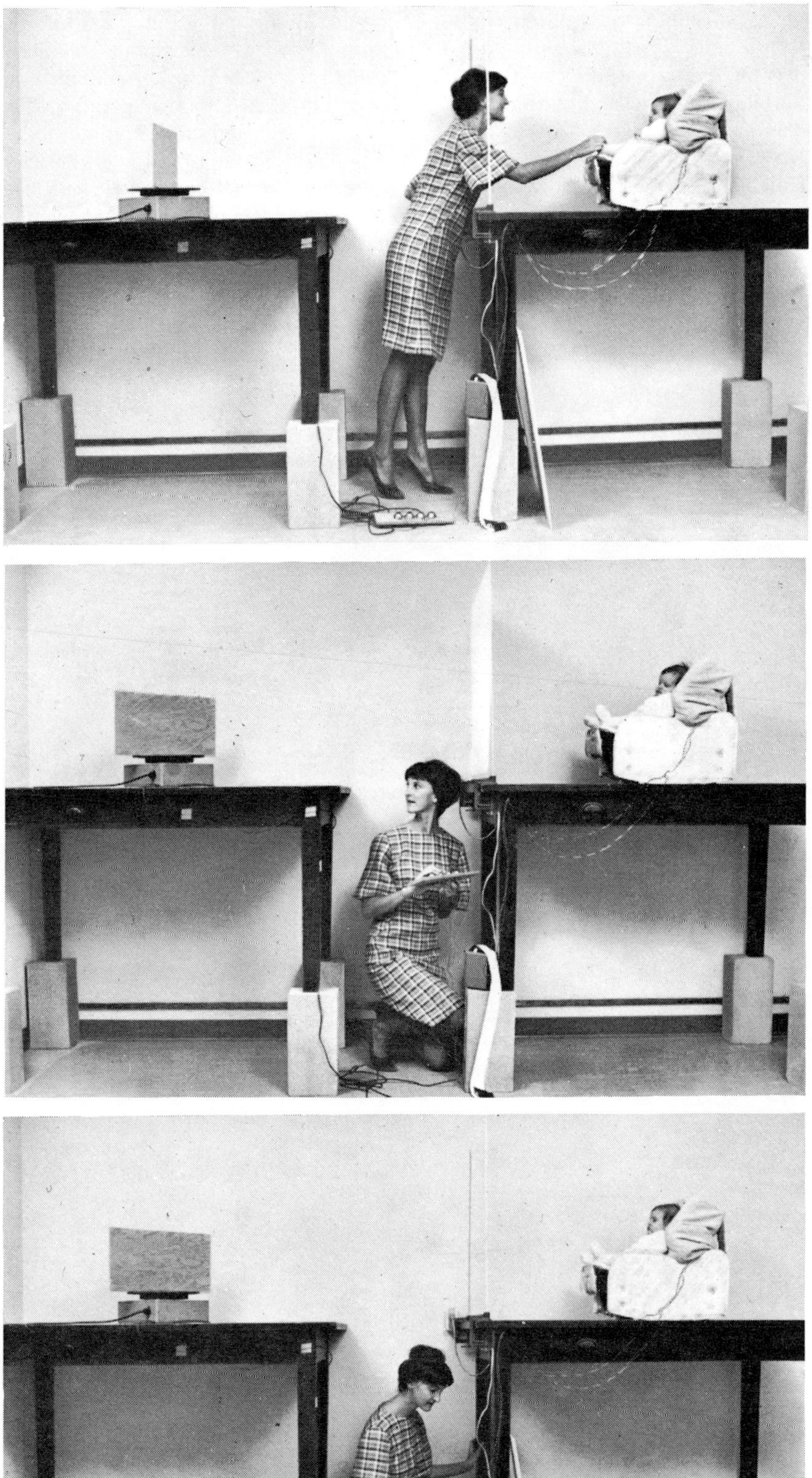

EXPERIMENTAL PROCEDURE begins with conditioning. The infant is trained to respond to a rectangle seen in a certain orientation and the response is reinforced by a "peekaboo" (*top*). Then a screen is interposed between the infant and the stimulus area while the experimenter changes the orientation (*center*). With the screen removed, the experimenter watches a recorder to see whether or not the infant responds to the test stimulus (*bottom*).

groups of infants on the size-constancy test. Infants in one group wore a patch over one eye so that they could not register binocular parallax but could register only motion parallax and pictorial cues. A second group viewed, instead of the real cubes, projected slides that were rich in pictorial cues but lacked both binocular and motion parallax entirely. A third group of infants wore specially constructed stereoscopic goggles and viewed projected stereograms of the various scenes; their presentation contained binocular parallax and pictorial cues but lacked motion parallax. The results were interesting. The monocular group performed just as the unrestricted group of the first experiment had. The conditioned stimulus elicited an average of 101 responses; stimulus 1 (the same cube farther away), 60 responses; stimulus 2 (the large cube at the distance of the conditioned stimulus), an average of 53 responses; stimulus 3 (the large cube set to be projectively equivalent to the conditioned stimulus), only 22 responses. The infants who viewed the slides performed quite differently: they produced 94 responses to the conditioned stimulus, 52 to stimulus 1, 44 to stimulus 2 and 96 to stimulus 3. Their behavior suggested that their responses were determined solely by the projective size of the cubes

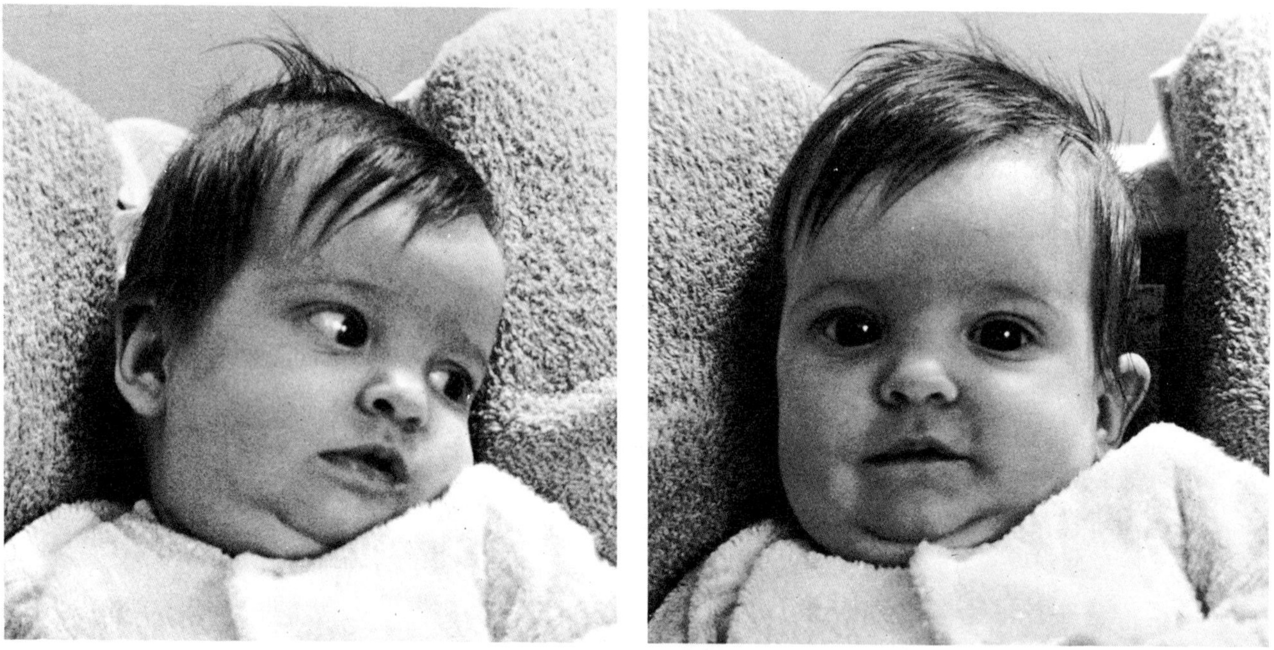

RESPONSE in these experiments was a head-turning motion that operated a switch in the cushions at the infant's head. At first the infants gave exaggerated responses (*left*); later they responded more economically, keeping their eyes on the stimulus (*right*).

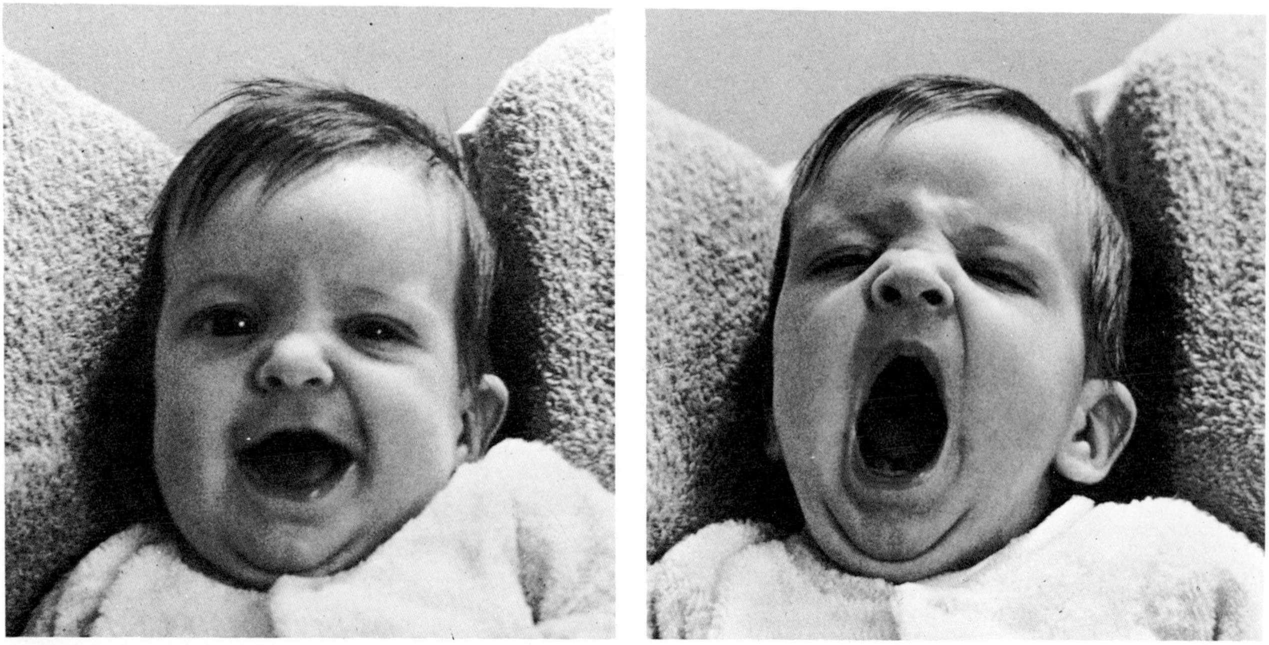

PLEASURE at the peekaboo reinforcement was manifest (*left*), and was sufficient to keep infants responding up to 20 minutes between reinforcements. The problem in experiments with infants is boredom; after a while even the peekaboo loses its charm (*right*).

in the various presentations; the pictorial distance cues in the slides were obviously not even being detected (or stimulus 3 could not have elicited as many responses as the conditioned stimulus), much less serving as cues to distance and size constancy. The infants in the stereogram group were different again. Their responses suggested some size constancy but less than the responses of either the unrestricted infants or the monocular group did. The values were: conditioned stimulus, 94 responses; stimulus 1, 44 responses; stimulus 2, 40 responses, and stimulus 3, 32 responses. It therefore appeared that motion parallax was the most effective cue to depth, followed by binocular parallax. The static pictorial cues in the retinal image seemed to be of no value.

A second set of experiments was carried out to investigate shape constancy and slant perception. The subjects were infants between 50 and 60 days old. The conditioned stimulus in this investigation was a wooden rectangle 25 by 50 centimeters (about 10 by 20 inches) placed two meters away and turned 45 degrees from the "frontoparallel plane," a plane at a right angle to their line of sight. The test stimuli were (1) the same rectangle placed in the infant's parallel plane, or at a right angle to the line of sight; (2) a trapezoid, placed in the parallel plane, that projected a retinal image of the same shape as the rectangle in the 45-degree position, and (3) this same trapezoid placed in the 45-degree position. The three test stimuli differed from the conditioned stimulus as shown in the bottom illustration on this page.

If infants are capable of shape constancy, stimulus 1 should be more effective than stimulus 3, which should be about the same as stimulus 2. If they are controlled by retinal shape only, on the other hand, stimulus 2 should get more responses than 3 or 1. The results were that the conditioned stimulus elicited an average of 51 responses; stimulus 1, the same rectangle in a different orientation, elicited 45.13 responses; stimulus 2, which projected the same retinal image as the conditioned stimulus, elicited only 28.50 responses, and stimulus 3 elicited 26 responses. There was no doubt that these infants had learned to respond to real shape, not retinal shape. Statistical analysis showed, moreover, that there was no significant difference between the number of responses elicited by the conditioned stimulus and the number elicited by test stimulus 1. It therefore appeared that the infants were responding to true shape and displaying shape constancy *without* having discriminated between different orientations of the same object.

This last result was extremely puzzling and we modified the experiment to examine it in more detail. There were three groups of infants aged 50 to 60 days, each with a different set of stimuli. One group was trained with the rectangle turned five degrees away from the parallel position. The three test stimuli were the same rectangle turned 15 degrees, 30 degrees and 45 degrees from the parallel plane. The second group of infants was trained with a trapezoid placed in the parallel plane whose shape was projectively equivalent to the rectangle in its five-degree position. The three test stimuli were trapezoids set up in the parallel position and projectively equal to the three test stimuli used for the first group. For the third group the

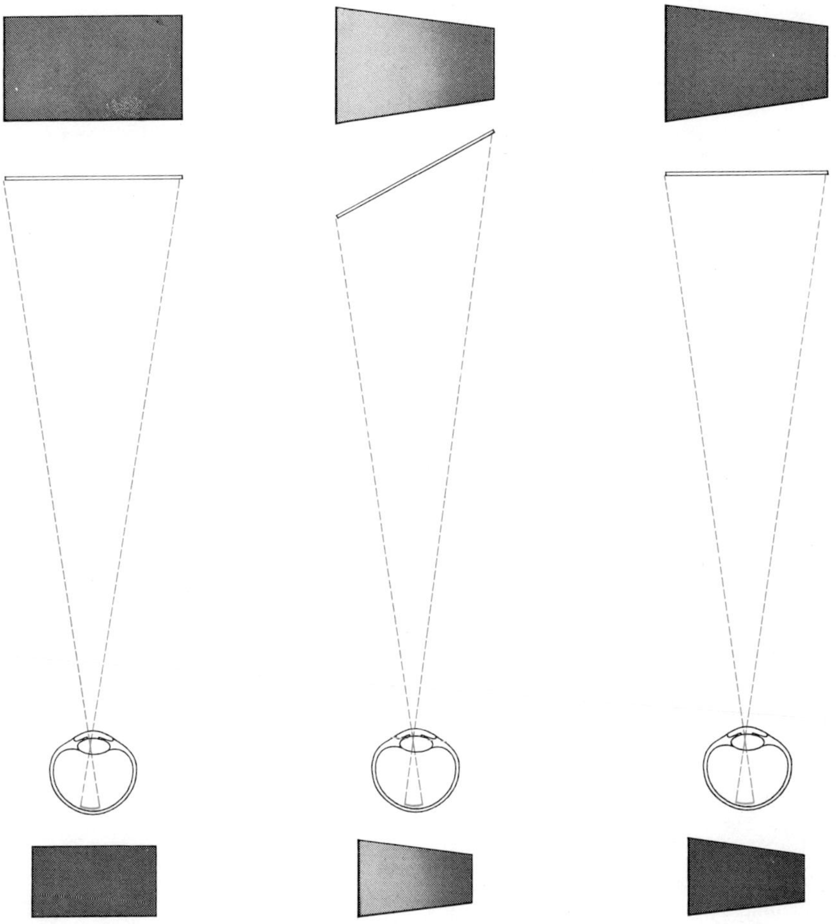

SHAPE CONSTANCY is illustrated by shapes in different orientations. A rectangle presented in the parallel plane (*left*) projects a rectangular image on the retina (*bottom*) and is seen as a rectangle. Presented at a slant, it projects a trapezoidal image (*center*), yet is usually seen as a rectangle. A trapezoid in the parallel plane projects the same shape (*right*).

STIMULUS	REAL SHAPE	ORIENTATION	RETINAL SHAPE
1	SAME	DIFFERENT	DIFFERENT
2	DIFFERENT	DIFFERENT	SAME
3	DIFFERENT	SAME	DIFFERENT

TEST STIMULI in the first shape-constancy experiment described in the text differed from the conditioned stimulus as shown. Retinal shape was expected to be the governing factor.

rectangles used for the first group were hidden by a screen with a rectangular hole cut in it so that the body of the rectangle was visible but its edges were not; the only information available on the difference between the conditioned stimulus and the test stimuli was therefore given by variations in orientation. To summarize the three viewing conditions, the stimuli viewed by group 1 varied in projective shape and orientation, with real shape constant. Those viewed by group 2 varied in real shape and projective shape, with orientation constant. Those viewed by group 3 varied in orientation only, with real shape and projective shape remaining constant.

This was a multipurpose experiment. It was intended, first of all, to discover whether or not infants can discriminate among different orientations of the same shape; hence group 1. If the answer to that question were negative, the experiment should show whether or not such infants could discriminate orientation as such; hence group 3. Moreover, a comparison of group 1 with groups 2 and 3 would bear on the idea, mentioned earlier, that spatial constancies are attained by a prediction from one retinal image in a perceived orientation to another image in another orientation. If it were true that infants see an object in space as a projective shape with an orientation, the infants in group 1 would give far fewer responses to the test stimuli than the infants in the other two groups, since the first group, viewing an object rotated in space, would have both projective shape and orientation available to differentiate test stimuli from conditioned stimulus, whereas the other two groups would have only one of these differentiating variables at their disposal.

On the contrary, the infants in group 1 showed the poorest discrimination; they responded as if the three test stimuli looked the same as the conditioned stimulus. The infants in groups 2 and 3 showed good discrimination, indicating that variations in real shape (and therefore in projective shape) can be registered by infants and that variations in orientation can also be registered. The poor discrimination shown by group 1 can only mean that real shape—which was the same in all four of the stimuli—was perceptually more salient than either orientation or projective shape. This finding seems very important, since it is a blow not only against empiricism but also against the idea (common to nativists and empiricists) that perception of simple variables is in some way developmentally earlier than perception of complex variables.

A third set of experiments was concerned with completion problems. Again the subjects were infants between 50 and 60 days old. The conditioned stimulus was a black wire triangle with a black iron bar placed across it. After training as before, four wire test stimuli were presented [*see illustration on this page*]. The complete triangle elicited an average of 42 responses. The other test stimuli elicited 18.25, 17.25 and 20 responses respectively. This can only mean that these infants saw the conditioned stimulus as a triangle with a bar over it. Since none of these infants had ever seen a triangle before the experiment, and since during the experiment it was only seen with a bar over it, the empiricist reliance on learning and experience cannot be justified. In a second experiment in which slides of these triangular objects were presented rather than the wire objects, the result was quite different: there was no preference for one test figure over any other. As in the case of space perception, the infants' performance appeared to depend not on static retinal cues but rather on the information contained in variables, such as motion parallax, that are available only to a mobile organism viewing a three-dimensional array.

Our investigation was originally directed to the nativism-empiricism controversy. The eight-week-old infants certainly were more capable of depth discrimination, orientation discrimination, size constancy, shape constancy and completion than an empiricist would have predicted. On the other hand, the babies were also less capable than a strict nativist would have predicted. They could not discriminate pictorial cues and they could not maintain shape constancy and orientation discrimination simultaneously. It cannot be stated, therefore, that the experiments have resolved the issue one way or another. Nor do they seem merely to indicate that the true position is a compromise—that there are some innate abilities and that these are

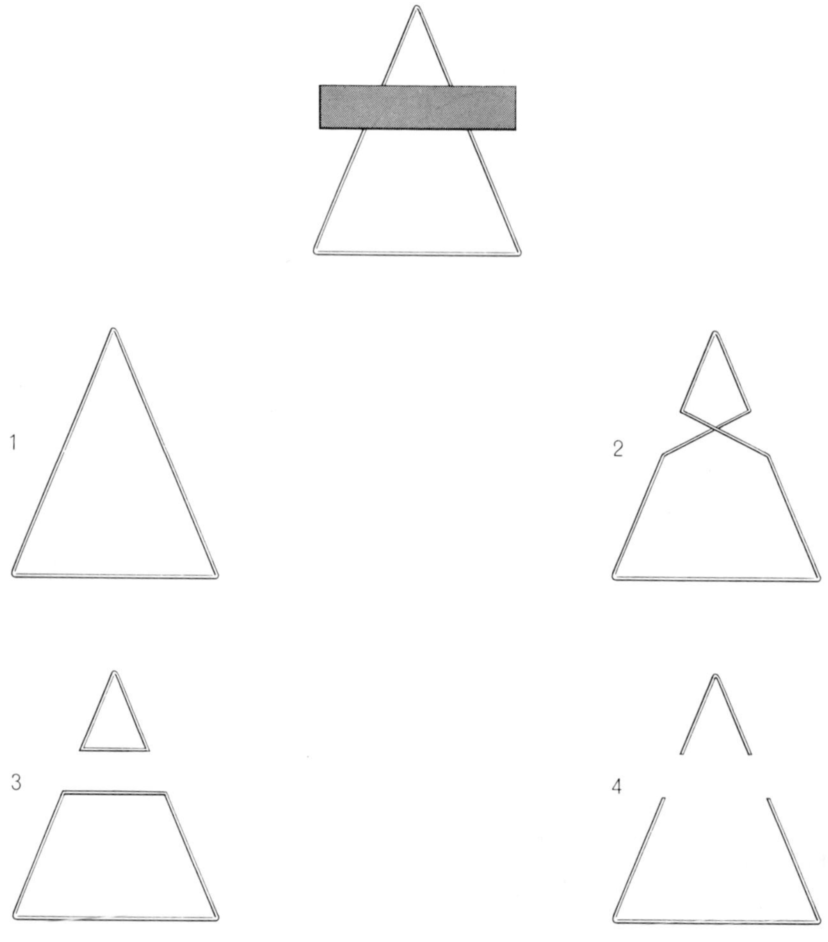

COMPLETION EXPERIMENT was conducted with these objects. The conditioned stimulus was a triangle with a bar attached to it, thus interrupting its shape. Of the test stimuli, *3* and *4* are more like the conditioned stimulus than *1* and *2* are. Actually infants seem to complete objects as adults do, as shown by the fact that *1* was the most effective stimulus.

elaborated by experience and learning. My impression is rather that these studies have added to the growing body of evidence that the whole controversy is based on false premises.

The most notable set of false premises stems from the belief that perception is caused by the momentary retinal image. What the experiments seem to show is that evolution has tuned the human perceptual system to register not the low-grade information in momentary retinal images but rather the high-fidelity information in sequences of images or in simultaneous complexes of images—the kind of information given by motion parallax and binocular parallax. The infants in these studies were obviously able to register variables containing complex information. Yet they were unable to use the information in the slide presentations of the first and third sets of experiments. This failure must surely mean that infants are not sensitive to the kind of information that can be frozen on the plane of a picture or locked into a momentary retinal image. A similar conclusion can be drawn from the fact that in none of these experiments did retinal similarity seem to make for more responses. Rather than being the most primitive kind of perceptual ability, it would seem, the ability to register the information in a retinal image may be a highly sophisticated attainment and may indeed have to be learned.

These results suggest a theory of perceptual and perceptual-motor development. It is obvious that an adult is capable of some responses these infants apparently lacked. For example, the infants in the second shape-constancy experiment seemed to be unable to register real shape and orientation simultaneously but able to register orientation in the case of a surface without limiting contours. The most plausible hypothesis is to assume that infants have a lower processing capacity than adults—that their perceptual systems can handle simultaneously only a fraction of the information they register. Infants can register the real shape of an object and they can also register its orientation. If they have limited processing capacity, however, they may be able to process only one of these variables even when both are present and are registered. This makes sense of the discrepancy between the behavior of group 1 and that of group 3 in the shape-constancy experiment. The infants of group 1 were presented with a real shape in various orientations, but they could process only the shape, which remained invariant, and so their discrimination appeared poor. Those in group 3 viewed a surface whose retinal shape stayed the same but whose orientation varied, and by choosing to process orientation and ignore retinal shape they were able to show good discrimination.

If capacity is limited, it also seems plausible that the infant perceptual system should give priority to information that has definite survival value. On this reasoning one would expect the shape of an object to have greater priority than its orientation and the orientation of a surface to have greater priority than its shape. Objects must be responded to, and their shape will often indicate the proper response, whereas surfaces are things to be landed on or used as supports, and their orientation is surely their most important attribute. One would also predict low priority for retinal shape and size, variables that are of no survival value except to a representational artist.

This evolutionarily oriented line of reasoning may also help one to understand the problem of perceptual-motor learning. The fact that infants will initially misreach has often been taken to show that they cannot perceive depth. If they can in fact perceive depth, the misreaching remains to be explained. A clue to an explanation is given by the fact that the most obvious change in an infant as he develops is a change in size. It seems likely that an infant who misreaches does so not because of poor depth perception but because he simply does not know how long his arm is. Since arm length is going to change drastically during development, it would be uneconomical—indeed, positively maladaptive—if the perceptual-motor system were geared at birth for a particular arm length.

The overall picture of perceptual development that is emerging is very different from traditional ones. It has long been assumed that perceptual development is a process of construction—that at birth infants receive through their senses fragmentary information that is elaborated and built on to produce the ordered perceptual world of the adult. The theory emerging from our studies and others not reported here is based on evidence that infants can in fact register most of the information an adult can register but can handle less of the information than adults can. Through maturation they presumably develop the requisite information-processing capacity. If this view is correct, the visual world of the infant may well be overwhelming at times, but it is probably not the meaningless buzz it has long been thought to be.

35

ARRESTED VISION

AUSTIN H. RIESEN
July 1950

MANY primitive organisms show immediate and highly uniform reactions to light from the moment of birth. In man vision is a much more complex skill that develops gradually through the years of infancy and childhood. How much of this capacity is innate and how much is acquired by learning or through the natural maturation of the eyes during the child's early years? What are the factors that determine visual perception? If we knew the answers to these questions we could do a great deal more than we can now to improve defective vision.

The task of separating the hereditary factors from the effects of experience in human vision obviously is not easy. For example, a newborn infant at first shows no clear indication of any response to a bright disk presented before its eyes. Only after several weeks does the growing infant begin to look at the disk. Is this the result of growth, of experience or of both? Does the change in response come about through practice in the use of the eyes, or through a natural maturation that occurs, quite independently of use, in the retina of the eye, in the eye or neck muscles, in fiber tracts of the central nervous system or in several of these parts combined?

Scientific studies of the growth of behavior have shown that certain abilities do develop without use as animals mature. Thus tadpoles raised under anesthesia to prevent swimming movements nevertheless improve in swimming ability. Chicks and rats kept in darkness for a time show some progress in vision-controlled behavior. Children also demonstrate a basic rate of maturation in some capacities: there is a limit to the degree of retardation or acceleration of these abilities that can be effected by restricting or expanding their training.

But some of these studies have revealed curious contradictions. Wendell Cruze at North Carolina State College found that after newly hatched chicks had been kept in darkness for five days, they were generally able to peck at and hit 24 of the first 25 grains presented to them; this score was 12 per cent better than the average of hits by chicks immediately after hatching. On the other hand, S. G. Padilla at the University of Michigan showed that if the period of darkness was extended to 14 days, the pecking response failed to appear, presumably because the instinct to peck at spots on the ground died out through disuse. The chicks began to starve in the midst of plenty. So it appears that lack of practice, at least if sufficiently prolonged, can interfere with the development of behavior which is basically instinctive or reflex in nature.

In human beings the most nearly pertinent evidence on this problem has come from studies of patients operated upon at advanced ages for congenital cata-

CHIMPANZEES WERE BLINDFOLDED when they were not kept in a darkroom (*left*). When the chimpanzees were brought into the light at the age of 16 months (*right*), they exhibited a serious retardation of vision.

racts. These patients, who have passed all their lives in near-blindness, ranging from the bare ability to tell day from night to some ability to distinguish colors and localize light, invariably report an immediate awareness of a change after a successful operation. They begin at once to distinguish differences in the parts of the visual field, although they cannot identify an object or describe its shape. After a few days' practice they can name colors. From this point on progress is slow, often highly discouraging, and some patients never get beyond the ability to distinguish brightness and color. Others, over a period of months and even years, develop the ability to identify simple geometric figures, read letters and numbers and, in rare cases, to identify complex patterns such as words, outline drawings and faces. During their efforts to improve their visual skill the patients go through a long period of picking out elements in an object and inferring the nature of the object from these elements—often erroneously. For example, a child of 12, some months after her operation, is reported by her doctor to have pointed to a picture and called it "a camel, because it has a hump." What she identified as a hump was the dorsal fin of a fish.

But such cases of congenital cataract do not give us very satisfactory evidence on the elementary problem of how disuse affects the development of visual behavior. There are too many other variables; we must take into account (1) the degree of the patient's previous blindness, since he was not in total darkness, (2) the limit that is imposed on his potentialities for improvement by the fact that the eye operated on lacks a lens, and (3) the circumstance that in all these cases there appears to be another visual handicap—jerky movements of the eyeballs known as spontaneous nystagmus. The effects of these combined difficulties are not readily calculable. For a more meaningful study it is highly desirable to eliminate these variables by setting up a controlled experiment that will determine the effects of disuse on normal eyes. Obviously such an experiment cannot be risked in human beings; no one would wish to impose permanent reading difficulties on any person having to adjust himself to a civilized society. The most logical subject for the experiment is another higher primate. The chimpanzee was chosen, because its behavior, like man's, is dominated by vision, and because it is intelligent and tractable.

In 1942 at the Yerkes Laboratories of Primate Biology in Orange Park, Fla., an infant male chimpanzee was separated from its mother on the day of birth and blindfolded with a gauze bandage and adhesive tape. This animal defeated the experimenters by loosening the tape at the side of his left nostril and habitually peeking down his nose with his left eye. By the age of 16 weeks he gained full freedom from facial bandages. Although he did not recognize his feeding bottle at this time, nor show fixation of persons or objects, he developed fairly adequate visual behavior within a few weeks.

In 1945 the experimenters tried again. This time two newborn chimpanzee infants, a male and a female respectively named Snark and Alfalfa, were housed in a completely darkened room. During the first 16 months the only light these infants experienced was an electric lamp turned on for intervals of 45 seconds several times daily for their routine care and feeding. When they were first tested for visual perception at the age of 16 months, both chimpanzees showed extreme incompetence. Their reflex responses indicated that their eyes were sensitive to light—the pupils constricted; sudden changes of illumination startled the animals; they responded to a slowly waving flashlight with jerky pursuit movements of the eyes and side to side following motions of the head. But both chimpanzees failed to show any visual responses to complex patterns of light until after they had spent many hours in illuminated surroundings. They did not respond to play objects or their feeding bottles unless these touched some part of the body. They did not blink at a threatening motion toward the face. When an object was advanced slowly toward the face, there was no reaction until the object actually touched the face, and then the animal gave a startled jump.

After the 16-month period of darkness, Alfalfa was placed on a limited light schedule until the age of 21 months and Snark until 33 months. When Alfalfa was later moved into a normal daylight environment, in the course of many months she developed normal recognition of objects, began to blink in response to threats and ceased to be startled by a touch. Snark was much more retarded. Between the ages of 20 and 27 months, while he was still on rationed light, he learned after many hundreds of trials to

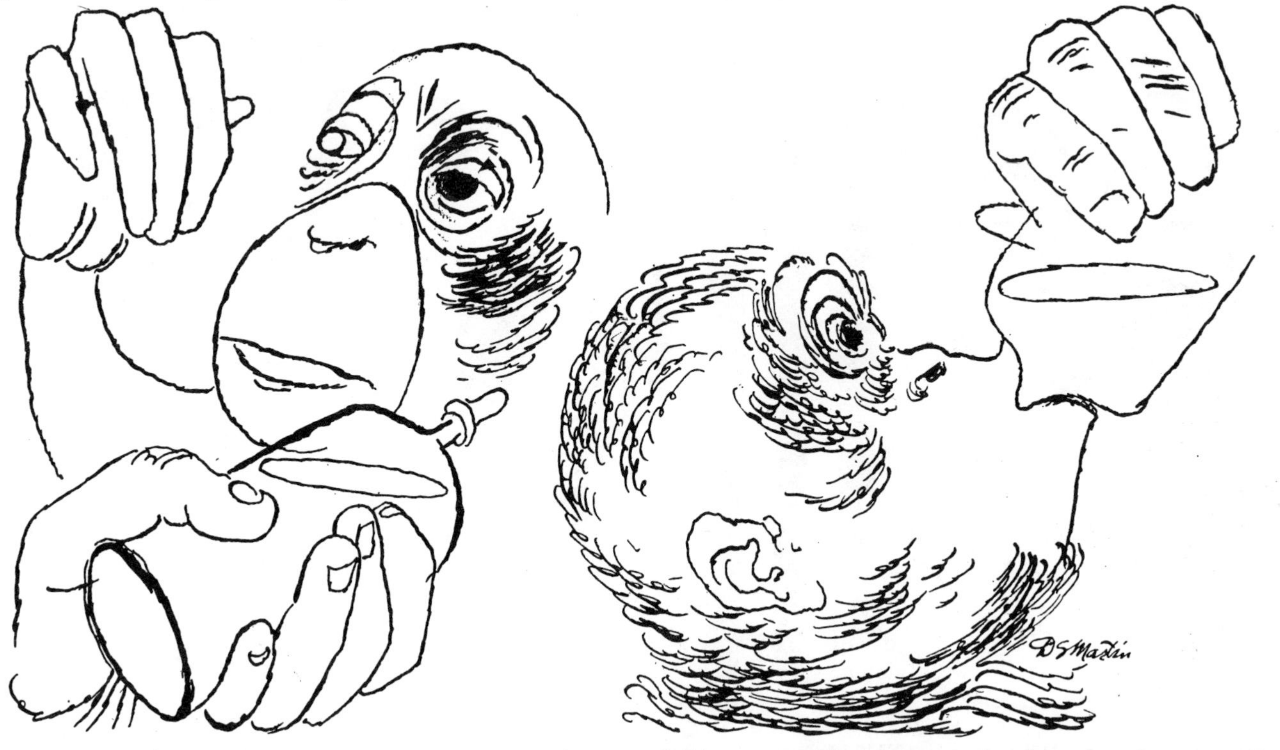

CHIMPANZEES WERE FED during tests of their visual development. Chimpanzee raised in the dark (*left*) was unable to grasp a bottle, even after several trials. Normal chimpanzee grasped it after one trial.

tell the difference between contrasting signs, differing in color or pattern, which indicated either food or a mild electric shock. His visual acuity, as measured by ability to discriminate between horizontal and vertical lines, was well below that of normally raised animals. At the end of 33 months he began to live in the normally lighted chimpanzee nursery and later out of doors with chimpanzees of his own age. It was expected that he would rapidly acquire normal visual behavior. He did improve slightly at first, but after this small initial improvement he actually lost ground in visual responsiveness, until even reflex activity began to die away.

What is the explanation of this deterioration? Had the development of his eyes been permanently arrested by the absence of light? There had been no previous evidence that stimulation by light is essential for the normal growth of the primate retina or optic nerve. It was a surprise to find that, while the eyes of these chimpanzees remained sensitive to light after 16 months in darkness, the retina and optic disk in both animals did not reflect as much light as normal chimpanzee eyes do. Snark later developed a marked pallor of the optic disk in both eyes. There is other evidence suggesting that fish and amphibians, at least, need light-stimulation for normal eye development. So the physiological effects of the lack of light may be part of the explanation for Snark's loss of visual function. But it is not the whole explanation for all the visual abnormalities in these two chimpanzees, nor does it explain the visual difficulties of the cataract patients. These patients have excellent color discrimination, and, incidentally, do not show pallor of the optic disk. Moreover, we now have clear evidence from further experiments with chimpanzees that not merely light itself but stimulation by visual patterns is essential to normal visual development.

In these experiments three other newborn chimpanzees, two females and a male, were put into the darkroom. Debi was raised for seven months in complete darkness, even during her feedings and other care. Kora was raised for the same period on a ration of an average of one and a half hours of light daily, but the light, admitted through a white Plexiglas mask, was diffuse and unpatterned. Lad was given one and a half hours of patterned light daily: he could observe the edges of his crib, the variations in pattern introduced by movements of his own body and appendages, and all the accompaniments of bottle-feeding, including the moving about of persons in the moderately lighted room.

At seven months, when the three subjects were removed to normal daylight surroundings, Lad's visual performance was indistinguishable from that of chimpanzees raised normally. Kora and Debi, however, showed the same kinds of retardation as had Snark and Alfalfa, with some minor exceptions. Kora did not develop the blink response to a moving object until six days after her removal from darkness, and Debi not until 15 days. It took Kora 13 days and Debi 30 days to acquire the ability to pursue a moving person with the eyes, and they did this by a series of refixations instead of following smoothly as normal animals of comparable age do; it took Kora 20 days and Debi 16 days to pursue visually a moving feeding bottle; Kora 13 days and Debi 30 days to fixate the image of a stationary person.

These differences between Debi and Kora may lie within the range of variation that would occur in a group of animals treated exactly the same as either Debi or Kora. This question could be checked only by repeating the experiment many times.

Between seven and 10 months of age Debi and Kora both showed a moderate and intermittent outward (wall-eyed) deviation of the eyes. This gradually was overcome. Both infants also showed an initial spontaneous nystagmus, *i.e.*, jerky eye movements. It appeared only sporadically, and was more pronounced under general excitement than when the animals were well relaxed.

Normal animals of seven months learn to avoid a large yellow and black striped disk after receiving one or two mild electric shocks from it. Debi and Kora, however, were shocked by the disk twice a day for six and nine days, respectively, before they so much as whimpered when it was shown. Only after 13 days in Kora's case and 15 days in Debi's did they consistently indicate by some sort of avoidance response that they saw the disk within five seconds of the time that it was raised in front of their eyes.

In still another study an infant chimpanzee named Kandy was put in the

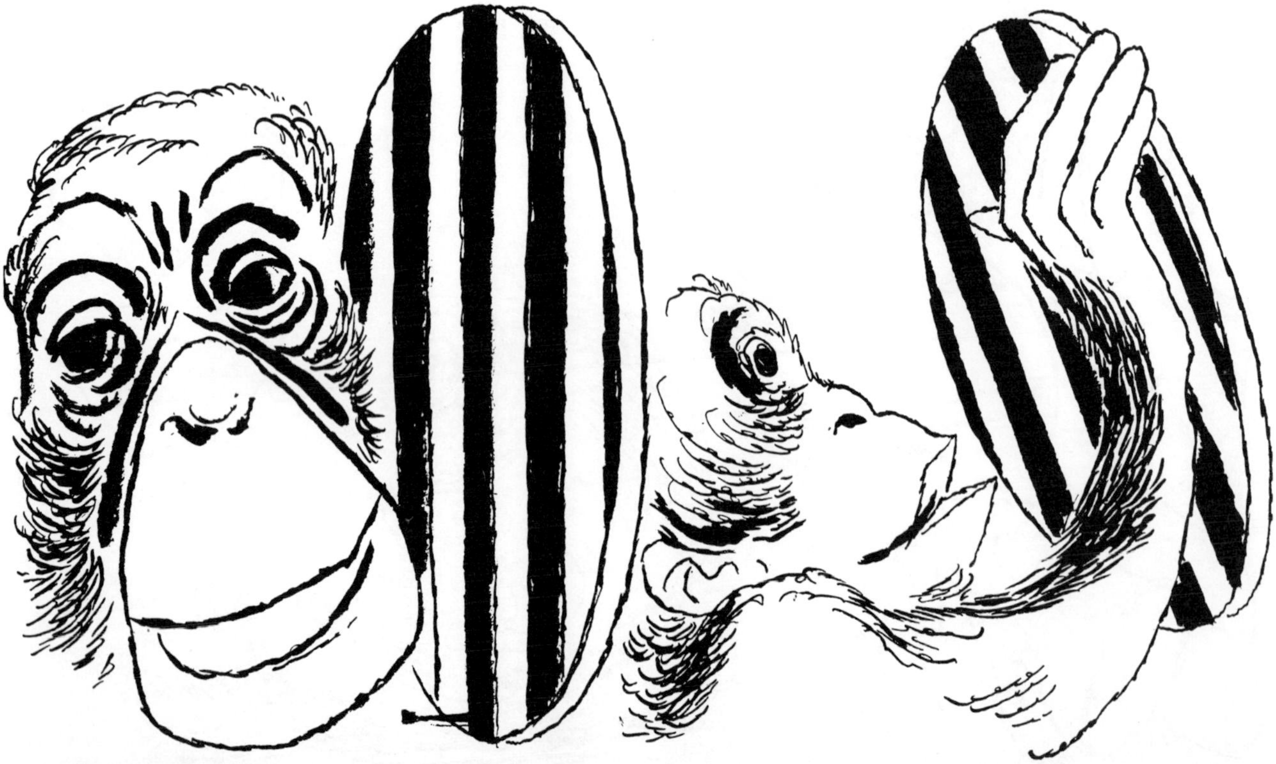

NORMAL AND ABNORMAL ANIMALS were subjected to the same stimuli. At the left an abnormal chimpanzee is given a mild electric shock by a disk with a contact at bottom. At right normal chimpanzee is shocked.

darkroom for only the first three months of life. After she was removed to daylight surroundings, her progress on the same tests was approximately parallel to that of Debi and Kora. There were three interesting differences: 1) Kandy showed a convergent squint (cross-eyes), which cleared up in a little less than two months; 2) she did not have spontaneous nystagmus; 3) she required 24 days, as compared with 13 or 15, to develop consistent avoidance of the black and yellow shock-disk. The last difference suggests that Kandy learned more slowly because of her younger age; in other words, that the development of visual discrimination was a matter of maturity as well as learning. This conclusion was strongly supported by the finding that an infant chimpanzee started through the same training at the age of two days failed to show avoidance in a month's time.

All these observations demonstrate that vision must be put to use if it is to develop normally, but they also indicate that during the first few months of an infant's life visual development is advanced by growth factors which are entirely independent of practice. Normally reared animals, for example, do not blink in response to the movement of objects across the visual field until they have reached the age of two months; the older darkroom animals, despite previous lack of experience, began to show this response within about two weeks after they were transferred to daylight surroundings.

The development and maintenance of normal visual functions in higher primates depends on a whole complex of interrelated factors, hereditary and environmental, and it can readily be disturbed at any stage of the individual's growth. This was shown in an experiment with a chimpanzee named Faik. Faik was raised in the normal light of the laboratory's nursery until the age of seven months. At that time the standard series of tests described above showed that he had excellent use of vision. Then from the age of eight to 24 months he was kept in the darkroom. He lived an active life filled with tactile, auditory, olfactory, gustatory and kinesthetic stimulation. He invited rough-house play from his caretakers at feeding times, and his general state of health remained entirely satisfactory.

When Faik was returned to daylight living quarters at 24 months, he had lost all ability to utilize vision in his interplay with the environment. He no longer recognized the feeding bottle, and failed to look at objects or persons, either stationary or moving. More than this, he possessed a strong spontaneous nystagmus and was even unable to follow a moving light in a darkroom until the fifth day after he was put back into a lighted environment. His first visual following movements, like those of all the darkroom-raised subjects, were not smooth but a series of jerky refixations, made even more jerky by the pronounced spontaneous nystagmus.

Even in direct sunlight Faik failed to grimace or close his eyelids; he gave no indication of the slightest discomfort when the sun shone in his eyes. (The chimpanzees raised in the darkroom from birth did close their lids in intense light.) Faik showed pallor similar to that of Snark and Alfalfa in his optic disks. His recovery of vision has been slow and is still only partial. Explanation of his case, and that of Snark, remains a challenge to further research.

These chimpanzee studies have established several fundamental points. They show that newborn animals, and older infants that have been kept in darkness for a time, exhibit visual reflexes when they are first subjected to light. Some responses that bear a close resemblance to reflex behavior, such as blinking at something rapidly approaching the face, become automatic only after considerable practice. Visual pursuit of moving objects, the coordination of the two eyes and convergent fixation, and the first recognition of objects come only after many hours or weeks of experience in use of the eyes. It takes the chimpanzee hundreds of hours of active utilization of the eyes to develop its vision to the stage where it can adequately guide locomotion and complex manipulations. The findings in the cases of two subjects that were kept in darkness for long periods indicate that the postponement of light exposure for too long can result in making the development of normal visual mechanisms extremely difficult if not impossible.

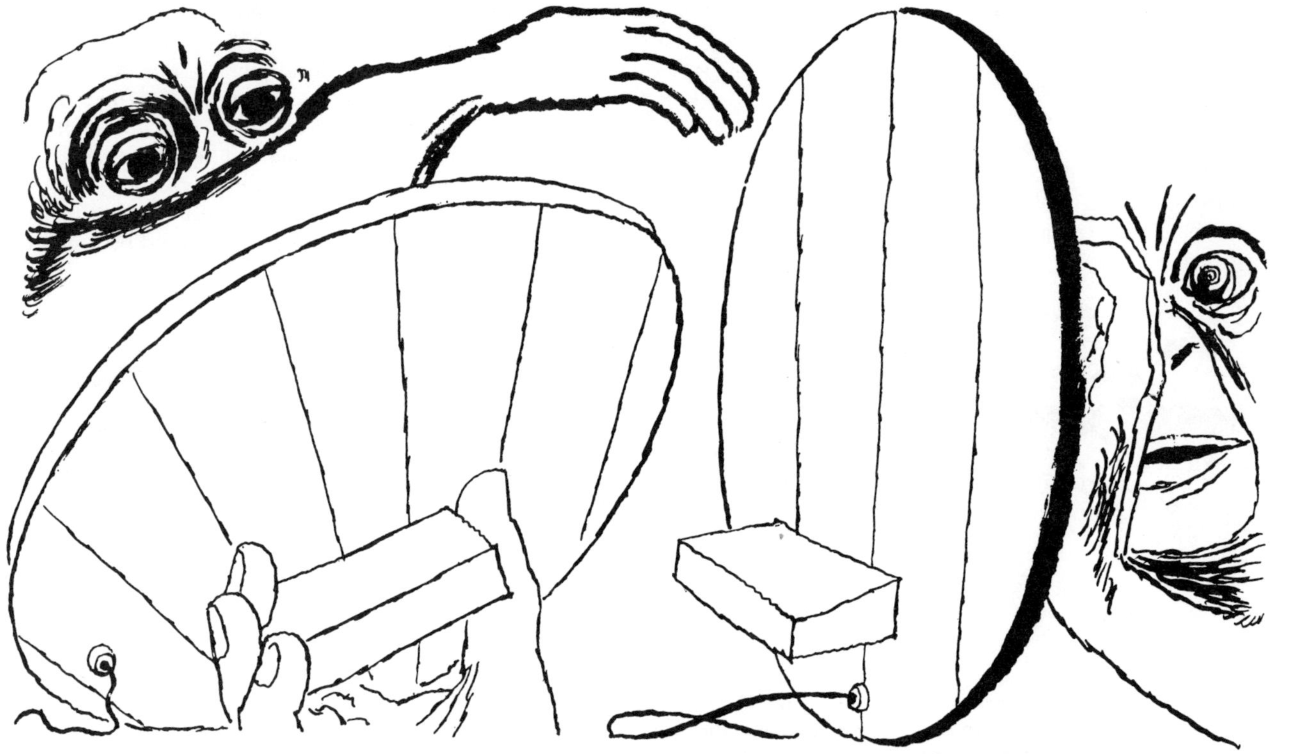

NORMAL AND ABNORMAL RESPONSE to shocking-disk was exhibited by animals. At left a normal chimpanzee responds violently after one shock. At right abnormal chimpanzee fails to avoid disk after many shocks.

36

THE EYE AND THE BRAIN

R. W. SPERRY
May 1956

Probably no question about the behavior of living things holds greater general interest than the age-old issue: Heredity versus Learning. And none perhaps is more difficult to investigate in any clear-cut way. Most behavior has elements of both inheritance and training; yet each must make a distinct contribution. The problem is to separate the contributions. We can take vision as a case in point. An animal, it is often said, must learn to see. It is born with eyes, but it matures in the use of them. The question is: Just where does its inborn seeing ability end and learning begin? To put the matter another way: Exactly what equipment and instinctive skills are we born with?

This article is an account of experiments which have given some new insight into the heredity-learning question. The behavior studied is vision, and the story begins 31 years ago.

In 1925 Robert Matthey, a zoologist of the University of Geneva, delivered to the Society of Biology in Paris an astonishing report. He had severed the optic nerve in adult newts, or salamanders, and they had later recovered their vision! New nerve fibers had sprouted from the cut stump and had managed to grow back to the visual centers of the brain. That an adult animal could regenerate the optic nerve (and even, as Matthey reported later, the retina of the eye) was surprising enough, but that it could also re-establish the complex network of nerve-fiber connections between the eye and a multitude of precisely located points in the brain seemed to border on the incredible. And yet this was the only possible explanation, for without question the newts had regained normal vision. They would stalk a moving worm separated from them by a glass wall in their aquarium; they were able to see a small object distinctly and follow its movements accurately.

A long series of confirmations of Matthey's discovery followed. He transplanted an eyeball from one newt to another, with good recovery of vision. Leon S. Stone and his co-workers at Yale University transplanted eyes successfully from one species of salamander to another, and grafted the same eye in four successive individuals in turn, each of which was able to use the eye to regain its vision. Eventually experimenters found that fishes, frogs and toads (but not mammals) also could regenerate the optic nerve and recover vision if the nerve was cut carefully without damage to the main artery to the retina.

The optic nerve of a fish has tens of thousands of fibers, most or all of which must connect with a specific part of the visual area of the brain if the image on the retina is to be projected accurately to the brain. The newt, whose retina is less fine-grained than a fish's, has fewer optic fibers, but still a great many. The system is analogous to a distributor's map with thousands of strings leading from a focal point to thousands of specific spots on the map. How can an animal whose optic fibers have all been cut near the focal point re-establish this intricate and precisely patterned system of connections? Matthey found that the regenerating fibers wound back into the

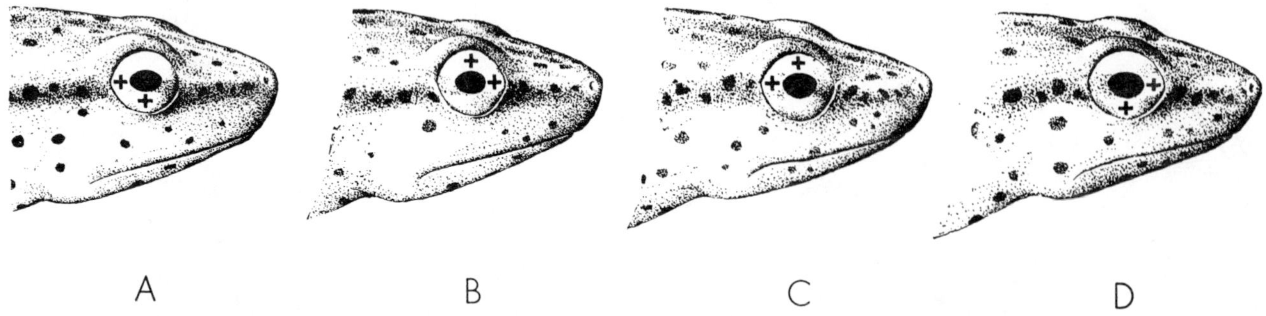

EYE OF THE NEWT was turned in various ways by the experiments described in this article. In A the normal position of the eye is marked with crosses. In B the eye has been turned so that its front-back and up-down axes are inverted. In C the eye on the opposite side of the head has been transplanted to the side shown with its up-down axis inverted. In D the eye on the opposite side of the head has been transplanted to the side shown with its front-back axis inverted. In each case the operation is done on both eyes.

brain in what looked like a hopelessly mixed up snarl. Yet somehow, from this chaos, the original orderly system of communications was restored.

Two possible explanations have been considered. The one that was long regarded as the more plausible is that the connections are formed again by some kind of learning process. According to this theory, as the cut nerve regenerates a host of new fibers, branching and crawling all over the brain, the animal learns through experience to make use of the fiber linkages that happen to be established correctly, and any worthless connections atrophy from disuse.

The second theory is that each fiber is actually specific and somehow manages to arrive at its proper destination in the brain and reform the connection. This implies some kind of affinity, presumably chemical, between each individual optic fiber and matching nerve cells in the brain's visual lobe. The idea that each of the many thousands of nerve fibers involved has a different character seemed so fantastic that it was not very widely accepted.

These were the questions we undertook to test: Does the newt relearn to see, or does its heredity, forming and organizing its regenerated fibers according to a genetic pattern, automatically restore orderly vision?

Our first experiment was to turn the eye of the newt upside down—to find out whether this rotation of the eyeball would produce upside-down vision, and if so, whether the inverted vision could be corrected by experience and training. We cut the eyeball free of the eyelids and muscles, leaving the optic nerve and main blood vessels intact, then turned the eyeball by 180 degrees. The tissues rapidly healed and the eyeball stayed fixed in the new position.

The vision of animals operated on this way was then tested. Their responses showed very clearly that their vision was reversed. When a piece of bait was held above the newt's head, it would begin digging into the pebbles and sand on the bottom of the aquarium. When the lure was presented in front of its head, it would turn around and start searching in the rear; when the bait was behind it, the animal would lunge forward. (Since its eyes are on the side of the head, a newt can see objects behind it.) As color-adapting animals, the newts with upside-down eyes even adjusted their color to the brightness above them instead of to the dark background of the aquarium bottom. Besides seeing everything up-

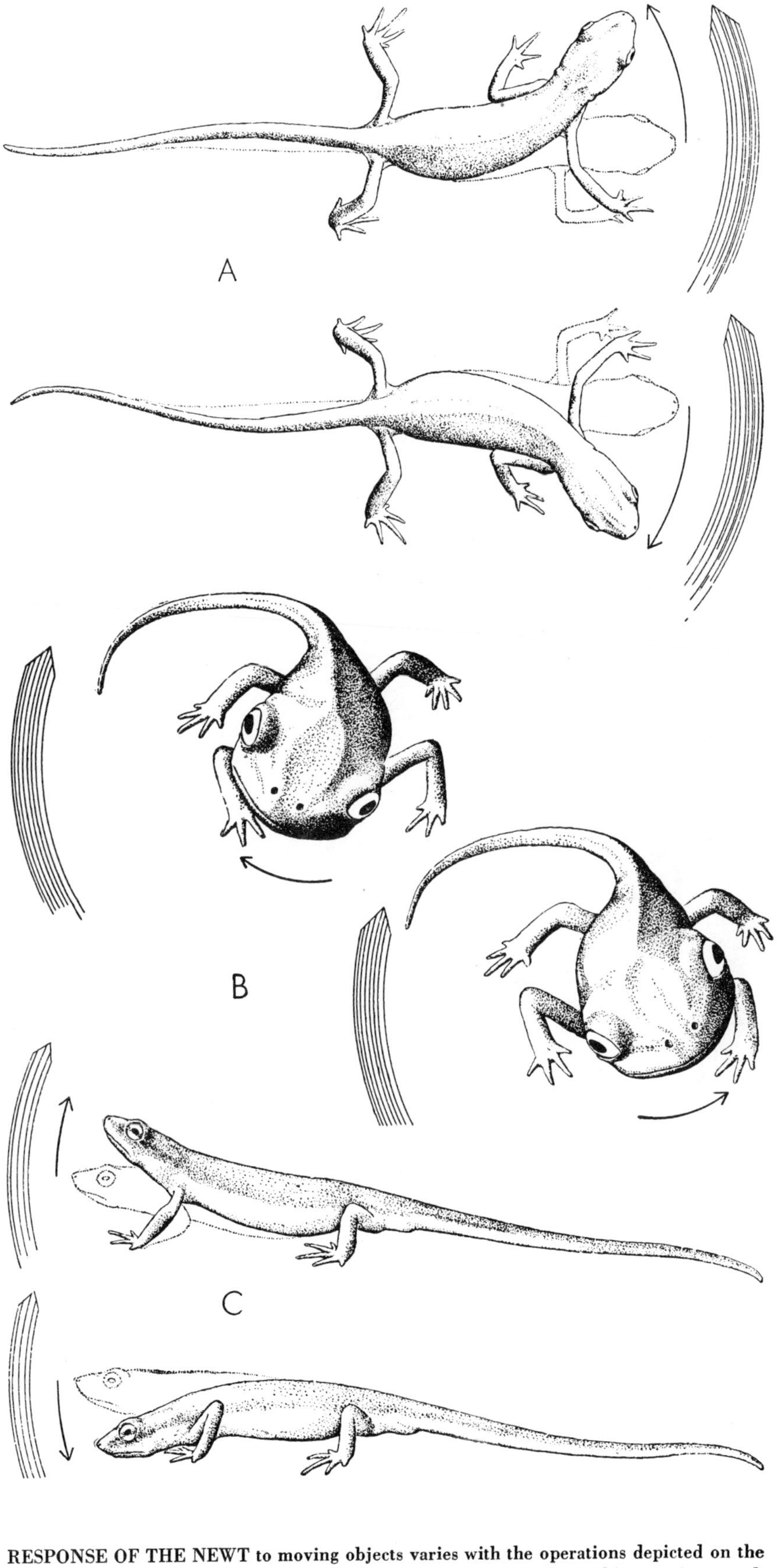

RESPONSE OF THE NEWT to moving objects varies with the operations depicted on the opposite page. The first newt in each of the three pairs of animals on this page is normal. When an object (*thick arrows*) is moved past the newt, the animal turns its head in the same direction (*thin arrows*). The second newt in each pair represents the behavior of the animal after one or more of the operations. The response of the second newt in A corresponds to operations B and D on the opposite page; in B, to operations B and C; in C, to C and D.

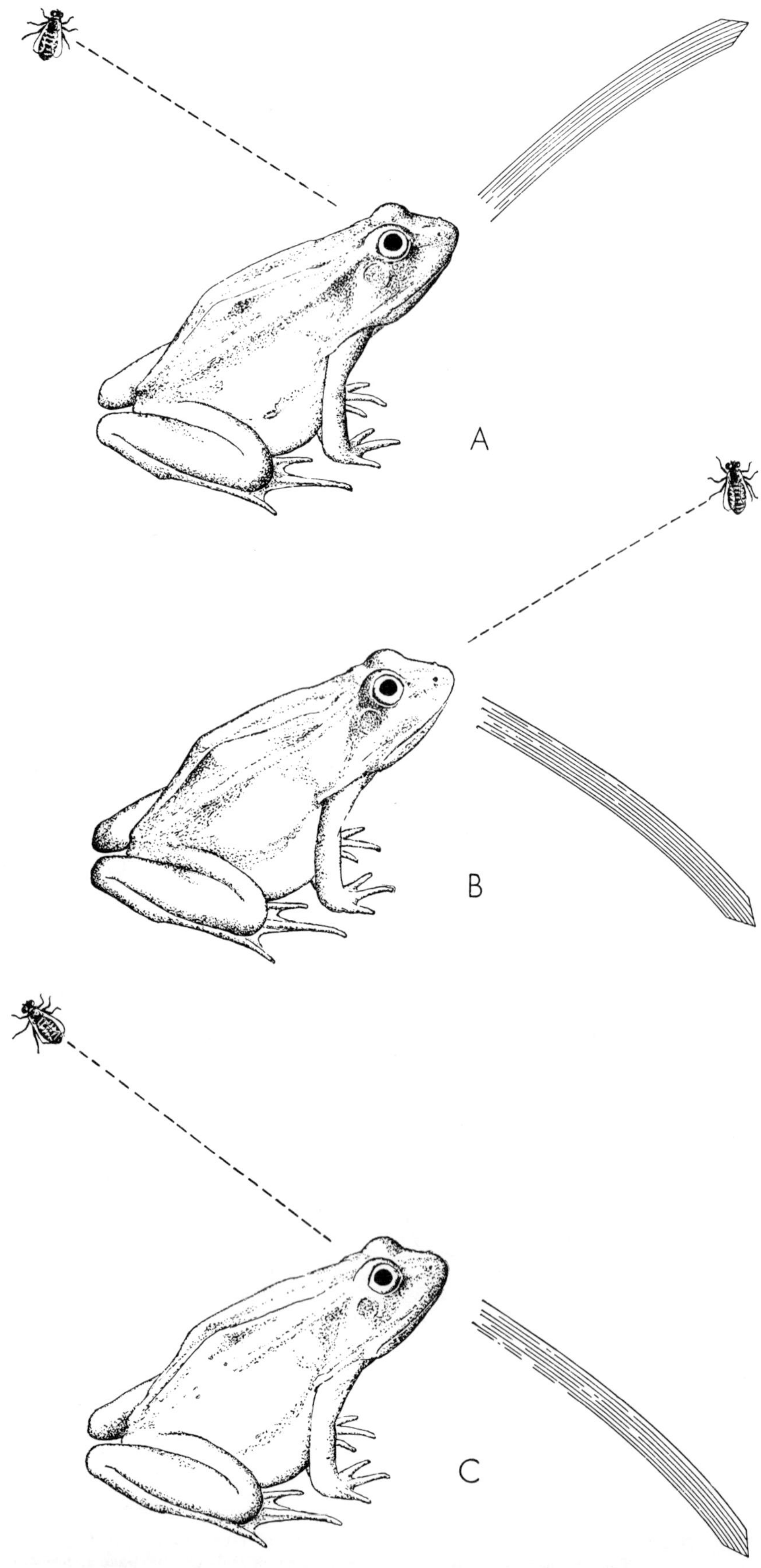

SAME OPERATIONS ON A FROG produce these effects when the animal strikes at a fly. In A the fly is above and behind a frog whose eyes have been turned by operation D on page 362; the animal strikes in the direction shown by the thick arrow. In B the eyes of the frog have been turned by operation C. In C the eyes of the frog have been turned by operation B.

side down and backward, the animals kept turning in circles, as if the whole visual field appeared to be whirling about them. Human subjects who have worn experimental lenses that invert the visual field have reported that any movement of the head or eyes tends to make everything seem to whirl around them.

The operated newts never relearned to see normally during the experiment. Some were kept with their eyes inverted for as long as two years, but showed no significant improvement. However, when rotated eyes were turned back to the normal position by surgery, the animals at once resumed normal behavior. There was no evidence that their long experience with inverted vision had brought about any change in the functioning of the central nervous system.

A second experiment bore out further the now growing suspicion that learning probably was not responsible for the recovery of vision by newts whose optic nerves had been cut. This time we rotated the eyeball and severed the optic nerve as well. The object was to find out whether the regenerating nerve fibers would give the newt normal vision, inverted vision or just a confused blur.

During the period of nerve regeneration the animals were blind. The first visual responses began to reappear about 25 to 30 days after the nerve had been cut. From the beginning these responses were systematically reversed in the same way as those produced by eye rotation alone. In other words, the animals again responded as if everything was seen upside down and backward. In these animals also the reversed vision remained permanently uncorrected by experience.

In another series of experiments we cut the optic nerves of the two eyes and switched their connections to the brain. Normally each optic nerve crosses to the side of the brain opposite the eye. We connected the cut nerve to the brain lobe on the same side. The result was to make the animals behave after regeneration as if the right and left halves of the visual field were reversed. That is, the animals responded to anything seen through one eye as if it were being viewed through the other eye. This switch too was permanent, uncorrected by experience. Frogs and toads responded to the experiment in the same way as newts.

By rotating the eyeball less than 180 degrees (*e.g.*, a 90-degree turn), and by combining eye transplantation from one side to the other with various degrees of rotation, we produced many

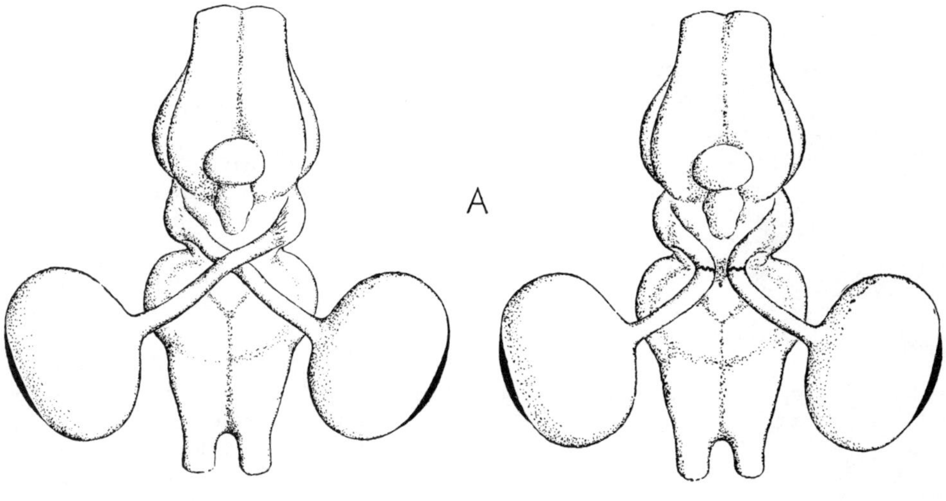

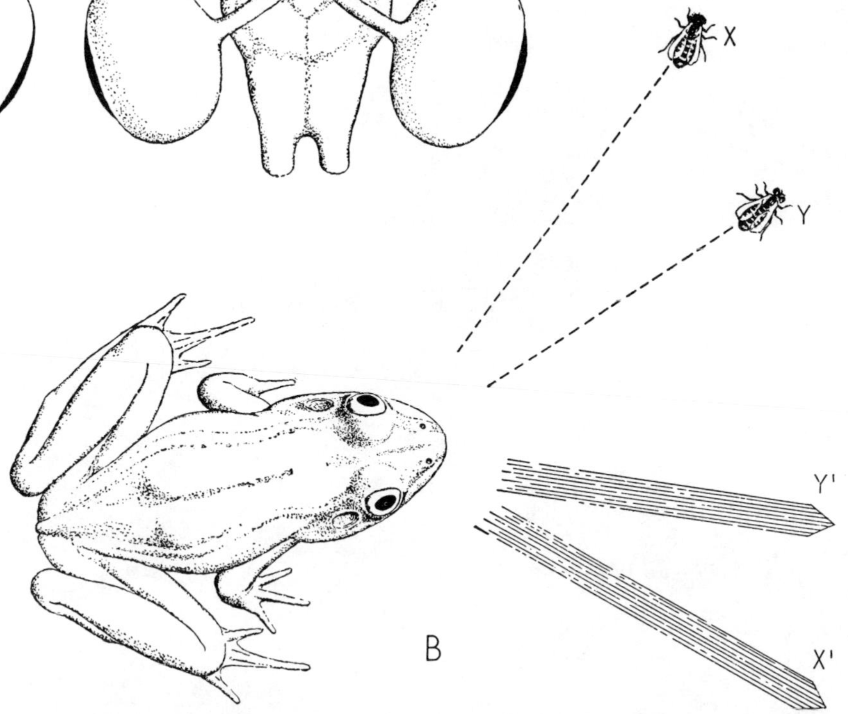

OPERATION ON THE OPTIC NERVES of a frog produced the effect shown at the lower right. At upper left the eyes of the frog are joined to the brain by the optic nerves. In the operation, which is depicted at top center, the nerves were cut and rejoined so that they did not cross. When a fly was at X, the frog struck at X'; when it was at Y, the frog struck at Y'.

other forms of abnormal spatial perception. But every experiment had the same basic outcome: the animal—newt, frog, toad or fish—always regenerated an organized pattern of vision. The visual field as a whole might be turned upside down, or inverted on another axis, or displaced from the left to the right side, but always the spatial organization within the visual field itself was restored in the normal pattern. Evidently the individual nerve fibers from the retina, after regeneration, all regained their original relative spatial functions in projecting the picture to the brain.

This orderly restoration of the spatial relations could hardly be based on any kind of learning or adaptation, under the conditions of our experiments. Animals don't *learn* to see things upside down and backward or reversed from left to right: reversed vision is more disadvantageous than no vision at all. The results clearly demonstrated that the orderly recovery of correct functional relations on the part of the ingrowing fibers was not achieved through function and experience, but rather was predetermined in the growth process itself.

Apparently the tangle of regenerating fibers was sorted out in the brain so as to restore the orderly maplike projection of the retina upon the optic lobe. If we destroyed a small part of the optic lobe after such regeneration, the animal had a blind spot in the corresponding part of its visual field, just as would be the case in normal animals. It was as if each regenerated fiber did indeed make a connection with a spot in the brain matching a corresponding spot in the retina.

It follows that optic fibers arising from different points in the retina must differ from one another in some way. If the ingrowing optic fibers were indistinguishable from one another, there would be no way in which they could re-establish their different functional connections in an orderly pattern. Each optic fiber must be endowed with some quality, presumably chemical, that marks it as having originated from a particular spot of the retinal field. And the matching spot at its terminus in the brain must have an exactly complementary quality. Presumably an ingrowing fiber will attach itself only to the particular brain cells that match its chemical flavor, so to speak. This chemical specificity seems to lie, as certain further experiments indicate, in a biaxial type of differentiation which produces unique arrays of chemical properties at the junction places.

Such chemical matching would account for recognition on contact, but how does a fiber find its way to its destination? There is good reason to believe that the regenerating fibers employ a shotgun approach. Each fiber puts forth many branches as it grows into the brain, and the brain cells likewise have widespreading branches. Thus the chances are exceedingly good that a given fiber will eventually make contact with its partner cells. We can picture the advancing tip of a fiber making a host of contacts as it invades the dense tangle of brain cells and their treelike expansions. The great majority of these contacts come to nothing, but eventually the growing tip encounters a type of cell surface for which it has a specific chemical affinity and to which it adheres. A chemical reaction then causes the fiber tip to stop advancing and to form a lasting functional union with the group of cells, presumably roughly circular in

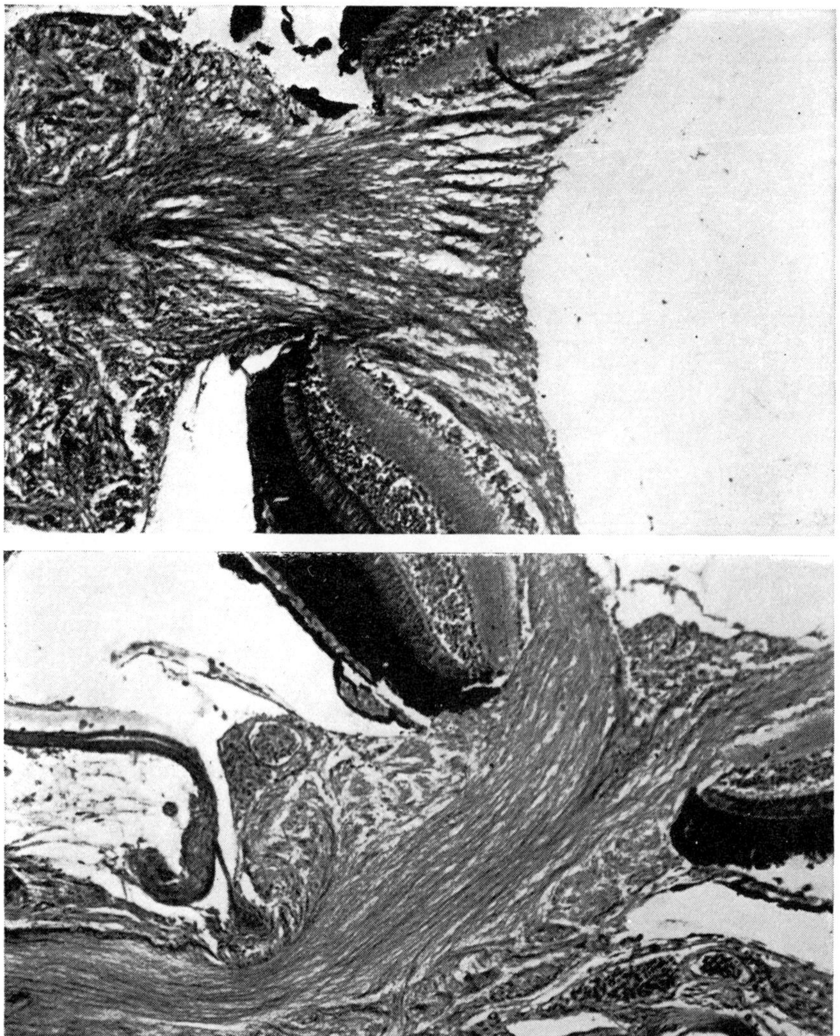

OPTIC NERVE of *Bathygobius soporator*, a fish of the goby family, was cut and allowed to regenerate. The regenerated nerve is shown in these three photomicrographic sections. In each photograph the eye is toward the right and the nerve runs from right to left. The top photograph shows a section of one nerve; the bottom two photographs show different sections of the same nerve. In all three sections the nerve fibers are tangled. Despite this apparent disorganization the fishes from which the sections were taken could see normally.

formation, which constitutes the spot in the brain matching the fiber's source spot in the retina.

The experiments on vision have been found to apply equally to other parts of the central nervous system. Normal function can be recovered through regeneration by general sensory nerves in the spinal cord, by the vestibular nerve in the ear mediating the sense of equilibrium and by other sensory and motor nerve circuits.

All the experiments point to one conclusion: the theory of inherent chemical affinities among the nerve fibers and cells is able to account for the kinds of behavior tested better than any hypothetical mechanism based on experience and learning. There is no direct proof of the theory, for no one has yet seen evidence of the chemical affinity type of reaction among nerves under the microscope. But an ever-growing accumulation of experimental findings continues to add support to the chemical theory.

We return to our original question: How big a role does heredity play in behavior? The experiments cited here show that in the lower vertebrates, at least, many features of visual perception—the sense of direction and location in space, the organization of patterns, the sense of position of the visual field as a whole, the perception of motion, and the like—are built into the organism and do not have to be learned. More general experiments suggest that the organization of pathways and associations in the central nervous system must be ascribed for the most part to inherent developmental patterning, not to experience. Of the thousands of circuit connections in the brain that have been described, not one can demonstrably be attributed to learning. Whatever the neural changes induced in the brain by experience, they are extremely inconspicuous. In the higher animals they are probably located mainly in the more remote byways of the cerebral cortex. In any case they are superimposed upon an already elaborate innate organization.

The whole idea of instincts and the inheritance of behavior traits is becoming much more palatable than it was 15 years ago, when we lacked a satisfactory basis for explaining the organization of inborn behavior. Today we can give more weight to heredity than we did then. Every animal comes into the world with inherited behavior patterns of its species. Much of its behavior is a product of evolution, just as its biological structure is.

SPACE PERCEPTION IN THE CHICK

ECKHARD H. HESS

July 1956

Suppose we observe that members of a particular species of birds always sing the same song. Is the song of this species innate or is it learned through the young bird's imitation of its parents? Let us isolate some young of this species from the adults so that no opportunity for learning is allowed. Will the young sing the song of their species? If the species selected is the nightingale, we shall discover that the young birds do not sing in the same way that the adults normally do, showing that the song is ordinarily learned through imitation. If, on the other hand, we isolate young robins, we shall find that they still sing the song of their kind, indicating the existence of an innate ability.

Why does a duckling or a gosling tag along after its mother? Until recent years it was believed that the young of a species possessed an inborn capacity for following only their own parents. It has now been shown for many species that the young animal will become attached to other objects in place of the parent if those objects are present during a critical

HOOD holds experimental goggles over the chick's eyes and leaves its beak free for pecking and eating. In one experiment the hood was fitted with prisms that caused the chick to see everything as though it were seven degrees to one side of its actual position.

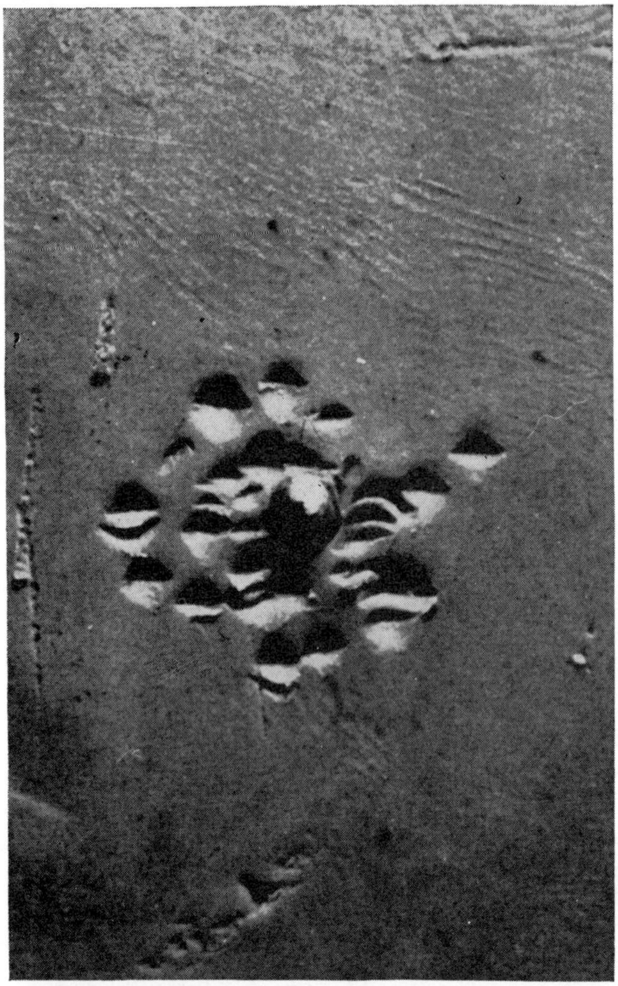

CONTROL CHICKS, wearing hoods fitted with pieces of flat plastic, were allowed to peck at a brass nail embedded in modeling clay. A chick one day old made the pattern at left; a chick four days old, the pattern at right. The patterns are centered on the nail.

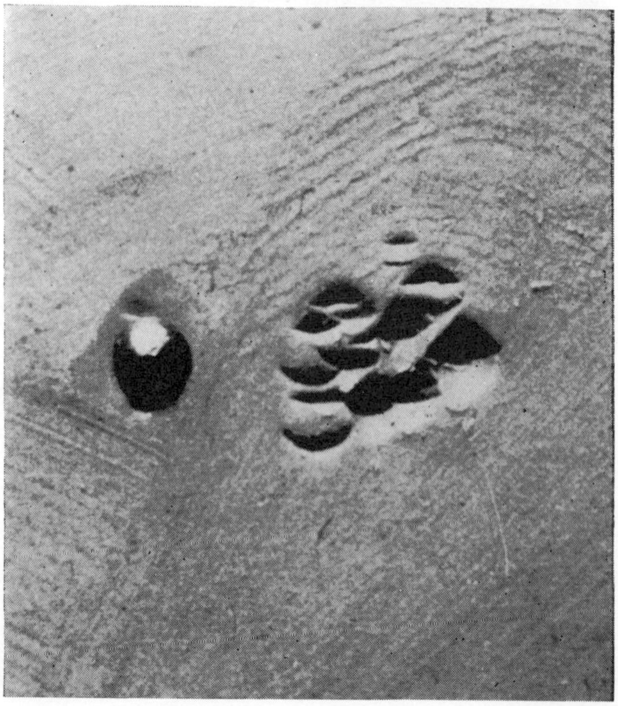

EXPERIMENTAL CHICKS wore hoods fitted with prisms that displaced objects seven degrees to the right. A chick one day old made the pattern at left; a chick four days old, the pattern at right. The pecks are more tightly clustered, but still displaced to right.

period shortly following its birth. A duckling may learn to follow a wooden decoy, a goose or even a human being if exposed to one of these objects instead of to its parent during this critical early period. Later it will follow that object in preference to its own mother.

Why is it important to know whether a certain behavior pattern is learned or innate? One reason is that once we have this information, we are well on our way to knowing under what circumstances the behavior can be changed. If it is learned, then we may alter the physical or psychological environment so that another behavior is learned in its place. If it is innate, we may not be able to modify the behavior unless we use the innate behavior pattern as a foundation upon which to build additional responses, so that the resulting composite behavior appears to be different.

Many psychologists believe that the ultimate aim of animal studies is to provide us with a better understanding of human behavior. Such an objective is not attained by generalizing from animal to human behavior—a practice of which comparative psychologists are commonly accused—although it is true that some hypotheses about man are occasionally suggested by the extension of behavioral trends observed in the progression from the lower to the higher animals. More likely, however, the understanding of human behavior is served through animal research in quite another fashion. That is to say, the animal laboratory is a testing ground for the evolution of techniques and the development of criteria which may ultimately be applied with ease and safety to humans.

If we can discover which of man's behaviors are learned and which are innate, we will know which ones may be readily changed and which can be modified, if at all, only within narrow limits. Such findings might explain why some experiences in an individual's early life affect his subsequent behavior whereas other early experiences apparently do not. We may learn how to create an environment in which desirable behaviors will be promoted and undesirable behaviors will be modified.

A further word should be said regarding innate and learned behavior. The simple fact that a behavior appears later than infancy does not necessarily mean that it is learned. It may represent the natural unfolding of innate processes occurring along with the individual's physiological development. We call this process maturation, and we may classify it as a special kind of innate behavior. Behavior which develops through maturation possesses, in all probability, the same resistance to modification that characterizes ordinary innate responses.

One problem which has for some decades been of interest to the comparative psychologist is the accurate localization of objects in space. When an organism first perceives the environment, can it accurately see where things are? A large number of experiments have been carried out on the development of pecking accuracy in chicks. The results, however, have been far from clear. Some investigators concluded that their experiments indicated a maturational process, others assumed that practice through trial and error led to this accuracy, and still others thought the entire process to be innately determined.

The experiments to be described were undertaken to ascertain whether a chick's visual perception of space—as measured through its accuracy in pecking at grain—depends upon learning or upon the maturation of an innate ability. One possible method for deciding this question would be to raise chicks to adulthood without permitting them the opportunity for normal visual experience and then expose them to a situation in which they might demonstrate their pecking ability. Prior to the experiment described here, experimenters who undertook this problem prevented young chicks from practicing the sensory-motor coordination involved in pecking by means of keeping them in dark enclosures or covering their heads with little hoods which masked their eyes but left their beaks free for eating. The results of these experiments were later laid open to question when it was suggested that in the absence of stimulation by light the eyes may fail to develop normally. Any inaccuracy in pecking might well have been the result of degeneration in the retina or the nerves.

To overcome this difficulty the author sought a method that would prevent normal visual experience and yet would not interfere with the normal physiological development of the eye. A solution to this problem was found in the technique of fitting the chicks' eyes with prismatic lenses which would displace the visual image to the right or to the left.

Suppose that a chick first sees the light of day wearing prisms which cause a displacement of the visual image seven degrees to the right. If the exact visual localization of objects in space is a totally learned ability, the chick's performance should be unaffected by the fact that it is wearing displacement prisms. When the chick sees a food object, it should start pecking but in a random fashion until, after trial and error, the object is eaten. Gradually, as sensory-motor associations are built up, the chick's accuracy should improve.

If, on the other hand, the chick is born with an innate ability to locate objects visually, the first pecks which such a chick directs toward objects seen through the displacement lenses should be about seven degrees to the right. Since the young chick starts its peck with its eyes about 25 to 30 millimeters away from the object, the actual displacement should be about 3 or 4 mm. With time and practice the chick might learn to correct for the displacement so that it would strike at objects seven degrees to the left of where they appeared to be. This, in fact, was the author's expectation.

In the actual experiment 28 Leghorn chicks were hatched in complete darkness and were immediately fitted with thin rubber hoods into which transparent plastic goggles had been inserted. The hoods were placed over their heads quickly in such a subdued light that the animals had essentially no normal light experience. The goggles in the hoods of 10 of the chicks were flat pieces of plastic which produced no image displacement. These 10 were the control animals. Twelve of the chicks had hoods which were fitted with plastic prisms which displaced the whole visual field seven degrees to the right. Six of the animals wore lenses which caused a similar displacement of the visual field to the left.

All of the animals were returned to darkness for a period of about six hours so that they could become accustomed to the hoods. Then, when they were about one day old, all of the animals were tested for pecking accuracy. They were allowed to strike at small objects embedded in modeling clay. The targets were small brass nails, embedded so that they could not be dislodged by pecking. The modeling clay provided a simple means of recording the accuracy with which the chicks pecked at the nails. By photographing the dented clay after such a pecking session and then tracing the actual dispersion of pecks from a projected image of the negative, it was possible to get a clear picture of the accuracy or inaccuracy of the chicks as they were tested.

The pecks made by all of the chicks were scattered. There was, however one fundamental difference in the performance of the control and experimental animals. In the control group the pecks were scattered about the target so that the target itself formed the center of the distribution. For those chicks wearing lenses which displaced the visual field to the right, the pecks were similarly scattered, but they were centered about a point seven degrees to the right of the target. Similarly, the group whose lenses displaced their visual images to the left showed a scattering of pecks to the left of the target. Some pecks of chicks in all groups actually hit the target.

Half of the control group and half of each of the two experimental groups were now placed in an enclosure in which grain had been loosely scattered on the floor. The other half of the three groups were placed in a box in which they had access to bowls of mash; accuracy in pecking was therefore not required. In the latter situation a chick which missed the grain at which it aimed would nevertheless hit other grains in the bowl almost every time it pecked. This was not true, of course, of those chicks which were pecking at individual grains scattered on the floor.

When the chicks were between three and four days old, they were tested again. The results showed a great increase in accuracy on the part of the control chicks: now their pecks clustered quite closely about the target. There was no detectable difference between the two subgroups of the control animals—those fed on scattered food and those fed on mash in bowls.

Among the animals wearing displacement prisms, improvement of a kind had also occurred. The pecks were clustered just as tightly as those of the controls, showing that increased accuracy had certainly been achieved. The centers of these clusters, however, were approximately 4 mm. to the right or to the left of the target, depending on which displacement glasses were worn by the experimental animal. Again there was very little difference in accuracy among the subgroups of experimental animals. But another difference was evident in the physical condition of the subgroups. Where the animals which had access to bowls of mash were as healthy as the control animals, the animals in the scattered grain situation were in poor physical condition and apparently would have died if they had been kept in the same situation. Two animals maintained in this situation died the following day.

We must conclude that the chick's visual apparatus for locating objects in space is innate and not learned. This conclusion is based on the fact that the chick wearing displacement prisms clustered its pecks about the spot where the object was seen. It did not simply peck at random until it struck the target.

Furthermore, the chick whose visual field was displaced appeared unable to learn through experience to correct its aim. Its only improvement was to increase the consistency of the distance by which it missed the target. Apparently the innate picture which the chick has of the location of objects in its visual world cannot be modified through learning if what is required is that the chick learn to perform a response which is antagonistic to its instinctive one.

The technique developed for the foregoing experiment seemed to offer an admirable opportunity for studying another aspect of bird vision—stereopsis, or binocular depth perception. The question to be answered was whether the bird possesses this capacity.

In man there is considerable overlap of the areas viewed by the two eyes. Since the pupils of the eyes are about two and a half inches apart, however, each eye gets a slightly different picture of the commonly shared view. In some way these two pictures are integrated in the brain so that objects viewed appear three-dimensional rather than flat.

In the chick, on the other hand, the eyes are at the sides of the head rather than at the front. Consequently, except for a relatively small area directly in front of the bird, the two eyes receive visual stimulation from different parts of the surroundings.

In man, optic fibers from each eye travel to both sides of the brain. In the bird this is not the case. The optic fibers from the chick's left eye presumably cross over completely to the right side of the brain and those from the right eye to the left side of the brain.

Essentially on the basis of these facts alone it was believed by some that the bird lacks binocular depth perception. In other words, it was thought that the bird's brain could not combine the two small overlapping images to produce an impression of depth or three-dimensionality. The bird's perception of depth and distance was believed to be entirely dependent upon monocular cues, *i.e.*, cues which can be utilized by one eye alone. One important monocular cue is received through the successive impressions of an object obtained by moving the head and viewing the object from various angles. Other monocular cues are the diminution of size with increased distance, the overlapping by nearer objects of more distant ones, and accommodation, or focus.

The author undertook the following experiment to determine whether the normal adult chicken uses binocular cues to localize objects in space. Rubber hoods were slipped over the heads of chickens six to eight weeks old. These hoods were fitted with prismatic lenses having their broad bases outward. If a man were to look through a similar, but larger, set of lenses, using binocular vision, objects would appear closer to him than they actually were. If he used his right eye alone, the object would appear to the left of its actual position. Similar results should be expected of chickens.

Of the six animals used, all pecked short at grains of mash placed before them. None struck the surface on which the grains rested. When the experimenter covered the right or the left eye of the chicken with masking tape, the bird struck the surface on which the grain rested but missed to the side away from the exposed eye. The conclusion to be drawn is that the normal adult chick-

VARIOUS HOODS used by the author in his experiments in the department of psychology at the University of Chicago are mounted in the laboratory. The hoods are made of rubber.

CONVERGING LENSES were also placed in the hoods, causing the chicks to peck short of objects. These chicks learned to peck accurately at objects on the ground, presumably benefiting from muscular cues, but continued to peck short at objects in the air.

en uses binocular cues to localize objects in space.

Later nine newly hatched chicks were outfitted with the same kind of prismatic lenses and were similarly tested. As with the adult chickens, the chicks struck in the direction of the grains but always short of them, thereby demonstrating that in the absence of any visual experience, binocular depth cues are still employed.

In the last of the three experiments on stereoscopic vision, nine chickens were raised to an age of two to three months with the opportunity of using only monocular vision. From the day of hatching they wore hoods, changed each day, which had openings for only one eye. In other words, on the first day they would wear a hood which would allow the use of only the right eye, on the second day a hood which exposed only the left eye, and so on. These hoods contained no lenses or prisms. The purpose of this procedure was simply to prevent experience with binocular vision, but at the same time to allow extensive use of both eyes. When these chickens were tested at the end of two or three months with binocular prisms having their broad bases outward, all nine animals pecked short of the grain. Apparently the lack of binocular experience did not prevent the appearance of binocular vision.

Summing up our results, we conclude that the naive chick as well as the experienced one possesses binocular depth perception. This innate organization for the perception of depth requires neither learning nor continued use for its presence in the adult animal.

38

PLASTICITY IN SENSORY-MOTOR SYSTEMS

RICHARD HELD
November 1965

Anyone who has worn eyeglasses is likely to have experienced distorted vision the first time he put them on. The distortion may have been severe enough to cause him trouble in motor coordination, as in reaching out to touch something or in being sure of where he stepped. Such a person will also recall, however, that in a day or two the distortion disappeared. Evidently his central nervous system had made some adjustment so that the things he saw through the glasses looked normal again and he could have renewed confidence in his touch and step.

This process of adjustment, particularly as it operates in recovery from radical transformations of vision (as when the world is made to appear upside down or greatly shifted to one side by special goggles), has attracted the attention of scientists at least since the time of the great 19th-century investigator Hermann von Helmholtz. What has intrigued us all is the finding that correct perception of space and accurate visually guided action in space are in the long run not dependent on unique and permanently fixed optical properties of the paths taken by light rays traveling from object to eye. This finding, however, must be squared with the normally high order of precision in spatial vision and its stability over a period of time. How can the visual control of spatially coordinated action be stable under normal circumstances and yet sufficiently modifiable to allow recovery from transformation? Recovery takes time and renewed contact with the environment. Adaptation must result from information drawn from this contact with the environment. If the end product of adaptation is recovery of the former stability of perception, then the information on which that recovery is based must be as reliable and unvarying as its end product. The investigations my colleagues and I have undertaken (first at Brandeis University and more recently at the Massachusetts Institute of Technology) have been directed toward discovering this source of information and elucidating the mechanism of its use by the perceiving organism. A useful tool in our work has been deliberate distortion of visual and auditory signals, a technique we call rearrangement.

Visual rearrangement can be produced experimentally with prisms [see the article "Experiments with Goggles," by Ivo Kohler, beginning on page 299]. Similarly, the apparent direction of sounds can be distorted in the laboratory by suitable apparatus. We have used such devices to show that in many cases the viewer or the listener subjected to these distortions soon adapts to them, provided that during the experiment he has been allowed to make voluntary use of his muscles in a more or less normal way.

The proviso suggests that there is more to the mechanism of perceptual adaptation than a change in the way the sensory parts of the central nervous system process data from the eyes and ears. The muscles and motor parts of the nervous system are evidently involved in the adaptation too—a revelation that has been very important in our efforts to discover the responsible source of information. The concept of a relation between sensory and motor activities in the adaptive process is reinforced by what happens when humans and certain other mammals undergo sensory deprivation through prolonged isolation in monotonous environments, or motor deprivation through prolonged immobilization. Their performance on perceptual and motor tasks declines. By the same token, the young of higher mammals fail to develop normal behavior if they undergo sensory or motor deprivation.

Taken together, these findings by various experimenters suggested to us that a single mechanism is involved in three processes: (1) the development of normal sensory-motor control in the young, (2) the maintenance of that control once it has developed and (3) the adaptation to changes or apparent changes in the data reported by the senses of sight and hearing. A demonstration that such a mechanism exists would be of value in understanding these processes. Moreover, it would help to explain a phenomenon that otherwise could be accounted for only by the existence of enormous amounts of genetically coded information. That phenomenon is the adjustment of the central nervous system to the growth of the body—on the sensory side to the fact that the afferent, or input, signals must change with the increasing separation between the eyes and between the ears, and on the motor side to the fact that the growth of bone and muscle must call for a gradual modification of the efferent, or output, signals required to accomplish a particular movement. This problem is especially critical for animals that grow slowly and have many jointed bones. The possibility that the need for genetically coded information has been reduced by some such mechanism is of course contingent on the assumption that the animal's environment is fairly stable. For these reasons it is not surprising that clear evidence for adaptation to rearrangement and for dependence of the young on environmental contact in developing coordination has been found only in primates and in cats.

Such, in brief, is the background of

our effort to discover the operating conditions of the suspected mechanism. Our conclusion has been that a key to its operation is the availability of "reafference." This word was coined by the German physiologists Erich von Holst and Horst Mittelstädt to describe neural excitation following sensory stimulation that is systematically dependent on movements initiated by the sensing animal; von Holst and Mittelstädt also used the word "exafference" to describe the result of stimulation that is independent of self-produced movement. "Afference" alone refers to any excitation of afferent nerves. These concepts should become clearer to the reader from the remainder of this article.

Among the contributions von Helmholtz made to science were many that were later incorporated into psychology. His experiments included work on the displacement of visual images by prisms. He was the first to report that the misreaching caused by such a displacement is progressively reduced during repeated efforts and that on removal of the prism the subject who has succeeded in adapting to this displacement will at first misreach in the opposite direction.

Helmholtz' findings and those of similar experiments by many other workers have often been interpreted as resulting from recognition of error and consequent correction. We doubted this interpretation because of our conviction that a single mechanism underlies both

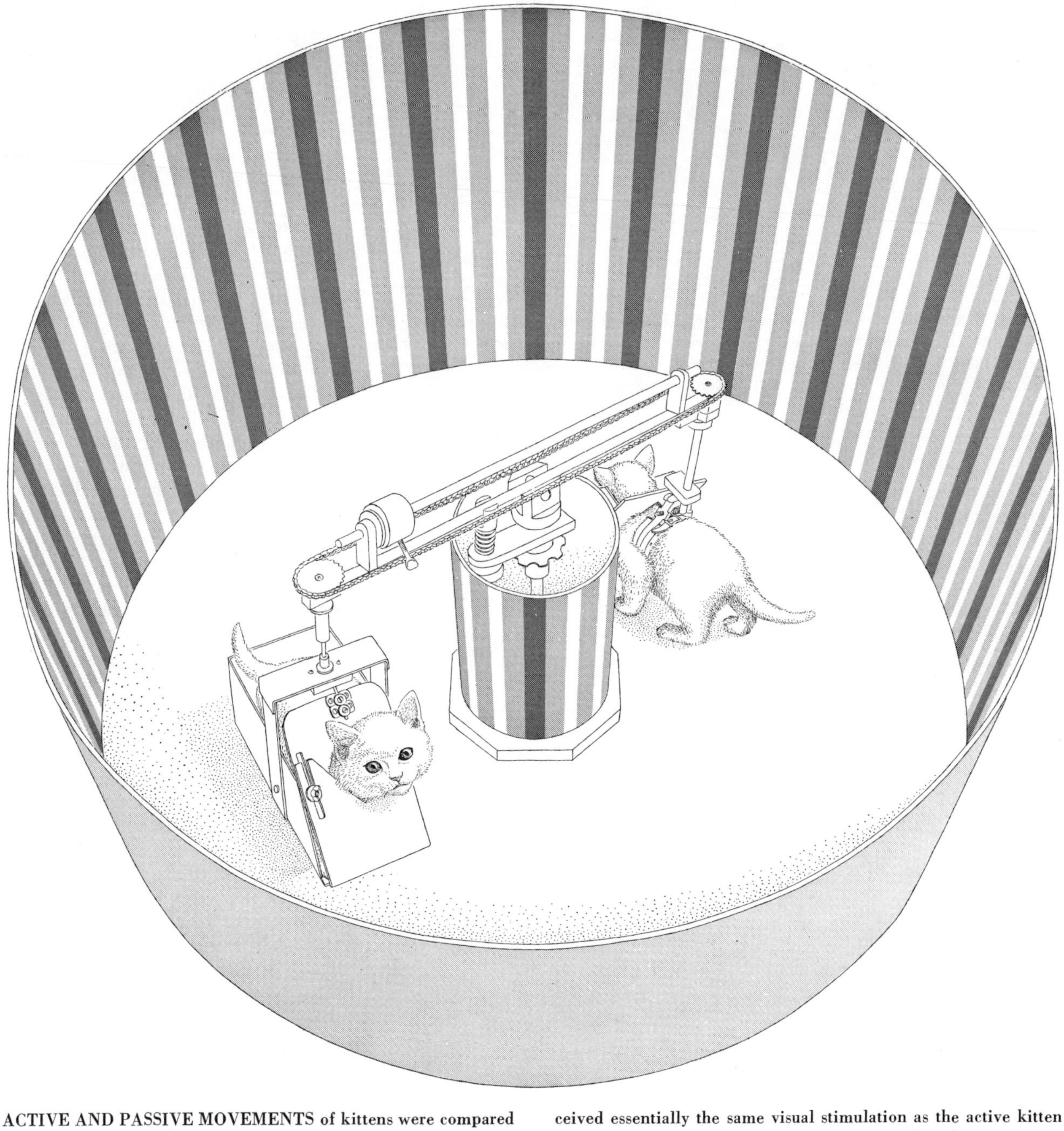

ACTIVE AND PASSIVE MOVEMENTS of kittens were compared in this apparatus. The active kitten walked about more or less freely; its gross movements were transmitted to the passive kitten by the chain and bar. The passive kitten, carried in a gondola, received essentially the same visual stimulation as the active kitten because of the unvarying pattern on the wall and on the center post. Active kittens developed normal sensory-motor coordination; passive kittens failed to do so until after being freed for several days.

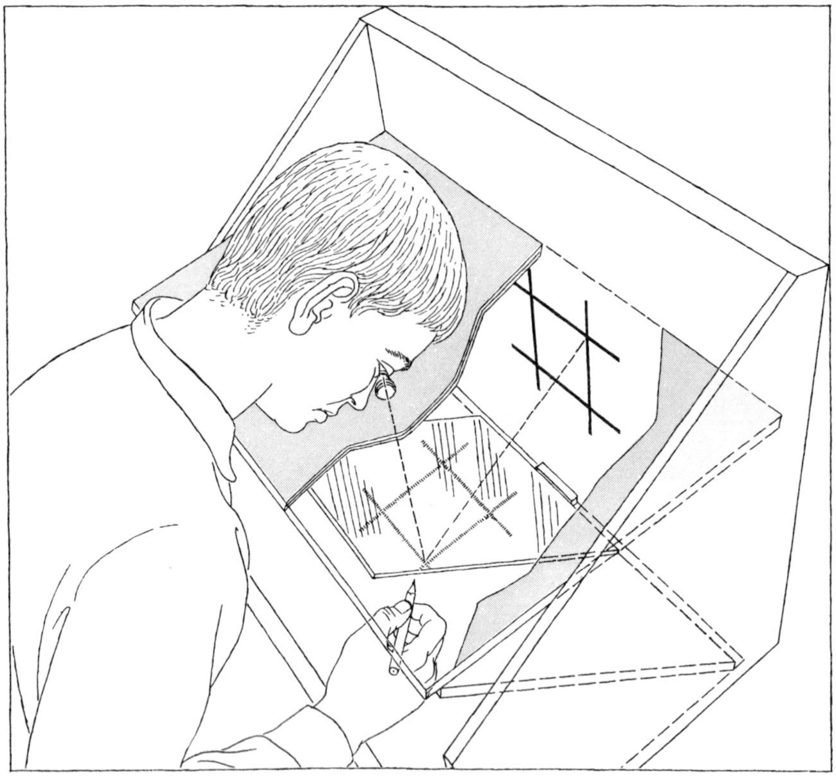

MIRROR APPARATUS tests subject's ability to guide his unseen hand to a visible target. Subject first marks under the mirror the apparent location of the corners of the square as he sees them in the mirror. He then looks through a prism, as depicted in the illustration below, after which he makes more marks. They show his adaptation to the prism effect.

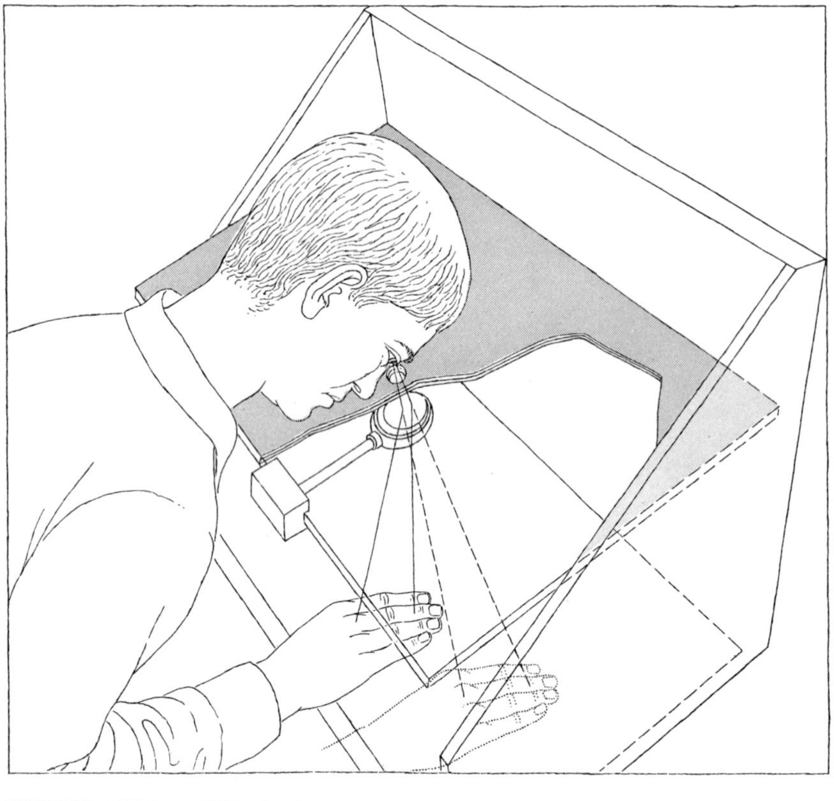

VIEW THROUGH PRISM displaces a visual image. Some subjects looked at their motionless hand, some moved the arm back and forth in a left-right arc, and some had the arm moved passively in a similar arc. They then made marks under the mirror as shown in the illustration at the top of the page. Typical results appear in illustrations on opposite page.

adaptation to rearrangement in the adult and the development of the young. An error-correcting process could hardly explain the original acquisition of coordination. If an infant initially has no sense of the spatial relation between his efforts to move his hand and their visual consequences, he cannot recognize a visible error in reaching. Yet infants do acquire eye-hand coordination in their earliest months. Hence we suspected that error recognition was no more necessary for adaptation in the adult than it was in the development of the infant's coordination. To test this assumption we designed an experiment that prevented the subject from recognizing his error. If he still managed to correct his reach to allow for a displaced image, it would be evident that there was more to the matter of adaptation than the simple fact that the subject could see his error directly.

With this objective in mind we designed the apparatus shown in the top illustration at the left. In this apparatus the subject saw the image of a square target reflected by a mirror and was asked to mark on a piece of paper under the mirror the apparent position of the corners of the square. Because of the mirror, he could see neither the marks nor his hand. After he had marked each point 10 times, withdrawing his hand between markings so that he would have to position it anew each time, the mirror and marking sheet were removed and a prism was substituted. Looking through the prism, the subject then spent several minutes moving his hand in various ways, none of which involved deliberate reaching for a target. Thereafter the original situation was restored and the subject made more marks under the mirror. These marks revealed that each of the subjects was making some correction for the displacement of image that had been caused by the prism.

Having thus established that at least partial adaptation can occur in the absence of direct recognition of error, we used the apparatus to test the role of motor-sensory feedback in adaptation. Our main purpose was to see what degree of adaptation would occur under the respective conditions of active and passive movement—in other words, under conditions of reafference and exafference in which the afference was equivalent. In these experiments the subject's writing arm was strapped to a board pivoted at his elbow to allow left and right movement. He then looked at his hand through a prism under three conditions: (1) no movement, (2) active movement, in which he moved the arm back and forth himself, and (3) passive movement, in which he kept his arm limp and it was moved back and forth by the experimenter. In each case he marked the apparent location of points under the mirror before and after looking through the prism.

Comparison of these marks showed that a few minutes of active movement produced substantial compensatory shifts [*see illustrations at right*]. Indeed, many of the subjects showed full adaptation, meaning exact compensation for the displacement caused by the prism, within half an hour. In contrast, the subjects in the condition of passive movement showed no adaptation. Even though the eye received the same information from both active and passive conditions, the evidently crucial connection between motor output and sensory input was lacking in the passive condition. These experiments showed that movement alone, in the absence of the opportunity for recognition of error, does not suffice to produce adaptation; it must be self-produced movement. From the point of view of our approach this kind of movement, with its contingent reafferent stimulation, is the critical factor in compensating for displaced visual images.

What about an adaptive situation involving movements of the entire body rather than just the arm and hand? We explored this situation in two ways, using an apparatus in which the subject judged the direction of a target only in reference to himself and not to other visible objects [*see top illustration on next page*]. This kind of direction-finding is sometimes called egocentric localization.

The apparatus consisted initially of a drum that could be rotated by the experimenter, after which the subject, sitting in a chair that he could rotate, was asked to position himself so that a target appeared directly in front of him. Later we dispensed with the drum and merely put the subject in a rotatable chair in a small room. After the experimenter had randomly positioned the target, which was a dimly illuminated slit, the subject rotated himself to find the target.

The first of the two ways in which we tested the role of reafferent stimulation involving movement of the whole body was an experiment in adaptation to short-term exposure to prisms. After several trials at locating the target, the subject put on prism goggles. He then

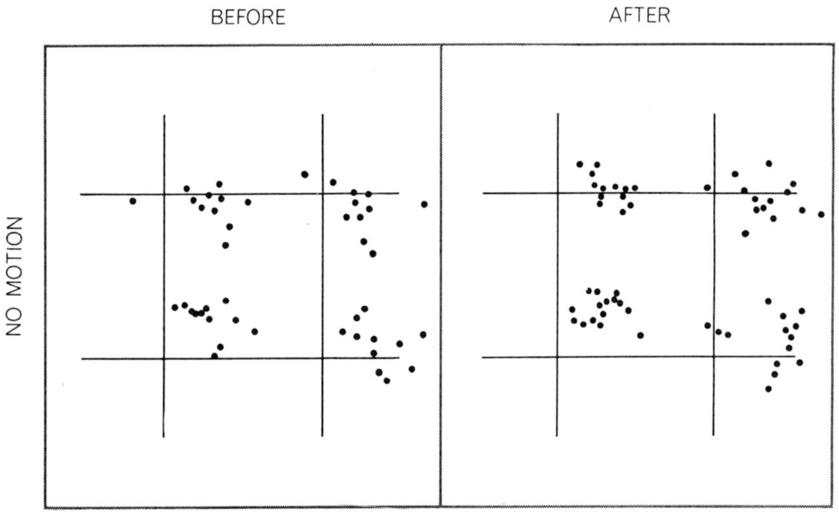

MARKINGS made by a subject before and after looking through a prism as described in illustrations on opposite page are shown. He kept hand still while viewing it through prism.

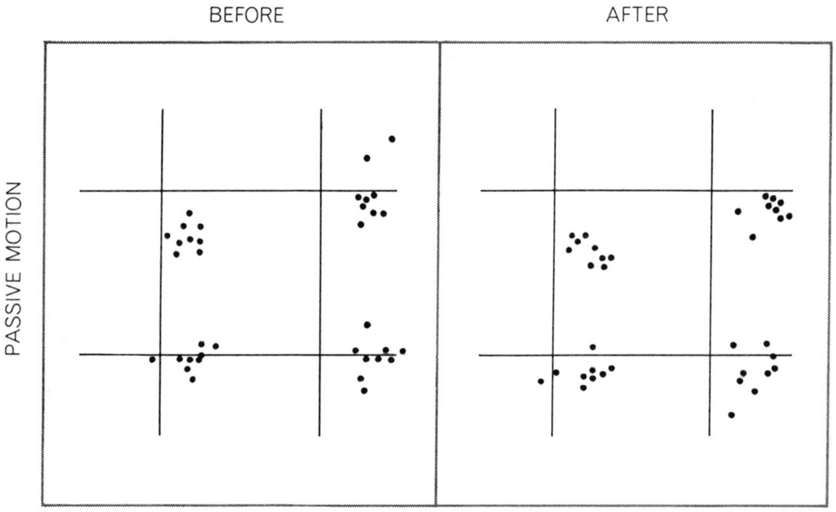

PASSIVE MOVEMENT of subject's hand as he viewed it through prism produced these marks. They show no adaptation to horizontal displacement of images caused by the prism.

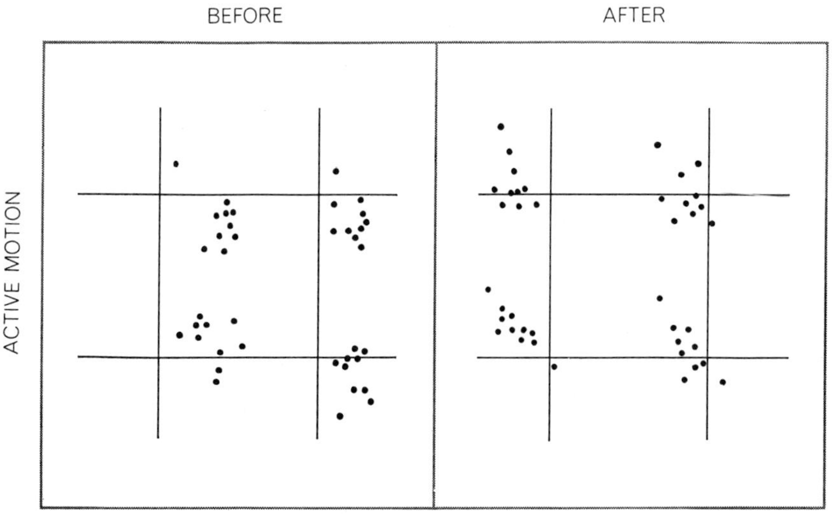

ACTIVE MOVEMENT of subject's hand produced a clear adaptation to displacement of images by prism. Tests showed importance of such movement in sensorimotor coordination.

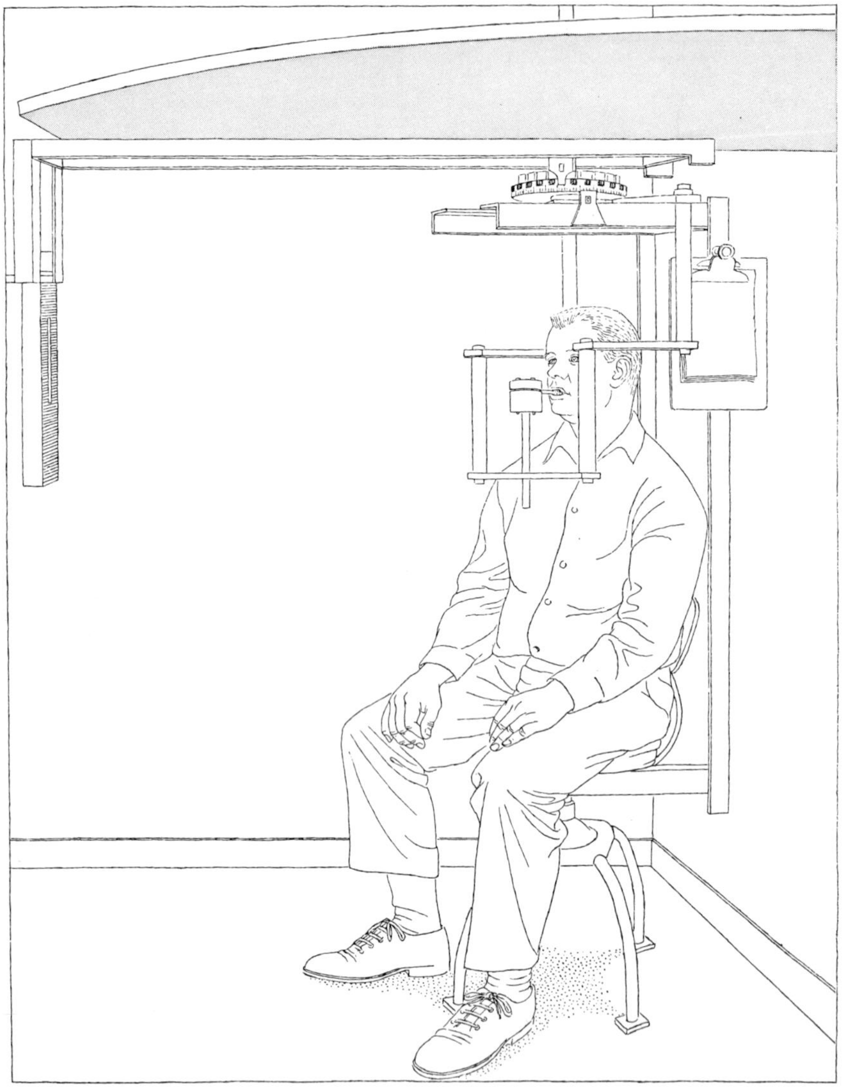

DIRECTION-FINDING by egocentric localization, in which a subject judges the direction of a target only in relation to himself and not to other visual cues, uses this apparatus. Target is randomly positioned at subject's eye level; he then rotates himself so that the target is directly in front of him. He does this before and after wearing prism goggles with which he either walks on an outdoor path or is pushed along the same path in a wheelchair. Change in direction-finding after wearing prisms measures adaptation to the prisms.

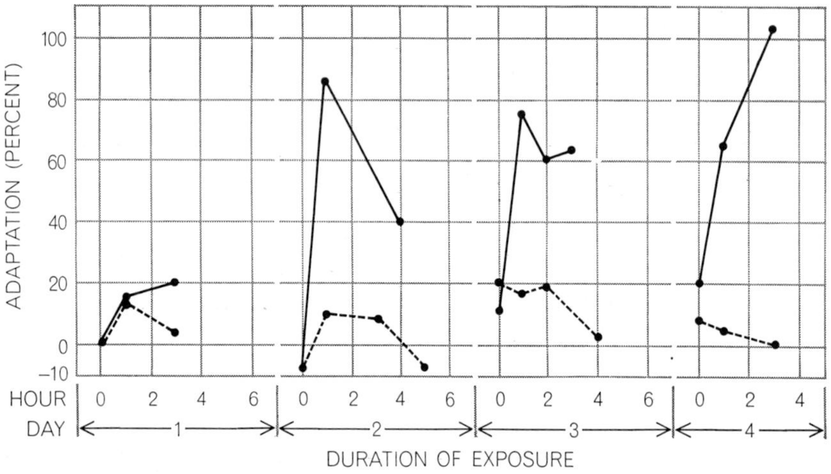

PROLONGED EXPOSURE to prisms produced varying degrees of adaptation to them depending on whether a subject's movement was active (*solid lines*) or passive (*broken lines*).

walked for an hour along an outdoor path or sat in a wheelchair that was pushed along the same path for the same length of time. Thereupon he removed the goggles and went back to the target-finding apparatus for more tests. Any error in target-finding after wearing the prism goggles would be a measure of the adaptation the subject had made to the visual displacements produced by the prisms.

Again the degree of adaptation achieved by the subjects who had been involved in active movement was far greater than that of the subjects who had been carried in the wheelchair. This was true both when one subject had been exposed to the active condition and another to the passive and when a single subject had been exposed successively to each condition. Even more striking contrasts appeared in our second test, which involved wearing prisms for several hours at a time under conditions of active and passive movement. In these circumstances several of the subjects who were able to move voluntarily achieved full adaptation, whereas subjects whose movements were passive achieved virtually no adaptation.

In this connection it will be useful to mention an experiment we conducted on directional hearing. The sound emanating from a localized source reaches the listener's nearer ear a fraction of a second sooner than it reaches his farther ear. This small difference in the time of arrival of the sound at the two ears is the first stage in ascertaining the direction from which the sound comes. If, then, a subject's ears could be in effect displaced around the vertical axis of his head by a small angle, he would err by an equivalent angle in his location of the sound. This effect can be produced artificially by a device called the pseudophone, in which microphones substitute for the external ears. Subjects who have worn a pseudophone for several hours in a normally noisy environment show compensatory shifts in locating sounds, provided that they have been able to move voluntarily. In addition they occasionally report that they hear two sources of sound when only one is present. When measurements are made of the two apparent directions of the source, they differ by approximately the angle at which the ears were displaced around the center of the head during the exposure period. I have called the effect diplophonia.

The reports of doubled localization

following adaptation suggest that compensation for rearrangement consists in the acquisition of a new mode of coordination that is objectively accurate for the condition of rearrangement but that coexists along with the older and more habitual mode. If this is true, the gradual and progressive course of adaptation usually found in experiments must be considered the result of a slow shift by the subject from the older direction of localization to the newer direction.

All these experiments strongly suggested the role in adaptation of the close correlation between signals from the motor nervous system, producing active physical movement, and the consequent sensory feedback. This correlation results from the fact that the feedback signals are causally related to movement and that in a stable environ-

PASSIVE TRANSPORT of a subject wearing prism goggles while viewing a random scene is depicted. Purpose of the apparatus was to test the hypothesis that subjects moving actively through such a scene, which looks the same with or without prisms, would show a degree of adaptation to the prisms whereas subjects moved passively would not. That is what happened. Tests showed a link between visual and motor processes in the central nervous system by altering the correlation between motor outflow and visual feedback.

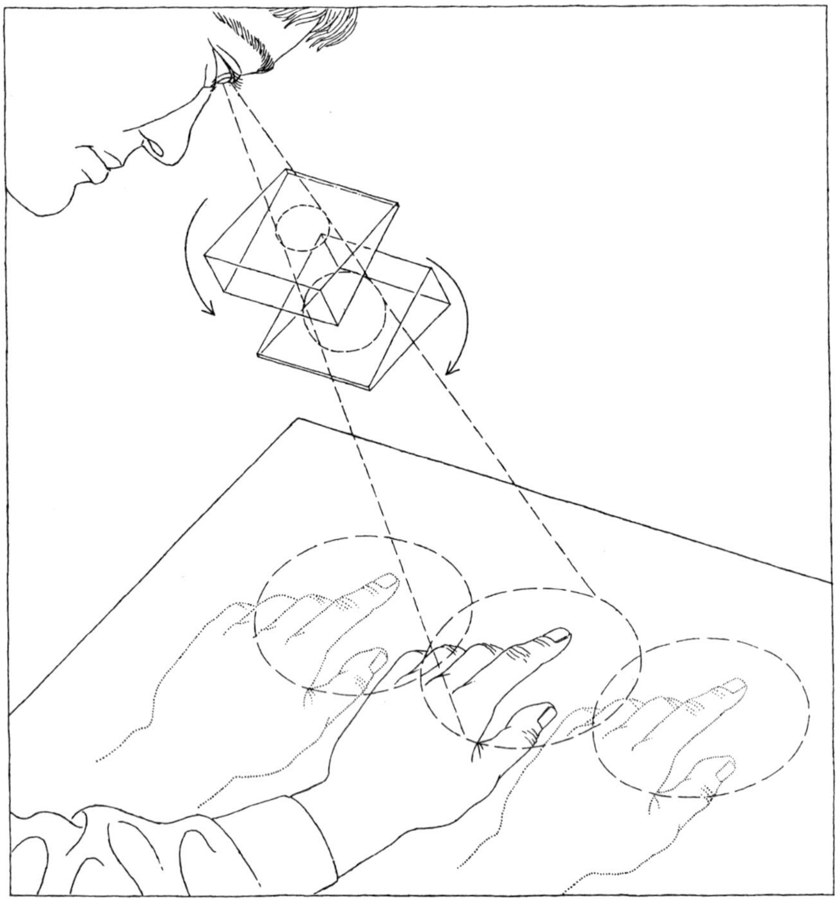

VERIFICATION EXPERIMENT sought to show role of correlation of sensory feedback and active physical movement by impairing it. Means of decorrelation was the rotating-prism apparatus shown here. It produces apparently continuous movement of subject's hand in one dimension, thus breaking the link between actual movement and visual feedback.

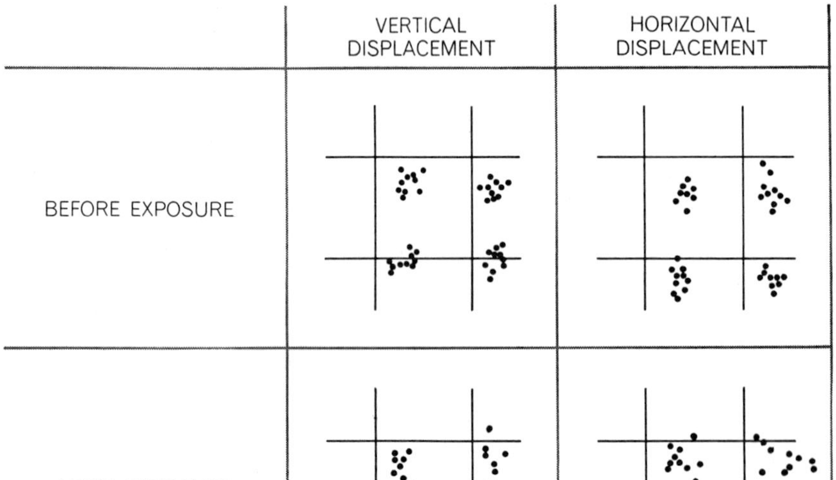

RESULTS OF DECORRELATION are shown in markings made by a subject before and after looking through rotating prism. In one condition (*left*) prisms displaced images vertically; in another (*right*), horizontally. Markings after long exposure are spread out in the direction of displacement, showing a loss of precision in visual-motor coordination.

ment there is a unique feedback signal for any particular movement. The correlation is reduced by environmental instability: the presence either of objects that themselves move or of passive movements of the body that are produced by external forces. Under these conditions more than one feedback signal may accompany any particular movement.

From a theoretical point of view the importance of body movement and particularly of self-produced movement derives from the fact that only an organism that can take account of the output signals to its own musculature is in a position to detect and factor out the decorrelating effects of both moving objects and externally imposed body movement. One way to verify the importance of the correlation would be to set up an experimental situation in which the correlation was impaired or deliberately decorrelated. If the consequence was a loss of coordination, evidence for the role of normally correlated reafference in maintaining normal coordination would be strengthened.

We conducted such an experiment in visual perception by means of an apparatus that provided a prism effect of continually varying power [*see top illustration at left*]. In such an apparatus an object such as the hand seems to move constantly, and the movement perceived is wholly independent of whatever actual motion may be taking place. The same arm movement made at different times will produce different retinal feedbacks. Since the subject does not control the continual changes in his visual input that are produced by the prism, his nervous system has no means of distinguishing these changes in the input from those that are self-initiated.

With this apparatus we conducted various experiments, again including active and passive arm movements of the type described previously. We found that the coordination between eye and hand was significantly degraded under conditions of active movement but not under conditions of passive movement. Similar results appeared in tests made by Sanford Freedman of Tufts University of the effect of decorrelation on hearing. Again the performance of subjects who were allowed to move actively during decorrelation deteriorated badly, whereas the performance of subjects whose bodily movements were restricted did not deteriorate. Both the visual and the auditory experiments confirmed the importance of the correlation between movement and sensory feedback in maintaining accurate coordination.

In another test of our hypothesis about reafference we undertook to see what would happen when subjects looked through prisms at a random scene, lacking in the lines and curves that provide normal visual cues. The straight lines characteristic of normal scenes look curved when viewed through a prism. When the prism is removed, such lines seem to curve in the opposite direction. What if straight lines looked curved after a subject had removed prism goggles through which he had viewed a random scene?

Our hypothesis was that such an effect would be produced in subjects who moved actively while viewing the random field but not in those whose movements were passive. If such a result occurred, we would have shown that the subjective geometry of the visual field can be altered by reafference. This finding would have the surprising implication that a motor factor is involved in a process traditionally regarded as purely visual. We would have demonstrated in another way the close, one-to-one correlation between movement and visual feedback and would have further evidence of a link between motor and visual mechanisms in the central nervous system.

Our apparatus for testing this hypothesis consisted of a large drum that had on its inside surface an irregular array of small spots [*see illustration on page 7*]. These spots looked the same whether viewed with a prism or not. Each subject, before putting on prism goggles and entering the drum, was tested for his perception of a vertical line; we did this by having him indicate when a grating of bars given varying curvatures by prisms appeared straight. Thereafter, entering the drum with the goggles on, the subject either walked around in the drum or was transported on a cart. He stayed in the drum for half an hour and then, after removing the goggles, again took the test with the grating of bars. Without exception the active subjects perceived curvature when looking at lines that were actually straight, whereas the passive subjects perceived little or none.

Having established by these various means the role of reafference in adaptation to changed sensory inputs, we decided to examine its role in the development of visually controlled coordination in the newborn. The contribution of experience to the development of perceived space and of spatially oriented behavior has been debated for some centuries. During the past few decades a number of experimental approaches to the issue have been made. The technique most often used involves depriving very young animals of sensory contact with the environment. It has been hoped that the procedure would decide whether or not sensory experience, as opposed to maturation alone in the absence of such experience, is required for the development of spatial discrimination.

In certain species of higher mammals, including man, various forms of visual deprivation ranging from total absence of light to mere absence of gross movement in a normally illuminated environment have all resulted in deficiencies in visually guided behavior. Unfortunately these deficiencies are not easily interpreted. They can be attributed, at least in part, to several alternative causes, including pathological changes in the anatomy of the retina and its projections to the brain. Since our findings implicated movement-produced stimulation, they enabled us to test this factor without depriving animals of normal visual stimulation.

The experiments my colleague Alan Hein and I have performed to study the earliest development of vision originated from observations made by Austin H. Riesen of the University of California at Riverside and his collaborators. Riesen's research demonstrated that kittens restrained from walking from the time of their earliest exposure to light develop marked deficiencies in the visual control of behavior compared with unrestrained animals reared normally. The deficiencies of Riesen's animals may have resulted either from the lack of variation in visual stimulation, which was the explanation he preferred, or from the lack of visual stimulation correlated with movement, which was our own hypothesis.

To decide between these alternatives we devised an apparatus in which the gross movements of a kitten moving more or less normally were transmitted to a second kitten that was carried in a gondola [*see illustration on page 373*]. These gross movements included turns to left and right, circular progress around the center post of the apparatus and any up-and-down motions made by the first kitten. The second kitten was allowed to move its head, since prior experimenters had reported that head movement alone was not sufficient to produce normal behavior in kittens, and it could also move its legs inside the gondola. Both kittens received essentially the same visual stimulation because the pattern on the walls and the center post of the apparatus was unvarying.

Eight pairs of kittens were reared in darkness until the active member of each pair had enough strength and coordination to move the other kitten in the apparatus; the ages at which that state was attained ranged from eight to 12 weeks. Two other pairs were exposed to patterned light for three hours a day between the ages of two and 10 weeks; during exposure they were in a holder that prevented locomotion. Thereafter all 10 pairs spent three hours a day in the apparatus under the experimental condition; when they were not in the apparatus, they were kept with their mothers and littermates in unlighted cages.

After an average of about 30 hours in the apparatus the active member of each pair showed normal behavior in several visually guided tasks. It blinked at an approaching object; it put out its forepaws as if to ward off collision when gently carried downward toward a surface, and it avoided the deep side of a visual cliff—an apparatus in which two depths, one shallow and the other a sharp drop, appear beneath a sheet of glass [see the article "The 'Visual Cliff,'" by Eleanor J. Gibson and Richard D. Walk, beginning on page 341]. After the same period of exposure each of the passive kittens failed to show these types of behavior. The passive kittens did, however, develop such types of behavior within days after they were allowed to run about in a normal environment.

In sum, the experiments I have described have led us to conclude that the correlation entailed in the sensory feedback accompanying movement—reafference—plays a vital role in perceptual adaptation. It helps the newborn to develop motor coordination; it figures in the adjustment to the changed relation between afferent and efferent signals resulting from growth; it operates in the maintenance of normal coordination, and it is of major importance in coping with altered visual and auditory inputs. The importance of the correlation in all these functions has been revealed by experiments that tamper with its normal operation. In the process these experiments have uncovered a fundamental role of the motor-sensory feedback loop.

BIBLIOGRAPHY

I THE ORGANIZATION OF PERCEPTUAL SYSTEMS

1. Early Concepts of the Senses and the Mind

DISCOURS DE LA METHODE PLUS LA DIOPTRIQUE ET LES METEORES. René Descartes. Henry Le Gras, 1658.

HELMHOLTZ'S TREATISE ON PHYSIOLOGICAL OPTICS. Edited by James P. C. Southall. Dover Publications, Inc., 1962.

THE OPUS MAJUS OF ROGER BACON. Translated by Robert Belle Burke. University of Pennsylvania Press, 1928.

2. Information and Memory

THE MAGICAL NUMBER SEVEN, PLUS-OR-MINUS TWO: SOME LIMITS ON OUR CAPACITY FOR PROCESSING INFORMATION. George A. Miller in *Psychological Review*, Vol. 63, No. 2, pages 81–97; March, 1956.

3. Attention and the Perception of Speech

CONTEXTUAL CUES AND SELECTIVE LISTENING. Anne M. Treisman in *Quarterly Journal of Experimental Psychology*, Vol. 12, No. 4, pages 242–248; November, 1960.

ON THE FUSION OF SOUNDS REACHING DIFFERENT SENSE ORGANS. D. E. Broadbent and Peter Ladefoged in *The Journal of the Acoustical Society of America*, Vol. 29, No. 6, pages 708–710; June, 1957.

PERCEPTION AND COMMUNICATION. D. E. Broadbent. Pergamon Press, Inc., 1958.

THREE AUDITORY THEORIES. J. C. R. Licklider in *Psychology: A Study of a Science*, edited by Sigmund Koch, Vol. 1, pages 41–144. McGraw-Hill Book Company, Inc., 1959.

4. The Split Brain in Man

CEREBRAL COMMISSUROTOMY. J. E. Bogen, E. D. Fisher and P. J. Vogel in *Journal of the American Medical Association*, Vol. 194, No. 12, pages 1328–1329; December 20, 1965.

CEREBRAL ORGANIZATION AND BEHAVIOR. R. W. Sperry in *Science*, Vol. 133, No. 3466, pages 1749–1757; June 2, 1961.

LANGUAGE AFTER SECTION OF THE CEREBRAL COMMISSURES. M. S. Gazzaniga and R. W. Sperry in *Brain*, Vol. 90, Part 1, pages 131–148; 1967.

MICROELECTRODE ANALYSIS OF TRANSFER OF VISUAL INFORMATION BY THE CORPUS CALLOSUM. G. Berlucchi, M. S. Gazzaniga and G. Rizzolati in *Archives Italiennes de Biologie*, Vol. 105, pp. 583–596; 1967.

OBSERVATIONS ON VISUAL PERCEPTION AFTER DISCONNEXION OF THE CEREBRAL HEMISPHERES IN MAN. M. S. Gazzaniga, J. E. Bogen and R. W. Sperry in *Brain*, Vol. 88, Part 2, pages 221–236; 1965.

II SENSORY SYSTEMS

5. Inherited Sense Defects

GENETICS. H. Kalmus. Penguin Books.

6. Taste Receptors

CHEMORECEPTOR MECHANISMS. V. G. Dethier in *Molecular Structure and Functional Activity of Nerve Cells*, edited by R. G. Grenell and L. J. Mullins, pages 1–30. American Institute of Biological Sciences, 1956.

ELECTROPHYSIOLOGICAL STUDIES OF ARTHROPOD CHEMORECEPTION. III: CHEMORECEPTORS OF TERRESTRIAL AND FRESH-WATER ARTHROPODS. Edward S. Hodgson in *Biological Bulletin*, Vol. 115, No. 1, pages 114–125; August, 1958.

PROBLEMS IN INVERTEBRATE CHEMORECEPTION. Edward S. Hodgson in *The Quarterly Review of Biology*, Vol. 30, No. 4, pages 331–347; December, 1955.

7. The Stereochemical Theory of Odor

THE CHEMICAL SENSES. R. W. Moncrieff. Leonard Hill, Limited, 1951.

THE NATURE OF THE UNIVERSE. Lucretius. Translated by R. E. Latham. Penguin Books, 1951.

THE SENSES OF ANIMALS AND MEN. Lorus and Marjory Milne. Atheneum, 1962.

THE STEREOCHEMICAL THEORY OF OLFACTION. John E. Amoore, Martin Rubin and James W. Johnston, Jr., in *Proceedings of the Scientific Section of the Toilet Goods Association*, Special Supplement to No. 37, pages 1–47; October, 1962.

8. Biological Transducers

THE GENERATION OF ELECTRIC ACTIVITY IN A NERVE ENDING. Werner R. Loewenstein in *Annals of the New York Academy of Sciences*, Vol. 81, Article 2, pages 367–387; August 28, 1959.

THE PHYSICAL BACKGROUND OF PERCEPTION. E. D. Adrian. Oxford University Press, 1947.

RECEPTORS AND SENSORY PERCEPTION. Ragnar Granit. Yale University Press, 1955.

9. The Ear

THE EARLY HISTORY OF HEARING—OBSERVATIONS AND THEORIES. Georg v. Békésy and Walter A. Rosenblith in *The Journal of the Acoustical Society of America*, Vol. 20, No. 6, pages 727–748; November, 1948.

HEARING: ITS PSYCHOLOGY AND PHYSIOLOGY. Stanley Smith Stevens and Hallowell Davis. John Wiley & Sons, Inc., 1938.

PHYSIOLOGICAL ACOUSTICS. Ernest Glen Wever and Merle Lawrence. Princeton University Press, 1954.

10. Eye and Camera

VISION AND THE EYE. M. H. Pirenne. The Pilot Press, Ltd., 1948.

THE RETINA. S. Polyak. University of Chicago Press, 1941.

THE PHOTOCHEMISTRY OF VISION. George Wald in *Documenta Ophthalmologica*, Vol. 3, page 94; 1949.

THE LIGHT REACTION IN THE BLEACHING OF RHODOPSIN. George Wald, Jack Durell and C. C. St. George in *Science*, Vol. 3, No. 2,877, pages 179–181; February 17, 1950.

11. Visual Pigments in Man

CHEMICAL BASIS OF HUMAN COLOUR VISION. W. A. H. Rushton in *Research*, Vol. 11, No. 12, pages 478–483; December, 1958.

THE VISUAL PIGMENTS. H. J. A. Dartnall. John Wiley & Sons, Inc., 1957.

VISUAL PIGMENTS IN MAN. W. A. H. Rushton. Liverpool University Press, 1962.

III PHYSIOLOGICAL ANALYZERS

12. Inhibition in Visual Systems

DISCHARGE PATTERNS AND FUNCTIONAL ORGANIZATION OF MAMMALIAN RETINA. Stephen W. Kuffler in *Journal of Neurophysiology*, Vol. 16, No. 1, pages 37–68; January, 1953.

INTEGRATIVE PROCESSES IN CENTRAL VISUAL PATHWAYS OF THE CAT. David M. Hubel in *Journal of the Optical Society of America*, Vol. 53, No. 1, pages 58–66; January, 1963.

RECEPTIVE FIELDS, BINOCULAR INTERACTION AND FUNCTIONAL ARCHITECTURE IN THE CAT'S VISUAL CORTEX. D. H. Hubel and T. N. Wiesel in *Journal of Physiology*, Vol. 160, No. 1, pages 106–154; January, 1962.

THE VISUAL PATHWAY. Ragnar Granit in *The Eye, Volume II: The Visual Process*, edited by Hugh Davson. Academic Press, Inc., 1962.

13. How Cells Receive Stimuli

INITIATION OF IMPULSES AT RECEPTORS. J. A. B. Gray in *Handbook of Physiology, Vol. I, Section I: Neurophysiology*, pages 123–145. American Physiological Society, 1959.

THE NEURAL MECHANISMS OF VISION. H. K. Hartline in *The Harvey Lectures, 1941–1942*. Series 37, pages 39–68; 1942.

RECEPTORS AND SENSORY PERCEPTION. R. Granit. Yale University Press, 1955.
SENSORY COMMUNICATION. Edited by Walter A. Rosenblith. John Wiley & Sons, Inc., 1961.

14. Retinal Processing of Visual Images

RECEPTIVE FIELDS, BINOCULAR INTERACTION AND FUNCTIONAL ARCHITECTURE IN THE CAT'S VISUAL CORTEX. D. H. Hubel and T. N. Wiesel in *The Journal of Physiology*, Vol. 160, No. 1, pages 106–154; January, 1962.
THE MECHANISM OF DIRECTIONALLY SELECTIVE UNITS IN RABBIT'S RETINA. H. B. Barlow and W. R. Levick in *The Journal of Physiology*, Vol. 178, No. 3, pages 477-504; June, 1965.
RECEPTIVE FIELDS OF SINGLE OPTIC NERVE FIBERS IN A MAMMAL WITH AN ALL-CONE RETINA. Charles R. Michael in *Journal of Neurophysiology*, Vol. 31, No. 2, pages 249–282; March, 1968.

15. The Visual Cortex of the Brain

DISCHARGE PATTERNS AND FUNCTIONAL ORGANIZATION OF MAMMALIAN RETINA. Stephen W. Kuffler in *Journal of Neurophysiology*, Vol. 16, No. 1, pages 37–68; January, 1953.
INTEGRATIVE PROCESSES IN CENTRAL VISUAL PATHWAYS OF THE CAT. David M. Hubel in *Journal of the Optical Society of America*, Vol. 53, No. 1, pages 58–66; January, 1963.
RECEPTIVE FIELDS, BINOCULAR INTERACTION AND FUNCTIONAL ARCHITECTURE IN THE CAT'S VISUAL CORTEX. D. H. Hubel and T. N. Wiesel in *Journal of Physiology*, Vol. 160, No. 1, pages 106–154; January, 1962.
THE VISUAL PATHWAY. Ragnar Granit in *The Eye, Volume II: The Visual Process*, edited by Hugh Davson. Academic Press, Inc. 1962.

16. Vision in Frogs

THE BIOLOGY OF THE AMPHIBIA. G. Kingsley Noble. Dover Publications, Inc., 1954.
EFFECTIVENESS OF DIFFERENT COLORS OF LIGHT IN RELEASING POSITIVE PHOTOTACTIC BEHAVIOR OF FROGS, AND A POSSIBLE FUNCTION OF THE RETINAL PROJECTION TO THE DIENCEPHALON. W. R. A. Muntz in *Journal of Neurophysiology*, Vol. 25, No. 6, pages 712–720; November, 1962.
SUMMATION AND INHIBITION IN THE FROG'S RETINA. H. B. Barlow in *The Journal of Physiology*, Vol. 119, No. 1, pages 69–88; January, 1953.

IV PERCEPTUAL PROCESSES

17. Stabilized Images on the Retina

THE ORGANIZATION OF BEHAVIOR. D. O. Hebb. John Wiley & Sons, Inc., 1949.
VISUAL EFFECTS OF VARYING THE EXTENT OF COMPENSATION FOR EYE MOVEMENTS. Lorrin A. Riggs and S. Ülker Tulunay in *Journal of the Optical Society of America*, Vol. 9, No. 8, pages 741–745; August, 1959.
VISUAL PERCEPTION APPROACHED BY THE METHOD OF STABILIZED IMAGES. R. M. Pritchard, W. Heron and D. O. Hebb in *Canadian Journal of Psychology*, Vol. 14, No. 2, pages 67–77; 1960.

18. Texture and Visual Perception

BINOCULAR DEPTH PERCEPTION WITHOUT FAMILIARITY CUES. Bela Julesz in *Science*, Vol. 145, No. 3630, pages 356–362; July, 1964.
THE OPTICAL SPACE SENSE. Kenneth N. Ogle in *The Eye, Vol. IV: Visual Optics and the Optical Space Sense*, edited by Hugh Davson. Academic Press, Inc., 1962.
STEREOPSIS AND BINOCULAR RIVALRY OF CONTOURS. B. Julesz in *Bell Telephone System Technical Publications Monograph 4609*, 1963.
TOWARDS THE AUTOMATION OF BINOCULAR DEPTH PERCEPTION. B. Julesz in *Information Processing 1962: Proceedings of IFIP Congress 62*. North-Holland Publishing Company, 1962.

19. The Fortification Illusions of Migraines

ON A DISTINCT FORM OF TRANSIENT HEMIOPSIA. Hubert Airy in *Philosophical Transactions of the Royal Society of London*, Vol. 160, Part 1, pages 247–264; 1870.
PATTERNS OF CEREBRAL INTEGRATION INDICATED BY THE SCOTOMAS OF MIGRAINE. K. S. Lashley in *Archives of Neurology and Psychiatry*, Vol. 46, No. 2, pages 331–339; August, 1941.
RECEPTIVE FIELDS AND FUNCTIONAL ARCHITECTURE OF MONKEY STRIATE CORTEX. D. H. Hubel and T. N. Wiesel in *The Journal of Physiology*, Vol. 195, No. 1, pages 215–243; March, 1968.
THE SENSATIONS PRODUCED BY ELECTRICAL STIMULATION OF THE VISUAL CORTEX. G. S. Brindley and W. S. Lewin in *The Journal of Physiology*, Vol. 196, No. 2, pages 479–493; May, 1968.

20. Auditory Localization

CORTICAL CORRELATES OF AUDITORY LOCALIZATION AND OF RELATED PERCEPTUAL PHENOMENA. Mark R. Rosenzweig in *The Journal of Comparative and Physiological Psychology*, Vol. 47, No. 4, pages 269–276; August, 1954.

21. Pattern Recognition by Machine

DISCUSSION OF PROBLEMS IN PATTERN RECOGNITION. W. W. Bledsoe, J. S. Bomba, I. Browning, R. J. Evey, R. A. Kirsch, R. L. Mattson, M. Minsky, U. Neisser and O. G. Selfridge in *Proceedings of the Eastern Joint Computer Conference*, pages 233–237; 1959.

HOW WE KNOW UNIVERSALS: THE PERCEPTION OF AUDITORY AND VISUAL FORMS. Walter Pitts and Warren S. McCulloch in *The Bulletin of Mathematical Biophysics*, Vol. 9, No. 3, pages 127–147; 1947.

MACHINE RECOGNITION OF HAND-SENT MORSE CODE. Bernard Gold in *IRE Transactions of the Professional Group on Information Theory*, Vol. IT-5, No. 1, pages 17–24; March, 1959.

THE ORGANIZATION OF BEHAVIOR. D. O. Hebb. John Wiley & Sons, Inc., 1949.

22. Eye Movements and Visual Perception

PATTERN RECOGNITION. Edited by Leonard M. Uhr. John Wiley & Sons, Inc., 1966.

CONTEMPORARY THEORY AND RESEARCH IN VISUAL PERCEPTION. Edited by Ralph Norman Haber. Holt, Rinehart & Winston, Inc., 1968.

A THEORY OF VISUAL PATTERN PERCEPTION. David Noton in *IEEE Transactions on Systems Science and Cybernetics*, Vol. SSC-6, No. 4, pages 349–357; October, 1970.

SCANPATHS IN EYE MOVEMENTS DURING PATTERN PERCEPTION. David Noton and Lawrence Stark in *Science*, Vol. 171, No. 3968, pages 308–311; January 22, 1971.

V ILLUSIONS AND CONSTANCIES

23. Visual Illusions

SENSATION AND PERCEPTION IN THE HISTORY OF EXPERIMENTAL PSYCHOLOGY. Edwin Garrigues Boring. D. Appleton-Century Company, 1942.

OPTICAL ILLUSIONS. S. Tolansky. Pergamon Press, Inc., 1964.

EYE AND BRAIN. R. L. Gregory. McGraw-Hill Book Company, Inc., 1966.

WILL SEEING MACHINES HAVE ILLUSIONS? R. L. Gregory in *Machine Intelligence I*, edited by N. L. Collins and Donald Michie. American Elsevier Publishing Co., Inc., 1967.

24. The Processes of Vision

THE KINETIC DEPTH EFFECT. H. Wallach and D. N. O'Connell in *Journal of Experimental Psychology*, Vol. 45, No. 4, pages 205–218; April, 1953.

THE RELATION OF EYE MOVEMENTS, BODY MOTILITY AND EXTERNAL STIMULI TO DREAM CONTENT. William Dement and Edward A. Wolpert in *Journal of Experimental Psychology*, Vol. 55, No. 6, pages 543–553; June, 1958.

THE SENSES CONSIDERED AS PERCEPTUAL SYSTEMS. James J. Gibson. Houghton Mifflin Company, 1966.

COGNITIVE PSYCHOLOGY. Ulric Neisser. Appleton-Century-Crofts, 1967.

25. The Moon Illusion

EXPERIMENTAL PSYCHOLOGY. Robert S. Woodworth and Harold Schlosberg. Henry Holt & Co., Inc., 1954. See pages 455–491.

THE MOON ILLUSION. Edwin G. Boring in *American Journal of Physics*, Vol. 11, No. 2, pages 55–60; April, 1943.

THE MOON ILLUSION AND THE ANGLE OF REGARD. Alfred H. Holway and Edwin G. Boring in *The American Journal of Psychology*, Vol. 53, No. 1, pages 109–116; January, 1940.

THE PERCEPTION OF THE VISUAL WORLD. J. J. Gibson. Houghton Mifflin Company, 1950.

26. Vision and Touch

ADAPTATION OF DISARRANGED HAND-EYE COORDINATION CONTINGENT UPON RE-AFFERENT STIMULATION. Richard Held and Alan Hein in *Perceptual and Motor Skills*, Vol. 8, No. 2, pages 87–90; June, 1958.

AN ESSAY TOWARDS A NEW THEORY OF VISION. George Berkeley. E. P. Dutton & Co., 1910.

THE NATURE OF PERCEPTUAL ADAPTATION. Irvin Rock. Basic Books, Inc., Publishers, 1966.

PERCEPTION. Julian Hochberg. Prentice-Hall, Inc., 1964.

PERCEPTUAL ADAPTATION TO INVERTED, REVERSED, AND DISPLACED VISION. Charles S. Harris in *Psychological Review*, Vol. 72, No. 6, pages 419–444; November, 1965.

27. The Perception of Neutral Colors

BRIGHTNESS CONSTANCY AND THE NATURE OF ACHROMATIC COLORS. Hans Wallach in *Journal of Ex-*

perimental Psychology, Vol. 38, No. 3, pages 310–324; June, 1948.

SOME FACTORS AND IMPLICATIONS OF COLOR CONSTANCY. Harry Helson in *Journal of the Optical Society of America*, Vol. 33, No. 10, pages 555–567; October, 1943.

A THEORY OF DEPRESSION AND ENHANCEMENT IN BRIGHTNESS RESPONSE. A. Leonard Diamond in *Psychological Review*, Vol. 67, No. 3, pages 168–199; May, 1960.

THE WORLD OF COLOUR. David Katz. Kegan Paul, Trench, Trubner & Co., Ltd., 1935.

28. Experiments in Color Vision

COLOR VISION AND THE NATURAL IMAGE. PART I. Edwin H. Land in *Proceedings of the National Academy of Sciences*, Vol. 45, No. 1, pages 115–129; January, 1959.

COLOR VISION AND THE NATURAL IMAGE. PART II. Edwin H. Land in *Proceedings of the National Academy of Sciences*, Vol. 45, No. 4, pages 636–645; April, 1959.

SYMPOSIUM ON NEW DEVELOPMENTS IN THE STUDY OF COLOR VISION. *Proceedings of the National Academy of Sciences*, Vol. 45, No. 1, pages 89–115; January, 1969.

SENSATION AND PERCEPTION IN THE HISTORY OF EXPERIMENTAL PSYCHOLOGY. Edwin G. Boring. Appleton-Century-Crofts, Inc., 1942.

29. Experiments With Goggles

ADAPTATION, AFTER-EFFECT AND CONTRAST IN THE PERCEPTION OF CURVED LINES. James J. Gibson in *Journal of Experimental Psychology*, Vol. 16, No. 1, pages 1–31; February, 1933.

SOME PRELIMINARY EXPERIMENTS ON VISION WITHOUT INVERSION OF THE RETINAL IMAGE. George M. Stratton in *The Psychological Review*, Vol. 3, No. 6, pages 611–617; November, 1896.

VISION WITHOUT INVERSION OF THE RETINAL IMAGE. George M. Stratton in *The Psychological Review*, Vol. 4, No. 4, pages 341–360; July, 1897.

VISION WITHOUT INVERSION OF THE RETINAL IMAGE. (CONCLUDED). George M. Stratton in *The Psychological Review*, Vol. 4, No. 5, pages 463–481; September, 1897.

30. The Perception of Motion

CONFIGURATIONS IN EVENT PERCEPTION. Gunnar Johansson. Uppsala, Almqvist & Wiksells, Boktryckeri, 1950.

THE VISUAL PERCEPTION OF VELOCITY. J. F. Brown in *Psychologische Forschung*, Vol. 14, No. 3–4, pages 199–232; March, 1931.

31. The Illusion of Movement

AN ANALYSIS OF THE VISUAL PERCEPTION OF MOVEMENT. H. R. De Silva in *British Journal of Psychology*, Vol. 19, Part 3, pages 268–305; January, 1929.

APPARENT MOVEMENT OF A NECKER CUBE. Paul A. Kolers in *American Journal of Psychology*, Vol. 77, No. 2, pages 220–230; June, 1964.

EXPERIMENTAL STUDIES ON THE SEEING OF MOTION. Max Wertheimer. Philosophical Library, 1961.

VI DEVELOPMENT AND MODIFICATION

32. The Origin of Form Perception

EFFECTS OF EARLY EXPERIENCE UPON THE BEHAVIOR OF ANIMALS. Frank A. Beach and Julian Jaynes in *Psychological Bulletin*, Vol. 51, No. 3, pages 239–263; May, 1954.

FORM PREFERENCES IN NEWLY HATCHED CHICKS. Robert L. Fantz in *The Journal of Comparative and Physiological Psychology*. Vol. 50, No. 5, pages 422–430; October, 1957.

ON THE STIMULUS SITUATION RELEASING THE BEGGING RESPONSE IN THE NEWLY HATCHED HERRING GULL CHICK. N. Tinbergen and A. C. Perdeck in *Behavior*, Vol. 3, Part 1, pages 1–39; 1950.

PATTERN VISION OF YOUNG INFANTS. Robert L. Fantz in *The Psychological Record*, Vol. 8, pages 43–47; 1958.

THE PERCEPTION OF THE VISUAL WORLD. James J. Gibson. Houghton Mifflin Company, 1950.

33. The "Visual Cliff"

BEHAVIOR OF LIGHT- AND DARK-REARED RATS ON A VISUAL CLIFF. E. J. Gibson, T. J. Tighe and R. D. Walk in *Science*, Vol. 126, No. 3,262, pages 80–81; July 5, 1957.

THE MECHANISM OF VISION. XI. A PRELIMINARY TEST OF INNATE ORGANIZATION. K. S. Lashley and J. T. Russell in *Journal of Genetic Psychology*, Vol. 45, No. 1, pages 136–144; September, 1934.

SPACE PERCEPTION OF TORTOISES. R. M. Yerkes in *The Journal of Comparative Neurology*, Vol. 14, No. 1, pages 17–26; March, 1904.

VISUALLY CONTROLLED LOCOMOTION AND VISUAL ORIENTATION IN ANIMALS. James J. Gibson in *The British Journal of Psychology*, Vol. 49, Part 3, pages 182–194; August, 1958.

34. The Visual World of Infants

NATIVISM AND EMPIRICISM IN PERCEPTION. J. E. Hochberg in *Psychology in the Making: Histories of Selected Research Problems*, edited by Leo Postman. Alfred A. Knopf, Inc., 1962.

THE PERCEPTION OF THE VISUAL WORLD. James J. Gibson. Hougton Mifflin Company, 1950.

SLANT PERCEPTION AND SHAPE CONSTANCY IN INFANTS. T. G. R. Bower in *Science*, Vol. 151, No. 3712, pages 832–834; February 18, 1966.

35. Arrested Vision

THE DEVELOPMENT OF VISUAL PERCEPTION IN MAN AND CHIMPANZEE. Austin H. Riesen in *Science*, Vol. 106, No. 2744, pages 107–108; August 1, 1947.

36. Space Perception in the Chick

THE EYE AND THE BRAIN. R. W. Sperry in *Scientific American*, Vol. 194, No. 5, pages 48–52; May, 1956.

THE VERTEBRATE EYE AND ITS ADAPTIVE RADIATION. Gordon Lynn Walls. Cranbrook Institute of Science, 1942.

VISION WITH SPATIAL INVERSION. F. W. Snyder and N. H. Pronko, University of Wichita Press, 1952.

37. The Eye and the Brain

MECHANISM OF NEURAL MATURATION. R. W. Sperry in *Handbook of Experimental Psychology*. John Wiley & Sons, Inc., 1951.

PATTERNING OF CENTRAL SYNAPSES IN REGENERATION OF THE OPTIC NERVE IN TELEOSTS. R. W. Sperry in *Physiological Zoology*, Vol. 21, No. 4, pages 351- 361; October, 1948.

38. Plasticity in Sensory-Motor Systems

MOVEMENT-PRODUCED STIMULATION IN THE DEVELOPMENT OF VISUALLY GUIDED BEHAVIOR. Richard Held and Alan Hein in *Journal of Comparative and Physiological Psychology*, Vol. 56, No. 5, pages 872–876; October, 1963.

NEONATAL DEPRIVATION AND ADULT REARRANGEMENT: COMPLEMENTARY TECHNIQUES FOR ANALYZING PLASTIC SENSORY-MOTOR COORDINATIONS. Richard Held and Joseph Bossom in *Journal of Comparative and Physiological Psychology*, Vol. 54, No. 1, pages 33–37; February, 1961.

PLASTICITY IN HUMAN SENSORIMOTOR CONTROL. Richard Held and Sanford J. Freedman in *Science*, Vol. 142, No. 3591, pages 455–462; October 25, 1963.

INDEX